Handbook of Behavior Therapy in Education

Handbook of Behavior Therapy in Education

Edited by

Joseph C. Witt
Louisiana State University
Baton Rouge, Louisiana

Stephen N. Elliott
University of Wisconsin-Madison
Madison, Wisconsin

and

Frank M. Gresham
Louisiana State University
Baton Rouge, Louisiana

Plenum Press • New York and London

Library of Congress Cataloging in Publication Data

Handbook of behavior therapy in education.

Includes bibliographies and index.

1. Behavior modification. 2. Behavior therapy for children. 3. School psychology. 4. Child psychotherapy. I. Witt, Joseph C. II. Elliott, Stephen N. III. Gresham, Frank.

LB1060.2.H36 1988 370.15'3 88-4191

ISBN-13:978-1-4612-8238-9 e-ISBN-13:978-1-4613-0905-5

DOI: 10.1007/978-1-4613-0905-5

Softcover reprint of the hardcover 1st edition 1988

A Division of Plenum Publishing Corporation

233 Spring Street, New York, N.Y. 10013

For three who taught me:

Robert M. Adams, who introduced me both to a science of human behavior and to Kantor and helped me learn to write

Lee Meyerson, who introduced me both to an ecological perspective and to Lewin and helped me learn to think

Nancy Kerr, who fully introduced me both to the O in the S-O-R paradigm and to Galileo and helped me learn to appreciate the uniquess and the power of the individual

JOSEPH C. WITT

Dedicated to my sons, Dustin Rhodes and Andrew Taylor, to my friend, Ed Argulewicz, and to my wife, Anita

STEPHEN N. ELLIOTT

To Gwen, Jennifer, Julie, and Jill, without whose tolerance above and beyond the call of duty this book would not have been possible

FRANK M. GRESHAM

Contributors

Kay Aldridge
Department of Psychology
University of Arizona
Tucson, Arizona

Teresa Kay Anderson
Ampitheater Public Schools
Tucson, Arizona

Donald M. Baer
Department of Human Development
University of Kansas
Lawrence, Kansas

Wendy K. Berg
Department of Pediatrics
University Hospital School
University of Iowa
Iowa City, Iowa

John R. Bergan
Department of Educational Psychology
University of Arizona
Tucson, Arizona

Michael P. Carey
Department of Psychology
Louisiana State University
Baton Rouge, Louisiana

Caryn L. Carlson
Department of Psychology
Virginia Polytechnic Institute and State University
Blacksburg, Virginia

Laura B. Carper
Department of Psychology
Louisiana State University
Baton Rouge, Louisiana

Joseph Corrao
Department of Psychology
University of Nebraska-Lincoln
Lincoln, Nebraska

Lucinda Cummings
Kennedy Memorial Hospital for Children
Brighton, Massachusetts

Carl J. Dunst
Human Development Research and Training Institute
Western Carolina Center
Morganton, North Carolina

Craig Edelbrock
Department of Psychiatry
University of Massachusetts Medical School
Worchester, Massachusetts

Stephen N. Elliott
Department of Educational Psychology
Univeristy of Wisconsin-Madison
Madison, Wisconsin

Ian M. Evans
Department of Psychology
SUNY-Binghamton
Binghamton, New York

Jason K. Feld
Department of Educational Psychology
University of Arizona
Tucson, Arizona

Michael Ferrari
Department of Individual and Family Studies
University of Delaware
Newark, Delaware

Cyril M. Franks
Graduate School of Applied and Professional Psychology
Rutgers University
Piscataway, New Jersey

Anthony J. Goreczny
Department of Psychology
Louisiana State University
Baton Rouge, Louisiana

Brandon F. Greene
Behavior Analysis and Therapy Program
Southern Illinois University
Carbondale, Illinois

Frank M. Gresham
Department of Psychology
Louisiana State University
Baton Rouge, Louisiana

Sandra L. Harris
Graduate School of Applied and Professional Psychology
Rutgers University
Piscataway, New Jersey

Alan E. Kazdin
Department of Psychiatry
Western Psychiatric Institute and Clinic
University of Pittsburgh School of Medicine
Pittsburgh, Pennsylvania

Mary L. Kelley
Department of Psychology
Louisiana State University
Baton Rouge, Louisiana

Phillip C. Kendall
Department of Psychology
Temple University
Philadelphia, Pennsylvania

Gloria S. Kishi
Division of Special Education and Rehabilitation
Syracuse University
Syracuse, New York

Rebecca Dailey Kneedler
Department of Curriculum, Instruction, and Special Education
University of Virginia
Charlottesville, Virginia

Thomas R. Kratochwill
Department of Educational Psychology
School Psychology Program
University of Wisconsin-Madison
Madison, Wisconsin

Jayne A. Kurkjian
Department of Psychology
SUNY-Binghamton
Binghamton, New York

Benjamin B. Lahey
Department of Psychology
Georgia Children's Center
University of Georgia
Athens, Georgia

Kathleen L. Lemanek
Department of Pediatrics
University of Miami School of Medicine
Miami, Florida

Francis E. Lentz, Jr.
College of Education
University of Cincinnati
Cincinnati, Ohio

F. Charles Mace
Graduate School of Applied and Professional Psychology
Rutgers University
Piscataway, New Jersey

Brian K. Martens
Department of Psychology
Syracuse University
Syracuse, New York

Johnny L. Matson
Department of Psychology
Louisiana State University
Baton Rouge, Louisiana

Sandra J. McKenzie
Department of Psychology
Louisiana State University
Baton Rouge, Louisiana

T. F. McLaughlin
Department of Special Education
Gonzaga University
Spokane, Washington

Ruth Lyn Meese
Department of Education, Special Education, and Social Work
Longwood College
Farmville, Virginia

Gary B. Melton
Department of Psychology
University of Nebraska-Lincoln
Lincoln, Nebraska

Luanna H. Meyer
Division of Special Education and Rehabilitation
Syracuse University
Syracuse, New York

Richard J. Morris
Department of Educational Psychology
School Psychology Program
University of Arizona
Tucson, Arizona

C. Michael Nelson
Department of Special Education
University of Kentucky
Lexington, Kentucky

Kathleen D. Paget
Department of Psychology
University of South Carolina
Columbia, South Carolina

Michael D. Powers
Department of Special Education
University of Maryland
College Park, Maryland

Robert B. Rutherford, Jr.
Department of Special Education
Arizona State University
Tempe, Arizona

Elizabeth A. Schaughency
Oregon Health Sciences Center
University of Oregon
Eugene, Oregon

Edward S. Shapiro
College of Education
Lehigh University
Bethlehem, Pennsylvania

Joyce C. Swarner
Department of Educational Psychology
University of Arizona
Tucson, Arizona

Carol M. Trivette
Human Development Research and Training Institute
Western Carolina Center
Morganton, North Carolina

Dorothy J. Van Buren
Department of Psychology
Louisiana State University
Baton Rouge, Louisiana

David P. Wacker
Department of Pediatrics
University Hospital School
University of Iowa
Iowa City, Iowa

Edward J. Watson-Perczel
Behavior Analysis and Therapy Program
Southern Illinois University
Carbondale, Illinois

Randy Lee Williams
Department of Special Education
Gonzaga University
Spokane, Washington

Donald A. Williamson
Department of Psychology
Louisiana State University
Baton Rouge, Louisiana

Joseph C. Witt
Department of Psychology
Louisiana State University
Baton Rouge, Louisiana

William H. Yeaton
ISR/SRC
University of Michigan
Ann Arbor, Michigan

Preface

What do we know about behavioral analysis and intervention in educational settings? Given that educational institutions were among the first to embrace the new technology of behavior change in the late 1950s and early 1960s, it is apparent that we have had the opportunity to learn a great deal. The evolution of the field of behavior therapy has witnessed a change in the behavior therapist from an adolescent fascination with repeatedly demonstrating the effectiveness of the new technology to a mature recognition of the complex implications of the behavioral paradigm for individuals, systems, and society.

Many "facts" now taken for granted were considered impossibilities a mere two decades ago. In her 1986 presidential address to Division 25 of the American Psychological Association, Beth Sulzer-Azaroff reviewed a number of changes in attitude in education that were strongly influenced by behavior therapy. Most educators now agree that (a) everyone can learn, (b) complex skills can be taught, (c) precise, general, and durable performance can be taught, and (d) barriers to learning can be overcome. In addition, we would add that behavior therapy is being applied to increasingly more complex human problems, such as social skill deficits, internalizing disorders, and dysfunctional systems and organizations.

Along with these accomplishments has come a growing recognition of the problems inherent in the application of behavioral technology. Among these problems have been frequent failures in the generalization and maintenance of change, unanticipated second- and third-order effects (i.e., side effects) of interventions, and legal challenges to some procedures. Concomitantly, there has been an increase in the resistance to behavioral procedures in education. Many teachers will not even consider using "behavior modification." For interventions that are attempted, there are frequent practical problems with treatment integrity and the maintenance of treatment at sufficient strength for a sufficient amount of time to be effective.

Within the context of these possibilities and complexities, it is the goal of this text to provide clear statements of what behavior therapy has to offer education. This analysis takes the form of providing not only a comprehensive synthesis of research and practice, but also provides the content and process for confronting the problems head on. If there is a singular aim of this book, it is to describe behavioral solutions to the most pressing educational problems, but to accomplish this by providing the reader with a new or renewed appreciation of the reciprocal relationship between behavioral technology and the ecology of the educational system into which the technology is placed.

The book is designed to advance research and practice. A primary audience will be professionals who work on a day-to-day basis with children, their families, and their teachers. It is designed to provide a summary of the available research pertaining to important educational issues and problems. Because it provides a synthesis of existing research with directions for the future, the book will also be of interest to researchers in the fields of school and clinical psychology as well as special education. In addition, the book is appropriate as a text for students in these related fields.

This book has come about as the result of generous contributions from many people. First, and most especially, we would like to thank the authors who made our work not only effortless but invigorating. As members of a supportive network of individuals who believe in a behavioral approach to education, we appreciate the collegiality and inertia created by a critical mass of like-minded individuals and we wish to acknowledge the importance of the Driftwood Society and our other friends who make our work not only better but more enjoyable. This work would not have been possible without the support of our editor, Eliot Werner, who expertly and patiently molded our early ideas into a coherent and comprehensive text. Our students have been a constant source of inspiration and we would like to note especially Brian K. Martens, William T. McKee, Kathleen Lemanek, Mary Boone Von Brock, Sally Evans, Timothy Turco, Michael P. Carey, Melissa Pardue, and Ramasamy Manikam. We must also gratefully acknowledge James Geer, Chairman of the Department of Psychology, and David Harned, Dean of the College of Arts and Sciences at Louisiana State University, for providing a supportive and comfortable environment containing the freedom and resources needed to accomplish our work. Numerous individuals served as reviewers for individual chapters and our heartiest thanks go to those who generously provided feedback to authors. Saving the best for last, we must say how much we appreciate the continued support and encouragement of our families.

Joseph C. Witt
Stephen N. Elliott
Frank M. Gresham

Contents

PART V THE PRACTICE OF BEHAVIOR THERAPY WITH SPECIFIC PROBLEMS AND POPULATIONS

PART VI THE FUTURE OF BEHAVIOR THERAPY IN EDUCATION

PART I

Foundations of Behavior Therapy

The foundation of behavior therapy is in the science of human behavior. In this section, the contributors describe the fundamental assumptions on which the field is based and provide a context into which the remaining chapters can be placed. In Chapter 1, Powers and Franks not only discuss the history and assumptions of behavior therapy, but also provide cogent insights into the changing role of behavioral practice within an educational context. Gresham and Carey, in Chapter 2, provide a comprehensive synthesis of major epistemological and methodological underpinnings of modern behaviorism. Chapters 3 and 4, by Shapiro and Edelbrock, respectively, describe the major issues surrounding assessment and diagnosis from a behavioral perspective.

CHAPTER 1

Behavior Therapy and the Educative Process

Michael D. Powers and Cyril M. Franks

Introduction

If behavior therapy is a relative Johnny-come-lately on the psychotherapeutic scene, the popular usage of reinforcement procedures stems back to antiquity. For thousands of years rewards and punishments had been used in one way or another to modify behavior with little recognition of the principles involved. If contemporary behavior therapy offers many procedures for the modification of behavior, cognition, affect, and even psychophysiological activity, it was not until the late 1950s that behavioral science had developed sufficiently to participate in the foundation of behavior therapy as we know it today. The present domain of behavior therapy is vast, its methodology sophisticated, and its influence impressive. However, with one possible exception, this has been accomplished without benefit of anything that could even remotely be described as a breakthrough. Virtually all progress can be attributed to ingenious developments in methodology, to more extensive behavioral training, and to growing sophistication in the behavioral sciences. In an understandable enthusiasm for behavioral therapy, this sobering fact is sometimes overlooked by the behavioral community.

It was not until the middle of the present century that behavioral principles were applied systematically in any area. In education, the main concern here, these principles were manifest chiefly in reinforcement-based procedures, such as teaching machines and token economies. The impetus was further generated by such advances as Thorndike's laws of learning and Skinner's operant conditioning. Nowadays, the influence of behavior therapy in education and child training extends far beyond these simple beginnings. Behaviorally oriented systems theory, cognitive strategies, psychophysiological technology, and the vast armamentarium of clinical behavior therapy are being successfully applied in a variety of settings involving young people. But once again, despite this sophistication and efficacy, basic principles remain few and relatively unchanged.

An in-depth examination of these matters is

Michael D. Powers • Department of Special Education, University of Maryland, College Park, Maryland 20742. **Cyril M. Franks** • Graduate School of Applied and Professional Psychology, Rutgers University, Piscataway, New Jersey 08854.

clearly not possible here. For this the reader is referred elsewhere (e.g., Franks and Wilson's ongoing *Annual Review of Behavior Therapy*, 1973; Kazdin's (1978) history of behavior modification, and Erwin's (1978) insightful appraisal of behavior therapy from the perspective of a philosopher).

The Roots and Rise of Behavior Therapy

Behavior therapy, a term used here interchangeably with behavior modification, does not designate a single or unified concept, theory, or practice. Its roots can be traced back to many schools of thought and philosophical systems, to different countries, and to pioneers in disciplines only peripherally related to psychology. As long ago as 1971, Krasner was able to identify at least 15 major streams of development that had joined together by the late 1960s to form a distinctive approach. This comprehensive list includes such diverse strains as behaviorism and the rise of experimental psychology, instrumental conditioning, classical conditioning, research in education institutions, and the advent of experimental social psychology. Doubtless, were Krasner to reformulate his list today, it would extend to include such influences as behavioral medicine, psychophysiology, applied cognitive theory technology, and more.

If psychologists now predominate in behavior therapy, many of the early leaders belonged to other disciplines—for example, the physiologist Pavlov and the psychiatrist Wolpe. Of equal significance is the diversity of behavior therapy, which owes its allegiance to no one country, leader, or school of thought. In the United States, for example, one early impetus stemmed from operant conditioning and its offshoots, culminating in the rise of what later came to be known as applied behavior analysis. In the United Kingdom, British psychologists such as Eysenck and his group at the Maudsley Hospital were painstakingly developing a viable, S-R-based learning theory alternative to psychodynamic therapy. Meanwhile, in South Africa, Wolpe and his associates were coping with the problem of how to use behavioral principles in the development of a therapeutic technique that would be as effective for the verbally sophisticated, intact client as the more primitive, institutionalized mentally impaired client to whom the principles of conditioning had hitherto been applied. It was the endeavor that led to the emergence of systematic desensitization and psychotherapy by reciprocal inhibition, the nearest thing to a breakthrough in behavior therapy that has emerged to date (Wolpe, 1958).

S-R learning theory is conditioning based and the underlying Pavlovian theory is central to both psychology and politics in the Soviet Union. This might lead to the expectation that behavior therapy would be firmly established and well accepted in the USSR. In reality the opposite is true. Behavior therapy is identified by Soviet scientists with an unacceptable mechanistic materialism, whereas Soviet psychology is equated with dialectic materialism. Thus, for Soviet scientists, behavior therapy is at best a misrepresentation of reality (Franks, 1984b). This is an important point to keep in mind in any discussion of the worldwide impact of behavior therapy.

Out of such diverse beginnings grew the many faceted behavioral framework of today. There are now more than several dozen national societies dedicated exclusively to some aspect of behavior therapy. In the United States the Association for Advancement of Behavior Therapy (AABT) has almost 4,000 members and the Association for Applied Behavior Analysis is approaching a membership of 2,000. The German equivalent of the AABT is larger yet. The World Association of Behavior Therapy has already held two international congresses, in Jerusalem and Washington, D.C., and some 40 to 50 journals devoted exclusively to behavior therapy are currently published. Intensive training programs proliferate and behavior therapy is becoming an integral component of psychiatric education and the training of allied professionals (Franks, 1982).

At first impression, many techniques in behavior therapy seem to have more in common with brief and relatively directive therapies such as Ellis's (1962) rational emotive therapy, Lazarus's (1981) multimodal therapy, and Beck's (1976) cognitive therapy, than with the behavior therapy movement *per se*. Those procedures that are unique to mainstream behavior therapy—such as thought stoppage, desensitization, token economies, cognitive restructuring, contracting, and behavior rehearsal—seem to have little in common with each other. Virtually anything can be and often is classified as behavioral by the addition of the right prefix or suffix. Consider, for example, the advent of behavioral medicine, behavioral psychopharmacology, and cognitive behavior therapy. Whether it is meaningful to include this diverse assemblage under one rubric and what the commonality between them is remains open to question.

Contemporary behavior therapy may arbitrarily but conveniently be classified under four broad headings: applied behavior analysis; neobehavioristic S-R theory; social learning theory; cognitive behavior modification (Wilson & Franks, 1982). Applied behavior analysis, a direct extension of Skinner's behaviorism, relies largely on the fundamental assumption of operant conditioning that behavior is a function of its consequences. Treatment then becomes a matter of developing procedures for the modification of relationships between overt behaviors and their consequences. To accomplish these changes, applied behavior analysis makes use of techniques based on the principles of positive and negative reinforcement, punishment, extinction, stimulus control, and procedures derived primarily from laboratory research. Cognitive processes and other private events are regarded as beyond the domain of scientific analysis. Another distinguishing facet of applied behavior analysis is the remarkably ingenious methodology that has been developed for both intervention and evaluation of treatment effects. It might also be noted that applied behavior analysis is primarily concerned with the intensive study of the individual.

The neobehavioristic mediational S-R model features classical and avoidance conditioning, with principles derived from Pavlov, Skinner, Mowrer, Miller, Hull, and Eysenck, among others. Mediational variables and hypothetical constructs are given prominence. Systematic desensitization and flooding, two procedures closely associated with this model, are directed primarily toward the extinction of the underlying anxiety that is believed to maintain most disorders. Imagery and other private events, including cognitive processes and covert conditioning techniques, are integral components of this approach. All are presumed to follow the laws of learning that govern overt behavioral activities.

Social learning theory was developed largely by Bandura and his associates. Three separate but interacting regulatory systems are postulated to control behavior. These are external stimulus events, external reinforcement, and cognitive mediational processes. These cognitive mediational processes determine which environmental influences are given due attention and how they are perceived and interpreted by the individual concerned. Most important, interactions between individual and environment are reciprocal. Social learning theory is based on a reciprocal determinism model of causal processes in human functioning. Behavior, cognitive processes, and environmental factors impinge on the individual in terms of a complex interactional process that determines outcome. The emphasis in social learning theory is on the individual as the agent of change. Self-control and self-direction are integral aspects of social learning theory. Classical conditioning is recognized but operant conditioning and modeling are given greater prominence.

The fourth major approach, cognitive behavior modification, is rapidly assuming a position of preeminance in the behavioral galaxy. For some, this so-called cognitive revolution heralds a paradigm shift, a new way of formulating the very essence of behavior therapy. For others, and we tend to fall into this category, it is debatable whether behavior therapy itself, much less cognitive behavior therapy, has achieved paradigmatic status. If this be so, then it is premature to think in terms of a paradigm shift. It is our contention that, although the attention given to cognitive processes in behavior therapy is salutary, the principles and methodology involved are common to behavior therapy at large, a direct outgrowth of research and development. All behavioral procedures have elements of cognition to greater or lesser extents. What is innovative are the creative strategies that have been evolved for the measurement, monitoring, modification, and evaluation of these cognitive components of behavioral change (see Franks, 1982, for further discussion).

All four approaches share a common core of basic concepts and assumptions. In particular, there is a commitment to the methodology of the behavioral scientist and an S-R learning model of human behavior that is fundamentally different to the traditional psychodynamic, intrapsychic, and quasi-disease model of mental illness that characterizes most other systems of therapeutic intervention. In all four approaches, treatment rests on a careful behavioral assessment of the problem and the development of appropriate procedures individually tailored toward specific needs. Although past events relevant to the present situation are not neglected, the emphasis is on current determinants of behavior. It is not regarded as essential to understand the origins of a psychological problem to bring about behavior change and, by the same token, successful behavior change does not necessarily tell us about etiology.

According to Kazdin (1978a), regardless of identification, behavior therapists share the following characteristics: a focus on current rather than historical determinants of behavior; an emphasis on overt behavior change as the main criterion by which treatment is to be evaluated; the specification of treament in objective terms so as to make replication possible; the reliance on basic research in psychology as a source of hypotheses about treatment and specific therapeutic techniques; and specificity in definition, treatment, and measuring target populations.

Some Problems and Fallacies in Behavior Therapy

There are many unresolved issues in behavior therapy, of which the following are but a few.

The Behaviorism in Behavior Therapy

It is erroneous to equate all behavior therapy with behaviorism and to assume that behaviorism is a monolithic concept (Franks, 1980). At least two major kinds of behaviorism need to be identified: methodological behaviorism and metaphysical or radical behaviorism. Methodological behaviorism is mediational, often mentalistic and inferential. It frequently employs hypothetico-deductive methodology and group designs. By contrast, metaphysical behaviorism deemphasizes mental states. It is nonmediational, antimentalistic, never inferential, and favors induction over hypothesis testing. Single-subject designs with repeated measurments are the preferred strategies of the metaphysical behaviorist. Understandably, the majority of practicing behavior therapists today are methodological behaviorists—because the dismissal of all cognitive and covert processes would necessarily lead to a rejection of virtually all current behavior therapy procedures. Be this as it may, metaphysical or radical behaviorism in its many forms is still in favor in certain circles (e.g., Fordyce, 1976; Rachlin, in press).

Then there are the less practice relevant but philosophically important related issues of the roles of determinism and self-control in behavior therapy. For many behavior therapists, a major goal of therapy is the development of some form of self-control in which the individual concerned is in command. For other behavior therapists, this is an illusion and there is no such thing as either a self or self-control. We know of no experimental procedure for a definitive resolution of these problems. Ultimately, it becomes a matter of philosophical preference.

The Importance of Conditioning in Behavior Therapy

For many behavior therapists, classical and operant conditioning in conjunction with some form of modeling is still the core of their therapeutic armamentarium. For others, any experimentally valid strategy is acceptable provided that it satisfies the canons of scientific inquiry. This diminished reliance on the principles of conditioning, either classical or operant, stems in part from the failure to demonstrate either general factors of conditionability or the central position occupied by conditioning mechanisms in behavioral change. When conditioning is suspect, the role of S-R learning theory in behavior therapy becomes open to question.

Other lesser, still unresolved but important issues in beahvior therapy pertain to the validity and usefulness of trait theory and the appropriateness of a dimensional model. With the notable exception of Eysenck and his followers (e.g., Eysenck, 1976) there are now few trait theorists in behavior therapy and it is a modified version of the notion of behavioral specificity that holds the day.

Another and closely related issue is the usefulness of personality as a concept in behavior therapy. Some behavior therapists make major use of personality theory and others reject the concept completely. Similar disagreements pertain to the relative impact of environmental as contrasted with constitutional or genetic influences. For some behavior therapists. behavior change is attributable entirely to some form of learning process and genetic influences are regarded as minimal. Others take quite the opposite point of view.

Given this diversity there can be no universally accepted definition of behavior therapy. Early notions about the nature of behavior therapy were elegantly simple. For example, in 1959, Eysenck defined behavior therapy in terms of the application of the "laws of modern learning theory" and let it rest at that. Since then a variety of increasingly complex definitions of behavior therapy have arisen, each stressing a favorite theory or principle of learning. Epistemologists characterize behavior therapy in terms of methodology rather than any allegiance to a specific unifying theory or set of principles. But this freedom carries with it the risk of failing to capture the uniqueness of whatever it is that behavior therapists do. By contrast, more doctrinaire definitions stress specific psychological principles and reject all others. But, in so doing, much of contemporary behavior therapy becomes excluded.

The definition of behavior therapy currently advocated by the Association for Advancement of Behavior Therapy is so broad that, for all practical purposes, it is nonexclusive. It reads as follows:

> Behavior therapy involves primarily the application of principles derived from research, experimental and social psychology for the alleviation of human suffering and the enhancement of human functioning. Behavior therapy involves a systematic evaluation of the effectiveness of these applications. Behavior therapy involves environmental change and social interaction rather than the direct alteration of bodily processes by biological procedures. The aim is primarily educational. The techniques facilitate improved self-control. In the conduct of behavior therapy, a contractual agreement is negotiated, in which mutually agreeable goals and procedures are specified. Responsible practitioners using behavior therapy are guided by generally accepted principles. (Franks & Wilson, 1975, p. 1)

By this definition, there is little that is not behavior therapy. Provided that the findings are data based and in accord with the canons of behavioral science, someone somewhere calls it behavior therapy. As noted in an article with a title that speaks for itself, "2081: Will We Be Many or One—or None?" behavior therapy could evolve into some highly developed entity or it could fragment into disparate fields (Franks, 1981). A narrow definition offers the advantage of ready exclusivity at the price of comprehensiveness. Conversely, a more broad-based definition, comprehensive but not exclusive, could wash out the uniqueness of behavior therapy altogether. Some would avow that this, in itself, need not necessarily be a bad thing and that, as scientists and clinicians, we are committed to understanding and the alleviation of suffering rather than doctrinaire labeling or partisanship.

The Present Status of Behavior Therapy

Behavior therapy is now in its third decade. If the first decade was characterized by ideology and polemics, and the second by consolidation, the present decade is the era of sophisticated methodology, innovative models, conceptual soul searching, and a quest for new horizons. Increasingly, while clinicians grapple with the resolution of everyday practical problems, attention is given to the consideration, if not necessarily the resolution, of problems such as those previously outlined. There are numerous other issues that could be discussed were this a book rather than a section of one chapter. For example, there is the ongoing debate about the possibility of rapprochement between behavior therapy and psychoanalysis—a position that we find untenable (see Franks, 1984). Then there is the problem of the increasing divergence between what behavior therapists actually do in clinical practice and what they write about and claim to be doing. The list is almost endless.

Some Misconceptions about Behavior Therapy

Perhaps because of the past behavior of a small number of behavior therapists, misconceptions about behavior therapy still arise in certain professional and lay circles. Fortunately, with increasing public sophistication and more mindful attention to their image by behavior therapists, these faulty notions are assuming increasingly less significance (see Franks & Barbrack, 1983, for a more extended discussion of these and related matters).

Among the more widely held misconceptions and their refutation are the following.

1. Behavior therapy is neither a superficial nor a symptomatic form of treatment. Certainly, the notion of underlying psychodynamic causes that have to be understood before specific problems can be corrected is alien to behavior therapy. But this does not mean that behavior therapists focus naively or exclusively on presenting symptoms *per se*. The sophisticated behavior therapist will make a thorough, detailed, and probing behavioral analysis of all possible determining contingencies prior to the development of a specific program for intervention. Throughout the intervention process, assessment and evaluation go hand in hand. As the incoming data dictate, the intervention strategy is modified accordingly. It is this continuous process of monitoring, evaluation, and strategic modification that characterizes contemporary behavior therapy, making it a far cry from the simplistic caricature evoked by its critics.

2. Behavior therapy as currently practiced is not an approach that rejects or even deemphasizes the importance of cognitive processes and other covert events. What the contemporary behavior therapist does attempt is the understanding of these processes within a framework that lends itself to scientific formulation (see the *Annual Review of Behavior Therapy* for a more detailed discussion of the changing scene vis-à-vis cognition and behavior therapy over the years).

3. Behavior therapy is neither mechanistic nor impersonal. The therapist–patient relationship is important in contemporary behavior therapy. The difference is that in behavior therapy there is an attempt to understand these relationships in behavioral terms and

thereby suggest ways in which they can be enhanced to facilitate therapeutic benefit. In so doing, it is important that the behavior therapist be emphathetic, ethical, humane, and warm. Behavior therapy is not a Machiavellian approach to society in which the goal is unidirectional influence over a client's behavior. Contemporary behavior therapy is characterized by an openness in which the goals of therapy are constantly discussed and reappraised as part of a process of mutual collaboration between therapist and client. The client has to be an informed participant in the therapeutic process and the goals of treatment subject to reevaluation as the therapy proceeds.

Conclusions

Such then is a brief overview of behavior therapy, its problems and its status. In less than three decades, behavior therapy has evolved from the status of a radical fringe alternative to an indisputable part of the therapeutic establishment. The appeal of behavior therapy as currently practiced is to those who prefer a coherent conceptual framework to a melange of intuition, anecdotal evidence, and personal endorsement. If behavior therapy has not become the single wave of the future that was predicted in a surge of enthusiasm by early behavior therapists, neither has it suffered the early demise that its enemies had gleefully foretold. What behavior therapy lacks as yet is some consistent and meaningful model or image of humanity, but then this lack is conspicuous in most therapeutic systems. If behavior therapy has not reached adulthood it seems to have progressed beyond the stage of adolescence and to have achieved merited respectability in the therapeutic arena. It should be noted, finally, that behavior therapy is still a relatively young psychological discipline and that learning theory itself is not very old. To expect definitive conclusions in such a new field when physics and chemistry have failed to do so after 2,000 years seems unreasonable. When all is said, and occasionally even done, it seems appropriate to conclude that, in one form or another, behavior therapy is here to stay. It is with this background that we turn now to a more detailed discussion of the matter at hand, namely the relevance of all of this for the educative process.

Obstacles to the Rise of Behavior Therapy in Educational Settings

Early applications of behavior modification to education emphasized enhancement of instructional outcomes (Gray, 1932). Skinner (1954, 1961, 1963) stressed the importance of interactive methods of instruction, and developed what he and his associates termed the experimental analysis of behavior as a means of ensuring interaction in the teaching-learning process. Early applications of operant learning theory with developmentally disabled children (e.g. Ferster, 1961; Orlando & Bijou, 1960) provided clear evidence that learning could be enhanced by manipulating consequences and contingencies of reinforcement. Although the emphasis on interaction was critical to teaching efforts with both handicapped and nonhandicapped learners, an understanding of the reciprocal effect of learner behavior on subsequent teacher behavior was only in its infancy. It was for future workers to determine the effects of target behavior change on the collateral behavior of the learner, on the behavior of peers, and the behavior of the instructor.

In those early, halcyon days, learning outcomes received considerable attention. The explication of applied behavior analysis techniques that were successful in increasing academic and prosocial behavior as well as decreasing undesirable behavior led to increased research activity in educational settings. However, availability of these techniques and clear demonstrations of their effectiveness did not lead to wholesale adoption, or even endorsement, by the educational community at large. In fact, with the noteworthy exception of the education of severely handicapped children, the process of change and rate of acceptance of behavioral psychology in education has been slower than might be expected given these early and dramatic successes. Possible reasons for this slow rate of change include the perceived arrogance of applied behavior analysts (see Baer & Bushnell, 1981), the absence of sufficient "system pain" to motivate change, and the absence of an ecological/systems perspective (Keogh, 1981). On a more encouraging note, according to some behavioral school psychologists and special educators, the perceived desirability of behavioral techniques and actual use of behavioral interventions in the schools have increased. Nevertheless, all of these factors represent possibly significant impediments to change within the organization and elaboration is warranted.

Perceived Arrogance

Since the mid- to late 1960s, behavioral interventions in educational settings have become widespread. As the number of proponents grew, so too grew the clamor that change was not coming quickly enough. Behavior analysts argued that they had a research basis to support changes in both the mission and method of education (Baer & Bushnell, 1981; Barlow, 1984; Bijou, 1970). Behavior analysts presented evidence that their methods could be used efficiently and effectively to enhance academic learning and teach prosocial behavior to children, and to teach teachers to use their own naturally occuring behavior to enhance learning (Baer & Bushnell, 1981). Spokespersons for behavioral applications to education promised positive outcomes and continued to demonstrate the means to achieve these outcomes in professional publications. When acceptance of the mission and method of applied behavior analysis by the educational community was not completely forthcoming, behavior therapists in education became polarized away from the mainstream.

System Pain

For change to be contemplated, perceived need for change must be experienced by individuals in the organization. Moreover, these individuals must have access to and credibility in the organizational system to translate their perceptions of need into policy changes and subsequent action (Liberman, 1983). These individuals must also have sufficient authority to motivate the organization to change (Liberman, 1979).

Schools are social organizations. They rely on collaborative, interdependent relationships between administrators, faculty, related services professionals, support staff, members of boards of education, local government officials, parents, and students. The introduction of new educational ideas or techniques implies a change in these basic relationships inasmuch as each of these individuals is involved in the delivery, receipt, or advocacy of educational services. However, the unique nature of schools as organized social systems creates two special problems for change that are different from those experienced by other organizational structures (e.g., businesses, for-profit hospitals): schools are less vulnerable to the effects of competition, and more vulnerable to community pressures on a day-to-day basis (Schmuck, 1982). For the most part, public schools do not have to compete with one another to remain viable. Their existence is guaranteed by legislative action and social mores. The absence of market forces allows educators in the school system to resist change if such change violates cherished philosophical, cultural, and social values.

Day-to-day problems and pressures from students, parents, and board of education members lead to different, more acutely felt system pain. Educators tend to respond much more quickly to the disequilibrium created by short-term crises. Their goals in responding to such crises are to quell the disturbance, satisfy the concerned parties, and get back to the business of teaching. However, these short-term crises are rarely of sufficient duration or magnitude to require major shifts in the educative process. Moreover, as members of an organizational system, school personnel would implicitly seek to maintain the structure, content, and process characteristic of the school before the crisis arose. This process can be explained in terms of the homeostatic pressure that living systems exert on themselves (Miller, 1978), or as a function of the absence of a change in the contingencies of reinforcement. Only increases in the magnitude or duration of demands for change, with the concomitant disequilibrium and explicit threat of changes in the contingencies of reinforcement, are likely to create sufficient system pain to motivate permanent changes in the form and function of the educative process. The impetus for change can arise from various levels. But it is not clear that those persons involved in administration, teaching, or advocacy feel sufficiently dissatisfied with current educational practices to demand large-scale change.

The special circumstances created by lack of competition as a motivator for change, coupled with inertia caused by attempting to maintain the homeostatic balance of the school as an organization, impede organizational development. Thus, the "special problem" faced by behavioral psychology in the schools is not really so special at all. One need only recall the educational system's resistance to the introduction of System of Multicultural Pluralistic Assessment (SOMPA, Mercer, 1973), the research from developmental psychology relevant to teaching, and to the overwhelming evidence that many severely handicapped children could learn, to recognize that the plight of behavior modification in the schools has as much to do with the school as an organizational system as with the efficacy of behavioral interventions (Franks, 1984a).

Ecological/Systems Perspective

Behavior therapy, particularly applied behavior analysis, has been rightly criticized for its lack of an ecological or systems perspective (Keogh, 1981; Powers & Handleman, 1984; Willems, 1974). School psychologists and educators using behavioral methods have been justifiably assailed for not giving sufficient consideration to the organizational aspects of schools, teachers' attitudes and perceptions related to the interventions, and the collateral effects of behavioral interventions (Keogh, 1981). Maher, Illback, and Zins (1985) extended the principles and methods of organizational behavior management to educational settings. The social validation of behavioral outcomes is an important advance in accounting for the perceptions of relevant others (parents, teachers) vis-à-vis the acceptability of those outcomes (Runco & Schreibman, 1983; Wolf, 1978). In similar fashion, Wahler (1975), Evans (1985), and Voeltz and Evans' (1982) work on behavioral interrelationships expand the scope of applied behavior analysis.

Unfortunately, these advances are not in widespread use in educational settings. Once again, behavioral educators and school psychologists have failed to adopt a systems perspective. In a thought-provoking paper, Baer and Bushnell (1981) argued that we should begin to apply behavior analysis procedures to society, investigating the manner in which findings from social science are applied and integrated into accepted practice. This may be a right approach as long as the investigation process includes different levels of analysis. In this way we might gain access to the social and organizational factors that motivate change and stagnation in schools.

These three reasons for less than optimal use of behavior therapy in the schools—perceived arrogance, the absence of system pain, and the failure to adopt a systems perspective—are interdependent and change in any one will reverberate through the educational system. We have available the models for understanding and the methods for implementation. In some ways the problem, how to apply behavioral approaches to education, is part of the solution. Behavior therapy provides many of the techniques for analyzing the effects of interventions as long as the questions asked have the flexibility to address a variety of levels within the school system.

Behavior Therapy and the Educative Process

Several areas in behavior therapy have special relevance to the educative process. Some relate directly to the enhancement of instructional outcomes. Others address educational process, organizational factors, and policy issues relevant to the acceptance and use of behavior therapy in educational settings.

Social Validity

Behavior therapists rely on empirically derived, observable data as a basis for clinical and educational decision making. Historically, significantly less emphasis has been placed on the social and clinical importance of intervention. In time, however, it became clear that persons not directly involved in treatment planning and execution, for example, teachers and parents, were evaluating the effects of behavioral interventions by different standards. Frequently, their evaluations directly affected project continuation and access to resources. Behavior analysts had demonstrated that they could deliver the goods (if allowed to control the contingencies), but had neglected to ask whether the goods were acceptable as delivered.

In recent years, behavior therapists and educators have attempted to rectify this problem by social validation and attention to consumer satisfaction. Do behavioral interventions produce changes that are also clinically and socially important? Three areas merit consideration in response to this question: (a) treatment goals or target behavior selection; (b) treatment procedures; and (c) effects of treatment (Wolf, 1978), including collateral positive changes in nontarget behaviors and negative effects. Numerous investigators have assessed the social acceptability of their interventions. By addressing the perceived clinical importance of behavioral interventions, therapists and educators will insure that their decisions, means, and end results are congruent with community standards (see Kent & O'Leary, 1976; Minkin *et al.*, 1976; Runco & Schreibman, 1983; Schreibman, Koegel, Mills & Burke, 1981).

Target behavior selection is important in behavior therapy (Kratochwill, 1985a). Moreover, the domain for selection of targets has expanded from the assessment of discrete, unitary behaviors to a systems approach (Evans, 1985; Mash, 1985). This change in focus is of significance for two reasons: first, schools are highly visible settings that may be scrutinized more closely than other public institutions. Their primary mission is the preparation of the young to be productive adult members of society. Second, community norms are local issues (Thurman & Fiorelli, 1979). Parents, teachers, and members of boards of education have implicit and explicit goals for their children's education. In some communities these goals are vocationally oriented, in others the emphasis is more on higher education. Thus, target behaviors selected for intervention must conform in some rational way to community standards. Further, these targets must be seen as socially significant and appropriate to the educational setting.

Van Houten (1979) described two methods for developing standards of competency against which target behavior selection and treatment efficacy can be compared: norm-based and experimentally based selection. Norm-based selection involves the identification of highly competent models and a determination of their levels of performance on given target behaviors. These performance criteria then become the standards against which the interventions are socially validated.

For example, having teachers and principal identify a seventh-grade male with superior conversational skills and then assessing the various verbal and nonverbal component behaviors of conversational skills (e.g., requesting elaborations, eye-contact with the speaker) provides an objective standard against which to evaluate the social validity of the intervention. By using a community-chosen global standard, social acceptability is ensured. By identifying component behaviors of the global target behavior, a more objective measure of social validation can be obtained. Indeed, the use of norms with direct observations may enhance the power of each as an assessment method (Nelson & Bowles, 1975).

The selection of standards of competence through experimentally based means utilizes two methods. The first involves the experimental manipulation of the target behavior across a wide range of responses, and a determination of the point at which relevant others deem the target behavior maximally useful. The second involves an examination of the effects of training a child to various behavioral standards on the acquisition of other, more difficult skills (Van Houten, 1979). In this way, the possibility of incidental learning or overlearning is addressed, and the problem of premature termination of training in preparatory skills (which themselves subsequently effect the acquisition of more complex behavior) is avoided.

Taken together, these procedures suggest that the social validation of target behaviors be viewed as an iterative process (Van Houten, 1979). That is, the process of using subjective and normative judgments with global evaluations leads to the specification of competency criteria and treatment levels for appropriate (i.e., socially valid) target behaviors. Notable examples exist of the use of social validation with junior high school students (Minkin *et al.*, 1976), autistic children (Runco & Schreibman, 1983), and mentally retarded adults (Vogelsberg & Rusch, 1979).

When evaluating the effects of behavioral interventions, two methods are relevant: social comparison and subjective evaluation (Kazdin, 1977). Social comparison involves the identification of nonimpaired peers who are similar to the client in subject and demographic variables. The client is subsequently compared to this normative standard to determine treatment effects. Subjective evaluation provides a global judgment as to whether the behavior changes observed are perceived as important by persons with whom the client interacts.

Social validation is an efficient method for determining the subjective impressions of significant others on target behavior selection, procedures, and treatment effects. When used with appropriate limitations (cf. Kazdin, 1982; Rusch, 1979; Wolf, 1978) it provides synthetic validity (Anastasi, 1976) for objectively derived data. By complementing traditional behavioral assessment techniques, social validation allows interventions to be evaluated against therapeutic and experimental criteria (Risley, 1970), thereby enhancing the value and generality of results obtained.

Implications for Education

Schools are social settings. They are scrutinized by parents and taxpayers, and evaluated by state departments of education. Their policies and procedures are reviewed by many for conformity to educational, philosophical, and social standards. Given that behavior modification is an often misunderstood discipline (see Pumroy, 1984; Woolfolk, Woolfolk, & Wilson, 1977), behavioral psychologists and educators are especially at risk for errors of social validity. Some of these risk factors are doubtless the results of confusion among educational administrators between philosophical issues and subsequent educational policy as contrasted with scientific issues (e.g., "We don't allow the use of punishment in our schools"). Others are caused by misunderstandings of behavior modification. Still others result from the fact that few teacher training programs provide didactic and supervised practicum experiences in the application of behavior therapy to education. These risk factors often lead to problems in application and acceptance. One solution is to educate others through teacher-training programs, in-service training, and direct example. Failures of social validation, however, are errors of omission for which the behavior therapist must assume responsibility. In some quarters, the judicious use of behavior modification techniques is merely tolerated, in others it is encouraged. Irrespective of acceptability it is incumbent on the behavioral psychologist and educator to determine which target behaviors, which intervention procedures, and which outcomes are perceived as socially valid for any given community.

Problems may exist when attempting social validation techniques with special populations. For example, the identification of a normative group for social comparison purposes with developmentally disabled students might be difficult. For children with severe developmental disabilities the task is even harder. In such cases, social comparison may be inappropriate, and subjective evaluation sufficient. Documenting that the target behavior is clinically important and that other less restrictive interventions fail to produce socially valid treatment gains may be the best one can do.

Sole reliance on the opinions of others (parents, teachers) for the selection of socially valid target behaviors and subsequent levels of those behaviors should be approached cautiously. Referrals for assistance in classroom child management are made by teachers, parents, or administrators. Thus, the likelihood exists that prospective targets for intervention will reflect the biases and values of the referral agent rather than the school or community as a social system. The facile assumption by the behavioral psychologist that the target behavior is socially valid because the referral source is a socially significant other may be erroneous. Further checking (with other teachers or administrators or children) may prove helpful.

Despite research showing that the opposite is more likely true (Kazdin, 1977), referral agents may erroneously assume that appropriate deportment in the classroom is a necessary precursor to academic achievement. This might lead to requests to increase various nonacademic classroom behaviors (e.g., staying in one's seat, remaining on task) rather than to increase academic performance. School referral agents may require guidance to ensure that the target behavior of most importance—that is, with the greatest social validity—is not misidentified.

When attempting to determine the social validity of a procedure one must first determine whom to approach. Conceivably, teachers, parents, administrators, and other children could be included. Some of these groups will have personal, sometimes predictable, agenda (imagine asking a "law-and-order" principal about the social validity of reducing shouting in a junior high school physical education class). In certain situations a homogeneous sample may be optimal, in others heterogeneity may be more appropriate.

Social validation of behavior therapy with the developmentally disabled warrants special consideration. Public Law 94:142 mandates the delivery of educational programs within the least restrictive environment for students eligible for special educational services. This mandate has been expanded to cover educational interventions, particularly behavior-reduction procedures. The least restrictive interventions should be tried before more invasive interventions are attempted. Although few individuals would have difficulty classifying behavioral procedures at the extremes on a continuum of restrictiveness (e.g., verbal reprimand vs. electric shock), subtler distinctions need to be made as one moves toward the midpoint. Moreover, continua are based on local norms, and variations in procedural placement will occur across community lines. What is needed are social validation data for various behavioral procedures and a determination of the social appropriateness of particular procedures for specific target behaviors. Although research exists demonstrating the social validity of various target behaviors and treatment outcomes for the developmentally disabled (cf. Runco & Schreibman, 1983; Schreibman, *et al.*, 1981), few studies document the social validity of the procedures used (see Schutz, Rusch, & Lamson, 1979, for a notable exception).

Educational Validity

Behavioral educators and psychologists must be prepared to document positive intervention outcomes if they wish to prosper in school settings. In the past, such documentation has borrowed heavily from methodologies developed in highly controlled laboratory settings or university-based model demonstration projects. The resources offered by these settings have often been substantial: for example, tight control over training teachers, and adequate data collectors. Although these projects advance the field, they also engender the notion that the only good design is a well-controlled, single-case design. For the practice of behavior modification in the schools, however, the imposition of clinical research methods onto applied educational problems is usually insufficient.

To address this issue, Voeltz and Evans (1983) introduced the concept of *educational validity*. Simply stated, this deals with questions of internal validity, educational integrity, and empirical and social validity of a given educational intervention. *Internal validation* is the process of determining whether observed changes in behavior have occurred as a function of the intervention offered. This is particularly important in educational settings because threats to internal validity, for example, the passage of time, intervention interference, adventitious reinforcement, punishment and modeling, are built-in to the educative process. Controlling these threats requires an expanded view of experimental interventions in educational settings. For example, Voeltz and Evans (1983) argued that educational interventions are typically not planned unless it is clear that the child does not have the skill and that the skill is necessary and important enough to teach. If this be so, then baseline data to indicate the absence of the behavior are superfluous. Time series analyses utilizing data probes across relevant environments are sufficient.

Teachers rarely have either the time or facilities to collect adequate data. Moreover, even if they did, the use of single-case designs on (presumed) unitary, discrete behaviors presents problems. Behavioral researchers frequently ignore behavioral interrelationships in their work with children (Voeltz & Evans, 1982). Further, single-case designs—particularly multiple baseline designs—are logically inconsistent for measuring such interrelationships because they assume that all target behaviors are somehow separate and unrelated to each other. Multivariate assessment and, less formally, asking caregivers to evaluate the status of nontarget behaviors before and after treatment as part of the social validation of treatment effects, are useful beginnings to the resolution of this response-interrelationship problem (see also Evans, 1985, and Voeltz, Evans, Derer, & Hanashiro, 1983).

Educational integrity addresses the issue of procedural reliability (Billingsley, White, & Munson, 1980). That is, did the implementor of the behavioral strategy carry out the program as intended? Billingsley *et al.* found that half the teachers studied erred in their delivery of the intervention as originally written. As a consequence, the child performance data were uninterpretable. To determine interobserver reliability, procedural reliability data are essential.

Voeltz and Evans (1983) extended this concept to special educational settings. They argued that teachers must first conduct ecological, functional analyses to determine those environmental conditions that are in effect during the behavioral intervention. Monitoring teacher behavior and ecological characteristics allows the evaluator to determine whether both implementor and environmental characteristics remain constant and true to the intervention plan. The amount of instructional time teachers spend implementing the behavioral intervention to students should also be assessed. The alleged failure of a procedure has little meaning if insufficient time is alloted for its use. Finally, behavioral procedures leading to successful outcomes for large numbers of learners need to be specified so that normative data can be accumulated. By using periodic peer evaluations of teacher behavior, environmental conditions, extent of programming time, and an aggregate of normative experiences with given interventions, judgments about educational integrity are possible within the realistic constraints of the educational system.

As noted earlier, *social validation* refers to the process of determining whether behavior change is meaningful to significant persons in a child's life. Moreover, skills taught must be functional and valued in the environment in which the child is expected to perform (Liberty, Haring, & Martin, 1981). Voeltz and Evans (1983) also suggested that *empirical validity*—whether the treatment will be beneficial to the student's eventual outcome—must be satisfied for a treatment program to be educationally valid. Interventions offered handicapped students must reflect appropriate developmental sequelae, but must also address the criterion of ultimate functioning (those functional skills needed by a handicapped adult to function as independently as possible in community settings). Christian and Luce (1985) added that ultimate training goals must also take into account generalization and maintenance across environments and environmental agents (i.e., teachers, parents, peers).

Educational validation is an important advance in the delivery of behavior therapy to children in schools. By emphasizing educational settings that differ from clinical environments, internal, experimental, and social validity and procedural reliability assure practical relevance.

Developmental Psychology and Child Behavior Therapy: Implications for the Educative Process

Harris and Ferrari (1983) documented the importance of developmental bases in the behavioral treatment of phobias and attention deficit disorder. The plasticity of child behavior, the social validity of certain age-appropriate behaviors, and parental perceptions based on parental developmental levels are all of direct relevance to the treatment process. Kendall, Lerner, and Craighead (1984) added that assumed homogeneity is imprudent. It obscures the fact that each child possesses varying cognitive, emotional, social, and behavioral abilities and capacities. Child behavioral assessment demands consideration of these domains as well as other environmental factors and is thus less effected by the criticism of Kendall *et al.* than other schools of intervention (Mash & Terdal, 1981).

Developmental psychology has much to offer child behavior therapy as applied to educational settings. In this respect, four areas within developmental psychology are noteworthy: diagnosis, assessment, treatment selection, and potential contributions from developmental psychopathology.

Diagnosis

Increasingly, child behavior therapists are recognizing the need to use a formal diagnostic framework, typically the *Diagnostic and Statistical Manual of Mental Disorders, Third Edition* (DSM-III; American Psychiatric Association, 1980). Educators, however, have been slower to adopt this diagnostic framework, relying instead on those categorical educational classifications required by state departments of education for special education placement and funding purposes. Both processes have similar goals: to provide nomothetic descriptions of a child upon which to base treatment decisions. Both approaches emphasize syndromal diagnosis. Certain behaviors that co-occur in a clinical presentation are grouped together and labeled (e.g., overanxious disorder, educably mentally retarded). Nomothetic data derived from syndromal diagnosis are valuable signposts for the further behavioral (idiographic) assessment of childhood problems. Moreover, the integration of nomothetic considerations from syndromal diagnosis with idiographic data gathered during behavioral assessment may enhance the clinical utility of each (Powers, 1984).

Unfortunately, diagnostic frameworks tend to underemphasize developmental issues. Although DSM-III makes scattered references to developmental factors in diagnostic decision making (Harris & Powers, 1984), it fails to acknowledge the importance of chronological age, cognitive development, and psychosexual development in any meaningful way (Kazdin, 1983). Because of their reliance on norm-referenced tests for diagnostic purposes, educational diagnosticians fare somewhat better. However, they too fall prey to the error of assumed homogeneity (Kendall *et al.*, 1984) when selecting special education placements.

Edelbrock (1984) proposed a normative-developmental perspective on diagnosis and assessment. By evaluating behavior against a normative group, more precise measures of deviance are obtained. It is important to document qualitative and quantitative changes in behavior over time. The Child Behavior Profile (Achenbach & Edelbrock, 1983) is a valid and reliable method for providing normative comparisons, assessing differences based on age, and determining response interrelationships within diagnostic subgroups.

Placing a behavior in behavioral and chronological contexts thereby facilitates appropriate treatment decisions. Where the child's behavior falls within the normative range, the opportunity exists to help parents or other referral agents modify their unrealistic expectations of child behavior. Such a perspective allows behavioral educators to evaluate a child's awareness of, and method of coping with, various age-appropriate developmental tasks (Srouf & Rutter, 1984).

Assessment

Child behavioral assessment has been described as a multimethod approach for gathering information about behavior using empirically validated and developmentally sensitive procedures (Ollendick & Hersen, 1984). The importance of a developmental basis for the behavioral assessment of children has been emphasized for developmentally disabled learners (Powers, 1984) and nonhandicapped individuals (Kendall *et al.*, 1984), a point made repeatedly in the *Annual Review of Behavior Therapy*

Behavioral assessment has a two-fold purpose: (a) to provide predictive information with respect to the potential efficacy of one intervention over another, and (b) to monitor and evaluate the effects of the intervention once implemented.

For Carr and Durand (1985a), some behavioral problems of children serve a communicative function. Drawing from research in pragmatics, a branch of psycholinguistics, these authors suggest that attention seeking and escape behavior are socially motivated and thereby serve a communicative function. Thus, Carr and Durand (1985b) taught four children socially acceptable verbal communications for soliciting positive attention or assistance from adults. High rates of functional communication and low rates of problem behavior were obtained by differentially reinforcing functional communication. Removing the functional utility of the communicative response led to increases in the problem behaviors.

This work demonstrates the importance of communicative function in maintaining disruptive behavior and the need to assess the function of the behavior prior to intervening. Unfortunately, most individuals working in educational settings will not have sufficient resources to conduct motivational analyses with high degrees of internal validity. A more practical solution would be to use the Motivation Assessment Scale of Durand and Crimmins (1983) to determine the conditions motivating disruptive behavior and subsequent behavioral treatments.

Assessing behavior problems prior to intervention necessitates consideration of contextual and temporal bases of the behavior (Mash & Terdal, 1981) and the use of multiple sources of data (Powers & Handleman, 1984). The assessor must take special care to understand the reciprocally determined nature of the child's behavior and refrain from describing the problem as residing solely "within" the child, teacher, parent, or environment. Rather, behavioral assessment should include the child's developmental status as a stimulus to others and as a processor of information, and the child as an agent, shaper and selector of change (Kendall *et al.*, 1984). Thus, the behavioral educator would consider: (a) physical and behavioral characteristics and the reactions and feedback from others to those characteristics, (b) present developmental status in cognitive, social, and emotional spheres, (c) the child's predictably upcoming developmental events and their potential influences, and (d) the child's ability to evaluate the particular demands of an upcoming developmental task and goodness-of-fit, psychologically and behaviorally, to meet those demands and perceive himself or herself as flexible and competent. The assessment of earlier developmental tasks maladaptively or discontinuously mastered might also be relevant to treatment planning (Sroufe & Rutter, 1984).

Children exhibit great plasticity of behavior, cognition, and affect. Thus, when assessing the effects of intervention over time one must remain mindful of the child's individual developmental trajectory, that is, the rate, pace, and manner in which developmental tasks are confronted and overcome or not overcome (Kendall *et al.*, 1984). The behavioral educator also has to face the dilemma of choosing whether to use the same measurement device throughout treatment despite the possibility that, because of changing developmental status, it may be measuring different things at different points in the treatment process (Baltes, Reese, & Nesselroade, 1977).

Special attention must also be paid to the collateral behavior of relevant others. Some traditional single-case designs, particularly the multiple baseline, obfuscate the effect of behavior on other relevant behaviors (Voeltz & Evans, 1982). Social learning theory purists would further argue that such designs are incompatible with one of their theoretical bedrocks, namely reciprocal determinism. Particularly in educational contexts, Voeltz and Evans' (1982, 1983) solutions rest on the more judicious use of single-case designs.

One solution to potential problems caused by rapidly changing developmental status has been proposed by Kendall *et al.* (1984) and Nelson and Bowles (1975). Treatment effects could be evaluated through the use of such multiple measures as direct observation, behavioral rating scales, and developmentally based normative rating scales. Change, when produced, would then be evaluated further against control children. Such an approach serves a dual purpose. The effects of the immediate intervention are evaluated, and normative developmental data would become available for potential aggregation with other studies using similar populations and similar interventions.

Treatment Selection

An individual's affective, behavioral, cognitive, and physical status determines which interventions may be effective, inefficient, or otherwise contraindicated (Sroufe, 1979). For example, Higa, Tharp, and Calkins (1978) found that children below age 6 may lack the prerequisite cognitive and verbal abilities (particularly comparing one's own behavior to a standard) required for the successful use of self-monitoring techniques. Similarly, McCandless and Marshall (1957) found that children under age 6 did not have the abstraction or reading skills to evaluate the sociometric status of peers. Presentation of rosters in pictorial form was more successful in obtaining valid and reliable measures. These studies suggest that children of different ages understand and experience the same event differently depending on a variety of organismic and interactional factors. Cognizance of these factors should contribute to the more effective individualization of treatment efforts by behavioral educators.

Research in developmental psychology can be very pertinent to educational settings. For example, Schleser, Cohen, Meyers, and Rodick (1984) found that 6-year-olds with the cognitive capacity for concrete operational thought learned and generalized self-instructional strategies significantly better than preoperational children. These results suggest that cognitive capacity be considered as a relevant developmental moderator of treatment outcome. Indeed, Kendler and Kendler (1962) suggested that the critical period for the development of mediational thinking—an essential component of self-instructional training—is age 5 to 7.

In their review of social and affective interventions with preschool-age children, Elias, Clabby, Ottaviano, and Kovaleski (1983) listed developmental tasks to consider in treatment programs designed for this group. These include development of (a) basic trust in the environment; (b) expectations of competence; and (c) the ability to balance frustrations and conflict with awareness of successes and competence. Elias *et al.* emphasized the need to incorporate these developmental tasks into intervention plans, and provide guidelines to this end (see also Eisenberg & Harris, 1984).

Katz, Kellerman, and Siegel (1980) identified a relationship between age and different behavioral and cognitive manifestations of anxiety in children with cancer. Older children expressed anxiety through descriptions of pain and muscle rigidity, whereas younger children expressed their anxiety through crying, screaming, and requesting restraint. Such findings could shed light on the appropriateness of muscle relaxation as a component of systematic desensitization with young children (see Kendall *et al.*, 1984).

Normative developmental data may provide useful criteria against which to compare child behavior prior to treatment selection. For example, school phobia most commonly occurs upon entry into school or after transitions in school or grade placement (Ollendick & Mayer, 1983). Awareness of this normative developmental sequence may help the behavioral educator to decide on the type and focus of treatment. Thus, rather than relying exclusively on the presumed social validity of the target behavior, the behavioral educator should be guided by both developmental markers and empirically validated treatments.

Developmental Psychopathology

Developmental psychopathology is defined as "the study of the origins and course of individual patterns of behavioral maladaptation" without regard to age of onset, cause, developmental pattern, or change in behavioral manifestation (Sroufe & Rutter, 1984, p. 18). More specifically, developmental psychopathology is concerned with the study of disordered behavior, relationships to nondisordered behavior, the origins of pathological behavior that do not evince until adulthood, and the time course, manifestations, antecedents, and sequelae of psychopathology. By providing descriptive data about the natural course, associated behavior changes, and sequelae of child psychopathology, developmental psychopathologists contribute an expanded perspective in which to understand and evaluate the behavior of children in schools.

That developmental psychopathologists seek to relate deviant behavior to nondisordered behavior is of special relevance to behavioral educators. This attention to a normative developmental base against which gradients of behavior can be compared permits the adjunctive use of such valid and reliable psychometric measures as the Child Behavior Profile (Achenbach & Edelbrock, 1983) and the Kaufman Assessment Battery for Children (Kaufman & Kaufman, 1983) in the determination of behavioral interrelationships and learning styles in these children.

If developmental psychopathology is to provide useful guidelines for the behavioral treatment of childhood problems, certain basic tenets of developmental psychology (Santostefano, 1978; Sroufe & Rutter, 1984) have to be reconciled with contemporary behavior therapy:

1. Behavior can be understood only within the larger psychological and behavioral contexts in which it is embedded. Although this ecological or systems view is consonant with some contemporary behavioral theorists (cf. Schwartz, 1982; Willems, 1977), it is eschewed by others (cf. Baer, 1974). Recent work on behavioral interrelationships (Voeltz & Evans, 1982), a systems model for target behavior selection (Evans, 1985), and the biobehavioral nature of chronic pain (Schwartz, 1982) are important advances in the move toward conceptual congruence with developmental theorists.

2. Throughout development, earlier forms of behavior become embedded within more complex forms of behavior, yet still remain potentially active. Thus, the concept of stage-related behavior is misleading in that earlier methods of coping, still available for use, may become manifest in periods of extraordinary stress or where stimulus conditions are insufficient to occasion the performance of more complex forms of behavior. The development of the capacity to be flexible—being able to adapt to the environment, or to change the environment—engenders competence (Block, 1982). Such perceived competence further solidifies new, learned behavioral repertoires and increases the likelihood of future performance of those behaviors.

For contemporary behavior therapists, acceptance of this proposition involves expansion of the concept of learning histories, those previous behavioral repertoires, stimulus and reinforcement events of a child's past that may impact on present behavior. To utilize research in developmental psychology fully, earlier cognitive styles, emotional characteristics, and the effects of previous physical conditions on the development of earlier behavior need to be considered together with behavioral responses learned under various stimulus conditions.

3. Behavioral organization increases in flexibility over time. As the child develops, awareness of multiple methods to achieve different goals expands. With increasing awareness comes the potential for added behavioral flexibility and adaptation. This is as important as more appropriate outcome measures (i.e., probes in a time series) that are better tailored and more forgiving of the multiplicity of conditions present in a classroom during behavioral treatments (Voeltz & Evans, 1983). Moreover, linear methods of tracking a behavior over several conditions of treatment may prove insufficient to document complex changes. Increasing flexibility and organization require simultaneous rather than sequential analysis. Kendall *et al.*'s (1984) suggested use of normative and observational data to evaluate treatment effects is an important step toward resolution of this problem. Kendall and Braswell (1982), for example, used normative and observational data to evaluate the effects of self-control training with children.

4. Children are active processors rather than passive reactors to environmental inputs, and remain agents, shapers, and selectors of environmental events (Kendall *et al.*, 1984; Santostefano, 1978; Sroufe, 1979). Although this may seem similar to the concept of reciprocal determinism, certain differences exist which create problems for the empirical validation of developmental change. As Sroufe and Rutter (1984) noted, development is not comprised of linear additions of new behavior, it is cumulative and interactive. Organization of new behaviors, cognitions, and

emotional states into existing repertoires occurs simultaneously with reorganization of old repertoires. A single behavior may have different meanings with each new development or in different contexts (Sroufe & Rutter, 1984). It remains to be seen whether behavioral researchers, with their emphasis on the acquisition, generalization, and maintenance of specific behaviors, will accept nonlinear measures.

5. The course of development across the lifespan is lawful. Aberrant development does not occur in a vacuum. Thus, whenever behavior therapists are concerned with past and future manifestations of a child's behavior, they are thinking developmentally.

Child Behavior Therapy: Changing Roles and Implications for Education

The educational system entrusts teachers with the twin responsibilities of evaluating and increasing academic performance, and controlling and enhancing prosocial classroom behavior. The unfortunate result has been that significant portions of teacher time are relegated to the task of behavior control, leaving less time for instruction (Lovitt, 1973).

Clinical psychology has played a formative role—along with special education, educational psychology, and counseling psychology—in the development of school psychology (Brown, 1982). In particular, child clinical psychology and the subarea of child behavior therapy have made important contributions to the amelioration of children's problems in educational settings. For example, school-based behavioral interventions for children exhibiting impulsivity (Kendall & Finch, 1978), fears and phobias (Morris & Kratochwill, 1983), poor social skills (Berler, Gross, & Drabman, 1982), and hyperactivity (O'Leary, 1980) all have their roots in child behavior therapy. To illustrate these developments and their implications for behavior modification in schools, we will consider three areas: cognitive behavior therapy, the communicative nature of disruptive behavior, and systems approaches to educating the developmentally disabled.

Cognitive Behavior Therapy

Cognitive behavior therapy aims to place behavior under the child's internal control. Procedures available include self-instruction training (Fish & Pervan, 1985), self-recording (Nelson, Lipinski, & Black, 1976), cognitive restructuring (Ollendick, 1979), modeling (Kendall & Finch, 1978), and self-reinforcement (Bolstad & Johnson, 1972). Comprehensive reviews of empirical and methodological issues have been provided elsewhere (cf. Franks & Wilson, 1973; Meador & Ollendick, 1984; O'Leary & Dubey, 1979; Rosenbaum & Drabman, 1979). The three issues to be discussed here as they relate to cognitive behavior therapy with children in schools are (a) the effects of the child as stimulus; (b) developmental factors; and (c) issues related to treatment effectiveness.

Child Effects

These are the reciprocal influences that a child's behavior exercises over the affect, cognition, or behavior of adults (Emery, Binkoff, Houts & Carr, 1983, p. 398). Researchers who adopt a systems perspective (e.g., Harris, 1983; Patterson & Fleischman, 1979; Wahler, 1980) tend to focus on the family as the relevant system of interaction. In many instances, this is appropriate. However, a systems or ecological approach to behavior therapy with children in schools should also consider the school as a system and the effects the target child's behavior during intervention has on the teacher and classroom peers. These interactions have received scant attention.

It has been hypothesized that such variables as age, IQ, attributional style, verbal ability, and cognitive style play a role in the success or failure of cognitive behavior therapy with children (Copeland, 1982). To the extent that the child brings these attributes into either the classroom *per se* or the school as a system, one can expect different teacher behaviors. The reactions of other children further complicate the scene. For example, Bugental, Collins, Collins, and Chaney (1978) provided self-instruction training to one group of hyperactive boys and teacher administered contingent social reinforcement to another. At 6-month follow-up, children given self-instruction training sustained significantly stronger attributions of personal control over behavior. However, the group of boys provided contingent social reinforcement by teachers were rated as significantly less impulsive and hyperactive by those teachers. Although not investigated in this study, child-effects in the social reinforcement groups must also be considered. The possibility of reciprocally reinforcing interactions between child and teacher cannot be disregarded. Moreover, there exists the possibility that teacher self-efficacy was enhanced by their interventions (rather than an experimenter providing the intervention). Finally, teacher attributional style and expectations of change may have influenced teachers' follow-up ratings on hyperactivity and impulsivity measures.

Emery *et al.* (1983) offered several solutions: first, perform a systems functional analysis during assessment. This involves a functional analysis of adult and child antecedent and consequent variables controlling child behavior. Second, when selecting initial target behaviors, identify those behaviors that the referring teacher finds reinforcing. In this way, teachers will be more likely to follow through with the intervention in order to bring about increases or decreases of behavior that are socially valid to them.

Developmental Factors

Increasing awareness of the role of child development in child behavior therapy has led to new interest in developmental factors associated with cognitive behavior modification. Substantial evidence for this link exists. For example, Borkowski, Levers, and Gruenfelder (1976) found that first grade children performed a learning task better when taught a cognitive mediational strategy combined with physical manipulation of the objects used in the task. A younger group, however, was unable to use this strategy to enhance performance on the same task. Their performance was enhanced by physical manipulation of the objects alone. Child behavior therapists need to consider the skills required from the child for use of a given cognitive strategy prior to application.

Luria (1961) noted that children are generally not able to use covert speech to guide overt behavior until age 5½. Various studies have investigated the effects of self-instructional training on task performance with children above and below this age cutoff. For example, Higa *et al.* (1978) found that 7-year-olds improved performance with self-instructional training whereas children under age 6 did not. These authors speculate that the dual requirement to perform the task and self-instruct may be confusing to the child. An alternative but compatible explanation is that the younger children were not yet able to make cognitive use of covert speech and that such training constituted a cognitive distraction.

Other relevant developmental factors in cognitive therapy with children include intellectual ability (Barkley, Copeland, & Sivage, 1980) and race (Genshaft & Hirt, 1979). In an early study, Ridberg, Parke, and Heatherington (1971), found that children with low IQs were more successful in modifying impulsivity when training models verbalized cognitive strategies that were used to solve a task. In contrast, high IQ children were more successful after viewing models perform the scanning strategy without verbalizing. Barkley *et al.* likewise found that children with higher mental ages were more successful with cognitive self-instructional training than their lower mental-age peers. Genshaft and Hirt (1979) found that impulsivity when responding to intellectual tasks was reduced when children were trained in self-instructional strategies by models of the same race. Unfortunately, studies of the effect of race on cognitive behavior modification are rare (cf. Copeland, 1981), and conclusions are premature.

The evidence supporting modifications in cognitive behavior therapy for children as a function of mental age is clearer. Children of lower mental age, whether by reason of chronology (e.g., preschoolers), or disability, are less likely to make effective use of cognitive mediational strategies unless the strategies are concrete and structured (Copeland, 1982). When employed, cognitive strategies with younger children should rely more on concrete exemplars (i.e., verbalization of the strategy by trainers; actual manipulation of materials) than abstract exemplars (i.e., models who are only observed to be carrying out the strategy). Children with higher cognitive levels (by virtue of age, IQ, or verbal ability) are more likely to respond to abstract and more complex self-instructional strategies (Copeland, 1982). Future studies should report chronological and mental ages as well as other relevant variables.

Issues Related to Treatment Effectiveness

Cognitive behavior therapy is of little use in the classroom unless learned strategies generalize and are maintained. Unfortunately, neither of these areas has received sufficient study to provide specific guidelines for practice. In the main, one must rely on generic guidelines for promoting generalization (cf., Stokes & Baer, 1977). The use of a generalization map (Drabman, Hammer, & Rosenbaum, 1979) to determine classes of generalization achieved might also be helpful. Stevenson and Fantuzzo (1984) provided an excellent example of the use of generalization maps with elementary school children. However, despite intuitive appeal, suggestions for enhancing generalization through the use of prompts and prompt fading (Fox & Kendall, 1983) await systematic investigation.

Various factors have been reported to exercise influence over maintenance of treatment gains in self-control training with children, including leniency of self-determined performance standards (Brownell, Coletti, Ersner-Hershfield, Hershfield, & Wilson, 1977) and self-monitoring (Nelson, Lipinski, & Boykin, 1978; Sagotsky, Patterson, & Lepper, 1978). Brownell *et al.* found that children who established more stringent performance criteria for themselves maintained their academic behaviors at a higher rate following removal of external contingencies than children adopting more lenient standards. Sagotsky *et al.* investigated a nonclinical group of elementary school children. These children successfully used self-monitoring to increase academic behavior and decrease off-task behavior. In contrast, other studies of self-assessment with problem children (Santogrossi, O'Leary, Romanczyk, & Kaufman, 1973; Turkewitz, O'Leary, & Ironsmith, 1975) found self-monitoring ineffective when used alone. When used in conjunction with other reward procedures, however, self-monitoring improves maintenance even after other procedures are withdrawn (O'Leary & Dubey, 1979).

Given the increasing interest in cognitive behavior modification among school psychologists (cf. Fish & Pervan, 1985), special care must be taken to learn from the work of child behavior therapists who have pioneered the use of this strategy and to distinguish those aspects of therapy that relate to educational settings from their clinical counterparts. On the one hand, generalization and maintenance can be confronted in a more expansive fashion in school settings because children are relatively captive for 6 hours each day. On the other hand, there are the experimental realities of educational settings: few schools have the resources to provide trained observers on an extended basis or even for briefer unobtrusive classroom observation. The school psychologist must adopt different methodological strategies, including perhaps the use of multiple time-series behavior probes over time (Voeltz & Evans, 1983) and case study research methods (Kratochwill, 1985b). One must think of intervention in the context of the total educational plan rather than as a discrete intervention. Although this presents vexing problems of control, it also opens new opportunities to study response interrelationships. Finally, teachers are but one of the variety of influential agents a child encounters over a 6-hour period. Others include bus drivers, principals, lunchroom monitors, peers, and older students in other grades. These add many potentially confounding ecological variables to the treatment plan, but they also add numerous opportunities to study success or failure in generalization and maintenance.

The Communicative Nature of Disruptive Behavior

The idea that behavior may have communicative intent is not new. Philosophers from Plato to Rousseau, family therapists (cf., Minuchin, 1974), behavioral clinicians (cf. Harris, 1983; Patterson, 1982), and observant parents have all noted the child's ability to communicate intentions through preverbal (e.g., crying) and nonverbal (e.g., tantruming) means.

Carr and Durand (1985a) proposed a theoretical basis for understanding and treating disruptive behavior in the severely developmentally disabled. Whereas it emphasizes the more severely handicapped learner, their work has clear relevance to behavioral educators treating less handicapped children.

Drawing from the fields of psycholinguistics, developmental psychology, and applied behavior analysis, Carr and Durand proposed that, when motivated by attention from others or escape/avoidance considerations, disruptive behavior in severely handicapped children may serve a communicative function. In so doing, these authors emphasized the importance of prior determination of the motivating conditions of behavior and subsequent training of a more appropriate (i.e., functional, socially valid) communication form to take the place of the disruptive behavior presently used to communicate. The newly trained communicative behavior must serve the same social function (i.e., attention, escape) as the disruptive behavior.

Empirical demonstrations of the communicative hypothesis are available. Durand and Carr (1982) determined that self-injurious behavior (SIB) in three developmentally disabled children was motivated either by attention or escape from demands. When the children were taught communicative behaviors that were discrepant in form but identical in function, rates of SIB decreased to near zero levels. In a related study, Carr and Durand (1985b) developed an assessment protocol for identifying conditions motivating tantrums, aggressions, and SIB in developmentally disabled children. Treatment emphasized the differential reinforcement of more appropriate communicative responses, and successfully suppressed targeted behavior problems in all children. Maintenance and generalization of learned communicative responses and concurrent suppression of SIB was examined by Durand and Carr (1983). At 18 months, two of three children had maintained learned responses and generalized them to new teachers and new classrooms. The third child required a brief booster session to facilitate generalization of low rates of SIB.

The communication hypothesis and resulting assessment and treatment implications have considerable heuristic and practical value. As school psychologists are increasingly being asked to provide a wide range of assessment, treatment, and consultative services for severely handicapped learners (see Powers & Harris, 1985), the relevance of these methods for less-involved and nonhandicapped children cannot be understated.

Implications for Assessment

The behavioral assessment of children in schools is a multifaceted enterprise, incorporating data from molecular, intraorganismic as well as molar, environmental, sources (Powers, 1985). The behavioral assessment of conditions motivating a target problem appropriately emphasizes the role of assessment in intervention planning and program monitoring. Thus, prior to developing treatments for alternative communicative behaviors, one must determine the form and social function of the target.

To assist in this task, Durand and Crimmins (1983) developed the Motivation Assessment Scale (MAS; 1983).[1] Consisting of 16 Likert-type items, this teacher-scored device permits discriminations between disruptive behavior motivated by four potential functions: escape, adult attention, sensory feedback, and access to tangible materials. Initial studies of validity and reliability of the MAS are satisfactory. Information obtained from the MAS assists the behavioral educator in selecting treatments that are functionally compatible with the social factors motivating the target behavior. Durand and Carr (1985) provided guidelines for use of the MAS in educational settings.

Implications for Treatment

The communication hypothesis points to the importance of training alternative means of communication that (a) have a higher likelihood of fulfilling the child's expressed needs; (b) are more socially valid; and (c) are more developmentally appropriate. Just as one would not expect a hungry infant to communicate his or her wish to be fed in any way other than crying, so too the behavioral educator must consider chronological and mental age, developmental status, and physical limitations when selecting alternative communication forms to replace maladaptive behavior. With severely handicapped children, this task is more obvious. Teaching the manual sign for help would clearly be more expeditious than training a child with little or no expressive vocal language to utter the word *help* in order to get adult attention during a difficult task involving less handicapped children.

Durand and Carr (1982, 1983) and Carr and Durand (1985b) have proposed a new technique, the Differential Reinforcement of Communication (DRC), as a means of systematically increasing novel, more functional and socially valid, communicative behaviors while concurrently decelerating disruptive behaviors. This procedure entails the training of a communicative response (vocal or manual) that is capable of eliciting the same reinforcer (i.e., motivating condition) as the disruptive behavior. For example, Carr and Durand (1985b) identified social attention as the motivator of disruptive behavior in some children. Previously, these children had elicited social attention from adults by means of tantrums, self-injury, etc. By teaching the child to emit the communicative behavior, "Am I doing good work?" in the presence of the teacher, with the teacher subsequently reinforcing this communication with adult attention, disruptive behavior was reduced and appropriate solicitation of social attention was increased.

Durand and Carr (1985) offered several guidelines for using DRC. First, the motivating conditions for the disruptive behavior should be identified through direct observation in analogue or naturalistic settings. The Motivation Assessment Scale (Durand & Crimmins, 1983) may be a useful adjunct. Next, a functionally appropriate alternative communication must be selected based on the motivating condition. Finally, that communication must be taught using reinforcement and shaping techniques and opportunities for appropriate use.

Theoretical Implications

The special emphasis placed on the form, function, and sequence of different skill areas by psycholinguistics may provide curricular guidance to behavior therapists already skilled in intervention methodology (see Carr,

[1] Available from V. Mark Durand, Ph.D., Department of Psychology, SUNY, Albany, New York 12222.

1985). Further basic and applied research is needed.

A Systems Approach to Educating the Developmentally Disabled

Various investigators have argued for an expansion of the domains of assessment and treatment when providing services to the developmentally disabled (Christian, Hannah, & Glahn, 1984; Emery *et al.*, 1983; Evans, 1985; Harris, 1983; Powers & Handleman, 1984; Voeltz & Evans, 1982). Although many adjectives have been used to characterize this approach (e.g., ecological, systems, molar, multi-level), all share a common element: the recognition that effective service delivery must occur within and take into account a multiplicity of contexts. This implies more than mere awareness of relevant factors; explicit consideration of child, family, environmental, interactional, and organismic variables in assessment and intervention are essential. Perhaps arbitrarily, we will use the term *systems* to describe this approach.

Characteristics of a Systems Approach

Systems approaches to the developmentally disabled borrow from general systems theory (cf., Miller, 1978). (See Powers, 1988, for a more comprehensive review of this topic.) One critical feature will be discussed here: the reciprocity between various components of the system, and its implications.

Numerous components in any given child converge to produce the highly individualized behavioral, cognitive, and environmental profile to which we respond. These include biological states, such as health, sensory acuity, hunger, and fatigue (Nelson & Hayes, 1979); genetic, biochemical, and neurological variables (Mash & Terdal, 1981); prior learning histories (Powers & Handleman, 1984); expectations of reward and punishment (Franzini, 1970); and expectations of personal efficacy (Bandura, 1977).

Environmental components include the family's readiness for change (Powers & Handleman, 1984); the family's technical skill in managing their child's behavior (Harris, 1984); the presence and capabilities of siblings (Lobato, 1983; McHale, Simeonsson, & Sloan, 1984); the family's response to raising a developmentally disabled child (Harris, 1982); the present position of the child within the family's life cycle (Harris & Powers, 1984a); classroom curriculum (Donnellan, 1980); classroom setting (Olley, 1980); and peer reactions (McHale & Simeonsson, 1980).

It is not our intent to imply that one must consider all organismic, family, and school-related variables with every child. We have not included additional factors, such as community reaction, maternal insularity, or physical characteristics of the living environment, all of which have been found to determine the behavior of some developmentally disabled children. Rather, we argue that these components deserve consideration in assessment and treatment decision making to the extent that each might provide information relevant to problem maintenance or problem resolution. Thus, the focal contribution of a systems approach to educating the developmentally disabled is that it provides for molecular and molar descriptions of the target behavior. Behavioral educators can work in several spheres if necessary, or in one sphere while simultaneously observing positive and negative effects in others. Moreover, such an approach emphasizes the need for interactions among professionals, whether through multidisciplinary teams or discipline-specific consultation.

As behavior therapy in educational settings continues to broaden, certain conceptual and theoretical inconsistencies will have to be addressed. For example, ecological applications of behavioral technology raise questions of verification of behavior change, of which behaviors are accessible for study and, most fundamental, of how to define and study triadic or quadratic interactions.

The Relevance of DSM-III and the Classification of Child Psychopathology to Behavior Therapy in Educational Settings

With all its limitations, the *Diagnostic and Statistical Manual of Mental Disorders, Third Edition* (DSM-III; American Psychiatric Association, 1980) is the most comprehensive attempt to classify child and adult psychopatholgy to date. (See Nathan & Harris, 1983, with adults, and Achenbach, 1980; Harris, 1979; Powers, 1984; Rutter & Shaffer, 1980, with children.) Although DSM-III has been available for over 7 years, its use has largely been restricted to clinicians and researchers. Only infrequently is DSM-III used in educational settings, and it is even less frequently taught in school psychology training programs.

We believe that increased usage would benefit research and behavioral practice in schools. The use of DSM-III would not supercede the need for educational diagnosis to group children for educational placement; rather, it would add to the diagnostic decision-making base. Kendall *et al.* (1984) note the need for normative data against which behavioral interventions with children can be evaluated. Syndromal diagnosis of participants in specific intervention procedures facilitates development of such a data base. To the extent that the various disciplines conducting behavioral interventions in schools subscribe to the practice of diagnosis as part of the cluster of variables investigated, the normative data base will accrue more quickly.

Adoption of a common diagnostic nomenclature facilitates comparisons of research findings in child behavior therapy with those of child psychiatry (Kazdin, 1983). Considering the amount and quality of behavioral research being conducted in educational settings, continued failure to adopt the dominant diagnostic scheme (DSM-III) could likewise impede integration of behavioral research in schools with the larger body of research findings in child psychology, psychiatry, and clinical social work.

DSM-III is a nomothetic tool. It focuses on the development of generalizations that apply to many people. In contrast, behavioral assessment is idiographic. It emphasizes specification of person, event, setting, and organismic controlling variables in the service of developing highly individualized treatment plans. Nomothetic data are useful adjuncts to idiographic data in that the former facilitate communication among professionals, guide the clinician's decision-making behavior, and suggest behavioral dimensions of particular importance to be assessed idiographically.

Integrating DSM-III diagnosis with child behavioral assessment practices offers both practical and heuristic advantages (Powers, 1984). DSM-III diagnosis serves an initial broad-band assessment function, with investigation of individual controlling variables subsequently undertaken using behavioral assessment techniques. Treatment plans are then based on the functional-analytic data obtained through behavioral assessment. Such a model allows the specificity and treatment planning capabilities of behavioral assessment to be brought to bear on syndromal diagnosis. Moreover, the behavior therapist gains access to various nomothetic considerations inherent in the use of syndromal diagnosis. Heuristically, this model emphasizes the importance of feedback loops and response interrelationships in the diagnosis-assessment-treatment-evaluation cycle. Information obtained at any phase of the behavioral assessment process will influence decision making at one or more points in the cycle.

Behavior therapists often reject syndromal diagnosis because of its less stringent reliability, psychodynamic assumptions, and questionable relevance to treatment (Mash & Terdal, 1981). Though still valid, these criticisms are much less appropriate for DSM-III than its earlier editions. Regulatory agencies are increasingly making funding levels contingent on specific diagnoses and the demonstrable efficacy of specific treatments for those diagnoses. As this trend shows no sign of reversing, it behooves behavior therapists and behavioral educators to participate in the development and use of more effective diagnostic systems.

Behavior Therapy and the Assumption of Educability

Will all school children profit from the use of some form of behavior therapy? It depends on whom you ask, the data you review, and for which populations. Over the past 20 years, an enormous data base attests to its efficacy. We have also become more aware of the circumstances surrounding possible negative effects of behavior therapy interventions with children (Barbrack, 1985) and what to do about it (Mays & Franks, 1985). In brief, we no longer need to defend the practice of behavior therapy in the schools.

Since the early 1980s, however, a new coda has been added to this basic question. That coda, born of Reaganomics, state-level budget cuts, and dwindling resources in schools, asks "At what cost?" and "Do the resources expended exceed even the most reasonable expectation of gain?" Some may oversimplify the question by asking, "Is behavior modification cost-beneficial?" This begs what we perceive to be the real question, namely "What are the limits of habilitation?"

To illustrate this issue, we will limit discussion to the question of benefits and costs of behavioral education for individuals with severe developmental disabilities. These children have been diagnosed as severely or profoundly mentally retarded, autistic, mentally retarded-blind, cerebral palsied-deaf, or a variety of other descriptions that communicate severe language, social, cognitive, and adaptive deprivations. All will require life-long care and habilitative efforts.

Consideration of the utility of behavioral education for the severely developmentally disabled involves complex legal, scientific, and ethical issues. To make this point, we will focus briefly on one of these issues: the concept of educability and its impact on behavior therapy in the schools and on social policy.

Special educators, school psychologists, and child behavior therapists generally agree that there is benefit to educating the severely developmentally disabled. Although classified as education, for many children the tasks offered may more commonly be construed as training (e.g., toileting, self-feeding). For our purposes, we will use the terms *educability* and *trainability* interchangeably and without reference to chronological or developmental age or diagnostic entity. Educability implies a potential for positive change. Such changes provide the building blocks for increasing independence in the task trained. If behavior modification does not cure such disorders as autism or profound mental retardation, well-planned behavioral interventions can substantially increase the life choices of both client and family. There are times, however, when the professional is confronted by limitations to positive change imposed by external forces (e.g., state or federal cutbacks) or by the pervasiveness of the client's condition. It is during these times that difficult questions are asked and difficult decisions made.

Ultimately, educability is a legal term. The courts have repeatedly guaranteed the child's right to an affirmative effort by educators to bring about educational growth. This implies a documented, appropriate, and sustained attempt at education (Martin, 1981). Some argue that we have been caught up (misled?) by the normalization movement, and that the data do not support the notion that all severely developmentally disabled clients are educable (Ellis, 1979). Others (e.g. Baer, 1981; Bricker, 1970; Favell, Risley, Wolfe, Riddle, & Rasmussen, 1981) argue equally compellingly that, because reported studies have failed to document procedural reliability and the validity of interventions in treatment failures, the resulting data are either uninterpretable or inconclusive. Effective arguments have been made that, in the absence of such data, we should "keep on trying." As Baer (1981) stated, given the fact that we cannot conclusively prove that all children are educable or the converse, that some children are not educable, the most defensible course of action, regardless of level of handicap, is to continue trying to educate all children.

Certain implications follow: for behavior therapists in educational settings, the policy that all children can benefit in some way from instruction demands continuing efforts at developing instructional techniques, exploration of the relationships between physiological condition, learning style, and learning objectives, and consideration of the multiplicity of modifiable factors that contribute to effective learning environments. For social policymakers, regardless of level of handicap, decisions must be made with respect to the priority to be given to the education of children and how to establish and motivate constituencies to carry out such policies. In addition, behavioral scientists and social policymakers must join forces to tackle the question: What should be done if best practice has failed to produce results in the most severely disabled child?

Bailey (1981) recommended a four-tiered system for providing educational programming for the profoundly retarded: skill teaching, behavior reduction, maintenance, and stimulation. This last tier provides educational therapy appropriate to the client's status, and physical and occupational therapy to improve range of motion and tactile, visual, and auditory stimulation. Wherever programming teaches prerequisite skills for entrance into a skill teaching program, the client is provided such training. Favell *et al.* (1981) emphasized that these clients require programs to maintain their current developmental levels and echo the suggestions of others (cf. Bailey, 1981; Ellis, 1979; Kaufmann & Krouse, 1981) that enrichment or stimulation programs be provided where skill training programs have been documented as unsuccessful. Importantly, Favell *et al.* (1981) suggested that delimiting conditions for programming be specified. Thus, even when documentation has been provided that a client presently cannot profit from skill training, changes in conditions need to be identified that, if evidenced at some future point, will demand reconsideration of educational objectives.

Presently, public policy and educational practice are guided by the legal position that all children are educable, a position based more on faith than evidence. To effect change, behavioral psychologists and educators must be prepared to participate in several arenas. These include legal testimony, participation in the legislative process, cost-benefit analysis, and social validation of treatment goals. Failure to participate is likely to lead to others setting the standards and developing policy.

Behavior Therapy and Education: Implications for the Future

In the past, school psychologists have relied on clinical psychology for their models and practices. This has led to a restrictive emphasis on the individual child and his or her problems, rather than on the child as an interactive participant in the school system. Moreover, the domain of school psychology as an applied science has been limited to problems faced by children and teachers in the school. Although the age limits have been expanding as school districts increase services to individuals aged 0 to 5 and 18 to 21, the types of problems considered have not changed significantly, nor have the foci of treatment kept pace with our understanding of the importance of families and community networks.

Two areas warrant elaboration: the expanding view of the province of school psychology, and the social psychology of behavior therapy in educational settings. Bardon (1982a,b, 1983) has been a major proponent of change within the school psychological community. Acknowledging the various crises facing professional school psychology, Bardon (1982b) proposed a shift in title and emphasis that would place practitioners of applied psychology in education in various arenas where education—broadly defined—is taking place. These include families, communities, higher education, adult education settings, and residential homes for the handicapped. This emphasis allows behavior therapists with special expertise in the educative process access to treatment across the life span. Behavioral educational psychologists would define their populations and settings by function rather than chronological age. In this manner, those skilled in promoting the teaching-learning process may be able to conceptualize learning processes and outcomes beyond the boundaries of the school *per se*. This would facilitate integration of theoretical and practical knowledge not traditionally within the armamentarium of school psychologists (e.g., family systems treatment methods, knowledge from behavioral pediatrics and health psychology).

Broader bases for intervention mean little if the same mistakes are repeated. Educational settings (be they schools, adult activity centers for the retarded, or group homes for delinquent boys) generate social forces that must be considered if the behavioral programs are to be successfully maintained. Liberman (1979), Reppucci (1973, 1977) and Reppucci and Saunders (1974) have elucidated several problems confronting behavior therapists trying to establish programs in organizations. They describe eight organizational constraints, each of which can impede optimal implementation of behavioral programs: institutional constraints, limited resources, perceived inflexibility, external pressure, two populations, language, labeling, and compromise. To this list Reppucci (1977) added the port-of-entry, existing institutional staff, and political realities. Liberman (1979) emphasized the need to demonstrate competence, goal setting, maintaining flexibility, conflict resolution, maintaining administrative support, and maintaining staff performance.

Institutional constraints refer to those administrative or bureaucratic policies which impact negatively on aspects of the program. *Limited resources* pertain to the discrepancies between financial, physical, personnel, and technological resources needed for a program and those allotted or available. Organization staff *perceptions of inflexibility* stem from the behavior therapist's attempt to maintain theoretical integrity in the face of organizational forces demanding excessive compromise. *External pressure* refers to the (sometimes different) agendas of administrative, economic, or political forces that influence the development or maintenance of behavioral programs. The problem caused by *two populations* is similar to that faced by any behavioral consultant when the consultee has direct care responsibility for clients. Ultimately, the behavior therapist must rely on someone else to control the contingencies. The problem of *language* refers to issues that arise and may compromise a program when the common vocabulary used is neither meaningful nor acceptable to members of the organization. When organizational staff respond to a *label* for an activity (e.g., recreational therapy) rather than the function that activity serves for a particular client (e.g., escape from a required task), problems ensue. *Compromise* refers to the fact that the behavior of behavior therapists is reciprocally determined by environmental contingencies. As such, the task of maintaining objectivity is more difficult. When a new behavioral program is to be started, the *port-of-entry* period must be negotiated before organizational sanctions are imposed on the newcomer (i.e., behavior therapist). During this period, *existing staff* seek to determine whether the potential impact of the newcomer will be positive or negative before responding with positive or negative sanctions. Such staff can become allies or nemeses, and often cannot be replaced if inefficient. Working through and around them becomes an important task. *Political realities*, similar to institutional constraints, include unions and internal politics of an organization as they relate to program development and maintenance.

When proposing a new program the behavior therapist often has to demonstrate competence in the methodologies involved before the staff will accept his or her role as a knowledgeable professional. Goal setting and attainment can be problems when other activities interfere with the timely completion of planned change. The need to maintain flexibility is actually the strategy of tolerating successive approximations of program behavior by organizational staff in the early phases of intervention. Conflict awareness and resolution become important proactive aspects of any behavioral program residing within a larger organizational structure because failure to identify and resolve conflicts can lead to unforseen alteration or dissolution of the program. Maintenance of administrative support is essential for program continuance. Equally important is maintenance of program staff performance. Both issues require systematic attention and cognizance of contingencies of reinforcement for the groups involved.

If the business of applying psychology to education takes the form envisioned by Bardon (1982b), then overcoming these various organizational pitfalls becomes integral to the process of carrying out the form and function of that mission. Although terms such as schooling, education, and training are often used synonomously, we suggest that the future of behavior therapy and the teaching-learning process will continue to develop fruitfully across the lifespan and across organizational structures if education, broadly conceived, becomes the conceptual centerpiece. In the process, a redefinition of behavioral school psychology may emerge: the application of empirically derived principles of learning to problems of learning outcome and process across the lifespan in educational, social, and organizational contexts.

As we have attempted to document, the science of behavior therapy has come a long way in a short time and progress is evident in many areas. At the same time, we have tried to make it clear that the time for complacency has not yet arrived. If we remain true to that spirit of continuous peer-minded constructive evaluation that is one of the hallmarks of behavior therapy, that day will never arrive.

References

Achenbach, T. M. (1980). DSM-III in light of empirical research on the classification of child psychopathology. *Journal of the American Academy of Child Psychiatry, 19,* 395–412.

Achenbach, T. M., & Edelbrock, C. S. (1983). *Manual for the Child Behavior Checklist and Child Behavior Profile.* Burlington, VT: Child Psychiatry, University of Vermont (1 South Prospect Street, Burlington, VT 05401).

American Psychiatric Association. (1980). *Diagnostic and Statistical Manual of Mental Disorders* (3rd Ed.). Washington, DC: Author.

Anastasi, A. (1976). *Psychological testing* (4th Ed.). New York: MacMillan.

Baer, D. M. (1981). A hung jury and a Scottish verdict: Not proven. *Analysis and Intervention in Developmental Disabilities, 1,* 91–97.

Baer, D. M., & Bushnell, D. (1981). The future of behavior analysis in the schools? Consider its recent past, then ask a different question. *School Psychology Review, 10,* 259–270.

Bailey, J. S. (1981). Wanted: A rational search for the limiting conditions of habilitation in the retarded. *Analysis and Intervention in Developmental Disabilities, 1,* 45–52.

Baltes, P. B., Reese, H. W., & Nesselroade, J. R. (1977). *Life-span developmental psychology: Introduction to research methods.* Monterey, CA: Brookes/Cole.

Bandura, A. (1977). *Social learning theory.* Englewood Cliffs, NJ: Prentice-Hall.

Barbrack, C. R. (1985). Negative outcome in behavior therapy. In D. T. Mays & C. M. Franks (Eds.), *Negative outcome in psychotherapy and what to do about it* (pp. 76–105). New York: Springer.

Bardon, J. I. (1982a). The psychology of school psychology. In C. R. Reynolds & T. B. Gutkin (Eds.), *The handbook of school psychology* (pp. 3–14). New York: Wiley.

Bardon, J. I. (1982b). School psychology's dilemma: A proposal for its resolution. *Professional Psychology, 13,* 955–968.

Bardon, J. I. (1983). Psychology applied to education. *American Psychologist, 38,* 185–196.

Barkley, R. A., Copeland, A. P., and Sirage, C. (1980). A self-control classroom for hyperactive children. *Journal of Autism and Developmental Disorders, 10,* 75–89.

Barlow, D. H. (1984). Editorial. *Behavior Therapy, 15,* 1–2.

Beck, A. T. (1976). *Cognitive therapy and the emotional disorders.* New York: International Universities Press.

Berler, E. S., Gross, A. M., & Drabman, R. S. (1982). Social skills training with children: Proceed with caution. *Journal of Applied Behavior Analysis, 15,* 41–53.

Bijou, S. W. (1970). What psychology has to offer education - Now. *Journal of Applied Behavior Analysis, 3,* 65–71.

Billingsley, F., White, O. R., & Munson, R. (1980). Procedural reliability: A rationale and an example. *Behavioral Assessment, 2,* 229–241.

Block, J. (1982). Assimilation, accomodation, and the dynamics of personality development. *Child Development, 53,* 281–295.

Bolstad, O. D., & Johnson, S. M. (1972). Self-regulation in the modification of disruptive classroom behavior. *Journal of Applied Behavior Analysis, 5,* 443–454.

Borkowski, J., Levers, G., & Gruenfelder, T. (1976). Transfer of mediational strategies in children: The role of activity and awareness during strategy acquisition. *Child Development, 47,* 779–786.

Bricker, W. A. (1970). Identifying and modifying behavioral deficits. *American Journal of Mental Deficiency, 75,* 16–21.

Brown, D. T. (1982). Issues in the development of professional school psychology. In C. R. Reynolds & T. B. Gutkin (Eds.), *The handbook of school psychology* (pp. 14–23). New York: Wiley.

Brownell, K. D., Coletti, G., Ersner-Hershfield, R., Hershfield, S. M., & Wilson, G. T. (1977). Self-control in children: Stringency and leniency in self-determined and externally imposed performance standards. *Behavior Therapy, 8,* 442–455.

Bugenthal, D. B., Collins, S., Collins, L., & Chaney, L. A. (1978). Attributional and behavioral changes following two behavior management interventions with hyperactive boys: A follow-up study. *Child Development, 49,* 247–250.

Carr, E. G. (1985). Converging perspectives in psycholinguistics and behaviorism. In E. Schopler & G. B. Mesibov (Eds.), *Communication problems in autism* (pp. 89–92). New York: Plenum Press.

Carr, E. G., & Durand, V. M. (1985a). The social-communicative basis of severe behavior problems in children. In S. Reiss & R. Bootzin (Eds.), *Theoretical issues in behavior therapy* (pp. 219–254). New York: Academic Press.

Carr, E. G., & Durand, V. M. (1985b). Reducing behavior problems through functional communication training. *Journal of Applied Behavior Analxsis, 18,* 111–126.

Christian, W. P., & Luce, S. C. (1985). Behavioral self-help training for developmentally disabled individuals. *School Psychology Review, 14,* 177–181.

Christian, W. P., Hannah, G. T., & Glahn, T. J. (Eds.). (1984). *Programming effective human services.* New York: Plenum Press.

Copeland, A. P. (1981). The relevance of subject variables in cognitive self-instructional programs for impulsive children. *Behavior Therapy, 12,* 520–529.

Copeland, A. P. (1982). Individual difference factors in children's self-management: Toward individualized treatments. In P. Karoly & F. H. Kanfer (Eds.), *Self-management and behavioral change* (pp. 207–239). Elmsford, NY: Pergamon Press.

Donnellan, A. M. (1980). An educational perspective of autism: Implications for curriculum development and personnel development. In B. Wilcox & A. Thompson (Eds.), *Critical issues in educating autistic children and youth* (pp. 53–88). Washington, DC: U.S. Dept. of Education, Office of Special Education.

Drabman, R. S., Hammer, D., & Rosenbaum, M. S. (1979). Assessing generalization in behavior modification with children: The generalization map. *Behavioral Assessment, 1,* 203–219.

Durand, V. M., & Carr, E. G. (1982, August). *Differential reinforcement of a communicative behavior: An intervention for the disruptive behaviors of developmentally disabled children.* Paper presented at the meeting of the American Psychological Association, Washington, DC.

Durand, V. M., & Carr, E. G. (1983, October). *Differential reinforcement of communicative behavior. Classroom intervention and maintenance.* Paper presented at the meeting of the Berkshire Association for Behavior Analysis and Therapy, Amherst, MA.

Durand, V. M., & Carr, E. G. (1985). Self-injurious behavior. Motivating conditions and guidelines for treatment. *School Psychology Review, 14,* 171–176.

Durand, V. M., & Crimmins, D. B. (1983, October). *The Motivation Assessment Scale: A preliminary report on an instrument which assesses the functional significance of children's deviant behavior.* Paper presented at the meeting of the Berkshire Association for Behavior Analysis and Therapy, Amherst, MA.

Edelbrock, C. (1984). Developmental considerations. In T. H. Ollendick & M. Herson (Eds.), *Child behavioral assessment: Principles and procedures* (pp. 20–37). Elmsford, NY: Pergamon Press.

Eisenberg, N., & Harris, J. D. (1984). Social competence: A developmental perspective. *School Psychology Review, 13,* 267–277.

Elias, M. J., Clabby, J. F., Ottaviano, D., & Kovaleski, J. F. (1983). Social and affective interventions with preschool children: Developmental issues and promising programs. *New Jersey Journal of School Psychology, 2,* 41–53.

Ellis, A. (1962). *Reason and emotion in psychotherapy.* New York: Lyle Stuart.

Ellis, N. R. (1979). The Partlow case: A reply to Dr. Roos. *Law and Psychology Review, 5,* 15–49.

Emery, R. E., Binkoff, J. A., Houts, A. C., & Carr, E. G. (1983). Children as independent variables: Some clinical implications of child-effects. *Behavior Therapy, 14,* 398–412.

Erwin, E. (1978). *Behavior therapy: scientific, philosophical and moral foundations.* Cambridge, England: Cambridge University Press.

Evans, I. M. (1985). Building systems models as a strategy for target behavior selection in clinical assessment. *Behavioral Assessment, 7,* 21–32.

Eysenck, H. J. (1959). Learning theory and behavior therapy. *Journal of Mental Science, 105,* 61–75.

Eysenck, H. J. (1976). Behavior therapy: Dogma or applied science. In M. P. Feldman & A. E. Brondhurst

(Eds.), *Theoretical and experimental bases of behavior therapies* (pp. 186–205). London: Wiley.

Favell, J. E., Risley, T. R., Wolfe, A. F., Riddle, J. I., & Rasmussen, P. R. (1981). The limits of habilitation: How can we identify them and how can we change them? *Analysis and Intervention in Developmental Disabilities, 1,* 37–43.

Ferster, C. B. (1961). Positive reinforcement and behavioral deficits of autistic children. *Child Development, 32,* 437–456.

Fish, M. C., & Pervan, R. (1985). Self-instruction training: A potential tool for school psychologists. *Psychology in the Schools, 22,* 83–92.

Fordyce, W. E. (1976). *Behavioral methods for chronic pain and illness.* St. Louis, MO: C. V. Mosby.

Fox, D. E., & Kendall, P. C. (1983). Thinking through academic problems: Application of cognitive-behavior therapy to learning. In T. R. Kratochwill (Ed.), *Advances in school psychology* (Vol. 3, pp. 269–301). Hillsdale, NJ: Erlbaum.

Franks, C. M. (1980). On behaviourism and behaviour therapy—Not necessarily synonymous and becoming less so. *Australian Behaviour Therapist, 7,* 14–23.

Franks, C. M. (1981). 2081: Will we be many or one - or none? *Behavioural Psychotherapy, 9,* 287–290.

Franks, C. M. (1982). Behavior therapy: An overview. In C. M. Franks, G. T. Wilson, P. C. Kendall, & K. D. Brownell (Eds.), *Annual review of behavior therapy: Theory and practice* (Vol. 8, pp. 1–38). New York: Guilford Press.

Franks, C. M. (1984a). Behavior therapy with children and adolescents. In C. M. Franks, G. T. Wilson, P. C. Kendall, & K. D. Brownell (Eds.), *Annual review of behavior therapy: Theory and practice* (Vol. 10, pp. 236–290). New York: Guilford Press.

Franks, C. M. (1984b). On conceptual and technical integrity in psychoanalysis and behavior therapy: Two fundamentally incompatible systems. In H. Arkowitz & S. B. Messer (Eds.), *Psychoanalytic therapy and behavior therapy* (pp. 223–247). New York: Plenum Press.

Franks, C. M., & Barbrack, C. (1983). Behavior therapy with adults: An integrative approach. In A. E. Kazdin, M. Hersen, & A. Bellack (Eds.), *The clinical psychology handbook* (pp. 507–529). Elmsford, NY: Pergamon Press.

Franks, C. M., & Wilson, G. T. (1974–1979). *Annual review of behavior therapy: Theory and practice* (Vol. 1–7, 1973–1978). New York: Bruner/Mazel.

Franks, C. M., & Wilson, G. T. (1975). Ethical and related issues in behavior therapy. In C. M. Franks & G. T. Wilson (Eds.), *Annual review of behavior therapy: Theory and practice* (Vol. 3, pp. 1–11). New York: Bruner/Mazel.

Franks, C. M., Wilson, G. T., Kendall, R. C., & Brownell, K. D. (1982–1985). *Annual review of behavior therapy: Theory and practice* (Volumes 8–10, 1982–1984). New York: Guilford Press.

Franzini, L. R. (1970). Neglected variables in behavioral case assessment. *Behavior Therapy, 1,* 354–358.

Genshaft, J. L., & Hirt, M. (1979). Race effects in modifying cognitive impulsivity through self-instruction and modeling. *Journal of Experimental Child Psychology, 27,* 185–194.

Gray, J. S. (1932). A biological view of behavior modification. *Journal of Educational Psychology, 23,* 611–620.

Harris, S. L. (1979). DSM-III—Its implications for children. *Child Behavior Therapy, 1,* 37–46.

Harris, S. L. (1982). A family system approach to behavioral training with parents of autistic children. *Child and Family Behavior Therapy, 4,* 21–35.

Harris, S. L. (1983). *Families of the developmentally disabled: A guide to behavioral intervention.* Elmsford, NY: Pergamon Press.

Harris, S. L. (1984). Intervention planning for the family of the autistic child: A multilevel assessment of the family system. *Journal of Marital & Family Therapy, 10,* 157–166.

Harris, S. L., & Ferrari, M. (1983). Developmental factors in child behavior therapy. *Behavior Therapy, 14,* 54–72.

Harris, S. L., & Powers, M. D. (1984a). Behavior therapists look at the impact of an autistic child on the family system. In E. Schopler & G. Mesibov (Eds.), *The effects of autism on the family* (pp. 207–224). New York: Plenum Press.

Harris, S. L., & Powers, M. D. (1984b). Diagnostic issues. In T. H. Ollendick & M. Herson (Eds.), *Child behavioral assessment: Principles and procedures* (pp. 38–57). Elmsford, NY: Pergamon Press.

Higa, W. R., Tharp, R. G., & Calkins, R. P. (1978). Developmental verbal control of behavior: Implications for self-instructional training. *Journal of Experimental Child Psychology, 26,* 489–497.

Katz, E. R., Kellerman, J., & Siegel, S. E. (1980). Behavioral distress in children with cancer undergoing medical procedures: Developmental considerations. *Journal of Consulting and Clinical Psychology, 48,* 356–365.

Kaufman, A. S., & Kaufman, N. L. (1983). *Kaufman Assessment Battery for Children.* Circle Pines, MN: American Guidance Service.

Kauffman, J. M., & Krouse, J. (1981). The cult of educability: Searching for the substance of things hoped for: the evidence of things not seen. *Analysis and Intervention in Developmental Disabilities, 1,* 53–60.

Kazdin, A. E. (1977). Assessing the clinical or applied importance of behavior change through social validation. *Behavior Modification, 1,* 427–451.

Kazdin, A. E. (1978a). Behavior therapy: Evolution and expansion. *The Counseling Psychologist, 23,* 34–37.

Kazdin, A. E. (1978b). *History of behavior modification: Experimental foundations of contemporary research.* Baltimore, MD: University Park Press.

Kazdin, A. E. (1982). Methodological strategies in behavior therapy research. In G. T. Wilson & C. M. Franks (Eds.), *Contemporary Behavior Therapy* (pp. 403–442). New York: Guilford Press.

Kazdin, A. E. (1983). Psychiatric diagnosis, dimensions of

dysfunction, and child behavior therapy. *Behavior Therapy, 14*, 73–99.

Kendall, P. C., & Braswell, L. (1982). Cognitive behavioral self-control therapy for children: A components analysis. *Journal of Consulting and Clinical Psychology, 50*, 672–689.

Kendall, P. C., & Finch, A. J. (1978). A cognitive-behavioral treatment for impulsivity: A group comparison study. *Journal of Consulting and Clinical Psychology, 46*, 110–118.

Kendall, P. C., Lerner, R. M., & Craighead, W. E. (1984). Human development and intervention in childhood psychopathology. *Child Development, 55*, 71–82.

Kendler, H. H., & Kendler, T. S. (1962). Vertical and horizontal processes in problem solving. *Psychological Review, 69*, 1–16.

Kent, R. N., & O'Leary, K. D. (1976). A controlled evaluation of behavior modification with conduct disordered children. *Journal of Consulting and Clinical Psychology, 44*, 586–596.

Keogh, B. K. (1981). Ask a different question: Expect a different answer. *School Psychology Review, 10*, 278–284.

Kratochwill, T. R. (1985a). Selection of target behaviors: Issues and directions. *Behavioral Assessment, 7*, 3–5.

Kratochwill, T. R. (1985b). Case study research in school psychology. *School Psychology Review, 14*, 204–215.

Krasner, L. (1971). Behavior therapy. In P. H. Mussen (Ed.), *Annual review of psychology* (Vol. 22, pp. 483–532). Palo Alto, CA: Annual Reviews.

Lazarus, A. A. (1981). *The practice of multimodal therapy*. New York: McGraw-Hill.

Liberman, R. P. (1979). Social and political challenges to the development of behavioral programs in organizations. In P. Sjoden, S. Bates, & W. S. Docken (Eds.), *Trends in behavior therapy* (pp. 369–398). New York: Academic Press.

Liberman, R. P. (1983). Guest Editor's preface. *Analysis and Intervention in Developmental Disabilities, 3*, iii–iv.

Liberty, K. A., Haring, N. G., & Martin, M. M. (1981). Teaching new skills to the severely handicapped. *Journal of the Association for the Severely Handicapped, 6*, 5–13.

Lobato, D. (1983). Siblings of handicapped children: A review. *Journal of Autism and Developmental Disorders, 13*, 347–364.

Lovitt, T. C. (1973). Self-management projects with children with behavioral disorders. *Journal of Learning Disabilities, 6*, 138–150.

Luria, A. R. (1961). *The role of speech in the regulation of normal and abnormal behavior*. New York: Liveright.

Maher, C. A., Illback, R. J., & Zins, J. E. (Eds.). (1985). *Organizational psychology in the schools: A handbook for school professionals*. Springfield, IL: Charles C Thomas.

Martin, R. (1981). All handicapped children are educable. *Analysis and Intervention in Developmental Disabilities, 1*, 5–11.

Mash, E. J. (1985). Some comments on target selection in behavior therapy. *Behavioral Assessment, 7*, 63–78.

Mash, E. J., & Terdal, L. G. (1981). Behavioral assessment of childhood disturbance. In E. J. Mash & L. G. Terdal (Eds.), *Behavioral assessment of childhood disorders*. New York: Guilford Press.

Mays, D. T., & Franks, C. M. (Eds.). (1985). *Negative outcome in psychotherapy and what to do about it*. New York: Springer.

McCandless, B. R., & Marshall, H. R. (1957). A picture sociometric technique for preschool children and its relation to teacher judgment of friendship. *Child Development, 28*, 139–148.

McHale, S. M., & Simeonsson, R. J. (1980). Effects of interaction on nonhandicapped children's attitudes toward autistic children. *American Journal of Mental Deficiency, 85*, 18–24.

Meador, A. E., and Ollendick, T. H. (1984). Cognitive behavior therapy with children: An evaluation of its efficacy and clinical utility. *Children and Family Behavior Therapy, 6*, 25–44.

Mercer, J. (1973). *Labeling the mentally retarded*. Los Angeles, CA: University of California Press.

Miller, J. G. (1978). *Living systems*. New York: McGraw-Hill.

Minkin, N., Braukmann, C. J., Minkin, B. S., Timbers, G. D., Timbers, B. J., Fixen, D. L., Phillips, E. L., & Wolf, M. M. (1976). The social validation and training of conversational skills. *Journal of Applied Behavior Analysis, 9*, 127–140.

Minuchin, S. (1974). *Families and family therapy*. Cambridge, MA: Harvard University Press.

Morris, R. J., & Kratochwill, T. R. (1983). *Treating children's fears and phobias: A behavioral approach*. Elmsford, NY: Pergamon Press.

Nathan, P. E., & Harris, S. L. (1983). The diagnostic and statistical manual of mental disorders: History comparative analysis, current status, and appraisal. In C. E. Walker (Ed.), *Handbook of clinical psychology: Theory, research, and practice* (pp. 303–343). Homewood, IL: Dow-Jones-Irwin.

Nelson, R. D., & Bowles, P. E. (1975). The best of two worlds—Observation with norms. *Journal of School Psychology, 13*, 3–9.

Nelson, R. D., & Hayes, S. C. (1979). Some current dimensions of behavioral assessment. *Behavioral Assessment, 1*, 1–16.

Nelson, R. D., Lipinski, D. P., & Black, J. L. (1976). The relative reactivity of external observations and self-monitoring. *Behavioral Therapy, 7*, 314–321.

Nelson, R. O., Lipinski, D. P., & Boykin, R. A. (1978). The effects of self-recorders training and the obtrusiveness of the self-recording device on the accuracy and reactivity of self-monitoring. *Behavioral Therapy, 9*, 200–208.

O'Leary, K. D. (1980). Pills or skills for hyperactive children. *Journal of Applied Behavior Analysis, 13*, 191–204.

O'Leary, S. G., & Dubey, D. R. (1979). Applications of

self-control procedures by children: A review. *Journal of Applied Behavior Analysis, 12,* 449–465.

Ollendick, T. H. (1979). Behavioral treatment of anorexia nervosa: A five-year study. *Behavior Modification, 3,* 124–135.

Ollendick, T. H., & Hersen, M. (1984). An overview of child behavioral assessment. In T. H. Ollendick & M. Hersen (Eds.), *Child behavioral assessment: Principles and procedures.* Elmsford, NY: Pergamon Press.

Ollendick, T. H., & Mayer, J. (1983). School phobia. In S. M. Turner (Ed.), *Behavioral treatment of anxiety disorders.* New York: Plenum Press.

Olley, J. G. (1980). Organization of educational services for autistic children and youth. In B. Wilcox & A. Thompson (Eds.), *Critical issues in educating autistic children and youth* (pp. 13–23). Washington, DC: U.S. Dept. of Education, Office of Special Education.

Orlando, R., & Bijou, S. W. (1960). Single and multiple schedules of reinforcement in developmentally retarded children. *Journal of the Experimental Analysis of Behavior, 3,* 339–348.

Patterson, G. R. (1982). *Coercive family process.* Eugene, OR: Castalia.

Patterson, G. R., & Fleischman, J. J. (1979). Maintenance of treatment effects: Some considerations concerning family systems and follow-up data. *Behavior Therapy, 10,* 168–185.

Powers, M. D. (1984). Syndromal diagnosis and the behavioral assessment of childhood disorders. *Child and Family Behavior Therapy, 6,* 1–15.

Powers, M. D. (1985). Behavioral assessment and the planning and evaluation of interventions for developmentally disabled children. *School Psychology Review, 14,* 155–161.

Powers, M. D. (Ed.). (1988). *Expanding systems of interaction for persons with developmental disabilities.* Baltimore, MD: Paul H. Brookes.

Powers, M. D., & Handleman, J. S. (1984). *Behavioral assessment of severe developmental disabilities.* Rockville, MD: Aspen Press.

Powers, M. D., & Harris, S. L. (1985). Guest editors' comments: Developmental disabilities: Current status and future directions. (Special Issue). *School Psychology Review, 14,* 140–141.

Pumroy, D. K. (April, 1984). *Why is it taking so long for behavior modification to be used in the schools - or am I being too impatient?* Paper presented at the Annual Meeting of the National Association of School Psychogists, Philadelphia, PA.

Rachlin, H. (in press). Pain and behavior. *The Behavioral and Brain Sciences.*

Reppucci, N. D. (1973). Social psychology and institutional change: General principles for intervention. *American Journal of Community Psychology, 1,* 330–341.

Reppucci, N. D. (1977). Implementation issues for the behavior modifier as institutional change agent. *Behavior Therapy, 8,* 594–605.

Reppucci, N. D., & Saunders, J. T. (1974). Social psychology of behavior modification. *American Psychologist, 29,* 649–660.

Ridberg, E. H., Parke, R. D., & Hetherington, E. M. (1971). Modification of impulsive and reflective cognitive styles through observation of film-mediated models. *Developmental Psychology, 5,* 369–377.

Risley, T. R. (1970). Behavior modification: An experimental-therapeutic endeavor. In L. A. Hamerlynck, P. O. Davidson, & L. E. Acker (Eds.), *Behavior modification and ideal mental health services* (pp. 137–151). Calgary: University of Calgary Press.

Rosenbaum, M. S., & Drabman, R. S. (1979). Self-control training in the classroom: A review and critique. *Journal of Applied Behavior Analysis, 12,* 467–485.

Runco, M. A., & Screibman, L. (1983). Parental judgments of behavior therapy efficacy with autistic children: A social validation. *Journal of Autism and Developmental Disorders, 13,* 237–248.

Rusch, F. R. (1979). Toward the validation of social/vocational survival skills. *Mental Retardation, 17,* 143–145.

Rutter, M., & Shaffer, D. (1980). DSM-III: A step forward or back in terms of the classification of child psychiatric disorders? *Journal of the American Academy of Child Psychiatry, 19,* 371–394.

Sagotsky, G., Patterson. C. J., & Lepper, M. R. (1978). Training children's self-control: A field experiment in self-monitoring and goal setting in the classroom. *Journal of Experimental Child Psychology, 25,* 242–253.

Santogrossi, D. A., O'Leary, K. D., Romanczyk, R. G., & Kaufman, K. F. (1973). Self-evaluation by adolescents in a psychiatric hospital school token program. *Journal of Applied Behavior Analysis, 6,* 277–287.

Santostefano, S. (1978). *A biodevelopmental approach to clinical child psychology.* New York: Wiley.

Schleser, R., Cohen, R., Meyers, A. W., & Rodick, J. D. (1984). The effect of cognitive level and training procedures on the generalization of self-instructions. *Cognitive Therapy and Research, 8,* 187–200.

Schmuck, R. A. (1982). Organization development in the schools. In C. R. Reynolds & T. B. Gutkin (Eds.), *The handbook of school psychology* (pp. 829–857). New York: Wiley.

Schreibman, L., Koegel, R. L., Mills, J. I., & Burke, J. C. (1981). Social validation of behavior therapy with autistic children. *Behavior Therapy, 12,* 610–624.

Schutz, R. P., Rusch, R. F., & Lamson, D. C. (1979). Evaluation of an employers procedure to eliminate unacceptable behavior on the job. *Community Services Forum, 1,* 4–5.

Schwartz, G. E. (1982). Integrating psychobiology and behavior therapy: A systems perspective. In G. T. Wilson & C. M. Franks (Eds.), *Contemporary behavior therapy* (pp. 119–141). New York: Guilford Press.

Skinner, B. F. (1954). The science of learning and the art of teaching. *Harvard Educational Review, 24,* 86–97.

Skinner, B. F. (1961). Why we need teaching machines. *Harvard Educational Review, 31*, 377–398.

Skinner, B. F. (1963). Reflections on a decade of teaching machines. *Teachers College Record, 65*, 1–8.

Sroufe, L. A. (1979). The coherence of individual differences. *American Psychologist, 34*, 834–841.

Sroufe, L. A., & Rutter, M. (1984). The domain of developmental psychopathology. *Child Development, 55*, 17–29.

Stevenson, H. C., & Fantuzzo, J. W. (1984). Application of the "generalization map" top a self-control intervention with school-aged children. *Journal of Applied Behavioral Analysis, 17*, 203–212.

Stokes, T. F., & Baer, D. M. (1977). An implicit technology of generalization. *Journal of Applied Behavioral Analysis, 10*, 349–367.

Thurman, S. K., & Fiorelli, J. S. (1979). Perspectives on normalization. *The Journal of Special Education, 13*, 339–346.

Turkewitz, H., O'Leary, K. D., & Ironsmith, M. (1975). Generalization and maintenance of appropriate behavior through self-control. *Journal of Consulting and Clinical Psychology, 43*, 577–583.

Van Houten, R. (1979). Social validation: The evolution of standards of competency for target behaviors. *Journal of Applied Behavior Analysis, 12*, 581–591.

Voeltz, L. M., & Evans, I. M. (1982). The assessment of behavioral interrelationships in child behavior therapy. *Behavioral Assessment, 4*, 131–165.

Voeltz, L. M., & Evans, I. M. (1983). Educational validity: Procedures to evaluate outcomes in programs for severely handicapped learners. *Journal of the Association for the Severely Handicapped, 8*, 3–15.

Voeltz, L. M., Evans, I. M., Derer, K. R., & Hamashiro, R. (1983). Targeting excess behavior for change: A clinical decision model for selecting priority goals in educational contexts. *Child and Family Behavior Therapy, 5*, 17–35.

Vogelsberg, R. T., & Rusch, F. R. (1979). Training three severely handicapped young adults to walk, look, and cross uncontrolled intersections. *AAESPH Review, 4*, 264–273.

Wahler, R. G. (1975). Some structural aspects of deviant child behavior. *Journal of Applied Behavior Analysis, 8*, 27–42.

Wahler, R. G. (1980). The insular mother: Her problems in parent–child treatment. *Journal of Applied Behavior Analysis, 13*, 207–219.

Willems, E. P. (1974). Behavioral technology and behavioral ecology. *Journal of Applied Behavior Analysis, 7*, 151–165.

Willems, E. P. (1977). Steps toward an ecobehavioral psychology. In A. Rogers-Warren & S. Warren (Eds.), *Ecological perspectives in behavioral analysis*. Baltimore, MD: University Park Press.

Wilson, G. T., & Franks, C. M. (Eds.). (1982). *Contemporary behavior therapy: Conceptual and empirical foundations*. New York: Guilford Press.

Wolf, M. M. (1978). Social validity: The case for subjective measurement or how applied behavior analysis is finding its heart. *Journal of Applied Behavior Analysis, 11*, 203–214.

Wolpe, J. (1958). *Psychotherapy by reciprocal inhibition*. Stanford, CA: Stanford University Press.

Woolfolk, A. E., Woolfolk, R. L., & Wilson, G. T. (1977). A rose by another name . . . : Labeling bias and attitudes toward behavior modification. *Journal of Consulting and Clinical Psychology, 45*, 184–191.

CHAPTER 2

Research Methodology and Measurement

Frank M. Gresham and Michael P. Carey

Scientific research refers to controlled, systematic, empirical, and critical investigation of natural phenomena that is guided by hypotheses and theory about supposed relations between such phenomena (Kerlinger, 1986). The *method of science* represents a method of knowing that is unique in that it possesses a self-correcting feature that verifies of disconfirms formally stated predictions (i.e., hypotheses) about natural phenomena. Cohen and Nagel (1934) identified three additional methods of knowing that are diametrically opposed to science: (a) the method of tenacity, (b) the method of authority, and (c) the method of intuition.

The *method of tenacity* describes a way of knowing based upon an individual's belief of what is true or not true. Truth in this case is defined as such simply because the individual believes something to be true irrespective of disconfirming evidence. The method of tenacity might be applied to some individuals (e.g., Mercer, 1979) who staunchly maintain that intelligence tests are biased against cultural and racial minorities in spite of compelling evidence to the contrary (see Reynolds, 1982, for a review).

The *method of authority* refers to the existence of truths that are based upon the statements, proclamations, and/or writings of established authority figures or organizations. For example, if fundamentalist churches decree that abortion is wrong, immoral, criminal, and sinful it is true because an authority organization has defined it as such. One problem with this method of knowing is that there exists more than one authority organization. For example, the Supreme Court has declared abortion a constitutional right that is not a criminal act. Historically, the method of science has conflicted with the method of authority. The statement by Copernicus that the sun rather than the earth was the center of the universe was disputed and considered false because it conflicted with party line authoritarian accounts of the time (i.e., the Church).

The *method of intuition* is based on a priori notions of logic and supposition rather than empirical data. The method of intuition is predicated upon rationalism, which defines phenomena as true simply because it "stands

Frank M. Gresham and Michael P. Carey • Department of Psychology, Louisiana State University, Baton Rouge, Louisiana 70803.

to reason" that they must be true. An excellent example of the method of intuition can be found in the area of psychoeducational evaluation where many professionals still maintain the belief that certain aptitudes interact with certain treatments to produce differential effects in learning (aptitude × treatment interactions or ATIs). A good example for ATI claims can be found in the work of Kaufman and Kaufman (1983), who rationally postulate that certain aptitudes (e.g., simultaneous or sequential processing) should interact with certain treatments. This rationally derived belief, however, has not been shown to be true using empirical (i.e., scientific) methods of investigation (Arter & Jenkins, 1977; Cronbach & Snow, 1977).

Levels of Scientific Investigation

Johnston and Pennypacker (1980) described three levels of scientific investigation, each of which tells us something different about natural phenomena. The first level is *demonstration* that yields statements of the "if—then" variety. Demonstration does not involve control of independent variables in order to observe their effects on dependent variables. Demonstration simply involves the observation of a phenomenon and recording facts about that phenomenon. For example, Pavlov's initial observation that dogs salivated when they heard their caretaker's footsteps led to extremely important controlled investigation of respondent conditioning.

The second level of scientific investigation is *correlation,* which requires the observation and quantification of variables. Correlational statements allow one to predict phenomena from knowledge of independent (predictor) variables with degrees of precision. Correlational statements are statements of the co-occurrence of events, but are not causal statements. That is, if two events co-occur this does not necessarily mean that one event caused the other event. Johnston and Pennypacker (1980) maintain that functional relations are scientifically stronger statements than correlational statements. *Functional relations* are statements that specify an event is determined, produced, or "caused" by a single independent variable. In contrast, correlational statements can specify the relation between two events, both of which may be caused by a third event. The difference between a functional relation and a correlation is that the former isolates a single event and demonstrates that this event in isolation is both necessary and sufficient to produce systematic changes in a second event.

The final method of scientific investigation is the *experimental method.* The experimental method differs from correlational/functional methods in that the independent variable(s) is under complete control and manipulation of the experimenter. For example, the experimenter can not only control the application of an independent variable to a certain phenomenon (e.g., reinforcement for on-task behavior), but also can assign different quantifications of that independent variable (e.g., variable interval 2-minute or VI 2 min.) and subsequently observe its effects. Correlational and functional relational approaches must take variables as they exist in nature and observe their effects on other variables. The experimental method represents the most conceptually elegant and powerful form of scientific investigation because of the control it affords the experimenter in investigating natural phenomena (Johnston & Pennypacker, 1980).

The purpose of this chapter is to provide a necessarily brief overview of research methodology and behavioral measurement. The topics discussed in this chapter represent domains of knowledge that are required in order to consume, evaluate, and produce research. The following sections address the origins and current status of the scientist-practitioner, the types of research questions being asked in educational settings from a behavioral perspective, research design, theories of behavioral measurement, and data analytic procedures. This chapter's objective is to provide readers with a conceptual overview of research methodology and behavioral measurement rather than step-by-step instructions for conducting behavioral research. We point readers to comprehensive and informative references for specific details where appropriate.

Scientist-Practitioner Model

The idea of the scientist-practitioner model of training, at least in clinical psychology, originated as an official policy of the American Psychological Association (APA) in 1947. Two years later, the Boulder Conference (1949) endorsed the scientist-practitioner model of training for clinical psychology training programs. Then, as now, there were two basic attitudes regarding the training of clinical psychologists. One group strongly holds to the position that research training distracts from the more appropriate emphasis in diagnostics and therapy. The other group strongly maintains that emphasis in diagnosis and therapy distracts from the time and effort necessary to train good researchers. Barlow, Hayes, and Nelson (1984) provided an in-depth discussion of this issue in their informative text.

Our sentiments are clearly with the latter position. We believe that effective practitioners must adopt a scientific attitude toward problems they encounter in educational settings. That is, practitioners should have the methodological skills to consume, evaluate critically, and produce research. Our position is that effective practitioners conceptualize referral problems like effective researchers in that they (a) identify problems in measurable terms; (b) formulate testable hypotheses; (c) test their hypotheses empirically; (d) accept or reject hypotheses; and (e) draw conclusions based on empirically tested hypotheses.

There have been several arguments against research training for applied psychologists over the years. For example, Albee (1970) suggested that the "game of science" is incompatible with clinical practice. In short, Albee (1970) believed that because the origin and maintenance of psychological problems could be traced to childhood, the practitioner must engage in "life history research" rather than experimental research. This argument, which seems to be based on the method of intuition, ignores the fact that behavior often has more temporally proximal causes. Moreover, historical factors (e.g., childhood experiences) are not amenable to manipulation, control, or functional analysis. As such, historical factors represent a class of variables that have dubious reliability because they are based on historical recollection and are fixed and immutable because they have already occurred.

Peterson (1976) argued that most clinical psychologists were not interested in research and that most students wished to be professionals rather than scientists. This led to the establishment of the doctor of psychology (Psy. D.) degree at the University of Illinois. Peterson (1976) indicated that over 40% of students' time was spent doing dissertation research and learning foreign languages, which represented an ineffective use of resources for persons planning to enter professional careers. Peterson (1976) concluded that the role of a practitioner is the provision of professional services concerned with assessment and behavior change. Peterson (1976) believed that there was no need for a psychologist to be trained as a producer of research in order to be an intelligent consumer of research.

Peterson's (1976) arguments against research training for psychologists contain several flaws. First, he uses the argument that since students were more interested in being professionals rather than scientists, then students should be trained as professionals. This logic can be questioned on two counts. One, if psychology is defined as the science of behavior, how can one be a psychologist without also being a scientist? Two, student preference for certain activities should probably never be used as the ultimate criterion for how they will be trained. If students know how they should be trained before they are trained, then they could perhaps as easily train themselves. A second logical error that Peterson (1976) makes is that he seems to equate the relevance of research training with the relevance of learning foreign languages. This argument seems at best to strain credibility. Three, Peterson (1976) frequently uses the term *professional* and sets up a false dichotomy between professionals and scientists. If so-called professionals are concerned with assessment and behavior change, then how can one be a professional without thorough knowledge and understanding of the theoretical, empirical, and technical bases of the techniques used to assess and change behavior?

Our basic position regarding research training is that because scientific research involves the controlled, systematic, and critical investigation of natural phenomena, practitioners who approach referral problems in a controlled, systematic, empirical, and critical fashion are more likely to identify and isolate those variables that can be manipulated to effect behavior change. We believe that good practitioners conceptualize problems much like good scientists. Like good scientists, good practitioners maintain an open and critical attitude toward their conclusions as evidenced by their willingness to entertain and test rival hypotheses at any time during the process of assessment and intervention.

Research Epistemology

This chapter is concerned with a conceptual approach of how scientists come to have knowledge of what is and what is not true about natural phenomena. That is, we are interested in providing readers with some of the issues involved in research epistemology. The purpose of this section is to present issues involved in the use of anologies and models in scientific research, operational definitions, the philosophies of logical positivism and radical behaviorism, and the value of the nomological network (Cronbach & Meehl, 1955) as a conceptual model for guiding research in psychology and education.

Scientific Analogies

One issue that seems to have plagued psychology since its inception is the use of analogies to describe how organisms behave. Psychology, perhaps more than any other science, is prone to analogical reasoning that often bears a remote resemblance to natural behavior. For example, Freud's structural division of the personality into the id, ego, and superego represented a rather loose analogy to what persons did and why. More recently, the work of cognitive psychologists in the area of artificial intelligence via computer simulations of human thought represents perhaps as great a conceptual strain as Freud's psychoanalytic theory.

Achinstein (1968) pointed out that analogies are often used in the physical sciences. For example, an analogy has been drawn between nuclear fission and the division of a liquid into smaller drops (Meitner & Frisch, 1939). Analogies are used in science to facilitate understanding of concepts or constructs. This understanding is made easier by specifying the similarities between the concept or construct and other concepts that are more easily grasp or with which individuals have had prior experience. The bases for these similarities may be abstract, physical, or functional.

In psychology and education, we typically utilize functional similarities to describe relations between concepts or constructs (e.g., human thinking and computer-simulated thinking). Unfortunately, there are a host of unknown (and hence, uncontrollable) variables that affect our concepts or constructs as well as basic differences between living organisms and nonliving machines. Analogies often are useful conceptual tools to promote understanding; however, they often do not accurately describe the phenomenon in which we are interested with enough precision to be scientifically useful.

Models in Science

Achinstein (1968) discussed three broad types of models used in science: (a) representational models, (b) theoretical models, and (c) imaginary models. *Representational models* are three-dimensional representations of an object that allow for the discovery of facts about the object it represents. Representational models are utilized primarily in engineering (e.g., models of buildings, cars, dams, etc.). *Imaginary models* are models that are designed to demonstrate what an object or event might be like if certain *a priori* assumptions of the model were in fact (but are not) true. Imaginary models describe what might be true under conditions that do not and probably cannot exist (e.g., assume that the earth had no gravitational pull). Imaginary models are used to investigate phenomena using assumptions that otherwise may be self-contradictory in order to shed light on a phenomenon we already have knowledge of under a different set of assumptions. In some sciences, such as astrophysics, imaginary models may have technical, theoretical, or even social benefit. For example, one could make the assumption that the earth had no ozone layer and postulate the effects this assumption would have on climate, food production, and even human life itself.

The social sciences, particularly psychology, use almost exclusively theoretical models. A theoretical model as a set of assumptions about some phenomenon or system. Guilford's (1959) structure of intellect model represents a theoretical model of the structure of human intelligence. Similarly, the Atkinson and Shriffin (1968) model of memory represents a theoretical model of the structure and function of human memory. Theoretical models are merely approximations to natural phenomenon, but their value lies in the fact that several theoretical models can be proposed and tested to confirm which model is a more accurate representation of nature. The primary value of theoretical models is that they can be empirically tested and either accepted, modified, or rejected to more closely estimate what is true or not true about some phenomenon.

Operational Definitions

Science represents a set of empirically testable propositions about some phenomenon of interest. Only those propositions based on public and repeatable observations are admissible to the domain of science. To investigate a phenomenon of interest, scientists must be careful to define that phenomenon in precise terms. This is known as an *operational definition*. An operational definition makes reference to operations involved in measuring the phenomenon of interest. Operational definitions may also be mathematical definitions as well. For example, the sample standard deviation is defined operationally (and mathematically) as the square root of the average squared deviations about the sample mean.

Operational definitions are not inconsistent with hypothesis generation, theory, or speculation. Operational definitions only seek to define specifically and measurably how terms are used in particular theories, hypotheses, or speculations so that there can be a common ground for agreement on what the scientist means by the concept being investigated. Operational definitions are not logically necessary nor logically sufficient definitions of a phenomenon. For example, a social psychologist may operationally define love as the frequency with which one individual tells another individual he/she loves them. Although this is certainly an operational definition of love, the frequency with which one person tells another person he or she loves them is neither a necessary nor a sufficient condition for love to exist.

No branch of study can legitimately be called a science if it does not employ operational definitions. As such, operational definitions are invaluable in the science of psychology whose theoreticians and practitioners are prone to habitate the roily, metaphysical underworld of undefined hypothetical constructs and pseudo-causes of these undefined constructs.

Logical Positivism and Behaviorism

Logical positivism as a research epistemology was initiated in the 1920s by scientists and philosophers who were concerned with the impossibility of speculative metaphysics as a way of knowing (Achinstein, 1968). Metaphysics represents a branch of inquiry dealing with phenomena beyond the realm of experience. Statements in metaphysics are incapable of empirical verification and, as such, are not within the domain of science.

Logical positivism offered a reconstruction of science in which all terms, constructs, and theories are directly observable (at least at some point) and hence can be empirically demonstrated. Logical positivists can talk of constructs and theories because they allow for relations between theoretical terms (i.e., unobservables) and nontheoretical terms (i.e., observables). The relations between theoretical and nontheoretical terms represent connections in a theory and are termed correspondence rules.

Methodological behaviorism represents a version of logical positivism that holds that because mentalistic events (e.g., thought, feelings, attitudes, etc.) are unobservable, then no truth can be gained from the study of unobservable events (Skinner, 1974). Methodological behaviorism maintains that unobservable events cannot be reliably measured and thus represent phenomena beyond the realm of experience (i.e., these phenomena are metaphysical). For example, we cannot measure a person's intelligence because it is unobservable, but we can measure the number of learning trials to some criterion on verbal or spatial tasks. In short, methodological behaviorism represents the most extreme form of operationalism.

In many ways, the logic of methodological behaviorism is hard to dismantle. For example, if we know that a person has not drunk water for 3 days we might say the person will feel thirsty. If the person feels thirsty, he or she will in all likelihood drink. Thus, a person drinks because he or she feels thirsty. The methodological behaviorist would say that the way a person feels in this case is irrelevant in a functional analysis of drinking behavior. All we need to know is the time elapsed since the person last ingested liquids (antecedent event). Knowing this is both necessary and sufficient to make a probablistic statement regarding a person's drinking behavior. No information for a functional analysis is lost by ignoring the intermediate, unobservable stage of how the person feels.

Skinner (1974) is the founder of a different form of behaviorism known as *radical behaviorism*. Radical behaviorism does not disavow the existence of internal events (e.g., thought, feelings, etc.) but rather questions the nature of the events. Skinner (1974) acknowledges the presence and possible functional relations between so-called internal events and external/observable behavior. The major difficulty internal events create for the empiricist is accurate measurement of these events in relation to observable behavior. The consideration of internal events in many ways frees behavioral researchers from the intellectual straitjacket of methodological behaviorism. This freedom, however, creates a "good news-bad news" situation. The good news is that it allows for the generation of hypotheses about a much broader range of variables that may affect behavior than is possible in methodological behaviorism. The bad news is that it provides a window for metaphysical terms and mentalistic fictions to be opened by fuzzy-headed researchers and practitioners. The rebirth of cognitive psychology in many ways represents a return to the metaphysics and structuralism of the past, but now wrapped in the euphemism of cognitive science.

The Nomological Network

Over 30 years ago, Cronbach and Meehl (1955) set forth a philosophy of science for the construct validation of tests that is applicable to all of scientific research. Construct validity refers to the degree to which a given measurement procedure (tests, observations, etc.) reflects the construct of interest and the meaning that is attached to the construct (i.e., how the construct is interpreted). Construct validity is represented by a set of empirically testable hypotheses that are used to accept or reject one's interpretation of the construct of interest.

Cronbach and Meehl (1955) stated that to make clear what something is requires that one set forth the laws in which it occurs. This interlocking system of laws is called a *nomological network*. The laws in a nomological network can relate (a) observable behaviors to observable behaviors, (b) theoretical constructs to observable behaviors, and (c) theoretical constructs to theoretical constructs. A requirement for a construct to be scientifically admissible is that it occur in a nomological network in which at least some of the laws are observable behaviors. This requirement bears a striking similarity to the use of correspondence rules in methodological behaviorism by which theoretical terms are linked to nontheoretical (observable) terms. Elaboration of a nomological network represents increased knowledge of the construct and the addition of more and more observables that, in turn, result in less and less inference about the meaning of the construct.

Scientific research, whether it be correlational, group differentiation, classification, or structural, can be conceptualized from the perspective of the nomological network. Research in psychology and education relates observables to observables (frequency of on-task behavior to accuracy of academic performance), observables to theoreticals (academic engaged time to intelligence), and theoreticals to theoreticals (self-efficacy to achievement motivation). Cronbach and Meehl (1955) pointed out that early on in the investigation of a phenomenon the nomological network will have few connections that are elaborated and revised on the basis of empirical relations demonstrated through the scientific method. We believe that the nomological network is a useful heuristic for conceptualizing, designing, and interpreting research in psychology and education.

Research Strategies

In spite of the emphasis in American psychology on training scientists-practitioners, applied psychologists typically spend only 10% to 15% of their time in research-related activities (Garfield & Kurtz, 1976). Moreover, the median number of lifetime publications of doctoral clinical psychologists is approximately one manuscript (Kelly, Goldberg, Fiske, & Kilkowski, 1978). The previous discussion of the so-called scientist versus practitioner split seems to exemplify the argument of the relevance/irrelevance of research training for psychologists. That is, given that doctoral-level psychologists are doing so little research in their careers, then it must be the case that research training is irrelevant for the day-to-day practice of applied psychologists. We vehemently disagree with this position and maintain, as do Martens and Keller (1987), that the scientist-practitioner model itself has not failed, but rather the failure has been with its implementation. The following sections will briefly review research strategies that may assist in the implementation of the scientist-practitioner model.

Single-Case Experimental Designs

Barlow (1980) suggested that applied psychologists may not necessarily be lacking on interest in or dedication to research, but rather they may simply be lacking specific strategies (i.e., methodologies) for conducting research. Hayes (1981) advocated training practitioners in the conception, design, and application of single-case or time-series methodology. Hayes (1981) offers several reasons why single-case methodology (a legitimate, controlled, and internally valid research tool) has been underutilized in applied settings.

First, single-case methodology is undertaught (or untaught) in training programs. Most research methodology courses are taught by statiticians who usually have no applied experience nor interest in applied research problems. In addition, there is often a strong bias against using single-subject designs to fulfill theses and dissertation requirements in training programs. Second, the time-series methodology has not been focused toward practitioners. Most published reports of single-case methodologies have used designs that contain many complexities that are not practical in everyday applied work (see the *Journal of Applied Behavior Analysis* for many such impractical examples). In short, many published reports of the single-case methodology through which one could model appropriate design strategies are simply user-unfriendly. Third, the single-case approach has been exclusively associated with a behavioral approach to intervention. This is understandable because behaviorists have been the prime utilizers of this approach. However single-case methodology, like group design methods, is atheoretical and can be used by any theoretical approach to intervention. Finally, agencies (e.g., school districts) provide little support for research endeavors. In fact, doing research may be perceived as incompatible with practice.

Hayes (1981) enumerated five core elements of single-case methodology: (a) repeated measurement, (b) analysis of intrasubject variability, (c) specification of treatment conditions or independent variables, (d) replication, and (e) design flexibility. Each of these core elements will be discussed briefly in the following sections.

Repeated Measurement

By definition, time-series research involves the repeated measurement of behavior over time. Unlike group repeated measures designs, the single-case approach uses more frequent measurements of the dependent variable and uses the subject's baseline levels of behavior as the criterion against which treatment effects are compared. Thus, each subject serves as his or her own control in time-series research. Repeated measurements can and often are taken on multiple dependent variables, such as direct observations of behavior, self-reports, ratings by others, and so forth. This represents the single-case analogue to multivariate designs in group research.

Intrasubject Variability

Variability within subjects is treated as error in group experimental designs (i.e., sum of squares within subjects) and, as such, represents a source of variance that cannot (or more accurately, is not) be explained. In contrast, intrasubject variability in the single-case approach is conceptualized as being amenable to a functional analysis. That is, intrasubject variability may be functionally related to specifiable environmental and/or physiological stimulus or setting events. In short, variability in the behavior of a single subject is viewed as data that can be identified, isolated, functionally analyzed, and controlled.

Specification of Conditions

Clear specification of all components of the independent variable differentiates single-case research from group-design research. Although group research may specify a treatment one group receives versus another group, it often does not specify in operational terms all components in enough detail for replication of the treatment by other researchers. For example, one group may receive client-centered therapy for depression whereas another group receives rational-emotive therapy. Although core elements of client-centered and rational-emotive therapy can be specified, they often are not specifically assessed in group research. This issue has received increased attention in applied research under the label of treatment integrity (Yeaton &

Sechrest, 1981). Treatment integrity refers to the degree to which treatments are implemented as planned. Obviously, poorly implemented treatments represent not only a threat to the internal validity of research design, but also the generalizability (i.e., external validity) of treatment effects.

Single-case research adheres to a clearer and more specific description of treatment components that is typical of group research. This, in part, is because single-case researchers have been behavioral in their orientation and as such adhere to a strong empirical, operational approach to research.

Replication

There are two types of replication in single-case research: (a) within-subject replication and (b) between-subject replication. Within-subject replication typifies the underlying logic of time-series methodology. That is, the effects of the independent variable on the dependent variable are replicated at various phases of the experiment. This replication allows one to attribute changes in the dependent variable to the independent variable, thus ensuring the internal validity of the design. Between-subject replication involves replicating treatment effects using the same treatment over several clients. For example, a classroom management program might be replicated across first, third, fifth, and seventh grades, thus ensuring the external validity of the treatment program.

Design Flexibility

Hayes (1981) indicated that the largest difference between group and single-case research is the flexibility and tentativeness of the single-case approach. Group-design research is fixed in that it is planned and carried out irrespective of the treatment effects observed. Single-case research, however, is always subject to change depending on the level, trend, and variability in the data. For example, a researcher might have planned to use response cost to reduce the frequency of classroom disruptive behavior. The response cost procedure may have minimal effects on disruptive behavior and, as such, the researcher adds a time-out contingency to the response cost contingency and observes substantial decreases in the target behavior. This flexibility allows researchers to change treatments in midstream to achieve maximal benefits yet still maintain the internal validity of designs (see Barlow & Hersen, 1984, for details).

Between-Group Designs

The foregoing discussion points out the value of single-case methodology for practitioners in applied settings. The advantages of repeated measurement, analysis of intrasubject variability, treatment specification, replication, and design flexibility have proven invaluable to researchers and practitioners in conducting an experimental analysis of behavior. However, there are several aspects of group designs that are clearly superior to single-case methodology (Kratochwill, Mace, & Mott, 1985).

One, group experimental designs are clearly superior to single-case designs when one wants to compare two or more treatments. There are a number of potential confounds and threats to internal validity when trying to compare the effects of two or more treatments for a single subject. For example, the sequential ordering of different treatments may explain effects on the dependent variable, thus making conclusions of one treatment's superiority over another's hazardous at best. Moreover, treatments may interact with each other in unknown ways to produce differential effects that may not have been observed if a single treatment had been used (multiple treatment interference). Even single-case designs that attempt to control for sequential or order effects (e.g., the alternating treatments design) have a number of problems with multiple treatment interference (Kratochwill *et al.*, 1985). Group experimental designs can clearly provide a more internally valid test of differences produced by two or more treatments primarily because well-designed group experiments satisfy the independence-of-error terms assumption in analysis of variance and/or the general linear model (see Cohen & Cohen, 1983).

A second advantage of between-groups designs is that they are more suitable for large-group studies than single-case designs. Studies concerned with effects of large-scale interventions for large groups of subjects are more appropriately investigated using between-groups experimental designs. Project Follow Through represents a good example of such a large-scale study using a between-groups experimental design (see Becker & Carnine, 1980, for a review).

A third advantage of group designs is when one is interested in studying behavior interrelationships. Single-case strategies are inadequate for investigating the covariation of a large number of responses in a group or groups of individuals (Voeltz & Evans, 1982). Wahler (1975) used cluster analytic techniques to study the behavior interrelationships of response class members in a group of school-age children. Strain and Ezzell (1978) used lag sequential analysis of 11 behavioral responses within and between subjects across three settings. Multivariate correlational analysis is preferable to visual inspection of graphed data to determine the degree of interrelationship between behaviors in a response class.

Finally, group designs allow for theoretical advances in building elegant causal models for problem behaviors by allowing for investigation of the many variables impacting on the occurrence and nonoccurrence of behavior. Patterson (1986) built a structural model to account for the antisocial behavior in children taking into account such predictor variables as parental discipline style, family stress, and coercive parent–child interactions. This type of investigation, which utilizes analysis of covariance structures (linear structural relations), is not possible using single-case methodology.

Measurement of Behavior in Psychology and Education

The measurement of phenomenon represents the life's blood of scientific activity. Measurement of behavior can be defined as the assignment of numbers to objects in such a way as to represent quantities of attributes (Nunnally, 1978). The term *attributes* suggests that objects themselves are not being measured, but rather particular features of objects. For example, two sticks may vary on the attribute of length. Length represents an abstraction that should not be confused with other attributes of sticks (e.g., color, density, weight, etc.). Similarly, behavior possesses several attributes or dimensions, such as frequency, temporality (duration, latency, and interresponse time), permanent by products, and intensity (Gresham, 1982).

The purpose of this section is to describe two distinct measurement strategies that have evolved, somewhat independently, in the fields of psychology and education. These two measurement strategies have acquired various labels in the measurement literature including, nomothetic-idiographic, normative-ipsative, or norm-referenced-criterion-referenced (Brown, 1983). The labels basically describe the issue of group versus individual sources of data, but do not capture the underlying issue of units of measurement. As such, we will describe what has been termed vaganotic or relative measurement strategies and idemnotic or absolute measurement strategies (Johnston & Pennypacker, 1980).

Relative (Vaganotic) Measurement

The basis of current psychometric theory as well as all parametric statistical analysis can be traced to the beginnings of probability theory, the development of calculus, and the study of measurement error. According to Johnston and Pennypacker (1980), the works of Newton, Legendre, Gauss, Leplace, and Quetelet all provided the foundation for modern measurement theory. Somewhat later, the work of early psychologists, such as Fechner and

Weber in psychophysics, provided additional information concerning measurement theory.

The measurement of attributes in vaganotic (relative) measurement systems is based on the variation in a set of underlying observations. Measurement scales (e.g., ordinal or interval) define attributes into existence on the basis of relative variability rather than the absolute values of the attributes under consideration. For example, a student's level of academic achievement on a standardized achievement test is commonly expressed as a T score ($m=50$; $s=10$). The T score, in turn, is based on the distance the student's raw score is from the mean. The score is standardized by subtracting the student's raw score from the raw score mean (based on the sample) and the difference divided by the standard deviation. The student's performance on the test is subsequently interpreted relative to the performance of others on the test rather than in the sense of the student's absolute level of academic proficiency.

The important issue to understand in relative (vaganotic) measurement is the meaning of the units of measurement. In our example, the T score represents a standard score with known properties. However, the score is standard with respect to a given sample and does not correspond to the absolute value of the attribute being measured (achievement). Clearly, the T score is defined on the basis of variability in a set of achievement scores. Johnston and Pennypacker (1980) suggested that this approach to measurement is unique to the social sciences and represents the most fundamental difference between the natural sciences and the social sciences. An example from the physical sciences may highlight the difference in measurement strategies. Suppose a scientist wished to measure the weight of a given object. Further suppose that the units of grams, kilograms, or pounds did not exist. The scientist using a relative measurement system might attempt to determine the weight of the object by collecting all objects in the lab and other buildings (to ensure a representative sampling of objects). The scientist subsequently presents all of the objects to a panel of judges and has them specify which object is heavier (presented two at a time). The scientist could assign scale values to all objects (e.g., T scores) and thus determine the relative weight of the object under consideration. This creates no problem until another scientist in another lab wishes to investigate the weight of the same object.

The major conceptual problem with relative measurement strategies is that the number assigned to the phenomenon under investigation bears no fixed relation to the absolute size of the phenomenon of interest. Thus, units of measurement are removed from the phenomenon and may not accurately portray the attribute under investigation.

Absolute (Idemnotic) Measurement

Absolute or idemnotic measurement refers to measurement that utilizes absolute and standard units whose existence is established independent of variability in the phenomenon being measured (Johnston & Pennypacker, 1980). The earliest absolute measurement strategies were developed for the description of physical parameters such as distance, mass, and time. Later, new concepts were defined into existence by forming various ratios and/or combinations of these three basic physical parameters. For example, velocity was defined as Distance/Time. The meter was defined as the distance from the equator to either pole $\times 10^{-6}$. These examples show that units of measurement were anchored to physical phenomena (primarily distance, mass, and time) and units of measurement were defined independently of the variance in the object being measured.

The use of absolute measurement has not been constrained to the physical or natural sciences. For example, Ebbinghaus used the number of words remembered from word lists as an indication of memory. Later, Thorndike used the time it took for cats to solve puzzles and the number of errors in puzzle solution as measures of animal intelligence. Finally, Pavlov used the amount of saliva secreted by animals (read from a graduated tube) in a given time frame as an index of the strength of the conditioned response. All of these early psychologists were similar in their insistence upon the use of standard and absolute-based measurement in their rather diverse areas of interest.

Today, behavioral psychologists, particularly those from the applied behavior analysis camp, utilize absolute unit-based measurement of behavior. As mentioned earlier, behavior has several dimensions that can be measured on an absolute scale. Frequency (the number of times a behavior occurs), duration (how long a behavior lasts), interresponse times (the time which elapses between responses), and permanent byproducts (i.e., the effects of behavior such as litter, vandalism, etc.) all represent absolute-based measurement. Combinations of the aspects of frequency and temporality can be used to define other dimensions of behavior such as *response rate* (Frequency/Time) or *celeration* (change in response rate as a function of time).

The use of absolute measurement in behavioral psychology has been applied to a seemingly endless variety of phenomena, including academic achievement, social skills, intelligence, creativity, perceptual-motor skills, psychopathological behavior, vandalism, traffic violations, safety, and so forth. The empirical literature in these diverse areas attests to the practicality and acceptance of idemnotic (absolute) measurement in psychology and education viewed from a behavior analytic perspective.

Objective measurement may be defined as a system of measurement in which the unit of measurement is defined independently of the distribution of the object being measured (Guion & Ironson, 1983). By definition, relative measurement strategies are not objective in this sense because these measurement strategies often use the standard deviation of the distribution of scores from a sample to standardize units of measurement. Clearly, this is only objective in relation to the particular sample upon which these units are based and cannot be generalized to other distributions of scores obtained from other samples without a questionable combination of data transformation (e.g., equating procedures) and a leap of faith.

Recent work in the area of latent trait theory appears to get around this sticky problem of sample-dependent units of measurement. Latent trait theory (to be discussed in detail later in this chapter) provides a means for constructing scales of measurement that can be fixed without reference to a specific sample of individuals (Guion & Ironson, 1983). In other words, the probability of a given response to an item does not depend on the distribution of the phenomenon being measured (i.e., the parameters are said to be invariant) (Hambleton & Cook, 1977). As such, the unit of measurement in latent trait theory can be said to be on a *ratio scale* because it does not depend on sample distributions for its meaning.

Integration of Relative and Absolute Measurement

The foregoing discussion of relative and absolute measurement strategies highlights the vast differences in the fundamental assumptions of each measurement approach. Based on the information presented, it would appear that the basic principles of each measurement approach represents a case of irreconcilable differences. Each measurement strategy has, however, contributed greatly to knowledge of human behavior and to the practices of classification, intervention, and evaluation of intervention outcomes. We believe strongly that researchers should retain both models of measurement depending on what research question needs to be answered at a particular time.

First, relative measurement is indispensible when one wishes to sample the same behaviors of a group of individuals and to determine deviant (i.e., different) responses of a given individual in the group. This approach has been advocated by several prominent behavioral psychologists under the rubric of social comparison (Kazdin, 1977; Walker & Hops, 1976; Wolf, 1978). For example, Walker and

Hops (1976) used normative observational data (i.e., absolute rates of 19 categories of observed classroom behavior) to assess the degree of treatment effectiveness in two classrooms. Normative data were collected on nonreferred classroom peers and target children's behavior rates were compared before and after intervention. Walker and Hops (1976) stated that normative peer data provides an operant measure of appropriate child behavior in a given classroom setting and provides a measure of variability and trends in this operant level over time as a function of changes in classroom stimulus conditions. Yeaton and Sechrest (1981) discussed a similar concept under the label of treatment effect norms.

Second, relative and absolute measurements are in fact tapping somewhat different dimensions of behavior in terms of the molar versus molecular distinction. Absolute measurement typically focuses on somewhat small or molecular units of behavior, such as the frequency of out-of-seat behavior, the duration of hitting others, or the number of chairs overturned in a temper tantrum. All of these responses could be statistically summarized using a relative measurement strategy (e.g., factor analysis) into a molar unit or *response class* labeled disruptive behavior. You will note in this example that the behavioral dimensions of frequency, duration, and behavioral by-products are all included in the response class of disruptive behavior. This creates no conceptual or theoretical problem from a behavioral perspective because all three behaviors could be members of the same *functional response class* (i.e., they could be controlled by the same antecedent and consequent events). Factor analysis of these behaviors merely represents an objective means of summarizing these behaviors.

Wahler (1975) studied behavioral covariation of 19 child behaviors and six social-environmental categories using cluster analysis procedures. Based on this analysis, Wahler (1975) found that children's behavioral repertoires contained responses that covaried predictably across school and home settings. It is important to note that the units of analysis in this study were direct observational records reflecting the percentage of occurrence of each behavior calculated on a moment-by-moment basis in a measurement session. Thus, absolute unit-based (idemnotic) measures were subjected to vaganotic statistical analyses (i.e., correlational and cluster analysis). This in no way detracted from the quality of information produced by the analyses and, in fact, provided invaluable information concerning the notion of response classes as well as controlling variables of specific responses within those response classes.

Finally, and perhaps most importantly, the decision to employ relative or absolute measurement should be dictated by the purposes one has for measuring behavior. If one's purpose is to select individuals for intervention, then one should use social comparisons (relative measurement) to determine the deviance of behavior rates of others (see Walker & Hops, 1976). Similarly, one could evaluate the effectiveness of intervention by the same process (see Yeaton & Sechrest, 1981). Voeltz and Evans (1982) suggested that multivariate statistical procedures represent a preferable strategy to be used to examine patterns among responses derived from systematically observed categories of behavior. These multivariate strategies have been utilized successfully in behavioral research with behaviorally disordered adolescents (Strain & Ezzell, 1978), aggressive children (Harris, 1980), and autistic children (Lichstein & Wahler, 1976). Subsequent sections of this chapter will describe these multivariate statistical procedures and will provide an outline for their use in answering major research questions.

Psychometric Theories and Measurement

Several psychometric theories have been proposed to evaluate the quality of assessment data. The most prominent of these is known as classical test theory, which is based on the notions of true and error scores. Variations of classical test theory include generalizability theory or domain sampling theory (Cronbach, Gleser, Nanda, & Rajaratnam, 1972) and the multitrait-multimethod matrix (Campbell & Fiske, 1959). More recently, item response theory based on the idea of latent traits and item characteristic curves, has received increased attention (Lord & Novick, 1968).

Behavioral assessment has traditionally lacked a theoretical structure from which to devise techniques to evaluate the quality of behavioral assessment data. Recently, the idea of accuracy (rather than reliability and validity) has emerged as a measurement criterion in the behavioral literature (Cone, 1981; Johnston & Pennypacker, 1980). Also, Staats (1981) and Burns (1980) have promulgated the idea of social behaviorism psychometrics to address the quality of behavioral assessment data using the concepts of basic behavioral repertoires and cumulative hierarchial learning.

The purpose of the following sections is to describe five frequently used psychometric approaches that have been employed to evaluate the reliability, validity, and/or accuracy of behavioral assessment data. These five approaches are (a) classical test theory, (b) generalizability theory, (c) multitrait-multimethod matrix, (d) item response theory, and (e) accuracy. These five approaches will be briefly described in the following sections along with examples from the behavioral literature to illustrate how behavioral psychologists utilize these diverse approaches in evaluating the psychometric quality of behavioral assessment data.

Classical Test Theory (CTT)

Overview

CTT is based on the notion of true and error scores first developed by Spearman (1904). The idea behind true and error scores is based on the concept of systematic and unsystematic variation in a set of scores. *Systematic variation* refers to predictable increases or decreases in scores that result from factors such as learning, training, development, fatigue, forgetting, and the like. Systematic variation in a set of scores can be detected by a regular or orderly arrangement of scores (e.g., decreases in test performance as a function of time/fatigue). For example, if a group of sprinters ran 20 consecutive 100 meter dashes, there would be a systematic (predictable) increase in times for each 100 meter dash. Similarly, if a group of individuals received 2 hours of instruction in geometry each day, there would be a systematic (orderly) increase in geometry test scores for the group.

Unsystematic variation refers to fluctuation of scores for individuals over time as a result of random (unpredictable) factors operating in the individual, in the environment, or in the individual and environment. The key difference in systematic and unsystematic variation is that the former produces orderly changes in a set of scores whereas the latter produces disorderly or haphazard changes in a set of scores. Basically, systematic variation is variation that can be explained or predicted.

Reliability and Validity

It should be obvious that reliability is based on the degree of systematic variation in a set of scores relative to the total variation in a set of scores. Thus, the reliability of measurement in CTT is the extent of unsystematic variation in the quantitative description of the same attribute of an individual when the same individual is measured a number of times. *Error* of measurement refers to the discrepancy between an individual's observed test score and his or her true score.

CTT is based on the conceptualization of a test score as a random variable. A given individual's score on a particular test or measurement occasion is viewed as a random sample of one of many possible test scores that a person could have earned on repeated administrations of the same test or, more accurately, a strictly parallel form of that test. In short, reliability is defined as the extent of unsystematic variation of one individual's scores on a series of parallel tests. The reliability coefficient is an index of the degree to which scores on one parallel test can predict scores on any other parallel test.

Various procedures have been developed for estimating the reliability (e.g., stability, alternate forms, internal consistency) and validity (e.g., content, construct, criterion-related) of scores in CTT. These are well known and will not be discussed here. For more detailed accounts of these procedures see excellent texts by Crocker and Algina (1986), Ghiselli, Campbell, and Zedeck (1981), and Nunnally (1978).

Assumptions

Ghiselli *et al.* (1981) specified three fundamental assumptions upon which CTT is based. The first of these assumptions has to do with true scores, another with error scores, and the last with the way in which these two scores are combined. These three assumptions are listed as follows:

1. The individual possesses stable characteristics or traits (i.e., true scores) that persist through time.
2. Error scores are completely random.
3. Fallible scores are the result of the addition of true and error scores.

The first assumption must necessarily be made if the ideas of true and error scores are to be meaningful. If a person's true score changed frequently and unsystematically, there would be no stability in the attribute under consideration. Frequently changing scores are unpredictable from one time to the next and are thus considered error.

The second assumption must follow from the first assumption in that errors of measurement are completely random (i.e., they result from unsystematic variation). Recall that unsystematic error represents changes in a distribution of scores in a disorderly or haphazard fashion. CTT assumes that variability of this sort is caused by random (as opposed to systematic) factors and, as such, reflects the unreliability of the measure.

Finally, CTT states that an individual's obtained score (i.e., fallible score) on a measure is simply the sum of the true score plus the error score. Thus, all scores on tests, inventories, questionnaires, and so forth represent a combination of true scores and error scores.

Relevance to Behavioral Assessment

The principles and assumptions underlying CTT would seem to be antithetical to the assumptions and purposes of behavioral assessment. For example, behavioral assessment assumes that responses or behaviors exhibited in an assessment are samples of behavior in a particular situation rather than a sign of an underlying construct. Further, behavior is assumed to be situation specific (Mischel, 1968) rather than cross situational (trait) as in CTT. Kazdin (1979), for example, presented evidence that behavior is determined by a variety of factors pertaining to how responses are assessed and the conditions under which assessment takes place.

Nelson (1983) argued that given the assumption that behavior is modifiable, then stability (test–retest reliability) should not be expected. Given the assumption that behavior is situation specific, then concurrent validity across assessment situations (e.g., school versus home) should not be expected. Finally, given that behavior varies across response systems or channels (e.g., cognitive-verbal, overt-motoric, and physiological-emotional), then convergent validity across methods should not be expected.

All of the previously cited arguments are legitimate based on the assumption in CTT that individuals possess characteristics or traits (i.e., true scores) that are stable over time. A closer look at this assumption may help clarify some of these inconsistencies between behavioral assessment and CTT.

First, CTT assumes that an individual's true score is stable over time. Behavioral assessment assumes that behavior is changeable over time, but does not address the concept of true score. If a behavioral program is designed to modify behavior in a given situation, then one would be producing predictable or systematic changes in behavior. Systematic changes in behavior in CTT are not viewed as error (unreliability) and do not create a problem of violating CTT assumptions. Therefore, Nelson's (1983) argument fails to differentiate between systematic and unsystematic variability in scores over time. Behavioral interventions are designed to produce systematic and predictable behavior changes and, as such, cannot be considered as error in CTT.

Second, although one sometimes finds low correlation among measures taken in different situations, this is not always the case. Patterson and Bank (1986) found that parent ratings of antisocial behavior (home situation) predicted teacher and peer ratings of antisocial behavior (school situation). Wahler (1975) found that behavioral clusters (response classes) were stable across four school situations or settings. The assumption that behavior does not occur cross-situationally disavows the concept of setting generalization. Stokes and Baer (1977) reviewed several studies in which behavior has been shown to occur in relevant nontraining situations. If the same controlling variables (i.e., antecedents and consequences) occur in other settings, then behavior will and should occur cross-situationally.

Finally, the independence of the three response systems could suggest the unreliability of measuring any one or combination of response systems. Cone (1979) suggested that the failure to find high correspondence between response systems may be caused by method–content confounds. That is, most studies have mixed method (e.g., self-report and direct observation) and content (e.g., fear of stimuli versus motoric or physiological responding in the presence of feared stimuli) dimensions. These method–content confounds are equivalent to adding error to measurement because different constructs are being assessed and the methods used to measure these constructs have widely ranging reliabilities.

Generalizability Theory (G Theory)

Overview

G Theory is based on the domain sampling model (DSM) of reliability and measurement error that arose in the mid-1950s (Tryon, 1957) in reaction to CTT or the model of parallel tests. The basic notion of the DSM is that a measure is composed of a random sample of items from a hypothetical domain or universe of items. In the DSM, a *trait* is conceptualized as a group of behaviors that have some property in common.

G Theory was developed by Cronbach and colleagues (Cronbach *et al.*, 1972) and represents a set of techniques for studying the degree to which a given set of measurements of an individual generalizes to a more extensive set of measurements of that individual. G Theory can best be conceptualized as a set of measurement conditions (independent variables) under which a test score (dependent variable) is obtained. As such, G Theory studies are usually analyzed statistically with ANOVA procedures.

Cone (1977) identified six universes of generalizability that are relevant to behavioral assessment: (a) scorer, (b) item, (c) time, (d) method, (e) setting, and (f) dimension. These universes of generalizability represent measurement conditions under which a given behavior for a given individual may be measured. For example, a behavior observed at one point in time, in one setting, by one observer, and by one method (e.g., direct observation) would be assessed by generalizability to other behaviors, other times, other settings, other observers, and by other methods.

One can see similarity between the universes of generalizability in G Theory and traditional notions of reliability and validity in CTT. Scorer generalizability is similar to interobserver reliability/agreement. Time generalizability is roughly equivalent to stability or test-retest reliability. Method generalizability is similar to convergent validity. Item generalizability is like internal consistency reliability. Setting generalizability is similar to criterion-related validity. Dimension generalizability is somewhat like discriminant validity. The key difference between G Theory and CTT is that the former views behavior (or scorers, methods, times, etc.) as a representative sample of the universe of similar behaviors (or scorers, methods, times, etc.), whereas the latter considers a set of behaviors to be strictly parallel to another set of behaviors (i.e., model of parallel tests).

Reliability and Validity

As previously noted, reliability and validity in G Theory are viewed as the different ways in which test scores can be generalized. The universes of generalizability such as scorer, item, method, time, setting, and dimension bear a correspondence in CTT to interrater reliability, internal consistency reliability, convergent validity, test-retest reliability, criterion-related validity, and discriminant validity, respectively.

The index of generalizability for a particular universe is defined by the generalizability coefficient, which is defined as the ratio of universe score variance to expected observed score variance. Readers should note the parallel to CTT in which reliability is indexed by the reliability coefficient, which is the ratio of true score variance to fallible or observed score variance. Another way of conceptualizing the generalizability coefficient is that it represents the squared correlation (i.e., percent of variance) between observed scores and universe scores or the degree to which observed scores predict (represent) universe scores.

Assumptions

Several assumptions underlie G Theory that differentiate it from the assumptions in CTT (Crocker & Algina, 1986; Ghiselli *et al.*, 1981). First, a domain or universe is defined as a set of measurement conditions that is more extensive than the conditions under which sample measurements were obtained. As such, a particular test or measurement procedure is viewed as a sample of items or behaviors from a domain or universe of interest. Second, domains are described statistically by their average characteristics, which include (a) averages of means of the scores on the components in the sample; (b) averages of variances of the scores on the components in the sample; (c) averages of covariances among the components in the sample; and (d) averages of covariances between the components and any other variable outside the domain. The basic assumption in G Theory is that given an adequate sample, the means, variances, and covariances in the sample accurately represent the domain or universe means, variances, and covariances.

A final assumption in G Theory is that universes or domains of interest include the following: (a) scorer, (b) item, (c) time, (d) setting, (e) method, and (f) dimension. Thus, a sample of scorers, items, times, settings, methods, and dimensions are said to accurately represent the universe of scorers, items, times, and so forth that might have been used. In other words, G Theory refers to the various ways in which scores might be generalized rather than in terms of reliability and validity.

Relevance to Behavioral Assessment

The principles and procedures of G Theory appear, on the surface, to be more consistent with the assumptions underlying behavioral assessment. Cone (1977) argued that all universes of generalizability are relevant to behavioral assessment. Essentially, the differences between traditional and behavioral assessment in the context of G Theory are philosophical rather than methodological or statistical. The concept of a domain in the DSM more closely corresponds to the behavioral notion of a response class than does the concept of a trait in CTT.

A *response class* can refer to a group of behaviors that have some property in common (e.g., a functional response class), which may mean the behaviors within the class are controlled by the same antecedent and/or consequent stimulus events (Voeltz & Evans, 1982). Response classes can also refer to a cluster or group of behaviors that covary or correlate with each other (Wahler, 1975). A *domain* is defined in the DSM as a group of behaviors that have some property in common. A homogenous domain of behaviors would be defined statistically as one that had relatively high interitem and item-total (domain) correlations. Given these descriptions of response class and domains, one can see the striking similarity between these two concepts.

Jones, Reid, and Patterson (1975) used the Behavior Coding System (BCS) to estimate what they termed the total deviant score. The BCS contains 14 behaviors that are summed to yield this total deviant score. These 14 behaviors are intercorrelated and each behavior correlates with the total deviant score. Behaviorally, these 14 behaviors can be viewed as members of a response class labeled total deviant behavior because all behaviors in this class covary with each other. The correlations between these 14 behaviors provide evidence of the generalizability of each behavior to other members in the response class. Moreover, the correlation between these 14 behaviors and other behaviors in other response classes in other settings, assessed through different methods, and at other times, provides evidence for dimension, setting, method, and time generalizability, respectively. An excellent example of behavioral data that can be conceptualized in terms of G Theory is the recent study by Patterson and Bank (1986) in which deviant child behavior assessed through different methods and in different settings was related to inadequate parental discipline.

Conceptually, G Theory is particularly relevant for behavioral assessment. A basic assumption in behavioral assessment is that behavior is influenced greatly by environmental events or situations in which behavior is assessed. G Theory assumes that the universes of domains of generalizability represent all conditions under which scores from assessment devices might be obtained. In short, G Theory assumes that scores are influenced by the conditions under which the scores are obtained. In this respect, behavioral assessment and G Theory share common conceptual bases.

Multitrait-Multimethod Matrix (MTMM)

Overview

The idea of the MTMM matrix was developed by Campbell and Fiske (1959) as an extention of CTT notions of reliability and validity. Central to the MTMM matrix are the ideas of convergent and discriminant validity. Convergent validity refers to the correlation between different methods of measuring the same trait. Discriminant validity refers to the degree different traits can be discriminated. According to Campbell and Fiske (1959), reliability is defined as the agreement between two efforts to measure the same trait using maximally similar methods. In contrast, validity is defined as the agreement between two attempts to measure the same trait using maximally different methods.

Convergent validation is based on the notion of multiple operationalism, which states that reality is more than any single measure or definition of reality. Thus, the MTMM matrix implies that any single operational definition of a behavior, response class, or trait is equivocal.

The MTMM matrix is comprised of four components. First, the reliability diagonal identifies the reliability of each trait measured by each method (monotrait-monomethod values). Second, the hetereotrait-monomethod triangle identifies several traits measured by the same method. The reliability diagonal and the hetereotrait-monomethod triangle make up the monomethod block. Third, the validity diagonal (monotrait-hetereomethod values) specifies a single trait measured by different methods. Finally, the hetereotrait-heteromethod triangle identifies the values of different traits measured by different methods.

These are several parallels of the MTMM matrix to both CTT and G Theory. For example, the correlation between different methods of measuring different traits (discriminant validity) would be an indication of criterion-related validity in CTT. Also, the correlation between different methods of measuring the same trait (convergent validity) would be taken as evidence of criterion-related and construct validity in CTT. In terms of G Theory, the method universe of generalizability corresponds directly to convergent validity in the MTMM matrix. Similarly, the dimension universe of generalizability parallels discriminant validity in the MTMM matrix.

Reliability and Validity

As previously mentioned, reliability and validity have slightly different conceptualizations in the MTMM matrix. For example, the correlation between the WISC-R and Stanford Binet intelligence tests would be interpreted as evidence of criterion-related (and construct) validity in CTT. The MTMM approach, however, would view this correlation more in terms of reliability because it represents the same trait being measured by similar methods (i.e., individually administered intelligence tests). One way of viewing reliability and validity in the MTMM conceptualization is the degree of similarity or dissimilarity between measurement methods. The more similar the methods are for measuring a given trait, the closer the correlation would be to a reliability coefficient. Alternatively, the more dissimilar the methods are for measuring a given trait, the closer the correlation would be to a validity coefficient. It should be noted that different sources of assessment information (e.g., teacher and parent ratings) are considered to be different methods of measurement in the MTMM matrix.

Campbell and Fiske (1959) specified four criteria for establishment of validity in the MTMM matrix. One, the coefficients in the validity diagonal (monotrait-heteromethod) should be significantly different from zero and sufficiently large to encourage further investigation. These values represent evidence for convergent validity. Two, the values in the validity and other variables having neither trait nor method in common. That is, convergent validity coefficients (i.e., values in the validity diagonal) should exceed the values in the heterotrait-heteromethod and heterotrait-monomethod triangles. Three, values in the validity diagonal should exceed the values obtained from different traits measured by the same method (heterotrait-monomethod triangle). Four, the same pattern of correlations between traits should be demonstrated for both monomethod and heteromethod blocks. In other words, the pattern of correlations between different traits should be relatively similar regardless of whether the traits are measured by the same or different methods.

The first requirement in the MTMM matrix represents evidence for convergent validity and the last three requirements provide evidence for discriminant validity. In spite of the conceptual beauty of the MTMM matrix, several statistical problems accrue from its use. First, evidence for convergent and discriminant validity is relative. That is, a researcher must view the correlations in the matrix relative to one another and make a somewhat qualitative judgment. Second, the correlations in the matrix may flucuate given the lack of perfect reliability of measurement (Jackson, 1969). Third, the liklihood of finding convergent validity is greater if the size of the MTMM matrix is large because of the probability of finding spuriously high correlations given a large number of comparisons (i.e., a Type I error). Finally, there is no way of separating method variance from content variance if researchers use different tests in the matrix. Cone (1979) referred to this as method–content confound. For example, one might be interested in comparing two methods of measuring intelligence and academic achievement (e.g., individual and group tests). It is likely that there would be large differences in content between individual and group intelligence and achievement tests.

Several alternatives have been proposed to overcome these statistical problems in the MTMM matrix. Schmitt, Coyle, and Saari (1977) reviewed several alternatives for analyzing MTMM matrices. These include (a) analysis of variance (ANOVA) models, (b) path analysis, (c) multimethod factor analysis, (d) principal components analysis, (e) three-mode factor analysis. More recently, Jorkeskog and Sorbom (1983) advocated the use of analysis of covariance structures to analyze MTMM data. A discussion of each of these methods is beyond the scope of the present chapter. Interested readers, however, are advised to consult the informative review by Schmitt *et al.* (1977) to determine the advantages and disadvantages of each method.

Assumptions

The basic assumptions in the MTMM matrix are more closely aligned with the assumptions in CTT. However, the notion of convergent validity in the MTMM approach bears a striking similarity to method generalizability in G Theory and the idea of discriminant validity corresponds to the G Theory concept of dimension generality. The assumptions in G Theory or the DSM differ from the assumptions in CTT or the model of parallel tests. That is, method generalizability assumes that the obtained correlation between two methods corresponds to all methods in the universe that might have been used. In contrast, convergent validity assumes that the correlations obtained from different methods only refers to the specific methods under consideration. In this sense, the MTMM matrix is based primarily on the assumptions from CTT.

The major difference in the assumptions of the MTMM approach is theoretical or philosophical rather than statistical. Campbell and Fiske (1959) stated that any conceptual formulation of a trait is a response tendency that can be observed under several experimental conditions and that a particular trait can be reliably differentiated from other traits. The MTMM approach is based on the philosophical notion of multiple operationalism, which purports that reality is more than a single measure of reality (i.e., singular operationalism). The MTMM matrix represents a means of multiplying operationalizing behavior such that it can be fixed or triangulated in "psychological space." Only to the extent that different methods of measuring a given construct agree with one another can the construct be said to exist in reality. That is, the construct exists as an entity regardless of the methods used to measure it. This logic is not unlike the logic used in our legal system in the sense of corroborating evidence (i.e., other or additional evidence).

Relevance to Behavioral Assessment

The logic of the MTMM approach appears to be entirely consistent with behavioral assessment given the emphasis in modern-day behavioral assessment on the use of multiple methods of assessment (Cone, 1978; Hersen & Bellack, 1981, Mash & Terdal, 1981). Cone's (1978) description of the Behavioral Assessment Grid (BAG) includes an ordering of behavioral assessment methods ranging from direct (e.g., direct naturalistic observations) to indirect (e.g., self-report). The key distinguishing feature of indirect versus direct behavioral assessment methods is the degree to which the method measures behavior at the time and place of its actual occurence. Behavioral assessment methods are defined as direct or indirect based on their temporal and physical proximity to the actual occurrence of behavior.

Behavioral assessment, of course, does not talk in terms of traits, however, the behavioral analogue to traits can easily be found in the literature under various names such as response classes (functional and topographical), response clusters, behavioral constellations, and basic behavioral repertoires (BBRs) (Burns, 1980; Staats, 1975; Voeltz & Evans, 1982). A key difference between traits and response classes/clusters is the assumption in the latter that the behaviors in the class or cluster measure nothing beyond itself (Voeltz & Evans, 1982). In contrast, the assumption made in terms of a trait is that the trait represents more than simply the behaviors comprising the trait (i.e., the trait measure relates to a larger construct or conceptualization of the trait).

Cone (1979) used the terminology multibehavior-multimethod (MBMM) matrix to refer to investigation of behavior–behavior relationships measured by different methods. Given the situation specificity assumption in behavioral assessment, it would be important from a behavioral perspective to control for setting or situational variables (e.g., school versus home) as well as content assessed by measurement procedures. For example, if one were to compare teacher and parent ratings of social skills, it would be difficult to rule out the effects of setting differences (i.e., setting variance) on these ratings. Moreover, one would also have to control for content variance by ensuring that exactly the same behaviors were included on the teacher and parent rating scales. In terms of tight experimental control, one would have to utilize a multibehavior-multimethod-multisetting-multicontent matrix to parcel out the variance due to different sources. This obviously becomes unwieldly as the number of behaviors, methods, settings, and contents increases. The advantage of considering these different influences on behavioral assessment data is primarily conceptual in that failure to find relations among measures may result from method differences, setting differences, content differences, or method × setting × content interactions.

Given that the MTMM approach is based primarily on the statistical assumptions of CTT, the same criticism of the CTT model described earlier also hold for the MTMM approach. The major assumption in CTT that an individual possesses stable traits that persist through time appears to be in direct violation of the assumption in behavioral assessment that behavior is situation specific. Moreover, the lack of convergent validity using behavioral assessment methods could be due to factors other than the inadequacy of the methods used in measuring a given response class. For example, the lack of correspondence between direct observations of classroom behavior and teacher ratings of classroom behavior could result from the difference between these two methods in terms of temporal proximity to the actual occurrence of behavior (i.e., direct versus indirect measurement of behavior), situational differences upon which each method is based (structured versus unstructured activities), or each method capturing or different behavioral dimension (e.g., frequency versus intensity).

The chief advantage of conceptualizing a behavioral assessment in the MTMM framework is that the potential it has for understanding similarities and differences may provide information useful for a functional analysis of behavior because each method is influenced by setting, temporal, and situational contingencies. In addition, the notion that multiple operationalism of behavior is theoretically consistent with a behavioral approach to assessment represents a useful rule-governed behavior for behavioral assessors that ensures comprehensive data and interpretive clarity.

Accuracy

Overview

The concept of measurement accuracy reflects a behavioral alternative to CTT and the DSM (G Theory) views of evaluating the quality of behavioral assessment measures. In fact, accuracy is totally antithical to traditional concepts of reliability and validity, which are based on the notions of true scores, fallible (observed) scores, and error scores. Johnston and Pennypacker (1980) suggested that CTT uses the concept of variability to define phenomena into existence. The mathematics of probability theory allow for an estimate of a true score based on the variability in a set of scores produced by a given measuring instrument. So-called true scores (which can never be known) are estimated from the reliability of measures. Reliability reflects the percentage of variance in test scores that is true score variance and the percentage of variance that is error score variance. Error variance is a way of saying we do not know the source of variance and, as such, we assume it results from random factors operating in the measurement situation.

Cone (1981) suggested that variability in observed performance on assessment devices is interpreted quite differently from a behavioral perspective than in a traditional (CTT) sense. In the behavioral view, variability is considered to be the window through which one can assess or evaluate functional relationships between behaviors and behavior–environment interactions. Johnston and Pennypacker (1980) advocated using principles of measurement found in the natural sciences for behavioral assessment. The natural sciences utilize methods that require units of measurement that are standard and absolute and that do not require variablility in the phenomena being studied to derive their meaning. Similarly, the physical sciences use standard and absolute units of measurement, such as time, distance, and force, which are established prior to studying new phenomena and that do not depend on the phenomena being studied.

Behavior can also be studied using standard and absolute units of measurement using concepts from the physical sciences. For example, frequency, duration, latency, interresponse times, intensity, and permanent products of behavior all can be measured using standard and absolute units of time, force, and frequency. As in the physical sciences, these behavioral dimensions can be combined to produce additional behavioral dimensions. For example, frequency divided by time results in an index of behavioral rate.

The adequacy of behavioral assessment is evaluated in relation to some standard of effective performance. In this sense, behavioral assessment is criterion referenced in that behavioral performances of individuals are compared to some criterion rather than to the performances of other individuals. Linehan (1980) discussed the relation between behavioral assessment and criterion-referenced testing as follows:

> criterion-referenced testing is a method designed to measure performance and to estimate a person's level (or in some cases the simple presence or absence of) skill, capability, or achievement in absolute rather than relative terms. (p. 149)

Accuracy, Reliability, and Validity

Cone (1981) indicated that accuracy is not equivalent to reliability or validity. *Accuracy* refers to how well a measure reflects the objective, topographic features of behavior. *Reliability* refers to the consistency with which repeated observations of the same phenomenon yield equivalent information. *Validity* (in the criterion-related sense) refers to the relation between observed behavior and some other variable.

Given these definitions, it is obvious that measures can be reliable and not be accurate. For example, two observers may agree on the occurence of behavior at high levels, but both observers may have drifted away from the objective, topographic definitions of behavior. Wolfe, Cone, and Wolfe (1986) demonstrated high levels of interobserver agreement (90% or greater), but relatively low levels of accuracy (50% to 60%). The converse, however, is not true in that measures cannot be accurate unless they are also reliable. It is not possible for each observer to be controlled by the objective, topographic features of behavior and not agree with each other.

Accurate measures of behavior may or may not be valid. It is well known that reliability sets the upper limit for validity (i.e., measures cannot be valid unless they are also reliable). However, validity does not necessarily influence the accuracy of a measure. For example, observers may record higher frequencies of positive social interaction for females than males when, in fact, the frequencies of these responses may be equal for the two sexes. If these response frequencies are correlated with teacher ratings of positive social interaction one could say that observed frequencies of positive social interaction are a valid index of positive social interaction. They would not, however, be an accurate index of positive social interaction, given that a child's sex acted as a moderater variable that decreased the accuracy of behavioral measurement.

Basic Assumptions

There are several implicit assumptions that underlie measurement accuracy from a behavioral perspective. First, units of measurement are standard and absolute in that their values are established independent of the phenomenon being studied. For example, standard units of time, distance, intensity, and frequency do not depend on definitions derived from the sample under investigation. Second, variability in behavior is considered to reflect real differences in behavior (as opposed to error) that are functionally related to environmental events. Hence, there is no concept of true score and error score in measurement accuracy because variability in behavior is not considered to be random or unsystematic. Instead, the degree of deviation (from a standard criterion) in measuring a behavior by a particular measuring instrument is considered to reflect the inaccuracy (as opposed to error in the traditional sense) of the instrument. By analogy, the failure to calibrate scales to a criterion (e.g., standard scales) would reflect the inaccuracy of the scales (i.e., the scales may overestimate or underestimate weight in relation to the criterion/standard). Third, an accurate behavioral assessment device is reflected in how sensitive it is to objective dimensional qualities of the behavior being measured. Thus, accuracy refers to the correspondence between a measurement device and the true state of nature.

Relevance to Behavioral Assessment

The notion of measurement accuracy appears to be the most theoretically consistent with behavioral theory. Cone (1981) stated that behavioral assessors are concerned with assessing facts about behavior that are (more or less) independently verifiable. The facts about behavior that must be established are (a) if a behavior occurs; (b) if it occurs repeatedly; (c) if it occurs in more than one setting; (d) if it can be measured in more than one way; and (e) if it is systematically related to the occurrence of other behaviors.

The accuracy of behavioral assessment data can be assessed if and only if the true values of observed behavioral events are known (Johnston & Pennypacker, 1980). The methodological problem this requirement presents is that it may be difficult to obtain true values of behavioral events. Several procedures have been recommended for establishment of true values of behavioral events. Cone (1981) suggested that a scripted behavioral performance in which actors are trained to emit different behaviors at various response rates might be used to establish the criterion or true value of behavioral events. For example, actors could display rates of out-of-seat behavior at a rate of .10 per minute, off-task at a rate of .05 per minute, and disturbing others at a .15 rate per minute. The accuracy of observers applying a behavioral code measuring these behaviors could be assessed by comparing their recording of behavior rates to the criterion/actual rates.

The accuracy of behavior rating scales could be established by having a panel of expert raters provide ratings of behaviors viewed on video tape or directly. A composite of these ratings across the various dimensions of rated behaviors could serve as the standard against which novices' ratings might be compared. Similar procedures could be developed for establishing the accuracy of interview, self-report, and behavioral role-play measures.

Cone (1981) indicated that the accuracy of assessment procedures can be quantified by using simple agreement percentages. For example, the accuracy of a behavioral observation code would be computed by dividing the observed rates (or durations, latencies, etc.) by the standard or criterion rates of the behavior. Different accuracies could be computed across settings, behaviors, times, and subjects.

Measurement accuracy appears to bear the closest correspondence to behavioral assessment and the assumptions upon which it is based. The key disguishing features of accuracy are its idiographic emphasis, the notion of a criterion or standard against which observed behavior rates are compared, and units of measurement that are established independently of the measurement procedure. Future research should more fully develop the technology of assessing measurement accuracy for behavioral assessment procedures.

Latent Trait Theory

Overview

Latent trait theory (LTT) was introduced by Lord (1952) as a means of determining the characteristics of test items, such as item difficulty and item discrimination. LTT assumes that performance on a test (or any other measuring device) can be predicted by defining characteristics of examinees referred to as traits. Scores on these traits are estimated and are subsequently used to explain test performance (Lord & Novick, 1968). Traits, by definition, are unobservable and thus are given the name latent traits. LTT specifies the relation between observable test performance and latent traits that are presumed to underlie test performance.

A central concept of LTT is the item characteristic curve (ICC), which depicts the probability of responding correctly to an item as a function of the latent trait. The latent trait is designated by the Greek symbol *theta* (θ). In LTT, ICCs are simply mathematical functions that describe the probability of correct or incorrect item responding as a function of theta. Thus, as theta increases, the probability of correct item responding increases and vice versa.

Hambleton and Cook (1977) provided an informative and understandable overview of LTT. These authors indicated that the utilization of LTT has been low because of the mathematical complexity of LTT, the lack of convenient computer programs for latent trait models, and the restrictive assumptions of LTT that limit practical use of latent trait models.

Research into the application of latent trait models in analyzing educational test data has increased dramatically over the past 10 years (Crocker & Algina, 1986). In contrast, there has been limited use of LTT to estimate item characteristics of test data other than intelligence and achievement tests. For example, there have been limited applications of latent trait models for behavioral domains (traits) of depression, anxiety, social skills, and the like.

Reliability and Validity

LTT and ICCs represent a means of determining certain characteristics of items on a test. As such, ICCs are used much like classical item statistics in the sense that items that have good discrimination and reliabilities (item-total correlations) are retained in a test.

The major differences between CTT and LTT are the assumptions each make about the data being analyzed. Hambleton and Cook (1977) indicated that the major advantage of latent trait models is that once a given set of test items have been fitted to a latent trait model, it is possible to estimate an individual's ability (score) on the same ability scale from any subset of items from the domain of items that have been fitted to the model. As such, estimation of the latent trait is independent of the particular choice and number of items selected. Latent trait models allow for comparisons among examinees who might have taken different subsets of items on a test.

Two concepts are crucial in understanding the use of LTT in evaluating test items: (a) item difficulty and (b) item discrimination. *Item difficulty* refers to the probability of answering an item correctly given a level of theta (i.e., the score on the latent trait). *Item discrimination* refers to the degree to which an item differentiates among examinees at different levels of theta. As theta increases, the probability of correct item responding and discrimination of items also increases and vice versa.

A given ICC is a member of a family of curves of the same general form, but that differ depending on the parameters used to define the curve. Several ICCs are used to evaluate item statistics and how these statistics relate to the latent trait under investigation. These ICCs include (a) the one-parameter logistic ogive or Rasch model, (b) the two-parameter logistic model, and (c) the three-parameter logistic model. The one-parameter or Rasch model assumes that items vary only in difficulty whereas the two-parameter model assumes that items vary in both difficulty and discrimination. The Rasch and two-parameter models assume further that guessing does not occur. As such, these models would not be appropriate for multiple-choice or true/false tests. The three-parameter model adds a *correction for guessing* which is useful for multiple-choice and true-false tests.

Assumptions

There are two basic assumptions underlying LTT: (a) unidimensionality of latent space and (b) local independence. *Unidimensionality* refers to the statistical dependence among items. It is assumed that the items in a test or domain are homogenous in the sense of measuring a single ability or latent trait. For example, it would be assumed on a test of mathematics that a single trait would underlie the items that comprise the math test (i.e., the items would be correlated with a single factor or trait). *Local independence* refers to the assumption that test item responses of a given examinee are statistically independent. In other words, an examinee's performance on one item does not affect performance on other items in the test.

Hambleton and Cook (1977) indicated that the local independence assumption does not mean that test items are uncorrelated over a group of examinees. Obviously, positive correlations between pairs of test items will result if there is variation among the examinees on the latent trait measured by the test items (Lord & Novick, 1968). The term local independence is used because it refers to the statistical independence between items for an examinee (or group of examinees) located at a single point on the latent trait scale. For example, an examinee located at +1 standard deviation on the latent trait scale (θ), all items would be assumed to be statistically (and locally) independent. This would not be true of a group of examinees located at different points on the latent trait scale (e.g., −1, −2, +1, 0, etc.).

Relevance to Behavioral Assessment

At first blush, latent trait models appear to be diametrically opposed to the assumptions underlying behavioral assessment. The most basic assumption in LTT is that the latent trait is not directly observable and is estimated by a person's responses to many items whose sum is used to estimate the latent trait for that individual. In LTT, three levels are used: (a) the test item, (b) the scale or summation of test items in a domain, and (c) the latent trait.

How then can LTT be useful in behavioral assessment that disavows the existence of underlying traits? Speaking from a theoretical perspective, LTT does not create particular problems for behavioral assessment. If one assumes that a collection of responses (all of which covary or correlate with one another) represents a response class, then one could use the mathematics of LTT to estimate difficulty and discrimination of behaviors for different levels of the response class (theta). Note that theta in behavioral assessment would not refer to the latent trait, but rather it would refer to a person's score on the response class. It would not refer to an unobservable or latent trait. Thus, LTT concepts (with the exception of the interpretation of theta) can be used to evaluate data from behavioral assessment. LTT models could be applied to direct observations of behavior, behavior rating scales, self-report measures, and behavioral role-play tests. Guion and Ironson (1983) presented a similar conception of LTT.

LTT models could be applied to all self-report measures used in behavioral assessment. For example, the Revised Children's Manifest Anxiety Scale (RCMAS) is a self-report measure of anxiety in which the child responds Yes or No to a series of 25 items (five of which are social desirability items). One could apply either a Rasch or two-parameter logistic ogive model to these data because guessing would not be a factor in the scale. Theta would simply be the sum of the 20 items on the scale and each item could be evaluated in terms of difficulty and/or discrimination by constructing an ICC. In this case, item difficulty would be interpreted as the probability of endorsing a Yes response (i.e., the direction of anxiety on the scale) as a function of theta (the total RCMAS score). Item discrimination would indicate how well each item differentiated individuals at each level of theta.

The Rasch, two-parameter, and three-parameter logistic test models can only be applied to test items that are scored dichotomously (Hambleton & Cook, 1977). Several researchers have developed LTT models that can be applied to item choices or response options (Bock, 1972; Samejima, 1973; Wang & Stanley, 1970). These models are called nominal response models and utilize the information contained in all response options. Each response option can be described by an item-option characteristic curve (IOCC).

Many behavioral rating scales use three, four, and five response options. As such, a nominal response model can be used to generate IOCCs for each response option or rating. For example, the Child Behavior Checklist (CBCL) (Achenbach & Edelbrock, 1983) employs a 3-point scale: 0- Not True; 1- Somewhat True: and 2- Very True. LTT could be used to develop IOCCs for each item on the CBCL. One would want to be sure to develop these IOCCs for each of the narrow-band factors on the CBCL because it is a multidimensional rating scale (recall that a basic assumption in LTT is unidimensionality). Latent trait models could be developed for each of the factors on the CBCL, such as Anxiety, Social Withdrawal, Depressed, Delinquent, Hyperactive, and so forth.

LTT models could also be applied to direct observational data. All interval observation systems employ a dichotomous scoring rule in which behaviors are scored as to occurrence or nonoccurrence in a particular interval. As such, a Rasch or two-parameter logistic model could be fitted to the data to determine the difficulty and discrimination of each behavior in a response class. Walker and Hops (1976) employed a 19-category classroom observation code in an investigation designed to collect classroom normative data. Eleven of the 19 behaviors measured what might be called Inappropriate Classroom Behavior (e.g., noisy, self-stimulation, physical negative, not attending, etc.) and eight of the 19 behaviors assessed Appropriate Classroom Behavior (e.g., attending, complies, volunteering, etc.). Each of these two response classes could be formed by summing the respective behaviors in each class to yield a total score (theta) for Inappropriate and Appropriate Classroom Behavior. Specific behaviors in each response class could have differing item difficulties and item discriminations at each level of theta. These LTT models could also be used for observational data scored by frequency, duration, latency, and permanent product recording systems.

Statistical Analysis and Behavioral Research

The most important basis for deciding which statistical technique to use in analyzing data is the nature of the research question(s) to be answered. Our earlier discussion of the nature and types of research questions should help in guiding one to choices of appropriate statistical analysis techniques. Tabachnick and Fidell (1983) categorized research questions into four basic types: (a) degree of relationship among variables, (b) group differentiation, (c) prediction of group differences, and (d) structure of measures. All of these statistical techniques associated with each of these research questions can be considered special applications of the general linear model (GLM).

The GLM is designed to deal with relations among variables that can be represented by a straight line (Cohen & Cohen, 1983). In addition to this linearity assumption, the GLM also assumes the additivity of variables in the linear model. That is, if a variable is to be predicted from a set of variables, the variables used to predict the criterion variable (or dependent variable) are additive in the prediction equation. The assumptions of linearity and additivity, however, do not preclude the investigation of variables with curvilinear, quadratic, or cubic relationships because these variables can be transformed or recoded such that they can be handled in the GLM.

Our purpose in this section is not to provide the reader with an in-depth review of univariate, bivariate, and multivariate statistical analysis techniques. Instead, we wish to present a conceptual algorithm for choosing a given technique based on the research question(s) to be answered. More comprehensive discussions of correlation/regression (Cohen & Cohen, 1983), univariate (Hays, 1985), and multivariate (Tabachnick & Fidell, 1983; Tatusoka, 1971) techniques are recommended for the interested reader.

Table 1 presents an outline of statistical analysis techniques that can be used to answer each of the four types of research questions mentioned earlier. As can be seen in Table 1, there are a variety of techniques that can be used to answer each of the four types of research questions. These techniques vary in terms of (a) the number of independent vari-

Table 1. Statistical Analysis Techniques for Research Questions

I. Degree of relationship between variables
   A. Bivariate correlation
      1. Pearson product moment correlation
      2. Point-biserial correlation
      3. Phi correlation
      4. Tetrachoric correlation
      5. Conditional probabilities
   B. Multivariate correlation
      1. Multiple regression
      2. Canonical correlation
      3. Multivariate multiple regression
      4. Path analysis
      5. Partial correlation
      6. Semipartial correlation
      7. Time series analysis
         a. Autoregressive moving averages models (ARIMA)
         b. Spectral analysis
         c. Lag sequential analysis
II. Group differentiation
   A. Univariate analyses
      1. One-way ANOVA
      2. Factorial ANOVA
      3. Student's t test
      4. One-way ANCOVA
      5. Factorial ANCOVA
   B. Multivariate analyses
      1. One-way MANOVA
      2. Factorial MANOVA
      3. Hotelling's T^2
      4. One-way MANCOVA
      5. Factorial MANCOVA
III. Prediction of group differences
   A. One-way discriminant analysis
   B. Hierarchial one-way discriminant analysis
   C. Factorial discriminant analysis
   D. Hierarchial factorial discriminant analysis
   E. Standard discriminant analysis
   F. Stepwise discriminant analysis
   G. Cluster analysis
IV. Structure of measures
   A. Item-total correlation
   B. Internal consistency
   C. Latent trait analysis
   D. Principal components analysis
   E. Factor analysis
   F. Analysis of covariance structures (linear structural relations)
   G. Cluster analysis
   H. Behavior structural analysis/path referenced assessment

ables (predictors); (b) the number of dependent variables (criteria); (c) the types of variables (continuous or categorical); (d) the ways in which the independent variables are ordered in the analysis; (e) the units of analysis (e.g., subjects versus things); and (f) the presence or absence of covariates.

References

Achenbach, T., & Edelbrock, C. (1983). *Manual for the Child Behavior Profile*. Burlington, VT: University of Vermont.

Achinstein, P. (1968). *Concepts of science: A philosophical analysis*. Baltimore, MD: The John Hopkins Press.

Albee, G. (1970). The uncertain future of clinical psychology. *American Psychologist, 25*, 1071–1080.

Arter, J. A., & Jenkins, J. R. (1977). Examining the benefits and prevalence of modality considerations in special education. *Journal of Special Education, 11*, 281–298.

Atkinson, R. C., & Shiffrin, R. M. (1968). Human memory: A proposed system and its control processes. In K. W. Spence & J. T. Spence (Eds.), *The psychology of learning and motivation* (2nd ed.). New York: Academic Press.

Barlow, D. H. (1980). Behavior therapy: The next decade. *Behavior Therapy, 11*, 315–328.

Barlow, D., & Hersen, M. (1984). *Single case experimental designs* (2nd ed.). New York: Pergamon Press.

Barlow, D., Hayes, S., & Nelson, R. (1984). *The scientist practitioner*. New York: Pergamon Press.

Becker, W. C., & Carnine, D. W. (1980). Direct instruction: An effective approach to educational intervention with the disadvantaged and low performers. In B. B. Lahey & A. E. Kazdin (Eds.), *Advances in clinical child psychology* (pp. 429–473). New York: Academic Press.

Bock, R. D. (1972). Estimating item parameters and latent ability when responses are scored in two or more nominal categories. *Psychometrika, 37*, 29–51.

Brown, F. G. (1983). *Principles of educational and psychological measurement* (3rd ed.). New York: Holt, Rinehart, & Winston.

Burns, L. (1980). Indirect measurement and behavioral assessment: A case for social behaviorism psychometrics. *Behavioral Assessment, 2*, 197–206.

Campbell, D. T., & Fiske, D. W. (1959). Convergent and discriminant validation by the multitrait-multimethod matrix. *Psychological Bulletin, 56*, 81–105.

Cohen, J., & Cohen, P. (1983). *Applied multiple regression/correlation analysis for the behavioral sciences* (2nd ed.). Hillsdale, NJ: Erlbaum.

Cohen, M., & Nagel, E. (1934). *An introduction to logic and scientific method*. New York: Harcourt.

Cone, J. D. (1977). The relevance of reliability and validity for behavioral assessment. *Behavior Therapy, 8*, 411–426.

Cone, J. D. (1978). The behavioral assessment grid (BAG): A conceptual framework and taxonomy. *Behavior Therapy, 9*, 882–888.

Cone, J. (1979). Confounded comparisons in triple response mode assessment. *Behavioral Assessment, 1*, 85–95.

Cone, J. (1981). Psychometric considerations. In M. Hersen & A. Bellack (Eds.), *Behavioral assessment: A practical handbook* (38–70). New York: Pergamon Press.

Crocker, L., & Algina, J. (1986). *Introduction to classical and modern test theory*. New York: Holt, Rinehart, & Winston.

Cronbach, L. J., & Meehl, P. E. (1955). Construct validity in psychological tests. *Psychological Bulletin, 52*, 281–302.

Cronbach, L. J., & Snow, R. (1977). *Aptitude and instructional methods: A handbook for research on interactions*. New York: Irvington.

Cronbach, L. J., Gleser, G. C., Nanda, H., & Rajaratnam, N. (1972). *The dependability of behavioral measurements*. New York: Wiley.

Garfield, L. L., & Kurtz, R. M. (1976). Clinical psychologists in the 1970s. *American Psychologist, 31*, 1–9.

Ghiselli, E., Campbell, J., & Zedeck, S. (1981). *Measurement theory for the behavioral sciences*. San Francisco: W. H. Freeman.

Gresham, F. M. (1982). A model for the behavioral assessment of behavior disorders in children: Measurement considerations and practical application. *Journal of School Psychology, 20*, 131–143.

Guilford, J. P. (1959). The three faces of intellect. *American Psychologist, 14*, 469.

Guion, R. M., & Ironson, G. H. (1983). Latent trait theory for organizational research. *Organizational Behavior and Human Performance, 31*, 54–87.

Harris, A. (1980). Response class: A Guttman scale analysis. *Journal of Abnormal Child Psychology, 8*, 213–220.

Hambleton, R. K., & Cook, L. L. (1977). Latent trait models and their use in the analysis of educational test data. *Journal of Educational Measurement, 14*, 75–96.

Hayes, S. C. (1981). Single case experimental design and empirical clinical practice. *Journal of Consulting and Clinical Psychology, 49*, 193–211.

Hays, W. (1985). *Statistics* (3rd ed). New York: Holt.

Hersen, M., & Bellack, A. (Eds.). (1981). *Behavioral assessment: A practical handbook* (2nd ed.). New York: Pergamon Press.

Jackson, D. N. (1969). Multimethod factor analysis in the evaluation of convergent and discriminant validity. *Psychological Bulletin, 29*, 259–271.

Jones, R. R., Reid, J. B., & Patterson, G. R. (1975). Naturalistic observation in clinical assessment. In P. McReynolds (Ed.), *Advances in psychological assessment* (Vol. 3). San Francisco: Jossey-Bass.

Johnston, J. M., & Pennypacker, H. S. (1980). *Strategies and tactics of human behavioral research*. Hillsdale, NJ: Erlbaum.

Jorkeskog, K. G., & Sorbom, D. (1983). *LISREL VI: Analysis of linear structural relationships by maximum liklihood and least squares methods* (2nd ed.). Chicago: Natural Education Resources.

Kaufman, A., & Kaufman, N. (1983). *K-ABC: Kaufman Assessment Battery for Children: Interpretive manual.* Circle Pines, MN: American Guidance Service.

Kazdin, A. E. (1977). Assessing the clinical or applied importance of behavior change through social validation. *Behavior Modification, 1,* 427–452.

Kazdin, A. E. (1979). Situational-specificity: The two-edged sword of behavioral assessment. *Behavioral Assessment, 1,* 57–75.

Kelly, E. L., Goldberg, L. R., Fiske, D. W., & Kilkowski, J. (1978). Twenty-five years later: A follow-up study of the graduate students in clinical psychology assessed in the VA Selection Research Project. *American Psychologist, 33,* 746–755.

Kerlinger, F. (1986). *Foundations of behavioral research* (3rd ed.). New York: Holt, Rinehart, & Winston.

Kratochwill, T., Mace, F. C., & Mott, S. (1985). Research methods from applied behavior analysis. In C. R. Reynolds & V. L. Willson (Eds.), *Methodological and statistical advances in the study of individual differences* (pp. 335–392). New York: Plenum Press.

Lichstein, K. L., & Wahler, R. G. (1976). The ecological assessment of an autistic child. *Journal of Abnormal Child Psychology, 4,* 31–54.

Linehan, M. M. (1980). Content validity: Its relevance to behavioral assessment. *Behavioral Assessment, 2,* 147–159.

Lord, F. M. (1952). The relationship of the reliability of multiple choice items to the distribution of item difficulties. *Psychometrika, 18,* 181–194.

Lord, F. M., & Novick, M. R. (1968). *Statistical theories of mental test scores.* Reading, MA: Addison-Wesley.

Martens, B. K., & Keller, H. R. (1987). Training school psychologists in the scientific tradition. *School Psychology Review, 16,* 329–337.

Mash, E. J., & Terdal, L. G. (Eds.) (1981). *Behavioral assessment of childhood disorders.* New York: Guilford Press.

Meitner, L., & Frisch, O. R. (1939). Disintegration of uranium by neutrons: A new type of nuclear reaction. *Nature, 143,* 239.

Mercer, J. (1979). In defense of racially and culturally nondiscriminatory assessment. *School Psychology Digest, 8,* 89–115.

Mischel, W. (1968). *Personality and assessment.* New York: Wiley.

Nelson, R. O. (1983). Behavioral assessment: Past, present, and future. *Behavioral Assessment, 5,* 195–206.

Nunnally, J. C. (1978). *Psychometric theory* (2nd ed.). New York: McGraw-Hill.

Patterson, G. R. (1986). Performance models for antisocial boys. *American Psychologist, 41,* 432–444.

Patterson, G. R., & Bank, L. (1986). Bootstrapping your way in the nomological thicket. *Behavioral Assessment, 8,* 49–73.

Peterson, D. R. (1976). Need for the Doctor of Psychology degree in professional psychology. *American Psychologist, 31,* 792–798.

Reynolds, C. R. (1982). The problem of bias in psychological assessment. In C. Reynolds & T. Gutkin (Eds.), *Handbook of school psychology* (pp. 178–208). New York: Wiley.

Samejima, F. (1973). Homogenous case of the continuous response model. *Psychometrika, 38,* 203–219.

Schmitt, N., Coyle, B. W., & Saari, B. B. (1977). A review and critique of analyses of multitrait-multimethod matrices. *Multivariate Behavioral Research, 12,* 447–478.

Skinner, B. F. (1974). *About behaviorism.* New York: Alfred A. Knopf.

Spearman, C. (1904). The proof and measurement of association between two things. *American Journal of Psychology, 15,* 72–101.

Staats, A. (1981). Paradigmatic behaviorism, unified theory construction methods, and the Zeitgeist of separtism. *American Psychologist, 36,* 239–256.

Stokes, T., & Baer, D. (1977). An implicit technology of generalization. *Journal of Applied Behavior Analysis, 10,* 349–367.

Strain, P. S., & Ezzell, D. (1978). The sequence and distribution of behavioral disordered adolescents' disruptive/inappropriate behaviors: An observational study in a residential setting. *Behavior Modification, 2,* 403–425.

Tabachnick, B. G., & Fidell, L. S. (1983). *Using multivariate statistics.* New York: Harper & Row.

Tatusoka, M. M. (1971). *Multivariate analysis: Techniques for educational and psychological research.* New York: Wiley.

Tryon, R. C. (1957). Reliability and behavior domain validity: Reformulation and historical critique. *Psychological Bulletin, 54,* 229–249.

Voeltz, L. M., & Evans, I. M. (1982). The assessment of behavioral interrelationships in child behavior therapy. *Behavioral Assessment, 4,* 131–165.

Wahler, R. G. (1975). Some structural aspects of deviant child behavior. *Journal of Applied Behavior Analysis, 8,* 27–42.

Walker, H. M., & Hops, H. (1976). Use of normative peer data as a standard for evaluating classroom treatment effects. *Journal of Applied Behavior Analysis, 9,* 159–168.

Wang, M., & Stanley, J. (1970). Differential weighting: A review of methods and empirical studies. *Review of Educational Research, 40,* 663–705.

Wolf, M. M. (1978). Social validity: The case for subjective measurement or how applied behavior analysis is finding its heart. *Journal of Applied Behavior Analysis, 11,* 203–214.

Wolfe, V. V., Cone, J. D., & Wolfe, D. A. (1986). Social and solipsistic observer training: Effects on agreement with a criterion. *Journal of Psychopathology and Behavioral Assessment, 8,* 211–226.

Yeaton, W. H., & Sechrest, L. (1981). Critical dimensions in the choice and maintenance of successful treatments: Strength, integrity, and effectiveness. *Journal of Consulting and Clinical Psychology, 49,* 156–167.

CHAPTER 3

Behavioral Assessment

Edward S. Shapiro

Although the development of behavior modification procedures have been popular for the past 20 years, the emergence of interest in behavioral assessment is a fairly recent phenomenon. For example, prior to 1977 a number of books and journals were available that described techniques for modifying behavior problems of children, adolescents, and adults. No specific volumes, however, were published that attended to the behavioral assessment process. From 1977 to the present, the number of publications in behavioral assessment has been significant, resulting in no less than 10 books and two journals devoted to this topic.

Despite the apparent upsurge of interest in behavioral assessment, it is important to note that most of the efforts toward developing the technology of behavioral assessment have emerged from research conducted in clinical settings. This was true of investigators describing the assessment of adult and child behavior problems (e.g., Barlow, 1981; Mash & Terdal, 1981). Few attempts were made to bring behavioral assessment into the school setting.

Edward S. Shapiro • College of Education, Lehigh University, Bethlehem, Pennsylvania 18015.

Recently, increasing interest in behavioral assessment in the school setting has become evident (Alessi & Kaye, 1983; Anderson, Cancelli, & Kratochwill, 1984; Shapiro, 1987; Shapiro & Lentz, 1985). School psychologists, in particular, are beginning to recognize the value of the behavioral assessment methodology for evaluating school-based problems. Although this is encouraging, bringing behavioral assessment into the school setting requires careful consideration of issues not common to the clinical settings in which behavioral assessment strategies have been developed. In particular, school-based evaluations require attention to academic and social/emotional responses. Schools, also present problems in assessment not typically encountered in clinical settings, such as not always providing direct access to observation of the behavior, their inability to control effectively the school environment for assessment, their inability to implement effectively intervention strategies derived from the assessment, and the presence of contingencies on the behavior of teachers and school administrators that may be incompatible with using behavioral assessment in educational settings.

The purpose of the present chapter is to examine the methods and use of behavioral assessment as applied to educational settings. A brief overview of the distinctions between traditional and behavioral assessment will be followed by a discussion of how these distinctions can be related to assessment in the schools. Methods of behavioral assessment will than be described with emphasis on the assessment of academic as well as behavioral problems. Finally, a discussion of potential barriers and limitations of using behavioral assessment in school settings will be presented.

Although this chapter will provide significant detail in applying behavioral assessment to educational settings, interested readers are encouraged to refer to publications by Alessi and Kaye (1983), Shapiro (1987), and Shapiro and Kratochwill (1988) for further information.

Traditional versus Behavioral Assessment

Contrasts of behavioral and traditional approaches to assessment have been extensively described by numerous authors (Arthur, 1969; Ciminero, 1977; Ciminero & Drabman, 1977; Cone & Hawkins, 1977; Goldfried, 1977; Goldfied & Kent, 1972; Mash & Terdal, 1976; Mischel, 1968; Wiggins, 1973) and have been clearly summarized by Hartmann, Roper, and Bradford (1977) (see Table 1). Any attempt to do so here would be highly redundant. Instead, a brief review of the most critical differences between these methods will be offered. Readers interested in more in-depth discussion of the distinctions between behavioral and traditional assessment are encouraged to examine any of the sources just noted.

Behavioral assessment was originally conceptualized as an alternative methodology for assessing personality (Mischel, 1968). One of the most critical distinctions, therefore, was in the conceptualization of personality *per se*. From a traditional perspective, personality refers to the collection of enduring states or characteristics that pervade the individual's interactions at all times. These traits are intrapsychic and derive from the combination of biological (genetic) and learned responses that are enduring and can be identified as underlying current behavioral difficulties.

In contrast, behavioral assessment does not employ personality constructs in explaining behavior. Observable behavior is discussed only in descriptive terms that relate the behavior to the environmental events surrounding the behavior. Causes of the behavior are related only to an examination of events that precede (antecedents) or follow (consequences) the occurrence of the behavior.

Directly linked to this distinction is the assumption of situational specificity. In traditional assessment it is assumed that an individual's behavior can be determined by understanding these underlying characteristics. As such, assessment methods are aimed only at uncovering these traits without regard for the setting in which the problem behavior is observed. For example, if a traditional personality assessment would suggest that a child is a passive-aggressive personality, it is assumed that the child will display passive-aggressive responses in school, at home, and with his or her friends.

In behavioral assessment, all behavior is assumed to be situationally specific. This implies that any particular behavioral problem is a function of the variables present in the setting in which it was observed. Attempts to suggest that the behavior represents a pattern that will occur in all (or most) situations are withheld pending empirical verification. In other words, before a behavior is deemed to be cross-situational, assessments must be conducted in a significant number of different and similar situations.

Nelson (1983) and Nelson and Hayes (1979) have pointed out the importance of this assumption for the behavioral assessment process. In particular, by assuming situational specificity, the evaluator is required to examine the influence of the environment and the individual's skills in understanding the behavior problem. Support for this position was first described by Mischel (1968), who found

Table 1. Differences between Behavioral and Traditional Approaches to Assessment

	Behavioral	Traditional
I. Assumptions		
1. Conception of personality	Personality constructs mainly employed to summarize specific behavior patterns, if at all	Personality as a reflection of enduring underlying states or traits
2. Causes of behavior	Maintaining conditions sought in current environment	Intrapsychic or within the individual
II. Implications		
1. Role of behavior	Important as a sample of person's repertoire in specific situation	Behavior assumes importance only insofar as it indexes underlying causes
2. Role of history	Relatively unimportant, except for, for example, to provide a retrospective baseline	Crucial in that present conditions seen as a product of the past
3. Consistency of behavior	Behavior thought to be specific to the situation	Behavior expected to be consistent across time and settings
III. Use of data	To describe target behaviors and maintain conditions	To describe personality functioning and etiology
	To select the appropriate treatment	To diagnose or classify
	To evaluate and revise treatment	To make prognosis; to predict
IV. Other characteristics		
1. Level of inferences	Low	Medium to high
2. Comparisons	More emphasis on intra-individual or idiographic	More emphasis on inter-individual or nomothetic
3. Methods of assessment	More emphasis on direct methods (e.g., observations of behavior in natural environment)	More emphasis on indirect methods (e.g., interviews and self-report)
4. Timing of assessment	More ongoing; prior, during, and after treatment	Pre- and perhaps posttreatment or strictly to diagnose
5. Scope of assessment	Specific measures and of more variables (e.g., of target behaviors in various situations of side effects, context, strengths as well as deficiencies)	More global measures (e.g., of cure, or improvement) but only of the individual

Note. From "Some Relationships between Behavioral and Traditional Assessment" by D. P. Hartmann, B. L. Roper, & D. C. Bradford, 1979, *Journal of Behavioral Assessment, 1*, pp. 3–21. Copyright 1979 by Plenum Press. Reprinted by permission.

that many personality traits did not remain stable over time. Further, Kazdin (1979) pointed to evidence from the behavioral assessment literature that suggests that assessment of the same behavior from different response modalities (i.e., cognitive, motor, physiological) do not commonly correspond. Additionally, informational cues, setting, and the presence of observers have all been found to influence behavioral outcomes.

The assumption of the situational specificity of behavior is critical in choosing the methodologies for assessing behavior. In traditional assessment, one assumes that traits or characteristics are stable across time and situations. As such, the typical method of assessment involves removing the person to a novel environment (usually the psychologist's office) and administering measures that will aide the psychologist in determining the traits that underlie the observed behavior. Once these characteristics are determined, they are used to explain the individual's responses in situations other than the one in which the problem behavior seems to be occurring.

Because behavioral assessment assumes all

behavior to be situationally specific, it requires that the assessment be conducted by directly observing the problem behavior in the environment in which it is occurring. Any decisions about the cross-situational nature of the behavior are withheld until assessments are conducted across a significantly representative sample of settings. Only if the behavior was found to occur in a number of settings different from and similar to the one in which the problem was first reported is the behavior considered as a generalized response (cross-situational).

Behavior is also considered to be multidimensional in behavioral assessment. It is recognized that each individual behavior problem may consist of motor responses (observable performance), verbal responses (what one says), covert responses (thoughts), and/or physiological responses (emotions). An effective behavioral assessment requires evaluation of all response types or modalities, although it is recognized that correspondence between modalities of behavior may not yield convergence (Cone, 1979).

Evaluation of traditional assessment measures is made using psychometric properties ascribed to tests such as adequate development of norms, reliability, and validity. Although the use of similar evaluation methods and the use of generalizability theory have been suggested for evaluating behavioral assessment (Cone, 1977; Hartmann, *et al.*, 1979), Nelson and her colleagues (Nelson, 1983; Nelson & Hayes, 1979; Nelson, Hay, & Hay, 1977) have argued that the differing nature of the assumptions that underlie traditional and behavioral assessment suggest that alternative techniques for evaluating behavioral assessment would be appropriate. Specifically, Nelson, (1983) and Nelson and Hayes (1979) have suggested the use of conceptual validity (enhancing the understanding of behavior and its controlling variables), treatment validity (the relationship between the assessment measures and the effectiveness of the selected treatment program), and interobserver agreement as some of the key measures in evaluating behavioral assessment.

In summary, some of the most critical differences between traditional and behavioral assessment lie in their basic conceptualization of personality. Where traditional assessment sees behavior as indicative of underlying traits and characteristics that need to be assessed, behavioral assessment concentrates on the observable behavior and its related antecedents and consequences. This basic difference results in varying methodologies for assessment with behavioral assessment relying more on direct observation of behavior in the setting where it is naturally occurring.

Although these distinctions between traditional and behavioral assessment do not specifically address evaluations in educational settings, they are equally applicable in schools for children evaluated for social/emotional problems. However, school-based referrals also require assessment of academic skills. Little attention has been given to the behavioral assessment of academic skills (Kratochwill, 1982). Although the conceptualization of traditional assessment in evaluating academic skills is somewhat different compared to assessing personality, similar comparisons between assumptions underlying traditional and behavioral assessment methodologies can be made.

Traditional assessment of academic skills usually involves the administration of a norm-referenced, standardized achievement test such as the Wide Range Achievement Test (WRAT) (Jastak & Jastak, 1978) or Peabody Individual Achievement Test (PIAT) (Dunn & Markwardt, 1970). In addition, the assessment may incorporate measures designed to evaluate information-processing skills related to school learning, such as the Illinois Test of Psycholinguistic Abilities (Kirk, McCarthy, & Kirk, 1971), or Bender-Gestalt Visual Motor Integration Test (Koppitz, 1963).

Results of norm-referenced achievement tests are designed to provide an indication of the child's academic achievement level in comparison to other children of similar age/grade. The test requires children to answer questions in basic skills, such as reading, math, or language arts. Although these measures may be somewhat useful for gross estimation of a child's ability, they may be misleading. Items contained on the measures are generally derived from many curricula and may contain questions at the child's grade level that they have not been afforded the opportunity to learn. Indeed, Jenkins and Pany (1978) and Leinhardt and Seewald (1981) have found evidence that most commonly used achievement tests have questionable overlap with what is taught in different basal reading series. In the same way as traditional personality assessment, where a child's responses on a particular test will be used to make general statements about personality, achievement tests will be used as representative samples of academic behavior. Thus, the interpretation of academic skills from achievement tests is analogous to the conceptualization of personality from traditional assessment measures.

Assessment of information processing clearly can be viewed as traditional assessment. In the same way that observable behavior is viewed as a sign of underlying pathology in traditional personality assessment, poor academic performance is seen as indicative of dysfunctional neuroprocessing.

Additional support for conceptualizing traditional methods of academic assessment as analogous to traditional assessment of personality is the lack of consideration given to the influence of environment. Neither achievement tests nor information-processing measures typically consider environmental variables in drawing conclusions about the child's skills. Instead, results on these tests are viewed primarily as indicative of the presence or absence of those skills that may underlie performance on the test. For example, a child's poor performance on a reading comprehension subtest of an achievement test may be ascribed to poor auditory processing if tests administered to specifically determine auditory processing skills likewise show deficient performance.

A behavioral assessment of academic skills would measure academic skills by examining performance where it is typically expected to occur, that is, within the curriculum materials in which the child is being instructed. In this way, academic abilities and deficits are based only on performance without inference to potential underlying processes that may be related to the skill deficiency.

Equally important, behavioral assessment of academic skills would involve the direct observation of the child in the setting where the problem behavior occurred. Variables that affect learning, such as teacher instruction, curriculum materials, feedback, and so forth would all be considered in the assessment.

Although strategies for behavioral assessment of academic skills are just emerging, Shapiro (1987), and Shapiro and Lentz (1985, 1986) have described a methodology useful for school psychologists in conducting this type of assessment. Detail regarding this method is provided later in this chapter.

In the next section, the general methods for conducting behavioral assessments are described. These methods underlie the assessment process for both academic and social/emotional problems. Following this section, the application of these methods are discussed when referral problems are specifically for social/emotional or academic difficulties.

Methods of Behavioral Assessment

Cone (1978) provided a conceptual framework for the methodology of behavioral assessment. Each strategy is considered on a continuum from direct to indirect assessment based on the relationship of the method of data collection to the actual occurrence of the behavior. For example, observing the child's behavior in the classroom under typical instruction would be the most direct form of observation. Interviewing an informant, such as a teacher, would be an indirect form of assessment since the data being collected (teacher verbal reports) are removed from the direct observation of the behavior.

Techniques of behavioral assessment include direct observation, self-monitoring, role-play tests, interviewing, checklists/rating scales, peer assessment, and physiological measures. Although each of these will be covered in some detail, interested readers are encouraged to examine one of many excellent available resources which elaborate these procedures.

Direct Observation

Perhaps the most defining characteristic of behavioral assessment, direct observation involves the collection of data by observing the specified target behavior as it actually occurs. This procedure results in a verifiable, empirical description of the behavior and serves as the criterion against which all other methods of assessment must be judged.

Various types of data can be obtained through direct observation. These include permanent products, event recording, duration recording, and time sampling. In addition, recording of those events surrounding the target behavior (antecedents and consequences) can also be obtained through direct observation. Choosing the type of data to collect is based on a number of variables, including the frequency of the behavior being observed, type of behavior observed, and how the behavior being observed is defined. Of critical importance is that the data collected are considered useful in understanding and explaining the referral problem.

Permanent Products

Certain behavioral responses result in permanent products. For example, if one wanted to monitor cigarette smoking on an inpatient psychiatric hospital unit, one could count the number of cigarette butts remaining in ashtrays at the end of the day. Cigarette butts are a permanent product of the response of smoking. In schools, children are often asked to perform behaviors that result in permanent products. For instance, a worksheet from a basal reading series workbook, a worksheet from a mathematics lesson, or the results of weekly spelling tests are all permanent products. These can be useful measures for assessing behaviors that occur in the natural environment.

A particular advantage of these measures is their simplicity in collection. A child's work can be compiled and examined at some later time convenient to the evaluator. In addition, the responses on the worksheets could be analyzed to evaluate carefully potential skills lacking in the child's repertoire. Still further, examination of the work for problems in accuracy as well as completion may be conducted.

The use of this measure is not restricted to academic behavior. For example, vandalism may be represented by keeping a weekly count on the number of windows broken or amount of new graffiti inscribed on walls. A child's absentee record provides a permanent product of potential school avoidance problems.

Although permanent products provide an excellent and unobtrusive means of collecting data that are occurring naturally, the measure has the disadvantage of requiring inference from the data to the behavior. Because the behavior is not directly observed, the resulting data are assumed to represent the actual behavioral response. For example, if the number of completed homework papers per week are used as the data for a child referred because of failure to complete assignments, an increase in the number of completed homework assignments may not necessarily mean that the referred child is actually completing his homework. Further investigation may reveal that the child's parents, sister, or friends are responsible. Clearly, the use of this type of data must be supported by additional data collection methods.

Event Recording

The type of data known as event recording requires the recording of individual instances of behavior. Typically, the observer records the number of times the specified behavior(s) occurs within a time interval. The exact interval chosen is based on the most reasonable and logical time frame for recording the behavior. For example, if a teacher was to record the number of times a child left the classroom without permission, one could record the frequency of the behavior across the entire day. If, however, one was recording the number of times students called out, it may make sense to record this behavior for only part of the day (during reading or math).

Event recording is most successful if the behavior recorded has a discrete beginning and end. Hand raising, calling out, and throwing wads of paper, all have definite starting and finishing points. Behaviors such as doing seatwork, rocking, and interacting with peers may be ambiguous as to when they begin and end. Critical to effective event recording is the development of an operational definition for observation. Although behaviors that do not have discrete starting and ending points can be defined to contain such parameters, other methods of recording data (time sampling) are suggested.

Event recording is particularly useful for low-rate behaviors. Such behaviors occur infrequently, but are of significant concern to warrant the development of behavioral intervention programs. For example, stealing or fighting in classrooms may occur infrequently, but are usually considered significant problems for which event recording may be employed.

Behaviors that occur in response bursts may also be good candidates for event recording. Certain behavior problems do not consist of a single, discrete behavior, but contain a set of multiple responses that usually coincide. For example, aggressive behavior of children may include hitting, kicking, swearing, and throwing objects. It would be inappropriate to count any one of these behaviors as indicative of aggression. More realistically, a definition for an entire outburst of aggressive behavior could be identified that included a criterion for when each outburst ended. Shapiro, Lentz, and Sofman (1984), in a study examining the aggressive behavior of emotionally disturbed adolescents, defined an episode of aggression as incorporating the occurrence of any of a list of behaviors, including hitting, spitting, swearing, throwing, and leaving the classroom. One aggression free minute was used as the criterion to decide when an episode ended.

The process of event recording is straightforward. Observers can use almost any device capable of counting, including paper-and-pencil, golf-counters, beads, grocery store counters, and so forth. Each occurrence of the behavior is recorded and the accumulated total is than reported. Because these events are obtained during a specific time period, they are usually reported in terms of rate (frequency/unit time). When rates are used, it is important for the evaluator to realize that most people do not clearly understand their meaning. For example, if the rate of interrupting is found to be .5/min, it would be important to communicate that this rate reflects that the child is interrupting approximately once every 2 minutes or 15 times in the course of 30 minutes. By offering meaningful interpretations of rate, the value of the measure becomes clear.

Although rates should be used in reporting most event recording, it may also be appropriate to report event recording in terms of frequency. For example, if data were collected over a 2-month period regarding a child's shoplifting arrests, the low-rate of the behavior would be accurately reflected by simply reporting that the child was arrested three times. It would be very misleading to break this rate down, for example, by dividing the number of arrests by the number of days to obtain a rate per day (3/60 days, rate=.005). In general, it seems sensible that only low-rate behaviors be reported in terms of frequency of occurrence.

Duration Recording

When a behavior does not occur as a single instance but instead persists for a period of time after its initiation, duration recording may be the appropriate response to be measured. The amount of time from the onset of the behavior to its termination is recorded. Each episode is recorded separately, and a mean duration per episode is determined.

Certain types of behaviors are best assessed using duration. For example, if the amount of after-school time devoted to doing homework was targeted, a good measure of the behavior would be obtained by having the youngster record the amount of study time during baseline, and subsequently, once the intervention program was begun.

Recording of duration can be important in reflecting behavior change. Some behaviors may show no change in frequency but may display changes in duration. For example, data being kept by a mother on a child's tantruming may show no reduction in number of tantrums over a 2-week period, but collection of duration (length of tantrums) may display a significant reduction. The examination of both event and duration recording would provide evidence that although the frequency of tantrums continues at a steady rate, the duration is substantially improved.

Although duration recording can be valuable, it does become somewhat cumbersome to obtain. When the behavior is of moderate to high rate, accurate duration recording usually requires the use of a stopwatch or some other timing device. This would most certainly be difficult for teachers and would not be recommended for use in classrooms. An alternative would be to have teachers record the actual time (hours:minute) a behavioral event begins and ends, rather than trying to keep track of the duration using a stopwatch. Again, if the behavior is low rate, this becomes a viable alternative. If the behavior is of moderate or high rate, the recording process remains too involved.

In general, duration recording is an important measure that can be added to event recording to reflect accurately the target behavior. In using duration, one must be acutely aware of its limitations given the often cumbersome nature of the recording mechanism. The measure can, however, remain sensitive to changes not always noticeable with event recording alone.

Time Sampling

Event and duration recording require that the behavior being observed contain a discrete beginning and ending. Although behaviors that are more continuous can be recorded using event recording by defining the starting and finishing parameters, it may be difficult always to obtain accurate recording using this method. In addition, it may not always be possible to observe behavior for an extended period of time. Teachers may find it difficult simultaneously to teach and record data when the behavior is occurring at a substantial rate. Likewise, observers may not be readily available to record behavior across a long time period, such as an entire day.

In those cases where event recording is not appropriate or possible, the use of time sampling procedures may be employed. Time sampling involves the recording of behavior within short intervals of time. The purpose of time sampling is not to provide a detailed account of exactly how often the behavior occurred, but to provide a best estimate of occurrence by sampling data during observational periods.

Observations using time sampling usually begin by dividing the observation period into smaller units. The actual interval selected is based on the most logical and practical time frame for observation. Behaviors that occur at very high rates would best be estimated by very short observation intervals. Those occurring at more moderate rates could be observed effectively by longer intervals. Although intervals could legitimately be of any duration, they are most often less than one minute, usually 10, 15, or 30 seconds.

Three types of time sampling observation procedures can be identified. Each is based on how one defines whether a behavior has occurred. Whole interval time sampling would require that the observed behavior be present for the entire interval to be recorded as present. Absence of the behavior for any time during the interval would result in the behavior being recorded as absent in that period.

Partial interval recording defines the behavior as present if it occurs at all during the interval. Thus, either single or multiple occurrences of behavior during an interval would cause the behavior to be recorded as present during the interval.

Momentary time sampling involves recording whether the behavior is present or absent at the instant the interval begins. In this method of recording, one is only interested in the behavior for a moment, ignoring the behavior throughout the rest of the interval. Unlike event or duration recording, time sampling only records behavior presence or absence and not its actual frequency. As such, one can only estimate the frequency by examining the percentage of intervals in which the behavior was present (or absent). It is important to recognize that the use of time sampling can introduce systematic bias into data obtained using these methods.

Whole interval sampling requires that behavior be continuous during a time interval to be recorded as present. Because any interruption in this behavior would cause the entire interval to be recorded as behavior absent, data recorded in this way may underestimate the actual occurrence of the behavior. Likewise, because partial interval recording causes behavior to be recorded as present when any single occurrence (no matter how brief) of the behavior appears, results may tend to overestimate the actual frequency of occurrence. Momentary time sampling may appear to be the best measure for estimating actual behavioral occurrences because one records only by observing for behavioral presence (absence) at preset intervals.

Numerous studies have examined the relationships between actual behavioral occurrence and time sampling methods (Green & Alverson, 1978; Powell & Rockinson, 1978; Powell, Martindale, Kulp, Martindale, & Bauman, 1977) and have consistently determined that whole interval recording tends to underestimate performance whereas partial interval recording gives an overestimate. Lentz (1982) compared partial and momentary time sampling in recording mother–child interactions and concluded that the degree of error introduced by momentary recording was substantially less than with partial interval recording.

Although the data suggests that momentary time sampling may be superior to whole interval or partial interval, other factors must be considered in choosing a time sampling technique. Some behaviors lend themselves to whole interval recording. These are responses that should be present for continuous periods of time to be considered socially valid (Kazdin, 1977; Wolf, 1978). For example, Ollendick, Shapiro, and Barrett (1981) used a whole interval time sampling procedure in recording the play behavior of severely, multihandicapped children. Using 10-second intervals, children had to play appropriately with defined toys throughout the entire period (allowing one second glances away from the toys) for the behavior to be considered present. The use of a whole interval recording system seems logical because playing is a behavior that must be sustained across time. Any changes in the behavior that are socially valid (Kazdin, 1977) must contain longer periods of sustained play activity. Partial interval recording would have permitted any instant of play behavior, no matter how brief, to be recorded as behavior present. Although this may have resulted in a measure more sensitive to behavior change, the data may have been misleading. Likewise, although the use of a momentary time sampling procedure would have been possible, changes in the data would not have been as socially valid as with whole interval recording because play is logically viewed as containing behavior that is sustained across time.

Use of partial interval recording is particularly warranted when any change in the behavior of interest, no matter how small, is of importance to the observer. This procedure might be used, for example, if one were trying to reduce self-injurious behavior where the effects of an intervention procedure needs to be demonstrated no matter how slight.

Another important consideration in using time sampling procedures is the variability of behavior. These strategies for observation are based on the assumption that behavior under observation is occurring at a steady rate across time. If a behavior occurs at variable rates across settings or time, it is important that data be obtained within each of these different settings or time periods. A child's responses during a small group reading assignment may be quite different when compared to the large group or when given individual seatwork to complete.

Recording Antecedents/Consequences

The direct observation of behavior often requires the collection of more than just the frequency or rate of behavioral occurrence. An important aspect of assessment is determining the variables that are functionally related to the occurrence of the target behavior. This requires that data be obtained on those events that precede and follow the target behavior. These events, known as antecedents and consequences, can be recorded in one of two ways.

The observer can simply write down and describe events as they occur. This narrative can then be analyzed to determine the antecedent and consequent events surrounding the behavior. For example, an observation may result in the following description:

> Johnny raises his hand, the teacher calls on someone else. Johnny calls out the answer to the question, the teacher reprimands Johnny, Johnny complains that he is never called on. Teacher tells him that she would call on him if he didn't always call out the answer.

From this brief observation, the targeted behavior (calling out) seems to have as its antecedent the teacher not calling on Johnny when his hand is raised and the consequence being teacher reprimands and attention. Although many more observations like this one would be needed to draw conclusions regarding potential antecedents and consequences, it is clear that one may begin to determine the events surrounding the behavior from this observation method.

A second means for identifying antecedents and consequences would involve predetermining categories for observation and collecting data using a time sampling procedure. For example, teacher attention is often found to be significantly related to student behavior. As such, the relationship of teacher attention to the target behavior may be recorded. Likewise, teacher questions or prompts usually serve as antecedent events for performance. These and other categories of behavior may be identified and recorded systematically.

In considering which teacher behaviors need to be observed, one should consider those aspects of instruction that are directly related to behavior change. Specifically, the use of effective pacing, prompts, frequent and immediate feedback, high rates of reinforcement, have all been found to be important in effective classroom management (e.g., Brophy, 1979). Additionally, those behaviors related to opportunities to respond, such as types and levels of questioning procedures, arrangement of academic tasks (e.g., peer tutoring), and instruction directly on the tasks to be learned, all have found to have significant influences on student performance (Brophy & Evertson, 1976).

Systematic Observation Systems

Direct observation can be conducted by devising one's own observation code or using an already existing system. In developing one's own code, two steps are required. First, the observer collects a narrative description of the behavior. This narrative is then analyzed to determine the appropriate responses to be observed systematically. For example, an initial narrative may find that it is important to collect data on a student's on-task behavior, question asking behavior, and calling out. In addition, data on the frequency and quality of student–teacher and student–student interaction are found to be important.

Once these behaviors are identified and defined, the observer than collects data systematically using one of the methods discussed earlier (permanent products, event recording, duration, time sampling). This provides quantitative data on the behaviors of interest.

Although the development of a behavioral observation code is not difficult, it can be time consuming. An alternative to making up one's own code is to use an already existing system specifically designed for use in the setting in which one is going to observe.

Many codes have appeared in the literature. Some have been developed specifically for assessing behavior in home settings (Reid, 1978) or schools (O'Leary, Romanczyk, Kass, Dietz, & Santogrossi, 1979). Others have developed codes specifically for assessing certain types of behavior problems (Greenwood, Todd, Walker, & Hops, 1978; Stanley & Greenwood, 1981). Certain codes are designed for use across settings (Wahler, House, & Stambaugh, 1976).

Among the many codes available for use in schools, Saudargas and Creed-Murrah (1980) published a code that was developed by and for the use of school psychologists. The code enables the observer to record at least 15 student and six teacher behaviors. Included are provisions for momentary time sampling as well as recording events within 30-second intervals.

After noting the conditions under which the observation was made (large group, teacher led; small group, teacher led; independent seatwork), and other general information about the observation (such as the seating arrangement in the class), one obtains data on two sets of behaviors. One set is called states and consists of behaviors that would vary in duration. These are collected by 30-second momentary time sampling. Included in these behaviors are schoolwork, out-of-seat, looking around, motoric movement, playing with objects, social interaction with another child, social interaction with the teacher, and other activity. The other data collected are events, discrete behaviors that are counted within intervals. These include seven child and six teacher categories. Child categories are raise hand, calling out, out-of-seat, object agression, noise making, approach child, and other child approach. Teacher categories are teacher approach student doing schoolwork, teacher approach off-task student, teacher direction followed by opposition, teacher direction followed by compliance, teacher approval, and teacher disapproval. Definitions for each behavioral category along with extensive examples of occurrence and nonoccurrence of the behavior are provided.

Observations are made by collecting data on events continuously throughout the observation period and time sampling states every 30-seconds. Additional behaviors not included on the observation form can be added for each individual case.

Data obtained from the Saudargas code can be very useful for understanding student problems and student–teacher interactions in classroom settings. Although research on the code is underway, preliminary findings suggest that the code can accurately predict children identified as learning disabled (Slate & Saudargas, 1984). In addition, the code has been used extensively in clinical decision making and found to be very useful in quantifying a number of school-based referral problems.

Although the code has distinct advantages, it is limited in its usefulness when one is making certain types of observations. The code was designed primarily for use in elementary classroom settings during academic instruction. It would be less useful for observing periods such as playground behavior. In addition, the code is aimed at the types of behavior problems generally encountered in young children and may not be applicable at a secondary level.

Self-Monitoring

Although it is common for data collection to be completed by observers, it is equally possible that the individual who is the subject of observation can observe and record the occurrences of his or her own behavior. This process is known as self-monitoring.

Two components are incorporated into self-monitoring. First, the individual must self-observe that the behavior under question has actually occurred. Once the individual acknowledges that the behavior has occurred, its occurrence is recorded using a recording device. Although it is possible for self-observation or self-recording to occur independently, they commonly are combined into self-monitoring.

An extensive literature exists regarding the theoretical and practical applications of self-monitoring (e.g., Ciminero, Nelson, & Lipinksi, 1977; Haynes, 1978; Mace & Kratochwill, this volume; McFall, 1977; Nelson, 1977; Shapiro, 1984). In general, the research has concerned itself with two issues regarding self-monitoring. The first is the effect that self-monitoring may have on behavior. Simply recording the presence or absence of behavior may substantially alter its frequency. Known as reactivity, much effort has been devoted to identifying the variables that may aide in predicting reactivity. Among the variables found that can significantly influence reactivity have been the motivation of the subject to change his or her behavior, whether the behavior self-monitored has a positive or negative valence, the nature of the target behavior, whether the self-recording of the behavior occurs immediately or is delayed, and the nature of the device used for self-monitoring (Nelson, 1977).

A second issue that has been addressed by researchers is the importance of accurate self-monitoring and its relationship to reactivity. Studies have shown that accuracy may not be a prerequisite for reactive self-monitoring. Nelson (1977), Ciminero *et al.* (1977), and Haynes (1978) have provided extensive reviews of this literature. Most research has found either very high or very low levels of accuracy with no predictable relationships to reactive self-monitoring.

Reactivity in self-monitoring is actually a two-edged sword. If one is using self-monitoring as an assessment strategy, such reactivity would be unwelcome because it would occur during baseline data collection. In contrast, self-monitoring may be an appropriate behavior change procedure and reactivity would be an indication of success. Given that accurate prediction of reactivity is questionable, the use of the procedure for assessment alone may be limited. However, self-monitoring may provide a valuable and useful adjunct for assessment and/or intervention once observer-based data have been collected.

The actual technique of self-monitoring is rather straightforward. Any of the procedures described for conducting direct observation could be employed including event recording, duration recording, or time sampling. Typically, self-monitoring is conducted by having the individual record events using either paper-and-pencil or a mechanical recording device like a grocery store counter.

Numerous applications of this technique to school settings have been reported. These include self-monitoring of academic responses (Piersel & Kratochwill, 1979), attention (Hallahan & Sapona, 1983), work productivity (Shapiro, Browder, & D'Huyvetters, 1984), and nondisruptive behavior (Rhode, Morgan, & Young, 1983; Robertson, Simon, Pachman, & Drabman, 1979).

There are many advantages to self-monitoring in school settings. From a practical standpoint, teachers often object to the time involved in conducting observations and implementing behavioral treatment programs. Because self-monitoring shifts the primary responsibility for data collection and treatment from the teacher to the student, the amount of teacher effort needed to maintain student behavior is significantly reduced.

Another advantage in self-monitoring is the self-awareness that monitoring one's own behavior may bring. Often, school psychologists observe children who do not appear to be aware that their behaviors are disruptive to others. By having these children record their own responses, they may begin to acquire the initial recognition of when their behavior needs to be altered.

A final advantage of self-monitoring comes in the potential of these procedures for use in mainstreaming. One of the reasons often given by teachers for maintaining children in more restrictive settings is the children's inability to display appropriate behavior in nonspecial education settings. A possible strategy for addressing this problem might be first to teach the children to self-monitor accurately their behavior in the special education setting. This assessment could be based on a simple 5-point global rating (1=awful, 5=super) that is completed at the end of each period or work assignment. Once this skill was learned, children could begin returning to regular education classes while continuing to self-monitor. Teachers in the regular education settings would only have to provide their ratings at the end of the period before the child returned to the special education class. A similar system was demonstrated to be effective in mainstreaming behaviorally handicapped students from resource rooms to regular education classes (Rhode *et al.*, 1983).

It has been the experience of the author that recommendations involving self-monitoring and other self-management strategies are usually well received by teachers who would like to see students display increased management of their own behavior. Clearly, self-monitoring has great potential for use as both an assessment and behavior change strategy in schools.

Role-Play Tests

Although the collection of data by directly observing behavior in the settings and under the conditions in which it naturally occurs represents the most desired approach of behavioral assessment, certain behaviors do not lend themselves to such observation. For example, children who have difficulties in social interaction may rarely display these behaviors in the classroom. Opportunities to observe such interaction may be present during recess or in the lunchroom; however, observation in those settings may be quite difficult. Additionally, behaviors of interest may occur primarily on the school bus, on the walk home, or in the community.

One means for assessing these types of behaviors involves the use of role-play tests. These measures attempt to simulate situations in which the behaviors occur and than observe them within the simulation setting. More than any other area, role-play tests have been used for assessing social skills.

One of the first role-play tests for children was developed by Bornstein, Bellack, and Hersen (1977) based on the work of Eisler, Hersen, Miller, and Blanchard (1975) with adults. The Behavioral Assertiveness Test for Children (BAT-C) involved developing a series of nine scenes that reflected typical problems requiring appropriate social skills among elementary school children. Instructions were given to children to pretend that these scenes were actually happening and for them to respond as they would in those situations. Scenes were read to the children with a prompt provided for their response. For example, one scene used was:

> Narrator: You're part of a small group in science class. Your group is trying to come up with an idea for a project to present to class. You start to give your idea when Amy begins to tell hers also.
>
> Prompt: Hey, listen to my idea. (Bornstein *et al.*, 1977, p. 186)

After each scene is presented, observers score the child's response on a number of predetermined variables. The specific variables assessed include various components of social skills, such as eye contact, duration of reply, smiles, and so forth. Van Hasselt, Hersen, Whitehill, and Bellack (1979) have provided an excellent summary of variables typically assessed in role-play tests of social skills.

Other investigators have used a somewhat different approach in developing role-play tests. Reardon, Hersen, Bellack, and Foley (1979) developed a more empirically derived version of the BAT-C called the Behavioral Assertiveness Test for Boys (BAT-B). This role-play test was constructed by having teachers rate each of 50 scenes regarding the degree to which the scene was common in the experience of elementary school boys. The 20 highest rated scenes (10 positive, 10 negative) were than used for the role-play test. Shapiro, Stover, and Ifkovitz (1983) and Shapiro, Gilbert, Friedman, and Steiner (1985) also used a similar procedure in deriving role-play tests.

In addition to using a more empirically derived set of scenes, the scenes selected can be based on the assessment of specific types of social skills. For example, Matson, *et al.* (1980) developed scenes specifically to assess giving compliments, giving help, and making appropriate requests. Williamson, Moody, Granberry, Lethermon, and Blouin (1983) derived scenes to assess giving praise, assertiveness, and accepting help. Matson and Senatore (1981), using a role-play test to assess social skills in mentally retarded adults, derived scenes designed to assess positive statements, acknowledging others, and complaining.

Although role-play tests involve collection of data through direct observation, the data are not obtained under the same conditions in which these behaviors occur in the natural setting. This type of assessment has been referred to as analogue assessment because the evaluation is conducted under related (analogous) but unnatural conditions. For the data obtained from this assessment to be considered valuable, the degree to which the results of role-play tests represent levels of responding actually present in the natural environment must be determined.

An increasing literature has been developing over the past few years that is addressing this issue in the assessment of adults and children. Most of these studies involve evaluations of the concurrent and predictive validity of role-play tests. Typically, results of role-play tests are compared to other measures alleged to be assessing social skills. These measures have included paper-and-pencil measures of assertiveness completed by both teachers and children, perspective-taking tasks, peer ratings, problem solving groups, dyadic direct observations, and extensions of role-play tests beyond single responses to scenes that include one-minute conversations (Matson *et al.*, 1980; Reardon *et al.*, 1979; Van Hasselt, Hersen, & Bellack, 1981; Williamson *et al.*, 1983). Results of these studies have converged on the findings that role-play tests are, at most, moderately correlated with some of these measures. In particular, most of these studies have not found significant correlations between role-play tests and the various paper-and-pencil measures.

Although these studies may suggest questionable concurrent validity of role-play tests, few studies have actually examined the degree of relationship between behaviors observed during role-play tests and rates of identical behaviors assessed within the natural environment. This is understandable given the difficulty in directly observing such behaviors as giving compliments, or asking for help. The low frequency nature of such responses makes direct observation quite difficult and costly.

Shapiro *et al.* (1983) and Shapiro *et al.* (1985) have described an alternative method to the role-play test that makes assessment of social skills within the natural setting potentially possible. Called the Contrived Test of Social Skills (CTSS), the procedure involves unobtrusively creating typical events that require the social skills being assessed. After scenes are constructed in the same way as typical role-play tests, teachers are prompted by observers to introduce such scenes during regular classroom instruction. For example, if one wanted to assess giving compliments, a scene might be constructed in which a confederate child is asked to show an "A" spelling paper to the child under observation and to say, "Look what I got on my spelling test." The targeted child's response is observed and recorded using the same measures typically used for role-play tests. Neither the confederate nor the target child are aware that the scene was contrived, thereby providing a potentially naturalistic measure for assessing social skills.

Shapiro *et al.* (1983) and Shapiro *et al.* (1985) have examined the concurrent validity of this measure among kindergarten children and emotionally disturbed children between 9 and 14 years. In these studies, the CTSS was compared to self- and teacher-reported paper-and-pencil measures of assertiveness and performance on role-play tests that used the identical scenes performed in the CTSS. Results of both studies have supported the findings of others that role-play tests and paper-and-pencil measures have marginal relationships. However, a particularly interesting finding is that role-play tests and the CTSS have moderate to strong relationships. This finding suggests that the questionable validity of role-play tests noted by others may be more a function of not assessing the identical behaviors across modes of assessment. Continued research is clearly needed to better clarify the value and function that role-play assessment may provide. At present, research shows that role-play tests can be sensitive to treatment gains when training is specifically given on the role play scenes. Whether these gains can be generalized to the natural environment is still questionable.

Interviewing

The use of interviewing as an assessment strategy represents a form of indirect assessment because data collected are primarily based on retrospective reporting. Although there are components of interviewing that include direct observation, the responses observed during interviews do not usually replicate those of interest in the natural environment. Despite the indirectness of interviewing, it remains as one of the most important components of behavioral assessment. Interestingly, the amount of research devoted to this procedure is far less than other behavioral assessment strategies (Gresham, 1984; Hay, Hay, Angle, & Nelson, 1979; Haynes & Wilson, 1979; Linehan, 1977). Additionally, where attention has been given to interviewing, few systematic approaches to conducting behavioral interviews have been offered.

One exception to this has been the work of Bergan (Bergan, 1977; Bergan & Tombari, 1975, 1976; Kratochwill & Bergan, 1978), who has developed a methodology for performing behavioral interviews. The interview process according to Bergan is seen as a set of verbal prompts and responses between the consultant and consultee. An elaborate scheme has been developed for classifying each verbalization along several dimensions, including who spoke, the context of the statement, the intention of the comment, and whether the comment calls for a response or not. Studies have showed that the specific types of verbal statements made by consultants will result in more effective identification of target problems and more likely development of solutions to problems (Bergan & Tombari, 1976).

Although Bergan (1977) provided the only well-defined, systematic approach to conducting behavioral interviews, a number of others have suggested general guidelines or categories for asking questions in a behavioral interview (e.g., Holland, 1970; Kanfer & Grimm, 1977; Kanfer & Saslow, 1969). Both Bergan's approach and these others are based on conducting interviews with either informants or with the subjects themselves when they are adults. Very little literature has appeared on conducting behavioral interviews directly with children.

Paget (1984) recently reviewed five systematic interview procedures for interviewing children. Scales selected for review used either structured or semistructured formats and were developed for use primarily in psychiatric settings. Excluded in her review were checklists/rating scales, parent interview procedures, and behavioral interviewing procedures designed for assessing less severe behavior problems. The five specific instruments examined were the Kiddie-Schedule of Affective Disorders (Kiddie-SADS) (Chambers, Puig-Antich, & Tabrizi, 1979), Children's Psychiatric Inventory (CPI) (Herjanic, Herjanic, Brown, & Wheatt, 1975), Mental Health Assessment Form (MHAF) (Kestenbaum & Bird, 1978), Interview Schedule for Children (ISC) (Kovacs, 1978), and the Isle of Wright Survey (IWS) (Rutter & Graham, 1968). Measures were compared on descriptive and psychometric properties of reliability and validity.

Results of Paget's (1984) review suggest that most of these measures present significant problems for use in schools. Current research strongly urges users of these interview formats to proceed cautiously with drawing conclusions from their findings. In particular, Paget noted the need for an effective interview format in schools to be capable of evaluating severely disturbed and behavior-disordered children. At present, no systematic measure analogous to those reviewed exists for school-based assessments.

Although verbal reports of parents and teachers remains as a primary source of data, several limitations of this method must be recognized. First, the reliability and validity of verbal reports has always been questionable. Research has often noted the influence of selective attention of past events, motivation to provide accurate data, and expectations of the interview process as potential problems (Linehan, 1977). Further, even in behavioral interviews, agreement between interviewers regarding the identification of specific behavior problems has not been consistently demonstrated (Gresham, 1984; Hay *et al.*, 1979). Interestingly, Bergan and his colleagues were able to demonstrate effective interater agreement when using the behavioral interviewing strategies defined in his model (Bergan & Tombari, 1975, 1976; Bergan, Byrnes, & Kratochwill, 1979; Brown, Kratochwill, & Bergan, 1982).

Despite the obvious limitations of interviewing, the strategy has several advantages. Among them, the flexibility of collecting specific information as well as observing nonverbal behaviors potentially indicative of problems are important in the assessment process (Linehan, 1977). Perhaps even more important, interviewing provides an opportunity to establish interpersonal relationships that will play an important part in securing the trust of the interviewee in any future interaction. This would be particularly important when interviewing teachers or parents who may be asked to implement a behavior change program.

In schools, interviewing plays an especially critical role in conducting behavioral assessments. Interviews with teachers are necessary for obtaining information about a child's behavioral and academic progress. Data such as instructional techniques, classroom contingencies, classroom schedules, and child teacher interactions can be provided through interviews. Although these data always need to be confirmed through some other assessment method, preferably direct observation, the interview can be a rich source of information.

Checklists/Rating Scales

Another indirect form of assessment involves the use of paper-and-pencil instruments that ask respondents about behavior. Some of these measures are designed as self-report scales whereas others are designed to be completed by informants. Additionally, these scales can be divided as assessing either global or specific categories of behavior.

Global behavior rating scales and checklists provide respondents with a large array of questions about many different types of behavior problems. Depending on the particular scale, individuals either rate the occurrence of an individual behavior or simply note its existence. These scales may be particularly useful as screening measures prior to conducting interviews. For example, after completing a behavior rating scale, the interviewer can concentrate his or her questions on the particular behaviors noted by the respondent instead of wasting time asking questions about areas not related to the individual's problem.

A large number of these scales have appeared in the literature. Walls, Werner, Bacon, and Zane (1977) and Haynes and Wilson (1979) have provided some of the most extensive listings of these measures. In addition, a special issue of *School Psychology Review* (Vol. 12(3), 1982) and Hoge (1983) serve as excellent reviews of a number of scales. Although some of these references are dated, these lists are the most comprehensive published.

One of the best and most comprehensive behavior rating scales applicable for use in schools is the set of instruments developed by Achenbach and his colleagues (Achenbach, 1978; Achenbach & Edelbrock, 1978, 1986; Edelbrock & Achenbach, 1984). Four different but related versions of these scales have been developed. The Child Behavior Checklist and Profile (CBCL) is for use by parents, the Teacher Report Form of the Child Behavior Checklist and Profile (TRF) is completed by teachers, the Direct Observation Form of the scale (DOF) is completed by the evaluator, and the Youth Self-Report Form (YSR) is used for individuals between 11 and 16 years as a self-report measure. Norms have been fully developed for the CBCL (ages 4 to 16) and TRF (ages 6 to 16). These norms are factor analyzed by age and sex grouping (4 to 5, 6 to 11, and 12 to 16 years) and represent over 2,000 randomly selected children from the Washington D C area.

A particularly attractive aspect of these scales is the possibility of comparing results between parents, teachers, direct observation, and self-report. Although limited work has currently been done with the DOF and YSR (Reed & Edelbrock, 1984), these instruments will most likely add a dimension not typically available with most rating scales. McConaughy (1985) presents an excellent description and demonstration of the application of these measures for use in school-based assessments.

Any attempt to mention or recommend specific scales would obviously omit others that are used by some evaluators. Global behavior rating instruments that have frequently been mentioned in the literature for use in school settings include the Conners Rating Scale (Conners, 1968, 1970, 1973; Goyette, Conners, & Ulrich, 1978), the Behavior Problem Checklist (Quay & Peterson, 1967), and the Walker Problem Identification Checklist (Walker, 1983). Each of these measures is designed to provide data for making normative comparisons of the target child to a standardized sample.

The use of global rating scales is primarily for screening. Once the potential target behaviors are identified, assessors may find it useful to administer another behavior rating scale designed to assess very specific areas of dysfunction. For example, initial interviewing or rating scales may suggest the possibility of depression. In addition to conducting direct observation, the evaluator may wish to have the child complete the Children's Depression Inventory (Kovacs, 1983).

A large number of these types of measures have appeared in the literature. Although many of them do not contain extensive psychometric evaluation or standardization, they may be useful in providing data regarding specific types of behavior problems. Again, any attempt to mention available scales would almost invariably omit others, however, several scales used by the author are the Self-Control Rating Scale (Kendall & Wilcox, 1979; Kendall, Zupan, & Braswell, 1981), the Anger Inventory for Children (Finch & Nelson, 1982; Nelson & Finch, 1978), Children's Assertiveness Behavior Scale (Wood, Michelson, & Flynn, 1978), Fear Survey Schedule for Children (Scherer & Nakamura, 1968), Children's Action Tendency Scale (Deluty, 1979), and the Children's Depression Inventory (Kovacs, 1983).

Among the advantages of these measures are their economic utility, comprehensiveness, and ability to quantify responses. These measure may provide valuable and effective means for assessing behavior that can supplement data obtained through more direct methods. Additionally, certain measures can offer quantifiable self-report on behaviors that may not be easily observed.

Despite the advantages of checklists/rating scales, they have several limitations. Data obtained through these methods are subject to the same biases of all indirect assessment. Demand characteristics, social desirability, and the expectations held by the respondent can affect the responses on these measures. In addition, the measures may only provide indications of perceptions of behavior and not reflect actual behavior rates.

A particularly important limitation of these measures is their general lack of psychometric quality in development. Most checklists/rating scales are based on small, homogeneous, samples not representative of general population characteristics. Although this is understandable given the expense of such standardization efforts, it is important to realize these limitations in interpreting data from these scales. Further, the lack of interrelationships between these measures and more direct assessment strategies typically found in many studies (e.g., Kazdin, Esveldt-Dawson, & Loar, 1984; Kendall & Wilcox, 1978; Shapiro, Lentz, & Sofman, 1984) suggests that these measures need to be supported by direct observation strategies.

Despite the disadvantages of checklists /rating scales, these measures can play an important part in behavioral assessments. Their economy allows for the collection of information that may be costly and impractical to collect otherwise. In schools, this is particularly true given the constraints on the teacher's and psychologist's time as well as potential access to parents for interviews. As the methodology continues to improve, it would be expected that these measures will remain as a major source of behavioral assessment.

Peer Assessment

Another assessment strategy often used in evaluating children's social behavior is to ask the child's peers what they think of each other. Often confused with sociometry that requires peers to state how they *feel* about each other (Kane & Lawler, 1978), peer assessment is conducted by having children provide either nominations, ratings, or rankings of their peers on specified dimensions of behavior.

Peer nominations involve asking children to nominate a set number of indivuals in response to a particular purpose. For example, children may be asked to list three children they would most like to sit next to at lunch (positive peer nomination) or three they would least like to play with (negative peer nomination). To avoid the problem of children not nominating others because they are forgotten, children are usually provided with a list of all names from which nominations can be made. When performed across a large number of children (for instance an entire classroom), the mean number of nominations received by each child can be obtained.

Peer ratings involve having children rate all peers on a specified dimension. For example, children may be asked to rate each member of their class on a 5-point Likert scale regarding how much they like them. This method is considered superior to nominations alone because it insures that all children receive some type of evaluation (Greenwood, Walker, & Hops, 1977).

Peer rankings combine nominations and ratings by having children rank order all class members on a specific characteristic. For example, children may be asked to list those they would like to sit near from the one they most would like to sit near to the least.

Measures obtained by peers are taken to be representative of peer acceptance and likability. Although the measures have psychometric limitations (see Kane & Lawler, 1977, for an extensive review), the measures can be useful in determining perceptions of change. Unfortunately, peer assessment measures have not often displayed significant changes when obtained pre- and posttreatment (e.g., Gottmann, Gonso, & Schuler,

1976; LaGreca & Santogrossi, 1980) nor have they been significantly correlated with role-play tests of social skills (e.g., Van Hasselt *et al.*, 1981) although such results have not been consistently found (Hobbs, Walls, & Hammersly, 1984). Clearly, further research is needed to determine more accurately the interrelationships between peer assessment measures and other methods of social skill assessment.

Despite the psychometric and correlational data suggesting the problems with these measures, peer assessment may be a particularly important measure for evaluating the effectiveness of social skills training programs. Children with poor social skills are often disliked and isolated from their peers (Gresham, 1981). It would be anticipated that programs designed to improve social skills would lead to changes in those measures reflecting peer acceptance. Although peer assessment measures are far from perfect, they do reflect what children say they think about each other. As such, changes in these measures might be good indicators of social validity. One potential explanation for the failure of peer assessment to show changes after treatment may be related to when the measures are taken. Documented and observable changes in social skills would probably not have an immediate impact in changing long-standing opinions about a disliked child. Only after a relatively long period of sustained appropriate social skills would these opinions begin to alter. Most studies employing a social skills training program obtain peer assessment measures immediately prior to and after treatment. As such, any change on these measures would not be anticipated. It would seem logical that given a long period of response maintenance, that changes in peer assessment might become evident. Few studies have actually provided empirical support for this hypothesis. Likewise, unless those behaviors specifically identified by peers as related to friendship and likability are targeted for change, few changes on peer assessment measures would be anticipated. Recent studies by Strain and his colleagues (Odom, Hoyson, Jamieson, & Strain, 1985; Strain, 1983) have specifically targeted those behaviors rated by peers as related to social acceptability. Results showed significant modification of these behaviors after interventions specifically aimed at these responses.

Given the current limitations of peer assessment measures, it is suggested that these measures be used only as supplemental to more direct forms of assessing social skills, such as role-play tests and direct observations. Continued research is clearly needed to examine the potential value that peer assessment might play in evaluation of long-term effectiveness of these procedures.

Physiological Assessment

The assessment of physiological responses is rarely used with children (e.g., Barrios, Hartmann, & Shigatomi, 1981; Johnson & Melamed, 1979). Yet, it seems logical that physiological assessment may be important, particularly when assessing and treating anxiety disorders. At present, there have been few discussions of the use of physiological measures for assessing children's fears (Barrios *et al.*, 1981; Johnson & Melamed, 1979; and Morris & Kratochwill, 1983, are exceptions) and even fewer published empirical studies where psychophysiological measures have been used to determine treatment outcome.

Among the various types of physiological measures, cardiovascular and electrodermal measures have been used in the few studies with children. Cardiovascular measures include heart rate, blood pressure, pulse, and respiration. Although few investigations involving cardiovascular responses in children's fears have been conducted, a number of studies have demonstrated the feasibility and importance of using this measure (Melamed, Yurcheson, Fleece, Hutcherson, & Hawes, 1978; Shapiro, 1975). Interestingly, some investigations have not found correspondence among varying cardiovascular measures (e.g., Van Hasselt, Hersen, Bellack, Rosenblum, & Lamparski, 1979)

Electrodermal measures usually involve assessing changes in skin conductance and resistance. Although very common in the evaluation of adult anxiety disorders, these measures are rarely used with children (Barrios *et al.*, 1981; Johnson & Melamed, 1979). Melamed and Siegal (1975) did report the use of this measure in evaluating the effects of filmed modeling on children undergoing elective surgery.

One may appropriately question the potential applicability of physiological measures for school-based problems. Although it seems premature to use these measures based on the limited research with children, such measures may prove to be potential adjuncts to treating anxiety disorders in children in the school setting. For example, a child with an identified public speaking phobia may be engaged in a desensitization treatment with the school counselor or psychologist. Simple physiological measures, such as pulse or heart rate, may be found to be correlated to perceived anxiety levels. As such, teaching the child to monitor and record these physiological responses may be a potential mechanism for evaluating successful treatment.

One needs to recognize, however, that the relationships between physiological, cognitive, and motoric measures of behavior are far from consistent. In particular, the few studies examining physiological measures with children have found no clear correspondence between the measures of self-reported anxiety and overt behavior (Morris & Kratochwill, 1983).

Although the use of physiological measures for some school-based problems may be appropriate, it is unlikely that this will be a primary means of conducting behavioral assessments in school settings. Both the potential expense and practical limitations of using physiological measures make them much more plausible within the clinical or private-practice setting. Still, it is important to remember the possible use of such measures when treating anxiety related problems within the school.

Behavioral Assessment of Academic Skills

When assessments are being conducted within the educational setting, it is necessary to attend to both the child's social-emotional and academic behaviors. The methods for behavioral assessment discussed earlier apply equally when addressing either of these problems. However, additional techniques are needed when evaluating academic skills. In this section, an examination of procedures for the behavioral assessment of academic skills will be discussed. In addition, the application of behavioral assessment specifically for school-based assessment of social-emotional problems will also be offered.

Assessing Academic Behavior

The evaluation of academic problems in children from a behavioral assessment perspective requires consideration of two major sets of variables. First, the academic environment must be assessed. Those events that serve as antecedents and consequences to academic responses, including instructional techniques, feedback mechanisms, curriculum materials, types of responses made, and teacher and student expectations are examined. Second, the individual skills of the child must also be determined. In particular, those skills within the curriculum that have been learned and are deficient need to be identified.

Assessing the Environment

The variables within the environment chosen for assessment should be those that reflect academic success in learning basic skills. Many years of systematic research have resulted in the clear identification of specific events that result in academic success. Rosenshine (1981), in a thorough review of this research, identified the following four variables as critical for academic performance: time allotted for instruction, time engaged in academic work, content covered, and a set of instructional procedures called direct instruction. His conclusions were based on the extensive review of the Beginning Teacher Education Project (Denham & Lieberman, 1980), Project Follow-Through (Stallings, 1975), and much of the traditional educational psychology research.

Other research has offered support for Rosenshine's conclusions, especially research on opportunities to respond (Greenwood, Delquadri, & Hall, 1984; Greenwood *et al.*, 1985; Thurlow, Ysseldyke, Graden, & Algozzine, 1984). In essence, Rosenshine (1981) concluded that the more time a student spends engaged in work making frequent, correct responses, and the more content covered, the more the student achieves.

Another set of variables related to achievement are the use of reinforcement contingencies. Accuracy of reading comprehension (Lahey & Drabman, 1973; Lahey, McNees, & Brown, 1973), oral reading (Lovitt, Eaton, Kirkwood, & Perlander, 1971), formation of letters and numbers (Hasazi & Hasazi, 1972; Stromer, 1975), arithmetic computation (McLaughlin, 1981), spelling (Lovitt, 1978) and creative writing (Campbell & Willis, 1978) have all been significantly improved by reinforcement contingencies. Likewise, the use of peer tutoring (Delquadri, Greenwood, Stretton, & Hall, 1983; Heron, Heward, Cooke, & Hill, 1983), previewing of material (Rose & Sherry, 1984), and avoidance of drill (Lovitt & Hansen, 1976a) have all been found to have potential effects on academic performance.

In addition to contingencies for performance affecting academic production, research has also shown the potential effects of monitoring academic performance. A number of studies employing data-based decision making for altering academic programs have shown such procedures to enhance student performance (Hallahan, Lloyd, Kneedler, & Marshall, 1982; Kosiewicz, Hallahan, Lloyd, & Graves, 1982; Lovitt, 1981; Stowitschek, Lewis, Shores, & Ezzel, 1981).

In general, an assessment of the learning environment must address several issues, including the teacher behaviors and contingencies for academic performance, the potential opportunities for making academic responses, the amount of time allotted for instruction, the degree to which the child is actually engaged in academic responding, the behaviors that are competing with engagement, and the mechanisms for monitoring student progress. In essence, one must examine those variables with functional relationships to academic performance.

Teacher interviews and direct observation are used to assess the academic environment. Although the basic structure of the teacher interview as described by Bergan (1977) is employed, the content for the interview is somewhat different. Shapiro and Lentz (1985) described a list of questions that need to be addressed when conducting a behavioral interview for academic problems. The information obtained in the interview should provide clear understanding of the type of problem, the instructional methods of the teacher, the amount of allotted time, the type of feedback and contingencies operating in the classroom, where the child is currently placed in the curriculum, and other information related to planning for an academic remediation program. Although no data are presently available on the psychometric accuracy of teacher interviews for collecting such information, much of the data obtained through teacher interview is subsequently confirmed through observational methods.

Direct observation of a student for an academic problem should reflect those variables that are related to academic success. Specifically, engaged time, contingencies for performance, teacher/student interaction, behaviors competing with academic performance (i.e., calling out, out-of-seat, etc.), and teacher instructional techniques need to be observed. Among the available observation codes mentioned earlier, the Saudargas State-Event Classroom Observation Code (Saudargas & Creed-Murrah, 1980) seems to have provisions for collecting data on most of these variables.

In summary, the behavioral assessment of the academic environment requires evaluation of those variables closely related to academic performance. Teacher interview and direct observation, specifically aimed at these variables, are used to provide the needed information.

Assessing the Individual

Academic performance is dependent on the academic environment in which the child is instructed and the child's particular skill level. Academic failure of a child indicates that the child has not learned material that they have been taught. It therefore seems logical that the assessment of academic skills should be derived from the curriculum materials in which the child has been instructed. Unfortunately, traditional assessment of academic skills does not follow this logic. Typically, evaluations of academic skills are conducted by administering standardized tests of achievement. These instruments consist of items that may or may not have been instructed in the child's specific curriculum. Jenkins and Pany (1978) and Leinhardt and Seewald (1981) have found that standardized achievement tests may have little overlap between what is taught and what is tested. Scores on these instruments may only reflect the failure of the child's curriculum to include the item in the instructional sequence rather than true deficiencies in performance.

Given the problems with overlap between what is tested and what is taught, one should take great care to insure that any assessment be linked to instructional strategies designed to remediate the problem. As such, the assessment measures must be able to serve as baseline measures against which change in behavior can be evaluated once treatment has begun. Standardized achievement tests clearly do not permit such use. These measures are largely influenced by practice effects and would not be sensitive to small increments in performance.

The behavioral assessment of academic skills requires that two pieces of data be identified that define a student's academic difficulty. First, where in the curriculum material in which the student is being instructed are they expected to be at the time of the assessment? Second, where in the same curriculum do the acquired skills of the child place him or her? The discrepancy between these points provides the content that must be mastered and, therefore, the skills needed to remediate the problem.

It is necessary to provide measures for assessing academic skills that are derived from the curriculum, can be frequently repeated without influence from practice effects, will be sensitive to behavior change, and are not too cumbersome to administer. Three types of measures of this nature have been identified. The first is criterion-referenced or mastery tests provided by the curriculum publisher. These tests usually assess instructional objectives in a book or level. Examination of these measures may then provide indications of academic performance. Recent research has found that for some basal reading series, these measures may be good quality tests (Tindal, *et al.*, 1985).

A second source of measures is published criterion-referenced tests not particularly linked to any curriculum. Some of these measures may be useful, particularly if they are linked closely to instructional objectives. One must be cautious in using these, however, in that many of these measures are not sensitive to behavior change.

The third source of measures, and the one given most attention, are skill probes. These measures meet the requirements of behavioral assessment of academic skills and appear to have excellent psychometric properties (Deno, Mirkin, & Chiang, 1982). The development of these measures is not new and have been discussed extensively by Lovitt and Hansen (1976b) and Deno and Mirkin (1977).

Essentially, measures used for assessment represent a "pulse" of the skill area. For example, in reading, oral reading rates and comprehension are used. The child is asked to read aloud short (100–300 words) excerpts from the beginning, middle, and end of a book in the basal reading series. Following each excerpt, a series of comprehension questions are asked. The procedure begins with the level in which the child is currently placed and progresses downward or upward until mastery is attained. Deno and Mirkin (1977), Starlin (1982), and Lovitt (1981) have all defined criterion reading rates for determining mastery, instructional, and frustration levels. Oral reading rate (words correct per minute), error rate (incorrect per minute), and comprehension (percentage of correctly answered questions) are used to determine levels.

Similar types of measures can be used for assessing any area of basic skills, including math (Deno & Mirkin, 1977), spelling (Deno, Mirkin, Lowry, & Kuehnle, 1980), or written language (Deno, Marston, & Mirkin, 1982). These measures have been found to be responsive to behavior change and can be repeated frequently. It is important to note that the use of these measures does not suggest that the skill chosen for assessment (e.g., oral reading rates in reading) should be targeted for instruction. These are simply metrics that have been found to be sensitive to improvements in academic abilities. For instance, although a child may be found to have a particularly low oral reading rate, the instructional strategies may involve improving silent reading, comprehension, and decoding skills. The instructional level, however, is based on the results of the assessment of oral reading rates. Likewise, continued monitoring of progress is conducted by repeated administration of oral reading probes.

Another goal of assessing academic skills using these methods is making recommendations for specific instructional objectives. For example, after determining the computational deficiencies of a student in math, it may become clear that the student lacks an understanding of regrouping rules. Assessment using skill probes would allow one to make very specific suggestions to teachers for setting goals and objectives.

An important component to the behavioral assessment of academic skills is the continual monitoring of performance. Graphic displays of behavior can be used to make decisions regarding the success or failure of intervention programs. In addition, they can serve as feedback to the student regarding performance.

In general, the behavioral assessment of academic skills incorporates the assessment of the instructional environment and the individual's academic abilities. Although the behavioral assessment of academic skills is more complicated than presented here, an increasing literature is emerging which describes the use of these measures in detail (Fuchs, Deno, & Marston, 1983; Fuchs, Deno, & Mirkin, 1984; Marston, Tindal, & Deno, 1984; Shapiro, 1987; Shapiro & Lentz, 1985, 1986; Shinn & Marston, 1985; Tindal, 1985; Tindal *et al.*, 1985; Tucker, 1985).

Assessing Social-Emotional Behavior

School-based assessments often require evaluations of the social and emotional functioning of children (Prout, 1983). School psychologists when conducting these evaluations do not typically rely on behavioral assessment strategies (Fuller & Goh, 1983; Prout, 1983). Evaluations are usually conducted using measures of personality such as projective and objective tests (Fuller & Goh, 1983). Despite this strategy, surveys have often reported that psychologists are uncomfortable with their ability to evaluate emotionally handicapped children (Ramage, 1979).

Gresham (1985) recently has called for a redefinition of behavior disorders. His proposal is for behavior disorders to be defined as follows:

1. Specification of excesses, deficits, and/or situational inappropriateness of behavior in operational terms;
2. Specification of objective features of behavior

and its multiple dimensions such as frequency, duration, intensity, etc.;
3. Specification of the behavior system or systems through which excesses and deficits are expressed (i.e., cognitive-verbal, overt-motoric, and/or physiological/emotional);
4. Demonstration of the occurrence of behavioral excesses and/or deficits across situations;
5. Occurrence of excesses and/or deficits over time;
6. Agreement upon the occurrence of excesses, deficits, and/or situational inappropriateness of behavior using multiple methods of assessment; and
7. The continuation of excesses, deficits, and/or situational inappropriateness of behavior at an unacceptable level subsequent to a school-based intervention. (pp. 499–500)

In Gresham's (1985) delineation of this definition, he essentially argues for a behavioral assessment methodology in determining behavior disorders in children.

The strategies described earlier can all be applied in conducting school-based assessments of social-emotional problems. Assessment can begin with either a behavioral interview of the referral source or the completion of a global behavior checklist. Once the behavior problems are defined, direct observation is conducted. Additional assessment in terms of specific behavioral checklists/rating scales, role-play tests, and/or peer assessments are conducted as needed.

Based on the data, recommendations for intervention programs can be developed. Data collected during the assessment can serve as baseline against which behavior change is measured. Further, a cross-situational examination of the behavior can be made to determine if the child meets the definition of behavior disorders suggested by Gresham (1985). If the criterion for the definition is met, a decision can be made whether the child's problem can be adequately handled in the present situation or a referral for special education is needed.

The behavioral assessment of social-emotional problems of children has an extensive literature (e.g., Mash & Terdal, 1981). Although application to school-based referrals are not directly addressed in this literature, there has recently been an increasing interest in bringing behavioral assessment technology to the school setting (e.g., Alessi & Kaye, 1983; Kratochwill, 1982; Shapiro, 1987). Continued efforts in this direction are clearly recommended to bring empirical documentation and validation to decisions regarding a child's social/emotional functioning.

Barriers to Behavioral Assessment in Educational Settings

Despite the extensive development of the behavioral assessment technology for application into schools, significant barriers to the implementation of these strategies exist. Shapiro and Kratochwill (1985) recently addressed these issues pointing to a number of significant factors that can affect the implementation and acceptance of behavioral assessment in the educational environment.

Three levels at which barriers are found can be identified. These are the practioner level, trainer level, and administrative/political level. The practioner level concerns those barriers that are present among practicing school psychologists. Any attempt to use behavioral assessment in schools must address the potential impediments that occur at this level. Among the many impediments to behavioral assessment which may be present among practioners are issues related to the model of service delivery, the lack of standardization of behavioral assessment techniques, perceptions of practicing school psychologists regarding their defined roles, the failure of research findings to alter the methods of service delivery, and the availability of resources to change behavior (Shapiro & Kratochwill, 1985).

One of the most salient barriers facing practioners is the ability to obtain retraining. Training in behavioral assessment is not a priority in the training of most school psychologists (Anderson *et al.*, 1984). Typically, emphasis is placed on more traditional forms of assessing personality, such as projective tests (Fuller & Goh, 1983). Given this lack of training, school psychologists who are genuinely interested in being trained in behavioral assessment may have few opportunities to learn effectively this technique. Attendance at professional conferences or short workshops is only able to introduce ideas to the practitioner. To learn actually to use behavioral assessment, practitioners need to have access to some type of an on-going training program where clinical supervision is provided. Unfortunately, short of returning to graduate school for a doctoral degree, few opportunities exist.

Very closely related to this point are the barriers evident at the trainer level. In particular, trainers of school psychologists are often slow to alter their methods of training based on research and continue to train individuals in traditional/diagnostic methods of assessment (Anderson *et al.*, 1984). The endorsement of such methods by the mentors of impressionable graduate students creates further impediments to behavioral assessment.

A related difficulty can occur even in training programs where behavioral assessment is strongly advocated and taught. Field supervisors, an extension of the training program, rarely share this approach to assessment. Being trained primarily in traditional methods, these individuals are not capable of providing direct supervision on a daily basis to students in training. As such, an unusually large burden of difficulty falls on the shoulders of the university supervisors. Additionally, the failure of students to see their field supervisors advocating behavioral assessment places the student into a somewhat uncomfortable position of possibly having to debate the merits of the approach to evaluation in which they were trained with their immediate supervisor.

The third level at which barriers to behavioral assessment exist is the administrative/political level. At this level, concerns are often related to the administration's perception of the school psychologist's role as a diagnostician, the political repercussions of not placing as many children into special education, which may be a by-product of using behavioral assessment, and the administrator's potential concerns about compliance with Public Law 94-142.

Although the later two concerns may be legitimate, the perceptual difficulties of administrators result primarily from the school psychologist who perpetuates this perception. Administrators are usually reactive, not proactive. School administrators often have expressed desires for school psychologists to perform in alternative roles (Kaplan, Clancy, & Chrin, 1977). Their perceptions are based on the observable actions of the professionals who work for them. Because traditional assessment remains the primary method by which psychologists deliver services, the administration assumes this to be the expected approach of all psychologists.

Barriers related to political issues are more difficult to address. School administrators must be responsive to pressure generated by parents and advocacy groups. Because the purpose of behavioral assessment is to design behavioral interventions and avoid classification, it is possible that the number of students actually placed in special education could be reduced. Groups who act as advocates for handicapped children may view this as an attempt to exclude certain children from receiving special education services. Administrators may have to be responsive to such pressure and require that diagnostic decision making continue.

Although it is possible that such advocacy could result in a barrier to behavioral assessment, the solution to the problem lies in educating the advocacy group. In keeping with the mainstreaming mandate of P.L. 94-142, the treatment of children within the regular education setting should be a priority. Recently, the National Association of School Psychologists presented a position paper representing the organization's view that services to regular education are important and critical in improving services to all children with school-related difficulties (NASP, 1985).

Further, the use of behavioral assessment provides empirical documentation when programs implemented in the regular education setting are failing and special education becomes warranted. Clearly, making these points to advocacy groups may begin to alter any concerns they may have about changing the service delivery model in school psychology.

At the training program level, changes in the philosophy and approach to training are needed. Programs need to emphasize the important link between assessment and intervention. Such linkages are readily possible when behavioral assessment is used. Likewise, training programs need to base instruction on empirical research. This would clearly suggest that teaching traditional methods of assessment should be de-emphasized.

Finally, at the administrative level, education and demonstration is needed that service delivery can be different than exists currently. Psychologists must demonstrate the value and cost-efficiency of consultation and behavioral assessment. Many administrators may find behavioral assessment to be a logical and valuable alternative to traditional assessment.

Future Considerations

Behavioral assessment has been discussed as a useful procedure for conducting evaluations within the school setting. Strategies for evaluating social-emotional and academic difficulties of children were described. Potential barriers and limitations to acceptance of behavioral assessment in schools were also noted.

The degree to which behavioral assessment is currently being employed in educational settings is still in question (Anderson *et al.*, 1984; Shapiro, Lentz, & Sofman, 1985). As such, the true value of the methodology is yet to be determined. Although research does seem to suggest that behavioral assessment could serve as a legitimate alternative to traditional/diagnostic methods of assessment (e.g., Mash & Terdal, 1981; Shapiro, 1987; Shapiro & Kratochwill, 1988), the acceptance of such a methodology within the educational environment is not clear.

The increased use of behavioral assessment in school settings must be based on the accumulation of research evidence suggesting that this methodology results in improved services to children. At present, little research supporting this position actually exists. Gradin, Casey, and Christenson (1985) and Graden, Casey, and Bonstrom (1985) have recently described an attempt to implement and evaluate a preplacement service delivery model that incorporated behavioral assessment and behavioral consultation as key components in the model. Results from Graden's studies were encouraging but significant methodological deficiencies in the study preclude drawing any definitive conclusions. Additionally, Lentz and Shapiro (1985) described a model for service delivery that incorporated behavioral assessment and behavioral consultation as key components but also included provisions for meeting federal guidelines for making decisions regarding eligibility for special education. At present, however, data are not available regarding the efficacy of the model.

Perhaps the best evidence that behavioral assessment in the schools can be valuable can be found in the results of large-scale projects that have incorporated a behavioral model of assessment and intervention. Included in these efforts are Behavior Analysis Follow Through (Stallings, 1975), the Direct Instruction program (Engelmann & Carnine, 1982), the Pine County Minnesota project (Tindal, Wesson, Deno, Germann, & Mirkin, 1985) and the Minneapolis School District project (Marston & Magnusson 1985). Results of these projects have consistently shown that students in these projects have higher achievement levels when compared to more traditional approaches (Becker & Carnine, 1981; Becker & Gersten, 1982; Gersten, 1985).

Despite the encouraging results of such programs, little research demonstrating the applicability and generalizability of these methods to the typical school district have emerged. Until such time as behavioral assessment is shown to be substantially better in meeting the needs of such districts, it is unlikely that widespread acceptance of these methods will occur.

Although the value of behavioral assessment in the schools is as yet untested, it is clear that current assessment methods are inadequate. Research examining the current state of assessment in special education (particularly in the classification of learning disabilities) conducted by the University of Minnesota Institute for Research in Learning Disabilities, led Ysseldyke to conclude that assessment as it is conducted is inadequate in making decisions about classification and intervention (Ysseldyke *et al.*, 1983). Behavioral assessment presents a potential alternative to traditional assessment. Continued research will be needed to clearly establish if this method results in better or more useful decision making.

References

Achenbach, T. M. (1978). The child behavior profile: I. Boys ages 6–11. *Journal of Consulting and Clinical Psychology, 46,* 478–488.

Achenbach, T. M., & Edelbrock, C. J. (1978). The classification of child psychopathology: A review and analysis of empirical efforts. *Psychological Bulletin, 85,* 1275–1301.

Achenbach, T. M., & Edelbrock, C. J. (1986). *Manual for the Teacher's Report Form and the Teacher Version of the Child Behavior Profile.* Burlington, VT: University of Vermont Department of Psychiatry.

Alessi, G., & Kaye, J. H. (1983). *Behavior assessment for school psychologists.* Kent, OH: National Association of School Psychologists.

Anderson, T. K., Cancelli, A. A., & Kratochwill, T. R. (1984). Self-reported assessment practices of school psychologists: Implications and practice. *Journal of School Psychology, 22,* 17–29.

Arthur, A. Z. (1969). Diagnostic testing and the new alternatives. *Psychological Bulletin, 72,* 183–192.

Barlow, D. H. (Ed.). (1981). *Behavioral assessment of adult disorders.* New York: Guilford Press.

Barrios, B. A., Hartmann, D. P., & Shigetomi, C. (1981). Fears and anxieties in children. In E. J. Mash & L. G. Terdal (Eds.), *Behavioral assessment of childhood disorders* (pp. 259–304). New York: Guilford Press.

Becker, W. C., & Carnine, D. W. (1981). Direct instruction: A behavior theory model for comprehensive educational intervention with the disadvantaged. In S. W. Bijou & R. Ruiz (Eds.), *Behavior modification: Contributions to education* (pp. 145–210). Hillsdale, NJ: Erlbaum.

Becker, W. C., & Gersten, R. (1982). A follow up of Follow-Through: The later effects of the direct instruction model on children in fifth and sixth grades. *American Educational Research Journal, 19,* 75–92.

Bergan, J. R. (1977). *Behavioral consultation.* Columbus, OH: Charles E. Merrill.

Bergan, J. R., & Tombari, M. L. (1975). The analysis of verbal interaction occurring during consultation. *Journal of School Psychology, 13,* 209–226.

Bergan, J. R., & Tombari, M. L. (1976). Consultant skill and efficiency and the implementation and outcomes of consultation. *Journal of School Psychology, 14,* 3–14.

Bergan, J. R., Byrnes, I. M., & Kratochwill, T. R. (1979). Effect of behavioral and medical models of consultation on teacher expectancies and instruction of a hypothetical child. *Journal of School Psychology, 17,* 306–316.

Brophy, J. E. (1979). Teacher behavior and its effects. *Journal of Educational Psychology, 71,* 733–750.

Brophy, J. E., & Evertson, C. *Learning from teaching: A developmental perspective.* Boston, MA: Allyn & Bacon.

Bornstein, M. T., Bellack, A. S., & Hersen, M. (1977). Social skills training for unassertive children: A multiple-baseline analysis. *Journal of Applied Behavior Analysis, 10,* 183–195.

Brown, D. K., Kratochwill, T. R., & Bergan, J. R. (1982). Teaching interview skills for problem identification: An analogue study. *Behavioral Assessment, 4,* 63–74.

Campbell, J. A., & Willis, J. (1978). Modifying components of creative behavior in the natural environment. *Behavior Modification, 2,* 549–564.

Chambers, W. J., Puig-Antich, J., & Tabrizi, M. A. (1979). *The ongoing development of the Kiddie-SADS.* Unpublished manuscript.

Ciminero, A. R. (1977). Behavioral assessment: An overview. In A. R. Ciminero, K. S. Calhoun, & H. E. Adams (Eds.), *Handbook of behavioral assessment* (pp. 3–14). New York: Wiley.

Ciminero, A. R., & Drabman, R. S. (1977). Current developments in the behavioral assessment of children. In B. B. Lahey & A. E. Kazdin (Eds.), *Advances in clinical child psychology* (Vol. 1, pp. 47–84). New York: Plenum Press.

Ciminero, A. R., Nelson, R. O., & Lipinski, D. P. (1977). Self-monitoring procedures. In A. R. Ciminero, K. S. Calhoun, & H. E. Adams (Eds.), *Handbook of behavioral assessment* (pp. 195–232). New York: Wiley.

Cone, J. D. (1977). The relevance of reliability and validity for behavioral assessment. *Behavior Therapy, 88,* 411–426.

Cone, J. D. (1978). The Behavioral Assessment Grid (BAG): A conceptual framework and a taxonomy. *Behavior Therapy, 9,* 882–888.

Cone, J. D. (1979). Why the "I've got a better agreement measure" literature continues to grow: A commentary on two articles by Birkimer and Brown. *Journal of Applied Behavior Analysis, 12,* 571–572.

Cone, J. D., & Hawkins, R. P. (1977). Current status and future directions in behavioral assessment. In J. D. Cone & R. P. Hawkins (Eds.), *Behavioral assessment: New directions in clinical psychology* (pp. 381–418). New York: Brunner/Mazel.

Conners, C. K. (1968). A teacher rating scale for use in drug studies with children. *American Journal of Psychiatry, 126,* 884–888.

Conners, C. K. (1970). Symptom patterns in hyperkinetic, neurotic, and normal children. *Child Development, 41,* 667–682.

Conners, C. K. (1973). Rating scales for use in drug studies in children. *Psychopharmacology Bulletin, 9,* 24–84.

Delquadri, J. C., Greenwood, C. R., Stretton, K., & Hall, D. V. (1983). The peer tutoring spelling game: A classroom procedure for increasing opportunity to respond and spelling performance. *Education and Treatment of Children, 6,* 225–239.

Deluty, R. H. (1979). Children's action tendency scale: A self-report measure of aggressiveness, assertiveness, and submissiveness in children. *Journal of Consulting and Clinical Psychology, 47,* 1061–1071.

Denham, C., & Lieberman, P. (Eds.). (1980). *Time to learn.* Washington, DC: National Institute of Education.

Deno, S. L., & Mirkin, P. (1977). *Data based program modification: A manual.* Reston, VA: Council for Exceptional Children.

Deno, S. L., Mirkin, P. K., Lowry, L., & Kuehnle, K. (1980). *Relationships among simple measures of spelling and performance on standardized achievement tests* (Research Report No. 21). Minneapolis, MN: University of Minnesota, Institute for Research on Learning Disabilities.

Deno, S. L., Marston, D., & Mirkin, P. (1982). Valid measurement procedures for continuous evaluation of written expression. *Exceptional Children, 48,* 368–371.

Deno, S. L., Mirkin, P. K., & Chiang, B. (1982). Identifying valid measures of reading. *Exceptional Children, 49,* 36–45.

Dunn, L. M., & Markwardt, F. C. (1974). *Peabody Individual Achievement Test.* Circle Pines, MN: American Guidance Service.

Edelbrock, C. S., & Achenbach, T. M. (1984). The teacher version of the child behavior profile: I. Boys aged 6–11. *Journal of Consulting and Clinical Psychology, 52,* 207–217.

Eisler, R. M., Hersen, M., Miller, P. M., & Blanchard, E. B. (1975). Situational determinants of assertive behavior. *Journal of Consulting and Clinical Psychology, 43,* 330–340.

Engelmann, S., & Carnine, D. W. (1982). *Theory of instruction.* New York: Irvington.

Finch, A. J., & Nelson, W. M. (1982, November). *The children's inventory of anger: A self-report measure.* Paper presented at the annual meeting of the Association for the Advancement of Behavior Therapy, Washington, DC.

Fuchs, L. S., Deno. S. L., & Marston, D. (1983). Improving the reliability of curriculum-based measures of academic skills for psychoeducational decision making. *Diagnostique, 8,* 135–149.

Fuchs, L. S., Deno, S. L., & Mirkin, P. K. (1984). The effects of frequent curriculum-based measurement and evaluation on pedagogy, student achievement, and student awareness of learning. *American Educational Research Journal, 21,* 449–460.

Fuller, G. B., & Goh, D. S. (1982). Current practices in the assessment of personality and behavior by school psychologists. *School Psychology Review, 12,* 240–243.

Gersten, R. (1985). Direct instruction with special education students: A review of evaluation research. *The Journal of Special Education, 19,* 41–58.

Goldfried, M. R. (1977). Behavioral assessment in perspective. In J. D. Cone & R. P. Hawkins (Eds.), *Behavioral assessment: New directions in clinical psychology* (pp. 3–22). New York: Brunner/Mazel.

Goldfried, M. R., & Kent, R. N. (1972). Traditional versus behavioral assessment: A comparison of methodological and theoretical assumptions. *Psychological Bulletin, 77,* 409–420.

Gottman, J. M., Gonso, J., & Schuler, P. (1976). Teaching social skills to isolated children. *Journal of Abnormal Child Psychology, 4,* 179–197.

Goyette, C. H., Conners, C. K., & Ulrich, R. F. (1978). Normative data on revised Conners parent and teacher rating scale. *Journal of Abnormal Child Psychology, 6,* 221–236.

Graden, J. L., Casey, A., & Bonstrom, O. (1985). Implementing a pre-referral intervention system: Part II. The data. *Exceptional Children, 51,* 487–496.

Graden, J. L., Casey, A., & Christensen, S. L. (1985). Implementing a pre-referral intervention system: Part I. The model. *Exceptional Children, 51,* 377–384.

Green, S. B., & Alverson, L. G. (1978). A comparison of indirect measures for long duration behaviors. *Journal of Applied Behavior Analysis, 11,* 530.

Greenwood, C. R., Walker, H. M., & Hops, H. (1977). Issues in social interaction/withdrawal assessment. *Exceptional Children, 43,* 490–501.

Greenwood, C. R., Todd, N. M., Walker, H. M., & Hops, H. (1978). *Social Assessment Manual for Preschool Level-SAMPLE.* Eugene, OR: Center at Oregon for Research in the Behavioral Education of the Handicapped.

Greenwood, C. R., Delquadri, J., & Hall, R. V. (1984). Opportunity to respond and student academic performance. In U. L. Heward, T. E. Heron, D. S. Hill, & J. Trap-Porter (Eds.), *Focus on behavior analysis in education* (pp. 58–88). Columbus, OH: Charles E. Merrill.

Greenwood, C. R., Dinwiddie, G., Terry, B., Wade, L.,

Stanley, S. O., Thibadeau, S., & Delquadri, J. C. (1984). Teacher- versus peer-mediated instruction: An ecobehavioral analysis of achievement outcome. *Journal of Applied Behavior Analysis, 17,* 521–538.

Gresham, F. M. (1981). Assessment of children's social skills. *Journal of School Psychology, 19,* 120–133.

Gresham, F. M. (1984). Behavioral interviews in school psychology: Issues in psychometric adequacy and research. *School Psychology Review, 13,* 17–25.

Gresham, F. M. (1985). Behavior disorder assessment: Conceptual, definitional, and practical considerations. *School Psychology Review, 14,* 495–509.

Hallahan, D. P., & Sapona, R. (1983). Self-monitoring of attention with learning disabled children: Past research and current issues. *Journal of Learning Disabilities, 16,* 616–620.

Hallahan, D. P., Lloyd, J. W., Kneedler, R. D., & Marshall, K. J. (1982). A comparison of the effects of self- versus teacher assessment of on-task behavior. *Behavior Therapy, 13,* 715–723.

Hartmann, D. P., Roper, B. L., & Bradford, D. C. (1979). Some relationships between behavioral and traditional assessment. *Journal of Behavioral Assessment, 1,* 3–21.

Hasazi, J. E., & Hasazi, S. E. (1972). Effects of teacher attention on digit reversal behavior in an elementary school child. *Journal of Applied Behavior Analysis, 5,* 157–162.

Hay, W. M., Hay, L. R., Angle, H. V., & Nelson, R. O. (1979). The reliability of problem identification in the behavioral interview. *Behavioral Assessment, 1,* 107–118.

Haynes, S. N. (1978). *Principles of behavioral assessment.* New York: Gardner Press.

Haynes, S. C., & Wilson, C. C. (1979). *Behavioral assessment: Recent advances in methods, concepts, and applications.* San Francisco: Jossey-Bass.

Heron, T., Heward, W., Cooke, N., & Hill, D. (1983). Evaluation of a classwide peer tutoring system: First graders teach each other sight words. *Education and Treatment of Children, 6,* 137–152.

Herjanic, B., Herjanic, M., Brown, F., & Wheatt, T. (1975). Are children reliable reporters? *Journal of Abnormal Child Psychology, 3,* 41–48.

Hobbs, S. A., Walls, D. L., & Hammersely, G. A. (1984). Assessing children's social skills: Validation of the Behavioral Assertiveness Test for Children (BAT-C). *Journal of Behavioral Assessment, 6,* 29–36.

Hoge, R. D. (1983). Psychometric properties of teacher-judgement measures of pupil aptitudes, classroom behaviors, and achievement levels. *The Journal of Special Education, 17,* 401–429.

Holland, C. (1970). An interview guide for behavioral counseling with parents. *Behavior Therapy, 1,* 70–79.

Jastak, J., & Jastak, S. (1978). *Wide Range Achievement Test.* Wilmington, DE: Jastak Associates.

Jenkins, J. R., & Pany, D. (1978). Standardized achievement tests: How useful for special education? *Exceptional Children, 44,* 448–453.

Johnson, S. B., & Melamed, B. G. (1979). The assessment and treatment of children's fears. In B. B. Lahey & A. E. Kazdin (Eds.), *Advances in clinical child psychology* (pp. 108–139). New York: Plenum Press.

Kane, J. J., & Lawler, E. E., III (1978). Methods of peer assessment. *Psychological Bulletin, 85,* 555–586.

Kanfer, F. H., & Grimm, L. G. (1977). Behavior analysis: Selecting target behaviors in the interview. *Behavior Modification, 1,* 7–28.

Kanfer, F. H., & Saslow, G. (1969). Behavioral diagnosis. In C. Franks (Ed.), *Behavior therapy: Appraisal and status* (pp. 417–444). New York: McGraw-Hill.

Kaplan, M. S., Clancy, B., & Chrin, M. (1977). Priority roles for school psychologists as seen by superintendents. *Journal of School Psychology, 15,* 75–80.

Kazdin, A. E. (1977). Assessing the clinical or applied significance of behavior change through social validation. *Behavior Modification, 1,* 427–452.

Kazdin, A. E. (1979). Situational specificity: The two-edged sword of behavioral assessment. *Behavioral Assessment, 1,* 57–75.

Kazdin, A. E., Esveldt-Dawson, K., & Loar, L. L. (1984). Correspondence of teacher ratings and direct observations of classroom behavior of psychiatric inpatient children. *Journal of Abnormal Child Psychology, 11,* 549–564.

Kendall, P. C., & Wilcox, L. E. (1979). Self-control in children: Development of a rating scale. *Journal of Consulting and Clinical Psychology, 47,* 1020–1029.

Kendall, P. C., Zupan, B. A., & Braswell, L. (1981). Self-control in children: Further analysis of the self-control rating scale. *Behavior Therapy, 12,* 667–681.

Kestenbaum, C. J., & Bird, H. R. (1978). A reliability study of the mental health assessment form for school-age children. *Journal of the American Academy of Child Psychiatry, 17,* 338–347.

Kosiewicz, M. M., Hallahan, D. D., & Lloyd, J. (1981). The effects of an LD student's treatment choice on handwriting performance. *Learning Disabilities Quarterly, 4,* 281–286.

Kirk, S. A., McCarthy, J., & Kirk, W. (1971). *Illinois test of psycholinguistic abilities.* Urbana, IL: University of Illinois Press.

Koppitz, E. M. (1963). *The Bender gestalt test for young children.* New York: Grune & Stratton.

Kovacs, M. (1978). *Interview Schedule for Children (ISC) Form C, 10th rev.* Pittsburgh: University of Pittsburgh School of Medicine, Western Psychiatric Institute and Clinic.

Kovacs, M. (1983). *The Children's Depression Inventory: A self-rated depression scale for school-aged youngsters.* Pittsburgh: University of Pittsburgh School of Medicine, Western Psychiatric Institute and Clinic.

Kratochwill, T. R. (1982). Advances in behavioral assessment. In C. R. Reynolds & T. B. Gutkin (Eds.), *The handbook of school psychology* (pp. 314–350). New York: Wiley.

Kratochwill, T. R., & Bergan, J. R. (1978). Evaluating programs in applied settings through behavioral consultation. *Journal of School Psychology, 16*, 375–386.

LaGreca, A. M., & Santogrossi, D. A. (1980). Social skills training with elementary school students: A behavioral group approach. *Journal of Consulting and Clinical Psychology, 48*, 220–227.

Lahey, B. B., & Drabman, R. S. (1973). Facilitation of the acquisition and retention of sight word vocabulary through token reinforcement. *Journal of Applied Behavior Analysis, 6*, 101–104.

Lahey, B. B., McNees, M. D., & Brown, C. C. (1973). Modification of deficits in reading for comprehension. *Journal of Applied Behavior Analysis, 6*, 475–480.

Leinhardt, G., & Seewald, A. (1981). Overlap: What's tested, what's taught. *Journal of Educational Measurement, 18*, 85–96.

Lentz, F. E., Jr. (1982). *An empirical examination of the utility of partial interval and momentary time sampling as measurements of behavior.* Unpublished doctoral dissertation, University of Tennessee, Knoxville, TN.

Lentz, F. E. Jr., & Shapiro, E. S. (1985). Behavioral school psychology: A conceptual model for the delivery of psychological services. In T. R. Kratochwill (Ed.), *Advances in School Psychology* (Vol. 4, pp. 191–222). Hillsdale, NJ: Erlbaum.

Linehan, M. N. (1977). Issues in behavioral interviewing. In J. D. Cone & R. P. Hawkins (Eds.), *Behavioral assessment: New direction in clinical psychology* (pp. 30–51). New York: Brunner/Mazel.

Lovitt, T. C. (1978). Arithmetic. In N. Haring, T. Lovitt, M. Eaton, & C. Hansen (Eds.), *The fourth R: Research in the classroom* (pp. 127–167). New York: Charles E. Merrill.

Lovitt, T. C. (1981). Charting academic performance of mildly handicapped youngsters. In J. M. Kauffman & D. P. Hallahan (Eds.), *Handbook of special education* (pp. 393–417). Englewood Cliffs, NJ: Prentice-Hall.

Lovitt, T. C., & Hansen, C. C. (1967a). The use of contingenty skipping and drilling to improve oral reading and comprehension. *Journal of Learning Disabilities, 9*, 481–487.

Lovitt, T. C., & Hansen, C. C. (1976b). Round one- placing the child in the right reader. *Journal of Learning Disabilities, 9*, 347–353.

Lovitt, T. C., Eaton, M., Kirkwood, M. E., & Perlander, A. (1971). Effects of various reinforcement contingencies on oral reading rate. In E. Ramp & B. L. Hopkins (Eds.), *A new direction for education: Behavior analysis* (pp. 54–71). Lawrence, KS: University of Kansas Press.

Marston, D., & Magnusson, D. (1985). Implementing curriculum-based measurement in special and regular education settings. *Exceptional Children, 52*, 266–276.

Marston, D., Tindal, G., & Deno, S. L. (1984). Eligibility for learning disability services: A direct and repeated measurement approach. *Exceptional Children, 50*, 554–556.

Mash, E., & Terdal, L. (1976). *Behavior-therapy assessment: Diagnosis, design, and evaluation.* New York: Springer.

Mash, E., & Terdal, L. (Eds.). (1981). *Behavioral assessment of childhood disorders.* New York: Guilford Press.

Matson, J. L., Esveldt-Dawson, K., Andrasik, F., Ollendick, T. H., Petti, T. H., & Hersen, M. (1980). Direct, observational, and generalization effects of social skills training with emotionally disturbed children. *Behavior Therapy, 11*, 522–531.

Matson, J. L., & Senatore, V. (1981). A comparison of traditional psychotherapy and social skills training for improving interpersonal functioning of mentally retarded adults. *Behavior Therapy, 12*, 369–382.

McConaughy, S. H. (1985). Using the child behavior checklist and related instruments in school-based assessment of children. *School Psychology Review, 14*, 479–494.

McFall, R. M. (1977). Analogue methods in behavioral assessment: Issues and prospects. In J. D. Cone & R. P. Hawkins (Eds.), *Behavioral assessment: New directions in clinical psychology* (pp. 152–177). New York: Brunner/Mazel.

McLaughlin, T. F. (1981). The effects of a classroom token economy on math performance in an intermediate grade class. *Education and Treatment of Children, 4*, 139–147.

Melamed, B., & Siegel, L. (1975). Reduction of anxiety in children facing hospitalization and surgery by use of filmed modeling. *Journal of Consulting and Clinical Psychology, 43*, 511–521.

Melamed, B., Yurcheson, R., Fleece, E. L., Hutcherson, S., & Hawes, R. (1978). Effects of filmed modeling on the reduction of anxiety-related behaviors in individuals varying in level of previous experience in the stress situation. *Journal of Consulting and Clinical Psychology, 46*, 1357–1367.

Mischel, W. L. (1968). *Personality and assessment.* New York: Wiley.

Morris, R. M., & Kratochwill, T. R. (1983). *Treating children's fears and phobias: A behavioral approach.* New York: Pergamon Press.

National Association for School Psychologists. (1985). Advocacy for appropriate educational services for all children. *NASP Communique, 13* (8), 9.

Nelson, R. O. (1977). Methodological issues in assessment via self-monitoring. In J. D. Cone & R. P. Hawkins (Eds.), *Behavioral assessment: New direction in clinical psychology* (pp. 217–240). New York: Brunner/Mazel.

Nelson, R. O. (1983). Behavioral assessment: Past, present, and future. *Behavioral Assessment, 5*, 195–206.

Nelson, R. O., & Hayes, S. C. (1979). Some current dimensions of behavioral assessment. *Behavioral Assessment, 1*, 1–16.

Nelson, R. O., Hay, L. R., & Hay, W. M. (1977). Comments on Cone's "the relevance of reliability and validity for behavioral assessment." *Behavior Therapy, 8*, 437–440.

Nelson, W. M., III, & Finch, A. J., Jr. (1978). *The Children's Inventory of Anger.* Unpublished manuscript, Xavier University.

Odom, S. L., Hoyson, M., Jamieson, B., & Strain, P. S. (1985). Increasing handicapped preschoolers' peer social interactions: Cross-setting and component analysis. *Journal of Applied Behavior Analysis, 18,* 3–16.

O'Leary, K. D., Romanczyk, R. G., Kass, R. E., Dietz, A., & Santogrossi, D. (1979). *Procedures for classroom observation of teachers and children.* Stony Brook, NY: Psychology Department, SUNY at Stony Brook.

Ollendick, T. H., Shapiro, E. S., & Barrett, R. P. (1982). Effects of vicarious reinforcement in normal and severely disturbed children. *Journal of Consulting and Clinical Psychology, 50,* 63–70.

Paget, K. D. ((1984). The structured assessment interview: A psychometric review. *Journal of School Psychology, 22,* 415–427.

Piersel, W. C., & Kratochwill, T. R. (1979). Self-observation and behavior change: Applications to academic and adjustment problems through behavioral consultation. *Journal of School Psychology, 17,* 151–161.

Powell, J., Martindale, B., Kulp, S., Martindale, A., & Bauman, R. (1977). Taking a closer look: Time sampling and measurement error. *Journal of Applied Behavior Analysis, 10,* 325–332.

Powell, J., & Rockinson, R. (1978). On the inability of interval time sampling to reflect frequency of occurrence data. *Journal of Applied Behavior Analysis, 11,* 531–532.

Prout, H. T. (1983). School psychologists and social-emotional assessment techniques: Patterns in training and use. *School Psychology Review, 12,* 377–383.

Quay, H. C., & Peterson, D. R. (1967). *Manual for the behavior problem checklist.* Champaign-Urbana, IL: University of Illinois.

Ramage, J. (1979). National survey of school psychologists: Update. *School Psychology Digest, 8,* 153–161.

Reardon, R. C., Hersen, M., Bellack, A. S., & Foley, J. M. (1979). Measuring social skill in grade school boys. *Journal of Behavioral Assessment, 1,* 87–105.

Reed, M. L., & Edelbrock, C. (1983). Reliability and validity of the direct observation form of the Child Behavior Checklist. *Journal of Abnormal Child Psychology, 11,* 521–530.

Reid, J. B. (Ed.). (1978). *A social learning approach to family intervention, Vol. 2: Observation in home settings.* Eugene, OR: Castalia Publishing.

Rhode, G., Morgan, D. P., & Young, K. R. (1983). Generalization and maintenance of treatment gains of behaviorally handicapped students from resource rooms to regular classrooms using self-evaluation procedures. *Journal of Applied Behavior Analysis, 16,* 171–188.

Robertson, S. J., Simon, S. J., Pachman, J. S., & Drabman, R. S. (1979). Self-control and generalization procedures in a classroom of disruptive retarded children. *Child Behavior Therapy, 1,* 347–362.

Rose, T., & Sherry, L. (1984). Relative effects of two previewing procedures on LD adolescents oral reading performance. *Learning Disabilities Quarterly, 7,* 39–44.

Rosenshine, B. V. (1981). Academic engaged time, content covered, and direct instruction. *Journal of Education, 3,* 38–66.

Rutter, M., & Graham, P. (1968). The reliability and validity of the psychiatric assessment of the child: I. Interview with the child. *British Journal of Psychiatry, 114,* 563–579.

Saudargas, R. A., & Creed-Murrah, V. (1980). *State-Event Classroom Observation System.* Unpublished manuscript, Department of Psychology, University of Tennessee, Knoxville, TN.

Scherer, M. W., & Nakamura, C. Y. (1968). A fear survey schedule for children (FSS-FC): A factor analytic comparison with manifest anxiety (CMAS). *Behavior Research and Therapy, 6,* 173–182.

Shapiro, A. H. (1975). Behavior of kibbutz and urban children receiving an injection. *Psychophysiology, 12,* 79–82.

Shapiro, E. S. (1984). Self-monitoring. In T. H. Ollendick & M. Hersen (Eds.), *Child behavior assessment: Principles and procedures* (pp. 148–165). New York: Pergamon Press.

Shapiro, E. S. (1987). *Behavioral Assessment in School Psychology.* Hillsdale, NJ: Erlbaum.

Shapiro, E. S., & Kratochwill, T. R. (1985, March). *Barriers to behavioral assessment in the schools.* Paper presented at the annual meeting of the National Association of School Psychologists, Las Vegas, NV.

Shapiro, E. S., & Kratochwill, T. R. (Eds.). (1988). *Behavioral assessment in the schools: Conceptual foundations and practical applications.* New York: Guilford Press.

Shapiro, E. S., & Lentz, F. E. Jr. (1985). Assessing academic behavior: A behavior approach. *School Psychology Review, 14,* 325–338.

Shapiro, E. S., & Lentz, F. E. Jr. (1986). Behavioral assessment of academic behavior. In T. R. Kratochwill (Eds.), *Advances in School Psychology, Vol. 5* (pp. 87–139). Hillsdale, NJ: Erlbaum.

Shapiro, E. S., Stover, J. E., & Ifkovits, G. A. (1983, December). *Predictive and concurrent validity of role-play and naturalistic assessment of social skills in kindergarten children.* Paper presented at the annual meeting of the Association for the Advancement of Behavior Therapy, Washington, DC.

Shapiro, E. S., Browder, D. M., & D'Huyvetters, K. K. (1984). Increasing academic productivity of severely multi-handicapped children with self-management: Idiosyncratic effects. *Analysis and Intervention in Developmental Disabilities, 4,* 171–188.

Shapiro, E. S., Gilbert, D., Friedman, J., & Steiner, S. (1985, November). *Concurrent validity of role-play and contrived tests in assessing social skills in disruptive adolescents.* Paper presented at the annual meeting of the Association for the Advancement of Behavior Therapy, Houston, TX.

Shapiro, E. S., Lentz, F. E., Jr., & Sofman, R. (1985). Validity of rating scales in assessing aggresive behavior in classroom settings. *Journal of School Psychology, 23,* 69–80.

Shinn, M., & Marston, D. (1985). Differentiating mildly handicapped, low-achieving, and regular education students: A curriculum-based approach. *RASE: Remedial and Special Eduction, 6*(2), 31–38.

Slate, J. R., & Saudargas, R. A. (1984, April). *Behaviors and behavior patterns of learning disabled, seriously emotionally disturbed, and average children in the regular classroom.* Paper presented at the annual meeting of the Southeastern Psychological Association, New Orleans, LA.

Stallings, J. (1975). Implementation and effects of teaching practices in follow through classrooms. *Monographs of the Society for research in Child Development, 40.*

Stanley, S. D., & Greenwood, C. R. (1981). *CISSAR: Code for instructional structure and student academic response.* Juniper Gardens Children's Project, Kansas City, KS.

Starlin, C. M. (1982). On reading and writing. *Iowa Monograph Series.* Des Moines, IA: Department of Public Instruction.

Stowitschek, C., Lewis, B., Shores, R., & Ezzel, D. (1981). Procedures for analyzing student performance data to generate hypothesis for the purpose of educational decision making. *Behavior Disorders, 5,* 136–150.

Strain, P. S. (1983). Identification of social skill curriculum targets for severely handicapped children in mainstreamed preschools. *Applied Research in Mental Retardation, 4,* 369–382.

Stromer, R. (1975). Modifying letter and number reversals in elementary school children. *Journal of Applied Behavior Analysis, 8,* 211.

Thurlow, M., Ysseldyke, J. E., Graden, K., & Algozzine, R. (1984). Opportunity to learn for LD students receiving different levels of special education services. *Learning Disabilities Quarterly, 7,* 55–67.

Tindal, G. (1985). Increasing the effectiveness of special education: An analysis of methodology. *Journal of Learning Disabilities, 18,* 101–112.

Tindal, G., Fuchs, L. S., Fuchs, D., Shinn, M. R, Deno, S. L., & Germann, G. (1985). Empirical validation of criterion-referenced tests. *Journal of Educational Research, 78,* 203–209.

Tindal, G., Wesson, C., Deno, S. L., Germann, G., & Mirkin, P. K. (1985). The Pine County model for special education delivery: A data-based system. In T. R. Kratochwill (Ed.), *Advances in School Psychology* (Vol. 4, pp. 223–250). Hillsdale, NJ: Erlbaum.

Tucker, J. A. (Ed.). (1985). Curriculum-based assessment [Special issue]. *Exceptional Children, 52*(3).

Van Hasselt, V. B., Hersen, M., Bellack, A. S., Rosenblum, N. D., & Lamparski, D. (1979). Tripartite assessment of the effects of systematic desensitization in a multi-phobic child: An experimental analysis. *Journal of Behavior Therapy and Experimental Psychiatry, 10,* 51–55.

Van Hasselt, V. B., Hersen, M., Whitehill, M. B., & Bellack, A. S. (1979). Social skill assessment and training for children: An evaluative review. *Behaviour Research and Therapy, 17,* 413–437.

Van Hasselt, V. B., Hersen, M., & Bellack, A. S. (1981). The validity of role play tests for assessing social skills in children. *Behavior Therapy, 12,* 202–216.

Wahler, R. G., House, A. E., & Stambaugh, E. E. II (1976). *Ecological assessment for child problem behavior: A clinical package for home, school, and institutional settings.* New York: Pergamon Press.

Walker, H. M. (1983). *Walker problem identification checklist* (Revised). Los Angeles: Western Psychological Services.

Walls, R. T., Werner, T. J., Bacon, A., & Zane, T. (1977). Behavioral checklists. In J. D. Cone & R. P. Hawkins (Eds.), *Behavioral assessment: New directions in clinical psychology* (pp. 77–146). New York: Brunner/Mazel.

Wiggins, J. S. (1973). *Personality and prediction: Principles of personality assessment.* Reading, MA: Addison-Wesley.

Williamson, D. A., Moody, S. C., Granberry, S. W., Lethermon, V. R., & Blouin, D. C. (1983). Criterion-related validity of a role-play social skills test for children. *Behavior Therapy, 14,* 466–481.

Wolf, M. M. (1978). Social validity: The case for subjective measurement or how applied behavior analysis is finding its heart. *Journal of Applied Behavior Analysis, 11,* 203–214.

Wood, R., Michelson, L., & Flynn, S. (1978, November). *Assessment of assertive behavior in elementary school children.* Paper presented at the annual meeting of the Association for the Advancement of Behavior Therapy, Chicago, IL.

Ysseldyke, J. E., Thurlow, M., Graden, J., Wesson, C., Algozzine, B., & Deno, S. (1983). Generalization from five years of research on assessment and decision making: The University of Minnesota Institute. *Exceptional Education Quarterly, 4*(1), 75–93.

CHAPTER 4

Diagnosis and Classification

Craig Edelbrock

Many practitioners, including psychologists working in educational settings, feel they have little need to classify the emotional and behavioral disorders manifested by the disturbed children they serve. Many see diagnosis as a pseudo-scientific exercise having little practical payoff. Some view classification as unnecessary labeling, which casts a negative stigma on children. The types of diagnostic categories embodied in the third edition of the American Psychiatric Association's (1983) *Diagnostic and Statistical Manual* (DSM-III), for example, often seem remote from everyday work with individual children. One might be tempted to ask "What use is diagnosis?"

This unfortunate situation has arisen in part from a lack of appreciation of the role of classification in the field of child mental health. The ability to differentiate accurately and reliably among emotional and behavioral disorders of childhood is essential to progress in research, clinical services, and training pertaining to disturbed children. Many research findings, for example, are simply generalizations about groups or classes. Statements such as "children having disorder *x* also tend to have characteristic *y*" and " group *x* differs significantly from group *y*," are elementary scientific laws. The ability to identify homogenous groups of disturbed children is essential not only to standardize research samples across studies but also as a prerequisite to establishing how such groups differ in systematic ways.

In clinical practice, implicit taxonomic assumptions shape decisions about whether a child has a disorder or not, is in need of treatment, has a good or bad prognosis, or will respond to a particular treatment. Taxonomies of childhood disorders also facilitate professional communication about childhood disturbances, shape the training of mental health professionals, and provide a framework for linking clinical experiences with individual cases.

The term *diagnosis* itself is also a stumbling block. In a narrow sense, diagnosis is simply classification—the grouping of phenomena into categories according to established criteria. Diagnosis thus involves differentiating among disorders of different types. In a broader sense, however, diagnosis involves an investigation of the underlying nature and causes of phenomena. In diagnosing engine

Craig Edelbrock • Department of Psychiatry, University of Massachusetts Medical School, Worcester, Massachusetts 01605. Preparation of this chapter was supported in part by a Faculty Scholar's Award from the William T. Grant Foundation.

trouble, for example, an auto mechanic may first consider observed signs and symptoms, but the ultimate goal is to determine the underlying cause of the mechanical difficulty. Diagnosis is more than simple classification of outward signs and symptoms, it involves getting to the heart of the matter.

In child mental health, diagnosis in the narrow sense of classification is equated with formal diagnosis or differential diagnosis. Psychopathological disorders are grouped into categories according to predetermined criteria, such as those offered in DSM-III. This is a taxonomic exercise: cases are classified on the basis of features that differentiate among various classes or *taxa*. In the broader sense, diagnosis involves a diagnostic formulation—the result of an in-depth investigation of an individual case. The diagnostic formulation goes beyond the sifting and sorting of outward signs and symptoms and addresses the nature and causes of dysfunction in an individual. It is easy to see why practitioners are less interested in formal diagnosis than diagnostic formulations. The former offers only classification of the case according to rigid rules: subtleties of the individual case are lost. The latter offers a more satisfying explanation of how and why the individual developed the disorder, and this translates more directly into guidelines for case management.

Although it may be tempting for practitioners to ignore formal diagnosis altogether and concentrate on diagnostic formulations, this would have many drawbacks. Diagnostic formulations are highly idiosyncratic. They depend heavily on the individual practitioner's personal training, clinical experiences, subjective impressions, and assumptions. Diagnostic formulations are of questionable reliability and validity, but they are rarely tested against any independent criteria. Diagnosis is an effective means of conveying information about a case only if the categories and criteria are explicit and operationally defined, reliably assessed, and have valid implications regarding etiology, course, prognosis, treatment response, and outcome.

Behavioral therapists also eschew diagnosis. The careful selection and precise quantification of target behaviors are hallmarks of behavioral assessment. The emphasis in behavior therapy, however, is on intraindividual changes in target behaviors that may vary from case to case. The necessities of grouping cases according to their distinguishing features and categorizing behaviors into broader syndromes and categories are overlooked. The behavioral approach to assessment and therapy cannot be faulted for the lack of explicit and operational procedures and the reliability and validity of behavioral assessments are usually well established. There is a growing realization, however, that the selection of target behaviors involves implicit taxonomic assumptions and that behaviors are interrelated in complex ways. As Voeltz and Evans (1982) pointed out, there is a need in child behavior assessment and therapy to relate specific target behaviors to broader behavioral patterns and syndromes.

The purpose of this chapter is to review diagnosis and classification of childhood psychopathology as they relate to research and clinical services in educational settings. The two major approaches to classifying child disorders, the medical approach and the psychometric approach, will be reviewed. Relations between these two approaches and prospects for future research will then be addressed.

Two Major Approaches to Classification

The classification of child psychopathology has been dominated by two major approaches: the medical and the psychometric. These two approaches differ in their assumptions regarding the nature of psychopathology, their conceptions of the purpose of classification, and their diagnostic methods. The medical paradigm, as illustrated by DSM-III, is founded on the assumption that psychopathological disorders are disease entities. The purpose of psychiatric diagnosis is to relate observed signs and symptoms to underlying brain pathology. Even if no organic etiology is identified, an underlying disease, defect, or deficit is still postulated to account for observed signs and symptoms. Clinical interviews, physical examinations, and laboratory tests are used to determine if a patient has a given disorder or not. The psychometric approach, in contrast, grew out of attempts to assess personality and intelligence. The goal is to describe individual differences in psychological traits, rather than to identify organic etiologies. Psychometric research has relied heavily on the use of standardized assessment instruments such as personality inventories, behavioral checklists, and rating scales.

The Medical Approach

The dominant diagnostic system in the United States is the third edition of the DSM (DSM-III: American Psychiatric Association, 1980). The first two editions of the DSM (1952, 1968) offered few diagnostic categories explicitly for children and were plagued by the lack of operational diagnostic criteria and low reliability (see Achenbach & Edelbrock, 1978, 1983, for reviews). The DSM-III is more highly differentiated in the area of "Disorders Usually First Evident in Infancy, Childhood, or Adolescence," and employs more explicit diagnostic criteria than its predecessors. The DSM-III is also multiaxial, with separate axes for coding clinical syndromes (Axis I), personality disorders, and specific development disorders (Axis II), physical disorders (Axis III), and for rating the severity of psychosocial stressors (Axis IV) and highest level of adaptive functioning in the past year (Axis V).

Axis I (clinical syndromes) covers an extremely broad range of emotional and behavioral disorders, including Conduct Disorder, Attention Deficit Disorder, Anxiety Disorders, Eating Disorders, Stereotyped Movements Disorders (tics), Pervasive Developmental Disorders, Other Disorders (e.g., oppositional disorder, elective mutism) and Other Disorders with Physical Manifestations (e.g., stuttering, enuresis, encopresis). There is no age limit applied to the disorders listed in the child section of the DSM-III. Childhood diagnoses can be applied to adults, and adult diagnoses—such as Schizophrenia and Affective Disorders—can be applied to children. Personality Disorders, coded on Axis II, are usually not applied to children under the age of 18, whereas Specific Developmental Disorders (such as Developmental Reading Disorder, Developmental Language Disorder, etc.) are usually not applied to adults.

Each category of Axis I disorders includes separate disorders or subtypes. Attention Deficit Disorder (ADD), for example, encompasses three subtypes: ADD with Hyperactivity, ADD without Hyperactivity, and ADD Residual Type. Anxiety Disorders, as a further example, include Separation Anxiety, Avoidant Disorder, and Overanxious Disorder. Each disorder is briefly described in a narrative format and, to the extent to which they are known, the associated features, age at onset, course, impairments, complications, predisposing factors, prevalence, sex ratio, and familial pattern are outlined. Guidelines for differential diagnosis are also provided.

Diagnostic criteria for each disorder are listed in a group format. For ADD, for example, diagnostic criteria are grouped into three sections: Inattention, Impulsivity, and Hyperactivity (see Table 1). To be diagnosed as having ADD with Hyperactivity, a child must manifest three of five symptoms of inattention; three of six symptoms of impulsivity, and two of five symptoms of Hyperactivity. The child must also have an age at onset before seven and a duration of at least 6 months. Exclusion criteria are also listed. For instance, the diagnosis of ADD is not warranted if the symptoms are due to Schizophrenia, Affective Disorder, or Severe or Profound Mental Retardation.

Reactions to the DSM-III have been mixed. There is little doubt that it encompasses many improvements over the DSM-II. Among the advantages are the multiaxial diagnostic framework and the more explicit diagnostic

Table 1. Diagnostic Criteria for Attention Deficit Disorder with Hyperactivity

A. Inattention. At least three of the following:
  1. Often fails to finish things he/she starts
  2. Often doesn't seem to listen
  3. Easily distracted
  4. Has difficulty concentrating on schoolwork or other tasks requiring sustained attention
  5. Has difficulty sticking to a play activity

B. Impulsivity. At least three of the following:
  1. Often acts before thinking
  2. Shifts excessively from one activity to another
  3. Has difficulty organizing work
  4. Needs a lot of supervision
  5. Frequently calls out in class
  6. Has difficulty awaiting turn in games or group situations

C. Hyperactivity. At least two of the following:
  1. Runs about or climbs on things excessively
  2. Has difficulty sitting still or fidgets excessively
  3. Has difficulty staying seated
  4. Moves about excessively during sleep
  5. Is always "on the go" or acts as if "driven by a motor"

D. Onset before age of seven.

E. Duration of at least six months.

F. Not due to schizophrenia, affective disorder, or severe or profound mental retardation.

Note. Adapted from the DSM-III (American Psychiatric Association, 1980).

criteria. Despite these advantages, many aspects of the DSM-III have been questioned. The decision to code mental retardation in Axis I with clinical syndromes, for example, has been criticized. Rutter & Shaffer (1980) argued that the assessment and diagnosis of mental retardation is completely different from that of mental illness. They have argued quite persuasively that mental retardation should be coded on a separate axis, as in the World Health Organization's (WHO) taxonomy of childhood disorders (Rutter, Shaffer, & Shepherd, 1975) and the International Classification of Diseases (WHO, 1978). The inclusion of specific developmental disorders (which are coded on Axis II) in a psychiatric taxonomy is also controversial, because children with reading or language difficulties are not necessarily psychiatrically disturbed and treatment of such problems usually involves nonpsychiatric interventions, such as educational remediation, tutoring, and special class placements.

A broader criticism involves the validity of many of the diagnostic categories applied to children. As Spitzer and Cantwell (1980) stated, disorders were included in the DSM-III primarily on the basis of "face validity," which is "the result of clinicians agreeing on the identification of a particular syndrome or pattern of clinical features as a mental disorder." Diagnostic criteria for each disorder were generated initially by asking clinicians to describe the essential features of the disorder. The DSM-III thus reflects current clinical wisdom rather than being based on empirical facts.

The DSM-III, like its predecessors, was formulated through consensual committee work. It has been said that "If a camel is a horse designed by a committee, then the DSM-III is psychiatry's camel." It no doubt represents lengthy deliberations, complex negotiations, and numerous compromises between different individuals and factions. The contributions of many clinicians to the development and field testing of the DSM probably increased its clinical utility, but with no solid empirical foundation, it stands on the shifting sands of clinical judgment and committee vote.

The DSM-III also offers a much more differentiated taxonomy of childhood disorders than its predecessors and many diagnoses have no counterparts in earlier editions. In other words, there are many more child diagnoses than ever before, and many are brand new. The question is whether certain diagnoses represent naturally occurring syndromes or are artificial concoctions of the committee process. Many diagnoses, particularly those without historical precedent, lack adequate empirical support.

The lack of empirical underpinnings to the DSM-III can be illustrated by considering the diagnosis of ADD. The DSM-II category of Hyperkinetic Reaction (Hyperactivity) was reformulated in the DSM III, largely because of the belief that attention deficits were a more central and persistent feature of the disorder than excess motor activity. The term *Minimal Brain Dysfunction,* which had been applied to childhood hyperactivity, is no longer endorsed by most authorities because most hyperactive children do not have any detectable brain malfunction and most children with bona fide brain abnormalities are not hyperactive. In this case, therefore, the DSM-III does not represent incremental refinements over the DSM-II. Rather, the DSM-III shares little common ground, either in how disorders are defined or labelled, with its predecessor. Contrast this with the revisions in the adult area, where many disorders have historical roots extending back to Kraepelin's (1883) original taxonomy of adult psychiatric disorders. The diagnosis of adult disorders is founded on a larger cumulative body of knowledge based on decades of research and trial-and-error experimentation. Cumulative progress is more difficult to establish in the child area, because the diagnostic system has shifted so radically from one edition of the DSM to the next.

The DSM-III went even further in revamping the diagnosis of Hyperkinetic Reaction and distinguished between ADD with Hyperactivity and ADD without Hyperactivity. This suggests (a) that some children manifest attention deficits but not hyperactivity, and (b) that ADD with and without Hyperactivity are subtypes of the same disorder. Both points were controversial and neither was supported by empirical data. A considerable amount of recent research has addressed the validity of the diagnosis of ADD and has explored differences between ADD subtypes (e.g., Edelbrock, Costello, & Kessler, 1984; Lahey, Schaughency, Strauss, & Frame, 1984). The construction of the DSM-III is thus akin to building a house first, then trying to place a foundation beneath it. Rather than basing the diagnostic system on empirical research, empirical research has been necessary to provide post hoc validation of the diagnostic system.

Diagnostic criteria for ADD were generated from clinical material and organized into three symptom clusters (see Table 1). Diagnostic thresholds for each cluster were established, presumably by committee process. For example, to be considered inattentive, a child must manifest at least three of five symptoms of inattention. How were these diagnostic thresholds selected? Do they represent optimal cutoff points that best discriminate children with ADD from other groups? Were they selected on the basis of the distribution of such behaviors in the general population of children? Unfortunately not. Diagnostic thresholds were selected arbitrarily, based solely on clinical judgment and committee vote.

Analysis of the diagnostic criteria for ADD raises two other key considerations. First, although the diagnostic criteria are certainly more explicit than those employed in the DSM-II, they are far from being truly operational. There are no prescribed assessment procedures in the DSM-III. In other words, the DSM-III lists what to assess, but not how to assess it. There is wide variability among diagnosticians in how to assess child symptoms, and this undoubtedly contributes much to diagnostic unreliability. Second, the DSM-III generally lacks a normative developmental perspective on childhood disorders. Many diagnoses, including ADD, Separation Anxiety, and Oppositional Disorder, are defined by behaviors that are quite common in normal children. The behaviors themselves are not pathognomonic, particularly if they are infrequent, mild, or unassociated with other problems. Moreover, many clinically relevant behaviors vary by sex and age, and some behaviors (e.g., bed wetting, temper tantrums, short attention span) may be considered normal at one age, but not another. The lack of attention to normal and developmental variations in children's behavior is a major shortcoming of the DSM.

Reliability

A key question concerning DSM-III has been its reliability. Diagnoses cannot represent valid distinctions among disorders unless they are reliable. Higher reliability was expected for the DSM-III than its predecessors, because (a) the multiaxial approach provides a framework for sorting out numerous aspects of a patient's functioning that would have otherwise been muddled together and (b) the diagnostic criteria for each disorder are more explicit. Several studies have tested the reliability of DSM-III diagnoses. In the field trials of the DSM-III (APA, 1980: Appendix F), interjudge reliability was tested first with the initial draft of the diagnostic criteria and then following revisions of the criteria. The statistic kappa, which corrects for chance level of agreement was used to quantify agreement between different clinicians who diagnosed the same cases. A kappa of zero corresponds to chance level of agreement, whereas a kappa of 1.00 indicates perfect agreement. Kappas less than .60 indicate less than acceptable reliability. In the first phase of field testing the overall interjudge reliability for Axis I was kappa = .68. Surprisingly, in the second phase of field testing (following the revisions of the diagnostic criteria), interjudge reliability declined (overall kappa = .51). Many of the most common disorders (e.g., ADD, Conduct Disorder, Anxiety Disorders, Affective Disorders) had unacceptably low reliabilities (less than .60). Moreover, reliabilities were reported only for major categories of disorders, not for subtypes. It seems likely that interjudge reliabilities were even lower for specific diagnoses than for general categories.

More recent studies have evaluated the reliability of diagnostic judgments based on case histories. Higher reliability would be expected because variability in the primary data on which the diagnoses were based is eliminated. Using case histories, Mezzich, Mezzich, and Coffman (1985) found that DSM-III diagnoses were somewhat more reliable than DSM-II diagnoses. Among the DSM-III Axis I disorders, only mental retardation was reliably diagnosed (kappa = .96). The reliabilities of the other Axis I disorders were low (average = .48, range .05 to .62). Interjudge reliabilities have been higher in studies of inpatient samples and have ranged from .71 (Werry, Methven, Fitzpatrick, & Dixon, 1983) to .74 (Strober, Green, & Carlson, 1981). However, reliabilities were again reported for broad categories rather than specific diagnoses.

Test–retest reliability, which involves the degree of agreement between diagnoses made on two occasions, has been determined in two recent studies. Both studies employed structured interviewing procedures that standardize the collection of diagnostic data (see Edelbrock & Costello, 1984, for a review of structured interviewing procedures). In one study, diagnoses were derived from a structured diagnostic interview (the K-SADS) with parent and child (Chambers et al., 1985). Short-term (2–3 day) test–retest reliabilities as measured by the intraclass correlation, averaged .55 for individual items and .68 for summary scales. Reliabilities of Axis I diagnoses ranged from kappa = .24 to .70. In the other study (Costello, Edelbrock, Dulcan, Kalas, & Klaric, 1984), diagnoses were derived from separate interviews with the parent and child using the Diagnostic Interview Schedule for Children. One-week test–retest reliabilities for symptom scores were much higher for the parent interview (average intraclass correlation = .76) than for the child interview (average intraclass correlation = .62). Reliabilities of Axis I diagnoses were also higher for the parent interview (average kappa = .55) than the child interview (average kappa = .37). Additionally, the reliability of the child interview was strongly related to age (Edelbrock, Costello, Dulcan, Kalas, & Conover, 1985). Children aged 6 to 9 were generally unreliable in reporting their own symptoms, whereas adolescents aged 14 to 18 were as highly reliable as their parents.

Overall, the reliability of the DSM-III is mediocre. The reliability of many diagnoses is low, although some diagnoses have achieved acceptable reliability. The standardization of diagnostic data in reliability studies, either through the use of case histories or structured interviewing procedures, has resulted in reliabilities that are generally higher than those obtaining in the initial DSM field trials. Reliabilities have been higher for broad groupings of diagnoses than for specific diagnoses. Furthermore, several studies indicate higher reliabilities for behavior and conduct disorders (e.g., ADD, Conduct Disorder, Oppositional Disorder) that involve overt, readily observable symptoms, than for affective and neurotic disorders (e.g., Anxiety Disorders, Affective Disorders), which involve more covert symptoms.

Validity

As discussed previously, the DSM-III embodies diagnoses that have been judged to have face validity and clinical utility. Given the fact that many DSM-III child diagnoses are new or have been totally reworked from the DSM-II, their predictive and discriminative validity is largely unknown. Considerable research is needed to determine whether the child diagnoses embodied in the DSM-III represent valid distinctions among disorders. Rutter (1977, 1978) has outlined the criteria for establishing the validity of diagnostic categories. An essential prerequisite is that the signs and symptoms that comprise the disorder must co-occur and form a distinct syndrome. The disorder must also constitute a handicapping condition and be reliably diagnosed. Lastly, and perhaps most importantly, the disorder must be related to a particular etiology, course, prognosis, treatment response, or outcome. For most DSM-III diagnoses applied to children, empirical research is needed in virtually every area of validation.

On balance, the DSM-III represents several important advances in child psychiatric diagnosis, despite many remaining limitations and flaws. Among the foremost advantages are the multiaxial framework, the use of more explicit diagnostic criteria, and the greater differentiation of disorders of childhood (even though adding more disorders of questionable validity is not helpful). Among the most pressing limitations are the lack of adequate empirical support for many diagnoses, the lack of truly operational procedures for the assessment of child characteristics, the inadequate consideration of normative and developmental issues in child psychopathology, and mediocre reliability.

The DSM-III was not offered as a final and definitive taxonomy of child psychiatric disorders, but is a provisional system: a temporary organizing framework for research, services, and training. In fact, the recent revision (DSM-III-R) was designed to correct major problems with certain child diagnoses. One flaw that was recognized early, for example was that the diagnostic criteria for Oppositional Disorder were far too lenient. Almost all children manifest some oppositional behaviors (e.g., stubbornness, arguing, temper tantrums, disobedience), at least sometimes or to some degree. The diagnostic threshold for Oppositional Disorder in the DSM-III was set too low: only two of five symptoms were required for the diagnosis and there are no guidelines for assessing the severity of each criterion. If applied literally, most children would warrant the diagnosis of Oppositional Disorder. In a recent study employing a highly structured diagnostic interview, for example, 79% of the children referred to a mental health facility met criteria for Oppositional Disorder (Costello *et al.*, 1984). The solution, which is still being worked out, will probably involve increasing the number of diagnostic criteria, raising the diagnostic threshold, and perhaps adding some severity index to each criterion. Other diagnoses currently being considered for revision include ADD (where the distinction between ADD with and without Hyperactivity is being questioned), and Conduct Disorder (where the distinctions between Aggressive/Non-Aggressive and Socialized/Undersocialized subtypes are being reconsidered).

The Psychometric Approach

The psychometric approach to the classification of childhood psychopathology has attempted to construct more reliable and valid taxonomies of childhood disorders than those offered by the DSM and other clinically derived diagnostic systems. In contrast to the clinical approach underlying the DSM, the psychometric approach has involved the quantitative analysis of empirical data. Psychometric research has involved multivariate statistical analysis of data obtained from behavioral checklists and rating scales and the quantitative scaling and standardization of such data. Major themes in psychometric research have been (a) identifying behavioral syndromes, (b) constructing empirically based typologies of childhood disorders, and (c) determining the reliability and validity of psychometrically based assessment and classification procedures.

Syndrome Identification

Numerous psychometric studies of child psychopathology have been aimed at identifying behavioral syndromes. Reports and ratings of children's emotional and behavioral problems are first obtained, usually from adults such as parents and teachers. Multivariate statistical procedures, such as factor analysis or cluster analysis, are then used to identify subgroups of behaviors that co-occur and form distinct syndromes. There are major methodological differences between studies, including differences in the instruments used, the informants who provide the ratings, the characteristics of the subject samples, and the type of statistical analysis employed. Not surprisingly, such efforts have produced very heterogenous results. Two crucial questions are (a) Is there convergence in findings across studies? and (b) Are disagreements in findings across studies due to methodological differences?

Number of Syndromes

One outstanding difference between studies is whether they have yielded a few global broad-band syndromes or numerous circumscribed narrow-band syndromes. The finding of a few broad-band syndromes, however, does not necessarily contradict the finding of numerous narrow-band syndromes. Second-order factor analysis, which involves analyzing correlations between narrow-band syndromes, has revealed higher-order groupings among narrow-band syndromes. In other words, narrow-band syndromes may be hierarchically related to broader and more inclusive syndromic patterns. Studies differ in their ability to resolve patterns of relations among behaviors into global versus circumscribed patterns of covariation.

A pertinent example is the factor analysis of parent ratings obtained with the Child Behavior Checklist (Achenbach & Edelbrock, 1983). Factor analysis of parent ratings of clinically referred boys aged 6 to 11 revealed nine narrow-band syndromes, which were labeled Schizoid or Anxious, Depressed, Uncommunicative, Obsessive Compulsive, Somatic Complaints, Social Withdrawal, Hyperactive, Aggressive, and Delinquent. Second-order factor analysis revealed that the first five syndromes were positively correlated with one another and formed a broad-band grouping (labeled Internalizing), whereas the last three syndromes were positively correlated with one another and formed a broad-band grouping (labeled Externalizing). The essential point is that no one level of syndrome differentiation is intrinsically correct, and it is probably an advantage to be able to score both narrow-band and broad-band syndromes from the same measure.

Convergence among Studies

Despite technical and methodological differences, there appears to be considerable convergence in findings across studies. Among studies that have yielded two or three broad-band syndromes there is good agreement regarding a dichotomy between affective and neurotic problems on one hand, and behavior and conduct problems on the other. The affective/neurotic syndrome, comprising primarily fear, anxiety, depression, obsessions/compulsions, withdrawal, and somatic complaints, has been variously labeled Internalizing, Personality Problem, Inhibition, Shy-Anxious, Apathy-Withdrawal, and Anxious-Fearful. The broad-band behavior/conduct syndrome, comprising primarily hyperactivity, oppositionalism, aggression, delinquency, and cruelty, has been labeled Externalizing, Conduct Problems, Aggression, Anger-Defiance, Acting Out, and Hostile-Aggressive (Achenbach, 1966, 1978; Achenbach & Edelbrock, 1979, 1983; Behar & Stringfield, 1974; Clarfield, 1974; Cowen *et al.*, 1973; Edelbrock & Achenbach, 1984, 1985; Kohn & Rosman, 1972; Miller, 1967; Peterson, 1961; Quay, 1966; Quay & Quay, 1965; Venables *et al.*, 1983). These findings also illustrate how syndromes comprising similar behaviors can be given different summary labels, which can obscure the similarities in findings across studies.

Among studies that have identified four or more syndromes, there appears to be good agreement regarding the existence of narrow-band aggressive, delinquent, hyperactive, schizoid, anxious, depressed, withdrawn, and psychosomatic syndromes. Syndromes comprising immaturity, obsessions-compulsions, sex problems, sleep problems, academic difficulties, and uncommunicativeness have also been identified in two or more studies (see Achenbach & Edelbrock, 1978, 1984, for detailed reviews).

Methodological Differences

It would be misleading to concentrate on agreements among studies and ignore the numerous disagreements. After all, no one study has identified all of the replicated syndromes, and no one syndrome has been precisely replicated in different studies. Why don't different studies yield the same behavioral syndromes? Variables that influence the results of factor analytic investigations of child psychopathology have been discussed in detail elsewhere (Achenbach & Edelbrock, 1978; Edelbrock, 1983, 1986). The most salient methodological differences include (a) the assessment instruments, (b) the informants who provide the reports and ratings, (c) the subject samples, and (d) the factoring technique.

Instrument differences alone account for much of variability among studies. Meta-analyses of factor analyses have shown that the number of syndromes identified is largely a function of the number of behaviors assessed (see Achenbach & Edelbrock, 1978). Measures comprising relatively few items have generally yielded only two or three syndromes, whereas measures comprising numerous items have tended to yield eight or more syndromes. Measures also differ in terms of degree of behavioral coverage. Some, such as Conners' Revised Teacher Rating Scale (Goyette, Conners, & Ulrich, 1978) are focused primarily on hyperactivity and conduct problems and therefore do not yield a broad range of syndromes. Others, such as the Child Behavior Checklist (Achenbach & Edelbrock, 1983) have broad behavioral coverage and yield many more narrow-band syndromes. A number of other instrument differences, including response scaling, time frame, and level of analysis (i.e., molar or molecular units of behavior) are also likely to influence multivariate results (see Edelbrock, 1983, 1986).

Differences between informants also account for discrepancies between studies. We would not necessarily expect parents, teachers, trained observers, and clinicians to report similar prevalence and patterning of child behaviors, because they observe and interact with children in different settings and situations. Each informant also embodies different perspectives and biases regarding child functioning and different adults no doubt influence children's behavior in different ways. In their review of empirical studies, Achenbach and Edelbrock (1978) concluded that separate analysis of ratings provided by parents, teachers, and mental health workers yielded broad-band syndromes corresponding to the affective/neurotic versus behavior/conduct dichotomy. However, some informant differences in narrow-band syndromes have emerged. In developing parallel parent and teacher versions of the Child Behavior Profile, for example, separate analysis of parent and teacher ratings of disturbed children revealed several syndromes similar enough to warrant the same summary labels: Aggressive, Depressed, Immature, Obsessive-Compulsive, and Social Withdrawal (see Achenbach & Edelbrock, 1983; Edelbrock & Achenbach, 1984, 1985). However, some syndromes derived from teacher ratings (e.g., Unpopular, Inattentive, Nervous-Overactive) had no counterparts in analyses of parents ratings. Conversely, some syndromes derived from parent ratings (e.g., Delinquent, Somatic Complaints) did not emerge consistently in analyses of teacher ratings. This suggests that parents and teachers differ in their opportunity to observe certain child behaviors, or perhaps differ in their sensitivity to, awareness of, or tolerance for different behaviors.

The findings of factor-analysis investigations are also likely to be influenced by the nature of the subject samples and the technique of factor analysis. Factor analyses of child behavior problems have generally been performed on haphazard and heterogenous samples of subjects. Clearly, analyses based on normative or mildly disturbed samples are limited in their ability to detect syndromes of extremely deviant behavior. Conversely, analyses based on samples of extremely disturbed children (e.g., inpatient samples) are unlikely to detect syndromes characterizing less severe psychopathology.

Factor analysis also entails numerous methodological alternatives. Although almost all published studies have employed principal components or principal factor analysis with varimax rotation, there are some important technical differences between studies. As one would expect, studies employing more stringent criteria for determining number of factors have tended to identify fewer syndromes than studies employing lenient criteria. The minimum cutoff point used to determine salient items on each factor have also varied widely (e.g., .20 to .50), as has the minimum number of salient items required to constitute a factor. These differences obviously influence the number and composition of the resulting syndromes.

In sum, empirical efforts to identify syndromes of child psychopathology have produced heterogeneous results. Despite numerous methodological differences between studies, there appears to be some consensus regarding the existence of two global broad-band syndromes and numerous narrow-band syndromes. Moreover, discrepancies between studies can largely be attributed to differences among the assessment instruments used, the informants, the subject samples, and the factoring technique. The consensus among studies, however, does not translate into one taxonomy of child disorders. Rather, the taxonomic implications of multivariate findings are instrument specific. Each instrument provides unique operational procedures for assessing a particular set of behaviors and syndromes. Such measures yield quantitative scores on two or more behavioral syndromes, rather than indicating whether a child has a given disorder or not. How are the results of such quantitative assessments translated into categorical distinctions?

From Syndromes to Categories

There are several approaches to translating quantitative assessments of child functioning into categorical distinctions. One of the simplest approaches is to employ a cutoff point, usually based on the distribution of scores obtained in a normative sample. The cutoff point may correspond, for example, to a particular percentile rank obtained in a normative sample or to a degree of deviation from the normative mean, as measured in standard deviations. Either way, the taxonomic procedure is similar. Scores at or below the normative cutoff point can be taken to represent the normal range of behavioral variations, whereas scores above the cutoff point can be interpreted as behavioral deviations. For instance,total behavior problem score computed from the

Child Behavior Checklist is a global index of maladjustment. The upper limit of the normal range of scores corresponds to the 90th percentile in a randomly selected normative standardization sample (see Achenbach & Edelbrock, 1981). To account for sex and age differences, separate cutoff points have been determined for boys and girls aged 4 to 5, 6 to 11 and 12 to 16. Scores above these cutoff points represent behavioral deviations relative to normal agemates. The validity of this procedure is supported by the finding that (by definition) only 10% of nonreferred children score above the cutoff point, compared to approximately 75% of clinically referred children.

Cutoff points can also be applied to more circumscribed behavioral syndromes to identify children with particular types of problems. Conners' Abbreviated Questionnaire, a 10-item rating scale covering hyperactivity, inattention, impulsivity, and aggression, has been widely used to identify hyperactive children (see Barkley, 1981). Children scoring at or above 1.5 standard deviations above the normative mean have been considered hyperactive, whereas those scoring below that cutoff point have been considered nonhyperactive. Alternatively, a score corresponding to 2.0 standard deviations above the mean for the child's sex and age group has been recommended as a cutoff point (Barkley, 1981).

In their simplest application, cutoff points are applied to only one scale at a time. This obviously works well when distinguishing between only two groups (e.g., normal versus disturbed or hyperactive versus nonhyperactive). But how can scores on several scales be translated into categorical decisions? One solution is to specify inclusion and exclusion criteria, which take two common forms. First, the difference between scores on two scales can be used to select children having particular patterns or scores. The Child Behavior Checklist, for example, yields scores on two broad-band syndromes labeled Internalizing and Externalizing. Although these two broad-band syndromes represent different types of behavioral problems, they are positively associated with one another. This situation is analogous to the distinction between Verbal IQ and Performance IQ. Across groups of subjects, Verbal IQ and Performance IQ are positively correlated with one another. Nevertheless, it is possible to identify individuals who have a sufficiently large Verbal /Performance discrepancy to suggest a distinct pattern of cognitive abilities. In a similar manner, the difference between Internalizing and Externalizing scores can be used to identify individual children who are primarily internalizers or primarily externalizers. A difference of 10 T-score points between Internalizing and Externalizing scores has been recommended as a minimum criterion, providing that the child's total behavior problem scores exceeds the 90th percentile for his or her sex and age group (Achenbach & Edelbrock, 1983, pp. 33–34).

The second type of inclusion/exclusion criteria involves the use of separate cutoff points on multiple scales. To obtain a relatively pure group of hyperactive children, for example, a researcher might specify that each child score above the normative cutoff point on a hyperactive scale and below the normative cutoff points on all other scales (e.g., anxiety, depression, aggression, etc.). Of course, one must specify combinations of inclusion and exclusion criteria carefully, or no individuals will fit the dictated pattern of scores.

A good example of the intelligent use of multiple cutoff points is the development of the Iowa version of Conners' (1969) Teacher Rating Scale. Items for a 10-item rating scale were selected that correlated with external criteria for either hyperactivity or aggression, but not both. Using a combination of cutoff points for the hyperactive and aggressive scales, three behavioral subtypes can be identified: pure hyperactive, pure aggressive, and mixed hyperactive and aggressive. This tripartite distinction has proven to be valuable in differentiating among clinically referred children (see Langhorne & Loney, 1979; Loney, Langhorne, & Paternite, 1978).

Many commonly used measures of child psychopathology, including the parent and teacher versions of the Child Behavior Checklist and Profile (Achenbach & Edelbrock, 1983; Edelbrock & Achenbach, 1984, 1985), the Revised Behavior Problem Checklist (Quay & Peterson, 1983) and Miller's (1967) School Behavior Checklist, yield scores on several narrow-band behavior problem syndromes. Scores can be portrayed on standardized profiles showing the child's standing on several behavioral dimensions at once. Simple cutoff points and inclusion/exclusion criteria do not easily capture all of the information contained in multidimensional profiles. More complex multivariate statistical procedures are required to identify subgroups of children manifesting similar profile patterns.

Cluster analysis is one multivariate statistical procedure that is well attuned to constructing empirically derived typologies from profile data (see Anderberg, 1973; Everitt, 1980; Lorr, 1983, for reviews of clustering methods). Cluster analysis is a relatively new statistical procedure in the behavioral sciences and only a few studies have used it to construct empirically based typologies of child psychopathology (Edelbrock & Achenbach, 1980; Eisenberg, Gersten, Langner, McCarthy, & Simcha-Fagan, 1976; Spivack, Swift, & Prewitt, 1971). These studies illustrate the promise and potential of taxonometric methods such as cluster analysis. Cluster-based typologies of childhood psychopathology are more properly viewed as experimental efforts and as heuristic devices for stimulating future research, than as definitive achievements.

A recently constructed typology of Child Behavior Profile patterns illustrates the cluster analytic approach (see Achenbach & Edelbrock, 1983; Edelbrock & Achenbach, 1980, for methodological details). The goal was to identify subgroups of disturbed children having similar patterns of scores on the narrow-band behavior problem scales of the Child Behavior Profile (which is scored from the Child Behavior Checklist completed by parents). To account for sex and age differences in the patterning of behaviors, the cluster analyses of Profile scores were conducted separately for boys and girls aged 4 to 5, 6 to 11, and 12 to 16. A hierarchical clustering algorithm, called centroid analysis, was used (a) to group together subjects having similar patterns of scores and (b) to arrange such groups in a hierarchial taxonomy. At low levels in the taxonomy, clusters of subjects had very specific profile patterns, whereas at higher levels clusters were combined into larger groups representing more global distinctions. Subjects having extremely low (25 or less) or high (100 or more) total behavior problem scores were not clustered, because their scores tend to be uniformly low or high across all scales. In other words, they tend to share similarity in profile elevation, rather than pattern.

Six profile types were identified for boys aged 6 to 11 and boys aged 12 to 16, whereas seven types were identified for boys aged 4 to 5 and girls aged 4 to 5, 6 to 11 and 12 to 16. For example, the profile types identified for girls aged 6 to 11 are shown in Figure 1, which depicts the mean profiles for each type that was reliably identified in the cluster analyses. (Each profile type in Figure 1 is portrayed in terms of standard scores based on clinically referred samples. A z-score of 0 thus corresponds to the mean score obtained by referred children, whereas a z-score of +1.0 corresponds to one standard deviation above the clinical mean, etc.). Each profile type was given a summary label based on its high points. Type A, for instance, had high points on the Depressed and Social Withdrawal scales, whereas type B had a single high point on the Somatic Complaints Scale, and so on.

The profile types portrayed in Figure 1 summarize the profile features shared by homogeneous subgroups of clinically referred girls aged 6 to 11. Figure 2 illustrates the percentage of girls classified according to each profile type. For example, 12.9% of the clinically referred girls in the sample had profiles resembling the Depressed-Social Withdrawal type, compared to 14% who resembled the Somatic

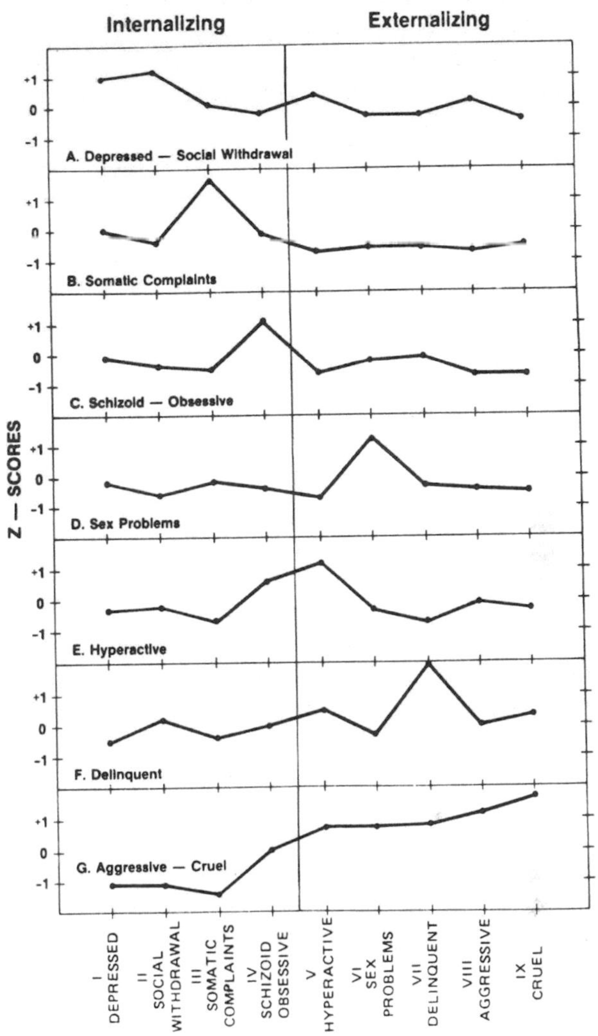

Figure 1. Child Behavior Profile types identified for girls aged 6–11 (adapted from Edelbrock & Achenbach, 1980).

Complaints profile types, and so on. Figure 2 also indicates the hierarchical relations among profile types. In the hierarchical cluster analysis, clusters representing types A, B, and C were combined into a higher-order grouping reflecting primarily Internalizing problems. Conversely, clusters representing types E, F, and G were combined into a higher-order grouping reflecting primarily Externalizing problems. The cluster representing type D (Sex Problems) did not reliably combine with either the higher-order Internalizing or Externalizing grouping, and is labeled as Mixed in Figure 2. Also shown in Figure 2 are the percentage of girls who were unclassified because they did not resemble any profile types (2.7%), and the percentages who had total behavior problem scores too low (10.6%) or too high (5.7%) to permit classification by profile pattern.

This typology of Child Behavior Profile patterns provides operational procedures for (a) classifying individual cases according to pattern and severity of parent-reported behaviors, (b) identifying homogeneous subgroups of children having similar profile features,

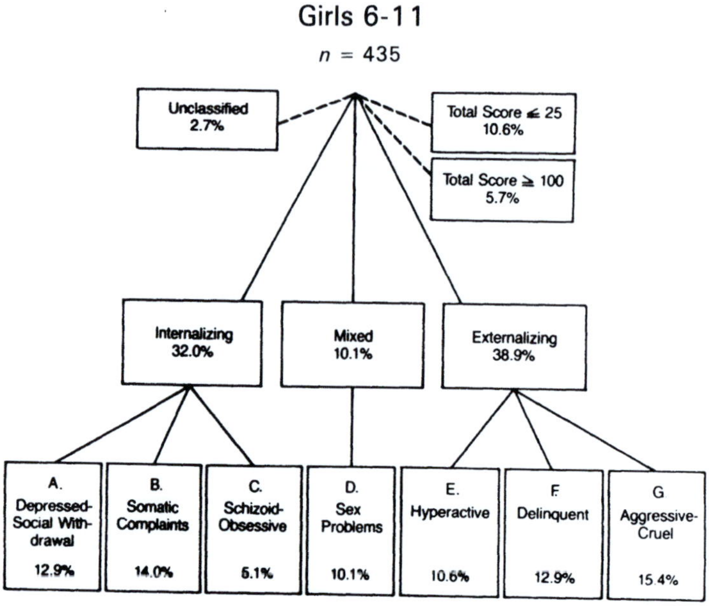

Figure 2. Hierarchical relations among Child Behavior Profile types identified for girls aged 6–11 (adapted from Edelbrock & Achenbach, 1980).

and (c) concisely summarizing the distribution of behavior problems among subject samples. The hierarchical nature of the typology provides the additional advantage of being able to group children according to either global or specific profile features. Further research is needed to determine how such categorizations relate to external criteria, such as etiologic factors, development course, treatment response, and outcome.

Reliability and Validity

Much psychometric research has been stimulated by the inadequate reliability and validity of clinically based taxonomies such as the DSM. To what extent has psychometric research improved the reliability and validity of child assessment and classification? Over short testing intervals (i.e., one week to one month), most child behavior rating scales completed by parents or teachers have yielded high test–retest reliabilities (r = .80 to .90). Reliabilities tend to be higher for overt, easily observable behaviors (e.g., aggression, hyperactivity), than for more covert phenomena (e.g., anxiety, depression). In a recent study employing the teacher version of the Child Behavior Checklist, for example, Edelbrock, Greenbaum, and Conover (1985) found that one-week test–retest reliabilities were higher for child aggression, inattention, and overactivity (average r = .91), than child anxiety and withdrawal (average r = .80). Several studies have also documented that over a short testing interval, ratings of the frequency and/or severity of child behavior problems tend to decline slightly from the first assessment to the second (Achenbach, 1978; Achenbach & Edelbrock, 1979; Evans, 1975; Miller, Hampe, Barrett, & Noble, 1972). This phenomenon has been attributed to practice effects (Werry & Sprague, 1974) and statistical regression to the mean (Milich, Roberts, Loney, & Caputo, 1980). This effect is rather small, however, and is probably not clinically meaningful. Over longer retesting intervals (i.e., one to six months), test–retest correlations tend to drop to about r = .50 to .70), but this may reflect true change in child behaviors over time rather than measurement error.

Children's ratings of their own emotional and behavioral problems tend to be less reliable than ratings by adults (r = .60 to .70). The reliability of children's self-reports vary according to the type of behavior and the age of the child. In general, reliabilities have been higher for behavior and conduct problems than for affective and neurotic symptoms. Not surprisingly, test–retest reliabilities have been much lower for younger children than for older children and adolescents (see Edelbrock, Costello *et al.*, 1985).

Interrater reliability, which reflects the degree of similarity between ratings provided by different informants, depends to a large extent on the raters having similar exposure to the child's behavior. Mother–father agreement tends to be moderately high (r = .60 to .80). Parent–teacher agreement tends to be low (r = .30 to .40), but this may reflect true differences in children's behavior at home and at school. Children's self-ratings do not correlate highly with ratings provided by adults. Parent–child agreement, for example, is usually low (r = .20 to .40). However, some studies have shown a clear pattern of discrepancies between parents and their children (Edelbrock *et al.*, 1986; Herjanic & Reich, 1982). In general, parents report more child behavior and conduct problems than their children, whereas children report more affective and neurotic symptoms than their parents.

The reliability of categorizations based on psychometric assessments of child psychopathology has received little research attention to date. It is tempting to assume that such reliabilities would be high, given the high reliabilities of quantitative assessments. However, the product-moment correlation reflects only similarity in the rank-ordering of pairs of scores. It is not sensitive to differences in the absolute magnitude of pairs of scores. A high degree of similarity in rank ordering of scores would not necessarily translate into high reliability of categorizations. For example, ratings of childhood hyperactivity obtained separately from mothers and fathers may correlate highly with one another, despite a large mean difference in magnitude. Such data would not yield highly reliable classifications if a cutoff point were used to classify children as hyperactive versus nonhyperactive. Considerable research is needed to evaluate the reliability of psychometrically based classifications of disturbed children. Preliminary studies indicate moderately high reliability of classifications derived from informants having a similar information base (see Edelbrock & Achenbach, 1980).

The validity of psychometric assessments of child psychopathology has been supported by several lines of evidence. For one, significant relations between scores derived from different instruments supports the concurrent validity of both measures (see Achenbach & Edelbrock, 1978, 1983). Many measures have also been shown to discriminate well between groups of children judged to be normal versus disturbed according to independent criteria (e.g., Achenbach & Edelbrock, 1981, 1983; Edelbrock & Achenbach, 1984; Goyette, Conners, & Ulrich, 1978; Miller, 1977; Werry & Quay, 1969). Additionally, some measures have been shown to discriminate significantly among diagnostic subgroups of disturbed children, including depressed, delinquent, hyperactive, and aggressive (see Achenbach & Edelbrock, 1984; Ross & Pelham, 1981). Broad-band and narrow-band syndromes have also manifested differential correlates. Children manifesting the broad-band behavior/conduct syndrome, for example, tend to have more disorganized families and have worse prognoses than children manifesting the broad-band affective/neurotic syndrome (see Achenbach & Edelbrock, 1978). Children manifesting various narrow-band syndromes have also been shown to differ in terms of numerous psychological, perceptual, familial, and interpersonal measures (see Achenbach & Edelbrock, 1978; Quay, 1979). Empirically based typologies of child psychopathology have also been shown to differentiate among children in terms of social competencies and demographic characteristics (see Edelbrock & Achenbach, 1980; Eisenberg *et al.*, 1976).

Relations between Medical and Psychometric Approaches

The medical and psychometric approaches to classifying child psychopathology embody quite different assumptions and methods. Nevertheless, some syndromes identified in multivariate studies have counterparts in the DSM-III (see Achenbach, 1980; Edelbrock, 1986). Multivariate syndromes resembling ADD with Hyperactivity have been identified in several studies (Achenbach, 1978; Achenbach & Edelbrock, 1979; Arnold & Smeltzer, 1974; Behar & Stringfield, 1974; Conners, 1973; Miller, 1967). ADD without Hyperactivity, which reflects inattention and impulsivity but not overactivity, also corresponds to multivariate syndromes identified in some studies (Conners, 1969; Edelbrock & Achenbach, 1984, 1985; Edelbrock, Costello, & Kessler, 1984; Quay & Quay, 1965; Walker, 1976). The distinction in the DSM-III between Aggressive and Non-Aggressive Conduct Disorder corresponds to the findings of separate syndromes reflecting overt aggression on one hand and more covert delinquency on the other (Achenbach, 1978; Achenbach & Edelbrock, 1979, 1983; Arnold & Smeltzer, 1974; Conners, 1973; Edelbrock & Achenbach, 1985; Jenkins, 1966; Miller, 1967). Several affective/neurotic disorders, including Overanxious Disorder, Dysthymia, Major Depression, Social Phobia, and Obsessive-Compulsive Disorder, parallel syndromes identified in multivariate studies (see Edelbrock, 1986).

Conversely, some multivariate syndromes do not have clear counterparts in the DSM-III. Syndromes reflecting cruelty, unpopularity, and social withdrawal, for example, have been identified in two or more empirical studies, but do not overlap with any one DSM-III diagnosis. Furthermore, many DSM-III diagnoses do not correspond to multivariate syndromes, but represent specific symptoms. Axis I diagnoses of pica, elective mutism, enuresis, encopresis, simple phobia, stuttering, sleepwalking, and minor motor tics, for instance, correspond to items on many behavioral checklists and rating scales.

Neither the medical or psychometric approach has offered definitive achievements and both have fallen short of producing a perfectly comprehensive, reliable, and valid taxonomy of childhood disorders. Both approaches have acknowledged strengths and weaknesses. The strength of the medical approach lies in its high degree of clinical relevance and widespread clinical use. The use of the DSM-III is mandated by insurance companies and other third-party payers of medical benefits. This dictates to a large extent that the DSM-III will shape clinical services for children and the training of child mental health professionals. Whether they like it or not, all child mental health professionals must be conversant with the DSM-III. The DSM-III also serves as the organizing framework for research in child psychiatry.

The major weaknesses of the DSM-III stem from its clinical, rather than empirical, foundations. Empirical support for many DSM-III diagnoses is lacking and validation efforts are the focus of many current research endeavors. The reliability of many DSM-III diagnoses is also mediocre, which imposes an inherent limitation on validity. The medical approach seems more useful and appropriate when dealing with rare and severe disorders (such as autism, Tourette's Disorder, gender identity disorder, dissociative disorders, etc.), which are qualitatively distinct from normal variations.

The major strength of the psychometric approach is its empirical foundation and methodologic rigor. This has perhaps limited its clinical utility to some degree, because some psychometric measures are difficult and cumbersome to administer, score, and interpret, and some empirically derived syndromes do not resemble familiar clinical constructs. Unlike the DSM, the psychometric approach has not yet yielded a consensual taxonomy of childhood disorders. Rather, each separate assessment instrument taps a unique set of behaviors and syndromes that are operationalized in different ways. Behavioral checklists and rating scales are widely used in child research, but they do not easily contribute to a cumulative body of knowledge because of the intrinsic differences between measures.

The validity of psychometric assessment of

child psychopathology have been subjected to more empirical tests than the DSM and, by and large, reliability is moderately high for most measures. The psychometric approach seems to be well attuned to assessment and classification of childhood disorders that represent quantitative deviations from the norm. Common behavioral deviations, such as hyperactivity, aggression, and anxiety, for example, seem more amenable to psychometric study than rare and extreme psychopathologies. Psychometric research has also addressed normative and developmental aspects of children's emotional and behavioral functioning in many ways (see Edelbrock, 1984). Behavioral measures, for example, are often standardized on normative samples comprising children of different ages. Additionally, some measures have been developed and standardized separately for different age groups.

Future Prospects

Several emerging trends are likely to characterize future research on the classification of childhood disorders. Within the medical paradigm, we can expect vigorous research aimed at boosting the reliability and validity of child psychiatric diagnoses. The recent revision of the DSM-III (DSM-III-R) addresses several major shortcomings in the child area and to a greater extent than ever before, revisions are being based on empirical data. These revisions will not solve all of the intrinsic limitations of the medical approach, but they will provide a somewhat firmer empirical foundation. Another trend will be towards systematizing and standardizing the collection of diagnostic data through the use of structured diagnostic interviews (see Edelbrock & Costello, 1984, for a review). Reducing the information variance inherent in the diagnostic process is likely to boost substantially diagnostic reliability. Research on the correlates and predictive value of DSM-III diagnosis will no doubt continue also.

The development of ways of translating quantitative assessments into categorical groupings will probably rank high among the priorities for psychometric research. Preliminary efforts suggest that cluster analysis is a promising taxonomic tool, but the reliability and validity of cluster-based taxonomies have not been thoroughly explored. The proliferation of new checklists and rating scales is also likely to wane, as researchers concentrate on using one or more of the handful of highly developed measures (see Barkley, in press). Lastly, we may expect more synergistic research combining the medical and psychometric approaches. Many research studies seek to capitalize on the strengths of both approaches and some new measures yield DSM-III diagnoses and quantitative indexes of child psychopathology (e.g., Costello *et al.*, 1984; Hodges, Kline, Cytryn, & McKnew, 1982).

References

Achenbach, T. M. (1966). The classification of children's psychiatric symptoms: A factor-analytic study. *Psychological Monographs, 80*, (7, Whole No. 615).

Achenbach, T. M. (1978). The Child Behavior Profile: I. Boys aged 6–11. *Journal of Consulting and Clinical Psychology, 46*, 478–488.

Achenbach, T. M. (1980). DSM-III in light of empirical research on the classification of child psychopathology. *Journal of the American Academy of Child Psychiatry, 19*, 395–412.

Achenbach, T. M., & Edelbrock, C. S. (1978). The classification of child psychopathology: A review and analysis of empirical efforts. *Psychological Bulletin, 85*, 1275–1301.

Achenbach, T. M., & Edelbrock, C. S. (1979). The Child Behavior Profile: II. Boys aged 12–16 and girls aged 6–11 and 12–16. *Journal of Consulting and Clinical Psychology, 47*, 223–233.

Achenbach, T. M., & Edelbrock, C. S. (1981). Behavior problems and competencies reported by parents of normal and disturbed children aged 4 through 16. *Monographs of the Society for Research in Child Development, 46* (1, Serial No. 188).

Achenbach, T. M., & Edelbrock, C. S. (1983). *Manual for the Child Behavior Checklist and Revised Child Behavior Profile.* Burlington, VT: Author.

Achenbach, T. M., & Edelbrock, C. S. (1984). Psychopathology of childhood. *Annual Review of Psychology, 35*, 227–256.

American Psychiatric Association. (1952). *Diagnostic and*

statistical manual of mental disorders. Washington, DC: Author.

American Psychiatric Association. (1968). *Diagnostic and statistical manual of mental disorders* (2nd ed.). Washington, DC: Author.

American Psychiatric Association. (1980). *Diagnostic and statistical manual of mental disorders* (3rd ed.). Washington, DC: Author.

American Psychiatric Association. (1987). *Diagnostic and statistical manual* (3rd ed., revised). Washington, DC: Author.

Anderberg, M. R. (1973). *Cluster analysis for applications.* New York: Academic Press.

Arnold, L. E., & Smeltzer, D. J. (1974). Behavior checklist factor analysis for children and adolescents. *Archives of General Psychiatry, 30,* 799–804.

Barkley, R. (1981). *Hyperactive children: A handbook for diagnosis and treatment.* New York: Guilford Press.

Barkley, R. (in press). A review of child behavior rating scales and checklists for use in research on child psychopathology. In M. Rutter, A. H. Tuma, & I. Lann (Eds.), *Assessment and diagnosis in child and adolescent psychopathology.* New York: Guilford Press.

Behar, L. B., & Stringfield, S. (1974). A behavior rating scale for the preschool child. *Developmental Psychology, 10,* 601–610.

Chambers, W. J., Puig-Antich, J., Hirsch, M., Paez, P., Ambrosini, P. J., Tabrizi, M. A., & Davies, M. (1985). The assessment of affective disorder in childhood and adolescence by semistructured interview. *Archives of General Psychiatry, 42,* 696–702.

Clarfield, S. P. (1974). The development of a teacher referral form for identifying early school maladaption. *American Journal of Community Psychology, 2,* 199–210.

Conners, C. K. (1969). A teacher rating scale for use in drug studies with children. *American Journal of Psychiatry, 126,* 884–888.

Conners, C. K. (1973). Rating scales for use in drug studies with children. *Psychopharmacology Bulletin,* (special issue), 24–84.

Costello, A. J., Edelbrock, C., Dulcan, M. K. Kalas, R., & Klaric, S. H. (1984). *Development and testing of the NIMH Diagnostic Interview Schedule for Children (DISC) in a clinical population.* Final report (Contract #RFP-DB-81-0027), Center for Epidemiologic Studies, NIMH, Rockville, MD.

Cowen, E., Dorr, D., Clarfield, S., Kreling, B., McWilliams, S. A., Pokracki, F., Pratt, D., Terrell, D., & Wilson, A. (1973). The AML: A quick screening device for early identification of school maladaption. *American Journal of Community Psychology, 1,* 12–35.

Edelbrock, C. (1983). Problems and issues in using rating scales to assess child personality and psychopathology. *School Psychology Review, 12,* 293–299.

Edelbrock, C. (1984). Developmental considerations. In T. H. Ollendick & M. Hersen (Eds.), *Child behavioral assessment: Principles and procedures* (pp. 20–37). New York: Pergamon Press.

Edelbrock, C. (1987). Psychometric research on children and adolescents. In M. Hersen & C. Last (Eds.), *Issues in diagnostic research* (pp. 219–240). New York: Wiley.

Edelbrock, C., & Achenbach, T. M. (1980). A typology of Child Behavior Profile patterns: Distribution and correlates for disturbed children aged 6–16. *Journal of Abnormal Child Psychology. 8,* 441–470.

Edelbrock, C., & Achenbach, T. M. (1984). The teacher version of the Child Behavior Profile: I. Boys aged 6–11. *Journal of Consulting and Clinical Psychology, 52,* 207–217.

Edelbrock, C., & Achenbach, T. M. (1985). *The teacher version of the Child Behavior Profile: II. Boys aged 12–16 and girls aged 6–11 and 12–16.* Unpublished manuscript.

Edelbrock, C., & Costello, A. J. (1984). Structured psychiatric interviews with children and adolescents. In G. Goldstein & M. Hersen (Eds.), *Handbook of psychological assessment* (pp. 276–290). New York: Pergamon Press.

Edelbrock, C., Costello, A. J., & Kessler, M. K. (1984). Empirical corroboration of Attention Deficit Disorder. *Journal of the American Academy of Child Psychiatry, 23,* 285–290.

Edelbrock, C., Costello, A. J., Dulcan, M. K., Kalas, R., & Conover, N. C. (1985). Age differences in the reliability of the psychiatric interview of the child. *Child Development, 56,* 265–275.

Edelbrock, C., Greenbaum, R., & Conover, N. C. (1985). Reliability and concurrent relations between the teacher version of the Child Behavior Profile and Conners' Revised Teacher Rating Scale. *Journal of Abnormal Child Psychology, 13,* 295–304.

Edelbrock, C., Costello, A. J., Dulcan, M. K., Conover, N. C., & Kalas, R. (1986). Parent–child agreement on child psychiatric symptoms assessed via structured interview. *Journal of Child Psychology and Psychiatry, 27,* 181–190.

Eisenberg, J. G., Gersten, J. C., Langner, T. S., McCarthy, E. D., & Simcha-Fagan. O. (1976). A behavioral classification of welfare children from survey data. *American Journal of Orthopsychiatry, 46,* 447–463.

Evans, W. R. (1975). The Behavior Problem Checklist: data from an inner city population. *Psychology in the Schools, 12,* 301–303.

Everitt, B. (1980). *Cluster analysis* (2nd ed.). New York: Halsted.

Goyette, C. H., Conners, C. K., & Ulrich, R. (1978). Normative data on Revised Conners Parent and Teacher Rating Scales. *Journal of Abnormal Child Psychology, 6,* 221–236.

Herjanic, B., & Reich, W. (1982). Development of a structured psychiatric interview for children: Agreement between child and parent on individual symptoms. *Journal of Abnormal Child Psychology, 10,* 307–324.

Hodges, K., Kline, J., Cytryn, L., & McKnew, D. (1982). The development of a child assessment interview for research and clinical use. *Journal of Abnormal Child Psychology, 10,* 173–189.

Jenkins, R. L. (1966). Psychiatric syndromes in children and their relation to family background. *American Journal of Orthopsychiatry, 36,* 450–457.

Kohn, M., & Rosman, B. L. (1972). A social competence scale and symptom checklist for the preschool child: Factor dimensions, their cross-instrument generality, and longitudinal persistence. *Developmental Psychology, 6,* 430–444.

Kraepelin, E. (1883). *Compendium der Psychiatrie.* Leipzig: Abel.

Lahey, B. B., Schaughency, E. A., Strauss, C. C., & Frame, C. L. (1984). Are Attention Deficit Disorders with and without Hyperactivity similar or dissimilar disorders? *Journal of the American Academy of Child Psychiatry, 23,* 302–309.

Langhorne, J. E., & Loney, J. (1979). A four-fold model for subgrouping the Hyperkinetic/MBD syndrome. *Child Psychiatry and Human Development, 9,* 153–159.

Loney, J., Langhorne, J. E., & Paternite, C. E. (1978). An empirical basis for subgrouping the hyperkinetic/minimal brain dysfunction syndrome. *Journal of Abnormal Psychology, 87,* 431–441.

Lorr, M. (1983). *Cluster analysis for social scientists.* San Francisco: Jossey-Bass.

Mezzich, A. C., Mezzich, J. E., & Coffman, G. A. (1985). Reliability of DSM-III vs. DSM-II in child psychopathology. *Journal of the American Academy of Child Psychiatry, 24,* 273–280.

Milich, R., Roberts, M., Loney, J., & Caputo, J. (1980). Differentiating practice effects and statistical regression on the Conners Hyperkinesis Index. *Journal of Abnormal Child Psychology, 8,* 549–552.

Miller, L. C. (1967). Louisville Behavior Check List for males 6–12 years of age. *Psychological Reports, 21,* 885–896.

Miller, L. C. (1977). *Louisville Behavior Checklist Manual.* Los Angeles, CA: Western Psychological Services.

Miller, L. C., Hampe, E., Barrett, C. L., & Noble, H. (1972). Test-retest reliability of parent ratings of children's deviant behavior. *Psychological Reports, 31,* 249–250.

Peterson, D. R. (1961). Behavior problems of middle childhood. *Journal of Consulting Psychology, 25,* 205–209.

Quay, H. C. (1966). Personality patterns in pre-adolescent delinquent boys. *Educational and Psychological Measurement, 26,* 99–110.

Quay, H. C. (1979). Classification. In H. Quay & J. Werry (Eds.), *Psychopathological disorders of childhood* (pp. 1–42). New York: Wiley.

Quay, H. C., & Peterson, D. (1983). *Manual for the Revised Behavior Problem Checklist.* Coral Gables, FL: Author.

Quay, H. C., & Quay, L. C. (1965). Behavior problems in early adolescence. *Child Development, 36,* 215–220.

Ross, A. O., & Pelham, W. E. (1981). Child psychopathology. *Annual Review of Psychology, 32,* 243–278.

Rutter, M. (1977). Classification. In M. Rutter & L. Hersov (Eds.), *Child psychiatry: Modern approaches* (pp. 359–386). Oxford: Blackwell.

Rutter, M. (1978). Diagnostic validity in child psychiatry. *Advances in Biological Psychiatry, 2,* 2–22.

Rutter, M., & Shaffer, D. (1980). DSM-III: A step forward or back in terms of the classification of child psychiatric disorders. *Journal of the American Academy of Child Psychiatry, 19,* 371–394.

Rutter, M., Shaffer, D., & Shepherd, M. (1975). *A multiaxial classification of child psychiatric disorders: An evaluation of a proposal.* Geneva: World Health Organization.

Spitzer, R. L., & Cantwell, D. P. (1980). The DSM-III classification of the psychiatric disorders of infancy, childhood, and adolescence. *Journal of the American Academy of Child Psychiatry, 19,* 356–370.

Spivack, G., Swift, M., & Prewitt, J. (1971). Syndromes of disturbed classroom behavior: A behavioral diagnostic system for elementary school. *Journal of Special Education, 5,* 269–292.

Strober, M., Green, J., & Carlson, G. (1981). Reliability of psychiatric diagnosis in hospitalized adolescents. *Archives of General Psychiatry, 38,* 141–145.

Venables, P. H., Fletcher, R. P., Dalais, J. C., Mitchell, D. A., Schulsinger, F., & Mednick, S. A. (1983). Factor structure of the Rutter Children's Behavior Questionnaire in a primary school population in a developing country. *Journal of Child Psychology and Psychiatry, 24,* 213–222.

Voeltz, L. M., & Evans, I. M. (1982). The assessment of behavioral inter-relationships in child behavior therapy. *Behavioral Assessment, 4,* 131–165.

Walker, H. M. (1976). *Walker problem behavior identification checklist.* Los Angeles, CA: Western Psychological Services.

Werry, J., Methven, R. J., Fitzpatrick, J., & Dixon, H. (1983). The inter-rater reliability of the DSM-III in children. *Journal of Abnormal Child Psychology, 11,* 341–354.

Werry, J., & Sprague, R. (1974). Methylphenidate in children: Effect of dosage. *Australian and New Zealand Journal of Psychiatry, 8,* 9–19.

Werry, J., & Quay, H. C. (1969). Observing the classroom behavior of elementary school children. *Exceptional Children, 35,* 461–470.

World Health Organization. (1978). *International classification of diseases* (9th ed.). Geneva: World Health Organization.

PART II

Technical Issues in the Use and Dissemination of Behavior Therapy

A large number of new technical and social developments have occured recently in the field of behavior therapy. These developments have taken the field from the fascination with the technology of behavior change to a deeper and more mature understanding of the complexites involved in the implementation of even the simplest interventions. In Chapter 5, Elliott addresses one of the more fundamental problems in the use of of a behavioral methodology: that is, whether the individuals involved in a particular setting will even allow them to be used. Elliott reviews the growing literature with respect to the acceptability of interventions. In Chapter 6, Harris and Ferrari challenge the behavior therapist to be cognizant of the interaction between a child's developmental level and the manner in which assessment and treatment data are interpreted. Yeaton's Chapter 7 on Treatment Effect Norms describes an intriguing new development in the selection of alternative treatments, that being the development of norms whereby strength of treatment for a particular problem can be evaluated relative to specific independent variables and subject characteristics. In Chapter 8, Evans, Meyer, Kurkjian, and Kishi provide an insightful analysis of the complex manner in which behaviors within an individual's repertoire are interrelated. This analysis has enormous implications for assessment and treatment. Anderson and Kratochwill, in Chapter 9, provide a comprehensive survey of the literature on training others in behavioral techniques. Finally, Bergan, Feld, and Swarner provide an update in Chapter 10 of the pioneering work initiated by Bergan in the mid-1970s on behavioral approaches to consultation. This chapter describes Bergan's work using a systematic consultation model on a national basis with the Head Start project.

CHAPTER 5

Acceptability of Behavioral Treatments in Educational Settings

Stephen N. Elliott

Numerous effective treatment procedures for children exhibiting learning and behavior problems have been developed and researched. However, many of the most effective treatments are often unacceptable and underutilized. The concern about the acceptability and utilization of treatments has been a persistent and central theme in behavioral psychology as attested to by O'Leary (1984), Reppucci and Saunders (1974), and Stolz (1981). Explanations for the poor acceptance and utilization of behavioral treatments have ranged from concerns about the potential for restricting individual rights (U.S. Congress 1974a, 1974b) to issues of terminology or jargon (Kazdin & Cole, 1981; Witt, Moe, Gutkin, & Andrews, 1984; Woolfolk, Woolfolk, & Wilson, 1977).

In many ways, Wolf's (1978) conceptualization of social validity can be used to subsume the wide range of explanations offered to account for society's frequent reluctance to use behavioral methods. Specifically, he suggested that society (i.e., teachers, parents, children) would need to validate behavioral treatments "on at least three levels: (a) the social significance of the *goals* . . . (b) the social appropriateness of the *procedures* . . . [and] (c) the social importance of the *effects*" (Wolf, 1978, p. 207, italics added). Collectively these judgments refer to social validity. Social validity has become an important consideration when selecting and evaluating treatment procedures. Kazdin's (1977) and Wolf's (1978) conceptual works on social validity have emphasized the influence consumers' perceptions of a treatment can have on the use and potential outcomes of a treatment.

Much of the empirical research that has followed from this conceptual work on social validity has focused on the acceptability of treatment procedures. Kazdin's (1980a) seminal research on the acceptability of alternative treatments for deviant children stimulated a series of investigations with clinical populations (Kazdin, 1980b, 1981, 1984; Kazdin, French, & Sherick, 1981) and disruptive school children (Elliott, Witt, Galvin, & Peter-

Stephen N. Elliott • Department of Educational Psychology, University of Wisconsin-Madison, Madison, Wisconsin 53706.

son, 1984; Martens, Witt, Elliott, & Darveaux, 1985; Witt, Elliott, & Martens, 1984; Witt, Martens, & Elliott, 1984). Focusing on social validity of target behaviors and treatment outcomes should be emphasized when psychologists are the treatment agents; however, it is also important to assess social validity of treatment procedures when psychologists function as consultants to teachers and parents.

According to Wolf (1978) "by giving the same status to social validity that we now give to objective measurement and its reliability we will bring the consumer . . . into our science [behavior modification]" (p. 207). The notion of "bringing the consumer into our science" emphasizes the need to understand treatment and consumer variables that influence the acceptance of behavioral treatments and brings us to the central purpose of this chapter. That is to review recent research concerning the acceptability and use of behavioral interventions for misbehaving school children. This review focuses primarily on teachers' reactions to treatments, but because children's and psychologists' reactions to school-based treatments have the potential to influence teachers' reactions they also are examined. Many readers will quickly realize the tripartite coverage of reactions to behavioral treatments is consistent with a behavioral consultation model (Bergan, 1977), whereby a psychologist works cooperatively with a teacher to analyze and treat a child's problem. This is by design, for one of the major components of behavioral consultation is selecting and implementing a treatment for an identified problem. Thus we believe much of the basic social validity research, especially that concerning the study of the acceptability of treatment procedures, contributes to the advancement of behavioral consultative methods, the development of a science of treatment selection, and to treatment evaluation methodology.

In addition to a scientific rationale for investigating treatment acceptability, there are strong pragmatic and legal/ethical rationales for this type of research. Wolf (1978) aptly captured the pragmatic perspective when he noted

> that if the participants don't like the treatment then they may avoid it, or run away, or complain loudly. And thus, society will be less likely to use our technology [behavior modification], no matter how potentially effective and efficient it might be. (p. 206)

Independent of this pragmatic rationale, courts have ruled out certain procedures that might be unacceptable because they infringe upon client rights (Budd & Baer, 1976). Institutional review committees, which often include laypersons, routinely are used to decide whether a treatment procedure is acceptable for a given problem. Finally, ethical codes and research on children's involvement in treatment decisions support involving children in selecting treatment procedures (Melton, 1983).

Overview of Acceptability Models and Research Methods

Kazdin (1981) defined treatment acceptability as "judgments by laypersons, clients, and others of whether treatment procedures are appropriate, fair, and reasonable for the problem or client" (p. 493). Although no theory of acceptability is well established, several factors that have been demonstrated empirically to influence individuals' judgments of treatment acceptability have been incorporated into conceptual models by Witt and Elliott (1985) and Reimers, Wacker, and Koeppl (1987).

Models of Treatment Acceptability

Witt and Elliott (1985) developed a working model of acceptability that stressed the interrelations among four elements: treatment acceptability, treatment use, treatment integrity, and treatment effectiveness (see Figure 1). The hypothesized relationships among these four elements can be characterized as

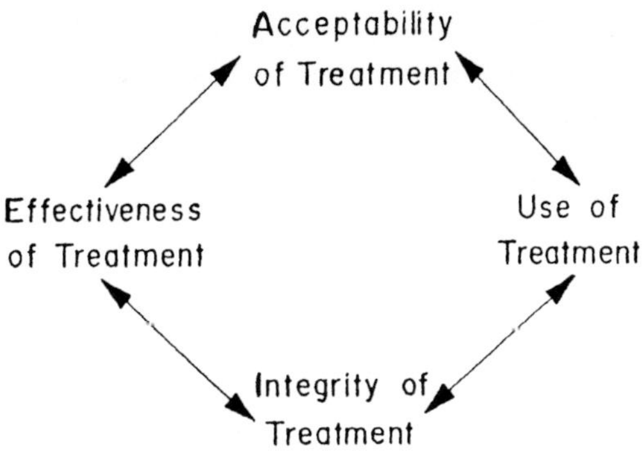

Figure 1. Witt and Elliott's (1985) "working" model of major variables that influence treatment acceptability. Reprinted with permission.

sequential and reciprocal. That is, acceptability is ultimately the initial issue in the sequence of treatment selection and use. Once a treatment is deemed acceptable, the probability of using the treatment is high relative to treatments rated lower. A central element hypothesized to link use and effectiveness is treatment integrity. If integrity is high, the probability of effecting a behavioral change is enhanced. Finally, if the effectiveness of the treatment meets or exceeds the expectations of the service provider, the probability of judging the treatment acceptable is enhanced. To date, empirical evidence has not been amassed in a single investigation to support or refute this model; however, researchers have provided evidence about several of the interrelationships among the four elements. The majority of this research will be reviewed later in this chapter.

Stimulated by the Witt and Elliott model, Reimers, Wacker, and Koeppl (1987) developed a more complex model of treatment acceptability (see Figure 2). These authors assumed a treatment must be well understood before acceptability is assessed, and therefore incorporated a treatment knowledge component into their decision-making flowchart concerning acceptability. According to the Reimers *et al.* model, when a proposed treatment is perceived to be low in acceptability, it

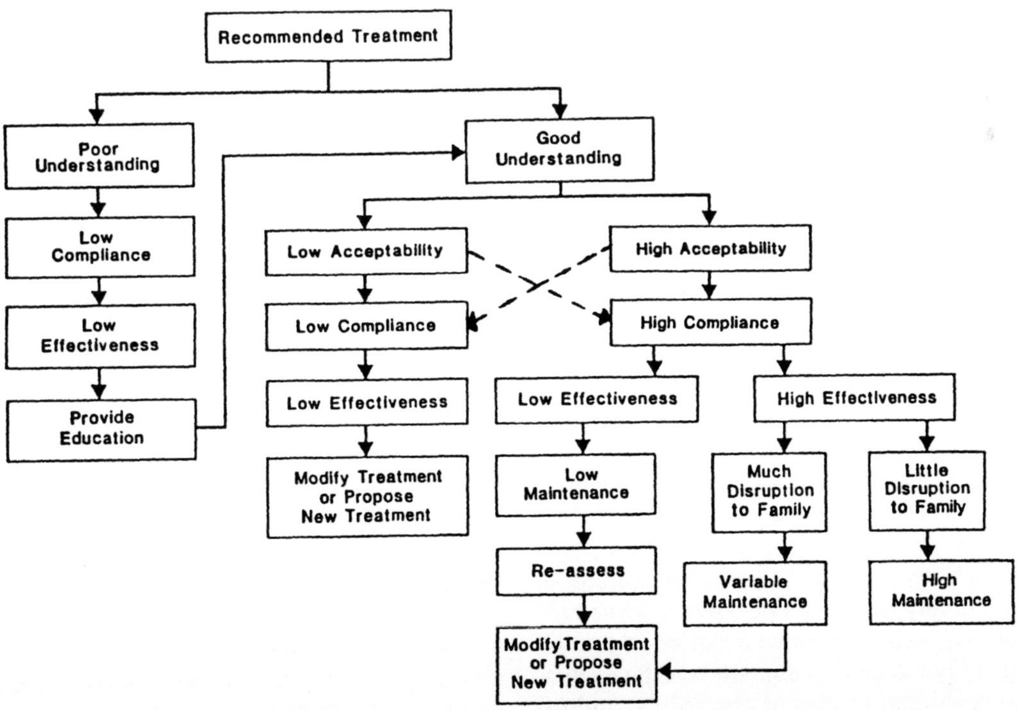

Figure 2. Reimers, Wacker, and Koeppl's (1987) proposed model of treatment acceptability. Reprinted with permission.

is likely poor compliance will follow, thus decreasing the probability of the treatment being effective. In this model, compliance represents a teacher's or parent's attempt to implement a treatment. Once a treatment has been attempted, maintenance (i.e., continued use of the treatment) is the major issue. If a treatment is rated as being high in acceptability, it is likely that compliance with the recommendations will be high. However, the effects of treatment can still range from not effective to highly effective. If the treatment is not effective, there will not be maintenance of treatment effects, and reassessment of the problem behavior, recommended procedure, or treatment integrity is probably warranted. If the problem behavior was identified correctly, and if the recommended treatment was implemented as prescribed, some modifications of the treatment may be warranted or another treatment might be proposed. At this point, then, the cycle would repeat itself. When a treatment is highly effective, it is assumed maintenance of treatment effects will also be high, provided a family or school routine was not significantly disrupted either by the resulting change in behavior, or by the changes brought about by implementing the procedure. Disruption can occur, for example, when unusual resources or amounts of time are needed to continue the treatment.

Neither the Witt and Elliott (1985) model nor the Reimers *et al.* model fully characterize the complex array of variables that potentially interact to influence the selection and implementation of behavioral treatments. Although imperfect, these models have been heuristic guides to stimulating research questions. Major research questions center around (a) the measurement of treatment acceptability, (b) the influence of child variables (e.g., type of behavior problem, severity of problem, age, sex, race) on teachers' ratings of acceptability, (c) the influence of teacher variables (e.g., years teaching experience, knowledge of behavioral treatments) on the evaluation of different types of treatments, and (d) the relationship between consumers' and clients' pretreatment acceptability evaluations and posttreatment effectiveness. Instrumentation and methods have been developed to begin answering these and other questions and will be discussed next.

Research Methods

Decisions about the social validity of a treatment consist of judgments by consumers of whether or not they like the treatment procedures or effects. In other words, it is the subjective evaluation of an individual's satisfaction with a treatment (Kazdin, 1981). The measurement of a subjective variable presents a significant challenge. On one hand, there is a bias in behavioral psychology to assess only those variables that can be reliably quantified; on the other hand, there is an increasing interest in relatively intangible constructs such as happiness, satisfaction, and gratification (Wolf, 1978).

A number of methods have been developed for assessing the social appropriateness of treatment goals (Kazdin, 1977; Willmer *et al.*, 1977; Wolf, 1978). The procedures of social comparison and subjective evaluation, developed by Kazdin, are illustrative. Social comparison involves the documentation of the skills displayed by normal children in various settings. Thus, the social and adaptive skills displayed by normal peers are considered to be socially appropriate educational goals. Subjective evaluation, the second method, involves formal and informal methods of asking opinions of others concerning the social appropriateness of treatment goals. Typically, the opinions of teachers and parents of a child and experts in the field are solicited.

The two methods of social validity developed by Kazdin have been used by researchers, particularly those interested in assessing and training social skills (e.g., Hersh & Walker, 1983; Minkin *et al.*, 1976). The development of methods to assess the acceptability of treatment procedures, however, has engendered the most research, although it has been analogue in nature. With the publication of two treatment acceptability studies in 1980, Kazdin (1980a, b) provided a paradigm that subsequent researchers have worked within. The essential elements of this paradigm have been a pencil and paper problem-treatment vignette followed by evaluative ratings about the treatment. Within this paradigm, the primary independent variables manipulated have been the severity of the target problem and the type of treatment employed. Other independent variables of interest have included an array of demographic indexes about the individual rating the treatments. For example, when teachers have been the treatment evaluators, information about years of teaching experience, type of training, and knowledge of behavioral principles and methods have been measured. In addition, some acceptability researchers (e.g., Elliott, Turco, & Gresham, 1987; Kazdin, French, & Sherick, 1981) have investigated how different consumers (i.e., parents, teachers, children, and hospital staff) of treatments evaluate them, thus invoking the rater as an independent variable. The primary dependent variable of interest in treatment acceptability research has been consumers' evaluative reactions to treatments as operationalized by one of several recently developed rating scales (i.e., Behavior Intervention Rating Scale or BIRS; Children's Intervention Rating Profile or CIRP; Intervention Rating Profile-20 or IRP-20; Intervention Rating Profile-15 or IRP-15; and Treatment Evaluation Inventory or TEI). A copy of each of these rating scales appears in the appendix of this chapter.

The first published objective measure of treatment acceptability was the Treatment Evaluation Inventory (TEI) (Kazdin, 1980a). The TEI has 15 questions where respondents use a 7-point Likert scale to rate the acceptability, fairness, suitability, etc., of intervention methods. Kazdin (1980a) reported that according to an unrotated principal components factor analysis based on a sample of 60 pilot college students, 15 of the 16 TEI items loaded highly (.67 to .94) on one factor. The first factor accounts for 51.4% of the variance. The TEI was originally written for and used in analogue research with adult populations (Kazdin, 1980a, b; 1981) The TEI, however, was later modified (audiotaped) and used in research with child psychiatric populations (Kazdin *et al.*, 1981). The complexity of the sentence structures of the TEI makes it virtually useless with primary school populations. Each question of the TEI has a different range of Likert responses. Therefore, respondents must reorganize their responses for each new question. This is a tedious task that makes using the TEI in nonadult populations difficult.

Witt and Martens (1983) reformulated the TEI to create a new treatment acceptability scale specifically designed for use in school settings and called it the Intervention Rating Profile (IRP) (Witt & Martens, 1983). The IRP was originally a 20-question scale containing five factors: (a) general acceptability (61% of the variance), (b) risk of the intervention to target child (12% of the variance), (c) amount of teacher time required (11% of the variance), (d) effect of the intervention on other children (7% of the variance), and (e) amount of teacher skill required (7% of the variance). A revision of the IRP, called the IRP-15, consisted of the 15 items from the IRP-20 that most specifically addressed various aspects of intervention acceptability (Martens *et al.*, 1985). Each question on the IRP is scored on a 6-point Likert scale. The scale remains the same from question to question, ranging from "Strongly Disagree" to "Strongly Agree." The IRP has been successfully used in analogue research with preservice and practicing teachers to assess the social validity of treatment methods (Elliott *et al.*, 1984; Martens *et al.*, 1985; Witt & Robins, 1985; Witt, Elliott, *et al.*, 1984; Witt, Martens, & Elliott, 1984). The length of the scale and item structure of both versions of the IRP makes them impractical to use with children.

Evidence for the validity and reliability of the IRP-15 is encouraging. Witt and Martens (1983) found the IRP correlated .86 with the evaluative dimension of the Semantic Differential. Further validity evidence can be inferred from a study (Martens *et al.*, 1985) in which the IRP-15 differentiated between two interventions (a teacher-implemented response cost and sending a child to the office) in terms of the degree to which they were acceptable to teachers. Reliability (as determined by Cronbach's alpha) of the IRP-15 was .98 (Witt & Martens, 1983).

To date, only one objective scale has been published that has been specifically designed to measure the treatment acceptability judgments of children, the Children's Intervention Rating Profile (CIRP) (Witt & Elliott, 1983). The CIRP is a seven-question, 6-point Likert scale of children's social acceptability ratings ranging from "I agree" to "I do not agree." The CIRP represents an objective instrument that has been validated on over 1,000 students in the fifth through tenth grades and found to have an average coefficient alpha of .86 (Turco & Elliott, 1986b). Several published studies have used the CIRP to assess the acceptability ratings of children (Elliott, Witt, Galvin, & Moe, 1986; Shapiro & Goldberg, 1986; Turco & Elliott, 1986a, b). The CIRP has seven questions that have been found consistently to load on two factors. Six of the questions load heavily on the first factor. One question, Number 2, concerning harshness of a teacher's actions, composes the second factor. The CIRP would benefit from refinements so as to eliminate the one-question factor.

As researchers become more cognizant of the need to assess treatment acceptability, we can expect modifications of existing scales and the development of new and perhaps more sophisticated measures. For example, Shapiro and Goldberg (1986) changed the number of items and scaling on the CIRP. Von Brock (1985) expanded the IRP-15 to create a new 24-question scale, the Behavioral Intervention Rating Scale (BIRS). Structurally, the BIRS has three factors: (a) the IRP-15 or Acceptability (15 questions and 63% of the variance), (b) Effectiveness (7 questions and 6% of the variance), and (c) Time (2 questions and 4.3% of the variance). The Acceptability factor was found to have a high positive relation with the Effectiveness factor (.79) and the Time factor (.65). The Effectiveness factor and the Time factor correlated moderately (.63). Consistent with previous studies comparing treatment acceptability measures and the evaluation factor of the Semantic Differential (SD) (Kazdin, 1980), there was a high correlation (.78) between the Acceptability factor of the BIRS and the Evaluation factor of the SD. Using a partial correlation, with the Time factor partialed from the Effectiveness factor, the correlation between Acceptability and Effectiveness was .49. When partialing the Time factor from both Acceptability and Effectiveness factors, the resulting correlation was .64. This demonstrated the importance of the two-item Time factor. A coefficient alpha was used to determine the reliability of each scale. The total BIRS (24 items) yielded an alpha of .97. The three factors of the BIRS, Acceptability, Effectiveness, and Time, yielded alphas of .97, .92, and .87, respectively.

To date, the research methods employed by investigators interested in studying the acceptability of various treatment procedures have been limited primarily to large *N*, quasi-experimental designs utilizing the problem-treatment vignette format outlined above. Although a few naturalistic studies have been completed where the social validity of the treatment goals and effects were considered, only one treatment study (Shapiro & Goldberg, 1986) has been reported where the treatment procedures were actually evaluated by the recipients of the treatment. Researchers interested in treatment acceptability have identified as major short-term research goals (a) the development of meaningful acceptability measures, (b) the cataloging of the relative acceptability of a wide range of treatments, and (c) the understanding of the lawful impact of a few basic variables, such as target problem severity and type of interventions on consumers' evaluation of treatment procedures. Before examining specific studies, it is important to highlight that the majority of published research on treatment acceptability has been analogue in nature and, with the exception of a few studies (e.g., McMahon & Forehand, 1983; Shapiro & Goldberg, 1986), has been predominantly concerned with pretreatment judgments of consultees (treatment agents) rather than clients. This emphasis on analogue, pretreatment acceptability research is warranted at this time. First, analogue research allows for more experimental control of salient variables and generally large samples under identical conditions. In the early stages of model building and instrument development, such an approach is fruitful. Second, the assessment of treatment agents' reactions to possible treatments prior to implementation reflects the typical treatment selection interactions of psychologists and teachers. At this time, applied researchers are beginning to transfer the methods and knowledge base from analogue research to naturalistic investigations and their practice in schools. In the next section, we examine specific studies and their major findings.

Review of Acceptability Research: An Examination of Variables That Influence Teachers' Treatment Selections

Upon a moment's reflection, a rather long list of variables can be generated that potentially influence a teacher's selection of a treatment for a misbehaving child. Based on a consultation service delivery framework where a psychologist interacts with a teacher to assess and treat a child, Table 1 was developed to characterize the variables that have been investigated by researchers interested in understanding pretreatment acceptability and the effects on treatment outcomes. Thus, this table serves as an advance organizer for our review of treatment acceptability studies.

Psychologist-Related Variables That Affect Treatment Acceptability

Two variables, jargon used in describing treatments and psychologists' involvement in treatments, are the major psychologist-related variables that have been studied within the treatment acceptability paradigm. The rationales psychologists provide for an atypical treatment (e.g., paradoxical procedures) have also been investigated; however, this research is reviewed in a latter section on types of treatments.

Psychological Jargon

Several researchers have demonstrated that individuals' evaluations of psychological treatments vary as a function of what the treatment is called and how it is described. For example, Woolfolk and her associates (Woolfolk & Woolfolk, 1979; Woolfolk *et al.*, 1977)

Table 1. Variables within a Consultative Framework That Can Influence Teachers' Evaluations of Treatment Acceptability

Consultant (psychologist) ---→	Consultee (teacher) ---→	Treatment ---→	Client (child)
Jargon	Years experience	Time required	Severity of problem
Involvement	Knowledge of behavior principles	Type of treatment	Type of problem
	Type of training	Reported effectiveness	
	Class management techniques used		

Note. The variables in this table have been investigated empirically. Many more variables, such as the race and sex of the consultant, consultee, and client, could be investigated. Most analogue research to date has been with female teachers and hypothetical male problem children because this is most representative of reality.

presented preservice teachers a videotape of a teacher who reinforced appropriate behavior, ignored inappropriate behavior, and used a backup token economy during an elementary school class. For one group of preservice teachers, the videotape was described as illustrative of behavior modification and for the other group it was called humanistic education. These researchers found the personal qualities of the teacher and the effectiveness of the teaching method were perceived more positively when the method was labeled humanistic education as opposed to behavior modification.

Kazdin and Cole (1981), in a follow-up investigation to Woolfolk, presented undergraduate college students written descriptions of treatments designed to alter classroom misbehavior. These two researchers concluded that interventions described in behavioral terms were evaluated less favorably than procedures labeled humanistic; however, simply labeling a treatment as behavior modification did not influence treatment evaluations.

As an extension of his acceptability research, Witt and several colleagues (Witt, Moe, *et al.*, 1984) investigated the effects of the type of language used to describe interventions on teachers' rating of the interventions' acceptability. Specifically, these researchers manipulated three types of jargon (behavioral, pragmatic, and humanistic) used to describe an intervention that required a target child to stay in at recess for his misbehavior. The behavioral description used terms emphasizing that staying in at recess involved the contingent application of punishment for the specific purpose of controlling a child's inappropriate behavior. The humanistic description emphasized the purpose of staying in at recess was to help the child understand and express his feelings by reading a book about feelings or talking with his teacher. In the pragmatic description, staying in at recess was presented as a "logical consequence" of the child's misbehavior. The research method employed by Witt *et al.* is typical of the problem-treatment paradigm outlined previously and the IRP-15 was used to operationalize the dependent variable of treatment acceptability. The major finding with regard to the jargon variable was that the intervention described in pragmatic terms was rated significantly more acceptable than the same intervention described in either humanistic or behavioral terms.

In summary, it can be concluded from the four studies reviewed that the jargon a psychologist uses to describe a treatment is clearly a salient variable to teachers and one that can influence overall perceptions of the acceptability and effectiveness of a given treatment. Unfortunately, it was also demonstrated that behavioral terminology did not serve to bias teachers' evaluations positively; rather, treatments described either in humanistic or pragmatic terms were preferred.

Psychologist Involvement in Treatment Implementation

To date, there have not been any published studies where researchers have directly manipulated the amount or type of treatment involvement exhibited by a psychologist, although we are aware of a study (i.e., Rhodes, in preparation) that will soon contribute information to this area. Intelligent inferences about the influence of psychologists' treatment involvement, however, can be gleaned from two investigations (i.e., Algozzine, Ysseldyke, Christenson, & Thurlow, 1983; Martens, Peterson, Witt, & Cirone, 1986). Using a case description methodology, Algozzine *et al.* investigated teachers' preferences among 40 treatment alternatives applied to three types of classroom problems. These researchers concluded that teachers preferred interventions that they could implement directly rather than those that require consultation with a psychologist and/or placing the child outside the classroom.

Martens *et al.* (1986) followed up on Algozzine and his work to investigate the treatment preferences of 2,493 teachers, both regular and special education, from Iowa and Nebraska. Using the Classroom Intervention Profile, a 65-item questionnaire that requires the rating of 49 classroom interventions on three scales (i.e., Effectiveness, Ease of Use, and Frequency of Use), these researchers were able to deduce several significant trends with regard to teachers' treatment preferences. Of interest here is their finding that consultation with other personnel was rated relatively low in terms of effectiveness and ease of use. By comparison, interventions involving verbal redirection, manipulation of a material reward, and in-class timeout were rated consistently higher than consultation with a specialist such as a psychologist. Martens *et al.* attributed this poor acceptance of consultation to the relatively large time involvement required. The variable of amount of time required for an intervention has been found consistently to influence teachers' acceptability ratings of interventions (Witt, Elliott, & Martens, 1984).

This time variable as it relates to a psychologist's involvement in treatment requires more detailed examination and clarification. Presently, we know from self-reports that teachers generally prefer to use treatments that can be conducted in their own classrooms requiring little time in consultation (indirect service) with specialists such as psychologists. It has not been empirically established, however, that teachers do not want psychologists to be highly involved in direct treatment of students within their classrooms.

Psychologists' Treatment Preferences

It is logical to assume that psychologists will suggest treatments they find acceptable to teachers who are requesting assistance with a misbehaving student. Surprisingly, very little data exists that documents psychologists' acceptability of treatments. In fact, within the scope of this chapter only one investigation has been published in which psychologists' pretreatment acceptability ratings have been collected and also compared to teachers' and children's ratings. Elliott *et al.* (1987) investigated fifth graders', teachers', and school psychologists' acceptability evaluations of three types of group contingencies (dependent, interdependent, and independent) with a consequence of positive reinforcement for appropriate behavior. The major conclusion of this study is that although the children, psychologists, and teachers found the use of group contingencies generally acceptable for treating disruptive classroom behavior, they preferred forms of group contingencies where the consequences for an individual were based on either the individual himself or herself (independent group contingency) or the entire group (interdependent group contingency). Letting a subset of a group (dependent group contingency) determine the consequences for the entire group was least acceptable for the fifth grade and teacher samples, and unacceptable for the psychologist respondents.

Teachers' Treatment Preferences and Variables That Influence These Preferences

Unlike the acceptability research with psychologist-related variables, the research with teachers is numerous and provides insights about the variables that impact treatment selection and use. In this section we review research that covers child variables (e.g., severity of problem, type of problem), treatment characteristics (e.g., time involved, punishment vs. reinforcement, group vs. individual contingencies, strong vs. weak treatment effects), and teacher background variables (e.g., years experience, special vs. regular education training, knowledge of behavioral principles).

Severity of Child's Problem

This variable has been of high interest to researchers and consequently it has appeared as an independent variable in many studies (Elliott *et al.* 1984; Elliott *et al.*, 1987; Frentz & Kelley, 1986; Kazdin, 1980a; Martens *et al.*, 1985; Von Brock & Elliott, 1987; Witt, Elliott, &

Martens, 1984; Witt, Martens, & Elliott, 1984; Witt, Moe, *et al.*, 1984). This severity variable has been operationalized by changes in the degree to which a target child behaves inappropriately or by the number of children who are behaving inappropriately. The vast majority of researchers have conceptualized problem severity as a child variable and thus have developed problem scenarios involving behaviors ranging from inattention or passive off-task to major disruptive and aggressive behavior toward others. In general, the collective results of these studies have demonstrated that the more severe a child's problem, the more acceptable any given treatment. Several specific studies concerning the problem severity variable follow.

Kazdin (1980a) had undergraduate students evaluate the acceptability of four treatment methods (reinforcement of incompatible behaviors, 10-minute time-out from reinforcement, drug treatment [methylphenidate (Ritalin)], and moderately painful contingent electric shock) to improve one of two severities of child misbehaviors. The results showed that college students rated treatments as significantly more acceptable for more severe case descriptions than for less severe case descriptions.

It appears that severity of a target problem influences how complex an acceptable treatment can be. For example, in a two-experiment study, Elliott *et al.* (1984) investigated experienced teachers' acceptability ratings for behavioral interventions. In the first part of the study, regular and special education teachers were asked to read one of three case descriptions of an elementary school student whose misbehaviors were of a low (daydreaming), moderate (obscene language), or severe (destruction of other's property) nature and to rate the acceptability of one of three positively oriented intervention methods that were either low in complexity (praise), of moderate complexity (home-based reinforcement), or highly complex (token economy). The results indicated that the least complex intervention (praise) was the most acceptable treatment for the least severe problem behavior (daydreaming). The most complex treatment (token economy) was rated as the most acceptable intervention for the most severe behavior problem (destroying property) (Elliott *et al.*, 1985). In the second part of the Elliott *et al.* (1985) study, all of the variables remained the same except that teachers were asked to evaluate the acceptability of one of three reductive intervention methods that were either low (ignoring), medium (response-cost lottery), or high (seclusion time-out) in complexity. The results indicated that the least complex intervention (ignoring) was the most acceptable treatment for the least severe behavior problem (daydreaming).

An investigation by Frentz and Kelley (1986) of parents' acceptability ratings of reductive treatments provides support and generalizability evidence for the conclusion that treatment acceptability is effected significantly by the severity of the target problem. Frentz and Kelley asked 82 mothers to rate, via the TEI, five treatment procedures (i.e., differential attention, response cost, timeout, spanking alone, timeout with spanking) as methods for resolving a mild or a severe child behavior problem. The results indicated that the sampled parents rated all treatments as being more acceptable when applied to the severe problem.

Type of Treatment

This variable has generally been characterized by treatments described as either positive (e.g., praise, DRO, DRL, token economy) or reductive (e.g., response cost, timeout, overcorrection). In the child clinical literature, treatments involving medication and electroshock have also been assessed with regard to acceptability. In general, researchers have found that the acceptability ratings of all varieties of consumers (teachers, parents, children) have been consistently higher for positive than reductive treatment procedures (Elliott *et al.*, 1984; Kazdin, 1980a, b, 1981; Martens *et al.*, 1986; Witt & Robins, 1985; Witt,

Elliott, & Martens, 1984). For example, in the first investigation with educators as subjects, Witt, Elliott, and Martens assessed 180 preservice teachers' acceptance of six treatments, three positive (praise, home-based reinforcement, token economy) and three negative (ignoring, response cost, seclusion timeout) for changing target behaviors of either daydreaming, obscene language, or destroying others' property. These researchers found significant main and interaction effects for both the treatment and problem severity variables, but of interest here is the fact that the positive treatments were evaluated consistently more acceptable on the IRP-20 than were the reductive treatments for the same problems.

In a replication and extention of the Witt, Martins *et al.* (1984) investigation, Elliott *et al.* (1984) provided empirical support for the assertion that acceptability varies as a function of treatment type. They assessed experienced teachers' acceptance for the same six interventions as Witt *et al.* (1984) and used the IRP-20 to operationalize acceptability. Again they found that the average acceptability ratings for the positive treatments were significantly more favorable than for the reductive treatments. In addition, there was a clear interaction between the variables of problem severity and treatment type with the least complex positive and negative treatments (i.e., praise and ignoring) being rated most acceptable for the mild problem (i.e., daydreaming) and the most complex treatments (i.e., token economy and seclusion timeout) being rated the most acceptable for the severe problem (i.e., destroying others' property).

Psychotherapy outcome research has demonstrated that paradoxical treatments are effective procedures for oppositional behavior (Strong, 1984; Wilson & Bornstein, 1984), yet they do not appear to be frequently used in school settings. Paradoxical treatments involve actions by a psychologist/therapist that are in apparent opposition to the acknowledged goals of treatment. As such, paradoxical treatments are counterintuitive and deviate from mainstream procedure used in schools. Because of this, Cavell, Frentz, and Kelley (1986a) recently examined teachers' reactions to such procedures. Specifically, they had 120 middle and high school teachers rate, via the TEI, one of five treatment conditions (four paradoxical procedures and a contingency contracting procedure). Teachers rated the paradoxical procedures as generally unacceptable and significantly lower than the continuation of an unsuccessful contingency contract. Some variability among the four paradoxical conditions was observed. When the psychologists' actual intentions were described and positive effects were predicted on the basis of a student's previous resistance to behavior change, teachers rated the treatment more acceptable (although in an absolute sense it was still unacceptable on the TEI) than the condition where no rationale for the paradoxical treatment was provided.

A final study for consideration within our examination of treatment types concerns teachers' reactions to the use of single case withdrawal designs. Cavell, Frentz, and Kelley (1986b) conducted a rather unique investigation to examine teachers' acceptance of six rationales justifying treatment withdrawal. Johnston (1972) provided a pragmatic rationale for this study when he questioned, "What teacher, seeing Johnny for the first time quietly seated for most of the day, would like to experience another week or two of bedlam just to satisfy the perverted whim of a psychologist?" (p. 1035). Using a sample of 126 middle and high school teachers, Cavell *et al.* (1986a) tested teachers' reactions to continuing the treatment and the following six rationales for using a withdrawal phase: (a) to see if the program was still necessary, (b) because the psychologist was not fully convinced that it was the treatment that changed the child, (c) because it would allow the child's teachers and parents to know whether or not it was the program that changed behavior, (d) it would help to further improve the child's behavior, (e) because the psychologist was handling the case like an experiment, and (f) no explanation. The results of the study indicated that teachers did not rate these six rationales as being significantly different. All mean total acceptability scores on the TEI indicated teachers found the rationales moderately acceptable with the "see if program is still necessary" rationale receiving the highest average rating and the "convincing others" rationale the lowest average rating. An examination of individuals' evaluative ratings, however, suggested that nearly a third of the teachers found some of the rationales unacceptable.

Acceptability research by Kazdin and his associates (Kazdin, 1980a, b; Kazdin *et al.*, 1981) attests to the generalizability of the finding that people generally rate positive treatment procedures as more acceptable than negative procedures for changing children's behavior. The specific results of these Kazdin studies are not directly applicable to education settings because the raters have been predominantly undergraduate psychology students and some of the treatments are rarely, if ever, used by teachers.

Time Required to Implement a Treatment

Time is a valuable asset to teachers who often are responsible for educating 25 or more children at once. Thus, it should not be surprising to find that when teachers evaluate a behavior change procedure prior to use, they are time conscious. The research on treatment acceptability has indicated that time is a very salient factor in teachers' pretreatment acceptability ratings of treatment procedures (Elliott *et al.*, 1984; Kazdin, 1982; Witt & Martens, 1983; Witt, Elliott, & Martens, 1984; Witt, Martens, & Elliott, 1984).

As means of illustrating the research on time, we will review one study in detail. Witt, Martens, and Elliott (1984) directly manipulated the variables of teacher time involvement, intervention type, and behavior problem severity in a factorial design to assess how 180 teachers would evaluate treatments on the IRP-20. Descriptions of the treatments included estimates of the amount of time required to implement the treatment. A treatment was classified as requiring low amounts of teacher time if it required less than 30 minutes per day, as requiring moderate amounts of teacher time if it required 1 to 2 hours to prepare and 30 to 60 minutes to maintain, and as requiring high amounts of teacher time if it necessitated more than 2 hours of start-up and approximately 1 hour per day to maintain. The results of the study indicated that time in itself affected acceptability ratings, and more importantly, time interacted significantly with both problem severity and treatment type. In summary, all things being equal teachers preferred treatments that were more time efficient. However, when confronted with a severe problem they seem to adjust their expectations upward about the strength of treatment and consequently the time involved to change the problem behavior. Based on this and other analogue studies, teachers appear to be time conscious but not time obsessed when selecting treatments.

Reported Effectiveness of a Treatment

After a treatment has been implemented the ultimate criterion for evaluating it is effectiveness. In other words, did the prescribed treatment change the target behavior in the desired direction and to the desired extent? As you realize by now, however, we have hypothesized that prior to selection and implementation of a treatment, acceptability is an important evaluation criterion. Given the existence of these two important treatment evaluation criteria, the relationship between them requires examination. Two possible direct causal relationships between acceptability and effectiveness exist. They are that (a) acceptability → effectiveness and (b) effectiveness → acceptability. These two forms of the relationship are testable with naturalistic and analogue methods and generally require pretreatment and posttreatment measures of acceptability to be correlated with posttreatment effectiveness. From a consultative perspective, however, one could also test the effectiveness → acceptability relation by providing a consultee treatment effectiveness information prior to selection of a treatment. Several researchers, in fact, have investigated the effect of treatment outcome or effectiveness information in consumers' ratings of treatment acceptability (Clark & Elliott, 1986; Kazdin, 1981; Von Brock & Elliott, 1987).

Kazdin (1981) conducted a two-experiment investigation testing the influence of treatment efficacy and adverse side effects on TEI ratings of acceptability and Semantic Differential ratings of potency, activity, and evaluation. Specifically, in the first experiment undergraduate college students rated each of four treatments (i.e., reinforcement or incompatible behavior, positive practice, timeout from reinforcement, and medication) for an aggressive or a hyperactive child. The treatments were described as having either strong or weak effects. In Experiment 2, Kazdin substituted a side effects variable for the treatment efficacy variable. In both experiments treatments were rated as consistently different, with the undergraduates rating reinforcement of incompatible behavior the most acceptable treatment followed by positive practice, timeout, and medication. The reported treatment effectiveness information (strong vs. weak effects) did not influence acceptability ratings, although it did influence perceptions of treatment potency. In contrast, the presence of undesired side effects markedly influenced acceptability ratings with stronger side effects reducing acceptability ratings of all treatments.

Von Brock and Elliott (1987) were interested in the impact of outcome information on teachers' ratings of treatment acceptability. They had 216 experienced teachers rate, via the BIRS, one of three treatments (token economy, response cost, or timeout) for changing a mild or severe classroom behavior problem. One of three types of effectiveness information accompany each problem-treatment scenario. Teachers received either no effectiveness information, teacher-satisfaction effectiveness information, or researcher-based effectiveness information. The results suggested that effectiveness information did influence ratings when the problem severity was taken into consideration. When there was a milder problem, information concerning an intervention's effectiveness from research sources influenced effectiveness and acceptability ratings more than if no information was given. This was a surprising finding. Logically, one would predict that with a severe problem, more information would be sought prior to implementing treatment. If considered analogous to a medical problem, with a mild illness, one might not consult a doctor, but with a more serious illness people usually seek out additional information to treat the problem. This study suggested that with classroom problems the *opposite* might be true: with severe problems, teachers rely more on their own judgments. This finding suggests teachers may be more amenable to interventions before a problem becomes too severe. Catching problems early may give psychologists more freedom in treatment choice with their consultees. Another explanation may be that teachers have preconceived notions about interventions. When presented with a mild problem, they feel there is more room for decision making concerning how to handle the problem, and therefore they are willing to experiment with different treatments. Thus, they are more influenced by information concerning these treatments. On the other hand, with severe problems, teachers may not be as comfortable with intervention experimentation and may rely more on past experience, or judgment. Another point that should be noted is that these teacher raters were all in graduate education classes and may have had more respect for research-based findings than would be true of the general teacher population.

In addition to providing insights about the influence of outcome information on pretreatment ratings of acceptability, the Von Brock and Elliott (1987) study also contributed new information about the covariation of pretreatment acceptability ratings with perceived effectiveness ratings. Specifically, these researchers used the BIRS, and were thus able to operationalize acceptability and effectiveness ratings concurrently. They found that when teachers viewed an intervention as less acceptable, they also rated it as less effective. Once again this provided support for the notion of a strong relationship between acceptability and effectiveness, but it also suggests that teachers' views on treatment acceptability influenced their views on treatment effectiveness. When teachers do not find a treatment acceptable they may also think of it as ineffective. The implication for consultation here is the importance of assessing perceived acceptability and effectiveness because of the impact these perceptions may have on outcome. In addition, it suggests that manipulating one of the constructs (acceptability or effectiveness) by providing information (e.g., "most teachers have liked this intervention" or "several of your colleagues have found this to be a very effective intervention"), one may be able to influence the treatment outcome.

In a follow-up investigation to the Von Brock and Elliott (1987) study, Clark and Elliott (1986) examined the effects of treatment strength information on teachers' pretreatment acceptability ratings of overcorrection and modeling-coaching procedures for social behavior deficits. The variables-of-treatment strength had two levels, strong and weak, and was presented in a treatment-description narrative accompanied by a graph illustrating the target child's and a comparison normal peer's behavior over a 12-week period. The results confirmed the hypothesis that meaningful treatment strength information does affect teachers' pretreatment ratings of acceptability. When given a treatment that was described as being strong and successful, teachers rated it higher than if the treatment had been described as weak and relatively unsuccessful. Thus, the effects of strength of outcome information on BIRS ratings appear strong. Given the relatively low level of acceptability of overcorrection, it was rated higher in terms of acceptability and effectiveness when teachers were informed that it had been effective. Conversely, teachers' ratings of modeling/coaching, which was viewed as highly acceptable, were reduced when informed that the treatment had minimum effects.

There have been numerous studies examining the effects of strength of treatment information on ratings of acceptability. Prior to the Clark and Elliott study, two investigators have studied specifically this relationship (Kazdin, 1981; Von Brock, 1985). In the Kazdin study, no relationship was found between the strength of therapeutic effects and ratings of pretreatment acceptability. Some researchers (McMahon & Forehand, 1983; Witt, Elliott, & Martens, 1984) have questioned Kazdin's methodology and believe that his treatment strength variable had a restricted range and his sample of college students was unrepresentative of individuals involved in treatment decisions. The Clark and Elliott study was conducted with the Kazdin study as a general paradigm so that more information concerning the relationship between treatment effectiveness and acceptability could be obtained. The primary difference between the Kazdin (1981) study and the Clark and Elliott study was the presentation of effectiveness information. Both strong and weak therapeutic effects of outcome information were presented; however, more detailed information was provided by Clark and Elliott than by Kazdin. Another major difference in the Clark and Elliott study and Kazdin's was the inclusion of a knowledge assessment and intervention use assessment. Kazdin used undergraduate students as subjects, who may have had little experience with the treatments being presented, whereas Clark and Elliott used classroom teachers knowledgeable of behavior change principles. Also, because these teachers had teaching experience they had developed personal biases about treatments that were measured and taken into account. It is primarily because of these differences, we believe, that the results of the two studies differed. In summary, the results from the Clark and Elliott study suggested that when classroom teachers clearly understand what is being presented to them, treatment strength information does affect their acceptability of a treatment.

In addition to the three pretreatment, analogue investigations of the effectiveness → acceptability relationship we have reviewed, there has been one actual treatment study (Shapiro & Goldberg, 1986) where the posttreatment acceptability and effectiveness relationship has been examined. Briefly, these researchers were interested in children's reactions to three types of group interventions that had been used to influence their spelling achievement. Using the CIRP to operationalize treatment acceptability, Shapiro and Goldberg reported that although no differences in effectiveness in promoting spelling were found among the three different group contingencies, the sixth graders rated the independent contingency more acceptable than either the interdependent or dependent group contingency. This naturalistic, posttreatment rating of group contingencies by children is consistent with the findings of Elliott, Turco, and Gresham's (1987) analogue investigation of pretreatment acceptability.

Teacher Background Variables

In the continuing search for explanations for differential acceptance of treatments, researchers have begun to measure, control, or manipulate rater variables, such as technical knowledge of treatments, past experience with treatments, and type of education. To date, however, only four published studies have systematically considered teacher background information and its effect on treatment acceptability ratings.

Several research teams (e.g., Jeger & McClure, 1979; McMahon, Forehand, & Griest, 1981) have suggested that more positive attitudes toward behavioral techniques follow increases in knowledge of such techniques. Based on this premise, McKee (1984) set out essentially to replicate Kazdin's (1980a) investigation of the acceptability of reinforcement of incompatible behavior, positive practice, timeout from reinforcement, and medication with a group of teachers who varied in their knowledge of behavioral principles. McKee measured teachers' knowledge using a modified 16-item version of the Knowledge of Behavioral Principles as Applied to Children test (KBPAC) (O'Dell, Tarler-Benlolo, & Flynn, 1979) and was able to assign teachers to a high or low knowledge group using a median-split technique. Like Kazdin, McKee employed a Latin-Square design and used both the TEI and the Semantic Differential to assess reactions to the four treatments. The results of this study supported McKee's hypothesis that there would be differences between the knowledge groups with regard to treatment evaluations. Specifically, the teachers in the high knowledge group generally rated all treatments more acceptable on the TEI than did the teachers in the low knowledge group. This data is supportive of the understanding component in the Reimers *et al.* (1987) model of treatment acceptability in that it suggests improved acceptability and potentially increased use of treatments may be facilitated through increased familiarity with basic behavioral intervention principles.

Clark and Elliott (1986) also measured teachers' knowledge of behavioral principles as part of their investigation of treatment strength and its impact on acceptability ratings. Knowledge, however, was not a selection criterion nor manipulated variable. Rather it was measured as a means of more completely understanding a group of regular and special educators from different states. These researchers developed their own 10-item multiple-choice test over basic behavioral principles and procedures. The results of this knowledge test demonstrated the various subgroups of subjects (i.e., Nebraska special educators, Louisiana special educators, and Louisiana regular educators) were relatively knowledgeable consumers of behavioral treatments and did not differ significantly among themselves. Although limited variation in total knowledge existed, Clark and

Elliott reported statistically significant, albeit moderate, correlations between teachers' knowledge and their treatment acceptability ratings on the BIRS. Consistent with McKee's (1984) findings, these data suggest that more knowledge of behavioral treatments is predictive of relatively higher acceptance ratings for behavioral treatments.

The results of the Clark and Elliott (1986) study support a hypothesis that special and regular educators do not as groups evaluate the acceptability of treatments differently. The Clark and Elliott study, however, was a weak test of this hypothesis because of the sample's size and its regional limitations. More, if not better, data to support this no-difference-in-training hypothesis was provided in an acceptability study by Epstein, Matson, Repp, and Helsel (1986). These researchers selected regular and special educators to investigate specifically the effects of a rater's educational status and student disability type on acceptability ratings of five approaches to treatment (i.e., medication, special education, counseling, behavior modification, and effective education). The results of this study indicated no differences in the mean acceptability ratings of regular and special educators, with both rating special education programming the most acceptable and medication the least acceptable.

A final teacher background variable of interest to some researchers has been teaching experience (Witt & Robins, 1985; Witt, Moe *et al.*, 1985). Witt and his associates have reported finding an inverse relation between years of teaching experience and treatment acceptability. Specifically, in the Witt, Moe *et al.* (1984) study, which was reviewed earlier when we examined the jargon variable, years of teaching experience was found to be a significant covariate with teachers' acceptability evaluations of behavioral, pragmatic, and humanistic treatments. In general, teachers with more experience in the field seem to find all treatments less acceptable. Many yet unexamined variables can be hypothesized to account for this high-experience, low-acceptability trend. For example, changes in teacher training, changes in societal expectations about what teachers should do, and/or individuals' learning histories with classroom interventions.

Children's Treatment Preferences and Variables That Influence These Preferences

Few researchers have investigated the acceptability of interventions from a child's perspective. Notable exceptions include treatment studies by Foxx and Jones (1978), Ollendick, Matson, Esveldt-Dawson, and Shapiro (1980), and Kirigin, Braukmann, Atwater, and Wolf (1982), where anecdotal information was collected about clients' satisfaction with a treatment. Kazdin *et al.* (1981) have assessed children's acceptability of psychological treatments more directly using the Treatment Evaluation Inventory (TEI). The Kazdin *et al.* (1981) investigation was an analogue study of how child psychiatric inpatients, their parents, and the institutional staff rated the acceptability of four treatments (i.e., positive reinforcement of incompatible behavior, positive practice, medication, and timeout from reinforcement) for children with severe behavior problems. The relative ratings of acceptability for the four treatments were identical for children, parents, and staff, although children rated all treatments as less acceptable than did parents or staff members. Specifically, reinforcement of incompatible behavior was evaluated as the most acceptable treatment for a child displaying a severe behavior problem. Positive practice, medication, and timeout from reinforcement followed reinforcement of incompatible behavior in terms of acceptability ratings. A secondary but interesting finding was that children above 10 years of age rated treatments significantly more acceptable than did children below 10 years of age.

Elliott *et al.* (1986) investigated normal sixth-grade children's reactions to 12 interventions for classroom misbehaviors involving a male student who either destroyed another student's property or frequently talked out of turn. The students' acceptability ratings were documented via the Children's Intervention Rating Profile or CIRP (Witt & Elliott, 1985). The alternative treatments that were rated by 79 sixth graders were private reprimand by teacher, public reprimand by teacher, private praise by teacher, public praise by teacher, individual loses recess, individual gains extra recess, whole class loses recess, whole class gains extra recess, individual stays in for recess, individual goes to a quiet room, individual goes to principal's office, and individual earns rewards via a point system. These 12 treatments were classified either as a verbal, a reinforcement, or a traditional intervention and were designed to vary on dimensions of individual-group and positive reinforcement-negative reinforcement. Elliott and his associates found sixth graders rated the acceptability of the 12 interventions very differently. Specifically, interventions that emphasized individual teacher–student interactions, or group reinforcement, or negative sanctions for the misbehaving child were rated as most acceptable. Public reprimands of an individual and negative contingencies for a group when only one child misbehaved were rated as unacceptable interventions by sixth graders. The four traditional interventions (i.e., principal's office, point system, staying in during recess, quiet room) as a group were rated the most acceptable methods when compared to the behavioral interventions. A final finding by Elliott *et al.* (1986) was that behavior problem severity did not significantly impact sixth-grade students' ratings of interventions except for the traditional interventions.

Following the Elliott *et al.* (1986) study, Turco and Elliott (1986) investigated the influence of children's developmental level and gender on their acceptability ratings of interventions. These researchers had 693 fifth-, seventh-, and ninth-grade students complete the CIRP in response to 12 intervention methods to correct classroom behavior problems. In general, students at all three grades rated home-based interventions as the most acceptable method and rated public reprimand as an unacceptable method for changing another student's behavior. The responses to the other interventions were variable across grades. For example, fifth graders rated private and public praise as highly acceptable methods for changing behavior, but seventh and ninth graders rated private praise as an unacceptable method. Self-monitoring is usually more desirable for older than younger children, yet only fifth graders rated it an acceptable treatment. Loss of free time or recess was evaluated as an unacceptable method for changing behavior by the fifth graders, but was rated as very acceptable by the seventh and ninth graders (these seventh graders had a free activities period, however, the ninth graders did not). Only ninth graders indicated a sensitivity to selecting intervention methods based on the severity of the problem and the gender of the respondent. The researchers concluded that caution is warranted when making generalizations about the acceptability of various intervention methods given the influence of grade, gender, and problem severity on acceptability ratings.

Given the perceived popularity of group contingency interventions among teachers' and children's differential acceptability responses to group contingency methods (Elliott *et al.*, 1986; Turco & Elliott, 1986), a more detailed investigation of various types of group contingency methods was undertaken by Elliott, Turco, Evans, and Gresham (1984). A sample of 660 black and white, male and female, fifth graders responded via the CIRP to one of three problem severities (i.e., two children being disruptive, half a class being disruptive, a whole class being disruptive) and one of the three group contingency methods. Significant results were observed for interactions between rater's gender and problem behavior severity and rater's race and problem behavior severity. The major new findings of this study of treatment acceptability were (a) female students rated the three forms of group contingency interventions less acceptable than males as the severity of the problem increased, (b) black students, in general, rated group contingency interventions significantly more acceptable than white students, and (c) the three forms of group contingency interventions were rated acceptable in an absolute sense and were not rated as significantly different. These findings highlight the impact of two basic individual differences, race and gender, on children's acceptability judgments of interventions, and reinforce a common perception that group contingency interventions are generally acceptable to children.

According to Elliott (1986), under the constraints of the research methodology one can offer the following integrative guidelines to summarize the research on children's treatment acceptability:

> (a) children differentially evaluate the acceptability of interventions with younger children preferring positive interventions and/or the interventions modeled by adults in their environment and older children rating more aversive and/or non-traditional interventions as acceptable; (b) children's sex and racial-ethnic background seem to affect intervention acceptability ratings differentially; and (c) the severity of the target problem generally is not important for younger children, but does influence adolescents' acceptability ratings. These conclusions are subject to further investigation and under varying methodologies. (Elliott, 1986, p. 31)

Summary of Past Research Findings with Recommendations for Future Research

The majority of the research on treatment acceptability has been published in the last 5 years. Much of this research has been concerned with simply measuring the construct of treatment acceptability and cataloguing consumers' acceptance of an array of treatments for children exhibiting inappropriate behavior. However, with each new study additional variables are being investigated. In this chapter, findings from 20 empirical studies of treatment acceptability and several secondary investigations that complement these studies were examined with the intent to understand further the specific variables that affect teachers' evaluations of treatments. These 20 studies are summarized in Table 2.

I acknowledge that acceptability research is at a rather rudimentary level; however, based on the studies reviewed, the following four general conclusions seem warranted. First, a meaningful methodology exists for quantifying consumers' and clients' evaluations of treatments. Second, treatment acceptability is a complex construct that is influenced by several salient child, teacher, and psychologist variables. Third, under most conditions the typical educational consumers evaluate positive treatments relatively more acceptable than reductive treatments. Fourth, a moderate to strong positive relation exists between pretreatment acceptability and perceived treatment effectiveness.

Research on consumers' acceptability of treatment procedures is relevant to successful consultation in education. Although the findings do not provide a direct prescription for selecting a treatment, they do provide a conceptual organizer and sensitize a consultant and consultee to a list of variables that require consideration prior to the implementation of a treatment. At a very basic level, treatments can be evaluated on two dimensions, acceptability and effectiveness. Witt and Elliott's (1985) Intervention Decision Matrix (see Figure 3) provides a picture of how these two dimensions interact and can serve as a starting point when initially brainstorming treatments with a teacher. Ideally, only those treatments with a history of documented effectiveness should be considered, thus narrowing pretreatment discussion to issues of acceptability. At this point a consultant can begin to assess the consultee's philosophy about treatments (e.g., reinforcement vs. punishment; teacher initiated vs. psychologist or parent initiated; individual vs. group), his or her treatment knowledge and skills, time and material resources, and past experience with treatments.

Table 2. Summary of Research on Treatment Acceptability

Authors	Year	Subjects	Type of study	Independent variable(s)	Dependent measure(s)	Major findings
Kazdin, A. E.	1980(a)	Undergraduate college students	Analogue	Four alternative behavior interventions	Treatment Evaluation Inventory (TEI); Semantic Differential	Interventions differed markedly in acceptability ratings, with positive treatments being rated more favorably than reductive.
Kazdin, A. E.	1980(b)	Undergraduate college students	Analogue	Four alternative behavioral interventions	Treatment Evaluation Inventory (TEI); Semantic Differential	In Exp. 1: Reinforcement of incompatible behavior and nonexclusionary forms of time-out were rated as more acceptable than isolation. In Exp. 2: Isolation was more acceptable when included in a contingency context, and when used to back up another form of time-out than when used by itself.
Kazdin, A. E.	1981	Undergraduate college students	Analogue	Four alternative behavioral interventions	Treatment Evaluation Inventory (TEI); Semantic Differential	In Exp. 1: Effectiveness of treatments in altering behavior did not influence acceptability ratings, but did influence strength of treatment. In Exp. 2: Presence of adverse side effects markedly influenced acceptability ratings.
Kazdin, A. E. French, N. H. Sherick, R. B.	1981	Child psychiatric inpatients; parents, and staff members.	Analogue	Four alternative behavioral interventions	Treatment Evaluation Inventory (TEI); Semantic Differential	Treatments varied in their overall acceptability, with positive treatments abeing rated as most acceptable. Children rated treatments as less acceptable than their parents.
Witt, J. C. Martens, B. K.	1983	Preservice and student teachers	Analogue	Six alternative behavioral interventions	Intervention Rating Profile (IRP)	Judgments of the acceptability of classroom interventions are comprised of one major and four secondary components. Results indicated that positive interventions requiring low amounts of teacher time and applied to a mild behavior problem were viewed as most acceptable.

(continued)

Table 2. *(Continued)*

Authors	Year	Subjects	Type of study	Independent variable(s)	Dependent measure(s)	Major findings
Witt, J. C. Elliott, S. N. Martens, B. K.	1984	Preservice and student teachers	Analogue	Intervention type (pos. vs. red.), teacher time involvement, and behavior problem severity	Intervention Rating Profile (IRP)	Those interventions that were positive and required less teacher time were viewed as most acceptable. Severity of the behavior problem did not significantly influence ratings of acceptability.
McKee	1984	Regular education teachers	Analogue	Teacher's knowledge of behavior principles, type of problem, and type of intervention	Treatment Evaluation Inventory (TEI); Semantic Differential	High knowledge group teachers rated treatments more acceptable than low knowledge group teachers. Treatments were rated differentially with reinforcement significantly more acceptable than time-out and positive practice. Ratings were not different for the different problem cases.
Witt, J. C. Martens, B. K. Elliott, S. N.	1984	School teachers (K-12)	Analogue	Intervention type, teacher time involvement, and behavior problem severity	Intervention Rating Profile (IRP)	Interventions which required more time to implement were viewed as least acceptable to teachers.
Elliott, S. N. Witt, J. C. Galvin, G. Peterson, R.	1984	Regular and special education teachers	Analogue	Intervention complexity, behavior problem severity	Intervention Rating Profile (IRP)	Acceptability ratings varied with severity of problem behavior. Interventions which required less time were viewed as most acceptable. Positive treatments were viewed as more acceptable than reductive techniques.
Witt, J. C. Moe, G. Gutkin, T. B. Andrews, L.	1984	Regular and special education teachers	Analogue	Jargon of Tx description, behavior problem severity, teacher experience	Intervention Rating Profile (IRP)	Pragmatic description was viewed as more acceptable than behavioral or humanistic descriptions. Interventions were rated as more acceptable when the problem was severe. Highly experienced teachers rated interventions as less aceptable.

Martens, B. K. Witt, J. C. Elliott, S. N. Darveaux, D.	1985	Regular and special education teachers	Analogue	Behavior problem severity, interventionist, case intervention modality	Intervention Rating Profile-15 (IRP-15); Semantic Differential	Intervention requiring moderate amounts of time were viewed as most acceptable. Interventions were rated as more acceptable when the problem behavior was severe.
Witt, J. C. Robbins, J. R.	1985	Regular education, preschool, and Headstart teachers	Analogue	Type of intervention, behavior problem severity, teacher experience, interventionist	Intervention Rating Profile (IRP)	Positive interventions were rated as more acceptable than reductive strategies. Teahcers with less experience rated interventions as more acceptable than experienced teachers.
Cavell, T. A. Frentz, C. E. Kelley, M. L.	1986a	Middle and high school teachers	Analogue	Paradoxical treatments	Treatment Evaluation Inventory (TEI)	Teachers rated paradoxical procedures generally unacceptable and significantly lower than an unsuccessful contingency contract. Ratings of the four paradoxical conditions varied according to rationale.
Cavell, T. A. Frentz, C. E. Kelley, M. L.	1986b	Middle and high school teachers	Analogue	Withdrawal of treatments	Treatment Evaluation Inventory (TEI)	Acceptability of withdrawal conditions varied with respect to rationale.
Epstein, M. H. Matson, J. L. Repp, A. Helsel, W. J.	1986	Regular and special educators	Analogue	Five alternative treatment approaches	Treatment Evaluation Inventory (TEI)	In two experiments, results indicated that teachers could distinguish between treatments on the basis of their acceptability. No differences were found between regular and special education teachers or between children labeled as mentally retarded or learning disabled.
Frentz, C. Kelley, M. L.	1986	Mothers of children between the ages of 2 and 12	Analogue	Five alternative (reductive) Tx interventions	Treatment Evaluation Inventory (TEI)	Treatments were rated as more acceptable when applied to a more severe behavior problem.

(continued)

Table 2. (*Continued*)

Authors	Year	Subjects	Type of study	Independent variable(s)	Dependent measure(s)	Major findings
Von Brock, M. B. Elliott, S. N.	1987	Regular education teachers	Analogue	Behavior problem severity, intervention type, outcome information	Behavior Intervention Rating Scale (BIRS); Semantic Differential	The BIRS reliably measures acceptability and effectiveness, and treatment outcome information was shown to influence ratings of treatments.
Elliott, S. N. Turco, T. L. Gresham, F. M.	1987	Regular education teacher	Analogue	Rater, behavior problem severity, intervention type, and sex of rater	Children's Intervention Rating Profile (CIRP); Intervention Rating Profile (IRP)	Children rated all 3 types of group contingencies acceptable, whereas teachers and psychologists rated dependent group contingencies unacceptable and independent and interdependent forms acceptable.
Clark, L. Elliott, S. N.	1987	Regular and special education teachers	Analogue	Behavior problem type, intervention type, outcome information, and teacher's intervention knowledge	Behavior Intervention Rating Scale (BIRS); Teacher's Intervention Use Assessment	Teachers preferred modeling-coaching to overcorrection for social skills problems, and treatment outcome information significantly influenced ratings of both acceptability and effectiveness.
Shapiro, E. S. Goldberg, R.	1987	Sixth graders	Naturalistic	Type of group contingency	Children's Intervention Rating Profile (CIRP); spelling performance	Group contingencies did not differentially effect spelling performance, however, sixth graders rated the independent group contingency more acceptable than the interdependent or dependent group contingency.

Note. From "Acceptability of Behavioral Treatment Interventions: A Review of the Literature" by T. M. Reimers, D. P. Wacker, and G. Koeppl, 1987, *School Psychology Review, 16*, pp. 212–227. Copyright 1987 by the National Association of School Psychologists. Adapted by permission.

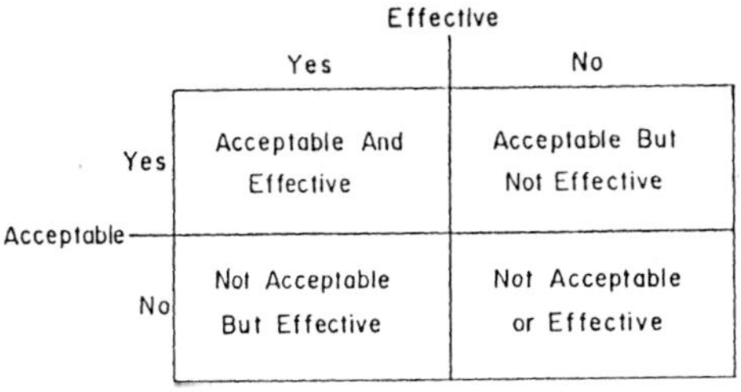

Figure 3. The Intervention Decision Matrix. Reprinted with permission.

Future researchers would contribute significantly to the refinement of treatment acceptability by investigating it naturalistically in a consultative context. Such a context affords information on variables that researchers have indicated affect consumers' evaluations of treatments, thus providing a strong test of the generalizability of analogue, pretreatment acceptability findings.

Most researchers have taken a majority approach (Garfield, 1983) to the study of treatment acceptability. With this approach we learn what treatments the majority of the consumers prefer, but are at risk of overlooking a significant minority of consumers' evaluations. We have learned that consumers varying in their knowledge of behavioral principles differentially rate the acceptability of treatments. This argues for much more attention to subjects' background information in our research and also for more single-subject investigations.

We still do not know enough about the pretreatment acceptability → posttreatment effectiveness link for a specific case, nor the average effectiveness → pretreatment acceptability link for cases in general. Knowledge of the causal relationships between these variables is central to the future vitality of acceptability research and to consultative practices with teachers.

Appendix

The Treatment Evaluation Inventory[1]

Please complete the items listed below. The items should be completed by placing a checkmark on the line under the question that best indicates how you feel about the treatment. Please read the items very carefully because a checkmark accidentally placed on one space rather than another may not represent the meaning you intended.

1. How acceptable do you find this treatment to be for the child's problem behavior?

___	___	___	___	___	___	___
Not at all acceptable			Moderately acceptable			Very acceptable

2. How willing would you be to carry out this procedure yourself if you had to change the child's problems?

___	___	___	___	___	___	___
Not at all willing			Moderately willing			Very willing

3. How suitable is this procedure for children who might have other behavioral problems than those described for this child?

___	___	___	___	___	___	___
Not at all suitable			Moderately suitable			Very suitable

[1]From "Acceptability of Alternative Treatments for Deviant Child Behavior" by A. E. Kazdin, 1980, *Journal of Applied Behavior Analysis*, 13, pp. 259–273. Copyright 1982 by *Journal of Applied Behavior Analysis*. Reprinted by permission.

4. If children had to be assigned to treatment without their consent, how bad would it be to give them *this* treatment?

______	______	______	______	______	______	______
Very bad			Moderately			Not bad at all

5. How cruel or unfair do you find this treatment?

______	______	______	______	______	______	______
Very cruel			Moderately cruel			Not cruel at all

6. Would it be acceptable to apply this procedure to institutionalized children, the mentally retarded, or other individuals who are not given an opportunity to choose treatment for themselves?

______	______	______	______	______	______	______
Not at all acceptable to apply this procedure			Moderately acceptable			Very acceptable to apply this procedure

7. How consistent is this treatment with common sense or everyday notions about what treatment should be?

______	______	______	______	______	______	______
Very different or inconsistent			Moderately consistent			Very consistent with everyday notions

8. To what extent does this procedure treat the child humanely?

______	______	______	______	______	______	______
Does not treat humanely at all			Treats them moderately humanely			Treats them very humanely

9. To what extent do you think there might be risks in undergoing this kind of treatment?

______	______	______	______	______	______	______
Lot of risks are likely			Some risks are likely			No risks are likely

10. How much do you like the procedures used in this treatment?

______	______	______	______	______	______	______
Do not like them at all			Moderately like them			Like them very much

11. How effective is this treatment likely to be?

______	______	______	______	______	______	______
Not at all effective			Moderately effective			Very effective

12. How likely is this treatment to make permanent improvements in the child?

______	______	______	______	______	______	______
Unlikely			Moderately			Very likely

13. To what extent are *un*desirable side effects likely to result from this treatment?

______	______	______	______	______	______	______
Many undesirable side effects likely			Some undesirable side effects likely			No undesirable side effects would occur

14. How much discomfort is the child likely to experience during the course of treatment?

______	______	______	______	______	______	______
Very much discomfort			Moderate discomfort			No discomfort at all

15. Overall, what is your general reaction to this form of treatment?

______	______	______	______	______	______	______
Very negative			Ambivalent			Very positive

Intervention Rating Profile—20 (IRP-20)[2]

The purpose of this questionnaire is to obtain information that wil aid in selection of classroom interventions. These interventions will be used by teachers of children with behavior problems. Please circle the number which best describes your agreement or disagreement with each statement.

	Strongly disagree	Disagree	Slightly disagree	Slightly agree	Agree	Strongly agree
1. Teachers are likely to use this intervention because it requires few technical skills.	1	2	3	4	5	6
2. Teachers are likely to use this intervention because it requires little training to implement effectively.	1	2	3	4	5	6
3. Most teachers would find the intervention suitable for the behavior problem described.	1	2	3	4	5	6
4. Most teachers would find this intervention appropriate for behavior problems in addition to the one described.	1	2	3	4	5	6
5. The child's behavior problem is severe enough to warrant use of this intervention.	1	2	3	4	5	6
6. This intervention would be appropriate for use *before* making a referral.	1	2	3	4	5	6
7. This intervention would not be difficult to implement in a classroom with 30 other students.	1	2	3	4	5	6
8. This intervention is practical in the amount of time required for parent contact.	1	2	3	4	5	6
9. This intervention is practical in the amount of time required for contact with school staff.	1	2	3	4	5	6

[2]From "Assessing the Acceptability of Behavioral Interventions Used in Classrooms" by J. C. Witt and B. K. Martens, 1983, *Psychology in the Schools, 20,* pp. 510–517. Copyright 1983 by *Psychology in the Schools*. Reprinted by permission.

	Strongly disagree	Disagree	Slightly disagree	Slightly agree	Agree	Strongly agree
10. This intervention is practical in the amount of time required for record keeping.	1	2	3	4	5	6
11. This intervention is practical in the amount of out-of-school time required for implementation.	1	2	3	4	5	6
12. This intervention would not be disruptive to other students.	1	2	3	4	5	6
13. It would not be difficult to use this intervention and still meet the needs of other children in a classroom.	1	2	3	4	5	6
14. This intervention should prove effective in changing the child's problem behavior.	1	2	3	4	5	6
15. This would be an acceptable intervention for the child's problem behavior.	1	2	3	4	5	6
16. This intervention would not result in negative side effects for the child.	1	2	3	4	5	6
17. This intervention would not result in risk to the child.	1	2	3	4	5	6
18. This intervention would not be considered a "last resort."	1	2	3	4	5	6
19. Overall, this intervention would be beneficial for the child.	1	2	3	4	5	6
20. I would be willing to use this intervention in the classroom setting.	1	2	3	4	5	6

Intervention Rating Profile—(IRP-15)[3]

The purpose of this questionnaire is to obtain information that will aid in the selection of classroom interventions. These interventions will be used by teachers of children with behavior problems. Please circle the number which best describes your agreement or disagreement with each statement.

	Strongly disagree	Disagree	Slightly disagree	Slightly agree	Agree	Strongly agree
1. This would be an acceptable intervention for the child's problem behavior.	1	2	3	4	5	6
2. Most teachers would find this intervention appropriate for behavior problems in addition to the one described.	1	2	3	4	5	6
3. This intervention should prove effective in changing the child's problem behavior.	1	2	3	4	5	6
4. I would suggest the use of this intervention to other teachers.	1	2	3	4	5	6

[3]From "Acceptability of Classroom Management Strategies" by J. C. Witt and S. N. Elliott, 1985. In T. R. Kratochwill (Ed.), *Advances in School Psychology* (Vol. 4, pp. 251–288). Copyright 1985 by Lawrence Erlbaum Associates, Inc. Reprinted by permission.

	Strongly disagree	Disagree	Slightly disagree	Slightly agree	Agree	Strongly agree
5. The child's behavior problem is severe enough to warrant use of this intervention.	1	2	3	4	5	6
6. Most teachers would find this intervention suitable for the behavior problem described.	1	2	3	4	5	6
7. I would be willing to use this intervention in the classroom setting.	1	2	3	4	5	6
8. This intervention would *not* result in negative side-effects for the child.	1	2	3	4	5	6
9. This intervention would be appropriate for a variety of children.	1	2	3	4	5	6
10. This intervention is consistent with those I have used in classroom settings.	1	2	3	4	5	6
11. The intervention was a fair way to handle the child's problem behavior.	1	2	3	4	5	6
12. This intervention is reasonable for the behavior problem described.	1	2	3	4	5	6
13. I liked the procedures used in this intervention.	1	2	3	4	5	6
14. This intervention was a good way to handle this child's behavior problem.	1	2	3	4	5	6
15. Overall, this intervention would be beneficial for the child.	1	2	3	4	5	6

The Children's Intervention Rating Profile (CIRP)[4]

	I agree					I do not agree
1. The method used to deal with the behavior problem was fair.						
2. This child's teacher was too harsh on him.						
3. The method used to deal with the behavior may cause problems with this child's friends.						
4. There are better ways to handle this child's problem than the one described here.						
5. The method used by this teacher would be a good one to use with other children.						
6. I like the method used for this child's behavior problem.						
7. I think that the method used for this problem would help this child do better in school.						

[4]From "Acceptability of Classroom Management Strategies" by J. C. Witt and S. N. Elliott, 1985. In T. R. Kratochwill (Ed.), *Advances in School Psychology* (Vol. 4, pp. 251–288). Copyright 1985 by Lawrence Erlbaum Associates, Inc. Reprinted by permission.

References

Algozzine, B., Ysseldyke, J. E., Christenson, S., & Thurlow, M. (1982). *Teachers' intervention choices for children exhibiting different behaviors in school.* Minneapolis, MN: University of Minnesota, Institute for Research on Learning Disabilities.

Bergan, J. R. (1977). *Behavioral consultation.* Columbus, OH: Merrill.

Budd, K. S., & Baer, D. M. (1976). Behavior modification and the law: Implications of recent judicial decisions. *Journal of Psychiatry and Law, 4,* 171–244.

Cavell, T. A., Frentz, C. E., & Kelley, M. L. (1986a). Consumer acceptability of the single case withdrawal design: Penalty for early withdrawal? *Behavior Therapy, 17,* 82–87.

Cavell, T. A., Frentz, C. E., & Kelley, M. L. (1986b). Acceptability of paradoxical interventions: Some nonparadoxical findings. *Professional Psychology: Research and Practice, 17,* 519–523.

Clark, L., & Elliott, S. N. (1986). *The influence of treatment strength information of knowledgeable teachers' pretreatment evaluations of social skills training methods.* Manuscript submitted for publication.

Elliott, S. N. (1986). Children's ratings of the acceptability of classroom interventions for misbehavior: Findings and methodological considerations. *Journal of School Psychology, 24,* 23–35.

Elliott, S. N., Witt, J. C., Galvin, G., & Peterson, R. (1984). Acceptability of positive and reductive interventions: Factors that influence teachers' decisions. *Journal of School Psychology, 22,* 353–360.

Elliott, S. N., Turco, T. L., Evans, S., & Gresham, F. M. (1984, November). *Group contingency interventions: Children's acceptability ratings.* Paper presented at the annual convention of the Association for the Advancement of Behavior Therapy, Philadelphia.

Elliott, S. N., Witt, J. C., Galvin, G. A., & Moe, G. L. (1986). Children's involvement in intervention selection: Acceptability of interventions for misbehaving peers. *Professional Psychology: Research and Practice, 17,* 235–241.

Elliott, S. N., Turco, T. L., & Gresham, F. M. (1987). Consumers' and clients' pretreatment acceptability ratings of classroom-based group contingencies. *Journal of School Psychology, 25,* 145–154.

Epstein, M. H., Matson, J. L., Repp, A., & Helsel, W. J. (1986). Acceptability of treatment alternatives as a function of teacher status and student level. *School Psychology Review, 15,* 84–90.

Foxx, R. M., & Jones, J. R. (1978). A remediation program for increasing the spelling achievement of elementary and junior high school students. *Behavior Modification, 2,* 211–230.

Frentz, C., & Kelley, M. L. (1986). Parents' acceptance of reductive treatment methods: The influence of problem severity and perception of child behavior. *Behavior Therapy, 17,* 75–81.

Garfield, S. (1983). Some comments on consumer satisfaction in behavior therapy. *Behavior Therapy, 14,* 237–241.

Hersh, R. H., & Walker, H. M. (1983). Great expectations: Making schools effective for all students. *Policy Studies Review, 23,* 147–186.

Jeger, A. M., & McClure, G. (1979). Attitudinal effects of undergraduate behavioral training. *Teaching of Psychology, 6,* 226–228.

Johnston, J. M. (1972). Punishment of human behavior. *American Psychologist, 27,* 1033–1054.

Kazdin, A. E. (1977). Assessing the clinical or applied significance of behavior change through social validation. *Behavior Modification, 1,* 427–452.

Kazdin, A. E. (1980a). Acceptability of alternative treatments for deviant child behavior. *Journal of Applied Behavior Analysis, 13,* 259–273.

Kazdin, A. E. (1980b). Acceptability of time-out from reinforcement procedures for disruptive child behavior. *Behavior Therapy, 11,* 329–344.

Kazdin, A. E. (1981). Acceptability of child treatment techniques: The influence of treatment efficacy and adverse side effects. *Behavior Therapy, 12,* 493–506.

Kazdin, A. E. (1984). Acceptability of aversive procedures and medication as treatment alternatives for deviant child behavior. *Journal of Abnormal Child Psychology, 2,* 289–302.

Kazdin, A. E., & Cole, P. M. (1981). Attitudes and labeling biases toward behavior modification: The effects of labels, content, and jargon. *Behavior Therapy, 12,* 56–68.

Kazdin, A. E., French, N. H., & Sherick, R. B. (1981). Acceptability of alternative treatments for children: Evaluation of inpatient children, parents, and staff. *Journal of Consulting and Clinical Psychology, 49,* 900–907.

Kirigin, K. A., Braukmann, C. J., Atwater, J. D., & Wolf, M. M. (1982). An evaluation of teaching-family (Achievement Place) group homes for juvenile offenders. *Journal of Applied Behavior Analysis, 15,* 1–16.

Martens, B. K., Witt, J. C., Elliott, S. N., & Darveaux, D. (1985). Teacher judgements concerning the acceptability of school based interventions. *Professional Psychology: Research and Practice, 16,* 191–198.

Martens, B. K., Peterson, R. L., Witt, J. C., & Cirone, S. (1986). Teacher perceptions of school-based intervention: Ratings of intervention effectiveness, ease of use, and frequency of use. *Exceptional Children, 53,* 213–223.

McKee, W. T. (1984). *Acceptability of alternative classroom treatment strategies and factors affecting teachers' ratings.* Unpublished master's thesis, University of British Columbia, Vancouver, Canada.

McMahon, R. J., & Forehand, R. L. (1983). Consumer satisfaction in behavioral treatment for children: Types, issues, and recommendations. *Behavior Therapy, 14,* 209–225.

McMahon, R. J., Forehand, R., & Griest, D. L. (1981).

Effects of knowledge of social learning principles on enhancing treatment outcome and generalization in a parent training program. *Journal of Consulting and Clinical Psychology, 49,* 526–532.

Melton, G. G. (1983). Decision making by children: Psychological risks and benefits. In G. B. Melton, G. P. Koocher, & M. J. Saks (Eds.), *Children's competence to consent* (pp. 137–159). New York: Plenum Press.

Minkin, N., Braukmann, J. C., Minkin, B. L., Timbers, G. D., Timbers, B. J., Fixen, D. L., Phillips, E. L., & Wolf, M. M. (1976). The social validation and training of conversation skills. *Journal of Applied Behavior Analysis, 9,* 127–139.

O'Dell, S. L., Tarler-Benlolo, L., & Flynn, J. M. (1979). An instrument to measure knowledge of behavioral principles as applied to children. *Journal of Behavior Therapy and Experimental Psychiatry, 10,* 29–34.

O'Leary, K. D. (1984). The image of behavior therapy: It is time to take a stand. *Behavior Therapy, 15,* 219–233.

Ollendick, T. H., Matson, J. L. Esveldt-Dawson, K. & Shapiro, E. S. (1980). Increasing spelling achievement: An analysis of treatment procedures utilizing an alternative treatments design. *Journal of Applied Behavior Analysis, 13,* 645–654.

Reimers, T. M., Wacker, D. P., & Koeppl, G. (1987). Acceptability of behavioral treatments: A review of the literature. *School Psychology Review, 16,* 212–227.

Reppucci, N. D., & Saunders, J. T. (1974). The social psychology of behavior modification: Problems of implementation in natural settings. *American Psychologist, 29,* 649–660.

Rhodes, M. (in preparation). *Influence of psychologist's involvement and jargon on teachers' ratings of treatments.* Study in progress.

Shapiro, E. S., & Goldberg, R. (1986). A comparison of group contingencies for increasing spelling performance among sixth grade students. *School Psychology Review, 15,* 546–557.

Stolz, S. B. (1981). Adoption of innovations from applied behavioral research: "Does anybody care?" *Journal of Applied Behavior Analysis, 14,* 491–505.

Strong, S. R. (1984). Experimental studies in explicitly paradoxical interventions: Results and implications. *Journal of Behavior Therapy and Experimental Psychiatry, 15,* 189–194.

Turco, T. L., & Elliott, S. N. (1986a). Assessment of students' acceptability of teacher-initiated interventions for classroom misbehaviors. *Journal of School Psychology, 24,* 307–313.

Turco, T. L., & Elliott, S. N. (1986b). Students' acceptability ratings of interventions for classroom misbehaviors: A developmental study of well-behaving and misbehaving youth. *Journal of Psychoeducational Assessment, 4,* 281–289.

U.S. Congress, House Committee on the Judiciary, Subcommittee on Courts, Civil Liberties, and the Administration of Justice (1974a). *Oversight hearing: Behavior modification programs in the Federal Bureau of Prisons.* 93rd Cong., 2nd sess., February 27, 1974 (Serial No. 26). Washington, DC: U.S. Goverment Printing Office.

U.S. Congress, Senate Committee on the Judiciary, Subcommittee on Constitutional Rights (1974b). *Individual rights and the federal role in behavior modification.* 93rd Cong., 2nd sess., November 1974. Washington, DC: U.S. Government Printing Office.

Von Brock, M. B. (1985). *The influence of effectiveness information on teachers' ratings of acceptability.* Unpublished master's thesis, Louisiana State University, Baton Rouge, LA.

Von Brock, M. B., & Elliott, S. N. (1987). The influence of treatment effectiveness information on the acceptability of classroom interventions. *Journal of School Psychology, 25,* 131–144.

Willner, A. G., Braukmann, C. J., Kirigin, K. A., Fixen, D. L., Phillips, E. L., & Wolf, M. M. (1977). The training and validation of youth-preferred social behaviors with child-care personnel. *Journal of Applied Behavior Analysis, 10,* 219–230.

Wilson, G. L., & Bornstein, P. H. (1984). Paradoxical procedures and single-case methodology: Review and recommendations. *Journal of Behavior Therapy and Experimental Psychiatry, 15,* 195–204.

Witt, J. C., & Elliott, S. N. (1983, August). *Assessing the acceptability of behavioral interventions.* Paper presented at the annual meeting of the American Psychological Association, Anaheim, CA.

Witt, J. C., & Elliott, S. N. (1985). Acceptability of classroom management strategies. In T. R. Kratochwill (Ed.), *Advances in school psychology* (Vol. 4, pp. 251–288). Hillsdale, NJ: Erlbaum.

Witt, J. C., & Martens, B. K. (1983). Assessing the acceptability of behavioral interventions used in classrooms. *Psychology in the Schools, 20,* 510–517.

Witt, J. C., & Robbins, J. R. (1985). Acceptability of reductive interventions for the control of inappropriate child behavior. *Journal of Abnormal Child Psychology, 13,* 59–67.

Witt, J. C., Elliott, S. N., & Martens, B. K. (1984). Acceptability of behavioral interventions used in classrooms: The influence of teacher time, severity of behavior problem, and type of intervention. *Behavioral Disorders, 10,* 95–104.

Witt, J. C., Martens, B. K., & Elliott, S. N. (1984). Factors affecting teachers' judgments of the acceptability of behavioral interventions: Time involvement, behavior problem severity, type of intervention. *Behavior Therapy, 15,* 204–209.

Witt, J. C., Moe, G., Gutkin, T. B., & Andrews, L. (1984). The effect of saying the same thing in different ways: The problem of language and jargon in school-based consultation. *Journal of School Psychology, 22,* 361–367.

Woolfolk, R. C., & Woolfolk, A. E. (1979). Modifying the

effect of the behavior modification label. *Behavior Therapy, 10,* 575–578.

Woolfolk, A. E., Woolfolk, R. C., & Wilson, G. T. (1977). A rose by any other name . . . : Labeling bias and attitudes toward behavior modification. *Journal of Consulting and Clinical Psychology, 45,* 184–191.

Wolf, M. M. (1978). Social validity: The case for subjective measurement or how applied behavior analysis is finding its heart. *Journal of Applied Behavior Analysis, 11,* 203–214.

CHAPTER 6

Developmental Factors and Their Relationship to the Identification and Treatment of Behavior Problems of Childhood

Sandra L. Harris and Michael Ferrari

A Chip off the Old Block

Larry, 4 years, 4 months old, is the third child of an intact family. He was a full-term baby born after a 5 hour labor. He weighed 8½ pounds at birth, had a strong cry, and good color. His general health has always been good and his developmental milestones well within normal limits.

Larry is upset by new changes and was distressed when his family moved to a new home about a year ago. He is reluctant to be left alone, seeking out his mother when the two of them are alone in the house. He does, however, stay with a familiar baby-sitter. His parents' major concerns are that his speech is poorly articulated and immature in content, and that he resists being taught by other people. He will not let people read to him nor does he seek answers to "why" questions.

It is of interest to note that Larry's paternal grandfather, now a judge, was slow in his language development. Family members say that Larry is much like his grandfather. The results of a Stanford-Binet revealed that Larry was functioning below age level in most areas, although his pattern was erratic with some skills far below age level and others closer to the expected performance of a 4-year-old.

It Is Hard to Find the Words

Greg is a good looking 5-year-old with a sweet smile whose speech is far below average for a boy his age. He attempts to communicate, but words come with great difficulty and he prefers to use gestures. Although he remained seated throughout the testing session, Greg had difficulty focusing on tasks for a sustained time. He glanced around a great deal, kept trying to explore the test kit, and had to be repeatedly brought back to the task at hand. His inattention seemed more suggestive of distractibility than negativism. When he was able to concentrate he gave evidence of trying quite hard to do well. After the structure of the testing situation was removed, Greg moved around the room in an almost random fashion.

Sandra L. Harris • Graduate School of Applied and Professional Psychology, Rutgers University, Piscataway, New Jersey 08854. **Michael Ferrari** • Department of Individual and Family Studies, University of Delaware, Newark, Delaware 19711.

Greg's birth and early development were uneventful. His milestones were within normal limits, although his speech was early in onset and yet never developed normally. His social skills and play behavior are immature and his behavior sometimes has a perseverative quality. He has become less of a management problem since his mother took a course in child behavior modification.

Will He Outgrow It?

At 2 years, 3 months Phil is a sturdy, good looking boy who is still in diapers. He has a history of body rocking and head banging to the point of tears. A time out procedure has decreased the self-injury. Phil is also capable of rather violent tantrums involving biting, screaming, and pinching.

Phil was the product of a full-term pregnancy. His mother did not seek medical attention until the 7th month of pregnancy. She was not conscious during the labor or delivery and is unable to provide any information about how he looked at birth. His medical history indicates he required surgery for a hernia nine hours after birth. He was a good eater, but a poor sleeper who was apparently overactive from birth. He resisted being held and was not a cuddly baby. He has always been difficult for his mother to manage. When Phil was about 12 months old his mother went to the hospital to have her appendix removed. When she came home he pushed her away and would not come close to her for days.

The family history is interesting in several respects. Phil's paternal grandmother and aunt have a history of psychosis; his mother describes herself as a poor student in school.

Phil's performance on the Bayley Scales of Infant Development showed that he was at an age-appropriate level for motor tasks and receptive language, but had almost no expressive language.

Comments

These three cases, drawn from our files of diagnostic assessments, reflect the kinds of developmental considerations the behavior therapist confronts when assessing children and their families for treatment. Larry's speech is immature. Close questioning reveals that his grandfather had a similar problem, but is now a successful judge. Is Larry likely to follow in his grandfather's footsteps? Or does his speech delay reflect other problems as well? Does the family's view of him as "just like his grandfather" intrude upon his development and create a prophesy of language delay that will be fulfilled? Or, does his being "a chip off the old block" make the family sympathetic and patient in a way they might otherwise not be?

Greg has a difficult time concentrating on the test materials during the assessment session and then wanders about the room unable to focus on any of the potentially interesting stimuli for more than a few seconds. Is this distractibility normal in a 5-year-old? Should he be given special treatment, or simply allowed to outgrow a phase of development?

Phil's background appears problematic. His mother has little income, a very limited education, and few skills for child care. There is a family history of psychosis. What shall we make of Phil's head banging, tantrums, and pronounced delay in expressive speech? Is he a child who has lacked appropriate stimulation at home? Is he genetically predisposed to psychosis? Will early intervention offer hope of avoiding later psychopathology?

Introduction

These kinds of issues make clear why it is essential for the behavior therapist to be familiar with developmental psychology. As the data base of psychology continues to grow it becomes vastly more likely that the adherents of each school of the discipline will be conscious mainly of their own body of evidence and at best aware only dimly that alternative views exist (cf. Pribram, 1977). As behavioral practitioners, we should become sensitive to this hazard and ensure that our data base enables us to evaluate behavior in its developmental context.

The purpose of the present chapter is to review some of the information available in the domain of developmental psychopathology and alert the reader to the valuable contributions of developmental psychologists to professional practice. To accomplish these objectives we will review some of the studies that have been done on the occurrence of problem behaviors in normal children. We will then focus on several specific normal problems—aggression, withdrawal, fearfulness, and overactivity—and consider how these behaviors manifest themselves in childhood and when they move into the realm of the deviant. We will also examine research on childhood predictors of adult deviance. Finally, we will discuss some guidelines for making decisions about when to intervene in a child's behavior problems.

The Prevalence of Problem Behaviors

Teachers, psychologists, and other mental health and educational personnel are frequently called on to decide whether or not a child's behavior is abnormal. Although making such discriminations when the behavior is extreme may be relatively easy, there are many situations where a more refined judgment is required. In these instances it would be useful to draw on research concerning the frequency of problem behaviors in the general child population. Although we have elsewhere criticized the lack of extensive normative data for such clinically important problem areas as assertiveness or social skills in children (Harris & Ferrari, 1983), nonetheless it is important to recognize and use normative data in those areas where they do exist.

Consider for example a teacher who complains that a child in his or her classroom is hyperactive. It is a matter of considerable significance to decide whether we ought to provide consultation for the teacher in developing a classroom program for the management of hyperactive behavior or help that teacher adjust his or her expectations about what constitutes an appropriate activity level for a child. Thus, one of our first responsibilities is to make an objective evaluation of the child's activity level and compare that to what we know about the normative behavior of children of the same age and sex. Our access to a broader data base than many teachers or parents allows us to give those individuals objective feedback about their concerns and then to work with them in planning appropriate changes in the child and/or themselves to cope with the perceived problem.

Normative Studies

One of the earliest compilations of developmental norms for children was the report of MacFarlane, Allen, and Honzik (1954), begun in 1928 in Berkeley, California. For many years this description of behavior problems among 252 children followed from birth to maturity was one of the primary sources of normative data for child's problems in growing. Many years have now passed since that early study and although some of its conclusions still offer insight into contemporary child behavior, it is important to turn to more recent surveys as well. It seems reasonable to expect that children who have grown up in an era of potential nuclear destruction, space shuttles, computer technology, televised violence, and so forth may differ in some important ways from their predecessors who lived most of their formative years before the Second World War.

When we consider the limitations of surveys on normative behavior, it is also important to note that many of these studies are based on maternal or teacher report rather than direct observation and thus may not reflect accurately the child's behavior. For example, Lapouse and Monk (1958) indicated that mothers tend to underestimate their child's fears when compared to the child's own report. There also are questions in the professional literature about differences in findings when one relies on cross-sectional as compared to longitudinal data to assess differences in children at various ages.

Infancy and Preschool Years

In spite of the methodological limits of studies on the prevalence of various problem behaviors in childhood, some consistencies do seem to emerge across studies. For example, several recent studies tend to agree that boys exhibit more behavior problems than girls and that the sheer frequency of problems declines with increasing age. Thus, Crowther, Bond, and Rolf (1981) in a survey of preschool children in Vermont day care settings found that boys demonstrated a greater frequency of externalizing and aggressive behavior than girls. They indicated that more than 20% of the boys 2 to 4 years old and 20% of 2-year-old girls exhibited very high activity levels. More than 20% of the 2- to 3-year-old boys were rated as inattentive and demanding constant adult attention. Many of these problem behaviors declined with age.

Some normative data on very young children are available from an extensive study of 418 preschool children in London (Jenkins, Bax, & Hart, 1980). In terms of sleep disturbances, there was an increase after 6 months of age with a peak at 12 to 18 months. Waking and difficulty settling down to sleep more than once most nights was found among 23% of 12-month-olds and 24% of 18-month-olds. Food fad and poor appetite appeared at around 18 months of age as children began to feed themselves and increased after 24 months of age as they gained increasing control over what they ate. At 36 months of age 7% of children were still in diapers during the day and 19% at night. By 48 months of age there were no more diapers, but 8% still wet the bed three times or more a week.

In this same study, Jenkins *et al.* (1980) found that the greatest degree of maternal concern about the child's behavior occurred at 3 years of age (23%). The percentage of children considered a problem by the child's physician as well as mother was likewise greatest at 36 months (16% mild problems, 10% moderate, 1% severe). The commonest parental complaints were difficulty in management, child needing too much attention, and tantrums. Once again, there was a higher ratio of problems for boys than girls.

Among 100 3-year-old nursery school children in an inner London borough, Coleman, Wolkind, and Ashley (1977) found that symptom scores decreased to a small extent with age. Five specific problem areas that showed a significant decline from 3 to 5 years of age were being taken into parents' bed, wet at night, wet in the day, nervous habits, and fears. They reported no prognostic significance for parental complaints at 3 and 4 years old and teacher ratings at age 5 years. There was some suggestion that overactivity in boys and difficulty in separation in girls may be predictive of problem behavior in school.

When Hughes, Pinkerton, and Plewis (1979) studied children entering infant school in inner London (mean age = 4 years, 10 months) they found 13% of them had difficulty coping with school. The most common problems, found in about 25% of the sample, were inability to stay on task without help from the teacher, problems in understanding and using language, and problems in fine motor control. Boys as a group had more problems than girls. A follow-up of these youngsters 18 months later suggested that problems in cooperation and concentration increased whereas coping with personal needs and fine motor control difficulties declined. The authors concluded that although the majority of difficulties experienced by children entering school are likely to be short-lived, there is a substantial subgroup of children for whom difficulties persist.

Elementary School Years

Among school aged children, as among preschool and kindergarten children, the pattern of greater frequency of problems for boys than girls continues (Werry & Quay, 1971). Acting out, disruptive, or immature behavior were found by Werry and Quay (1971) to be uniformly more common among boys than girls. According to the results of their survey of kindergarten through second grade children in Urbana, Illinois, 49% of the boys were described as restless, 46% as disruptive, 43% as inattentive, and 48% as distractible. The reports from other surveys of declining frequency of problems with age were likewise verified in the Werry and Quay (1971) research with findings of fewer symptoms in both boys and girls after age 5 years, and a sharp drop between 5 and 6 years of age. They conclude that there is a high frequency of problem behavior among the general population of children 5 to 8 years of age, with boys showing an average of 11.4 symptoms and girls an average of 7.6.

This finding of a high frequency of problems in the general population was likewise observed by Lapouse and Monk (1958) in an earlier survey of 6- to 12-year-old children in Buffalo, New York. They found that 43% of these children had seven or more fears or worries, 17% had wet their beds within the past year, 28% experienced nightmares, 48% lost their tempers twice a week or more, 49% were overactive, and 30% were restless. Trites, Dugas, Lynch, and Ferguson (1979) similarly reported that 20.6% of the kindergarten through sixth grade boys they surveyed in Ontario, Canada met the criteria for hyperactivity. Such repeated findings raise the question of whether these behaviors reflect psychopathology, or simply transient developmental events. It is difficult to construe a behavior observed in one quarter to one half of all children as abnormal.

Common Behavior Problems

Social Withdrawal

Shy, socially withdrawn children create concern for parents, teachers, and others who are distressed by the youngster's apparent discomfort. But do these children merit our professional concern? As Conger and Keane (1981) pointed out, although shy and withdrawn children are frequent targets of social skills training, there is little evidence that shyness *per se* is predictive of adult psychopathology. On the other hand, some forms of isolated withdrawn behavior may have more serious implications, and so it is important to make refined discriminations within the broad category of social withdrawal.

Normative Data

A cautious, somewhat withdrawn approach to new situations is common in early childhood. For example, Feldbaum, Christenson, and O'Neal (1980) watched children become assimilated into a preschool setting and noted the initially isolated style adopted by boys and girls. In the first few weeks the children were largely observers, with little parallel or cooperative play, and little verbalization to peers. Within 4 weeks the boys' activity level approximated their peers, whereas the girls were still not fully assimilated.

In terms of developmental norms for kindergarten through second grade, Werry and Quay (1971) found 16.7% of the boys and 15.5% of the girls described as withdrawn, and 14.2% of boys and 14.7% of girls called aloof. It has also been noted that there is moderate stability of isolate and social behavior from kindergarten to first grade (Rubin, Daniels-Beirness, & Bream, 1984). Nonetheless, preschool children who exhibit severe internalizing symptoms are no more likely to continue to be severely shy 7 years later than are children not labeled as disturbed preschoolers (Fischer, Rolf, Hasazi, & Cummings, 1984) thus questioning the behavioral continuity of even extreme shyness in children.

In their early study, MacFarlane and her colleagues (1954) reported shyness as a quality in 11.4% of boys and 24.1% of girls between ages 7 and 14. The peak age of shyness for boys was 12 years, with 22% of boys being described as shy, whereas for girls the peak was 11 years of age, with 37% called shy.

A more recent study by Rutter, Tizard, and Whitmore (1981) on the Isle of Wight surveyed all of the 10- to 12-year-olds living on that island in 1964 and 1965. According to parental report, 29.8% of the boys and 16.7% of the girls in the general population were described as solitary. Among those children with psychiatric diagnoses these percentages rose to 44.4% of the boys and 48.6% of the girls. Teachers gave somewhat reduced estimates with 17% of the boys and 10.1% of the girls in the general population identified as solitary, and 32.4% of the boys and 27.9% of the girls in the psychiatric population so designated.

Defining the Term

In determining the clinical significance of withdrawn, isolated behavior it is important to consider what one means by the terms. As Wanlass and Prinz (1982) point out, social isolation can be defined in terms of absence of social interaction, low sociometric status, rejection by peers, social skills deficits, active avoidance of peers, day dreaming, and passive-unassertive style. They argue that the data do not support the notion that every child with a low level of social interaction has other clinical concomitants of social withdrawal. Some socially isolated youngsters are unhappy and rejected by their peers, others may be shy but not disliked by other children, and others may be anxious and oversensitive (Wanlass & Prinz, 1982).

The Aggressive-Withdrawn Child

The value of discriminating subcategories of social withdrawal is illustrated by the research of Ledingham and Schwartzman (1984), who for 3 years followed children identified by their peers as aggressive, withdrawn, or aggressive and withdrawn. The aggressive-withdrawn and aggressive children were more likely to have failed a grade or to be in special classes on follow-up than were the withdrawn children.

In another study, Ledingham (1981) found the frequency of occurrence of aggressive-withdrawn behavior decreased with age, and that teachers regarded aggressive-withdrawn children as more deviant than normal controls or aggressive children in terms of external reliance, inattention-withdrawal, inability to change tasks easily, and slowness to complete work. Their mothers said they were more deviant in distractibility, pathological use of sense, and need for adult contact.

When Milich and Landau (1984) compared aggressive and aggressive-withdrawn children in terms of peer reactions they found the aggressive children were disruptive, popular, assertive and controlling, whereas the aggressive-withdrawn youngsters were immature, unpopular, and poorly controlled.

Based on this research it appears that a combination of aggression and withdrawal places a child in a high-risk category that merits careful attention. Ledingham (1981) speculated that some of these children may be preschizophrenics because their behavior resembles that reported about the childhood behavior of some schizophrenic adults.

Aggression

Whether in combination with behavioral withdrawal or when seen by itself, aggressive behavior in children often commands rapid professional attention, perhaps because of its overt nature and unpleasant impact on others. In fact, aggressive behavior has been characterized as one of the most easily recognized behavioral excesses of childhood (Ross, 1981).

Acts of aggression take many forms and, as we have seen, are often associated with other behaviors that in the extreme may represent serious life disturbances for a child and others in the environment. The central theme of aggression refers to intentional behavior that results in injury or destruction of an animate or inanimate object. As such, aggressive behavior may involve a physical gesture toward another person, theft or destruction of another's property, a physical attack with intention to inflict injury, or behavior characterized as verbal abuse.

It is clear from retrospective and follow-up studies (e.g., Kohlberg, LaCrosse, & Ricks, 1972; Robins, 1974; Roff & Wirt, 1984; Watt, Stolorow, Lubensky, & McClelland, 1970; Wittman & Steinberg, 1944) that overaggressive behavior in childhood can be an important predictor of overaggression, delinquency, and other psychopathological conditions in the adolescent and adult years. Thus, substantial aggression in a child has contemporaneous and long-term implications that may warrant clinical intervention.

Normative Data

As with many areas of behavioral decision making, the clinician's task of distinguishing between aggressive behavior that merits attention and aggressive behavior that can be considered normative is not simple. Once again, developmental considerations loom as important.

There is some evidence that aggressive behavior peaks in early childhood and then declines (Maccoby, 1980). However, how one defines an aggressive incident can greatly influence the interpretation of developmental trend data. For this reason, developmental psychologists have divided the spectrum of aggressive behavior into instrumental and hostile aggression (cf. Rule, 1974; Sears, Maccoby, & Levin, 1957).

In the infant to toddler years, true intentional hostile aggressive behavior is not frequent, and is primarily instrumental in nature (Dawe, 1934; Flake-Hobson, Robinson, & Skeen, 1983; Hartup, 1974). From the age of 2 to 5 years, there is a gradual decline in instrumental aggression with a concomitant increase in hostile aggression (Hartup, 1974). The appearance of elaborate threatening gestures and the focusing of aggression toward specific targets is also more commonly observed at this age (Maccoby, 1980). By the early middle-childhood years (ages 6 to 8) there is less "total" aggression than earlier, but a higher proportion of hostile than instrumental aggression (Flake-Hobson *et al.*, 1983; Hartup, 1974). Other studies suggest a greater propensity toward more stable patterns of physical aggression beyond the early childhood years and a greater likelihood that older children will use more distal forms of aggression (e.g., verbal abuse, name calling) than younger children (Feshbach, 1970; Kagan & Moss, 1962; Olweus, 1979).

Sex Differences

The identification of sex differences in patterns of aggressive behavior appears reliable and important in clinical decision making. Maccoby and Jacklin's (1974) review found boys consistently more aggressive than girls in a broad range of studies employing observational methods (e.g., McIntyre, 1972; Pedersen & Bell, 1970), experimental controls (e.g., Liebert & Baron, 1972; Rau, Stover, & Guerney, 1970), and self-rating and projective measures (e.g., Manosevitz, Prentice, & Wilson, 1973).

Many of these findings have been replicated more recently (e.g., Crowther *et al.*, 1981; Olweus, 1979; Strayer & Strayer, 1976), although the robust nature of the findings once reported in this area may no longer be as readily apparent (cf. Maccoby, 1980). This was illustrated in a recent study by Moore and Mukai (1983) of the in-home aggressive behavior of normal and control-problem children. Measures of aggressive/aversive child behavior were derived from family interaction data including physical aggression, verbal aggression, passive-dependent behavior, disobedience, and total aversive behavior. Although the study replicated many of the previous developmental findings that show decreases in total aggressive behavior beyond the preschool period, only physically aggressive behavior yielded a significant sex difference. Overall differences in the display of aggression across sex were not found.

Some of the discrepancies between earlier and more recent research on sex differences in childhood aggression may be due to cultural and cohort changes, and changes in methodologies; other mechanisms may also be operative (Achenbach, 1982). For example, Achenbach and Edelbrock (1981) suggested that data on aggression for clinical and nonclinical populations of boys and girls have often been combined and reported by sex without consideration for clinical status. In their study they found that among children referred for mental health services, boys substantially outnumbered girls in parental reports of a variety of aggressive behaviors (e.g., bullying, meanness to others, getting into fights). Interestingly, the sex differences for nonreferred children were small, showing only a slightly higher frequency of aggression in boys.

Fearfulness

Big dogs, darkness, and imaginary creatures populate the world of children, and for many youngsters generate fearful behavior. We are hardly surprised at these transient fears of early childhood and typically would not suggest professional intervention to remediate them. Nonetheless, some children do experience fears such as school phobia, social fears, and other specific phobias that move from the domain of normal childhood distress to behavior that would benefit from treatment.

Normative Data

In general, the number and kind of fears a child reports are related to age. According to MacFarlane and her colleagues (1954), the frequencies of fears show a decided downward trend over time, with an increase at age 11. As MacFarlane *et al.* (1954) noted, the subjects in their sample were 11 years old when World War II began and this may have affected the children's level of fear. Angelino and Shedd (1953) found a similar pattern of increased fears at around ages 9 to 11 years; however, more recent studies have failed to replicate this pattern (e.g., Croake, 1969; Lapouse & Monk, 1958; Russell, 1967).

In the survey by MacFarlane *et al.* (1954), boys had the highest number of fears at 3½ years (56%) and girls peaked at 3 years (67%). Across all age groups, 33.7% of boys and 25.4% of girls were reported to have specific fears.

In the Isle of Wight study (Rutter *et al.*, 1981) of 10- to 12-year-old children, the frequency of fearfulness in boys from the general population was 26.2% and for girls it was 26.8% according to parental report. Among children with a psychiatric diagnosis these figures rose to 42.9% for boys and 45.9% for girls. The estimates made by teachers were somewhat different, with 17.6% of the boys and 6% of the girls in the general population called fearful, and 24.3% of the boys and 48.8% of the girls in the psychiatric population.

The picture that emerges in terms of change in the objects of fearful behavior across ages is more consistent than the data concerning frequency of fears. Thus, MacFarlane *et al.* (1954) found fear of dogs and darkness to be the most pronounced fears of small children. Older children are less afraid of small animals (Angelino, Dollins, & Mech, 1956) and have fewer fears of darkness and imaginary creatures (Bauer, 1976) than do the younger children. As children grow older their fears tend to focus more on social situations and school (Angelino *et al.*, 1956).

Eme and Schmidt (1978) followed 27 fourth-grade children over one year and found considerable stability in terms of the number and kind of fears they expressed. The three most common fears of children in this sample were: (a) bodily harm; (b) robbers, kidnappers, or death; and (c) animals. According to the authors, 83% of the fears reported by these children were present one year later. This stability of fearfulness bears clinical significance, because it has been argued that a fear that persists for longer than 5 months merits clinical intervention (Pozanski, 1973). Were this true, most of the fourth graders in Eme and Schmidt's sample would require treatment.

A striking example of the impact of social issues on children's development is found in research on children's reactions to the threat of nuclear war or accident. Thus, Schwebel (1982) indicated that in the early 1960s, around the time of the Berlin and Cuban crises, 44% of children surveyed expected war and 95% said they cared about the danger of war. Following the Three Mile Island nuclear accident in 1979, 70% of the children studied expected a nuclear plant accident (Schwebel & Schwebel, 1981). More than half of the children anticipated serious physical consequences from such an accident.

There are few data on the question of intensity, as opposed to frequency or object, of fearfulness. Graziano, DeGiovanni, and Garcia (1979) indicated that we have no data-based way of knowing whether small children experience more global or intense fears than older children.

Sex may also be an important factor in the reporting of fearful behavior. Some research suggests that girls are more fearful than boys (e.g., Angelino *et al.*, 1956; Bamber, 1974). Nonetheless, MacFarlane and her colleagues (1954) found a somewhat higher mean level of reported fear for boys as compared to girls across all ages, and Rutter and his colleagues (1981) did not identify significant sex differences for fearfulness among children in the general population. Factors such as the nature of the questionnaire or interview used to collect data, and the definition of fearfulness, may account for these differences.

It appears to us that one of the least studied dimensions of children's fears—intensity—may be one of the most important factors in deciding whether clinical intervention is appropriate. Mild to moderate fears are a common phenomenon of childhood and typically have only a transient and superficial impact on the child's life. For some children the intensity of the fear and/or nature of the feared object assumes a central role in the child's life and dictates the need for treatment.

Overactivity

As was the case in the study of aggressiveness or fearfulness in children, the clinician monitoring the presence of overactivity, or hyperactivity as it is more often called, would do well to consult the developmental literature before deciding to intervene with this behavioral excess. Complaints from parents (e.g., "He literally climbs the walls when he has nothing to do.") cannot be our sole guide in designating overactive behavior as maladaptive. Just as we would not steadfastly use behavior checklists, reports from teachers, or results of psychometric evaluations in isolation, we cannot ignore the developmental context of activity level.

As we have seen repeatedly, many behaviors appropriate at one age are clearly inappropriate and maladaptive at a later age. Activity level is an important illustration of this concept because it is affected by many different variables (e.g., reinforcement history; O'Leary, Pelham, Rosenbaum, & Price, 1976) and is relatively unstable at early ages (Battle & Lacey, 1972; Maccoby & Feldman, 1972). Thus, it is essential that overactivity be viewed in a developmental matrix.

Normative Data

Despite a large literature concerned with the hyperactive child (e.g., Cantwell, 1975; Kenny, 1980) and the often diagnosed correlates of hyperactivity, such as attention deficit disorder (e.g., McMahon, 1984), only a few studies have tracked the developmental course of activity level in hyperactive children and most of these have examined only a narrow age range. Nonetheless, a developmental trend does seem to emerge from normative studies that suggests a decrease in activity level with increasing age. For example, in a widely cited series of studies Abikoff, Gittelman-Klein, and Klein (1977) observed classroom activity level in normal and hyperactive children and found significant negative correlations between age and gross and fine motor activity patterns. They later replicated these findings (Abikoff, Gittelman, & Klein, 1980).

Routh, Schroeder, and O'Tuama (1974), observing free-play activity level of children 3 to 9 years old, found a developmental effect of age, with older children showing decreased levels of free-play activity relative to younger children. Crowther *et al.* (1981) likewise showed a decrease of activity level in children from 2 to 4 years old. Most recently, Milich (1984) followed 47 boys ages 6.9 to 12.9 years for 2 years and found a significant negative correlation between measures of gross motor activity (fidgetiness, ankle actometer, being out of seat) and increasing age. In addition to replicating earlier findings showing a developmental trend of decrease in activity level with increasing age in middle childhood, Milich's (1984) findings are especially important as they represent one of the few longitudinal studies in the area.

In light of consistent developmental findings on activity level it is surprising that most diagnostic conceptualizations of hyperactivity do not take developmental trends into account. Even though hyperactive children may be distinguished as hyperactive more by a "lack of effectiveness in purposeful activities" (Kanter, 1982) than simple overactive motor behavior, the lack of attention to developmental data on activity level is distressing. This ignorance of developmental data is especially worrisome when combined with the tendency of some practitioners to advocate pharmacologic treatment of children at very young ages (cf. Donaldson, 1983). It does not seem an exaggeration to suggest that in some hyperactive children the efficacious component of treatment may be reducible to an overriding effect of increasing age!

Achenbach (1982) has suggested that greater attention be paid to etiological considerations in identifying and treating overactive children; he cites the examples of success of drug treatment in studies focusing on organic influences (Wender, 1971) and the success of behavioral methods in studies of environmental influences (Wolraich, Drummond, Solomon, O'Brien, & Sivage, 1978). Achenbach's (1982) suggestion might be expanded to include a recognition of developmental influences as well.

It is difficult to know how often overactivity occurs as a problem behavior. Studies of the incidence rates differ markedly in their estimates. Cantwell (1977) indicates that the diagnosis is applicable to 4% of the school-age population. The *Diagnostic and Statistical Manual* (DSM-III) (American Psychiatric Association, 1980) cites a prevalence figure of 3% for prepubertal children. Other estimates range considerably upward of these figures to a high of 10% (See Shaywitz, Kopper, & Gordon, 1978).

In addition to within-culture differences, rates of incidence of hyperactivity may vary across cultures as well. In the Isle of Wight studies (Rutter, Tizard, & Whitmore, 1970) the incidence of hyperactivity was less than 0.1%. Taylor (1980), based on a British survey, reported a 1.5% incidence rate. In a more recent study, Taylor and Sandberg (1984) used the Conners Teacher Rating Scale to compare behavior of 437 English school children to data from Australia and the United States. Surprisingly, they found English school children received higher "hyperactivity" scores than the comparison group. Taylor and Sandberg (1984) concluded that diagnostic inconsistency rather than true differences in children's behavior account for most of the anomolies in the cross-cultural rates of incidence.

Other variables beyond age are important in understanding the impact of development on activity level. A child's sex appears to be as important in this area as in some of the others we reviewed. Boys often display a higher activity level than girls, although it is not clear when this difference emerges. Despite some reports specifying boys as more active and likely to engage in gross motor and vigorous activity than girls as early as the first year (Goldberg & Lewis, 1969; Pedersen & Bell, 1970) there is not a consensus that boys are more active than girls until the preschool years (Smith & Connolly, 1972).

In the school age period boys do appear to be more active than girls (Macoby & Jacklin, 1974) and to be far more likely to receive a diagnosis of hyperactivity (Cantwell, 1975; Kanter, 1982). The sex ratio of hyperactivity varies dramatically from one source to another. The DSM-III lists 10 boys for every 1 girl as hyperactive. Many estimates of sex ratio are considerably lower, with the mean approximately four males to every one female (Barkley, 1981). Given this information is is evident that we will see far fewer hyperactive girls than boys.

Other developmental factors such as the cooccurrence of attentional problems (Harris & Ferrari, 1983) need to be underscored as important for their impact on the adjustment difficulties and treatment of the hyperactive child.

Predicting Future Psychopathology

If behavior problems are not uncommon among the general child population, it is important to know which behaviors merit our professional attention as having the power to identify children who will be troubled adults and which behaviors are simply transient developmental events. Although our data base for making prognostic statements is limited, there is some research suggesting a few consistent patterns.

One difficulty that arises when doing research in this area is that researchers often work with adults having a known diagnosis and try to reconstruct information about their childhood behavior. Such research may rely on memories of people whose recall is biased by their knowledge of the subject's current diagnosis. One improvement in this regard has been to go to impersonal records, such as school reports, to obtain the retrospective data.

Another approach to research on predictive factors in psychopathology is to follow children to adulthood. Such research requires large numbers of children to increase the likelihood of having a substantial group of disordered adults for study years later. The probability of having sufficient numbers of psychopathological adults can be increased by tracking children, such as the offspring of adult schizophrenics, who are known to be at risk for adult disorders. Although it is a long process to follow children to adulthood, one can obtain useful data along the way by looking at early childhood predictors of later childhood and adolescent behavior.

General Studies

Although many of the behavior problems of the preschool years are transient in nature, attachment behavior at one year of age does have some predictive power. Lewis, Feiring, McGuffog, and Jaskir (1984) found that boys with insecure attachment to their mothers at one year were more vulnerable to psychopathology at 6 years than were securely attached boys. This relationship was not found for girls. The authors indicate that other factors, including stressful life events and family demographic variables also influenced the later development of symptoms.

In a similar fashion, nursery school behavior has some predictive power. Chazan and Jackson (1974) followed children entering school and found that 42.5% of the youngsters initially rated as poorly adjusted still had serious problems 2 years later. When Westman, Rice, and Bermann (1967) examined the school records of 130 children from nursery school through high school they discovered that children with problems in nursery school tended to have similar problems in later school life. The most useful predictors were the child's relationships with other people, signs of behavioral eccentricity, and observed pathological family relations.

Likewise, when Fisher and her colleagues (1984) followed a group of children from preschool through elementary and junior high school they found positive correlations between internalizing and externalizing behavior in preschool years and similar behavior in later childhood. There was also a negative correlation between internalizing and externalizing preschool symptoms and later social competence. In all cases the correlations were significant, but small and therefore of limited clinical significance.

In their examination of stability and change in behavior over a 5-year period among urban children ages 6 to 18 years, Gersten, Langer, Eisenberg, Simcha-Fagan, and McCarthy (1976) concluded that it was important to intervene in cases of aggressive behavior toward family or peers, disturbances in speech, thought, or intellect before the child turned 6.

Schizophrenia

There is an interesting body of research examining the children of schizophrenic parents. Since these youngsters are at risk for the development of schizophrenia as adults, it may be especially fruitful to follow them to adulthood.

It has been demonstrated that the children of schizophrenic parents are more distractible (Harvey, Winters, Weintraub, & Neale, 1981), have lower mean perceptual sensitivity (Nuechterlein, 1983), exhibit more cognitive and attentional deficits (Winters, Stone, Weintraub, & Neale, 1981), and have more deviant speech (Harvey, Weintraub, & Neale, 1982) than do control groups of normal children. It will of course be important to follow these children to determine to what extent these deviations predict psychopathology of adulthood. Interestingly, children of unipolar, but not bipolar depressives, show a pattern similar to the children of schizophrenics (e.g., Harvey *et al.*, 1981; Harvey *et al.*, 1982; Winters *et al.*, 1981).

In a predictive study with Danish children of schizophrenic parents, teachers completed a 29-item questionnaire on the child's school behavior (John, Mednick, & Schulsinger, 1982). A 10-year follow-up identified important patterns of behavior for the children who later demonstrated marked psychopathology. Boys who later became schizophrenic were described by their teachers as presenting inappropriate school behavior and discipline problems. They were called anxious, lonely, and restrained. Borderline schizophrenic boys had been characterized as anhedonic, isolated, and distant when they were children. The pattern was somewhat different for girls. Both schizophrenic and borderline schizophrenic girls were called anhedonic, withdrawn, disengaged, and isolated. The schizophrenic girls were poorly controlled whereas the borderline schizophrenic girls were described as overly restrained.

In a retrospective study of social competence among schizophrenic and psychotically depressed adults, Lewine, Watt, Prentky, and Fryer (1980) found that the schizophrenics had received low ratings of social competence as school children. The psychotically depressed adults did not differ from the normal controls in terms of childhood social competence. Females were more socially skilled than males during childhood, regardless of adult diagnosis.

Hyperactivity

Another area of diagnostic prediction that has generated a useful literature is activity level. For example, Buss, Block, and Block (1980) studied preschool children, and on a 4-year follow-up observed a relative stability of activity level. On a personality measure the highly active children were described as taking advantage of others and asserting themselves more than the less active youngsters, who were described as shy, obedient, and compliant. Campbell, Schleifer, and Weiss (1978) similarly reported considerable stability of ratings of activity level between ages 4½ years and 6½ years for both hyperactive and normal control subjects. These authors noted that problems in infant sleep pattern were related to higher scores for conduct problems, anxiety, and dislike for school in early childhood. Infant feeding problems showed no such predictive power.

In a longer follow-up, Halverson and Waldrop (1976) reported continuing stability in activity level over 5 years for children first assessed in preschool. High activity was negatively related to cognitive and intellectual performance at age 7½ years. On the other hand, intense social participation was positively related to intellectual performance and it is therefore important to discriminate high social interaction from high motor activity.

The finding of continued problems for hyperactive preschool children in elementary school was verified by Campbell, Endman, and Bernfeld (1977), who observed that children originally identified as hyperactive had more negative feedback from elementary school teachers, were more disruptive, were rated by their teachers as hyperactive, and had lower self-esteem.

Unhappily, the school problems of hyperactive youngsters persist into adolescence. Weiss, Minde, Werry, Douglass, and Nemeth (1971) did a 5-year follow-up into adolescence and noted that although hyperactive behavior decreased with time, the social, emotional, attentional and learning problems of these youngsters persisted. Although restlessness had been a problem for all the children when they were younger, only 30% were so described in adolescence. Their hyperactive behavior became less gross or disturbing with time, but distractibility remained a major problem for many of the children.

Another important finding of Weiss *et al.* (1971) was that those hyperactive youngsters rated high on aggression during childhood had a higher risk of exhibiting antisocial behavior in the follow-up period. Children from more pathological families also had a higher risk of delinquency during the follow-up assessment. Consistent with this finding, Milich and Loney (1979) argued that aggressive behavior may be a more important predictor of adolescent behavior problems, such as antisocial behavior and low self-esteem, than hyperactivity *per se*.

One study that followed hyperactive children into young adulthood noted that employers tended to see these young people as competent, whereas teachers rated them as inferior to normal controls (Weiss, Hechtman, & Perlman, 1978). Thus, it is important whether we are attempting to predict the hyperactive child's behavior in a work or school setting. The demands of the classroom create an especially difficult context for these youngsters. Given the opportunity to choose compatible employment they become less conspicious than they had been in school.

Delinquency and Antisocial Behavior

The presence of aggressive behavior in childhood is not only important for predicting antisocial conduct among hyperactive youngsters, but others as well. In a review of early predictors of male delinquency, Loeber and Dishion (1983) found that problem behaviors and low academic performance were important predictors of later delinquent behavior. From age 9 years onward, antisocial referrals, aggression, and predelinquent behavior are the best predictors of later delinquency. Roff and Wirt (1984), following a sample of 2,453 children through school records, identified childhood aggression as the most important predictor of delinquency among boys, but not girls.

In an important study of the relationship between antisocial behavior in childhood and adulthood, Robins (1966) followed 524 patients of a child-guidance clinic for as long as 30 years. She concluded that children who had initially been referred for antisocial behavior exhibited the highest rates of adult antisocial behavior. These people were poorer, more alienated socially, and had more complaints of poor physical health than other subjects. From these findings it appears that the prognosis for antisocial children is quite poor. In contrast, children who had suffered from neurotic symptoms such as fearfulness, withdrawal, hypersensitivity, or temper tantrums did not differ from normal control subjects in adulthood (Robins, 1966).

Deciding to Intervene

As our discussion has demonstrated, identifying significant deviations in children is probably more difficult than making the same discriminations among adults. By their very nature children are in a constant process of change, experimentation, and testing of their personal and social realities. They sample a variety of behaviors, adopting some, dropping others, and making modifications along the way, contingent on subtle and gross reinforcement and punishment from other people and themselves.

We have already discussed the value of long-term prognosis as a variable in deciding to intervene in a child's problems. Marked hyperactivity, the aggressive-withdrawn behaviors that appear to mark some preschizophrenic children, or a consistent pattern of antisocial behavior all merit our close professional attention. But, is long-term prognosis alone a sufficient basis for making a decision to intervene, or should other factors be considered as well?

In our view, although the statistical power of some prognostic factors cannot be overlooked, there are additional issues to consider in making a treatment decision. We believe that even if a child ultimately outgrows a problem, this does not justify allowing a condition causing pain and discomfort for parents and/or child to persist for a prolonged period when psychological intervention might terminate the difficulty more quickly.

Social Factors

Social class has some impact on the likelihood that parents will seek help for their child. Parents who are more affluent tend to bring their children for help sooner and for less serious problems than do families with more restricted incomes (Harris, 1974). Shechtman (1971) found that lower-income black children are likely to be referred to clinics only when their behavior is disruptive to the school or community. When she compared mothers' descriptions of 20 black children who were referred to a clinic with a normal control group of black youngsters, she found that the two samples differed on only three items: disobedience, fighting, and poor school work. A parallel study with white children (Schechtman, 1970) identified many more behaviors distinguishing the control and clinic populations. Social and cultural factors can have a substantial impact on the referral process.

Parental Judgment

It is rare for a young child to initiate a clinic contact. Typically parents or teacher are the first to identify a behavior as problematic and suggest the need for professional help. Clinicians tend to rely heavily on parental judgment in making a decision to treat a child (McCoy, 1976). In other words, if a behavior bothers the adults in his or her world, the child is likely to be labeled as problematic.

It is encouraging to note that at least one study suggests that parents are fairly good judges of their child's need for help. Thompson and Bernal (1982), searching for inappropriate parental referrals to clinics, were led to conclude that most of the parents in their study perceived their child's behavior reasonably accurately. Nonetheless, parents are not perfect perceivers of a child's distress. In comparing the outcome of separate, structured psychiatric interviews with mothers and with children, Herjanic and Reich (1982) found highest agreement between the two generations about concrete, observable, severe, and unambiguous child symptoms. Mothers tended to report more behavioral symptoms than the children, whereas children revealed more subjective symptoms than their mothers related.

There are other data suggesting that under some conditions, parental perception is not wholly accurate. For example, Jacobs, Grounds, and Haley (1982) found only moderate agreement between mothers and fathers when describing their child's behavior. There was less agreement between the parents of distressed than nondistressed samples. Similarly, Griest, Forehand, Wells, and McMahon (1980) indicated that mothers of nonclinic children were better predictors of their child's behavior than were mothers of clinic-referred children. Piers (1972) found that parents of normal children overestimated their child's self-esteem, whereas parents of clinic-referred children underestimated their child's own sense of self-worth. Similarly, Ferrari (1984) found mothers to be better predictors of their child's self-esteem than fathers, with fathers more likely to overestimate their daughter's self-esteem than their son's.

In a broad look at diagnostic conclusions based on talking to a mother alone or a child alone, Reich, Herjanic, Welner, and Gandhy (1982) found considerable disagreement between these two sources. Antisocial personality and enuresis were most reliably diagnosed from the two sources of input. Girls' interviews were more often suggestive of neurotic disorder and possible depression than were mothers' interviews, whereas the mothers' interviews suggested behavior disorder more often than did the sons'. Older children (12 to 16 years of age) were in closer agreement with their mothers than were the younger children. These data make it impossible to conclude whether the mothers or the children were more accurate informants. It is quite possible that for some conditions maternal report may provide a more accurate evaluation, whereas for other problems, the child's impressions may bear greater validity.

Guidelines for Intervention

Rutter (1975) offered some useful suggestions to the clinician deciding whether to intervene in a child's life. He raised two basic questions: (a) Is the child's behavior abnormal in statistical terms, and (b) Does the behavior impair the child's social functioning? In regard to statistical factors one needs to consider the child's age and sex, the persistence and situation specificity of the behavior, the life circumstances of the child, the sociocultural setting, extent of disturbance, and the type, severity, and frequency of symptoms. When evaluating social impairment one examines such dimensions as the child's suffering, social restrictions created by the behavior, the extent to which the behavior interferes with normal development, and the effect of the behavior on other people.

Summary

We have reviewed the general literature concerning the impact of developmental factors on common behavior problems of childhood. In general this research suggests that as children get older the frequency and intensity of their behavior problems declines and that those problems that persist over time have more significant prognostic implications than those that emerge only briefly. A consideration of developmental factors is essential in reaching a diagnostic decision, although treatment planning must consider other factors such as subjective discomfort and impact upon the family as well.

It is our hope that although an abundance of research data is forcing most of us to become increasingly narrow in our sphere of competency, behavior therapists will not ignore vital research on developmental factors that should inform our clinical decision making. The loss of a developmental perspective could lead to inefficient and inappropriate treatment decisions.

References

Abikoff, H., Gittelman-Klien, R., & Klein, D. F. (1977). Validation of a classroom observation code for hyperactive children. *Journal of Consulting and Clinical Psychology, 45,* 772–783.

Abikoff, H., Gittelman, R., & Klein, D. F. (1980). Classroom observation code for hyperactive children: A replication of validity. *Journal of Consulting and Clinical Psychology, 48,* 555–565.

Achenbach, T. M. (1982). *Developmental psychopathology.* New York: Wiley.

Achenbach, T. M., & Edelbrock, C. S. (1981). Behavioral problems and competencies reported by parents of normal and disturbed children aged 4 through 16. *Monographs of the Society for Research in Child Development, 46*, Serial 188.

American Psychiatric Association. (1980). *Diagnostic and statistical manual of mental disorders* (3rd Ed.). Washington, DC: Author.

Angelino, H., & Shedd, C. (1953). Shifts in the content of fears and worries relative to chronological age. *Proceedings of the Oklahoma Academy of Science, 34*, 180–186.

Angelino, H., Dollins, J., & Mech, E. V. (1956). Trends in the "fears and worries" of school children as related to socioeconomic status and age. *Journal of Genetic Psychology, 89*, 263–276.

Bamber, J. H. (1974). The fears of adolescents. *Journal of Genetic Psychology, 125*, 127–140.

Barkely, R. (1981). The use of psychopharmacology to study reciprocal influences in parent–child interaction. *Journal of Abnormal Child Psychology, 9*, 303–310.

Battle, E. S., & Lacey, B. A. (1972). A context of hyperactivity in children over time. *Child Development, 43*, 757–773.

Bauer, D. H. (1976). An exploratory study of developmental changes in children's fears. *Journal of Child Psychology and Psychiatry, 17*, 69–74.

Buss, D. M., Block, J. H., & Block, J. (1980). Preschool activity level: Personality correlates and developmental implications. *Child Development, 51*, 401–408.

Campbell, S. B., Endman, M., & Bernfeld, G. (1977). A three-year follow-up of hyperactive preschoolers into elementary school. *Journal of Child Psychology and Psychiatry, 18*, 239–250.

Campbell, S. B., Schleifer, M., & Weiss, G. (1978). Continuities in maternal reports and child behaviors over time in hyperactive and comparison groups. *Journal of Abnormal Child Psychology, 6*, 33–45.

Cantwell, D. F. (1975). *The hyperactive child: Diagnosis, management, and current research.* New York: Spectrum.

Cantwell, D. F. (1977). Genetics of hyperactivity. *Journal of Child Psychology and Psychiatry, 16*, 181–197.

Chazan, M., & Jackson, S. (1974). Behaviour problems in the infant school: Changes over two years. *Journal of Child Psychology and Psychiatry, 15*, 33–46.

Coleman, J., Wolkind, S., & Ashley, L. (1977). Symptoms of behaviour disturbance and adjustment to school. *Journal of Child Psychology and Psychiatry, 18*, 201–210.

Conger, J. C., & Keane, S. P. (1981). Social skills intervention in the treatment of isolated or withdrawn children. *Psychological Bulletin, 90*, 478–495.

Croake, J. W. (1969). Fears of children. *Human Development, 12*, 239–247.

Crowther, J. H., Bond, L. A., & Rolf, J. E. (1981). The incidence, prevalence, and severity of behavior disorders among preschool-aged children in day care. *Journal of Abnormal Child Psychology, 9*, 23–42.

Dawe, H. C. (1934). An analysis of two-hundred quarrels of preschool children. *Child Development, 5*, 139–157.

Donaldson, J. Y. (1983). Disorders usually evident in infancy, childhood or adolescence. In W. H. Reid (Ed.), *Treatment of DSM-III psychiatric disorders* (pp. 5–33). New York: Brunner/Mazel.

Eme, R., & Schmidt, D. (1978). The stability of children's fears. *Child Development, 49*, 1277–1279.

Feldbaum, C. L., Christenson, T. E., & O'Neal, E. C. (1980). An observational study of the assimilation of the newcomer to the preschool. *Child Development, 51*, 497–507.

Ferrari, M. (1984). Chronic illness: Psychosocial effects on siblings. I. Chronically ill boys. *Journal of Child Psychology and Psychiatry, 25*, 459–476.

Feshbach, S. (1970). Aggression. In P. H. Mussen (Ed.), *Carmichael's manual of child psychology* (pp. 159–259). New York: Wiley.

Fischer, M., Rolf, J., Hasazi, J. E., & Cummings, L. (1984). Follow-up of a preschool epidemiological sample: Cross-age continuities and prediction of later adjustment with internalizing and externalizing dimensions of behavior. *Child Development, 55*, 137–150.

Flake-Hobson, C., Robinson, B. E., & Skeen, P. (1983). *Child development and relationships.* Reading, MA: Addison-Wesley.

Gersten, J. C., Langer, T. S., Eisenberg, J. G., Simcha-Fagan, O., & McCarthy, E. D. (1976). Stability and change in types of behavioral disturbance of children and adolescents. *Journal of Abnormal Child Psychology, 4*, 111–128.

Goldberg, S., & Lewis, M. (1969). Play behavior in the year-old infant: Early sex differences. *Child Development, 40*, 21–31.

Graziano, A. M., DeGiovanni, I. S., & Garcia, K. A. (1979). Behavioral treatment of children's fears: A review. *Psychological Bulletin, 86*, 804–830.

Griest, D. L., Forehand, R., Wells, K. C., & McMahon, R. J. (1980). An examination of differences between nonclinic and behavior-problem clinic-referred children and their mothers. *Journal of Abnormal Psychology, 89*, 497–500.

Halverson, C. F., & Waldrop, M. F. (1976). Relations between preschool activity and aspects of intellectual and social behavior at age 7½. *Developmental Psychology, 12*, 107–112.

Harris, S. L. (1974). The relationship between family income and number of parent-perceived problems. *International Journal of Social Psychiatry, 20*, 109–112.

Harris, S. L., & Ferrari, M. (1983). Developmental factors in child behavior therapy. *Behavior Therapy, 14*, 54–72.

Hartup, W. W. (1974). Aggression in childhood: Developmental perspectives. *American Psychologist, 29*, 336–341.

Harvey, P., Winters, K., Weintraub, S., & Neale, J. M. (1981). Distractibility in children vulnerable to psychopathology. *Journal of Abnormal Psychology, 90*, 298–304.

Harvey, P. D., Weintraub, S., & Neale, J. M. (1982). Speech competence of children vulnerable to psychopathology. *Journal of Abnormal Child Psychology, 10,* 373–388.

Herjanic, B., & Reich, W. (1982). Development of a structured psychiatric interview for children: Agreement between child and parent on individual symptoms. *Journal of Abnormal Child Psychology, 10,* 307–324.

Hughes, M., Pinkerton, G., & Plewis, I. (1979). Children's difficulties in starting infant school. *Journal of Child Psychology and Psychiatry, 20,* 187–196.

Jacobs, T., Grounds, L., & Haley, R. (1982). Correspondence between parents' reports on the Behavior Problem Checklist. *Journal of Abnormal Child Psychology, 10,* 593–608.

Jenkins, S., Bax, M., & Hart, H. (1980). Behaviour problems in pre-school children. *Journal of Child Psychology and Psychiatry, 21,* 5–17.

John, R. S., Mednick, S. A., & Schulsinger, F. (1982). Teacher reports as a predictor of schizophrenia and borderline schizophrenia: A Bayesian decision analysis. *Journal of Abnormal Psychology, 91,* 399–413.

Kagan, J., & Moss, H. A. (1962). *Birth to maturity.* New York: Wiley.

Kanter, D. R. (1982). Etiological considerations in childhood hyperactivity. In P. Karoly, J. J. Steffen, & D. J. O'Grady (Eds.), *Child health psychology: Concepts and issues* (pp. 211–227). New York: Pergamon Press.

Kenny, T. J. (1980). Hyperactivity. In H. E. Rie & E. D. Rie (Eds.), *Handbook of minimal brain dysfunction* (pp. 437–455). New York: Wiley.

Kohlberg, L., Lacrosse, J., & Ricks, D. (1972). The predictability of adult mental health from childhood behavior. In B. B. Wolman (Ed.), *Manual of childhood psychopathology* (pp. 1217–1286). New York: McGraw-Hill.

Lapouse, R., & Monk, M. A. (1958). An epidemiological study of behavior characteristics in children. *American Journal of Public Health, 48,* 1134–1140.

Ledingham, J. E. (1981). Developmental patterns of aggressive and withdrawn behavior in childhood: A possible method for identifying preschizophrenics. *Journal of Abnormal Child Psychology, 9,* 1–22.

Ledingham, J. E., & Schwartzman, A. E. (1984). A 3-year follow-up of aggressive and withdrawn behavior in childhood: Preliminary findings. *Journal of Abnormal Child Psychology, 12,* 157–168.

Lewine, R. R. J., Watt, N. F., Prentky, R. A., & Fryer, J. H. (1980). Childhood social competence in functionally disordered psychiatric patients and normals. *Journal of Abnormal Psychology, 89,* 132–138.

Lewis, M., Feiring, C., McGuffog, C., & Jaskir, J. (1984). Predicting psychopathology in six-year-olds from early social relations. *Child Development, 55,* 123–136.

Liebert, R. M., & Baron, R. A. (1972). Some immediate effects of televised violence on children's behavior. *Developmental Psychology, 6,* 469–475.

Loeber, R., & Dishion, T. (1983). Early predictors of male delinquency: A review. *Psychological Bulletin. 94,* 68–99.

Maccoby, E. E. (1980). *Social development, psychological growth, and the parent-child relationship.* New York: Harcourt, Brace, Jovanovich.

Maccoby, E. E., & Feldman, S. S. (1972). Mother-attachment and stranger-reactions in the third year of life. *Monographs of the Society for Research in Child Development, 37.*

Maccoby, E. E., & Jacklin, C. N. (1974). *The psychology of sex differences.* Stanford, CA: Stanford University Press.

MacFarlane, J. W., Allen, L., & Honzik, M. (1954). *A developmental study of the behavior problems of normal children between twenty-one months and fourteen years.* Berkeley, CA: University of California Press.

Manosevitz, M., Prentice, N. M., & Wilson, F. (1973). Individual and family correlates of imaginary companions in preschool children. *Developmental Psychology, 8,* 72–79.

McCoy, S. A. (1976). Clinical judgments of normal childhood behavior. *Journal of Consulting and Clinical Psychology, 44,* 710–714.

McIntyre, A. (1972). Sex differences in children's aggression. *Proceedings of the 80th Annual Convention of the American Psychological Association, 7,* 93–94.

McMahon, R. C. (1984). Hyperactivity as dysfunction of activity, arousal, or attention: A study of research relating to DSM-III's attention deficit disorder. *Journal of Clinical Psychology, 40,* 1300–1308.

Milich, R. (1984). Cross-sectional and longitudinal observations of activity level and sustained attention in a normative sample. *Journal of Abnormal Child Psychology, 12,* 261–276.

Milich, R., & Landau, S. (1984). A comparison of the social status and social behavior of aggressive and aggressive/withdrawn boys. *Journal of Abnormal Child Psychology, 12,* 277–288.

Milich, R., & Loney, J. (1979). The role of hyperactive and aggressive symptomatology in predicting adolescent outcome among hyperactive children. *Journal of Pediatric Psychology, 4,* 93–112.

Moore, D. R., & Mukai, L. H. (1983). Aggressive behavior in the home as a function of the age and sex of control-problem and normal children. *Journal of Abnormal Child Psychology, 11,* 257–272.

Nuechterlein, K. H. (1983). Signal detection in vigilance tasks and behavioral attributes among offspring of schizophrenic mothers and among hyperactive children. *Journal of Abnormal Psychology, 92,* 4–28.

O'Leary, K. D., Pelham, W. E., Rosenbaum, A., & Price, G. H. (1976). Behavioral treatment of hyperkinetic children: An experimental evaluation of its usefulness. *Clinical Pediatrics, 15,* 510–515.

Olweus, D. (1979). Stability of aggressive reaction patterns in males. A review. *Psychological Bulletin, 86,* 852–876.

Pedersen, F. A., & Bell, R. Q. (1970). Sex differences in preschool children without histories of complications of pregnancy and delivery. *Developmental Psychology, 3,* 10–15.

Piers, E. (1972). Parent prediction of children's self-concept. *Journal of Consulting and Clinical Psychology, 38,* 428–433.

Pozanski, E. (1973). Children with excessive fears. *American Journal of Orthopsychiatry, 43,* 438–439.

Pribram, K. (1977). Some observations on the organization of studies of mind, brain, and behavior. In N. E. Zinberg (Ed.), *Alternate states of consciousness* (pp. 220–229). New York: Free Press.

Rau, M., Stover, L., & Guerney, B. G. (1970). Relationship of socioeconomic status, sex, and age to aggression of emotionally disturbed children in mother's presence. *Journal of Genetic Psychology, 116,* 95–100.

Reich, W., Herjanic, B., Welner, Z., & Gandhy, P. R. (1982). Development of a structured psychiatric interview for children: Agreement on diagnosis comparing child and parent interviews. *Journal of Abnormal Child Psychology, 10,* 325–336.

Robins, L. (1966). *Deviant children grown up.* Baltimore, MD: Williams & Wilkins.

Robins, L. N. (1974). *Deviant children grown up.* Huntington, NY: Krieger.

Roff, J., & Wirt, R. D. (1984). Childhood aggression and social adjustment as antecedents of delinquency. *Journal of Abnormal Child Psychology, 12,* 111–126.

Ross, A. O. (1981). *Child behavior therapy: Principles, procedures, and empirical basis.* New York: Wiley.

Routh, D. K., Schroeder, C. S., & O'Tuama, L. A. (1974). Development of activity level in children. *Developmental Psychology, 10,* 163–168.

Rubin, K. H., Daniels-Beirness, T., & Bream, L. (1984). Social isolation and social problem solving: A longitudinal study. *Journal of Consulting and Clinical Psychology, 52,* 17–25.

Rule, B. G. (1974). The hostile and instrumental function of human aggression. In W. W. Hartup & J. deWit (Eds.), *Determinants and origins of aggressive behaviors* (pp. 128–149). The Hauge: Mouton.

Russell, G. W. (1967). Human fears: A factor analytic study of three age levels. *Genetic Psychology Monographs, 76,* 141–162.

Rutter, M. (1975). *Helping troubled children.* New York: Plenum Press.

Rutter, M., Tizard, J., & Whitmore, K. (1970). *Education, health, and human behavior.* London: Longman Press.

Rutter, M., Tizard, J., & Whitmore, K. (1981). *Education, health and behaviour.* London: Longman Press.

Schwebel, M. (1982). Effects of the nuclear war threat on children and teenagers: Implications for professionals. *American Journal of Orthopsychiatry, 52,* 608–618.

Schwebel, M., & Schwebel, B. (1981). Children's reactions to the threat of nuclear plant accidents. *American Journal of Orthopsychiatry, 51,* 260–270.

Sears, R. R., Maccoby, E. E., & Levin, H. (1957). *Patterns of child rearing.* New York: Harper.

Shaywitz, B. A., Klopper, J. H., & Gordon, J. W. (1978). Methylphenidate in 6-hydroxydopamine treated developing rat pups. *Archives of Neurology, 35,* 463–469.

Shechtman, A. (1970). Psychiatric symptoms observed in normal and disturbed children. *Journal of Clinical Psychology, 26,* 38–41.

Shechtman, A. (1971). Psychiatric symptoms observed in normal and disturbed black children. *Journal of Clinical Psychology, 27,* 445–447.

Smith, P. K., & Connolly, K. (1972). Patterns of play and social interaction in preschool children. In N. B. Jones (Ed.), *Ethological studies of child behavior* (pp. 65–95). London: Cambridge University Press.

Strayer, F. F., & Strayer, K. (1976). An ethological analysis of social agonism and dominance relations among preschool children. *Child Development, 47,* 980–989.

Taylor, E. (1980). Brain damage: Evidence from measures of neurological function in children with psychiatric disorder. In E. F. Purcell (Ed.), *Psychopathology of children and youth* (pp. 219–248). New York: Josiah Macey, Jr., Foundation.

Taylor, E., & Sandberg, S. (1984). Hyperactive behavior in English school children: A questionnaire survey. *Journal of Abnormal Child Psychology, 12,* 143–156.

Thompson, R. J., & Bernal, M. E. (1982). Factors associated with parent labeling of children referred for conduct problems. *Journal of Abnormal Child Psychology, 10,* 191–202.

Trites, R. L., Dugas, E., Lynch, G., & Ferguson, H. B. (1979). Prevalence of hyperactivity. *Journal of Pediatric Psychology, 4,* 179–188.

Wanlass, R. L., & Prinz, R. J. (1982). Methodological issues in conceptualizing and treating childhood social isolation. *Psychological Bulletin, 92,* 39–55.

Watt, N. F., Stolorow, R. D., Lubensky, A. W., & McClelland, D. C. (1970). School adjustment and behavior of children hospitalized for schizophrenia as adults. *American Journal of Orthopsychiatry, 40,* 637–657.

Wender, P. (1971). *Minimal brain dysfunction in children.* New York: Wiley-Interscience.

Weiss, G., Minde, K., Werry, J. S., Douglass, V., & Nemeth, E. (1971). Studies on the hyperactive child—VII. Five year follow-up. *Archives of General Psychiatry, 24,* 409–414.

Weiss, G., Hechtman, L., & Perlman, T. (1978). Hyperactives as young adults: School, employers, and self-rating scales obtained during ten-year follow-up evaluation. *American Journal of Orthopsychiatry, 48,* 438–445.

Werry, J. S., & Quay, H. C. (1971). The prevalence of behavior symptoms of younger elementary school children. *American Journal of Orthopsychiatry, 41,* 136–143.

Westman, J. C., Rice, D. L., & Bermann, E. (1967). Nursery school behavior and later school adjustment. *American Journal of Orthopsychiatry, 37,* 725–731.

Winters, K. C., Stone, A. A., Weintraub, S., & Neale,

J. M. (1981). Cognitive and attentional deficits in children vulnerable to psychopathology. *Journal of Abnormal Child Psychology, 9*, 435–453.

Wittman, M. P., & Steinberg, L. (1944). A study of prodromal factors in mental illness with special reference to schizophrenia. *American Journal of Psychiatry, 100*, 811–816.

Wolraich, M., Drummond, T., Salomon, M., O'Brien, M., & Sivage, C. (1978). Effects of methylphenidate alone and in conjunction with behavior modification procedures on the behavior and performance of hyperactive children. *Journal of Abnormal Child Psychology, 6*, 149–161.

CHAPTER 7

Treatment Effect Norms

William H. Yeaton

The wide diversity of problems in educational settings poses a formidable challenge to behavior therapists. Indeed, the multitude of behavior change strategies in the second part of this volume probably reflects the degree of creativity required to confront such a diverse set of problems. At some point, however, the clinician and the researcher may wish to look beyond these multiple and seemingly separate problems and strategies to gain a more unified perspective of the field of behavior therapy. One fundamental purpose in this chapter is to create such a unified perspective by discussing the notion of treatment effect norms. Although the concept of norm necessarily implies a more catholic view than would otherwise emerge from one's own research or experience, it also offers an opportunity to integrate and to focus, yet also cast a broad net.

Examples from outside the field of education will be utilized to illustrate particularly important issues intrinsic to treatment effect norms. Especially common will be examples from psychology, health, and medicine. In the same way that other substantive areas reflect concerns parallel to those of the behavior therapist, normative approaches in other substantive areas are instructive in illustrating principles germane to all treatment effect norms. Thus, the generality of the normative approach is reflected by some natural linkages between behavior therapy in education and psychology, health and medicine. Furthermore, there are many parallels between the normative approach and recent developments in meta-analysis and data synthesis (Light, 1983). Those meta-analysis procedures that inform the normative approach will be utilized to structure this discussion of treatment effect norms.

An air of caution and good judgment is vital to correct interpretation of treatment effect norms. Simply put, the results of treatment effect norms are no better than the data on which they are based. This chapter takes a strong stand on this point and argues that methodological issues are fundamental to establishing veridical norms and critical for making valid inferences from normative data. The validity approach of Campbell (e.g., Campbell & Stanley, 1966; Cook & Campbell, 1979) provides the unifying structure to the methodological critique of treatment effect norms discussed in this chapter.

The ultimate questions of therapy (e.g., "What treatment, by whom, is effective for

William H. Yeaton • ISR/SRC, University of Michigan, Ann Arbor, Michigan 48106.

this individual with that particular problem, under which set of circumstances, and how does it come about?" [Paul, in press, p. 1]) are precisely the same questions for which one seeks answers when establishing treatment effect norms. Thus, the answers that emerge from establishing treatment effect norms will also inform the fundamental goals of therapy. And, of course, the methods of producing norms and the recognition of their shortcomings will qualify the answers that emerge.

Aggregating Treatment Effects

The concept of norm conveys a sense of typicalness, some kind of mean or standard. More formally, a *norm* is an average of two or more scores or quantitative measurements—number of headaches, weight loss, IQ scores, days of school attended, number of new friends. The phrase *treatment effect norm* refers to the outcomes of a particular intervention or a family of interventions whose intent is to alleviate or terminate a particular problem. The effect or effects that are produced by treatments imply that there is some basis of comparison for the effect—say the difference between the number of cigarettes smoked by a group of adolescents who have received an educational program and a group that has not received the program. Although this basis of comparison may change in obvious ways (different comparison groups may be substituted—current smokers and those who have never smoked, or different outcome measures used—the percentage of adolescents who have successfully quit smoking or have never begun to smoke), a treatment effect is implied nonetheless.

A theme later developed in this chapter is that treatment effects cannot be correctly interpreted without knowledge of other contextual factors that may enhance or diminish effectiveness. Supplementary information, also in normative form, such as the number of hours of therapy or the one-to-one or group nature of therapy will provide a vital context for interpreting normative results within a particular setting. In judging the effectiveness of an intervention intended to reduce teacher absenteeism, it would probably be important to provide additional normative information on various characteristics of teachers, such as age and number of years of experience.

The fundamental data from which treatment effect norms are established are most likely to be found in the published research literature. Although it is possible and often desirable to aggregate data such as proportions (Yeaton & Wortman, 1984) or correlations (Hunter, Schmidt, & Jackson, 1982), the examples used in this chapter will be limited to group averages. Using the previous examples to illustrate, separate treatment effect norms might be established from the literature by aggregating effects for group versus individualized therapy or for teachers with 5 or less years versus those with more than 5 years of experience. Of course, the ability to produce these stratifications presumes that relevant information has been reported in each or most of the published research studies that have been used to establish treatment effect norms. In the absence of this relevant information, normative results and their interpretation should be qualified by stating the percentage of studies in which relevant information was reported.

Though this chapter emphasizes treatment effect norms established from the published research literature, there is no intrinsic requirement that this limitation be made. It is quite feasible and often highly desirable to develop norms within any logical unit (e.g., schools, classes, districts). In fact, one could argue that the more local the normative data, the more useful the results will be to potential users in those units.

Establishing Norms

The fundamental guidepost in establishing a treatment effect norm is the specific question that is to be answered by the normative data. To illustrate, suppose that a researcher or practitioner is interested in determining whether a particular social skills training program works. As stated, the question of program effectiveness is much too general. In practical terms, choice of the comparison or control group will be dictated by the question being asked (Kazdin & Wilson, 1978), which will, in turn, affect the size of the treatment effect that results. If by "Does the treatment work?" we mean does it work better than no program, then obviously we would want to aggregate results in studies that compared a social skills training group to a group that did not receive treatment. If, instead, we mean, "Does the social skills training program work better than the best alternative?" (perhaps a program that emphasized a participant's cognitive understanding of their social skills problems), then a completely different set of studies and effects would be aggregated. Perhaps by "Does this treatment work?" we mean "Does the treatment improve social skills functioning?" In this case we would be interested in comparing initial functioning to performance subsequent to treatment. If a more theoretical question, "Why does the treatment work?", is to be answered, results of studies comparing treatment and placebo groups would be aggregated.

The question being asked should be specific enough to dictate that a particular subset of studies is scrutinized to identify pertinent effects. For example, the effects of token programs in normal classrooms are quite likely to be different than those in special education classrooms. In other instances, the context may be time related. For example, many questions require that close attention be given to effects over considerable time periods. Educational programs whose intent is to prevent smoking initiation in preteens will require lengthy follow-ups to establish their effectiveness. Again, the exact question being asked will determine the effects that should be aggregated to establish an appropriate norm.

Veridical Norms

In the same way that well-established criteria guide the conduct of individual research studies, so too should accepted criteria guide the establishment of veridical normative data. In fact, it is difficult to imagine criteria for conducting individual studies that are not in some way relevant to establishing veridical norms. The examples listed in the following illustrate how three aspects of individual studies, bias, reliability, and statistical analysis, also apply to developing high quality norms. Normative data should be selected with minimal bias from the relevant research literature. Chalmers and his colleagues (Chalmers, Celano, & Sacks, 1983) have tried to avoid another sort of potential bias in coding information by requiring that coders be blind to all parts of the research report except the results section. Orwin and Cordray (1985) called attention to the potentially low reliability of information extracted from primary research studies. And Hedges (1984) suggested that conventional statistical analyses of aggregate data are problematic and has developed alternatives.

Using Norms

Although there are a myriad of uses of norms, one convenient way to organize these uses is to identify their respective audiences. In the following section, the utilization of norms by three user groups is discussed.

Use of Norms by Therapists

Behavior therapists may use normative data as a rationale that a particular problem exists, though such data will almost certainly be specific to that individual and his or her circumstances. For example, a young child may be called shy by his parents and a therapist may determine that there is a problem by virtue of the fact that the child plays alone on most occasions and infrequently talks with other children either in the classroom or on the playground. That is, measures of interaction occurrence are well below normative rates for a same-sex peer group across a variety of situations.

Of course, it would be naive to ignore the

critical role of judgment by the therapist in determining that a problem exists. Normative data must be assessed in the context in which it is embedded, otherwise interpretation is likely to be irrelevant.

Using the previous example to illustrate, a comparative deficiency in the frequency of social interaction may not be problematic if it occurs in the first month of the school year. Simply waiting may solve the problem. There is a similar temporal aspect to a problem such as swearing because a young child who swears far more than his peers may be severely reprimanded. However, at a later time the same rate of swearing may be tolerated as typical teenager spunk. (The opposite would occur with conformist behavior—young children are often expected to copy others, but the same rate of conforming behavior in a later period may be judged harshly because a child is supposed to become more individualistic over time). In the context of a summer camp when a new group of campers arrives every couple of weeks, an apparent deficiency may not be judged as problematic because, in most social situations, one is likely to encounter the same group of persons over a more extended period of time.

Behavior therapists not only utilize normative data to suggest that a problem exists but also to indicate the degree to which a problem has been solved or needs resolution. Low rates of school attendance may be increased to a point near the school average and, thus, no longer be seen as a problem by school personnel. Wolf (1978) uses the phrase *social validity of effects* to describe this strategy (Kazdin, 1977; Yeaton, 1982), which will be discussed more completely later.

Use of Norms by Researchers

The research audience may use normative data to determine the current status of a given field of study. The National Institutes of Health's consensus development program (Wortman, 1981) aims to assess the research evidence for various medical procedures (e.g., coronary artery bypass graft surgery, breast cancer screening) from a normative perspective. Though the consensus process does not currently use the normative data from published studies in a systematic manner, the approach is clearly normative in that an informal aggregation of the efficacy and safety of these medical procedures is an integral part of the consensus process. In the event that insufficient data exists on which to base a consensus statement, future research can be targeted to answer questions that have consistently been avoided in the research literature.

Use of Norms by Consumers

Most typically, research findings are targeted toward other researchers and providers of treatment. Seldom do normative data exist that can be utilized directly by consumers. Yet, if these norms were readily available, they might prove very useful in important consumer decisions.

Take, for example, a woman faced with the choice of several alternative treatments for positively diagnosed breast cancer. Though the research evidence had not been clear-cut, radical mastectomy was the treatment of choice up until the last several years. However, recent evidence (Fisher, Bauer *et al.*, 1985; Fisher, Redmond *et al.*, 1985) suggests that there are few differences in survival between radical mastectomy and a more conservative surgery for women with early breast cancer. Thus, the evidence for minimal differences in survival indicates that quality of life issues and patient preference should play a vital role in treatment decisions.

Unfortunately, normative data do not currently exist that provide appropriate information on which a woman can make an informed choice regarding appropriate treatment. If outcomes from all controlled studies that compared various breast cancer treatment options were made available to patients (and also to surgeons and radiologists), a much more informed choice could be made, especially if these data were stratified to reflect the particular characteristics of the individual patient (e.g., outcomes broken down by age, location, and size of tumor). Furthermore, it is probably accurate to say that most consumers do not even consider the potential utility of normative data regarding prior success rates of individual doctors when choosing a physician to treat a specific problem.

A similar use might be made of normative data by teachers faced with several alternative interventions to decrease disruptive classroom behavior. Again, normative data comparing results of these alternatives could be made available to these potential teacher consumers and a decision could be made based on norms as well as personal preference and expected competency in conducting a particular treatment. Separate norms reflecting outcomes stratified by, say, problem severity and teacher experience might be of additional use in choosing among treatment alternatives. It is not difficult to imagine similar uses of treatment effect norms that would prove useful to other, relevant consumer groups such as parents, administrators, and legislators.

Misuses of Normative Data

There are numerous ways in which normative data may be misused and the reader should be aware of these potential problems. Campbell's notion of the corruptibility of measurement is particularly pertinent here.

> The more any quantitative social indicator is used for decision making, the more subject it will be to corruption pressures and the more apt it will be to distort and corrupt the social processes it is intended to monitor. (Campbell, 1979, p. 85)

Thus, if normative data on school attendance or achievement test scores were used to establish merit pay levels, one would predict that the measures on which the norms are based would begin to be distorted (teachers may count children present even if they miss several hours of class time and teachers may change the allocation of class activities to increase the odds that students will attain higher scores on standardized tests).

For years height and weight charts have been consulted to determine what a given person with a given body frame should weigh. These charts reflect the weights associated with the lowest death rate for given heights. A recently updated version of the chart indicated that the ideal poundage had increased for each of the height and weight classes, much to the delight of most dieters. Unfortunately, the ideal weights are likely to be skewed upward by the fact that cigarette smokers, who die at significantly younger ages, are included in the chart, thus rendering those normative data suspect.

Another potential misapplication of normative data exists when normative behavior is intrinsically deficient (Sechrest & Yeaton, 1981). For example, an expert panel has recently judged as abnormally high what until now had been considered normal levels of cholesterol in the diet (Kolata, 1985). Rather than regarding existing dietary levels as acceptable because they are commonly found in the diet of Americans, the panel recommended that a reduced normative level was more desirable.

Standardized Treatments

The term *treatment effect norms* infers that the effects of a single treatment strategy are averaged. Because the user of a treatment effect norm may wish to predict the utility of a very specific version of treatment, he or she will be most interested in the effects of that particular treatment, not some other treatment, or a different version of that particular treatment.

Treatments will vary along many dimensions that are likely to alter their effects, however. The skill of the behavior therapist, the number and length of training sessions, and the magnitude of the reinforcers utilized are aspects of treatment strength (Yeaton & Sechrest, 1981) that may alter the effects produced. Even when similar versions of treatment are planned to be administered, treatments may vary in the integrity with which they are given (Salend, 1984; Yeaton & Sechrest, 1981). Such departures from planned implementation can also be expected to alter treatment effects. Unfortunately, qualifications of study effects based on departures from treatment protocols presuppose that authors have monitored and reported treatment integrity. Without standardizing treatments at given levels of strength and integrity, normative data will possess a great deal of variability and lead to inaccurate assessment of the predicted effectiveness of treatment.

The Efficacy–Effectiveness Distinction

It would be incorrect to conclude from the previous discussion that all treatments should be given in some fixed, standardized manner. Rather, the critical point is that one should construct norms that reflect specific conditions of treatment implementation (a given level of treatment strength and integrity) and use these data to make predictions about potential treatment effects.

A different way to look at the problems posed by standardizing treatments has been articulated by the Office of Technology Assessment (OTA, 1978) in making a distinction between the efficacy and effectiveness of treatment. *Efficacy* refers to the outcomes of treatments implemented under ideal conditions, whereas *effectiveness* deals with effects likely to be found in more real-world applications. If efficacy is in question, then normative data should be taken from studies where integrity is likely to be high, often as a result of direct researcher involvement. Issues regarding effectiveness will likely point one in the direction of research studies conducted with minimal researcher involvement.

The OTA conceptualization of effects makes it clear that there are two distinct and separable dimensions regarding treatment standardization and, additionally, infers that there is a preferred order to ask questions regarding effects. First, does the treatment work when implemented under ideal conditions? If the answer is no, it makes little sense to ask further questions. But if the answer is yes, the second question addresses outcomes when conditions of implementation are likely to be compromised. Norms that reflect the second question should not include studies that ask the first question.

Behavior therapists would seem to be more interested in questions of effectiveness because educational settings may preclude interventions far from the ideal. Given this preference, there are several ways in which normative data might be stratified. Certainly the treatment itself will present a source of potential variability. Results should be separated for different versions of treatment—the more variable the treatment, the greater the need for stratification. A token economy with clear contingencies for performance and reward would seem to possess less inherent variability than a parent training program with various feedback, modeling, and verbal praise components. Effects resulting from professional therapists are likely to be different from those produced by parent therapists (see Durlak, 1979, for an apparent contradiction), at least for some sorts of problems. Certainly, the setting in which treatment is given and performance is assessed (e.g., in the office or in the classroom) should be carefully noted.

For the researcher who wishes to utilize normative data, the focus will be on the degree to which treatment has been uniformly implemented in the studies from which norms have been established. As mentioned earlier, the degree of standardization will almost certainly vary as a function of whether the treatment question pertains to efficacy or effectiveness. From a broader perspective, however, the goal of treatment standardization also focuses attention on the possible roles of the behavior therapist (Yeaton, 1982a). In the interest of maximizing effectiveness, it might be argued that therapists should implement most treatments or at least serve in a consultant capacity to ensure that treatment is not degraded when given by appropriate change agents. This direct role may, unfortunately, result in minimal systemwide impact because there are a relatively limited number of behavior therapists who would confront a large number and wide diversity of problems. Another possibility would seek to achieve uniform effects rather than uniform treatments. In this approach, treatments would be designed and empirically tested that are robust to degradation. That is, programs may be developed that can be given in nonstandardized ways without diminishing treatment effects.

Levels of Normative Aggregation

In an earlier portion of this chapter, care was taken to point out the importance of aggregating data that consistently addressed the same empirical question. In addition, the question being asked plays another important role, namely to influence the level of aggregation most appropriate to a particular answer.

Natural Levels of Aggregation

Nationwide data would be most relevant when the number of mathemetics majors in college during the past 10 years are to be compared to the number of majors in other countries. Individual states vary widely in the average number of dollars allocated per student as well as in their average SAT scores. A question regarding the relationship between teacher salaries and absenteeism would likely focus on data within particular cities or school districts. CAT scores for boys and girls of male and female teachers might reasonably be studied for different grade levels. Certain questions regarding curriculum are often directed to individual schools in cities and districts. Questions surrounding merit pay can be asked using an individual class and teacher as the unit of aggregation. Various teaching strategies can be directed at particular students or types of students to assess relative effectiveness. It is also possible to aggregate data within specific subjects or even within particular skills for a given subject to assess, say, the effectiveness of peer tutoring.

Variability within Aggregation Units

Choosing the appropriate unit of aggregation is likely to be critical given the inherent variability within the classes of units mentioned earlier. For example, a comparison of behavioral and nonbehavioral approaches to enhance academic productivity would be problematic if different approaches were implemented in different cities and cities varied widely in the academic abilities of students. Contrasts between measures of productivity for behavioral and nonbehavioral approaches within grades of a particular school district in similar cities would be far more conducive to interpretation. By removing the extraneous between-city source of variability, the presence of an intervention effect would be much more evident. In the event of no apparent difference between the two approaches, it will also be much easier to interpret the absence of an intervention effect.

Thus, it is apparent that a judicious choice of the unit of aggregation will enhance the inferential power of questions asked by the behavior therapist. Unfortunately, other aspects of the research context may possess sources of variability that will alter treatment effects and, therefore, the normative data that are obtained. Time is a conspicuous culprit among these sources of variability. Because there are pronounced changes in academic, physical, and social skills during the years of schooling, care must be taken to ensure that comparable chronological ages and abilities are present in the units of aggregation that are being studied. Given the increasing rate of maturation in school age children, it may also be critical to update existing norms or at least to avoid direct comparisons of normative data from two very different time periods.

Even within a given yearly period, however, there may be quite different amounts of variability that can be expected, which lends further caution to the kinds of inferences that should be made. For example, there is a great deal of variance in the age in which children first walk and talk. Because most developmental laggards soon equal their peers in physical and verbal skills, there should be little concern if a young child is not talking several months later than the average. However, the same lag in language at a much later time period is likely to be viewed as permanent and therefore perceived as a problem by a concerned parent.

Methodological Levels of Aggregation

Besides the more obvious ways in which treatment effects can be aggregated (by locale and by time periods), it may also be very useful to consider the influence of various methodological issues and to stratify treatment effects within these levels of aggregation. In fact, Light (1984) argued that one of the most important advantages of an approach that aggregates effects from different studies is that certain issues can be addressed and questions can be asked that cannot be resolved or answered within a single study. Kavale and Glass (1984, p. 216) find this advantage to be critical in making policy decisions in education. "Although many physical sciences reveal strong main effects, special education is likely to reveal higher order interactions in abundance and main effects but rarely."

Effects can be stratified by treatment type, either general classes such as behavioral or nonbehavioral or more specific therapies such as Gestalt, Adlerian, or rational-emotive (Smith & Glass, 1977). Although this aggregation scheme seems straightforward, one could further ascertain subtypes of a given therapy (e.g., the different versions of psychodynamic therapy).

Another possibility is to aggregate results by presenting problem. In Scovern and Kilmann's (1980) review of the outcome literature on electroconvulsive therapy, effects were considered separately for depressives, schizophrenics, and a broad category termed "other." In cases for which there is no clear distinction between problem types, this strategy would be impractical, but, in general, one might anticipate that treatment effects would be quite variable among types of presenting problems.

Characteristics of patients or clients can be used as a stratifying variable for reporting treatment effects. Kavale and Glass (1984) reported treatment effects separately for children with differing IQs in testing the effects of special education classes. Their work also illustrates the possibility of aggregating treatment effects in more than one way within a given data set as they also reported results by different grade levels.

The specific outcome measures may be an important source of variability, and, therefore, a dimension on which to stratify. Sulzbacher (1973) reviewed 753 studies on the effects of psychotropic medicine with children and reported results separately as direct measures of behavior, psychological testing, rating scales, and clinical impressions. He found a wide disparity between the percentage of studies reporting no statistically significant difference across measurement types. In studies whose outcomes were of the clinical impression variety, only 12% reported no statistical difference, whereas 83% of the studies using psychological tests reported no statistical difference. Carlberg and Kavale (1980) found differences in treatment effects in their review of regular and special class placement for measures of achievement and social/personality, though the differences were much more modest than those found by Sulzbacher.

One way to categorize studies is by the general category of outcome measures they report—subjective or qualitative and objective or quantitative. However, this somewhat simplistic and artificial dichotomy is gradually being replaced by an orientation that includes both kinds of measures within a given study (Cook & Reichardt, 1979). This approach assumes that measures are complementary in their strengths and weaknesses (e.g., reactive and nonreactive measures may be aggregated separately and examined for the consistency of their outcomes) and that each may be appropriate to one of the varied questions that are asked within a given study. Analagously, the consumer of treatment effect norms is unlikely to hold particular allegiance to one outcome measure and therefore may wish to examine the effectiveness of a treatment across a number of distinct measures. Because treatments can safely be assumed to have multiple effects, it certainly makes considerable sense to aggregate intended and potentially unintended effects.

Measures of attitude may be quite important if they represent a general satisfaction with a treatment because they may also predict future compliance. In medicine, quality of life is absolutely essential to an assessment of treatment effectiveness (McPeek, Gilbert, & Mosteller, 1977), because there often will be trade-offs between the quantity and quality of life. This is the case with laryngeal cancer (McNeil, Weichselbaum, & Pauker, 1981), where preservation of normal speech and likelihood of survival work in opposition. Ideally, we wish to develop treatments such as coronary artery bypass graft surgery that enhance both survival and life quality (Wortman & Yeaton, 1985).

Often, treatments will be targeted either directly or indirectly to cognitive skills. Certainly, part of the rationale of the desegregation movement was to alter the achievement levels of black children, a goal that has apparently been achieved (Bryant & Wortman, 1984). It is probably not an exaggeration to say that most interventions in education ranging from Head Start programs to Job Training aim to change some apsect of cognitive ability or performance.

Treatments in medicine and health are often aimed at changing some physiological or behavioral outcome. For example, reduction of blood pressure may potentially be achieved by reducing the amount of salt in the diet (Brown *et al.*, 1984). Educational interventions may attempt to alter attendance rates (Barber & Kagey, 1977) or perceptual and sensory motor skills (Kavale & Glass, 1984). Though not always measured, a tacit goal of these medical and educational interventions might also be to change simultaneously a participant's attitude (e.g., to like school more) and to enhance achievement levels (e.g., to increase scores on standardized tests).

The length of the follow-up period might be expected to be associated with the size of the treatment effect one finds. Smith and Glass found a statistically significant, negative relationship between the length of follow-up and the magnitude of treatment effect—the longer the follow-up the smaller the treatment effect. In contrast, Nicholson and Berman (1983) reviewed the literature on psychotherapeutic treatments for neurosis and found no systematic relationship between the treatment effects reported and the length of follow-up.

Methodological Confounds

Whereas it seems clear that various methodological dimensions of a study must be considered in the interpretation of study results, it is equally clear that unambiguous conclusions about the effects of methodology are seldom possible. This shortcoming often results from the fact that many methodological dimensions vary simultaneously within a given study. In few instances can one safely assume that two studies differ only in that methodological dimension in which one is interested. If effects are aggregated separately by outcome measure, one should be cautious not to overinterpret differences in treatment effects because the same set of outcome measures are seldom reported in each of the studies in the review.

Thus, methodological factors affecting treatment effects may vary unsystematically along with the outcomes reported. In the Sulzbacher study discussed earlier, if children with more severe problems happened to be included in studies utilizing psychological tests, then problem severity rather than the reactivity of the measurement might account for much of the outcome difference. Landman and Dawes (1982) reanalyzed the Smith and Glass data base and reported treatment effects at post-test and two subsequent, follow-up periods. Here again care must be taken in interpreting effects because the relationship between treatment effects and length of follow-up may be confounded with other study dimensions (e.g., more reactive measures may be associated with shorter follow-up times, producing a spurious relationship between length of follow-up and treatment effect size).

In other instances, there may be consistent methodological flaws present in many of the studies being aggregated. This was the case in the randomized controlled trials comparing groups of patients who had received coronary artery bypass graft surgery and patients remaining on a drug regimen (Detre & Peduzzi, 1982). In each study substantial numbers of medical patients dropped out of the drug condition and subsequently received surgery to alleviate severe angina. The biasing effect of these crossovers (treatment effects are underestimated) and also be directly reflected in treatment effect norms established from those studies. Although some authors have discussed the advantage of aggregating studies with complementary weaknesses (because biases are assumed to be self-canceling) (e.g., Staines, 1974), special efforts will need to be taken to address the problem of consistent flaws with each unique data set. For example, Yeaton, Wortman, and Langberg (1983) developed a statistical procedure to estimate the maximum effect of crossovers in controlled trials of coronary artery bypass surgery.

Using the Validity Approach to Establish Treatment Effect Norms

Rather than aggregating treatment effects on a myriad of levels that simply make sense, it is preferable to be guided by current theory and a conceptual base within a given area of study. A unifying structure also provides direction for those researchers who wish to ascertain the influence of methodological issues. Campbell and colleagues (Campbell & Stanley, 1966; Cook & Campbell, 1979) have discussed just such an approach in the social sciences for the last 20 years or so. Their approach centers around four different types of validity: external, construct, internal, and statistical conclusion. These validity types have considerable heuristic value in directing the kinds of normative strata that one should seriously consider (Wortman, 1983).

External validity is concerned with the generality of the research findings for different persons, occasions, settings, responses, and so forth. As such, it focuses one's efforts on the possible differential effects of treatment for each of these logically different units. Thus, in studying the effects of coronary artery bypass graft surgery on survival in patients with coronary artery disease, outcomes are often stratified by severity of the initial disease state (e.g., one, two, or three vessel disease). Similarly, sex of patient is an important stratifying variable in the treatment of threatened stroke by aspirin (e.g., Canadian Cooperative Study Group, 1978).

Construct validity is actually broken up into two subtypes, construct validity of cause and construct validity of effect. Construct validity of cause is concerned with the precise mechanism and active elements by which treatments have their effects. Quite naturally, then, it directs one to aggregate the same or conceptually similar treatments within different studies. Miller and Berman (1983) followed this strategy in reporting results separately for individual and group cognitive behavior therapies.

Construct validity of effects refers to the extent that an outcome variable as operationalized actually measures the conceptual variable in question. For example, does the percentage of time that a child spends on task in a classroom actually mirror the more general variable of student learning with its implicit assumptions regarding attentiveness and productivity? Thus, in assessing the effects of open classrooms on student learning, one may wish to look at standardized test scores as well as teacher-made test results and quality of completed homework assignments as separate measures of learning because none, alone, completely captures the more general variable of student learning.

Internal validity focuses on the degree in which it is legitimate to make causal statements relating independent and dependent variables. Studies high in internal validity allow strong claims about causality; studies low in internal validity do not allow such claims. To assess the internal validity of a particular study, one should pay particular attention to its experimental design because the design is crucial to causal inference. From the perspective of treatment effect norms, internal validity and experimental design are not simply logical or philosophical niceties because there is considerable evidence that the experimental design directly affects the size of the treament effect that contributes to a normative data base (Wortman & Yeaton, 1983). For example, when studies comparing patients receiving coronary artery bypass graft surgery and a medical regimen were partitioned into randomized controlled trials and controlled trials that utilized matching without randomization, there were considerable differences in mortality (Wortman & Yeaton, 1983) between the two types of studies, with smaller effects, generally, being associated with the randomized studies.

This so-called design effect (Yeaton, 1982b) seems to be quite robust. Smith and Glass (1977), in their meta-analysis of psychotherapy outcome studies, found a statistically significant, positive relationship between ratings of internal validity and treatment effect size—larger effects were associated with greater internal validity and smaller effects related to lesser internal validity. In education, Kulik and his colleagues (e.g., Kulik, Kulik, & Cohen, 1980) have consistently noted the lack of a design effect in their meta-analyses of education research. In contrast, Wortman and Bryant (1985) found that quasi-experiments using a matching strategy had larger effects than randomized studies in their integrative review of desegregation research. Thus, the direction and the existence of a design effect is quite variable but certainly represents a potentially important source of variation in establishing norms.

A separate but not unrelated aspect of experimental design and internal validity deals with the specific control group used as a basis of establishing effectiveness. Sacks, Chalmers, and Smith (1982) found that in each of the six distinct areas of medicine they examined, studies that compared treatment results to those in a historical control group (patients treated for the same disorder but at some previous point in time) consistently overestimated treatment effects relative to those studies using randomized, concurrent controls. Landman and Dawes (1982), in their reanalysis of the meta-analysis of Smith and Glass (1977), found that a significant portion of the treatment effect could be attributed to the placebo effect of treatment. That is, the effect found by comparing placebo groups to no-treatment controls was a significant portion of the treatment versus no-treatment effect. Though noted previously with respect to the particular question being asked (cf. Cordray & Bootzin, 1983), the choice of the particular comparison group is absolutely critical to the inferences made, in this case with respect to the magnitude of the treatment effect likely to be found.

Statistical conclusion validity refers to the legitimacy of conclusions based on any statistical analysis of the findings. Although treatment effect data are descriptive in nature and, thus, will not necessarily be tested for statistical significance, the power or sensitivity of statistical tests is pertinent to sample size, which is relevant to inference from normative data. The reliability of conclusions based on treatment effect norms is directly proportional to the number of participants that make up the average treatment effect within a particular study and to the number of study effects that are aggregated. Either a small number of participants within studies or a small number of studies would potentially limit the strength of conclusions one can make. As Hunter, Schmidt, and Jackson (1982) noted, however, if the individual study is not used as the unit of analysis (cf. Whiting-O'Keefe, Henke, & Simborg, 1984) but estimated results are determined by the total number of participants across all studies, then even a relatively small number of studies may have a large, overall sample size.

In a later section of this chapter the case will be made that statistical criteria should not be the sole basis for establishing the effectiveness of treatment. Although this argument should and soon will be elaborated, it is also appropriate to mention it here because the size of sample plays such an integral role in tests of significance, though clinical significance and practical importance should be the more relevant criteria for judging the applied effectiveness of treatment.

Use of Treatment Effect Norms in Planning Research

For those conducting research, normative data from treatment outcome studies may be particularly useful in planning future studies. For example, Cordray and Orwin (1983) illustrated how information on attrition in treatment and comparison groups from previous studies can be utilized to ensure that *achieved* sample size goals are met. By anticipating dropout rates in similar studies and settings, researchers can oversample from the pool of participants to achieve a particular sample size. In fact, a current volume (Cordray, 1985) discusses several ways in which normative data can be utilized in planning, as well as some of the impediments for implementing these strategies.

Interpretation of Norms

Much of the emphasis in this paper has been placed on the quality of information included in a given norm. Methodological concerns such as validity, research design, study outcomes, and control groups have assumed a central position in this discussion. Nonetheless, equal attention must be given to the interpretation of treatment effect norms because data do not speak for themselves.

A norm is more than a score, more than a mean treatment effect. Indeed, it is more than a mean and a standard deviation, more than a mean plus a *z*-score or percentile. Missing is the context in which the finding exists—the substantive area, the perceived importance of change to the reader, and the behavioral implications of the finding. Perhaps interventions with disadvantaged high school students alter their mean reading score by half a grade level in reported instances in the research literature. Will this difference make it easier to find and keep a job? Will the job significantly enhance the quality of their life? And will the difference make it any less likely that they will be a part of the welfare system in 20 years?

These are indeed difficult questions, but the behavioral implications of outcomes are well worth the extra efforts to find out. For example, would interventions whose aim is to change children's safety behaviors be of legitimate importance if they did not reduce deaths and injuries (Yeaton, Greene, & Bailey, 1981)? The behavior analysts have been particularly sensitive to these issues because their outcome measures were often indicted as being readily quantifiable but of little social relevance. If the percentage of the time spent on task as a result of a particular treatment has been increased from 50% to 80%, what difference does it really make to the student? To answer the question, measures of social validity (Kazdin, 1977; Wolf, 1978) should be included along with measures of on-task behavior. Teachers may be asked to assess general impressions of a student's performance before and after an intervention. Measures of productivity (e.g., homework assignments completed) and quality (e.g., percentage of correct answers) may also be noted. Together, these measures allow a much more informed conclusion about the effectiveness of treatment.

Establishing Important Effects

Experts within a substantive field may be quite adept at judging the applied importance of treatment effects (Sechrest & Yeaton, 1982). This ability is most probably due to their familiarity with the field. More specifically, these experts may possess a kind of intuitive metric that allows comparative relationships to be made with some basis in reality. It is as if they carry with them a personal treatment effect norm based on the literature that they have read and remembered.

The absolute size of an effect may not be indicative of its importance. A cogent example of this has been noted by Rosenthal (1984) in his report of a study of the drug propranolol by the National Heart, Lung, and Blood Institute. The early results of the study were so favorable that it was judged unethical to continue. Using percentage of variance accounted for as a measure of effect size, the use of propranolol accounted for one fifth of one percent of the variance in death rates. Although one might not be accustomed to viewing such seemingly small effects as important, a moment's pause for reflection on the fact that human life is the outcome measure and that such an effect may be much larger than available from other drugs makes the interpretation more understandable.

In the same way that absolutely small effects may turn out to be quite important, absolutely large effects may be relatively unimportant. Treatments that cause statistically significant weight loss (Brownell, 1982) may be trivial if there is no concurrent improvement in health status. If the loss is not likely to be noticed by others, there may be little chance of maintaining the loss (important social reinforcers will be lacking). The social importance of interventions to reduce blood pressure may depend on the initial blood pressure level—large changes at some places in the scale may have little impact on the patient's health.

Some outcomes are not important in and of themselves but rather become important when aggregated. A treatment for obesity that decreased intake by 50 calories a day would be important over a period of months and years. An educational intervention that raised the protein intake of each poor child by 1% might have a large, potential health effect on the population of poor children.

Although it is important to establish the importance of treatment effects, it may be equally critical to establish the nonimportance of treatment effects. In fact, the substantiation of no difference can be particularly enlightening and of considerable applied importance (Sechrest & Yeaton, 1985). An especially apt example of this can be taken from the treatment outcome literature on interventions for breast cancer. For years a controversy has been raging over the most appropriate treatment for breast cancer while in its early stages. Very recent evidence on the subject (Fisher, Bauer *et al.*, 1985; Fisher, Redmond *et al.*, 1985) indicates that there is little difference in survival rates between radical mastectomy and less invasive surgeries either alone or combined with radiotherapy and that the differences that exist may actually favor the more conservative interventions. Had treatment effect norms been utilized, this conclusion might have been reached long ago.

Caveats

Normative data may be deficient if the treatment for which effects are being aggregated is in the process of change. The author has become quite aware of this influence because of his interest in the assessment of new medical technologies (e.g., Yeaton & Wortman, 1985). The time-dependent nature of treatments is not unique to medicine and health, however.

Witness the introduction of new educational procedures or the reinvention of old educational technologies.

Temporal Aspects

To illustrate the various ways that time may influence the normative outcomes of treatment effects in a literature, the author will refer to his work on the evaluation of coronary artery bypass graft surgery (CABGS) (Yeaton & Wortman, 1984). In this medical procedure a vein from a patient's leg is typically used to bypass one or more occluded arteries in the heart. This medical technology has been rapidly disseminated in the last 15 years and has evolved considerably as surgeons have gained more experience with it. Computer technologies in the classroom are currently going through a similar period of rapid dissemination and evolution (Johnston, 1984). Normative data on the effects of medical and educational technologies are likely to be outdated unless this technological change is taken into account. If we take seriously Skinner's (1984) and other critics' suggestions to introduce computer technologies in the classroom even more quickly, then normative data on acquisition of new knowledge and concepts should most definitely reflect changes in the technology itself.

The situation is yet more complex because changes in the treatment are often accompanied by parallel changes that influence treatment effect size. For example, the target population being studied is likely to change over time. In this case the relative percentage of patients with one, two, and three vessel coronary artery disease receiving CABGS has changed considerably in the last 15 years. Supplementary technologies have also evolved. For example, life-support systems have steadily improved during this period, thus influencing mortality otherwise attributable to surgery. Perhaps most important has been the rapid changes in the medical regimen patients are likely to receive. The introduction of beta blockers and calcium channel blockers (Johnson *et al.*, 1981) has improved the prognosis of the comparison group, coronary heart disease patients who receive only drugs.

It is not difficult to cite parallel aspects in the evaluation of a mental health treatment (Yeaton, 1982b). The author is currently involved in an assessment of the effectiveness of implosion therapy (IT) (Nurius & Yeaton, 1987). Certainly, the treatment labeled implosion therapy in 1985 is different than the treatment with the same name in 1965. The set of problems to which IT has been applied is much more diverse than in previous periods. New drugs and behavioral techniques now exist to deal with secondary symptoms. And the group to which IT results are compared is much more likely to be a variety of systematic desensitization or some other rival treatment rather than an untreated control group.

There is no single, weakness-free way to attack the temporal dimension problem in establishing valid treatment effect norms. Given the influence of time, and its potential influence on treatment effects, however, the capacity to update norms in an efficient and ongoing way is critical. This function is particularly well suited to computer and microcomputer technology, and the author is currently conducting research on the assessment of new cardiovascular technologies that will utilize a microcomputer to produce and update normative data.

One option is to cast normative data in a variety of ways, each with its own advantage. The data can be cumulated over years, starting with the earliest data in which treatment effects were reported. This approach allows determination of the first time point in which statistically or clinically significant effects were present. Yearly data can be cumulated starting with the most recent results and working backward in time. Here, one can assess the more current status of the treatment uninfluenced by earlier results, either positive or negative. Finally, norms can simply be given on a yearly basis, which allows one to pinpoint specific periods when dramatic shifts in effectiveness occurred, and thus identify potentially important changes in the research context (e.g., patient mix, particular version of treatment given, comparison group composition) that may produce these shifts.

Implicit Standards

Oftentimes, there will be implicit standards that must be considered in establishing and interpreting normative data. For example, treatment goals created by clients and therapists act as a standard against which progress is compared. In many areas of medicine, questions relative to the maintenance of effects have reasonably well agreed on standards. For instance, the effectiveness of treatments for breast cancer is typically ascertained with a follow-up period of at least 10 years. Similar standards in education or behavior therapy are rare (Wortman, 1984), though interventions for cigarette smoking are a possible exception.

Another implicit standard relates to the perception of effectiveness of treatments or research on treatment in their early stages of development. In justifying the failure to teach home safety skills to children at less than perfect acquisition levels, Peterson (1984, p. 291) stated "that less than 100% criterion responding may be acceptable in this preliminary study, with better performance a reasonable goal for future work in this area."

Sometimes, normative data is judged relative to an implicit standard of attainability. Trowbridge (1982) addressed the question of attainable standards for norms with regard to the growth of Western and non-Western children, arguing that assessment of nutritional status is more adequate if the attainability of certain heights is taken into account.

The notion of implicit standards is intrinsic to the perennial argument within universities regarding salary raises. In the 1983–1984 academic year at the University of Michigan a full professor's salary was 87.8% of that given by 10 peer, private schools and 108.1% of the average salary at 6 peer, public schools (CESF Newsletter, 1985). Depending on which standard is applied, a case can be made for or against the need for salary increments for full professors.

Research by Wolf and his colleagues at Achievement Place also illustrates the use of implicit standards quite nicely (Minkin *et al.*, 1976). Conversational skills were taught to predelinquent girls and ratings of performance were obtained. The average posttraining rating was 4.3 for study participants, 3.7 for a sample of junior high females, and 5.0 for university females. Because the most appropriate, implicit standard of comparison is the sample of junior high females and not the university females, the treatment would likely be judged successful.

Concluding Thoughts

Normative data possess considerable intuitive appeal but are fraught with potential difficulties. The process of establishing veridical norms requires expertise in a number of different methodological areas. The completeness of the normative sample draws attention to possible bias in selecting studies. Issues such as research design, choice of comparison group, and the validity and reliability of aggregated outcome measures are all of vital importance. This chapter has offered the threats to validity approach as a useful heuristic in structuring the development of norms. Researchers have been encouraged to interpret norms with a view toward relevant theory and the substantive area in which the results are embedded. And finally, the question of whether meaningful change has been achieved cannot be ignored in any responsible set of conclusions based on treatment effect norms.

References

Barber, R. M., & Kagey, J. R. (1977). Modification of school attendance for an elementary population. *Journal of Applied Behavior Analysis, 10,* 41–48.

Brown, J. J., Lever, A. F., Robertson, J. I. S., *et al.* (1984). Salt and hypertension. *Lancet, ii,* 456.

Brownell, K. D. (1982). Obesity: Understanding and treating a serious, prevalent, and refractory disorder. *Journal of Consulting and Clinical Psychology, 50,* 820–840.

Bryant, F. B., & Wortman, P. M. (1984). Methodological issues in the meta-analysis of quasi-experiments. In W. H. Yeaton & P. M. Wortman (Eds.), *Issues in data synthesis* (pp. 5–24). Beverly Hills, CA: Sage.

Campbell, D. T. (1979). Assessing the impact of planned social change. *Evaluation and Program Planning, 2,* 67–90.

Campbell, D. T., & Stanley, J. C. (1966). *Experimental and quasi-experimental designs for research.* Chicago, IL: Rand McNally.

Canadian Cooperative Study Group. (1978). A randomized trial of aspirin and sulfinpyrazone in threatened stroke. *New England Journal of Medicine, 299,* 61–67.

Carlberg, C., & Kavale, K. (1980). The efficacy of special versus regular class placement for exceptional children: A meta-analysis. *Journal of Special Education, 14,* 295–309.

CESF Newsletter (1985). The University of Michigan, Ann Arbor, *3,* 2.

Chalmers, T. C., Celano, P., & Sacks, H. S. (1983). Bias in treatment assignment in controlled clinical trials. *New England Journal of Medicine, 309,* 1358–1361.

Cook, T. D., & Campbell, D. T. (1979). *Quasi-experimentation: Design and analysis issues for field settings.* Chicago, IL: Rand McNally.

Cook, T. D., & Reichardt, C. S. (Eds.). (1979). *Qualitative and quantitative methods in evaluation research.* Beverly Hills, CA: Sage.

Cordray, D. S. (Ed.). (1985). *Utilizing prior research in evaluation planning.* San Francisco: Jossey-Bass.

Cordray, D. S., & Bootzin, R. R. (1983). Placebo control conditions: Tests of theory or effectiveness? *The Brain and Behavioral Sciences, 2,* 286–287.

Cordray, D. S., & Orwin, R. C. (1983). Improving the quality of evidence. Interconnections among primary evaluation, secondary analysis, and quantitative synthesis. In R. J. Light (Ed.), *Evaluation studies review annual* (Vol. 8, pp. 91–119). Beverly Hills, CA: Sage.

Detre, K., & Peduzzi, P. (1982). The problems of attributing death of non-adherers: The VA coronary bypass experience. *Controlled Clinical Trials, 3,* 355–364.

Durlak, J. A. (1979). Comparing effectiveness of paraprofessional and professional helpers. *Psychological Bulletin, 86,* 80–92.

Fisher, B., Bauer, M., Margolese, R., *et al.* (1985). Five-year results of a randomized clinical trial comparing total mastectomy with or without radiation in the treatment of breast cancer. *The New England Journal of Medicine, 312,* 665–673.

Fisher, B., Redmond, C., Fisher, E. R., *et al.* (1985). Ten-year results of a randomized clinical trial comparing radical mastectomy with or without radiation. *The New England Journal of Medicine, 312,* 674–681.

Hedges, L. V. (1984). Advances in statistical methods for meta-analysis. In W. H. Yeaton & P. M. Wortman (Eds.), *Issues in data synthesis* (pp. 25–42). Beverly Hills, CA: Sage.

Hunter, J. E., Schmidt, F. L., & Jackson, G. B. (1982). *Meta-analysis: Cumulating research findings across studies.* Beverly Hills, CA: Sage.

Johnson, S. M., Mauritson, D. R., Corbett, J. R., Woodward, W., Willerson, J. T., & Hillis, L. D. (1981). Double-blind, randomized, placebo-controlled comparison of propranolol and verapamil in the treatment of patients with stable angina pectoris. *American Journal of Medicine, 71,* 443–451.

Johnston, J. (Ed.). (1984). *Evaluating the new information technologies.* San Francisco: Jossey-Bass.

Kavale, K. A., & Glass, G. V. (1984). Meta-analysis and policy decisions in special education. In B. E. Keogh (Ed.), *Advances in special education* (Vol. 4). Greenwich, Connecticut: JAI Press.

Kazdin, A. E. (1977). Assessing the clinical or applied importance of behavior change through social validation. *Behavior Modification, 1,* 427–452.

Kazdin, A. E., & Wilson, G. T. (1978). *Evaluation of behavior therapy: Issues, evidence, and research strategies.* Lincoln, NE: University of Nebraska Press.

Kolata, G. (1985). Heart panel's conclusions questioned. *Science, 227,* 40–41.

Kulik, J. A., Kulik, C.-L. C., & Cohen, P. A. (1980). Effectiveness of computer based college teaching: A meta-analysis of findings. *Review of Educational Research, 50,* 525–544.

Landman, J. T., & Dawes, R. M. (1982). Psychotherapy outcome. Smith and Glass' conclusions stand up under scrutiny. *American Psychologist, 37,* 504–516.

Light, R. J. (Ed.). (1983). *Evaluation Studies Review Annual* (Vol. 8). Beverly Hills, CA: Sage.

Light, R. J. (1984). Six evaluation issues that synthesis can resolve better than single studies. In W. H. Yeaton & P. M. Wortman (Eds.), *Issues in data synthesis* (pp. 57–73). San Francisco: Jossey-Bass.

McNeil, B. J., Weichselbaum, R., & Pauker, S. G. (1981). Speech and survival. Tradeoffs between quality and quantity of life in laryngeal cancer. *New England Journal of Medicine, 305,* 982–987.

McPeek, B., Gilbert, J. P., & Mosteller, F. (1977). The end result: Quality of life. In J. P. Bunker, B. A. Barnes, & F. Mosteller (Eds.), *Costs, risks, and benefits of surgery* (pp. 170–175). New York: Oxford University Press.

Miller, R. C., & Berman, J. S. (1983). The efficacy of cognitive behavior therapies: A quantitative review of the research evidence. *Psychological Bulletin, 94,* 39–53.

Minkin, N., Braukmann, C. J., Minkin, B. L., Timbers, B. J., Fixsen, D. L., Phillips, E. L., & Wolf, M. M. (1976). The social validation and training of conversational skills. *Journal of Applied Behavior Analysis, 9,* 127–140.

Nicholson, R. A., & Berman, J. S. (1983). Is follow-up necessary in evaluating psychotherapy? *Psychological Bulletin, 93,* 261–278.

Nurius, P. S., & Yeaton, W. H. (1987). An illustrated critique of "hidden" judgments, choices, and compromises. *Clinical Psychology Review, 7,* 695–714.

Office of Technology Assessment. (1978). *Assessing the efficacy and safety of medical technologies.* Washington, DC: U.S. Government Printing Office (Stock No. 052-003-00593-0).

Orwin, R. G., & Cordray, D. S. (1985). Effects of deficient reporting on meta-analysis: A conceptual framework and reanalysis. *Psychological Bulletin, 97,* 134–147.

Paul, G. L. (in press). Can pregnancy be a placebo effect?—Terminology, designs, and conclusions in the study of psychological and pharmacological treatments of behavioral disorders. In L. White, B. Tursky, & G. F. Schwartz (Eds.), *Placebo: Clinical phenomena and new insights.* New York: Guilford Press.

Peterson, L. (1984). Teaching home safety and survival skills to latch-key children: A comparison of two manuals and methods. *Journal of Applied Behavior Analysis, 17,* 279–293.

Rosenthal, R. (1984). *Meta-analytic procedures for social research.* Beverly Hills, CA: Sage.

Sacks, H., Chalmers, T. C., & Smith, H. (1982). Randomized versus historical controls for clinical trials. *American Journal of Medicine, 72,* 233–240.

Salend, S. J. (1984). Integrity of treatment in special education research. *Mental Retardation, 22,* 309–315.

Scovern, A. W., & Kilmann, P. R. (1980). Status of electroconvulsive therapy: Review of the outcome literature. *Psychological Bulletin, 87,* 260–303.

Sechrest, L., & Yeaton, W. (1981). Assessing the effectiveness of social programs: Methodological and conceptual issues. In S. Ball (Ed.), *Assessing and interpreting outcomes* (pp. 41–56). San Francisco: Jossey-Bass.

Sechrest, L., & Yeaton, W. H. (1982). Magnitudes of experimental effects in social science research. *Evaluation Review, 6,* 579–600.

Sechrest, L., & Yeaton, W. H. (1985). *Role of no-difference findings in applied research.* Manuscript submitted for publication.

Skinner, B. F. (1984). The shame of American education. *American Psychologist, 39,* 947–954.

Smith, M. L., & Glass, G. V. (1977). Meta-analysis of psychotherapy outcome studies. *American Psychologist, 32,* 752–760.

Staines, G. L. (1974). The strategic combination argument. In W. Leinfellner & E. Kohler (Eds.), *Developments in the Methodology of Social Science* (pp. 417–430). Dordrecht, Holland: D. Reidel.

Sulzbacher, S. I. (1973). Psychotropic medication with children: An evaluation of procedural biases in results of reported studies. *Pediatrics, 51,* 513–517.

Trowbridge, F. L. (1982). Attainable growth. *Lancet, 1,* 232.

Whiting-O'Keefe, Q. E., Henke, C., & Simborg, D. W. (1984). Choosing the correct unit of analysis in medical experiments. *Medical Care, 22,* 1101–1114.

Wolf, M. M. (1978). Social validity: The case for subjective measurement or how applied behavior analysis is finding its heart. *Journal of Applied Behavior Analysis, 11,* 203–214.

Wortman, P. M. (1981). Consensus development. In P. M. Wortman (Ed.), *Methods for evaluating health services* (pp. 1–22). Beverly Hills, CA: Sage.

Wortman, P. M. (1983). Evaluation research: A methodological perspective. *Annual Review of Psychology, 34,* 223–260.

Wortman, P. M. (1984). Evaluation at the frontier: Some timely comments for future use. *Evaluation Network, 5,* 35–44.

Wortman, P. M., & Bryant, F. B. (1985). School desegregation and black achievement. An integrative review. *Sociological Methods and Research, 13,* 289–324.

Wortman, P. M., & Yeaton, W. H. (1983). Synthesis of results in controlled trials of coronary artery bypass graft surgery. In R. J. Light (Ed.), *Evaluation studies review annual* (Vol. 8, pp. 536–551). Beverly Hills: Sage.

Wortman, P. M., & Yeaton, W. H. (1985). Cumulating quality of life results in controlled trials of coronary artery bypass graft surgery. *Controlled Clinical Trials, 6,* 289–305.

Yeaton, W. H. (1982a). A critique of the effectiveness of applied behavior analysis research. *Advances in Behavior Research and Therapy, 4,* 75–96.

Yeaton, W. H. (1982b, August). *An evaluation research perspective for assessing new psychotherapeutic techniques.* Paper presented at the meeting of the American Psychological Association, Washington, DC.

Yeaton, W. H., & Sechrest, L. (1981). Critical dimensions in the choice and maintenance of successful treatments: Strength, integrity, and effectiveness. *Journal of Consulting and Clinical Psychology, 49,* 156–167.

Yeaton, W. H., & Wortman, P. M. (1984). Evaluation issues in medical research synthesis. In W. H. Yeaton & P. M. Wortman (Eds.), *Issues in data synthesis* (pp. 43–56). San Francisco: Jossey-Bass.

Yeaton, W. H., & Wortman, P. M. (1985). Medical technology assessment: The evaluation of coronary artery bypass graft surgery using data synthesis techniques. *International Journal of Technology Assessment in Health Care, 1,* 125–146.

Yeaton, W. H., Greene, B. F., & Bailey, J. S. (1981). Behavioral community psychology: Strategies and tactics for teaching community skills to children and adolescents. In A. E. Kazdin & B. B. Lahey (Eds.), *Advances in Clinical Child Psychology,* (Vol. 4, pp. 243–282). New York: Plenum Press.

Yeaton, W. H., Wortman, P. M., & Langberg, N. (1983). Differential attrition: Estimating the effect of crossovers on the evaluation of a medical technology. *Evaluation Review, 7,* 831–840.

CHAPTER 8

An Evaluation of Behavioral Interrelationships in Child Behavior Therapy

Ian M. Evans, Luanna H. Meyer, Jayne A. Kurkjian, and Gloria S. Kishi

Introduction

Although William James's evocative metaphor for describing consciousness as a stream is still often quoted, the continuities of behavior that characterize everyday life seem equally noteworthy. In the early development of behavior therapy, or behavior modification, it was convenient to de-emphasize the descriptive complexity of the intermingling flow of individual repertoires, and concentrate instead on the identification of discrete behavioral events. This selective focus clearly served the field well, judging from the scientific and professional success of behavior modification. However, it imposed three conceptual restrictions on the field, all of which have become recognized in recent years. One of these is that the behavior identified as problematic tends to have high face validity (it is the problem as identified by the complainants), but may be superficial as the primary target for intervention. This is the issue of target behavior selection (Hawkins, 1986; Nelson & Hayes, 1979). Second, as frequency is the primary metric for reporting discrete behavioral events, the outcome of an intervention is expressed, and evaluated, in terms of changes in frequency that may or may not clarify the clinical value of the outcome. This is the issue of social validity (Kazdin, 1977; Voeltz & Evans, 1983; Wolf, 1978). And third, the causal variables for isolated behaviors are typically sought in environmental antecedents and consequences, without sufficient atten-

Ian M. Evans and Jayne A. Kurkjian • Department of Psychology, SUNY-Binghamton, Binghamton, New York 13901. **Luanna H. Meyer and Gloria S. Kishi** • Division of Special Education and Rehabilitation, Syracuse University, Syracuse, New York 13244–2280. Preparation of this chapter was supported in part by Contract 300-82-0363 from the Office of Special Education Programs, U.S. Department of Education, which was awarded to the University of Minnesota with a subcontract to Syracuse University. The opinions expressed herein do not necessarily reflect the position or policies of the U.S. Department of Education, and no official endorsement should be inferred.

tion to the role of other behaviors within the organism as independent variables (Staats, 1975).

Although all three issues are closely connected, this chapter will focus on the third concern. By analyzing the way responses are interrelated within individual repertoires, and by having a clearer understanding of the principles of response organization, we should be in a better position to design direct and indirect interventions that will be associated with long-term benefits and short-term behavior change. Short-term demonstrations of behavior change have been valued because, of course, they offer convincing and immediate evidence regarding the success of an intervention designed to alleviate a specified problem. It should not be surprising, therefore, that immediate effects on the target behavior have remained, for the most part, the commonly accepted and frequently used evaluation criterion in clinical practice and journal publications. This is true even though a closer look often reveals that the artificial treatment conditions are still in place and are difficult to remove without a return to the original, referral difficulties: Children remain in and return to special behavioral facilities and schools with predictable and disappointing regularity.

Continuing concern for generalization, maintenance, and, now, collateral behavior changes reveals the eventual confrontation with issues such as the meaningfulness and permanency of behavior change. Thus far, however, the field has viewed generalization and maintenance primarily as processes that take place after acquisition (Wildman & Wildman, 1975). There are signs we are becoming more analytical and creative in confronting such issues (Horner, Bellamy, & Colvin, 1984), but an alternative perspective to address continuing clinical intervention difficulties would require a more holistic view of behavioral events (Evans, Weed, Brown, & Weld, in press). We should be able to effect beneficial therapeutic change in complete personal repertoires, not just piecemeal behaviors. We should also be able to insure that unintended, negative collateral behaviors—or side effects—do not materialize. And, as Baer (1986) recently noted, we must document what else has happened: Do children still remain in special units and treatment facilities, or can they be returned to their families and communities? To accomplish outcomes such as these, behavior modification must adhere to its original, theoretical emphasis on the functional organization of the organism's repertoire in relationship to the environment. This in turn will require the design of interventions that do more than manipulate single target behaviors and the evaluation of outcomes that move beyond frequency, duration, and rate.

Some years ago, two senior authors published a detailed examination of response interrelationships in child behavior therapy (Voeltz [Meyer] & Evans, 1982). In some ways the present analysis is an update of that article, so we shall not repeat descriptions of the basic theoretical concepts and issues involved. In the 1982 paper, we surveyed the literature up to 1980 that provided evidence for the prevalence of collateral effects. In this chapter, we report a similar review of more recent studies. However, it no longer appears necessary to argue the point that positive and negative collateral effects do occur with regularity, whether planned for or not: this reality has become increasingly recognized. The information in the updated review is intended instead to utilize the more recently available data to specify further the different types of collateral effects that have been observed and their implications for understanding response interrelationships. This review does support the clinical relevance of considering response interrelationships in the design of interventions for children, but also reveals little progress in the use of methodologies that would allow us to do so more systematically. For reasons that will become apparent, the concept of response organization and the principles that determine it have special significance for behavioral interventions in educational contexts. Why this is so and how this information is relevant will be the focus of the chapter.

General Concepts

There are many organizing principles whereby behaviors can be considered to relate to each other, and a variety of behavioral constructs that imply response organization within repertoires. However, there are few agreed on methodologies for analyzing response interrelationships, and the elaborate observational and recording techniques that have been developed within behavior modification are designed for identifying individual behaviors. The types of relationships that may be observed within repertoires depend heavily on the specific behavioral measurement procedures and the descriptive statistics used for their analysis. To illustrate this point and to introduce some of the general methodological issues, consider the following description of behavior:

> Jim, a third-grade boy, is being observed on the school playground during recess. He is standing at the edge of the playground, talking to his friends and at the same time kicking up a little pile of dirt with his left foot. While still in the group of boys, he reaches into his pocket and pulls out a packet of gum. He does not offer it to his companions but unwraps one stick which he pops into his mouth and then drops the wrapper on the ground. At that moment, he turns and sees some other boys beginning to set up an impromptu game of soccer with a tennis ball. He runs over to join in and participates for a while, kicking the ball if it comes to him and shouting directions to some of the other players. After a few moments, he suddenly bends down and re-ties his shoelaces. One of the other boys yells at him to get up. When Jim does so, he runs over and punches his critic in the stomach. Shortly after that, a teacher appears and blows a whistle, calling out the usual command for everyone to line up as recess is over. Jim does not respond to the whistle, and instead kicks the ball in the opposite direction. He then runs off to retrieve it.

An important thing to remember about such a description is that although it is a fairly standard description of behavior, it contains numerous different levels of analysis from relatively molecular, physical units of motor behavior (kicking, standing) to very molar categories (participates in a game) with varying levels of inference (runs to retrieve the ball). As long as different levels of analysis are used in the original description and identification of behaviors, there are various ways, taxonomically, that some behaviors can be subsumed by others. For instance, kicking the ball is subsumed by the general category playing soccer as a necessary element. Kicking the dirt and taking out gum, however, are subsumed within the category talking to friends, but are not necessary components of that category: they simply fall within the temporal boundaries of the more general description of the activity.

Despite these complexities, if a researcher or clinician was interested in a single behavioral category, such as aggression, littering, or noncompliance, then the situation just described is relatively simple. In this case, what we are calling single behaviors are really single categories of behavior, each one covering a wide range of given instances or exemplars. To record these categories, the observer would have to be provided with operational definitions of aggression, littering, and noncompliance that would allow punching, dropping the gum wrapper on the ground, and not responding appropriately to the whistle to be included in their respective categories. With the exception of a few highly specific acts that are defined topographically, almost all behavioral intervention in educational or clinical settings is directed toward categories of responses. Although there could be any number of rules for including responses within a class, the typical one applied in behavioral analyses is to specify the common function of the different behaviors for the individual. Thus, behaviors that are physically very different from one another, such as kicking, punching, and pulling hair would all be considered exemplars of the concept of aggression if they shared the function of coercing others. And behaviors that are physically similar, like a playful punch or kicking a ball, would be excluded from that same category of behavior. Simply because an organizational rule can be specified for the observer does not necessarily imply that behaviors that follow the rule will represent a true class for the individual being observed. Thus, punching and kicking might be socially accepted aggressive behaviors in the boy's subculture, whereas hair pulling might be considered nonmasculine and therefore not part of a class of aggressive behaviors for that individual.

Personality is another organizational principle that is imposed by the observer. If a researcher were interested in a general personality level of description, the connection among behaviors would be based on the frequency of their occurrence within an individual in comparison to some reference group. Thus a teacher who had observed Jim on many different occasions might—if the behavior described earlier was typical—have formed the judgment that relative to other third-grade boys, Jim was more aggressive and less compliant. When asked to rate a group of children, this observer would then rate Jim as high on aggression and noncompliance. This does not mean that the behaviors co-occur, but simply that if many other children rated as highly aggressive were also rated as noncompliant, then statistical clustering techniques would support a relationship between aggressive behavior and noncompliant behavior. Assuming that we can be sure that the class of noncompliant behavior is not just a subset of the class of aggressive behaviors, then this type of approach has the potential to reveal that certain behavioral characteristics tend to be seen within individuals—and a syndrome has been identified. Although we argued earlier (Voeltz & Evans, 1982) that the notion of a syndrome implies recognition of response interrelationships, we would not agree with those who suggest that the syndrome is itself an organizational construct with much validity (e.g., Kazdin, 1983).

In the syndrome construct, the assumption of some kind of relationship between classes of behavior is derived from their tendency to be high or low (typical or atypical) within individuals relative to others. The same logic is applied to a relationship between behaviors within the individual: when one behavior is high (relative to an established baserate) the other behavior will be high (relative to its own baserate in the same individual). The parameters of high or low refer to frequencies within some time interval, and the correspondence between the behaviors is based on a series of intervals. Covariation of behaviors is always unique to the particular time windows of these two intervals, and all methodological problems in this area relate to this fact. To illustrate this temporal window for understanding response interrelationships, consider the girl who likes either to ride her bike or to watch TV during her free time. As she cannot do both things at once, a short interval used to represent an observation occasion—say 5 minutes—would reveal no relationship between the two activities or a negative one, as she would either be riding her bike or watching TV or doing something else entirely during most intervals. A slightly longer interval of perhaps a day would show that only on weekends or school holidays does she have much free time, and on these days TV watching and bike riding will be elevated. If the interval is made still longer—perhaps relative frequencies within given months—the relationship again changes because during winter months her bike riding is restricted and the covariation between these two functionally similar behaviors would not be noticeable.

It will be important to consider these methodological issues as we discuss some of the possible models for the way in which responses may be organized or interrelated within individual repertoires.

Models of Response Interrelationships

When we talk of response interrelationships we are usually not directly concerned with structural relationships, such as the way a series of responses are coordinated by the central nervous system into a smooth sequence. There are also homeostatic relationships between overt actions and the mobilization required to sustain and regulate these actions by the sympathetic and parasympathetic processes of the autonomic nervous system. Such physiological mechanisms do give rise to many interactions between response systems (Evans, 1986). However, we are here more concerned with functional, not organic, interactions that can be accounted for by psychological principles.

Behavioral Chains

One of the most obvious organizational principles is that of the response chain, in which one behavior immediately follows another. The early behavior may be thought to set the occasion for the next response, essentially functioning much like a discriminative stimulus. This is a familiar concept because many everyday tasks or routines consist of a series of actions learned in a sequence. Training children with disabilities to perform such tasks has typically involved a task analysis in which each discernible link in the chain is taught—either in a forward or backward sequence (cf. Snell, 1983).

In the case of an inappropriate activity, the evidence for a chained relationship is a high degree of consistency in the steps of the sequence, so that the occurrence of behaviors early in a chain (e.g., agitation) predict the rapid occurrence of others in fixed sequence (e.g., crying, task refusal, and then finally throwing the task materials). The importance of this concept for the design of interventions is, as recognized by classical learning theorists such as Hull and Guthrie, that the earlier responses in the chain, being furthest from the reinforcement that terminates the sequence, are the weakest habits. Distracting, redirecting, or otherwise extinguishing responses early in the stimulus–response chain is, therefore, considerably easier.

Behavioral Sequences

The difference between this concept and that of a chain is that the occurrence of one behavior does not trigger or *elicit* the occurrence of the next, but does increase the probability of the second behavior occurring sometime in the future. Descriptively these relationships are fairly easily identified by sequential analysis (Sackett, 1979). As the exact sequence of events does not inevitably occur, the metric of interest is the expected probability of the next response appearing in the next measured time interval, or the one after that, and so forth. Sackett and his colleagues have described a number of lagged sequential analysis procedures for establishing the conditional probability of one event following another, even when the behavior alters the future probability of a response that is quite far away in time.

The concept of the predictable sequence or order of events separated in time is easier to describe than to explain. In fact, it is not really a principle of response organization but a description of a response relationship that has many possible causes. One of these could be creating a physiological change by the first response, which increases the need for the second, or makes it more likely to occur, such as the relationship between binge eating and subsequent purging. In a study described by Borreson and Anderson (1982), a young man with profound mental retardation had a characteristic behavior that invariably preceded ruminative vomiting. This consisted of a series of tongue, mouth, and throat movements that began immediately following a meal and steadily increased in frequency until the vomiting occurred. When these early responses were consequated the rumination was eliminated, whereas when the vomiting alone was consequated the rumination was simply reduced. Another type of relationship occurs when the early response makes the later response more likely through mechanical means, such as setting an alarm clock so as to wake up at a particular time the next day. A common causal mediator is that the first behavior results in some social interaction which in turn influences the later behavior. For example, a student's inappropriate classroom behavior might result in a teacher ignoring the child who then engages in a more directed form of attention-seeking behavior later in the class. In cases like this the sequence may be highly predictable, but there is no intrinsic organizational principle linking the two undesirable behaviors.

Behavioral Hierarchies

Other than response chaining linked by the proprioceptive cue properties of the first behavior, the organizational concept of behavioral hierarchies was one of the few that was used frequently in classical learning theory (e.g., Hull, 1934). As a result of the individual's learning history, a variety of different responses are acquired in a given situation or stimulus context. Circumstances of reward, nature of the deprivation, and other motivational factors determine that some responses are more probable than others, thus creating a hierarchy of response probabilities. The response with the highest probability will be performed most regularly in that stimulus situation. If it is blocked in some way—physically, for example, or through extinction—then the next most probable response would be expected to occur (Cahoon, 1968). This is why the concept of behavioral hierarchies is so important for avoiding negative, unintended side effects. It is often assumed that the responses in this hierarchy constitute a response class and that they all potentially serve the same function. In reality, the minimal requirement is that they may all be elicited by the same situation. Furthermore, some responses that may have been reinforced in the past may cease to be functional, and thus would no longer be used by the organism.

Concomitant Responses

A fundamental assumption of the response hierarchy position is that only one complex behavior can occur at any given time, so that the individual must select a response for that situation. Consequently, no other response in the hierarchy can occur at the same time. However, there are many simpler responses that can literally co-occur—for example, as in the familiar joke, it *is* possible to walk and chew gum simultaneously. In our research (Evans & Voeltz, 1982) we typically found true co-occurrence with minor stereotypic behavior engaged in by students while they were also involved in instructional tasks. For instance, a child might be completing worksheets and at the same time swinging his or her legs and humming. In our observational system, we coded these instances as "excess behavior while on task," and found that this code occurred often in young children with severe handicaps who attended public school programs. In one-to-one instruction, for example, the category accounted for 26% of the total observation time, compared to 42% of the time in which the child engaged in academic tasks without any excess behavior occurring.

It is not clear exactly why these behaviors should be concurrent with activities and tasks requiring sustained attention and concentration, but it seems reasonable to assume that they serve some kind of arousal modulation function. As such they are integral to the dominant activity. Given that these elements are universal—watch any group of college students, for example, taking a difficult exam—the appropriate goal would be to limit their intrusiveness rather than eliminate them from the student's repertoire. In contrast, behavior such as sitting quietly with hands on lap or on the desk is sometimes demanded of special education students by their teachers; this may not only be an unnatural requirement—differing significantly from accepted levels of such self-stimulatory behaviors by nonhandicapped children and adults—but may also seriously interfere with the child's ability to do the primary task. If the behavior (e.g., pencil tapping) is being used to regulate attention, it may actually help the child to stay on task (e.g., complete the worksheet). The consequences of disallowing such a behavior could result in a reduction of on-task activities (Evans & Meyer, 1985). To use a familiar example: each of the chapter authors of this book and its readers has most likely deliberately arranged for or will use idiosyncratic behavioral props and aids to assist in the task of sharing knowledge by reading and writing. Drinking a cup of coffee while writing or snacking while reading can be effective strategies to maintain the motivation and level of attention needed to complete such a task.

Physical and anatomical conditions limit the true co-occurrence of behavioral events. However, there are entire classes of behavior that permit simultaneous occurrence once we look beyond motor activities. The most obvious examples are language and related cognitive activities that can take place in parallel with other activities that are often not even slightly related. Talking to a friend while driving a car is a good example. Occasionally, when some unusual event happens in relationship to driving, cessations in the speech flow or conversation reveal that attentional mechanisms and cognitive "executive" processes have been directed back to the driving activity. Similarly, those who are in the early stages of mastering a new motor skill—such as learning to walk—do not engage in some parallel cognitive or language activities without suffering negative consequences (e.g., the toddler who falls when distracted by a novel object). For the most part, the response systems involved do permit simultaneous activities, unrestricted by the physics of the motor system once fluency of behaviors has been developed. Thus it is possible to dictate a letter and drive a car at the same time, but difficult if not impossible to switch off the dictaphone and shift gears simultaneously.

When we see clusters of motor responses ostensibly occurring together, it is difficult to discern whether they are truly concomitant responses or simply elements of one response that have been identified as different by the observer. Because of the discrepant physical topographies involved, a student with severe disabilities who body rocks and slaps his face at the same time might be thought of as engaging in two behaviors at once. The meaning of this behavior pattern may be more complex if this represents a unitary activity, such as posting and holding the reins while riding a horse (which could be done separately) or shifting weight to one foot while kicking with the other (which could not). Experimental studies have attempted to separate the elements of a complex ritual, and if any of the elements can exist independently it follows that they are not simply parts of an integrated pattern that has been broken up into arbitrary units by the observer.

We have used, for instance, automated electronic data recording devices (MOREs) to observe excess behavior in real time (Evans & Voeltz, 1982). The internal clocks of the MORE record the durations of up to five different behaviors simultaneously, with the observer entering the codes for the child's behavior any time it changed (i.e., any time a response began, or an ongoing response ceased). Thus the MORE, in this real time mode, functioned like a multichannel event recorder. By sectioning this stream of behaviors every second, we were able to look at the true co-occurrence of responses and thus ascertain whether certain excess behaviors always stopped and started together (in which case they were probably elements of the same general action) or whether they occurred independently. Although the cost of gathering real time data is prohibitive, this methodology is really the only way applied researchers can determine co-occurrence of behavior, because the inference is more usually drawn from behaviors being seen to occur within the same, rather lengthy time window of the typical 5-, 20-, and 30-second observe/record interval used in direct observation.

Response Class

An opposite organizational pattern is when two or more responses cannot co-occur or be integrated into a more complex unit and represent equivalent behaviors that perform virtually identical functions. These may be considered substitutable (Rachlin & Burkhard, 1978). It is interesting to note that in correlational analysis, the behaviors would negatively correlate, assuming that an appropriate time window has been selected. This is not always clear from the literature. For example, Dehaven, Rees-Thomas, and Benton (1980) suggested that stereotyped responding could be defined as a response class whose members covary together. If responses form a class, it is likely that one will predominate until blocked or prevented in some way, and then another will be initiated. If they form a cluster of concurrent behaviors (such as rocking, head slapping, and teeth grinding), then they may indeed covary.

Building on the concept of response classes and depending upon the substitutability of behaviors, Carr, Durand, and others have designed interventions to deal with severe behavior problems that emphasize communicative behaviors as functional substitutes for negative responses. In this work, the negative responses are viewed as socially undesirable (though somewhat effective, for the child) strategies to obtain certain preferred consequences, such as obtaining food, materials, and/or social attention, or to escape from an unpleasant task or situation (Carr & Durand, 1985; Durand & Kishi, 1987). To the extent that communication behaviors are taught to accomplish the desired consequences in a socially acceptable but equally effective way, the behavior problems should be reduced and eliminated (thus displaying a negative correlation between the two types of behavior).

The concept of response class has been one of the most prominent in any discussion of response organization in behavior modification; Staats (1961), for example, used the notion of response classes to provide a behavioral analysis of language acquisition. In the operant laboratory, the fact that behaviors are defined very strictly in terms of their effects means that a variety of different, but equally effective, forms of behavior are reinforced, eventually forming a set (response class) of functionally equivalent responses. In an important paper challenging the entire presumption of response structure as a necessity, Baer (1982) argued that the "hallmark of a response class is that behavior changing procedures applied to a subset of the class produce similar results on all members of the class" (pp. 240–241). However, the examples he gives, of compliance training, imitational training, and so forth, are very different from the principle of simple functional equivalence and are more readily thought of as instances of rule learning or rule-governed behavior. Just as the observer must be given a rule for the inclusion and coding of many different behaviors as exemplars of the concept of aggression, compliance, and so forth, the natural contingencies of reinforcement and punishment provide children with information as to which behavioral classes are acceptable or unacceptable. Whenever social disapproval is expressed for some specific behavior, it is through verbal specification of the principle that results in entire classes of prosocial behavior being influenced in the child.

Responses Linked by a Common Influence

In this organizational concept, two behaviors that are not directly related to each other are nevertheless seen to covary (over relatively lengthy time periods) because both are influenced by some common factor that could be either a response or a behavioral state. An example might be two behaviors by a high school student that are not generally connected—smoking and damaging property—that tend to covary over time because both behaviors become more probable on days when the student cuts classes and leaves the school without authorization. The initial behavior of truancy created environmental opportunities that increased the probability of two otherwise unrelated activities.

Very often the common link is some behavioral state produced by one behavior. An elementary example is that of fatigue induced by vigorous exercise. After the exercise experience, a variety of generally unrelated physical activities may all be reduced. This effect, incidentally, has been observed by investigators attempting to reduce self-stimulatory and other excess behaviors in students with developmental disabilities, especially autism (e.g., Lancioni, Smeets, Ceccarani, Capodaglio, & Campanari, 1984; Watters & Watters, 1980). Some have suggested that the effect is not so much fatigue as some more direct mechanism involving the central nervous system, because the type and duration of exercise is important for reducing autistic behaviors (Kern, Koegel, & Dunlap, 1984). By the same token, if some autistic behavior problems are possibly related to the regulation of arousal, the performance of an activity that influences general arousal level would influence a number of other responses. Some of these influences are emotional states, such as depression: a family argument might result in a student experiencing depression, which influences studying behavior, responsiveness to friends and other social interactions, and appetite. Thus, very different behaviors, such as eating and studying, become linked over time when they are both negatively influenced by an event—an argument with parents that has generated criticism and resulted in general punishment of a variety of activities and behaviors.

Dynamic Interactions

Once emotional responses or emotional states are includes in our analysis of response repertoires, a wide array of dynamic interactions among responses becomes apparent. Although the experimental analysis of behavior has paid relatively little attention to such response interactions, they have been extensively examined in classical learning theory and have been incorporated generally in behavior therapy as a discipline. The basic assumption of this principle is that some behaviors—especially emotional responses—create motivational states such that the reduction in the behavior is reinforcing. This is the standard two-factor theory, which has proved invaluable in explaining a vast set of response relationships in adult behavior therapy (Levis, 1981). The reinforcing effect of emotional increase or decrease creates some of the most significant response interrelationships one is likely to observe.

A good example of such a dynamic interaction would be the behaviors involved in the eating disorder known as bulimia. Excessive eating or binging is typically regulated by appetite variables as well as by a concern over weight gain. A major source of internal regulation or control of eating (i.e., knowing that restricting eating results in weight loss and/or maintenance) is lost when a teenager learns that vomiting permits one to eat a great deal but not gain weight. Similarly, if the adolescent has major concerns about appearance and not gaining weight, then overeating generates feelings of anxiety that are immediately reduced by purging (voluntarily vomiting). However unpleasant the vomiting may be, the reinforcement from the anxiety reduction is much stronger. Binging behavior itself is controlled by other variables: there is a great deal of evidence to suggest that when an individual is experiencing stress, depression, rejection, and similar emotions, the tendency to binge is much higher (e.g., Chiodo, 1985). External factors thus play a complex role in eliciting the behavior, but the binge–purge pattern itself is closely interlinked in a dynamic system whereby the purging is strongly reinforced by reduction in the anxiety arising from the binging, and the binging is made more possible by the availability of the purging response. (We have presented this model as though it is factual; however, it is obviously a theoretical model for which there is good support but no definitive proof.)

In many cases of child behavior therapy, elaborate networks of interactive or dynamically related behaviors can be discerned (Evans, 1985), thus a major task confronting the clinician is to map out this complicated network of response interrelationships.

Reciprocal Relationships

The previous discussion has considered response interrelationships from the perspective of positive connections, that is, how one response in a repertoire somehow increases the probability of another. Of course, in the short term, two responses with similar functions might tend to alternate so that as the probability of one decreases the other would increase. Over a broader time frame, however, the two behaviors would show a more direct relationship, as would occur when all examples of that response class are reduced. Next, however, we shall examine the issues surrounding the nonoccurrence of a behavior and the true negative relationship that exists when the occurrence of one response reliably predicts the nonoccurrence of another.

What makes these relationships seem so paradoxical is our convention of talking about increasing and decreasing behaviors. In actuality, we change only the relative frequency of behaviors within a fixed repertoire. When an inappropriate behavior is reduced in frequency, some other behavior must fill the void and replace the excess behavior; this is a question of simple logic, based on the premise that a living organism must always be engaging in behavior. What is the opposite of, say, aggressive behavior as a response class? Basically there are three possibilities: (a) nonaggressive behavior that is not restricted in any way, such as playing the piano or watching TV—that is, anything other than aggression; (b) nonaggressive behavior that is appropriate and achieves the same or similar function, such as assertive behavior; and (c) a specific alternative response that does not achieve the function but that is maladaptive or inappropriate, such as self-injury. (If only one exemplar within the response class of aggression were reduced, then a fourth possibility is that another equally aggressive response would become more likely: the student consequated for hitting others might start pinching them instead.)

In learning theory, it has been recognized for some time that extinction or punishment contingencies that reduce the frequency of some responses raise the frequency of other behaviors in the individual's repertoire. These can be relatively passive behaviors such as, for a rat in an operant chamber, sitting still or increasing grooming instead of pressing the lever. Whether a variety of other behaviors all increase their probability slightly or one other alternative behavior increases greatly is a function of three influences: the exact contingency conditions of extinction, whether an alternative response is made available, and the prior organization of behavior within the individual's repertoire. From this analysis, the various intervention options follow: in reducing an excess behavior, one can simply impose an extinction (or negative consequences) contingency, in which case the form of the alternative behaviors that will emerge is left unspecified and will depend on prior reinforcement history relative to the other available responses in the child's repertoire, intrinsic response organization, or adventitious positive contingencies. Conversely, one can simultaneously impose the extinction contingency and a positive reinforcement contingency for a specified alternative behavior(s), which could be behavior the child already has and/or ones that must be concurrently taught.

The range of the latter option is considerable. At least the following versions can be identified (remembering that in each case an extinction or negative consequences contingency *is* in effect for the targeted excess behavior): (a) omission training, in which reinforcement is delivered contingent on a period of time in which any behaviors other than the targeted excess occur; (b) DRO (differential reinforcement of other behavior), in which any set of other behaviors not including the target behavior is reinforced; (c) DRI (differential reinforcement of incompatible behavior) in which an explicit behavior that is not the target behavior and is considered incompatible with it is reinforced.

Incompatibility itself varies. Some behaviors are topographically incompatible with the targeted excess and thus cannot be performed at the same time. Others are just alternative behaviors that fill time but are not topographically incompatible. Still others are incompatible but also functionally equivalent to the target behavior, so that they are good alternatives or substitutes for the excess behavior. We could therefore derive a fourth category, the differential reinforcement of other (preferably incompatible) behavior that serves the same function as the targeted behavior in a more socially acceptable manner. These other, incompatible behaviors that are functionally equivalent but more socially acceptable could be ones the child already has but is not using appropriately or they could be ones that the child does not have and that therefore must be taught. With children who have severe disabilities and behavior problems, it is far more likely that the child has no incompatible skill to readily substitute, without instruction, for negative behavior—a probability that led Staats (1975) to observe many years ago that punishment seems theoretically indefensible as a major and viable intervention mechanism for these individuals. Instead, instruction to build new responses must receive major emphasis if lasting behavior change is to be a possibility.

Along these lines, educative or curricular approaches are currently receiving major attention as the appropriate interventions for reducing excess behavior (Meyer & Evans, 1986). One of the most interesting features of this approach is that it necessitates a good understanding of what the functions of various excess behaviors are: this will require a serious reconsideration of strategies for a functional analysis of behavior that go beyond the simple identification of immediate antecedents and consequences. Careful assessments of the learner's abilities and needs will also be required to provide input into the identification of alternative skills that can feasibly be acquired by the child to replace excess behavior. From this educative perspective, it is surprising that many behavior modification experts have argued that excess behavior interferes with instruction, so that before any new, more adaptive alternative behavior can be taught, excess behaviors must first be reduced. To us, this mistaken argument has subtly contributed to the use of more and more intrusive and aversive contingencies or negative consequences. This occurs because the educator or clinician struggles to reduce a behavior that serves some function without providing an explicitly adaptive alternative skill that the child can use. If the function is important (which it must be for the child) and he or she is taught no alternative ways to accomplish it, it seems obvious that it will be extremely difficult to extinguish the techniques that he or she does have to meet continuing needs (no matter how socially inappropriate or costly to the child in other ways). Furthermore, even if such negative behaviors are reduced by an intervention, they are highly likely to reappear in the future if, again, no equally powerful alternative has been acquired.

Clearly, modifying an excess through teaching an adaptive alternative may take a certain amount of time, and during this time period some tactics may be needed to interfere with the occurrence of the negative behavior. This is crucial, for example, with life-threatening and dangerous behaviors. Evans and Meyer (1985) discussed these needs and tactics in some detail. Once the new skill is acquired, it must also become the most probable response for a given situation, occur spontaneously, and be reinforced by the natural environment so that it is truly functional as a substitute for the old problem behavior. If behaviors such as screaming and throwing objects are found to be serving the function of escape from aversive tasks and the student is therefore taught an appropriate communication signal for "I want to stop this activity" or "I need a break," then that alternative and preferable form (which might be a single word or a sign) must be understood by all controlling adults in the student's environment and must be reinforced by them. Because this is not always possible or even desirable (e.g., not all tasks can be permanently avoided), the new communication skill creates a further situational opportunity. It reveals an additional educational need in the individual's repertoire, such as an inability to tolerate unpleasant or difficult tasks. As suggested earlier these skill deficit explanations do not really represent organizational concepts, but they do illustrate instances in which a response (or actually lack of a response) is a causal or independent variable for the behavior of concern.

In terms of collateral effects, a logical conclusion of the present argument is that behavioral events will always fill the void when an excess behavior's probability is reduced. Thus, there are always collateral effects. These new probabilities may not be measured, particularly if they are simply extensions of former activities, but they will certainly be present. If a new behavior that has been planned for emerges (and is recorded), then it might be considered as a collateral effect but it is certainly directly related to the treatment. For example, it has now become quite common to reduce stereotypic responding by teaching toy play or some other constructive way to spend leisure time, especially when alone (e.g., Meyer, Evans, Wuerch, & Brennan, 1985). This is based on the premise that much stereotypic behavior serves a self-stimulatory function. Assuming that appropriate play does not include self-stimulations with the toys or leisure materials, appropriate play is an incompatible alternative that could appear as a collateral effect but should more correctly be thought of as a mediating variable, establishing the integrity of the intervention (Yeaton & Sechrest, 1981). First, was the clinician successful in teaching the alternative leisure skill (treatment integrity), and second, did this strategy result in the elimination of self-stimulation (treatment outcome)? In these situations, it is of great importance to monitor the appearance of the appropriate behavior and its concomitant effect on the inappropriate behavior revealed in settings other than the treatment environment in which the new activities were explicitly introduced. Otherwise, the apparent effect of the treatment is really no more than a physical artifact of the intervention, producing a variety of behaviors that occupy time and thus inevitably reduce the frequency of the excess behavior.

Other Causes of Collateral Effects

In the previous comments, we made it clear that there are consequences of interventions that are not collateral effects arising from principles of response organization. In this section, we shall briefly review some of these, because although best described as treatment artifacts, some may still be useful sequelae of well-designed interventions. Probably the most dramatic of these effects is when the intervention establishes a new response in the individual's repertoire or greatly increases the frequency of an existing behavior. For instance, Wolfe, Mendes, and Factor (1984) decreased children's TV viewing time and noted an increase in time spent reading and doing homework. These activities just filled the time void, but it is also likely that far less positive behaviors could have increased rather than these. There might have been, for example, an increase in the amount of time spent roughhousing in the living room or talking on the phone to a friend, conceivably representing negative side effects (collateral behavior).

A second, common cause of collateral effects is more superficial. This is the direct effect of the intervention on the student. Negative effects often occur if the intervention is aversive in some way, by causing pain, humiliation, and so forth. In such instances the aversive intervention itself will elicit emotional responses (screaming, crying, temper tantrums), aggressive responses that are escape motivated (such as lashing out at the teacher or intervention agent), and withdrawal/avoidance behaviors (such as bolting from the situation or avoiding that adult or task in the future, or, in more competent students, such elaborate tactics as running away, truancy, and unemployment). If the original excess behavior served an escape function, these negative collateral effects of treatment may be even more extreme.

Positive collateral consequences of the intervention also occur, especially in children who might not be receiving very high densities of social interaction or positive reinforcement in their natural environment. The introduction of a treatment program often provides new opportunities for reward, social contact, and other situational changes that increase positive affect. A good illustration of this is provided in Matson and Stephens (1981). The target behavior identified in a person with severe retardation was patting the walls while walking from place to place. With the introduction of an overcorrection procedure that did reduce wall patting, there was a concomitant increase in smiling and conversing. This positive change appeared to be the direct consequence of the social contact between the client and the therapist administering the overcorrection. Overcorrection did have immediate effects on behavior: wall patting was, of course, physically prevented during the overcorrection, whereas the social contact increased the client's smiling and conversing with the therapist. What has occurred in this instance is not a direct relationship between appropriate and inappropriate behavior, but an indirect chain in which incidents of wall patting evoked overcorrection, which required that the therapist approach and initiate physical exercise, which, in turn, was related to smiling and conversing in the context of increased social contact. Thus, as the authors pointed out, when the target behavior decreased and overcorrection was then used less often, appropriate social responses declined accordingly. During the maintenance phase, when wall patting had been extinguished, social responses also reverted once again to zero levels.

A third mechanism that has been frequently reported in the literature is one in which the positive outcome of the improvement in behavior begins to have a snowballing or ripple effect on the individual's repertoire and his or her interactions with others (Evans, 1985). This happens through a series of slightly different influences. One, closely related to the social intervention just described, is that the improved behavior serves to change the way the individual is treated by others, so that reductions in negative behavior allow for more approval behavior from others. This generates an entire series of more positive social interactions. Another influence is more direct: the new behavior allows the student to do things he or she could not do before. For example, Bornstein and Knapp (1981) reported how a reduction in self-expressed fear resulted in or permitted more effective social interactions and more regular school attendance. A related direct influence is the logical or natural sequelae to certain behaviors, such as a reduction in chronic vomiting resulting in weight gain (Apolito & Sulzer-Azaroff, 1981).

These are not really collateral effects based on response organization as much as the natural consequences of precipitating a new set of causal influences. Hawkins (1986) discussed the value of access behaviors, which are important because they increase the likelihood of gaining access to environments, situations, and interactions that are reinforcing and provide opportunities for further learning and rewards. Hence, children with severe disabilities might be taught to play with the kinds of leisure materials enjoyed by their nonhandicapped peers in order to develop a shared interest and skill repertoire that is more supportive of social interactions between children with and without disabilities than developmentally appropriate activities would be (Meyer & Putnam, in press). Finally, improvement in certain behavioral areas have the potential of changing the individual's own appraisal of self and his or her capabilities, enhancing self-esteem, increasing confidence, and positively influencing mood and self-image.

Collateral Effects Reported in Recent Studies

In order to examine the direct, indirect, and intervention-induced collateral effects of the kind described thus far, we surveyed the recent literature, following the same format as was used in the earlier review (Voeltz & Evans, 1982). Nineteen journals in child psychology, behavioral psychology, special education, and/or developmental disabilities were comprehensively searched to identify all studies in which a successful effort to reduce an excess behavior included some information that concomitant nontargeted behavior changes also occurred. Table 1 summarizes this information for the 65 studies located for the 5-year time period from summer 1980 through summer 1985 that met the following criteria: (a) a negative excess behavioral target was modified, through either a behavior reduction effort or skill instruction; (b) the subject(s) was kindergarten age through age 19; and (c) internal validity of the study results (as opposed to the reported behavioral interrelationship) was supported by a demonstration of experimental control, generally through the use of an acceptable within-subject design. With one difference, these criteria are the same as those used to identify the 29 studies reporting collateral effects that were published prior to summer 1980 and reviewed earlier (Voeltz & Evans, 1982). The only difference between the two sets of studies is that the earlier review—and the corresponding table in that review—included preschool studies as well. Thus, the increase in total number of studies reporting collateral effects (from 29 over the 10-year period 1970–1980 to 65 for 1980–1985) is substantial.

Unfortunately, the quality of this information does not appear to be increasing as well. In fact, there are noticeable declines in the number of studies that support claims of collateral effects with either reference to a potentially verifiable written record or behavioral observation rather than simply anecdoctal report. In addition, support for the collateral behavior change as a function of the intervention to change the target behavior—evidenced by information on the collateral response(s) collected across all phases of the experimental design—is provided in slightly fewer studies than was true in our earlier review. Table 2 summarizes these data. In contrast to these disappointing trends, the sheer number of studies now being done that include substantive documentation of the collateral effects has increased greatly (see Table 2). In the earlier survey we found a strong tendency for authors to report collateral improvements incidentally in the discussion section of the articles, whereas many more investigators now seem to be aware of collateral effects and to look for them. There are fewer reports of negative collateral or side effects; if this decrease in reporting reflects a decrease in occurrence of such negative effects, it indicates a growing sensitivity in behavior modification to the very real problem that some interventions may effectively reduce excess behavior and/or increase skills, but do so at considerable cost to the student.

This latter sensitivity is important because it seems hard for educators and clinicians to recognize the possibility that well-intentioned interventions could actually have negative consequences for children. There must always be costs (not necessarily financial, which is another issue) to clients whenever treatments are planned: in terms of how educational resources, time, instructional opportunity and so on are allocated, and in terms of the outcomes—of positive behaviors and opportunities lost or negative behaviors increased.

Table 1. Reported Nontarget Changes Produced by Interventions Designed to Reduce Excess Behavior

Study	Intended excess target behavior[a]	Concurrent nontarget behavior changes[b]	Type[c]	I.V.?[d]	Design
Adams (1980)	Hair pulling	+ Closer proximity to classmates (+) + Initiates play (+) + Initiates conversation (+) + Independence in self-help (+) + Relaxed and outgoing (+)	1	No	Multiple treatment following baseline
Altman, Grahs, & Friman (1982)	Thumb-sucking	− Hair-pulling (−)	4	Yes	ABAB, then CBC
Altman, Haavik, & Higgins (1983)	Self-injurious behavior	+ Mouthing (−)	1	No	ABCBC
Ball, Purna, Rios, & Constantine (1985)	Finger biting	Noted increased willingness and ability to engage in therapy and educational activities	1	No	ABAB
Barmann (1980)	Hand-mouthing (resulting in rumination)	− Rumination	?	?	ABAB
Barmann & Vitali (1982)	Trichotillomania	+ Appropriate interaction w/other family members (+)	3	No	Multiple baseline across subjects
Barrett, Matson, Shapiro, & Ollendick (1981)	A. Sucking finger behaviors	− Topographically similar	4	No	Alternating treatment design
	B. Tongue protrusion	− Topographically similar behaviors			
Barrett & Linn (1981)	Toe walking	+ Ankle dorsiflexion	2	Yes	ABABC
Baumeister & MacLean (1984)	A. Self-injury	+ Interactions with others − Self-stimulatory behavior	2,3	Yes	ABA with changing criterion
	B. Self-injury	+ Interactions with others − Self-stimulatory behavior			
Belacher, Conetta, Cole, Iannotti, & McGovern (1982)	Tantrum behavior	+ Appropriate social behavior (+)	3	No	AB
Bierly & Billingsley (1984)	Stereotypic manipulation of objects	+ Appropriate toy play	3	Yes	ABAB
Blount, Drabman, Wilson, & Stewart (1982)	Diurnal bruxism	+ Laughing (+) + Playing (+) + Sociable behavior (+)	1	No	AB
Bornstein & Knapp (1981)	Fear-related verbal remarks Self-reported fears	+ Regular school attendance (+) + Effective interaction w/peers (+) + Involvement in appropriate activities (+)	4	No	AB

(*continued*)

Table 1. (*Continued*)

Study	Intended excess target behavior[a]	Concurrent nontarget behavior changes[b]	Type[c]	I.V.?[d]	Design
Chambers, Sanok, & Striefel (1980)	Running away				ABCBCD
Clements, Ditchburn, & Grumm (1982)	Spitting and playing with saliva	− Masturbation (−) − Poking (−) + Engagement (+) − Tapping (−)	3	Yes	ABAB
Cordle & Long (1980)	Hair-pulling	+ Confidence (+) + Assertiveness (+)	1	No	AB
Czyzewski, Barrera, & Sulzer-Azaroff (1982)	Stereotyped hand movements	− Tantrum screaming (−) + Child initiated interactions (+)	3	Yes	ABAB
Dehaven, Rees-Thomas, & Benton (1980)	A. Hand & finger waving, rocking B. Staring, rocking C. Throwing head back, aggressive behaviors	+ Toy touching (+)	3	Yes	ABAB
DeLuca & Holborn (1984)	Hair-pulling Nail biting	+ Interest in boys (+) + Interest in school-related activities (+) − Absences from school (−) + Enjoyment of social events (+)	1	No	ABC
Durand (1982a)	Hitting face and head Flicking nose	+ Play behavior (+)	3	Yes	Multiple baseline
Durand (1982b)	Hitting self	+ Fine motor tasks (+) − Drooling (−)	3	Yes	Withdrawal design
Eason, White, & Newsom (1982)	A. Finger flicking, kicking legs B. Waving head, biting hands C. Rocking body, banging hand on floor, banging object on leg or floor D. Staring upward, twirling object E. Lining up blocks, staring at objects, flicking fingers F. Twirling objects, finger-flicking	A. + Toy play (+) B. + Toy play (+) C. + Toy play (+) D. + Toy play (+) E. + Toy play (+) F. + Toy play (+)	3	Yes	Multiple baseline across subjects
Favell, McGimsey, & Schell (1982)	A. Hand-mouthing B. Eye-poking C. Eye-poking D,E,F. Pica	A. + Toy play (+) + Interaction w/staff (+) B. + Toy play (+) C. + Toy play (+) D,E,F. + Toy chewing + Eating popcorn (+) + Toy holding (+)	4	Yes	A. ABABCBC B. ABAB C. ABAB D,E,F. Multielement design

Table 1. *(Continued)*

Study	Intended excess target behavior[a]	Concurrent nontarget behavior changes[b]	Type[c]	I.V.?[d]	Design
Fellner, Larouche, Sulzer-Azaroff (1984)	Self-stimulation	+ Toy play (+) + Then—novel self-stimulation (−)	3	Yes	ABAB
Framer & Sanders (1980)	Fitful sleeptalking, sleepwalking, nightmares, improvement in family communication/interaction	− Disturbed sleep (−)	1	No	AB
Gaylord-Ross, Weeks, & Lipner (1980)	Biting self	+ Noted soft vocalizations (+) + Noted loud vocalizations (−)	1	Yes	ABAB across task conditions
Gaylord-Ross, Weeks, Lipner, & Gaylord-Ross (1983)	Self-injury ($n = 22$)	+ Instructional task completed (+)	3	Yes	Group design (6 exp'l't conditions)
Graziano & Mooney (1982)	Nighttime fears	+ Occurrence of new psychological problems (−)	1	No	Extended follow-up of original study
Greene, Bailey, & Barber (1981)	Excessive noise-making on the school bus	− Out of seat (−) − Roughhousing (−)	3	Yes	ABABC ex 1 ABAB exp 2
Gross, Farrar, & Liner (1982)	Hair-pulling	+ Toy play (+)	1	No	Modified reversal design ABABCD
Gunter, Brady, Shores, Fox, Owen, & Goldzweig (1984)	A. Stereotypic vocalizations B. Stereotypic vocalizations	A. − Rocking (−) − Mouthing (−) − Hand movements (−) − Lip mouthing (−) B. − Rocking (−) − Mouthing (−) − Gazing (−)	3	Yes	Multiple baseline across activities
Hayashida (1982)	O-C rituals	+ Then—2 non-targeted rituals (−)	2	Yes	Multiple baseline
Johnson, Baumeister, Penland, & Inwald (1982)	A. Self-injury (20-yr.-old) B. Self-injury (44-yr.-old)	A. − Self-hitting (−) − Hand-mouthing (−) − Head to chair (−) − Inappropriate vocalizations (−) − Foot stomping (−) − Stereotypy (−) B. − Pinching (−) − Biting (−) − Leg hitting (−) − Chair slapping (−) − Stereotypy (−) − Tongue chew (−) − Verbalization (+) − Inappropriate verbalization (−)	3	Yes	A. ABACA B. ABCBA

(continued)

Table 1. (*Continued*)

Study	Intended excess target behavior[a]	Concurrent nontarget behavior changes[b]	Type[c]	I.V.?[d]	Design
Johnson *et al.* (1982) (*continued*)	C. Stereotypy (13-yr.-old)	C. − Hand and finger stereotypy (−) − Self-hitting (−) − Hyperventilation (−) − Body rocking and head rolling (−) − Biting (−) − Lap slapping (−) − Crying (−) − Yelling (−) − Self-restraint (−)			C. ABCDEA
Kellerman (1980)	Nightmares, nocturnal anxiety	+ General assertiveness (+)	1	No	Not clear
Kerr, Strain, & Ragland (1982)	Negative social interaction	+ Social interaction (+)	3	Yes	ABABCBC
Lancioni, Smeets, Ceccarani, & Gossens (1983)	Task-related responses (all subjects) and: A. Hand-flapping B. Head-weaving C. Finger-playing	A,B,C. − Non-targeted self-stimulatory behaviors (−)	3	No	ABACB
Lochman, Burch, Curry, & Lampron (1984)	Off-task behavior	+ Subjective feelings of self-esteem (+)	1	No	Group design (2 × 2)
Lockwood & Bourland (1982)	A. Finger biting B. Arm biting, face slapping	A. + Toy play (+) B. + Toy play (+)	3	Yes	A. AB B. ABAB
Luce & Hall (1981)	A. Inappropriate verbalizations	None	1	No	A. ABAB
	B. Inappropriate verbalization	B. − Escape behaviors (−)	1	No	B. ABCAB
	C. Inappropriate verbalization	Noted crying and complaining when contingent exercise introduced . . . reduced number of stand-ups required	1	No	C. Multiple baseline across time period
Luiselli (1980)	A. Running from ?B. Room to room, loud screaming	Parents noted that reprimands prior to T.O. acquired aversive properties/parents reported child more responsive to their requests	1	No	A. AB B. ABAB
Luiselli (1984)	Aggressive and destructive acts	+ Appropriate display of anger (+) + Expression of sadness and sympathy (+)	2	No	AB
Luiselli & Rice (1983)	Inappropriate peer interactions	+ Toy play (+)	3	Yes	ABAB
Luiselli, Myles, & Littman-Quinn (1983)	Aggression	+ Screaming, kicking banging door while in T.O. (−)	4	No	Multiple baseline across behaviors & settings

Table 1. (*Continued*)

Study	Intended excess target behavior[a]	Concurrent nontarget behavior changes[b]	Type[c]	I.V.?[d]	Design
MacLean & Baumeister (1982)	Abnormal stereotyped movements	+ Visual regard for people and objects + Playing w/people, toys, pets	1	No	ABAB *S* 1/2 AB *S* 3/4
McGonigle, Duncan, Cordisco, & Barrett (1982)	A. Self-stimulation B. Self-stimulation C. Self-stimulation D. Self-stimulation	A. + Spontaneous play (+) B. None C. None D. None	3	No	C,D. Multiple baseline across *Ss* (*Ss* C/D) and behaviors (*Ss* A/B)
Michelson, DiLorenzo, Calpin, & Williamson (1981)	Excessive noise in lunchroom	+ Appropriate lunchroom behaviors (+)	3	Yes	ABAB
Miles & Cuvo (1980)	Disruptive behaviors	+ Task completion (+)	1	Yes	A-BC-A-BC -A-CD-A-CD-BC
Mulick, Schroeder, & Rojahn (1980)	Rumination	+ Toy play	3	Yes	Multiple treatment following baseline
Page, Finney, Parrish, & Iwata (1983)	A. Food stealing	During treatment: + weight gain (−) Follow-up: − weight gain (+)			
	B. Food stealing	During treatment: + weight gain (−) Follow-up: − weight gain (+)	2	No	Multiple baseline across subjects For each S, multiple baseline across 3 settings
Polvinale & Lutzker (1980)	Nonsexual assaultive behavior Inappropriate interpersonal sexual behavior	+ Social interactions with peers (+)	2	No	Modified multiple baseline across time of day and settings
Rapoff, Altman, & Christophersen (1980)	Self-hitting	Teacher reported *S* more compliant following treatment	1	No	ABAB
Reilich, Spooner, & Rose (1984)	Stereotypic behavior	+ Workshop production (+) + Enhanced learning (+)	2 1	No	AB
Rincover & Devany (1982)	A. Head banging B. Face scratching C. Head banging	A. + Discrimination skills (+) C. + Readiness activities (+)	4	No	A. ABC B. ABAB C. ABAB Treatments introduced at one time

(*continued*)

Table 1. (*Continued*)

Study	Intended excess target behavior[a]	Concurrent nontarget behavior changes[b]	Type[c]	I.V.?[d]	Design
Rincover & Devany (1982) (*continued*)					for (A) and (C) and then for (B) in quasi multiple baseline design
Riordan, Iwata, Wohl, & Finney (1980)	Food refusal, food selectivity	− Disruptive behavior (−)	3	Yes	Multiple baseline across food items
Rosen & Rosen (1983)	Stealing	− Physical aggression (−) − Verbal aggression (−) − Property destruction (−) − Teasing (−) − Leaving assigned area (−)	2	Yes	ABABC
Simpson & Swenson (1980)	A. Rumination	+ Proximity to others (+) + Appropriate toy play (+) − Face slapping (−) − Body rocking (−) − Thumb sucking (−)	3	Yes	ABAB
	B. Repetitive vocalizations	+ Proximity to others (+) + Appropriate play (+) − Jumping (−) − Hand clapping (−) − Body spinning (−)			
Singh, Dawson, & Manning (1981)	Stereotypic behavior	+ Smiling (+) + Communicating (+) + Laughing in response to staff playing or talking to subject (+)	3	Yes	ABAB
Singh, Manning, & Angell (1982)	Rumination	+ Stereotyped behavior (−) + Socially appropriate behavior (+)	3	Yes	AB
Thorbecke & Jackson (1982)	Drooling	+ Spontaneous statements about her drooling (?)	1	No	ABAB
Tomporowski (1983)	Withdrawal, self-stimulation, rigidity	+ Self-initiated responses (+)	3	Yes	AB
Watters & Watters (1980)	Self-stimulatory behaviors design ($n = 5$)	+ Correct responses on learning tasks (+)	3	Yes	Group
Wesolowski & Zawlocki (1982)	Eye-gouging	+ Responding to simple verbal instructions (+) + Responding to their names (+) + Reaching out to touch staff (+) + Involvement in SPED classes and other activities (+)	3	No	ABAB exp 1 AB exp 2

Table 1. *(Continued)*

Study	Intended excess target behavior[a]	Concurrent nontarget behavior changes[b]	Type[c]	I.V.?[d]	Design
Williamson, Calpin, DiLorenzo, Garris, & Petti (1981)	Hyperactive behavior	+ Spelling/arithmentic performance (+)	4	No	ABAB
Wolfe, Mendes, & Factor (1984)	Excessive TV viewing time	+ Time spent reading (+) + Time spent on homework (+)	3	Yes	Multiple baseline across families
Woods (1982)	Head banging, hand biting, aggression	Reported to be greatly improved in performance and interactions	1	No	ABA

[a]Alphas indicate different subjects and/or experiments.
[b]Each behavior is followed by (+) or (−) where + = positive behavior and − = excess behavior. Positive collateral effects would include increases for + behaviors and decreases for − behaviors, whereas negative effects include decreases for + behaviors and increases for − behaviors.
[c]In each case, the nature of the reported data on nontargeted behavior change has been classified according to one of three major types: 1 = anecdotal records (usually verbal reports); 2 = verifiable written records (such as skill acquisition data, new placement, and so forth), though not reported in the study; 3 = behavioral observation of the nontarget behaviors; and 4 = other (that is, collateral effects were described but no data source could be determined).
[d]If the monitoring of the nontarget behavior change is included within the experimental design, the I.V.? (internal validity) column lists a "yes." If "no" is marked, the reported nontarget behavior change (regardless of type) cannot be attributed to the intervention.

Table 2. Studies of Excess Behavior Change Reporting Collateral Effects in Major Journals in Child Psychology, Behavioral Psychology, Special Education, and/or Developmental Disabilities

Information	Number/percentages of studies[a]: A: Through summer 1980	B: Summer 1980 through summer 1985[b]
Total no. meeting criteria	29	65
Collateral effects supported by:		
• Anecdotal report	10(34%)	22(34%)
• Verifiable report	7(24%)	8(12%)
• Behavioral observation	20(69%)	30(46%)
Internal validity of collateral behavior change supported by design?	16(55%)	32(49%)

[a]The number and percentages across the coding categories total more than 65 studies and 100% respectively, because of multiple data sources and/or more than one subject specified for some studies.
[b]Collateral changes were reported for an additional 8 studies but the data source was unspecified.

A few years ago, in attempting to study teachers' decision-making processes surrounding such costs and benefits, we (Evans and Meyer) designed a study based on decision theory to see whether teachers would judge the increase in a negative behavior worse or better than the decrease in a positive behavior as a result of an intervention. The study failed, essentially because we were unable to find any teacher subjects who were willing to rate either type of cost as more or less acceptable; both were considered totally unacceptable by our special education teacher sample. Admirable as this is, it does not remove the problem, so in our manual recommending decision strategies to teachers we have a procedure in which we ask them to consider the collateral costs and benefits and from that information decide whether a planned intervention should be implemented as designed. From our survey of published studies, however, one would have difficulty deriving much guidance for teachers—this seems to be a clear instance of the published research literature being less advanced than the best practices of master teachers and other clinicians.

In another way the studies listed do not provide a particularly useful set of guidelines regarding response organization. Although collateral effects were indeed reported, the great variety of type of effect makes it impossible to see any specific pattern. All of the hypothesized mechanisms of response organization are present in the effects noted, including, and more predominantly, those types of collateral effects we referred to as artifacts of the intervention. However, there is certainly not enough consistency in the findings for us to be able to abstract any rules that would guide practitioners confronting certain specific types of excess behavior. There are no predictable collateral effects observed when the targeted behavior is head-banging, or phobic behavior, or self-stimulatory finger and hand mannerisms. There is certainly not a single instance in which a collateral effect could have been predicted from the type of response covariation implied by syndrome theory and the global interactions depicted in child psychopathology research. In our own research on response interrelationships, in which we were dealing with a fairly narrow range of self-injurious and self-stimulatory behaviors in young students with severe developmental delays, we found no consistent patterns related to any particular type of response or response topography and even a great deal of variability within individual children in the way their response repertoires were organized over time.

It appears unavoidable to have to conclude at this juncture that there are not going to be any nice simple patterns of excess behavior—syndromes—that will hold up across students and across development. What then, can we generalize from the literature? In our opinion what can be generalized are some rules about some possible types of response organization and some behavioral principles that could yield an infinite variety of actual response clusters and relationships. This means that the focus for the designer of interventions will have to be on idiographic patterns discovered by careful assessment in which the total response pattern or repertoire of the individual is taken into account, just as patterns of interaction between environment and behavior are being taken into account in ecobehavioral approaches (Greenwood, Schulte, Kohler, Dinwiddie, & Carta, 1986). In fact this has always been the way of behavior therapy—the generalizable concepts are not specific rules about behavioral phenomena but principles of behavioral regulation—the knowledge of which provides the clinician with a structure for looking at unique, idiographic instances of behavior.

Few of the papers cited in our table conducted prior analyses of response relationships or formulated specific hypotheses about the collateral effects they would expect as a result of taking response organization into account. The few that did so, however, seemed to be well reinforced. For example, Johnson, Baumeister, Penland, and Inwald (1982) were able to demonstrate the importance of reinforcement for positive behavior after a punishment contingency resulted in substantial increases in explicitly measured collateral behavior. By analyzing response interactions and taking these principles of organization into account we are confident that educators and clinicians will be able to design substantially more effective interventions, not only in terms of their impact on the target behavior but in terms of their actual impact on students' lives and development. The various studies reviewed in this chapter do not yet prove this assertion, but the prognostications look excellent.

Summary

The continued escalation of positive benefits of the kind described here represent collateral effects that are extremely important but may or may not be a true function of the organization of behavior. At the same time it seems that emphasizing the creation of ripple effects and improvements—so that natural environmental contingencies can begin to take over and maintain as well as enhance improvement—represents the kind of outcome concerns that should be our goal in the design of behavioral interventions. In this sense, there are clearly some intervention targets that are more likely to produce ongoing collateral benefits than others. Other factors being equal, these should be selected for intervention. Thus Wahler's (1975) concept of the keystone behavior is a useful one, in spite of our present lack of sophistication in identifying such behaviors through experimental discovery procedures. Our limited success in documenting how behaviors are truly organized and what kinds of behaviors might serve as keystones or access behaviors should not dissuade us from pursuing such questions. It is unfortunate that, to date, the evidence that such phenomena may indeed exist and have important treatment implications comes primarily from the idiosyncratic accumulation of data regarding unintended behavioral changes in studies where the primary focus was on manipulating a single target behavior (Voeltz & Evans, 1982).

What must now occur is a major shift in the focus of these interventions with children. We must move from measuring and manipulating behaviors one at a time to developing methodologies for making decisions regarding children's total repertoires. We must similarly develop criteria to evaluate the success of our efforts that deal with real outcomes—those that result in positive consequences for the lives of the children and their families. Our present intervention and evaluation procedures seem ill suited to address complex repertoires and long-term outcomes, and the problem is not likely to be solved by substituting trait and personality measures (as with the new interest in DSM-III) for frequency counts of single target behaviors. Nor is it as simple as polling the community to support the meaningfulness of the target behavior selected and/or the degree of behavior change that has taken place, which has become a commonly used application to reflect concerns for social validation. This minor paradigm shift seems helpful and does represent a recognition that change is needed to protect behavior therapy from charges of triviality. What we have attempted to do in this chapter, however, is to present the theoretical and empirical support for the importance of assuming a broader look at that application and evaluation of behavior modification with children in education settings.

References

Adams, W. (1980). Treatment of assaultive hair pulling in a multihandicapped youth. *Journal of Autism and Developmental Disorders, 10,* 335–342.

Altman, K., Grahs, C., & Friman, P. (1982). Treatment of unobserved trichotillomania by attention-reflection and punishment of an apparent covariant. *Journal of Behavior Therapy and Experimental Psychiatry, 13,* 337–340.

Altman, K., Haavik, S., & Higgins, S. T. (1983). Modifying the self-injurious behavior of an infant with spina bifida and diminished pain sensitivity. *Journal of Behavior Therapy and Experimental Psychiatry, 14,* 165–168.

Apolito, P. M., & Sulzer-Azeroff, B. (1981). Lemon-juice therapy: The control of chronic vomiting in a twelve-year-old profoundly retarded female. *Education and Treatment of Children,* 4(4), 339–347.

Baer, D. M. (1982). The imposition of structure on behavior and the demolition of behavioral structures. In D. J. Bernstein (Ed.), *Response structure and organization. Nebraska Symposium on Motivation, 1981* (pp. 217–254). Lincoln, NE: University of Nebraska Press.

Baer, D. M. (1986). Exemplary service to what outcome? [Review of *Education of learners with severe handicaps: Exemplary service strategies*]. *Journal of The Association for Persons with Severe Handicaps, 11,* 145–147.

Ball, T., Purna, D., Rios, M., & Constantine, C. (1985). Flexible arm splints in the control of a Lesch-Nyhan victim's finger biting and a profoundly retarded client's finger sucking. *Journal of Autism and Developmental Disorders, 15,* 177–184.

Barmann, B. C. (1980). Use of contingent vibration in the treatment of self-stimulatory hand-mouthing and ruminative vomiting behavior. *Journal of Behavior Therapy and Experimental Psychiatry, 11,* 307–311.

Barmann, B. C., & Vitali, D. L. (1982). Facial screening to eliminate trichotillomania in developmentally disabled persons. *Behavior Therapy, 13,* 735–742.

Barrett, R., Matson, J., Shapiro, E., & Ollendick, T. (1981). A comparison of punishment and DRO procedures for treating stereotypic behavior of mentally retarded children. *Applied Research in Mental Retardation, 2,* 247–256.

Barrett, R., & Linn, D. M. (1981). Treatment of stereotyped toe-walking with overcorrection and physical therapy. *Applied Research in Mental Retardation, 2,* 13–21.

Baumeister, A. A., & MacLean, W. E. (1984). Deceleration of self-injurious and stereotypic responding by exercise. *Applied Research in Mental Retardation, 5,* 385–393.

Belacher, T. L., Conetta, C., Cole, C., Iannotti, E., & McGovern, M. (1982). Eliminating a severely retarded blind adolescent's tantrums using mild behavioral interruption: A case study. *Journal of Behavior Therapy and Experimental Psychiatry, 13,* 275–260.

Bierly, C., & Billingsley, F. (1984). An investigation of the educative effects of overcorrection on the behavior of an autistic child. *Behavioral Disorders, 9,* 11–21.

Blount, R. L., Drabman, R. S., Wilson, N., & Stewart, D. (1982). Reducing severe diurnal bruxism in two profoundly retarded females. *Journal of Applied Behavior Analysis, 15,* 565–571.

Bornstein, P. H., & Knapp, M. (1981). Self-control desensitization with a multi-phobic boy: A multiple baseline design. *Journal of Behavior Therapy and Experimental Psychiatry, 12,* 281–285.

Borreson, P., & Anderson, J. (1982). The elimination of chronic rumination through a combination of procedures. *Mental Retardation, 20,* 34–38.

Cahoon, D. D. (1968). Symptom substitution and behavior therapies: A reappraisal. *Psychological Bulletin, 69,* 149–158.

Carr, E. G., & Durand, V. M. (1985). Reducing behavior problems through functional communication training. *Journal of Applied Behavior Analysis, 18,* 111–126.

Chambers, J. H., Sanok, R. L., & Striefel, S. (1980). Using contingent decreased freedom-of-movement to eliminate classroom running away: A case study. *Education and Treatment of Children, 3,* 123–132.

Chiodo, J. (1985). The assessment of anorexia nervosa and bulimia. In M. Hersen, R. M. Eisler, & P. M. Miller (Eds.), *Progress in behavior modification* (vol. 19, pp. 255–292). Orlando, FL: Academic Press.

Clements, J. C., Ditchburn, C., & Grumm, D. (1982). A brief correction procedure for the management of high rate spitting in a profoundly retarded girl. *Journal of Behavior Therapy and Experimental Psychiatry, 13,* 353–356.

Cordle, C. J., & Long, C. G. (1980). The use of operant self-control procedures in the treatment of compulsive hair-pulling. *Journal of Behavior Therapy and Experimental Psychiatry, 11,* 127–130.

Czyzewski, M. J., Barrera, R. D., Sulzer-Azaroff, B. (1982). An abbreviated overcorrection program to reduce self-stimulatory behaviors. *Journal of Behavior Therapy and Experimental Psychiatry, 13,* 55–62.

Dehaven, E., Rees-Thomas, A., & Benton, S. (1980). The use of omission training to reduce stereotyped behavior in three profoundly retarded adults. *Education and Training of the Mentally Retarded, 15*(4), 298–305.

DeLuca, R. V., & Holborn, S. W. (1984). A comparison of relaxation training and competing response training to eliminate hair pulling and nail biting. *Journal of Behavior Therapy and Experimental Psychiatry, 15,* 67–70.

Durand, V. M. (1982a). Analysis and intervention of self-injurious behavior. *Journal of The Association of the Severely Handicapped, 7*(4), 44–53.

Durand, V. M. (1982b). A behavioral/pharmacological intervention for the treatment of severe self-injurious behavior. *Journal of Autism and Developmental Disorders, 12,* 243–251.

Durand, V. M., & Kishi, G. S. (1987). Reducing severe behavior problems among persons with dual sensory impairments: An evaluation of a technical assistance model. *Journal of The Association for Persons with Severe Handicaps, 12,* 2–11.

Eason, L. J., White, M. J., & Newsom, C. (1982). Generalized reduction of self-stimulatory behavior: An effect of teaching appropriate play to autistic children. *Analysis and Intervention in Developmental Disabilities, 2,* 157–169.

Evans, I. M. (1985). Building systems models as a strategy for target behavior selection in clinical assessment. *Behavioral Assessment, 7,* 21–32.

Evans, I. M. (1986). Response structure and the triple response mode concept in behavioral assessment. In R. O. Nelson & S. C. Hayes (Eds.), *Conceptual foundations of behavioral assessment* (pp. 131–155). New York: Guilford Press.

Evans, I. M., & Meyer, L. H. (1985). *An educative approach to behavior problems: A practical decision model for interventions with severely handicapped learners.* Baltimore, MD: Paul H. Brookes.

Evans, I. M., & Voeltz, L. M. (1982). *The selection of intervention priorities in educational programming of severely handicapped preschool children with multiple behavioral problems.* (Final Report, Grant No. G00-790-1960). Honolulu, HI: University of Hawaii Departments of Psychology and Special Education. (ERIC Document Reproduction Service No. ED 240 765 and Exceptional Child Education Resources No. EC 161-828).

Evans, I. M., Weed, K. A., Brown, F. A., & Weld, E. M. (in press). Differential generalization of component behaviors within routines: An experimental analysis of functional competence. *Child and Family Behavior Therapy.*

Favell, J. E., McGimsey, J. F., & Schell, R. M. (1982). Treatment of self-injury by providing alternate sensory activities. *Analysis and Intervention in Developmental Disabilities, 2,* 83–104.

Fellner, D. J., Laroche, M., & Sulzer-Azaroff, B. (1984). The effects of adding interruption to differential reinforcement on targeted and novel self-stimulatory behaviors. *Journal of Behavior Therapy and Experimental Psychiatry, 15,* 315–321.

Framer, E. M., & Sanders, S. H. (1980). The effect of family contingency contracting on disturbed sleeping behaviors in a male adolescent. *Journal of Beahvior Therapy and Experimental Psychiatry, 11,* 235–237.

Gaylord-Ross, R. J., Weeks, M., & Lipner, C. (1980). An analysis of antecedent, response, and consequence events in the treatment of self-injurious behavior. *Education and Training of the Mentally Retarded, 15,* 35–42.

Gaylord-Ross, R., Weeks, M., Lipner, C., & Gaylord-Ross, C. (1983). The differential effectiveness of four treatment procedures in suppressing self-injurious behavior among severely handicapped students. *Education and Training of the Mentally Retarded, 18,* 38–44.

Graziano, A. M., & Mooney, K. C. (1982). Behavioral treatment of "night fears" in children: Maintenance of improvement at 2½- to 3-year follow-up. *Journal of Consulting and Clinical Psychology, 50,* 598–599.

Greene, B. F., Bailey, J. S., & Barber, F. (1981). An analysis and reduction of disruptive behavior on school buses. *Journal of Applied Behavior Analysis, 14,* 177–192.

Greenwood, C. R., Schulte, D., Kohler, F., Dinwiddie, G., & Carta, J. (1986). Assessment and analysis of ecobehavioral interaction in school settings. In R. J. Prinz (Ed.), *Advances in behavioral assessment of children and families* (Vol. 2, pp. 68–98). Greenwich, CT: JAI Press.

Gross, A. M., Farrar, M. J., & Liner, D. (1982). Reduction of trichotillomania in a retarded cerebral palsied child using overcorrection, facial screening, and differential reinforcement of other behavior. *Education and Treatment of Children, 5,* 133–140.

Gunter, P., Brady, M., Shores, R., Fox, J., Owen, S., & Goldzweig, I. (1984). The reduction of aberrant vocalizations with auditory feedback and resulting collateral behavior change of two autistic boys. *Behavioral Disorders, 9,* 254–263.

Hawkins, R. P. (1986). Selection of target behaviors. In R. O. Nelson & S. C. Hayes (Eds.), *Conceptual foundations of behavioral assessment* (pp. 331–385). New York: Guilford Press.

Hayashida, M. (1982). Successful response prevention of rituals producing increase then decrease of untreated rituals. *Journal of Behavior Therapy and Experimental Psychiatry, 13,* 225–228.

Horner, R. H., Bellamy, G. T., & Colvin, G. T. (1984). Responding in the presence on nontrained stimuli: Implications of generalization error patterns. *Journal of The Association for Persons with Severe Handicaps, 9,* 287–295.

Hull, C. L. (1934). The concept of the habit-family hierarchy and maze learning. *Psychological Review, 41,* 33–52.

Johnson, W. L., Baumeister, A., Penland, M. J., & Inwald, C. (1982). Experimental analysis of self-injurious, stereotypic, and collateral behavior of retarded persons: Effects of overcorrection and reinforcement of alternative responding. *Analysis and Intervention in Developmental Disabilities, 2,* 41–66.

Kazdin, A. E. (1977). Assessing the clinical or applied importance of behavior change through social validation. *Behavior Modification, 1,* 427–452.

Kazdin, A. E. (1983). Psychiatric diagnosis, dimensions of dysfunction, and child behavior therapy. *Behavior Therapy, 14,* 73–99.

Kellerman, J. (1980). Rapid treatment of nocturnal anxiety in children. *Journal of Behavior Therapy and Experimental Psychiatry, 1,* 9–11.

Kern, L., Koegel, R. L., & Dunlap, G. (1984). The influence of vigorous versus mild exercise on autistic stereotyped behaviors. *Journal of Autism and Developmental Disorders, 14,* 57–67.

Kerr, M. M., Strain, P. S., & Ragland, E. U. (1982). Teacher-mediated peer feedback treatment of behaviorally handicapped children: An analysis of effects on positive and negative interactions. *Behavior Modification, 6,* 277–290.

Lancioni, G. E., Smeets, P. M., Ceccarani, P. S., Capodaglio, L., & Campanari, G. (1984). Effects of gross motor activities on the severe self-injurious tantrums of multihandicapped individuals. *Applied Research in Mental Retardation, 5,* 471–482.

Lancioni, G. E., Smeets, P. M., Ceccarini, P. S., & Goosens, A. J. (1983). Self-stimulation and task-related responding: The role of sensory reinforcement in maintaining and extending treatment effects. *Journal of Behavior Therapy and Experimental Psychiatry, 14,* 33–41.

Levis, D. J. (1981). Extrapolation of two-factor learning theory of infrahuman avoidance behavior and psychopathology. *Neuroscience and Behavioral Review, 5,* 355–370.

Lochman, J. E., Burch, P. R., Curry, J. F., & Lampron, L. B. (1984). Treatment and generalization effects of cognitive-behavioral and goal-setting interventions with aggressive boys. *Journal of Consulting and Clinical Psychology, 52,* 915–916.

Lockwood, K., & Bourland, G. (1982). Reduction of self-injurious behaviors by reinforcement and toy use. *Mental Retardation, 20,* 169–173.

Luce, S. C., & Hall, R. V. (1981). Contingent exercise: A procedure used with differential reinforcement to reduce bizarre verbal behavior. *Education and Treatment of Children, 4,* 309–327.

Luiselli, J. K. (1980). Controlling disruptive behaviors of an autistic child: Parent-mediated contingency management in the home setting. *Education and Treatment of Children, 3,* 195–203.

Luiselli, J. K. (1984). Treatment of an assaultive sensory-impaired adolescent through a multi-component behavioral program. *Journal of Behavior Therapy and Experimental Psychiatry, 15,* 71–78.

Luiselli, J. K., & Rice, D. M. (1983). Brief positive practice with a handicapped child: An assessment of suppressive and re-educative effects. *Education and Treatment of Children, 6,* 241–250.

Luiselli, J. K., Myles, E., & Littman-Quinn, J. (1983). Analysis of a reinforcement/time-out treatment package to control severe aggressive and destructive behaviors in a multihandicapped rubella child. *Applied Research in Mental Retardation, 4,* 65–78.

MacLean, W. E., Jr., & Baumeister, A. A. (1982). Effects of vestibular stimulation on motor development and stereotyped behavior of developmentally delayed children. *Journal of Abnormal Child Psychology, 10,* 229–245.

Matson, J. L., & Stephens, R. M. (1981). Overcorrection treatment of stereotyped behaviors. *Behavior Modification, 5,* 491–502.

McGonigle, J. J., Duncan, D., Cordisco, L., Barrett, R. R. (1982). Visual screening: An alternative method for reducing stereotypic behaviors. *Journal of Applied Behavior Analysis, 15,* 461–467.

Meyer, L. H., & Evans, I. M. (1986). Modification of excess behavior: An adaptive and functional approach for educational and community contexts. In R. H. Horner, L. H. Meyer, & H. D. B. Fredericks (Eds.), *Education of learners with severe handicaps: Exemplary service strategies* (pp. 315–350). Baltimore, MD: Paul H. Brookes.

Meyer, L. H., Evans, I. M., Wuerch, B. B., & Brennan, J. M. (1985). Monitoring the collateral effects of leisure skill instruction: A case study in multiple-baseline methodology. *Behaviour Research and Therapy, 23,* 127–138.

Meyer, L. H., & Putnam, J. (in press). Social integration. In V. B. Van Hasselt, P. S. Strain, & M. Hersen (Eds.), *Handbook of developmental and physical disabilities.* New York: Pergamon Press.

Michelson, L., DiLorenzo, T. M., Calpin, J. P., & Williamson, D. A. (1981). Modifying excessive lunchroom noise. *Behavior Modification, 5,* 553–564.

Miles, C. L., & Cuvo, A. J. (1980). Modification of the disruptive and productive classroom behavior of a severely retarded child: A comparison of two procedures. *Education and Treatment of Children, 3,* 113–121.

Mulick, J., Schroeder, S., & Rojahn, J. (1980). Chronic ruminative vomiting: A comparison of four treatment procedures. *Journal of Autism and Developmental Disorders, 10,* 203–213.

Nelson, R. O., & Hayes, S. C. (1979). Some current dimensions of behavioral assessment. *Behavioral Assessment, 1,* 1–16.

Page, T., Finney, J. W., Parrish, J. M., & Iwata, B. A. (1983). Assessment and reduction of food stealing in Prader-Willi children. *Applied Research in Mental Retardation, 4,* 219–228.

Polvinale, R., & Lutzker, J. (1980). Elimination of assaultive and inapprorpiate sexual behavior by reinforcement and social-restitution. *Mental Retardation, 18,* 27–30.

Rachlin, H., & Burkhard, B. (1978). The temporal triangle: Response substitution in instrumental conditioning. *Psychological Review, 85,* 22–48.

Rapoff, M. A., Altman, K., & Christophersen, E. R. (1980). Elimination of a retarded blind child's self-hitting by response-contingent brief restraint. *Education and Treatment of Children, 3,* 231–236.

Reilich, L. L., Spooner, F., & Rose, T. L. (1984). The effects of contingent water mist on the stereotypic responding of a severely handicapped adolescent. *Journal of Behavior Therapy and Experimental Psychiatry, 15,* 165–170.

Rincover, A., & Devany, J. (1982). The application of sensory extinction procedures to self-injury. *Analysis and Intervention in Developmental Disabilities, 2,* 67–81.

Riordon, M. M., Iwata, B. A., Wohl, M. K., & Finney, J. W. (1980). Behavioral treatment of food refusal and selectivity in developmentally disabled children. *Applied Research in Mental Retardation, 1,* 95–112.

Rosen, H. S., & Rosen, L. A. (1983). Eliminating stealing: Use of stimulus control with an elementary student. *Behavior Modification, 7,* 56–63.

Sackett, G. P. (1979). The lag sequential analysis of contingency and cyclicity in behavioral interaction research. In J. D. Osofsky (Ed.), *Handbook of infant development* (p. 623–649). New York: Wiley.

Simpson, R., & Swenson, C. (1980). The effects and side-effects of an overcorrection procedure applied by parents of severely emotionally disturbed children in a home environment. *Behavioral Disorders, 5,* 79–85.

Singh, N. N., Dawson, M. J., & Manning, P. (1981). Effects of spaced responding DRL on the stereotyped behavior of profoundly retarded persons. *Journal of Applied Behavior Analysis, 14,* 521–526.

Singh, N. N., Manning, P. J., & Angell, M. J. (1982). Effects of an oral hygiene punishment procedure on chronic rumination and collateral behaviors in monozygous twins. *Journal of Applied Behavior Analysis, 15,* 309–314.

Snell, M. E. (1983). Developing the IEP: Selecting and assessing skills. In M. E. Snell (Ed.), *Systematic instruction of the moderately and severely handicapped* (2nd ed., pp. 76–112). Columbus, OH: Charles E. Merrill.

Staats, A. W. (1961). Verbal habit families, concepts, and the operant conditioning of word classes. *Psychological Review, 68,* 190–204.

Staats, A. W. (1975). *Social behaviorism.* Homewood, IL: Dorsey Press.

Thorbeck, P. J., & Jackson, H. J. (1982). Reducing chronic drooling in a retarded female using a multi-treatment package. *Journal of Behavior Therapy and Experimental Psychiatry, 13,* 89–93.

Tomporowski, P. D. (1983). Training an autistic client: The effect of brief restraint on disruptive behavior. *Journal of Behavior Therapy and Experimental Psychiatry, 14,* 169–173.

Voeltz, L. M., & Evans, I. M. (1982). The assessment of behavioral interrelationships in child behavior therapy. *Behavioral Assessment, 4,* 131–165.

Voeltz, L. M., & Evans, I. M. (1983). Educational validity: Procedures to evaluate outcomes in programs for severely handicapped learners. *Journal of The Association for the Severely Handicapped, 8*(1), 3–15.

Wahler, R. G. (1975). Some structural aspects of deviant child behavior. *Journal of Applied Behavior Analysis, 8,* 27–42.

Watters, R. G., & Watters, W. (1980). Decreasing self-stimulatory behavior with physical exercise in a group of autistic boys. *Journal of Autism and Developmental Disorders, 10,* 379–387.

Wesolowski, M. D., & Zawlocki, R. J. (1982). The differential effects of procedures to eliminate an injurious self-stimulatory behavior (digito-ocular sign) in blind retarded twins. *Behavior Therapy, 13*, 334–345.

Wildman, R. W. II, & Wildman, R. W. (1975). The generalization of behavior modification procedures: A review—with special emphasis on classroom applications. *Psychology in the Schools, 12*, 432–448.

Williamson, D. A., Calpin, J. P., DiLorenzo, T. M., Garris, R. P., & Petti, T. A. (1981). Treating hyperactivity with dexadrine and activity feedback. *Behavior Modification, 5*, 339–416.

Wolf, M. M. (1978). Social validity: The case for subjective measurement or how applied behavior analysis is finding its heart. *Journal of Applied Behavior Analysis, 11*, 203–214.

Wolfe, D. A., Mendes, M. G., & Factor, D. (1984). A parent-administered program to reduce children's television viewing. *Journal of Applied Behavior Analysis, 17*, 267–272.

Woods, T. (1982). Reducing severe aggression and self-injurious behaviors: A nonintrusive, home based approach. *Behavioral Disorders, 7*, 180–188.

Yeaton, W. H., & Sechrest, L. (1981). Critical dimensions in the choice and maintenance of successful treatments: Strength, integrity, and effectiveness. *Journal of Consulting and Clinical Psychology, 49*, 156–167.

CHAPTER 9

Dissemination of Behavioral Procedures in the Schools

Issues in Training

Teresa Kay Anderson and Thomas R. Kratochwill

Introduction

The delivery of psychological services in educational settings has in recent years centered increasingly on the consultative role and the teacher's direct involvement in the intervention process with students. Influences leading to this shift in emphasis from that of the more traditional psychometric focus originated in legal as well as professional arenas. The passage and implementation of Public Law 94-142, The Education for All Handicapped Children Act of 1975, and its requirement that a child be educated in the appropriate "least restrictive environment," has led to an increase in consultative activities of mental health professionals. In conformance with the letter and the intent of this statute, greater care has been taken that children experiencing difficulties in school are removed from the regular classroom and educated in a more specialized setting only after other educational alternatives have been carefully explored. In the professional arena more emphasis has been placed on prevention of mental health problems in educational settings (Knoff, 1984). Prevention can be aimed at primary, secondary, or tertiary services as conceptualized in the community mental health arena (Clarizo, 1979). Primary prevention programs focus on school resources that can be used to increase awareness of mental health needs of students. A main goal of such programs is to educate care providers (parents, teachers) so that serious mental health problems never develop. Secondary prevention programs typically are aimed at a group that is at risk of developing more severe problems. An attempt is made to eliminate existing problems (e.g., classroom disruption) so that serious problems (e.g., conduct disorders) do not develop. Tertiary prevention programs focus on students who already have serious learning and/or behavioral problems that significantly influence their school adjustment.

A number of psychological service delivery

Teresa Kay Anderson • Ampitheater Public Schools, 701 West Wetmore Road, Tucson, Arizona 85705. **Thomas R. Kratochwill** • Department of Educational Psychology, University of Wisconsin-Madison, Madison, Wisconsin 53706.

approaches have been designed to increase the teacher's role in the prevention process. Major goals of these approaches include making available a much broader range of psychological services in the schools, decreasing the time for which children and teachers must wait for consultative input, increasing the likelihood that the needs of children can be met in the regular classroom environment, and increasing the numbers of children served by working with teachers and other school personnel in further developing their educational problem solving and classroom management skills. Inservice training for personnel within the school setting can be an extremely valuable tool in this regard, both in the facilitation of the consultation role and developing consultee skills necessary for the implementation of intervention plans developed. Consultees within the schools need to be aware of procedural entry steps involved in obtaining consultation, the nature of the consulting relationship itself, and the kinds of responsibilities likely to be involved. In addition, teacher knowledge of behavior modification principles and skill in their classroom applications are vital to effective consultation and management of student learning and behavior difficulties.

Classroom-based behavior modification programs can be used to improve diverse child behavior difficulties, including performance in academic skills, social interaction, classroom management, and numerous other problems that may interfere with academic progress (Kazdin, 1982). The teacher-training literature reveals, in addition, that teachers have been trained successfully in a wide variety of behavior management skills and in the principles of behavior on which those techniques are based (Allen & Forman, 1984; Bernstein, 1982). Training methods found in the empirical literature to be particularly effective include modeling, role playing, and feedback, as well as didactic instructional techniques (written material, lecture, and discussion) when used in combination with one or more of the other methods.

An important aspect to consider in the facilitation of teacher's involvement in direct intervention in educational settings is that they must assume new roles: namely, those of consultee and behavior change agent (Grieger, 1972). Moreover, empirical investigations have shown that attitudes toward behavior modification can have a significant impact upon the effectiveness of behavior program outcomes (e.g., Kazdin & Cole, 1981; Woolfolk & Woolfolk, 1979; Woolfolk, Woolfolk, & Wilson, 1977). Although very little attention has been paid to this issue in the literature, the success of behavioral consultation and the implementation of behavioral interventions in the classroom may depend heavily on teacher attitudes toward behavioral principles and concepts (Kazdin, 1980a; Kazdin & Cole, 1981; Witt & Elliott, 1985).

Although the applications of behavior consultation and therapy within the educational setting have been extensive, a major concern pertains to the effective dissemination and extension of existing procedures and techniques to the large number of settings that would profit from their use (Fawcett, Mathews, & Fletcher, 1980; Kazdin, 1981b; Stolz, 1981). Inservice teacher training is an excellent way in which to approach the accomplishment of this goal. It cannot be assumed, however, that sufficient knowledge and skill in the use of behavioral methods can be taught in brief training workshops to insure the proper teacher application of these procedures. Inservice teacher training must be viewed not as an end, but as a facilitating agent for the effective use of a behavioral consultative model in the schools. Ongoing consultation with teachers following the introduction of these training packages is considered essential. This chapter reviews some issues in dissemination within the context of the teacher-training literature in educational settings. We first describe some conceptual issues in the dissemination of psychological information in educational settings, with a special emphasis on the consultation role. Thereafter, we provide an overview of the teacher-training literature in the context of the various methodologies employed to investigate the training outcomes. Relevant parent-training research is also reviewed with implications for teacher training presented. Finally, a number of conceptual issues are discussed in terms of the bearing they have on facilitating the dissemination of psychological information.

Issues in Dissemination

Regardless of the type of service delivery model utilized in a particular educational setting, a number of psychologist-initiated activities can serve to facilitate the implementation of interventions. Dissemination of information is one vital aspect in this facilitation process, and a number of ways in which to approach this type of activity in the schools have been suggested (Lolli, 1980). There are several prime interest groups within a school district that must be informed of the range of potential psychological services. Included among these groups are administrators, teachers, parents, and the students themselves. Lolli pointed out the importance of meeting with each of these interest groups and keeping them abreast of available school psychological services for which their general awareness and input are essential. Speaking to students as a classroom group, at parent organization meetings, or in parent-training groups are excellent ways of reaching these interest groups. The opportunity to offer inservice programs through which faculty members can be apprised of available programs and procedures as well as interesting innovations is another avenue that should be considered (Conoley & Conoley, 1982a; Lolli, 1980).

Inservice training for personnel within the school setting can be an extremely valuable tool in the facilitation of psychological services and in developing needed teacher awareness and skills. For example, if the mental health professional is to meet successfully the needs of children in the least restrictive environment, the means must be found for disseminating as much information and developing as many effective child management skills as possible (Gutkin & Curtis, 1982; White & Pryswansky, 1982). Because it is the classroom teacher who has the most direct contact with students in the school setting, inservice teacher training is a promising way in which to approach the attainment of these goals.

In addition to skill development, teachers need to be aware of procedural entry steps involved in obtaining services, the nature of these services, and the kinds of contracts that are likely to be involved. It is very important, in other words, that teachers not only acquire the skills necessary to implement intervention plans developed, but that they be apprised in advance of their prerogatives and responsibilities (Reynolds, 1982; Sandoval, Lambert & Davis, 1977).

Teacher training has been viewed as an integral part of the consultation process in the schools (Bardon & Bennett, 1974). Two consultant objectives identified by Bergan (1977) for the plan-implementation phase of behavioral consultative problem solving are important in this context: (a) determining the skill adequacy of the consultee and/or other plan executors, and (b) ascertaining the feasibility of conducting skills training. If the consultant determines that training is needed and feasible, a third plan-implementation objective of designing procedures to enhance the mastery of needed skills is included (see Chapter 5 for a more detailed discussion of the consultation process).

An inservice training area vital to the effective management of learning and behavioral difficulties in the classroom is that of teacher training in the principles and application of classroom intervention procedures. Classroom-based behavior management programs can be utilized to improve diverse child behavior difficulties, including performance in traditional academic skills, social interaction, classroom management, and other special problems that may interfere with academic progress (Kazdin, 1982). The extensive literature on behavior modification with children leaves little doubt that contingency management can effectively be used to increase desirable and decrease undesirable social and academic child behaviors (Kazdin, 1981b; Ross, 1981; Sulzer-Azaroff, 1981). A substantial body of evidence also exists supporting the efficacy of training teachers in the application of these child behavioral management procedures (Allen & Forman, 1984; Bernstein, 1982; Kazdin, 1980c, Ross, 1981). Indeed, a most efficient way in which to alter learning and behavioral difficulties in the classroom is to educate teachers in a set of procedures for systematic behavior change, which then, with ongoing professional input, can be used as a basis for handling a variety of classroom behavior problems (O'Leary & O'Leary, 1977; Patterson, 1971).

Teacher Training/Education

Teachers have been educated successfully in a wide variety of behavior management skills as well as in the principles of behavior underlying those procedures. However, inadequate training can lead, not only to a failure in obtaining effective classroom behavior control, but even to serious misapplication of procedures and abuse if cautions are not observed (Farnham-Diggory, 1981; Kazdin, 1981c; Stein, 1975). In order for behavioral procedures to be effective in obtaining student behaviors that are conducive to learning in the classroom, they must be implemented carefully, systematically, and consistently. In order to determine the techniques most likely to promote the acquisition and responsible application of behavior change skills, a substantial number of research investigations have been conducted. Most teacher-training research reports the efficacy of combinations of various training procedures, but a few studies have attempted to evaluate training component effectiveness (Bernstein, 1982; Kazdin, 1980c). Among the methods frequently studied are written manuals, lectures, discussion, modeling, role playing, cuing, and feedback.

The written manual has been a particularly popular training approach for presentation of basic principles and introduction to behavior management procedures. A great variety of child behavior management manuals are available (Bernal & North, 1978). However, there is little evidence of adequate evaluation of this type of training (McMahon & Forehand, 1980). Other didactic instructional methods frequently utilized include lectures and discussion of principles and practices. One of the most consistent findings reported for didactic instruction in general is that it is not sufficient when application of skill is the goal of training (Bernstein, 1982). Although instruction appears to contribute to knowledge of behavioral principles as assessed verbally, it is apparently inadequate in achieving actual classroom performance of behavior management skills.

The effects of observational learning on skill acquisition have been studied extensively (Bandura, 1977; Rosenthal & Zimmerman, 1978), and the efficacy of modeling and role playing in the training of behavior change agents has been consistently reported (Bernstein, 1982). Modeling training has been conducted in analogue situations, on videotape or film, and in actual classrooms. Role playing frequently accompanies modeling in training, particularly when new skills are being taught (Bois, 1972). Modeling involves the demonstration of skills by someone already competent in their application, and role playing allows teachers the opportunity to rehearse those skills in the training setting before their actual use is attempted in the classroom. One of the most frequently reported training methods is feedback. Feedback training involves providing individuals with verbal, written, videotaped, or graphically displayed information about their own behavior. Table 1 provides a summary of the research related to various teacher training techniques.

Table 1. Summary of Teacher-Training Research

Studies demonstrating training method effectiveness	Package/component	*N*	Design
Didactic instruction			
Carnine & Fink, 1978	Package	13	Multiple baseline
Clark, Macrae, Ida, & Smith 1975	Package	2	Multiple baseline
Cossairt, Hall, & Hopkins, 1973	Package	3	Multiple baseline
Greenwood, Hops, Walker, Guild, Stokes, & Young, 1979	Package	50	Group
Hall, 1971	Package	1	Reversal
Hall, Fox, Willard, Goldsmith, Emerson, Owen, Davis, & Portia, 1971	Package	6	Reversal
Hall, Panyan, Rabon, & Broden, 1968	Package	3	Reversal
Hundert, 1982	Package	2	Multiple baseline
Johnson & Sloat, 1980	Package	13	Group
Kazdin, 1974	Package	6	Group
Koegel, Russo, & Rincover, 1977	Package	11	Multiple baseline
Madsen, Madsen, Saudargas, Hammond, Smith, & Edgar, 1970	Package	32	Group
McKeown, Adams, & Forehand, 1975	Package	20	Group
Rollins, McCandless, Thompson, & Brassell, 1974	Package	16	Group
Speidel & Tharp, 1978	Package	6	Multiple baseline
Modeling			
Carnine & Fink, 1978	Package	13	Multiple baseline
Clark, Macrae, Ida, & Smith, 1975	Package	2	Multiple baseline
Hall, 1971	Package	1	Reversal
Hall, Fox, Willard, Goldsmith, Emerson, Owen, Davis, & Portia, 1971	Package	6	Reversal
Koegel, Russo, & Rincover, 1977	Package	11	Multiple baseline
Madsen, Madsen, Saudargas, Hammond, Smith, & Edgar, 1970	Package	32	Group
Nagle & Gresham, 1979	Component	1	A-B-C
Ringer, 1973	Component	1	Multiple baseline/Reversal
Rutherford, 1973	Component	20	Group
Sloat, Tharp, & Gallimore, 1977	Component	5	Multiple baseline
Speidel & Tharp, 1978	Package	6	Multiple baseline
Role playing			
Burka & Jones, 1979	Package	3	Multiple baseline
Carnine & Fink, 1978	Package	13	Multiple baseline
Greenwood, Hops, Walker, Guild, Stokes, & Young, 1979	Package	50	Group
Jones & Eimers, 1975	Package	2	Multiple baseline
Jones, Fremouw, & Carples, 1977	Package	12	Pyramid
Jones & Miller, 1977	Package	4	Reversal
Madsen, Madsen, Saudargas, Hammond, Smith, & Edgar, 1970	Package	32	Group
McKeown, Adams, & Forehadn, 1975	Package	20	Group
Feedback			
Carnine & Fink, 1978	Package	13	Multiple baseline
Clark, Macrae, Ida, & Smith, 1975	Package	2	Multiple baseline

(continued)

Table 1. (*Continued*)

Studies demonstrating training method effectiveness	Package/component	*N*	Design
Feedback (*continued*)			
Cooper, Thompson, & Baer, 1970	Package	2	Multiple baseline
Cossairt, Hall, & Hopkins, 1973	Package	3	Multiple baseline
Greenwood, Hops, Delquadri, & Guild, 1974	Package	3	Multiple baseline
Hall, Panyon, & Rabon, 1968	Package	3	Reversal
Horton, 1975	Package	2	Multiple baseline
Hundert, 1982	Package	2	Multiple baseline
Kazdin, 1974	Package	6	Group
Koegel, Russo, & Rincover, 1977	Package	11	Multiple baseline
Madsen, Madsen, Saudargas, Hammond, Smith, & Edgar, 1970	Package	32	Group
Parsonson, Baer, & Baer, 1974	Component	2	Multiple baseline
Rutherford, 1973	Package	20	Group
Sloat, Tharp, & Gallimore, 1977	Component	3	Multiple baseline
Speidel & Tharp, 1978	Package	6	Multiple baseline
Thomson, Holmberg, & Baer, 1978	Component	24	Multiple baseline

Training Research Using Teacher-Reported Classroom Interventions

Several teacher-training researchers have conducted inservice workshops or some other type of training program with teachers and then collected data on child classroom behaviors targeted by those teachers for behavioral intervention. Frequently, in this type of study, data collection has been conducted by the teacher trainees themselves as part of the training package without the use of any type of check on observer reliability or adequate research design. Because of these methodological inadequacies, inferences regarding the effectiveness of these teacher-implemented interventions are frequently limited. A more serious criticism, however, relates to the fact that no child behavior data were collected before teacher training, and no teacher behavior data were collected over time during training. Thus, even when objective baseline and postintervention data on child behaviors have been collected, it is unknown what changes in teacher behavior have occurred specifically as a result of training, if any, and whether or not successful child behavior intervention programs carried out by teachers were actually the result of training received. Essentially, researchers have failed to ensure the integrity of the treatment/training program.

One study utilizing this approach to the evaluation of teacher training was conducted by Anderson, Fredericks, Baldwin, Dalke, and McDonnell (1978). These investigators trained teachers in a data-based inservice training model involving group presentation of behavior management principles and individual teacher instruction in the application of these principles to the classroom; however, the nature of these training procedures were not specified clearly. Data were collected by teachers without provision for interobserver reliability assessment, and the data were reported only in terms of the number of behavioral programs considered by the authors to be successful in decreasing inappropriate student behavior. Although it was reported that 17 teachers conducted 34 behavioral programs and that 88% of these programs resulted in decreased inappropriate child behavior, no evaluation can be made regarding the effectiveness of either the training program or any of the teacher-implemented child behavior interventions.

A study conducted by Zimmerman and Zimmerman (1971) also reported numbers of teacher-conducted behavior modification projects after a training program had been presented. Training included background reading, discussion of behavior problems and classroom management techniques, lectures, and presentation and discussion of individual classroom projects. That a respectably large number of these teacher projects (26) were carried out utilizing a wide variety of behavioral techniques was advanced as evidence of training success; yet, no formal attempt was made to evaluate the success or failure of these interventions.

Inferences about the effectiveness of a training package developed by Andrews (1970) were based on three case studies conducted by teacher trainees. This investigator reported that 14 teacher volunteers from elementary classrooms were trained with a written manual, lectures, and individual instructions in the classroom application of behavior modification principles. Homework assignments for the inservice training program included data collection and intervention with target children in the respective teachers' classrooms. These studies reported pre- and postintervention repeated observational assessments and dramatic child behavior improvements, but interobserver agreement was not assessed and no teacher behavior data were gathered. Because the only teacher-related data that were collected were subjective course evaluation reports related to satisfaction with the training, no firm conclusions can be drawn about the actual effectiveness of this training package.

Similarly, a consultation seminar was conducted by Canter and Paulson (1974) in which teachers were trained in the implementation of functional-behavioral intervention skills. Training methods utilized included didactic instruction (readings, lectures, and discussions), approximately an hour of instructor observation and feedback within the classroom setting, and homework assignments in which teachers conducted behavioral intervention projects with children in their classes. Evaluative data included teacher records kept on these child behavior interventions and teacher responses to attitudinal questionnaires. These data supported the effectiveness of the training model. However, only one case study example was reported. These authors correctly noted a need for more direct in-class observation of teachers, audiovisual aids to demonstrate appropriate intervention approaches, and more evaluative data measuring the effectiveness of the teacher training package.

An inservice training package involving the presentation of information through readings, lectures, and discussion was also reported by Martin (1975). Unfortunately, incompletely defined student and teacher behaviors were measured in an A-B design format with only a few data points included. Observer agreement was assessed, but no generalization measures were collected. An increase in teacher approval behaviors of 15% was reported with a slight increase in teacher disapproval as well. Pupil on-task behavior showed no substantial change during the experiment. Martin (1975) reported another teacher training study in which lectures, modeling, role playing, graphed feedback, and index card reminders were utilized. Several categories of teacher behavior were recorded in this study, and observer reliability was assessed. Teacher "positive actions" were found to increase from 30% at baseline to 52% after training had been conducted. The methodological characteristics in both of these studies make the effectiveness of these training packages difficult to determine.

Teacher training in which readings, classroom management projects, and the use of university student "mini-consultants" was investigated by Tyler (1981). Teacher reports on behavior modification results indicated that of 44 attempts to decrease specific undesirable behaviors, 77% showed a decrease of 50% or more. Twenty attempts to increase positive behavior rates resulted in a 100% success rate with increase of greater than 50%. Overall, 13 teachers successfully changed behaviors in their classrooms in 60 to 70 attempts. These results are interpreted by the authors as demonstrating the effectiveness of their training consultation package. Design and data collection procedures are unclear, however, making interpretation of this study difficult.

A more sophisticated research design was reported by Hall (1971) and Hall *et al.* (1971). However, these studies were again limited to child behavior data in experiments carried out by teachers who had been trained in child behavior management. These investigators trained elementary and junior high school teachers in the use of contingent attention and ignoring through the use of reading assignments, lectures, discussion, modeling, individual and group consultation, homework, graphed and quiz feedback, and reinforcement through academic credit. Behavioral intervention projects were conducted by teachers in A-B-A-B designs with observation of particular student target behaviors and interobserver agreement reliability assessments. Reversal phases in these studies were extremely short (only two data points in some cases) minimizing the potential disadvantage of this design yet effectively demonstrating that the interventions were responsible for changes in child behavior. Although these results do not show clear evidence of training package effectiveness, the experiments did demonstrate that teachers in a variety of classroom settings were able to obtain reliable observation records and carry out experimental manipulations successfully utilizing the types of resources available in most school settings.

In summary, a variety of teacher-training techniques have been investigated with teacher-collected child behavior data included as the only measure of effectiveness for teacher-conducted classroom intervention projects. It is very important in this type of research that data on teacher behavior be collected and analyzed so it can be determined what changes, if any, have occurred in the responses of the individuals trained. Additional child behavior data provided valuable information regarding the actual effects of changes in teacher behavior on classroom interactions; however, these data should be collected by independent observers and assessed carefully for interobserver reliability.

More adequate experimental designs are also essential for the evaluation and future utilization of these training methods. The methodological weaknesses found in the studies reviewed make it impossible to evaluate the efficacy of the training packages described. Two general categories of experimental designs that have been used to handle more adequately these methodological issues include single-subject time-series designs and between-groups comparison designs.

Time-Series Designs

Single-case time-series research designs have frequently been employed in the evaluation of teacher-training techniques. The most effective utilization of these designs for that purpose is to collect data on training-relevant teacher behaviors before, during, and after the introduction of the training component(s). It is advisable also to collect data on student behaviors that would presumably be influenced by expected changes in teacher behavior. If teacher responses change significantly after training, the efficacy of those training methods will have been demonstrated. If, in addition, student classroom behaviors show definite improvements, as would certainly be the goal of any teacher-training program, further evidence of training expediency will have been obtained. The advantages of this type of research design are that only a small number of teachers and classrooms are required and important sources of individual variability in relation to the various techniques can be revealed.

Time-series designs generally rule out such basic threats to validity as history, maturation, and testing by varying the order in which different treatment and control conditions are implemented, as in the case of behavior reversals, or by introducing the intervention(s) to different individuals or behaviors at different points across time, as in the multiple baseline design. In either case, significant behavioral effects can be attributed to the intervention or training rather than to extraneous events (Hersen & Barlow, 1976; Kazdin, 1982). Multiple baseline designs have been particularly popular for evaluation of teacher-training research, undoubtedly because of the impossibility of withdrawing most training conditions completely, as well as the ethical and practical limitations of reversal design utilization.

An A-B-C time-series design was utilized by Nagle and Gresham (1979) in their evaluation of two teacher-training strategies in which modeling alone and modeling with information feedback were employed. Dependent measures in this study include length of teacher commands (number of words) and student compliance rate as a function of commands. The results of this study were that whereas modeling alone dramatically reduced the number of words in teacher commands, with a concomitant effect of an increased child compliance rate, modeling with informational feedback had little additional effect. It was noted by these authors that such threats to internal and external validity as multiple treatment interference and reactive effects of experimental arrangements were weaknesses in the study and that the use of reversal, multiple baseline, or control groups designs would be necessary to clarify their experimental effects.

A substantial number of investigators have chosen the multiple baseline experimental design for evaluation of entire teacher-training packages. Koegel, Russo, and Rincover (1977) utilized the multi-response baseline design to determine the effectiveness of the combination of a written manual, videotape, and teaching performance feedback in training teachers in behavior modification techniques selected for individual target children. Student and teacher behaviors were observed, and observer agreement and maintenance after training were assessed. The training procedures were found to be effective for all 11 teachers in increasing behavior management skills. After training, the teachers' correct use of the procedures generalized to new target behaviors and different children. It was also demonstrated that when the teachers consistently used the procedures correctly, their teaching was effective in modifying student behavior.

Another teacher training package was evaluated by Spiedel and Tharp (1978). Lectures, discrimination training, modeling, guided practice, and feedback were combined by these investigators and evaluated with a multiple baseline design across six experienced classroom teachers. Six teacher behaviors were observed and coded, and observations were checked for reliability. Two of these teacher behaviors were specifically trained, and four were observed but not trained so that generalization could be assessed. Follow-up data were also collected to test training durability. Training effects were found to be significant, specific to those behaviors trained, and maintained for 5 months.

A training package utilized by Clark, Macrae, Ida, and Smith (1975) included written instructions, modeling, verbal feedback, and graphed feedback. Subjects participating in this study were undergraduates in a practicum training situation with quizzes and grades operating as performance contingencies. This study took place in a training center, and observational data were collected in a classroom for the mentally retarded. A multiple baseline design across teaching behaviors was used in this study with categories of teacher behavior including the appropriate use of teacher praise, correction, and response cost procedures. Observer agreement was assessed, but no follow-up data were collected. The data suggested that the package was effective in establishing the use of a variety of teaching skills and in increasing teacher praise rates. Teachers demonstrated the appropriate use of most of the skills trained before any contact with feedback, quizzes, or grades so it was inferred that these contingencies may not have been a necessary part of this training package.

Jones and his associates (Burka & Jones,

1979; Jones & Eimers, 1975) utilized a role playing training package to train teachers in a broad range of behavior management procedures emphasizing limit setting, prompting, and differential reinforcement of other (DRO) more appropriate behaviors. The training package included explanation and modeling of skills, discussion, role playing in a simulated classroom environment in which participants alternated playing the roles of teacher and good and bad students, feedback on performance, and rearrangement of classroom furniture. Both studies utilized multiple baseline designs and collected observational data on student behaviors before, during, and after completion of teacher training. A limitation of both of these studies was that no direct assessments of teacher behavior were conducted. Observer agreement was assessed in both studies but neither study addressed generalization or maintenance issues. The results of these studies indicated that teacher training was instrumental in reducing disruptive student behavior and increasing productivity (Jones & Eimers, 1975) and appropriate verbal participation (Burka & Jones, 1979).

Jones and Miller (1977) collected behavioral data on students as well as teachers trained with the same role playing package described earlier. A reversal design (A-B-A) for implementation of appropriate teacher responding to student behavior demonstrated that training significantly changed teacher responding and that appropriate teacher consequences for student behaviors resulted in reduced disruptiveness in the target classroom. Follow-up data collected 3 months later indicated that skills learned by the teachers were still being used effectively. Jones, Fremouw, and Carples (1977) demonstrated that teachers trained in their classroom management skill package could then successfully train other teachers in the same manner. It was found through the use of a pyramid training research design that student disruptiveness had decreased at least as much for the group of teachers trained by other teachers as for the students of the originally trained teachers. Serving as trainers appeared to benefit teachers, especially those who had benefitted least from the original training sessions. This study is limited, however, in the respect that only student behavior data were collected.

Horton (1975) trained teachers to discriminate behavior-specific praise from general praise by having teachers read a definition of the target behavior, discuss that definition with an instructor, and score correct and incorrect videotaped teacher behaviors until a criterion of 100% accuracy had been attained. Following this training sequence, teachers were asked to increase their behavior-specific praise rates in the classroom, and daily audiotaped feedback was made available to them regarding their success. The first experimental phase involved classroom instruction in reading only; a second experimental phase included language arts and math as well. A multiple baseline design across two fourth grade teachers was utilized in an A-B-A-C intervention format with the second baseline phase consisting of removal of experimenter feedback. The teacher behaviors measured in this study indicated that behavior-specific praise rates had increased after training; however, these effects were restricted to subject-matter areas in which training had been conducted.

Carnine and Fink (1978) trained one teacher and two aides in a class for the developmentally delayed and evaluated the effects of their training program through the use of a multiple baseline across subjects design. These investigators trained two direct instruction techniques, rate of presentation and signaling, with a written manual, live modeling, and videotape feedback. Teacher responses were coded in terms of a specified sequence of teacher-child-teacher interactions, and child achievement was assessed on the Wild Range Achievement Test (WRAT). Follow-up data were collected as were interobserver reliability assessments. One possible limitation of this study was that teachers were given and asked to read the written manual while baseline data were being collected. A descriptive research investigation conducted in conjunction with this study provided information on the performance of intensively trained teachers. Their performance was monitored and used as a standard of comparison for untrained teacher and teacher aides. With implementation of the training package, all three subjects increased their levels of appropriately signaling pupil responses and accelerated their rates of presentation well above the comparison standard. Observations made one week and 4 weeks after completion of training indicated that performance levels had been maintained.

The use of a manual, training exercises, and feedback were investigated by Hundert (1982) for training two teachers of the multihandicapped deaf in measurement skills (setting objectives and measuring pupil performance) and behavior modification programming skills. A multiple baseline design was utilized by this author with dependent measures on teacher behavior modification program writing and implementation for target student behaviors. Behavior modification programs were written by teachers and entered on forms to facilitate their evaluation, and teacher approval, prompting, instructing, and correcting responses were observed in the classroom. Teacher ratings of pupils on an adaptive behavior scale were also obtained. Observer agreement was assessed, and generalization measures across pupils and target student behaviors were collected. It was found that measurement training had little general effect on either teacher or pupil behavior, but after programming training, teachers increased both their program writing and correct use of behavior modification procedures. This training was generalized across pupils and target behaviors, and along with these effects, improvement in student behavior was demonstrated. Because the same package of teacher training methods were used in measurement and programming training, the effectiveness of these methods apparently interacted with the types of skills being trained in this study.

A multiple baseline study across three teachers conducted by Cossairt, Hall, and Hopkins (1973) evaluated the component and package effectiveness of instructions, feedback, and feedback plus social praise in the training of teachers to utilize more praise in the classroom. Dependent measures in this study included teacher verbal praise, pupil attending and productivity in the form of permanent products, and even experimenter verbal interactions with teachers. Observer agreement was assessed on these data collection procedures, and 3-week follow-up data were collected as well. The results of this study indicated that introduction of the entire package to one teacher in a single experimental condition produced more teacher praise for student attending behavior, and postchecks indicated that high rates of teacher praise and student attending were maintained. Component analysis results were not as clear. Feedback increased teacher praise more effectively than instructions with one subject and not with the other. Feedback plus social praise produced more teacher praise for student attending behavior with both of these teachers, but postchecks indicated a decrease in praise rates from those previously attained.

Van Houghten and Sullivan (1975) investigated the relative effectiveness of instructing teachers in the use of counting and graphing their own behaviors with specific criterion praise rates to be attained, and the use of auditory cues delivered via the school P.A. system. These authors reported the use of a multiple baseline design across three classroom teachers with training introduced in an A-B-C-A-C-A format. Specific teacher praise categories were observed, and interobserver reliability assessments were conducted. It was found that the introduction of auditory cues markedly increased teacher praise rates but that self-recording was relatively ineffective with these teachers. No follow-up data were collected.

Cooper, Thompson, and Baer (1970) studied the combined efficacy of four types of feedback on teacher delivery of contingent attention. Examples of appropriate attending behavior, daily success and failure rates feedback, and more frequent reports of appropriate attending rates were provided as training. A multiple baseline across two Head Start teachers was utilized in an A-B-A format. Disruptive and appropriate pupil responses were observed as well as four specific categories of teacher attending behavior; observer agreement checks were also conducted. Both teachers showed an increase in attending to appropriate child responses after feedback regarding those behaviors was provided. The data indicated that training increased only those specific attending behaviors trained and not all attending behaviors in general.

Parsonson, Baer, and Baer (1974) provided two teacher aides in a program for the institutionalized mentally retarded with frequent observer feedback on their use of contingent attention for generalized child behaviors. A multiple baseline experimental design was utilized across teachers, and five categories of teacher attending behaviors were observed. The categories of appropriate and inappropriate child behaviors were also coded, and observer reliability checks were conducted. These investigators conducted follow-up observations for 11 weeks after feedback was withdrawn to determine training maintenance. For both teacher aides, the effect of training was an increase in appropriate child behavior attention that was apparently durable.

Ringer (1973) combined the multiple baseline and reversal experimental designs in examining the training effects of live modeling in a teacher's fourth grade classroom. A token reinforcement approach to decreasing the disruptive, inappropriate behaviors of 10 target children was designed cooperatively by the teacher and the experimenter to be particularly transferrable to management by that teacher. This behavioral program was then modeled for and assessed by that teacher in an A-B-A-C reversal format, demonstrating the effectiveness of the environmental contingencies implemented as well as the ability of the teacher to implement the procedures independently. Teacher and pupil behaviors were observed and observer reliability assessed. It was found that when the token helper withdrew from the classroom, the teacher was able to manage the token system and maintain disruptive behaviors at lower than baseline levels. Specific increases of teacher social attention to appropriate pupil behavior did not occur, however.

The use of classroom behavior management assignments, immediate (bug-in-the-ear) observer feedback, graphed daily feedback, and self-monitoring were investigated by Thompson, Holmberg, and Baer (1978) in a multiple baseline design across 24 teachers with reversal design formats for child behavior intervention evaluation. These authors trained preschool student teachers in a laboratory setting as well as Head Start teachers and orphanage day care workers in field school settings in the effective use of priming and reinforcement procedures in the classroom. Dependent measures included teacher behaviors as well as student verbal behaviors and peer interactions. Observer agreement assessments were conducted, and generalization measures across settings, children, and time were collected. It was found that the self-monitoring and immediate observer feedback methods were the most successful training techniques; assignments and graphed feedback were found to be much less effective. The authors suggested that although none of these methods was evaluated in combination with any of the others, certain combinations of these techniques might be better than any of them in isolation.

Sloat, Tharp, and Gallimore (1977) investigated the incremental effectiveness of six classroom-based teacher training techniques through the use of a multiple baseline design in which training was staggered across two small groups of teachers and baseline data collected before and after each training component. Training techniques investigated were didactic instruction, modeling and role playing, videotape feedback, direct coaching, graphed feedback, and graphed feedback with goals. The five elementary classroom teachers who participated in this study were observed during their regular teaching activities and assessed on 18 specific teacher praise behavior categories. Interobserver agreement was assessed, and follow-up data were collected one week after completion of training. These authors reported training effects for modeling plus role playing, video feedback, and graphed feedback with goals, but not for direct coaching or graphed feedback without goals.

To summarize, single-subject time-series designs have been used widely to evaluate teacher training programs. Multiple baseline and reversal designs and combinations of these two design approaches have been utilized to demonstrate the package and component effectiveness of a number of teacher-training techniques. It has been found that didactic instruction can be used effectively for teacher training in combination with a variety of other teacher training methods including modeling (e.g., Hall, 1971), role playing (e.g., Greenwood *et al.*, 1979), and feedback (e.g., Hundert, 1982). Component analyses reveal that modeling and feedback can be effective training methods in isolation as well (e.g., Nagle & Gresham, 1979; Parsonson *et al.*, 1974; Sloat *et al.*, 1977). A role playing training package developed by Jones and his associates has been found to be very effective in training (e.g., Jones & Eimers, 1975), and the combination of all four training methods, instruction, modeling, role playing, and feedback, has been found to be an effective training package (e.g., Carnine & Fink, 1978).

Although single-case designs provide an excellent way to conduct preliminary investigations of training technique effectiveness, it is not possible to determine the relative effectiveness of treatment packages in this manner (Kazdin, 1982). For comparisons of packages of training procedures, group designs are most appropriate. Teacher training studies utilizing between-group comparison designs have been reported in the literature and are reviewed next.

Training Research Utilizing Between-Groups Comparison Designs

Another major research methodology category employed in the evaluation of teacher-training techniques is the between-groups design in which groups receiving different training packages and/or components are compared. Individuals are selected and assigned to groups in such a way as to minimize differences prior to training, and threats to internal validity are ruled out primarily through the use of randomization and various types of control groups (Kazdin, 1980c). A group design is particularly appropriate when the purpose of a study is to determine the effectiveness of a given procedure or set of procedures on a well-defined group.

Madsen *et al.* (1970) evaluated the success of a teacher-training package including discussion, role playing, videotape and observer feedback with 32 elementary school teachers in the application of rules, approval, ignoring, and disapproval in the classroom. A posttest-only control group design was utilized with control group teachers matched with experimental group teachers on years of teaching experience and grade level taught. Posttraining observational data were collected on four categories of teacher behavior and one category of student behavior; no observer reliability assessments were made. The authors reported that the results of this investigation indicated training package effectiveness in decreasing inappropriate student behaviors, but only percentages of the various behavior categories were presented.

Brown, Frankel, Birkimer, and Gamboa (1966) found that didactic instruction alone may improve teacher performance. In one condition children displayed a reduction in problem behaviors after teachers ($N = 30$) received handouts on how to define problems and record data and two 2½ hour workshops over 2 days. On the other hand, no changes occurred in children of teachers ($N = 25$) who received handouts only.

Ward and Baker (1968) trained teachers in

the use of contingent attention in the classroom and collected pre- and posttraining data on four categories of teacher behavior and disruptive and appropriate student behaviors. Other children in the same classes as the teachers' target children were used as controls for student data, and one teacher not included in training served as a control for teacher behavior data. Four teachers and 12 first grade children served as experimental subjects in the study. Teacher training consisted of discussion of behavior modification principles and feedback on appropriateness of attention delivered in the classroom. The behavior of students whose teachers had participated in training showed a significant improvement from baseline treatment levels whereas no significant changes were found for the same-class control children. The amount of teacher attention to target children remained the same from baseline to training conditions; however, the proportion of attention to task-relevant child behavior increased.

A pretest-posttest control group design was utilized by Rutherford (1973) to investigate the effects of training procedures that included a modeling videotape, a feedback videotape, combined modeling and feedback videotapes, and a no-training control condition. This investigator collected observational data on the number of positive and negative responses teachers gave to children, and interobserver reliability assessments were conducted. Results of this study indicated that the modeling videotape alone and the modeling and feedback videotapes combined were effective, whereas the feedback videotape in isolation was not effective in changing teacher behaviors. No generalization or follow-up measures were included in this study.

Greenwood *et al.* (1979) also utilized the pretest–posttest control group design and analysis of covariance procedures in their evaluation of a comprehensive teacher training package. In their behavior management training package were included a written manual, instruction sessions, consultant prompts, feedback and praise, role playing, and teacher payment contingencies. They observed and recorded behaviors in 50 elementary school classrooms on four categories of teacher behavior, several categories of individual student behaviors, and two categories of class behavior as a whole. Student measures of social adjustment and achievement and teacher training participant satisfaction data were also obtained. Results indicated significant effects for the experimental group for increases in teacher approval and student appropriate classroom behavior, and decreases in four categories of student inappropriate behavior. Program satisfaction ratings were positive, and continued use of the program was reported a year later.

Teacher training designed to increase the appropriate use of reinforcement in the classroom was investigated by Kosier and Severson (1971). Training components consisting of didactic instruction (lecture and discussion), instruction plus individual feedback and consultation, and instruction plus video feedback and consultation were presented to 20 elementary school teachers in three experimental groups. A no-training control group was also included. Dependent measures included observational data on teacher and student responses, and interobserver agreement was assessed. It was found that whereas teacher praise to the class as a whole increased, teachers in the experimental groups increased only slightly their amount of praise to disruptive students. A significant difference was not demonstrated between the instruction-only training group and the groups trained with instruction plus feedback and consultation.

Bowles and Nelson (1976) trained teachers ($N = 13$) in the use of praise and prompts through an inservice training workshop consisting of lectures and discussion, modeling, videotapes, and practice in classroom behavior management, and compared the effectiveness of this package of training components with in-class bug-in-the-ear feedback training. The teachers were assessed before and after training on a paper-and-pencil test of behavior modification principles as well as on several specific in-class response categories. Observer agreement was assessed, and generalization data from the training setting to the classroom was obtained. The workshop apparently did not produce significant classroom behavior changes because the only measure that reflected a difference between experimental and control groups as a result of the inservice training package was the paper-and-pencil test. Increased teacher praise and contingency statements were produced, however, with the bug-in-the-ear direct classroom training component.

Walker and Buckley (1972) conducted a teacher training study as part of a larger investigation on the effective use of the token economy in the classroom. Their teacher-training package included a written manual, discussion, "direct training" in behavior modification techniques (not well specified), and consultation with and monitoring of classroom teachers. Teacher behaviors were observed in the classroom. In this study significant differences were not obtained for teacher training and control group means.

The use of information, instructions to practice, and performance feedback as a package for training teachers in the use of classroom behavior management techniques was investigated by Johnson and Sloat (1980). These investigators collected seven specific categories of observational behavior data on teacher behaviors in the classroom and anonymous teacher evaluations of the training staff. Significant increases in positive teacher behaviors and decreases in negative teacher behaviors after completion of the training program were found. However, these performance levels were found to be not maintained at follow-up 5 months later.

Hay, Nelson, and Hay (1977) investigated the efficacy of simply training teachers in classroom observational procedures through written instruction and discussion for improvement in classroom behavior management. Eight elementary school teachers were observed before and after training for frequency of praise, prompts, and criticisms delivered in the classroom in response to appropriate, disruptive, and passive student behaviors exhibited. Observer reliability checks were conducted, and a repeated-measures analysis of variance was conducted on the frequency of each teacher verbalization over the experimental phases. An analysis of variance was also conducted on student behavior change. The results indicated that the frequency of prompts (but not praise or criticism) to students systematically observed by the teacher increased significantly after training. Students observed by the teacher also showed more appropriate behavior in the classroom than students who were not observed.

An inservice training workshop was conducted by Rollins, McCandless, Thompson, and Brassel (1974) before the start of the school year in which readings on behavior modification, discussion sessions, classroom practice with videotaped feedback and peer observation, and practice in data collection, behavior identification, and programming were utilized to train the effective use of reinforcement, extinction, and a token system in the classroom of 16 teachers. After school started, four categories of teacher positive reinforcement behavior and five categories of punishment behavior were observed in the classroom as well as attentive and disruptive student responses. Intellectual and achievement child measures were also obtained. Checks on the reliability of observational data collection were gathered as well as follow-up data the following school year. The authors found that compared with matched control teachers and classes, the teachers who had participated in the inservice training showed higher frequencies of positive reinforcement and lower incidences of punishment. The experimental classes were significantly less disruptive and more attentive. It was also reported that the experimental classes demonstrated more gain on intellectual and achievement measures.

Kazdin (1974) utilized a factorial design to determine the efficacy of a training package including lectures and discussion, reading assignments on operant principles, signaling when to reinforce in the classroom, and daily feedback. The six elementary school teachers included in this study were observed on two specific approval and disapproval response categories as well as physical contact, verbal comment, and facial attention. The results indicated definite individual changes in teacher behavior as a result of the training package. No assessment was conducted on child behavior change or behavior generalizations.

McKeown, Adams, and Forehand (1975) utilized a factorial design also to compare teacher training in behavior modification via a written manual, with training via lectures and role playing, and training including all three components. A no-instruction control group was also included in this study. Dependent measures collected before and after training included classroom observations of student disruptive behaviors and a written assessment of teacher knowledge of behavior modification principles. Observer agreement checks were made during data collection, and an analysis of variance was conducted on the data as well as a correlational procedure between increases in teacher knowledge of behavior modification and decreases in student disruptive behavior. The results indicated that teachers receiving lectures and role-playing training gained more in knowledge of behavior principles. It was also found that disruptive student behavior decreased only in the classrooms of those teachers receiving that combination of training component, either alone or with the training manual component added.

Some studies have examined the relation between training in behavior modification and consultation services to the classroom teacher (e.g., Anderson, Kratochwill, & Bergan, 1986; White & Pryzwansky, 1982). Anderson *et al.* (1986) evaluated the relative effectiveness of two teacher training packages under two analogue consultation dependent measures in a two treatment × two levels of consultation completely randomized factorial design. The subjects in the study included elementary school teachers ($N = 56$) in an urban school district. The conditions included training in classroom behavior modification and consultation, and training in consultative service delivery procedures and general multidisciplinary team processes (a nonspecific control). Analogue consultation dependent measures included specific and general problem identification, problem analysis, and problem evaluation behavioral consultation elicitors from the Bergan (1977) behavioral consultation model.

The effectiveness of the four conditions was evaluated on knowlege of behavior modification principles and concepts, and the frequency of specific categories of consultee (teacher) verbal behaviors. Results suggested that the active experimental training package was effective in increasing teacher knowledge of behavioral procedures and in increasing the frequency of teacher verbalizations regarding overt child behaviors, behavior observation techniques, and behavioral intervention plans during the problem identification and problem analysis phases of analogue consultation. It was also found that even after training, specific consultant questions were important in eliciting consultee statements related to environmental conditions surrounding behavior. In contrast, the use of more general consultant verbal behaviors resulted in significantly more vague, unspecified, and irrelevant types of consultee verbalizations.

White and Pryzwansky (1982) investigated the effects of teacher training on consultation with classroom learning disabilities (LD) teachers. In the study, 12 LD resource teachers received different types of training: four received communication skills training, four received conceptual assumptions training, and four served as a control group. Each resource teacher conducted three 20- to 30-minute conferences with each of five elementary school teachers ($N = 60$). The outcome measures consisted of classroom teacher ratings of satisfaction with services, joint ratings of child progress toward goals, percentage of recommendations implemented, and classroom teacher ratings of joint responsibility, and of resource teacher respect, empathy, and congruence.

The authors found that there were no differences resulting from either type of training at posttest for classroom teacher respect, resource teacher congruence, joint responsibility, or joint ratings of the child's progress. Moreover, training resource teachers in communication skills resulted in higher classroom teacher ratings of resource teacher empathy. Also, differences due to resource teacher experiences prior to this study were found with classroom teacher ratings of the child's progress, and the number of recommendations implemented.

In summary, the group studies reviewed were found to demonstrate the effectiveness of teacher training packages utilizing didactic instruction plus role playing (e.g., Greenwood *et al.*, 1979; McKeown *et al.*, 1975), didactic instruction plus feedback (e.g., Johnson & Sloat, 1980; Kazdin, 1974), modeling plus feedback (e.g., Rutherford, 1973), and didactic instruction plus role playing, modeling, and feedback (e.g., Madsen *et al.*, 1970). These studies were generally adequate methodologically, using appropriate dependent measures, controls for extraneous variables, and experimental designs, and analyses. One major limitation found in the studies utilizing group designs for evaluation of teacher training is the failure to demonstrate adequately skill maintenance and generalization.

Summary of Teacher Training Research

A number of teacher training studies reported in the literature utilized only the child behavior data collected by teacher trainees for assigned classroom intervention projects in evaluation of the teacher training procedures. Because of the lack of teacher behavior data and adequate experimental design, these studies provide only minimal evidence for the efficacy of teacher training methods. More sophisticated empirical support has been reported in the literature, however, through the use of a variety of single-case time-series and between-group designs. Single-subject designs utilized in teacher training research include reversals, multiple baselines, A-B-C designs, and combinations of these various evaluation approaches (see Table 1). These experimental designs provide a wealth of information regarding the effectiveness of a variety of teacher-training methods. Between-group designs have also been used to demonstrate the efficacy of teacher training procedures. In this type of design, randomization and the use of various types of control groups are generally utilized to provide valid evidence of training effects.

Overall, the teacher training research points to a number of effective training options. Didactic instruction, modeling, role playing, cuing, and feedback techniques have all been used effectively to train teachers in the use of classroom behavior management techniques. Didactic instruction should be used only in combination with other training methods, such as modeling, role playing, and feedback. Didactic instruction alone has been found to be effective in at least two studies (i.e., Andrews, 1970; Brown *et al.*, 1976). However, several studies that included didactic instruction as part of a component analysis, did not find any evidence for its effectiveness (e.g., Bowles & Nelson, 1976; Cossairt *et al.*, 1973; Johnson & Sloat, 1980; Sloat *et al.*, 1977). Moreover, the better measures used in the latter studies would suggest that this component needs to be evaluated further. Nevertheless, it is probable that some form of didactic training is a prerequisite to other forms of successful teacher training.

Cuing has been investigated relatively infrequently. In the Bowles and Nelson (1976) study didactic instruction and cuing were effective during training.

Role playing training generally includes a

modeling component. Based on our review, role playing and role playing combined with modeling provided effective instructional procedures. However, differences among studies, such as amount of training time and focus of outcome measure, may be a factor in determining how successful these procedures are independently, and in combination. In research on feedback procedures, we find considerable support, but most feedback is provided within the context of other components, such as didactic instruction and modeling. However, modeling and feedback appear to be effective when used in isolation as well as in combination with other methods. The use of didactic instructional techniques (written materials, lectures, and discussions) in combination with modeling, role playing, and feedback have been found effective in single-case time-series designs and between-group comparison research (e.g., Carnine & Fink, 1978; Madsen *et al.*, 1970).

Surprisingly, few studies have used specific reinforcement procedures independently of other instructional procedures. This is surprising in view of the relative efficacy of this tactic with a wide range of effective target responses, settings, and subjects (Kazdin, 1982). A limitation common to the teacher training research overall, appears to be a dearth of evidence for generalization and maintenance of teacher training effects. In a review of the generalization ,of behavioral teacher training, Robinson and Swanton (1980) reported only six studies that attempted to establish that training had resulted in generalized change and three studies providing convincing evidence of that.

Generalization was defined by Robinson and Swanton (1980) as occurring:

> if and only if either one of two possibilities holds: Either (a) similar effects are demonstrated in a nontraining condition where no controlling events are scheduled, or (b) similar effects are demonstrated in a nontraining condition where the events scheduled are (1) less costly than the training events, and (2) not similar to those scheduled in the training condition. (p. 487)

The three studies found by these reviewers to demonstrate generalized behavior change were described in some detail earlier. Koegel *et al.* (1977) evaluated a training package that included the use of a written manual, videotaped modeling, and trainer feedback. This combination was found to be effective in training skills that generalized to a variety of children and target behaviors. Horton (1975) increased rates of specific teacher praise through the use of feedback that generalized to subject areas other than that in which it was trained, and Parsonson *et al.* (1974) also utilized feedback to train preschool teachers to apply correct social contingencies to several classes of child behaviors. Generalization in these studies appeared to be related to two variables: the type of training provided and teachers' attitudes toward the training. Generalization appeared to be promoted by extensive training involving a wide range of conditions in which skills can be learned. It was also found that teachers whose training generalized to other situations and subjects held more favorable attitudes toward their training than those who did not (Robinson & Swanton, 1980).

Relevant Parent-Training Research

Research that has implications for the dissemination of behavioral procedures through teacher training includes studies in which parents have been trained to use behavioral management techniques. Behavioral training studies have been conducted investigating the use of didactic instruction, modeling, role playing, and feedback approaches for parents. Because of the somewhat more advanced state of the parent-training research area, some of these studies are particularly relevant for consideration here. The reader interested in a more detailed and comprehensive overview of the parent-training literature should consult some major reviews of this area (e.g., Forehand & McMahon, 1981;

Griffin, 1979; Henry, 1981; McLoughlin, 1982; O'Dell, 1974).

An evaluation of four training techniques including written presentation, lecture presentation, videotaped modeling, and modeling plus role playing was conducted in a between-group experimental design by Nay (1975). The dependent measures utilized were a multiple-choice questionnaire assessing all aspects of behavioral information presented, and an audiotaped analogue in which typical behavior problems were presented for which appropriate multiple-choice responses were required. Nay found that the written assessment revealed no significant differences among treatment groups. However, in the audio-simulated situations, modeling and role playing were found to be superior to written and lecture presentations, but not to modeling alone.

Component analyses of parental feedback training were conducted in time-series experimental designs by Budd, Green, and Baer (1976) and Doleys, Doster, and Cartelli (1976). Both of these studies demonstrated significant behavior changes after introduction of a feedback training component. Doleys and his associates found that preliminary training via written materials, lecture, and role playing resulted only in small behavioral changes, and that parental feedback was a necessary training procedure.

A between-group study conducted by Flanagan, Adams, and Forehand (1979) investigated parent training via written presentation, lecture presentation, videotaped modeling, and role playing. Three response measures were utilized in this study: a multiple-choice questionnaire assessing knowledge of principles and procedures presented, an audiotape analogue assessing performance skill in the application of behavioral procedures, and an at-home trial of parental skill involving interaction with a child. These investigators reported that all treatment groups were superior to the control group on the questionnaire knowledge assessment. Differences between treatment groups were apparent on the audiotape analogue assessment in which role playing was found to be superior to the lecture presentation groups, and on the at-home assessment where modeling was found to be more effective than the written presentation.

The effectiveness of written manual instruction, filmed modeling, filmed modeling plus a brief individual check out, and individual modeling and rehearsal training methods were investigated by O'Dell, Mahoney, Horton, and Turner (1979) in a group experimental study. The dependent variables assessed were skills demonstrated in a role-playing situation and a consumer satisfaction measure. These authors reported no differences among training models in parent attitude responses. Measures of parent skills attained showed all training models to be significantly better than no treatment. Filmed modeling plus the brief individual check out were found to be superior to all of the other training approaches.

O'Dell, Krug, Patterson, and Faustman (1980) conducted another between-group study that investigated the use of a take-home written manual, individual modeling plus manual, and filmed modeling plus manual. A multiple-choice assessment instrument and in-home observations were utilized to assess dependent variables in this study. It was found that all three training methods were superior to no treatment; however, no significant differences between groups were demonstrated.

Hudson (1982) investigated parental training via verbal instruction, verbal instruction plus systematic training of behavioral principles, and verbal instruction plus modeling and role playing in a between-group experimental design. Several dependent measures were collected in this study, including a multiple-choice assessment of knowledge of behavior principles, videotaped behavioral assessment of skill application, completion of home child skill training, child development as assessed on the Denver Developmental Screening Test, and two assessment procedures related to parental satisfaction with training procedures. It was reported that inclusion of training in general behavior principles did not improve the performance of the parents participating in this study and that it was necessary to include modeling and role-playing components that more directly shaped parental behavior.

A study investigating modification of mothers' behaviors and attitudes through a videotape modeling group discussion program was conducted by Webster-Stratton (1981). This between-group study examined the effectiveness of a training package in which standardized modeling vignettes and therapist-led discussions were utilized. Dependent measures included observations of parent–child interactions in an analogue setting, an attitudinal measure assessing five dimensions characterizing parental perceptions of parent–child interactions, and a consumer satisfaction questionnaire. The results of this study indicated that treatment and control groups differed significantly on observational measures, but not on the attitudinal variables assessed.

Acquisition of parenting skills via four training methods as predicted on the basis of parent characteristics was investigated by O'Dell *et al.* (1982). The training methods utilized a written manual, an audiotape, videotaped modeling, and live modeling and rehearsal with a child. Outcome was assessed via an in-home observation of parental reinforcement skills. It was found that all training methods were superior to a minimal instructions control group. The audiotaped manual was less effective than the written manual or live modeling with rehearsal. There were no significant differences among the written, videotaped, or live modeling rehearsal training methods. Parent reading level and demographic characteristics were significantly related to training effectiveness in the control group and in groups receiving written or live modeling plus rehearsal training. These characteristics did not affect outcome in the group receiving videotaped modeling training, so it was concluded that videotaped modeling training more consistently taught a wider range of parents.

An instrument to assess parental knowledge of behavioral principles has been developed by O'Dell, Tarler-Beniolo, and Flynn (1979). This instrument, entitled Knowledge of Behavioral Principles as Applied to Children (KBPAC), is a 50-item multiple-choice test designed to assess verbal understanding of basic behavioral principles. A Kuder-Richardson reliability coefficient of .94 was reported for this instrument as well as a split-half correlation of .93. These data were collected from a large sample (147 persons) including teachers, parents, mental health professionals, and graduate students in psychology. Thus, the instrument appears to possess satisfactory content validity and good internal consistency. It appears to be useful for future research in the area of child behavior management where a general measure of this type of knowledge is needed.

In a review of behavioral parent-training generalization and maintenance research, Sanders and James (1983) concluded that only limited aspects of these important variables have been addressed. Although the efficacy of parent training has been supported on the basis of generalization over time and maintenance of training effects, generalization across settings, behaviors, and individuals has not been extensively researched. The predominant behavioral training generalization strategy within the field appears to remain "train and hope" (Sanders & James, 1983; Stokes & Baer, 1977).

In summary, empirical support for training methods involves written manuals (O'Dell *et al.*, 1980; O'Dell *et al.*, 1982), modeling (Flanagan *et al.*, 1979; Nay, 1975; O'Dell *et al.*, 1979; O'Dell *et al.*, 1982), role playing (Flanagan *et al.*, 1979), feedback (Budd *et al.*, 1976; Doleys *et al.*, 1976), modeling plus manual (O'Dell *et al.*, 1980), and modeling plus discussion (Webster-Stratton, 1981). Parent training studies have been conducted investigating the relationship between subject characteristics and attitudes and training outcome as well (O'Dell *et al.*, 1979; O'Dell *et al.*, 1982; Webster-Stratton, 1981). Videotaped modeling was found to reach a wider range of parents (O'Dell *et al.*, 1982); however, research results involving the interaction of attitudes and trainee skill acquisition have been inconclusive.

The parent-training literature, therefore, like the teacher-training literature, indicates that didactic instruction in various combinations with modeling, role playing, and feedback can be used to provide effective training in the management of child behavior. Videotaped/filmed modeling appears to be a particularly promising training method; however, its usefulness with teachers of varying characteristics has been less well established than with parents at this point. A neglected variable in the parent- and teacher-training research appears to be that of trainee attitudes toward behavior modification and the possible interaction of attitudes with training outcomes. Further examination of this important variable is warranted.

Further Considerations

Integrity of Intervention Programs

A major issue that must be addressed in teacher training research refers to the integrity of the intervention process and procedures. Increasingly, researchers have been concerned with evaluating treatment programs to ensure their integrity. That is, researchers have emphasized that when a treatment is being implemented it must be implemented as originally intended (Peterson, Homer, & Wonderlich, 1982; Yeaton & Sechrest, 1981). In the implementation of teacher intervention programs there are basically two concerns that must be addressed. First of all, in the process of training teachers in intervention programs the researcher must ensure that teachers are introduced to programs in a way that the researcher designed them. For example, a multicomponent intervention package must be introduced with each of the components specified and outlined in great detail. Thus, steps must be taken to ensure that the teachers are presented with the complete package and in the correct order.

In addition, when teachers implement intervention programs in applied settings, researchers must check to determine that the program is being implemented as originally designed and taught. This is a crucial step as many factors in the natural environment might militate against the program being implemented as designed. For example, teachers might find the program difficult to integrate into the regular classroom routine, they might find it very inconvenient to distribute tokens to students, or they might find it difficult in terms of their time to be involved in monitoring components of the program. Thus, there could be some type of slippage in the process of implementing the intervention program. The point is that steps must be taken to ensure that what is really being called an intervention program as conceived by the designers or researchers is what is actually being implemented.

A case example from the experience of the authors is noteworthy in this regard. The second author has had an opportunity to review a number of assertive discipline programs that have been implemented in elementary school settings. In one particular case, teachers were provided with written information at a workshop on how the assertive discipline program would be carried out. Once the program was put into place, teachers were requested to complete the program as originally designed. However, many variations occurred. For example, teachers in one first grade classroom decided that it was not a good idea to use intermediate steps before sending a child home with a note and decided that this step could be used immediately for rather serious discipline problems. Thus, although the program might be in place, it was not being carried out as designed.

A major concern in monitoring the integrity

of treatment programs is that the investigator must have a reliable and valid estimate of the program's implementation. This obviously has an important bearing on whether or not the program was actually being tested or whether some variation is being examined. Ultimately, research needs to examine this process to determine what type of natural degradation of programs occurs and under what conditions we can expect these problems to occur. Of course, there is much to learn from this implementation process that might have a bearing on designing better programs in applied settings.

Teacher Attitudes

The use of behavior modification techniques in the classroom has been found to provide a practical and viable method for establishing behavior change in children experiencing learning and behavioral difficulties. The success of these procedures and of intervention models generally, however, depends heavily on teacher awareness, skill, and cooperation in handling the roles of the behavior change mediator. Because teachers are asked to assume these responsibilities, consideration must be given, not only to procedural and skill level issues, but also to whether or not the classroom teacher really accepts the concepts and principles of behavior theory. Although very little attention has been addressed to this issue in the published empirical literature, teacher attitude toward behavior modification is an important variable in the implementation of classroom-based behavioral programs (Grieger, 1972; Musgrove, 1974).

Attitudes toward behavior therapy have been found to impact significantly on the effectiveness of behavioral program outcomes. Research has suggested that the label *behavior modification* itself can result in negative evaluations of treatment procedures (Kazdin & Cole, 1981). Describing classroom behavior modification procedures as humanistic education has been found to result in more favorable outcome evaluations (Woolfolk, Woolfolk, & Wilson, 1977). Whether sources of bias originate from reactions to operant conditioning philosophy, from reports of unsavory behavioral practices, or simply from inaccurate notions about behavioral procedures themselves, attitudes appear to have a definite impact on the successful application of behavior management procedures (Woolfolk & Woolfolk, 1979).

Attitudes have been conceptualized by Baron and Byrne (1977) as consisting of three components: (a) the cognitive component (b) the affective component, and (c) the behavioral component. The *cognitive component* consists of categories used to classify subject stimuli and beliefs associated with those categories; the *affective component* involves feelings of like or dislike toward a subject; and the *behavioral component* comprises particular predispositions toward action in regard to a subject. Questionnaires and attitude scales have typically been used to assess each of these attitudinal components; however, the degree of congruence among them is essentially unknown (Hannah & Pliner, 1983).

Relatively little research has been conducted in which the attitudes of teachers and the impact of those attitudes on the educational process has been examined. Even less attention has been focused on teacher attitudes specifically toward behavior modification. Teacher attitudes have been measured in essentially an evaluation of consumer satisfaction related to behavior modification training programs (e.g., Ryan, 1976; Vane 1972). Armer and Thomas (1978) conducted a study investigating attitudes toward interdisciplinary collaboration in pupil personnel services teams. Investigations have been also conducted on teacher attitudes toward students, especially those with handicaps, and the behavioral effects of those attitudes in the classroom and on mainstreaming efforts (Good & Brophy, 1972; Hannah & Pliner, 1983; Horne, 1979).

Grieger (1972) suggested that several teacher attitudes potentially have an impact on behavior modification consultation, but this work is speculative and based on the author's professional experience rather than empirical research. Attitudes believed by Grieger to interfere with behavior modification problem-solving attempts include the following: (a) *the child needs fixing,* in which teachers perceive child behavior as relatively independent of situational variables, with the stimulus for action perceived as coming primarily from within the child; (b) *it is wrong to express negative feelings,* where teachers consider it inappropriate to bring child difficulties in the classroom to the attention of the school psychologist or other professional; (c) *children must not be frustrated,* in which as few demands as possible are placed on a child experiencing learning, behavioral, or emotional difficulties; (d) *the should-ought syndrome,* where it is assumed that without training, children can be expected to acquire a behavioral repertoire conforming to societal standards; (e) *the he makes me syndrome,* in which the child is held responsible both for the child's actions and the teacher's behavioral and emotional responses; and (f) *children are blameworthy for their actions,* in which it is suggested that children freely choose to do unacceptable things. Each of these attitudes is suggested as possibly interfering significantly with successful learning of behavior management principles and procedures and with their implementation in the classroom.

Although empirical research related to teacher attitudes toward behavior modification in the classroom is extremely scarce, Musgrove (1974) developed a scale to measure attitudes toward behavior modification and administered it to teaching faculties of elementary schools in Florida. This instrument consists of 20 Likert scale items with a 5-point scale of strongly agree, agree, neutral or undecided, disagree, and strongly disagree. The absolute range of scores possible on the scale was a low of 20 and a high of 100, with a score of 60 indicating a neutral or undecided attitude. Musgrove obtained in his sample a range of scores from 20 to 96 with a mean of 64 and a standard deviation of 13. The standard error of measurement was 3.2, and a Kuder-Richardson reliability coefficient of .94 was obtained. An average interitem correlation was found to be .44, and no validity coefficients are available. An item analysis comparing the scores of the top 27% with those of the lowest 27% of the sample indicated discriminations between the two groups at a significant level ($p < .001$). The standardization sample for this instrument consisted of elementary school teachers who were predominantly female, and Musgrove cautions against generalizing to the general population of teachers at all levels. The scale does appear to possess content and face validity, and the data indicate that the scale discriminates varying teacher attitudes.

Acceptability of Behavior Modification

It is important that the effects of interventions be evaluated on the basis of the applied or social significance of behavioral goals, procedures, and effects (Kazdin, 1977; Wolf, 1978). Do behavioral changes effected actually make a difference in the lives of the individuals involved? Given the importance of the teacher as consultee and behavior change agent in the schools, the attitudes and characteristics of these individuals would appear to be important variables to investigate.

In recent years there has been a growing empirical research base on the acceptability of behavioral interventions (Witt & Elliott, 1985). This acceptability has been typically conceptualized under the rubric of social validation. Kazdin (1981a) refers to treatment acceptability as "judgments by persons, clients, and others of whether treatment procedures are appropriate, fair, and reasonable for the problem or client" (p. 493). Research in this area has focused on clinical/instructional and school/educational settings. In the former area Kazdin and his associates (Kazdin, 1980a,b, 1981a; Kazdin, French, & Sherick, 1981) developed a procedure in which various individuals (e.g., undergraduate psychology majors; institutionalized children and their parents, and hospital staff) were requested to rate various interventions (e.g., time out, reinforcement of incompatible behavior, positive practice, and drug therapy) for a certain child problem. Kazdin and his associates have found that treatments can be distinguished in terms of acceptability (i.e., positive treatments are rated more acceptable) and that the severity of the problem influenced acceptability in that all treatments were rated as more acceptable with the more severe problems. The work of Kazdin and his associates has included a number of analogue dimensions that may limit generalizability to school/educational settings.

Witt, Elliott, and their associates (Elliott, Witt, Galvin, & Peterson, 1984; Martens, Witt, Elliott, & Darveaux, 1985; Witt & Martens, 1983; Witt, Elliott, & Martens, 1984; Witt, Martens, & Elliott, 1984) have focused their work on educational settings. Research in this area has suggested that positive interventions are usually regarded as more acceptable than negative interventions and that teacher's decisions to use an intervention are influenced by such factors as time involved, implementation skills, and resources required for treatments.

Acceptability of behavioral treatments is a high priority for future research especially with regard to applications in educational settings. Based on existing research in the field it appears that acceptability is a complex construct. However, even though current research has elaborated on the various dimensions of acceptability, information is needed about the various factors that influence acceptability of treatments as they are usually presented in educational settings. Basically, this means that researchers will need to move from more analogue to more clinical research in this area in order to understand more accurately the nature of acceptability (Kratochwill & Van Someren, 1985).

Summary and Conclusion

A perusal of the teacher training literature available at this time suggests several things. First, the teacher-training literature reveals that teachers have been trained successfully in a wide variety of behavior management skills as well as in the principles of behavior on which those techniques have been based. Training methods found to be particularly effective include modeling, role playing, and feedback as well as didactic instructional techniques, such as written material, lectures, and discussion when used in combination with one or more of the procedures listed above.

Second, it has been noted that the success of behavioral procedures in the classroom may depend heavily on teacher attitudes toward and acceptability of behavior modification concepts and techniques. Teacher acceptability is an issue receiving more empirical attention and one worthy of future investigation.

Finally, concerns must be raised over the *process* of dissemination of behavioral procedures. The applications of behavior therapy and consultation in educational settings have been extensive, major contributions, including the development of a large number of techniques with solid empirical support. As noted by Kazdin (1981b), a major limitation in the successful application of behavior modification to the education of children pertains to the effective dissemination and extension of existing procedures and techniques to the large number of settings that could profit from their use. As discussed in this chapter, inservice teacher training is an excellent way in which to accomplish this goal. Some caution must be noted with the adoption of this type of approach, however.

The question has been raised as to whether or not enough information can be disseminated in short-term teacher inservice workshops to allow these participants to apply properly the principles taught. The possibility of serious misapplication of procedures by teacher trainees whose only exposure to behavioral methods has been at this type of training session is viewed by Stein (1975) as a potentially serious ethical issue. Although the behavioral approach to the solution of human behavior problems has been advanced as possibly the most ethical means of accomplishing a client change, this argument can be based only on the premise that applications of empirically validated principles will be precise and systematic, fully explicated to behavior change agents, and careful monitoring on process and outcome. It cannot be assumed that a brief introduction of behavioral principles and procedures to educational personnel will in any way accomplish these basic ethical requirements without carefully structured approaches aimed at increasing the probability of the appropriate application of behavioral methods (Stein, 1975).

One possible approach to the solution of this problem is that of making available to all behavior modification students the opportunity for ongoing consultative follow-up for the development and implementation of any behavior program attempted by these individuals (Sattler, 1982; Stein, 1975). Inservice training, essentially, should be viewed not as an end, but simply as a means for facilitating the more effective utilization of behavior modification in the schools (Conoley & Conoley, 1982a).

ACKNOWLEDGMENTS

The authors wish to express their appreciation to Ms. Karen Kraemer for word processing the manuscript.

References

Allen, C. T., & Forman, S. G. (1984). Efficacy of methods of training teachers in behavior modification. *School Psychology Review, 13*, 26–32.

Anderson, R., Fredericks, H. D. B., Baldwin, V. L., Dalke, B., & McDonnell, J. J. (1978). A data-based inservice teacher training model for public school systems. *Education and Training of the Mentally Retarded, 13*, 224–228.

Anderson, T. K., Kratochwill, T. R., & Bergan, J. R. (1986). Training teachers in behavioral consultation and therapy: An analysis of verbal behaviors. *Journal of School Psychology, 24*, 229–241.

Andrews, J. K. (1970). The results of a pilot program to train teachers in the classroom application of behavior modification techniques. *Journal of School Psychology, 8*, 37–42.

Armer, B., & Thomas, B. (1978). Attitudes toward interdisciplinary collaboration in pupil personnel services. *Journal of School Psychology, 16*, 167–176.

Bandura, A. (1977). *Social learning theory*. Englewood Cliffs, NJ: Prentice-Hall.

Bardon, J. I., & Bennett, V. D. (1974). *School psychology*. Englewood Cliffs, NJ: Prentice-Hall.

Baron, R. A., & Byrne, D. (1977). *Social psychology*. Boston, MA: Allyn & Bacon.

Bergan, J. R. (1977). *Behavioral consultation*. Columbus, Ohio: Charles E. Merrill.

Bernal, M. E., & North, J. A. (1978). A survey of parent training manuals. *Journal of Applied Behavior Analysis, 11*, 533–544.

Bernstein, G. S. (1982). Training behavior change agents: A conceptual review. *Behavior Therapy, 13*, 1–23.

Bois, K. G. (1972). Role playing as a behavior change technique: Review of the empirical literature. *Psychotherapy: Theory, Research and Practice, 9*, 185–192.

Bowles, P. E., & Nelson, R. O. (1976). Training teachers as mediators: Efficacy of a workshop versus the bug-in-the-ear techniques. *Journal of School Psychology, 14*, 15–26.

Brown, J. H., Frankel, A., Birkimer, J. C., & Gamboa, A. N. (1966). The effects of a classroom management workshop on the reduction of children's problematic behavior. *Corrective and Social Psychiatry and Journal of Behavior Technology, Methods and Therapy, 22*, 39–41.

Budd, K. S., Green, D. R., & Baer, D. M. (1976). An analysis of multiple misplaced parental social contingencies. *Journal of Applied Behavior Analysis, 9*, 459–470.

Burka, A. A., & Jones, F. H. (1979). Procedures for increasing appropriate verbal participation in special elementary classrooms. *Journal of Applied Behavior Analysis, 3*, 27–48.

Canter, L., & Paulson, T. (1974). A college credit model of in-school consultation: A functional behavioral training program. *Community Mental Health Journal, 10*, 268–275.

Carnine, D. W., & Fink, W. J. (1978). Increasing the rate of presentation and use of signals in elementary classroom teachers. *Journals of Applied Behavior Analysis, 11*, 35–46.

Clarizio, H. F. (1979). School psychologists and the mental health needs of students. In G. D. Phye & D. J. Reschly (Eds.), *School psychology: Perspectives and issues* (pp. 309–341). New York: Academic Press.

Clark, H. B., Macrae, J. W., Ida, D. M., & Smith, N. R. (1975). The role of instructions, modeling, verbal feedback and contingencies in the training of classroom teaching skills. In E. Ramp & G. Semb (Eds.), *Behavior analysis: Areas of Research and application*. Englewood Cliffs, NJ: Prentice-Hall, Inc.

Cossairt, A., Hall, R. V., & Hopkins, B. L. (1973). The effects of experimenter's instructions, feedback and praise on teacher praise and student attending behavior. *Journal of Applied Behavior Analysis, 6*, 89–100.

Conoley, J. C., & Conoley, C. W. (1982a). *School consultation: A guide to practice and training*. New York: Pergamon Press.

Conoley, J. C., & Conoley, C. W. (1982b). The effects of two conditions of client-centered consultation on student–teacher problem descriptions and remedial plans. *Journal of School Psychology, 20*, 323–328.

Cooper, M. L., Thompson, C. L., & Baer, D. M. (1970). The experimental modification of teacher attending behavior. *Journal of Applied Behavior Analysis, 3*, 153–157.

Doleys, D. M., Doster, J., & Cartelli, L. M. (1976). Parent training techniques: Effects of lecture-role playing followed by feedback and self-recording. *Journal of Behavior Therapy and Experimental Psychiatry, 7*, 359–362.

Elliott, S. N., Witt, J. C., Galvin, G. A., & Peterson, R. (1984). Acceptability of positive and reductive behavioral interventions: Factors that influence teacher decisions. *Journal of School Psychology, 22*, 353–360.

Farnham-Diggory, S. (1981). But how do we shape up rigorous behavioral analysts? *Developmental Review, 1*, 58–60.

Fawcett, S. B., Mathews, R. M., & Fletcher, R. K. (1980). Some promising dimensions for behavioral community technology. *Journal of Applied Behavior Analysis, 13*, 505–518.

Flanagan, S., Adams, H. E., & Forehand, R. (1979). A comparison of four instructional techniques for teaching parents to use time-out. *Behavior Therapy, 10*, 94–102.

Forehand, R. L., & McMahon, R. J. (1981). *Helping the noncompliant child: A clinician's guide to parent training*. New York: Guilford Press.

Good, T., & Brophy, J. (1972). Behavioral expression of teacher attitudes. *Journal of Educational Psychology, 63*, 617–624.

Greenwood, C. R., Hops, H., Delquadri, J., & Guild, J. (1974). Group contingencies for group consequences in classroom management: A further analysis. *Journal of Applied Behavior Analysis, 7*, 413–425.

Greenwood, C. R., Hops, H., Walker, H. M., Guild, J. J., Stokes, J., & Young, K. R. (1979). Standardized classroom management program: Social validation and replication studies in Utah and Oregon. *Journal of Applied Behavior Analysis, 12*, 235–253.

Grieger, R. M. (1972). Teacher attitudes as a variable in behavior modification consultation. *Journal of School Psychology, 10*, 279–287.

Griffin, M. W. (1979). Training parents of retarded children as behavior therapists. *Australian Journal of Mental Retardation, 5*, 18–27.

Gutkin, T. B., & Curtis, M. J. (1982). School-based consultation: Theory and techniques. In C. R. Reynolds & T. B. Gutkin (Eds.), *The handbook of school psychology* (pp. 796–828). New York: Wiley.

Hall, R. V. (1971). Training teachers in classroom use of contingency management. *Educational Technology, 11*, 33–38.

Hall, R. V., Panyan, M., Rabon, D., & Broden, M. (1968). Instructing beginning teachers in reinforcement procedures which improve classroom control. *Journal of Applied Behavior Analysis, 1*, 315–322.

Hall, R. V., Fox, R., Willard, D., Goldsmith, L., Emerson, M., Owen, M., Davis, F., & Porcia, E. (1971). The teacher as observer and experimenter in the modification of disrupting and talking-out behaviors. *Journal of Applied Behavior Analysis, 4*, 141–149.

Hannah, M. E., & Pliner, S. (1983). Teacher attitudes toward handicapped children: A review and synthesis. *School Psychology Review, 12*, 12–25.

Hay, L. R., Nelson, R. O., & Hay, W. M. (1977). The use of teachers as behavioral observers. *Journal of Applied Behavior Analysis, 10*, 345–348.

Henry, S. A. (1981). Current dimensions of parent training. *School Psychology Review, 10*, 4–14.

Hersen, M., & Barlow, D. H. (1976). *Single case experimental designs: Strategies for studying behavior change*. New York: Pergamon Press.

Horne, M. (1979). Attitudes and mainstreaming. A literature review for school psychologists. *Psychology in the Schools, 16*, 61–67.

Horton, G. O. (1975). Generalization of teacher behavior as a function of subject matter specific discrimination training. *Journal of Applied Behavior Analysis, 8*, 311–319.

Hudson, A. M. (1982). Training parents of developmentally handicapped children: A component analysis. *Behavior Therapy, 13*, 325–333.

Hundert, J. (1982). Training teachers in generalized writing of behavior modification programs for multihandicapped deaf children. *Journal of Applied Behavior Analysis, 15*, 111–122.

Johnson, J. L., & Sloat, K. C. (1980). Teacher training effects: Real or illusory? *Psychology in the Schools, 77*, 109–115.

Jones, F. H., & Eimers, R. C. (1975). Role playing to train elementary teachers to use a classroom management "skill package." *Journal of Applied Behavior Analysis, 8*, 421–433.

Jones, F. H., & Miller, W. H. (1977). The effective use of negative attention for reducing group disruption in special elementary school classrooms. In K. D. O'Leary & S. C. O'Leary, (Eds.), *Classroom management: The successful use of behavior modification*. New York: Pergamon Press.

Kazdin, A. E. (1974). The assessment of teacher training in a reinforcement program. *The Journal of Teacher Education, 25*, 266–270.

Kazdin, A. E. (1977). Assessing the clinical or applied significance of behavior change through social validation. *Behavior Modification, 1*, 427–452.

Kazdin, A. E. (1980a). Acceptability of alternative treatments for deviant child behavior. *Journal of Applied Behavior Analysis, 13*, 259–273.

Kazdin, A. E. (1980b). Acceptability of time-out from reinforcement procedures for disruptive child behavior. *Behavior Therapy, 11*, 329–344.

Kazdin, A. E. (1980c). *Behavior modification in applied settings.* Homewood, IL: The Dorsey Press.

Kazdin, A. E. (1981a). Acceptability of child treatment techniques: The influence of treatment efficacy and adverse side effects. *Behavior Therapy, 12,* 493–506.

Kazdin, A. E. (1981b). Behavior modification in education: Contributions and limitations. *Developmental Review, 1,* 34–57.

Kazdin, A. E. (1981c). Uses and abuses of behavior modification in education: A rejoinder. *Developmental Review, 1,* 61–62.

Kazdin, A. E. (1982). Applying behavioral principles in the schools. In C. R. Reynolds & T. B. Gutkin, (Eds.). *The handbook of school psychology* (pp. 501–529). New York: Wiley.

Kazdin, A. E., & Cole, P. M. (1981). Attitudes and labeling biases toward behavior modification: The effects of labels content, and jargon. *Behavior Therapy, 12,* 56–68.

Kazdin, A. E., French, N. H., & Sherick, R. B. (1981). Acceptability of alternative treatments for children: Evaluations by inpatient children, parents, and staff. *Journal of Consulting and Clinical Psychology, 49,* 900–907.

Knoff, H. M. (1984). A conceptual review of discipline in the schools: A consultation service model. *Journal of School Psychology, 22,* 335–345.

Koegel, R. L., Russo, D. D., & Rincover, A. (1977). Assessing and training teachers in the use of behavior modification with autistic children. *Journal of Applied Behavior Analysis, 10,* 197–205.

Kosier, K. P., & Severson, R. A. (1971, February). *Effects of teacher inservice and consultation on pupil task-oriented behavior.* Paper presented at the meeting of the American Education Research Association, New York.

Kratochwill, T. R., & Van Someren, K. R. (1985). Barriers to treatment success in behavioral consultation: Current limitations and future directions. *Journal of School Psychology, 23,* 225–239.

Lolli, A., Jr. (1980). Implementing the role of the school psychologist. *Psychology in the Schools, 17,* 70–75.

Madsen, C. H., Madsen, C. K., Saudargas, R. A., Hammond, W. R., Smith, J. B., & Edgar, D. E. (1970). Classroom RAID (Rules Approval, Ignore, Disapproval): A cooperative approach for professionals and volunteers. *Journal of School Psychology, 8,* 180–185.

Martens, B. K., Witt, J. C., Elliott, S. N., & Darveaux, D. X. (1985). Teacher judgments concerning the acceptability of school-based interventions. *Professional Psychology, 16,* 191–198.

Martin, F. (1975). Increasing teachers' positive actions in the classroom. *Psychological Reports, 37,* 335–338.

McKeown, D., Jr., Adams, H. E., & Forehand, R. (1975). Generalization to the classroom of principles of behavior modification taught to teachers. *Behavior Research and Therapy, 13,* 85–92.

McLoughlin, C. S. (1982). Procedures and problems in behavioral training for parents. *Perceptual and Motor Skills, 55,* 827–838.

McMahon, R. J., & Forehand, R. (1980). Self-help behavior therapies in parent training. In B. B. Lahey & A. E. Kazdin (Eds.) *Advances in clinical child psychology* (Vol. 2, pp. 149–176). New York: Plenum Press.

Musgrove, W. J. (1974). A scale to measure attitudes toward behavior modification. *Psychology in the Schools, 11,* 392–396.

Nagle, R. J., & Gresham, F.M. (1979). A modeling-based approach to teacher consultation: A case study. *Psychology in the Schools, 16,* 527–532.

Nay, R. W. (1975). A systematic comparison of instructional techniques for parents. *Behavior Therapy, 6,* 14–21.

O'Dell, S. (1974). Training parents in behavior modification: A review. *Psychological Bulletin, 8,* 418–433.

O'Dell, S. L., Mahoney, N. D., Horton, W. G., & Turner, P. E. (1979). Media-assisted parent training: Alternative models. *Behavior Therapy, 10,* 103–110.

O'Dell, S. L., Tarler-Beneolo, L., & Flynn, J. M. (1979). An instrument to measure knowledge of behavioral principles as applied to children. *Journal of Behavioral Therapy and Experimental Psychology, 10,* 29–34.

O'Dell, S. L., Krug, W. W., Patterson, J. N., & Faustman, W. O. (1980). An assessment of methods for training parents in the use of time-out. *Journal of Behavior Therapy and Experimental Psychiatry, 11,* 21–25.

O'Dell, S. L., O'Quin, J. A., Alford, B. A., O'Briant, A. L., Bradlyn, A. S., & Giebenhain, J. E. (1982). Predicting the acquisition of parenting skills via four training methods. *Behavior Therapy, 13,* 194–208.

O'Leary, K. D., & O'Leary, S. G. (1977). *Classroom management: The successful use of behavior modification.* New York: Pergamon Press.

O'Leary, D. K., & Schneider, M. K. (Producers). (1983). *Catch 'em being good* [Film]. Champaign,IL: Research Press.

Parsonson, B. S., Baer, A. M., & Baer, D. M. (1974). The application of generalized correct social contingencies: An evaluation of a training program. *Journal of Applied Behavior Analysis, 7,* 427–437.

Patterson, G. R. (1971). Behavioral intervention procedures in the classroom and in the home. In A. E. Bergin & L. Garfield (Eds.) *Handbook of psychotherapy and behavior change* (pp. 751–775). New York: Wiley.

Peterson, L., Homer, A. L., & Wonderlich, S. A. (1982). The integrity of independent variables in behavior analysis. *Journal of Applied Behavior Analysis, 15,* 477–492.

Reynolds, M. C. (1982). The rights of children: A challenge to school psychologists. In T. R. Kratochwill (Ed.), *Advances in school psychology* (Vol. 2, pp. 97–118). Hillsdale, NJ: Erlbaum.

Ringer, V. M. J. (1973). The use of a "token helper" in the management of classroom behavior problems and in teacher training. *Journal of Applied Behavior Analysis, 6,* 671–677.

Robinson, V., & Swanton, C. (1980). The generalization of behavioral teacher training. *Review of Educational Research, 50,* 486–498.

Rollins, H. A., McCandless, W. R., Thompson, M., &

Brassel, W. R. (1974). Project success environment: An extended application of contingency management in inner-city schools. *Journal of Educational Psychology, 66,* 167–178.

Rosenthal, T. L., & Zimmerman, B. J. (1978). *Social learning and cognition.* San Francisco: Academic Press.

Ross, A. O. (1981). *Child Behavior Therapy: Principles, procedures and empirical basis.* New York: Wiley.

Rutherford, R. B.(1973). The effects of a model videotape and feedback videotapes on the teaching styles of teachers in training. *Journal of Experimental Education, 42,* 64–69.

Ryan, B. (1976). Teacher attitudes toward behavior modification one year after an in-service training program. *Behavior Therapy, 7,* 264–266.

Sanders, M. R., & James, J. E. (1983). The modification of parent behavior: A review of generalization and maintenance. *Behavior Modification, 7,* 3–27.

Sandoval, J., Lambert, N. M., & Davis, J. M. (1977). Consultation from the consultee's perspective. *Journal of School Psychology, 15,* 334–342.

Sattler, J. M. (1982). *Assessment of children's intelligence and special abilities* (2nd ed.). Boston, MA: Allyn & Bacon, Inc.

Sloat, J. C. M., Tharp, R. G., & Gallimore, R. (1977). The incremental effectiveness of classroom based teacher training techniques. *Behavior Therapy, 8,* 810–811.

Spiedel, G. E., & Tharp, R. G. (1978). Teacher-training workshop strategy: Instructions, discrimination training, modeling, guided practice, and video feedback. *Behavior Therapy, 9,* 735–739.

Stein, T. J. (1975). Some ethical considerations of short-term workshops in the principles and methods of behavior modification. *Journal of Applied Behavior Analysis, 8,* 113–115.

Stokes, T. F., & Baer, D. M. (1977). An implicit technology of generalization. *Journal of Applied Behavior Analysis, 10,* 349–367.

Stolz, S. B. (1981). Adoption of innovations from applied behavioral research: "Does anybody care?" *Journal of Applied Behavior Analysis, 14,* 491–505.

Sulzer-Azaroff, B. (1981). Issues and trends in behavior modification in the classroom. In S. W. Bijou & R. Ruiz (Eds.), *Behavior modification: Contributions to education* (pp. 63–93). Hillsdale, NJ: Erlbaum.

Thompson, C. L., Holmberg, M. C., & Baer, D. M. (1978). An experimental analysis of some procedures to teach priming and reinforcement skills to preschool teachers. *Monographs of the Society for Research in Child Development, 43*(4).

Tyler, V. O. (1981). Aggressive consultation in the schools with miniconsultants, college credits—And a show of power. *Psychology in the Schools, 18,* 341–348.

Vane, J. R. (1972). A school behavior modification program: Teacher attitudes a year later. *Behavior Therapy, 3,* 41–44.

Van Houghton, R., & Sullivan, K. (1975). Effects of an audio cuing system on the rate of teacher praise. *Journal of Applied Behavior Analysis, 8,* 197–201.

Walker, H. M., & Buckley, N. K. (1972). Programming generalization and maintenance of treatment effects across time and across settings. *Journal of Applied Behavior Analysis, 5,* 209–224.

Ward, M. H., & Baker, B. L. (1968). Reinforcement therapy in the classroom. *Journal of Applied Behavior Analysis, 1,* 323–328.

Webster-Stratton, C. (1981). Modification of mothers' behaviors and attitudes through a videotape modeling group discussion program. *Behavior Therapy, 12,* 634–642.

White, G. W., & Pryzwansky, W. B. (1982). Consultation outcome as a result of in-service resource teacher training. *Psychology in the Schools, 19,* 495–501.

Witt, J. C., & Elliott, S. N. (1985). Acceptability of classroom intervention strategies. In T. R. Kratochwill (Ed.), *Advances in school psychology* (Vol. 4, pp. 251–287). Hillsdale, NJ: Erlbaum.

Witt, J. C., & Martens, B. K. (1983). Assessing the acceptability of behavioral interventions. *Psychology in the Schools, 20,* 510–517.

Witt, J. C., Elliott, S. N., & Martens, B. K. (1984). Acceptability of behavioral interventions used in classrooms: The influence of amount of teacher time, severity of behavior problem, and type of intervention. *Behavioral Disorders, 10,* 95–104.

Witt, J. C., Martens, B. K., & Elliott, S. N. (1984). Factors affecting teachers' judgments of the acceptability of behavioral interventions: Time involvement, behavior problem severity, and type of intervention. *Behavior Therapy, 15,* 204–209.

Wolf, M. (1978). Social validity: The case for subjective measurement or how applied behavior analysis is finding its heart. *Journal of Applied Behavior Analysis, 11,* 203–214.

Woolfolk, R. L., & Woolfolk, A. E. (1979). Modifying the effect of the behavior modification label. *Behavior Therapy, 10,* 575–578.

Woolfolk, A. E., Woolfolk R. L., & Wilson, G. T. (1977). A rose by any other name . . . Labeling bias and attitudes toward behavior modification. *Journal of Consulting and Clinical Psychology, 45,* 184–191.

Yeaton, W. H., & Sechrest, L. (1981). Critical dimensions in the choice and maintenance of successful treatment: Strength, integrity, and effectiveness. *Journal of Consulting and Clinical Psychology, 49,* 156–167.

Zimmerman, J., & Zimmerman, E. (1971). Doing your own thing with precision: The essence of behavior management in the classroom. *Educational Technology, 11,* 26–32.

CHAPTER 10

Behavioral Consultation

Macroconsultation for Instructional Management

John R. Bergan, Jason K. Feld, and Joyce C. Swarner

Introduction

Gerald Caplan (1970) formally introduced consultation into psychological services to cope with the problem of serving a large number of children with a small staff. Caplan's work in Israel following World War II centered on the provision of psychological services to children who had spent their early lives in European concentration camps. In the late 1940s, large numbers of these children came to Israel bearing the deep and lasting psychological scars of war. Caplan simply did not have the staff necessary to provide direct services to these children. Out of necessity, he hit upon the idea of offering consultation to the adults providing care for the newly arrived children of Europe. By this means he was able to meet the pressing demands for psychological care that were the legacy of the preceding dark years of conflict.

The efficiency of consultation as a service delivery technique derives from the tripartite structure of consultation interactions. The consultant, who possesses a higher level of knowledge and skill, works with one or more consultees. The consultees in turn provide services directly to clients. A consultant may work with many consultees and each consultee may work with many clients. There is thus a multiplier effect that enables more clients to benefit from a consultant's expertise than is the case when services are rendered directly from a consultant to a client. This multiplier effect is one of the principal service delivery advantages offered by consultation.

Although one of the major benefits of consultation is its efficiency, the multiplier effect inherent in consultation is generally not fully exploited in educational settings. Consultation in the schools is typically rendered on an individual case basis to a teacher or parent consultee for the purpose of dealing with the problems of one or a small number of children (see, for example, Bergan, 1977). Moreover, consultation has generally focused on a relatively narrow range of student and teacher

John R. Bergan, Jason K. Feld, and Joyce C. Swarner • Department of Educational Psychology, University of Arizona, Tucson, Arizona 85721.

needs and has been practiced as a remedial intervention to solve adjustment problems and remediate social and emotional difficulties (Gallessich & Davis, 1981; Reschly, 1976). Even in those instances in which cognitive skills are involved, the focus is generally on remediation. The emphasis on problem remediation is congruent with the rendering of service on an individual-case basis. Consequently, although immensely valuable in resolving individual child problems, consultation practices have not fully been incorporated into the organizational routines of schools or widely utilized by teachers and other educational staff to facilitate the teaching/learning process.

A fuller use of consultation technology would be to adapt the procedures to encompass a broader range of instructional management processes and consequently to extend services to all students and teachers. This type of expansion could markedly broaden the impact of consultation services. The potential multiplier effect inherent in consultation would then make it possible to render services to large numbers of consultees and children. The term *macroconsultation* seems appropriate to describe this expanded conceptualization of the consultation process.

Macroconsultation can help in planning learning activities, in identifying curriculum needs, and in promoting learning. All these functions can occur in addition to the traditional use of consultation for remediation.

This chapter introduces a technology for macroconsultation that facilitates the management of instruction for large numbers of children and for children in remote locations. Macroconsultation, as is shown in this chapter, is not merely a straightforward extension of individual-case consultation. The nature of goals, the strategies for achieving goals, and the communication techniques used in macroconsultation are markedly different from those of individual-case consultation.

The macroconsultation technology discussed in this chapter is being developed at the Center for Educational Evaluation and Measurement in the College of Education at the University of Arizona for use with the Head Start organization. This Head Start application will be used extensively to illustrate macroconsultation principles. However, the general approach illustrated here can be applied in other settings.

Macroconsultation in Head Start

Macroconsultation is being provided by the Center for Educational Evaluation and Measurement to Head Start programs as part of a planning and assessment system aimed at promoting the development of Head Start children. The heart of the system is the *Head Start Measures Battery* (HSMB), which comprises six scales assessing cognitive and social development (Bergan & Smith, 1985). The HSMB provides information on children's development that can be used to plan learning experiences to promote growth. In addition, the HSMB scales offer information on the amount of development that has occurred during the Head Start program year. This information is used by teachers to evaluate growth.

Consultants in the Program Services Division of the Center consult with Educational Coordinators, who manage the Head Start educational programs in local Head Start programs throughout the nation. They work directly with teachers to provide learning experiences for children to facilitate growth. Thus, in this case macroconsultation has a double multiplier effect. Each consultant in the Center works with several classroom teachers, who, in turn, work directly with children in Head Start classrooms.

Macroconsultation is used to guide an educational assessment and planning cycle. This cycle is an ongoing decision-making process that occurs throughout the Head Start program year. Macroconsultation occurs in four phases and can be implemented one or several times during the program year (see Figure 1).

Each phase of macroconsultation is briefly described here to exemplify the decision-mak-

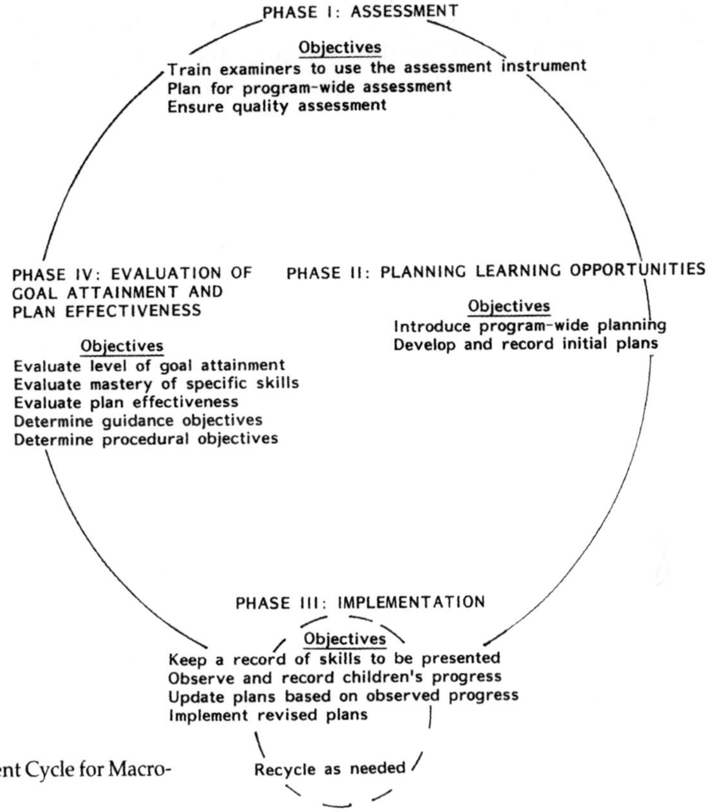

Figure 1. The Instructional Management Cycle for Macroconsultation.

ing steps required in instructional management. An example from Head Start demonstrates the implementation of the macroconsultation process.

The first phase of macroconsultation focuses on assessment. The aim is to guide assessment with the HSMB to identify children's learning needs. The second phase occurs when programs receive assessment results following administration of the HSMB. The focus at this time is on using the results to plan learning experiences appropriate to children's developmental levels. The third phase occurs midway in the program year. At this time plans are revised based on the children's observed progress. The fourth phase of consultation is an evaluation phase occurring at the end of the year. Consultants work with coordinators to interpret the assessment results which show what growth children have made during the course of the year. The aim at this time is to determine the extent to which educational goals have been met, and to evaluate the effectiveness of the plans designed to achieve those goals.

The phases of macroconsultation for instructional management described here follow a similar pattern to those used in the problem-solving process for individual case consultation widely used in school settings (see, for example, Bergan, 1977). There are, however, several features of macroconsultation that distinguish it from the traditional problem-solving approach. Describing macroconsultation in Head Start programs will highlight these differences.

Distinctive Features of Macroconsultation

Macroconsultation for instructional management differs from individual case consultation in several significant aspects. The first difference is in the nature of the assessment technology. The second involves the medium of communication. The third involves the goals and objectives, and the fourth, the communication techniques used.

Assessment Technology for Head Start Macroconsultation

Effective macroconsultation for instructional management requires the support of developmentally based assessment technology. Assessment provides the information needed to formulate goals and objectives and thus, guides the course of macroconsultation. In addition, assessment plays an important role in maximizing the efficiency of communication. Macroconsultation services for Head Start rely on assessment information provided by the HSMB.

Functions of Assessment

Assessment serves two important functions in macroconsultation for Head Start. First, it is a tool for planning learning experiences for children. The importance of assessment in instructional planning has been long recognized (see, for example, Gagne & Briggs, 1974; Glaser & Nitko, 1971). Assessment provides a benchmark for determining children's current level of functioning. The teacher who knows a child's current developmental level can plan learning experiences that are appropriate for that child (Bergan, Stone, & Feld, 1985). The HSMB is administered in the fall to obtain information used in planning for Head Start children.

The second function of assessment is the evaluation of children's progress. Assessment following instruction indicates whether or not the goals of instruction have been achieved. In addition, assessment may offer information regarding the effectiveness of plans implemented to attain instructional goals. Information on goal attainment and plan effectiveness is essential in determining the course that consultation should take (Bergan, 1977). For example, failure to achieve the goals of consultation suggests that either the goals should be revised and/or the plans made to achieve goals should be modified. Spring administration of the HSMB provides information to evaluate these questions.

Path-Referenced Assessment in Macroconsultation

Macroconsultation services being offered in the Head Start program make use of path-referenced assessment technology (Bergan, 1987; Bergan, Stone, & Feld, 1985). This technology was incorporated into the development of the HSMB (Bergan & Smith, 1985). Path-referenced assessment links performance to position in an empirically validated developmental sequence or path.

Path-referenced assessment technology is based on a model of development derived from latent trait theory (Bock & Aitkin, 1981; Lord, 1980). The general latent trait model holds that the probability of performing a test correctly is a function of examinee ability and characteristics of the item. An item characteristic of particular importance for path-referenced assessment is item difficulty. Developmental sequences of tasks can be determined using latent trait estimates of item difficulty. Hypotheses regarding task sequences can be tested using difficulty estimates (Bergan & Stone, 1985).

Latent trait technology places item difficulty and person ability on the same scale. This makes it possible to relate individual ability (developmental level) to a specific position in a developmental sequence of tasks. A child's latent ability or developmental level score can be used to estimate the probability that the child will be able to perform each of the various tasks in the progression.

Path-referenced assessment has a number of advantages related to its use in macroconsultation. First, because the path-referenced approach indicates position along a developmental path, it facilitates educational planning. The teacher who knows a child's developmental level knows the skills that have been mastered in the past and the challenges that lie ahead in order for progress to occur. Thus it is possible to plan learning experiences that the child can profit from, and that, on the other hand, are not so easy that nothing new is learned.

A second advantage of the path-referenced approach is that it links ability to the probability of correctly performing specific tasks in a developmental sequence. For a century norm-referenced assessment technology has linked ability to position in a norm group, thus obscuring the relationship between ability and the performance of specific skills taught in educational environments. Criterion-referenced assessment (e.g., Glaser, 1963; Nitko, 1980) offered assessment information on the performance of specific tasks, but it totally ignored the construct of ability. Clearly, the ability construct is important to teachers because they have continued to use it to evaluate children's progress. Not surprisingly, there has never been a clear relationship between what is measured on ability tests and what is taught in educational settings. Path-referenced assessment offers a way to relate ability to the performance of specific tasks.

There is good reason to establish the relationship between ability and tasks mastered. A question of critical concern in education is the influence of teaching on the acquisition of broad systems of knowledge rather than on specific isolated skills. The ability construct provides a tool for conceptualizing how individual skills are related to each other within knowledge systems. When one teaches a set of developmentally related tasks, one is teaching ability rather than influencing the performance of isolated, unrelated competencies.

The relationship between developmental level and task performance is shown in Figure 2. The figure illustrates an Individual Developmental Profile from the Math scale of the HSMB. A list of the skills assessed appears at the left side of the profile. Skills are ordered by difficulty within categories such as Counting and Ordering and Addition. A column of Mastery Level Codes is just to the right of the skill list. At the right side of the profile the child's developmental level (DL) is indicated by a vertical line of letters (F's for fall, S's for spring). Each skill description is followed by a shaded bar. The variations in shading are used to designate mastery level and to show its relationship to developmental level. If the child's DL line crosses the darkest shaded part of the bar for a skill, the child is at the Mastery Level (+) for that skill. If the child's DL line crosses the medium shaded part of the bar, the child is at one of the Partial Mastery Levels (× or /). When the DL line crosses the lightest shaded part of the bar, the child is at the Nonmastery (−) Level.

Response probabilities are divided into mastery levels for ease of interpretation. The Nonmastery level includes probabilities from 0 to .24, Low Partial Mastery ranges from .25 to .49, High Partial Mastery from .50 to .74, and Mastery goes from .75 to 1. For example, the DL of 50 for the hypothetical child in the figure indicates Mastery of the first three skills in the Counting and Ordering category, Low Partial Mastery for the fourth skill, and Nonmastery for the last two skills.

An Individual Development Profile is provided after Fall HSMB assessment, for each child and for each scale administered. It is useful as a permanent record in the child's file and for providing information to parents. By using the spring profile, the teacher can determine the amount of progress the child has made and can compare the level of the teaching goals with the child's DL.

A Class Development Profile is also provided to the teacher and shows the class DL information for each scale administered (see Figure 3). It gives the same kind of information for the class as is on the profile for the individual child. In addition, it provides (a) a list of all the children's names and their individual DLs; (b) an average DL for the class for each scale; (c) a line of letters on the chart that gives a picture of the ability of the total class; and (d) the average Mastery Level Codes printed next to the skill descriptions.

Communication Technology for Head Start Macroconsultation

Macroconsultation generally involves communication with several educational programs, some of which may be located in

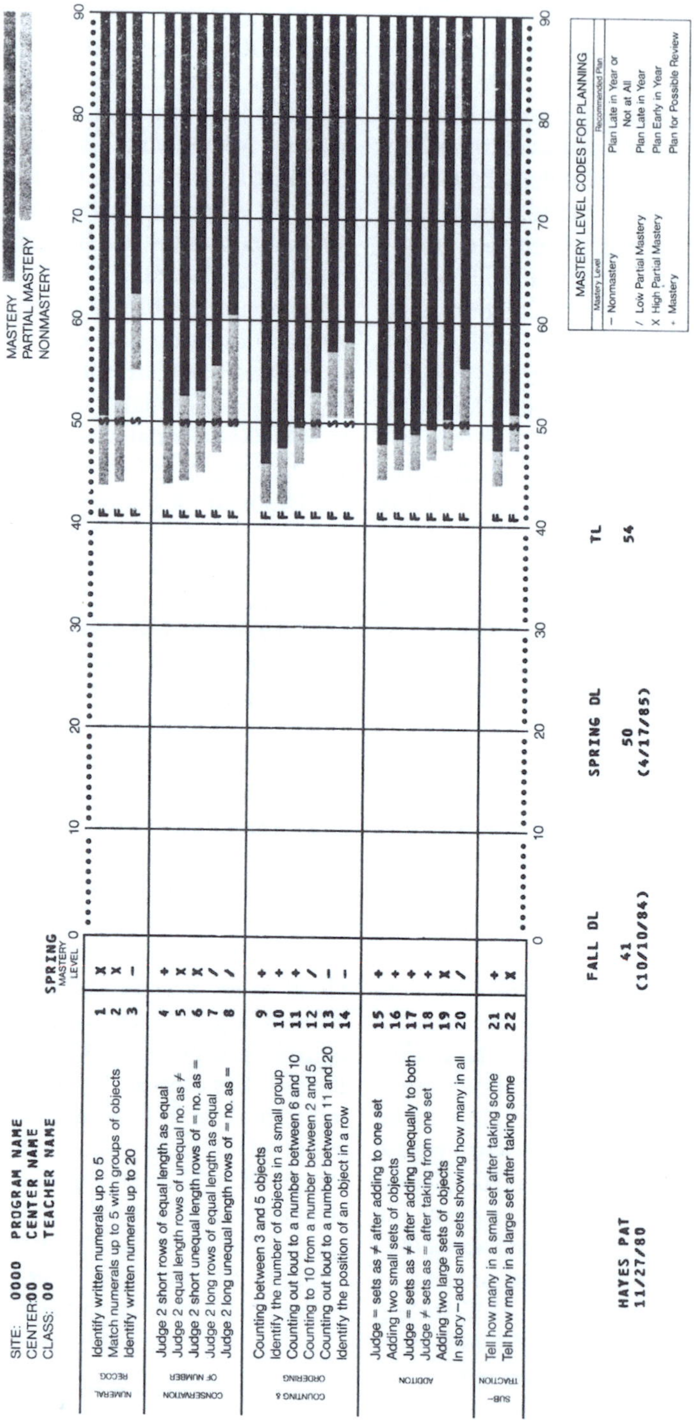

Figure 2. HSMB Individual Developmental Profile for Math.

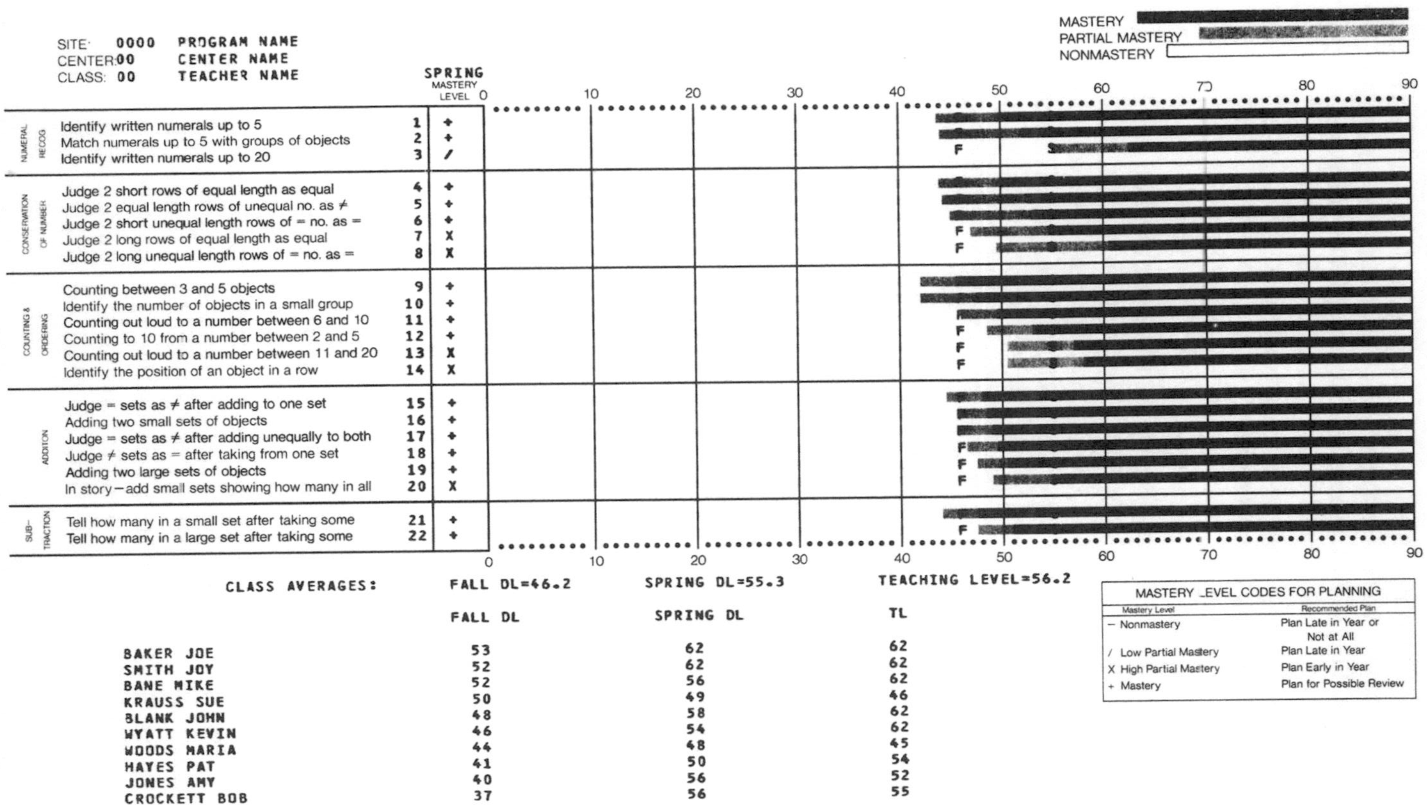

Figure 3. HSMB Development Profile Math scale.

remote areas. To facilitate communication, the Program Services Division at the Center conducts teleconferencing sessions with several programs at one time. The Center also maintains two toll-free telephone lines to answer questions and concerns that arise in Head Start programs between teleconferencing sessions.

Teleconferencing connects the consultant with consultees at different locations. Usually five consultees participate in an hour-long prescheduled teleconferencing session. Guided by scripts, consultants at the Center instruct consultees and answer questions on the administration of the HSMB and the use of assessment information for instructional management. Examples of these scripts are provided in the following section.

Participating programs benefit from teleconferencing in several ways. First, teleconferencing reduces or eliminates travel time. Second, it facilitates decision making and problem solving by enabling administrative issues to be handled expeditiously. Third, it allows policy issues to be simultaneously discussed and allows a cross-fertilization of ideas. Fourth, in remote areas it increases accessibility to outside experts who are otherwise inaccessible. Fifth, it provides an opportunity to use new technology and up-to-date consultation techniques.

Teleconferencing can also benefit the consultant in several ways. The consultant who uses teleconferencing increases effectiveness, reduces travel time, and has greater access to other experts. This can broaden the consultant's resources and contributes to his/her professional development. It allows consultation to take place on relatively short notice and may allow problems to be handled rapidly and at an early stage. It provides an opportunity to use a new technology and to become familiar with new service delivery techniques.

Macroconsultation Goals and Objectives

The goals and objectives of macroconsultation have three distinctive characteristics. First, there invariably will be a set of long-range goals to be achieved through consultation. Second, the goals and objectives will likely be developmental ones, and third, they will usually apply to large numbers of children.

Long-Range Goals

Macroconsultation for instructional management can be expected to focus on cognitive accomplishments and to do so over an extended time span. For example, the goals of an educational program typically involve enhancing children's learning during the course of a program or school year. The initial educational needs of children are identified at the beginning of the program year by one or more assessment instruments, and growth is measured by assessment during and at the end of the program year.

Because of the long-range character of macroconsultation goals it is reasonable to expect that they will be stated in rather general terms. These general goals will, of course, be made up of subordinate goals related to more specific and shorter-term objectives. An example of a general macroconsultation goal might be to promote the development of math skills of children. That broad goal can be divided into subordinate goals, such as the development of counting and ordering skills, addition skills, subtraction skills, conservation skills, and numeral recognition skills. These subordinate goals are related to specific objectives, such as counting objects, counting to 10 from a number greater than one, and identifying the ordinal position of an object in a sequence of objects. The development of math skills is pursued throughout the course of the program year. Specific objectives related to that goal are pursued at various times during the program year.

Developmental Nature of Goals and Objectives

A second significant feature of macroconsultation goals is that they emphasize the acquisition of new competencies, like math skills, rather than focusing on the remediation of deficits. The focus on new competencies implies a point of view about children that is radically different from the remedial point of view typically associated with individual-case consultation.

A child can be seen as functioning at a particular developmental level. The child moves to a higher developmental level through the attainment of competencies defined by objectives included in the goal. The chapter later details how developmental goals for large numbers of children can be identified through use of the HSMB assessment and planning system, and how these goals can be achieved by incorporating developmentally sequenced educational objectives into learning activities. As mentioned earlier, the HSMB provides information on children's development in six areas of cognitive and social development. The developmental sequences of skills measured by the HSMB are empirically validated. A child's score indicates his or her current position in the sequence (i.e., developmental level). As new skills are acquired, the child progresses in the sequence. The aim is to provide learning experiences that assist children in moving from their current developmental level to a more advanced level of development.

There is a subtle, but important implication that arises from basing macroconsultation goals on the acquisition of developmentally sequenced skills. In the absence of a developmental sequence, consultation has generally been terminated when goals have been attained (Bergan, 1977). For example, a teacher may decide in consultation that the children in her class should have certain minimal competencies. When these minimal competencies are attained, efforts may be considered to have been successful and the consultation would typically be terminated. On the other hand, when goals are based on a developmental sequence, essentially the entire sequence becomes a goal. A teacher may set goals for each child based on each child's position in that sequence (developmental level). As each child masters a skill in a sequence, the next skill in the sequence becomes an appropriate goal. In this way, goals are being continuously revised as the child becomes ready for more challenging activities. Consequently, macroconsultation is an ongoing decision-making process that occurs throughout an educational program year.

Relating goals to development sensitizes the consultant and the teacher to the needs of the individual child. The task of the consultee is to set goals that are neither too far above nor too far below the developmental level of the individual child. This can be accomplished only if goals for individual children are based on their level of development.

Goals for an Entire Program

The third significant feature of macroconsultation goals is that they generally involve most, if not all, of the children in an educational program. Macroconsultation affords the opportunity to apply psychological principles to the management of instruction for an entire educational program. Although consultation is now widely practiced in educational settings (see, for example, Ramage, 1979), the possibility of using it as a vehicle for applying psychological principles in an entire program has not been adequately recognized.

The focus in macroconsultation on large numbers of children has implications for the type of assessment techniques used to determine children's educational needs. First, effective macroconsultation requires assessment techniques that can be used in a cost-effective way with large numbers of children. In order for goals and objectives to be established for all children it is helpful to use an assessment device that yields information that can be used to set general educational goals for the program and one that also provides a common basis for program staff to communicate these goals with one another. The assessment device should also provide explicit information on the educational needs of each child within the program so that these needs can be considered when implementing educational plans in the classroom.

Because macroconsultation focuses on large numbers of children, the strategy should maximize the amount of assessment information obtained while minimizing the amount of staff time required to obtain such information. Assessing learning needs through the use of traditional interviewing techniques, as is generally done in consultation, could require an excessive amount of time. Using an assessment device like the HSMB reduces assessment time and at the same time yields useful information based on path-referenced developmental sequences. This facilitates formulating programwide consultation goals and objectives and also provides assessment information on individual needs.

Macroconsultation Communication Techniques

The fact that macroconsultation generally involves many consultees who in turn serve many children imposes certain constraints on the kinds of communication that can reasonably be expected to occur in this form of consultation. There is a great deal of information to communicate to a great many people and a limited amount of time to do so. Consequently, the techniques used must be able to convey large amounts of information in a short time. Five major techniques that are useful in promoting efficiency of communication are (a) communication control, (b) categorization, (c) implication, (d) summarization, and (e) validation.

Communication Control

The consultant's control of communication during macroconsultation allows him or her to guide the course of the process to meet consultee needs. Communication control may be achieved through the use of questions and imperative statements (Bergan, 1977). For example, a consultant may use the imperative, saying: "Plan to teach all the skills for which the children are high partial masters." He or she may also use the question format by saying: "Which skills will you include in the first lesson plan?" To achieve communication control the consultant must make extensive use of these kinds of utterances. Effective use of communication control is particularly important in macroconsultation because of the need to communicate efficiently. For example, as indicated earlier, consultation with Head Start programs occurs over long distance phone lines, and time is limited.

Communication in macroconsultation requires limiting the number of topics covered in an interview. This can be done by refining the questions that the consultant uses in guiding the course of the interview. One way to accomplish this is through the use of a script specifying the questions to be covered during an interview session. Scripts enhance communication efficiency in two ways: first, they ensure that essential topics are covered. Second, they minimize interview length by helping to avoid digressions. Although scripts need not be followed slavishly, they can provide the consultant with general guidelines for directing the course of the interview. Scripts are used extensively in macroconsultation for Head Start and some examples of them will be given later in the chapter.

Categorization

Information can be communicated at different levels of generality. For example, one might talk in broad terms about the development of social skills. On the other hand, one might discuss a more narrow topic, such as sharing toys with other children. In macroconsultation, there is an advantage to communicating in broader categories. The use of broad categories increases the amount of information communicated in a given utterance. For example, when one talks about promoting the development of math skills, many skills are included in the category. On the other hand, when one talks about enhancing counting skills, far fewer skills are included.

There is, however, a potential drawback to using broad categories in consultation communications. Ambiguity in communication may increase as category inclusiveness increases. For instance, there may be greater agreement on what is included in the category of counting skills for preschoolers than on what is included in math skills for them. The problem of ambiguity can be solved to a degree by using constructs that clearly link broad categories to specific skills. For example, in Head Start consultation the construct of developmental level (DL) is linked to specific skills on the various HSMB reporting forms that communicate children's performance. For instance, a DL score of 53 on the Math scale not only conveys the child's overall developmental level, it also determines the probability of the child's passing each of the various items on the scale. Thus, the DL score for the Math scale can be used to provide information on approximately 30 skills. Additionally, the mastery level codes provide information on all of the skills associated with a particular mastery class for a child. This information can be used to communicate planning information in a highly efficient fashion. For example, a consultant might suggest that a teacher plan learning experiences for all of the skills in the High Partial Mastery category for a given child or for a group of children.

Implication

Another way to increase communication efficiency is to gather information that conveys other information by implication. For example, if a consultant says to a consultee: "How many teachers have you trained to administer the HSMB?" he or she may be able to determine not only the number of people trained, but also that training was scheduled for a group and did occur.

Implication is a useful interview technique to gain information about an activity that involves a series of steps or preconditions. To employ implication effectively, it is useful to list in advance those activities that include steps or preconditions. The consultant can then determine the point in the sequence at which a question can most effectively be targeted. Questions that are closer to the end of a sequence tend to yield more information. However, the amount of information obtained will also depend on the nature of the answer given. For example, suppose that the response to the earlier question about how many people came to training was that "No one came." In this case, there would be some uncertainty as to whether training was scheduled. If the consultant wanted information about training, a question would then have to be targeted at a higher point in the sequence; for example "Was training scheduled?"

Summarization

A third way to increase communication efficiency during macroconsultation is by using summary statements. Summary statements are used in macroconsultation in essentially the same way they are in individual-case consultation. After a number of communication control statements have been made, the consultant summarizes what has been said. Summaries serve several useful purposes in macroconsultation. First, they assist in recalling what has been said. A great deal of information is communicated in macroconsultation, and not all of it is written down. Accordingly, it is important to review the contents of conversation periodically during the course of the interview.

A second function of the summary is to provide direction for the interview. There is always the possibility in macroconsultation that conversation may drift aimlessly from one topic to another. This is especially a concern when conducting macroconsultation by teleconference. The summary provides a way to keep consultation focused on the topic at hand. For instance, if the consultee(s) brings up information that is not relevant to the topic under discussion, the consultant may respond with a summary of previous information that does deal with the topic intended for discussion. The summary will bring the discussion back to the topic and may stimulate further discussion. The third use of summary statements is to set the stage for establishing agreement as to what has been communicated in macroconsultation. This involves the validation of information communicated during the interview.

Validation

Macroconsultation requires a collaborative effort in which the parties involved understand each other's point of view and are clear as to the nature of agreed on actions to be implemented during the instructional management cycle. In order to achieve this consensus, it is necessary to validate the information that has been communicated, and to do so frequently during the course of macroconsultation interviews. For instance, suppose that a consultant said: "We said that I would call you next week to see how assessment was going." A summary of this kind sets the stage for validating arrangements made during an interview. In many instances, consultees may respond to a summary as though it were a request for validation. For instance, a consultee might respond to the above summary by saying: "Yes, that's right." When validation does not occur, the consultant should explicitly request validation. Thus, a consultant might follow a summary by saying: "Is this what we agreed upon?"

Using a Prototypic Case

A fifth way to increase communication efficiency in macroconsultation is to make use of a prototypic case. For example, suppose that a consultant wanted to assist a teacher to plan learning experiences for each of the children in her class. Doing this would not necessarily require a separate consultation interview for each child. The consultant could use, as an example, the information on one or more children who reflect different developmental levels in the class. For example, the consultant and teacher might choose three typical children: one with a relatively high DL, one with an average DL, and one with a low DL. Planning strategies developed for these prototypic children could then be generalized to other children functioning at similar levels.

These communication techniques are used extensively in scripts developed for macroconsultation. The scripts define the strategies and procedures used in each phase of the instructional management cycle and are discussed in the next section.

Macroconsultation in the Instructional Management Cycle

Phase 1: Assessment

As mentioned at the beginning of the chapter, macroconsultation is implemented in four phases during the program year. The first phase of instructional management cycle involves assessment. The purpose of assessment is to identify learning needs for initial program planning. Assessment and planning are inextricably related processes. Assessment requires an assessment tool that provides information about learning needs. With this kind of assessment tool, educational goals and objectives can be established for the entire program and for children in each of the classrooms within the program. The assessment phase of macroconsultation covers topics that include: (a) training examiners in the administration of the assessment instrument; (b) planning, scheduling, and managing programwide assessment; and (c) ensuring quality assessment through monitoring procedures. The script implemented during this phase of consultation is designed to elicit information from the consultee regarding these topics and to assist in formulating solutions to issues that may arise. The following script describes the steps used in conducting the first phase of macroconsultation and provides examples of questions asked. This phase and subsequent phases are conducted either during the teleconference session or when a caller uses the toll-free number to contact the center.

I. Training Examiners on HSMB Administration
   A. Initiate discussion to determine if caller conducted training at the participating program. This will help to determine if consultation can be conducted with the caller or if another individual is responsible for managing assessment activities. It also establishes the extent to which training has been planned and executed.
      1. Who did the training in your program?
   B. Initiate discussion to determine if any problems occurred during training. This will help to identify concerns or problems that the consultee may be encountering in training examiners to conduct assessment. It also helps the consultant in identifying programs needing additional supervision and monitoring throughout the instructional management cycle.
      1. How did local training go?
      2. Tell me about your training sessions.
   C. Initiate discussion to determine if training is being conducted in a timely and effective way. This will help determine if assistance is required to streamline and modify training procedures.
      1. How long was training time for each examiner?
   D. Summarize and validate discussion to ensure that technical assistance provided for planning and conducting training is agreed on.
      1. We agree then that additional teachers will be trained and that they will read the training material beforehand. We also said that you will distribute an agenda and a list of goal statements indicating what training will accomplish. Is that an accurate summary?

II. Planning for Programwide Assessment
   A. Initiate discussion to establish consultees plans for programwide assessment. This will help to clarify the procedures to be used in conducting assessment with large numbers of children in a timely fashion and allow the consultant to offer suggestions for managing assessment.
      1. Can you describe the procedures you are going to use to assess the children?
      2. Who is doing the testing in your program?
      3. Were you able to locate a quiet testing area?
      4. Have you scheduled a date for testing to begin?
      5. Have you scheduled a completion date for testing?
   B. Summarize and validate discussion to ensure that technical assistance provided for program-wide assessment is agreed upon.
      1. You said that the teachers will set up a quiet area in the classroom where each child will be assessed. You also said that they will assess 10 children each day starting Monday and will finish in two weeks. Is that correct?

III. Ensuring Quality Assessment
   A. Initiate discussion to determine quality control procedures during assessment activities. This helps to determine whether quality control

procedures have been established and implemented. It also provides information so that the consultant can offer suggestions to ensure quality assessment.

1. When you monitored during training did you find that examiners were proficient enough to conduct assessment?
2. Tell me about your plans to follow-up during testing.

B. Summarize and validate discussion to ensure that technical assistance provided for ensuring quality assessment is agreed upon.

1. So you feel that the examiners are proficient to conduct assessment and you will continue to monitor them by shadow scoring during actual assessment to provide follow-up suggestions. Is that an accurate summary of what you will do?

C. Ask questions to determine if there is a need for any additional technical assistance for the topics covered during this phase.

1. Are there any aspects of training, testing or management that I can further assist you with?

D. Initiate discussion to arrange a contact for ensuring that data collection is going as planned and also to arrange for the second phase of consultation.

1. I'll call you next Friday to see how things are going with the assessments.
2. As you will have completed the assessments in two weeks it would be a good idea if we also talk the Friday after that to review the results of assessment and to begin planning learning activities. Is this O.K. with you?

Phase 2: Planning Learning Opportunities

The second phase following assessment focuses on planning learning experiences appropriate to children's developmental levels as determined through assessment using the HSMB. Goals and objectives for the program and for individual children are transformed into learning activities designed to promote competency in skills and concepts. Macroconsultation during this phase focuses on sequencing the presentation of these skills and concepts in a way that will maximize successful outcomes. Once plans are made they are implemented by the classroom teacher. The teacher then keeps a record of the skills presented in learning activities and notes the progress made by each child in the classroom.

The Class Development Profile and Planning Guide

For Head Start, a Class Development Profile and Planning Guide (see Figure 4) has been developed to be used in conjunction with the HSMB to assist teachers in formalizing their plans for the content of instruction. Teachers use the Guide to record content plans for an entire program year in each of the HSMB content areas. The design of the guide makes it possible to specify instructional plans in a short period of time. The guide is accompanied by an Interpretation Guide (Swarner, 1985), which discusses how the Planning Guide may be used and presents detailed descriptions of the skills included in each of the content areas. The guide organizes the content of instruction in two ways: first, specific capabilities are nested within successively broader categories of competence. This organization is congruent with the framework discussed in the earlier section on goals and objectives in which specific objectives were linked to subordinate goals and subordinate goals were related to general goals. For instance, in the area of math, counting aloud to 10 is nested within the larger category of Counting and Ordering skills. Counting and

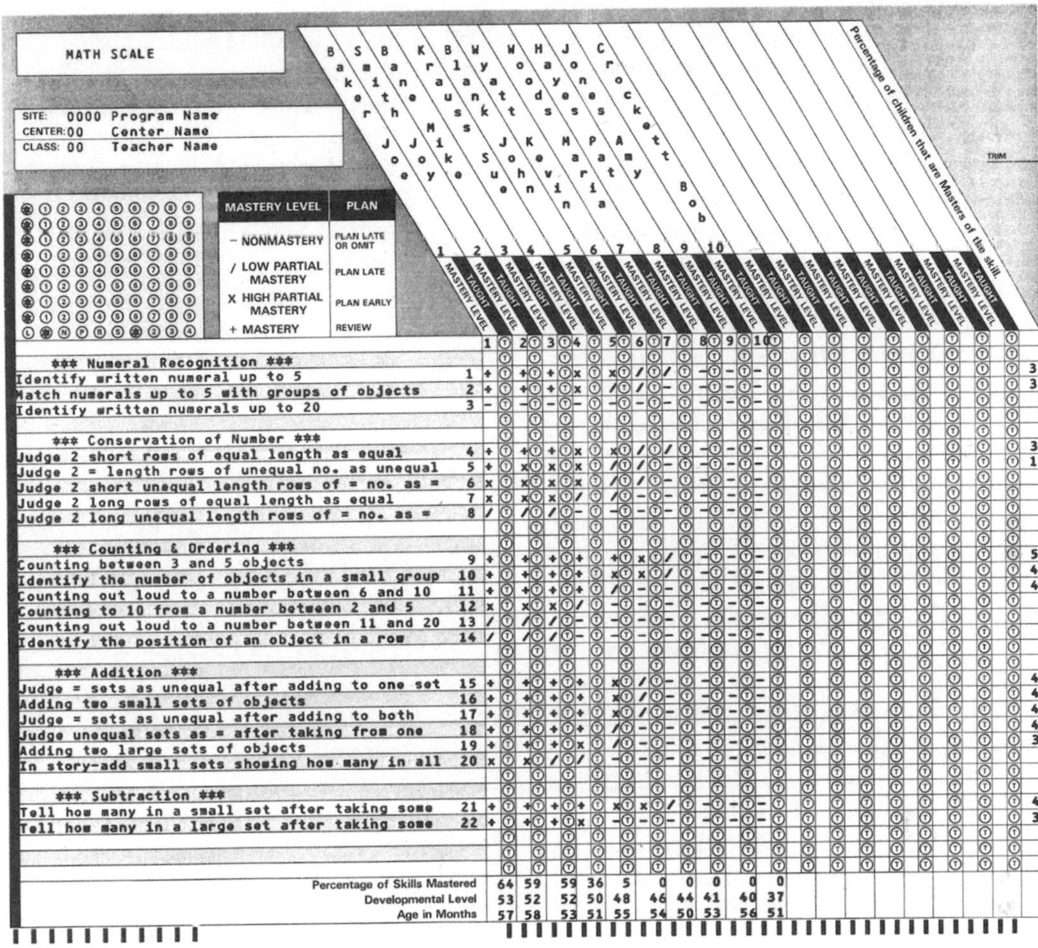

Figure 4. The HSMB Class Development Profile and Planning Guide.

Ordering skills are in turn placed in the Working With Numbers category.

Each of the content categories in the planning guides can be linked to an instructional activity. For example, a category such as Counting and Ordering skills can be linked to instructional activities involving various types of counting tasks. Each of the content categories in the planning guides can also be linked to an instructional goal or objective. For instance, the Counting and Ordering category can be linked to the goal of developing children's counting skills. In macroconsultation, the linking of content to instructional activity, and to goals and objectives provides a way to make instruction congruent with stated program goals and objectives.

Relating specific competencies to more general skill categories in the guide affords a way to relate long-range instructional goals and plans to specific instructional objectives and to concrete lesson-planning activities. This helps to ensure that lesson plans will be directed toward an overall end.

The second type of organization used in the guide is developmental. As mentioned earlier, planning for effective instructional management may be enhanced by considering the developmental sequencing of skills. The categories of competence identified in the planning guides are associated with validated developmenal sequences. Each skill in the guides can be described in terms of its position in one or more developmental progressions. For example, counting forward to 10 is identified as being subordinate to other counting skills, such as counting backward.

The Profile and Planning Guide is the primary tool that the teacher will use for planning. It combines individual and class Mastery Level information in a way that allows the teacher to use the HSMB results for continuous planning. A plastic overlay page provides the teacher with a way of recording: (a) what skills are to be taught to which children, and (b) changes in the children's Mastery Levels during the year. The teacher later reports on the printed copy of the profile which of the skills were taught during the course of the program year.

A short description of each skill is at the left side of the profile. Each skill is numbered so that it can be linked to a teacher's lesson plan. As mentioned earlier, the skills are grouped in categories and listed in order of difficulty. The first skill in each category is the easiest one of the group, and the last one is the most difficult.

Each child's name is printed in the slanted spaces at the the top. Below each child's name there are two columns. The first column shows the child's Mastery Level Code for each skill. The second is a column of T's. This column is used during the year to indicate which skills have been taught to a child. The symbols (+, ×, /, −) in the Mastery Level column show how likely the child is to perform each of these skills.

Other information on the profile that is helpful in planning includes: (a) the percentage of skills that each child has mastered; (b) the child's DL; and (c) the child's age (in months). A column at the far right side of the page indicates the percentage of children who have mastered each skill. Following fall assessment, booklets containing the Class Development Profile and Planning Guide for the scales in the HSMB system are sent to the consultee. There is a separate guide for each participating class.

As mentioned earlier, the results of the HSMB assessment provide two types of scores. Each type of score is calculated for the individual child and for the class. Every child and class receive a Mastery score for each skill on a scale. In addition, every child and class receive an overall DL score for each scale. These scores can help the teacher identify the skills that the child is ready to learn. These two scores are described below.

Mastery Scores and Levels

A Mastery score is computed for each child for each skill on the six HSMB scales (Language, Math, Nature & Science, Perception, Reading, and Social Development). This Mastery score indicates how likely it is that the child will be able to perform a skill correctly. For example, a Mastery score of 55 indicates that the child will perform the skill correctly 55% of the time. The Mastery scores are grouped into Mastery, High Partial Mastery, Low Partial Mastery, and Nonmastery Levels so that teachers can use them to plan class activities. The Mastery Levels suggest what kinds of learning activities and experiences are most likely to enhance the child's development. In addition, they help to point out which skills would be too easy or too difficult for the child. The teacher can use each child's Mastery level to determine which skills would be appropriate to teach the child next. Each of these Levels is identified on the guide by a code symbol. The Mastery Levels, their codes, and definitions are defined as follows.

Mastery (+): The child will perform the skill correctly 75% to 100% of the time. This skill should be considered already learned.

High Partial Mastery (×): The child will perform the skill correctly 50% to 74% of the time. This skill provides a moderate challenge for the child. The teacher should teach as many of these skills as possible, as soon as possible.

Low Partial Mastery (/): The child will perform the skill correctly 25% to 49% of the time.

This skill provides a greater challenge to the child. The teacher should teach these skills after the child has mastered a fair number of the High Partial Mastery skills.

Nonmastery (−): The child will perform the skill correctly less than 25% of the time. The child would probably have difficulty learning it if it was presented before High and Low Partial Mastery skills.

Developmental Level (DL) Score

A Developmental Level (DL) score is computed for each child for each of the six scales administered. The DL score is based on the child's performance on each scale and represents the child's ability level across all the skills on that scale. The DL is shown graphically on the HSMB Development Profile and on the Profile and Planning Guide. It shows the child's position on a developmental path of skills that are arranged according to difficulty. A child will usually have a different DL for each of the HSMB scales.

The Planning Interview

The Class Development Profile and Planning Guide is the core of the planning system. It presents individual and class information that the teacher can use for planning throughout the year. It is designed to help teachers provide learning activities that are appropriate for children's developmental levels. Teachers can identify: (a) what combinations of skills are appropriate for each child during different planning periods, and (b) which children can be grouped for similar activities. The profile, with its plastic overlay, helps the teacher plan appropriate activities for individual children, follow progress, update mastery levels, and update and revise plans for learning activities.

The planning interview makes extensive use of the planning guides. The guides are designed to assist consultees to carry out planning activities with a minimum of assistance. As consultees become familiar with the guides, the amount of interview time devoted to eliciting information will be shortened and the focus of macroconsultation during this phase will shift to summarizing and validating information provided by consultees. At the start of the planning interview, the consultant should provide an introduction to the consultees regarding the purpose and utility of the interview. The following script describes the steps used in conducting the planning phase of macroconsultation.

I. Introduction to Program Planning
   A. Initiate discussion to ensure consultee has appropriate material at hand.
      1. I'm calling to follow-up on the recent mailing of HSMB Profiles and Planning Guide to your program and to assist you in using them for planning. Have you received the Profiles and Planning Guide?
      2. Would you take out the Planning Guide and Individual Profile?

   B. Introduce the nature of the program planning phase and prepare the consultees for what will follow.
      1. As you know, teachers may use the Planning Guide for four important teaching objectives. It may be used to identify individual learning needs for initial planning, keep a record of the types of skills presented, observe and record children's progress, and update lesson plans based on progress. As we talk I will describe each of these objectives and the procedures for accomplishing them. Do you have any questions at this point?

II. Initial Planning
   A. Initiate discussion to establish some ground rules of communication with consultees.
      1. Let's start with the first objective, identifying learning needs. As

you can see on the Planning Guide, a Developmental Level score is provided for each child assessed with the HSMB. The Developmental Level score can be thought of as an indicator of a child's overall ability in the content area. The DL determines the level of mastery for each skill that makes up the ability. The Planning Guide shows each child's mastery level for each skill. Mastery of a skill is indicated by the code "+", high partial mastery by an "×", low partial mastery by a "/", and nonmastery by a "–". Do you see these?

B. Initiate discussion to establish the sequence of planning and teaching.
   1. Teachers may want to review skills that children have already mastered and present new skills that the children are ready to learn. Which mastery code would show the teacher the skills appropriate for review?
   2. Which mastery code would show new skills that the children are ready to learn?
   3. Teachers may also want to include some of the skills indicated by a "/". Look at the Individual Development Profile. Picture an imaginary line dividing the medium shaded green areas for each skill in half. Teachers may wish to include those "/" skills for which the column of "Fs", that is, the Fall developmental level falls close to the left side of the imaginary line. These will be skills that children can perform accurately close to 50% of the time. Do you have any questions about that?

C. Summarize and validate discussion to ensure plans are agreed upon.
   1. To summarize then, "+" skills will be presented for review and "×" skills would be presented as new skills for the children to learn. O.K.?
   2. As the children learn these skills the teachers will begin to include some of the "/" skills in learning activities. Do we agree?

Phase III: The Implementation Interview

To keep children interested in activities, and to keep them progressing, it is important to have them taking part in activities that are at their ability level. The third phase of macroconsultation helps to ensure continuity in planning and instruction throughout the year so that children continue to progress. This phase of macroconsultation focuses on three important consultation objectives: (a) observing and recording children's progress; (b) revising plans based on observed progress; and (c) implementing revised plans. Observing children's progress provides the information needed in macroconsultation for redefining and restructuring teaching activities. Revising and implementing new plans based on progress serves further to enhance development. This phase may be implemented several times throughout the program year (see Figure 1).

I. Keeping a Record of Skills to Be Presented
   A. Initiate discussion to establish recording of skills presented to children.
      1. The next objective is to keep a record of the skills presented in learning activities. Teachers can use the Profile and Planning Guide for this. As the teachers identify and present "+", "×", and some of the "/" skills they can show this on the plastic overlay. This is done by placing a check mark in the Taught column under the child's name and next

to the skill that is being presented. Do you see where this check mark would go?

B. Initiate discussion to establish management activities directed by the consultee to ensure accurate recording of skills presented.
   1. What would be some of the things that you could do to assist teachers in using the planning guide for identifying learning needs and keeping a record of the skills presented?

C. Summarize and validate discussion to ensure recording plans are agreed on.
   1. So to summarize, you will be setting aside some time to meet with your teachers to discuss the benefits of using the Planning Guide. Then you can then have them identify, and mark on the overlay the skills that they will include in their lesson plans. Is that an accurate summary of what you plan to do?

D. Initiate discussion to establish timely and accurate recording procedures.
   1. It would be a good idea to do this as soon as possible so that your assessment information can be used to help the children progress. When do you think would be a good time for you to work with the teachers in using the information for planning?

E. Summarize and validate discussion to ensure recording procedures are carried out as agreed on.
   1. So the teachers will plan next week and then begin to include the skills in their activities. O.K.?

II. Observing and Recording Children's Progress
   A. Initiate discussion to establish observation and recording of children's progress.
      1. The next objective is to observe and keep a record of the children's progress. Teachers may use the overlay for this by placing a "+" in the Mastered column under the child's name and next to the skill that has been learned. Of course, this should only be done when, in the teacher's judgment, the child has learned the skill. Do you see where this would go on the guide?

   B. Initiate discussion to establish management activities directed by the consultee to ensure accurate observation and recording of progress.
      1. What are some things that you might want to do to assist teachers in using the planning guide to observe and keep a record of the children's progress?

   C. Summarize and validate discussion to ensure procedures for observing and recording progress are agreed on.
      1. So to summarize, you'll meet with the teachers once a week to review the children's progress and to assist them in recording this information on the planning guide. Is that an accurate summary?

III. Updating Lesson Plans
   A. Initiate discussion to establish procedures for updating lesson plans based on progress.
      1. As your teachers observe and record children's progress they can decide which skills to present next. They can, of course, continue to present skills from the first lesson plan that have not yet been learned. As the children learn the "+", "×", and some of

the "/" skills, what other skills might the teacher want to include?

B. Summarize and validate discussion to ensure procedures for updating lesson plans are agreed on.
   1. So as the children begin to learn the easier skills the teacher can present the more difficult "/" skills and the "−" skills. Agreed?

C. Summarize and validate discussion to ensure that recording, observation, and lesson plan update procedures are agreed upon.
   1. When teachers update lesson plans they can use the overlay as they did in their initial planning to record this information. They can also record children's continued progress as they did before. O.K.?

IV. Recycling the Implementation Phase
A. Initiate discussion to review the objectives of the instructional management cycle and to identify any issues.
   1. So to summarize, the Planning Guide will be used to identify learning needs, keep a record of the types of skills presented, observe and record progress, and revise lesson plans where needed. Would you like to discuss any of these four objectives in greater detail?

B. Initiate discussion to emphasize the importance of proceeding through these four objectives several times throughout the program year.
   1. As you know, teachers should implement these objectives several times throughout the program year. This will help to establish continuity in planning and instruction throughout the year. By doing this, children will remain interested in activities and will continue to progress.

C. Initiate discussion to arrange for subsequent contacts in order to ensure that the cycle is being implemented several times.
   1. I would like to set up a time that we can talk again to review how the teachers are doing and to take a look at the progress that the children are making. When would be a good time for me to call you again?

D. Summarize and validate discussion to ensure date of the next consultation is agreed on.
   1. So I will call you on Friday, the 15th at 3:00 to review the progress that the children have made and how the teachers are doing in updating their lesson plans. O.K.?

Phase IV: The Evaluation of Goal Attainment and Plan Effectiveness

The final phase of macroconsultation is an evaluation occurring at the end of the year. Consultants work with Education Coordinators to interpret the results of HSMB assessment showing children's growth during the course of the year. Two questions are addressed. One involves the extent to which the goals of instruction have been attained. The other has to do with the effectiveness of plans put into operation to achieve these goals.

Assessment results are used in instructional evaluation to provide feedback to teachers, educational coordinators, and program administrators that can be applied to future instructional planning. It is this feedback mechanism that relates assessment directly to instruction, which does so in a manner designed to foster program improvement.

In reality, the evaluation process begins earlier in the year with the identification of learning needs. Needs identification provides one of two major pieces of information used in the evaluation process. The second source of information comes from assessment at the end of the instructional management cycle. For example, in Head Start, combining information from HSMB assessment at the beginning of the year with information on achievement and teaching obtained toward the end of the year makes it possible to evaluate goal attainment and plan effectiveness.

Evaluating Goal Attainment

The evaluation of goal attainment involves an examination of the level of goal attainment and the level of mastery of the specific skills targeted for instruction. In macroconsultation, the process of evaluating the level of goal attainment and level of skill mastery may be conducted for an individual child, a class, a group of classes forming a program, or a group of programs. Performing goal level and skill mastery evaluations at different levels in the instructional organization affords a rich variety of information that can facilitate the efforts of each segment of the organization. The data necessary to implement evaluations at different levels in the instructional organization can be obtained by aggregating information from classes and programs.

Evaluating the Level of Goal Attainment

Evaluating the level of goal attainment typically focuses on the question of whether or not instructional goals have been met. Although this question is central, it is not the only question of importance. Path-referenced assessment instruments such as the HSMB determine not only whether goals have been met, but also the degree to which they have been met, or even exceeded. This capability to determine whether children's expected performance level is above or below an established goal level is a valuable one that provides information on the appropriateness of goals as well as on the nature of goal attainment.

Two types of information must be considered in determining the level of goal attainment during macroconsultation. One is the developmental level of the children in the group. Developmental level may be assessed in terms of the overall level of achievement of each individual child in the group or for the group as a whole. For example, consider the problem of determining the achievement level of the entire class in the area of math. Overall class achievement in math can be determined in the following way. First the path score, the child's developmental level, for the math scale of the HSMB is calculated for each child in the class. Next, these path scores are averaged to give an indication of the developmental level of the group as a whole.

A second type of information is necessary to evaluate level of goal attainment. This is a Teaching Level (TL) to a child. Within the HSMB system, whenever a skill is taught to a child or to a group of children, the teacher indicates this on the Class Development Profile and Planning Guide. This information is analyzed at the end of the program year by the University of Arizona and a Teaching Level (TL) score is computed for each child. As with the DL, Teaching Level can also be averaged to yield a classroom average Teaching Level.

Figure 5 illustrates information on the level of goal attainment in the math area for an entire class. The table includes information on Fall and Spring class developmental level and on Teaching Level. Fall DL is indicated by a column of Fs, Spring DL by a column of Ss, and TL by a column of Ts. As with the DL for the class, the TLs for all the children in the class are averaged to give a class TL.

The first question to be addressed in evaluating level of goal attainment is the congruence between teaching level and developmental level. Teaching level should be about

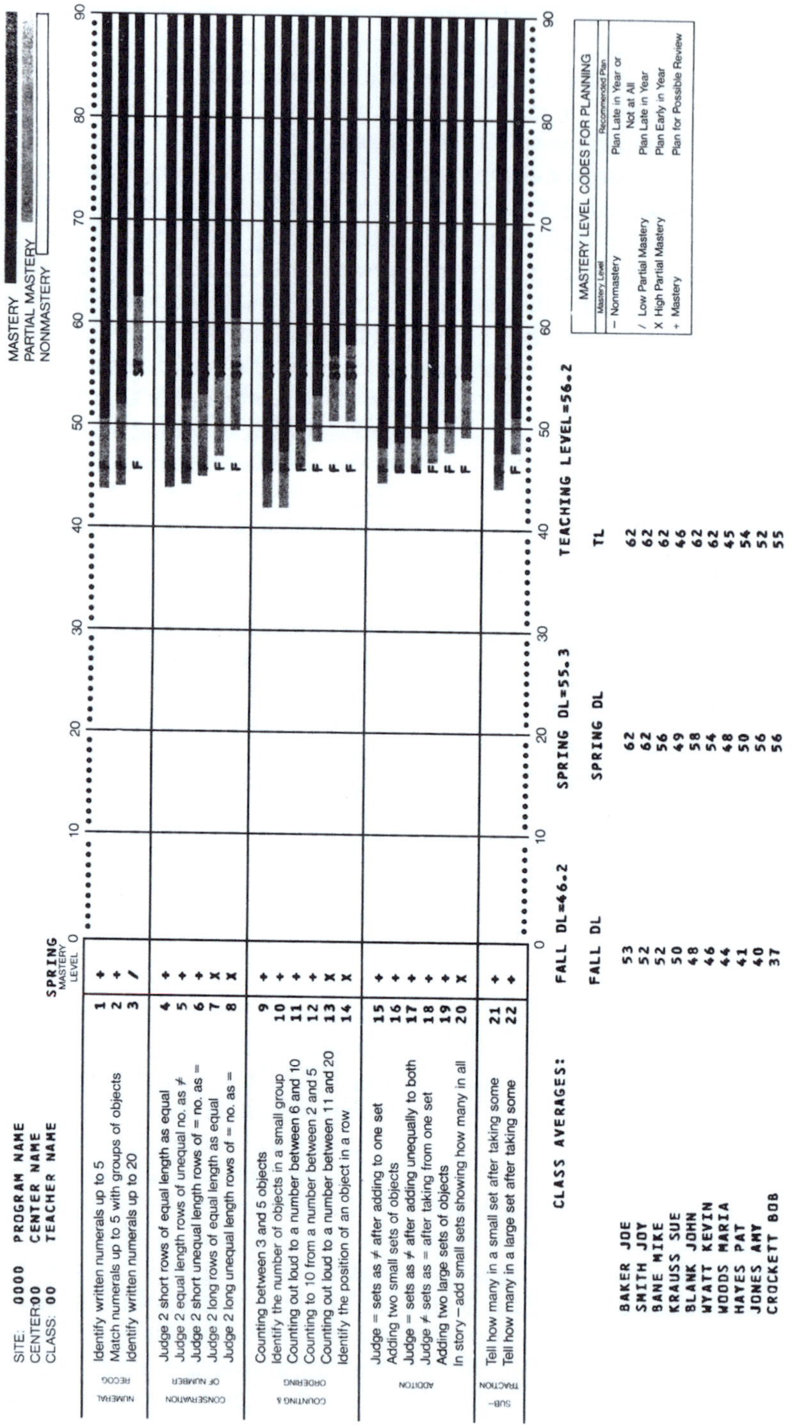

Figure 5. HSMB Development Profile Math scale—fall and spring.

the same as spring developmental level. Comparisons can be made between the TL and the DL for each child and for the class. These comparisons indicate how successfully particular skills have been taught. The closer the DL and TL are, the more accurately the teacher has targeted his or her teaching on the child's ability level. Discrepancies between the two signal the need for changes in planning strategies. When teaching level is substantially higher than developmental level, large numbers of skills are being taught that the children are not learning. This suggests either that the skills are too difficult for the children or that the instructional procedures are not effective in promoting skill acquisition. In macroconsultation, an examination of information aggregated across programs may throw some light on these alternatives. For example, if children of similar ages are functioning at a higher developmental level than that reflected in a given class, then it may be useful to identify the factors that could promote a higher level of skill acquisition in that class.

When teaching level is well below spring developmental level, the children are not being challenged in the content area under consideration. This suggests a need to examine the goals of instruction. For example, it could happen that a teacher would underestimate the learning capabilities of the children in the class. Under these circumstances, the teacher would probably want to revise instructional plans and implement them to increase teaching level.

Evaluating Skill Mastery

The evaluation of the level of goal attainment provides a global indication of the relationship between developmental level and the goals of instruction carried out in teaching activities. The evaluation of the mastery of specific skills provides an in-depth look at the capabilities that make up the developmental level and teaching level. As in evaluating the level of goal attainment, two kinds of information are needed to evaluate the level of skill mastery. The first is the skills actually taught, and the second is the level of skill mastery for each of these skills.

For Head Start, the Skill Level Progress Report (Figure 6) is used to evaluate the level of skill mastery. This report shows the fall-to-spring progress of each child in a class. A short description of each skill on the scale is at the left side of the page. Each child's name is printed in the slanted spaces at the top. Below each child's name there are two columns. The first column shows the child's fall Mastery Score for a particular skill, and the second column shows the child's spring Mastery Score. The child's overall Developmental Levels for the fall and spring assessments are printed at the bottom of these columns. The report also indicates whether or not the skill was taught to that child. If a skill was taught, there is a star (*) between the fall and spring mastery scores. This report provides a detailed account of the skills taught and learned by a group of children. For example, the results may reveal large blocks of skills in a given content area that were inadvertently left out of instructional plans for a given class. It may show further that children are not mastering the overlooked skills during the course of instruction. Information of this kind has clear implications for instructional decision making.

Evaluating Plan Effectiveness

It is important to realize that goal attainment and plan effectiveness are not inextricably linked. It is quite possible for the goals of instruction to be attained in the absence of any instructional plan. For example, maturational influences or learning occurring outside of the instructional environment may be responsible for observed developmental progress. Likewise, instruction may be effective in the absence of goal attainment. For example, it is possible that certain instructional goals may not be achieved even though children may make substantial progress resulting from instruction.

SITE: 0000 PROGRAM NAME
CENTER: 00 CENTER NAME
CLASS: 00 TEACHER NAME

MATH SCALE

MASTERY SCORE	TRANSLATES TO	MASTERY LEVEL CODE
75 - 100		+
50 - 74		X
25 - 49		/
0 - 24		-

	BAKER JOE		SMITH JOY		BANE MIKE		KRAUSS SUE		BLANK JOHN		WYATT KEVIN		WOODS MARIA		HAYES PAT		JONES AMY		CROCKETT BOB	
TESTING TIMES	OCT 85	APR 86	OCT 85	APR 86	OCT 85	APR 86	OCT 85	APR 86	OCT 85	APR 86	OCT 85	APR 86	OCT 85	APR 86	OCT 85	APR 86	OCT 85	APR 86	OCT 85	APR 86
*** NUMERAL RECOGNITION ***																				
IDENTIFY WRITTEN NUMERAL UP TO 5	86*	99	84*	99	83*	95	70*	63	53*	97	42*	91	26*	60	13*	73	8*	95	4*	95
MATCH NUMERALS UP TO 5 WITH GROUPS OF OBJECTS	80*	98	77*	98	75*	91	62*	56	47*	94	38*	85	25	53	14*	65	10*	91	5*	91
IDENTIFY WRITTEN NUMERALS UP TO 20	16*	74	13*	74	12*	34	7*	5	4*	45	2*	22	1*	5	1*	8	0*	34	0*	34
*** CONSERVATION OF NUMBER ***																				
JUDGE 2 SHORT ROWS OF EQUAL LENGTH AS EQUAL	88*	99	86*	99	85*	96	73*	66	56*	98	44*	93	27*	63	13*	76	9*	96	4*	96
JUDGE 2 = LENGTH ROWS OF UNEQUAL NO. AS UNEQUAL	77*	97	74*	97	72*	89	59	53	45*	92	36*	83	24	51	13*	62	10	89	5	89
JUDGE 2 SHORT UNEQUAL LENGTH ROWS OF = NO. AS =	73*	97	69*	97	67*	87	53*	47	38*	91	30*	80	19	44	10*	56	7*	87	4	87
JUDGE 2 LONG ROWS OF EQUAL LENGTH AS EQUAL	60*	94	57*	94	55*	79	40*	35	28*	85	21*	69	13*	32	7*	43	5*	79	3*	79
JUDGE 2 LONG UNEQUAL LENGTH ROWS OF = NO. AS =	39*	80	36*	80	35*	56	25*	22	18*	63	14*	46	9	20	6*	27	4*	56	3*	56
*** COUNTING & ORDERING ***																				
COUNTING BETWEEN 3 AND 5 OBJECTS	99*	100	99*	100	98*	100	95	92	85*	100	72*	100	44	90	16*	96	8*	100	3*	100
IDENTIFY THE NUMBER OF OBJECTS IN A SMALL GROUP	96*	100	95*	100	95*	99	88	83	75*	99	63*	98	40*	81	19*	90	12*	99	5	99
COUNTING OUT LOUD TO A NUMBER BETWEEN 6 AND 10	96*	100	95*	100	94*	100	77	65	44*	100	24*	99	6	58	1*	82	0*	100	0*	100
COUNTING TO 10 FROM A NUMBER BETWEEN 2 AND 5	74*	100	68*	100	64*	94	36	27	16*	97	9*	86	3	23	1*	42	0*	94	0*	94
COUNTING OUT LOUD TO A NUMBER BETWEEN 11 AND 20	40*	94	36*	94	33*	69	19*	15	10*	78	6*	53	3	13	1	22	1*	69	0*	69
IDENTIFY THE POSITION OF AN OBJECT IN A ROW	38*	91	34*	91	32*	65	19	15	11*	74	7*	50	4	14	2*	21	1	65	1*	65
*** ADDITION ***																				
JUDGE = SETS AS UNEQUAL AFTER ADDING TO ONE SET	98*	100	97*	100	97*	100	89	82	68*	100	49*	99	20	79	5*	91	2*	100	1*	100
ADDING TWO SMALL SETS OF OBJECTS	98*	100	97*	100	96*	100	86*	77	59*	100	37*	99	12*	72	2*	89	1	100	0*	100
JUDGE = SETS AS UNEQUAL AFTER ADDING TO BOTH	97*	100	96*	100	95*	100	82	73	55*	100	35*	99	12	68	3*	86	1*	100	0*	100
JUDGE UNEQUAL SETS AS = AFTER TAKING FROM ONE	97*	100	95*	100	94*	100	77	64	42*	100	22*	99	6	57	1*	82	0*	100	0*	100
ADDING TWO LARGE SETS OF OBJECTS	93*	100	90*	100	88*	99	61	46	27*	100	13*	97	3	40	1	69	0	99	0*	99
IN STORY-ADD SMALL SETS SHOWING HOW MANY IN ALL	56*	97	51*	97	48*	81	29	23	16*	88	11*	68	5	21	2	33	1	81	1*	81
*** SUBTRACTION ***																				
TELL HOW MANY IN A SMALL SET AFTER TAKING SOME	98*	100	97*	100	96*	100	89	83	71*	100	53*	99	25	80	7*	91	4*	100	1*	100
TELL HOW MANY IN A LARGE SET AFTER TAKING SOME	88*	100	84*	100	81*	98	53	41	25*	99	13*	94	4	35	1*	61	0*	98	0*	98
DEVELOPMENTAL LEVEL	53	62	52	62	52	56	50	49	48	58	46	54	44	48	41	50	40	56	37	56
TEACHING LEVEL	62		62		62		46		62		62		45		54		52		55	

Figure 6. The HSMB Skill Level Progress Report. The star (★) indicates that the skill was taught.

Developmental Change

Several types of information may be useful in determining plan effectiveness during macroconsultation. Among the most basic of these is information on developmental change. It is important to determine the extent to which children have advanced their skills during the course of instruction. Developmental progress is a sign that instruction may have been effective. Lack of progress or regression to a previous level suggests a lack of instructional effectiveness.

When using the HSMB, developmental change may be assessed by computing path scores at the beginning of instruction in the fall and again toward the end of the instructional year. The amount of change is determined simply by subtracting the fall score from the spring score. It is worth noting that both the fall and spring scores will contain a small amount of measurement error. No assessment tool is entirely free from errors in measurement. For example, a child may respond to one or more items correctly without possessing the skills presumably measured by those items. Thus, the child's score does not give a completely accurate assessment of his or her capabilities. Although the fall and spring scores will contain measurement error, the difference between them is an unbiased estimate of true change, that is uncontaminated by measurement error (Rogosa, Brandt, & Zimowski, 1982). That is not to say that change scores do not have important limitations (Rogosa *et al.*, 1982). Nonetheless, they can be used to provide a simple and direct measure of development occurring during the course of instruction.

Teaching and Skill Performance

Although developmental change is a necessary condition for assuming the effectiveness of an instructional plan, it is not a sufficient condition. Change occurring during the course of a program year could result from factors other than instruction.

It is not always possible to say what has brought about improvement or lack of improvement in the child, class, or program, but it is helpful to think over the possible causes and see if they may apply to a particular child or class. For example, if a child or class has made progress and:

1. The TL is much lower than the DL; it is possible that the children are learning skills from sources other than the classroom.
2. The TL and DL are close; this suggests that the teacher has accurately targeted his or her teaching on the children's ability levels.

If however, a child or class has made little progress between fall and spring, and:

1. The TL is much lower than the DL; raising the teaching goals, that is, teaching more difficult skills may result in children showing greater progress.
2. The TL and the DL are close; teaching goals were probably set at a good level at the beginning of the year, but the activities themselves may not be effective ones. Activities may need to be revised, or replaced with others that are more effective.
3. The TL is much higher than the DL; the teacher may have set his or her goals too high. The skills may be too difficult and the children may become discouraged. The teacher may also have moved ahead to more difficult skills before the children had mastered less difficult ones.

Guidance Objectives

As indicated in the discussion of the evaluation process, data on goal attainment and plan effectiveness can be used to guide the course of instructional management. Such guidance generally takes place in the evaluation interview. For example, an evaluation interview conducted at the end of the instructional year can be used to address instructional management issues of concern for the following fall. The consultant uses goal attainment and plan effectiveness information to determine the need to direct discussion to other phases of the instructional management process. It may be useful to shift the discussion from evaluation to identification of learning needs, or to questions involving planning.

Procedural Objectives

The final set of objectives for the evaluation interview concern making the necessary arrangements to proceed with additional cycles of the macroconsultation process. For example, consider the situation in which an evaluation interview is being conducted with an educational coordinator toward the end of an instructional year. Under these circumstances, there may be a need to make plans for identification of those learning needs which might occur the following fall. If this is the case, the consultant must make plans to follow-up the discussion at a future date.

The Evaluation Interview

During the evaluation interview the consultant and consultees determine the extent to which the goals of instruction have been attained and whether or not the plans implemented to achieve those goals have been effective. The evaluation interview leads to a reiteration of the macroconsultation process. Thus, at some point in the interview, discussion will usually shift to the identification of learning needs. At this point the interviewing techniques associated with needs identification will be implemented. Evaluation may also signal the need to engage in the techniques associated with the planning phase of macroconsultation. When this occurs, the interviewing procedures associated with these two phases are employed.

In summary, objectives of the evaluation interview fall into four major categories. The first is to evaluate goal attainment. The second to evaluate plan effectiveness. The third relates to the guidance of the instructional management process, and the fourth to procedures for future macroconsultation sessions. The evaluation interview may be conducted at the child, class, and program level. The example presented here is at the class level.

I. Evaluate Level of Goal Attainment
   A. Initiate discussion on goal attainment at the classroom level by having the consultees summarize information on teaching level and developmental level.
      1. Look at the Classroom Development Profile. What are the spring developmental and teaching levels for your classroom?
   B. Summarize and validate goal attainment at the classroom level by establishing agreement with the consultee on the extent to which goals have been achieved. This would include any discrepancies between teaching level and spring developmental level.
      1. Because your teaching level is just about the same as the spring developmental level for the children, do we agree that the goals for the class as a whole have been met in the math area?

II. Evaluate Mastery of Specific Skills
   A. Initiate discussion on level of skill mastery by examining the relationship between skills taught and skill mastery.
      1. Look at the Skill Level Progress Report for math. Can you tell me some things about the progress children made on skills that were taught and skills that were not taught?
   B. Summarize and validate the attainment of objectives reflected in the data on the mastery of specific skills.

1. Do we agree that all of the children mastered the objectives related to counting and the recognition of math symbols? However, there were some children who were nonmasters of the addition and subtraction tasks. Also, there were five children who mastered several of the addition tasks that were not targeted for instruction.

III. Determine Whether to Proceed to the Next Phase of the Interview or to Earlier Phases in Macroconsultation
   A. If the information derived from the evaluation of goal attainment and mastery of specific skills suggests progressing to the next phase in the interview, indicate to the consultee the need to move on.
      1. Let's consider the effectiveness of teaching procedures that you used to assist the children in learning the skills that you taught in math.

   B. If information derived from the evaluation of goal attainment and mastery of specific skills suggests the need to return to the identification of learning needs or to another previous phase, indicate to the consultee the need to go back to an earlier phase of macroconsultation.
      1. Let's spend a little more time reviewing how to teach for mastery of skill in addition and subtraction.

IVa. Evaluate Plan Effectiveness
   A. Initiate discussion to determine the extent to which children have advanced their skills during the course of instruction by looking at change in developmental level from fall to spring.
      1. Look at the Class Development Profile. Is the spring DL higher than the fall DL for the class?

   B. Summarize and validate change in developmental level from fall to spring.
      1. So the class as a whole has moved from an average developmental level of 45 in the fall to 55 in the spring. Is that accurate?

   C. Initiate discussion to determine the extent to which the teaching level was targeted to the children's ability levels.
      1. Look at the teaching level for the class. How close is it to the spring development level for the class?

   D. Summarize and validate the plan effectiveness in relationship to spring development level.
      1. The teaching level and developmental level are close. This suggests that the teacher has accurately targeted his or her teaching on the children's ability levels.

IVb. Determine Guidance Objectives
   A. Summarize goal attainment findings and determine whether or not it will be necessary to shift discussion from evaluation to identification of learning needs. If a shift to learning needs identification is warranted, validate the need with the consultee.
      1. Earlier we saw that the teaching level in this class is well below the developmental level of the children. Do you agree that we ought to take another look at the learning needs in this class?

   B. Determine whether or not there is a need to direct discussion to planning. If a shift to planning is warranted, validate the need with the consultee.

1. Earlier we saw that the goals for instruction in this classroom have not been achieved by most of the children and that the children are not learning the skills you have taught. Do you agree that we ought to go back and identify the things that need to be done in this classroom in order to achieve instructional goals?

V. Determine Procedural Objectives
   A. Make the necessary arrangements to proceed with additional cycles of the macroconsultation process, if necessary, then summarize and validate these arrangements.
      1. We said that we will talk again two weeks from today to see if the changes that we made in teaching plans had an effect on children's learning. Is that right?

Conclusion

We have introduced macroconsultation as a new form of consultation service and described its application in the Head Start program. Macroconsultation for instructional management provides a potentially useful service that does not now exist in most educational programs. Macroconsultation applies consultation techniques in a way that can benefit every child in an educational program. It does not replace individual-case consultation; rather, it provides needed instructional management services that are not provided by individual case consultation.

Implementation in Head Start provides a unique opportunity to demonstrate the application of macroconsultation. Head Start is a national project with a variety of programs. We have had the opportunity to use macroconsultation in settings representing every region of the country, and to observe the implementation of macroconsultation principles in a variety of conditions.

Our observations suggest a number of possible applications for macroconsultation techniques outside of Head Start. We feel that macroconsultation could be used effectively in other large early childhood programs. For example, it could be applied in large-scale day care programs operated in either the public or the private sector. Macroconsultation techniques might also be applied in public school settings, particularly in large school systems. Application in the schools would be somewhat different than the demonstration described in this chapter in that services would not need to be provided by long-distance phone. Face-to-face meetings would undoubtedly play a more prominent role in consultation within a school setting than it does in consultation rendered across the entire nation.

Macroconsultation requires the communication of a large amount of information in a short period of time. In part, this is accomplished by using communication techniques that condense information and focus on information specific to the assessment and planning cycle. The use of categorization, implication, and prototypic cases discussed in the early part of this chapter are examples of how information may be condensed. These techniques alone are not sufficient to make consultation with large numbers possible.

Macroconsultation requires products including assessment instruments and planning materials. These products act as information reservoirs that reduce the burden of communicating vast quantities of information in macroconsultation. As demonstrated previously, a consultant using the HSMB may refer to a large number of specific skills in relation to a group of children by indicating that the skills of concern are those in the high partial mastery category. There are two potentially negative consequences associated with the need for products. One is that product development is expensive and time consuming. However, the cost in time and money may be more than offset by the gain in efficiency and impact of macroconsultation services when the number of clients to be served is sufficiently large. The second negative feature of products is that they limit the scope of macroconsultation. For example, consultation using the HSMB is limited by the skills included in the battery. The effects of this kind of limitation can be minimized if provisions are included for revising products based on expressed program needs.

Macroconsultation is a new approach to consultation services, and there is a particularly pressing need for research on macroconsultation techniques. Needed research includes studies of macroconsultation interview procedures and the overall effects of the macroconsultation process on program implementation and on the outcomes of implementation.

References

Bergan, J. R. (1977). *Behavioral consultation*. Columbus, Ohio: Charles E. Merrill Publishing Co.

Bergan, J. R. (in press). Path-referenced assessment. In C. R. Reynolds (Ed.), *Encyclopedia of special education: A reference for the education of the handicapped and other exceptional children and youth* (p. 1159). New York: Wiley.

Bergan, J. R. (Ed. and Project Director), & Smith, A. N. (Government Project Officer). (1985). *Head Start Measures Battery*. Tucson, Arizona: University of Arizona, Center for Educational Evaluation & Measurement.

Bergan, J. R. & Stone, C. A. (1985). *Restricted item response models for developmental assessment*. Paper presented at annual meeting of American Educational Research Association, Los Angeles, CA.

Bergan, J. R., Stone, C. A., & Feld, J. K. (1985). Replacement and component rules in hierarchically ordered mathematics rule learning tasks. *Journal of Educational Psychology, 74*, 39–50.

Bock, R. D., & Aitkin, M. (1981). Marginal maximum likelihood estimation of item parameters: Application of an algorithm. *Psychometrika, 46*, 443–459.

Caplan, G. (1970). *The theory and practice of mental health consultation*. New York: Basic Books.

Gagne, R. M. & Briggs, L. J. (1974). *Principles of instructional design*. New York: Holt, Rinehart & Winston.

Gallessich, J. & Davis, J. (1981). Consultation: Prospects and retrospects. In J. C. Conoley (Ed.), *Consultation in schools: Theory, research, procedures* (pp. 295–302). New York: Academic Press.

Glaser, R. (1963). Instructional technology and the measurement of learning outcomes. *American Psychologist, 18*, 519–521.

Glaser, R. & Nitko, A. J. (1971). Measurement in learning and instruction. In R. L. Thorndike (Ed.), *Educational measurement* (2nd ed., pp. 625–670). Washington, DC: American Council on Education.

Lord, F. M. (1980). *Applications of item response theory to practical testing problems*. Hillsdale, NJ: Erlbaum.

Nitko, A. J. (1980). Distinguishing the many varieties of criterion referenced tests. *Review of Educational Research, 50*, 461–485.

Ramage, J. C. (1979). National survey of school psychologists: Update. *School Psychology Digest, 8*, 153–161.

Reschly, D. J. (1976). School psychology consultation: "Frenzied, faddish, or fundamental." *Journal of School Psychology, 14*, 105–113.

Rogosa, D., Brandt, D., & Zimowski, M. (1982). A growth curve approach to the measurement of change. *Psychological Bulletin, 92*, 720–748.

Swarner, J. (1985). *Interpretation guide for the Head Start Measures Battery*. Tucson, AZ: University of Arizona.

PART III

Problems and Challenges for Behavior Therapy

Chapters in this section address the multifaceted complexities involved in utilizing behavioral procedures in educational settings. It has been a very large, and not always graceful, step from the animal laboratory to the classroom. Behaviorists have encountered problems with maintaining appropriate control, issues with treatment integrity, client and consultee resistance, and many other social and technical difficulties present in imperfect human systems. Almost from the start, behaviorists recognized and anticipated problems with the generalization and maintenance of treatment once intensive intervention is terminated. Rutherford and Nelson (Chapter 11) describe the various methods that have been used to solve generalization and maintenence problems and provide a comprehensive literature review of studies addressing these topics. The next two chapters deal in large part with the side effects of change. In Chapter 12, Martens and Witt provide an analysis of the complex ramifications for an ecological system when change is introduced into that system and provide a methodology that may assist in anticipating and planning for side effects. Dunst and Trivette in Chapter 13 provide a thoughtful analysis of the conditions under which it is useful to provide help or assistance to an individual. Although there is a natural human inclination to help someone in need, Dunst and Trivette's review of the help-seeking literature suggests that very often even the most benevolent interventions can sometimes do more harm than good by creating dependency and attenuating self-esteem. Finally, in Chapter 14, Corrao and Melton provide a well-organized review of the major legal issues that affect the use of a behavioral methodology in schools and institutions.

CHAPTER 11

Generalization and Maintenance of Treatment Effects

Robert B. Rutherford, Jr. and C. Michael Nelson

For the past two decades, applied behavior analysts have developed increasingly effective interventions for modifying undesired or maladaptive social and academic behaviors of students in tightly controlled and structured learning environments. The applied behavior analysis literature, which is reported in a score of journals and hundreds of textbooks (Rutherford, 1987), contains numerous demonstrations of the law of effect in educational settings with students whose behaviors have been brought under teacher control. However, many applied studies have failed to result in desired changes in target behaviors that persist and generalize to nontreatment settings where therapeutic contingencies are not in effect. The failure to accomplish the maintenance and generalization of intervention effects imposes a critical limitation on this research. Historically, behavioral maintenance and generalization are frequently called for in applied studies (Baer, Wolf, & Risley, 1968; Gelfand & Hartmann, 1984; Stokes & Baer, 1977; Wildman & Wildman, 1975) but seldom is it systematically assessed or programmed.

An important set of questions regarding behavior change intervention includes the following: Will desired behavior changes maintain when students leave structured, highly controlled training settings? Will students emit newly learned behaviors in a variety of nontraining settings, across a number of teachers or trainers, and over time? In addition, will the effects of learning new prosocial or adaptive academic responses facilitate the acquisition of similar behaviors that were not originally targeted for acquisition in the training setting?

The failure to achieve generalization of desired behavior changes in applied behavior analysis studies has been described as an "albatross" (O'Leary & O'Leary, 1976) and a "challenge" (Gelfand & Hartmann, 1984). Hayes, Rincover, and Solnick (1980) stated "one might argue that generality is not so much an essential aspect of applied behavior analysis as it is one of the foremost challenges to it" (1980, p. 283). The question is one of whether behavior change without generalization is of any applied value; that is, whether

Robert B. Rutherford, Jr. • Department of Special Education, Arizona State University, Tempe, Arizona 85287. **C. Michael Nelson** • Department of Special Education, University of Kentucky, Lexington, Kentucky 40506.

behavior change without generalization is merely the implementation of prosthetic rather than therapeutic control. If students do not continue to emit newly acquired behaviors following the completion of training or are unable to perform these new behaviors in settings other than those in which they were initially trained, these learned behaviors have, in most cases, little functional value. If behavior change is not durable across time and settings, applied behavior analysis will "probably cease to exist by default because it will not have provided permanent solutions to social problems" (Holman, 1977, p. 79).

Much of the early applied behavior analysis research in education either failed to address the issue of generalization altogether or approached it from a procedural point of view in terms that Stokes and Baer (1977) described as "train and hope." Early research addressing generalization, as well as many current studies, may be characterized by an emphasis on changing target behaviors in treatment settings, and hoping for serendipitous maintenance and generalization of the behavior once training or intervention is completed. In fact, the most frequent strategy for assessing generalization in the 270 applied behavior analysis studies reviewed by Stokes and Baer (1977) consisted of post hoc reports of unplanned generalization effects. In a more recent analysis of behavioral intervention research literature with seriously emotionally disturbed children, Nelson and Rutherford (1987) found that of the 48 studies they analyzed, 31 addressed the issue of maintenance and generalization; however, 19 of these studies only assessed these effects. An emphasis on generalization effects appears to be increasing in the applied behavior analysis literature since Stokes and Baer (1977) called for a "technology of generalization," but the evidence for planned and programmed generalization remains insufficient and scattered.

The purpose of this chapter is to review the maintenance and generalization literature in education since Stokes and Baer (1977) outlined a technology of generalization. The questions addressed are: (a) Has this technology developed in the past decade? (b) Have behavior analysts established maintenance and generalization procedures that enable students to perform socially and academically effective behaviors beyond the controlled settings where these behaviors were initially trained or taught? (c) What strategies contribute to the technology of maintenance and generalization? and (d) What are the barriers to the development of effective procedures for ensuring the maintenance and generalization of behavior change in educational settings?

Definitions

Generality, or the maintenance and generalization of newly acquired behaviors following treatment, can be measured through several means. "A behavior change may be said to have generality if it proves durable over time, if it appears in a wide variety of possible environments, or if it spreads to a wide variety of related behaviors" (Baer *et al.*, 1968, p. 96). These aspects of generality are equivalent to the terms response maintenance, stimulus generalization, and response generalization.

Response Maintenance

Response maintenance involves the continuation of behavior in treatment settings following the withdrawal of an intervention program. Response maintenance of behavioral procedures is measured in terms of the strength or durability of learned behaviors once the initial contingencies are withdrawn.

This durability or persistence of behavior across time when treatment variables are no longer in effect is a crucial issue for behaviorists and educators (Warren, 1977). Achieving maintenance involves designing therapeutic environments where change continues beyond treatment conditions, as opposed simply to designing prosthetic environments where behavioral change is manifested only when treatment conditions are in effect.

Stimulus Generalization

Stimulus generalization, or transfer of training, refers to those situations where behaviors are emitted in settings or in the presence of stimuli other than those in which they were originally taught. This generalization across situations involves the continuation or transfer of behaviors to new settings or to new teachers. Stimulus generalization occurs when behavior that is modified in one stimulus situation generalizes to stimuli that are not directly associated with treatment contingencies (Sulzer-Azaroff & Mayer, 1977). This has been referred to as a spread of effects to other stimulus situations.

In education, applied behavior analysts are concerned with the generalization and transfer of behaviors to other classrooms and settings as well as the transfer of these behaviors to the control of other teachers or trainers. For example, mainstreaming exceptional students from special to regular classrooms often involves programming stimulus generalization (Rose, Lessen, & Gottlieb, 1982). In education, the purpose of generalization programming is to transfer behaviors learned in special treatment settings to regular classrooms or other less restrictive environments.

Response Generalization

Response generalization involves a change in behaviors not specifically planned for in the original intervention program. This concomitant or concurrent behavior change involves alterations in behaviors in the same response class as the target behaviors, but these behaviors have not received the treatment intervention. This generalization across behaviors involves changes in untrained responses that covary with changes in trained responses. It is a spread of effects to other classes of behavior from the class of behavior that is modified (Sulzer-Azaroff & Mayer, 1977).

The spread of effects to related behaviors not originally targeted for behavior change is a fundamental concern of all educators. Without such generalization, instruction would involve tedious repetition of learning trails across every single behavior. The literature on language training and generalized imitative behavior illustrates the importance of response generalization (Garcia, 1974; Garcia, Bullet, & Rust, 1977).

Stimulus Control

Stimulus control is said to occur when antecedent stimuli systematically affect or control the probability that behavior will occur. The purpose of maintenance and generalization programming of behavior across time, situations, or behaviors is to weaken stimulus control in the training setting and expand the control of behavior to stimuli in the maintenance and generalization setting.

Applied behavior analysis research has demonstrated repeatedly that students' academic and social behaviors can be brought under stimulus control in a variety of structured classroom environments. The problem with regard to maintenance and generalization of these behaviors is one of either transferring the controlling discriminative stimuli to new classroom settings or shifting stimulus control to other discriminative stimuli in these new classroom settings.

The following review of the research literature on generality of behavior change in educational settings focuses on the strategies behavioral researchers have implemented to shift stimulus control from training to natural learning environments. We present an analysis of the literature that has contributed to a technology of generalization (Stokes & Baer, 1977) to promote the transfer of social and academic behaviors in education.

Review Methodology

The initial context of this review was established by previous reviews and summaries of behavioral research in the literature pertaining to the maintenance and generalization of behavior change. First, we reviewed 53 secondary sources, for example, texts and review articles, that directly addressed maintenance and generalization in education. We then attempted to update this data base through a comprehensive ERIC search of literature pertaining to behavioral interventions in educational settings which addressed the issues of maintenance and generalization. Concurrently, we undertook a systematic search of published educational maintenance and generalization research since 1977 in the following journal indexes: the *American Journal of Mental Deficiency; Behavioral Disorders; Behavior Modification; Behavior Therapy; Child and Family Behavior Therapy; Education and Treatment of Children; Education and Training of the Mentally Retarded; Journal of Applied Behavior Analysis; Journal of the Association for Persons with Severe Handicaps* (formerly the *AAESPH Review*); *Journal of Autism and Developmental Disorders* (formerly the *Journal of Autism and Childhood Schizophrenia*); *Journal of Learning Disabilities; Journal of Special Education Technology; Journal of School Psychology; Learning Disabilities Quarterly;* and *Remedial and Special Education* (formerly *Exceptional Education Quarterly*). Articles meeting the following research and procedural criteria were selected for inclusion:

1. Subjects were preschool, elementary, and secondary students who initially exhibited social or academic behavioral excesses or deficits.
2. One or more behavioral intervention procedures were used.
3. Intervention, maintenance, and generalization procedures were school based, or were applied to behavior occurring in school and/or affecting school performance.
4. A valid single-subject or control group experimental design was used.
5. An objective data base of direct measures of overt behavior was employed.

Eighty-seven articles were identified that addressed maintenance and generalization in educational settings. These articles were drawn from the approximately 5,300 articles published in the surveyed journals between 1977 and the present. These primary sources were divided into those articles reporting studies that dealt with normal or mildly handicapped students and articles that reported studies that dealt with moderately or severely handicapped students. Thirty-eight articles containing 46 studies fell into the former category; 51 articles containing 57 studies fell into the latter category.

A number of components and characteristics of each study were identified and analyzed in an attempt to determine commonalities and differences among the studies in each group. These components and characteristics included: (a) the subject(s) of the study and the setting(s) where intervention, maintenance, and generalization procedures occurred; (b) the target behaviors that were the focus of the intervention, maintenance, and generalization procedures employed; (c) the initial intervention procedures in the training setting, including the types of reinforcers used; (d) the group or single-subject design used to assess the effects of the initial intervention; (e) the outcome of the intervention in the training setting (successful: behavior change across settings, subjects, responses, stimulus conditions, or time; partially successful: some behavior change across settings, subjects, responses, stimulus conditions, or time; unsuccessful: failure to achieve behavior change across settings, subjects, responses, stimulus conditions, or time); (f) methods used to assess maintenance and generalization effects (i.e., across settings, subjects, responses, stimuli, or time); (g) whether specific maintenance and generalization procedures were employed and the types of procedures used; and (h) the outcome of the study in terms of maintenance and generalization of the target behaviors (successful: significant behavior change over pretest or baseline conditions; partially successful: significant behavior change for some target behaviors or for some subjects over pretest or baseline conditions; unsuccessful: no significant behavior change over pretest or baseline conditions).

Results

Studies with Normal or Mildly Handicapped Students

The components and characteristics of studies that reported maintenance and generalization of normal and mildly handicapped students' behaviors are reported in Table 1. In 23 of the 46 studies, training and maintenance and generalization took place in regular preschool or elementary school classrooms; 16 measured training, maintenance, and generalization in special resource, self-contained, or clinic classrooms or settings, and in nine studies training took place in special settings with maintenance and generalization effects measured in regular classrooms or in the home. A variety of academic and social behaviors were targeted for modification. Specific academic skills, such as reduction in subtraction inversion errors, words read correctly, improvisation with tools, comprehension and production of correct coin labels, oral and written spelling performance, handwriting, and multiplication, division, and subtraction problems correct were modified, and maintenance and generalization of these skills were assessed. The specific social behaviors targeted for modification and maintenance and generalization assessment included classroom survival skills, on-task behaviors, appropriate verbal behaviors, reduction in classroom disruptive behaviors, social cooperation, sharing and peer proximity responses, cues to others to invite praise, appropriate peer tutoring behaviors, and correspondence between saying and doing.

The intervention procedures employed in this group of studies included a number of behavior change strategies used in combination with a variety of reinforcers. Cuing, demonstration, modeling, rehearsal, feedback, and role playing; teacher, self-, and peer reinforcement; packaged intervention programs such as PASS, PREP, and PEERS; and correspondence training, behavioral contracting, and the good behavior game were implemented in conjunction with a variety of edible, tangible, activity, monetary, token, or social reinforcers to change target behaviors.

Experimental designs used in these studies included control group and single-subject designs. Withdrawal or reversal designs, multielement designs, and multiple-baseline designs across settings, behaviors, subjects, trainers, instructional programs, and tutor–tutee dyads were employed. Two of the studies (Barton & Ascione, 1979; Greenwood Hops, & Walker, 1977) used a control group, 16 studies implemented a reversal or withdrawal phase, three studies employed a multielement design, and 27 studies used a multiple-baseline design either singly or in combination with other designs to analyze treatment effects.

The outcome of the intervention procedure on target behaviors in the training setting was overwhelmingly successful in the studies analyzed in this group. Forty-five of the studies reported successful outcomes and only Fantuzzo and Clement (1981) reported a partially successful outcome where successful behavior change was achieved for six of the nine subjects in the study.

A variety of procedures were used to assess maintenance and generalization in this group of studies. Twenty-seven studies initiated maintenance and generalization probes across settings either concurrently or immediately following training (stimulus generalization); 16 studies probed across similar responses (response generalization); six studies probed across trainers or probers (stimulus generalization); one study probed across instructional tasks; and 26 studies probed across time with a range of follow-up measures from three sessions to 10 months following the completion of the intervention program (response maintenance). Fifteen studies provided follow-up data for 3 weeks or less, eight studies reported approximately one month follow-up, and 11 studies reported from one and one-half to 10-month follow-up data.

The procedures implemented to establish maintenance and generalization of the behav-

Table 1. Studies Reporting Maintenance and Generalization: Normal and Mildly Handicapped

Authors/ date	Subjects/ settings	Target behaviors	Intervention procedures	Design	Outcome in training setting	Maintenance/ generalization assessment	Maintenance/ generalization procedure	Maintenance/ generalization outcome
Greenwood, Hops, & Walker (1977)	60 1st–3rd-grade students. Regular classrooms.	Survival skills (attending to task, working, volunteering and looking around).	PASS Program with token and social reinforcers.	Control group	Successful: Survival skills increased significantly for PASS group.	Across settings and time (9-week follow-up).	Programmed indiscriminable contingencies (increased schedule requirements, thinned reinforcers, natural setting and teacher praise, and faded reinforcers and program materials).	Successful: Survival skills maintained across time for PASS group.
Marholin & Steinman (1977)	4 10–12-year-old academic and behavior problem males and 4 10–12-year-old academic and behavior problem females. Regular classrooms.	On-task academic rate and accuracy and disruptive behaviors.	Token reinforcers.	ABCBC	Successful: On-task, academic rate and accuracy increased.	Across settings (teacher present or absent).	Probed but not programmed.	Partially successful: On-task did not maintain but academic rate and accuracy maintained in teacher's absence.
Polirstok & Greer (1977)	8th-grade behavior problem female. Regular classrooms.	Student verbal and nonverbal approval/ disapproval of teachers.	Tape-recorded cues and token reinforcers.	ABABA	Successful: Student approval of teachers increased.	Across time (6-week follow-up)	Probed but not programmed.	Successful: Students' approval responses maintained across time.
Blankenship (1978)	7 male and 2 female 9–11-year-old learning disabled students. Special day school classroom.	Subtraction inversion errors.	Demonstration plus feedback.	AB with follow-up condition.	Successful: Inversions decreased for all subjects.	Across responses and time (15 and 29 or 30-day follow-up).	Trained multiple exemplars.	Partially successful: 5 of 9 students' responses generalized to each of the uninstructed problem types and maintained across time.

Diaddigo & Dickie (1978)	10-year-old emotionally disturbed male. Special residential school classroom.	Classroom behavior points earned.	Contract for contingent home visits.	ABAB	Successful: Classroom behavior points increased.	Across responses.	Probed but no programmed.	Successful: Generalization across points and completion of academic assignments.
Epstein & Goss (1978)	10-year-old disruptive male. Regular classroom.	Talking-out, in-seat and on-task behaviors.	Token reinforcers.	ABABCD	Successful: Disruptive behaviors decreased.	Across time (6-week follow-up).	Mediated generalization (self-control).	Successful: Nondisruptive behaviors maintained across time.
Jenkins, Barksdale, & Clinton (1978)	3 11-year-old learning disabled males. Resource and regular classrooms.	Words read correctly per minute and percent correct comprehension.	Monetary reinforcers.	ABAB and multiple baseline across settings and behaviors.	Successful: Reading comprehension increased.	Across settings, responses, and time (8-week follow-up).	Probed but not programmed.	Partially successful: Minimal generalization from reading comprehension to reading rate but generalization from resource to regular classroom increased for 1 student and maintenance across time occurred for 2 of the 3 students.
Parsonson & Baer (1978)	2 male and 1 female 3-year-old normal students and 2 male 5- and 6-year-old language and behavior problem students. University preschool classroom.	Improvise with tools.	Trained with multiple exemplars and distractors.	Multiple baseline across behaviors and subjects.	Successful: Improvisations increased.	Across responses and time (up to 12 session and 3-month follow-up).	Trained multiple exemplars and trained to generalize.	Successful: Improvisations generalized within the trained class and maintained across time.
Reisinger (1978)	1 male and 2 female 3- and 4-year-old disruptive oppositional students. Special preschool classroom.	Cooperative behavior and proximity to peers.	Activity reinforcers.	ABAB and multiple baseline across subjects.	Successful: Cooperative behavior and proximity to peers increased.	Across settings (concurrent).	Probed but not programmed.	Successful: Cooperative responses and proximity to peers increased in free play setting.

(*continued*)

Table 1. (*Continued*)

Authors/ date	Subjects/ settings	Target behaviors	Intervention procedures	Design	Outcome in training setting	Maintenance/ generalization assessment	Maintenance/ generalization procedure	Maintenance/ generalization outcome
Stokes, Fowler, & Baer (1978)	3 male and 1 female 4- and 5-year-old normal students. University preschool classroom.	Cues to trainer inviting praise.	Instructions, role-playing, feedback and social reinforcers.	Multiple baseline across subjects.	Successful: Student cues to trainer increased.	Across settings and probers.	Introduced to natural community of reinforcers (recruiting teacher praise and reinforcement).	Successful: Cuing generalized across settings and probers.
	4 6-year-old academic and behavior problem males. Regular preschool classroom.	Cues to probers inviting praise.	Same as Exp. 1.	Same as Exp. 1.	Successful: Student cues to probers increased.	Same as Exp. 1.	Same as Exp. 1.	Successful: Cuing generalized across settings and probers.
Barton & Ascione (1979)	32 3–5-year-old normal students. University preschool classrooms.	Verbal and physical sharing.	Instructions, modeling, behavioral rehearsal, prompting, and social reinforcers.	ABA plus control group.	Successful: Verbal and physical sharing increased.	Across settings (concurrent), responses, and time (4-week follow-up).	Probed but not programmed.	Partially successful: Stimulus generalization, response maintenance, and response generalization were treatment and response specific.
Holman & Baer (1979)	2 male and 1 female 3–7-year-old normal students and 2 male and 1 female 3–7-year-old academic and behavior problem student. Special and regular classrooms.	On-task, off-task and disruptive behaviors.	Self-monitoring bracelet plus social reinforcers.	Multiple baseline across subjects plus reversal in follow-up.	Successful: Time on-task increased and disruptive behavior decreased. Off-task decreased for normal students only.	Across settings (concurrent) and time (5-and 10-month follow-up).	Mediated generalization (self-monitoring).	Successful: Responses generalized to classroom setting and maintained across time.

Sanok & Striefel (1979)	11-year-old electively mute female. Clinic, home and regular classroom.	Verbal responses.	Monetary reinforcers and response cost.	Multiple baseline across behaviors, settings and trainers.	Successful: 4 of 5 verbal responses increased.	Across settings (concurrent), responses, probers, and time (10 month follow-up).	Programmed indiscriminable contingencies (stimulus fading).	Successful: Verbal responses generalized across responses, to novel settings and to new individuals and maintained across time.
Anderson & Redd (1980)	2 male and 2 female 6-year-old distractible and reading deficient students. Regular classroom.	Appropriate verbal, motor and orientation behaviors and correct verbalization and matching.	Individual tutoring with prompts and social reinforcers.	Multi-element.	Successful: Social and academic behaviors increased.	Across settings.	Programmed indiscriminable contingencies (faded prompts and reinforcement during instruction, faded teacher presence and programmed intermittent reinforcement).	Successful: Social and academic responses generalized across settings.
Cuvo & Riva (1980)	5 male and 5 female ($\bar{X}$ age = 16.2 years) mentally retarded and 6 male and 4 female ($\bar{X}$ age = 4.4 years) normal students. Special schools or institutions.	Coin label comprehension and production.	Modeling training, proficiency testing and rehearsal plus social and tangible reinforcers.	Three factor mixed design plus multiple baseline across behaviors.	Successful: Coin comprehension and production increased for all subjects.	Across responses and time (1 and 4-weeks follow-up).	Probed but not programmed.	Successful: Generalization across responses (comprehension to production and production to comprehension repsonses) and maintained across time.
Fenrick & McDonnell (1980)	Male 15-year-old and 3 female 12–13-year-old normal peer "teachers." 2 male 12- and 13-year-old and 2 female 6- and 13-year-old trainable retarded students. Special school classroom.	Appropriate peer teaching behaviors.	Modeling and feedback for peer teaching behaviors.	Multiple baseline across subjects (peer teachers) and across instructional programs.	Successful: Appropriate peer teaching behaviors increased.	Across instructional tasks.	Probed but not programmed.	Successful: Peer teaching responses generalized across to untrained instructional tasks.

(continued)

Table 1. (*Continued*)

Authors/ date	Subjects/ settings	Target behaviors	Intervention procedures	Design	Outcome in training setting	Maintenance/ generalization assessment	Maintenance/ generalization procedure	Maintenance/ generalization outcome
Reese & Filipczak (1980)	4 8th- and 9th-grade normal students. Regular classrooms.	Attendance and work rate.	PREP Program with contracted reinforcers.	ABA	Successful: Attendance and work rate increased.	Across settings, responses, and time (3-week, 4-week and 1-month follow-up).	Probed but not programmed.	Successful: Attendance and work rate generalized across settings, responses and maintained across time.
Anderson-Inman (1981)	12-year-old behavior and academic problem female. Resource and regular classrooms.	Oral and written spelling performance.	Individualized spelling instruction in resource classroom.	ABAB	Successful: Spelling performance improved.	Across settings (concurrent).	Programmed common stimuli (spelling materials).	Successful: Spelling performance generalized across settings.
Baer, Holman, Stokes, Fowler, & Rowbury (1981)	4 male and 2 female 3–7-year-old normal and behavior problem students. University preschool classrooms and experimental room.	On-task, off-task and disruptive behaviors.	Self-monitoring (bead bracelet) plus social reinforcers.	Multiple baseline across subjects.	Successful: On-task increased and off-task and disruptive behaviors decreased.	Across settings (concurrent) and time (5-month and 3-month follow-up).	Mediated generalization (self-control).	Successful: Increased on-task and reduced off-task and disruptive responses generalized across settings and maintained across time.
	3 male and 1 female 4–5-year-old normal students. University preschool classroom.	Social interaction (student cues and and teacher praise). Academic production (handwriting tasks).	Role-playing, feedback, and social and tangible (toy) reinforcers.	Same as Exp. 1.	Successful: Cues and correct handwriting tasks completed increased.	Across trainers.	Introduced to natural community of reinforcers.	Successful: Social interaction and handwriting generalized across trainers.

Barton & Bevirt (1981)	6 male and 5 female 3–5-year-old normal students. Headstart summer preschool classroom.	Sharing with other children.	Verbal instructions, modeling, rehearsal, prompts and social reinforcers.	ABA	Successful: Sharing increased.	Across subjects (trained and nontrained pairs).	Programmed common stimuli (peers).	Successful: Sharing generalized across subjects.
Fantuzzo & Clement (1981)	10 7–9-year-old second grade normal students. Child development clinic classroom.	Attending, glancing and academic achievement.	Teacher and self-administered edible, social and token reinforcers.	ABAB	Partially successful: Attending and academic achievement increased and glancing decreased for 6 of 9 subjects.	Across subjects, responses, and subject-responses.	Mediated generalization (self-control).	Successful: Self-administered contingencies promoted generalization across subjects, responses and subject-responses.
Fishbein & Wasik (1981)	25 fourth-grade "disruptive" students. Regular school library.	Task-relevant, off-task and disruptive behaviors.	Good behavior game - teams earned token reinforcers exchangable for teacher time.	ABCB (C = game but no reinforcers).	Successful: Task-relevant behaviors increased and off-task and disruptive behaviors decreased.	Across settings.	Probed but not programmed.	Successful: Increased task relevant and reduced off-task and disruptive behaviors generalized across settings.
Fowler & Baer (1981)	2 4–5-year-old behavor problem females and 2 female and 3 male 4–5-year-old normal students. University preschool classroom and experimental room.	Offers to share, activity praise, study posture and conversation to target peers.	Early vs. late feedback with token and tangible (toy) reinforcers.	Multiple baseline across subjects.	Successful: Social behaviors increased in contingent settings.	Across settings.	Programmed indiscriminable contingencies (delayed reinforcement).	Successful: Social responses generalized across settings.

(continued)

Table 1. (*Continued*)

Authors/ date	Subjects/ settings	Target behaviors	Intervention procedures	Design	Outcome in training setting	Maintenance/ generalization assessment	Maintenance/ generalization procedure	Maintenance/ generalization outcome
Lebsock & Salzberg (1981)	15-year-old male and 14-year-old female behavior disordered students. Special classroom.	Denial, talking back and verbal reaction.	Role-playing, feedback and social reinforcers.	Multiple baseline across behaviors and subjects.	Successful: Criterion of decreased inappropriate verbal behaviors reached on role-playing probes.	Across settings (concurrent) and time (10-and 12-day follow-up).	Sequential modification (intervention transferred to generalization setting for 8 of 9 sessions).	Successful: Reduced inappropriate verbal responses generalized across settings and maintained across time.
Lloyd, Saltzman, & Kauffman (1981)	4 male 8–9-year-old learing disabled students. Special self-contained classroom.	Multiplication problems correct.	Preskills, strategy, and cue training with token reinforcers.	Multiple baseline across subjects.	Successful: Multiplication problems correct increased.	Across responses and time (3-session follow-up).	Mediated generalization (self-instruction).	Successful: Multiplication problems correct generalized across responses and maintained across time.
	3 male 8–9-year-old learning disabled students. Special self-contained classroom.	Division problems correct.	Same as Exp. 1.	Same as Exp. 1.	Successful: Division problems correct increased.	Across responses and time (4-session follow-up).	Same as Exp. 1.	Successful: Division problems correct generalized across responses and maintained across time.
Berler, Gross, & Drabman (1982)	6 male 8–10-year-old learning disabled students. Special day school classroom.	Eye contact and appropriate verbal content with peers.	Social skills training with peer trainers.	Multiple baseline across behaviors plus control group.	Successful: Eye contact and appropriate verbalizations increased.	Across trainers, settings, and time (1-month follow-up).	Trained multiple exemplars and programmed common stimuli (peers).	Partially successful: Eye contact and appropriate verbal content generalized across trainers and maintained across time but did not generalize across settings.
Blankenship & Baumgartner (1982)	5 male and 4 female 8–11-year-old learning disabled stu-	Percent of correctly computed subtrac-	Demonstration and modeling plus feed-	Multiple baseline across subjects.	Successful: Percent of subtraction problems	Across settings and time (2-week fol-	Probed but not programmed.	Partially successful: Increased percent of subtraction problems correct gener-

	dents. Resource room, cafeteria, and another room in elementary school.	tion problems.	back and token reinforcers.		correct increased.	low-up).		alized across settings and maintained across time for 3 of 9 subjects.
	6 students from Exp. 1 whose behavior failed to generalize.	Same as Exp. 1.	Same as Exp. 1.	ABA	Successful: Percent of subtraction problems correct increased.	Same as Exp. 1.	Trained to generalize, trained multiple exemplars, mediated generalization (used a verbal rule) and programmed indiscriminable contingencies.	Partially successful: Increased percent of subtraction problems correct generalized across settings and maintained across time for 5 of the 6 remaining subjects.
Greer & Polirstok (1982)	3 male 14–15-year-old delinquent or predelinquent tutors and 15 8th-grade tutees. Remedial reading classroom.	Tutor's on-task and use of social reinforcers.	Peer tutoring plus token reinforcers.	Multiple baseline across subjects and ABCBC.	Successful: Tutor and tutee behaviors increased.	Across settings and time (2-week follow-up).	Probed but not programmed.	Successful: On-task and use of social reinforcers generalized across settings and maintained across time.
	3 male 13–16-year-old low reading/on-task tutors and 15 7th-grade tutees. Remedial reading classroom.	Tutor approval of tutees, tutee attention to tutors, reading responses of tutees, reading responses of tutors in own reading class, and SAT scores.	Same as Exp. 1.	Same as Exp. 1.	Successful: Tutor and tutee behaviors increased.	Same as Exp. 1.	Same as Exp. 1.	Successful: Tutor and tutee responses generalized across settings and maintained across time.

(*continued*)

Table 1. *(Continued)*

Authors/ date	Subjects/ settings	Target behaviors	Intervention procedures	Design	Outcome in training setting	Maintenance/ generalization assessment	Maintenance/ generalization procedure	Maintenance/ generalization outcome
Paine, Hops, Walker, Greenwood, Fleischman, & Guild (1982)	1 male and 2 female 1st- and 4th-grade socially withdrawn students. Recess period in regular school.	Increased peer interaction.	PEERS Program. Teacher-mediated peer pairing in academic or play setting in classroom with teacher social reinforcers for interacting.	ABABABA	Successful: Peer interaction increased.	Across time (6-month follow-up and during baselines).	Sequential modification (intervention "booster shots").	Unsuccessful: Social interaction failed to maintain across time.
	1 male and 1 female 1st-grade socially withdrawn students. Recess period in regular school.	Same as Exp. 1.	Same as Exp. 1.	Same as Exp. 1.	Successful: Peer interaction increased.	Same as Exp. 1.	Same as Exp. 1.	Partially successful: 1 of 2 subjects' social interaction maintained across time.
	1 male and 1 female 4th graders and 2 male 3rd-grade socially withdrawn students. Recess period in regular school.	Same as Exp. 1.	Same as Exp. 1.	Same as Exp. 1.	Successful: Peer interaction increased.	Across time (during baselines).	No intervention "booster shots."	Partially successful: 1 of 4 subjects' social interactions maintained across time.
Schumaker & Ellis (1982)	1 male and 2 female adolescent learning disabled students. High school resource classroom.	Social skills performed correctly.	Role-playing and individual instruction from teacher plus stu-	Modified multiple baseline across behaviors.	Successful: All social skills were mastered.	Across settings.	Probed but not programmed.	Partially successful: Some social skills generalized to contrived role-playing and natural environment.

			dent confederates (paid - monetary reinforcers) in natural setting.					
Stowitschek, Hecimovic, Stowitschek, & Shores (1982)	6 male and 6 female 14–17-year-old behaviorally disordered students. State psychiatric hospital classroom.	Peer tutor use of records and graphs and learner spelling performance.	Peer tutoring package using modeling.	Multiple baseline across tutor-tutee dyads.	Successful: Tutor record keeping and graphing and tutee spelling performance increased.	Across settings (dyads).	Trained multiple exemplars.	Partially successful: Some record keeping, graphing and spelling performance generalized across dyads.
Tofte-Tipps, Mendonca, & Peach (1982)	Male 11-year-old and female 14-year-old with poor interpersonal relationships. Outpatient psychology clinic.	Conversational skills.	Social skills training with instruction, role-playing, modeling, rehearsal and feedback.	Multiple baseline within children and across behaviors.	Successful: All social skills increased in training scenes.	Across settings (scenes), familiar and unfamiliar adults and peers, and across responses.	Probed but not programmed.	Partially successful: Majority of behaviors generalized across settings, adults and peers, and responses.
Baer, Osnes, & Stokes (1983)	4-year-old normal male. University preschool classroom.	Correspondence between "saying" and "doing" (pick up clothes after bath and choose fruit for dessert).	Correspondence training with social and tangible reinforcers (hugs, etc.).	Multiple baseline across behaviors.	Successful: Correspondence achieved between "saying" and "doing."	Across responses and time (8-day follow-up).	Programmed indiscriminable contingencies.	Successful: Correspondence generalized across responses and maintained across time.

(*continued*)

Table 1. (*Continued*)

Authors/ date	Subjects/ settings	Target behaviors	Intervention procedures	Design	Outcome in training setting	Maintenance/ generalization assessment	Maintenance/ generalization procedure	Maintenance/ generalization outcome
Larsson & Larsson (1983)	6-year-old electively mute female. Regular 1st-grade classroom.	Verbal responding in regular classroom.	Single-peer reading sessions.	Multi-element (baseline, treatment, probe).	Successful: Verbal behaviors increased.	Across settings (concurrent) and time (3-session follow-up).	Trained multiple exemplars (peer presence).	Successful: Verbal responding generalized across settings and maintained across time.
	11-year-old educable mentally retarded electively mute female. Regular classroom.	Verbal compliance and spontaneous verbal responses in group setting.	Same as Exp. 1.	Multi-element and multiple baseline across behaviors.	Successful: Appropriate verbal behaviors increased.	Across settings (concurrent), responses, and time (3-session follow-up).	Same as Exp. 1.	Successful: Appropriate verbal behaviors generalized across responses and settings and maintained across time.
Mitchell & Milan (1983)	4 male and 3 female 5-year-old noncompliant students. Regular preschool classrooom.	Prosocial behaviors (self-recording, cleaning-up, theme participation and group-time behavior).	Modeling and token, social and activity reinforcers.	Multiple baseline across subjects and behaviors.	Successful: Imitation of prosocial behaviors increased.	Across responses.	Trained to generalize.	Successful: Generalized imitation increased across responses.
Rhode, Morgan, & Young (1983)	6 6–10-year-old behaviorally disordered students. University resource and regular classrooms.	Appropriate classroom behavior.	Phase I-Training in resource room with token re-	Multiple baseline across pairs of subjects.	Successful: Appropriate classroom behaviors increased.	Across settings and time (23- to 32-day follow-up).	Mediated generalization (self-evaluation).	Partially successful: 4 of 6 subjects' appropriate classroom behaviors generalized across settings and

			inforcers and systematic verbal feedback plus self-evaluation training. Phase II - Self-evaluation training and fading.					maintained across time.
Baer, Williams, Osnes, & Stokes (1984)	3 male and 1 female 4–5-year-olds with low verbal correspondence. Regular preschool playroom.	Correspondence between "saying" and "doing" (play and social behaviors).	Correspondence training with token and activity reinforcers.	Multiple baseline across behaviors.	Successful: Correspondence between "saying" and "doing" increased.	Across responses and time.	Programmed indiscriminable contingencies (delayed reinforcement of verbalization generalization and maintenance).	Successful: Correspondence generalized across responses and maintained across time.
Stevenson & Fantuzzo (1984)	2 5th-grade disruptive male students. Regular classroom and home.	Math problems completed and disruptive behavior.	Self-control training with token reinforcers.	ABAB	Successful: Math problems completed increased and disruptive behavior decreased.	Across subjects, settings (concurrent), responses, and time (9 to 15-week follow-up).	Mediated generalization (self-control).	Partially successful: Math problems completed and reduced disruptive responses generalized across students, responses and settings and limited maintenance across time.

iors established in the training settings included a number of the generalization promotion techniques suggested by Stokes and Baer (1977). Fifteen of the studies probed for maintenance and/or generalization without specifically programming for these effects. The studies using this approach, which Stokes and Baer labeled train and hope (1977), reported either success (nine studies) or partial success (six studies) in terms of achieving generality of results.

The second generalization enhancement strategy identified by Stokes and Baer (1977), sequential modification, was used in three studies with normal or mildly handicapped students. Lebsock and Salzberg (1981) initiated the training intervention in the generalization setting for eight or nine sessions to facilitate successful generalization and maintenance across settings and time. Paine *et al.* (1982) successfully programmed maintenance of increased peer interaction by scheduling "booster shots" of the packaged PEERS intervention program following training. In a second study, one of the two subjects' social interactions with peers maintained following intervention booster shots (Paine *et al.*, 1982).

Stokes and Baer's (1977) third generalization promotion technique, introduction of the subject to natural maintaining contingencies, was employed in three of the studies in this group. These studies, contained in two articles (Stokes, Fowler, & Baer, 1978, and Baer, Holman, Stokes, Fowler, & Rowbury, 1981), reported success in training normal and academic and behavior problem preschool students to cue and recruit teacher praise and reinforcement. These responses generalized across trainers and settings.

Training sufficient exemplars, the fourth technique proposed by Stokes and Baer (1977) to promote generalization, was used in seven of the studies reported here. Four of these studies reported successful generalization and three studies were partially successful. Of the latter studies, five of nine students' correct subtraction responses generalized across uninstructed problem types (Blankenship, 1978), five of six students' correct subtraction responses generalized across settings and time (Blankenship & Baumgartner, 1982), and eye contact and appropriate verbal content with peers generalized across trainers and time but failed to generalize across settings (Berler, Gross, & Drabman, 1982).

The fifth generalization strategy is to train loosely: that is, train with relatively little control over the stimuli presented and the correct responses allowed. Stokes and Baer (1977) proposed several strategies for loosening experimental control, including training different examples concurrently, and varying instructions, discriminative stimuli, social reinforcers, and backup reinforcers. None of the studies reviewed here reported the use of this strategy. Stokes and Baer's (1977) study reasoned that very few examples of training loosely are found because this strategy represents the antithesis of typical behavioral studies where attempts are made to maintain thorough control and careful restriction and standardization of research and training procedures. Apparently, this tradition still holds true today.

Programming indiscriminable contingencies, Stokes and Baer's (1977) sixth strategy for promoting generalization, was reported in seven of the studies analyzed. Six of the seven studies reported successful maintenance and generalization of responses. In the only study reporting partial success, Blankenship and Baumgartner (1982) combined a programming-indiscriminable-contingencies strategy in a generalization package to maintain and generalize the percent of correctly computed subtraction problems by six learning disabled students. Five of the six subjects' responses maintained and generalized across settings and time.

The seventh strategy suggested by Stokes and Baer (1977) is to program common stimuli in the training and generalization settings. Three of the studies reviewed here implemented this strategy using peers (Barton &

Bevirt, 1981; Berler, Gross, & Drabman, 1982); and spelling materials (Anderson-Inman, 1981) as the stimuli common to both settings. The first two studies reported successful generalization of oral and written spelling performance across settings, and sharing with other children across subjects, respectively. Berler *et al.* (1982) reported maintenance and generalization across time and trainers but failed to achieve generalization across settings.

Stokes and Baer's (1977) eighth generalization enhancement technique is to mediate generalization where the subject is taught a response in the training setting that is likely to be used in other settings as well. Mediated generalization is commonly achieved by programming either specific verbal or language responses or self-control responses common to training and generalization settings. Nine studies employed this strategy. As part of a generalization package, Blankenship and Baumgartner (1982) programmed a common verbal rule in two settings to bring about the maintenance and generalization of correctly computed subtraction problems for five of six students. Self-evaluation, self-instruction, self-monitoring, and other self-control strategies were successfully used in promoting generalization in six of the studies employing these techniques. In two other self-control studies, Rhode, Morgan, and Young (1983) found that a self-evaluation strategy enhanced maintenance and generalization of appropriate classroom behaviors of four of the six subjects in their study. Stevenson and Fantuzzo (1984) found that self-control enhanced generalization across students, responses, and settings but provided only limited maintenance across time.

The final generalization strategy proposed by Stokes and Baer (1977) is to train to generalize, where the ability to generalize is reinforced as a discrete response. Three studies used this generalization promotion technique. Again, as part of Blankenship and Baumgartner's (1982) generalization package, five of the six subjects were successfully trained to generalize. Also, Parsonson and Baer (1978) were successful in training preschool students to improvise with various tools and maintain these improvisations across time. Improvisation was successfully reinforced as a generalization response. Mitchell and Milan (1983) increased and maintained prosocial behaviors through modeling plus reinforcement of generalized imitation as a response class.

Studies with Moderately or Severely Handicapped Students

The components and characteristics of the research studies which investigated the maintenance and generalization of moderately or severely handicapped students' behaviors are reported in Table 2. Four of these 57 studies were conducted in regular public school classrooms; 29 took place in special public school classrooms, special day schools, or special laboratory settings; nine studies conducted training sessions in special settings and measured maintenance and generalization of subjects' responses in a variety of home, regular classroom, or community settings; and 15 studies were conducted in residential schools and institutions.

A number of academic, language, social, and self-help, leisure, and community-living skills were modified in this group of studies. These included academic behaviors such as tracing, arithmetic computation, printing, phonics pronunciation, use of a ruler, and completing assembly tasks; language behaviors such as verbal imitation, abstraction, initiation, labeling, self-instructions, responses to commands and questions, requests, yes-no mands, and conversation and nonverbal signing; social and play behaviors such as sharing, cooperative behaviors, and initiating social interactions; self-help, leisure, and community-living skills such as putting on hearing aid, pinball, videogame, and vending machine operation; and inappropriate behaviors such as noncompliance, aggression, clothes strip-

Table 2. Studies Reporting Maintenance and Generalization: Moderately and Severely Handicapped

Authors/ date	Subjects/ settings	Target behaviors	Intervention procedures	Design	Outcome in training setting	Maintenance/ generalization assessment	Maintenance/ generalization procedure	Maintenance/ generalization outcome
Garcia, Bullet, & Rust (1977)	17-year-old TMR male and 17-year-old TMR female. Special classroom and home.	Labeling using complex sentences.	Imitation training plus token and social reinforcers.	Multiple baseline across subjects.	Successful: Complex sentences increased.	Across settings and trainers concurrent to training (probes).	Sequential modification.	Successful: But confounded by successive manipulations prior to generalization effect for the first trained response.
Kissel & Whitman (1977)	17-year-old profoundly retarded male. Residential treatment center	Play responses and self-stimulation.	Play training and overcorrection.	Multiple baseline across settings and behaviors.	Successful: Play increased and self-stimulation decreased.	Across settings and responses.	Sequential modification.	Partially successful: Play responses failed to generalize across settings but 2 of 3 self-stimulatory responses generalized across settings and responses.
Koegel & Rincover (1977)	3 autisitc 7–11-year-old autistic males. Special training laboratory.	Nonverbal imitation or following verbal instructions.	Edible and social reinforcers.	Multiple baseline across subjects.	Successful: Study began following initial acquisition.	Across settings and trainers concurrent to training.	Probed but not programmed.	Partially successful: Some generalized imitation and instruction following during treatment but no generalization after treatment.
	6 7–12-year-old autistic males. Special training laboratory.	Same as Exp. 1.	Same as Exp. 1.	Same as Exp. 1.	Successful: Study began following initial acquisition.	Across time (up to 500-trial follow-up).	Programmed indiscriminable contingencies (thinning reinforcement schedules in training setting and intermittent noncontingent reinforcers in extra-training setting).	Successful: Imitation and instruction following maintained across time.

Russo & Koegel (1977)	5-year-old autistic female. Regular classroom.	Social behavior, self-stimulation and verbal responses to command.	Token reinforcers, response-cost and verbal reprimands.	Multiple baseline across behaviors.	Successful: Social behaviors and verbal responses increased and self-stimulation decreased.	Across settings, trainers, and time (40- to 47-week follow-up).	Programmed common stimuli (trained teachers in posttreatment settings) and programmed indiscriminable contingencies (thinned reinforcement schedule in training setting).	Successful: Increased social and verbal responses and decreased self-stimulation generalized across settings, trainers and maintained across time.
Zifferblatt, Burton, Homer, & White (1977)	12 9–14-year-old autistic males. Special day school classroom.	Following instructions, washing, wiping bottom and sharing toys.	Token reinforcers.	AB	Successful: Following instructions, self-help and sharing behaviors increased.	Across settings.	Programmed indiscriminable contingencies (arranged similar though unreinforced trials in different settings).	Successful: Instruction-following, self-help and sharing behaviors generalized across settings.
Gable, Hendrickson, & Strain (1978)	11-year-old multihandicapped male and 10-year-old multihandicapped female. Special school classroom.	Approach gestures, positive physical contact and cooperative play.	Prompting and social reinforcers.	Equivalent time samples.	Successful: All social behaviors increased.	Across settings and time (5-day follow-up).	Programmed common stimuli (reinforced spontaneously exhibited previously trained behaviors).	Partially successful: Social behaviors partially generalized across settings and maintained across time.
Luiselli, Colozzi, Donellon, Helfen, & Pemberton (1978)	10-year-old moderately retarded male. Special classroom.	Appropriate verbal responses.	Token and social reinforcers.	Multiple baseline across behaviors.	Partially successful: 3 of 4 appropriate verbal responses increased.	Across responses, trainers, and time (1-month and 3-month follow-up).	Probed but not programmed.	Partially successful: Appropriate verbal responses failed to generalize across responses but generalized across trainers and maintained across time for 3 of 4 responses.
Marholin & Townsend (1978)	10-year-old autistic female. Residential school.	Self-stimulatory behaviors.	Overcorrection (physical restraint).	ABCB	Successful: Self-stimulation decreased.	Across settings (concurrent).	Probed but not programmed.	Unsuccessful: Reduction in self-stimulation failed to generalize across settings.

(*continued*)

Table 2. (*Continued*)

Authors/ date	Subjects/ settings	Target behaviors	Intervention procedures	Design	Outcome in training setting	Maintenance/ generalization assessment	Maintenance/ generalization procedure	Maintenance/ generalization outcome
Mithaug (1978)	16-year-old severely retarded male. Special school.	Instruction-following responses to preposition-noun combinations.	Direct instruction and social reinforcers.	Multiple baseline across behaviors.	Successful: Instruction following increased.	Across responses.	Programmed indiscriminable contingencies (trained to relevant and irrelevant verbal cues).	Successful: Instruction-following generalized to untrained instructions.
Panyan & Hall (1978)	19- and 22-year-old severely retarded females. Residential school.	Vocal imitation and tracing.	Concurrent and serial training with edible and social reinforcers.	ABAB	Partially successful: Both subjects reached criterion on vocal imitation and one subject reached criterion on tracing.	Across responses and time (1-, 2-, and 6-month follow-up).	Sequential modification.	Partially successful: Generalization increased after concurrent training but decreased or remained the same after serial training.
Whitman, Hurley, Johnson, & Christian (1978)	10-year-old severely retarded male. Residential institution.	Following instructions, noncompliance, inappropriate manipulation of objects, aggression, clothes stripping, and inappropriate verbalizations.	Edible and social reinforcers plus physical restraint.	ABAB and multiple baseline across behaviors.	Successful: Instruction following increased and noncompliance and inappropriate manipulation of objects decreased.	Across responses and time (2-, 5-, and 16-week follow-up).	Trained multiple exemplars.	Partially successful: Reduced aggression and clothes stripping generalized but inappropriate vocalizations, instruction-following, noncompliance and inappropriate manipulation of objects remained at training levels.

Coleman, Whitman, & Johnson (1979)	17-year-old profoundly retarded male. Residential institution.	Appropriate play and self-stimulation.	Edible reinforcers and overcorrection.	Multiple baseline across trainers and settings.	Successful: Appropriate play increased and self-stimulation decreased.	Across settings (concurrent) and trainers.	Programmed common stimuli (teacher behaviors and materials) and sequential modification.	Unsuccessful: Increased appropriate play and decreased self-stimulation failed to generalize across settings or trainers.
Halle, Marshall, & Spradlin (1979)	5 male and 1 female 11–15-year-old severely and profoundly retarded students. Residential institution dining facility.	Meal requests.	15-second delay in giving subject food tray plus modeling.	Multiple baseline across settings and subjects.	Successful: Meal requests increased.	Across settings (concurrent) and trainers.	Programmed indiscriminable stimulus (15 second delay).	Partially successful: 4 of 5 subjects requested meals across trainers and 3 of 4 subjects requested meals across trainers and meals.
Handleman (1979)	4 6–7-year-old autistic males. University special school and home.	Verbal repsonses to specified questions.	Training in restricted vs multiple-natural settings with edible and social reinforcers.	Multiple baseline across sets of questions and settings.	Successful: Verbal responses increased.	Across settings.	Programmed common stimuli (multiple-natural settings).	Successful: 1 subject's verbal responses generalized across a restricted setting to home and 3 subjects' responses generalized across multiple-natural settings to home.
Kohl, Karlan, & Heal (1979)	4 11–16-year-old severely handicapped students. Residential facility.	Following instructions.	Pair manual signs with verbal instructions plus social reinforcers.	3 × 3 Latin square.	Successful: Instructions followed correctly increased.	Across responses.	Probed but not programmed.	Partially successful: Generalization of receptive training to expressive behaviors varied among students and instructional conditions.
Peterson, Austin, & Lang (1979)	1 male and 2 female visually impaired, severly and profoundly retarded adolescents. Special classroom.	Motor-gestural and vocal-verbal social behaviors to peers.	Prompting and social reinforcers.	Multiple baseline across subjects and ABAB.	Successful: Peer directed social behaviors increased.	Across settings (concurrent).	Probed but not programmed.	Successful: Peer directed social responses increased in generalization setting.

(continued)

Table 2. (*Continued*)

Authors/ date	Subjects/ settings	Target behaviors	Intervention procedures	Design	Outcome in training setting	Maintenance/ generalization assessment	Maintenance/ generalization procedure	Maintenance/ generalization outcome
Strain, Kerr, & Ragland (1979)	3 male and 1 female 9–10 year-old autistic students. Special school classroom.	Motor-gestural and vocal-verbal social behaviors to peers.	Peer trainers. Prompting, social reinforcers and social initiations.	ABAC and ACAB.	Successful: Peer directed social behaviors increased.	Across settings (concurrent).	Probed but not programmed.	Unsuccessful: Peer directed social responses did not generalize across settings.
Burgio, Whitman, & Johnson (1980)	2 male and 3 female 9–14-year-old mentally retarded students. Special classroom.	Self-instructional verbalizations, off-task and arithmetic, printing and phonics performance tasks.	Self-instruction training with modeling and distractors plus social reinforcers.	Multiple baseline across subjects.	Successful: Self-instructional and academic behaviors increased.	Across settings, subjects, responses, and time (15-day follow-up).	Mediated generalization (self-instruction).	Partially successful: Self-instruction and academic responses generalized across settings and maintained across time but did not generalize across subjects and responses.
Dorow (1980)	15-year-old severely retarded female. Residential training center.	Following commands.	Edible, music and social reinforcers plus ignoring.	Multiple baseline across behaviors plus ABA.	Successful: Following instructions increased in all conditions.	Across responses, reinforcers, and time (9-day follow-up).	Probed but not programmed.	Successful: Following commands generalized across behaviors and reinforcers and generalized across time.
Handleman & Harris (1980)	3 6–9-year-old autistic males. University special school and home.	Verbal responses to sequential questions.	Training in restricted *vs* multiple natural settings with edible and social reinforcers.	Multiple baseline across sets of questions plus counter-balanced design across training conditions.	Successful: Verbal responses increased.	Across settings (concurrent).	Programmed common stimuli (multiple-natural settings).	Successful: Verbal responses generalized across multiple-natural settings to home.

Hung (1980)	8-year-old autistic male and 10-year-old autistic female. Special classrooms.	Yes/no mands in response to offered food.	Prompting, modeling and fading plus social and edible reinforcers.	ABAB	Successful: Yes/no mands reached criterion.	Across stimuli and time (12 and 21 blocks of trials follow-up).	Probed but not programmed.	Successful: Yes/no mands generalized across stimuli and maintained across time.
Smeege, Page, Iwata, & Ivancic (1980)	3 17–23-year-old moderately retarded and emotionally impaired students. Multihandicap center classroom.	Use of ruler for measuring.	Task analysis with component instruction plus social reinforcers.	Multiple baseline across behaviors.	Successful: Correct measuring behaviors increased.	Across responses and time (2 to 3 week follow-up).	Probed but not programmed.	Partially successful: Use of rules generalized across behaviors for 2 of 3 subjects but was not maintained across time.
Tucker & Berry (1980)	5 male and 1 female 15–22-year-old severely multiply handicapped students. Residential institution.	Putting on hearing aids.	"No help," verbal instruction, demonstration and physical guidance plus social reinforcers.	Multiple baseline across subjects and multiple probe.	Successful: Putting on hearing aids increased.	Across settings, trainers, and time (3-week follow-up).	Probed but not programmed.	Partially successful: Putting on hearing aids generalized across settings for 4 of 6 subjects and maintained across time.
Wacker, Carroll, & Moe (1980)	2 male and 2 female 6–9-year-old trainable mentally retarded students. Special summer program.	Assembling a three-piece tagboard figure.	Train to verbalize task components plus social reinforcers.	Multiple baseline across subjects.	Successful: Number of correct assemblies increased.	Across settings and time (3–6-day follow-up).	Probed but not programmed.	Successful: Assembly task completion generalized across settings and maintained across time.
Welch & Pear (1980)	2 male 6- and 9-year-old and 2 female 5- and 14-year-old moderately retarded students. Residential center.	Naming objects.	Train using picture-cards, photographs or real objects with edible reinforcers.	ABCABC	Successful: Object naming increased.	Across stimulus modalities.	Programmed common stimuli (real objects) and trained multiple exemplars.	Partially successful: Generalized naming across all stimulus modalities for 1 subject and to real objects when trained with real objects for 3 of 4 subjects.

(*continued*)

Table 2. (*Continued*)

Authors/ date	Subjects/ settings	Target behaviors	Intervention procedures	Design	Outcome in training setting	Maintenance/ generalization assessment	Maintenance/ generalization procedure	Maintenance/ generalization outcome
Burger, Blackman, & Clark (1981)	43 male and 37 female educable mentally retarded children and adolescents. Public schools.	Verbal abstraction strategies.	Strategy training using self-instruction and modeling plus social reinforcers.	Control group.	Successful: Abstraction scores increased.	Across settings (stimuli) and time (2- to 3-day and 7- to 10-day follow-up).	Probed but not programmed.	Successful: Use of verbal abstraction strategies generalized across settings (stimuli) and maintained across time.
Coon, Vogelsberg, & Williams (1981)	20-year-old moderately to severely handicapped female. Special classroom and public buses.	Bus boarding and bus departing skill sequences.	Verbal instructions, modeling and social reinforcers.	Multiple baseline across behaviors and settings.	Successful: Skill sequences mastered.	Across settings and time (5-session follow-up).	Probed but not programmed.	Partially successful: Some bus skill sequences generalized across settings and maintained across time.
Oliver & Scott (1981)	6 male and 2 female 19–21-year-old mentally retarded students. Special school classroom.	Verbal adjective concepts.	Individual training (direct instruction plus edible and social reinforcers. Group training: same as above plus modeling).	Randomized block design.	Partially successful: 7 of 8 students reached criterion on verbal adjective concepts.	Across untrained stimuli.	Trained multiple exemplars.	Successful: Verbal adjective concepts generalized to more untrained stimuli following group training.
Warrenfeltz, Kelly, Salzberg, Beegle, Levy, Adams, & Crouse (1981)	2 male and 2 female 15–16-year-old behavior disordered students. Short-term residential facility.	Appropriate responses to instruction and to critical feedback and conversation.	Didactic training, role-playing and self-monitoring plus social reinforcers.	Multiple baseline across pairs of subjects.	Successful: Appropriate responses increased.	Across settings (concurrent), responses, and time (1-month follow-up).	Mediated generalization (self-control).	Successful: Appropriate responses generalized across settings, responses and maintained across time.

Campbell & Stremel-Campbell (1982)	10- and 12-year-old moderately language delayed males. Special classroom.	Initiation of language responses.	Token and social reinforcers.	Multiple baseline across behaviors.	Successful: Initiation of language responses increased.	Across settings (concurrent), responses, and time (3- to 8-day follow-up).	Trained loosely.	Partially successful: Initiation of language responses was inconsistent across responses, settings and time.
Hill, Wehman, & Horst (1982)	21-year-old profoundly retarded and 14- and 18-year-old severely retarded males. Special public school and community recreation centers.	Use of age-appropriate leisure skill (pinball) and inappropriate social behavior.	Verbal prompting, modeling, gesturing or physical guidance plus social reinforcers.	Multiple baseline across subjects. AB for inappropriate social behavior.	Successful: Pinball playing increased and inappropriate social behaviors decreased.	Across settings (concurrent).	Trained multiple exemplars.	Successful: Pinball playing maintained in community setting.
Lancioni (1982)	1 male and 2 female 8–10-year-old retarded students. Regular school.	Delayed initiation, cooperative play, verbalizing "that's good" and "thank you."	Peer tutoring with direct edible and social reinforcers.	Multiple baseline across behaviors.	Successful: All social behaviors increased.	Preintervention and postintervention probes and across settings.	Probed but not programmed.	Successful: Social responses maintained across settings.
	3 9–12-year-old retarded girls. Regular school.	Same as Exp. 1.	Peer tutoring with vicarious and direct social reinforcers.	Same as Exp. 1.	Successful: All social behaviors increased.	Same as Exp. 1.	Same as Exp. 1.	Successful: Social responses maintained across settings.
	2 male and 1 female 10–13-year-old retarded students. Regular school.	Same as Exp. 1.	Peer tutoring with vicarious and direct social reinforcers.	Same as Exp. 1.	Successful: All social behaviors increased.	Same as Exp. 1.	Same as Exp. 1.	Successful: Social responses maintained across settings.

(*continued*)

Table 2. (*Continued*)

Authors/ date	Subjects/ settings	Target behaviors	Intervention procedures	Design	Outcome in training setting	Maintenance/ generalization assessment	Maintenance/ generalization procedure	Maintenance/ generalization outcome
Sedlack, Doyle, & Schloss (1982)	1 male and 2 female 18–19-year-old severely retarded students. Special school.	Video game scores and percentage of game steps completed.	Modeling and cueing.	Multiple baseline across subjects.	Successful: Percentage of game steps and scores increased.	Across settings and time (3-month follow-up).	Probed but not programmed.	Successful: percentage of game steps completed and game scores generalized across settings and maintained across time.
Whitman, Scibak, Butler, Richter, & Johnson (1982)	9-year-old educable mentally retarded female. Special classroom.	Out-of-seat.	Correspondence training with edible and social reinforcers.	ABAB	Successful: Out-of-seat decreased.	Across time (8-month follow-up).	Probed but not programmed.	Successful: In-seat maintained across time.
	4 11–12-year-old educable mentally retarded males. Special classroom.	Appropriate sitting posture.	Correspondence training with privileges and social reinforcers.	Multiple baseline across subjects.	Successful: Sitting posture improved.	Across settings, trainers, and time (2-week follow-up).	Introduced to natural community of reinforcers (classroom teachers' social reinforcement).	Successful: Appropriate posture maintained across time and transferred to teacher control.
	2 male and 2 female 10–13-year-old nonverbal educable or trainable mentally retarded students. Special classroom.	On-task.	Correspondence training with visual cuing plus social reinforcers.	Multiple baseline across subjects.	Successful: On-task increased.	Across trainers and time (2-week follow-up).	Introduced to natural community of reinforcers (classroom teachers' social reinforcement).	Successful: On-task behavior maintained across time and transferred to teacher control.
Carr & Kologinsky (1983)	3 9–14-year-old autistic males. Special school.	Spontaneous signing and self-stimulation.	Edible, tangible and tactile reinforcers.	Multiple baseline across subjects plus ABAB.	Successful: Signing increased and self-stimulation decreased.	Across trainers, responses, and time (4-session follow-up).	Probed but not programmed.	Successful: Signing generalized across trainers, responses and maintained across time.

	3 10–14-year-old autistic males. Special school.	Spontaneous signing.	Edible reinforcers.	ABCBCD	Successful: Signing increased.	Across settings (concurrent) and trainers.	Trained multiple exemplars and programmed common stimuli (adult monitors).	Partially successful: All subjects generalized across trainers but only one subject maintained
Handleman & Harris (1983)	5 4–8-year-old autistic males. Special school and regular classroom.	Verbal responses to set questions.	Edible and social reinforcers.	AB	Successful: Verbal responses increased to criterion.	Across settings.	Sequential modification.	Partially successful: 4 of 5 subjects verbal responses generalized across settings.
Kelly, Salzberg, Levy, Warrenfeltz, Adams, Crouse, & Beegle (1983)	2 male and 2 female 15–17-year-old severely behaviorally disordered students. Residential treatment facility.	Following instructions.	Verbal training, role-playing, and self-monitoring.	Multiple baseline across subjects.	Successful: All subjects reached criterion on following instructions.	Across settings.	Mediated generalization (self-monitoring).	Successful: Following instructions generalized to vocational training setting.
Neef, Shafer, Egel, Cataldo, & Parrish (1983)	3 male and 3 female 6–8-year-old severely behaviorally disordered students. Special school.	Compliance with "do" and "don't" requests in analogue setting.	Compliance training with edible and social reinforcers plus physical guidance for noncompliance.	Multiple baseline across subjects.	Successful: Compliance increased.	Across "do" and "don't" responses and time (3- to 10-session follow-up).	Probed but not programmed.	Partially successful: Compliance failed to generalize across "do" and "don't" responses of students but maintained following training.
	5 male and 5 female 6–8-year-old developmentally delayed students. Special school.	Compliance with "do" and "don't" requests in natural classroom setting and teacher reinforcement of compliance.	Same as Exp. 1.	Multiple baseline across behaviors.	Successful: Compliance and teacher reinforcement of compliance increased.	Across "do" and "don't" responses and time (7- to 20-session follow-up) for teacher reinforcement.	Same as Exp. 1.	Partially successful: Compliance failed to generalize across "do" and "don't" responses of students but teacher reinforcement of compliance maintained across time.

(*continued*)

Table 2. (*Continued*)

Authors/ date	Subjects/ settings	Target behaviors	Intervention procedures	Design	Outcome in training setting	Maintenance/ generalization assessment	Maintenance/ generalization procedure	Maintenance/ generalization outcome
McGee, Krantz, Mason, & McClannahan (1983)	12-year-old autistic male and 15-year-old autistic female. Group home.	Compliance with "Give me ___" requests.	Social reinforcers.	Multiple baseline across sets of objects.	Successful: Compliance increased.	Across settings (concurrent).	Probed but not programmed.	Successful: Compliance generalized across settings.
Richmond & Lewallen (1983)	15- and 22-year-old profoundly retarded females. Special clinic classroom.	Verbal labeling of pictures and letters.	Single vs. dual trainers using edible and social reinforcers.	Alternating treatments.	Successful: Correct labeling increased more with dual trainers.	Across responses and time (3- and 4-session follow-up).	Probed but not programmed.	Successful: Correct labeling maintained across time and increased for nontrained responses.
Gaylord-Ross, Haring, Breen, & Pitts-Conway (1984)	17- and 20-year-old autistic males. Special classroom.	Initiation and elaboration of social interactions.	Social skills training package.	Multiple baseline across stimuli.	Successful: Correct social responses increased.	Across nonhandicapped peers and across time (4-month follow-up).	Trained multiple exemplars.	Partially successful: Correct social responses generalized across peers and maintained across time for 1 subject.
	18-year-old autistic male. Special classroom.	Same as Exp. 1.	Same as Exp. 1.	Multiple baseline across training objects.	Successful: Correct social responses increased.	Across handicapped peers and time (4-month follow-up).	Same as Exp. 1.	Successful: Correct social responses generalized across peers and maintained across time.
Haavik, Spradlin, & Altman (1984)	3 male and 1 female 3–5-year-old moderately handicapped students. Special preschool and home.	Verbal labeling of pictures.	Edible, tangible and social reinforcers.	Multiple baseline across training tasks plus ABA.	Successful: Correct verbal labeling of pictures increased.	Across settings and trainers.	Programmed common stimuli (contingencies).	Successful: Verbal labeling of pictures generalized to home setting.

Kiburz, Miller, & Morrow (1984)	18-year-old behaviorally disordered male. Residential mental health center.	Greeting, thanking and conversation behaviors.	Social skills training with modeling, role-playing, performance feedback and self-rewarding.	Multiple baseline across skills plus ABCDCA	Successful: Greeting and thanking behaviors increased.	Across settings, responses, and time (6-day follow-up).	Mediated generalization (self-control).	Successful: Social responses generalized across responses and settings and greeting behavior maintained across time.
McDonnell, Horner, & Williams (1984)	3 male and 1 female 16–19-year-old moderately to severely retarded students. Special classrooms and grocery stores.	Grocery item purchasing behaviors.	Simulation and in vivo training.	Multiple baseline across subjects.	Partially successful: Purchasing behaviors failed to increase in simulation but increased with simulation plus in vivo training.	Across settings and time (4-month follow-up - anecdotal).	Introduced to natural community of reinforcers (in vivo training).	Successful: Purchasing responses maintained across probe settings and time.
Neef, Walters, & Egel (1984)	3 male and 1 female 4–6-year-old autistic students. Special classroom.	"Yes" and "No" responses to set questions.	Embedded instruction plus edible, tangible and social reinforcers.	Multiple baseline across subjects.	Successful: Correct responses increased when instruction embedded in classroom activities.	Across different types of questions.	Introduced to natural community of reinforcers (embedded instruction).	Successful: "Yes" and "No" responses generalized to different types of questions.
Nietupski, Clancy, & Christiansen (1984)	3 male and 1 female 7–10-year-old moderately retarded students. Special classroom and community settings.	Vending machine use.	Picture-prompt prosthetic.	Multiple probe.	Successful: all subjects reached criterion on all three vending machines.	Across settings (nontrained vending machines) and time (6-week follow-up).	Trained multiple exemplars.	Partially successful: Vending machine skills partially generalized across settings and maintained across time.

(*continued*)

Table 2. (*Continued*)

Authors/ date	Subjects/ settings	Target behaviors	Intervention procedures	Design	Outcome in training setting	Maintenance/ generalization assessment	Maintenance/ generalization procedure	Maintenance/ generalization outcome
Shafer, Egel, & Neef (1984)	3 male and 1 female 5- and 6-year-old autistic students. Special classroom.	Positive social interactions with nonhandicapped peers.	Peer training with direct prompting and modeling.	Multiple baseline across subjects.	Successful: Positive social interactions increased in number and duration.	Across settings.	Programmed common stimuli (toys) and sequential modification.	Partially successful: Positive social interactions generalized only after specific programming.
Sprague & Horner (1984)	6 15–19-year-old moderately and severely retarded males. Integrated public school classrooms and community settings.	Vending machine use.	Picture-prompt prosthetic.	Multiple baseline across subjects.	Successful: All subjects reached criterion on vending machines.	Across settings (nontrained vending machines) and across time (18-month follow-up).	Trained multiple exemplars.	Partially successful: Vending machine skills generalized across all probe machines and maintained across time for 5 of 6 subjects.
Maag, Wolchik, Rutherford, & Parks (1986)	7- and 12-year-old autistic males. Residential school.	Self-stimulatory behaviors.	Sensory extinction.	Multiple baseline across behaviors and ABA.	Successful: Self-stimulatory behaviors decreased.	Across responses (concurrent) and settings.	Probed but not programmed.	Partially successful: Some corresponding reduction in other self-stimulatory behaviors.

ping, inappropriate manipulation of objects, inappropriate verbalizations, out-of-seat, off-task, and self-stimulatory behaviors were the responses targeted for modification, maintenance, and generalization.

The intervention procedures used included behavior enhancement strategies such as prompting, cuing, modeling, demonstration, feedback and fading; direct instruction, verbal instruction, embedded instruction, component instruction, signs paired with verbal instruction, and self-instruction, self-monitoring, and self-reward; concurrent versus serial training, individual versus group training, simulation versus in vivo training, play training, correspondence training, compliance training, and social skills training; and using picture-prompt prosthetics, peer tutors, role playing, physical guidance, and distractors. A variety of tactile, edible, tangible, token, and social reinforcers were used concurrently with these behavior enhancement strategies. The behavior reduction strategies used in a number of these studies included overcorrection, response-cost, verbal reprimands, physical restraint, planned ignoring, and sensory extinction.

The experimental designs used included group (e.g., control group, randomized block, and Latin square) and single-subject (e.g., reversal, AB, multiple-probe, alternating treatments, equivalent time samples, and multiple-baseline). Burger, Blackman, and Clark (1981) used a control group to analyze the effects of a self-instruction plus modeling intervention on the development of verbal abstraction strategies by educable mentally retarded students. Oliver and Scott (1981) and Kohl, Karlan, and Head (1979) used a randomized block design and a 3×3 Latin square design to evaluate treatment effects. Eleven studies employed a reversal or withdrawal phase, four collected baseline and intervention data but failed to initiate a reversal or withdrawal phase, two studies (Tucker & Berry, 1980, and Nietupski, Clancy, & Christiansen, 1984) used multiple probes, one study (Richmond & Lewallen, 1983) used alternating treatments, one study (Gable, Henrickson, & Strain, 1978) used equivalent time samples, and 42 studies used a multiple baseline design, either singly or in conjunction with another design to assess the effects of intervention on subjects' target behaviors.

The outcome of intervention procedures on target behaviors in training settings was again overwhelmingly successful in these studies with moderately and severely handicapped students. Fifty-three studies reported successful behavior enhancement or behavior reduction effects. Only four studies reported partially successful outcome data. Luiselli, Colozzi, Donellon, Helfen, and Pemberton (1978) reported that the subject mastered three of four target verbal responses; Panyan and Hall (1978) successfully modified vocal imitation for the two subjects and tracing for one of the subjects in their study; Oliver and Scott (1981) reported that seven of eight students reached criterion on vocal imitation and tracing responses; and McDonnell, Horner, and Williams (1984) found that subjects' grocery item purchasing responses failed to increase in simulation but increased with simulation plus *in vivo* training.

Maintenance and generalization assessment was accomplished through a variety of procedures. Stimulus generalization was assessed across concurrent or subsequent settings in 37 studies, across trainers in 12 studies, across various stimuli and stimulus modalities such as probes, questions, subjects, reinforcers, and peers in 11 studies; response generalization was assessed across similar responses in 13 studies; and response maintenance or follow-up data across time were collected in 29 of these studies. Fifteen studies reported follow-up data for 21 days (or sessions or trials) or less; four studies reported one month follow-up; and 15 studies provided from one and one-half to 18-month follow-up data. Koegel and Rincover (1977) reported maintenance of treatment effects for up to 500 trials for autistic students' nonverbal imitation or following verbal instruction responses.

Again, as in studies with normal or mildly handicapped students, the largest number of investigations in this group could be characterized as falling in the train-and-hope category. In 24 studies, generalization was assessed but not specifically programmed. Generalization and maintenance outcome in 14 of these studies was successful, in eight studies outcome was partially successful, and in two studies (Marholin & Townsend, 1978, and Strain, Kerr, & Ragland, 1979) learned responses failed to generalize across settings.

Sequential modification was implemented in six studies in this group. Garcia *et al.* (1977) systematically trained the use of complex sentences and programmed for generalization of these responses by initiating training in the generalization settings. Kissel and Whitman (1977) sequentially implemented overcorrection and positive reinforcement procedures across a series of behaviors and situations. Generalization efforts were marginally effective across settings and responses. Although Panyan and Hall (1978) reported limited generalization following serial training of the tracing and vocal imitation responses of two severely retarded students, Handleman and Harris (1983) reported that the correct verbal responses of four of the five autistic students in their study generalized across settings following sequential modification. Shafer, Egel, and Neef (1984) also found that autistic students' positive social interactions with nonhandicapped peers only generalized across settings after specific sequential programming of these interactions. Finally, Coleman, Whitman, and Johnson (1979) were unsuccessful in promoting generalization of appropriate play and reduced self-stimulation of a profoundly retarded student. Although they initiated a generalization package of programmed common stimuli and sequential modification, trained responses failed to generalize across settings or trainers.

Introduction to natural maintaining contingencies was used as a transfer strategy in four studies in this group. In two studies conducted by Whitman, Scibak, Butler, Richter, and Johnson (1982), appropriate sitting posture and on-task responses successfully generalized across settings and trainers and maintained across time in the first instance and across trainers and time in the second instance. Whitman *et al.* (1982) brought maintenance and transfer of students' continued responding under control of the classroom teachers' social reinforcers. Likewise, McDonnell, Horner, and Williams (1984) successfully programmed the maintenance and generalization of grocery item purchasing behaviors of moderately and severely retarded adolescents by providing training in grocery stores. The naturally maintaining contingencies of the in vivo setting facilitated the transfer of purchasing behaviors across a range of nontrained probe stores. Finally, Neef, Walters, and Egel (1984) used instruction embedded in regular classroom activities to trap appropriate "yes" and "no" responses of autistic preschool students in the natural community of reinforcers available within these regular classroom activities.

The training-sufficient-exemplars generalization technique was used in nine studies. In studies demonstrating successful maintenance and generalization outcome, Oliver and Scott (1984) reported that group training with multiple training models resulted in the transfer of verbal adjective concepts by mentally retarded students to untrained stimuli, and Hill, Wehman, and Horst (1982) promoted pinball playing in a community setting by training on a series of pinball machines. Also, Gaylord-Ross, Haring, Breen, and Pitts-Conway (1984) reported that correct social responses maintained and generalized following exposure to multiple peer exemplars for one of two autistic students in their first study and for one autistic student in their second study.

In two studies, vending machine skills partially generalized to nontrained vending machines for four subjects (Nietupski *et al.*, 1984) and generalized to nontrained machines for five of six subjects (Sprague & Horner, 1984) following exposure to multiple examples of vending machines. Whitman, Hurley, Johnson, and Christian (1978), Welch and Pear (1980), and Carr and Kologinsky (1983) reported partially successful generalization following exposure to multiple-punished response, object, and sign exemplars respectively.

Campbell and Stremel-Campbell (1982) conducted the only study we reviewed that assessed the effects of the strategy for promoting generalization identified by Stokes and Baer (1977) as training loosely. Campbell and Stremel-Campbell (1982) programmed language generalization by conducting language training within the context of an academic training task and programming a functional reduction in stimulus control by allowing the student to initiate language responses based on a wide array of naturally occurring stimulus events. Maintenance and generalization of initiated language responses was inconsistent across responses, settings, and time.

Five studies programmed indiscriminable contingencies to prevent the ready discrimination of the training contingencies in the maintenance and generalization setting. Russo and Koegel (1977) thinned the reinforcement schedule in the training setting whereas Koegel and Rincover (1977) combined thinned reinforcement schedules and intermittent noncontingent reinforcement in an extratraining setting to promote successfully response maintenance following training. Zifferblatt, Burton, Homer, and White (1977) successfully programmed generalization across settings by arranging similar, though unreinforced, trials in different settings. Mithaug (1978) successfully programmed response generalization through training the subject to follow instructions by responding to relevant and irrelevant verbal cues. Halle, Marshall, and Spradlin (1979) were partially successful in programming generalization of severely and profoundly retarded subjects' verbal meal requests across settings and trainers by establishing a 15-second delay in giving subjects food trays. Four of the five subjects requested meals across trainers and three of four subjects verbally requested meals across trainers and meals.

Programming common stimuli in training and posttraining setting was used to facilitate maintenance and generalization in nine studies with moderately and severely handicapped students. Five studies were at least partially successful in programming maintenance and generalization by establishing common stimuli in both settings such as toys, adult monitors, contingencies, real objects (i.e., as opposed to picture-cards or photographs as cues for naming objects), and teacher behaviors.

Handleman (1979) and Handleman and Harris (1980) programmed the generalization of autistic students' verbal responses to specified questions across multiple natural settings. Training took place within a school in a number of natural settings that were designed to resemble stimuli common to the student's home, the posttreatment setting. Gable *et al.* (1978) found that some student social behaviors maintained and generalized across settings following reinforcement of spontaneously exhibited previously trained behaviors in the posttreatment setting.

In the only study where the programming of common stimuli in training and posttraining settings was unsuccessful, Coleman *et al.* (1979) found planning common teacher behaviors and materials across settings did not facilitate generalization. Although the student's appropriate play increased and self-stimulation decreased in training, these behavior changes failed to generalize across settings or trainers.

Stokes and Baer's (1977) generalization promotion technique of mediated generalization was used in four studies in this group. Warrenfeltz *et al.* (1981) and Kiburz, Miller, and Morrow (1984) successfully instituted self-control procedures to maintain and generalize the social behaviors of behaviorally disordered adolescents across settings, responses, and time. Kelly *et al.* (1983) used a self-monitoring procedure to program successfully the generalization of four behaviorally disordered adolescents' instruction following behaviors across settings. Burgio, Whitman, and Johnson (1980) found that self-instruction training for five mentally retarded students promoted generalization and maintenance of self-instructional and academic responses across settings and time but failed to facilitate generalization of these responses across subjects or responses.

There were no studies with moderately or severely handicapped students that trained students to generalize.

Analysis and Discussion

More than 15 years ago, Baer, Wolf, and Risley (1968) stressed that "generalization should be programmed, rather than expected or lamented" (p. 97). A number of subsequent reviewers of the behavior analysis literature have found it to be woefully inadequate with regard to the demonstration of successful behavioral maintenance and generalization effects. For example, Anderson-Inman, Walker, and Purcell (1984) concluded that

> the failure of newly acquired skills to generalize across settings has become a major topic of concern to behavior analysts and educators alike . . . although a variety of possible strategies to promote the transfer of training have been proposed, we are still a long way from the systematic and data-based technology so needed in our schools. (p. 18)

Similarly, Gelfand and Hartmann (1984) observed that "the production of appropriately generalized and durable treatment effects is one of the remaining, major challenges for behavior therapy" (p. 155).

No less than six separate reviews of studies addressing the transfer of treatment effects across settings, responses, trainers, and/or time (Bailey & Lessen, 1984; Hayes *et al.*, 1980; Kauffman, Nussen, & McGee, 1977; Keeley, Shemberg, & Carbonell, 1976; Stokes & Baer, 1977; Warren, 1977) reported a limited number of studies in which maintenance and generalization effects were successfully programmed. The proportion of studies reporting follow-up data of at least one month ranged from 6.2% (Keeley *et al.*, 1976) to 28% (Kauffman *et al.*, 1977); studies assessing generalization effects across settings ranged from 2.7% (Keeley *et al.*, 1976) to 31.8% (Hayes *et al.*, 1980). The proportion of studies reporting response generalization ranged from 4.8% (Keeley *et al.*, 1976) to 13.6% (Hayes *et al.*, 1976). Warren (1977) found that 30% and Bailey and Lessen (1984) found that 27% of the articles they reviewed directly measured the occurrence of generalization. Stokes and Baer (1977) reported that 50% of the 270 studies they reviewed that specifically addressed the generalization of treatment effects failed to program for these effects.

Drabman, Hammer, and Rosenbaum (1979) developed a generalization map to categorize outcomes produced by generalization training. They found that, of the studies they reviewed in the child behavior modification literature published between 1960 and 1977 that addressed generalization, 51% measured generalization across time, 25% across settings, 29% across behaviors, and 8% across subjects. Fifty-seven percent of the studies analyzed in the present review assessed generalization across time, 74% across settings (including across trainers), 33% across behaviors, and 4% across subjects. The only substantial difference between Drabman *et al.* (1979) data and the present data appears to be the increase in the number of studies reporting assessment of generalization across settings in our analysis. This increase in across-setting generalization may be due in part to the inclusion of across-trainers data in this group. However, the current study analyzed generalization studies in education settings where emphasis is often placed on transfer of educational treatment effects to other classrooms or to other teachers.

The results of the current review of the maintenance and generalization literature parallel those of these earlier efforts. Educational research studies that specifically program for maintenance and generalization currently are quite limited in number. Of the approximately 5,300 articles published in the educational and behavioral psychology journals reviewed between 1977 and the present, less than 1% systematically programmed for maintenance and generalization of educational treatment effects across settings, responses, trainers, or time. Although not all of the articles contained in these studies met the research and procedural criteria for inclusion in this review, the fact that only 103 studies addressed the maintenance and generalization of the effects of educational programs indicates that the technology of generalization called for by Stokes and Baer in 1977 is still in the formative stages. Of the studies analyzed in this review that programmed for generalization, only 37% assessed generalization across settings, 19% programmed for response generalization, 15% programmed for generalization across trainers, and 37% programmed for behavioral maintenance across time. An additional 38% of these studies probed for, but failed to program, generalization effects. On the other hand, the studies analyzed in this review, though limited in number, suggest some strategies for successful programming of maintenance and generalization of treatment effects and point out some factors that may limit or impede successful transfer of these effects.

Strategies for Programming Maintenance and Generalization

A number of authors have suggested strategies for programming behavioral maintenance across time (Egel, 1984; Foxx, 1982; Powers & Handleman, 1984; Walker, 1979) and strategies for programming generalization of behaviors across settings, responses, subjects, or trainers (Egel, 1984; Foxx, 1982; Gelfand & Hartmann, 1984; Kazdin, 1984; Kazdin & Bootzin, 1972; Marholin & Siegel, 1978; McLaughlin, 1979; Rose, Lessen, & Gottlieb, 1982; Sulzer-Azaroff & Mayer, 1977; Walker, 1979; Wildman & Wildman, 1975). These strategies generally correspond to those suggested by Stokes and Baer (1977). Table 3 shows that when the 103 studies reviewed by the authors were analyzed with regard to which of Stokes and Baer's techniques have been used in educational settings to promote maintenance and generalization of treatment effects, we found that 39 studies employed a train-and-hope strategy and 8 studies used sequential modification. Although Stokes and Baer (1977) and Baer (1982) questioned the efficacy of these two procedures as true generalization promotion techniques, these procedures account for almost half of the studies we analyzed. Generalization was either not specifically planned, as in the first case, or intervention techniques were sequentially implemented in a number of settings until generalization occurred, as in the second case.

The strategies that Stokes and Baer (1977), Alberto and Troutman (1982), and Baer (1982) suggested have the greatest potential for promoting maintenance and generalization were used in few of the studies analyzed by the authors. Seven percent of the studies introduced students to a natural community of reinforcers; 14% of the studies trained multiple

Table 3. Studies Reporting the Use of Stokes and Baer's Strategies

Strategies	Studies: Normal or mildly handicapped students	Studies: Moderately or severely handicapped students
Train and hope	15	24
Sequential modification	3	5
Introduce to natural maintaining contingencies	3	4
Train sufficient exemplars	7	8
Train loosely	0	1
Use indiscriminable contingencies	7	5
Program common stimuli	3	9
Mediate generalization	9	4
Train to generalize	3	0

exemplars; 1% trained loosely; 12% programmed indiscriminable stimuli between training and generalization settings; 10% successfully programmed common stimuli in training and generalization settings; 12% mediated generalization by teaching various self-control strategies; and 2% of the studies trained students to perform a generalization response.

Generalization and maintenance strategies can be divided into those techniques aimed at programming the individual student to transfer new behaviors to posttreatment settings and those strategies aimed at programming the posttreatment environment to support and maintain new behaviors (O'Leary & O'Leary, 1976). Strategies designed to program the individual's behavior include mediating generalization, where students are taught self-control techniques (Baer *et al.*, 1981; Gelfand & Hartmann, 1984; O'Leary & Dubey, 1979), and reinforcing generalization as an independent response class (Blankenship & Baumgartner, 1982; Mitchell & Milan, 1983; Parsonson & Baer, 1978). In the latter case, students are taught the skill of generalization to take into the posttraining environment. For example, Blankenship and Baumgartner (1982) reinforced elementary students to generalize from instructed to noninstructed types of arithmetic problems. Twelve percent of the studies in the current review relied on programming the individual to achieve generalization.

Related to programming the student to facilitate transfer of training are the strategies of training student behaviors that trap natural reinforcers in the posttreatment setting (Baer & Wolf, 1970), and teaching students how to modify and control the behaviors of teachers, parents, and peers in the generalization setting (Graubard, Rosenberg, & Miller, 1971). Seven studies in the current review used behavior trapping techniques to introduce students to natural maintaining contingencies, such as teacher and peer reinforcers. For example, Whitman *et al.* (1982) demonstrated that a "say-do" correspondence training technique could be used with mentally retarded students to improve classroom behavior. Students' ability to follow through with what they said they would do allowed students to trap teacher praise and attention. None of the studies reviewed specifically taught students applied behavior analysis techniques to modify and control the behaviors of others in their natural environment.

Strategies for reprogramming the posttreatment environment include training significant others (e.g., parents, teachers, peers) as behavior change agents (Marholin, Siegel, & Phillips, 1976) and reducing differences between training and generalization settings, fading reinforcers, and redirecting peer and teacher attention to the student's appropriate behaviors (O'Leary & O'Leary, 1976). Another procedure involves systematically introducing aspects of the training setting into the posttraining setting (Walker & Buckley, 1972), such as reprogramming peers in the regular classroom to support students' appropriate behavior, equating stimulus conditions between the special and regular classrooms, and trapping regular classroom teachers to reinforce and support students' generalized behavior. The strategies of introducing the subject to a natural community of reinforcers, training sufficient exemplars, training loosely, programming indiscriminable contingencies, and programming common stimuli across settings are all examples of reprogramming the environment to achieve maintenance and generalization of treatment effects. Forty-three percent of the studies analyzed in this review reprogrammed the posttraining environment to facilitate generalization. Less than 2% of the studies combined programming the individual and reprogramming the environment to achieve generalization and maintenance of treatment effects.

Factors That Limit Maintenance and Generalization

There appear to be several factors that may limit or impede successful transfer of treatment effects to posttreatment settings. These potential limitations include: (a) failure to program natural components into the treatment plan; (b) single-subject design features which may, in fact, impede generalization and maintenance; and (c) problems inherent in collecting generalization and maintenance data in the natural or posttraining setting.

Natural Programming Limitations

Baer *et al.* (1968) observed that applied behavior analysis research involves, whenever possible, "the study of those (socially important) behavior in their usual social settings, rather than in a laboratory setting" (p. 92). The focus of programming is generally on conducting treatment programs in natural environments (Strain *et al.*, 1977) and developing natural contingencies to maintain and generalize behavior change to posttreatment settings. As Baer and Wolf (1970) stressed, the emphasis of applied behavior analysis is to assure the entry of the student's behavior into "natural communities of reinforcement" (p. 319) by adherence to "the relevance of behavior rule" (Ayllon & Azrin, 1968, p. 56), which emphasizes teaching behaviors that will continue to be reinforced after training. As Marholin and Siegel (1978) noted, the relevance of behavior rule "further implies that the natural environment must contain reinforcers of sufficient strength and frequency to maintain target behaviors" (p. 402).

The three components of natural programming most likely to facilitate maintenance and generalization include: (a) focusing on natural or relevant behaviors; (b) establishing natural contingencies to train and maintain behaviors; and (c) conducting training and/or posttraining programs in natural settings.

The types of behaviors targeted for change in the studies reviewed generally were relevant in that they involved student behaviors that had a high probability of being maintained by contingencies in the natural environment. Many of these behaviors had the potential to trap natural social contingencies in the posttreatment or natural setting. Social skills and appropriate speech and language behaviors are two classes of responses most likely to be maintained in the natural environment. Social skills, such as cooperative play (Gable *et al.*, 1978), initiating and elaborating social interactions (Gaylord-Ross *et al.*, 1984), eye contact with peers (Berler *et al.*, 1982), cooperative behaviors and proximity to peers (Reisinger, 1978), offers to share (Fowler & Baer, 1981), and a number of other social interaction behaviors were taught students in 31% of the studies in this review. Verbal behaviors, such as student verbal approval of teachers (Polirstok & Greer, 1977), verbal responses to questions (Larsson & Larsson, 1983; Sanok & Striefel, 1979), conversational skills (Tofte-Tipps, Mendonca, & Peach, 1982), vocal imitation (Panyan & Hall, 1978), meal requests (Halle *et al.*, 1979) and other speech and language behaviors were targeted in 26% of the studies reviewed.

In addition, increased academic and survival skills, and reduced maladaptive behaviors frequently bring about increased positive consequences in the natural environment. Academic behaviors were targeted in 17% of the studies reviewed and increased self-help, leisure, community and school survival skills were trained in 21% of the studies. Reduction of disruptive, off-task, or self-stimulatory behaviors was programmed in 23% of the studies.

The contingencies of reinforcement in the posttreatment setting should be consistent with contingencies present in the treatment environment to facilitate maintenance and generalization (Marholin & Siegel, 1978). Teacher or trainer social reinforcement of student behaviors, used either alone or in combination with other interventions, is the most frequently cited example of a contingency that is potentially available in the training and posttraining environment (Egel, 1984; Kazdin, 1984; Strain, Cooke, & Apolloni, 1976; Walker & Buckley, 1972). Whereas a variety of edible reinforcers (used in 20% of the studies), token reinforcers (21%), and tangible, monetary, contract, and tactile reinforcers (9%) were used as part of the intervention package in a number of the studies reviewed, over 63% of the studies included specific teacher social reinforcers and/or feedback to modify students' behaviors.

In addition to facilitating the training and transfer of students' behaviors with social reinforcers, other methods of programming common contingencies include using peers, who are potentialy available in both the training and posttraining settings, to teach behaviors (Walker & Buckley, 1972) or using a number of teachers or trainers across settings (Foxx, 1982; Kazdin, 1984) to program maintenance and generalization of treatment effects. Seventeen percent of the studies used peer tutors and 16% used multiple adult trainers.

Another procedure for programming common contingencies across training and posttraining settings is to teach students to self-instruct, self-monitor, self-evaluate, and/or self-reinforce their own behaviors. Behaviors that are under self-control contingencies are more likely to transfer across settings (Baer, Stokes, Holman, Rowbury, & Fowler, 1981; Loper & Hallahan, 1982; Rose, Lessen, & Gottlieb, 1982). For example, Baer *et al.* (1981) taught students to monitor their on-task behavior by means of a leather bracelet containing wire strands with movable beads. Students were instructed to move a bead each time a page of work was completed. Following successful self-monitoring in the treatment setting, students used the bracelet to monitor their behavior in the generalization setting. Ten percent of the studies we reviewed used self-monitoring, self-instruction, self-evaluation, or self-control as the primary intervention component.

The third component of natural programming to facilitate maintenance and generalization of treatment effects involves conducting training, whenever possible, in the natural environment (Gelfand & Hartmann, 1984; Powers & Handleman, 1984). Twenty percent of the studies in our review conducted intervention, maintenance, and generalization programming in the natural setting of the regular classroom and an additional 18% of the studies initiated intervention in special classroom settings and measured for behavioral maintenance and generalization in such natural settings as the regular classroom, the home, or the community. An additional 35% of the studies measured maintenance and generalization effects across internal settings such as different areas of the same school (Fowler & Baer, 1981); in the same classroom with the teacher present or absent (Marholin & Steinman, 1977); across meals in the same residential dining facility (Halle, Marshall, & Spradlin, 1979); and in a number of other settings within the same school or program.

Design Limitations

Baer *et al.* (1968) suggested two single-subject designs to evaluate functional relationships between target behaviors and experimental or treatment conditions. Reversal or withdrawal and multiple baseline designs are the most commonly used designs in applied behavior analysis research (Zucker, Rutherford, & Prieto, 1979). The reversal design shows the effect of the treatment by alternately presenting and removing the treatment over time. The multiple baseline design demonstrates the effect of the treatment on target behaviors by introducing the treatment at different points in time. The three types of multiple baseline designs are multiple baseline across behaviors, multiple baseline across subjects, and multiple baseline across settings or stimuli. Of the studies reviewed here, 17% employed a reversal or withdrawal phase, 58% used a multiple baseline design, and 9% used a combined multiple baseline and reversal design to assess treatment effects.

An interesting paradox in the use of single-subject designs and the assessment of maintenance and generalization effects is the fact that the use of the typical ABA design may operate against producing generalization (O'Leary & O'Leary, 1976). The question is whether outcomes are the result of treatment control or are due to a lack of generalization. Kendall (1981) phrased the question as follows:

> When the behavior does not reverse, or when baselines other than the one being treated show variation with a treatment, is this due to the generalization of the treatment to no-treatment conditions, or is it due to a lack of treatment control where the intervention is not having an effect? (p. 309)

The purpose of single-subject designs is to demonstrate the discrimination between treatment and nontreatment times; the purpose of maintenance and generalization programming is to weaken the discrimination between treatment and nontreatment. As Hartmann and Atkinson (1973) stated, the "generalization process is at once desired and claimed as necessary for successful therapy, and feared and denied, depending upon the time at which it takes place" (p. 590).

Greenwood *et al.* (1975) noted the paradoxical nature of ABA designs in which behavior reversal is required to demonstrate experimental or treatment control yet maintenance at some posttreatment point is required to show durability over time. Similarly, O'Leary and O'Leary (1976) pointed out that reversals may inhibit generalization and maintenance across time, settings, or responses.

Kendall (1981) addressed the issue of treatment control versus lack of generalization in single-subject research by describing a methodology for examining generalization within single-subject designs. Stimulus and response generalization, as well as response maintenance, were examined for reversal, multiple baseline, and multielement designs. *Problematic* generalization referred to cases where examining a certain type of generalization might contradict a demonstration of treatment control; *nonproblematic* generalization referred to those cases where examining a type of generalization would not contradict a demonstration of treatment control. For the reversal design, examining stimulus generalization and response maintenance would be problematic and examining response generalization would be nonproblematic. For multiple baseline across situations, examining stimulus generalization and response maintenance would be problematic and examining response generalization would be nonproblematic. For the multiple-baseline across behaviors design, assessing response generalization would be problematic and testing for stimulus generalization and response maintenance would be nonproblematic. Finally, for multielement designs, testing for stimulus generalization and response maintenance would be problematic whereas examining response generalization would be nonproblematic.

When we analyzed the studies in our review with regard to Kendall's (1981) criteria, we found that (a) of the 20 studies that initiated a reversal, 15 were problematic in terms of whether results could be attributed to insufficient treatment control or to stimulus generalization or response maintenance, and five studies were nonproblematic in that they assessed response generalization; (b) of the 12 studies that used a multiple baseline across situations, 11 were problematic in that they tested for either stimulus generalization or response maintenance; (c) for the 32 studies using a multiple baseline across behaviors design, 14 were problematic in that response generalization was assessed and 18 were nonproblematic because stimulus generalization or response maintenance was assessed; (d) of the four studies employing a multielement design, three were problematic due to the assessment of stimulus generalization and response maintenance and one study was nonproblematic in that response generalization was tested.

Six additional studies were nonproblematic in that they employed a combined multiple baseline and reversal design (Rusch & Kazdin, 1981). Haavik, Spradlin, and Altman (1984) and Kiburz *et al.* (1984) initiated a reversal phase within a multiple baseline design across training tasks and skills respectively. Whitman *et al.* (1978), Dorow (1980), and Maag, Wolchik, Rutherford, & Parks (1986) combined periods of reversal or treatment withdrawal with a multiple baseline across behaviors design. The Jenkins, Barksdale, and Clinton (1978) study, which Rose, Koorland, and Epstein (1982) identified as among the scientifically rigorous, combined a reversal design with a multiple baseline across situations and behaviors design.

Therefore, of the studies that used reversal designs, multiple baseline designs across situations or across behaviors, combined reversal and multiple baseline designs, and multielement designs in our review, 57% were problematic with regard to clear attribution of outcome to the effects of maintenance and generalization programming.

Data Collection Limitations

A third factor that may limit effective maintenance and generalization programming concerns the potential problems inherent in collecting maintenance and generalization data in posttreatment settings. Two variables that may impede the collecting of meaningful transfer or follow-up data in the natural environment include the failure to collect long-term follow-up data after treatment has been terminated and the existence of competing variables in the natural environment that preclude collecting accurate posttreatment data.

In addressing the failure of many applied behavior analysts and educators to collect long-term follow-up data, Warren (1977) stated,

> the issue of long-term durability is perhaps the most crucial one facing behavioral researchers and practitioners. If durability of treatment effects proves elusive, and no pragmatic technology is developed to insure it, then the ultimate value of a behavior technology is highly questionable. There is little to be gained from investing large amounts of time and money developing a technology that produces only short-term effects only under highly controlled conditions. (p. 184)

Keeley *et al.* (1976), Holman (1977), and Kauffman *et al.* (1977) have lamented the lack of documented long-term changes in applied behavior analysis research. Warren (1977) suggested that general standards defining valid follow-up data collection procedures are nonexistent. He proposed that minimum time periods of at least 2 to 6 months follow-up and some form of covert follow-up assessment need to be established. A limited number of the educational intervention studies since 1977 that addressed maintenance and generalization effects met these standards. Although some form of durability data was collected in 53% of the studies, only one third of these collected at least 2 months follow-up data. Although covert follow-up data collection procedures may have been used in some of the studies reporting these data, none of the investigators described these procedures in the studies reviewed here.

Competing variables in the natural and posttreatment environment may preclude collecting accurate transfer and follow-up data. Kauffman *et al.* (1977) suggested that educational follow-up data are difficult to collect because of classroom variables such as rapid change in children's behavior due to normal development processes and frequent changes in children's classroom environments (e.g., at least every 9 months) and the methodological problems of observer reliability and reactivity in naturalistic observation after passage of time. In addition, there are often institutional constraints in the natural environment that mitigate against collecting accurate transfer and follow-up data (Reppucci & Saunders, 1974).

A primary institutional constraint in collecting classroom-based transfer and follow-up data is the failure of teachers to continue to collect reliable data once treatment has been completed. Nelson and Rutherford (1987) and Walker (1979) pointed out that student behavior changes often do not maintain because teacher behaviors that produced the changes do not maintain. Because teachers generally are not reinforced for continuing data collection in posttreatment settings, there is often simultaneous decay in both teacher and student behaviors.

Conclusions

Baer *et al.* (1968), in establishing the parameters of applied behavior analysis, stated, "A behavior change may be said to have generality if it proves durable over time, if it appears in a wide variety of possible environments, or if it spreads to a wide variety of related behaviors" (p. 96). A decade later Stokes and Baer (1977) reviewed the generality literature and suggested an implicit technology of generalization. The purpose of this chapter has been to review the maintenance and generalization literature in education from 1977 to the present to determine whether this technology has developed.

The results of this review suggest that an implicit technology of generalization is still in its formative stages. Less than 2% of the approximately 5,300 articles published in the journals reviewed contained studies that addressed maintenance and generalization of educational treatment effects and less than 1% contained studies that systematically programmed for maintenance and generalization of these effects across settings, responses, trainers, or time.

In addition to the small percentage of educational research articles in the literature that have dealt with programming maintenance and generalization, there appear to be several factors that have limited effective transfer of treatment effects to posttreatment settings. Natural programming limitations, design limitations, and data collection limitations may have contributed to the small number of studies found in the recent literature that addressed maintenance and generalization effects.

Despite the small number of educational studies that programmed for generality and the limitations imposed on some of the studies that programmed for transfer and maintenance of treatment effects, a technology of generalization is forming and developing. Sixty-four studies contained procedures that programmed systematically for maintenance and generalization of educational treatment effects.

Acknowledgments

The authors wish to acknowledge Susan Bigelow for her assistance in the preparation of this chapter.

References

Alberto, P. A., & Troutman, A. C. (1982). *Applied behavior analysis for teachers: Influencing student performance.* Columbus, OH: Merrill.

Andersen, B. L., & Redd, W. H. (1980). Programming generalization through stimulus fading with children participating in a remedial reading program. *Education and Treatment of Children, 3,* 297–314.

Anderson-Inman, L. (1981). Transenvironmental programming: Promoting success in the regular class by maximizing the effect of resource room instruction. *Journal of Special Education Technology, 4,* 3–12.

Anderson-Inman, L., Walker, H. M., & Purcell, J. (1984). Promoting the transfer of skills across settings: Transenvironmental programming for handicapped students in the mainstream. In W. L. Heward, T. E. Heron, D. S. Hill, & J. Trap-Porter (Eds.), *Focus on behavior analysis in education* (pp. 17–37). Columbus, OH: Merrill.

Ayllon, T., & Azrin, N. H. (1968). *The token economy: A motivational system for therapy and rehabilitation.* New York: Appleton-Century-Crofts.

Baer, D. M. (1982). The role of current pragmatics in the future analysis of generalization technology. In R. B. Stuart (Ed.), *Adherence, compliance and generalization in behavioral medicine* (pp. 192–212). New York: Brunner/Mazel.

Baer, D. M., & Wolf, M. M. (1970). The entry into natural communities of reinforcement. In R. Ulrich, T. Stachnik, & J. Mabry (Eds.), *Control of human behavior: From cure to prevention* (Vol. 2, pp. 319–324). Glenview, IL: Scott, Foresman.

Baer, D. M., Wolf, M. M., & Risley, T. R. (1968). Some current dimensions of applied behavior analysis. *Journal of Applied Behavior Analysis, 1,* 91–97.

Baer, D. M., Holman, J., Stokes, T. F., Fowler, S. A., & Rowbury, T. G. (1981). Uses of self-control techniques in programming generalization. In S. W. Bijou & R. Ruiz (Eds.), *Behavior modification: Contributions to education* (pp. 39–61). Hillsdale, NJ: Erlbaum.

Baer, R. A., Osnes, P. G., & Stokes, T. F. (1983). Training generalized correspondence between verbal behavior at school and nonverbal behavior at home. *Education and Treatment of Children, 6,* 379–388.

Baer, R. A., Williams, J. A., Osnes, P. G., & Stokes, T. F. (1984). Delayed reinforcement as an indiscriminable contingency in verbal/nonverbal correspondence training. *Journal of Applied Behavior Analysis, 17,* 429–440.

Bailey, S. L., & Lessen, E. I. (1984). An analysis of target behaviors in education: Applied but how useful? In W. L. Heward, T. E. Heron, D. S. Hill, & J. Trap-Porter (Eds.), *Focus on behavior analysis in education* (pp. 162–176). Columbus, OH: Merrill.

Barton, E. J., & Ascione, F. R. (1979). Sharing in preschool children: Facilitation, stimulus generalization, response generalization, and maintenance. *Journal of Applied Behavior Analysis, 12,* 417–430.

Barton, E. J., & Bevirt, J. (1981). Generalization of sharing across groups: Assessment of group composition with preschool children. *Behavior Modification, 5,* 503–522.

Berler, E. S., Gross, A. M., & Drabman, R. S. (1982). Social skills training with children: Proceed with caution. *Journal of Applied Behavior Analysis, 15,* 41–53.

Blankenship, C. S. (1978). Remediating systematic inversion errors in subtraction through the use of demonstration and feedback. *Learning Disability Quarterly, 1,* 12–22.

Blankenship, C. S., & Baumgartner, M. D. (1982). Programming generalization of computational skills. *Learning Disability Quarterly, 5,* 152–162.

Burger, A. L., Blackman, L. S., & Clark, H. T. (1981). Generalization of verbal abstraction strategies by EMR children and adolescents. *American Journal of Mental Deficiency, 85,* 611–618.

Burgio, L. D., Whitman, T. L., & Johnson, M. R. (1980). A self-instructional package for increasing attending behavior in educable mentally retarded children. *Journal of Applied Behavior Analysis, 13,* 443–459.

Campbell, C. R., & Stremel-Campbell, K. (1982). Programming "loose training" as a strategy to facilitate language generalization. *Journal of Applied Behavior Analysis, 15,* 295–301.

Carr, E. G., & Kologinsky, E. (1983). Acquisition of sign language by autistic children II: Spontaneity and generalization effects. *Journal of Applied Behavior Analysis, 16,* 297–314.

Coleman, R. S., Whitman, T. L., & Johnson, M. R. (1979). Suppression of self-stimulatory behavior of a profoundly retarded boy across staff and settings: An assessment of situational generalization. *Behavior Therapy, 10,* 266–280.

Coon, M. E., Vogelsberg, R. T., & Williams, W. (1981). Effects of classroom public transportation instruction generalization to the natural environment. *Journal of the Association for Persons with Severe Handicaps, 6,* 46–53.

Cuvo, A. J., & Riva, M. T. (1980). Generalization and transfer between comprehension and production: A comparison of retarded and nonretarded persons. *Journal of Applied Behavior Analysis, 13,* 315–331.

Diaddigo, M., & Dickie, R. F. (1978). The use of contingency contracting in eliminating inappropriate classroom behaviors. *Education and Treatment of Children, 1,* 17–23.

Dorow, L. G. (1980). Generalization effects of newly conditioned reinforcers. *Education and Training of the Mentally Retarded, 15,* 8–14.

Drabman, R. S., Hammer, D., & Rosenbaum, M. S. (1979). Assessing generalization in behavior modification with children: The generalization map. *Behavioral Assessment, 1,* 203–219.

Egel, A. L. (1984). Programming the generalization and maintenance of treatment gains. In R. L. Koegel, A. Rincover, & A. Rincover, (Eds.), *Educating and understanding autistic children* (pp. 281–299). San Diego, CA: College-Hill.

Epstein, R., & Goss, C. M. (1978). A self-control procedure for the maintenance of nondisruptive behavior in an elementary school child. *Behavior Therapy, 9,* 109–117.

Fantuzzo, J. W., & Clement, P. W. (1981). Generalization of the effects of teacher- and self-administered token reinforcers to nontreated students. *Journal of Applied Behavior Analysis, 14,* 435–447.

Fenrick, N. J., & McDonnell, J. J. (1980). Junior high school students as teachers of the severely retarded: Training and generalization. *Education and Training of the Mentally Retarded, 15,* 187–194.

Fishbein, J. E., & Wasik, B. H. (1981). Effect of the good behavior game on disruptive library behavior. *Journal of Applied Behavior Analysis, 14,* 89–93.

Fowler, S. A., & Baer, D. M. (1981). "Do I have to be good all day?": The timing of delayed reinforcement as a factor in generalization. *Journal of Applied Behavior Analysis, 14,* 13–24.

Foxx, R. M. (1982). *Decreasing behaviors of severely retarded and autistic persons.* Champaign, IL: Research Press.

Gable, R. A., Hendrickson, J. M., & Strain, P. S. (1978). Assessment, modification, and generalization of social interaction among severely retarded, multihandicapped children. *Education and Training of the Mentally Retarded, 13,* 279–286.

Garcia, E. E. (1974). The training and generalization of a conversational speech form in nonverbal retardates. *Journal of Applied Behavior Analysis, 7,* 137–149.

Garcia, E. E., Bullet, J., & Rust, F. P. (1977). An experimental analysis of language training generalization across classroom and home. *Behavior Modification, 1,* 531–550.

Gaylord-Ross, R. J., Haring, T. G., Breen, C., & Pitts-Conway, V. (1984). The training and generalization of social interaction skills with autistic youth. *Journal of Applied Behavior Analysis, 17,* 229–247.

Gelfand, D. M., & Hartmann, D. P. (1984). *Child behavior analysis and therapy* (2nd ed.). New York: Pergamon Press.

Graubard, P. S., Rosenberg, H., & Miller, M. B. (1971). Student applications of behavior modification to teachers and environments or ecological approaches to social deviancy. In E. A. Ramp & B. L. Hopkins (Eds.), *A new direction for education: Behavior analysis* (Vol. 1, pp. 80–101). Lawrence, KS: University of Kansas Press.

Greenwood, C. R., Hops, G., & Walker, H. M. (1977). The durability of student behavior change: A comparative analysis of follow-up. *Behavior Therapy, 8*, 631–638.

Greer, R. D., & Polirstok, S. R. (1982). Collateral gains and short-term maintenance in reading and on-task responses by inner-city adolescents as a function of their use of social reinforcement while tutoring. *Journal of Applied Behavior Analysis, 15*, 123–139.

Haavik, S. F., Spradlin, J. E., & Altman, K. I. (1984). Generalization and maintenance of language responses: A study across trainers, schools, and home settings. *Behavior Modification, 8*. 331–359.

Halle, J. W., Marshall, A. M., & Spradlin, J. E. (1979). Time delay: A technique to increase language use and facilitate generalization in retarded children. *Journal of Applied Behavior Analysis, 12*, 431–439.

Handleman, J. S. (1979). Generalization by autistic-type children of verbal responses across settings. *Journal of Applied Behavior Analysis, 12*, 273–282.

Handleman, J. S., & Harris, S. L. (1980). Generalization from school to home with autistic children. *Journal of Autism and Developmental Disorders, 10*, 323–333.

Handleman, J. S., & Harris, S. L. (1983). Generalization across instructional settings by autistic children. *Child and Family Behavior Therapy, 5*, 73–83.

Hartmann, J. P., & Atkinson, C. (1973). Having your cake and eating it too: A note on some apparent contradictions between therapeutic achievements and design requirements in N = 1 studies. *Behavior Therapy, 4*, 589–591.

Hayes, S. C., Rincover, A., & Solnick, J. V. (1980). The technical drift of applied behavior analysis. *Journal of Applied Behavior Analysis, 13*, 275–285.

Hill, J. W., Wehman, P., & Horst, G. (1982). Toward generalization of appropriate leisure and social behavior in severely handicapped youth: Pinball machine use. *Journal of the Association for Persons with Severe Handicaps, 6*, 38–44.

Holman, J. (1977). The moral risk and high cost of ecological concern in applied behavior analysis. In A. R. Warren & S. F. Warren (Eds.), *Ecological perspectives in behavior analysis* (pp. 63–99). Baltimore, MD: University Park.

Holman, J., & Baer, D. M. (1979). Facilitating generalization of on-task behavior through self-monitoring of academic tasks. *Journal of Autism and Developmental Disorders, 9*, 429–446.

Hung, D. W. (1980). Training and generalization of yes and no as mands in two autistic children. *Journal of Autism and Developmental Disorders, 10*, 139–152.

Jenkins, J. R., Barksdale, A., & Clinton, L. (1978). Improving reading comprehension and oral reading: Generalization across behaviors, settings, and time. *Journal of Learning Disabilities, 11*, 5–15.

Kauffman, J. M., Nussen, J. L., & McGee, C. S. (1977). Follow-up in classroom behavior modification: Survey and discussion. *Journal of School Psychology, 15*, 343–348.

Kazdin, A. E. (1984). *Behavior modification in applied settings* (3rd ed.). Homewood, IL: Dorsey.

Kazdin, A. E., & Bootzin, R. R. (1972). The token economy: An evaluative review. *Journal of Applied Behavior Analysis, 5*, 343–372.

Keeley, S. M., Shemberg, K. M., & Carbonell, J. (1976). Operant clinical intervention: Behavior management or beyond? Where are the data? *Behavior Therapy, 7*, 292–305.

Kelly, W. J., Salzberg, C. L., Levy, S. M., Warrenfeltz, R. B., Adams, T. W., Crouse, T. R., & Beegle, G. P. (1983). The effects of role-playing and self-monitoring on the generalization of vocational social skills by behaviorally disordered adolescents. *Behavioral Disorders, 9*, 27–35.

Kendall, P. C. (1981). Assessing generalization and the single-subject strategies. *Behavior Modification, 5*, 307–319.

Kiburz, C. S., Miller, S. R., & Morrow, L. W. (1984). Structured learning using self-monitoring to promote maintenance and generalization of social skills across settings for a behaviorally disordered adolescent. *Behavioral Disorders, 10*, 47–55.

Kissel, R. C., & Whitman, T. L. (1977). An examination of the direct and generalized effects or a play-training and overcorrection procedure upon the self-stimulatory behavior of a profoundly retarded boy. *AAESPH Review, 2*, 131–146.

Koegel, R. L., & Rincover, A. (1977). Research on the difference between generalization and maintenance in extra-therapy responding. *Journal of Applied Behavior Analysis, 10*, 1–12.

Kohl, F. L., Karlan, G. R., & Heal, L. W. (1979). Effects of pairing manual signs with verbal cues upon the acquisition of instruction-following behaviors and the generalization to expressive language with severely handicapped students. *AAESPH Review, 4*, 291–300.

Lancioni, G. E. (1982). Normal children as tutors to teach social responses to withdrawn mentally retarded schoolmates: Training, maintenance, and generalization. *Journal of Applied Behavior Analysis, 15*, 17–40.

Larsson, D. G., & Larsson, E. V. (1983). Manipulating peer presence to program the generalization of verbal compliance from one-to-one to group instruction. *Education and Treatment of Children, 6*, 109–122.

Lebsock, M. S., & Salzberg, C. L. (1981). The use of role play and reinforcement procedures in the development of generalized interpersonal behavior with emotionally disturbed-behavior disordered adolescents in a special education classroom. *Behavioral Disorders, 6*, 150–163.

Lloyd, J., Saltzman, N. J., & Kauffman, J. M. (1981). Predictable generalization in academic learning as a result of preskills and strategy training. *Learning Disability Quarterly, 4*, 203–216.

Loper, A. B., & Hallahan, D. P. (1982). A consideration of

the role of generalization in cognitive training. *Topics in Learning and Learning Disabilities, 2,* 62–67.

Luiselli, J. K., Colozzi, G., Donellon, S., Helfen, C. S., & Pemberton, B. W. (1978). Training and generalization of a greeting exchange with a mentally retarded, language-deficient child. *Education and Treatment of Children, 1,* 23–39.

Maag, J. W., Wolchik, S. A., Rutherford, R. B., & Parks, B. T. (1986). Response covariation of self-stimulatory behaviors during sensory extinction procedures. *Journal of Autism and Developmental Disorders, 16,* 83–87.

Marholin, D., & Siegel, L. J. (1978). Beyond the law of effect: Programming for the maintenance of behavioral change. In D. Marholin (Ed.), *Child behavior therapy* (pp. 397–415). New York: Gardner.

Marholin, D., & Steinman, W. M. (1977). Stimulus control in the classroom as a function of the behavior reinforced. *Journal of Applied Behavior Analysis, 10,* 465–478.

Marholin, D., & Townsend, N. M. (1978). An experimental analysis of side effects and response maintenance of a modified overcorrection procedure. *Behavior Therapy, 9,* 383–390.

Marholin, D., Siegel, L. J., & Phillips, D. (1976). Treatment and transfer: A search for empirical procedures. In M. Hersen, R. M. Eisler, & P. M. Miller (Eds.), *Progress in behavior modification* (Vol. 3, pp. 294–342). New York: Academic Press.

McDonnell, J. J., Horner, R. H., & Williams, J. A. (1984). Comparison of three strategies for teaching generalized grocery purchasing to high school students with severe handicaps. *Journal of the Association for Persons with Severe Handicaps, 9,* 123–133.

McGee, G. G., Krantz, P. J., Mason, D., & McClannahan, L. E. (1983). A modified incidental-teaching procedure for autistic youth: Acquisition and generalization of receptive object labels. *Journal of Applied Behavior Analysis, 16,* 329–338.

McLaughlin, T. F. (1979). Generalization of treatment effects: An analysis of procedures and outcomes. *Corrective and Social Psychiatry and Journal of Behavior Technology Methods and Therapy, 25,* 33–38.

McLaughlin, T. F. (1980). A critical analysis of some possible strategies to shift behavioral control from programmed reinforcers to consequences in the natural environment. *Behavioral Engineering, 6,* 25–31.

Mitchell, Z. P., & Milan, M. A. (1983). Imitation of high-interest comic strip models' appropriate classroom behavior: Acquisition and generalization. *Child and Family Behavior Therapy, 5,* 15–30.

Mithaug, D. E. (1978). Case study in training generalized instruction-following responses to preposition-noun combinations in a severely retarded adult. *AAESPH Review, 3,* 231–245.

Neef, N. A., Shafer, M. S., Egel, A. L., Cataldo, M. F., & Parrish, J. M. (1983). The class specific effects of compliance training with "do" and "don't" requests: Analogue analysis and classroom application. *Journal of Applied Behavior Analysis, 16,* 81–99.

Neef, N. A., Walters, J., & Egel, A. L. (1984). Establishing generative yes/no responses in developmentally disabled children. *Journal of Applied Behavior Analysis, 17,* 453–460.

Nelson, C. M., & Rutherford, R. B. (1988). Behavioral intervention with seriously emotionally disturbed students. In M. C. Wang, H. J. Walberg, & M. C. Reynolds (Eds.), *Handbook of special education: Research and practice* (Vol. 2, pp. 125–153). Oxford, England: Pergamon Press.

Nietupski, J., Clancy, P., & Christiansen, C. (1984). Acquisition, maintenance and generalization of vending machine purchasing skills by moderately handicapped students. *Education and Training of the Mentally Retarded, 19,* 91–96.

O'Leary, S. G., & Dubey, D. R. (1979). Applications of self-control procedures by children: A review. *Journal of Applied Behavior Analysis, 12,* 449–465.

O'Leary, S. G., & O'Leary, K. D. (1976). Behavior modification in the school. In H. Leitenberg (Ed.), *Handbook of behavior modification and behavior therapy* (pp. 475–515). Englewood Cliffs, NJ: Prentice-Hall.

Oliver, P. R., & Scott, T. L. (1981). Group versus individual training in establishing generalization of language skills with severely handicapped individuals. *Mental Retardation, 19,* 285–289.

Paine, S. C., Hops, H., Walker, H. M., Greenwood, C. R., Fleischman, D. H., & Guild, J. J. (1982). Repeated treatment effects: A study of maintaining behavior change in socially withdrawn children. *Behavior Modification, 6,* 171–199.

Panyan, M. C., & Hall, R. V. (1978). Effects of serial versus concurrent task sequencing on acquisition, maintenance, and generalization. *Journal of Applied Behavior Analysis, 11,* 67–74.

Parsonson, B. S., & Baer, D. M. (1978). Training generalized improvisation of tools by preschool children. *Journal of Applied Behavior Analysis, 11,* 363–380.

Peterson, G. A., Austin, G. J., & Lang, R. P. (1979). Use of teacher prompts to increase social behavior: Generalization effects with severely and profoundly retarded adolescents. *American Journal of Mental Deficiency, 84,* 82–86.

Polirstok, S. R., & Greer, R. D. (1977). Remediation of mutually aversive interactions between a problem student and four teachers by training the student in reinforcement techniques. *Journal of Applied Behavior Analysis, 10,* 707–716.

Powers, M. D., & Handleman, J. S. (1984). *Behavioral assessment of severe developmental disabilities.* Rockville, MD: Aspen.

Reese, S. C., & Filipczak, J. (1980). Assessment of skill generalization: Measurement across setting, behavior, and time in an educational setting. *Behavior Modification, 4,* 209–224.

Reisinger, J. J. (1978). Generalization of cooperative behavior across classroom situations. *The Journal of Special Education, 12,* 209–217.

Reppucci, N. D., & Saunders, J. T. (1974). Social psychology of behavior modification: Problems of implementation in natural settings. *American Psychologist, 29,* 649–660.

Rhode, G., Morgan, D. P., & Young, K. R. (1983). Generalization and maintenance of treatment gains of behaviorally handicapped students from resource rooms to regular classrooms using self-evaluation procedures. *Journal of Applied Behavior Analysis, 16,* 171–188.

Richmond, G., & Lewallen, J. (1983). Facilitating transfer of stimulus control when teaching verbal labels. *Education and Training of the Mentally Retarded, 18,* 111–116.

Rose, T. L., Koorland, M. A., & Epstein, M. H. (1982). A review of applied behavior analysis interventions with learning disabled children. *Education and Treatment of Children, 5,* 41–58.

Rose, T. L., Lessen, E. I., & Gottlieb, J. (1982). A discussion of transfer of training in mainstreaming programs. *Journal of Learning Disabilities, 15,* 162–165.

Rusch, F. R., & Kazdin, A. E. (1981). Toward a methodology of withdrawal designs for the assessment of response maintenance. *Journal of Applied Behavior Analysis, 14,* 131–140.

Russo, D. C., & Koegel, R. L. (1977). A method for integrating an autistic child into a normal public-school classroom. *Journal of Applied Behavior Analysis, 10,* 579–590.

Rutherford, R. B. (1987). *Books in behavior modification and behavior therapy.* Tempe, AZ: Arizona State University.

Sanok, R. L., & Striefel, S. (1979). Elective mutism: Generalization of verbal responding across people and settings. *Behavior Therapy, 10,* 357–371.

Schumaker, J. B., & Ellis, E. S. (1982). Social skills training of LD adolescents: A generalization study. *Learning Disability Quarterly, 5,* 409–414.

Sedlak, R. A., Doyle, M., & Schloss, P. (1982). Video games: A training and generalization demonstration with severely retarded adolescents. *Education and Training of the Mentally Retarded, 17,* 332–336.

Shafer, M. S., Egel, A. L., & Neef, N. A. (1984). Training mildly handicapped peers to facilitate changes in the social interaction skills of autistic children. *Journal of Applied Behavior Analysis, 17,* 461–476.

Smeege, M. E., Page, T. J., Iwata, B. A., & Ivancic, M. T. (1980). Teaching measurement skills to mentally retarded students: Training, generalization, and follow-up. *Education and Training of the Mentally Retarded, 15,* 224–230.

Sprague, J. R., & Horner, R. H. (1984). The effects of single instance, multiple instance, and general case training on generalized vending machine use by moderately and severely handicapped students. *Journal of Applied Behavior Analysis, 17,* 273–278.

Stevenson, H. C., & Fantuzzo, J. W. (1984). Application of the "generalization map" to a self-control intervention with school-aged children. *Journal of Applied Behavior Analysis, 17,* 203–212.

Stokes, T. F., & Baer, D. M. (1977). An implicit technology of generalization. *Journal of Applied Behavior Analysis, 10,* 349–367.

Stokes, T. F., Fowler. S. A., & Baer, D. M. (1978). Training preschool children to recruit natural communities of reinforcement. *Journal of Applied Behavior Analysis, 11,* 285–303.

Stowitschek, C. E., Hecimovic, A., Stowitschek, J. J., & Shores, R. E. (1982). Behaviorally disordered adolescents as peer tutors: Immediate and generative effects on instructional performance and spelling achievement. *Behavioral Disorders, 7,* 136–148.

Strain, P. S., Cooke, T. P., & Apolloni, T. (1976). *Teaching exceptional children: Assessing and modifying social behavior.* New York: Academic Press.

Strain, P. S., Kerr, M. M., & Ragland, E. U. (1979). Effects of peer-mediated social initiations and prompting/reinforcement procedures on the social behavior of autistic children. *Journal of Autism and Developmental Disorders, 9,* 41–54.

Sulzer-Azaroff, B., & Mayer, G. R. (1977). *Applying behavior-analysis procedures with children and youth.* New York: Holt.

Tofte-Tipps, S., Mendonca, P., & Peach, R. V. (1982). Training and generalization of social skills: A study with two developmentally handicapped, socially isolated children. *Behavior Modification, 6,* 45–71.

Tucker, D. J., & Berry, G. W. (1980). Teaching severely multihandicapped students to put on their own hearing aids. *Journal of Applied Behavior Analysis, 13,* 65–75.

Wacker, D. P., Carroll, J. L., & Moe, G. L. (1980). Acquisition, generalization, and maintenance of an assembly task by mentally retarded children. *American Journal of Mental Deficiency, 85,* 286–290.

Walker, H. M. (1979). *The acting-out child: Coping with classroom disruption.* Boston, MA: Allyn & Bacon.

Walker, H. M., & Buckley, N. K. (1972). Programming generalization and maintenance of treatment effects across time and across settings. *Journal of Applied Behavior Analysis, 5,* 209–224.

Warren, S. F. (1977). A useful ecobehavioral perspective for applied behavior analysis. In A. R. Warren & S. F. Warren (Eds.), *Ecological perspectives in behavior analysis* (pp. 173–196). Baltimore, MD: University Park.

Warrenfeltz, R. B., Kelly, W. J., Salzberg, C. L., Beegle, C. P., Levy, S. M., Adams, T. A., & Crouse, T. R. (1981). Social skills training of behavior disordered adolescents with self-monitoring to promote generalization to a vocational setting. *Behavioral Disorders, 7,* 18–27.

Welch, S. J., & Pear, J. J. (1980). Generalization of naming responses to objects in the natural environment as a function of training stimulus modality with retarded children. *Journal of Applied Behavior Analysis, 13,* 629–643.

Whitman, T. L., Hurley, J. D., Johnson, M. R., & Christian, J. G. (1978). Direct and generalized reduction of inappropriate behavior in a severely retarded child through a parent-administered behavior modification program. *AAESPH Review, 3,* 67–77.

Whitman, T. L., Scibak, J. W., Butler, K. M., Richter, R., & Johnson, M. R. (1982). Improving classroom behavior in mentally retarded children through correspondence training. *Journal of Applied Behavior Analysis, 15*, 545–564.

Wildman, R. W., & Wildman, R. W. (1975). The generalization of behavior modification procedures: A review—with special emphasis on classroom applications. *Psychology in the Schools, 12*, 432–444.

Zifferblatt, S. M., Burton, S. D., Horner, R., & White, T. (1977). Establishing generalization effects among autistic children. *Journal of Autism and Childhood Schizophrenia, 7*, 337–347.

Zucker, S. H., Rutherford, R. B., & Prieto, A. G. (1979). Teacher directed interventions with behaviorally disordered children. In R. B. Rutherford & A. G. Prieto (Eds.), *Severe behavior disorders of children and youth* (Vol. 2, pp. 49–61). Reston, VA: Council for Children with Behavioral Disorders.

CHAPTER 12

On the Ecological Validity of Behavior Modification

Brian K. Martens and Joseph C. Witt

> The influences go backward and forward, up and down, round and round, compounding and branching as they go. All that is certain is that an error introduced anywhere in the network ramifies all over the place, and each consequence breeds further consequences. But it seems unlikely that an error can ramify endlessly. It spreads by way of the connections of the network, but sooner or later it must also begin to break them. We are talking, obviously, about a circulatory system, and a disease of a circulatory system tends to first impair circulation and then to stop it altogether.
>
> —Wendell Berry

Perhaps the single most significant characteristic of the 20th century has been the logarithmic development and unbridled application of new technology. Technological advances in sciences such as chemistry, physics, and biology have been promulgated at an outstanding rate, bringing with them dramatic increases in the perceived quality of life. Spurred by public demand and often supported by monies appropriated for research and development, scientists have grasped hungrily at new innovations, adopting the maxim "if it can be done, it should be done."

Recently, however, as problems have arisen from the unforeseen and unplanned long-term impacts of this technology, the unrestricted proliferation of scientific advancements has been moderated by a cautious concern over their ecological consequences. A major impetus for this concern has been the growing realization that the planet upon which we live is a closed system, and that once unleased upon this system, technological intrusions do not just go away. Nowhere has this realization been more evident than in the areas of pesticide development and industrial waste disposal. Unforeseen consequences,

Brian K. Martens • Department of Psychology, Syracuse University, Syracuse, New York 13244. **Joseph C. Witt** • Department of Psychology, Louisana State University, Baton Rouge, Louisiana 70803.

such as the overpopulation of certain insect species resulting from the killing of their natural predators, and the contamination of ground water caused by long-term decay of toxic waste containers, have resulted in the spending of countless dollars on the restoration of natural areas adversely affected by side effects of seemingly benign interventions.

As a result of increased experience with the long-term effects of intrusions into the ecological system, it has become increasingly apparent that in terms of the application of technology, we can never "do just one thing" (Willems, 1974). There is a growing body of evidence in all fields of applied science indicating that the use of technology, even in the most prudent and focused manner, may have widespread and long-term consequences (Sarason, 1984). Recognition of these difficulties has resulted in a closer alignment of applied scientists with what has become labeled as the ecological perspective. Slowly, psychologists too have begun to join the ranks of the ecologically minded, the most notable influences being apparent in the application of technologies for behavior change. As Willems (1974) asserted in his commentary on the then largely inductive approach to research in applied behavior analysis,

> if we think of the implications of such phenomena [that result from adoption of an ecological perspective] and what they suggest about human behavior in general, and if we think about the growing pressure to apply known behavioral technologies, the following observation emerges: we have become fairly conservative and sophisticated about introducing new biotic elements and new chemicals into our ecological systems, but we display almost childish irresponsibility in our attitudes toward behavioral and behavioral-environment systems. (p. 154)

Since Willems' article appeared in 1974, numerous changes have occurred with respect to the ways in which behavioral technologies have come to be perceived and applied in naturalistic settings. Paticularly noticeable have been changes occurring in the application of school-based behavior management techniques.

This chapter discusses major trends in the application of behavioral technology that have contributed to the emergent ecological perspective in the treatment of children's classroom behavior problems. In addition, assumptions of the ecological perspective in behavior analysis are presented and implications for the development of ecologically valid interventions are discussed.

The Ecological Perspective in Applied Behavior Analysis: Causal Trends

Behavioral interventions have a long history of successful application in the classroom setting. Utilizing treatment effectiveness as a criterion, behavior management strategies have been used successfully in response to a diverse array of problems (Kazdin, 1982; Reynolds, Gutkin, Elliott, & Witt, 1984). Recently, however, several factors within and outside the field of applied behavior analysis have encouraged the adoption of an ecological perspective in the evaluation of treatment success. Increased emphasis on an ecological perspective in the application of classroom behavior management techniques has resulted from four primary developments: (a) increased reports of intervention side effects, (b) frequent failure to obtain treatment generalization and maintenance, (c) increased popularity of consultation as a model of psychological service delivery, and (d) increased focus on consumer satisfaction as a criterion for treatment evaluation.

Reports of Intervention Side Effects

A major impetus for adoption of an ecological perspective has been the increase in reports of intervention side effects in which simultaneous changes have occurred in untreated behaviors and/or nontargeted individuals following the application of behavioral interventions to a single response (Ayllon & Roberts, 1974; Becker, Turner, & Sajwaj, 1978; Kazdin, 1973; Johnson, Baumeister, Penland, & Inwald, 1982; Russo, Cataldo, & Cushing, 1981; Witt, Hannafin, & Martens, 1983). With these reports of unforeseen intervention side effects has come the growing awareness that traditional assessment techniques employed by applied behavior analysts seeking treatment impact in relation only to a single response are inadequate as methodologies for evaluating treatment efficacy. Behavior analysts have therefore begun to expand their scope of inquiry into the effects of behavioral interventions in the classroom setting to include measurement of multiple behavior categories (Martens & Witt, 1984; Wahler, 1975), reciprocal behavior change between teachers and students (Bates, 1976), and collateral behavior change in nontarget peers (Kazdin, 1973).

Consistent with the old adage "if you go looking for trouble, you're likely to find it," behavior analysts have uncovered numerous unanticipated effects of behavioral interventions following adoption of these broader and more ecologically minded assessment techniques. For example, Sajwaj, Twardosz, and Burke (1972) reported increases in disruptive behavior for a young retarded child when excessive conversation with the teacher was placed on extinction. In another instance, Forehand, Breiner, McMahon, and Davies (1981) found a parent-training program that was effective in reducing oppositional behavior at home, inadvertantly resulted in increases in appropriate behavior at school. Results such as these have suggested that, just as in other areas of applied science, the application of behavioral technology, even with its traditionally molecular focus, is likely to result in widespread and often negative consequences in the behavior–environment system in which it is employed. However, as Willems (1974) asserts, application of the term *side effect* to these unanticipated results is probably inaccurate because

> When we think in terms of environment–behavior *systems,* we can see that there is a fundamental misconception embedded in the term "side effect" . . . What we so glibly call side effects no more deserve the adjective "side" than does the "principal" effect—they are all aspects of the interdependencies that we need so badly to understand. (Willems, 1974, p. 155)

Failure to Obtain Treatment Generalization

A second impetus for adoption of an ecological perspective has been the limited and frequently nonexistent generalization of treatment impact. Treatment generalization refers to collateral improvements similar to those realized in the targeted behavior that occur in a variety of settings, that spread to related problem behaviors, and that are maintained over time (Baer, Wolf, & Risley, 1968). In the field of applied behavior analysis, there currently exists a consensus of opinion that generalization of all three types can only occur through its explicit programming separate from implementation of the treatment proper (Meichenbaum, Bowers, & Ross, 1968; Miller & Sloane, 1976; Redd & Birnbauer, 1969; Wahler, 1969). Although the parameters of generalization programming have yet to be fully uncovered, Wahler, Berland, and Coe (1979), in their extensive review of generalization processes in child behavior therapy, state that "clearly, there is reason to voice doubts about the outcomes of mixing imposed (programmed) contingencies within the natural contingencies of environments" (p. 52).

In relating the possible outcomes of imposed and existing stimulus events on desired changes in behavior, the following 2 × 2 table can be generated (see Table 1). Imposed stimulus events (i.e., behavioral interventions) can either be in support of or operate against existing environmental contingencies. If the two sets of consequences operate to alter behavior in the same direction, then initial treatment impact and generalization across time are likely to be facilitated. If neither the inter-

Table 1. Outcomes of the Interaction between Imposed and Naturally Occurring Stimulus Events on Desired Behavior Change

		Imposed stimulus events	
		Facilitate change	Impede change
Naturally occurring stimulus events	Facilitate change	Initial impact high and generalization likely	Initial impact low with desired change occurring gradually
	Impede change	Inital impact high but generalization unlikely	Initial impact low and generalization unlikely

vention nor the existing forces in the environment act to promote desired behavior change, then initial treatment impact and generalization will in all probability fail to occur. However, if the imposed stimulus events are organized in such a way as to compete with existing contingencies in a particular setting, generalization across time will be unlikely to occur, even though initial treatment impact is present.

In one sense, generalization and maintenance of treatment imposed behavior change from one setting or set of stimulus conditions to another can be viewed as a form of responding under concurrent schedules. At any given instant a child can engage in a number of possible responses to environmental stimuli. According to Herrnstein's interpretation of the law of effect (McDowell, 1982), the child will engage in behavior for which the richest ratio of reinforcement is provided. During treatment a great deal of reinforcement is introduced into the child's environment contingent on one or more appropriate responses. In the simplest case, then, the child has a two-choice discrimination. He or she can continue responding in inappropriate ways and receive whatever reinforcement is available for those responses (e.g., peer attention) or the child can respond appropriately. Initial treatment success occurs because the child is likely to make the response associated with the richer schedule of reinforcement. If the functional analysis is conducted properly, the child will engage in more appropriate responses during treatment.

Now consider what occurs during the generalization process within the context of the simple case of two reward schedules (i.e., one for appropriate responding and one for inappropriate responding) operating concurrently. With the introduction of treatment, the schedule for appropriate responding is richer, but during generalization this schedule is considerably leaner or nonexistent. As a result, the probability of the child switching to the other schedule increases. Therefore, if the child's natural environment cannot be programmed to support the target behavior, then generalization of this behavior beyond the treatment phase will not occur. To take a handy and obvious example of this situation, there is a tremendous problem with recidivism in the incarceration of juvenile delinquents. This should not be surprising to anyone familiar with the nature of responding under concurrent schedules. In prison or other structured residential facilities, juvenile delinquents have an environment that supports appropriate behavior and punishes inappropriate behavior. When they leave prison, there is little or no generalization of appropriate responding because the environment to which they are returning (e.g., delinquent peer groups) encourages inappropriate behavior and in many cases punishes behavior that is societally approved. For the juvenile delinquent, the choice of schedules under which to respond is an easy one in prison and on the street. For most classroom management programs, the same pattern occurs, although not in as dramatic a fashion.

It may be more appropriate, then, to talk about generalization and maintenance of treatments rather than generalization and maintenance of behavior change. To the extent that treatment resembles the child's normal routine, gains made are more likely to endure. In a true ecological sense, the introduction of intrusive interventions that are foreign to the classroom and really do not belong there are counterproductive because typically the system cannot maintain them for very long and once they are removed the behavior patterns that occurred previously are likely to return.

The exception to this general rule is in cases where the problem is more appropriately termed a skill deficit rather than a performance deficit. If the environment is naturally supportive of a particular behavior and that behavior is not occuring because of a skill deficit, then an intensive intervention that results in skill acquisition is likely to be successful. In the case of social skills, for example, training programs that teach children to be more socially skilled are often successful in the long run because the environment is supportive of this class of behaviors. Parent training programs such as the one developed by Forehand and McMahon (1981) are often successful because, in a sense, they teach skills to the child's environment (i.e., the parents).

In their call for a broadened view of child behavior in naturalistic settings, Wahler *et al.* (1979) set the stage for an ecological perspective in applied behavioral analysis.

> From the laboratory era to the present-day ecobehavioral orientation, the child-clinical field has not gained a great deal of useful information on generalization phenomena. There is no doubt that some sort of process or processes govern those general outcomes of man-made and natural changes in child behavior. But we are just beginning to unearth the network behind these outcomes. Despite our own frustration at this state of affairs, we must also voice a guarded optimism for the future. Clinicians will (and should) continue their intervention efforts as if it were now possible to ensure appropriate generalization effects. In our view, the current ecobehavioral research emphasis will gradually add techniques and conceptual guidelines to these efforts. (p. 64)

Increased Popularity of Consultation as a Model of Service Delivery

Consultation has become one of the major professional functions of psychologists working in applied settings (Gutkin & Curtis, 1982). Faced with increasing numbers of children requiring some form of psychological service and decreasing numbers of personnel to meet these needs, psychologists were urged to "give psychology away" to nonpsychologists in order to "promote human welfare" (Miller, 1969, p. 1071). Consultation then has been implicated as a necessity rather than a luxury in the armamentarium of psychological service delivery.

Although there are many different approaches to consultation, several characteristics are common to virtually all consultation models. The characteristic most relevant to our discussion here is the active involvement of the consultee as a coequal professional in the consultation process.

> The active involvement of the consultee in the consultation process is seen as a crucial element in successful consultation. . . . For one thing, it is believed that "the consultant can seldom learn enough about the classroom, teacher(s), or the various human ecological systems operating to 'really' know what a better course of action would be in order to improve a particular environment" (Pyle, 1977, p. 193). Furthermore, failure to involve the consultee in the consultation process might result in the consultee's failure to "own" resulting treatment plans and may thus decrease the probability that the consultee will probably carry out agreed-on interventions. (Gutkin & Curtis, 1982, p. 801)

Explicit in the involvement of teachers in the consultation process is the assumption that, as an integral part of the classroom ecology, they are in a better position (than consultants) to judge the ultimate appropriateness of behavioral interventions. Furthermore, because teachers themselves are the individuals most likely to hold responsibility for long-term intervention implementation, behavioral strategies that are generated during the consultative interaction must meet their approval. Gone are the days when behavioral interventions developed with university funding in experimental classrooms are hailed on the basis of effectiveness alone. Instead, with increased utilization of the consultative model, behavioral interventions must now demonstrate effectiveness and ready application to the classroom ecology lest they be rejected out of hand by the guardian of the classroom ecology, the teacher.

Consumer Satisfaction as a Criterion for Treatment Evaluation

Closely related to increased use of the consultation model in the application of behavioral technology has been a growing emphasis on assessment of consumer satisfaction as a variable in treatment success. Falling under the general rubric of social validity, determination of whether behavioral interventions are acceptable has become an important area of research in applied behavior analysis (Kazdin, 1980, 1981; Martens, Witt, Elliott, & Darveaux, 1985; Witt, Elliott, & Martens, 1984). In general, acceptability refers to judgments by consumers as to whether treatment is fair in relation to a given problem, reasonable or intrusive in its application, and consistent with conventional notions of what treatment should be (Kazdin, 1980). Although all three criteria carry implications for the use of behavioral technology in applied settings, the dimension of intervention intrusiveness has the greatest relevance in terms of the present discussion. Acceptability research has suggested interventions that are excessively complicated, require unusually large amounts of teacher time to implement, or call for materials and equipment not easily procurable in the educational environment (e.g., light and buzzer apparatuses, time-out rooms) are likely to be perceived as intrusive when attempts are made to implement them in the classroom setting. As a result, behavior change agents are seeing the need to take a more system-level orientation when suggesting interventions for use in the classroom setting, placing greater consideration on existing characteristics of the classroom ecology for use as intervention alternatives.

Assumptions of the Ecological Perspective in the Use of Behavioral Interventions

In the previous section, we discussed global trends in the use of behavioral technology that have contributed to increased emphasis on adoption of an ecological perspective. In this section, we examine the major characteristics of the classroom setting as an ecological system, discuss similarities between behavioral assessment and ecological assessment, present the major assumptions of the ecological perspective in the use of behavioral interventions, and discuss the constraints under which ecologically minded behavior analysts operate. Although it is not the purpose of this section to identify specific interventions dictated by the emergent ecological perspective, it is our hope that the reader will come away from the discussion with a useful conceptual framework with which to make competent decisions of when to intervene and in what manner.

Within the biological sciences, ecological systems can be identified by several distinguishing characteristics. Perhaps the most notable characteristic of plant and animal habitats, or ecosystems, is the complex and interactional nature of their component parts. For example, it is not uncommon for a fresh water pond and its surrounding bank area to contain and support numerous forms of plant and algae growth, countless microorganisms, and various species of small animal life. The needs of all participants in the habitat are met only through complex interactions of chemical, physical, and behavioral processes such as carbon decay, photosynthesis, soil erosion, and hierarchical predation.

A second characteristic of ecological systems is their tendency to strive for homeostasis. Homeostasis refers to the achievement of a relatively stable condition between interdependent elements. Thus, in the absence of outside intrusions, our small pond area will exhibit a kind of "natural wisdom," ensuring that elements required for continuation of the habitat are kept in balance. Brief periods of animal overpopulation may be kept in check by the resulting depletion of food supplies. Eventually, as animals die from a lack of food needed to support their increased numbers, balance is restored to the animal–plant ratio.

The third and final characteristic of ecological systems is their relatively self-contained status. That is, with a few exceptions such as sunlight and rainfall, the business of life in an ecosystem is maintained on a largely intrasystem level. This will be referred to as *system integrity* throughout the remainder of the chapter. Ecological systems exhibit a finite capacity to achieve homeostasis among their component parts. As a result, intrusions into the system from the outside may have devastating consequences as the ability of the system to compensate proves inadequate.

To what extent does life in a school classroom exhibit characteristics similar to those of an ecological system? What are the components of the classroom ecology? Although a great deal of information has been accumulated concerning behavioral and academic activities that go on inside the classroom setting, these questions are just recently being addressed. Despite the paucity of direct empirical investigation, several general conclusions can be drawn in response to the questions on the basis of careful observation. The first characteristic of an ecological system is the complex and interactional nature of its component parts. If we consider the variety of appropriate and inappropriate behaviors that children exhibit in the classroom, the interactions between the behaviors of children and the behaviors of teachers, and the interactions between the behaviors of children and teachers with curriculum materials and physical components of the classroom setting, common sense alone suggests that the classroom is in fact a complex and interactional system.

In order for a classroom to be considered an ecological system, it must also show a tendency to strive for homeostasis. As mentioned previously, components of the classroom ecology include the behaviors of children and teachers and the interaction of these behaviors with curriculum materials and physical objects present in the setting. Homeostasis may therefore be provisionally defined as the establishment of relatively consistent patterns of behavior that enable students and teachers to satisfy their educational needs. Sarason (1984) referred to these consistent patterns of behavior as behavioral regularities and his conceptualization is germane to the present discussion.

To understand the concept of behavioral regularities, a personal reflection from Sarason (1984) is instructive:

> I remember as a child being puzzled and annoyed that no one could satisfactorily explain to me why one could not eat fried chicken for breakfast. It was obvious what the existing regularities were, but I could not understand why the alternative of chicken aroused such a strong feeling. (Sarason, 1984, p. 97)

A *behavioral* regularity then is the regular occurence or nonoccurence of a behavior or some series of behaviors. As Sarason points out, it is a regularity in our culture that we do not have chicken for breakfast. Many regularities can be observed within schools. These include the fact that schools are in session for five days and then are off for two days; that teachers are responsible for teaching and students are responsible for being taught; and that teaching usually occurs with teachers doing most of the talking in front of a class while children sit in orderly rows and listen (Sarason, 1971). In certain classrooms, specific regularities may exist such that children who misbehave are punished in a particular way or that children who demonstrate exemplary behavior are rewarded using predetermined methods. Wahler (1975) demonstrated that there are even regularities at the individual child level. That is, behaviors covary in orderly ways within the behavioral repertoires of individual children (Martens &

Witt, 1984; Voeltz & Evans, 1982). The point is that any classroom may have a number of regularities between which there exist complex relationships.

Because of a preoccupation with the development and implementation of effective interventions, we do not usually consider the effects that an intervention may have on the already existing behavioral regularities. We sometimes ask teachers to alter the existing regularities in the classroom without first knowing what those regularities are, without knowing the effects and side effects of changing the existing regularities, and without knowledge that what is being replaced is inferior to what is being suggested. Even among those who would admit side effects, there is an optimism that we will be able to control those problems when they arise. Always the assumption is that we can first set demons at large, and then, somehow, become smart enough to control them. This does not represent simply a lack of professionalism, it does not even strictly represent a lack of knowledge; it is a kind of idiocy that will have to be conquered if applied behavior analysis is to continue to advance as a science.

From the standpoint of behavioral regularities within an ecological model, it is obvious why the refer-test-place sequence is relatively more popular with teachers than the refer-consult-intervene sequence. Interventions typically require change in the existing regularities. More specifically, interventions usually require a change in teacher behavior. Changes in teacher behavior may have widespread and unanticipated effects on children who are not the target of intervention. Placing a child in a special education classroom has a relatively minor effect on the ecology of the classroom because teacher behavior does not have to be altered. Thus, following removal of a deviant child, teachers can continue teaching using the same methods as before within an ecology that is very similar and can expect results that are relatively predictable. Those that try new techniques must be willing to tackle the ambiguities that are the likely result of the restructuring of behavioral regularities.

Finally, that classrooms exist as relatively self-contained entities (at least for certain time periods each day) is a point that requires little elaboration. Not only are classrooms typically equipped with all the materials needed to engage in a variety of educational and play behaviors (in some cases, restroom facilities are even provided), children are typically expected to spend 6 hours, 5 days a week in this setting under the care of a single adult (who also is allowed minimal contact with outside individuals).

Ecological Behavior Assessment

Historically, the goal of behavioral assessment has been to identify meaningful response units and their controlling environmental variables (of an antecedent and consequential nature) for the purposes of understanding and altering behavior (Nelson & Hayes, 1980). Methodologies employed in behavioral assessment are based on Skinnerian assumptions that behavior can be measured in terms of its frequency, intensity, or duration, that behavior is setting specific, and that behavior is a function of its environmental consequences.

Representing what is essentially an expansion of traditional behavior assessment techniques, ecological behavior assessment shares all the aforementioned assumptions, with two important additions. First, in ecological behavior assessment, emphasis is placed on the quantification of behavior and its controlling environmental factors from a systems-level perspective. That is, rather than focusing exclusively on molecular units of targeted behavior and consequences directly responsible for their maintenance, the goal of ecological behavior assessment is to generate an understanding of the total behavior–environment system. This sytem mapping is typically accomplished through the measurement of behaviors and persons other than those to which an intervention is to be applied (Wahler & Fox, 1981). For example, research conducted by Wahler and his associates (Kara & Wahler, 1977; Wahler, 1975; Wahler, Sperling, Thomas, Teeter, & Luper, 1970) in which observational data were taken on a variety of child behaviors has suggested that behavioral interventions targeted at a single response are likely to result in complex patterns of collateral and inverse changes in behavior within a child's repertoire. In a similar expansion of traditional behavioral assessment techniques, Nelson and Bowles (1975) suggested that observational data taken on a target child in the classroom setting should be joined by identical data taken on nontarget peers. In this way, information can be obtained enabling the normative comparison of baseline and posttreatment levels of behavior, resulting in more realistic expectations for treatment success and providing a more accurate picture of intervention effectiveness.

Second, in ecological behavior assessment, emphasis is placed on the measurement of existing patterns of teacher and student behavior (i.e., behavioral regularities) with the goal of utilizing this information in the development of intervention alternatives. It is here that the ecological perspective in behavioral assessment most emulates the ecological perspective in other fields of applied science. Accordingly, it is this characteristic of ecological behavior assessment that distinguishes it most from more traditional forms of behavioral assessment.

The traditional assessment–intervention paradigm in applied behavior analysis has been to identify existing environmental factors that maintain a given pattern of deviant behavior, and then to apply an intervention that has been empirically demonstrated in previous research to have the highest efficacy rate in response to such problem behavior. Unfortunately, because of the recent developments in the application of behavioral technology discussed earlier, the adoption of such empirical-rational orientations to intervention implementation have proven extremely naive in relation to the complexity of the classroom ecology (Owens, 1971; Sarason, 1984; Willems, 1974; Witt & Elliott, 1985). Therefore, in contrast to the traditional assessment–intervention paradigm, behavioral assessment techniques resulting from adoption of an ecological perspective involve (a) the additional measurement of systemwide patterns of behavioral regularities, their frequencies, and their consequences; and (b) utilization of this information to structure intervention alternatives containing elements already existing in the classroom setting.

Given the complexity of the classroom ecology, how then is it possible to adequately assess the myriad interactions between behaviors of students, behaviors of students and teachers, and behaviors of students and teachers and the physical environment? With the finite nature of the assessment process and the functionally infinite possibilities for behavior–setting interactions, such a task would indeed be formidable. Fortunately, by drawing on concepts employed in the area of statistical analysis, our task need not be that of documenting all interactions but merely observation of those that contribute to a significant proportion of variance in possible classroom behavior.

The following steps then are presented as helpful suggestions in the ecological assessment of behavior in any classroom setting. First, it is important to assess teacher expectations for what constitutes good and bad regularities in classroom behavior. Because teachers are typically the rule makers for such behavior, and because they are the individuals most responsible for making decisions regarding behavior appropriateness, assessment of their expectations is likely to provide an important criterion by which to evaluate intervention success. Second, once teacher expectations for student behavior have been identified, the next step is to assess student behavioral regularities that actually exist in the classroom setting. Here, it is necessary to identify and observe multiple categories of student behavior at the individual and group level. Because of the emphasis of ecological behavior assessment on molar units of student behavior (i.e., patterns of behavior that occur across students), techniques such as momentary time sampling (Sulzer-Azaroff & Mayer, 1977), sequential interval time sampling of several students chosen at random, self-monitoring (Mahoney & Thoresen, 1974), and review of permanent products may be useful in obtaining frequency measures at the group level. An additional and somewhat creative method that can be used to observe behavior for the total class is termed the freeze approach. As Blackham and Silberman (1980) suggested:

> Essentially, the freeze approach requires the students in the classroom to stop and stay still when the teacher yells "Freeze." To illustrate the method, let us suppose that a teacher is bothered by the fact that students do not come right in to the room and sit down at their desks. She notices that many walk around the room for quite a while before being seated. The teacher then instructs her students that when she yells "Freeze", they are to stop and maintain a statuelike position. Once the students are still, the teacher then places a mark by the name of each student seated. This observational method can be used in the recording of other types of behavior, such as not doing assignments, talking to one's peers without permission, not being in line, etc. (p. 89)

Whatever the technique employed, one goal of ecological behavioral assessment is to identify relative frequencies of appropriate and inappropriate classroom behaviors that are descriptive for the class as a whole.

The third and perhaps most important task in the ecological assessment of classroom behavior is the identification of regularities in teacher behaviors. Whether they are aware of it or not, teachers play critical roles in the establishment of the classroom ecology. They generate rules for behavior that are specific to the classroom setting and deliver consequences to children in accordance with these rules. In an extensive investigation of 28 third-grade teachers, Emmer and Evertson (1981) reported the following:

> More effective managers spent considerable time during the first several weeks helping students learn how to behave in their classrooms. They had carefully thought out procedures for getting assistance, contacting the teacher, lining-up, turning work in, and standards for conduct during seatwork, group work, and whole class activities. Thus, these teachers knew what children needed to function in the classroom setting and in its activities, and they proceeded to teach these "survival" skills as part of the content at the beginning of the year. Better managers were also more careful monitors of student behavior and dealt with inappropriate behavior, when it occurred, more quickly than did less effective managers. The usefulness of this type of with-itness at the beginning of the year, before a pattern of inappropriate behavior becomes established, is evident. (p. 345)

In a system developed by Kaufman and O'Leary (1972), teacher behavior is observed for 20-second intervals followed by 10-second recording periods and classified into 11 categories (see Table 2). Again, regardless of the coding system used, the goal of systematic teacher observation is to identify the relative frequencies of behavioral regularities that are used to measure the behavior of students.

The fourth and final step in the ecological assessment of classroom behavior involves the assessment of behavioral processes. Specifically, once regularities in teacher and student behavior have been identified, the issue becomes one of determining just how the behaviors in which the teacher engages are used to consequence the behaviors in which students engage. Through an ecological mapping of contingencies common to classroom settings, it then becomes possible to draw comparisons between behaviors that teachers would like to encourage in students and behaviors that they actually do encourage through their interactions. For example, suppose that it has been determined that a teacher, Mr. Henry, spends over 80% of his time in the classroom either working quietly behind his desk or engaging in verbal interactions with students in close proximity to their work stations. Suppose further that behavioral reg-

Table 2. Categories of Teacher Behavior Using the Kaufman and O'Leary Observation System

Category: Description
1. Reprimand to the class: Making disapproving remarks to a small group or the whole class
2. Praise to the class: Making positive comments to a small group of students or the entire class
3. Loud reprimand to individuals: Negative verbal comments of disapproval made to an individual that can be heard by other members of the class
4. Soft reprimands to an individual: Negative verbal comments of disapproval to an individual that cannot be heard by other class members
5. Loud praise to an individual: Verbal comments of approval given to an individual that can be heard by other class members
6. Soft praise to an individual: Positive verbal comments made to an individual that cannot be heard by other class members
7. Educational attention—close: Providing a child aid with an academic task (answering a question, correcting a paper, etc.) within three feet—praise or disapproval not included in this category
8. Educational attention—far: Aid is provided from a distance of three feet or more
9. Negative facial attention: Frowning without an accompanying verbal reprimand
10. Touching a child: Any physical contact with the child
11. Redirecting attention: Diverting the child's disruptive or inappropriate behavior without commenting on the child's particular act

ularities observed in the students of Mr. Henry's class include relatively low frequencies of actual assignment completion, but generally high frequencies of out-of-seat behavior and peer interaction. When asked to describe expectations for the behavior of students in his class, Mr. Henry reports that students are expected to work independently at their desks, raise their hands when assistance is required, and complete an average of one assignment in each of six subject areas per day. Suppose further, that when observing the times in which Mr. Henry is working behind his desk or interacting with the students (behaviors that account for over 80% of his time during the day), we discover the following. When the students are working quietly at their desks, Mr. Henry is working quietly at his desk. In addition, Mr. Henry is only observed to engage in interaction with the students at their work stations in response to disruptive behavior or periods of loud noise resulting from peer interaction. If we assume that interaction with Mr. Henry is rewarding for the students, results of our ecological behavioral assessment would suggest that Mr. Henry is doing all the right things for all the wrong reasons. It then becomes a simple matter to help Mr. Henry redistribute his existing behavioral regularities in order to achieve the desired outcomes in student behavior.

The Ecological Validity of Behavioral Intervention

Armed with an ecological map of the classroom setting with its composite regularities in student and teacher behavior and their contingent use, what are the implications for development of behavioral interventions? Although we have to some extent anticipated the answer to this question in our discussion of ecological behavior assessment, in this section major assumptions of the ecological perspective in behavioral intervention are presented and constraints under which the ecologically minded behavior change agent operates are discussed.

Assumption 1: As an Ecology, Setting–Behavior Systems Strive toward Homeostasis

As discussed previously, ecological systems can be broadly defined as relatively self-contained settings comprised of elements in complex interaction. To the extent that elements within an ecological system are able to function harmoniously on a continuous basis, that system is said to have reached a state of homeostasis. Consequently, the classroom as a behavior–setting system may be viewed as an ecology in the sense that it is relatively self-contained (at least for certain time periods each day), is comprised of complex interactions between behaviors, and is characterized by the establishment of relatively consistent rules for behavior that enable the harmonious functioning of both students and teachers. Thus, the extent to which consistent behavioral regularities are observed within the classroom setting, that setting may be said to have reached a state of homeostasis. In contrast, classrooms in which rules for behavior are inconsistent, or in which the consequencing of behavior is inconsistent may be said to be in a state of flux. According to the assumption that ecologies strive for homeostasis, the behavior of children and teachers in a classroom in flux will increase in variability until some level of consistency is achieved in the manner by which individuals satisfy their behavioral needs (i.e., achieve reward).

Two opportunities for ecological intervention result from consideration of Assumption 1. First, the classroom teacher, as a critical determiner of regularities in children's classroom behavior, may not have a consistent set of rules by which behavior is consequenced. In this case, the development of rules for behavior which are consistent with teacher expectations may facilitate establishment of the desired behavioral regularities. Behavioral programming packages, such as assertive discipline, rely heavily on this type of ecological intervention and have gained immense popularity among educational personnel. Second, if consistent rules for behavior already exist in the classroom setting, intervention may be required to ensure that such rules are consistently enforced. Rules for behavior that do not lead to consistent consequences provide children with confusing messages about what is expected of them in the classroom.

Corollary 1: Change in One Behavioral Regularity Is Likely to Require Change in Other Regularities for Homeostasis to Be Maintained

Because of the interactional nature of elements within an ecological system, change in one element must be compensated for by some level of change in elements with which it interacts. Accordingly, changes in either student or teacher behavior will likely impact the behavior of all students in the classroom either directly or indirectly. For example, Scott and Bushell (1974) reported that teacher inattention to students resulting from extended contacts with another student led to higher rates of classroom off-task behavior. Thus, in the absence of such data identifying the widespread effects of a given behavioral intervention, it is better to choose intervention alternatives that are least disruptive to existing classroom regularities.

Assumption 2: Setting–Behavior Systems as Ecologies Maintain Finite Tolerance to Stress

Assumption 2 acknowledges that behavioral regularities in the classroom setting often do change and can be changed by manipulation of certain components. However, because ecological systems strive for homeostasis, change can be accomodated on a systemwide basis only up to a certain point before existing regularities in behavior decay. That is, ecological systems such as classrooms have finite tolerances to stress that, when exceeded, result in the loss of system integrity. Loss of system integrity can be observed in the cessation of existing behavioral regularities and corresponding increases in behavior variability (i.e., characteristics of a system in flux). So frequently, we as psychologists are approached by teachers who not only have been unable to control a certain child's behavior, but who report that other students in the class are becoming increasingly disruptive making it more difficult for the teacher to teach.

Corollary 1: Systems May Be Stressed from Within or from Without

Not only do ecological systems receive stress from changes occurring within them, when there is a superordinate system of which the ecology is a part, stress may also come from outside the system. With the exception of intrusions manufactured by man, stress in natural ecological systems frequently results from spontaneous happenings such as electrical storm fires or flooding. In terms of the classroom, such spontaneous sources of system stress may result from unresolved issues in the home environment that adversely affect children's classroom behavior, or from interstudent conflicts. Unless the resulting inappropriate behavior is particularly disruptive or chronic, existing forces in the classroom ecology (e.g., contingent teacher attention, proximity control, manipulation of material rewards) typically prove effective in regaining control over the problem behavior. Unfortunately, when faced with occurrences of inappropriate behavior that are atypical for a given student, teachers often unwittingly subvert their own carefully constructed classroom ecology by failing to adhere to previously identified contingencies.

Although not typically considered as such, a very significant source of external stress on the classroom ecology may also include attempts to implement interventions arising from interaction with a behavioral consultant. As discussed previously, issues concerning the stress that is often placed on teachers by the amount of time, materials, or extra personnel required to implement an intervention has played a major role in the emergent ecological perspective in behavioral technology. Research in this area has suggested interventions that demand a minimum of teacher time and resources are not only more acceptable but are more likely to be implemented and implemented correctly (Witt & Martens, 1983; Witt, Martens, & Elliott, 1984).

Corollary 2: System Integrity Takes Priority over Component Change as a Criterion for Intervention Success

Traditionally, the sole criterion for evaluating intervention success has been that of intervention effectiveness. Recently, however, support has increased for expanding the criteria by which behavioral interventions are evaluated to include dimensions such as consumer satisfaction, ease of implementation, and impact on nontargeted individuals (Barlow, 1981; Garfield, 1978; Voeltz & Evans, 1982; Wolf, 1978). Increased experience with the long-term use of behavior management strategies ranging from token economy systems to home-based reinforcement has resulted in emphasis on system integrity (i.e., the ability to maintain regularities in classroom behavior over long periods of time) as a means of evaluating treatment adequacy. For example, Martens, Peterson, Witt, & Cirone (1986) in an extensive survey of 2,279 regular and special education teachers found that interventions involving the early redirection prompting of misbehavior were rated as easier to use, more frequently used, and more effective than interventions involving manipulation of material rewards, time-out, or various other formal intervention programs. Because early redirection of student misbehavior requires significantly less time and extra teacher behavior than the other categories of intervention alternatives, and because an extensive body of literature exists attesting to the efficacy of contingency management, it seems that effectiveness alone was not the criterion on which the subjects based their ratings.

The implications for selecting behavioral interventions for use in the classroom setting are clear. Given the option of utilizing one of several intervention alternatives, it is more desirable from an ecological perspective to implement the strategy in which required teacher behaviors are most similar to existing teacher behaviors. Thus, if interventions designed to effect changes in student behavior can be implemented successfully without altering drastically the existing regularities in teacher behavior, negative side effects (i.e., unwanted changes in the behavior of other students) are likely to be minimized.

In choosing an appropriate manner in which to intervene in the classroom setting, it may be useful to make the distinction between the behaviors that teachers have in their repertoire and how these behaviors are used. From an ecological standpoint, behavior analysts are frequently guilty of throwing the baby out with the bath water when they suggest that teachers implement interventions requiring new behaviors and the contingent use of these new behaviors. Were the teacher's old behaviors inappropriate (i.e., inherently nonrewarding or nonpunishing), or were his or her behaviors merely being used inappropriately or noncontingently? If the behaviors employed by the teacher to manage student misbehavior were utilized in a contingent manner but were not found by the students to be rewarding (or punishing), the teacher may benefit from the addition of new behaviors that when used in a similar fashion are more likely to result in the desired effect. If the teacher's behaviors were merely being used noncontingently or in an inconsistent fashion, new behaviors need not be suggested, but rather the teacher may benefit from instruction and modeling on how to make his or her behavior contingent on the behavior of the students. From an ecological standpoint, this redistribution of existing teacher behavior is, whenever possible, the intervention of choice because it requires little change of existing classroom regularities.

Assumption 3: Behavioral Ecologies Are Closed Systems, and What Has Been Done Cannot Be Undone

This final assumption reflects what may be the most significant feature of the ecological perspective in the application of new technology. Specifically, Assumption 3 suggests that once a technological innovation has been unleased on an ecological system, remnants of that innovation will be reflected in the system for some time (Sarason, 1984). Although this assumption has become clearly evident in the biological sciences with the collective impact of industrial waste on the earth's environment, applied behavior analysts are just starting to become aware of its importance in the application of behavioral technology. McDowell (1982) addressed this issue as it related to the use of behavioral interventions through the mathematical application of Herrnstein's law of effect.

According to Herrnstein's law of effect, frequencies of responding increase hyperbolically with increases in reinforcement, and the rapidity with which the hyperbola approaches its asymptote (i.e., maximum levels of responding are reached) is a function of the ratio of reinforcment contingent on the target response to all reinforcement (either contingent or noncontingent) that is present in the environment. Thus, a given rate of reinforcement supports a higher rate of behavior in a barren environment than in an environment rich with background reinforcement. As McDowell (1982) observed:

> Herrnstein's hyperbola evidently requires a new approach to conceptualizing cases behaviorally and to applying reinforcement principles in therapy. In particular, the equation requires broader environmental conceptualizations of problem behavior that take into account sources of reinforcement other than the one in direct contact with (i.e., contingent upon) the behavior. . . . For example, lavish reinforcement procedures may be unnecessary in a lean environment, since minimal amounts of reinforcement can support large amounts of behavior when re [extraneous reinforcement] is small. Conversely, reinforcement procedures may be relatively unsuccessful in rich environments, because responding approaches its asymptote only at extremely high reinforcement rates when re is large. (p. 776)

With respect to the cumulative effects of behavioral technology on an ecological system, these findings would suggest that once a reinforcement procedure has been implemented in the classroom setting, subsequent reinforcement programs must employ reinforcers at a higher rate or employ reinforcers that are more lavish than those being currently used. Accordingly, when selecting intervention strategies, it would be ecologically unwise to introduce systems of new reward into an already reward-rich classroom. Rather, some form of response cost or a restructuring of existing contingencies would be likely to prove more effective.

Corollary 1. What Can Be Done Should Not Necessarily Be Done

Just because behavioral technologies have been developed, this does not grant carte blanc to the use of such technologies (Sarason, 1984; Willems, 1974). Every classroom in which the problem behaviors of children exist need not become a proving ground for the latest token economy system. As behavior change agents develop more effective means of altering children's classroom behavior, and attempts are made to give this technology away to professionals in other fields, the question must be asked as to how such innovations will ultimately fit into the educational ecology. It is quite possible that by choosing not to implement the newest innovation in classroom management, but to do nothing or to restructure the existing behavioral regularities, we as behavior change agents may actually prevent the production of more problems than existed in the classroom initially.

Concluding Comments

Society has come to expect that the application of technology can and will fix virtually any problem from curing disease to traveling in space. A similar mentality also exists with respect to the fixing of social and psychological problems. It is assumed that through the development and application of a new intervention or treatment program that virtually any problem can be ameliorated. The purpose of this chapter has been to provide an ecological view of this process and to examine what problems should be fixed, how should they be fixed, what the consequences of fixing them are, and even whether they should be fixed at all. For too long we have lived in the kingdoms of efficiency and effectiveness and it is time to follow the lead of the ecologist for whom the restoration of system balance is the loftier goal. To accomplish this we will need to know far more about behavioral regularities and interrelationships than is currently known, and more importantly we will need to examine our mind set that treatment efficacy in research studies is the criterion by which our success will be judged.

References

Ayllon, T., & Roberts, M. D. (1974). Eliminating discipline problems by strengthening academic performance. *Journal of Applied Behavior Analyses, 7,* 71–76.

Baer, D. M., Wolf, M. M., & Risley, T. R. (1968). Some current dimensions of applied behavior analysis. *Journal of Applied Behavior Analysis, 1,* 91–97.

Barlow, D. H. (1981). On the relation of clinical research to clinical practice: Current issues, new directions. *Journal of Consulting and Clinical Psychology, 49,* 137–145.

Bates, J. E. (1976). Effects of children's nonverbal behavior upon adults. *Child Development, 47,* 1079–1088.

Becker, J. V., Turner, S. M., & Sajwaj, T. E. (1978). Multiple behavioral effects of the use of lemon juice with a ruminating toddler-age child. *Behavior Modification, 2,* 267–278.

Blackham, G. J., & Silberman, A. (1980). *Modification of Child and Adolescent Behavior.* Belmont, CA: Wadsworth.

Emmer, E. T., & Evertson, C. M. (1981). Synthesis of research on classroom management. *Educational Leadership, 38,* 342–347.

Forehand, R. L., & McMahon, R. J. (1981). *Helping the noncompliant child.* New York: Guilford.

Forehand, R., Breiner, J., McMahon, R. J., & Davies, G. (1981). Predictors of cross-setting behavior change in the treatment of child problems. *Journal of Behavior Therapy and Experimental Psychiatry,* 12, 311–313.

Garfield, S. L. (1978). Research problems in clinical diagnosis. *Journal of Consulting and Clinical Psychology, 46,* 596–607.

Gutkin, T. B., & Curtis, M. J. (1982). School based consultation: Theory and techniques. In C. R. Reynolds & T. B. Gutkin (Eds.), *The handbook of school psychology* (pp. 796–828). New York: Wiley.

Johnson, W. L., Baumeister, A. A., Penland, M. J., & Inwald, C. (1982). Experimental analysis of self-injurious, stereotypic, and collateral behavior of retarded persons: Effects of overcorrection and reinforcement of alternative responding. *Analysis and Intervention in Developmental Disabilities, 2,* 41–66.

Kara, A., & Wahler, R. G. (1977). Organizational features

of a young child's behavior. *Journal of Experimental Child Psychology, 24,* 24–39.
Kaufman, K. F., & O'Leary, K. D. (1972). Reward, cost, and self-evaluation procedures for disruptive adolescents in a psychiatric hospital school. *Journal of Applied Behavior Analysis, 5,* 293–309.
Kazdin, A. E. (1973). The effect of vicarious reinforcement on attentive behavior in the classroom. *Journal of Applied Behavior Analysis, 6,* 71–78.
Kazdin, A. E. (1980). Acceptability of alternative treatments for deviant child behavior. *Journal of Applied Behavior Analysis, 13,* 259–297.
Kazdin, A. E. (1981). Acceptability of child treatment techniques: The influence of treatment efficacy and adverse side-effects. *Behavior Therapy, 12,* 493–506.
Kazdin, A. E. (1982). Applying behavioral principles in the schools. In C. R. Reynolds & T. B. Gutkin (Eds.), *The handbook of school psychology* (pp. 501–529). New York: Wiley.
Mahoney, M. J., & Thoresen, C. E. (1974). *Self-control: Power to the person.* Monterey, CA: Brooks/Cole.
Martens, B. K., & Witt, J. C. (1984). Assessment and prediction in an ecological system: Application of the general linear model to the response class concept. *Journal of Behavioral Assessment, 6,* 197–206.
Martens, B. K., Witt, J. C., Elliott, S. N., & Darveaux, D. X. (1985). Teacher judgments concerning the acceptability of school-based interventions. *Professional Psychology, 16,* 191–198.
Martens, B. K., Peterson, R. L., Witt, J. C., & Cirone, S. (1986). Teacher perceptions of school-based interventions. *Exceptional Children, 53,* 213–223.
McDowell, J. J. (1982). The importance of Herrnstein's mathematical statement of the law of effect for behavior therapy. *American Psychologist, 37,* 771–779.
Meichenbaum, D. H., Bowers, X. S., & Ross, R. R. (1968). Modification of classroom behavior of institutionalized female adolescent offenders. *Behavior Research and Therapy, 6,* 343–353.
Miller, G. A. (1969). Psychology as a means of promoting human welfare. *American Psychologist, 24,* 1063–1075.
Miller, S. J., & Sloane, H. N. (1976). The generalization effects of parent training across stimulus settings. *Journal of Applied Behavior Analysis, 9,* 355–370.
Nelson, R. O., & Bowles, P. E. (1975). The best of two worlds—observations with norms. *Journal of School Psychology, 13,* 3–9.
Nelson, R. O., & Hayes, S. C. (1980). Some current dimensions of behavioral assessment. *Behavioral Assessment, 1,* 1–16.
Owens, R. G. (1981). *Organizational behavior in education.* Englewood Cliffs, NJ: Prentice-Hall.
Pyle, R. R. (1977). Mental health consultation: Helping teachers help themselves. *Professional Psychology, 8,* 192–198.
Redd, W. H. & Birnbrauer, J. S. (1969). Adults as discriminative stimuli for different reinforcement contingencies with retarded children. *Journal of Experimental Child Psychology, 1,* 440–447.
Reynolds, C. R., Gutkin, T. B.. Elliott, S. N., & Witt, J. C. (1984). *School psychology: Essentials of theory and practice.* New York: Wiley.
Russo, D. C., Cataldo, M. F., & Cushing, P. J. (1981). Compliance training and behavioral covariation in the treatment of multiple behavior problems. *Journal of Applied Behavior Analysis, 14,* 209–222.
Sajwaj, T., Twardosz, S., & Burke, M. (1972). Side effects of extinction procedures in a remedial preschool. *Journal of Applied Behavior Analysis, 5,* 163–175.
Sarason, S. B. (1971). *The culture of the school and the problem of change.* Boston, MA: Allyn & Bacon.
Sarason, S. B. (1984). If it can be studied or developed, should it be? *American Psychologist, 39,* 477–485.
Scott, J., & Bushell, D. (1974). The length of teacher contacts and students' off task behavior. *Journal of Applied Behavior Analysis, 7,* 39–44.
Sulzer-Azaroff, B., & Mayer, G. R. (1977). *Applying behavior analysis procedures with children and youth.* New York: Holt, Reinhart, & Winston.
Voeltz, L. M., & Evans, I. M. (1982). The assessment of behavioral interrelationships in child behavior therapy. *Behavioral Assessment, 4,* 131–165.
Wahler, R. G. (1969). Setting generality: Some specific and general effects of child behavior therapy. *Journal of Applied Behavior Analysis, 2,* 239–246.
Wahler, R. G. (1975). Some structural aspects of deviant child behavior. *Journal of Applied Behavior Analysis, 8,* 27–42.
Wahler, R. G., & Fox, J. J. (1981). Setting events in applied behavior analysis: Toward a conceptual and methodological expansion. *Journal of Applied Behavior Analysis, 14,* 327–338.
Wahler, R. G., Sperling, K. A., Thomas, M. R., Teeter, N. C., & Luper, H. L. (1970). The modification of childhood stuttering: Some response-response relationships. *Journal of Experimental Child Psychology, 9,* 411–428.
Wahler, R. G., Berland, R. M., & Coe, T. D. (1979). Generalization processes in child behavior change. In B. B. Lahey & A. E. Kazdin (Eds.), *Advances in clinical child psychology* (Vol. 2, pp. 35–69).
Willems, E. P. (1974). Behavioral technology and behavioral ecology. *Journal of Applied Behavior Analysis, 7,* 151–165.
Witt, J. C., & Elliott, S. N. (1985). Acceptability of classroom intervention strategies. In T. R. Kratochwill (Ed.), *Advances in school psychology* (Vol. IV, pp. 251–288). Hillsdale, NJ: Erlbaum.
Witt, J. C., & Martens. B. K. (1983). Assessing the acceptability of behavioral interventions used in classrooms. *Psychology in the Schools, 20,* 510–517.
Witt, J. C., Hannafin, M. J., & Martens, B. K. (1983).

Home-based reinforcement: Behavioral covariation between academic performance and inappropriate behavior. *Journal of School Psychology, 21*, 337–348.

Witt, J. C., Elliott, S. N., & Martens, B. K. (1984). Acceptability of behavioral interventions used in classrooms: The influence of amount of teacher time, severity of behavior problem, and type of intervention. *Behavior Disorders, 9*, 95–104.

Witt, J. C., Martens, B. K., & Elliott, S. N. (1984). Factors affecting teachers' judgements of the acceptability of behavioral interventions: Time involvement, behavior problem severity, and type of intervention. *Behavior Therapy, 15*, 95–104.

Wolf, M. M. (1978). Social validity: The case for subjective measurement or how applied behavior analysis is finding its heart. *Journal of Applied Analysis, 11*, 203–214.

CHAPTER 13

Helping, Helplessness, and Harm

Carl J. Dunst and Carol M. Trivette

The extent to which help-seeking and help-giving have either positive or negative consequences depends on the intertwining of a host of intrapersonal and interpersonal factors. These include one's perception of the need for help, the manner in which help is offered, the source of help, the response costs involved in accepting help, and the sense of indebtedness the recipient feels toward the help provider (DePaulo, Nadler, & Fisher, 1983; Fisher, Nadler, & DePaulo, 1983; Nadler, Fisher, & DePaulo, 1983). Human service practitioners who offer help to their clients do so in the hope that it will do some good. However, there is strong evidence that certain types of help, and the manner in which it is provided, can produce helplessness (Coates, Renzaglia, & Embree, 1983) and have other harmful consequences, including attenuation of self-esteem (Fisher, Nadler, & Whitcher-Alagna, 1983), dependency on the donor (Merton, Merton, & Barber, 1983), and increased stress (Wortman & Conway, 1985).

Not all help-seeking and help-giving exchanges have harmful effects. Indeed, many help exchanges have positive influences (Cohen & Syme, 1985). The fact that some helping relationships have positive consequences whereas others have negative ones suggests that different conditions set the occasion for these differential outcomes (Brickman *et al.*, 1983). In this chapter we examine the help-seeking and help-giving relationship with particular emphasis on the characteristics of donor–recipient exchanges that are likely to produce positive and negative outcomes. Empirical and clinical evidence suggest that many treatment programs that are labeled successful oftentimes have negative side effects when other aspects of help-receiver behavior are taken into consideration.

In this chapter we employ a social system model (Dunst, 1985; Dunst & Trivette, in press) to illustrate how helping relationships can often go astray. We develop our notion of the broader-based context of helping relationships by proposing a social systems model that integrates formulations from the help-seeking (Brickman *et al.*, 1982; DePaulo *et al.*, 1983) and social support (Broadhead *et al.*, 1983; Cohen & Syme, 1985) literatures. Social systems theory views social units and the relationships among their members as interdependent, so that actions in one social unit or

Carl J. Dunst and Carol M. Trivette • Human Development Research and Training Institute, Western Carolina Center, Morganton, North Carolina 28655. Preparation of this chapter was supported in part by a grant (MH38862) from the U.S. Department of Health and Human Services, National Institute of Mental Health, Center for Prevention Research.

subunit reverberate and impact directly and indirectly on the behavior of the members of other social units. Systems theory is rooted in the German-European tradition of viewing persons as whole, integrated organisms whose behavior is affected by and has meaning within the contexts in which individuals function as members of different ecological settings and social units (Lewin, 1931, 1936; Reese & Overton, 1970). The direct and indirect influences affecting behavior are referred to as first- and second-order effects to emphasize the fact that persons and events beyond the immediate setting can and do influence behavior (Bronfenbrenner, 1979).

The chapter is divided into five major sections. In section one, we review a number of aspects of help-seeking and help-giving (social support) relationships with particular emphasis on factors that affect as well as are affected by the exchange of aid and resources. In section two, we propose an integrated view of help-seeking and social support. In section three, we examine the manner in which help-seeking and help-giving can produce helplessness as well as have other negative consequences. In section four, we examine those aspects of helping relationships that are likely to produce positive effects. In so doing, we propose a number of principles of helping relationships that may be used as guideposts for professionals to follow as part of help-seeking and help-giving exchanges. In the final section, we discuss the implications of the help-seeking and help-giving literature for practice in family support programs and behavior therapy.

Help-Seeking and Social Support

Most help-seeking models (see Brickman *et al.*, 1982; Gross & McMullen, 1983) focus on (a) perceptions of problems or needs, (b) decisions about the course of actions taken to alleviate a problem or meet a need, and (c) help-seeking itself (DePaulo, 1983). Social support theory attempts to explain how aid and resources provided by others affects the health and well-being of the recipient of support (Cohen & Syme, 1985). Although help-seeking and social support are theoretically related areas, only recently have these different conceptual frameworks been viewed as unique perspectives of the same type of social relationship (Antonucci & Depner, 1982; Gourash, 1978; Wilcox & Birkel, 1983). In this section, we examine the help-seeking process and the manner in which social support (help-giving) affects the behavior of the help-seeker. The material we review is used in the following section of the chapter to propose an integrated model of help-seeking and help-giving.

The Help-Seeking Process

Help-seeking is a complex behavioral process that is influenced by a multitude of personal and situational factors. However, the needs-based help-seeking model proposed by Gross and McMullen (1983) is a pragmatic approach that has direct implications for practice as well as understanding the conditions that may lead to decisions about help-seeking and the consequences of help-giving. According to these investigators, the choice of whether or not one is likely to seek help is influenced by the help-seeker's responses to three questions:

1. Do I have a problem that help will alleviate?
2. Should I ask for help?
3. Who is most capable of providing the kind of aid I need? (Gross & McMullen, 1983, p. 47)

Gross and McMullen (1983) proposed a three-stage model that they believe help-seekers follow in alleviating a problem or meeting a need. The three stages are (a) recognition of a problem or need, (b) the decision whether or not to seek help, and (c) the activities or actions taken to solve the problem or meet the need. Although their stage model implies that a help-seeker follows a sequential series of steps, Gross and McMullen (1983) note that

> it is unlikely that such serial process approximates the tortuous route of many help-seeking decisions. In actuality, these separate stages, though analytically distinct, often interact experimentally. Each subsequent step in the sequence is at least partially dependent on the manner in which preceding steps are resolved, and later stages often have an anticipating effect on earlier stages. For example, it is quite possible for second- and third-stage considerations to influence and interact with each other. The specific sources of help chosen in the third stage may often be associated with costs and benefits influencing whether or not help is sought in the first place (second stage). Furthermore, in making a complex decision such as deciding to seek help, some stages may be reversed in order, cycled several times, or omitted altogether. (p. 48)

Figure 1 graphically depicts the three steps in the Gross and McMullen (1983) model, how determinants define problems and needs, and how response costs influence decisions about help-seeking and acting upon advice. We now examine each of these steps in more detail.

Perceptions of Problems and Needs

The recognition of a problem or need sets the occasion for the decision to seek help. A problem or need is a relative phenomenon, and may be defined as an individual's perception of the discrepancy between actual states or conditions and what is considered normative. Gross and McMullen (1983) emphasize the need to distinguish between symptomatology and whether or not symptoms are seen as problematic. Epidemiological studies consistently show that a large percentage of the general population evidence symptoms that professionals would label as aberrant or deviant, yet very few people view these symptoms as necessarily problematic (e.g., Zola, 1966).

Nelson (1980) noted that symptomatology does not define the problems that individuals have.

> The mere recognition of some difficulty or unusual symptom is often insufficient to lead an individual to decide to take action and seek help. Unless the individual further identifies the condition as problematic or as potentially harmful, it is unlikely that outside help will be sought. (Gross & McMullen, 1983, p. 51)

Consequently, symptomatology may be a necessary but not a sufficient condition for explaining help-seeking behavior.

An extensive examination of the factors that

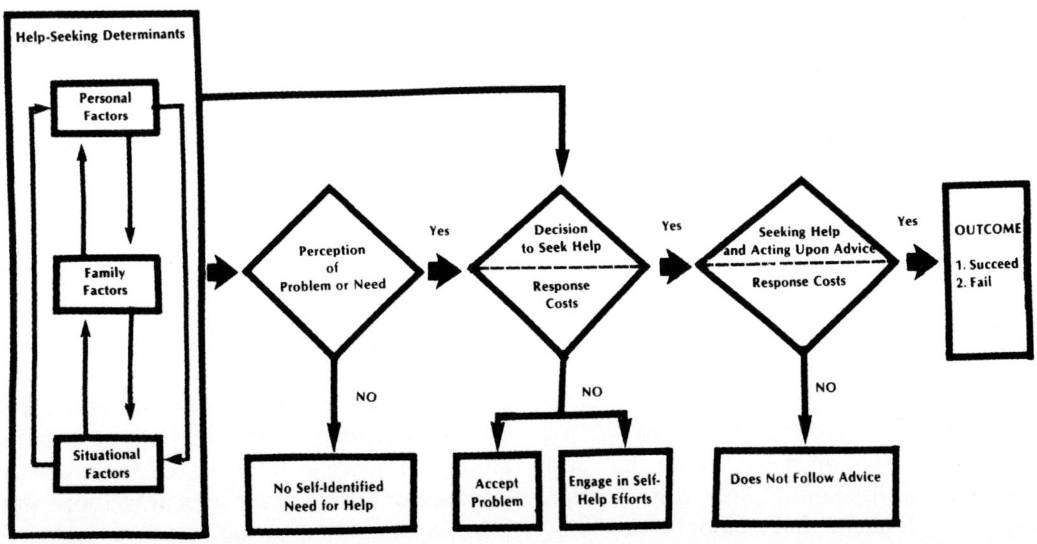

Figure 1. A conceptual framework for depicting major decision points in the help-seeking process (modeled after Gross & McMullen, 1983).

influence the perceptions of problems and needs is beyond the scope of this chapter (see e.g., Dovidio & Gaertner, 1983; McMullen & Gross, 1983; Nadler, 1983). Suffice it to say that cultural norms and values, intrapersonal characteristics, and social class and ethnicity as well as other psychological, social, and situational factors affect the extent to which conditions are viewed as problematic. For example, Zola (1966) found that conditions that persons view as "relevant for action" are generally defined by cultural and ethnic beliefs and norms. Consequently, it is not surprising that lower SES background persons are less likely to see symptomatology as problematic (Hollingshead & Redlich, 1958), and thus are less likely to see their condition as relevant for action. One of the major determinants of problem recognition is whether or not an individual sees him or herself as having behavior reactions or deviations in excess compared to other persons in his or her the subculture (Wills, 1983).

The Decision to Seek Help

Once symptomatology and its associated conditions are perceived to be a problem that is amendable, the next step involves the decision whether or not to seek help. According to Gross and McMullen (1983), the potential help-seeker may (a) accept the problem and thus do nothing, (b) attempt to resolve the difficulty him or herself, or (c) seek help from others. "For those problems that are judged insoluble or extremely unlikely to be resolved, the unfortunate victim can only suffer and/or learn to accept and live with a continuing or inevitable problem" (Gross & McMullen, 1983, pp. 53–54). For problems deemed amenable to self-help, the person is likely to involve their full range of intrapersonal coping and problem-solving mechanisms that bear on an acceptable solution (Pearlin & Schooler, 1978). For problems that cannot be solved by oneself, the person is likely to consider the various options for selecting the appropriate persons, social groups, or agencies that one might consider as potential sources of help.

The decision to do nothing, take care of matters oneself, or ask others for help, is influenced, in part, by the personal, social, and psychological costs of different courses of action (Gross & McMullen, 1983). One may do nothing, for example, if the calculated response costs are so great that a perceived problem or potential problem is less devastating than expending time and energy that is judged to be hazardous to one's health and self-preservation. For example, in our own work with low SES background pregnant teenagers and teenage mothers, we find that the failure to seek prenatal care and obtain well baby checks from public health agencies oftentimes has less to do with immaturity and inabilities on the part of these young women, and more to do with the fact that health agencies make these help-seeking and help-receiving experiences so punishing that the teenagers avoid contact at almost any cost. Pregnant teenagers are often made to feel guilty about their pregnancies and teenage mothers are assumed to be incompetent caregivers based on their social background and ages. By behaving in this manner, professionals are generally unaware that the way they treat these young women can have harmful effects (see Dunst, Vance, & Cooper, 1986).

One of the major personal response cost factors influencing a decision to seek help from others is the damage to self-esteem (Fisher, Nadler, & Witcher-Alagna, 1983). If a person perceives help-seeking as an admission of incompetence or inadequacy, he or she is less likely to admit to a problem or seek help from others. Similarly, if help-seeking and help-receiving involves an inequitable exchange, and thus results in a sense of indebtedness, a decision to seek help is often attenuated (Greenberg & Westcott, 1983). A host of intrapersonal and interpersonal factors enter into an evaluation of the response costs involved in help seeking (Piliavin & Piliavin,

1973), and impinge on whether or not help is sought.

Acting on Advice and Accepting Help

In instances where a decision is made to seek help from others, the advice or help offered may result in either alleviation of the problem or a failure to resolve or reduce the problem state. In our own work, for example, we find an interesting relationship between the presenting problem and the type of aid and assistance that is provided. In instances where there is a match between the nature of the help sought and the type of assistance provided, the help-seeking and help-receiving process is likely to have positive influences. For example, if a parent asks for some type of respite care for his or her handicapped child, and indeed some type of child care relief is provided, the help is likely to have beneficial influences. In contrast, where there is a mismatch between the nature of help sought and the type of assistance provided, the advice is not likely to be acted on and in some cases may have harmful effects. For example, if a parent asks for respite care for his or her child, but the helping professional perceives the help-seeking as some intrapsychic manifestation of rejection, and defines the problem in this manner, the help may be resented and the parent may withdraw from the helping relationship. Playing out the scenario, the family may not receive the respite they need, the time demands involved in caring for the child may exceed the parents' ability to cope, which in turn may result in harmful consequences such as abuse or a decision to institutionalize the child (see Dunst, Cooper, & Bolick, 1987).

In addition to influencing a decision to seek help, response costs influence decisions about acting on advice offered by help-givers. Specifically, once help is sought and advice is given, the help seeker must evaluate the costs of adhering to the prescribed regimen. Consider the following case study that recently came to our attention.

> A family consisting of a husband, wife, 8-year-old twins, and a 12-year-old sibling, requested child care assistance and advice in dealing with the behavior problems of one of the twins who was profoundly retarded. The handicapped youngster was totally dependent and placed excessive time demands on all the family members. The youngster displayed aggressive acts (hitting, biting, etc.) toward the other family members, which disrupted family functioning even more. The members of the family were obviously physically exhausted, and the need for rest was clearly indicated. The family was referred to a behavior specialist who noted that the aggressive acts occurred about 3 to 5 times per hour and that the aberrant behavior was displayed in order to gain social attention from other family members. The specialist prescribed a "treatment procedure of choice." The parents were instructed in how to apply time-out procedures for eliminating the problem behaviors. The procedures required that all the family members apply the time-out procedures, and that no family member was to interfere with one another's use of the time-out techniques. The parents, however, responded by indicating that they did not feel they could emotionally and physically follow through with the recommendations and that to do what the therapist recommended would be more disruptive to family functioning than tolerating the child's difficult behavior. The parents chose not to follow the prescribed treatment and decided to accept and live with the child's condition.

This vignette illustrates that the extent to which advice is followed depends on the response costs involved in adhering to a prescribed regimen. In this case example, the therapist failed to consider the broader-based context of the family in prescribing a treatment, and lost the opportunity to provide the type of help the family was in fact seeking. Had some type of child care relief been arranged, perhaps the family's well-being would have been enhanced, which in turn may have increased the probability of the family implementing the behavior treatment (Dunst & Trivette, in press).

The help-seeking process is a complex one that is influenced by as well as influences the behavior of the person seeking aid and resources. The help-seeking model briefly described earlier (see Gross & McMullen, 1983, for a more extensive discussion) underscores the fact that help-seeking behavior is multiply determined and varies as a function of help-seeking stage and response costs. The examples of help-seeking behavior provided as part of the discussion of the model illustrated that we must look beyond the immediate behavior of the help-seeker if we are to understand fully what (a) defines a problem or need, (b) influences a decision to alleviate the problem, (c) from whom advice is secured, and (d) whether the advice is followed. We now turn to a discussion of what it is that help-givers do that is supportive and affects the behavior of the help-seeker.

Social Support and Help-Giving

"Social support is defined as the resources provided by other persons" (Cohen & Syme, 1985, p. 4). More specifically, social support includes the emotional, psychological, physical, informational, instrumental, and material assistance provided by others that influences either directly or indirectly the behavior of the recipient of the help and assistance. Social support as used here refers to what help-givers do that affects the behavior of others, and is used synonymously with help-giving. To the extent that the support provided by network members is compatible with the recipient's perceptions of him or herself and the need for help, the assistance and aid is likely to be beneficial (Brickman *et al.*, 1982).

The Social Support Construct

Social support is a multidimensional construct that includes at least five components (Dunst & Trivette, in press; Hall & Wellman, 1985; House & Kahn, 1985). These are relational, structural, functional, and constitutional support, and support satisfaction. *Relational support* refers to the existence and quantity of social relationships, including such things as marital and work status, number of persons in one's social network, and membership in social organizations such as the church. *Structural support* refers to the characteristics of social networks, including network density, the stability and durability of relationships, the intensity of feelings toward network members, and reciprocity of relationships (see House & Kahn, 1985; Mitchell & Trickett, 1980). *Functional support* refers to the source, type, and quantity and quality of help and assistance. *Constitutional support* refers to the perceived need for help, the availability of the specificity type support needed, and the congruence (match) between the type of support needed and the type of support offered. *Support satisfaction* refers to the extent to which assistance and aid are viewed as helpful and useful.

Figure 2 shows the potential connections among the different components of the social support domain. This conceptualization is derived, in part, from the work of Hall and Wellman (1985) and House and Kahn (1985) and has evolved from our own work on explicating the components of the social support construct (Dunst & Trivette, in press). The existence or quantity of relational support is a necessary condition for and hence a partial determinant of (a) defining needs (constitutional support), (b) the structural characteristics of one's social network, and (c) the types of help and assistance available from network members. Similarly, constitutional needs and network structure may partially determine the particular types of support that are procured and offered. Finally, the types of support provided, especially the relationship between constitutional and functional support, will in part determine the degree to which one finds the aid and assistance helpful, and thus the extent to which one is satisfied with the support. Taken together, these five components and the potential connections among them provide a basis for understanding the temporal and mediational rela-

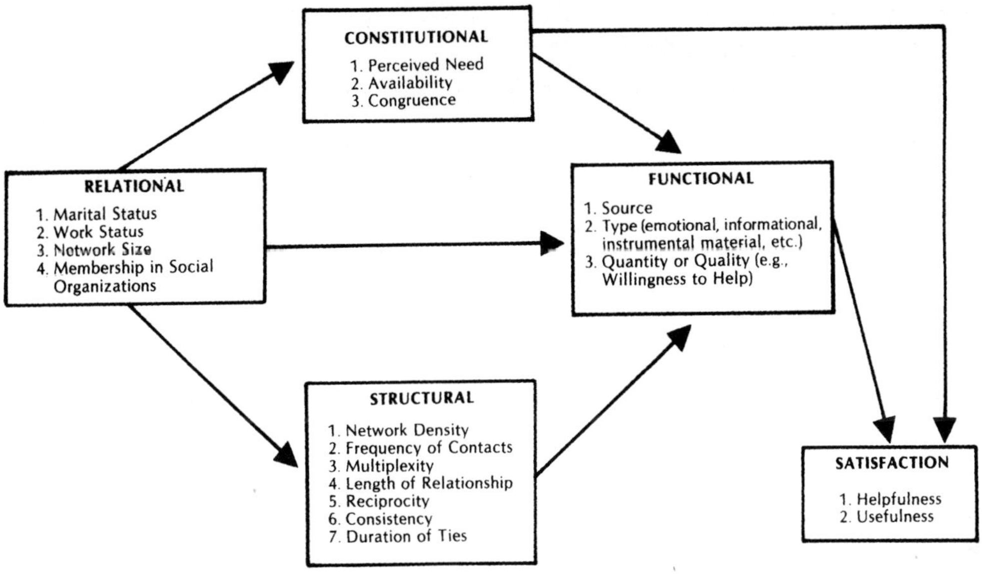

Figure 2. A conceptual framework for depicting five major components of social support and the potential relationships among the components (modeled after House & Kahn, 1985).

tionships that set the occasion for supportive exchanges.

The Effects of Social Support on Well-Being and Other Behavior

A sizable body of evidence indicates that social support has positive influences on personal and familial health and well-being (e.g., Cohen & Syme, 1985; Dean & Lin, 1977; McCubbin *et al.*, 1980; Mitchell & Trickett, 1980). Recent work has demonstrated that positive effects of social support go beyond promotion of intrapersonal and intrafamily physical and psychological health to include influences on parenting, family interactions, and child behavior. There is a growing body of evidence that social support directly and indirectly influences attitudes toward parenting (Crnic, Greenberg, Ragozin, Robinson, & Basham, 1983); parental styles of interaction (Crnic *et al.*, 1983; Crockenberg, 1981; Embry, 1980; Philliber & Graham, 1981; Weinraub & Wolf, 1983); parental attitudes, expectations, and aspirations for their children (Lazar & Darlington, 1982); and child behavior and development (Crnic *et al.*, 1983; Crnic, Greenberg, & Slough, 1986; Crockenberg, 1981).

The role that social support plays in (a) buffering families from the negative effects of the birth and rearing of a handicapped child and (b) promoting parent, family, parent–child, and child functioning has been the focus of a series of studies in our own program (Dunst, 1985; Dunst & Trivette, 1984, 1986; Dunst, Trivette, & Cross, 1986a,b, in press; Trivette & Dunst, 1987, in press). Collectively, our findings suggest the pattern of direct and indirect influences depicted in Figure 3 (see Dunst & Trivette, in press). The results from our studies show that (a) social support is the principle determinant of health and well-being, (b) social support and well-being are partial determinants of family integrity and functioning, (c) social support, well-being, and family functioning affect the styles of interactions parents use with their children, and (d) social support, well-being, and interactional styles influence parental perceptions of child functioning, and to a smaller degree, actual child development.

One particularly interesting set of findings

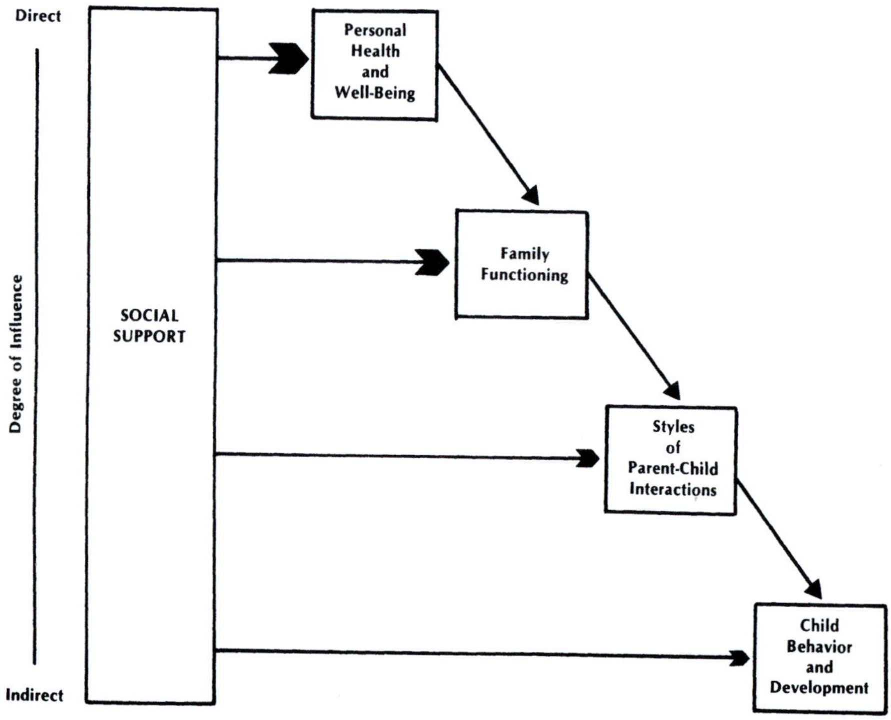

Figure 3. A graphic display for showing the direct and indirect influences of social support on personal well-being, family functioning, parental interactional styles, and child behavior and development.

may help illustrate these patterns of direct and indirect influences. In a number of studies, we have assessed how support, well-being, and parental styles of interaction affect the extent to which a parent perceives his or her child as having "behavior problems or difficulties" (Dunst *et al.*, 1986b, Dunst & Trivette, in press; Trivette & Dunst, 1987). We consistently find that parents are less likely to indicate their child's behavior is troublesome or difficult in instances where social support, well-being, and interactional patterns moderate the parent's perceptions. That is, in cases where social support enhanced well-being, and social support and well-being affected the display of positive interactional styles, parents were less likely to view their child's behavior as aberrant or deviant.

Social support seems to exert several types of influence on parental perceptions. First, where child-care responsibilities are shared among family members, friends, and relatives, or are fully or partially assumed by a day care or preschool program, the burden of care does not rest solely with one person (typically the mother), and thus excessive time demands are minimized. This in turn reduces the probability that well-being will be negatively affected (Bronfenbrenner, 1979). Second, the members of a parent's social network appear to serve as models that affect child-rearing attitudes and practices where parents adopt or modify their parenting styles if esteemed network members demonstrate effective and nuturing behavior (Cochran & Brassard, 1979). Third, the opportunity to share the trials and tribulations of rearing a child, whether handicapped or not, with other parents helps one understand that child rearing is often a difficult and demanding enterprise, and that no one person can do it alone.

The above pattern of relationships is found even when severity of the child's level of functioning is the same for two different children.

Thus, for two children with similar behavior characteristics, parents' appraisals of their child's behavior may vary considerably depending on the type of supportive experiences available to them. On the one hand, our findings indicate that behavior difficulty is a relative phenomenon, and on the other hand, indicate that we must look beyond the immediate setting for identifying the determinants of parents' perceptions of behavior. In the case example cited earlier, our behavior therapist would have perhaps been more successful if he or she had taken this broader-based perspective of the child and family, and suggested the need to consider respite in order to reduce time demands and promote well-being, which in turn would have increased the likelihood of the family being receptive to the prescribed treatment. Thus, even though a particular behavioral intervention is effective in reducing a problem behavior, the probability of *implementation* is reduced if the intervention does not fit into the overall ecology of family functioning.

An Integrated Model of Help-Seeking and Help-Giving

In many respects, help-seeking and help-giving (i.e., social support) may be considered opposite sides of the same coin. The help-seeking process considers the help-seeker's behavior and the conditions that set the occasion for perceiving a problem and the need for help and assistance. The notion of social support and help-giving considers the manner in which members of one's social support network are mobilized and provide help and assistance to the help-seeker. Several investigators have recently attempted to integrate help seeking and social support notions (Antonucci & Depner, 1982; Gourash, 1978; Wilcox & Birkel, 1982).

Gourash (1978) made one of the first attempts to integrate the help-seeking literature with particular emphasis on how provision of help from members of a person's informal social network influence help-seeking from formal support sources. According to Gourash (1978),

> social networks can affect help-seeking in a number of ways: (a) by buffering the experience of stress which alleviates the need for help, (b) by precluding the necessity for professional assistance through the provision of instrumental and affective support, (c) by acting as screening and referral agents to professional services, and (d) by transmitting attitudes, values, and norms about help-seeking. (p. 416)

This set of conditions suggests an inverse relationship between the need for help from members of formal support sources and the extent to which members of informal support networks can provide or mediate the resources and help necessary to affect personal and family well-being and functioning. It is now known, for example, that in most cases people turn to professionals for help only when assistance is not available from members of their personal social networks (Gurin, Veroff, & Feld, 1960), and that help from esteemed network members who convey a sense of "we" rather than "you" and "I" in dealing with problems is more likely to produce beneficial effects (Clark, 1983).

Figure 4 shows a model that integrates the help-seeking and social support models described earlier and that includes those factors that enter into a decision to seek help in response to normative and nonnormative life events. The model is based substantially on the work of Gross and McMullen (1983), Hall and Wellman (1985), House and Kahn (1985), and Wilcox and Birkel (1983). According to this model, personal (e.g., age, education level, self-esteem, psychological adjustment, sex), familial (e.g., SES, income), and situational (e.g., living arrangements, proximity to friends and relatives, "neighborhood" values, etc.) factors are considered partial determinants of one another. These three sets of characteristics collectively define an individual's subcultural patterns, and taken together are considered partial determinants of social support and help-seeking. Help-seek-

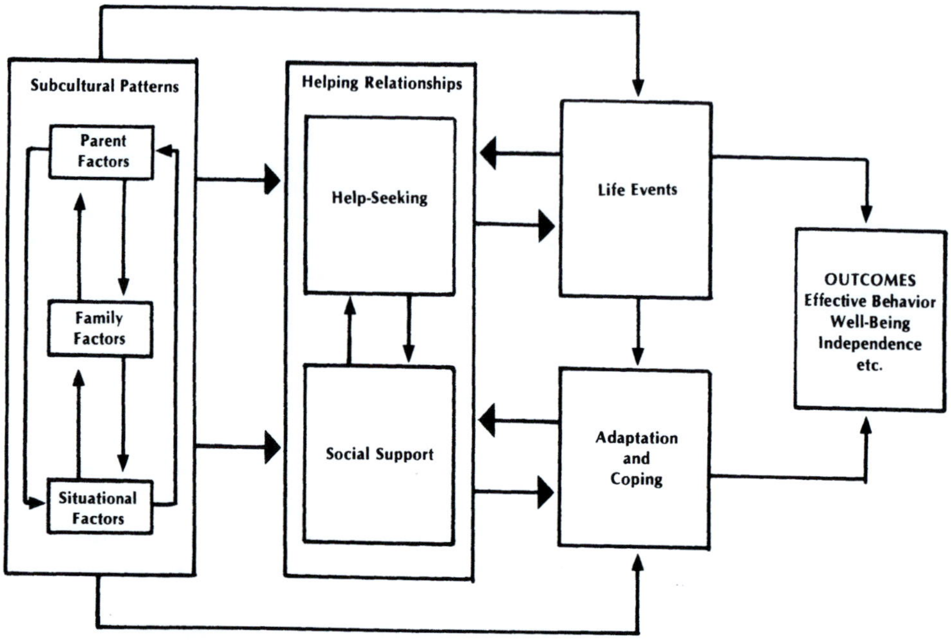

Figure 4. A conceptual framework for integrating the help-seeking and social support models as a basis for understanding the multiple determinants of behavior outcomes (modeled after Hall & Wellman, 1985).

ing and help-giving (social support) are seen as reciprocal and interdependent. The relationships and potential connections among the components of help-seeking and help-giving are as described earlier. Subcultural patterns, help-seeking, and social support are seen as partial determinants of coping mechanisms employed in response to normative and nonnormative life events. Collectively, subcultural patterns, helping relationships, and coping mechanisms are seen as directly and indirectly influencing the full range of a person's behavior, including self-esteem, locus-of-control, health and well-being, and other intrapersonal and interpersonal behaviors. For example, attenuation and enhancement of self-esteem have been found to be influenced by help-seeking decisions (DePaulo, 1982), reactions to help-giving and social support (Fisher, Nadler, & Whitcher-Alagna, 1983), and coping mechanisms employed in response to negative life events (Snyder, Higgins, & Stucky, 1983).

The intertwining of the various sets of factors displayed in Figure 4 will partially determine the extent to which help-seeking and help-giving exchanges are likely to have beneficial or harmful effects. In the following section, we examine several conditions for which help-seeking and help-giving have a probability of producing negative consequences.

The Negative Consequences of Help-Seeking and Help-Giving

Helping involves the distribution or redistribution of "resources by giving services, goods, money, information, or esteem" to others (Brickman *et al.*, 1983). By definition, support means "A favoring of someone or something, either by giving aid or merely by approving or sanctioning" (Guralnik, *Webster's New World Dictionary*, 1974, p. 1431). Help-givers, whether friends, relatives, neighbors, or professionals, offer aid and assistance in the hope that it will have positive influences. Research on the effects of social support and help-giving are generally disposed to find positive effects (Cohen & Syme,

1985). However, findings also suggest that help-giving can backfire and have deleterious effects under certain conditions (e.g., Fiore, Becker, & Coppel, 1983; Wortman & Lehman, 1985). In many instances well-intentioned help-givers do more harm than good (see especially Coates *et al.*, 1983).

In this section, we examine some of the potentially debilitating consequences of help-seeking and help-giving. None of the consequences or situations are mutually exclusive, and indeed there is considerable overlap in both the nature of the helping relationships that we describe and the harmful effects that may occur. We discuss the precipitating and consequent conditions separately for illustrative purposes only. Moreover, it should be explicitly recognized that no single donor–recipient exchange is likely to produce catastrophic negative effects. Rather, it would seem that repeated encounters that set the occasion for negative effects have cumulative and interactive consequences that are detrimental and debilitating.

Some Harmful Effects of Helping Relationships

Certain types of helping relationships have been found to have negative consequences, and four of these negative effects are addressed here: helplessness, dependency, lowered self-esteem, and indebtedness. Other negative consequences of helping not discussed include ambivalence (Hatfield & Sprecher, 1983), embarrassment (Shapiro, 1983), and perceived inadequacy (Rosen, 1983).

Learned Helplessness

In a seminal paper by Coates *et al.* (1983), the investigators used learned helplessness theory (Abramson, Seligman, & Teasdale, 1978) as a framework for explaining how help may undermine competence and a sense of personal control (Bandura, 1977; Lefcourt, 1981). The learned helplessness phenomenon refers to situations where people believe they have little or no control over events in their environments and lives, which in turn produces disruptions in behavior, including depression, lowered self-esteem, and attenuation of motivational responses (Abramson *et al.*, 1978).

According to Coates *et al.* (1983), there are at least four ways help can undermine competence and control.

> First of all, the help may be so overwhelming that it directly reduces the control that recipients have over their own lives. . . . [Second,] even the little acts of kindness we perform for one another can be killing by directly undermining the acquisition of new skills or the maintenance of old ones. . . . [Third,] even when help does not directly reduce control or impair the development of certain abilities, it can directly undermine the perceived self-efficacy of recipients [when] help carries with it the implication that recipients are relatively inferior and incapable of solving problems on their own. . . . Finally, help can undermine competence and control by creating confusion as to who should get credit or blame for the way things turn out. If the help is successful in resolving or lessening the problem, the recipients may attribute this outcome to the helper, with the result that they feel no more capable of dealing with problems on their own. (pp. 253–255)

The extent to which control and competence are undermined in helping relationships is likely to be influenced by the particular model of helping to which the help-seeker and help-giver subscribes. Brickman *et al.* (1982, 1983) delineate four helping models (moral, compensatory, enlightenment, & medical), each of which differs in attributions about the causes and solutions to problems, and thus the extent to which helping is likely to produce helplessness.

In the *moral model*, help-seekers are seen as responsible for creating problems and for solving them. According to Brickman *et al.* (1982), people who see their problems and needs from this perspective feel that others are "neither obligated to help (since everyone's troubles are of their own making) nor capable of helping (since everyone must find their own solutions)" (p. 370). In the *compensatory model*, help-seekers are seen as innocent victims of prior experiences and thus not responsible for their problems, but are responsible for solutions. Programs like Head Start and CETA (Comprehensive Educational Training Association) are based substantially on this model of helping. In the *enlightenment model*, help-seekers are seen as responsible for their problems but are not viewed as capable of solving them, at least on their own (e.g., Alcoholics Anonymous). The ability to actively engage in self-sustaining behavior is seen as beyond the control of the help-seeker, and thus the person's behavior must be shaped and guided by others who continually remind the person of his or her past wrong doings, and the need to depend on others for maintaining corrective behavior. In the *medical model*, help-seekers are seen as responsible for neither their problems nor their solutions. Persons who subscribe to this model believe that physical or mental problems are illnesses and diseases that only experts can fully understand, and thus are capable of treating and correcting.

Coates *et al.* (1983) hypothesized that "recipients who hold more strongly to models that reduce their responsibility for solutions (enlightenment and medical) will be most likely to respond to help by becoming helpless" (p. 258). The findings from a study conducted by Coates *et al.* supported this contention. Adherence to a model that reduced the help-seeker's responsibility for solving problems was more likely to result in a greater display of helplessness following donor–recipient exchanges. Corroborative evidence from studies by Langer and Benevento (1978) and Morrison, Bushell, Hanson, Fentiman, and Holdridge-Crane (1977) bolster these findings. In addition to finding a greater display of learned helplessness type behaviors, the investigators in both studies found a greater degree of dependence on the help-givers after help was provided to them.

Dependency on the Help-Giver

Merton *et al.* (1983) described those conditions that produce dependency on help-givers, and how such dependency contributes to the debilitation of the help-seeker. Dependency is created when help-givers, typically professionals as part of client–professional relationships, take relative and in some cases absolute control over the client's fate, and occurs most often in response to help-seeking for acute medical or psychological problems.

> [Because] the professional consulted when the client needs help may never [have] seen the client in a state of general well-being, [he or she] can therefore have only an indirect sense of the client's capability and strengths. This limited perspective reinforces the already ingrained tendency for the professional to exercise paternalistic authority. (Merton *et al.*, 1983, p. 21)

Somewhat ironically, the more "supportive and positive" the paternalistic tendencies, the more likely dependency will occur (see Fisher, Nadler, & Whitcher-Alagna, 1983, pp. 68–70).

In situations where help-givers usurp control and expect clients to surrender autonomy, or where clients freely or coercively give up decision-making authority, one is likely to find that the help exchange interferes with and postpones the client's acquisition of effective behavior (Brickman *et al.*, 1982). This in turn perpetuates the continued need for help and only reinforces a client's dependency on help-givers (Skinner, 1978).

The usurpation of control over decision making is not an uncommon occurrence in helping relationships. Professionals often tell clients (or the parents of clients if the latter happen to be children) what is wrong with them, what needs to be done to correct the deficits and weaknesses, where and how interventions ought to be carried out, how long they should see the professional and follow professional prescriptions, and so on. Surrender of decision-making power and usurpation of control cannot but foster a sense of dependency and powerlessness, and in many instances may defer or prevent the acquisition of behavior competencies that eventually make the person self-sustaining (Bandura, 1978; Brickman *et al.*, 1983). The major deficiency of helping relationships that foster dependency is a shift in locus of decision making and responsibility away from the help-seeker toward the help-giver.

In our own program, we have unfortunately found long-term negative consequences of fostering dependency. When our early intervention program began some 15 years ago, we adopted a traditional treatment model in which parents of handicapped, retarded, and developmentally at-risk infants were implicitly assumed to lack the necessary knowledge and skills to educate their infants, and consequently were instructed in how to intervene with their children in order to enhance the children's developmental competencies. Parents were visited weekly in their homes, told what was wrong with their children, what needed to be done to correct weaknesses, how they should teach their children, when and how long they should work with their children, and so on. These are the very conditions that we now know create dependencies because they take away control and decision making from the parents.

As it so happens, we kept contact with many of the families long after services were terminated and the children went into other service delivery systems (typically the public schools). For many families, we discovered a number of harmful consequences in follow-up interviews with the parents, who were often quite depressed and in some instances distraught about themselves and their children. They reported to us how "comfortable" it was to have someone from our early intervention program to "depend on" to tell them what, when, and how to treat their children, but when services were terminated and they were "on their own" they felt "lost" and incapable of "doing things independently." It is unfortunate that our treatment program may have unintentionally produced this type of dependency and its consequent conditions. Fortunately, we have used this type of evidence as a basis for rethinking early intervention that emphasizes enabling and empowering parents with the knowledge and skills that permit them to perform their parenting roles in a competent, self-sustaining manner (Dunst, 1985; Dunst & Trivette, in press).

Attenuation of Self-Esteem

One of the major negative consequences of certain types of help-giving is attenuation of self-esteem (see e.g., Nadler & Mayseless, 1983). Fisher, Nadler, and Whitcher-Alagna (1983) recently proposed a "Formalized Threat to Self-Esteem Model" that specifies those helping conditions that led to enhanced or depressed self-esteem. Their model "assumes that (a) most aid situations contain a mixture of positive and negative self-related elements, and (b) situational conditions and recipient characteristics determine whether a particular receipt of aid is predominately threatening or supportive" (p. 74).

The Fisher, Nadler, and Whitcher-Alagna (1983) model focuses on three types of interpersonal factors that pose threats to self-esteem: (a) self-relevant messages contained in aid itself, (b) values instilled during the socialization history of the help-seeker, and (c) the instrumental qualities of help and aid. The "messages" contained in the donor–recipient exchange may be either threatening or positive. To the extent that help-giving behavior conveys a sense that the help-seeker is inferior, incompetent, or inadequate, or that the help-giver disdains or is patronizing to the help-seeker, the aid and help will be threatening. On the other hand, if the help-giver conveys a sense of warmth, caring, and worthiness, the help is likely to have positive influences.

Whether or not aid and help are congruent with the help-seeker's values and socialized norms is also likely to enhance or threaten self-worth. Independence, self-reliance, and treating others fairly, and expecting to be treated fairly, are socialized values fundamental to western culture. "Aid that limits freedom of action is threatening, [whereas] aid that fosters it is supportive" (Fisher, Nadler, & Whitcher-Alagna, 1983, p. 75). In addition, help-seekers who enter into helping relationships with a sense of fairness to the donor (those who expect to "pay" for the help, reciprocate when the help-giver needs assistance, etc.) are likely to experience increased self-worth, but those that do not will find the experience self-threatening. Help-giving that "exploits or otherwise takes advantage of recipients . . . contains threatening elements, [whereas] aid that constitutes fair treatment . . . contains supportive elements" (Fisher, Nadler, & Whitcher-Alagna, 1983, p. 76).

The nature of the help itself will also affect the help-seeker's self-esteem. Aid and assistance will be supportive if it

> (a) decreases threats associated with one's current condition, and (b) increases the probability of future success. . . . In contrast, aid that [does not] relieve one's need state (e.g., because it is insufficient or ineffective) will be threatening because (a) one continues to bear both the failure that caused the current need state and the prospect of future problems, (b) persisting problems often become more embarrassing, (c) ineffective help may suggest one is being exploited, and (d) accepting ineffective help may call into question one's judgment, states, means, or power. (Fisher, Nadler, & Whitcher-Alagna, 1983, p. 76)

Some years ago one of us noted the inadvertent attenuation of self-esteem while working in an infant and toddler intervention program. The program operated a preschool classroom for normally developing, handicapped, retarded, and developmentally at-risk children, and offered a behavior management training program for the parents. The participants attended a 12-week training session that focused on observing, counting, charting, prompting, shaping, and reinforcing behavior. Parents whose children were enrolled in the classroom program were required to attend the training sessions.

After completion of the training, the parents could competently apply the behavior principles, but incidental comments made by a number of the parents after the training showed that self-esteem and a sense of parental competence were in some instances unintentionally attenuated. One mother of a normally developing child, for example, said that "Before participating in this program, I thought that I was a good parent. Now I know otherwise. I didn't realize I needed to know all these things in order to teach my child." The fact is she did not. She was already a competent parent that the program failed to recognize and acknowledge. Observations of the mother prior to participation in the training program indicated that she already displayed the types of parenting behavior that are known to optimize child development (Mahoney, Powell, Finnegan, Fors, & Wood, 1986; Uzgiris, 1986; Wenar, 1972; White & Watts, 1973), and indeed her child had a D.Q. (Developmental Quotient) of nearly 140 at 22 months of age. The assumption was made that she needed training, but such an assumption proved to be wrong and had negative consequences. What she really needed were experiences that supported and encouraged her parenting behavior.

Indebtedness

Helping relationships in which a help-giver provides aid or assistance to a help-seeker often results in a sense of indebtedness (a state of obligation to repay or help another) to the help-giver by the help-seeker. According to Gouldner (1960), indebtedness is based on the existence of the social norm of reciprocity what states that "(a) people should help those who have helped them, and (b) people should not injure those who have helped them" (p. 171). Greenberg and Westcott (1983), who have extensively reviewed the indebtedness literature (see also Greenberg, 1980), note that it is a "psychological state having motivational properties such that the greater the magnitude of indebtedness, the greater the arousal and, hence, the stronger the ensuing attempt to deal with or to reduce the indebtedness" (pp. 85–86).

According to Greenberg and Westcott (1983), help-seeking and the help-seeker's awareness of, or felt obligation to repay, may produce either positive or negative consequences depending on the nature of donor–recipient exchanges. At least four factors determine the magnitude of indebtedness: (a) response costs, (b) the locus of causality, (c) the donor's motives, and (d) the comparative value of the help-giver's aid and assistance. A help-seeker is likely to feel a greater sense of indebtedness if (a) the benefits derived from the donor–recipient exchange favor the help-seeker, (b) the onus of help-seeking resides in the person needing aid and assistance, (c) the help-giver's behavior is perceived as altruistic, and (d) comparisons with others leads one to conclude that the help was judged to be something for which the help-seeker should be grateful. In addition to these four factors, social class, intrapersonal values and beliefs, and the preexisting relationships between the donor and recipient are also likely to affect a sense indebtedness (see Greenberg & Westcott, 1983).

The negative consequences of indebtedness include threats to self-esteem, displays of negative affect (e.g., depression), dependence upon the help-giver, embarrassment, a sense of inferiority, negative feelings toward the help-giver, avoidance of the help-giver, and resistance to offers of help by others (Broll, Gross, & Piliavin, 1974; Greenberg & Westcott, 1983; Nadler, Shapiro, & Ben-Itzhak, 1983; Williams & Williams, 1983). These various psychological responses are likely to be worsened in situations where reciprocity is impeded, blocked, or unacknowledged (Greenberg & Westcott, 1983).

Generally, individuals feel less indebted when help is offered to them rather than requested in response to a problem or need state (Broll *et al.*, 1974). This suggests that offers of help may alleviate or prevent negative consequences. In contrast, a sense of indebtedness as well as negative feelings associated with the felt obligation increase as a function of both the help-seeker's request for help and the response costs of accepting help (Greenberg, 1980).

A major determinant of help-seeking and responses to it is the help-seeker's self-esteem. In a review of the relevant literature, Nadler and Mayseless (1983) found that high-esteem persons (a) seek less help when help-seeking is perceived as a personal inadequacy, (b) seek help less if receiving help does not include the opportunity to reciprocate, and (c) engage in more self-help behavior directed toward solving problems or meeting needs. Collectively, the findings reviewed by Nadler and Mayseless (1983) were interpreted as meaning that

> only high self-esteem individuals invest in self-help efforts after the receipt of self-threatening help, [which] leads to some intriguing implications for interpersonal helping relations. In fact, it suggests that for the high self-esteem individual, receiving help motivates self-help efforts that are likely to result in improved performance and renewed independence. On the other hand, for the low self-esteem individual, the *receipt of help fosters relative passivity and dependency* [italics added]. (p. 178)

This set of conditions brings us full circle in terms of the potentially debilitating consequences of helping relationships, and illustrates the interdependencies among the negative effects of help-seeking and help-giving, and how events beyond the immediate setting have first- and second-order influences in terms of producing adverse reactions. The phenomenon of help-seeking and help-giving is a complex psychological event that has multiple antecedents and multiple consequences. Our treatment of these complex sets of relationships has necessarily been superficial; however, when placed within the context of our integrated model of help-seeking and help-giving, we can begin to see that certain characteristics of help-seekers and help-givers, and the manner in which problems and needs are identified and help is requested or offered, set the occasion for the types of negative consequences that we have examined. We now turn to a discussion of several situational factors that affect helping relationships that also set the occasion for negative consequences.

Some Situational Considerations

In addition to those determinants described earlier, various situational conditions partly determine whether help is likely to have positive or negative consequences. A complete treatment of situational conditions is beyond the scope of this chapter (see e.g., Fisher, Nadler, & Whitcher-Alagna, 1983). We focus on four situational considerations (noncontingent help-giving, unsolicited help, incongruent help, and unnecessary help) because these conditions have been clinically and empirically found to have negative consequences under certain circumstances. Again, none of the conditions are mutually exclusive.

Noncontingent Help-Giving

Noncontingent help-giving, perhaps more than any other aspect of helping relationships, sets the occasion for increased passivity and dependence. The negative consequences of noncontingent help-giving are even more pronounced than those resulting from indebtedness situations because reciprocity is neither sanctioned or approved, and in many cases is not permissible. This type of noncontingent helping is most characteristic of social agencies serving the poor (e.g., health and social services departments), and is perhaps best exemplified by such programs and services as well-baby clinics, Aid to Families of Dependent Children (AFDC), and other social welfare programs (e.g., food stamps) (see Pettigrew, 1983). Skinner (1978) called this type of noncontingent help unethical because it "postpones the acquisition of effective behavior and perpetuates the need for help" (p. 251). To the extent that "Help supplies a needed resource but leads the person to see the production of that resource as contingent on what the helpers do rather than on his or her own behavior" (Brickman *et al.*, 1983, p. 34), the helping relationship is likely to have harmful consequences. Indeed, meeting needs and solving problems is likely to have long-term positive effects only when persons "take pride in their accomplishments [and] ascribe successes to their own abilities and efforts" (Bandura, 1978, p. 349). Noncontingent giving may seem expedient in terms of solving problems and meeting needs, but in the long run it may deprive the help-seeker of experiences that are important for future learning, acquisition of independent and problem-solving behaviors, and enhancement of self-esteem.

Many of the types of help offered noncontingently by social and human service agencies not only postpone and interfere with the acquisition of self-sustaining and other self-preservating behaviors, but often implicitly (and sometimes explicitly) reinforce the help-seeker's sense of inadequacy and incompetence. This in turn further attenuates efforts to acquire coping and problem-solving behaviors, and results from the interactions among a number of variables, most notably the help-seeker's lack of control and the recipient's awareness that he or she is not permitted to repay the benefactor. Accordingly, one would expect to find a greater sense of helplessness, dependency, and/or negative feelings toward a donor resulting from noncontingent provisions of aid and assistance.

Although noncontingent helping is most likely to be found in helping relationships involving publicly operated human service programs, one finds many examples of this type of help in less formal donor–recipient exchanges (Morse, 1983). Noncontingent giving may on the surface appear to meet the needs of the help-seeker, but again is likely to interfere with acquisition of instrumental behaviors and only attenuate a sense of competence and adequacy. Noncontingent giving by friends, neighbors, relatives, the church, etc., in response to help-seeking requests thus may do more harm than good, at least under certain conditions. If the help does not require the recipient to acquire effective behavior, and thus renders the person helpless or dependent, the immediate needs of the person may be met, but the ability to teach and foster effective behavior would be diminished.

Unsolicited Help

In situations where a person views him or herself as having a problem or need, and help is offered rather than requested, the help giving is likely to have beneficial influences (Fisher, Nadler, & Whitcher-Alagna, 1983). However, there are certain conditions in which unsolicited help may have harmful consequences. These include situations in which the aid or assistance cannot be refused (Fisher, Nadler, & Whitcher-Alagna, 1983) and where one sees the help-giving as a threat to already negative perceptions of oneself (Rosen, 1983).

Goranson and Berkowitz (1966) showed that involuntarily administered aid and assistance is likely to produce negative and defensive reactions. The type of situation where persons are given aid and assistance that is difficult or near impossible to refuse has been noted in our work with families who have been accused of child abuse or neglect. These families are often told that they must participate in our early intervention program, and that their failure to do so will result in the removal of the child from their custody. This type of helping relationship only serves to reinforce the parents' perceptions of themselves as inadequate and incompetent caregivers, and results in extreme dislike and sometimes hatred toward the individual establishing the contingency. These types of reactions are consistent with predictions derived from reactance theory (Brehm & Brehm, 1981), which states that negative feelings and attributions are likely to be greatest when freedom and control are restricted or eliminated (Worchel & Andreoli, 1974).

Unsolicited help is also likely to have negative consequences when it only reinforces already negative feelings toward oneself, and is likely to be greatest when advice or aid are offered by those whom the recipient does not know or does not wish to have advice from (e.g., a meddling neighbor who gives unsolicited child-rearing advice). Not only is the person unlikely to accept the aid, he or she is likely to react negatively to the person's efforts to be helpful.

Incongruent Help

Help that is sought and help that is offered is most likely to be beneficial if there is a match between what the help-seeker thinks he or she needs and the type of aid and resource that are offered (Fisher, 1983). In contrast, where there is incongruence or a mismatch between what is sought and what is offered, the occasion is set for negative outcomes. One of the consequences of incongruent help is that the recipient is less likely either to accept the help or adhere to prescribed regimens.

In a study recently completed in our own program, we examined the relationships between parents' perceived needs and adherence to carrying out child-level educational and therapeutic interventions. We found that parents were less likely to follow the regimens if other personal and family needs took precedence and dominated the person's behavior (Dunst & Leet, 1987). Specifically, parents were more likely to indicate that they did not have the time, energy, and personal investment to conduct child-level interventions if other needs were seen as more important, and thus deserving of their time and energy. Consequently, aid and assistance that is incongruent with what the help-seeker sees as the problem or need is not likely to be taken seriously, and the probability of adherence to the advice is lowered.

A second consequence of incongruent help occurs in situations where advice is given and the help-giver occupies a higher position in a social structure (client vs. professional, child vs. teacher, child vs. parent), and the failure to follow the prescribed regimen of the "powerful others" results in guilt and ambivalence. In our work with families involved in home-based early intervention programs, parents often report that they feel guilty and at fault for not carrying out prescribed treatments that they neither understand nor see the value of, despite the fact that they are asked to do things that are personally taxing and interfere with normative family functioning. In many cases, parents avoid contact with the intervention program staff by canceling home visits, not being home for scheduled visits, etc. They know quite well that they will be asked by the staff "Did you get a chance to try such and such activities?" for which they do not want to give an answer. Some parents have reported to us that they lied to staff about carrying out prescribed activities because the personal response costs and consequences are less severe than admitting to noncompliance.

In situations where incongruent offers of help are made, a potential range of negative responses are likely to be felt by the recipient. In addition, the failure to follow and adhere to prescribed treatments is likely to result in the professional viewing the recipient as resistant, uncooperative, oppositional, and apathetic. Attributions of this sort are in turn likely to change how the professional behaves toward the recipient, which is only likely to create or attenuate a tense helping relationship. This type of condition cannot but help set the occasion for eliciting negative and defensive reactions from the recipient (Fisher, Nadler, & Whitcher-Alagna, 1983).

Unnecessary Help

In situations where help is noncontingent, unsolicited, and incongruent, the help-seeker perceives a need or recognizes a problem, but the help that is offered either weakens the capacity to function independently or evokes extreme negative reactions from the recipient. Offers of help are also likely to have debilitating effects and elicit negative reactions when others see a person's condition as problematic but the person him or herself perceives no problem and has no identified need. We term this type of situation unnecessary help. An awareness of need for help is a major determinant of the consequences of helping relationships, and offers of unnecessary help only serve to increase the probability of resentment.

Many families referred to our program by professionals convey a sense of urgency and despair about the parents and their child(ren). In many cases they are labeled "multiproblemed." Yet when we interview the families, they report no problems or needs (or at least none that match those that the professionals have identified), and are puzzled as to why they might need our services. When the parents find out the reason(s) they were referred, one generally finds that the families see these issues as "none of their business." In some cases, the parents become very upset with the referring agency and show resentment toward the person making the referral. It has generally been our experience that in situations where a family has no identified problems or needs, and unnecessary help is offered, negative reactions are likely to ensue.

Many of the characteristics of effective help (donor responsiveness to needs, enhancement of instrumental capabilities, voluntary aid, normative assistance and resources, etc.) are blocked and impeded by situational conditions, including noncontingent, unsolicited, incongruent, and unnecessary help. To the extent that helping relationships include these types of situational characteristics, the likelihood of negative responses and reactions are increased considerably. Collectively, the material presented in this section suggests the conditions that should be avoided in helping relationships, and lead us to propose a set of principles that are likely to result in positive responses resulting from donor–recipient exchanges.

Enablement, Empowerment, and Euphoria

Taken together, the material reviewed thus far indicates that at least under certain circumstances, there are a number of potentially debilitating consequences of help-seeking and help-giving. The title of our chapter— "Helping, Helplessness, and Harm"—reflects this emphasis on the potentially harmful influences of helping relationships. We took this approach in the hope that pointing out negative consequences would bolster help-givers' attempts to avoid situations where provision of help might have first- and second-order negative effects. It was not our intention to paint a gloom and doom picture of donor–

recipient exchanges. Indeed, we could have titled our chapter "Enablement, Empowerment, and Euphoria" to emphasize those characteristics of helping relationships that have positive influences.

In this section of the chapter, we address those features of donor–recipient exchanges that serve to produce positive effects resulting from helping relationships, and in doing so offer a list of characteristics that may serve as principles for professionals to follow. The material presented in this section is based substantially on the work of Brickman *et al.* (1982, 1983); Fisher, Nadler, and Whitcher-Alagna (1983), and Hobbs *et al.* (1984), and their contributions deserve special recognition.

The principles that we have selected emphasize enabling persons to acquire effective behavior, and thus become empowered. Helping behavior that enables individuals to become competent and empowered should in turn strengthen functioning and promote physical and emotional well-being, a greater sense of self-worth, and foster other positive intrapersonal responses. To the extent that helping relationships meet all or at least most of conditions set forth by the principles, the greater the probability of positive outcomes. The principles include the following:

1. People respond better to help when donor characteristics are positive and proactive (Fisher, 1983). Help-givers who display a sincere sense of caring, warmth, and encouragement when offering or responding to requests for help are more likely to have health promoting and competency producing influences in the help-seekers behavior. "When positive donor motives are attributed (e.g., the donor is perceived to act out of kindness or generosity), aid is more supportive and results in more favorable reactions" (Fisher, Nadler, & Whitcher-Alagna, 1983, p. 73). This is especially the case where emphasis is placed on a person's strengths, and using them as a basis for solving problems or meeting needs.

2. Help is more likely to be favorably received if it is offered rather than requested, and the recipient has the choice of whether or not to accept the help (Fisher, Nadler, & Whitcher-Alagna, 1983). Help-seeking may be implicit or explicit, and the help-giver's sensitivity to verbal, nonverbal, and paraverbal messages displayed by the help-seeker is a key to being able to read a person's behavior and respond appropriately. Active and reflective listening are the types of techniques that are useful for reading requests and offering help. To be maximally effective, the help must be offered voluntarily, and the individual needing the help must be permitted to have final decision making about whether to accept it. The ability to refuse the help should be explicitly recognized by the donor, the decision sanctioned, and the opportunity for future exchanges left often as an option for the help-seeker to use. Aid that implies few lost freedoms is most likely to have positive effects in response to help-giving.

3. Help is more likely to be beneficial if recipients are personally not held responsible for their needs or problems, but are held responsible for solutions and their own maintenance (Brickman *et al.*, 1983). Moreover, the help is more likely to be beneficial if donors see themselves as responsible for outcomes. The latter sets the occasion for joint responsibility (see Principle Number 4) for identifying solutions and acting as "we" and not "you and I." The premise of this principle is not to blame recipients for the past, but rather to make them capable and accountable for being able to cope with and solve problems in the future. Enabling persons to become responsible means empowering them with the knowledge, skills, and resources necessary to face the world and its many demands and expectations, and come out of life's small and large battles better off than before.

4. Helping relationships are more likely to promote positive responses when the donor conveys a sense of cooperation and joint responsibility (partnership) for meeting needs and solving problems (Hobbs *et al.*, 1984). Donor–recipient exchanges that promote participatory decision making and shared re-

sponsibility among the help-seeker and help-giver set the occasion for the help-seeker to feel valued, important, and an equal. This represents the conditions par excellence for enabling and empowering people with the knowledge, skills, and resources to feel competent and in control over their lives and environment.

5. Help is more likely to be beneficial if the donor bolsters the self-esteem of the recipient, and helps the individual experience immediate success in solving a problem or meeting a need (Nadler & Mayseless, 1983). One of the major paradoxes of helping, especially in donor–recipient exchanges involving low self-esteem help-seekers, is that if you

> want help given to a low self-esteem person to work, [you] need to devise ways to raise the recipients' self-esteem, even temporarily, before providing the help. . . . If help is given after efforts toward self-esteem enhancement have been successful, it is more likely to precipitate adaptive behaviors (e.g., self-help efforts and subsequent improved performance) than if given before such efforts are attempted. (Nadler & Mayseless, 1983, p. 178)

Bolstering self-esteem can be accomplished by pointing out how the person already uses his or her strengths in other areas (Principle Number 1), and helping the person solve small problems and experience immediate success before tackling more difficult problems.

6. "Effective help leaves the recipient better off after the help than before, and maximally effective help leaves the recipient no longer in need of help" (Brickman *et al.*, 1983, p. 29). For help to be effective, the recipient must not only see that problems have been solved or needs have been met, but that he or she functioned as an active, responsible agent who played a significant role in improving his or her own life since it is the "recipient's own belief in (him or herself) as a causal agent that determines whether the gains made will last or disappear" (Brickman *et al.*, 1983, p. 32). Recipients must therefore perceive improvement, see themselves as no longer in need of help, and see themselves as responsible for producing the observed changes and maintenance of these changes, if donor-recipient exchanges are to be effective (Bandura, 1977). This sense of intra- and interpersonal control is most likely to be acquired as a function of learning effective, instrumental behavior.

7. Help is more likely to be beneficial if it promotes the acquisition of effective behavior that decreases the need for help, and thus makes the person capable and competent (Skinner, 1978). This type of help "enables the recipient to become more self-sustaining and less in need of future help" (Brickman *et al.*, 1983, p. 19), thus promoting independence (Fisher, Nadler & Whitcher-Alagna, 1983) and problem-solving capabilities (DePaulo *et al.*, 1983). To be fair and effective, help-giving must be contingent on the help-seeker's active attempts to meet needs and solve problems, and result in the acquisition of competencies that permit greater independence that in turn decreases the need for continued aid and assistance. Promoting effective behaviors, perhaps more than any other aspect of helping relationships, is the cornerstone of beneficial donor–recipient exchanges. To the extent that behavior competencies can be taught or facilitated that reduce the need for future help, the helping relationship will have been successful.

8. Help is more likely to be favorably received if it can be reciprocated, and the possibility of repaying the help-giver is sanctioned and approved but not expected (Fisher, Nadler, & Whitcher-Alagna, 1983). "Reciprocity is [most] likely to be the preferred mode of reducing indebtedness to the extent that recipients are made aware of this option and they perceive that the opportunity to reciprocate exists" (Greenberg & Westcott, 1983, p. 95). Repaying need not be material in nature, and in fact is often informational and emotional (e.g., sharing a recipe in exchange for services rendered to a child or family, or giving a tutor a paper demonstrating improvement in reading skills). A help-giver who provides aid and assistance and accepts aid and assistance makes the exchanges fair and equitable, which in turn bolsters the help-seeker's sense that he or she has as much to give as to take.

9. Help is maximally effective when the aid and assistance is congruent with the help-

seeker's appraisal of his or her problem or need (Fisher, 1983). Needs and need states are one set of conditions that motivate people to see the need for and seek help. Perceptions of problems and needs constitute forces that steer and propel behavior in certain directions (Garbarino, 1982). Positive reactions to help-giving is more likely to occur when aid and assistance is appropriate and matches one's appraisal of problems or needs. Insuring that help-giving is appropriate requires an assessment of the help-seeker's needs and problems in order to be sure there is congruence between what is needed and what is offered.

10. People are more likely to accept aid and assistance when the response costs of seeking and accepting help do not outweigh the benefits (Gross & McMullen, 1983). The most obvious cost involved in accepting help is the financial obligation to pay for the resources or services rendered by the help-giver. Many response costs are much more subtle, and enter into decisions about seeking or not seeking help, and accepting and not accepting help. Help-giving that reduces threats to self-esteem, moderates obligations to pay, protects behavior freedoms (decision making), and promotes competence and a sense of adequacy, are more likely to be seen as personally cost-effective.

Implications for Policy and Practice

The previously cited principles and the enabling and empowering characteristics that they embody suggest ways in which helping relationships can optimize the acquisition of self-sustaining behavior and thus strengthen intra- and interpersonal functioning. In this section of the chapter we describe the utility of the principles for policy decisions and family support programs, and discuss the implications of the principles for behavioral therapists.

Developing and Assessing Public Policy

Nicholas Hobbs and his associates (1984) in their book *Strengthening Families* proposed a framework for developing and assessing public policy designed to enhance community support, strengthen family functioning, and promote human development. They raised four value-based questions and then developed associated criteria that serve as a blueprint for establishing and evaluating family support programs. The programmatic characteristics that Hobbs *et al.* (1984) argued for, albeit in a different terminology, are embodied in the 10 principles outlined earlier. To the extent that policy and the manner in which services are rendered to families are consistent with the criteria set forth by Hobbs *et al.* (1984), a program would have high grades in terms of enabling and empowering families. The four value questions and associated criteria are:

1. Does the policy enhance community? Policies that enhance a sense of community (a) increase shared heritage, mutual aid, and community building; (b) promote a sense of individual and group adequacy and competence; (c) apply equally to all community members; and (d) do not separate people or bestow resources based solely on

> age, sex, racial and ethnic group membership, socioeconomic status, religious preference, educational level, handicapping condition, and the like. . . . Policies that promote the coming together of people around shared values and the pursuit of common cause enhance community [and promote] well-being. (Hobbs *et al.*, 1984, pp. 46–48)

2. Does the policy strengthen families? Policies that strengthen families recognize the family unit as the "foundation of meaningful community and . . . the context for the human development of their members" (Hobbs *et al.*, 1984, p. 49). Such policies (a) improve the capacity of families and their members to master a broad range of developmental tasks, including child rearing, growth and development, and health and nutrition; (b) promote and strengthen the capacity of families to identify and make use of their informal support networks; and (c) neither intrude into or restrict a family's capacity to make informed decisions about what is best for the family and its members.

3. Does the policy enable parents to adequately perform their parenting roles? "Policies that enable parents to make competent decisions for their family strengthen the family and enhance the well-being, developmental status, and rights of all family members" (Hobbs *et al.*, 1984, p. 50). The ability to accomplish these goals is most likely to occur by (a) promoting well-being through provision and mediation of support that ensures that parents have the necessary resources to carry out their parenting roles where (b) identification and access to needed resources occurs in a participatory, shared-responsibility fashion between the families and members of their informal and formal social networks.

4. Does the policy enhance individual development and protect the rights of family members? Policies that (a) promote competence and self-sustaining behavior and (b) protect individual family members from abuse and neglect are extremely important if parents are to have the opportunity to optimize their own growth and development as well as that of other family members. The promotion of individual and family functioning through protection of fundamental human rights is viewed by Hobbs *et al.* (1984) as encompassing all three previous values and criteria. Enhancement of community, strengthening families, and enabling parents are seen as ways of promoting individual development in a positive, proactive manner.

The work of Hobbs and his colleagues illustrate how one can go about establishing policies that are likely to result in the development of programs that produce positive outcomes. We now turn to a description of two exemplary family support programs that illustrate the operationalization of our enabling and empowering principles.

Family Support Programs

Family Matters

The Family Matters project in Syracuse, New York, is an excellent example of how theory, values, beliefs, and empirical evidence can form the basis for implementing a program designed to empower parents so that they can adequately perform their parenting roles (Cochran & Woolever, 1983). A social systems, human ecology framework forms the conceptual basis of the project (Bronfenbrenner, 1979; Cochran & Brassard, 1979). According to this perspective, social units and their members are seen as interdependent, so that events and changes in one unit reverberate and affect the behavior of persons in other social units. As noted by Cochran and Woolever (1983),

> it is important to keep all . . . aspects of family ecology in mind while developing a program and . . . to look constantly for ways in which those systems interact to affect the lives of certain families or individuals. (p. 228)

Family Matters is based on four major beliefs about families that illustrate the manner in which the enabling and empowering principles can guide program development. These include: (a) the belief that all families have strengths that can form the basis for proactively affecting behavior change; (b) the belief that the most valid and useful information and skills about child rearing resides within the informal social networks of the families (i.e., community in the Hobbs *et al.*, 1984, framework); (c) the belief that access to essential forms of support and resources necessary for performing parenting roles (and not personal or family characteristics *per se*) are the major determinants of successful child rearing; and (d) the belief that differences among cultural and ethnic groups are not deficiencies but rather indicators of important belief systems that need to be sustained to the extent that they promote individual and family functioning. Collectively, these beliefs guide the operationalization of efforts designed to empower parents to take control over their family's life so that they can act in an informed and responsible manner.

The six major goals of the project reflect this proactive, empowering orientation:

1. To reduce isolation (within and between families)

2. To give recognition to parents as experts
3. To reinforce and encourage parent–child activities
4. To share information about children, neighborhood, service, and work
5. To encourage the exchange of resources among neighboring families
6. To facilitate concerted actions by project participants on behalf of their children (Cochran & Woolever, 1983, pp. 230–231)

The project activities used to accomplish these goals are carried out as part of two major program components: home visits and neighborhood cluster groups. The home visiting component is "designed to give recognition to the parenting role, reinforce and enrich parent–child activities, and share information about child care and community services" (Cochran & Woolever, 1983, p. 232). Home visiting staff assist parents in identifying concerns, needs, interests, and strengths, and then use needs and strengths as a basis for promoting a sense of parenthood as a fundamentally important function for the future well-being and competence of all family members.

The cluster component is designed to

> reduce feelings of isolation by bringing families together at the neighborhood level, to encourage the sharing of information and resources among families, and, when parents voice a need for change in the neighborhood, to facilitate action in pursuit of those changes. (Cochran & Woolever, 1983, p. 233)

The neighborhood clusters form a basis for fostering linkages and mediating support among persons with similar concerns about child rearing, community issues, etc. The emphasis is on promoting a sense of community support in order to optimize experiences that are good for family functioning and child development.

The thing that makes Family Matters different from other programs, and consequently unique, is the emphasis on supporting and enabling families by taking a positive stance toward individual family members, the family unit, and community. This proactive approach is perhaps best reflected in Cochran and Woolever's (1983) contention that "Information, advice, connections, baby-sitting, emotional support, response to crisis—this is the stuff of informal support and that elusive sense of community" (p 237). It is not the activities *per se* that make Family Matters an exemplary program, but rather the style and the manner in which the activities are carried out.

Family, Infant, and Preschool Program

We have used the material and evidence presented in this chapter for conceptualizing, developing, implementing, and evaluating a social systems, family-oriented approach to early intervention (Dunst, 1985; Dunst & Trivette, in press). The Family, Infant and Preschool Program (FIPP) is guided by a philosophy that is called Proactive Empowerment through Partnerships (PEP). The PEP model places major emphasis on (a) identifying and strengthening child and family capabilities using a proactive rather than a deficit approach; (b) enabling and empowering parents with the necessary knowledge, skills, and resources needed to perform family and parenting functions in a competent manner; by (c) using partnerships between parents and professionals as the means to strengthen, enable, and empower families.

Our program is proactive in the sense that we take a positive stance toward children and their families. A proactive approach focuses on the child's and family's strengths and not their weaknesses, and promotes positive functioning by supporting families (Zigler & Berman, 1983). As Stoneman (1985) pointed out, "Every family has strengths and, if the emphasis is on supporting strengths rather than rectifying weaknesses, chances for making a difference in the lives of children and families are vastly increased" (p. 462). Although this means neither blaming the family nor holding them entirely or even primarily responsible for their problems or conditions, it does mean holding them responsible for identifying solutions and maintenance of newly acquired behavior (Brickman *et al.*,

1983; Rappaport, Davidson, Wilson, & Mitchell, 1975; Solomon, 1985).

Our program enables and empowers families by creating opportunities that permit a greater understanding and control over resources and decision making. Rappaport (1981) stated this in the following manner:

> Empowerment implies that many competencies are already present or at least possible. . . . Empowerment implies that what you see as poor functioning is a result of social structure and lack of resources which make it impossible for the existing competencies to operate. It implies that in those cases where new competencies need to be learned, they are best learned in a context of living life rather than in artificial programs where everyone, including the person learning, knows that it is really the expert who is in charge. (p. 16)

An individual or social unit (e.g., family) that is empowered knows what physical and psychological resources they have, how to go about getting resources they do not have, and understands that they played a major role in gaining access and control over those resources (Bandura, 1977).

Our program enables and empowers parents within the context of partnerships between families and professionals that avoids the paternalism characteristic of most client–professional relationships. Enabling and empowering families "requires a breakdown of the typical role relationship between professionals and community people" (Rappaport, 1981, p. 19). Partnerships imply that partners are capable individuals who become more capable by sharing knowledge, skills, and resources in a manner that leaves each person better off after entering into the cooperative endeavor.

FIPP uses a needs-based, social systems approach to provision and mediation of both child- and family-level support and resources. Family concerns, issues, and problems are first identified using a variety of needs-based assessment procedures (e.g., Leet & Dunst, 1985; Trivette & Dunst, 1986). Once family selected needs have been identified, the parents together with staff "map" the family's social support network in terms of both existing sources of support, and potential but untapped sources of aid, assistance, and resources. Options for meeting needs are explored, and the things the family and its members already do well are used as a base for exploring ways in which their network can be mobilized to meet the needs. "The goal [of intervention] is to *strengthen* normal socializing agencies (the family, the school, the church, the neighborhood), *not to replace them*" (Hobbs, 1975, p. 114, italics added).

The roles that staff play in this process are quite different than the expert role assumed by most professionals as part of early intervention and family support programs (see especially Solomon, 1985; Slater & Winkler, 1986). The primary staff function is to help families "identify needs, locate the informal and formal resources necessary for meeting those needs, and help link families with the identified resources" (Hobbs *et al.*, 1984; p. 50). In this capacity the staff perform a number of roles, including linking people, mobilizing existing resources and support, facilitating the establishment of new support structures, moderating exchanges among network members, consulting with families about problems or concerns, preparing the family and social network for transition across microsystems, and teaching parents competencies that will permit them to carry out their parenting roles in a more competent manner.

The implementation of the PEP model occurs through two transdisciplinary intervention teams, a specialized intervention team, a community resources component, nine model-demonstration projects, four training and technical assistance projects, and five research laboratories and projects (see especially Dunst & Trivette, in press). (A document entitled "Directory of Projects and Services of the Family, Infant and Preschool Program" describes the direct services, special projects, technical assistance and training activities, and research efforts of the program in more detail. It may be obtained by writing Community Resource Services, Family, Infant and Preschool Program, Western Carolina Center, Morganton, NC 28655.) The manner in which the empowerment and enabling principles are put into practice varies as a function of the goals of the individual project and program components, family needs, and the intended outcomes of provision and mediation of support. The PEP model, needs-based approach to intervention, emphasis on social support networks as the primary source of aid and resources, and the shift in roles that staff play in "making the system work" reflect a distinctive style of working with families. This distinctive style emphasizes enabling and empowering parents by directly translating our 10 principles into practice.

Implications for Behavior Therapy

A cursory search of the help-seeking and help-giving literature finds little mention of either the positive or negative consequences of behavior therapy. This is unfortunate because examining behavior therapy from the helping relationships perspective might provide some clues about why clients drop out of therapy, why they fail to comply with prescribed regimens, why there may be little or no maintenance or generalization of what is taught, and consequently why we need look beyond the immediate target behavior to judge the success or failure of a treatment program. In this final subsection of the chapter we explore some of the implications of the material presented herein for understanding the broader-based context of behavior therapy, and illustrate how our helping-relationships perspective might be used as a basis for conceptualizing and implementing behavioral treatments.

Behavior Therapy and Models of Helping

The reader may find it instructive to view behavior therapy from the four models of helping described by Brickman *et al.* (1982) and Brickman *et al.* (1983) because to do so provides some clues about the conditions that affect and maintain behavior change. As the reader will remember, each of these models differs in terms of the extent to which the help-seeker is held responsible for causing problems and whether or not they are responsible for solving problems. Additionally, each model differs with respect to attributions about locus of responsibility affecting and maintaining behavior change (Bandura, 1977; Brickman *et al.*, 1982).

In the moral model, people are responsible for their problems and solutions to them. This model seems entirely inconsistent with behavior therapy because persons are seen as undeserving of any type of help.

In the medical model, persons are neither responsible for their problems nor solutions. The reader may be surprised to find that Brickman *et al.* (1982) view a strict Skinnerian approach to behaviorism as a version of the medical model because "human behavior is determined by rewards and punishments in a way that makes it foolish to blame people for their problems or give them credit for solutions" (p. 373).

Although we do not entirely agree with this interpretation, it is possible to think of many situations in which a therapist might view problems (e.g., maladaptive behavior) as related not to the person's own doings and see him or herself (i.e., the therapist) as responsible for rearranging contingencies, making rewards available only in the presence of the therapist, and controlling behavior in a manner seen as appropriate by the therapist. In such cases, the client is likely to ascribe changes in behavior to the therapist and in turn (a) decrease efforts toward self-efficacious behavior (Bandura, 1977); (b) become more dependent on the therapist (Brickman *et al.*, 1982); and (c) may even lose the ability to do things they previously did well (Langer & Benevento, 1978). To the extent that a client or therapist, or both, subscribe to the medical model of helping, one would expect to find behavior change during therapy but very little maintenance. This is the case because the client has come to learn that the therapist and not the client him or herself was the agent responsible for affecting the change.

In the enlightenment model, people are seen as responsible for their problems and conditions but not capable of solutions at least on their own. On the one hand, this model requires people to accept a negative image of themselves because they have no one to blame but themselves for their problem, and on the other hand, to improve, they must submit to and follow regimens prescribed by "experts." "Since solutions to problems lies outside the [client], the solution can be maintained only so long as the relationship with the external authority . . . is maintained" (Brickman *et al.*, 1982, p. 374).

Many of the parent-training programs for behaviorally disordered children seem to be carried out from an enlightenment perspective to the extent that emphasis is placed on decreasing inappropriate behavior rather than promoting prosocial behavior (see especially the discussion to follow on moving behavior therapy beyond a deficit model). Accordingly, care givers whose children display aberrant behavior and who either implicitly or explicitly are made to feel incompetent as parents (otherwise why would they need help), must be instructed as to how to manage their children's behavior. The implicit or explicit inference regarding the parents' lack of parenting competencies cannot but be detrimental to their self-esteem, and although behavior change is likely to occur, the parents are more likely to attribute responsibility for the change to the therapist even though the parents indeed become more capable as a result of training efforts. Moreover, the "more extensive the situational aids for performance, the greater are the chances that behavior will be ascribed to external factors" (Bandura, 1977, p. 201). Under such conditions, one would expect to find very little maintenance of behavior change.

In the compensatory model, people are not responsible for their problems but are responsible for solutions. On the one hand, this model de-emphasizes attention to the past and consequently reduces the probability of increasing guilt or attenuation of self-esteem, and on the other hand, it emphasizes the client's acquisition of self-sustaining behaviors as well as a sense of self-efficacy (Bandura, 1977). Therapy or training is

> designed to *empower* [clients] to deal more effectively with their environment. A . . . therapist who approaches a [client] in the spirit of the compensatory model says to the [client], in effect, "I am your servant. How can I help you?" rather than "Do what I say." The typical response of observers who assume the compensatory model is to *mobilize* on behalf of the [client] . . . until the missing resources have apparently been supplied and the person can (and should) be responsible for his or her own fate. (Brickman *et al.*, 1982, p. 372, italics added).

To the extent that therapy promotes behavior change together with a sense of self-efficacy, the client is more likely to attribute responsibility for maintaining change to him or herself, and the success of the therapy should be enhanced considerably.

As can be seen from this brief discussion of helping models, the compensatory model is the approach of choice because it not only focuses on affecting behavior change but also explicitly attempts to enhance a sense of self-efficacy that conceptually, at least, appears to be one determinant of maintenance of change (Bandura, 1977).

Behavior Therapy, Help-Seeking, and Help-Giving

The integrated model of help-seeking and help-giving described earlier seems useful for understanding the conditions that are likely to result in behavior therapy being successful or unsuccessful, having harmful or enabling consequences, and so on. According to our helping-relationships model, behavior therapy (i.e., what a therapist does and the manner in which it is done) is a help-giving (social support) act and what the client asks for or is asked to do is part of the help-seeking process. Our model predicts that the extent to which a client is likely to acquire and maintain target behaviors and display changes in related response class categories (Kazdin, 1982) is multiply determined, and is the consequence of complex interactions among a host of intra- and interpersonal variables and of the historical experiences the recipient brings to the helping relationship. Evidence is accumulating that differences in treatment efficacy may be accounted for, in part, by taking the broader-based, social systems perspective advocated for in this chapter.

A recent study by Webster-Stratton (1985) is a nice demonstration of the advantage of taking this type of broader-based perspective for understanding the conditions that set the occasion for the differential efficacy of a treatment program. The study assessed the efficacy of a parent training program for affecting changes in parent and child behavior. The investigator examined the extent to which socioeconomic status (maternal education level, income, marital status, and referral status), maternal depression, and negative life experiences (life events) prior to implementation of the parent training program were related to both the short-term (one-month posttreatment) and long-term (one-year posttreatment) success of the treatment effort. The dependent measures (treatment outcomes) included self-report and observational measures of child and maternal behaviors, including child compliance, negative maternal demands, and mothers' perceptions of child behavior difficulty. The results showed that socioeconomic status and negative life events were significantly related to immediate and long-term success on nearly all the treatment outcomes. As one would expect, higher socioeconomic status and fewer negative life events were related to more successful treatment outcomes. The findings are not surprising because negative life events (death of a relative, divorce, the birth of a handicapped child, etc.) are the types of experiences that steer behavior in certain directions (Garbarino, 1982), and are likely to interfere with adherence to behavioral prescriptions if they are not related to the life event and reactions to it (which in turn is likely to determine treatment success). The Webster-Stratton (1985) findings corroborate those of other investigators who also found that various parent, family, and situational variables influenced treatment success (e.g., Griest, Forehand, & Wells, 1981; McMahon, Forehand, Griest, & Wells, 1981; Wahler & Afton, 1980; Wahler & Graves, 1983).

The results from studies that show that behavior therapy is likely to have differential influences depending on broader-based, ecological variables indicate a need to take these factors into consideration when deciding on the best course of action as part of donor–recipient exchanges. To the extent that personal, family, situational, and helping-relationships variables influence treatment outcomes, explicit attention to these antecedents seems necessary as part of behavior therapy and the manner in which it is conducted. More specifically, assessment of adequacy of resources, social support, life events, stress and well-being, and so on seems necessary as a basis for deciding the probability of treatment success. If conditions are such that the probability of success is low, therapy would need to focus on broader-based changes in the child's ecology before more specific client treatments were tried. Wahler's (1980) work on insularity is an excellent example of this approach to behavior therapy.

Some Potentially Harmful Consequences of Behavior Therapy

Kazdin (1982) pointed out that any type of treatment procedure, including behavior therapy, may produce positive and negative outcomes "depending on the behaviors that ordinarily covary with the target problem" (p. 349). Theoretically, behavioral treatment could have positive effects in terms of changes in targeted behavior but produce negative consequences in a related response class (e.g., increased in targeted behavior together with attenuation of self-esteem and internal locus of control). Accordingly, treatment outcomes

> may be deleterious (e.g., as implied by symptom substitution and deterioration effects) or beneficial (e.g., as implied by generalization) or both. Whether changes are 'negative' or 'positive' introduces an important but separate dimension (into

> treatment programs), namely, how the changes are viewed or evaluated. (Kazdin, 1982, p. 353)

When couched within our integrated help-seeking model shown in Figure 4, this refers to the multiple influences different causal and mediational antecedent conditions have in terms of producing multiple changes (either positive or negative, or both) in the help-seeker's behavior.

There is a large literature concerning the negative side effects of aversive control techniques (Kazdin, 1980) and a literature is beginning to be amassed concerning the negative side effects of reward (Balsam & Bondy, 1983). For example, Bandura (1975) noted that "When (people) know what they are being reinforced for, they may respond in accommodating or oppositional ways depending upon how they value the incentives, the influencers, and the behavior itself, and how others respond" (p. 14). There is, for instance, evidence that the use of extrinsic rewards with intrinsically motivated persons alters stimulus control so that removal of the extrinsic rewards results in less rather than more self-sustaining behavior (Deci, 1974).

Steiner's (1970) work on reactance shows that attempts to bring behavior under control is sometimes perceived to be a threat to personal freedom, which, as we have already noted, produces negative reactions (e.g., Brehm & Brehm, 1981). Similarly, one is more likely to find increased dependency and a greater display of learned helplessness in situations where one person holds all or most of the contingencies, and the delivery of reinforcers is possible only in the presence of that individual. In these instances, "it is not unusual to find that the improved behavior is under control (and thus dependent upon) the presence of the therapeutic agent or that the behavior does not generalize from one aspect of the environment to another" (Balsam & Bondy, 1983, p. 290).

In the earlier discussion of helping models and behavior therapy, we noted that depending on the stance therapists take in approaching donor–recipient exchanges, attenuation of self-esteem and self-efficacy may occur, and thus result in negative effects. Broadly speaking, behavior therapy, like any approach to treatment, can have harmful effects depending on *how* the therapy is conducted.

Bandura's (1975) excellent discussion of the ethics of behavior therapy and modification includes numerous examples of the potentially harmful consequences of different types of treatment. But as he so aptly points out, it is not the principles that are at fault, but rather how they are interpreted and applied that sets the occasion for negative effects. Rather than dwell on the negative, and keeping in line with the positive, proactive position that has evolved in the course of our examination of the characteristics of donor–recipient exchanges, we turn to a discussion of the implications of our empowerment and enablement principles for behavior therapy.

Behavior Therapy, Enablement, and Empowerment

The enabling and empowering principles described earlier appear to have utility for treatment provision by behavior therapists as well as other human service professionals. These principles embody the conditions that set the occasion for acquisition of self-sustaining behavior and attributions about self-efficacy. Thus, to the extent that behavior therapy can be conducted in a manner that takes into consideration all or most of the principles, the probability of broad-based success should be enhanced considerably. Close inspection of Bandura's (1975) exposition of the ethics of behavior therapy finds, interestingly enough, many of the very principles that we have arrived at from a different conceptual orientation. Several examples may help illustrate the similarities.

According to Bandura (1975), "behavioral approaches achieve their successes by the joint efforts of participants, not through unilateral control [by therapists]" (p. 15). This is precisely what Principle 4 states as the conditions for creating partnerships in meeting needs and solving problems. On the relative efficacy of reinforcers and rewards, he notes that "Consequences alter behavior through the intervening influence of thoughts and valuations" (p. 14) of the donor (therapist) and the recipient (client). This condition embodies the criteria of Principles 1, 2, and 5 to the extent that therapists display positive characteristics, clients attribute kindness and generosity to the offers of help, and therapists promote a sense of self-worth as part of the donor–recipient exchange. Additionally, he notes that therapeutic efforts are most likely to be successful if "the clients . . . choose what they wished changed . . . [and] the therapists help clients to overcome the problems from which they seek relief" (p. 14) and emphasis is placed on fostering the acquisition of behavior that "advances self-determination and enhancement of personal potentialities" (p. 19). The former is part of Principles 2 and 9 and the latter part of Principles 3, 6, and 7. Elsewhere, Bandura (1978) has discussed the role that reciprocal determinism plays in affecting behavior change, and how it influences behavior in a manner posited in Principle 8. Collectively, the characteristics of behavior therapy that Bandura suggests are most likely to result in broad-based positive influences are the same type of characteristics that are germane to our enabling and empowering principles. These principles suggest a unique, positive style of helping, attention to behavior change and self-efficacy, participatory involvement by client and therapist, and broader-based methods and goals for determining the success of treatment programs.

Moving Behavior Therapy beyond a Deficit Model

Most therapeutic methods, including behavior therapy, are conducted from a deficit perspective and are reactive rather than proactive. Indeed, the very term *therapy* means the treatment of a problem or disorder. A cursory review of any number of prominent behavioral journals finds the preponderance of articles reporting the results of studies designed to correct behavior excesses and inappropriate behavior. Furthermore, there tends to be an emphasis on fostering compliant and obedient rather than self-sustaining, independent, and self-efficacious behavior (e.g., Winett & Winkler, 1972). This is unfortunate because operant principles represent perhaps the most powerful technology for affecting change, and "if applied to proper ends, behavioral approaches can support a humanistic morality" (Bandura, 1975, p. 19).

Prevention models are typically advanced as alternatives to treatment programs (see e.g., Heller, Price, & Sher, 1980) although their conceptual and methodological soundness have been questioned (Lamb & Zusman, 1979). Conceptually, treatment and prevention models take a deficit stance toward behavior change. Treatment programs correct problems or disorders, whereas prevention programs decrease the risk of problems or disorders. The unifying theme of both treatment approaches is their emphasis on reducing negative outcomes. Consequently, both violate many of the enabling and empowering principles that we have proposed, and thus reduce the probability that interventions will be successful.

A third approach, and one that we believe holds the greatest promise for altering the manner in which we conduct interventions, including behavioral approaches, is the promotion model. In this model, emphasis is placed on promoting and strengthening functioning by fostering the acquisition of prosocial, self-sustaining, self-efficacious, and other positive behaviors. On the one hand, a promotion approach embodies most of our enabling and empowering principles, and on the other hand, provides the type of framework that encourages a proactive approach to defining outcomes and structuring interventions designed to promote these attributes.

The distinction we make between reactive versus proactive and treatment/prevention versus promotion is neither trivial nor semantic. These are differences that set the occasion for how we go about intervening with clients. Take, for example, school children who show difficulty in mastering academic material. In contrast to a treatment program that might focus on supplemental assistance (e.g., a resource room) designed to improve performance directly, a promotion program would assume an already existing level and set of competencies, and find ways to promote functioning using existing strengths. In a number of investigations that have taken this approach, children having learning difficulties were asked to teach younger children in the subject areas in which they were having difficulty (see Allen, 1976). The results showed that the youngsters improved their academic performance significantly as a function of serving in the tutor (helper) role (Allen & Feldman, 1974; Erickson & Cromack, 1972).

Moving behavior therapy beyond a deficit model is going to require a shift in how therapists approach helping relationships. A proactive, promotion model seems to have the greatest potential for therapists enabling and empowering clients in the manner described in this chapter. To the extent that therapists take pride in and derive rewards from seeing others become more competent and self-sustaining, application of the enabling and empowering principles seem to be a way to attain this type of success.

ACKNOWLEDGMENTS

Appreciation is extended to Pat Condrey, Pam Lowman, and Peggy Mankinen for assistance in preparation of this manuscript.

References

Abramson, L. Y., Seligman, M. E. P., & Teasdale, J. C. (1978). Learned helplessness in humans: Critique and reformulation. *Journal of Abnormal Psychology, 87,* 49–74.

Allen, V. L. (1976). *Children as teachers: Theory and research on tutoring.* New York: Academic Press.

Allen, V. L., & Feldman, R. S. (1974). Learning through tutoring: Low-achieving children as tutors. *Journal of Experimental Education, 42,* 1–5.

Antonucci, T. C., & Depner, C. E. (1982). Social support and informal helping relationships. In T. A. Wills (Ed.), *Basic processes in helping relationships* (pp. 233–254). New York: Academic Press.

Balsam, P. D., & Bondy, A. S. (1983). The negative side effects of rewards. *Journal of Applied Behavioral Analysis, 16,* 283–296.

Bandura, A. (1975). The ethics and social purposes of behavior modification. In C. M. Franks & G. T. Wilson (Eds.), *Annual review of behavior therapy theory and practice* (pp. 13–22). New York: Brunner/Mazel.

Bandura, A. (1977). Self-efficacy: Toward a unifying theory of behavioral change. *Psychological Review, 84,* 191–215.

Bandura, A. (1978). The self system in reciprocal determinism. *American Psychologist, 33,* 344–358.

Brehm, S. S., & Brehm, J. W. (1981). *Psychological reactance: A theory of freedom and control.* New York: Academic Press.

Brickman, P., Rabinowitz, V., Karuza, J., Coates, D., Cohn, E., & Kidder, L. (1982). Models of helping and coping. *American Psychologist, 37,* 368–384.

Brickman P., Kidder, L. H., Coates, D., Rabinowitz. V., Cohn, E., & Karuza, J. (1983). The dilemmas of helping: Making aid fair and effective. In J. D. Fisher, A. Nadler, & B. M. DePaulo (Eds.), *New directions in helping: Vol. 1. Recipient reactions to aid* (pp. 18–51). New York: Academic Press.

Broadhead, W. E., Kaplan, B. H., James, S. A., Wagner, E. H., Schoenbach, V. J., & Grimson, S. H. (1983). The epidemiologic evidence for a relationship between social support and health. *American Journal of Epidemiology, 117,* 521–537.

Bronfenbrenner, U. (1979). *The ecology of human development.* Cambridge, MA: Harvard University Press.

Broll, L., Gross, A. E., & Piliavin, I. (1974). Effects of offered and requested help on help-seeking and reactions to being helped. *Journal of Applied Social Psychology, 4,* 244–258.

Clark, M. (1983). Reactions to aid in communal and exchange relationships. In J. D. Fisher, A. Nadler, & B. M. DePaulo (Eds.), *New directions in helping: Vol. 1. Recipient reactions to aid* (pp. 281–304). New York: Academic Press.

Coates, D., Renzaglia, G. J., & Embree, M. C. (1983). When helping backfires: Help and helplessness. In J. D. Fisher, A. Nadler, & B. M. DePaulo (Eds.), *New directions in helping: Vol. 1. Recipient reactions to aid* (pp. 251–279). New York: Academic Press.

Cochran, M., & Brassard, J. (1979). Child development and personal social networks. *Child Development, 50,* 601–616.

Cochran, M., & Woolever, F. (1983). Beyond the deficit model: The empowerment of parents with information and informal supports. In I. E. Sigel & L. M. Laosa (Eds.), *Changing families* (pp. 225–246). New York: Plenum Press.

Cohen, S., & Syme, S. L. (Eds.). (1985). *Social support and health.* New York: Academic Press.

Crnic, A., Greenberg, M., Ragozin, A., Robinson. J., & Basham, R. (1983). Effects of stress and social support on mothers of premature and full-term infants. *Child Development, 54,* 209–217.

Crnic, K. A., Greenberg, M. T., & Slough, N. M. (1986). Early stress and social support influences on mothers' and high-risk infants' functioning in late infancy. *Infant Mental Health Journal, 7,* 19 48.

Crockenberg, S. (1981). Infant irritability, mother responsiveness and social influences on the security of infant-mother attachment. *Child Development, 52,* 857–865.

Dean, A., & Lin, N. (1977). The stress-buffering role of social support. *The Journal of Nervous and Mental Disease, 165* (16), 403–417.

Deci, E. L. (1974). *Intrinsic motivation.* New York: Plenum Press.

DePaulo, B. M. (1982). Social psychological processes in informal help-seeking. In T. A. Willis (Ed.), *Basic processes in helping relationships* (pp. 255–279). New York: Academic Press.

DePaulo, B. (1983). Perspectives on help-seeking. In B. M. DePaulo, A. Nadler, & J. Fisher (Eds.), *New directions in helping: Vol. 2. Help-seeking* (pp. 3–12). New York: Academic Press.

DePaulo, B. M., Nadler, A., & Fisher, J. (1983). *New direction in helping: Vol. 2. Help-seeking.* New York: Academic Press.

Dovidio, J. F., & Gaertner, S. L. (1983). Race, normative structure, and help-seeking. In B. DePaulo, A. Nadler, & J. Fisher (Eds.), *New directions in helping: Vol. 2. Help-seeking* (pp. 285–302). New York: Academic Press.

Dunst, C. J. (1985). Rethinking early intervention. *Analysis and Intervention in Developmental Disabilities, 5,* 165–201.

Dunst, C. J., & Leet, H. E. (1987). Measuring the adequacy of resources in households with young children. *Child: Care Health and Development, 13,* 111–125.

Dunst, C. J., & Trivette, C. M. (1984, August). *Differential influences of social support on mentally retarded children and their families.* Paper presented at the annual meeting of the American Psychological Association, Toronto, Canada.

Dunst, C. J., & Trivette, C. M. (1986). Looking beyond the parent-child dyad for the determinants of caregiver styles of interaction. *Infant Mental Health Journal, 7,* 69–80.

Dunst, C. J., & Trivette, C. M., (in press). Toward experimental evaluation of family-level interactions: Experiences from the Family, Infant and Preschool Program. In H. Weiss & F. Jacobs (Eds.), *Evaluating family programs.* New York: Aldine Press.

Dunst, C. J., Trivette, C. M., & Cross, A. H. (1986a). Mediating influences of social support: Personal, family, and child outcomes. *American Journal of Mental Deficiency, 90,* 403–417.

Dunst, C. J., Trivette, C. M., & Cross, A. H. (1986b). Roles and support networks of mothers of handicapped children. In R. Fewell & P. Vadasy (Eds.), *Families of handicapped children's needs and support across the lifespan* (pp. 167–192). Austin, TX: PRO-ED.

Dunst, C. J., Vance, S. D., & Cooper, C. S. (1986). A social systems perspective of adolescent pregnancy: Determinants of parent and parent–child behavior. *Infant Mental Health Journal, 7,* 34–48.

Dunst, C. J., Cooper, C. S., & Bolick, F. A. (1987). Supporting families of handicapped children. In J. Garbarino & K. Authier (Eds.), *Special children, special risk: The maltreatment of children with disabilities* (pp. 17–46). New York: Aldine.

Dunst, C. J., Trivette, C. M., & Cross, A. H. (in press). Social support networks of Appalachian and nonAppalachian families with handicapped children: Relationship to personal and family well-beings. In S. Keefe (Ed.), *Mental health in Appalachia.* Lexington: University of Kentucky Press.

Embry, L. (1980). Family support for handicapped preschool children at risk for abuse. *New Directions for Exceptional Children, 4,* 29–58.

Erickson, M. R., & Cromack, T. (1972). Evaluating a tutoring program. *Journal of Experimental Education, 41,* 27–31.

Fiore, J., Becker, J., & Coppel, D. (1983). Social network interactions: A buffer or a stress. *American Journal of Community Psychology, 11,* 423–439.

Fisher, J. D. (1983). Recipient reactions to aid: The parameters of the field. In J. D. Fisher, A. Nadler, & B. M. DePaulo (Eds.), *New directions in helping: Vol. 1. Recipient reactions to aid* (pp. 3–14). New York: Academic Press.

Fisher, J. D., Nadler, A., & DePaulo, B. M. (1983). *New directions in helping: Vol. 1. Recipient reactions to aid.* New York: Academic Press.

Fisher, J. D., Nadler, A., & Whitcher-Alagna, S. (1983). Four theoretical approaches for conceptualizing reactions to aid. In J. D. Fisher, A. Nadler, & B. M. DePaulo (Eds.), *New directions in helping: Vol. 1. Recipient reactions to aid* (pp. 51–84). New York: Academic Press.

Garbarino, J. (1982). *Children and families in the social environment.* New York: Aldine.

Goranson, R. E., & Berkowitz, L. (1966). Reciprocity and responsibility reactions to prior help. *Journal of Personality and Social Psychology, 3,* 227–232.

Gouldner, A. W. (1960). The norm of reciprocity: A preliminary statement. *American Sociological Review, 25,* 161–178.

Gourash, N. (1978). Help seeking: A review of the literature. *American Journal of Community Psychology, 6,* 499–517.

Greenberg, M. S. (1980). A theory of indebtedness. In K. Gergen, M. S. Greenberg, & R. H. Willis (Eds.), *Social exchange: Advances in theory and research* (pp. 3–26). New York: Plenum Press.

Greenberg, M. S., & Westcott, D. R. (1983). Indebtedness

as a mediator of reactions to aid. In J. D. Fisher, A. Nadler, & B. M. DePaulo (Eds.), *New directions in helping: Vol. 1. Recipient reactions to aid* (pp. 85–112). New York: Academic Press.

Griest, D. L., Forehand, R., & Wells, K. C. (1981). Follow-up assessment of parent behavioral training: An analysis of who will participate. *Child Study Journal, 11,* 221–229.

Gross, A. E., & McMullen, P. A. (1983). Models of the help-seeking process. In B. M. DePaulo, A. Nadler, & J. Fisher (Eds.), *New directions in helping: Vol. 2. Help-seeking* (pp. 45–70). New York: Academic Press.

Guralnik, D. B. (Ed.). (1974). *Webster's New World dictionary of the American language* (2nd college ed.). Cleveland, OH: William Collins & World.

Gurin, G., Veroff, J., & Feld, S. (1960). *Americans view their mental health.* New York: Basic Books.

Hall, A., & Wellman, B. (1985). Social networks and social support. In S. Cohen & S. L. Syme (Eds.), *Social support and health* (pp. 23–42). New York: Academic Press.

Hatfield, E., & Sprecher, S. (1983). Equity theory and recipient reactions to aid. In J. D. Fisher, A. Nadler, & B. M. DePaulo (Eds.), *New directions in helping: Vol. 1. Recipient reactions to aid* (pp. 113–141). New York: Academic Press.

Heller, K., Price, R. H., & Sher, K. J. (1980). Research and evaluation in primary prevention: Issues and guidelines. In R. H. Price, R. F. Ketterer, B. C. Bader, & J. Monahan (Eds.), *Prevention in community mental health: Research policy and practice* (pp. 285–313). Beverly Hills, CA: Sage.

Hobbs, N. (1975). *The futures of children: Categories, labels, and their consequences.* San Francisco: Jossey-Bass.

Hobbs, N., Dokecki, P. R., Hoover-Dempsey, K. V., Moroney, R. M., Shayne, M. W., & Weeks, K. H. (1984). *Strengthening families.* San Francisco: Jossey-Bass.

Hollingshead, A., & Redlich, F. (1958). *Social class and mental illness.* New York: Wiley.

House, J. S., & Kahn, R. L. (1985). Measures and concepts of social support. In S. Cohen & S. L. Syme (Eds.), *Social support and health* (pp. 83–108). New York: Academic Press.

Kazdin, A. E. (1980). *Research design in clinical psychology.* New York: Harper & Row.

Kazdin, A. E. (1982). Symptom substitution generalization, and response covariation: Implications for psychotherapy outcome. *Psychological Bulletin, 91,* 349–365.

Lamb, H. R., & Zusman, J. (1979). The seductiveness of primary prevention. *American Journal of Psychiatry, 136,* 12–17.

Langer, E. J., & Benevenuto, A. (1978). Self-induced dependence. *Journal of Personality and Social Psychology, 36,* 866–893.

Lazar, I., & Darlington, R. (1982). Lasting effects of early education. *Monographs of the Society for Research in Child Development, 47,* (2–3, Serial No. 195).

Leet, H. E., & Dunst, C. J. (1985). *Family Resource Scale: Reliability and validity.* (Available from Family, Infant and Preschool Program, Western Carolina Center, Morganton, NC 28655.)

Lefcourt, H. M. (Ed.). (1981). *Research with the locus of control construct: Vol. 1. Assessment methods.* New York: Academic Press.

Lewin, K. (1931). Environmental forces in child behavior and development. In C. Murchison (Ed.), *Handbook of child psychology* (pp. 94–127). Worcester. MA: Clark University Press.

Lewin, L. (1936). *Principles of topological psychology.* New York: McGraw-Hill.

Mahoney, G., Powell, A., Finnegan, C., Fors, S., & Wood, S. (1986). *The transactional intervention program: Theory, procedures. and evaluation.* Unpublished paper, Department of Special Education, University of Michigan, Ann Arbor, MI.

McCubbin, H. I., Joy, C. B., Cauble, A. E.. Comeau, J. K., Patterson, J. M., Needle, R. H. (1980). Family stress and coping: A decade of review. *Journal of Marriage and the Family, 42,* 855–871.

McMahon, R. J., Forehand, R., Griest, D. L., & Wells, K. C. (1981). Who drops out of therapy during parent behavioral training? *Behavioral Counseling Quarterly, 1,* 79–85.

McMullen, P. A., & Gross, A. E. (1983). Sex differences, sex roles, and health-related help-seeking. In B. DePaulo, A. Nadler, & J. Fisher (Eds.), *New directions in helping: Vol. 2. Helping-seeking* (pp. 233–263). New York: Academic Press.

Merton, V., Merton, R. K., & Barber, E. (1983). Client ambivalence in professional relationships: The problem of seeking help from strangers. In B. DePaulo, A. Nadler, & J. Fisher (Eds.), *New directions in helping: Vol. 2. Help-seeking* (pp. 13–44). New York: Academic Press.

Mitchell, R. E., & Trickett, E. J. (1980). Task force report: Social networks as mediators of social support. *Community Mental Health Journal, 16,* 27–43.

Morrison, J. K., Bushnell, J. D., Hanson, G. D., Fentiman, J. R., & Holdridge-Crane, S. (1977). Relationships between psychiatric patients' attitudes toward mental illness and attitudes of dependence. *Psychological Reports, 41,* 1194.

Morse, S. J. (1983). The nature of the help-related interchange as a determinant of a person's attitude toward other. In J. D. Fisher, A. Nadler, & B. M. DePaulo (Eds.), *New directions in helping: Vol. 1. Recipient reactions to aid* (pp. 305–332). New York: Academic Press.

Nadler, A. (1983). Personal characteristics and help-seeking. In B. DePaulo, A. Nadler, & J. Fisher (Eds.), *New directions in helping: Vol. 2. Help-seeking* (pp. 303–340). New York: Academic Press.

Nadler, A., & Mayseless, O. (1983). Recipient self-esteem and reactions to help. In J. D. Fisher, A. Nadler. & B. M. DePaulo (Eds.), *New directions in helping: Vol. 1. Recipient reactions to aid* (pp. 167–188). New York: Academic Press.

Nadler, A., Fisher, J. D., & DePaulo, B. M. (1983). *New directions in helping: Vol. 3. Applied perspectives on help-seeking and -receiving*. New York: Academic Press.

Nadler, A., Shapiro, R., & Ben-Itzhak, S. (1983). Good looks may help: Effects of helpers' physical attractiveness and sex of helper on males' and females' help-seeking behavior. *Journal of Personality and Social Psychology, 42*, 90–99.

Nelson, B. J. (1980). Help-seeking from public authorities: Who arrives at the agency door? *Policy Sciences, 12*, 175–192.

Pearlin, L. I., & Schoder, C. (1978). The structure of coping. *Journal of Health and Social Behavior, 19*, 2–21.

Pettigrew, T. F. (1983). Seeking public assistance: A stigma analysis. In A. Nadler, J. D. Fisher, & B. M. DePaulo (Eds.), *New directions in helping: Vol. 3. Applied perspectives on help-seeking and -receiving* (pp. 273–292). New York: Academic Press.

Philliber, S., & Graham, E. (1981). The impact of age of mother and mother–child interaction patterns. *Journal of Marriage and Family, 43*, 109–115.

Piliavin, J. A., & Piliavin, I. (1973). *The Good Samaritan: Why does he help?* Unpublished manuscript, University of Wisconsin.

Rappaport, J. (1981). In praise of paradox: A social policy of empowerment over prevention. *American Journal of Community Psychology, 9*, 1–25.

Rappaport, J., Davidson, W. S., Wilson, M. N., Mitchell, A. (1975). Alternatives to blaming the victim or the environment: Our places to stand have not moved the earth. *American Psychologist, 30*, 525–528.

Reese, H., & Overton, W. (1970). Models of development and theories of development. In L. Goulet & P. Baltes (Eds.), *Life span developmental psychology: Research and commentary* (pp. 116–145). New York: Academic Press.

Rosen, S. (1983). Perceived inadequacy and help-seeking. In B. DePaulo, A. Nadler, & J. Fisher (Eds.), *New directions in helping: Vol. 2. Help-seeking* (pp. 73–107). New York: Academic Press.

Shapiro, E. G. (1983). Embarrassment and help-seeking. In B. DePaulo, A. Nadler, & J. Fisher (Eds.), *New directions in helping: Vol. 2. Help-seeking* (pp. 143–163). New York: Academic Press.

Skinner, B. F. (1978). The ethics of helping people. In L. Wispe (Ed.), *Sympathy, altruism, and helping behavior*. New York: Academic Press.

Slater, M. A., & Wikler, L. (1986). "Normalized" family resources for families with a developmentally disabled child. *Social Work, 31*, 385–390.

Snyder, C. R., Higgins, R. L., & Stucky, R. J. (1983). *Excuses: Masquerades in search of grace*. New York: Wiley.

Solomon, B. B. (1985). How do we really empower families? New strategies for social work practitioners. *Family Resource Coalition Report*, No. 3., 2–3.

Steiner, I. (1970). Perceived freedom. In L. Berkowitz (Ed.), *Advances in experimental social psychology* (Vol. 5). New York: Academic Press.

Stoneman, Z. (1985). Family involvement in early childhood special education programs. In N. H. Fallen & W. Umansky (Eds.), *Young children with special needs* (2nd ed., pp. 442–469). Columbus, OH: Charles E. Merrill.

Trivette, C. M., & Dunst, C. J. (1986). *Inventory of social support: Reliability and validity*. (Available from Family, Infant and Preschool Program, Western Carolina Center, Morganton, NC 28655.)

Trivette, C. M., & Dunst, C. J. (1987). Proactive influences of social support in families of handicapped children. In H. G. Lingren, L. Kimmons, P. Lee, G. Rowe, L. Rottmann, L. Schwab, & R. Williams (Eds.), *Family strengths: Vol. 8–9. Pathways to well-being* (pp. 391–405). Lincoln: University of Nebraska Press.

Trivette, C. M., & Dunst, C. J. (in press). Characteristics and influences of role division and social support among mothers of handicapped preschoolers. *Parenting Studies*.

Uzgiris, I. (1986, May). *Interaction as context for early intervention*. Paper presented at the Third Annual Eric Denhoff Memorial Symposium on Child Development, Brown University, Providence, RI.

Wahler, R. G. (1980). Parent insularity as a determinant of generalization success in family treatment. In S. Salzinger, J. Antrobus, & J. Glick (Eds.), *The ecosystem of the "sick" child: Implications for classification and intervention for disturbed and mentally retarded children* (pp. 187–199). New York: Academic Press.

Wahler, R. G., & Afton, A. D. (1980). Attentional processes in insular and noninsular mothers: Some differences in their summary reports about child problem behavior. *Child Behavior Therapy, 2*, 25–41.

Wahler, R. G., & Graves, M. G. (1983). Setting events in social networks: Ally or enemy in child behavior therapy? *Behavior Therapy, 14*, 19–36.

Webster-Stratton, C. (1985). Case studies and clinical replication series: Predictors of treatment outcome in parent training for conduct disordered children. *Behavior Therapy, 6*, 223–243.

Weinraub, M., & Wolf, B. (1983). Effects of stress and support on mother–child interactions in single- and two-parent families. *Child Development, 54*, 1297–1311.

Wenar, C. (1972). Executive competence and spontaneous social behavior in one-year-olds. *Child Development, 43*, 256–260.

White, B., & Watts, J. C. (1973). *Experience and environment* (Vol. 1.). Englewood Cliffs, NJ: Prentice-Hall.

Wilcox, B. L., & Birkel, R. C. (1983). Social networks and the help-seeking process: A structural perspective. In A. Nadler, J. D. Fisher, & B. M. DePaulo (Eds.), *New directions in helping: Vol. 3. Applied perspectives on helping-seeking and -receiving* (pp. 235–253). New York: Academic Press.

Williams, K. B., & Williams, K. D. (1983). A social-impact perspective on the social inhibition of help-seeking. In B. DePaulo, A. Nadler, & J. Fisher (Eds.), *New directions in helping: Vol. 2. Help-seeking* (pp. 187–204). New York: Academic Press.

Wills, T. A. (1983). Social comparison in coping and help-seeking. In B. DePaulo, A. Nadler, & J. Fisher (Eds.), *New directions in helping: Vol. 2. Help-seeking* (pp. 109–141). New York: Academic Press.

Winett, R. C., & Winkler, R. C. (1972). Current behavior modification in the classroom: Be still, be quiet, be docile. *Journal of Applied Behavioral Analysis, 5,* 499–504.

Worchel, S., & Andreoli, V. (1974). Attribution of causality as a means of restoring behavioral freedom. *Journal of Personality and Social Psychology, 29,* 237–245.

Wortman, C. B., & Conway, T. L. (1985). The role of social support in adaptation and recovery from physical illness. In S. Cohen & S. L. Syme (Eds.), *Social support and health* (pp. 281–302). New York: Academic Press.

Wortman, C., & Lehman, D. (1985). Reactions to victims of life crises: Support that doesn't help. In I. G. Sarason & B. R. Sarason (Eds.), *Social support: Theory, research, and application.* The Hague: Martinus Nijhof.

Zigler, E., & Berman, W. (1983). Discerning the future of early childhood intervention. *American Psychologist, 38,* 894–906.

Zola, I. K. (1966). Culture and symptoms: An analysis of patients presenting complaints. *American Sociological Review, 31,* 615–630.

CHAPTER 14

Legal Issues in School-Based Behavior Therapy

Joseph Corrao and Gary B. Melton

Introduction

The use of behavioral treatments in schools may at first glance seem to present no particular legal questions. However, the variety of potentially conflicting interests involved in decisions to employ such techniques renders this area legally complex. In this chapter, we will examine some of the basic legal interests involved when behavior modification techniques are used in the classroom, or as an adjunct to classroom instruction. First, we will introduce three basic dichotomies of interests as conceptual tools useful in understanding the complexity of these areas of law. We will then explore, in order, issues surrounding consent to treatment, confidentiality, the rights to treatment and education, legal limits on behavioral treatments, and avenues through which the child or the child's advocate may seek redress of violations of the child's rights.

One prefatory note: this chapter is intended to sensitize professional educators to the legal issues surrounding the use of behavioral treatments. It is not intended to answer legal questions that may arise in specific situations. Only consultation with a legal professional familiar with recent developments in the law of schools, minors, and civil liberties can adequately address such questions. It is hoped that this chapter will provide psychologists and educators with an introduction to the legal issues relevant to behavior therapy and a sense of when to consult a legal professional with questions concerning the use of behavioral treatments.

Three Basic Dichotomies

The Constitution guarantees certain rights to all "persons," including minors (*In re Gault*, 1967; *Tinker v. Des Moines Independent School District*, 1969). Among the rights and liberties relevant to this discussion are the freedom of speech, freedoms from unreasonable search and involuntary servitude, and the guarantees of due process, equal protection, and privacy. Despite constitutional protections, state governments may infringe on these rights in certain circumstances. In general, the state

Joseph Corrao and Gary B. Melton • Department of Psychology, University of Nebraska-Lincoln, Lincoln, Nebraska 68588.

has power to infringe on rights in order to achieve a compelling or extremely important goal, if this goal can be achieved by no less drastic means. Historically, the state's interest in the safe and healthy upbringing of its citizens has been recognized as compelling. Consequently, in order to promote the health or welfare of a minor individual, the state may act on the minor in ways that would be prohibited if the individual were an adult. The state power to act to protect dependent persons, including minors, is called the *parens patriae* power, the power of the state to act as if it were a parent.

This, then, is our first dichotomy of interests: the interest of individual children and youth in the fullest reasonable expression of their civil rights, balanced against the state's interest in the healthy socialization of its citizens. School itself provides an example of these forces counterpoised. The 15-year-old who wishes to quit school to work in a department store is compelled by the state to remain in school, constitutional guarantees of freedom of association and movement notwithstanding (cf. *Wisconsin v. Yoder,* 1972). Of course, the state's power over most adults does not extend this far.

Recognizing that individuals have rights and freedoms that may at times run counter to state goals, the law establishes mechanisms whereby affected individuals may have some input into the formulation or implementation of state action affecting them. In the school setting, who shall have this input on behalf of the student is the question at the heart of our second dichotomy of interests.

Generally the student's parents are allowed input into goals and plans affecting the child's education, though the input to which they are entitled may be minimal. The family is entitled to choose, within limits, where the child will attend school (*Pierce v. Society of Sisters,* 1925). Parents are not entitled to specify details of the education that occurs in the public schools; school officials, as representatives of the state's interest in the proper education of minors, are entrusted with this responsibility. However, school officials must determine the details of educational curricula in a reasonable manner, and reasonable parental requests may be granted by the courts over the officials' objections (*Abrahamson v. Hershman,* 1983; *State ex rel. Kelley v. Ferguson,* 1914). Also, some aspects of education are sufficiently special that statutes expressly provide for greater parental involvement. The law also notes that the interests of parents do not always coincide with the best interests of the minor student. When parental interests seem likely to diverge from minors' interests in potentially detrimental ways, a legally designated third party, such as a family court judge, may be empowered to make decisions on behalf of minors. In special circumstances, minors may be allowed to decide certain things for themselves. These are questions of control, and they often raise related questions of privacy: whose privacy is to be protected, that of the individual student, or that of the student's family, or perhaps that of the school district official? Our second dichotomy, then, is one that embraces the issues of control and privacy. On one hand, the individual has power to control his or her own destiny, whereas on the other hand, parents (or some third entity, such as school district or family court judge) are empowered to control details of the individual child's education. Similarly, individual students may exercise control over information relevant to their education (such as assessment reports), or their parents (or some third party) may control access to this information.

Finally, we must bear in mind the distinction between ordinary schools and treatment centers for youthful offenders or disturbed youth. As Gardner (1982) pointed out, the state may have greater power to act in the face of countervailing individual interests when its action is for purposes of treatment or remediation than when its action is for purposes of punishment or crime prevention. Gardner's thesis suggests, for example, that a teacher in a public school setting may be able to satisfy constitutional due process requirements somewhat differently than may a teacher in a residential treatment setting for juvenile delinquents, as both face the decisions of whether and how to employ behavior modification techniques in their classrooms.

We have outlined three basic dichotomies: the liberty interests of the individual versus the *parens patriae* interests of the state; minors' personal interests in privacy and autonomy versus interests (which minors may share) in family privacy and parental autonomy; and the distinction between ordinary schools and treatment centers as the different purposes of each may shade legal analysis of the various interests involved.

We turn next to explorations of the most important issues raised when the school behavior therapist turns to the use of behavior modification techniques in the classroom, or as an adjunct to classroom work. We will examine how the law balances interests involving the three dichotomies identified earlier with respect to consent to treatment, confidentiality, and the rights to treatment and education. Later, we will examine aspects of behavior modification technology that the law regulates most closely. Finally, we will explore avenues of redress available to those whose rights have been violated by improper or impermissible use of behavioral treatments.

Consent to Treatment

General Principles

The dichotomies we have introduced are of particular importance in the question of consent to treatment. Should the state be able to compel minors' participation in treatment in order to enhance their education and socialization into productive citizens? Should minors be able to consent independently of their parents? How special must school-based treatment be before it requires consent?

In general, it is well established that treatment may not take place without the individual's informed consent (see, for reviews, Katz, 1984; Lidz *et al.*, 1984). This requirement is intended to protect clients' autonomy and privacy—prevention of unwanted intrusion into body or mind—and to humanize the professional–client relationship. To be valid, consent must be informed. That is, the consent must be based on disclosure of relevant information to the prospective competent client, who then makes a voluntary decision. To use legal jargon, the consent must be knowing, intelligent, and voluntary.

The rule in the majority of jurisdictions is that, for disclosure to be adequate, the professional must provide information a reasonable person would want to know about the nature, risks, and benefits of the proposed treatment and the alternatives (*Canterbury v. Spence*, 1972). However, some courts have held the objective, reasonable-person standard to be insufficiently respectful of clients' autonomy. They have adopted a subjective standard according to which the clinician must provide the information the particular client would want to know, given his or her own values (*Scott v. Bradford*, 1979).

The standard for competence is even less clear than the standard for disclosure. There are four types of tests (Roth, Meisel, & Lidz, 1977), and neither statutes nor courts often specify the prevailing test. The type of test most respectful of personal autonomy is simply whether the client expresses a preference. Only if the client is so low functioning or ambivalent as to be unable to indicate a preference would proxy consent be necessary. Given a somewhat higher standard, the client might be required to indicate not simply a preference, but understanding of the information disclosed. Under this test, a question arises of how much clients must understand and whether they must also appreciate the significance of the information in their own cases (Roth, Appelbaum, Sallee, Reynolds, & Huber, 1982). The third type of test requires not simply understanding, but a reasonable process of decision making—weighing risks and benefits. Finally, the test least respectful of autonomy is whether there is a reasonable outcome—the decision a reasonable person would have made, regardless of the actual quality of the decision-making process.

Minors are generally presumed to be incompetent to make treatment decisions, and their parents are empowered to make decisions on their behalf. The purposes of consent thus become confused (Melton, 1983a; Mnookin, 1978). Clearly, parental consent serves neither to protect the autonomy and privacy of the minor nor to equalize the status of professional and child-client. Informed consent by parents does, however, preserve parental autonomy, perhaps protect the minor from unnecessary or unwise treatment, and prevent the parents' assumption of financial liability for treatment to which they have not agreed.

The issue of fairness in assumption of financial liability is raised because minors are generally *per se* incompetent to make contracts. There are two common exceptions to this rule. First, under the common law, minors may contract for "necessaries" (e.g., food and lodging). The purpose of this exception is primarily to protect business owners (e.g., minors must pay for the Big Macs they purchase). Second, emancipated minors may make contracts independently. The standard for emancipation varies across jurisdictions, but it often includes some combination of military service, marriage, parenthood, and independent domicile. Although there are obvious practical justifications for emancipation statutes, the results of such statutes that seem to equate financial independence and competence can be disquieting. Why should a 14-year-old runaway who has a child be permitted to make decisions independently when the 17-year-old straight-arrow member of the Beta Club cannot?

Exceptions

No Consent Required

Common-Law Exceptions. Although the usual rule is that a parent must provide informed consent before treatment of a minor can take place, consent is unnecessary in some circumstances. In common law, there are two exceptions to the general rule that informed consent is necessary. First, under the *emergency exception,* treatment can take place without consent if death or serious bodily injury would otherwise result. Second, *therapeutic privilege* permits professionals to withhold information about patients' condition or the risks of treatment if, in reasonable clinical judgment, disclosure is deemed harmful. Because of the obvious disrespect for patients' autonomy it implies, therapeutic privilege is eroding in favor of full disclosure.

State-Compelled Treatment. In some other circumstances, the client has no choice about whether to participate in treatment. In such a circumstance, it is actually disrespectful of autonomy to solicit consent, which is merely a ruse. Clients' consent should be sought only if refusal will be honored. Parental control over minors is obviously not absolute. For example, it is well settled that minors may be compelled to attend school, even though compulsory attendance laws clearly intrude on the minor's freedom of association and choice of exposure to ideas and the parents' freedom to rear their children as they see fit. It may be a small step from compulsory education to compulsory treatment designed to assist students to benefit from education. The problem is especially acute for behavior therapy because of the similarity between application of principles of learning for the purpose of treatment and such application as part of ordinary teaching. If a teacher systematically applies behavioral techniques to increase student's on-task behavior, is parental consent required? Would it matter if the teacher did so on the advice of a consulting psychologist? What if the psychologist administered rewards directly?

Perhaps the best rule of thumb is that parental consent should be obtained if a special intervention—one that diverges from ordinary, expectable schooling—is planned, especially if the intervention involves matters that are generally acknowledged to involve personal or family privacy. For example, a federal district court (*Merriken v. Cressman*, 1973) held that school authorities had violated the parent's constitutional right to privacy by requiring students to take a personality test to screen for potential drug users and those who were identified to participate in a purportedly preventive intervention, such as confrontational group therapy. The court did not reach the question of whether the student's own right to privacy had been violated (see, for commentary, Bersoff, 1983; Melton, 1983c).

A federal statute (Hatch Amendment, 1978) requires parental consent before a student can be required

> to submit to psychiatric examination, testing, or treatment, or psychological examination, testing, or treatment, in which the primary purpose is to reveal information concerning:
> 1. Political affiliations;
> 2. Mental and psychological problems potentially embarrassing to the student or his family;
> 3. Sex behavior and attitudes;
> 4. Illegal, anti-social, self-incriminating and demeaning behavior;
> 5. Critical appraisals of other individuals with whom respondents have close family relationships;
> 6. Legally recognized privileged and analogous relationships, such as those of lawyers, physicians, and ministers; or
> 7. Income

The regulations implementing the Hatch Amendment (Department of Education, 1985b) define a "psychiatric or psychological examination or test" to include any "method of obtaining information, including a group activity, that is not directly related to academic instruction and that is designed to elicit information about attitudes, habits, traits, opinions, beliefs or feelings" [§ 98.4(c)(1)] and "psychiatric or psychological treatment" to mean "an activity involving the planned, systematic use of methods or techniques that are not directly related to academic instruction and that is designed to affect behavioral, emotional, or attitudinal characteristics of an individual or group" [§ 98.4(c)(2)]. The meaning of "direct[] relat[ionship] to academic instruction" is unclear. However, when a social studies teacher asks students about politics, the teacher may be administering a "psychological test" under the Hatch Amendment.

Psychological services in the schools will often be administered pursuant to the Education for All Handicapped Children Act of 1975. The Act itself requires schools to provide written notice to parents about evaluation, development of an Individualized Educational Program (IEP), and placement. However, the implementing regulations appear to require fully informed consent (Department of Education, 1985a, §§ 300.500, 300.504, and 300.505), although they do permit evaluation, planning, and placement without parental consent if state law does not absolutely require parental consent and a hearing officer approves. The standard that the hearing officer is to use in deciding whether to permit school officials to intervene without parental consent is not specified.

The Act permits children themselves to participate in the IEP meeting "whenever appropriate" [EAHCA, 1975, § 602(19)]. The Department of Education (1981) has interpreted this provision to mean that parents have discretion whether to permit the child to attend and that the child's attendance should be contingent on whether it "will be helpful in developing the IEP and/or directly beneficial to the child" (para. 21). The Department also suggests that "older handicapped children," particularly those at the secondary level, be encouraged to participate. In short, though, the EAHCA gives children themselves no right of consent, assent, or even notice of assessment, planning, or placement.

Implied Consent. Taken together, the Hatch Amendment (1978) and the EAHCA (1975) show clear Congressional intent to require parental consent to school-based psychological services. However, consent to each individual intervention may not be required. For example, if informed consent has been given to a course of treatment, consent for individual sessions may be implied. Separate affirmative consent would not be required. Similarly, if parents have agreed to placement in a class for behaviorally impaired children, they may reasonably expect the class to include interventions to increase their child's self-control, especially if such a goal is expressly included in the IEP. However, the wise practice is to err on the side of obtaining consent more frequently than may be required. For example, the evaluation of risks and benefits of treatment will almost inevitably change over the course of treatment, because some of the consequences of treatment will be known. "Blanket consent" is inherently invalid because it cannot be informed. The parents would not know to what consent was being given.

Minors' Consent Sufficient

Mature Minor Rule. Under some circumstances, the usual rule of *per se* incompetence may not apply. In common law, a mature minor rule has been applied to "technical batteries" in which a competent older minor has given consent without parental involvement (Wadlington, 1973). A battery occurs when there is touching without legally recognized consent. The mature minor rule was developed to prevent obviously unjust results when, prior to the lowering of the age of majority to 18, college-age minors consented to minor medical procedures. The mature minor rule is based on inferences from a small number of cases, and psychologists are probably ill-advised to rely on it.

However, in one context—minors' abortion decisions—the mature minor rule has been elevated to a standard of constitutional law. In a series of cases (see, for review, Melton & Pliner, 1986), the Supreme Court has held that mature minors must be permitted to make abortion decisions independently, and the Court has indicated in dicta that they (unlike immature minors) must be permitted to do so without parental knowledge. The Court has given little indication of the standard to be used in assessing maturity.

Statutory Exceptions. All states have adopted statutes abrogating *per se* incompetence in at least some contexts. Typically, these statutory exceptions involve one or more of the following assumptions about deleterious effects of failure to permit minors to provide independent consent: (a) failure to obtain evaluation or treatment necessary for the public health or safety; (b) failure to obtain treatment necessary for the minor's healthy socialization; (c) intrusion on the mature minor's privacy. Thus, states may permit minors to consent to evaluation and treatment for venereal disease, pregnancy, mental disorder, and substance abuse. The particular exceptions adopted and their implementation is often a patchwork without coherent purpose (Melton, 1983a; Wadlington, 1983). For example, Nebraska permits minors to consent, without parental knowledge, to evaluation and treatment of venereal disease, but then, in the same statute, makes parents financially liable for the treatment. It is unclear how billing is to take place in a way that confidentiality will be preserved. Nebraska also allows competent minors to consent independently to treatment for substance abuse, provided that an attempt has been made to involve parents, but not to other mental health treatment.

When statutory exceptions are made, they typically leave many unanswered questions, particularly in regard to their implications for school authorities. For example, Virginia permits minors to consent to outpatient treatment of mental disorders. However, the state and federal education laws give parents authority to consent. In a state like Virginia, should a school psychologist refuse to treat students without parental consent? The statute also leaves unclear whether a minor may refuse to consent to treatment. In Virginia, if a competent minor is brought to the therapist by his or her parents, is refusal of treatment legally binding? The answer probably depends on the theory on which the statutory right to consent is based. If it is based on respect for minors' privacy, then a right to consent independently should imply a right to refuse (see, e.g., *Melville v. Sabatino*, 1973). On the other hand, if based on state interests in protecting minors or the community, a right to consent would not imply a right to refuse. Suppose that the former interpretation is correct. Could a child refuse to participate in desensitization to alleviate test anxiety, if the treatment were a part of an IEP that a parent had signed? In such ambiguity or conflicts of laws, school-based psychologists might seek an attorney general's opinion and legislative action to clarify the law.

In one circumstance, a minor's participation in decision making is required, but his or her consent is legally unrecognized. Parents may give permission for minors' participation in research, but their consent is insufficient, too (Department of Health and Human Services, 1985). Children must assent to participate in research not for their own benefit. The limitation on parental authority in such a context is based on the fact that participation is not for the participants' own benefit. Therefore, the usual presumption of parents acting in their children's interest is not tenable. Children, in effect, have a veto power. To protect minors, however, parent's permission is also required.

Psychological and Ethical Issues

In recent years, numerous commentators have attacked the rule of minors' *per se* incompetence to consent to treatment (see, e.g., King, 1984–85; Melton, 1983d; Weithorn, 1982). This argument has been based on a substantial body of evidence that most older minors do not differ from adults in their competence to make decisions about treatment (see generally Grisso & Vierling, 1978; Koocher, 1983; Melton, 1981a; Melton, Koocher, & Saks, 1983). A frequently cited study by Weithorn and Campbell (1982) is illustrative. In their responses to hypothetical vignettes about various health dilemmas, 14-year-olds' responses were undifferentiable from adults' according to all four tests of competence to consent. Although they demonstrated incomplete understanding of alternatives and weighing of risks and benefits, 9-year-olds did not differ from the older groups in their ability to express a preference or in the decision itself. These laboratory findings are consistent with the results when elementary-school children are in fact given the power to consent to routine health care (Lewis, 1983).

Similar findings have been generated in a program of research in the therapeutic school at UCLA (Adelman, Kaser-Boyd, & Taylor, 1984; Adelman, Lusk, Alvarez, & Acosta, 1985; Kaser-Boyd, Adelman, & Taylor, 1985; Taylor, Adelman, & Kaser-Boyd, 1985). Students generally desired to participate in psychoeducational planning, and they were typically judged as effective participants by teachers, parents, and themselves. Their express consent to interventions resulted in fewer responses of frustration when faced with difficult problems, and their resistance to treatment, when it occurred, was based on actual risks or negative aspects of psychotherapy (cf. Roth & Roth, 1984).

The finding that elementary-school children typically make presumptively reasonable, adult-like decisions is important in that it suggests little risk of bad decisions and consequent harm. Taken together with research and theory indicating benefits of participation in decision making, such evidence supports permitting marginally incompetent minors, as well as those who are de facto competent, to consent independently to some treatments. Participation in decision making heightens treatment compliance and achievement, increases sense of personal control and individuation, inoculates against treatment-related stress, and fosters legal socialization (Melton, 1983b).

This body of research and theory not only rebuts the assumption underlying the legal presumption of incompetence, it also calls into question prevailing professional ethical standards. Psychologists have a primary ethical obligation to "respect the dignity and worth of the individual and strive for the preservation and protection of fundamental human rights" (APA, 1981, Preamble). Consistent with this overriding principle and the evidence showing minimal risk of harm from permitting at least older minors to participate in treatment decisions, Division 37 of the American Psychological Association (Division of Child, Youth, and Family Services, 1982b) has proposed revisions of the Ethical Principles of Psychologists (APA, 1981) to require consideration of minors' wishes even when minors are "prevented by law or psychological capacity from providing valid informed consent" (DCYFS, 1982b, Proposed Principle 6b). If the minor objects to treatment requested by his or her parents, factors to be considered in

> determining whether to provide services [include]: (a) the age and psychological maturity of the child. The older, and consequently, the more mature the child to make autonomous decisions, the more that child's preferences should be given weight. Most normal adolescents have the requisite psychological skills to make competent treatment decisions; (b) the degree to which coercive provision of a treatment proposed by parents or failure to provide services requested by a child might result in an abridgement of the child's basic human or constitutional rights (e.g., rights of liberty, privacy of body or mind); (c) the degree to which it appears that the parents' judgment regarding what is in the child's best interests may be mitigated by other factors. (DCYFS, 1982a)

The Division 37 recommendations were drafted by Lois Weithorn, and they have been endorsed by most of the relevant boards, committees, and divisions of APA. Weithorn (1983) has also discussed ways in which models of shared decision making may be applied (see also Melton, 1981a).

Psychologists who attempt to increase recognition of children's privacy and autonomy must keep in mind that children are unlikely to believe that they really are entitled to make an independent decision. Such disbelief is apt to be particularly pronounced among lower-class and minority-group children who have few experiences with entitlement (Lewis, 1983; Melton, 1980). Psychologists should, therefore, model decision making (Belter & Grisso, 1984), provide instruction in decision making (Lewis, 1983), and consciously provide repeated experiences with self-determination (Tapp & Melton, 1983). Issues about increasing sense of control over the decision apply, of course, even when the child has legal as well as ethical rights to self determination (Melton, 1981b). Psychologists should make affirmative efforts to involve children in the decision, and they should be careful to avoid ploys, perhaps inadvertent, that may serve to reduce the voluntariness of the decision. For example, in obtaining consent, psychologists should neither use a stepwise procedure (i.e., the foot-in-the-door technique) nor manipulate the timing of the decision or the disclosure of information so as to maximize compliance (Saks, 1983).

Confidentiality

Privacy extends, of course, beyond protection against intrusion into personal matters. Privacy also demands maintenance of control over personal information, even if it has been voluntarily disclosed to a second party. Although this principle is formally recognized by the mental health professions (see, e.g., APA, 1981, Principle 5), its implementation in treatment of children raises special ethical and legal problems.

The behavior therapist is likely to participate in several sorts of communication in the course of treatment, including conversations with teachers and other involved professionals, with the student, and with the student's family. Each of these communications presents a teacher or behavioral professional with at least three potential dilemmas. At any time, agencies of the state may demand disclosure of the content of these communications; may or must these demands be honored? At any time, professional or lay individuals may request information, or the teacher or behavioral professional may wish to share information with other service providers; is this proper? Finally, if the communication in question was one between child and professional, may this information be shared with the child's parents; must parental requests to know what the child said be granted?

In the following discussion of confidentiality and the use of behavior therapy in schools, we will distinguish between legal demands for information, other professionals' requests for information, and parental requests for information. The professional's duty of confidentiality, if one exists, varies depending on who is to share access to information. Further, the extent to which a statement or record is legally protectable as a confidence varies depending on the relationships among the parties to the communication.

We begin by focusing on legal demands for information, usually by subpoena. All 50 states have enacted statutes or rules, called *privilege* laws, that protect communications between lawyer and client from compelled disclosure in judicial or administrative contexts. Most states have extended similar protection to communications between doctor and patient, somewhat fewer to communications between clients and psychologists, psychotherapists and/or psychiatrists. A few states (Michigan, Montana) have extended full privilege protection to communications between teacher and student; in several other states, teacher–student communications enjoy limited protection. In Connecticut and Nevada, for example, only information regarding drug or alcohol abuse is privileged by statute. In California, Idaho, Indiana, Kentucky, North Carolina, North Dakota, Ohio, Pennsylvania, South Dakota, and Virginia, communications with school counselors (defined slightly differently in each state) are protected.

In the 30 or so states that appear to have no teacher–student or school counselor–student privilege statutes, communications between school psychologist and student are probably within the protection of the psychologist/client privilege. Some states that extend the privilege to psychologists or psychotherapists define the terms *psychologist* and *psychotherapist* fairly broadly to include many professionals involved in the direct provision of psychotherapeutic services. Under these statutes, behavior therapists may fall within the scope of the law, even if their degrees are in related disciplines such as social work or child guidance. Other states define *psychologist* or *psychotherapist* rather narrowly to mean only persons with particular graduate degrees or state licenses or certification.

Privilege laws have the effect of granting the client or patient, not the professional, some control over access to the content of the communication. In situations in which these laws apply, the professional cannot be compelled to testify or hand over certain documents over the objection of the client. If the client consents to the testimony, the professional has no independent power to withhold testimony or documents regarding communication with the client. These laws apply generally to civil suits, criminal prosecutions, and most hearings before administrative bodies.

Only information necessary to the provision of treatment services is within the scope of the privilege statutes. Information not related to the creation or implementation of a treatment plan, but communicated to the professional incident to the creation of such a plan, is not privileged, and must be disclosed on demand. For example, assume the treatment professional must know if a child uses marijuana in order to develop a proper treatment plan. If the child tells the treatment professional (and if the treatment professional is within the scope of the privilege law, and certain other requirements are met), this information may not be disclosed to a legal authority over the objection of the child (or, more often, of the child's parents or guardian). However, if knowledge of the child's marijuana use is not required by the professional to create a proper treatment plan, but the child nevertheless mentions it to the treatment professional, the information may be subject to disclosure in a legal proceeding. This apparent technicality serves the basic purpose of privilege law: to facilitate complete and candid necessary communication between helping professionals and persons in need of their help, without putting too high a barrier between the court and the truth.

Other service providers may come within the scope of the privilege statute, if the primary treatment professional is within that scope, and reasonably believes disclosure to these persons is necessary to accomplish the planned treatment. These other service providers are legally viewed as agents of the primary treatment professional. The client or patient may prevent any of these treatment agents from testifying, just as if each were the primary treatment professional. To illustrate this point, let us return to the marijuana-smoking child, and assume a treating psychologist who is within the protection of the privilege statute. The treating psychologist may disclose to teachers, or may ask the child to disclose to teachers, information necessary to the accomplishment of the child's treatment plan. If disclosure to the teacher of the child's marijuana use is required for successful treatment of the child, and if the teacher is subsequently called to testify against the child about this marijuana use before a body covered by the privilege statute, the child may prevent the teacher from testifying. Of course, to protect confidentiality as much as possible, the treating psychologist must caution all others to whom disclosure must be made against any further disclosure.

Thus far our discussion has focused on oral communications between treatment professional and client or patient. When such communications, and any other relevant data, are recorded either on paper or on other media such as computer disks, other issues arise. Our purpose here is not to survey the law of evidence. Suffice it to say that assessment and treatment records may be treated differently than oral communications by the law of privilege. Depending on variations among the states, clients or patients may find it more difficult to prevent disclosure of the contents of records made in the routine course of a treatment professional's day than to prevent disclosure of the same information if it is not contained in a routine report or log.

As mentioned earlier, privilege law applies only when certain authorities with subpoena power, such as courts and certain administrative hearing bodies, demand disclosure of confidences. The law of privileged communications does not address situations in which another service provider requests information regarding a child's assessment or treatment, or in which the treating professional wishes to share information with other professionals. In these latter situations, the treatment professional may share information with certain others, notwithstanding the patient's or client's wish to maintain confidentiality. The Family Educational Rights and Privacy Act of 1974 (commonly known as FERPA, or simply the Buckley Amendment), a federal law that grants parents broad control over the educational records of their minor children, specifically exempts from parental-consent requirements disclosure of records to other educators who have a legitimate educational interest in the child. Shortly, we will examine the provisions of the Buckley Amendment more closely.

Common law may offer greater protection to the confidentiality of treatment information than the statutory provisions discussed thus far. Common law is the judicially created, historically followed case law of civil relations. Common law varies from state to state. Under the common law of all states, certain professionals who disclose their client's or patient's confidences may face civil liability to their clients for harm done by the disclosure. Teachers and behavioral professionals are among those who may face civil liability for violating professional confidences by disclosing assessment data or results, diagnoses, treatment plans, treatment reports, or other personal information acquired in the course of treatment. Codes of ethics or other standards of the relevant profession may be used as legal yardsticks in determining whether the professional's conduct gives rise to liability under the common law. Both the prevailing Ethical Principles of Psychologists (APA, 1981) and recently proposed revisions (Division of Child, Youth, and Family Services, 1982b) state that "information obtained in clinical or consulting relationships [with], or evaluative data concerning children, students, employees or others, is discussed only for professional purposes and only with persons clearly concerned with the case" (Principle 5a). Such ethical principles may have the force of civil law in states that allow evidence of professional standards to be used in establishing the legal duty owed by a professional to a client.

In many states, statutes have been enacted that mandate reporting certain kinds of information, regardless of any other statutory or common laws that might grant privileges or otherwise work to prevent disclosure. The scope of these mandatory disclosure laws is limited to information bearing on specific events. For example, laws in many states compel disclosure to a state agency of all information concerning suspected instances of child abuse. This sort of law generally requires disclosure regardless of the relationship in which the communication occurred, and regardless of the client's expectation of confidentiality. Similar rules in many states cover instances of drug or alcohol abuse, and venereal disease. Information on other topics may be included in some state mandatory disclosure laws. Mandatory disclosure laws typically apply to many classes of persons likely to acquire such information, including teachers. Persons required to make disclosures incur no civil liability by complying with these statutory requirements, and may incur civil or criminal liability for failure to comply.

Thus far, we have considered issues raised when a legal authority demands confidential information from a teacher or other professional, and when another professional requests such information. We have also considered issues raised when a teacher or other professional wishes to share a client's, patient's, or student's confidences with a third party. We turn now to consider special issues raised when the third party is the parent or guardian of the minor under treatment.

Generally, the child has no right to privacy against the parent or guardian. Historically, the law has recognized the parents' right to control of their children. Only when this control is exercised in a manner that seriously conflicts with the child's development into a contributing member of society does the state deny parents this right of control. Consequently, in most circumstances, the concerned parents' or guardians' requests for information regarding the treatment of their children must be honored. This applies to the full range of information regarding a behavioral treatment: the nature of the presenting problem and its identification, assessment data and interpretations, treatment planning, treatment inplementation and records of progress, and any other information gathered along the way to completion of the treatment.

However, as we noted in the previous section, some states have empowered minors to consent for themselves to certain treatments. In most such statutes, the problem of control over records is not expressly addressed. A plausible argument can be made that, when minors consent to treatment independently, they should control their records. Otherwise, if the statute is based on protection of minors' privacy, the state's interests would be frustrated. Such a relationship would apply regardless of whether the respect for privacy is based on respect for minors' personhood or a utilitarian promotion of psychotherapy for minors who otherwise would not seek it. However, it should also be noted that a right to consent independently to psychotherapy does not necessarily imply a right to consent without parental knowledge. In fact, some states expressly place this limitation by statute (see, e.g., Nebraska's statute on substance abuse counseling).

Federal law grants parents or legal guardians broad rights of access and control regarding the educational records of children under the age of 18. The Family Educational Rights and Privacy Act (also known as the Buckley Amendment) was enacted in 1974. Since that time, many states have passed similar laws, most of which are directly modeled on the provisions of the Buckley Amendment. Under the terms of the Buckley Amendment and similar laws, parents and guardians have the right to review the educational records of their children, the right to request corrections in those records, and, if no change is made in the offending record, the right to insert an explanation of that record in the child's files. However, this right of access does not extend to any notes or records made solely for the use of "instructional, supervisory, and administrative personnel, and educational personnel ancillary thereto," if these notes are in the sole possession of the person who made them, or of a substitute temporarily filling in for that person. This exemption probably covers treatment notes that the school behavior therapist maintains, and does not file with the child's other school records.

In addition, the Buckley Amendment grants parents and guardians the right to control access to their minor child's educational records. We have already noted one of two exceptions to this right: parents need not give consent before educational records are shared with "other school officials, including teachers within the educational institution or local educational agency, who have been determined by such agency or institution to have legitimate educational interests" (Family Education Rights and Privacy Act, 1974). Further, parental consent is not required before educational records are shared with

> officials of other schools or school systems in which the student seeks or intends to enroll, upon condition that the student's parents be notified of the transfer, receive a copy of the record if desired, and have an opportunity for a hearing to challenge the content of the record. (Family Education Rights and Privacy Act, 1974)

The several other exceptions to the parental right of control over a child's educational records do not concern us here.

Parents and guardians have these rights of access and control to the exclusion of the child. The child has virtually no right to review or control access to his or her records until age 18, whereupon these rights of access and control become the child's, and are lost to parents and guardian. An educational agency or institution that denies parents or guardians their rights of access and control under the Buckley Amendment risks the loss of federal funds.

The Rights to Treatment and Education

Thus far, we have discussed negative rights, that is, rights designed to ensure freedom from government encroachment into the private lives of children or their families. We turn now to positive rights, that is, rights to government support. Positive rights might best be construed as providing opportunities, in this instance as a duty of the state, whereas negative rights place limitations on the state's intrusion into how opportunities are used. Two sorts of possible positive entitlements are especially relevant to school-based treatment—the purported rights to treatment and education. Such entitlements are sometimes argued as *human rights* owed children because of their dependent, vulnerable status and basic human needs (see, e.g., Joint Commission, 1969; United Nations, 1959).

Constitutional Law

Whatever their ethical status as guideposts for policy or even as natural rights, entitlements need not be—and typically are not—recognized in the Constitution. Successful arguments for recognition of entitlements have been based not on universal rights but instead the corollaries to other state action. These arguments have been of two types. First, if the state infringes on liberty, the due process clause of the fourteenth amendment requires that the nature of the intervention must, at a minimum, bear a "reasonable relation" to its purpose (*Jackson v. Indiana*, 1972). Thus, for example, a state probably could not require students to attend school but then provide no teachers. Second, if the state bestows a property benefit on its citizens, such as the opportunity for education (cf. *Goss v. Lopez*, 1975), then the equal protection clause requires equitable distribution of the benefit (see, e.g., *Brown v. Board of Education*, 1954).

It is important to keep in mind the general principle that the rights to treatment and education, when they exist, are derived from other, *fundamental* rights (i.e., rights implicitly or expressly embedded in the Constitution; see *San Antonio Independent School District v. Rodriguez*, 1973). Therefore, even the most ardent advocates of judicial activism are apt to construe the constitutional rights to treatment and education as substantially more limited than the terms may imply.

Right to Treatment

The right to treatment was originally proposed as a quid pro quo for institutionalized persons who had been civilly committed for the purpose of treatment (Birnbaum, 1960). The quid pro quo theory has also been applied to juvenile correctional facilities in jurisdictions in which juvenile incarceration is purported to have treatment as its purpose (see e.g., *Morales v. Turman*, 1974). Because the issue has tended to be raised in institutions that have violated any decent standard of humane care, the treatment that has been held to be constitutionally required has often been at the level of basic care (e.g., provision of nutritious meals, laundry services, and an adequate number of toilets). In the most famous and expansive application of the quid pro quo theory (*Wyatt v. Stickney*, 1971), the federal district court posited three broad entitlements: a humane psychological and physical environment, qualified staff in numbers sufficient to render adequate treatment, and individualized treatment plans. Thus, even in *Wyatt*, recognition of the right to treatment did not result in an order for good treatment.

The Supreme Court has had several opportunities to recognize a constitutional right to treatment. On each occasion, it has expressly avoided the issue. Former Chief Justice Burger made clear that he, at least, found the concept untenable. He argued that the state may legitimately require hospitalization for the purpose of mere custodial care (*O'Connor v. Donaldson*, 1975, concurring opinion). He feared that a right to treatment would imply a duty to be treated. There are other conceptual problems. Would a right to treatment be available to an untreatable person? Would any treatment suffice? Must the treatment be optimal? Moreover, the quid pro quo theory does not clearly apply to institutionalized minors, who typically have been voluntarily admitted by their parent or guardian. Even if it did apply, it might be a false victory. The clearest remedy for violation of the right to treatment is release. The right applies only if the state deprives one of liberty for the purpose of treatment. Simply put, if the state does not assume the duty to treat, it has no such duty because the constitution does not impose it. (The same simple principle also applies to education and social welfare programs; see, e.g., *San Antonio Independent School District v. Rodriguez*, 1973.)

A different legal theory, again applicable only to those persons in the state's care and custody, is at once narrower and more expansive. In litigation involving Willowbrook State School in New York (*New York State Association for Retarded Children, Inc. v. Rockefeller*, 1975), the federal district court rejected the quid pro quo theory because the mentally retarded residents had been voluntarily admitted. The court did hold, though, that the residents had a constitutional right to protection from harm. The court reasoned that confinement of mentally retarded persons in an environment so inhumane and bereft of habilitative programs as to resemble penal conditions violates the eighth amendment's prohibition of cruel and unusual punishment. Although the protection from harm standard requires no positive intervention, the court did construe it to require habilitative services so as to prevent regression or further developmental delay. Ultimately, the court was sufficiently frustrated in its efforts to make Willowbrook a benign environment that it ordered closing of Willowbrook (action that was eventually reversed) and establishment of community-based group homes (see Rothman & Rothman, 1984, for a comprehesive history of the *Willowbrook* litigation). Although the theory relied on by the *Willowbrook* court was narrow, the result was not.

The particular constitutional theory in *Willowbrook* is probably not viable outside correctional settings, because the Supreme Court has since held the eighth amendment to be inapplicable to noncriminal settings (*Ingraham v. Wright*, 1977). However, it is still of interest because the Supreme Court also has subsequently adopted the protection from harm standard in institutional litigation, although the Court neither relied on the same constitutional theory nor even cited *Willowbrook* (*Youngberg v. Romeo*, 1982). Relying on the due process clause of the fourteenth amendment, the Court held that habilitation (in this instance, behavioral training to prevent self-injury) is constitutionally required if it would permit a resident to live in safety free from undue restraint. The same theory could be applied to justify habilitation and treatment necessary for deinstitutionalization and, therefore, less intrusive state intervention. That the narrow *Youngberg* holding has the potential for expansive results, like *Willowbrook*, was indicated by a concurring opinion written by Justice Blackmun and joined by Justices Brennan and O'Connor. Blackmun indicated that he, at least, would be prepared to extend the Court's holding to include training to prevent deterioration of self-care skills.

The Right to Education

The right to treatment applies only to institutionalized persons, obviously a smaller population than the class of children who may need treatment. Although not constitutionally required to do so (*San Antonio Independent School District v. Rodriguez*, 1973), all states have made public education universally available. Because they have conveyed a right, the equal protection clause requires its equitable application. Litigation under this theory has focused on exceptional children's exclusion from school because of lack of special services or, conversely, minority children's exclusion from equal educational opportunity because of inappropriate placement in special education. Although appellate courts have never ruled on the issue, two federal district courts entered landmark decisions (*Mills v. Board of Education*, 1972; *PARC v. Pennsylvania*, 1971) that exceptional children have a right to education, including procedures designed to ensure access to adequate educational services.

Statutory Law

Constitutional litigation on the rights to treatment and education has subsided, in part because legislatures have enacted statutory guarantees that are clearer and often broader than constitutional requirements. State statutes frequently provide for a right to treatment for persons residing in state hospitals and schools, and a right to education, including special educational services, for all handicapped children.

In addition to provisions in state law, the federal Education for All Handicapped Children Act (1975) provides exceptional children through age 21 with a right to a free appropriate public education. Of particular interest to school-based therapists, the schools are required to provide exceptional children with "related services," including psychological services, required to assist them to benefit from special education (see, e.g., *In re A Family*, 1979; *Papacoda v. Connecticut*, 1979; cf. *Irving Independent School District v. Tatro*, 1984). The key issue is whether the services are for the purpose of education or treatment *per se*. If the latter, schools are not financially liable under the EAHCA. For example, courts have been reticent to require school systems to pay for psychiatric hospitalization, because they have regarded hospitalization as medical treatment (*Darlene L. v. Illinois State Board of Education*, 1983; *McKenzie v. Jefferson*. 1983).

The Supreme Court has interpreted the meaning of "appropriate" education under the EAHCA narrowly, despite the Act's guarantee of "special education and related services designed to *meet their unique needs*" [EAHCA, 1975, § 601(c), emphasis added]. In *Board of Education v. Rowley* (1982), the Court held that the IEP need only be "reasonably calculated to enable the child to receive educational benefits" (p. 207), with one measure of benefit for children in regular classrooms to be whether they are receiving passing marks and advancing from grade to grade. The Court also admonished lower courts to "be careful to avoid imposing their view of preferable educational methods upon the States" (p. 207). However, this restraint may not extend to a large proportion of cases. *Rowley* involved a particularly controversial problem in special education: the best method of education for children who are hearing-impaired (i.e., lip reading versus sign language). Issues about whether a child needs behavior therapy to achieve "educational benefits" rarely will involve such pedagogical controversies. Although the federal courts are presently reluctant to put tight strings around states' means of meeting requirements for receiving federal funds (*Pennhurst State School v. Halderman*, 1981), the EAHCA still is the most important piece of entitlement legislation for children and certainly the major federal legislation providing access to school-based therapies. Moreover, states can adopt broader entitlements to special education—something closer to optimal individualized education—and many have done so. These broader state policies may be enforceable in federal court under the EAHCA (*Geis v. Board of Education*, 1985).

Impermissible Interventions

In recent years, several landmark federal and state court cases have begun to establish the boundaries of legally permitted behavioral treatments (see Wexler, 1981, for detailed review). These cases have considered issues which behavior therapists recognize as token economies, negative reinforcement, aversive conditioning, and time out. In legal terms, these have been regarded as issues of mistreatment, abuse, and neglect, and older rules governing these issues have informed the courts' opinions regarding behavioral treatments. Though they constrain the behavior therapist's discretion slightly, the resulting rules probably do so little more than common sense would in most cases, while serving to protect the health, safety, and welfare of minors in behavior modification treatment programs.

We will examine these rules in the context of the behavior therapist's categories, dealing first with token economies, followed by negative reinforcement, aversive conditioning, and time out. Most of these cases have involved residential treatment settings. There is little reason to suspect that courts will be less vigorous in protecting the rights of minors in day school, though the legal reasoning employed may differ somewhat from that found in institutional cases. Note that the guidelines presented in this section represent minimal legal requirements of general applicabiity. In some cases, state education regulations, social service regulations, and mental health or juvenile justice regulations may impose more stringent requirements and afford the individual greater protection.

Token economies, which use points or credits as secondary reinforcers, are common in residential facilities and special education classrooms. In the token economy treatment, clients have the opportunity to earn points or credits, which they may then exchange for items of their choice at a store or canteen. Clients' desirable behaviors are reinforced by presentation of the point or credit (secondary reinforcement), and by acquisition of the desired object for which the points or credits are exchanged (primary reinforcement). These treatments present two special legal issues: the nature of primary reinforcers, and the nature of the work clients do to earn points or credits.

With respect to primary reinforcers, the items for which clients may exchange their credits, no stricture may be placed on a client's access to necessities of life. The client's access to reasonable quantities of the following may not be made contingent upon acquisition of points or credits in a token economy: wholesome, nutritious food; clothing appropriate to the season; shelter against the elements; and medical care, as well as opportunities for daily periods of exercise and rest of reasonable duration. This conclusion rests on the Supreme Court's determination that institutionalized minors have a right to reasonably safe conditions of confinement (*Youngberg v. Romeo*, 1982). Under *Youngberg* the courts show great deference to the decisions of trained professionals. Nevertheless, a decision to make access to necessities contingent on certain behaviors probably compromises the minor's safety sufficiently that most courts will have little difficulty restraining implementation of such a program.

Access to luxuries or privileges may be made contingent upon acquisition of credits or points in a token economy system. In order to fall within the category of privileges, however, the acts or items must be clearly unrelated to the health, safety, or welfare of the minor client. Such items as a minimum opportunity for phone conversations with close family members are related to the minor's welfare, and so may not be denied the (residential) client by categorizing them as phone privileges. However, extra phone call opportunities beyond the minimum may be controlled or denied as privileges. Parenthetically, minor clients are also entitled to privacy in their mail (*Milonas v. Williams*, 1982) and phone communications. Violation of these privacy rights exposes the violating individuals and agencies to liability for civil penalties. Similarly, requiring minors to submit to periodic polygraph (lie detector) examinations as a precondition to progress in an institution's level system has been ruled an illegal violation of the privacy of the minor client's thought (*Milonas v. Williams*, 1982).

The manner in which clients earn credits or points in token economies also presents a legal concern. Many treatment programs award points for purely personal behaviors such as polite speech or proper dress. Programs may also award points for light housekeeping duties such as making one's bed, and for duties more closely involved with institutional maintenance, such as washing cafeteria dishes, tables, or floors. Finally, some programs award points for behaviors best characterized as nonpersonal, child labor experiences, such as mowing lawns, cleaning streets as part of a community service project, or refurbishing houses for senior citizens.

In general, awarding points contingent upon the accomplishment of purely personal behaviors probably presents no problem in most jurisdictions. Points may be awarded or withheld on the basis of polite speech, proper dress, and other aspects of personal conduct, including purely personal light housekeeping, such as making one's bed or clearing one's desk. However, awarding points contingent upon activities having the character of institutional maintenance may run counter to state child labor laws in many jurisdictions, and may also run counter to constitutional protections against involuntary servitude. To participate in activities having the character of institutional maintenance, minors should be of the age allowed by the applicable state child labor law to go to work; they should agree to work in a truly voluntary, uncoerced fashion, and they should be paid the going wage for labor of the type and skill level they are involved in. Points may be awarded for this work, if doing so does not compromise the voluntariness of the minor's decision to participate. However, awarding points cannot substitute for payment at the going wage. Token economies that award points for participation in community development projects such as street sweeping, house painting, or land clearing in state parks, should meet the same requirements, or risk running counter to state restrictions on child labor and federal guarantees against involuntary servitude.

The term *negative reinforcement* refers to the termination of an uncomfortable condition contingent upon an appropriate response. For example, the client might be kept in an uncomfortably cold room until he or she enacts certain behavior, whereupon the client would be allowed into a comfortably warm room. Negative reinforcement should not be confused with punishment (which we will examine later) nor with ordinary (positive) reinforcement. The use of negative reinforcement requires creation of a state of discomfort in the client. The termination of this discomfort serves as the reinforcing stimulus in the operant paradigm.

As a general rule, treatment based on negative reinforcement should be avoided. The law might allow this sort of treatment to proceed if the following conditions are met: the state of discomfort will be relatively mild and brief; the treatment by negative reinforcement is highly likely to confer some benefit on the client; this benefit outweighs the harm done to the client (the state of discomfort); this benefit cannot be conveyed through some less harmful means; and further, there is some overriding social reason for conferring the benefit on the client (cf. *Milonas v. Williams*, 1982; *Youngberg v. Romeo*, 1982; but see *Santana v. Collazo*, 1983). Even appropriately documented consent may not protect the therapist or agency from liability for the harm (discomfort) caused by the negative reinforcement treatment (cf. *Milonas v. Williams*, 1982). Many courts may find the consent not truly informed where less discomforting alternatives existed but were not chosen.

Punishment stands on somewhat different ground. Punishment is the administration of an uncomfortable stimulus, or denial of a pleasurable one, contingent upon the performance of some negative behavior. Generally, common law permits the use of reasonable corporal punishment as a corrective measure in schools (see *Ingraham v. Wright*, 1975). According to Prosser (1971), the teacher's common law privilege to use corporal punishment

> extends to the infliction of any corporal punishment which is reasonable under the circumstances; but [not to] . . . any force which goes beyond that reasonably necessary for the purpose to be accomplished. All of the circumstances are to be taken into consideration, including the nature of the offense, the age, sex and strength of the child, his past behavior, the kind of punishment, and the extent of the harm inflicted [by the punishment].

Some states have enacted statutes codifying this common law teacher's privilege. These statutes specifically empower teachers to use corporal punishment to achieve certain classroom goals, principally the maintenance of order.

Reasonable noncorporal punishments are, of course, also allowed. Punishments such as the denial of an expected movie pass in the face of negative behavior, withdrawal of a previously granted extra phone call, denial of access to a favorite toy, are all instances of punishment that the law will allow. However, very severe punishments, corporal and noncorporal, will not be allowed. Punishments such as forcing a minor client to stand at attention for long periods of time, or picking the minor client up by simultaneous arm twisting and hair pulling, have been outlawed by at least one court (*Milonas v. Williams*, 1982). Punishments that restrict the client's access to visits from close family members, or opportunities to consult privately with legal counsel, are probably also impermissible.

Frequently confused with negative reinforcement, *aversive conditioning* involves the presentation of discomforting stimuli contingent upon the client's behaving in an undesirable fashion. Generally speaking, the rules regarding punishment apply to aversive conditioning. These techniques may be applied to minor clients only if the aversive stimulus is not physically harmful nor too intensely discomforting, and if the benefits to the client clearly outweigh the discomfort induced by the treatment. For example, a landmark case on a related issue (*Youngberg v. Romeo*, 1982) involved a profoundly retarded young adult male who inflicted injuries on himself and others. To prevent injury, therapists had to restrain the young man with soft shackles; essentially, the young man was tied to his bed with knotted sheets. In a case as extreme as this, an aversive conditioning program aimed at controlling the injurious behavior is likely to win court approval, if less intrusive methods (such as positive reinforcement of competing behaviors) prove unsuccessful. The court regards freedom from physical restraint as very important, and so will give the therapeutic goal of discontinuing use of soft shackles great weight in determining the appropriateness of aversive conditioning.

Even in such extreme cases, therapists considering the use of aversive conditioning techniques are advised to seek review of the proposed treatment plan, including peer review and citizen review where available, before implementing the plan. This review should determine whether the proposed treatment is, in fact, the least restrictive or least intrusive treatment likely to achieve the desired behavior change, and whether the proposed treatment is itself reasonably likely to achieve this change.

Time out is the practice of removing a client from a scene in which inappropriate behaviors are being acted out. Typically the client is acting in an aggressive or threatening manner, and is removed to a place of detention apart from the rest of the client population. The detention place is often a quiet room; when the client is inside, the door is frequently locked. Time out is not properly a form of punishment. Properly used, time out represents an opportunity for the client to regain control over behavior, a chance to settle down in a setting apart from the demand pressures of the peer group.

Time out also represents an opportunity for abuse of the minor client. Court cases reviewing specific instances of time out have held that detention in the time out area may not continue longer than is reasonably necessary for the client to regain composure (*Pena v. New York State Division for Youth*, 1976; *Milonas v. Williams*, 1982). Improper decisions to place a child into, and to retain a child in, a locked time out area expose the agency and individual personnel involved to liability for false imprisonment. Consequently, institutions using time out should adopt clear procedures for the initiation of time out detention, and for periodic review of the appropriateness of continued detention. The criteria for initiation and continuation of detention should be generally applicable to all cases, and should be clear to all personnel involved. The reasons for continuation of detention in a given case should be clearly documented each time review occurs.

While in the time out area, minor clients must be monitored by treatment personnel at regular intervals; the duration of these intervals will vary case by case, but probably should not exceed one hour. More frequent contacts with treatment personnel are called for in cases where the client is violent and may pose a danger to self. This monitoring should not be confused with the periodic reassessment of the continuation of time out discussed earlier. Though physically the two acts may occur together, they serve different purposes, the former serving to guard the client's liberty interest in time out that does not continue longer than necessary, the latter serving to guard the client and the facility against harm inflicted while time out continues.

The time out room must not be so spartan as to be unnecessarily uncomfortable, nor so lavishly furnished as to provide opportunities for the agitated client to inflict injuries on self or others. The client in time out must be accorded access to the necessities of life and the usual amenities, including at least wholesome food, proper clothing, and access to sanitary facilities including bathing facilities when time out continues for a lengthy time. The time out room must be reasonably heated, cooled, and ventilated. (But see *Santana v. Collazo*, 1983, for a different perspective on the use of isolation.) When time out continues for extended periods, the client must be given opportunities for reasonable periods of rest and exercise.

Finally, the movement of clients into time out areas should be accomplished without the use of unnecessary roughness (*Milonas v. Williams*, 1982; *Nelson v. Heyne*, 1974). Unnecessary or unreasonable use of force in these settings, as in any other setting, exposes the person using the force to civil liability for assault or battery, and to potential criminal liability for the same acts. The agency or facility may face similar liability, if it can be shown to have been negligent in screening, training, or supervising the overly rough employee.

Remedies for Violations of Minors' Rights

Remedies for violations of rights fall into two general categories: administrative remedies and civil actions. Criminal actions do not redress violations of rights in the sense that they usually do not result in compensation to the victim of the violation, and so will not be considered here. Administrative remedies often involve compensation, occasionally in pecuniary terms, more frequently in terms of making available opportunities that had been denied by the improper acts complained of. Civil actions, meaning lawsuits, commonly result in pecuniary compensation to victims, and may also give victims access to opportunities denied by the improper acts complained of.

Most courts require plaintiffs to seek administrative redress, when available, before hearing suits complaining of rights violations in school settings. Reflecting this judicial practice, we will first consider administrative remedies available in such cases, and later we will briefly discuss civil actions.

Administrative remedies usually take the form of appeals, formal or less so, to administrative supervisors or hearing boards. Because school-based behavioral treatments sufficiently elaborate to inspire complaint will likely arise in the context of special education, we look to the provisions of the Education For All Handicapped Children Act (EAHCA, 1975). This federal law applies to all agencies and programs that provide special educational services and receive federal funds, and its provisions are sufficiently generic to serve as models of what the states have implemented to handle similar complaints regarding non-federally funded programs.

Before a child may be assessed for placement in behavioral treatment as part of a special education program, the EAHCA requires that the parents or guardian be notified in writing, and consent must be obtained, either from parents or guardian, or from a judge, before the assessment can occur. The law places various restrictions on the conduct and use of assessment techniques. If the parents or guardian disagree with the results of this assessment, they have the right to request an independent assessment, which will be conducted at school district expense unless the district can demonstrate to a court that its own assessment was complete and accurate.

Upon completion of the assessment, school district officials are required to meet with the parents or guardian to draw up an Individualized Education Program (IEP). The district's special education administrator or a designee must attend on behalf of the district, as must the child's teacher. The district and the parents or guardian may invite other interested persons to attend. The child must be included, if considerations such as age, cognitive ability, and desire to participate suggest this is not inappropriate. As we noted earlier, participation by the child usually is desirable.

This meeting results in creation of the child's IEP, a document that details the child's present level of performance, and any supplementary aids and services to be included in treatment. The IEP also specifies who shall be responsible for implementation of each phase of the program, how progress will be measured, and when services will be initiated and terminated.

The parent or guardian who is dissatisfied with the IEP at any point in its negotiation or implementation can call the IEP group together to reconsider the program, as may the school district. In any case, the IEP group must meet at least annually to examine progress and reevaluate the program. If the parents or guardian feel the IEP meetings do not result in an appropriate treatment plan, they may appeal this group's decisions in an administrative fair hearing. In this hearing, school district and parents or guardian present their positions to an impartial hearing officer. This hearing represents the final level of administrative appeal under the EAHCA. If either the school district, or the parents or guardian, remain dissatisfied with the resulting IEP, either may sue in court to challenge it. The threat of resort to a fair hearing has apparently proven sufficient to cause many school districts to modify proposed IEPs. Baker and Brightman (1984) noted that "very few cases actually go to fair hearing."

The Buckley Amendment mentioned earlier in this chapter sets up administrative hearing mechanisms to handle cases in which parents or children challenge a school's use of educational records. This law applies to all educational agencies and institutions that receive federal funds either directly (for example, in the form of federal grants or contracts) or indirectly (for example, in the form of federally guaranteed student loans to students). The provisions of the Buckley Amendment, and of state laws patterned after it, are quite similar in outline to those of the EAHCA.

Typically, once one's administrative avenues have been exhausted, one may turn to the courts for help. We turn now to a brief discussion of civil actions, lawsuits, as avenues for the redress of violations of rights. We note, however, that recent decisions have made recourse to courts more difficult for plaintiffs seeking protection or vindication of minor's rights. The Supreme Court ruled recently that successful plaintiffs are not entitled to attorney's fees under the EAHCA (*Smith v. Robinson*, 1984).[1] This means that persons who bring such cases on behalf of minors must bear significant legal costs in order to mount their cases: these costs may not be recovered even if the case is won. The Court has also held that states are immune from suit under section 504 of the federal Rehabilitation Act of 1973 (*Atascadero State Hospital v. Scanlon*, 1985) and that in cases where section 504 of the Rehabilitation Act and the EAHCA are applicable, plaintiffs must proceed under the EAHCA only (*Irving Independent School District v. Tatro*, 1984).

Further, several lower federal courts have held that the Buckley Amendment does not give parents, guardians, or students a private cause of action against school districts that violate the provisions of that law (*Girardier v. Webster College*, 1977; *Price v. Young*, 1983). In jurisdictions that accept this holding, private parties cannot sue school districts or district personnel for use of a child's educational records inconsistent with the Buckley Amendment. Under the Amendment, these schools do face loss of federal funds. The application of this penalty is at the discretion of the Secretary of Education.

Despite these limitations, the private lawsuit remains a potent weapon. In the foregoing sections of this chapter, we have noted the various kinds of liability behavioral professionals may expose themselves and their agencies to by failing to follow the rules regarding various treatments. The person whose rights have been violated by a failure to follow the rules may bring a private, civil suit in any court with jurisdiction to hear such cases. These suits may take any of several forms, including malpractice (professional negligence) complaints, common negligence complaints, or intentional tort complaints.

In bringing a malpractice complaint, the plantiff alleges impermissibly sloppy professional behavior, such as poor assessment or improper implementation of a behavior modification technique. Courts have not viewed the complaint of educational malpractice favorably, and educational malpractice suits against teachers and schools have generally failed (see, e.g., *Helm v. Professional Children's*

[1]Congress has since enacted a statute providing for award of attorney's fees to parents prevailing in actions brought under the EAHCA (Handicapped Children's Protection Act of 1986).

School, 1980). However, the behavior therapist may be more closely analogized to the medical treatment professional, rather than the teacher, for purposes of a malpractice action. Courts that accept this analogy to the medical professional may be more willing to hear malpractice suits against behavior therapists couched in terms of medical malpractice than they have been to hear suits against teachers couched in terms of educational malpractice. Civil suits may also take the form of common negligence suits, as when the plaintiff complains, for example, that culpable inattention to the child's safety by a teacher allegedly resulted in harm to the child.

In malpractice and common negligence suits, the plaintiff must show that the defendant had a specific legal duty to act in a certain way with regard to the plaintiff (the way this is demonstrated is one factor distinguishing malpractice from common negligence); that the defendant failed to live up to that legal standard; that there exists a legally sufficient causal link between the defendant's failure to live up to the legal duty and some consequence to the plaintiff, and that the consequence to the plaintiff was some legally meaningful harm done. Failure on any of these points—duty, breach, causation, or damages—dooms the plaintiff's case. Failure of any point can be caused either by insufficiency of the plaintiff's proof, or by the defendant's successful interposition of a legitimate defense to a sufficiently proven point.

Civil suits may also allege intentionally inflicted harm, as when the plaintiff complains of assault, battery, or false imprisonment. In these cases, the plaintiff must show, among other things, that the defendant intended the act that caused the harm. Tortious intent is more than a mere "contraction of the muscles" (Prosser, 1971, p. 31) yet less than intending the harm done. For example, in a suit alleging battery resulting from the use of excessive force while placing a minor into a time out room, the plaintiff must show that the defendant intended to touch the minor, not that the defendant intended to cause a bruise or broken bone with that touch. However, because the staff member who placed the minor in time out is legally privileged reasonably to touch the minor in performance of the duties of employment, something more than a reasonable intent to touch must be shown. Although plaintiff need not prove an intent to break bones or cause injuries, an intent to touch in a manner unreasonably forceful must be demonstrated.

Civil suits involve certain costs to plaintiffs and defendants, and uncertain rewards. Plaintiffs certainly face the likelihood of lost work, and lost sleep, as they help prepare their cases. Defendants face bad publicity, which may jeopardize funding sources and embarrass employees, coworkers, and colleagues. Plaintiffs and defendants also face the pecuniary costs of filing fees, expert witness fees, and of course attorneys' fees. Yet civil suits are undeniably among the most potent weapons in the arsenal of the private citizen battling to protect rights, particularly the rights of those unable, by reason of age or disability, to fight their own battles unaided.

In closing, we suggest that the professionals using behavioral technology on the one hand, and children and their families on the other, have great incentives in the costs of lawsuits to work to prevent rights violations before they occur. With adequate legal guidance, planning and common sense, and just a bit of compassion, behavioral treatment can routinely deliver the benefits to clients described in other chapters of this book, without fear of compromise of civil rights.

References

Abrahamson v. Hershman, 701 F.2d 223 (1st Cir. 1983).

Adelman, H. S., Kaser-Boyd, N., & Taylor, L. (1984). Children's participation in consent for psychotherapy and their subsequent response to treatment. *Journal of Clinical Child Psychology*, 13, 170–178.

Adelman, H. S., Lusk, R., Alvarez, V., & Acosta, N. K. (1985). Competence of minors to understand, evaluate, and communicate about their psychoeducational problems. *Professional Psychology: Research and Practice*, 16, 426–434.

American Psychological Association. (1981). Ethical principles of psychologists. *American Psychologist, 36,* 633–638.

Atascadero State Hosp. v. Scanlon, 105 S.Ct. 3142 (1985).

Baker, B. L., & Brightman, R. P. (1984). Access of handicapped children to educational services. In N. D. Reppucci, L. A. Weithorn, E. P. Mulvey, & J. Monahan (Eds.), *Children, mental health, and the law* (pp. 289–307). Beverly Hills, CA: Sage.

Belter, R. W., & Grisso, T. (1984). Children's recognition of rights violations in counseling. *Professional Psychology: Research and Practice, 15,* 899–910.

Bersoff, D. N. (1983). Children as participants in psychoeducational assessment. In G. B. Melton, G. P. Koocher, & M. J. Saks (Eds.), *Children's competence to consent* (pp. 149–177). New York: Plenum Press.

Birnbaum, M. (1960). The right to treatment. *American Bar Association Journal, 46,* 499–505.

Board of Education v. Rowley, 458 U.S. 176 (1982).

Brown v. Board of Education, 347 U.S. 483 (1954).

Cantebury v. Spence, 464 F.2d 772 (D.C. Cir. 1972).

Darlene L. v. Illinois State Board of Education, 568 F.Supp. 1340 (N.D.Ill. 1983).

Department of Education. (1981). Assistance to states for education of handicapped children; interpretation of the individualized education program (IEP). *Federal Register, 46,* 5460–5474.

Department of Education. (1985a). Assistance to states for education of handicapped children. 34 CFR pt. 300.

Department of Education. (1985b). Student rights in research, experimental programs, and testing. 34 CFR pt. 98.

Department of Health and Human Services. (1985). Additional protections for children involved as subjects in research. 45 CFR pt. 46(D).

Division of Child, Youth, and Family Services, American Psychological Association. (1982a, March). *Position statement: Standards regarding consent for treatment and research involving children.* Washington, DC: Author.

Division of Child, Youth, and Family Services, American Psychological Association. (1982b, March). *[Proposed revisions of the Ethical Principles of Psychologists.]* Washington, DC: Author.

Education for All Handicapped Children Act of 1975, Pub. L. 94-142, 89 Stat. 355.

Family Educational Rights and Privacy Act of 1974, Pub. L. 90-247, § 438, 88 Stat. 571.

Gardner, M. (1982). Punishment and juvenile justice: A conceptual framework for assessing constitutional rights of youthful offenders. *Vanderbilt Law Review, 35,* 791–847.

Geis v. Board of Education, 54 U.S.L.W. 2193 (3d Cir. Sept. 30, 1985).

Girardier v. Webster College, 563 F.2d 1267 (8th Cir. 1977).

Goss v. Lopez, 419 U.S. 565 (1975).

Grisso, T., & Vierling, L. (1978). Minors' consent to treatment: A developmental perspective. *Professional Psychology, 9,* 412–427.

Handicapped Children's Protection Act of 1986, Pub. L. 99-372, 100 Stat. 796.

Hatch Amendment, Pub. L. 95-561, § 1250, 92 Stat. 2355 (1978).

Helm v. Professional Children's School, 103 Misc.2d 1053, 431 N.Y.S.2d 246 (App. Term 1980).

In re "A" Family, 602 P.2d 157 (Mont. 1979).

In re Gault, 387 U.S. 1 (1967).

Ingraham v. Wright, 403 U.S. 651 (1977).

Irving Independent School District v. Tatro, 104 S.Ct. 3371 (1984).

Jackson v. Indiana, 406 U.S. 715 (1972).

Joint Commission on the Mental Health of Children. (1969). *Crisis in child mental health: Challenge for the 1970's.* New York: Harper & Row.

Kaser-Boyd, N., Adelman, H. S., & Taylor, L. (1985). Minors' ability to identify risks and benefits of therapy. *Professional Psychology: Research and Practice, 16,* 411–417.

Katz, J. (1984). *The silent world of doctor and patient.* New York: Free Press.

King, P. A. (1984–85). Treatment and minors: Issues not involving lifesaving treatment. *Journal of Family Law, 23,* 241–265.

Koocher, G. P. (1983). Competence to consent: Psychotherapy. In G. B. Melton, G. P. Koocher, & M. J. Saks (Eds.), *Children's competence to consent* (pp. 111–128). New York: Plenum Press.

Lewis, C. E. (1983). Decision making related to health: When could/should children act responsibly? In G. B. Melton, G. P. Koocher, & M. J. Saks (Eds.), *Children's competence to consent* (pp. 75–92). New York: Plenum Press.

Lidz, C. W., Meisel, A., Zerubauel, E., Carter, M., Sestak, R. M., & Roth, L. H. (1984). *Informed consent: A study of decisionmaking in psychiatry.* New York: Guilford Press.

McKenzie v. Jefferson, 566 F.Supp. 404 (D.D.C. 1983).

Melton, G. B. (1980). Children's concepts of their rights. *Journal of Clinical Child Psychology, 9,* 186–190.

Melton, G. B. (1981a). Children's participation in treatment planning: Psychological and legal issues. *Professional Psychology, 12,* 246–252.

Melton, G. B. (1981b). Effects of a state law permitting minors to consent to psychotherapy. *Professional Psychology, 12,* 647–654.

Melton, G. B. (1983a). Children's competence to consent: A problem in law and social science. In G. B. Melton, G. P. Koocher, & M. J. Saks (Eds.), *Children's competence to consent* (pp. 111–128). New York: Plenum Press.

Melton, G. B. (1983b). Decision making by children: Psychological risks and benefits. In G. B. Melton, G. P. Koocher, & M. J. Saks (Eds.), *Children's competence to consent* (pp. 21–40). New York: Plenum Press.

Melton, G. B. (1983c). Minors and privacy: Are legal and

psychological concepts compatible? *Nebraska Law Review, 62*, 455–493.
Melton, G. B. (1983d). Toward "personhood" for adolescents: Autonomy and privacy as values in public policy. *American Psychologist, 38*, 99–103.
Melton, G. B., Koocher, G. P., & Saks, M. J. (Eds.). (1983). *Children's competence to consent*. New York: Plenum Press.
Melton, G. B., & Pliner, A. J. (1986). Adolescent abortion: A psycholegal analysis. In G. B. Melton (Ed.), *Adolescent abortion: Psychological and legal issues* (pp. 1–39). Lincoln NE: University of Nebraska Press.
Melville v. Sabatino, 30 Conn. 320, 313 A.2d 886 (1973).
Merriken v. Cressman, 364 F.Supp. 913 (E.D.Pa 1973).
Mills v. Board of Education, 348 F.Supp. 866 (D.D.C. 1972).
Milonas v. Williams, 691 F.2d 931 (10th Cir. 1982).
Mnookin, R. H. (1978). *Child, family and state: Problems and materials on children and the law*. Boston: Little, Brown.
Morales v. Turman, 383 F.Supp. 52 (E.D.Tex. 1974), *rev'd*, 535 F.2d 864 (5th Cir. 1976), *rev'd per curiam*, 430 U.S. 322 (1977), *reh'g denied*, 430 U.S. 988 (1977), *remanded*, 562 F.2d 993 (5th Cir. 1977).
Nelson v. Heyne, 491 F.2d 352 (7th Cir. 1974).
New York State Association for Retarded Children, Inc. v. Rockefeller ("*Willowbrook*"), 357 F.Supp. 752 (E.D.N.Y. 1975), *enforced sub nom*. New York State Association for Retarded Children, Inc. v. Carey, 393 F.Supp. 606 (1976), *aff'd*, 596 F.2d 27 (2d Cir. 1979), *enforced*, 492 F.Supp. 1099 (E.D.N.Y. 1980).
O'Connor v. Donaldson, 442 U.S. 563 (1975).
Papacoda v. Connecticut, 528 F.Supp. 68 (D.Conn. 1981).
PARC v. Pennsylvania, 334 F.Supp. 1257 (E.D.Pa. 1971) *and* 343 F.Supp. 279 (E.D.Pa. 1972).
Pena v. New York State Division for Youth, 419 F.Supp. 203 (S.D.N.Y. 1976).
Pennhurst State School v. Halderman, 41 U.S. 1 (1981).
Pierce v. Society of Sisters, 268 U.S. 510 (1925).
Price v. Young, 580 F. Supp. 1 (D.Ark. 1983).
Prosser, W. (1971). *The law of torts*. St. Paul, MN: West.
Rehabilitation Act of 1973, Pub. L. 93-112, 87 Stat. 355.
Roth, E. A., & Roth, L. H. (1984, April). *Children's feelings about psychiatric hospitalization: Legal and ethical implications*. Paper presented at the meeting of the American Orthopsychiatric Association, Toronto.
Roth, L. H., Appelbaum, P. S., Sallee. R.. Reynolds, C. F., & Huber, G. (1982). The dilemma of denial in the assessment of competency to refuse treatment. *American Journal of Psychiatry, 139*, 910–913.
Roth, L. H., Meisel, A., & Lidz, C. W. (1977). Tests of competency to consent to treatment. *American Journal of Psychiatry, 134*, 279–284.
Rothman, D. J., & Rothman, S. M. (1984). *The Willowbrook wars*. New York: Harper & Row.
Saks, M. J. (1983). Social psychological perspectives on the problem of consent. In G. B. Melton, G. P. Koocher, & M. J. Saks (Eds.), *Children's competence to consent* (pp. 41–53). New York: Plenum Press.
San Antonio Independent School District v. Rodriguez, 411 U.S. 1 (1973).
Santana v. Collazo, 714 F.2d 1172 (1st Cir. 1983).
Scott v. Bradford, 606 P.2d 554 (Okla. 1979).
Smith v. Robinson, 104 S.Ct. 3457 (1984).
State ex rel. Kelley v. Ferguson, 144 N.W. 1039 (Neb. 1914).
Tapp, J. L., & Melton, G. B. (1983). Preparing children for decision making: Implications of legal socialization research. In G. B. Melton, G. P. Koocher, & M. J. Saks (Eds.), *Children's competence to consent* (pp. 215–234). New York: Plenum Press.
Taylor, L., Adelman, H. S., & Kaser-Boyd, N. (1985). Exploring minors' reluctance and dissatisfaction with psychotherapy. *Professional Psychology: Research and Practice, 16*, 418–425.
Tinker v. Des Moines Independent School District, 393 U.S. 503 (1969).
United Nations. (1959). *Declaration of the rights of the child*. Resolution adopted by the General Assembly.
Wadlington, W. J. (1973). Minors and health care: The age of consent. *Osgoode Hall Law Journal, 73*, 115–125.
Wadlington, W. J. (1983). Consent to medical care for minors: The legal framework. In G. B. Melton, G. P. Koocher, & M. J. Saks (Eds.), *Children's competence to consent* (pp. 57–74). New York: Plenum Press.
Weithorn, L. A. (1982). Developmental factors and competence to consent to treatment. In G. B. Melton (Ed.), *Legal reforms affecting child and youth services* (pp. 85–100). New York: Haworth.
Weithorn, L. A. (1983). Involving children in decisions affecting their own welfare. In G. B. Melton, G. P. Koocher, & M. J. Saks (Eds.), *Children's competence to consent* (pp. 235–260). New York: Plenum Press.
Weithorn, L. A., & Campbell, S. B. (1982). The competency of children and adolescents to make informed treatment decisions. *Child Development, 53*, 1589–1598.
Wexler, D. B. (1981). *Mental health law: Major issues*. New York: Plenum Press.
Wisconsin v. Yoder, 406 U.S. 205 (1972).
Wyatt v. Stickney, 324 F.Supp. 781 (M.D.Ala. 1971), *enforced*, 344 F.Supp. 373 *and* 344 F.Supp. 387 (1972), *modified sub nom*. Wyatt v. Aderholt, 503 F.2d 1305 (5th Cir. 1974).
Youngberg v. Romeo, 457 U.S. 307 (1982).

PART IV

Behavior Change Strategies

The behavior therapist in an educational setting has a wide array of intervention options available. The chapters in this section each provide a comprehensive review of specific classes of intervention procedures. In most cases, each procedure is applicable to a wide range of problems. Because of the extremely large number of intervention procedures available, it was not possible to include a review of them all. The decision to include a particular class of strategies was based on a judgment that there existed a body of literature pertaining to the strategy that demonstrated efficacy when applied across a wide variety of problems. Thus, in this section, reviews are provided on cognitive-behavioral procedures (Kendall & Cummings, Chapter 15), home–school interventions (Kelley & Carper, Chapter 16), reductive procedures for decreasing inappropriate behaviors (Lentz, Chapter 17), token economies (McLaughlin & Williams, Chapter 18), self-monitoring (Mace & Kratochwill, Chapter 19), and social skills training (Gresham, Chapter 20). In addition to these procedures, which are used routinely in schools and other educational settings, we have also included a review of the literature pertaining to the use of biofeedback (Williamson, McKenzie, & Goreczny, Chapter 21). This technology shows considerable promise for use in educational settings.

CHAPTER 15

Thought and Action in Educational Interventions

Cognitive-Behavioral Approaches

Philip C. Kendall and Lucinda Cummings

Schools have always played a major role in the development of children, as a setting in which academic skills and information are acquired and as the context for socialization by teachers and peers. Whereas the former function has been generally recognized as the major goal of the educational system, others (e.g., Hagen, 1973; Zigler & Trickett, 1979) have argued that the school's socialization function is of equal or even greater importance in terms of the lifelong adjustment of the child. Socialization processes occurring in the eductional context include the acquisition and development of social skills crucial to successful peer relations, moral development, and the development of impulse control, the acquisition of thinking and problem-solving skills applicable across cognitive and social domains, and the development of attitudes and self-perceptions that influence effectance motivation and confidence levels in the child's approach to academic and social tasks.

Applications of behavior therapy to problems within educational settings have encompassed the academic and socialization functions of the school, proving an undeniably powerful means of modifying maladaptive behavior and enhancing academic performance. The evolution of cognitive-behavioral interventions has added new possibilities to our work in educational settings, in terms of their impact on socialization processes occurring in schools and in terms of their potential to provide greater maintenance and generalization of target skills.

The Cognitive-Behavioral Perspective

The cognitive-behavioral perspective on child psychopathology and psychotherapy places major emphasis on (a) the learning process, performance-based procedures, and the influence of the contingencies and models in the environment while (b) underscoring the centrality of mediating/information process-

Philip C. Kendall • Department of Psychology, Temple University, Philadelphia, Pennsylvania 19122. **Lucinda Cummings** • Kennedy Memorial Hospital for Children, Brighton, Massachusetts 02135.

ing factors in the development and remediation of academic and social disorders in children (Kendall, 1985). As noted elsewhere (Kendall, 1985), the model does not concern itself with efforts to uncover unconscious early trauma, nor does it belabor biological, neurological, and genetic aspects of pathology. Rather, these later factors are accepted as influential in certain disorders (e.g., Downs Syndrome), but of less concern in many others. Affective processes, family systems, and social contexts are not given primary emphasis, but these factors are recognized and integrated. Thus, cognitive-behavioral analyses involve considerations of numerous features of the child's internal and external environment and represent an integrationist perspective. As will become evident, cognitive, affective, social, and developmental processes are given meaningful roles alongside behavioral procedures in understanding etiology and prescribing remediation.

Basic to the cognitive-behavioral perspective are several guiding principles (see also Kendall, 1985; Mahoney, 1977). Learning for children involves cognitive mediation. And, as part of this learning, the child responds primarily to cognitive representations of environmental experiences rather than to the exact physical environment *per se*. Given this assigned role, ignoring cognitive factors, even if unwittingly, would be ill-advised.

Cognition includes several information processing features: cognitive events, processes, products, and structures (see Ingram & Kendall, 1986). For instance, an individual's self-talk (event), expectancies (processes), attributions (products), and schemata (structures) are involved in understanding and predicting maladjusted behavior and the effects of interventions. These dimensions are related, but can be viewed along a temporal dimension (Kendall & Braswell, 1982a) where expectancies precede behavioral events, self-talk and other cognitive events are concurrent with behavioral events, and attributions follow behavior. Cognitive structures (beliefs, schemata) develop after multiple behavioral events.

The cognitive-behavioral therapist serves as an educator, diagnostician, and consultant. Intervention is viewed as reeducation and the therapist is the educator. Diagnostic functions involve the careful functional analyses of the client's deficient and/or distorted cognitive activities. As a consultant, the therapist does not tell the student what to think but informs him or her of efficient ways to think. Although the expert, the therapist does not interact errorlessly but serves as a coping model (demonstrating strategies to overcome difficulties and frustrations). Thus, the cognitive-behavioral perspective holds that (a) cognition plays a part in learning, (b) there are multiple roles for cognitive features, and (c) the therapist serves as a coping model in the style of an educator, diagnostician, and consultant.

Cognitive-behavioral approaches provide a means of addressing socialization processes, cognitive skills, and developmental variables typically not highlighted by traditional behavioral interventions. One such set of variables involves the cognitive skills and attitudes that are prerequisites to the acquisition and maintenance of social or academic skills taught through standard behavioral means. For example, remediating the aggressive behavior of an impulsive child may require teaching a set of social skills, which can be done through standard behavioral techniques like modeling and behavioral rehearsal. However, before the impulsive child can profitably participate in social skills training sessions, he or she may well need to learn to attend to the instruction and to avoid responding impulsively to social stimuli. It is precisely these skill areas in which cognitive-behavioral techniques, such as verbal self-instruction and self-monitoring of attention (combined with modeling, rewards, and role plays), can be most effective, providing a set of prerequisite skills which then enable the child to make effective use of other interventions. Prerequisite attitudes may also be important in remediating children's social or academic problems. For instance, the learning disabled child with an overlay of reactive depression and the shy, withdrawn child may engage in negative, defeating self-talk that prevents him or her from taking full advantage of therapeutic techniques such as self-monitoring or social skills training. For these children, a cognitive-behavioral intervention that focuses on the development of coping self-statements and feelings of self-efficacy would provide them with attitudes and self-perceptions that are prerequisites to optimal skill development. Thus, the cognitive-behavioral model can provide therapeutic access to those processes and skills that are necessary to the effective use of more standard behavioral strategies, and the use of such prerequisite interventions may lead to better maintenance and generalization of target behaviors as well.

Another potentially major contribution of the cognitive-behavioral perspective is its assumption that cognitive processes, such as problem solving skills, reflectivity, attention, and other metacognitive or executive functions, are amenable to therapeutic intervention based on behavioral principles. This proposal is particularly important in the school setting, as it provides educators with a set of strategies for effecting change in these superordinate cognitive processes that can so pervasively affect the way in which a child acquires concrete skills and information. To teach a child through cognitive-behavioral techniques a set of conceptual problem-solving strategies that can be applied across a variety of academic and social tasks is to move that child closer to the important educational goal of learning how to learn (Brown, Bransford, Ferrara, & Campione, 1983).

Introducing cognition as an important variable has the additional benefit of forcing us to take account of the child's cognitive developmental level in designing interventions, whereas traditional behavioral therapies have not adequately considered developmental variables (Cummings, 1984; Furman, 1980; Kendall, 1984a). Behavioral approaches have tended to be applied across age groups of children and adolescents, or even in some cases to be developed for use with adults and applied to children without modification (Furman, 1980; Kendall, 1984a). Kendall (1984b) has referred to this problem as the "developmental uniformity myth" (p. 143). The assumption that children with the same referral problem can be treated with the same intervention, no matter what their age, is problematic for two reasons.

First, the nature of the problem may vary with age and therefore requires that the content of the treatment be age appropriate. Second, the child's cognitive developmental level may affect how well he or she can learn from a given intervention, and this would require age-appropriate variations in the treatment technique. The social skills training literature provides an example of the need to vary treatment content according to developmental level (Conger & Keane, 1981; Furman, 1980; Gresham & Lemanek, 1983). As detailed by Cummings (1984), developmental changes in children's friendship expectations and behavior seem to move from early situational concerns, such as propinquity and physical possessions, to an increasing emphasis on contextual and normative expectations, such as mutual sharing, and ultimately to a recognition of the personality characteristics and interests of the friend and emphasis on mutual understanding and intimacy. These developmental changes occur between 6 and 13 years of age and demonstrate the inappropriateness of teaching the same target social skills to elementary school children of different ages. Clearly the demands of social context change across childhood and the effectiveness of social skills interventions in terms of altering social status and behavior is likely to be compromised by the selection of developmentally inappropriate target skills. Interventions that focus on social congition as well as behavior are in a position to take developmental variables into account more effectively.

Demonstrations of the need to vary treatment technique according to cognitive developmental level are numerous in the cognitive-behavioral literature. For example, it has been shown that older children are able to generate spontaneously verbal self-instructional strategies in order to delay gratification, whereas younger children require explicit examples on which to model their verbalizations (Miller, Weinstein, & Karniol, 1978; Toner & Smith, 1977). Developmental differences in the use of verbalizing versus exemplary models have also been found (Bem, 1967; Denney, 1975). Indeed, the field of self-instructional training is built on the developmental premises of Luria (1961) and Vygotsky (1962) concerning private speech and its increasing role in mediating self-control as children grow older. Thus, cognitive-behavior therapists are in a unique position in terms of their ability to explore relations between a child's cognitive-developmental level and the relative efficacy of various treatment techniques, such as modeling, self-instruction, and imagery. Although this avenue of research has not been adequately explored, noteworthy beginnings have been made by Meyers and his colleagues (cf. Meyers & Cohen, 1984), and Wasserman (1983) has suggested a hypothetical developmental sequence of cognitive-behavioral techniques that could be empirically tested. The hypothesized continuum places modeling interventions at the preoperational phrase of cognitive development, with self-instructional techniques being considered more appropriate for children who have reached the concrete operational stage. Interventions involving imagery (e.g., systematic desensitization) are placed at the formal operational level in this model, and the semantically based therapies such as rational-emotive therapy (Ellis, 1971) are also considered to require formal operational thought. We might add to this hypothetical continuum the coaching techniques used in social skills training, which would seem to fall at the concrete operational stage in terms of their earliest efficacy. Research designed to test this set of hypotheses would contribute significantly to efforts to individualize treatments for children.

A final contribution of the cognitive-behavioral approach lies in its attention to attitudinal and affective variables. Feelings of low self-efficacy, test anxiety, math anxiety, phobias, and depression have all begun to receive attention in the child cognitive-behavioral literature (Cooley & Spiegler, 1980; Craddock, Cotler, & Jason, 1978; Genshaft, 1982; Kanfer, Karoly & Newman, 1975; Kendall, 1987; Stark, Brookman, & Frazier, 1988). Although this research is just beginning, it offers the possibility of developing more effective interventions for emotional problems whose impact is often evident in terms of decreased academic and social competence in the school setting.

Thus the cognitive-behavioral perspective has given rise to therapeutic approaches that have the potential to affect prerequisite skills and attitudes, to help children to develop broadly applicable thinking skills, and to take account of affective and developmental variables with respect to the treatment content and techniques. As the following illustrative review will show, cognitive-behavioral interventions in educational settings touch all of the academic and socialization functions of the school.

We will begin by discussing interventions aimed at children's academic functioning, including strategies for learning to solve problems systematically, decrease impulsivity and improve attention, and fostering confidence and self-efficacy in the student's approach to tasks. The review will then focus on cognitive-behavioral strategies in the social sphere, including techniques for overcoming social withdrawal, reducing impulsivity in social situations, modifying aggressive behavior, and preventing problem behavior though training in social problem solving.[1]

Areas of Application

Academic Interventions

Cognitive-behavioral techniques have begun to be utilized in attempts to improve students' approaches to academic tasks of all kinds. Although this line of research is relatively underdeveloped at this point, the over-

[1]Therapy manuals for the treatment of children/adolescents with problems in the areas of (a) impulsivity and (b) anxiety are available from the first author.

all goal seems to be the teaching of metacognitive or task-specific thinking skills that will help the student to approach an academic task in a more organized, efficient manner. These interventions have been applied to reading, writing, and math tasks with varying degrees of success; although their efficacy has not been clearly demonstrated, these strategies show the promise needed to warrant further investigation.

Cognitive-behavioral interventions in the area of reading instruction have been reviewed by Lloyd, Kosiewicz, and Hallahan (1982), and they include strategies for improving attention, increasing accuracy and fluency of decoding, and improving comprehension. Intervention efforts have focused on comprehension primarily, with strategies including literal questions, paraphrasing skills, and learning to anticipate questions (Lloyd *et al.*, 1982). A promising strategy for teaching children to answer literal questions involves having students underline facts in a story, number the facts, and place them in order according to the sequence of the story; underachievers and educable mentally retarded children have been shown to improve their accuracy in answering literal questions based on this strategy (Carnine, Prill, & Armstrong, in Lloyd *et al.*, 1982). Bommarito and Meichenbaum (cited in Meichenbaum & Asarnow, 1979) tested a multiple-components strategy for improving the comprehension of junior high school students with poor reading comprehension. They were taught a set of comprehension strategies (e.g., picking out salient themes, character motives, etc.) and the use of self-statements to cope with frustration. Relative to a no-treatment control group and practice-placebo controls, the experimental group demonstrated significantly better reading comprehension at posttest and one-month follow-up. These results suggest that cognitive-behavioral strategies may be effective in increasing reading comprehension skills, but replication and long-term follow-up evaluations are needed.

Application of cognitive-behavioral strategies to writing tasks has been more limited. Robin, Armel, and O'Leary (1975) worked with kindergarten children with writing deficiencies using either a self-instruction strategy, direct instruction, or a no-treatment control. Results were disappointing in terms of poor generalization to the writing of untrained letters and no demonstrable relationship between self-instructional behavior and letter-writing accuracy. Graham's (1983) application of a similar cognitive-behavioral technique with learning disabled children was equally disappointing in terms of transfer to the classroom. These results, though not conclusive, suggest that handwriting may not be an appropriate area for interventions of this type. Considering the multitude of factors mediating handwriting skills (e.g., visual perceptual skills, motor ability, visual-motor integration), it is not surprising that poor handwriting is not remediable by self-instruction alone. However, in those cases where impulsivity and poor attention can be shown to play a role in the deficiency, self-instructional techniques would be worth testing further.

Interventions in the area of math functioning have tended to focus more on affective variables than have studies in other academic areas. The work of Genshaft (Genshaft, 1982; Genshaft & Hirt, 1980) with young women suffering from math anxiety exemplifies this approach. Genshaft and Hirt (1980) compared tutoring, tutoring plus self-instruction, and a no-treatment control condition in treating 36 seventh-grade girls whose math achievement was below grade level and reading achievement was above grade level. The self-instructional intervention included self-monitoring of attention, learning to make positive self-statements, and reduction of arousal. Whereas all three groups made improvements on the Stanford Diagnostic Math Test, the self-instruction group showed greater gains on the computations subtest and made significant gains in terms of improving their attitudes toward math. Other studies have been similarly successful in alleviating academic anxiety through cognitive-behavioral techniques, including work in the areas of speech anxiety (Craddock *et al.*, 1978) and test anxiety

(Cooley & Spiegler, 1980), but evaluations of outcome in these studies were limited to analog situations and it is unclear whether these treatment effects would transfer to classroom situations (Lahey & Strauss, 1982). If one were to feel comfortable extrapolating from the work of Kendrick and colleagues (Kendrick, Craig, Lawson, & Davidson, 1982), where a cognitive-behavioral program was successful in reducing performance anxiety for pianists, then similar comprehensive interventions may indeed produce similar changes in other performance arenas.

Taken together, these studies suggest that cognitive-behavioral approaches hold promise in terms of their ability to improve students' approaches to academic tasks, but it is far too early to conclude that these approaches are uniformly effective. As Wong (1985) points out, there are many unresolved issues with respect to generalization of skills. Also, a cost-benefit analysis of using these techniques in the schools should be undertaken once there is more evidence to support their clinical effectiveness. The fact that some learning disabled children have been shown to have fewer metacognitive strategies for learning and recall of information (Hallahan & Sapona, 1983) suggests that cognitive interventions of this type may be particularly beneficial to this population and research in this area should be pursued. However, researchers and educators should be wary of unrealistic expectations and overzealous misapplication of cognitive-behavioral techniques to all types of learning disabilities, given the multiplicity of etiological factors underlying these disorders. For example, handwriting difficulties, especially in the young child, may be based on neurodevelopmental factors that are not accessible to cognitive-behavioral interventions, and attempts to apply these techniques with such children are likely to result in poor generalization (e.g., Graham, 1983; Robin *et al.*, 1975). Prudent researchers will select learning disabled subjects only after complete psychological evaluations have shown the problem to be one with which cognitive-behavioral interventions focusing on task approach behaviors might be beneficial.

Social Interventions

Overcoming Social Withdrawal

The recent burgeoning of intervention studies focusing on childhood social isolation may be traced to the literature that attests to the negative long-term consequences of social maladjustment in childhood (Van Hasselt, Hersen, Whitehill, & Bellack, 1979). Social isolation has been shown to predict a greater likelihood of dropping out of school (Ullmann, 1957), bad-conduct military discharges (Roff, 1961), juvenile delinquency (Roff, Sells, & Golden, 1972), and psychiatric disturbance in adulthood (Cowen, Pederson, Babigian, Izzo, & Trost, 1973). One reason for the predictive power of social acceptance with regard to later adjustment is the fact that peer relationships provide context and stimuli for the child's accomplishment of many cognitive, social, and moral developmental tasks (Hartup, 1970, 1983); without peer relationships, the socially isolated child may be delayed in important areas of functioning. Prevalence data have suggested that between 6% and 12% of elementary school children report having no friends in their classrooms (Gronlund, 1959; Hymel & Asher 1977). Thus training in social skills becomes an important intervention for the alleviation of a childhood problem of some magnitude as well as a potential technique for prevention of problems in adulthood.

One of the earliest applications of cognitive-behavioral techniques to the problem of social isolation involved an investigation of the self-guiding role of private speech in modeling interventions for withdrawn preschool children (Jakibchuk & Smeriglio, 1976). These researchers compared the effects of modeling films accompanied by third-person narrations with films accompanied by first-person narrations; both narrations were spoken by a child. The results indicated that the first-person narration had superior effects at both posttreatment and 3-week follow-up. Both modeling groups improved significantly relative to controls on three measures of peer interaction, but interaction levels for the third-person narration group returned to baseline at follow-up. These results suggested that incorporating an element of verbal self-instruction might improve maintenance of treatment effects beyond that which had been achieved by modeling alone.

The majority of social skills training studies have combined modeling and reinforcement strategies with techniques grouped under the rubric of coaching, which includes such interventions as instruction by an adult, rehearsal (role play with peers or adults), and feedback regarding one's performance. Coaching techniques have been more readily adaptable than modeling to the teaching of more complex, verbally mediated social skills (Combs & Slaby, 1977), but the development of specifically cognitive-behavioral approaches to social skills coaching has been limited. In an early coaching study that utilized a small number of subjects ($N = 4$), Gottman, Gonso, and Schuler (1976) developed a treatment for children low in peer-rated social acceptance that included some cognitive-behavioral strategies. Subjects learned to improve referential communication skills by playing a word game, practiced giving more positive social reinforcement through role plays, and learned to initiate interaction by watching a modeling tape that included first-person narration and coping self-statements of the type described by Meichenbaum and Goodman (1971). Children in the treatment group showed improved social acceptance at posttreatment and those in the attention control group did not. Another example of a cognitive-behavioral coaching strategy is Ladd's (1981) use of self-evaluation as a component of his coaching intervention with third grade children low in peer social acceptance. He has suggested that the ability of his coaching subjects to maintain gains in sociometric status and social skills over a 4-week follow-up interval was due to the inclusion of a self-evaluation component (Ladd, 1981). This was employed after sessions in which children practiced target skills with a peer during a structured game observed by the therapist. The therapist then met with each child individually to administer feedback and to ask the child to describe the consequences of each instance in which the target skill was used during the game. If the consequences had been negative, the child was then asked to suggest alternative strategies. Children were also asked to evaluate their own performance in terms of target skills they did not use and to suggest ways to incorporate them in the future. Thus children received guided practice in evaluating their own behavior and its consequences, and in generating alternative strategies when needed.

In a study focusing on shy children, Harris and Brown (1982) compared a cognitive-behavioral treatment to an informed teacher intervention that involved giving teachers the names of students high in self-reported shyness and suggesting techniques for reducing shyness in the classroom. The cognitive-behavioral group was taught to recognize negative self-statements in social or public speaking situations and to replace them with coping self-statements; this group also underwent muscle relaxation training and systematic desensitization. Significant decreases in self-reported social and public speaking anxiety were found in the cognitive-behavioral group, whereas the informed teacher and control groups did not show this change. Although there was no follow-up assessment and change was demonstrated only on a self-report measure, this study is noteworthy in terms of its attempt to alter the negative cognitions of shy children. Given the inclusion of such potent interventions as muscle relaxation and systematic desensitization in the cognitive-behavioral treatment, it is difficult to know the relative contribution of the cognitive component, but this type of intervention appears worthy of further investigation.

Despite the promising results achieved by the social skills training studies that have incorporated cognitive-behavioral strategies, there have been few attempts to develop systematically cognitive-behavioral treatments for social isolation. Ladd and Mize (1983) proposed a cognitive-social learning model of social skills training that highlights the importance of such variables as skill knowledge, knowledge of appropriate social goals, understanding of appropriate contexts in which skills can be applied, the ability to self-evaluate and adjust skill performance, attributions regarding social failure, and feelings of self-efficacy. All of these variables are accessible to cognitive-behavioral interventions and should be carefully considered in future efforts to remediate social withdrawal. Attention to these cognitive variables may improve the ability of traditional social skills interventions to change sociometric status and to effect long-term behavioral improvement.

Reducing Impulsivity

Children are not known for their ability to delay or their willingness to consider alternatives before taking action. Indeed, some degree of childhood spontaneity is desired. However, when rapid action leads to social difficulties, or when children do poorly, not because of a lack of ability but due to a failure to take their time, then impulsivity requires the attention of an educator or mental health professional.

Cognitive and behavioral impulsivity involve acting without thinking and remediating impulsivity must involve thought in the action sequence. Impulsive children can be taught, via cognitive-behavioral therapy, to inhibit fast and inaccurate actions, entertain various possible courses of action, and undertake the selected plan of action.

The details of the work on the reduction of cognitive impulsivity have been reviewed in detail elsewhere (Kendall & Braswell, 1985; see also Meador & Ollendick, 1984). Though not without its limitations and need for further development, this work and interventions based on it have been found to be effective in reducing unwanted impulsiveness. Interventions with a combination of self-instructional training, careful modeling, affective education, and behavioral contingencies and role plays are the most efficacious, whereas programs lacking one or several of these features have had more limited outcomes (cf. Abikoff & Gittelman, 1985: Camp, Blom, Hebert, & van Doorninck, 1977; Kendall & Braswell, 1982b). For instance, the added effectiveness of cognitive-behavioral training over behavioral training alone (Kendall & Braswell, 1982b) supports the need for the multifaceted intervention. In the Kendall and Braswell study, teacher-referred non-self-controlled (impulsive) children were provided 12 hours of treatment (cognitive-behavioral; behavioral; attention control). The cognitive-behavioral program improved teachers' blind ratings of self-control, and cognitive-behavioral and behavioral treatments improved teachers blind ratings of hyperactivity. Although several other measures showed changes for all groups and parents' ratings did not evidence treatment gains, the cognitive-behavioral program increased children's self-concept and was associated with reduction in off-task verbal and off-task physical behaviors in the classroom.

Other valuable conclusions can be drawn from the literature. For instance, the degree of the child's involvement in the treatment program shows a strong relationship to outcome (Braswell, Kendall, Braith, Carey & Vye, 1985). Added support for this position is evident in the work of Meyers and Cohen (1985) and their colleagues who have achieved desired gains from an intervention that provides the child-client with guided discovery. Getting the children to be involved seems to be a prerequisite to successful treatment.

Attributional factors contribute to outcome as well. Bugental and collegues (Bugental, Whalen, & Henker, 1977; Bugental, Collins, Collins, & Chaney, 1978) reported that children with a strong sense of personal control (and who were not receiving medication treatment) benefited more from self-control intervention than a reinforcement program.

Braswell, Koehler, and Kendall (1985) found that increasing levels of positive change on teacher ratings of classroom behavior were associated with attributions to personal effort. Accordingly, future work should address involvement and the child's perception of the fact that effort can produce the desired payoff.

Modifying Aggressive Behavior

Aggressive behavior in school children is both disruptive to the educational environment and likely to earn the aggressive child the censure of both peers and adults; moreover, childhood aggressive behavior has been shown to predict a greater likelihood of academic failure and psychopathology in adulthood (Kennedy, 1982; Wilson, 1984). Although contingency management interventions have been fairly successful thus far in terms of reducing classroom aggressive behavior, the ability of these programs to produce generalized, sustained behavior change has been questioned (Kennedy, 1982). The failure of contingency management programs to produce lasting change in aggressive children has been hypothesized by some to be the result of their failure to remedy skill deficits and teach alternative behaviors to the aggressive child, and indeed there is some evidence to suggest that aggressive children are deficient in verbal mediational skills (e.g., Camp, 1977), social skills, and interpersonal-problem-solving skills, such as perspective taking (Kennedy, 1982; Spivack, Platt, & Shure, 1976). Thus a series of cognitive-behavioral interventions aimed at remediating presumed problem-solving deficits in aggressive children have been developed; they include such approaches as stress inoculation, verbal self-instruction, rational-emotive therapy, affective imagery, social problem solving, and several combined approaches.

Verbal self-instruction techniques developed by Meichenbaum (Meichenbaum & Goodman, 1971; see also Kendall, 1977) for the treatment of impulsivity have been extended to children identified on the basis of their aggressive behavior. The majority of these investigations have combined verbal self-instruction with other techniques (see discussion of combined approaches below).

Another approach that incorporates some of the elements of verbal self-instruction is the stress inoculation paradigm. This approach is based on work with anxious adults (Meichenbaum, 1977) and adults who have difficulty controlling anger (Novaco, 1975) and was applied to impulsive, angry children by Goodwin and Mahoney (1975). This intervention involves teaching children to cope with situations in which they might feel threatened and therefore behave aggressively (e.g., taunting by peers) by teaching them to make coping self-statements in response to perceived threats. Goodwin and Mahoney (1975) used this technique with three boys judged to be aggressive at school, teaching them to use coping self-statements through a modeling tape and providing practice in using the technique during a series of taunting exercises in which they stood inside a circle of children who attempted to provoke them verbally. The boys' coping behavior improved across trials and their observed disruptive behavior in the classroom decreased, but the lack of a control group limits conclusions that can be drawn from this study. This treatment was tested in a better controlled study with 41 children ages 7 to 12 who were selected on the basis of their observed aggressive behavior at a day camp that was affiliated with a residential treatment center (Kettlewell & Kausch, 1983). The treatment consisted of 4 weeks of group and individual training in using coping self-statements and verbal self-instruction, with opportunities to practice alternative responses through role plays and taunting exercises similar to those used by Goodwin and Mahoney (1975). Treated subjects improved relative to controls on measures of interpersonal problem solving and frequency of being disciplined for aggression, but observed aggression and peer-rated aggression showed no change. Thus, based on the limited studies to date, it appears that stress inoculation may require more extended application and/or additional strategies to be a truly potent means of altering aggressive behavior in children.

Another treatment for aggression that bears some similarity to verbal self-instruction is Block's (1978) adaptation of rational-emotive therapy (Ellis, 1977). When applied to underachieving, aggressive high school students, modeling of rational-emotive self-statements and role plays of conflict situations resulted in improved academic achievement and decreased aggression, whereas no-treatment and attention control groups showed no such gains. These treatment-related changes persisted over the one-semester follow-up interval as well. This intervention seems to differ from verbal self-instruction and stress inoculation techniques in that it focuses on the aggressive child's cognitive attributions and appraisals regarding interpersonal situations and substitutes a set of rational self-statements for the presumed misperceptions of the child, whereas the former techniques emphasize maintaining self-control once provoked. The apparent potency of Block's (1978) intervention suggests that it might be combined with self-control techniques to produce a particularly effective treatment. However, Block's treatment has not been used with preadolescents and it is not clear whether it would be as effective with this age group, given the cognitive developmental differences and the formal operational demands of some of Ellis's techniques.

The affective imagery training described by Garrison and Stolberg (1983) is another intervention that is based on the idea that aggressive children tend to make misattributions in emotionally arousing situations (see Dodge, 1985). These authors reviewed some evidence which suggests that aggressive boys tend to misattribute anger to any state of emotional arousal, and they proposed to teach these children to make better emotional differentiations by attending to both physiological and cognitive cues. Thirty children in grades 3 to 5 were selected on the basis of high teacher ratings on the aggression scale of Achenbach's Child Behavior Checklist (Achenbach & Edelbrock, 1981) and randomly assigned to one of three treatment groups: affective imagery training, attention control, or no-treatment control. The affective imagery group received three sessions of training that included imagining emotionally arousing experiences they had experienced, noting physiological responses, and labeling the associated affect. Situations included fear, anger, happiness, and sadness. Subjects who received affective imagery training showed a significant decrease in observed aggressive behavior in the classroom relative to controls and their responses to an affect questionnaire tended to shift from angry to sad; these effects were maintained at 2-week follow-up.

Social-problem-solving training focuses on perspective-taking and alternative thinking and has also been demonstrated to be of some benefit with aggressive children. A group of 8-year-old boys who were shown film strips of interpersonal conflicts and allowed to role play and evaluate a variety of alternative solutions showed a decrease in aggressive behavior relative to controls of laboratory tasks, but behavior in a naturalistic context was not observed (Pitkanen, 1974). Chandler (1973) trained early adolescent delinquent boys in perspective-taking skills by having them rotate through all of the roles in skits they wrote concerning adolescent social situations. The treated group showed improved role-taking skills and significantly fewer delinquency contacts during an 18-month follow-up period (Chandler, Greenspan, & Barenboim, 1974).

Given the suggested (but often short-lived) efficacy of these cognitive-behavioral techniques for modifying aggression, it is not surprising that researchers have begun to combine these interventions in attempts to strengthen maintenance and generalization of outcomes. Robin, Schneider, and Dolnick (1977) combined muscle relaxation and problem-solving strategies (alternative thinking and evaluation of consequences) in developing an intervention called the Turtle Technique. Children were coached in self-control of aggression by teaching them to imitate a turtle and temporarily withdraw into a shell when threatened, according to a verbal cue given by a peer or teacher. When this technique was applied to two classrooms of emotionally disturbed, aggressive children, it resulted in significantly decreased observed aggressive behavior in the classroom. However, aggressive behavior had begun to decrease before the treatment began, so it is difficult to determine the cause of change (Meyers & Cohen, 1984). A similar treatment package called the Think Aloud program (Camp *et al.*, 1977) includes elements of Spivack and Shure's (Spivack *et al.*, 1976) problem solving training as well as self-instructional training. Children learned a set of four questions that were cues for steps in problem solving. Training in this technique with aggressive boys by regular classroom teachers resulted in improvements on the Matching Familiar Figures Test and increased prosocial behavior, but there was no observable improvement in problem-solving skills and no decrease in teacher-rated aggressive behavior. Thus, attempts to combine cognitive techniques into package treatments for younger aggressive children have met with moderate success.

Combined treatments have been somewhat more effective with adolescents. In a single case study of a 16-year-old boy who had multiple aggressive outbursts at school and at home, McCullough and colleagues (McCullough, Huntsinger, & Nay, 1977) trained the subject to use instructive self-talk to inhibit subvocal cursing and muscle relaxation and withdrawal in order to cope with situations in which he became angry. This treatment was quite successful in reducing the frequency of his aggressive behavior. Snyder and White (1979) worked with five teenage delinquents who had been nonresponsive to a token economy. Using a variety of techniques including imaginal rehearsal, role playing, and modeling, they taught them to reevaluate conflict situations and to use coping self-statements in response to frustration. This intervention resulted in improvements in academic and social behavior and decreased aggression relative to untreated controls, and these gains were maintained up to 6 weeks after treatment.

Recently some effort has been made to compare cognitive-behavioral interventions with other techniques in order to evaluate their relative efficacy, but thus far comparison studies have been restricted to preadolescent populations. Forman (1980) compared a combined treatment that included self-instruction, role taking, and problem-solving techniques, with a response-cost intervention. The results showed that both were more effective than an attention control condition but the cognitive-behavioral treatment was no more effective than response-cost in reducing aggressive behavior assessed by teacher ratings and classroom observations. Another comparison study focused on the relative efficacy of a cognitive-behavioral anger coping intervention, a goal-setting treatment with rewards for reaching self-determined behavioral goals, the combination of anger coping and goal setting, and a no-treatment control (Lochman, Burch, Curry, & Lapron, 1984). Subjects were 76 boys ages 9 to 12 with high teacher-rated aggression. The anger coping intervention involved social-problem-solving and self-instructional techniques for the self-control of anger in conflict situations. Comparisons among the four conditions 4 to 6 weeks after treatment showed that both anger coping groups improved on observation measures of disruptive and aggressive off-task behavior and on parent-rated aggression but not on teacher and peer ratings of aggressive behavior. Subjects in the goal setting group did not make such improvements. The authors concluded that anger coping resulted in generalized positive treatment effects and that the addition of goal setting meant stronger classroom effects.

The final comparison study we reviewed focused on hyperactive, aggressive children in evaluating the relative efficacy of methylphenidate (vs. a placebo) and a self-instructional, social-problem-solving treatment for anger control (Hinshaw, Henker, & Whalen,

1984). Outcome was assessed in terms of observed behavior during a set of provacation exercises in which the subject was verbally taunted by peers; videotapes of the exercises were scored in terms of self-control, intensity, and a variety of verbal and motoric behaviors. The results showed that methylphenidate was effective in reducing the intensity of the subject's behavior but had no effect on self-control. The cognitive-behavioral treatment increased general self-control and the use of coping behaviors relative to a control treatment that focused on increasing empathy. The drug-cognitive treatment combination was no more beneficial than cognitive-behavior therapy alone. This study provides a powerful demonstration of the effectiveness of self-instructional procedures in controlling anger in a stressful laboratory setting, but whether these treatment effects can be generalized to real-world settings remains to be investigated.

Overall it appears that cognitive-behavioral interventions are less effective with preadolescents than with adolescents in modifying aggressive behavior. Studies with aggressive children in elementary school have been generally disappointing in terms of demonstrated maintenance and generalization of treatment gains. This pattern of results points again to the importance of developmental factors in designing interventions. The only exceptions to this trend have been seen in more recent studies where combined treatments like anger coping and goal setting have shown some potential for long-term, generalized change (Lochman *et al.*, 1984); replications and extensions of this work appear to be worth undertaking. If some of these treatment packages prove beneficial to younger aggressive children, it would then be appropriate to undertake systematic components analyses and further comparison studies.

Caveats and Directives

Although there exists sufficient evidence to warrant continued interest, enthusiasm, and research, some of the promise of cognitive-behavioral interventions has been unfulfilled. That is, there remains the need to demonstrate better maintenance and generalization of treatment effects. The possibility that such effects are difficult to attain would require greater intervention intensity and longevity. The possibility that truly lasting effects take longer to consolidate would require that longer follow-ups be undertaken. To test the potency of these interventions will require longer follow-up intervals and more ecologically valid evidence of change.

Those who are involved in or will become active in the study of cognitive-behavioral procedures for change should pay added attention to the need for proper assessments (Kendall & Korgeski, 1979; Kendall, Pellegrini, & Urbain, 1981). If we are working to change cognitions, then we should be measuring these factors to determine if there are indeed changes. Correspondingly, with added attention being paid to the affect that is involved in treatment there is a growing need for assessments of affect. It is through these added assessments (e.g., measurements of cognition and affect along with more standard behavioral measures) that we may come to learn the mechanism/process of change and the best methods for further enhancing the existing change procedures.

Developmental factors have, quite simply, been ignored for too long. As was evident in our discussion, strategies for interventions with children require modifications to best fit the level of the child: developmental factors contribute directly to this individualization. Children below a certain age or not yet at a certain developmental stage may be unprepared for and incapable of using certain strategies. For instance, it has been argued on several occasions (Copeland, 1983; Kendall, 1977; Kendall & Braswell, 1985) that self-instructional procedures are best matched to children whose behavior evidences an absence of forethought and whose cognitive capacities allow for such reflective self-direction. Similarly for the social skills training efforts, different target behaviors are dictated by the developmental level of the target child.

Methodologically, there have been improvements in the general approach to the evaluation of interventions. However, we must restate the necessity of proper control conditions in the examination of treatment efficacy and we must buttress this with the call for *normative comparisons*. The outcomes of programs may seem quite positive only to have their impact wane as the lack of proper controls undermines the ability of the researcher to make conclusive recommendations. Normative comparisons (e.g., Kendall & Grove, in press; Kendall & Norton-Ford, 1982) provide an opportunity for examination of the clinical as well as statistical changes that may take place. By using the data on nondisturbed cases, the methodology of normative comparisons provides an opportunity to compare the treated cases to the rate (intensity; extremes) of the target behaviors in nonproblem cases. When treated cases (those identified as deviant from norms) return to within nondeviant limits after treatment then there is added evidence for the clinical significance of the desirable gains.

Rapid endorsement, like rapid disillusionment, has potential drawbacks. Cognitive-behavioral procedures have enjoyed and continue to enjoy a warm reaction from the majority of practitioners. However, do the data document the merits of such a warm welcome? In some other instances the procedures are rapidly tried, without proper care in implementation and without cautious matching of the style of the intervention to the type of disorder being treated, and there is a quick dismissal . . . "I tried it once and it didn't work." We recommend that the bandwagon tendency be avoided and that practitioners either refrain from applying cognitive-behavioral this or that to this or that problem or proceed with proper caution. Let us learn more about the cognitive deficits and distortions associated with the behavioral dysfunctions and then proceed toward reasoned applications to educational problems.

ACKNOWLEDGMENT

The authors wish to thank Jane Burrell for her secretarial assistance in the preparation of this manuscript.

References

Abikoff, H., & Gittelman, R. (1985). Hyperactive children treated with stimulants: Is cognitive training a useful adjunct? *Archives of General Psychiatry, 42,* 953–961.

Achenbach, T. M., & Edelbrock, C. S. (1981). Behavioral problems and competencies reported by parents of normal and disturbed children aged 4 through 16. *Monographs of the Society for Research in Child Development,* Serial No. 188.

Bem, S. L. (1967). Verbal self-control: The establishment of effective self-instruction. *Journal of Experimental Psychology, 74,* 485–491.

Block, J. (1978). Effects of a rational-emotive mental health program on poorly achieving high school students. *Journal of Counseling Psychology, 25,* 61–65.

Braswell, L., Kendall, P. C., Braith, J., Carey, M. P., & Vye, C. S. (1985). "Involvement" in cognitive-behavioral therapy with children: Process and its relationship to outcome. *Cognitive Therapy and Research, 9,* 611–630.

Braswell, L., Koehler, C., & Kendall, P. C. (1985). Attributions and outcomes in child psychotherapy. *Journal of Social and Clinical Psychology, 3,* 458–465.

Brown, A. L., Bransford, J. D., Ferrara, R. A., & Campione, J. C. (1983). Learning, remembering, and understanding. In J. Flavell E. M. Markman (Eds.), *Carmichael's manual of child psychology* (Vol. 1). New York: Wiley.

Bugental, D. B., Whalen, C. K., & Henker, B. (1977). Causal attributions of hyperactive children and motivational assumptions of two behavior-change approaches: Evidence for an interactionist position. *Child Development, 48,* 874–884.

Bugental, D. B., Collins, S., Collins, L., & Chaney, L. A. (1978). Attributional and behavioral changes following two behavior management interventions with hyperactive boys: A follow-up study. *Child Development, 49,* 247–250.

Camp, B. (1977). Verbal mediation in young aggressive boys. *Journal of Abnormal Psychology, 86,* 145–153.

Camp, B., Blom, G., Hebert, F., & van Doorninck, W. (1977). "Think aloud": A program for developing self-control in young aggressive boys. *Journal of Abnormal Child Psychology, 5,* 157–169.

Chandler, M. (1973). Egocentrism and antisocial behavior: The assessment and training of social perspective-taking skills. *Child Development, 9,* 326–443.

Chandler, M., Greenspan. S. & Barenboim, C. (1974). Assessment and training of role-taking and referential communication skills in institutionalized emotionally disturbed children. *Developmental Psychology, 10*, 546–553.

Combs, M. L., & Slaby, D. A. (1977). Social skills training with children. In B. Lahey & A. Kazdin (Eds.), *Advances in clinical child psychology* (Vol. 1, pp. 161–203). New York: Plenum Press.

Conger, J. C., & Keane, S. P. (1981). Social skills intervention in the treatment of isolated or withdrawn children. *Psychological Bulletin, 90*, 478–495.

Cooley, E. J., & Spiegler, M. D. (1980). Cognitive versus emotional coping responses as alternatives to test anxiety. *Cognitive Therapy and Research, 4*, 159–166.

Copeland, A. P. (1983). Children's talking to themselves: Its developmental significance, function, and therapeutic promise. In P. C. Kendall (Ed.), *Advances in cognitive-behavioral research and therapy* (Vol. 2, pp. 242–279). New York: Academic Press.

Cowen, E. L., Pederson. A., Babigian, H., Izzo, L. D., & Trost, M. A. (1973). Long-term follow-up of early detected vulnerable children. *Journal of Consulting and Clinical Psychology, 41*, 438–446.

Cradock, C., Cotler, S. & Jason, L. A. (1978). Primary prevention: Immunization of children for test anxiety. *Cognitive Therapy and Research, 2*, 389–396.

Cummings, L. (1984). *Social skills training for withdrawn children: Toward a developmental perspective*. Unpublished manuscript, University of Minnesota.

Denney, D. R. (1975). The effects of exemplary and cognitive models and self-rehearsal on children's interrogative strategies. *Journal of Experimental Child Psychology, 19*, 476–488.

Dodge, K. (1985). Attributional bias in aggressive children. In P. C. Kendall (Ed.), *Advances in cognitive-behavioral research and therapy* (Vol. 4). New York: Academic Press.

Ellis, A. (1971). *Growth through reason*. Palo Alto, CA: Science and Behavior Books.

Ellis, A. (1977). *How to live with and without anger*. New York: Reader's Digest Press.

Forman, S. (1980). A comparison of cognitive training and response cost procedures in modifying aggressive behavior of elementary school children. *Behavior Therapy, 11*, 594–600.

Furman, W. (1980). Promoting social development: Developmental implications for treatment. In B. B. Lahey & A. E. Kazdin (Eds.), *Advances in clinical child psychology*, (Vol. 3). New York: Plenum Press.

Garrison, S. R., & Stolberg, A. L. (1983). Modification of anger in children by affective imagery training. *Journal of Abnormal Child Psychology, 11*, 115–129.

Genshaft, J. L. (1982). The use of cognitive behavior therapy for reducing math anxiety. *School Psychology Review, 11*, 31–34.

Genshaft, J. L., & Hirt, M. (1980). The effectiveness of self-instructional training to enhance math achievement in women. *Cognitive Therapy and Research, 4*, 91–97.

Goodwin, S., & Mahoney, M. J. (1975). Modification of aggression through modeling: An experimental probe. *Journal of Behavior Therapy and Experimental Psychiatry, 6*, 200–202.

Gottman, J., Gonso, J., & Schuler, P. (1976). Teaching social skills to isolated children. *Child Development, 47*, 179–197.

Graham, S. (1983). The effect of self-instructional procedures on LD students' handwriting performance. *Learning Disability Quarterly, 6*, 231–234.

Gresham, F. M., & Lemanek, K. L. (1983). Social skills: A review of cognitive-behavioral training procedures with children. *Journal of Applied Developmental Psychology, 4*, 239–261.

Gronlund, N. E. (1959). *Sociometry in the classroom*. New York: Harper.

Hagen, O. A. (1973). *Changing world, changing teachers*. Pacific Palisades, CA: Goodyear.

Hallahan, D. P., & Sapona, R. (1983). Self-monitoring of attention with learning disabled children: Past research and current issues. *Journal of Learning Disabilities, 16*, 616–620.

Harris, K. B., & Brown, R. D. (1982). Cognitive behavior modification and informed teacher treatments for shy children. *Journal of Experimental Education, 50*, 137–143.

Hartup, W. W. (1970). Peer interaction and social organization. In P. H. Mussen (Ed.), *Carmichael's manual of child psychology* (Vol. 2, pp. 361–456). New York: Wiley.

Hartup, W. W. (1983). The peer system.. In P. H. Mussen & E. M. Hetherington (Eds.), *Carmichael's manual of child psychology*, (4th ed., Vol. 4). New York: Wiley.

Hinshaw, S. P., Henker, B., & Whalen, C. K. (1984). Self-control in hyperactive boys in anger-inducing situations: Effects of cognitive-behavioral training and of methylphenidate. *Journal of Abnormal Child Psychology, 12*, 55–77.

Hymel, S., & Asher, S. R. (1977). *Assessment and training of isolated children's social skills*. Paper presented at the biennial meeting of the Society for Research in Child Development, New Orleans (ERIC Document Reproduction Service No. ED 136930).

Ingram, R., & Kendall, P. C. (1986). Cognitive clinical psychology. In R. Ingram (Ed.), *Information processing approaches to clinical psychology* (pp. 3–22). New York: Academic Press.

Jakibchuk, L., & Smeriglio, V. L. (1976). The influence of symbolic modeling on the social behavior of preschool children with low levels of social responsiveness. *Child Development, 47*, 838–841.

Kanfer, F. H., Karoly, P., & Newman, A. (1975). Reduction of children's fear of the dark by competence related and situational threat related verbal cues. *Journal of Consulting and Clinical Psychology, 43*, 251–258.

Kendall, P. C. (1977). On the efficacious use of verbal self-instructional procedures with children. *Cognitive Therapy and Research, 1*, 331–341.

Kendall, P. C. (1984a). Cognitive processes and procedures in behavior therapy. In G. T. Wilson, C. M. Franks, K. D. Brownell, & P. C. Kendall, *Annual review of behavior therapy* (Vol. 9, pp. 132–180). New York: Guilford Press.

Kendall, P. C. (1984b). Social cognition and problem solving: A developmental and child-clinical interface. In B. Gholson & T. Rosenthal (Eds.), *Applications of cognitive developmental theory* (pp. 115–149). New York: Academic Press.

Kendall, P. C. (1985). Toward a cognitive-behavioral model of child psychopathology and a critique of related interventions. *Journal of Abnormal Child Psychology, 13*, 357–372.

Kendall, P. C. (1987). Cognitive processes and procedures in behavior therapy. In G. T. Wilson, C. M. Franks, P. C. Kendall, & J. Foreyt, *Review of behavior therapy* (Vol. 11). New York: Guilford Press.

Kendall, P. C., & Braswell, L. (1982a). On cognitive-behavioral assessment: Model, method, and madness. In C. D. Spielberger & J. N. Butcher (Eds.), *Advances in personality assessment* (Vol. 1, pp. 35–82). Hillsdale, N.J.: Erlbaum.

Kendall, P. C., & Braswell, L. (1982b). Cognitive-behavioral self-control therapy for children. A components analysis. *Journal of Consulting and Clinical Psychology, 50*, 672–689.

Kendall, P. C., & Braswell, L. (1985). *Cognitive-behavioral therapy for impulsive children*. New York: Guilford Press.

Kendall, P. C., & Grove, W. (in press). Normative comparisons in therapy outcome. *Behavioral Assessment*.

Kendall, P. C., & Korgeski, G. P. (1979). Assessment and cognitive-behavioral interventions. *Cognitive Therapy and Research, 3*, 1–21.

Kendall, P. C., & Norton-Ford, J. D. (1982). Therapy outcome research methods. In P. C. Kendall & J. N. Butcher (Eds.), *Handbook of research methods in clinical psychology* (pp. 429–460). New York: Wiley.

Kendall, P. C., Pellegrini, D., & Urbain, E. S. (1981). Assessment methods for cognitive-behavioral interventions with children. In P. C. Kendall & S. D. Hollon (Eds.), *Assessment strategies for cognitive-behavioral interventions* (pp. 227–286). New York: Academic Press.

Kendrick, M. J., Craig, K. D., Lawson, D. M.. & Davidson, P. O. (1982). Cognitive and behavioral therapy for musical performance anxiety. *Journal of Consulting and Clinical Psychology, 50*, 353–362.

Kennedy, R. E. (1982). Cognitive-behavioral approaches to the modification of aggressive behavior in children. *School Psychology Review, 11*, 47–55.

Kettlewell, P. W., & Kausch, D. F. (1983). The generalization of the effects of a cognitive-behavioral treatment program for aggressive children. *Journal of Abnormal Child Psychology, 11*, 101–114.

Ladd, G. W. (1981). Effectiveness of a social learning method for enhancing children's social interaction and peer acceptance. *Child Development, 52*, 171–178.

Ladd, G. W., & Mize, J. (1983). A cognitive-social learning model of social-skill training. *Psychological Review, 90*, 127–157.

Lahey, B. B., & Strauss, C. C. (1982). Some considerations in evaluating the clinical utility of cognitive behavior therapy with children. *School Psychology Review, 11*, 67–74.

Lloyd, J. W., Kosiewicz, M. M., & Hallahan. D. P. (1982). Reading comprehension: Cognitive training contributions. *School Psychology Review, 11*, 35–41.

Lochman, J. E., Burch, P. R., Curry, J. F., & Lampron, L. B. (1984). Treatment and generalization effects of cognitive-behavioral and goal-setting interventions with aggressive boys. *Journal of Consulting and Clinical Psychology, 52*, 915–916.

Luria, A. R. (1961). *The role of speech in the regulation of normal and abnormal behavior*. New York: Liveright.

Mahoney, M. J. (1977). Reflections on the cognitive-learning trend in psychotherapy. *American Psychologist, 32*, 5–13.

McCullough, J. P., Huntsinger, G. M., & Nay, W. R. (1977). Self-control treatment of aggression in a 16-year-old male. *Journal of Consulting and Clinical Psychology, 45*, 322–331.

Meador, A. E., & Ollendick, T. H. (1984). Cognitive-behavior therapy with children: An evaluation of its efficacy and clinical utility. *Child and Family Behavior Therapy, 6*, 25–44.

Meichenbaum, D. (1977). *Cognitive-behavior modification: An integrative approach*. New York: Plenum Press.

Meichenbaum, D., & Asarnow, J. (1979). Cognitive-behavior modification and metacognitive development: Implications for the classroom. In P. C. Kendall & S. D. Hollon (Eds.), *Cognitive-behavioral interventions: Theory, research, and procedures*. New York: Academic Press.

Meichenbaum, D., & Goodman, J. (1971). Training impulsive children to talk to themselves. *Journal of Abnormal Psychology, 77*, 115–126.

Meyers, A. W., & Cohen, R. (1984). Cognitive-behavioral interventions in educational settings. In P. C. Kendall (Ed.), *Advances in cognitive-behavioral research and therapy* (Vol. 3, pp. 131–167). New York: Academic Press.

Miller, D. T., Weinstein, S. M., & Karniol, R. (1978). Effects of age and self verbalization on children's ability to delay gratification. *Developmental Psychology, 14*, 569–570.

Novaco, R. W. (1975). *Anger control: The development and evaluation of an experimental treatment*. Lexington, MA: Lexington Books.

Pitkanen, L. (1974). The effect of simulation exercises on the control of aggressive behavior in children. *Scandinavian Journal of Psychology, 15*, 169–177.

Robin, A., Armel, S., & O'Leary, K. D. (1975). The effects of self-instruction on writing deficiencies. *Behavior Therapy, 6*, 178–187.

Robin, A., Schneider, M., & Dolnick, M. (1977). The turtle technique: An extended case study of self-control in the classroom. In K. D. O'Leary & S. G. O'Leary (Eds.),

Classroom management: The successful use of behavior modification (2nd ed.) Oxford: Pergamon Press.

Roff, M. (1961). Childhood social interactions and young adult bad conduct. *Journal of Abnormal Social Psychology, 63,* 333–337.

Roff, M., Sells, S. B., & Golden, M. M. (1972). *Social adjustment and personality development in children.* Minneapolis, MN: University of Minnesota Press.

Snyder, J., & White, M. (1979). The use of cognitive self-instruction in the treatment of behaviorally disturbed adolescents. *Behavior Therapy, 10,* 227–235.

Spivack, G., Platt, J. J., & Shure, M. B. (1976). *The problem-solving approach to adjustment.* San Francisco: Jossey-Bass.

Stark, K. D., Brookman, C. S., & Frazier, R. (1988). *A comprehensive school-based treatment program for depressed children.* Unpublished manuscript, University of Texas, Austin, TX.

Toner, I. J., & Smith, R. A. (1977). Age and overt verbalization in delay-maintenance behavior in children. *Journal of Experimental Child Psychology, 24,* 123–128.

Ullman, C. A. (1957). Teachers, peers and tests as predictors of adjustment. *Journal of Educational Psychology, 48,* 257–267.

Vygotsky, L. S. (1962). *Thought and language.* New York: Wiley.

Wasserman, T. H. (1983). The effects of cognitive development on the use of cognitive-behavioral techniques with children. *Child and Family Behavior Therapy, 5,* 37–50.

Wilson, R. (1984). A review of self-control treatments for aggressive behavior. *Behavioral Disorders, 9,* 131–140.

Wong, B. Y. L. (1985). Issues in cognitive-behavioral interventions in academic skill areas. *Journal of Abnormal Child Psychology, 13,* 425–442.

Zigler, E., & Trickett, P. K. (1979). The role of national social policy in promoting social competence in children. In M. W. Kent & J. E. Rolf (Eds.), *Primary prevention of psychopathology III: Social competence in children.* Hanover, NH: University Press of New England.

CHAPTER 16

Home-Based Reinforcement Procedures

Mary L. Kelley and Laura B. Carper

Introduction

Over the past 20 years, behavior therapists have become more reliant on the use of parents and teachers to implement interventions with children. The use of adult caretakers as contingency managers has proven to be an efficient and effective method of remediating children's behavior problems.

A key example of this trend is in the area of parent training. The approach provides parents with skills to effect change in their children and to cope with everyday family problems (Berowitz & Graziano, 1972; Mash, Hammerlynck, & Handy, 1976; Moreland, Schwebel, Beck, & Wells, 1982; O'Dell, 1974; Reisinger, Ora, & Frangia, 1976). Typically, parents are taught to reduce their children's misbehavior by giving clear instructions and by providing consistent consequences through their use of such techniques as differential attention, reward procedures, and time out. Parents provided with such training have reduced a variety of their children's behavior problems in the home, including noncompliance (Bernal, Klinnert, & Schultz, 1980; Forehand & King, 1977), verbal and physical aggression (Patterson, Chamberlain, & Reed, 1982; Wahler & Fox, 1980), and stealing (Stumphauzer, 1976).

In the field of education, there has been a trend in the same direction; teachers are being trained to improve children's academic performance and classroom behavior through their use of contingency management techniques. Teachers have remediated children's classroom problems through their systematic use of praise and ignoring (McAllister, Stachowiak, Baer, & Conderman, 1969), time out (Porterfield, Herbert-Jackson, & Risley, 1978), overcorrection (Foxx & Jones, 1978), as well as reward and response cost procedures (Long & Williams, 1973).

Behavioral techniques have been applied successfully to individual children and to entire classrooms of students. As with parents, teachers' use of contingency management techniques has proven effective with a variety of behavior problems. For example, teachers have successfully increased academic behaviors including studying, staying on task, and assignment completion. Classroom conduct

Mary L. Kelley and Laura B. Carper • Department of Psychology, Louisiana State University, Baton Rouge, Louisiana 70803.

problems, including talking out of turn and fighting, also have been reduced through teachers' application of behavioral techniques.

Often, communication between parents and teachers is rather informal and intermittent, usually taking the form of parent–teacher conferences or report cards. In these situations feedback given to parents often is negative, and parents, who lack special training, are unsure how to improve their children's classroom behavior effectively. Recently, however, there has been an increase in the collaboration between teachers and parents in remediating children's academic deficits and classroom conduct problems. With the emergence of Public Law 94-142, teachers have realized a legal and professional obligation to include parents in the education and socialization of their children. In addition, professionals working with children have become more aware of the benefits of effective parent–teacher collaboration (Guidubaldi, 1982). With this new awareness, there has been an attempt to join systematically the home and school in a cooperative effort between teachers and parents. One outcome of this effort has been the creation and utilization of home-based reinforcement programs for modifying classroom behavior. Such programs have provided parents with information about their children's school performance as well as with specific opportunities to assist in improving classroom behavior.

The purpose of this chapter is to present an overview of the relevant literature on home-based contingencies for academic performance. The review includes research dealing with the collaborative effort of parents and teachers toward modifying children's academic or classroom behavior.

Home-Based Reinforcement

Home-based reinforcement represents the combined effort of parents and teachers in modifying children's classroom behavior. The communication between parents and teachers typically takes the form of a school–home note. An example of such a note is presented in Figure 1. The procedure requires teachers to monitor children's performance of selected classroom behaviors and to communicate the information to parents. Parents are then responsible for providing appropriate consequences.

Home-based reinforcement programs have several advantages over classroom interventions. Further, some researchers have sug-

Figure 1. Sample school–home note for use with adolescents and older children.

Name________________ Date________________

Subject________

Was prepared for class	yes no NA	Homework assignment
Used class time well	yes no NA	
Participated in class	yes no NA	
Handed in homework	yes no NA	
Homework grade	F D C B A NA	
Test grade	F D C B A NA	Teacher's initials________

Comments

gested that home-based programs produce benefits in addition to desired behavior change (Budd, Leibowitz, River, Mindell, & Goldfarb, 1981; Fairchild, 1976; Gresham & Lemanek, 1987). The following summarizes the advantages and benefits of home-based contingency systems noted by these authors.

1. Home-based reinforcement programs may serve to establish communication between parents and teachers, and thus promote parent involvement within the school. In addition, because teachers and parents are working together and communicating often, children are less able to play one against the other.

2. Home-based contingency management programs are time and cost efficient in that teachers are responsible for administering only a component of the intervention. Therefore, teachers may be more likely to carry out the program effectively and to veiw the procedure as acceptable.

3. Teachers do not have to alter their teaching style significantly when employing school–home note programs; they simply evaluate students' behavior at regular intervals.

4. Home-based reinforcement programs do not create many of the problems associated with in-class reinforcement. In particular, teachers' concerns over the inequity of giving special rewards to only a few students can be eliminated.

5. Parents often have access to and control over a wider variety of privileges to serve as reinforcers than do teachers. Thus, the procedure is likely to be more effective due to the greater availability of rewards in the home.

6. In most home-based programs, children are provided with substantial increases in parental praise. Parental reinforcement, may not only function to increase appropriate classroom behavior, but may also bolster children's self-esteem.

7. Some researchers have suggested that delayed reinforcement (via a home-based treatment program) may enhance generalization of treatment by teaching children to behave appropriately in the absence of immediate gratification.

Parent–Teacher Communication Procedures

In order to be effective, school–home notes must provide parents with sufficient information about their children's classroom behavior so that appropriate, effective consequences can be delivered at home (Broughton, Barton, & Owen, 1981). Consequently, several key features of the procedure have been consistently included across studies. For example, the target responses included in the school–home note generally have been preselected by the teacher and have not varied from one day to the next. Typically, the teacher is required to evaluate frequently and routinely whether the child has performed the target responses. Specifically, parents have been provided with information about their children's classroom behavior on either a daily or weekly basis. In all of the studies reviewed, parents and children were aware of the purpose of the procedure and the consequences associated with positive and negative evaluations. Finally, although some school–home note programs have included punishing consequences for poor evaluations, opportunities for reinforcement always have been included and emphasized. Thus, in many ways the school–home note procedure is similar to a token economy system in that children contingently earn or lose tokens that represent rewards to be received at a later point in time (Broughton *et al.*, 1981).

In spite of these commonalities, a great deal of variability exists in the content of and procedures for using the school–home note. Perhaps the most notable variation is the degree of specificity of the target responses. The level of detail provided in the note has ranged from very specific to very global. For example, Karraker (1972) provided parents of second grade children with a daily card that indicated only whether or not the child had exhibited satisfactory performance in mathematics. A study conducted by Bailey, Wolf, and Phillips (1970) also provided parents with relatively global evaluations. The subjects of this study were five adolescent males, who resided in a group home for predelinquent youths. All had histories of poor academic performance. The teacher provided daily feedback to the boys' caretakers as to whether or not each boy had studied and complied with classroom rules. The procedure resulted in substantial improvements in the students' classroom behavior when they were provided with privileges for satisfactory reports.

Several studies that employed successful school–home note programs provided parents with very detailed descriptions of their children's classroom behavior. Lahey, Gendrich, Gendrich, Schnelle, & McNees (1977), for example, provided parents of kindergarten children with information about their children's naptime behavior, work completion, instruction following, and peer interactions. Very specific teacher evaluations also were provided to parents of five seventh graders who exhibited a variety of classroom behavior problems (Schumaker, Hovell, & Sherman, 1977). In the Schumaker *et al.* study, teachers evaluated the students' performance of 13 academic and social classroom behaviors. For example, the teacher recorded whether or not the student was prepared for class, paid attention during class, completed classwork, and turned in homework. Students were responsible for obtaining daily ratings from all of their instructors. The procedure resulted in marked improvement in the students' classroom behavior and moderate improvement in their grades.

The degree to which teachers have evaluated children's classroom behavior using specific, objective criteria also has varied considerably. For example, although Karraker (1972) provided parents with only global descriptions of their children's behavior, the performance criteria upon which the teachers evaluated the children were very specific; a satisfactory evaluation was earned when the child increased or maintained either his class rank in mathematics or the percentage of problems he completed correctly. Similarly, Allyon, Garber, & Pisor (1975) provided parents with nonspecific letters on days their children exhibited low levels of disruptive behavior. However, the criteria for earning a "Brag Sheet" were operationally defined as no more than two disruptions within a 15-minute block of time. In contrast, although Schumaker *et al.* (1977) required teachers to evaluate students' performance of an array of responses, the criteria for determining whether or not the behaviors occurred were not specified precisely.

Several studies that employed school–home notes operationalized the evaluation criteria and provided parents with very specific information (Blechman, Kotanchik, & Taylor, 1981; Budd *et al.*, 1981; Lahey *et al.*, 1977). For example, Blechman, Kotanchik, and Taylor (1981), increased the academic performance in students who performed inconsistently in either mathematics or reading by providing parents with objective feedback. Specifically, one week prior to the initiation of the note procedure, each student and their parent met individually with the teacher to review the student's baseline performance and to negotiate a contract. The contract specified the level of assignment accuracy required to earn rewards. On days when a child achieved his or her goal, the teacher recorded the percentage of problems completed correctly by the child. The procedure resulted in increased accuracy and consistency in the students' academic performance. Thus, the school–home note procedure employed by Blechman, Kotanchik, and Taylor (1981) not only included objective evaluation criteria and detailed feedback, but assisted parents in delineating the specific criteria for earning rewards.

The degree to which teachers have evaluated children according to operationally defined criteria or provided parents with detailed feedback has not appeared to be systematically related to treatment outcome. School–home notes typically have been effective irrespective of the specificity of the performance criteria or feedback. However, it is very likely that some level of objectivity and detail are necessary for the school–home procedure to be effective. It also is quite possible that treatment outcome would be differentially effected by the level of detail contained in the note. Finally, as other authors have suggested (Broughton *et al.*, 1981), it is possible that the importance of specificity and objectivity in teacher ratings and communication to parents may be related to the subject's characteristics such as age or type of behavior problem and to the parent's educational level or parenting skills. Clearly, research is needed that systematically manipulates the objectivity of performance criteria and the quality of information contained in the school–home note.

The comprehensiveness of home based contingency systems has varied considerably. Numerous studies were designed to alter only one behavior during a specific class period. For example, work accuracy in one academic subject has frequently been the only dependent measure (Karraker, 1972; Blechman, Kotanchik, & Taylor, 1981; Blechman, Taylor, & Schrader, 1981). Several studies, however, evaluated children's behavior throughout the entire school day (e.g., Budd *et al.*, 1981; Schumaker *et al.*, 1977). Budd *et al.* (1981), for example, employed a comprehensive school–home note procedure with preschool- and kindergarten-aged children. The subjects came from low socioeconomic backgrounds and attended a remedial summer school program for children who had displayed high levels of disruptiveness in previous school settings. The students' performance of several inappropriate behaviors were monitored throughout the school day. The school day was divided into 12 intervals during each of which the children could earn a sticker if they had not engaged in a target response. Thus, although the intervention encompassed behavior performed throughout the day, the children were given many opportunities to achieve small goals.

Although a few studies attempted to modify children's behavior throughout an entire school day, the majority of school–home note interventions were designed to change the frequency of a single behavior during a portion of the day. In some instances it appeared that only a single behavior deficit or excess existed. However, children frequently display more pervasive behavior problems that are not limited in occurrence to a specific academic period or subject. Consequently, logistical and methodological issues involved in the comprehensive use of a school–home note procedure have not been adequately addressed. For example, broadening the comprehensiveness of the school–home note to include children's behavior throughout the day might require the selection of target behaviors that are easily and accurately monitored by teachers.

Although teachers typically have evaluated students on a daily basis, several studies reported that notes were sent home only when the child behaved satisfactorily. Ayllon, Garber, and Pisor (1975), for example, provided parents with a good behavior letter on days when the child engaged in low levels of disruptiveness. Parents were not given feedback when the children behaved unsatisfactorily. However, parents were informed that the absence of a note indicated that their child was a severe problem and were told to reprimand accordingly. Other studies in which feedback was given to parents only when children achieved criterion included Lahey *et al.* (1979), who rewarded children with Brag Sheets, and Blechman, Kotanchik, and Taylor (1981) and Blechman, Taylor, & Schrader (1981), who provided congratulatory letters.

Saudargaus, Madsen, & Scott (1977) examined the effects of fixed versus variable time feedback using a school–home note. In the fixed-time condition, all students received a weekly report card on Friday, which contained information regarding the student's work performance for the week. In the variable-time conditions, a randomly selected subset of students received daily report cards with the same information. Parents were not told to provide home contingencies. This study found that the variable-time condition produced much higher rates of assignment completion than the fixed-time condition. The teachers in the study also preferred the variable-time reporting system.

Rationales for providing daily reports versus feedback only when children behave satisfactorily typically have not been provided. It is possible that the use of positive feedback only might diminish the likelihood that children will be severely punished for poor performance (Lahey *et al.*, 1979). The procedure also may result in greater teacher satisfaction as the teacher potentially would complete fewer notes. However, providing parents with positive evaluations only is, in a sense, partial communication. Such a system might prevent parents from fully monitoring, and thus consistently consequating, their children's behavior. Whether the two forms of feedback are differentially effective or socially valid can only be speculated as empirical evaluations addressing the issue have not been conducted.

Subjects and Target Behaviors

Subjects

School–home notes have been used to improve the academic performance and classroom conduct of kindergarteners (e.g., Budd *et al.*, 1981; Lahey *et al.*, 1977), elementary-aged children (e.g., Imber, Imber, & Rothstein, 1979; Saudergas *et al.*, 1977; Todd, Scott, Buston, & Alexander, 1976) and junior high and high school students (e.g., Alexander, Corbett, & Smigel, 1976; Heaton, Safer, Allen, Spinnato, & Prumo, 1976; Schumaker *et al.*, 1977). However, compared to the number of studies conducted with younger children, relatively few studies employed adolescents as subjects. This is particularly true for older adolescents. When high school students were the recipients of school–home note programs, they typically resided in an institutional or group-home setting.

Subjects in home-based reinforcement studies also have varied in their baseline performance levels. Several studies employed children who were not identified as having any specific academic or conduct problems (Dougherty & Dougherty, 1977; Lahey *et al.*, 1977 and Saudargaus *et al.*, 1977). Typically, these studies used school-home notes with entire classrooms of students. Other studies applied the procedure with subjects identified as having such problems as poor academic skills (Anesko & O'Leary, 1983; Imber *et al.*, 1979) or excessive disruptiveness (Budd *et al.*, 1981 & Heaton *et al.*, 1976). Studies that employed behavior problem children as the subjects have used school–home notes effectively with entire classrooms of such children as well as with individual students.

Target Behaviors

The behaviors modified with school–home notes have been as extensive and varied as those altered with school-based contingency management interventions (Broughton *et al.*, 1981). Numerous studies focused on academic-related behaviors. Several studies targeted academic process responses, such as studying (Bailey *et al.*, 1970) and staying on task (Coleman, 1973). Other studies employed home-based contingencies to increase academic outcomes or products, such as the amount or quality of completed classwork (Blechman, Taylor, & Schrader, 1981; Dougherty & Dougherty, 1977; Imber *et al.*, 1979; Saudargaus *et al.*, 1977).

A variety of disruptive classroom behaviors also have been reduced through the use of school–home notes. The procedure has been used to decrease classroom rule violations (Bailey *et al.*, 1970), disruptiveness (Ayllon, Garber, & Pisor, 1975), inappropriate behavior during naptime (Lahey *et al.*, 1979), and talking out during class (Dougherty & Dougherty, 1977).

Several researchers have combined academic-related and disruptive behaviors in defining target behaviors for their home-based interventions. For example, Heaton *et al.* (1976) used achievement scores, grades, and discipline problems as the dependent measures in their study. Likewise, Schumaker *et al.* (1977) targeted adherence to classroom rules, completion of classwork, and test grades.

Although there have not been any studies that compared the effects of school-home notes on academic process versus outcome variables, considerable support exists for targeting the latter. First, several researchers have suggested that outcome variables, such as work completion and work accuracy, should be targeted as they are the ultimate goals for any student (Winett & Winkler, 1972). Likewise, few teachers or parents would argue against the value of academic productivity; however, considerable disagreement might exist over what constitutes appropriate classroom conduct. Secondly, academic outcomes, such as the percentage of problems completed correctly, can be quickly and objectively monitored by teachers. Thus, teachers may be more willing to provide parents with such information for lengthy periods of time or for as long as is necessary. Third, parents can easily interpret information about work completion, and thus, are able to provide consequences in a consistent manner. For example, most parents are familiar with academic products, such as satisfactory and unsatisfactory work and grades. Finally, and perhaps most importantly, when children are rewarded for increased academic productivity, improvements in classroom conduct occurs simultaneously. Specifically, studies that compared the effects of teacher administered interventions applied to academic process behavior versus academic outcomes have shown that improved productivity resulted in decreased disruptiveness (Ayllon, Layman, & Kandel, 1975; Kirby & Shields, 1972). In contrast, studies targeting disruptiveness have not always found improvements in academic performance (Ferritor, Buckholdt, Hablin, & Smith, 1972; Wagner & Guyer, 1971).

Parent–Teacher Training

Parent Involvement and Training

When parents are trained to improve their children's behavior at home, they often are taught a variety of skills. Parents commonly are taught to select target behaviors, to monitor the occurrence of the target responses, and to use a variety of behavior change strategies (e.g., time out and reward procedures). However, because school–home notes are designed to modify classroom behavior, the procedure often requires parents to provide only appropriate consequences. Thus, parents' role in administering the school–home note intervention can be greatly reduced compared to their involvement in other home-based contingency programs.

Numerous studies have employed successful school–home note programs involving very minimal contact with, or training of, the children's parents. Several studies simply provided parents with a letter that explained the purpose of the school–home note procedure and specific strategies for providing effective consequences (Dougherty & Dougherty, 1979; Karraker, 1972; Lahey *et al.*, 1977; Saudargaus *et al.*, 1977). Lahey *et al.* (1977), for example, provided parents with a letter that instructed them to praise satisfactory school performance but to avoid punishing their child. Although contacts with the parents were very minimal, the procedure was effective in improving kindergarteners' behavior during naptime. Similarly, Saudargaus *et al.* (1977) informed parents only of how many assignments their children should complete daily and how many they actually completed. Apparently, the parents were not given any information on providing consequences for goal achievement.

Several studies successfully instituted school-home notes with behavior problem children by providing only a moderate amount of parent training (Ayllon, Layman, & Kandel, 1975, Blechman, Kotanchik, & Taylor, 1981; Budd *et al.*, 1981). For example, Ayllon, Layman, and Kandel (1975) provided parents of 23 highly disruptive boys with a single 2-hour training session. The session focused on training the parents to provide effective consequences contingent on their children's classroom behavior. The school–home note procedure resulted in a substantial decrease in disruptive behavior.

Parents also have been provided with relatively extensive training in establishing and providing home-based contingencies for academic performance (Bailey *et al.*, 1977; Blechman, Taylor, & Schrader, 1981; Schumaker *et al.*, 1977). For example, parents of adolescent boys were provided weekly training sessions on the administration of a relatively complex school–home token economy system (Schumaker *et al.*, 1977).

Two studies have compared the effects of amount and type of parent training on the effectiveness of school–home notes. Karraker (1972) trained parents of second graders in the use of a school–home note by providing either a descriptive letter, a 15-minute conference, or two 1-hour training sessions. Irrespective of training condition, all parents were told to provide positive consequences when their children performed satisfactorily and to avoid comment when notes were unsatisfactory. Parents who received 2 hours of parent training were given a more detailed lecture on providing appropriate consequences and additional information on general child management techniques. The results indicated that all training methods were effective in increasing the children's mathematics performance. However, due to the small number of children in each condition and the variability of baseline performance, differential treatment effects could not be ascertained.

Blechman, Taylor, and Schrader (1981) conducted a well-controlled treatment outcome study that compared the effects of different parent-training programs. The study is novel in terms of its experimental rigor and comprehensiveness and in its evaluation of relatively unique treatment procedures. The subjects were elementary-school-aged students from 17 classrooms. Students who performed inconsistently in mathematics were identified through statistical analyses and were then assigned randomly to one of two treatment conditions or to an untreated control condition. Children in both treatment conditions received a Good News Note on days when their mathematics performance was satisfactory. However, parents of children in one treatment group were instructed in the purpose of the school–home note and how to reward satisfactory performance via a brief letter. Children and parents assigned to the alternate treatment were taught to negotiate a contingency contract. The contract specified the mathematics performance criteria necessary to earn rewards and what rewards were earned for goal achievement. Parents who participated in the family-problem-solving session also were telephoned weekly to monitor contract compliance. The results indicated that both treatments produced significance reductions in classwork variability compared to the untreated control condition. However, children in the family-problem-solving condition completed their work more accurately than did children in the letter-only condition. Importantly, only children who received family-problem-solving demonstrated response maintenance on days that the treatment was briefly withdrawn.

The results of Karraker (1977) and Blechman, Taylor, and Schrader (1981) both indicated that the school–home note procedure produced substantial changes in children's mathematics performance when parents were provided with minimal training. However, Blechman, Taylor, and Schrader (1981) found that more extensive parent training produced a greater number of changes in performance. In general, significant improvements in children's classroom behavior have occurred when parents are provided with only minimal instruction in the use of a school–home note. However, with the exception of Blechman *et al.* (1981b) studies that supplied parents with only brief, written instructions, typically employed the school–home note procedure with entire classrooms of elementary-school-aged children. In addition, the subjects' academic and interpersonal classroom behavior generally were not described as particularly problematic. Thus, it is not clear whether parents of older children or children who exhibit behavior problems would be sufficiently trained to implement the school–home procedure if provided only with brief, written instructions. The Blechman, Taylor, and Schrader (1981) study suggests that this may not be the case.

In addition to the possibility that minimal training may be less effective, there appear to be other rationales for providing more extensive training to parents of behavior problem children. Given that many children who exhibit problem behavior at school display similar behavior at home (Patterson, 1982), expecting parents to provide appropriate consequences for satisfactory school performance may be unrealistic. Furthermore, as parents of behavior problem children frequently rely heavily on punishment to induce behavior change, caution in the use of brief, impersonal training with parents of such children appears warranted. Clearly, additional research is needed that examines the effects and side effects of different types and amounts of parent training on the success of school–home notes.

Teacher Involvement and Training

Teachers' involvement in the administration of home-based reinforcement programs has varied considerably. For example, in the study by Dougherty and Dougherty (1977), the teacher recorded only homework completion and talking without permission. In contrast, the teachers in the study by Schumaker *et al.* (1977) monitored a variety of behaviors for each student, including whether or not he or she came to class on time, brought supplies, stayed seated, talked inappropriately, followed directions, and paid attention. The majority of studies required teachers to monitor some aspect of their students' behavior. Some researchers have provided observers to monitor the classroom behavior so that teachers were required only to complete the report card each day (Bailey *et al.*, 1970).

The use of observers certainly is more convenient for teachers; however, it would seem that in the interest of generalizability, home-based reinforcement programs should be designed so that the procedures can be assumed completely by the teacher when the experimenter leaves. In addition, the ease of monitoring and time of teacher involvement are important to teachers. Witt, Martens, and Elliott (1984) found that the amount of time involvement affected teachers' judgments of the acceptability of behavioral intervention; for children with mild to moderate behavior problems, teachers view interventions that require little teacher time as more acceptable. Therefore, teachers may be more likely to implement the simple interventions with integrity. Broughton *et al.* (1981) also noted that complex monitoring and observational systems are important for research but sometimes impractical for the teacher. An informative and objective, yet simple system is probably best for clinical application.

Few studies have collected reliability data on teachers' monitoring of classroom behavior; however, the studies that have monitored teachers' reliability with observers (Budd *et al.*, Lahey *et al.*, 1977) generally have found that teachers are reliable in their monitoring. Reliability is an important part of a controlled study that many researchers have omitted.

With regard to teacher training, most studies do not address this point at all. Although researchers generally described teachers' duties in implementing the school–home note, they do not report on training techniques used to acquaint the teacher with the intervention. Only a few studies addressed the topic of teacher training. Schumaker *et al.* (1977) and Todd *et al.* (1976), for example, held conferences with the teachers involved in their studies to draw up the rules for the school–home note. In the study by Lahey *et al.* (1977), teachers were given instructions on how to fill out the daily report card; these teachers also were instructed to be positive when presenting the cards. Dougherty and Dougherty (1977) provided teachers with written instructions on rating target behaviors. Finally, although Saudargaus *et al.* (1977) did not discuss specific teacher training procedures, they did report that the teachers involved in their study had received previous training in the use of behavioral techniques.

The topic of teacher training has been neglected in the literature. Certainly, teacher training is an important part of this type of intervention. Researchers and clinicians should be cautioned against implementing this type of program with poorly trained teachers. Several problems are likely to occur if the teacher administering the home-note program is not properly instructed. First, teachers may be likely to respond to children identified as behavior problems in a negative way; teachers should be made aware that most home-based reinforcement programs are positive in nature. Second, if target behaviors are poorly defined, the teacher is less likely to be able to monitor these behaviors and implement the system properly; teachers should be instructed in, and be a part of, operationally defining these behaviors. Finally, if teachers are unaware of basic behavioral principles behind the reinforcement program, they may fail to provide appropriate consequences, which may decrease effectiveness.

In summary, although researchers may have provided adequate training for their teachers, many have not included a description of training techniques. Given that teacher training is such an important part of the home-based reinforcement system, more attention should be given to the description of the training techniques.

Consequences

Appropriate parental consequences are perhaps the most important aspect of the school–home note. Implicit in the design of any contingency management program is the assumption that appropriate behavior will be reinforced and inappropriate behavior ignored or punished. A variety of consequences have been offered to children contingent on satisfactory or unsatisfactory notes. Consequences have included praise, tangible rewards, responses cost, and various combinations thereof. Although most studies included praise as a component, several studies encouraged parental praise as the only home-based consequence for appropriate classroom behavior (Dougherty & Dougherty, 1977; Lahey *et al.*, 1977). In these studies, parents were instructed to praise their children contingent on satisfactory school reports. These studies were conducted with entire classrooms of students, none of whom exhibited any serious behavior problems. Lahey *et al.* (1977) simply informed parents to praise their children when the school–home note indicated satisfactory performance and to avoid punishing poor performance. These procedures were effective in increasing students' appropriate behavior.

Schumaker *et al.* (1977) compared the effects of parental praise with praise plus privileges on an adolescent's academic performance and classroom conduct. Praise alone was ineffective; in fact, on most days during that condition, the subject did not bring the card home. However, with the introduction of praise and privileges, the subject's classwork and adherence to classroom rules improved substantially.

Several studies offered tangible home rewards in addition to praise for good behavior at school (Alexander *et al.*, 1976; Blechman, Taylor, & Schrader, 1981). Numerous types of home rewards have been used, including allowance, later bedtime, and activity reinforcers such as bike riding and TV time. In one study, school attendance counselors contacted adults who controlled the reinforcers for six frequently truant adolescents (MacDonald, Gallimore, & MacDonald, 1970). The counselors negotiated deals between the adult and the student, such that reinforcers were contingent on school attendance. A novel aspect of the study was the fact that the adults contacted were not always parents; in one case the adult was a pool hall proprieter who controlled the youth's access to the pool hall. The intervention generally was effective in increasing the students' attendance.

Alexander *et al.* (1976) compared the effects of group versus individual consequences in modifying adolescents' class attendance. They found that the group consequences (which were delivered only if all members of the group attended all classes) were more effective than individual consequences in increasing class attendance.

Heaton *et al.* (1976) conducted a study using school and home rewards. In this study, teacher praise and points were made contingent on working behavior. In addition, attractive afternoon activities at school were contingent on a specified number of points. The students could also earn contingent home rewards for acquiring the correct number of points. This combination of consequences was effective in increasing classroom working behavior.

Several studies compared school-based with home-based contingency systems. Karraker (1972), for example, compared a performance feedback condition with a home reward condition in which rewards were given for satisfactory school performance. The results indicated that academic productivity increased only when students were provided with home rewards. Aylon, Garber, and Pisor (1975) found that school-based reinforcement (points that earned tangible rewards) was only temporarily effective in modifying academic and disruptive behavior in a highly disruptive classroom. However, a Good Behavior letter with home rewards was more effective in reducing disruptive behavior than the classroom-based intervention. Imber *et al.* (1979) compared teacher praise with home praise. In this study, students first received verbal praise from their teacher based on completion of seatwork. Following this phase, students received praise notes to take home contingent on work performance. Parents were instructed to praise their child for the note and to express the hope that the child might receive a praise note on the following day. A multiple baseline design revealed marked increases in work completion during each phase. Thus, home notes were more effective than teacher praise alone.

Finally, Budd *et al.* (1981) compared the relative effects of three types of consequences on students' disruptive behavior. The consequences were (a) stickers and teacher praise, (b) home rewards based on stickers earned at school, and (c) home and school rewards for low levels of disruptiveness. The study was conducted using three separate groups of six children. The results obtained with two groups of children revealed that home rewards produced a significant decrease in disruptive behavior. Similar decreases were not obtained when stickers and teacher praise were employed. The third group of children were introduced to the sticker condition immediately. This condition was followed by home privileges and then school plus home privileges. For four of the six children the first two conditions were mildly effective. However, a more striking decrease in the target behavior (off-area) was found with the school plus home privileges condition. For the remaining two subjects, no systematic decrease in behavior was found until school and home reinforcement was provided.

Response cost procedures also have been used to increase appropriate classroom behavior. In the study by Bailey *et al.* (1970), students earned extra privileges at home for satisfactory classroom behavior. In addition, students lost privileges contingent on unsatisfactory notes. Similarly, Todd *et al.* (1976)

provided a response cost in the form of a one-day suspension from school following three undesirable daily report cards. Finally, students in the Ayllon, Garber, and Pisor (1975) study earned and lost points contingent on classroom behavior.

One study in which parents were not told to provide home contingencies based on a school–home note was conducted by Saudargaus *et al.* (1977). In this study, no requirements were made to insure that the children's parents received or read the cards; therefore, one cannot be certain that the children received any feedback from their parents at all.

In conclusion, the research indicates that the school–home note program may be more effective than school-only or praise interventions; in studies comparing praise or school-only rewards with home rewards, the home rewards produced greater changes in behavior. Although praise should always be paired with rewards, praise alone does not seem to be a particularly potent reinforcer. This appears to be especially true for very disruptive children (Schumaker *et al.*, 1977).

A major shortcoming of the research on school–home notes has been the lack of evaluation of parents' appropriate delivery of consequences; rarely do researchers report data on parent consequences. An exception to this is the study by Budd *et al.* (1981), who asked parents to record consequences on the back of the report card and return it to school. However, this study is the exception to the rule. Clearly more research is needed that evaluates the consistency with which home consequences are given.

Treatment Maintenance and Follow-Up

The importance of employing techniques for ensuring treatment maintenance in the use of home-based reinforcement has been noted by several authors (Atkeson & Forehand, 1979; Broughton *et al.*, 1981). However, in spite of this attention, few treatment studies have even addressed the issues of maintenance and fading. Lahey (as cited in Gresham & Lemanek, 1987) recommended a specific fading procedure whereby daily report cards are faded to weekly cards and then faded out completely. Several studies have used such a fading technique; Bailey *et al.* (1970) faded daily cards to bi-weekly cards. Likewise, Dougherty and Dougherty (1977) faded their daily cards to weekly cards, which reported the week's performance. Schumaker *et al.* (1977) recommended a fading procedure whereby the student would carry a shortened version of the daily report card; however, this procedure was not implemented in any of their three experiments.

Other studies briefly discussed informal maintenance strategies. Imber *et al.* (1979) used praise cards "intermittently" after the study was concluded. The authors reported that the procedure effectively maintained student performance; however, no data were reported.

It is difficult to assess the long-term success of home-based reinforcement programs due to the lack of studies that collected follow-up data. Atkeson & Forehand (1979) noted in their review of home-based reinforcement programs that only 16% of the studies included follow-up measures. It also is difficult to examine the issue of response maintenance, as most studies were concluded at the end of the school year or semester and did not report later progress of the student. Studies that did report the use of a fading technique reported maintenance of treatment results; therefore, these studies reveal that results are maintained with such a fading strategy; however, little is known about maintenance in studies without fading techniques. More systematic research is needed to assess the importance of maintenance or fading techniques. This research would also help to answer the questions about the long-term effects and generalizability of home-based interventions.

Treatment Efficacy

With few exceptions, use of school–home notes has resulted in substantial improvements in students' classroom behavior. The results from several studies suggested that the procedure was more effective than an intervention conducted entirely within the school setting. For example, Ayllon, Garber, and Pisor (1975) successfully reduced children's disruptive behavior with school–home notes after a token economy previously employed in the classroom had failed. However, studies that directly compared school–home note interventions with alternative treatments have been reported only rarely. For example, experimental comparisons of classroom interventions, such as group contingencies or positive practice, have not been conducted. Until such evaluations take place little can be concluded about the comparative effectiveness of school-home notes and more traditional school-based interventions.

Although uncommon, several studies commented on instances in which school–home notes were not effective. Budd *et al.* (1981) reported that the intervention was ineffective with two of the 18 children treated. As noted by the authors, factors that may have contributed to the ineffectiveness of the treatment were a high base rate of misbehavior, social immaturity relative to peers, and inadequate implementation in the home. MacDonald *et al.* (1970) also noted that the procedure failed to produce increased attendance in several of the adolescent subjects apparently was due to adult mediators' inability or unwillingness to dispense rewards contingently.

As with any other body of research, studies that employed school–home notes often contained several methodological weaknesses. The studies reviewed sometimes failed to provide adequate measurement of the independent and dependent variables or follow-up data. Atekson and Forehand (1979) described several additional shortcomings of the procedure, including the lock of adequate experimental design, failure to use multiple outcome measures, and failure to monitor parent and teacher behavior. For further discussion of the methodological shortcomings of school–home notes, the reader is directed to the excellent review provided by Atkeson and Forehand (1979).

Social Validity

Researchers have become increasingly concerned with the validity of behavioral interventions from a social or societal perspective. Assessments of social validity have considered the importance of treatment goals and effects and the appropriateness of treatment procedures (Elliott, 1986; Wolf, 1978). Typically, the social validity of a treatment is determined through the evaluations of relevant judges such as the treatment recipients.

Very few studies have assessed the social validity of school–home notes. Although limited, the data have supported the social validity of the procedure. For example, parents' responses to a questionnaire administered 7 weeks after the treatment began indicated that they viewed the intervention very positively (Lahey *et al.*, 1977). The parents reported that they believed the intervention was important to their children's education and had resulted in improved parent–teacher communication. Parent satisfaction with the school–home note procedure also was indicated anecdotally in several studies. However, systematic evaluations of teachers' and students' satisfaction with the treatment or treatment outcome have not been conducted.

Several studies have compared the acceptability of school–home notes to other classroom management techniques. These studies have obtained judgments of treatment acceptability from potential consumers of the treatment, namely students and teachers. Witt *et al.* (1984) obtained evaluations of the acceptability of six classroom interventions from 180 teachers. The subjects were presented with written case descriptions of a behavior problem child and were asked to evaluate the acceptability of a single treatment using a 20-item scale. Although the study was designed to assess the main and interaction effects of teacher time, behavior problem severity, and treatment valence (positive versus reductive interventions), overall mean ratings for each of the treatments could be calculated from the data presented in the article. These means could range from 20 to 120 with higher scores indicating greater treatment acceptability. The data indicated that home-based reinforcement was perceived to be quite acceptable ($M = 78$) and received higher ratings than a token economy ($M = 61$), time out ($M = 56$) or ignoring ($M = 72$). However, school–home notes were not rated as highly as praise ($M = 82$) or response cost ($M = 88$).

Using similar methodology, Turco and Elliott (1985) evaluated children's acceptability of home versus school-based contingency management procedures. Students from grades 5, 7, and 9 evaluated the acceptability of a single treatment as applied to a written case vignette of a student with behavior problems. Treatment evaluations were obtained using a seven-item scale (total score range = 7 to 42). Overall, the students preferred home-based praise ($M = 30$) over home-based reprimands ($M = 28$), public teacher praise ($M = 27$), or public teacher reprimands ($M = 24$).

Although few in number, studies that examined the social validity of school–home notes have supported the use of the procedure. Parents have reported a high degree of satisfaction with the intervention. The results of Witt *et al.* (1984) and Turco and Elliott (1985) suggest that teachers and students view home-based contingencies as a highly acceptable method for remediating children's classroom behavior problems.

Definitive statements about the social validity of school–home notes can not be made because many unanswered questions remain. For example, it is unknown whether experience with the intervention would influence teachers' or students' ratings of acceptability. It seems quite possible that students (particularly adolescents) might view the procedure differently once they had been required to obtain publicly teacher evaluations on a daily basis. It also is unknown whether any number of variations in subject characteristics, school–home note format, or parent/teacher training would differentially effect acceptability ratings or consumer satisfaction.

Clinical Applications

School–home notes have been very effective in improving children's academic performance and classroom conduct. The literature attests to the robustness of the procedure; school–home notes have been used successfully with children of all ages and with a wide range of classroom problems. The procedure has been employed with individual students as well as with entire classrooms. Given that a great deal of variability exists in the development and administration of school–home notes, is one method better than another?

From our point of view, the answer to this question is both no and yes. No, the literature does not strongly suggest that a particular treatment package is superior to another; yes, the realities of clinical practice have taught us that some school–home note procedures are more likely to produce significant, socially valid changes in behavior than are others.

The vast majority of clinical uses of school–home notes are directed toward modifying the behavior of a particular child rather than all students in a given classroom. In order to warrant referral to a psychologist or educational consultant the child is very likely to be exhibiting behavior problems pretty much throughout the day. The child may not be completing his work satisfactorily or may be disrupting the classroom routine in some significant way. Chances are the child does both.

Assuming this typical child is able to do the work and on some occasions does so, a number of procedures are recommended in order to increase the likelihood that a school–home note will be implemented with integrity and will produce meaningful changes in behavior. Many of these recommendations are described in the Appendix, which presents the guidelines we typically follow when setting up a school–home note. As described in the Appendix, it often is necessary to monitor the child's behavior throughout the day. If this is to be done, the recording procedure must be easy for the teacher to use and require only a very brief period of time. Evaluation criteria must be clearly specified so that parents, teachers, and children are aware of the topography of the target behavior.

When determining appropriate target responses, we suggest that work productivity and accuracy be chosen over academic process behavior, such as remaining on task. As mentioned earlier in this chapter, responses such as the amount of work completed correctly can be quickly and objectively monitored by teachers; evaluations of the responses can be easily interpreted by parents. Although it may be necessary to intervene directly with classroom conduct problems, we recommend that target responses associated with classroom conduct be included only after obtaining satisfactory levels of academic productivity, as increased productivity often produces decreases in disruptiveness. However, when a child's disruptiveness significantly interferes with the classroom routine (e.g.,, excessive talking out during classroom discussions), the teacher may demand or the behavior may require an intervention directed specifically toward remediating conduct problems.

As illustrated in Figure 1, we have found it useful and at times necessary to include a space for the child or teacher to record homework assignments. This allows parents to know exactly what the child is to complete at home. With older children or adolescents, we have asked teachers to record the dates of upcoming tests on the day they are announced. When this is done parents can encourage their children's studying for tests across a number of days.

Good clinical practice dictates that parents and teachers be provided with adequate training in the use of the school–home note. The consultant should assist in establishing evaluation criteria and rewards for satisfactory performance. It often is helpful to provide parents and teachers with information on the principles of behavior in order to help ensure appropriate implementation of the program and effective problem solving. It also is sometimes necessary to augment a school–home note intervention with an in-school contingency management program. For example, with a very disruptive child, we sometimes add contingency procedures that provide immediate consequences for inappropriate classroom behavior along with the use of a school–home note for academic and conduct problems.

In order to establish appropriate criteria for earning rewards, it is important to collect at least a week of baseline data. This information can be used to establish criteria in individual academic subjects and will yield information on patterns of behavior. We often reward children for bringing home the note during baseline.

Consequences for behavior should primarily be reinforcing rather than punishing. Ideally, parents and children should work together to develop a list of reinforcers to be delivered daily and larger reinforcers to be given for consistently good performance during the week. Often the child engages in a number of reinforcing evening activities that can be made contingent on satisfactory school performance. Although punishing consequences should never be the primary method of behavior management and should be deemphasized with parents, we have found such aversive consequences as extra chores or early bed time delivered contingent on poor performance to be a useful way to augment a reward procedure. From a practical point of view, if children are not allowed to engage in their regular evening activities, they need something to do. Punishment in the form of completing extra chores or requiring mediational essays provides children with alternative activities.

After the school–home note is in place, parents should consistently reward children for appropriate behavior. Furthermore, parents should be instructed to expect a school–home note every day and to treat the lack of note as equivalent to an unsatisfactory note. Teachers should be made aware of this contingency and develop a plan for letting parents know when a note is not to be expected (e.g., teacher absences).

Fading school–home notes can be a tricky problem. We have encountered instances in which school–home notes were prematurely removed and the behavior quickly returned to baseline levels. This can occur even after a lengthy period of satisfactory performance. We suggest that the cards be faded in such a way that parents intermittently require their child to have the note completed. In this way parents know when to expect to receive a note. In addition, we suggest that with older children or adolescents that they be required to complete the note themselves on days when the teacher is not expected to complete it. In this way, they are required to write down their assignments and evaluate whether or not they behaved in a satisfactory manner. If the students' self-evaluations differ substantially from those of the teachers or if performance is not satisfactory, return to a daily procedure.

Another way of fading feedback is to abbreviate the school–home note so that less specific information is provided. For example, the teacher could begin providing information on overall academic performance rather than information about performance in individual subjects.

Summary and Discussion

The use of school–home notes has several advantages over traditional, classroom contingency management systems. The procedure promotes parent–teacher communication and collaborative problem solving. School–home notes make use of the wide range of incentives available in the home. Because teachers are responsible for only a component of the treatment, use of teacher time is minimal. Finally, the intervention, as it typically is used, encourages parental consistency and positive interactions between parents and their children.

An examination of the literature revealed a great deal of variability in the procedures for using the school–home note. For example, the specificity of the evaluation criteria employed by teachers and the feedback provided to parents has ranged from very detailed to global. Likewise, training of parents and teachers in the use of the school–home note has varied from minimal to comprehensive. The relationship between these and other variables and treatment outcome was not apparent as all of the studies reviewed reported that school–home notes were effective. Furthermore, very few studies have systematically examined the influence of procedural variations on treatment outcome. However, the importance of conducting component analyses was underscored by the results of Blechman, Taylor, and Schrader (1981), who found that more extensive parent training was related to favorable treatment outcome.

Several additional issues regarding the clinical utility of school–home notes were raised throughout this review. First, it is unclear whether school–home notes can be easily and effectively applied to children's behavior throughout the entire school day, as most studies employed the intervention during only a portion of the day. Secondly, very few studies described the rationales given and the methods employed to obtain teacher and parent cooperation. A third, related issue was the paucity of studies that specified the procedures used to train teachers to monitor objectively and reliably children's performance. Finally, strategies for fading treatment rarely were discussed and even more rarely, evaluated.

In many instances, the clinical utility of

school–home notes might be enhanced if the target responses are academic outcomes rather than behavior associated with the academic process. For example, responses such as work accuracy can be easily and objectively monitored by teachers. In contrast, when behaviors such as studying or paying attention are targeted, teacher training and involvement often are relatively extensive. Attempts to increase academic outcomes also represent socially significant goals, the importance of which can be easily understood by parents and teachers. Thus, targeting outcomes might enhance cooperation from adults responsible for administering the program.

The social validity of school–home notes rarely has been assessed; hence, definitive statements regarding procedures for enhancing the utility of school–home notes cannot be made. Results from the few studies that examined the social validity of school–home notes supported the use of the procedure. However, additional evaluations that compare the social validity of school–home notes to other behavioral interventions clearly are needed.

Research that evaluated the use of school–home notes generally has contained a number of methodological flaws. In several cases, the studies lacked adequate measurement of the dependent and independent variables. Very few studies assessed the integrity with which the intervention was employed through the monitoring of teacher and parent behavior. Finally, follow-up data were reported only rarely.

Taking a broader perspective, we note that a number of alternatives to the typical procedures included in school–home notes have not yet been explored. Usually, the procedure is developed through consultation with teachers and parents. Such consultation often involves several time-consuming visits to the school. Although frequent consultation often is necessary from a research perspective, clinicians who attempt to develop school–home note interventions may find the time commitment prohibitive. An alternative to this common practice might be to train parents in consultative and behavior management skills. Such skills would enable parents to work collaboratively with teachers in order to specify the target responses, monitoring procedures, and contingencies of reinforcement. Such training could be conducted with groups of parents and thus minimize the need for individualized parent training. As numerous studies have demonstrated that parents can be taught to modify their children's behavior problems in the home, their increased involvement in managing their children's school problems appears to be a topic worthy of investigation.

In general, research that employed school–home notes did not involve the target child in the development or administration of the intervention. However, self-control procedures have several advantages over interventions conducted solely by adults. Self-management interventions may encourage children's independence and maintenance of desired behavior change in the absence of external contingencies (O'Leary & Dubey, 1979). In addition, the procedures can function to reduce adults' involvement in remediating behavior problems. Given these advantages it appears worthwhile to expand the typical school–home note procedures to include self-control training as a component of the intervention. For example, adult control over the administration of the procedure could gradually be replaced with the use of self-control strategies, such as student goal setting or self-reinforcement.

In sum, school–home notes have been quite effective in remediating children's school problems. However, numerous methodological and clinical issues warrant the continued evaluations of the use of the procedure.

Appendix

Parent–Teacher Handout for Implementing a School–Home Note

Home-Based Rewards for Classroom Behavior: Use of School–Home Notes

Like regular academic report cards, school–home notes are a means by which parent and teacher can monitor the child's behavior in school. School–home notes are behavior records designed through a cooperative effort of parents, teachers, and sometimes consultants like psychologists. The notes are completed daily by the teacher and given to the child to bring home. Parents are responsible for rewarding children for satisfactory school performance. School–home notes are designed to increase desirable school behaviors such as classwork completion, attending class, being on time for class, and bringing required materials to class. There are several important steps in the design and use of the school–home note.

1. *Plan a Parent–Teacher Conference.* The first step in designing a school home note is for parents and teachers to conduct a conference. At this meeting, the teacher should describe to the parent the behaviors of the child that are a problem for him/her in school. The teacher and parent should also discuss what they consider to be acceptable and desirable behaviors in the child. Both teacher and parent should avoid blaming, and should try to make the correspondence as pleasant as possible.

3. *Define Target Behaviors.* Using the information that both parent and teacher have generated regarding the child's behavior at school, define behaviors that both parent and teacher would like to see the child perform more often. Whenever possible, define target behaviors in terms of increasing good behavior rather than decreasing bad behavior. This will make interactions with the child concerning the school–home note more positive. For example, instead of targeting number of times tardy to class, target number of times *on time* to class.

Define the behaviors as *specifically* as possible. The more specific, the more likely it is that you will get an accurate picture of the child's behavior. The target behaviors chosen should be relevant to important classroom behaviors such as work completion. For example, for an elementary school child, teacher and parent may break down "good" behavior into the following four behaviors:

1. Followed directions well
2. Turned in completed homework
3. Completed all classwork
4. Stayed in chair when asked

By defining behaviors specifically, parents can more easily identify those behaviors that should be rewarded at home.

3. *Set Small Goals.* Set goals for target behavior change small enough so that the child is likely to achieve them quickly. This will ensure that parent and teacher have opportunities to reinforce small changes toward desirable behavior and increase the likelihood that changes for the better will continue. As the child's behavior improves, you can gradually increase the amount of desirable behavior necessary to receive rewards.

4. *Designing the School–Home Note.* Each note should have a place for the child's name, the date, and the teacher's signature. The target behaviors should be stated clearly with a space on the side for the teacher to check whether or not the behavior occurred. (Some examples are provided in Table 1.)

5. *Establish Responsibilities.* Before beginning the use of the school-home note, the teacher, parent, and child should meet to establish responsibilities. It should be the parent's responsibility to provide the child with a note each day. It should be the child's responsibility to give the note to the teacher in the morning and to return the card to the parent after it is filled out. It should be the parent's responsibility to reward desirable behavior at home.

6. *Collect Baseline.* Before beginning the reward procedure, the teacher should complete the note for about a week *without* the parent providing rewards. This will let both parent and teacher know how the child is performing in school, and will help in setting up the specific target behaviors and criteria for rewards.

7. *Set Up Reinforcers.* With the help of the child, decide on a set of reinforcers from which the child can choose when he or she brings home a good school–home note. It should be very clear to the child exactly what criteria need to be met for a "good" note. Praise should always accompany the delivery of the rewards. The parents should set up both daily and weekly rewards for good reports.

8. *Carry Out the Promised Consequences.* It is very important to follow through with the promised consequences each time the child brings home a school home note that meets the daily goal for a reward. If the child fails to meet the daily goal or does not bring home the report card, the reinforcers are simply not given. Do *not* punish, unless a specific response cost procedure has been recommended. The purpose of the school–home note is to set up opportunities for you to reward and increase desirable school behavior.

9. *Fading Out the Note as Behavior Improves.* When behavior improves to appropriate levels, the school-home note should be faded out. A good way to do this is to shift to a weekly note. With a weekly

note, the teacher rates the child for the entire week and the child can earn the full week's consequences. If behavior worsens during this time, go back to the daily note. If the weekly system is successful for a few weeks, the child should be able to earn going off the system entirely (but should still receive the rewards noncontingently). Again, if behavior worsens, go back to the weekly note.

Remember, the key to the school–home note is *cooperation*. Parents and teachers should maintain communication during all phases of the procedure.

References

Alexander, R. N., Corbett, T. F., & Smigel, J. (1976). The effects of individual and group consequences on school attendance and curfew violations with pre-delinquent adolescents. *Journal of Applied Behavior Analysis, 9,* 221–226.

Atkeson, B. M., & Forehand, R. (1979). Home-based reinforcement programs designed to modify classroom behavior: A review and methodological evaluation. *Psychological Bulletin, 86,* 1298–1308.

Ayllon, T., Garber, S., & Pisor, K. (1975). The elimination of discipline problems through a combined school-home motivational system. *Behavior Therapy, 6,* 616–626.

Ayllon, T., Layman, D., & Kandel, H. J. (1975). A behavioral-educational alternative to drug control of hyperactive children. *Journal of Applied Behavior Analysis, 8,* 137–146.

Anesko, K. M., & O'Leary, S. G. (1983). The effectiveness of brief parent training for the management of children's homework problems. *Child and Family Behavior Therapy, 4,* 113–126.

Bailey, J. S., Wolf, M. M., & Phillips, E. L. (1970). Home-based reinforcement and the modification of pre-delinquents' classroom behavior. *Journal of Applied Behavior Analysis, 3,* 223–233.

Bernal, M. E., Linnert, M. D., & Schultz, L. A. (1980). Outcome evaluation of behavioral parent training and client-centered parent counseling for children with conduct problems. *Journal of Applied Behavior Analysis, 13,* 677–691.

Berowitz, B. P., & Graziano, A. M. (1972). Training parents as behavior therapists: A review. *Behavior Research and Therapy, 12,* 308–319.

Blechman, E. A., Kotanchik, N. L., & Taylor, C. J. (1981). Families and schools together: Early behavioral intervention with high risk children. *Behavior Therapy, 12,* 308–319.

Blechman, E. A., Taylor, C. J., & Schrader, S. M. (1981). Family problem solving versus home notes as early intervention with high-risk children. *Journal of Consulting and Clinical Psychology, 6,* 919–926.

Broughton, S. F., Barton, E. S., & Owen, P. P. (1981). Home based contingency systems for school problems. *School Psychology Review, 10,* 26–36.

Budd, K. S., Leibowitz, J. M., Riner, L. S., Mindell, C., & Goldfarb, A. L. (1981). Home-based treatment of severe disruptive behaviors: A reinforcement package for preschool and kindergarten children. *Behavior Modification, 5,* 273–298.

Coleman, R. G. (1973). A procedure for fading from experimenter-school-based to parent-home-based control of classroom behavior. *Journal of School Psychology, 11,* 71–79.

Dougherty, E. H., & Dougherty, A. (1977). The daily report card: A simplified and flexible package for classroom behavior management. *Psychology in the Schools, 14,* 191–195.

Elliott, S. N. (1986). Children's acceptability of classroom interventions for misbehavior: Findings and methodological considerations. *Journal of School Psychology, 24,* 23–35.

Fairchild, T. N. (1976). Home-school token economies: Bridging the communication gap. *Psychology in the Schools, 13,* 463–467.

Ferritor, D. E., Buckholdt, D., Hamblin, R. L., & Smith, L. (1972). The noneffects of contingent reinforcement for attending behavior on work accomplished. *Journal of Applied Behavior Analysis, 5,* 7–17.

Forehand, R., & King, H. E. (1977). Noncompliant children. *Behavior Modification, 1,* 93–108.

Foxx, R. M., & Jones, J. R. (1978). A remediation program for increasing the spelling achievement of elementary and junior high school students. *Behavior Modification, 2,* 211–230.

Gresham, F. M., & Lemanek, K. L. (1987). Parent education. In C. A. Maher & S. G. Forman (Eds.), *Providing effective educational services in school organizations: A behavioral approach* (pp. 153–181). Hillsdale, NJ: Erlbaum.

Guidubaldi, J. (1982). Transcending future shock: Invariant principles for school psychology. *School Psychology Review, 11,* 127–131.

Heaton, R. C., Safer, D. J., Allen, R. P., Spinnato, N. C., & Prumo, F. M. (1976). A motivational environment for behaviorally deviant junior high school students. *Journal of Abnormal Child Psychology, 4,* 263–275.

Imber, S. C., Imber, R. B., & Rothstein, C. (1979). Modifying independent work habits: An effective teacher–parent communication program. *Exceptional Children, 45,* 218–221.

Karraker, R. J. (1972). Increasing academic performance through home-managed contingency programs. *Journal of School Psychology, 2,* 173–179.

Kirby, F. D., & Shields, F. (1972). Modification of arithmetic response rate and attending behavior in a seventh grade student. *Journal of Applied Behavior Analysis, 5,* 29–84.

Lahey, B. B., Gendrich, J. G., Gendrich, S. I., Schnelle, J. F., Gant, D. S., & McNees, M. P. (1977). An evaluation of daily report cards with minimal teacher and parent contacts as an efficient method of classroom intervention. *Behavior Modification, 1,* 381–394.

Long, J. D., & Williams, R. L. (1973). The comparative effectiveness of group and individually contingent free time with inner-city junior high school students. *Journal of Applied Behavior Analysis, 6,* 465–474.

MacDonald, W. S., Gallimore, R., & MacDonald, G. (1970). Contingency counseling by school personnel: An economical model of intervention. *Journal of Applied Behavior Analysis, 3,* 175–182.

Mash, E. J., Hammerlynck, L. A., & Handy, L. C. (Eds.). (1976). *Behavior modification and families.* New York: Brunner/Mazel.

McAllister, L. W., Stachowiak, J. G., Baer, D. M., & Conderman, L. (1969). The application of operant conditioning techniques in a secondary school classroom. *Journal of Applied Behavior Analysis, 2,* 277–285.

Moreland, J. R., Schwebel, A. T., Beck, S., & Wells, R. (1982). Parents as therapists: A review of the behavior therapy parent training literature—1975–1981. *Behavior Modification, 6,* 250–276.

O'Dell, S. L. (1974). Training parents in behavior modification: A review. *Psychological Bulletin, 81,* 418–433.

O'Leary, S. G., & Dubey, D. R. (1979). Applications of self-control procedures by children: A review. *Journal of Applied Behavior Analysis, 12,* 449–465.

Patterson, G. R. (1982). *Coercive family process.* Eugene, OR: Castalia.

Patterson, G. R., Chamberlain, P., & Reed, J. B. (1982). A comparative evaluation of a parent-training program. *Behavior Therapy, 13,* 638–650.

Porterfield, J. K., Herbert-Jackson, E., & Risley, T. R. (1976). Contingent observation: An effective and acceptable procedure for reducing disruptive behavior of young children in group settings. *Journal of Applied Behavior Analysis, 9,* 55–64.

Reisinger, J. J., Ora, J. D., & Frangia, G. W. (1976). Parents as change agents for their children: A review. *Journal of Community Psychology, 4,* 103–123.

Saudargaus, R. W., Madsen, C. H., & Scott, J. W. (1977). Differential effects of fixed- and variable-time feedback on production rates of elementary school children. *Journal of Applied Behavior Analysis, 10,* 673–678.

Schumaker, J. B., Hovell, M. F., & Sherman, J. A. (1977). An analysis of daily report cards and parent-managed privileges in the improvement of adolescents' classroom performance. *Journal of Applied Behavior Analysis, 10,* 449–464.

Stumphauzer, J. S. (1976). Elimination of stealing by self-reinforcement of alternative behavior and family contracting. *Journal of Behavior Therapy and Experimental Psychiatry, 7,* 265–268.

Todd, D. D., Scott, R. B., Bostow, E., & Alexander, S. B. (1976). Modification of the excessive inappropriate classroom behavior of two elementary school students using home-based consequences and daily report card procedures. *Journal of Applied Behavior Analysis, 9,* 106.

Turco, T. L., & Elliott, S. N. (1985). *Students' acceptability rating of interventions for classroom misbehaviors: A developmental study of well-behaving and misbehaving youth.* Paper presented at the Annual Convention of the National Association of School Psychologists, Las Vegas, NV.

Wahler, R. G., & Fox, J. J. (1980). Solitary toy play and time out: A family treatment package for children with aggressive and oppositional behavior. *Journal of Applied Behavior Analysis, 13,* 23–39.

Wagner, R. F., & Guyer, B. D. (1971). Maintenance of discipline through increasing children's span of attending by means of a token economy. *Psychology in the Schools, 8,* 285–289.

Wolf, M. M. (1978). Social validity: The case for subjective measurement or how applied behavior analysis is finding its heart. *Journal of Applied Behavior Analysis, 11,* 203–214.

Winett, R. A., & Winkler, R. C. (1972). Current behavior modification in the classroom: Be still, be quiet, be docile. *Journal of Applied Behavior Analysis, 5,* 499–504.

Witt, J. C., Martens, B. K., & Elliott, S. N. (1984). Factors affecting teachers' judgements of the acceptability of behavioral interventions: Time involvement, behavior problem severity, and type of intervention. *Behavior Therapy, 15,* 204–209.

CHAPTER 17

Reductive Procedures

Francis E. Lentz, Jr.

This chapter will review the issues and effects of externally managed behavioral procedures applied to the reduction of undesirable behavior of regular or mildly handicapped children in school settings. Although there is a recognized overlap between classification categories, the examination of interventions in similar settings, with similar goals and objectives, similar populations, and similar procedures for instruction creates a more defined dimension for generalizable conclusions. Further, this type of review may provide an overview currently missing in the literature.

A number of other chapters in this volume complement this focus on reductive techniques, and an effort will be made not to overlap excessively. For example, chapters on generalization, token economies, and self-management are closely and critically related to the topic of reducing misbehavior in schools, and will provide greater detail in these areas. These chapters may also provide rationales for redesigning classrooms to prevent misbehavior. It is to be hoped that information on reductive techniques will provide valuable additional information to professionals who need to design and implement change programs in the schools.

Francis E. Lentz, Jr. • College of Education, University of Cincinnati, Cincinnati, Ohio 45221.

Introduction

To a large extent, behavior control is part of the institution of education, although the means for exercising control have generated heated discussions for probably as long as schools have existed. In the United States, disruptive or rule-breaking behavior has been a notable concern of teachers since surveys have existed (Sabatino, 1983). Further, it appears that the types of behaviors of concern may have drastically increased in seriousness over the last 40 years (Sabatino, 1983), perhaps accounting for the fact that the most prevalent public concern about education expressed in recent Gallup polls is discipline.

Given these fears and concerns, it is unfortunate that classroom personnel rely heavily on the use of contingent aversive attention, such as sarcasm or reprimands, to attempt to control behavior (Heller & White, 1975; Johnson, 1985; White, 1975). Conversely, teacher praise in classrooms becomes increasingly scarce as children get older (White, 1975). It hardly seems likely that such procedures, as they are applied, are very effective given the apparent discipline problems.

Because the public is strongly concerned about conduct problems, it would seem logical that educational researchers would be busily empirically examining various interventions. However, in a recent survey of various journals, Wyatt, Hawkins, and McCoy (1984) found practically no interest in conduct-oriented interventions in two major educational journals (*American Educational Research Journal* and *Exceptional Children;* 0% and 5% of articles over the last 20 years respectively). On the other hand, two behavioral journals (*Journal of Applied Behavior Analysis* and *Education and Treatment of Children*) devoted a large percentage of their space to classroom interventions in general, and to those targeting conduct problems in particular. There has been a large accumulation of empirical studies in these and other behaviorally oriented journals, indicating that a wide variety of behavioral procedures can reduce problem behaviors in schools. In fact, behavioral approaches may be the single best documented class of school-based psychological interventions. Thus, effective discipline is not lacking a strong research-oriented knowledge base.

Conduct Problems as Targets for Change

If you can think of a problem of excessive behavior in the schools, there has likely been an empirically investigated behavioral program applied to its reduction. Targets have ranged from mild disruptions (e.g., out of seat, call outs, off task, distracting interactions) (Broden, Bruce, Mitchell, Carter, & Hall, 1970), to more serious problems like aggression (Sallis, 1983), stealing (Rosen & Rosen, 1983), and truancy (Bizzis & Bradley-Johnson, 1981). Perhaps because of this coverage, Winett and Winkler (1972) criticized behavioral researchers for being interested in keeping children "still, quiet, and docile." At that time the charge was refuted by O'Leary (1972) as ignoring the literature on increasing deficit behaviors, many of which include academic performance. Presently the cumulative applications of behavioral procedures contains an impressive body of research on the treatment of deficit student behaviors, such as those related to academic achievement (e.g., Haring, Lovitt, Eaton, & Hansen, 1978); children's positive social skills (Cartledge & Milburn, 1980); and treating the socially withdrawn (e.g., Strain, 1977).

Wyatt *et al.* (1984) give several excellent reasons for a continuing emphasis on conduct problems by behavioral researchers. First, earlier behavioral literature made a major contribution to the psychological and educational literature by demonstrating the clear ability to control numerous behaviors in the classroom through manipulating external variables. Second, there is an apparent void in other educational literature; and behavioral interventions fill that void and are highly socially valid (Wolf, 1978), given the serious public concern. Finally, conduct problems lend themselves to behavioral research because of their relative ease of measurement; empirical resolutions continue to add to the general knowledge about human behavior.

The reduction of behavior problems does not need to be the only goal of a treatment procedure. As will be seen, procedures targeting the improvement of other behaviors, such as academic performance, may be quite effective in reducing disruptions. The establishment of treatment goals, however, may also be affected by the fact that people differ widely in their tolerances for different behaviors in children, in when they feel interventions are necessary, and in potential willingness to initiate a formal intervention. As will be seen, one of the roles of a behavior change consultant must be to insure appropriate consideration of treatment targets and methods (Sulzer-Azaroff & Mayer, 1977).

The basic issue remains that disruptions do not enhance the efficacy of a setting where important academic and social goals are addressed; and their reduction has benefits for other children and teachers, as well as for the target child. This point is made because many published interventions may directly target only a few behaviors (Kazdin, 1984), and accompanying overall benefits may tend to get ignored.

A final benefit for appropriate application of reductive techniques is in the potential prevention of the classification of children as emotionally disturbed. School psychologists currently report that half of their referrals are related to behavior problems (Prout, 1983); similarly there has been a virtual explosion in classifications of children as behavior disordered (Grosenick & Huntze, 1983). Gresham (1985) cogently suggests that a well-structured classroom intervention should precede the necessity for classification as behavior disordered or emotionally disturbed. Therefore there remains a great need for school-based professionals to understand the reductive techniques and to apply them appropriately.

Problem Behaviors in the School Environment

Behavioristic theories hold that problem behaviors are learned like any other behavior, and that they are maintained through the same environment–behavior interactions as desirable behaviors (Carr, 1981). Behavioral assessment typically contains a phase for direct analysis of the environmental events that are maintaining the identified behavior problem. (Sulzer-Azaroff & Mayer, 1977). Unfortunately, simple antecedent-behavior-consequent analysis (Sulzer-Azaroff & Mayer, 1977) may be insufficient for understanding the potential environmental arrangements that maintain or elicit excessive problem behaviors. A brief description of the basic arrangements that are functional in behavior maintenance will be made prior to a review of the various techniques.

Functional Paradigms of Environmental Maintenance

The most commonly considered reinforcer in the classroom may be attention (Kazdin, 1984; Sulzer-Azaroff & Mayer, 1977). Contingent, positive teacher (Becker, Madsen, Arnold, & Thomas, 1967) or peer (Solomon & Wahler, 1973) attention has been clearly shown to act as a positive reinforcer for appropriate and inappropriate student behavior. It should not be surprising, then, that contingent teacher reprimands can be either punishers or reinforcers, depending on the situation and the child (Van Houten & Doleys, 1983).

Conversely, a child's aggressive or unpleasant behavior may be negatively reinforced when it leads to the child avoiding some activity (e.g., a particular academic subject) or because it results in access to a desirable activity (e.g., free time) (Carr, 1981). Likewise, adult commands to alter or change behavior may be avoided by tantrums or whining (Carr & Newsom, 1985). Patterson (1976) conceptualized this as coercive behavior, and emphasized that the giving in of the adult is negatively reinforced when the child terminates aversive behavior.

Certain serious behaviors like stealing or aggression can generate tangible rewards for the actor, as well as the positive attention of certain peers (Emsdorf, Davis, & Davidson, 1983). Certainly, a truant child may access activities that are far more reinforcing than spending the day at school. Thus, with many children suspension may act as a reinforcer.

A critical issue in the selection of appropriate interventions involves the potential absence of adequate social or problem-solving skills in the repertoire of the student (Goldstein, 1981a,b). Although these problems are often conceptualized as related to problems like excessive anger or aggression, the lack of appropriate alternative behaviors that are instrumental in receiving social attention seems logically related to a number of classroom behavior problems, such as showing off or attention-getting behaviors.

Observation of others' behavior–environment interactions may relate to inappropriate behavior (Bandura, 1977). The processes involving acquisition of positive and negative behavior through imitation, and the effects of vicarious reinforcement and punishment have been clearly demonstrated in laboratory

(Bandura, 1978) and applied settings (Kazdin, 1973, 1977, 1979).

It is becoming increasingly clear that not only is behavior in natural settings affected by multiple antecedent or consequent events but that clusters of functional response classes may exist (Wahler, 1975). Such response classes appear to be idiosyncratic across individuals and settings within individuals. Further, there is some evidence that careful selection of target behaviors within response classes may facilitate the reduction of undesirable behaviors in the same class (Wahler & Fox, 1980).

Setting events, a class of stimuli that may be different from concurrent discriminative stimuli, have been emphasized in recent applied behavioral literature (Wahler & Fox, 1981; Wahler & Graves, 1983). Although not heavily investigated, setting events may relate to behavior problems by altering the probabilities of subsequent setting–behavior relationships. For example, Krantz and Risley (1977) demonstrated that if a high-activity period preceded a sedentary activity greater rates of disruption resulted during the less active period. On the other hand, Bachman and Fugua (1983) found that antecedent exercise reduced misbehavior. Different ecologies appear to be differentially related to the same basic setting events.

Implications for Change Agents

In summary, a choice of intervention procedures should occur only after a careful analysis of the environmental variables that evoke and maintain inappropriate behavior. Failure to diagnose accurately the prevailing maintenance conditions surrounding the exhibition of problem behaviors may well result in selection of treatment procedures that are likely to fail, or even make things worse. There are already enough variables impacting on the success of classroom interventions without compounding difficulties from the beginning. Where possible, this review will attempt to clarify the environmental functions of various interventions in terms of the naturally maintaining conditions related to intervention selection.

Specific Intervention Procedures

Separate discussions will occur for individually oriented versus group-oriented interventions, although group contingencies will be discussed only briefly. Even though events affecting individuals may be similar for both types of interventions, examination of the parameters of single cases should illuminate subtle but important issues.

Further, interventions have been grouped for review along three dimensions: individual procedures involving reinforcement or extinction; individual procedures involving punishment; and group-oriented procedures. Where there are overlaps (multiple treatment comparisons) within a particular article, it will be mentioned in all relevant sections, but discussed in detail in only one. For each set of conceptually similar procedures care will be taken to describe clearly the functional (a sometimes neglected issue) and topographical features of procedures for reducing excessive behaviors. To the extent that data exist, maintenance and generalization of results will be summarized for each section.

This review is not meant to be exhaustive (although over 100 empirical studies were reviewed) and detailed coverage is precluded by space considerations. Important issues like ethical selection of targets and treatment, complex treatment effects, and side effects will be generally summarized within separate sections.

Reduction of Behavior through Reinforcement

Appropriately, behavior analysts have been particularly sensitive to the ethics of modifying behavior through the use of aversive procedures (e.g., Kazdin, 1984; Sulzer-Azaroff & Mayer, 1986). The impetus for this concern comes from several sources. First, there is the premise that use of aversives is ethical only if other procedures are not available (Sulzer-Azaroff & Reese, 1982). This position is modified by issues like the potential danger of the behavior to the client or others, and by estimation of the effect of disruptions on others in the same environment. Second, singular application of aversives contingent on the target behavior may have undesirable side effects, and do not address what the desirable behavior may be (Heron, 1978). Thus, a number of procedures have been developed and applied to problems in school settings that involve, to various extents, the use of reinforcers to reduce problem behavior.

Four classes of reductive procedures using reinforcers will be discussed: (a) differential reinforcement of low rates of behavior (DRL)—reinforcers are made available providing that during a specified period the rate of the targeted undesirable behavior is less than a specified criteria; (b) differential reinforcement of other behavior (DRO)—reinforcers are made available if during a specified period the undesirable behavior does not occur; (c) differential reinforcement of incompatible behavior (DRI)—the opposite of the undesirable behavior is reinforced, for example reinforcement is contingent on hand raising when call outs are the target for reduction; (d) differential reinforcement of alternative behavior (DRA)—a positive behavior is contingently reinforced that is not necessarily incompatible with the undesirable behavior(s). For example, the accuracy and completion of math problems is reinforced and call outs, student talking, and out of seat are concurrently reduced. Several of these procedures, DRL and DRA in particular, have been applied in a dependent-group format and will be discussed in that section.

These four techniques can be further divided into two different functional paradigms. DRO and DRL, when carefully analyzed, have similarities to the operant paradigm of punishment because both often involve contingent removal or delay of a reinforcer. DRI and DRA, on the other hand, specifically target desirable behaviors to reinforce. Depending on the additional contingencies (if any) applied to the problem behavior, these latter two procedures can involve all positive procedures.

DRL

The majority of published studies using DRL for particular individuals have involved the provision of a reinforcer following the emission of fewer than a specified number of the targeted behavior during a specified time interval. However, the original laboratory concept of DRL (Kramer & Rilling, 1970) involved reinforcing interresponse times (IRT) of greater than a specified interval; thus the first response following an IRT of a specified length was reinforced. Responses with shorter IRTs are not reinforced; rather, they reset the IRT timer. The applied version of DRL is sometimes modified so that during a specified interval, if the criteria is set at greater than one, responses are ignored until the criterion is reached, then the next response results in delay or removal of the reinforcer. The latter paradigm appears, then, to be partially punishment.

Deitz (1977) labeled three different DRL paradigms for applied settings. The first, called spaced responding DRL, is the classic model. The second, called full interval DRL, sets the upper limit for responses and at the end of the period provides a reward if the criteria is not exceeded. The third, called interval DRL, sets the criteria at greater than one response for an interval, but resets the interval as soon as the criteria is exceeded.

Classic DRL

Deitz (1977) implemented a classic DRL paradigm to reduce inappropriate questioning by three 7- to 10-year-old behavior-disordered children. The procedure involved setting a criterion IRT for student questions, and not answering questions until the interval had elapsed. Then, the first question was answered, with praise for waiting, and the interval began once more. IRTs ranged from initial values of 3 to 5 minutes to subsequent values of 9 to 20 minutes. Results indicated a very positive effect. This also provides a good example of a procedure to reduce a behavior to a less than zero level. The asking of no questions would have been undesirable.

Full Session DRL

Deitz and Repp (1973) targeted talk outs (talking, singing, humming to oneself, or making unrelated statements) of an 11-year-old mentally retarded boy in a special public school classroom. The contingencies were in effect for only 50 minutes per day; if the child had three or fewer talk outs, he was given 5 minutes of play time at the end of the day. During the period no feedback was provided the student, but at the end he was told whether he met the requirement.

Talk outs were reduced from a mean of six in baseline to less than one during treatment. Subsequent return to baseline resulted in apparent maintenance of gains, although only seven days of data are reported. Aside from the problem of nonreturn to baseline (an experimental problem only, not a treatment problem!), the procedure was immediately effective. Although one may question the seriousness of the problem, the demonstration of effectiveness is clear.

Deitz and Repp (1974), Deitz, Repp, and Deitz (1976), and Deitz (1977) replicated the previous results with two regular school fifth grade boys, a 12- and a 15-year-old EMR boy, and a regular sixth grade girl. Talkouts and/or out of seat behaviors (and yelling for the EMR boy) were targeted, and nonexchangeable stars were used as contingent awards. Again, no feedback was provided during the treatment periods (45 minutes). Notably, the teacher recorded data on the target behavior during the latter study.

Both DRL and a response cost procedure were evaluated separately during the intervention with two adolescents swearing during resource room (Trice & Parker, 1983). During each instructional period, a marker was given to each student contingent on swearing. If the number of markers was less than the mean of baseline, the students were explicitly praised by an aide. In response cost, 5 minutes of after school detention were required if more than three markers per period were collected. Each procedure was effective, although response cost was quicker. It was noted that one student reacted very negatively to the initiation of the markers, perhaps indicating that they had the quality of punishers, and that even this DRL procedure was not totally positive.

Interval DRL

More serious behavior problems were targeted for a 7-year-old learning disabled (LD) boy by Deitz *et al.* (1978). Target behaviors during a 30-minute period included aggression toward other students, rolling on the floor, pounding on desks, throwing objects, yelling, and several other disruptive behaviors. The treatment was also different. First, the period was divided into shorter periods (2 minutes) and more than one behavior per interval resulted in resetting the timer. Secondly, stars were awarded for each interval, not just at the end of the period. Finally, the length of the interval was increased in a second treatment phase. From a baseline average of 19 target responses, the second treatment phase resulted in a decrease to a mean of approximately one.

As in Deitz and Repp (1973), removal of treatment did not result in a return of behaviors to baseline levels. The authors mention that the level of behavior achieved was acceptable to the teacher, and that the behavior "no longer interfered with ongoing academic activity." Unlike the previous types of DRL, this procedure provided implicit feedback to the student (short intervals, stars, reset the timer). Deitz (1977) drastically reduced talk outs of a first grade girl with interval DRL, and also found that withdrawal of treatment did not result in return to baseline levels (although there was regression).

Summary

It has been demonstrated that DRL can be an effective procedure in reducing mild and more serious problems for individuals. There are several issues that merit investigation. First, the duration of the apparent maintenance of gains achieved after treatment withdrawal deserves attention. Perhaps the more elaborate procedures could be faded to just feedback, and then to either self-monitoring or less frequent feedback for long-term maintenance. Given the strong need for generalization and maintenance research (Drabman, Hammer, & Rosenbaum, 1979; Stokes & Baer, 1978) this is very appropriate.

Secondly, it is unclear if immediate feedback (Trice & Parker, 1983) may not function as a contingent punisher, thus partially obviating the "positive" reduction effect. This particular phenomena could be dependent on the contingencies related to the feedback, although in Trice and Parker (1982) contingencies during the period with side effects to the feedback involved reinforcement. Hall *et al.* (1971) provided praise at the end of the day if a child's talk outs were low (not defined) without apparent feedback, so it seems clear that feedback during the DRL period is not crucial.

Although the procedures discussed here were used for only short periods, the group procedures to be discussed were often used for a full day. If DRL involves short intervals and frequent resetting of timers, then continuous efforts by teachers are required. Whether this would make them less palatable remains to be seen. Finally, DRL serves several environmental functions (Deitz, 1977). First, either at short or longer intervals, specific feedback concerning access to reinforcers is provided, and may bring appropriate behavior under explicit stimulus control. Secondly, additional positive reinforcers are explicitly added to the environment, and if they are more potent, provide competition with the contingencies that have supported the misbehavior. This latter issue is a serious concern and change agents must carefully consider the quality of any contingencies that are chosen for the individual target child.

DRO

The classic definition of DRO involves providing reinforcement contingent on not responding for a specified period, with a contingent resetting of a timer, thus delaying reinforcement contingent on a response before the interval ends (Homer & Peterson, 1980; Poling & Ryan, 1982). This procedure has been widely investigated in the laboratory and with the severely handicapped (Homer & Peterson, 1980; Poling & Ryan, 1982). Strangely the non-group reserach in regular or mildly handicapped classrooms is relatively sparse, and does not typically match the original paradigm.

Repp, Barton, and Brulle (1983) investigated two DRO procedures they refer to as whole interval or momentary DRO. In the former, reinforcers were provided at the end of brief intervals if the targeted behavior had not occurred; in the latter, student behavior was sampled at the specific moment the interval ends. If the targeted behaviors were not occurring, then a reinforcer was provided; the interval was not reset if a response occurred too soon.

For three mildly retarded 7-year-old males, the whole interval procedure was clearly more effective than momentary DRO in reducing mild disruptive behaviors (e.g., talk outs, out of seat, throwing or tapping objects, interrupting), although if whole interval preceded momentary DRO, momentary DRO would continue to suppress the behavior.

A second experiment, with a single subject, verified the superiority of the whole interval procedure. An additional experiment with another EMR student replicated the effect of whole interval DRO, although no comparison was made to the momentary procedure (Deitz *et al.*, 1976). Although the procedures were quickly effective, the authors remark that resetting the interval may have improved the procedure. It should be noted, however, that resetting the interval brings DRO much closer to the punishment paradigm (Poling & Ryan, 1982).

Severe running away in an emotionally disturbed boy was successfully treated with a procedure that combines a DRO procedure with time out (Chambers, Sanok, & Striefel, 1980). In this very interesting study, one-hour periods of not running away resulted in decreased restrictions on the child's in-school activity. Basically, the child moved through a hierarchy of six levels of increasingly less restrictive environments. If he attempted to run away, he was immediately moved to the most restrictive level. The procedure was modified several times as the behavior improved and reduced the problem from more than five times per week to an almost zero level. This was an extremely staff-intensive procedure, but appears to have been necessary for the boy's safety.

A brain-injured boy's hyperactive behavior was reduced by a DRO procedure that was partially conducted in a laboratory (Patterson, Jones, Whittier, & Wright, 1965). The boy was first treated in the laboratory with the aid of a wireless transmitter (during 10-minute sessions) by signaling him every 10-second period he was not off task, and providing a piece of candy. The second phase moved the procedure to the classroom, where he earned rewards for himself and his peers. Observations taken in the classroom, apparently not during conditioning periods, indicated that this procedure was successful.

Finally, in a study of the effects of a treatment package including a DRO procedure, the very disruptive school bus behavior of a moderately retarded 10-year-old was reduced to zero levels (Chiang, Iwata, & Dorsey, 1979). As part of the package, a point was awarded for every interval (one tenth of the trip between home and school) that no disruptive behavior occurred. Points were later exchanged at home and at school. Verbal reprimands were given for all inappropriate behavior, and points were lost for more than two reprimands per interval. Poor performance (not specified) resulted in withholding of backups, and/or time out. Although this procedure was very effective, the effectiveness of the various punishment or reinforcement components is unknown.

Summary

It is too bad that there are not more published studies of this promising procedure in classroom settings. Likewise, the absence of more research utilizing the resetting procedure indicates the need for additional investigation. The major drawback to DRO is the initial necessity for short periods, resetting the timer (if that is part of the procedure), and the requirement for constant teacher vigil (Poling & Ryan, 1982). However, it is an alternative to aversive procedures that has been quite successful with mild and more serious problems.

DRI

DRI represents a very different procedure from DRL and DRO, with the prime difference being that DRI involves specifically reinforcing desirable behaviors rather than involving the disruptive behaviors in the contingency. DRI procedures, usually involving teacher attention as reinforcers, were among the earliest published investigations by applied behavioral researchers. They are also, because of designs and a clear interest in demonstration of behavioral control by teachers, illustrative of the function of everyday classroom contingencies, especially contingent teacher attention. Further, as will be seen, teacher attention of any sort, even if it appears aversive, may indeed act as a reinforcer.

As a final note, it is equally valid to discuss

this class of interventions not as reductive techniques, but as techniques for increasing incompatible behavior. Whether you see a half full or a half empty glass, however, targeted disruptive behaviors are in fact reduced.

Differential Attention in the Classroom

Becker *et al.* (1967) investigated the effects of classroom rules, structured ignoring of mild disruptions, and praise for appropriate behavior in a number of elementary classrooms. Their procedure is typical for this type of research. First, they found that it was necessary to train carefully teachers to ignore and praise, even to give direct classroom feedback at first. The normal classroom often involves high use of reprimands and similar verbalizations, most of which are contingent on inappropriate behavior. Secondly, several of the inadequacies in the required dependence on teacher attention were found—attention not being very reinforcing or making attention contingent on behaviors for which children do not have prerequisite skills.

Classwide procedures for rules, ignoring mild disruption, and differential praise of appropriate behaviors were implemented across five elementary school teachers, in addition to special rules for especially problematic children. Results were very positive for the majority of children, drastically reducing off-task or mildly disruptive behaviors. However, there were also instructive failures. One boy's behavior was only slightly affected by differential praise because his academic skills were too low to meet academic requirements. Only after the initiation of tutoring was the praise effective. For one girl, nothing was particularly effective for long, including a token economy. She was verbally resistive as well; the authors describe it as a failure to find adequate reinforcers. For a final boy, praise was not particularly effective until combined with contingent, exchangeable points. These latter problems all occurred in one classroom, described as being one of the most positive; thus it appears that there are a number of children/problems who may not be initially responsive to this type of intervention.

Copeland, Brown, and Hall (1974) used differential principal attention for attendance to decrease truancy. Schutte and Hopkins (1970) increased compliance to instructions with differential teacher attention. Hall, Lund, and Jackson (1968) replicated Becker *et al.* (1967), using teacher attention and reducing "dawdling" and "non-study" behavior. In this case, the authors indicate that all students had the prerequisite academic skills to do the work. Hall *et al.* (1968) provided details of their teacher-training procedures, procedures that involved didactic and in-class training in using differential attention. In several cases data following termination of formal training are provided, indicating that teachers maintained effects.

Although Skiba, Pettigrew, and Alden (1971) were successful in reducing thumb sucking in three third grade girls by praising incompatible behaviors (writing, hands on desk, etc.) and ignoring thumb sucking, they were unable to demonstrate reduction to zero levels. Likewise, they pointed up the problems with insuring that, with a behavior like thumb sucking, differential reinforcement and ignoring last across the entire day.

All of the previously noted procedures are essentially a combination of structured ignoring of the undesirable behavior (extinction) and differential praise. Madsen, Becker, and Thomas (1968) investigated the separate effects of extinction and extinction plus praise. For their two subjects, mere ignoring of disruptions only served to increase them. With the addition of praise, rates were lowered. This potential problem with extinction in the absence of reinforcement will be discussed in a later section.

Baer, Rowbury, and Baer (1973) reported the same relative impotence of praise alone for some students that was reported by Becker *et al.* (1967). In their case, teacher attention and praise were contingent on student compliance with instructions. For two of three subjects, a brief time out for noncompliance was a necessary addition to achieve full effects. Workman, Kindall, and Williams (1980) also compared praise plus ignoring to praise plus a mild reprimand for student misbehavior. Although both procedures were effective, the reprimand condition was more rapidly effective whereas the ignore condition was more durable after withdrawal of treatment.

A number of studies indicate that differential attention for one student may have collateral effects on other students. In the clearest demonstration of this phenomenon, Witt and Adams (1980) examined the vicarious effects of two different teacher praise conditions—general praise and labeled praise. The latter contained a description of the behavior on which praise was contingent. For four kindergarten girls, mild disruptions were indirectly affected by observation of peers being attended to by the teacher, as well as affected by direct differential attention. Direct attention with a label was most effective in reducing misbehavior, followed by direct attention alone, and then vicarious attention. Interestingly, both misbehavior and desirable behavior were sequentially modified, providing a very clear example of the effects of teacher attention on different behaviors.

Boyd, Keilbaugh, and Axelrod (1981) did not fully replicate the results of Witt and Adams (1982). Approximately one half of their eight subjects were affected by observing teachers differentially attend to peers; for seven students the direct condition was far more effective in reducing mild misbehavior. Other studies indicate a consistent vicarious effect of teacher attention (Broden *et al.*, 1970; Kazdin, 1973; 1977; 1979; Kazdin & Klock, 1973). Although the effects were generally in a predicted direction, attention for off task vicariously increased the on task behavior of an observing peer in one case (Kazdin, 1977).

Two studies utilized differential adult attention (including more tangible activities) for attendance to decrease truancy (Bizzis & Bradley-Johnson, 1981; MacDonald, Gallimore, & MacDonald, 1970) in adolescents. Rosen and Rosen (1983) combined tokens and praise to reinforce an emotionally disturbed boy for only possessing his own objects with fines for possessing others to reduce stealing. Diaggio and Dickie (1978) used contingent home visits (contingent on earning tokens during the day for appropriate behavior) to reduce disruptive behavior of a student already on a token economy.

Peer Attention

Solomon and Wahler (1973) provided an excellent demonstration of the effects of differential peer attention. During baseline, 100% of peer attention to target disruptive students was contingent on misbehavior. Peers were then trained to ignore disruptions and to attend only to appropriate behavior and disruptions decreased greatly. Clearly a variety of differential contingencies for appropriate behavior in addition to teacher attention are effective.

Home-Based Contingencies

Trice, Parker, Furrow, and Iwata (1983) used notes to home with information concerning the days behavior to decrease disruptions and improve completion of classwork. Todd, Scott, Bostow, and Alexander (1976) sent notes home concerning student behavior where positive and negative contingencies were implemented. Disruptions were greatly reduced. These procedures combine positive and negative contingencies; attribution of effects to one or the other is not possible.

However, two studies investigated the effects of home reinforcement for good notes with kindergarten children. Lahey *et al.* (1977) sent brag sheets to parents, and Budd, Leibowitz, Riner, Mindell, and Goldfarb (1981) gave stars for no disruptive behavior for each of 12 school periods and sent the sheets home. In both cases school disruptions were reduced to very acceptable levels for all but two children in the Budd *et al.* (1981) study (out of 18 students).

Summary

DRI (teacher attention, peer attention, or other types) has been shown to be effective across a wide range of behaviors and students. Home school contingencies appear particularly effective. In the section on group behavior, additional successful applications will be examined. However, there are a number of caveats about DRI. First, teacher attention may not be a powerful contingency for more severe problems and for some students (e.g., Baer *et al.*, 1973; Becker *et al.*, 1967). In these cases additional reinforcers or aversive contingencies may be needed. Secondly, the application of differential reinforcement for behavior that is not in the repertoire, academic skills for example, is ineffective, or even creates disruptions (Center, Deitz, & Kaufman, 1982) because it offers reinforcers that are unobtainable.

Third, it is often difficult to train teachers to be consistently positive and to ignore mild misbehavior. Yet, it is clear that consistency is necessary for differential reinforcement to be effective. Fourth, descriptive praise may be more effective than general (Witt & Adams, 1983), and if teachers are to be trained, this may be a better objective. Fifth, there may well be positive side effects of differential attention during groups (e.g., Witt & Adams, 1983). Unusual vicarious effects were demonstrated when Pinkston, Reese, Leblanc, and Baer (1973) used contingent reinforcement of the victim following aggression combined with ignoring of the aggressor to decrease aggression in a preschool child; a seemingly vicarious effect.

Finally, structured ignoring (extinction) of misbehavior in the absence of misbehavior may well increase the problem (Madsen *et al.*, 1968), even though it has been an integral part of the differential reinforcement paradigm. In fact, it is doubtful, or at least unknown, if reinforcement of desirable behaviors without structured ignoring would have any effect at all. Irrespective of these concerns, DRI is a very easy procedure to use if teachers can learn to ignore mild disruptions. It seems that employment of DRI interventions may be applicable to almost any type of behavior problem.

DRA

The final type of positive reduction procedure has the greatest potential for routine improvement of classroom conduct because it not only reduces disruptive behavior, but can improve academic performance. Most of the studies to be discussed in this section examined the collateral effects of providing reinforcement for academic performance on inappropriate classroom behavior. The overall results of this research have great implications for teachers and classroom consultants who are interested in the most logistically simple procedure to intervene with behavior problems. Likewise, there are clear implications for the notion of engineering classrooms (Bushell, 1978) so that inappropriate behavior seldom occurs, and then seldom needs clinical interventions.

In-Class Procedures

Ferritor, Buckholdt, Hamblin, and Smith (1972) provided one of the earliest examples of the differential effects of rewarding on-task or appropriate behavior, versus directly reinforcing academic outcomes. In several third grade classrooms, a token economy was implemented, along with differential teacher attention and ignoring procedures (see the preceding). Two targeting procedures were examined, attending and tokens for being on task, and/or points and attention for academic performance. Significantly, they measured on task separately from disruptions. In general, they found that contingencies for on task and academics drastically lowered disruptions; on task was superior to academics for disruptions, but only academic contingencies had a significant effect on academic performance; a combination of both was superior to either alone. Thus, a classroom where contingencies were specifically directed to good behavior and academics had the best academic performance and the best behavior. However, attention to academics alone still had a significant effect on disruptive behavior.

Marholin and Steinman (1977) found similar results to Ferritor *et al.* (1972) in that reinforcement for on-task or academic performance reduced disruptions, but that on-task reinforcement was slightly superior. However, probes taken when the teacher was not in the room indicated that contingencies for academic performance maintained lower disruption levels than reinforcement for on-task (that could only be given by the teacher being present).

Hay, Hay, and Nelson (1977) also compared reinforcement of on-task with reinforcement of academics for five elementary school boys. Although they only measured a general on task category where disruptions were not differentiated, they demonstrated that reinforcement of on-task or academics increased on task, but only academic reinforcement increased academic performance to a significant degree. Hundert, Bucher, and Henderson (1976) report a similar study and found the same results.

In a series of studies, Ayllon and his associates (Ayllon & Roberts, 1974; Ayllon, Layman, & Burke, 1972; Ayllon, Layman, & Kandel, 1975) systematically replicated the effects of tokens for academic performance on disruptive behavior and academics. Results were consistent for four EMR boys, five disruptive regular class elementary school boys, and three hyperactive school children in a special class. Reinforcement of academics alone drastically reduced the level of disruptive behavior while improving classroom performance. Ayllon *et al.* (1975) demonstrated that academic reinforcement reduced disruptive behavior to a degree equal or better than that achieved with medication.

Three other studies indicate similar effects of altering academic procedures or contingencies on disruptive behavior. Van Houten, Hill, and Parsons (1975) in an examination of the effects of public posting of student performance scores, found that on-task behavior increased as well as academic performance (disruptions were not measured separately). Thomas, Nielson, Kuypers, and Becker (1968) reported that adding an academic tutor to an intervention examining the effects of differential teacher attention on appropriate behavior increased on-task behavior. Finally, Kelly and Stokes (1982) examined the effects of individual contracts with high school students in an alternative school. During baseline students were paid for their attendance at the school. Later, payment was made contingent on greed levels of academic performance. Attendance was even better under the academic contingencies than under direct reinforcement of attendance.

Home–School Contingencies

Witt, Hannafin, and Martens (1983) investigated the effects of sending a daily note from school to home concerning the students performance on a daily academic assignment. Parents were to provide praise and privileges contingent on the number of correct assignments and cross time improvement. Results indicate that the procedure was not only effective with the academic assignment, but that drastic improvements were made in disruptive behavior. This procedure is perhaps the most logistically simple procedure possible for a teacher because attention must only be given to scoring work, a normal process, to enjoy the benefits of improved student behavior.

Summary

Reinforcement of academic behavior has consistently been demonstrated to effect very positive changes in student on-task or disruptive behaviors. Although several studies indicated that direct attention to appropriate behavior was slightly superior to reinforcement of academics for disruptive behavior, the collateral effects of academic reinforcement on disruptive behavior were impressive (Ferritor *et al.*, 1972; Marholin & Steinman, 1977). All studies examined found that reinforcement of academics was quite effective in reducing inappropriate behavior; the collateral effects of reinforcing appropriate behavior on academics was variable, however. For that reason, the target of choice is academic performance. Another reason for such a selection is the ease of administration by teachers.

Although appropriate behavior and academics are related, it is not at all impossible to remain disruptive and complete assignments, making this procedure conceptually different from DRI, where a clearly incompatible positive behavior was reinforced. Thus it is not entirely clear why the effects on disruptive behavior of contingent reinforcement of academic performance are so consistent. One reason might be indicated by the results of Marholin and Steinman (1977), where academic work may have become a discriminative stimulus (with accompanying reinforcing value) for appropriate behavior.

Whatever the reason, direct reinforcement of academic behavior ought to be prime candidate in every case an intervention for inappropriate behavior is being considered. Caution not to offer reinforcement for behaviors not in student repertoires is made (Center *et al.*, 1982), as this may only increase disruptive behavior. Otherwise reinforcing academic performance increases academic performance, decreases disruptive behavior, has no demonstrated negative side effects, is totally positive in nature, and is a procedure that can be maintained across the year.

Extinction

As discussed earlier, ignoring of misbehavior is generally a part of procedures to reduce behavior through positive means. This is properly classified as extinction. It is different from time out (see following) because time out involves contingent removal of attention, whereas extinction is the general absence of reinforcement for a certain behavior.

Ignoring apparently has also been suggested as a behavior modification technique in the absence of targeting specific positive behaviors (Drabman, Jarvie, & Archbold, 1976). As Drabman *et al.* (1976) pointed out, extinction to be effective must be absolute, teachers must be prepared to see the misbehavior increase at first or in bursts, and should expect only a gradual change. Increases in behavior were certainly verified by Madsen *et al.* (1969) in their examination of extinction. For these reasons extinction by itself requires careful preparation of the teacher, and careful monitoring (Drabman *et al.*, 1976). It seems more reasonable to include in a package with a specific positive component unless after careful assessment of the maintaining conditions, the change agent judges there is sufficient positive reinforcement already present in the environment.

Summary

Most forms of classroom conduct problems appear to be amenable to interventions using positive reinforcement. Two procedures, DRL and DRO, may be more difficult to implement, especally with interval DRL or DRO with short monitoring periods and resetting of timers. In these cases requirements are heavy on classroom personnel, perhaps too heavy for a regular classroom teacher with 25 to 35 students. There are, however, a number of alternatives that utilize normal classroom activites as focus; notably the DRA procedures discussed earlier. In the case of DRA, implementation is not difficult at all, in fact management of reinforcers can even be delayed until the child gets home (Witt *et al.*, 1983).

All of these positive procedures share some general qualities. They all alter the absolute or relative relationship between positive contingencies for inappropriate behavior and positive contingencies for positive behavior.

Typically, either misbehavior is ignored or another attempt is made to reduce reinforcement (differential attention for example) or additional reinforcers are provided to desirable behaviors (DRA for example, or some forms of DRI). In the latter case it is then perhaps the relative reinforcement density that is altered, because reinforcement may still remain for the misbehavior (peer attention for example). This relative relationship can also be altered because the contingent reinforcers for positive behavior are more powerful than natural reinforcement for the undesirable behavior. In cases where procedures are not initially effective, and where other contingencies are in effect, this may be a result of a ratio that is not heavily in favor of the desired behavior in terms of frequency and potency.

The implication for change agents is that reinforcers should be carefully considered for the possible new reinforcers and for ones likely to remain in the environment. Likewise, if misbehavior is being negatively reinforced because it results in avoidance of commands or undesirable activities, then additional aspects of the treatment package must be added. Finally, it should be obvious by now that these interventions are not singular component phenomena; they are literally packages, and as such the composition must always be carefully planned.

If teachers are willing to work on changing their styles in the classroom toward increased use of praise and ignoring of minor disruptions, then positive results are also likely. However, consultants might seriously consider the necessity for adequate training and monitoring of teachers when interventions only involve differential attention and structured ignoring. An interesting approach to resolving a referred conduct problem might be to go ahead and implement a procedure like DRI or DRA, and then provide training on increasing differential and positive teacher attention. The result of such a procedure might be to reduce the need for future referrals, while solving the problems at hand. Finally, the research discussed so far goes a long way to providing most of the information needed to design and implement classroom models that are engineered to support positive student behavior without having to result in frequent clinical interventions. However, there may be a clear need with some students to use procedures involving aversive contingencies, a number of which have been investigated in the behavioral literature. As will be discussed, the use of aversive procedures may be justified only if more positive interventions have been tried and found ineffective, or if a clear danger to the student or others is judged.

Reduction of Behavior through Contingent Use of Aversive Procedures

There may be no more emotionally charged issue for behavioral approaches to treatment than the use of punishment (Axelrod & Apsche, 1983). Part of the problem is the difference between the technical and popular connotations of the term *punishment;* although a bigger part of the problem is violent disagreements over the appropriate uses of more aversive forms of punishment, especially in the treatment of the severely handicapped. (See Axelrod & Apsche, 1983, for a very thorough examination of the issues surrounding punishment.) However, regular and special classrooms for the mildly handicapped have not escaped the controversy, especially over such issues as time out (Polsgrove, 1983).

This chapter will review four classes of procedures that are technically considered punishment: use of reprimands or negative verbal feedback; response cost; time out; and overcorrection. To make it clear from the onset, the use of positive procedures to reduce classroom misbehavior is generally preferable; however, there may be situations and behaviors that may require punishment. When those situations occur, then professionals must understand and use aversive procedures appropriately. The reader will have to decide if softly spoken teacher reprimands require the same consideration as isolation time out; however, the two procedures serve the same function. That function is the reduction of behavior by making aversive events contingent on its occurrence.

Defining Punishment and Aversives

Technically punishment is "a reduction of the future probability of a specific response as a result of the immediate delivery of a stimulus for that response"; (Azrin & Holz as cited in Van Houten, 1983). In addition, the removal of a stimulus contingent on a response which also reduces future probabilities is considered punishment (Van Houten, 1983). Heron (1978) further specified three general types of punishment that are applicable to this discussion: the presenting of an aversive, or unpleasant stimulus contingent on a response (aversive is ultimately a relative issue); the withdrawal of a positive event (a penalty, fine, or as it is typically called, response cost); or the withdrawal of the opportunity to be reinforced (i.e., time out). There are very complex technical issues surrounding these general definitions, but they will serve for the current discussion.

Negative Verbal Feedback and Reprimands

Teacher reprimands and negative verbalizations are extremely common in classrooms; more common by far than praise (Heller & White, 1977; White, 1975). Typically, such verbalizations are made contingent on some student behavior that is aversive to the teacher. However, like any type of contingent teacher attention, reprimands can serve as either reinforcers or punishers. Given the frequency of these behaviors, it seems reasonable to determine what effect they may have, just as examining positive attention increased our knowledge about the classroom.

Thomas, Becker, and Armstrong (1968) demonstrated that increasing the disapproving statements of a teacher greatly increased the rate of student misbehavior. Others, however, have found certain forms of verbal reprimands to reduce the frequency of misbehavior. If they serve that function, then technically they are punishers.

O'Leary, Kaufman, Kass, and Drabman (1970) found that soft reprimands, given in close proximity to the student, did in fact decrease inappropriate behavior in elementary school children. Loud reprimands, however, accelerated misbehavior. Hall *et al.* (1971) demonstrated that a teacher saying "no" and pointing a finger at a handicapped student acted as a punisher. None of these studies, however, examined the full range of particular qualities that might differentiate reprimands that punish from reprimands that reinforce.

Jones and Miller (1974) observed teachers of emotionally disturbed children to determine which were the most effective at leading "orderly discussions." Such qualities as correctly identifying potentially disruptive behavior, a repertoire of gestures and verbalizations to indicate displeasure, proximity, quick responding, and subsequent positive attending were identified. Two target teachers were trained to deliver mild reprimands in a similar fashion, and disruptions in their groups decreased. Van Houten, Nau, MacKenzie-Keating, Sameoto, and Colavecchia (1982) conducted perhaps the most complete analysis of reprimands and found the following: reprimands delivered with eye contact and a grasp of the student were more effective than those without; otherwise closer reprimands were more effective than more distant ones; and finally, reprimands of one student may also decrease misbehavior of another.

Finally, several studies examined the effects of feedback, both positive and negative, about student behavior. Lobitz and Burns (1977) and Drabman and Lahey (1974) found that public feedback to a student about behavior was an effective procedure in reducing misbehavior. Kerr, Strain, and Ragland (1982) found that teacher-directed peer evaluations about very disruptive student behavior were quite effective in reducing it. Feedback was a routine part of a daily group meeting to discuss behavioral goals in a school for behavior disordered children. Goals alone were not very effective.

In summary, reprimands delivered in certain ways are an effective social punisher. The available research is rather thin (Van Houten & Doleys, 1983), and this is unfortunate given the apparent teacher preference for this procedure. Likewise, the differential effects of different types of reprimands should be considered in classroom research because it may confound results (Van Houten & Doleys, 1983). It is also unknown whether reprimands would even be necessary in a classroom that was predominantly positive. For example, in the Behavior Analysis Follow Through model, teachers were trained to give no negative feedback as part of the model, and on-task rates in classrooms implementing the model were very high (Jackson, 1976). Nevertheless, reprimands and negative verbal feedback can serve as mild punishers.

Response Cost

Response cost involves the removal of some earned reinforcers (Pazulinec, Meyerrose, & Sajwaj, 1983). It is different from time out because there is no restriction from earning reinforcers following the contingent removal. Three general procedures have been used: giving students points or tokens at the beginning of a period and taking away a certain number contingent on misbehavior; earning points or tokens for good behavior and losing them for bad; and group procedures (Pazulinac *et al.*, 1983). Typically, response cost has been used in very structured environments, given the need for careful control (Walker, 1983). The majority of studies on response cost involve token economies or group procedures and the reader is referred to those chapters in this volume. There are, however, some more individually applied investigations.

Witt and Elliot (1982) developed a procedure called a response cost lottery. For three fourth grade boys a lottery was established with activities and prizes as awards. Slips of paper were given them at the beginning of a specific period, and if they emitted one of several disruptive behaviors a slip was taken away from them. Remaining slips were turned in and became tickets for an end-of-week drawing for the rewards. Results indicated that the procedure increased on-task behavior for all boys (unfortunately disruptive behavior was not measured) to within group norms. This is a very low cost procedure for a teacher once established, although it involves extra privileges and some planning. There were no reported negative side effects.

Salend and Allen (1985) studied teacher- and self-managed response cost procedures to reduce the out-of-seat behavior of several learning disabled second graders. Tokens were given to students at the beginning of a period, and taken away contingent on the student leaving his seat. Out of seat behavior was reduced to near zero under both conditions.

Rapport, Murphy, and Bailey (1982) compared a response cost system to ritalin in increasing the on-task behavior of two hyperactive boys. During arithmetic the teacher would either flip a numbered card down, or activate a signalling device when the students were observed not to be working. Twenty points were given initially, each representing one minute of free time; each card or signal deducted one minute. Response cost was equal to or superior to ritalin in reducing off task.

In summary, response cost appears to be an effective procedure appropriate for classroom use (Walker, 1983). Given the required control and attention on the part of the teacher, choosing it as an intervention may be warranted only if positive procedures are ineffective or only partially effective. One exception to this may be the response cost lottery (Witt *et al.*, 1983). Procedures like those of Salend and Allen (1985) also seem simple to implement, especially if students can partially manage it themselves.

Time Out

Time out is a reductive procedure that generally involves changing the environment of the student from a more to a less reinforcing one contingent on particular student behavior (Harris, 1985). This may not require removing an individual from the environment; in fact there is a continuum of time out procedures that ranges along a dimension of restrictiveness (Brantner & Doherty, 1983; Gast & Nelson, 1977; Harris, 1985). Because of the potential abuse (and unfortunately actual abuse, Polsgrove, 1983) of this procedure, and beause of the ethical issues surrounding its use, time out has been extensively reviewed (Brantnor & Doherty, 1983; Gast & Nelson, 1977; Harris, 1985; Hobbs & Forehand, 1977; MacDonald & Forehand, 1973; Nelson & Rutherford, 1983). Likewise, several legal decisions concerning its use, primarily in institutions, have appeared (Griffith, 1983). The current review will not be exhaustive, but will provide coverage of examples of the various types of time out applied in the targeted settings.

The bulk of research on time out appears to be in situations other than classrooms for regular or mildly handicapped children. However, there are published studies on nearly all forms of time out for individuals and within interdependent group contingencies in the targeted classroom settings. This review will conclude with a discussion of ethical considerations and suggestions for use. The literature review will be grouped along the dimensions of restrictiveness, going from least restrictive to most restrictive, as follows: ignoring; removal of reinforcing stimuli or materials; contingent observation (the first three have all been called nonexclusionary); exclusion short of isolation; and isolation. It is recognized that the differences among some of these procedures may be small (Harris, 1985); however, examination through the hierarchy should facilitate the ethical discussion.

Nonexclusion

Lovitt, Lovitt, Eaton, and Kirkwood (1973) used a peer confederate and a contingent "natural consequences" to reduce the highly inappropriate or obscene verbalizations of a 9-year-old behavior-disordered youngster. When the child would emit a targeted verbalization, his peer, who sat beside him, would get up and move away, after informing him why he was moving. The peer would only come back when the target child made an appropriate comment. This procedure involved several aversives: first the peer comments as he left, and second the removal of possible peer reinforcement. The second part is essentially a nonexclusionary form of time out (the target child is not removed from the room) that involves ignoring and removal of reinforcing stimuli. Whichever of the components was effective is unclear; however, the comments reduced to near zero. The role of peer ignoring was, however, illuminated when a new child came into class, gave lots of attention to the target during the time out and drastically accelerated the misbehavior. This ceased when the teacher and peer explained to the new boy what the procedures were.

Kubany, Weiss, and Sloggett (1971) intervened with a regular first grade boy who was receiving high rates of peer attention for misbehavior. Each 2 minutes without disruption earned a potential treat for the class and the target child at the end of the day. Whenever the child misbehaved, the clock was turned off (thus removing the reinforcing signal); the child distributed the treats at the end of the day. Implementation of this procedure was highly effective at first, until a "blow up"; after that the teacher made sure the target did not give himself the first treat at the end of the day; on days he was bad there were not enough treats to go around. No other problems were noted. Although the clock served a time out function, it is clear that end of day treats were quite powerful in their own right; thus this procedure is similar to DRO.

Spitalnik and Drabman (1976) placed an orange card on the desk of two EMR children for 10 minutes contingent on misbehavior. This served as a signal that randomly given tangible reinforcers would not be given to the child with the orange card. Misbehavior during time out resulted in lengthening the interval and additional orange cards. This was highly effective. The authors note that because the card was given with a teacher comment about why, this reprimand may have caused the decrement in student behavior; however, reprimands were common in the classroom before time out.

The final type of nonexclusionary time out has been called contingent observation (Harris, 1985). Porterfield, Herbert, Herbert-Jackson, and Risley (1976) implemented a hierarchy of procedures contingent on the disruptive behavior of preschool children (aggression, crying, tantrums, etc.). Contingent on these behaviors a child was told what he or she had done, moved to the edge of the activity, and told to observe good behavior. The child was moved back to the group when the child could, on a prompt, tell what they should do. Refusal to cooperate, or continuance of disruption resulted in an exclusionary time out, that is, being moved to a quiet place. The procedure was very effective across 26 different children, caregivers continued to use it correctly, and staff and parents judged the procedure to be acceptable. This latter social validity assessment is critical with exclusionary time out procedures. In a similar procedure, Foxx and Shapiro (1978) used a time out ribbon with more seriously retarded children. When the child lost his ribbon, all attention was withdrawn, including the ability to earn edibles. Harris (1985) considers this a form of contingent observation because the child remains within the group.

The common thing with all of these procedures is that the child's environment is made less reinforcing contingent on the targeted behavior without any other type of exclusion. It was noted, however, that there are several possible potent components to these procedures, including teacher reprimands, and the possibility of reinforcement from other sources. It also seems likely that some backup procedure is necessary if the less exclusionary procedure results in student resistance (Porterfield *et al.*, 1976). These issues must be carefully considered before implementation of this type of procedure, or the environment may not in fact become less reinforcing. Nonexclusionary time out appears to have been effective, although the research into the crucial parameters is sparse. Certainly this type of time out is the least restrictive form of time out, and therefore may be accompanied by the fewest ethical objections.

Exclusion

The next level of time out involves removing a child from an activity to a less reinforcing part of the classroom, but not into isolation. Contingent observation (Porterfield *et al.*, 1976) included this as a backup to nonexclusionary time out. It appears (see the following discussion) that back ups in case of a failure of less exclusionary time out procedures typically involve more exclusionary time out.

Burchard and Barrera (1972), Devine and Tomlinson (1976), and Firestone (1976) all used some form of in-class time out chair to reduce serious disruption and aggression (Burchard & Barrera; Firestone) and less serious off task (Devine & Tomlinson). Devine and Tomlinson (1976) employed a work clock that ran when all children were on task and stopped when disruption occurred, resulting in a strike against the offending child. Three strikes resulted in the time out chair for one minute. Continued disruption or refusal to go to the chair resulted in removal from the classroom to the principal's office. (Whether that was time out is unclear). The procedures were effective, although there is little data.

For the other two studies, isolation time out was the back up for resistance. Both procedures drastically reduced serious problem behaviors. Again, the necessity for a fall back procedure is obvious; and it is unclear what the effects of exclusionary time out would have been without that threat. Thus although ostensibly less restrictive, more restrictive procedures seem to be built into the treatment package. Those using these procedures must seriously consider that particular issue from an ethical and logistical viewpoint.

Isolation Time Out

The contingent removal of a child from the natural environment to an isolated room is a procedure that has perhaps received the most negative press of the time out procedures (Polsgrove, 1983). Because it results in a highly aversive consequence, which has overtones of jail, this is perfectly understandable. This procedure can certainly not be used unless staff are physically capable of removing the offending student if he or she is uncooperative; and the dangers for abuse seem great. This procedure has been used with the populations of interest in this chapter with clear effects and several examples will be discussed in the following. All of the examples chosen involve serious problem behaviors by the students, primarily aggression toward others or destructive behavior.

Lahey, McNees, and McNees (1973) used isolation time to reduce the high-rate obscene verbal tic of an EMR boy. These behaviors were seriously interfering with his school progress (over 150 per hour). Prior to time out, a positive practice procedure was attempted; however, staff and subject expressed extreme dislike for this procedure. During treatment, the subject was placed in an isolation time out room contingent on any obscenity. The effects were dramatic, and a reversal was attempted. Because his rates went up immediately, time out was reinstated. Subsequently the observed rate went to zero. The parents reported generalization to the home, allowing them to take the child out of the home for the first time in years. It should be noted, however, that during the last phase there were periods when the time out room was used for other purposes, and rates went up drastically. Thus, it appears that the presence of the time out room was a necessary stimulus.

Webster (1976) reported the use of isolation time out to reduce the highly aggressive behaviors of an emotionally disturbed boy. The boy had a long history of aggression, and had recently injured other children; psychotherapy had been previously tried without effect. First, the teachers explained the problems to the boy, and discussed why his behavior should improve; then, for 5 days, warnings were given contingent on misbehavior; finally time out was instituted. Note that time out was potentially lengthy, the only parameter was that he remain in time out for the rest of the period, taking only his school books with him. Time out was not apparently immediately effective, and the child spent approximately an hour per day in time out. By the third week, however, drastic positive changes occurred and he only spent an average of 18 minutes per day in time out; by the 7th week no aggressive episodes were occurring. It is noted that his homework and classroom participation were very positively affected. It seems clear that the time out procedure was an effective punisher.

Conclusions and Recommendations

The various forms of time out are clearly effective in reducing misbehavior. Also, they often have positive generalization effects (Brantner & Doherty, 1983); however, they may also cause children to physically resist teachers. Their common function involves making a child's environment less reinforcing contingent on a misbehavior. There are a number of practical and ethical concerns with this procedure that must be fully understood by those who consider the use of time out.

First, before any form of time out can be effective, the normal environment must be positive (Nelson & Rutherford, 1983). Given the low praise and high disapprovals in some classrooms, this may be a problem. It is suggested that time out never be used except in a package that includes reinforcement for appropriate behavior (Gast & Nelson, 1977). A related environmental problem is that putting a child into the more restrictive time out may reinforce the teacher (a very aversive child is now removed) and increase the potential for inappropriate use.

Secondly, even mild time out procedures can require a more restrictive back up, thus not avoiding the potential problems. Similarly, the teacher may not be able to physically remove the child if required, resulting in a very dangerous physical confrontation (Nelson & Rutherford, 1983).

Given the problems with time out, it should be continuously evaluated. It is a procedure that may require extensive teacher attention and may lead to potential nonimplementation. Failure to evaluate may be a common problem with all interventions (Nelson & Rutherford, 1983); however, it has greater potential for harm in this case.

A number of recommendations have been made to insure the nonabuse of time out, especially isolation time out. They include (all are taken from Gast & Nelson, 1977; Harris, 1985; and Nelson & Rutherford, 1983):

1. Use positive reductive procedures first. Use mild forms of time out (nonexclusionary) if those do not work. If exclusionary or isolation time out is to be used (even as a back up), then the next procedures should be followed.
2. The maintaining variable in the environment must be carefully analyzed to insure that time out might be effective.
3. Always use time out with other explicitly positive procedures.
4. Carefully define the target behaviors and time out procedures in writing, and insure that staff are trained in the use of time out. The physical ability of the staff to take the student to time out must be explicitly considered.
5. Collect data and evaluate the procedure for effects.
6. Insure that an isolation room is safe for the student and that time out is implemented as written.

In the judgment of this author, isolation time out is unlikely to be an effective common procedure in most regular schools because of the logistical and physical requirements. Unfortunately, it is only too common to see teachers move problem children away from other children in an inconsistent effort to control misbehavior. It is highly doubtful if these procedures are typically effective; they may often be abused. Milder forms of time out may be particularly effective with younger children and are a likely tool for those attempting interventions. However, it is a tool that should be at the bottom of the toolbox and used only when others do not work.

Overcorrection

Overcorrection is a procedure that has been widely used with more severely handicapped clients (Axelrod, Brantner, & Meddock, 1978; Foxx & Bechtel, 1983; Miltenberger & Fuqua, 1981) and very infrequently in the schools with normal or mildly handicapped children. Two major types of overcorrection include restitutional overcorrection and positive practice overcorrection. The former requires the offender to make the environment like it was, or to make restitution. The latter typically involves requiring the subject to practice repeatedly the correct behavior, or simply make repeatedly some designated series of movements. As a procedure, it has proven effective in reducing such serious behaviors as aggression, self-abuse, and self-stimulation (Foxx & Bechtel, 1983). It has also been part of several toileting training programs (Foxx & Bechtel, 1983).

Bornstein, Hamilton, and Quevillon (1977) used a mild form of overcorrection to reduce the out of seat behaviors of a behavior-problem boy. While out of seat behaviors were targeted, the child exhibited a wide range of more severe behavior problems when he was out of his seat. The procedure included remaining in the classroom during a noon period and for every infraction, the child had to state the rule and raise his hand properly and ask permission to leave the seat. Practice lasted 3 minutes. The effects were quite drastic; interestingly, a reversal involving mild reprimands and differential praise was not effective. A final phase, with overcorrection, also had the child self-counting, and if he matched closely the teacher he earned the class a reward. Posttreatment follow-up found that he still had low levels of out of seat.

Summary

Certainly, aversive procedures have been widely used and are effective reductive techniques. Equally certainly they create more of an ethical dilemma for the change agent in selecting treatment to match problems. Careful analysis should be used to insure that there is a positive support system in place to support the reduction of problem behavior. If not, then the introduction of reinforcement procedures should be part of the treatment plan.

Like other reductive procedures with school populations, the evidence for generalization is sparse. One frequent concern, that of negative side effects, is real enough in some cases; however, positive side effects are as often reported (Newsom *et al.*, 1983).

Aversive procedures have often been used alone or in conjunction with positive procedures to reduce undesirable behavior in the classroom (e.g., Baer *et al.*, 1973; Barrish, Saunders, & Wolf, 1969; Chiang *et al.*, 1979; Rosen & Rosen, 1983). As will be seen later, they are generally acceptable if the behavior problem is judged severe enough, although positive reductive procedures are more acceptable to teachers (e.g., Elliott, Witt, Galvin, & Peterson, 1984).

It would seem important, however, to plan on withdrawing any aversive procedure and substituting a positive one once the behavior is under control. On the other hand, if the behavior is dangerous to the child or others, then it may need to be reduced quickly. Aversive procedures often achieve a quicker reduction. Finally, those who choose aversive procedures as the first treatment of choice have the responsibility to insure that the goals of treatment warrant such a choice.

Group Contingencies

There have been an increasing number of published evaluations of classroom contingencies that are applied concurrently to groups. Gresham and Gresham (1982) listed several advantages of group contingencies for behavior management over individual contingencies, including efficiency in teacher administration and effectiveness. Three types of group contingencies have been identified, and often compared (Gresham & Gresham, 1982; Litow & Pumoy, 1975): interdependent, where the overall behavior of the entire group determines if the group will receive reinforcement; independent, where the same contingencies are applied to the group, but each individual's behavior determines individual reinforcement; and dependent, where the behavior of several select group members determines reinforcement for the entire group.

Group contingencies have been developed to improve academic behavior (Bushell, 1978) and social behavior (Barrish *et al.*, 1969), and they have been implemented to reduce problem behaviors across the entire classroom (see the following discussion). The following discussion will be brief and is oriented to analyzing several reductive procedures that have been applied in a group format.

Group Reductive Techniques Using Positive Reinforcement

Group interventions have employed the previously discussed positive reductive techniques—DRO, DRI, and DRL—in interdependent and independent formats. For example, Schmidt and Ulrich (1969) used a group DRO procedure to reduce noise in a school gym. During gym, for every 10-minute period where noise did not exceed a particular decibel level, additional gym time and breaks were awarded the group. If noise at any time exceeded the limit, the timer was reset. Eleftherios, Shoudt, and Strang (1972) used a 30-second DRO procedure to reduce out of seat behavior in a class of first graders. If any child got out of his seat inappropriately, the timer was reset; otherwise a class token was earned, exchangeable for class recess time and a party. Wolf, Hanley, King, Lachowicz, and Giles (1970) used a timer with a momentary DRO procedure in reducing out of seat behavior, whereas Salzberg, Hopkins, Wheeler, and

Taylor (1974) used a whole interval DRO to reduce disruptive lunchroom behavior.

Although these DRO procedures were in an interdependent format, Epstein, Repp, and Cullinan (1978) used classwide DRL in an independent format to reduce effectively obscene language. On the other hand, Greene, Bailey, and Barber (1981) used an interdependent procedure very similar to DRL to reduce school bus misbehavior. Each day middle school students received rewards, providing the number of high noise outbursts did not exceed a specified level of outbursts. Finally, Gendrich, McNees, Schnelle, Beegle, and Clark (1982) provided schoolwide rewards depending on the amount of litter on school grounds remaining under a specified criteria for the week.

Perhaps the best replicated dependent group DRL procedure has been the Good Behavior Game (Barrish *et al.*, 1969; Darveaux, 1984; Fishbein & Wasik, 1981; Harris & Sherman, 1973; Medland & Stachnik, 1972; Saigh & Umar, 1983). Basically, the class is divided into teams, rules and inappropriate behaviors are carefully defined, and then each time a student breaks a rule, it is recorded (and usually displayed). Either the group with the fewest marks (below a criterion) or any team below the criterion is rewarded. This procedure has been extremely effective across a wide variety of ages, students, and even nationalities. Likewise, it appears to be simple to operate once the initial planning is over.

One of the easiest group DRI procedures has been the home–school note, or letter. Dougherty and Dougherty (1977) and Ayllon, Garber, and Pisor (1975) sent notes home for each student depending on appropriate behavior. Both were highly successful in reducing behavior problems in classrooms. Principal attention was delivered in a dependent group format to various classroom teams if they earned sufficient points; and then in an independent format to individual teams members for individual behavior (Darch & Thorpe, 1977). Both procedures were effective.

Just as group contingencies to reduce misbehavior can involve positive contingencies, there have been procedures involving dependent group punishment, primarily nonexclusionary time out. Ritschel, Mongrella, and Presbie (1972) played rock and roll music on a school bus as long as all students were in their seats. As soon as any student left his or her seat, the music was turned off for 5 seconds. This corresponds to nonexclusionary time out in that the reinforcing stimulus is removed contingent on the targeted behavior. Wasserman (1977) let a clock run as long as no students were misbehaving in a class; misbehavior resulted in turning the clock off and turning a light on for as long as the misbehavior continued. Rewards were contingent on the amount of elapsed time; thus the reinforcing stimulus (the clock) was removed contingent on the targeted behavior.

Summary

Group contingencies can be programmed along parameters similar to individual contingencies. Such contingencies, because they are not individualized, may have their special problems given the complex nature of the classroom environment. Either group or individual contingencies can reduce misbehavior. However, as long as the general classroom environment does not support desirable behaviors, clinical interventions must remain in place. It would seem more desirable to create a normal classroom environment, essentially a set of independent group contingencies, that obviate the need for individual interventions. The author would agree with others (Gresham & Gresham, 1981; Kazdin, 1984) that group contingencies are more efficient than individual contingencies. However, it is the essential arrangement of the classroom and its routine impact on individual behaviors that is critical. The ideal would be for whatever arrangement exists in the classroom to support continually the desired behaviors. Such an arrangement could lessen the need for frequent clinical interventions to reduce behavior—the normal classroom environment would not support them. This idea goes beyond the notion of teacher verbal behavior or attention *per se*, and involves the idea of engineering classroom environments; most engineered environments may well involve group contingencies.

Acceptability of Treatments to Reduce Behavior

Recently, a number of investigations into the acceptability of reductive treatments have been reported (Elliott *et al.*, 1984; Kazdin, 1980a,b, 1981; Witt & Martens, 1983; Witt, Martens, & Elliott, 1984; Woolridge & Richman, 1985). Although the investigations were conducted among different audiences (educators or undergraduates) the results appear relatively consistent. First, positive reductive procedures are generally more acceptable than such procedures as time out or overcorrection. With one study (Elliott *et al.*, 1984), a mild aversive procedure, the response cost lottery (see previous discussion), was also rated very highly. Secondly, the severity of the case affects treatment acceptability, with more severe behavior problems justifying more severe treatments. Third, the amount of time required on the part of teachers was a significant factor in treatment acceptability; although it was accepted that more severe problems were more time consuming.

Relatedly, more complex treatments were rated as less acceptable, given the severity of the problem factor. Other factors that play a part included the risk to the child, and the race and gender of the potential subject (Woolridge & Richman, 1985). In the latter case, white males rated more severe punishment. Although, except for the last example, none of these findings are surprising, they provide necessary social validity (Wolf, 1978) assessments for reductive techniques.

Basically, more positive treatments are the first choice, especially if the problem behavior is judged mild, and the procedures are not too complicated. Such procedures as DRI, differential attention, and reinforcement of academics would seem highly acceptable under both of these criteria. If the behavior problem is judged very serious, then more restrictive, and perhaps aversive procedures are acceptable. This certainly coincides with the previous recommendations concerning time out for example. Finally, the reference groups do not appear to equate all forms of aversive use in terms of acceptability. Thus, the technical distinction between punishment and reinforcement is not entirely a socially valid distinction. However, it would be interesting to see what the public opinion would be about a teacher-training program that emphasized the use of effective reprimands over the use of differential attention. Certainly, professionals using the various guidelines in this chapter would seem to be on safe ground. The personal opinion of the author is that less complex, and less time-consuming procedures are the one most likely to be implemented.

A Final Comment on Treatment Maintenance

Problem behaviors in the classroom can be reduced in a variety of ways. Nearly all of the procedures involve making reinforcement available for desired behavior and simultaneously reducing reinforcement for undesirable behavior. If such changes are not explicitly part of a procedure, as in time out, then recommendations for using the procedure involve altering reinforcement conditions.

Maintenance and generalization of treatment effects are issues with the reduction of classroom problems, just as with most areas of behavioral treatment. Most of the articles reviewed in this chapter did not explicitly examine maintenance after treatment was withdrawn. Given that a chapter in this volume is devoted to these issues, this section will be oriented toward particular classroom issues.

One type of classroom intervention is oriented toward changing the classroom environment more or less permanently; for example, those training teachers to use differential attention or to ignore appropriately (e.g., Hall *et al.*, 1968). In these cases a goal is to maintain those environmental changes in posttreatment, as well as maintaining student behavior changes at the same time. These are two separate issues of maintenance that may or may not be related.

On the other hand, there are reductive techniques that one would hope were temporary—time out or some forms of DRO for instance. Once they have served their purpose (i.e., to reduce behavior to acceptable levels) it is desirable, because of ethics or logistics, to withdraw them, although as mentioned, the typical suggestion for use is to continue to provide at least contingent attention on the desirable behaviors—not always an easy task. The goal in any case is to maintain acceptable levels of student behavior. Stokes and Baer (1977) and Kazdin (1984) have discussed explicit procedures for this purpose.

In classrooms it is quite clear that it is necessary to choose maintenance procedures idiosyncratically, depending on the nature of the classroom environment after treatment. For example, teacher A commonly attends to misbehavior, does not praise much, and plans no contingencies for academic performance. Teacher B has good rules, enforces them, uses differential attention satisfactorily, but does not plan contingencies for academic performance. If both successfully implement a DRL procedure to reduce disruption in a child, would withdrawal of treatment result in the same maintenance? Would the same maintenance plan be necessary? The author does not think so; but there is little empirical guidance available and the questions match a number of real life questions facing any classroom consultant. The question is, What particular environmental conditions, in what relationships, are likely to maintain good behavior after a reductive technique is withdrawn? It is unlikely, therefore, that there are generalizable statements about treatment procedures in terms of general maintenance expectations.

This also means that research in classrooms already operating with a good support system, a token economy for example, may not be comparable to research in classrooms that have more general management problems. Certainly, expanded research into classroom academic ecologies has begun (see Greenwood, Delquadri, & Hall, 1984), and there are clear demonstrations that maintenance of gains from complex treatment programs can be planned (Walker, Hops, & Johnson, 1975). What appears to be lacking is guidance for those change agents who must implement clinical interventions in a wide variety of classrooms. It is easy enough to talk of planning for maintenance, but how easy is it to get teachers to agree? The acceptability data discussed earlier would indicate that more complex interventions were less acceptable; and the alteration of treatments is often a complex process.

Perhaps the major need is a procedure for the behavioral assessment of maintenance conditions. If so, there have already been suggestions about analyzing the classroom environment for academic assessment (Lentz & Shapiro, 1986), and suggestions for assessing mainstreaming requirements from special education settings (Anderson-Inman, Walker, & Purcell, 1984) that may be related. Nevertheless, research into postreduction maintenance requirements for clinical behavior interventions in regular classrooms is badly needed.

Conclusion

There are numerous reductive procedures that are effective in the classroom. Choice of which one to use should be guided by a clear understanding of the potential ways in which problem behaviors can be maintained. Positive reductive procedures have been well investigated, and appear to be more acceptable than aversive procedures. However, for severe problems, aversive techniques may prove necessary, although they must be carefully monitored. The reader is referred to chapters on self-management and the token economy because such procedures offer exciting alternatives to the procedures discussed earlier. They may be especially relevant if classrooms are to be restructured, and if procedures that are less costly to teachers are to be selected.

References

Anderson-Inman, L., Walker, H., & Purcell, J. (1984). Promoting the transfer of skills across settings: Trans-environmental programming for handicapped students in the mainstream. In W. Heward, T. Heron, D. Hill, & J. Trap-Porter (Eds.), *Focus on behavior analysis in education* (pp. 17–38). Columbus, OH: Merrill.

Ayllon, T., & Roberts, M. (1974). Eliminating discipline problems by strengthening academic performance. *Journal of Applied Behavior Analysis, 7*, 71–76.

Ayllon, T., Layman, D., & Burke, S. (1972). Disruptive behavior and reinforcement of academic behavior. *The Psychological Record, 22*, 315–323.

Ayllon, T., Garber, S., & Pisor, K. (1975). The elimination of discipline problems through a combined school-home motivational system. *Behavior Therapy, 6*, 616–626.

Ayllon, T., Layman, D., & Kandel, H. (1975). A behavioral-educational alternative to drug control of hyperactive children. *Journal of Applied Behavior Analysis, 8*, 137–146.

Axelrod, S., & Apsche, S. (Eds.). (1983). *The effects of punishment on human behavior*. New York: Academic Press.

Axelrod, S., Brantner, J., & Meddock, T. (1978). Overcorrection: A review and critical analysis. *Journal of Special Education, 12*, 367–391.

Bachman, J. E., & Fuqua, R. W. (1983). Management of inappropriate behaviors of trainable mentally impaired students using antecedent exercise. *Journal of Applied Behavior Analysis, 16*, 477–484.

Baer, A., Rowbury, T., & Baer, D. (1973). The development of instructional control over classroom activities of deviant preschool children. *Journal of Applied Behavior Analysis, 6*, 289–298.

Bandura, A. (1977). *Social learning theory*. Englewood Cliffs, NJ: Prentice-Hall.

Barrish, H., Saunders, M., & Wolf, M. (1969). Good behavior game: Effects of individual contingencies for group consequences on disruptive behavior in a classroom. *Journal of Applied Behavior Analysis, 2*, 119–124.

Becker, W., Madsen, C., Arnold C., & Thomas, D. (1967). The contingent use of teacher attention and praise in reducing classroom behavior problems. *Journal of Special Education, 1*, 287–308.

Bizzis, J., & Bradley-Johnson, S. (1981). Increasing the school attendance of a truant adolescent. *Education and Treatment of Children, 4*, 149–155.

Bornstein, P., Hamilton, S., & Quevillon, R. (1977). Behavior modification by long distance: Demonstration of functional control over disruptive behavior in a rural classroom setting. *Behavior Modification, 1*, 369–380.

Boyd, L., Keilbaugh, W., & Axelrod, S. (1981). The direct and indirect effects of positive reinforcement on on-task behavior. *Behavior Therapy, 12*, 80–92.

Brantner, J., & Doherty, M. (1983). A review of timeout: A conceptual and methodological analysis. In S. Axelrod & J. Apsche (Eds.), *The effects of punishment on human behavior* (pp. 87–132). New York: Academic Press.

Broden, M., Bruce, C., Mitchell, M., Carter, V., & Hall, R. (1970). Effects of teacher attention in attending behavior of two boys at adjacent desks. *Journal of Applied Behavior Analysis, 3*, 199–203.

Budd, K., Leibowitz, J., Riner, L., Mindall, C., & Goldfarb, A. (1981). Home based treatment of severe disruptive behaviors: A reinforcement package for preschool and kindergarten children. *Journal of Behavior Modification, 5*, 273–298.

Burchard, J., & Barrera, F. (1972). An analysis of timeout and response cost in a programmed environment. *Journal of Applied Behavior Analysis, 5*, 271–282.

Bushell, D. (1978). An engineering approach to the elementary classroom: The Behavior Analysis Follow Through Project. In A. Catania & T. Brigham (Eds.), *Handbook of applied behavior analysis: Social and instructional processes* (pp. 525–563). New York: Irvington.

Carr, E. (1981). Contingency management. In A. Goldstein, E. Carr, W. Davidson, & P. Wehr (Eds.), *On aggression* (pp. 1–65). New York: Pergamon Press.

Carr, E., & Newsome, C. (1985). Demand-related tantrums: Conceptualization and treatment. *Behavior Modification, 9*, 403–426.

Cartledge, G., & Milburn, J. (1980). *Teaching social skills to children*. New York: Pergamon Press.

Center, D., Deitz, S., & Kaufman, M. (1982). Student ability, task difficulty, and inappropriate classroom behavior. *Behavior Modification, 6*, 355–374.

Chiang, S., Iwata, B., Dorsey, M. (1979). Elimination of disruptive bus riding behavior via token reinforcement on a "distance-based" schedule. *Education and Treatment of Children, 2*, 101–109.

Chambers, J., Sanok, R., & Striefel, S. (1983). Using contingent decreased freedom of movement to eliminate classroom running away: A case study. *Education and Treatment of Children, 6*, 123–132.

Copeland, R., Brown, R., & Hall, R. (1974). The effects of principal-implemented techniques on the behavior of pupils. *Journal of Applied Behavior Analysis, 7*, 77–86.

Darch, C., & Thorpe, H. (1977). The principal game: A

group consequence procedure to increase classroom on-task behavior. *Psychology in the Schools, 3,* 341–347.

Darveaux, D. (1984). The good behavior game plus merit: Controlling disruptive behavior and improving student motivation. *School Psychology Review, 13,* 510–514.

Deitz, S. (1977). An analysis of programming DRL schedules in educational settings. *Behavior Research and Therapy, 15,* 103–111.

Deitz, A., & Repp, A. (1973). Decreasing classroom misbehavior through the use of DRL schedules of reinforcement. *Journal of Applied Behavior Analysis, 6,* 457–463.

Deitz, S., & Repp, P. (1974). Differentially reinforcing low rates of misbehavior with normal elementary school children. *Journal of Applied Behavior Analysis, 7,* 622.

Deitz, S., Repp, A., & Deitz, D. (1976). Reducing inappropriate classroom behavior of retarded students through three procedures of differential reinforcement. *Journal of Mental Deficiency Research, 20,* 155–170.

Deitz, S., Slack, D., Schwarzmueller, E., Wilander, A., Weatherly, L., & Hilliard, G. (1978). Reducing inappropriate behavior in special classrooms by reinforcing average interresponse times: Interval DRL. *Behavior Therapy, 1,* 37–46.

Devine, V., & Tomlinson, J. (1976). The "Workclock": An alternative to token economies in the management of classroom behaviors. *Psychology in the Schools, 13,* 163–170.

Diaddigo, M., & Dickie, R. (1978). The use of contingency contracting in eliminating inappropriate classroom behaviors. *Education and Treatment of Children, 1,* 17–23.

Dougherty, E., & Dougherty, A. (1977). The daily report card: A simplified and flexible package for classroom behavior management. *Psychology in the Schools, 2,* 191–195.

Drabman, R., & Lahey, B. (1974). Feedback in classroom behavior modification: Effects on the target and her classmates. *Journal of Applied Behavior Analysis, 7,* 491–498.

Drabman, R., Jarvie, G., & Archbold, J. (1976). The use and misuse of extinction in classroom behavioral programs. *Psychology in the Schools, 13,* 470–476.

Drabman, R., Hammer, D., & Rosenbaum, M. (1979). Assessing generalization in behavior modification with children: The generalization map. *Beahvioral Assessment, 1,* 203–219.

Eleftherios, C., Shoudt, J., & Strang, H. (1972). The game machine: A technological approach to classroom control. *Journal of School Psychology, 10,* 55–60.

Elliott, S., Witt, J., Galvin, G., & Peterson, R. (1984). Acceptability of positive and reductive behavioral interventions: Factors that influence teacher's decisions. *Journal of School Psychology, 22,* 353–360.

Emsdorf, J., Davis, D., & Davidson, W. (1983). Social support and aggression. In A. Goldstein, E. Carr, W. Davidson, & P. Wehr (Eds.), *On aggression* (pp. 402–446). New York: Pergamon Press.

Epstein, M., Repp, A., & Cullinan, D. (1978). Decreasing "obscene" language of behaviorally disordered children through the use of a DRL schedule. *Psychology in the Schools, 3,* 419–422.

Ferritor, D., Buckholdt, D., Hamblin, R., & Smith, L. (1972). The noneffects of contingent reinforcement for attending behavior on work accomplished. *Journal of Applied Behavior Analysis, 5,* 7–17.

Firestone, P. (1976). The effects and side effects of timeout on an aggressive nursery school child. *Journal of Behavior Therapy and Experimental Psychiatry, 6,* 79–81.

Fishbein, J., & Wasik, B. (1981). Effect of the good behavior game on disruptive library behavior. *Journal of Applied Behavior Analysis, 14,* 89–93.

Foxx, R., & Bechtel, D. (1983). Overcorrection: A review and analysis. In S. Axelrod, & J. Apsche (Eds.), *The effects of punishment on human behavior* (pp. 133–220). New York: Academic Press.

Foxx, F., & Shapiro, S. (1978). The timeout ribbon: A nonexclusionary timeout procedure. *Journal of Applied Behavior Analysis, 11,* 125–136.

Gast, D., & Nelson, C. M. (1977). Legal and ethical considerations for the use of timeout in special education settings. Journal of Special Education, 11, 457–467.

Gendrich, J., McNees, M., Schnelle, J., Beegle, G., & Clark, H. (1982). A student-based anti-letter program for elementary schools. *Education and Treatment of Children, 5,* 321–325.

Goldstein, A. (1981a). Social skill training. In A. Goldstein, E. Carr, W. Davidson, & P. Wehr (Eds.) *On aggression* (pp. 159–218). New York: Pergamon Press.

Goldstein, A. (1981b). Problem solving training. In A. Goldstein, E. Carr, W. Davidson, & P. Wehr (Eds.), *On aggression* (pp. 219–252). New York: Pergamon Press.

Greene, B., Bailey, J., & Barber, F. (1981). An analysis and reduction of disruptive behavior on school busses. *Journal of Applied Behavior Analysis, 14,* 177–192.

Greenwood, C., Delquadri, J., & Hall, R. (1984). Opportunity to respond and student academic performance. In W. Heward, T. Heron, D. Hill, & J. Trap-Porter (Eds.), *Focus on behavior analysis in education* (pp. 58–88). Columbus, OH: Merrill.

Gresham, F. (1985). Behavior disorder assessment: Conceptual, definitional, and practical considerations. *School Psychology Review, 14,* 495–509.

Gresham, F., & Gresham, G. (1982). Interdependent, dependent, independent group contingencies for controlling disruptive behavior. *Journal of Special Education, 16,* 101–110.

Griffith, R. (1983). The administrative issues: An ethical and legal perspective. In S. Axelrod & J. Apsche (Eds.), *The effects of punishment on human behavior* (pp. 317–338). New York: Academic Press.

Grosenick, J., & Huntze, S. (1983). *More questions than answers: Review and analysis of programs for behaviorally disordered children and youth.* Columbia, MO: Dept. of Special Education, University of Missouri-Columbia.

Hall, R., Lund, D., & Jackson, D. (1968). Effects of teacher attention or study behavior. *Journal of Applied Behavior Analysis, 1,* 1–12.

Hall, R. V., Axelrod, S., Foundopoulos, M., Shellman, J., Campbell, R. A., & Cranston, R. (1971). The effective use of punishment to modify behavior in the classroom. *Educational Technology, 11,* 24–26.

Hall, R. V., Fox, R., Williard, D., Goldsmith, L., Emerson, M., Owen, M., Davis, F., & Porcia, E. (1971). The teacher as observer and experimenter in the modification of disputing and talking-out behavior. *Journal of Applied Behavior Analysis, 4,* 141–149.

Haring, N., Lovitt, T., Eaton, M., & Hansen, C. (1978). *The fourth R: Research in the classroom.* Columbus, OH: Merrill.

Harris, K. (1985). Definitional, parameteric, and procedural considerations in timeout interventions and research. *Exceptional Children, 51,* 279–288.

Harris, V., & Sherman, J. (1973). Use and analysis of the "good behavior game" to reduce disruptive classroom behavior. *Journal of Applied Behavior Analysis, 6,* 405–417.

Hay, W., Hay, L., & Nelson, R. (1977). Direct and collateral changes in on-task and academic behavior resulting from on-task versus academic contingencies. *Behavior Therapy, 8,* 431–441.

Heller, M., & White, M. (1975). Rates of teacher verbal approval and disapproval to higher and lower ability classes. *Journal of Educational Psychology, 67,* 796–800.

Heron, T. (1978). Punishment: A review of the literature with implications for the teacher of mainstreamed children. *Journal of Special Education, 12,* 243–252.

Hobbs, S., & Forehand, R. (1977). Important parameters in the use of timeout with children: A re-examination. *Journal of Behavior Therapy and Experimental Psychiatry, 8,* 365–370.

Homer, A., & Peterson, L. (1980). Differential reinforcement of other behavior: A preferred response elimination procedure. *Behavior Therapy, 11,* 449–471.

Hundert, J., Bucher, B., & Henderson, M. (1976). Increasing appropriate classroom behavior and academic performance by reinforcing correct work alone. *Psychology in the Schools, 13,* 195–200.

Jackson, D. (1976). Behavior analysis certification: A plan for quality control. In T. Brigham, R. Hawkins, J. Scott, & T. McLaughlin (Eds.), *Behavior analysis in education: Self control and reading* (pp. 7–15). Dubuque, Iowa: Kendall/Hunt.

Johnson, N. (1985). *West Haven: Classroom culture and society in a rural elementary school.* Chapel Hill, NC: University of North Carolina Press.

Jones, F., & Miller, W. (1974). The effective use of negative attention for reducing group disruptions in special elementary school classrooms. *The Psychological Record, 24,* 435–448.

Kazdin, A. (1973). The effect of vicarious reinforcement on attentive behavior in the classroom. *Journal of Applied Behavior Analysis, 6,* 71–78.

Kazdin, A. (1977). Vicarious reinforcement and direction of behavior change in the classroom. *Behavior Therapy, 1,* 57–63.

Kazdin, A. (1979). Vicarious reinforcement and punishment in operant programs for children. *Child Behavior Therapy, 1,* 13–36.

Kazdin, A. (1980a). Acceptability of time out from reinforcement procedures for disruptive child behavior. *Behavior Therapy, 11,* 329–344.

Kazdin, A. E. (1980b). Acceptability of alternative treatments for deviant child behavior. *Journal of Applied Behavior Analysis, 13,* 259–273.

Kazdin, A. E. (1981). Acceptability of child treatment techniques: The influence of treatment efficacy and adverse side effects. *Behavior Therapy, 12,* 493–506.

Kazdin, A. E. (1984). *Behavior modification in applied settings.* Homewood, IL: Dorsey Press.

Kazdin, A., & Klock, J. (1973). The effect of nonverbal teacher approval on student attentive behavior. *Journal of Applied Behavior Analysis, 6,* 643–654.

Kelley, M., & Stokes, T. (1982). Contingency contracting with disadvantaged youths: Improving classroom performance. *Journal of Applied Behavior Analysis, 15,* 447–454.

Kerr, M., Strain, P., & Ragland, E. (1982). Teacher-mediated peer feedback treatment of behaviorally handicapped children. *Behavior Modification, 6,* 277–290.

Kramer, T., & Rilling, M. (1970). The differential reinforcement of low rates: A selective critique. *Psychological Bulletin, 74,* 225–254.

Krantz, P., & Risley, T. (1977). Behavioral ecology in the classroom. In K. O'Leary & S. O'Leary (Eds.), *Classroom management* (pp. 349–366). New York: Pergamon Press.

Kubany, E., Weiss, L., & Sloggett, B. (1971). The good behavior clock: A reinforcement/time out procedure for reducing disruptive classroom behavior. *Journal of Behavior Therapy and Experimental Psychiatry, 2,* 173–177.

Lahey, B., McNees, M. P., & McNees, M. C. (1973). Control of an obscene "verbal tie" through timeout in an elementary school classroom. *Journal of Applied Behavior Analysis, 6,* 101–104.

Lahey, B., Gendrich, J., Gendrich, S., Schnelle, J., Gant, G., & McNees, P. (1977). An evaluation of daily report cards with minimal teacher and parent contacts as an efficient method of classroom intervention. *Behavior Modification, 1,* 381–394.

Lentz, F., & Shapiro, E. (1986). The functional analysis of the classroom environment. *School Psychology Review, 15,* 346–357.

Litow, L., & Pumoy, D. (1975). A brief review of classroom group-oriented contingencies. *Journal of Applied Behavior Analysis, 8,* 341–347.

Lobitz, W., & Burns, W. (1977). The "least intrusive intervention" strategy for behavior change procedures: The

use of public and private feedback in school classrooms. *Psychology in the Schools, 1,* 89–94.
Lovitt, T., Lovitt, A., Eaton, M., & Kirkwood, M. (1973). The deceleration of inappropriate comments by a natural consequence. *Journal of School Psychology, 2,* 149–158.
MacDonald, W., Gallimore, R., & MacDonald, G. (1970). Contingency counseling by school personnel: An economical model of intervention. *Journal of Applied Behavior Analysis, 3,* 175–182.
MacDonough, T., & Forehand, R. (1973). Response-contingent time-out: Important parameters in behavior modification with children. *Journal of Behavior Therapy and Experimental Psychiatry, 4,* 231–236.
Madsen, C., Becker, W., & Thomas, D. (1968). Rules, praise, and ignoring: Elements of elementary classroom control. *Journal of Applied Behavior Analysis, 1,* 139–150.
Marholin, D., & Steinman, W. (1977). Stimulus control in the classroom as a function of the behavior reinforced. *Journal of Applied Behavior Analysis, 5,* 465–478.
Medland, M., & Stachnik, T. (1972). Good behavior game: A replication and systematic analysis. *Journal of Applied Behavior Analysis, 5,* 45–51.
Miltenberger, R., & Fuqua, R. (1981). Overcorrection: A review and critical analysis. *The Behavior Analyst, 4,* 123–141.
Nelson, C., & Rutherford, R. (1983). Time-out revisited: Guidelines for its use in special education. *Exceptional Education Quarterly, 3,* 56–67.
Newsom, C., Favell, J., & Rincover, A. (1983). Side effects of punishment. In S. Axelrod, & J. Apsche (Eds.), *The effects of punishment on human behavior* (pp. 285–316). New York: Academic Press.
O'Leary, K. (1972). Behavior modification in the classroom: A rejoinder to Winett and Winkler. *Journal of Applied Behavior, 5,* 505–511.
O'Leary, K., Kaufman, K., Kass, R., & Drabman, R. (1970). The effects of loud and soft reprimands in the behavior of disruptive students. *Exceptional Children, 37,* 145–155.
Patterson, G. (1976). The aggressive child: Victim and architect of a coercive system. In E. Mash, L. Hamerlynck, & L. Handy (Eds.), *Behavior modification and families: Vol. 1. Theory and Research* (pp. 267–316). New York: Brunner/Mazel.
Patterson, G., Jones, R., Whittier, J., & Wright, M. (1965). A behavior modification technique for the hyperactive child. *Behavior Research and Therapy, 2,* 2217–2226.
Pazulinec, R., Meyerrose, M., & Sajwaj, T. (1983). Punishment via response cost. In S. Axelrod (Ed.), *The effects of punishment on human behavior* (pp. 71–86). New York: Academic Press.
Pinkston, E., Reese, N., LeBlanc, J., & Baer, D. (1973). Independent control of a preschool child's aggression and peer interaction by contingent teacher attention. *Journal of Applied Behavior Analysis, 6,* 115–124.
Poling, A., & Ryan, C. (1982). Differential reinforcement of other behavior schedules. *Behavior Modification, 6,* 3–21.
Polsgrove, L. (1983). Foreword. *Exceptional Education Quarterly, 3,* x–xi.
Porterfield, J., Herbert, Herbert-Jackson, E., & Risley, T. (1976). Contingent observation: An effective and acceptable procedure for reducing disruptive behavior of young children in a group setting. *Journal of Applied Behavior Analysis, 9,* 55–64.
Prout, H. (1983). School psychologists and social-emotional assessment techniques: Patterns in training and use. *School Psychology Review, 12,* 377–383.
Rapport, M., Murphy, A., & Bailey, J. (1982). Rotalin vs. response cost in the control of hyperactive children: A within-subject comparison. *Journal of Applied Behavior Analysis, 15,* 205–216.
Repp, A. C., Barton, L. E., & Brulle, A. R. (1983). A comparison of two procedures for programming the differential reinforcement of other behavior. *Journal of Applied Behavior Analysis, 16,* 435–445.
Ritschel, D., Mongrella, J., & Presbie, R. (1972). Group time-of-out-seat behavior of handicapped children while riding a school bus. *Psychological Reports, 31,* 967–973.
Rosen, H. S., & Rosen, L. D. (1983). Eliminating stealing: Use of stimulus control with an elementary student. *Behavior Modification, 7,* 56–63.
Sabatino, A. (1983). Discipline: A national issue. In D. Sabatino, A. Sabatino, & L. Mann (Eds.), *Discipline and behavioral management* (pp. 1–28). Rockville, MD: Aspen Publications.
Saigh, P. A., & Umar, A. M. (1983). The effects of a good behavior game on the disruptive behavior of Sudanese elementary school students. *Journal of Applied Behavior Analysis, 16,* 339–344.
Salend, S., & Allen, E. (1985). Comparative effects of externally managed and self-managed response cost system on inappropriate classroom behavior. *Journal of School Psychology, 23,* 59–67.
Sallis, J. (1983). Aggressive behaviors of children: A review of behavioral interventions and future directions. *Education and Treatment of Children, 6,* 175–191.
Salzberg, B., Hopkins, B., Wheeler, A., & Taylor, L. (1974). Reduction of kindergarten children's disruptive behavior with delayed feedback and delayed contingent access to play. *Journal of School Psychology, 12,* 24–30.
Schmidt, G., & Ulrich, R. (1969). Effects of group contingent events upon classroom noise. *Journal of Applied Behavior Analysis, 2,* 171–179.
Schutte, R., & Hopkins, B. (1970). The effects of teacher attention on following instructions in a kindergarten class. *Journal of Applied Behavior Analysis, 3,* 117–122.
Skiba, E., Pettigrew, E., & Alden, S. (1971). A behavioral approach to the control of thumbsucking in the classroom. *Journal of Applied Behavior Analysis, 4,* 121–125.
Solomon, R., & Wahler, R. (1973). Peer reinforcement control of classroom problem behavior. *Journal of Applied Behavior Analysis, 6,* 49–56.
Spitalnik, R., & Drabman, R. (1976). A classroom timeout

for retarded children. *Journal of Behavior Therapy and Experimental Psychiatry, 7*, 17–21.

Stokes, T., & Baer, D. (1977). An implicit technology of generalization. *Journal of Applied Behavior Analysis, 10*, 349–367.

Strain, P. (1977). An experimental analysis of peer social initiations on the behavior of withdrawn preschool children: some training and generalization effects. *Journal of Abnormal Child Psychology, 5*, 445–455.

Sulzer-Azaroff, B., & Mayer, G. (1977). *Applying behavior analysis procedures with children and youth.* New York: Holt, Rinehart, & Winston.

Sulzer-Azaroff, B., & Mayer, G. (1986). *Achieving educational excellence.* New York: Holt, Rinehart, & Winston.

Sulzer-Azaroff, B., & Reese, E. (1982). *Applying behavioral analysis: A program for developing professional competence.* New York: Holt, Rinehart, & Winston.

Thomas, D., Becker, W., & Armstrong, M. (1968). Production and elimination of disruptive classroom behavior by systematically varying teacher's behavior. *Journal of Applied Behavior Analysis, 1*, 35–45.

Thomas, D., Nielsen, L., Kuypers, D., & Becker, W. (1968). Social reinforcement and remedial instruction in the elimination of a classroom behavior problem. *Journal of Special Education, 2*, 291–306.

Todd, D., Scott, R., Bostow, D., & Alexander, S. (1976). Modification of the excessive inappropriate classroom behavior of two elementary school students using home based consequencies and daily report card procedures. *Journal of Applied Behavior Analysis, 9*, 465–478.

Trice, A., & Parker, F. (1983). Decreasing adolescent swearing in an instructional setting. *Education and Treatment of Children, 6*, 29–35.

Trice, A., Parker, F., & Iwata, M. (1983). An analysis of home contingencies to improve school behavior with disruptive adolescents. *Education and Treatment of Children. 6*, 389–399.

Trice, A., Parker, F., Furrow, F., & Iwata, M. (1983). An analysis of home contingencies to improve school behavior with disruptive adolescents. *Education and Treatment of Children, 6*, 389–399.

Van Houten, R. (1983). Punishment: From the animal laboratory to the applied setting. In S. Axelrod & J. Apsche (Eds.), *The effects of punishment on human behavior* (pp. 13–44). New York: Academic Press.

Van Houten, R., & Doleys, D. (1983). Are social reprimands effective? In S. Axelrod (Ed.), *The effects of punishment on human behavior* (pp. 45–70). New York: Academic Press.

Van Houten, R., Hill, S., & Parsons, M. (1975). An analysis of a performance feedback system: The effects of timing and feedback, public posting, and praise upon academic performance and peer interaction. *Journal of Applied Behavior Analysis, 8*, 449–457.

Van Houten, R., Nau, P., MacKenzie-Keating, S., Sameoto, D., & Colavecchia, B. (1982). An analysis of some variables influencing the effectiveness of reprimands. *Journal of Applied Behavior Analysis, 15*, 65–83.

Wahler, R. (1975). Some structural aspects of deviant child behavior. *Journal of Applied Behavior Analysis, 8*, 27–42.

Wahler, R., & Fox, J. (1980). Solitary toy play and time out: A family treatment package for children with aggressive and oppositional behavior. *Journal of Applied Behavior Analysis, 13*, 23–39.

Wahler, R., & Fox, J. (1981). Setting events in applied behavior analysis: Toward a conceptual and methodological expansion. *Journal of Applied Behavior Analysis, 14*, 327–338.

Wahler, R., & Graves, M. (1983). Setting events in social networks: Ally or enemy in child behavior therapy? *Behavior Therapy, 14*, 19–36.

Walker, H. (1983). Applications of response cost in school settings: outcomes, issues, and recommendations. *Exceptional Education Quarterly, 3*, 47–55.

Walker, H., Hops, H., & Johnson, S. (1975). Generalization and maintenance of classroom treatment effects. *Behavior Therapy, 6*, 188–200.

Wasserman, T. (1977). The utilization of a clock-light cueing device to signal group progress towards reinforcement in a classroom setting. *Psychology in the Schools, 4*, 471–479.

Webster, R. (1976). A time-out procedure in a public school setting. *Psychology in the Schools, 13*, 72–76.

White, M. (1975). Natural rates of teacher approval and disapproval in the classroom. *Journal of Applied Behavior Analysis, 8*, 367–377.

Winett, R., & Winkler, R. (1972). Current classroom behavior modification in the classroom: Be still, be quiet, be docile. *Journal of Applied Behavior Analysis, 5*, 499–504.

Witt, J., & Adams, R. (1980). Direct and observed reinforcement in the classroom: The interaction between information and reinforcement for socially approved and disapproved behavior. *Behavior Modification, 4*, 321–336.

Witt, J., & Elliott, S. (1982). The response cost lottery: A time efficient and effective classroom intervention. *Journal of School Psychology, 20*, 155–161.

Witt, J., & Martens, B. (1983). Assessing the acceptability of behavioral interventions used in classrooms. *Psychology in the Schools, 4*, 510–517.

Witt, J., Hannafin, M., & Martens, B. (1983). Home-based reinforcement: Behavioral covariation between academic performance and inappropriate behavior. *Journal of School Psychology, 21*, 337–348.

Witt, J., Martens, B., & Elliot, S. (1984). Factors affecting teachers' judgements of the acceptability of behavioral interventions: Time involvement, behavior problem severely, & type of intervention. *Behavior Therapy, 15*, 204–209.

Wolf, M. (1978). Social validity: The case for subjective measurement, or how applied behavior analysis is finding its heart. *Journal of Applied Behavior Analysis, 11*, 203–214.

Wolf, M., Hanley, E., King, L., Lachowicz, J., & Giles, D. (1970). The timer game: A variable interval contingency for the management of out-of-seat behavior. *Exceptional Children, 37,* 113–117.

Woolridge, P., & Richman, C. (1985). Teacher's choice of punishment as a function of a student's gender, age, race, and IQ level. *Journal of School Psychology, 23,* 19–29.

Workman, E., Kindall, L., & Williams, R. (1980). The consultative merits of praise-ignore versus praise-reprimand instruction. *Journal of School Psychology, 4,* 373–381.

Wyatt, W., Hawkins, R., & McCoy, P. (1984). Classroom interventions from 1963 to 1982: A twenty year look at differences in published research by behavior analysts, regular educators and special educators. *Education and Treatment of Children, 7,* 215–235.

CHAPTER 18

The Token Economy

T. F. McLaughlin and Randy Lee Williams

Overview

The essential parts of a token economy include only a few basic components (Kazdin, 1977) that are found in most behavioral interventions in the schools. Token systems include (a) tokens themselves, (b) determination of target behaviors, (c) specification of rules for how tokens are earned or lost, (d) specification of back-up consequences and their cost, and (e) method for exchanging tokens for back-up consequences (Kazdin, 1977; McLaughlin, 1975; K. D. O'Leary & Drabman, 1971).

The Tokens

The types of tokens used in classroom settings has varied greatly. Items such as points (McLaughlin, 1981a; McLaughlin & Malaby 1972a, 1975, 1976), currency (Logan, 1970; Payne, Polloway, Kauffman, & Scranton, 1975), chips (Bushell, 1978), stars, ratings (K. D. O'Leary & Becker, 1967) and check marks (Drabman, Spitalnik, & O'Leary, 1973) have been used most frequently.

T. F. McLaughlin and Randy Lee Williams • Department of Special Education, Gonzaga University, Spokane, Washington 99258.

Target Behaviors

The effectiveness of token economies for social behavior in classroom settings has been well documented for the last 18 years. These effects have been thoroughly reviewed elsewhere (Kazdin, 1977; K. D. O'Leary, 1978; K. D. O'Leary & Drabman, 1971; and S. G. O'Leary & K. D. O'Leary, 1976). The wide variety of inappropriate social behaviors that have been controlled by token economies have included talk outs (McLaughlin & Malaby, 1972b), out of seat (Barrish, Saunders, & Wolf, 1969), off task (Broden, Hall, Dunlap, & Clark, 1970), playground behavior (Holland & McLaughlin, 1982), hyperactivity (Christensen, 1975; Christensen & Sprague, 1973), overall classroom behavior (Hall, Panyan, Rabon, & Broden, 1968), and attendance (Hargreaves & McLaughlin, 1981). In addition to improving social behaviors, the token system has also been successfully implemented to modify a large number of academic behaviors (Kazdin, 1977). The academic behaviors improved have included reading (Ayllon & Roberts, 1974; Ayllon, Layman, & Burke, 1972; Bippes, McLaughlin, & Williams, 1986; Wolf, Giles, & Hall, 1968), arithmetic (McLaughlin, 1981b), and creative writing (Brigham, Graubrad, & Stans, 1972; Maloney & Hopkins, 1973). Token programs have been successfully employed to improve assignment completion (Clark, Lachowicz, & Wolf, 1968; McLaughlin & Malaby, 1972a, 1975, 1976), accuracy of performance (Ayllon & Roberts, 1974; Brigham, Frinfrock, Breunig, & Bushell, 1972; Chadwick & Day, 1971), and the rate of academic output (Lovitt & Curtiss, 1969; Lovitt & Esveldt, 1970; McLaughlin, 1981b).

Rules for Earning or Losing Tokens

Most token programs include the specification of explicit rules for the earning or losing of tokens. The goals of some token programs were to reduce disruptive behaviors (K. D. O'Leary & Becker, 1967) and/or other rule violations (Iwata & Bailey, 1974), whereas the goal of many recent token economies in the schools has been improving academic performance (Ayllon & Roberts, 1974; Ayllon *et al.*, 1972; McLaughlin & Malaby, 1972a, 1975, 1976). Typically the rules for earning or losing tokens are posted in the classroom (McLaughlin & Malaby, 1972a) or are discussed by the teacher with the class before each academic period (Bushell, 1974, 1978). The rules and/or discussion clearly specify the target behaviors and the number of tokens that will be earned or lost contingent on the behaviors' occurrence. Tokens have been awarded based on the behavior of an individual student (McLaughlin & Malaby, 1974a) a group of students (Bushell, 1978; Iwata & Bailey, 1974; McLaughlin, 1981c, 1982a), and the entire classroom of students or the entire school population (Holland & McLaughlin, 1982).

Consequences and Pricing

A wide array of items has been made available for which students have been able to exchange their tokens. Back-up consequences have included edibles such as candy, snacks, and cereals (Lovitt, Guppy, & Blattner, 1969; McKensie, Clark, Wolf, Kothera, & Benson, 1968). Other material objects have included toys, trinkets, and money (Drabman *et al.*, 1973; McKensie *et al.*, 1968; Turkewitz, O'Leary, & Ironsmith, 1975). Activity consequences have included such things as recess, extra recess, talking to a peer, after school sports, and movies (Ayllon & Roberts, 1974; Ayllon *et al.*, 1972; McLaughlin, 1981a). Some token systems in classroom environments have allowed students to leave school early (Swain & McLaughlin, in press; Truhlicka, Swain, & McLaughlin, in press). Typically, a wide variety of back-up consequences has been employed to ensure student responsiveness to the token program (Kazdin, 1977). A wide variety of back-up consequences makes it more likely that at least one item will function as a positive reinforcer; however, in some token systems, only one back-up consequence has been employed, such as free time. Free time may be particularly effective because it allows students to engage in a variety of self-determined activities (Osborne, 1969).

Many token programs in school settings have employed elaborate systems to inform students about the price of various backup activities. Early token programs developed for special needs children (Ayllon & Roberts, 1974; McKensie *et al.*, 1968; K. D. O'Leary & Becker, 1967) and regular elementary school students (McLaughlin & Malaby, 1972a) employed clearly specified contingencies between the target behaviors and contingent back-up consequences. The students earned a certain number of tokens for the occurrence of each target behavior and back-up consequences required a specific number of tokens. Other token programs have relied on a more graduated contingency between behavior and consequences, with more behavior earning more of a particular consequence, for example, more on-task behavior results in more earned free time (Long & Williams, 1973; Lovitt *et al.*, 1969).

Exchanging Tokens

Depending on the particular token economy, tokens may be exchanged (a) immediately after they have been earned (Ayllon *et al.*, 1972), (b) at the end of a specified period of time (K. D. O'Leary, Becker, Evans, & Saudargas, 1969), (c) after a variable amount of time (McLaughlin & Malaby, 1976) or (d) weekly (McLaughlin & Malaby, 1972a, 1975). Students are usually allowed to consume edible back-up items immediately after the exchange process. Typically, students are allowed to engage in activity back-up consequences for a specified amount of time immediately following the exchange (Bushell, 1978). In some instances, where only weekly exchange periods occur, the student retains the particular activity during specified back-up periods until the next weekly exchange takes place (McLaughlin & Malaby, 1972a). A wide variety of options in the exchange process has been employed in classroom token programs without a decrement in student performance (Kazdin, 1977; McLaughlin, 1975).

History

The token economy is not a new phenomenon. Historically, token economy systems have been documented as far back as the early middle ages (K. D. O'Leary & Drabman, 1971). In the 1880s, children in the New York schools were rewarded with praise, badges, and tickets that could be exchanged for toys (Ravitch, 1974). However, the systematic development of token economy programs in classrooms did not occur until the middle to late 1960s (S. G. O'Leary & K. D. O'Leary, 1976). Classroom token programs in the 1960s began to focus on improving social behavior (K. D. O'Leary & Becker, 1967) and academic behavior (Lovitt *et al.*, 1969). The publication of research pertaining to the token economy increased greatly until the late 1970s, but has declined steadily since that time. This decrease is probably a function of the token economy's well-documented effectiveness and reluctance of some professional journals to publish research similar to previous publications. In addition, in many recent studies token economies have been employed in conjunction with or were secondary to other behavioral procedures, such as public posting (Holland & McLaughlin, 1982), performance feedback systems (Van Houten, 1979), and daily report card programs (Smith, Williams, & McLaughlin, 1983). Some of the more recently developed management systems, such as public posting, performance feedback, and daily report cards, when used alone do not require as much monitoring and recording as classroom token systems. This consequent decrease in time needed to manage these newer systems may have made their use more appealing to some teachers and other professionals.

Classroom Token Economy: An Example

The following is a concrete example of the step-by-step implementation of a token economy (McLaughlin & Malaby, 1972a). As indicated previously the teacher should decide on (a) what the tokens will be, (b) the target behaviors, (c) back-up consequences and cost, and (d) the rules governing the relationships between target behaviors and tokens. In this study the teacher selected numerical points as the tokens and points earned by students were written on a recording sheet.

Points were chosen because they were easy to administer, impossible to steal, and their relative point values were understood by the students. A special form was developed for the students to record their points. The teacher typed the various behaviors that earned points on the left side of the page with enough squares so the students could record their earned points for each assignment and for their social behavior. The right side of the sheet contained areas for students to record the number of points lost for misbehaviors. This point sheet was taped to each student's desk. The teacher kept two separate records: one in a gradebook to record academic performance and one attached to a clipboard to record social behavior.

Nineteen different behaviors were targeted in their program. The behaviors that earned points included behaviors such as assignment completion, appropriate noon hour behavior, listening, studying, making art projects, taking notes, writing neatly, etc. Additionally, a response cost component was employed in which failing to complete work, chewing gum, eating candy, talking out, getting out of seat, fighting, and cheating resulted in losing points. The number of points earned or lost was determined by the student's performance, for example, a 90% accuracy on a 10-point assignment earned the student nine points, whereas 100% accuracy earned 10 points. Some behaviors resulted in more points being earned than others. For instance, a perfectly answered math assignment was worth 10 points, but listening to the teacher's presentation paid only one or two points. The same was also true for the loss of points: students lost more points for fighting (100) than they did for talking out (15 points).

To determine which back-up activities to employ, the teacher observed activities that the students appeared to enjoy. A meeting was held and the teacher, with the assistance of the students, listed the various activities that the students seemed to like very much. From this list, the students ranked the various activities in terms of their preference. The activity students said they preferred most was after school sports, so a high cost was placed on this activity (60 points), whereas the less preferred activity of taking out a ball at recess had a low cost (5 points). Twelve such activity back-up items were listed on a bulletin board with the price of each listed beside each activity. These activities included playing with classroom pets, sharpening pencils, writing on the board, playing games, coming in early, and so on.

During the first token economy condition, the students earned points each day of the week and these were exchanged each Friday. Later, this was changed to a variable number of school days. On the day prior to the exchanging of points for back-up activities, the teacher collected all the point charts and a student in the room totaled the points for all other students. The student totals for academic and social behavior were compared to the teacher's records to ensure accurate self-monitoring of points earned and lost. If a student failed to self-record enough points, the student was given the missing points. If a student recorded more points than earned, then the student lost the opportunity to exchange points for that week.

When the exchange took place (at a time convenient to the teacher), students took their point sheets to designated desks where other students subtracted the number of points required for the activity from the students' accumulated points. Any points that remained could be placed in a savings bank. A student could withdraw from the savings only if the student had missed some classes due to illness and had points saved in the bank. The entire exchange process took only 10 to 15 minutes. The students retained the purchased activities during daily designated back-up times until the next weekly exchange took place.

The token program developed by McLaughlin and Malaby (1972a) was effective in improving assignment completion for an entire class of fifth and sixth grade students. Later replications of this token system (McLaughlin & Malaby, 1975, 1976) generated similar results. Also, exchanging points after a variable number (average of five) of school days produced higher and more stable rates of assignment completion than did fixed interval exchanges after five days.

Practical Considerations

A great many variations on token economies have been implemented successfully in various classroom settings with a very wide range of students and target behaviors (Kazdin, 1982). Many of the aspects of an individual token system may be chosen somewhat arbitrarily or by preference, whereas other aspects are determined by practical considerations depending on the type of classroom, population of students served, number of students who will be involved directly with the token system, target behaviors, and the like.

The Token

One of the first decisions is to determine what to use as a token. The choice should be affected by the age and capability of the students, cost factors, and practical considerations. Poker chips have been used frequently and have several practical advantages. They stack together easily, are highly visible, and the colors can be used to reflect a different number of tokens (e.g., white equals one token, red equals five, etc.). Also, different colors can be designated for different children to control stealing (Gates, 1972). Unfortunately, using poker chips for large numbers of students can be quite expensive. Cardboard discs, pieces of paper, match sticks, paper clips, marbles, check slips, and written points have also been used. Some plastics and plumbing factories discard large quantities of plastic discs that can be used as tokens (Bushell, 1978).

For very young school-aged children, it is probably best to use a tangible form of token so that it is clear to the child when a token is earned and how many tokens have been earned (Stainback, Payne, Stainback, & Payne, 1973). With some young pupils, the teacher may feel it is better not to use items that are sharp, such as match sticks, or that are small and can be put in the mouth easliy, such as marbles or paper clips. For older students, these considerations are usually unwarranted. Simulated checks can be very useful and are not easily duplicated by students. The amount of the checks can be the same or varied. Teacher initials can also be used if there is concern that checks might be obtained other than through appropriate academic and social behavior.

Points have been used effectively with intermediate elementary students (McLaughlin & Malaby, 1972a, 1975, 1976) and are probably more socially acceptable to older students than more tangible tokens, such as poker chips or marbles (Swain & McLaughlin, in press). Points can be tally marks, one per appropriate behavior, or can be written in numerical form with various values for specific academic and social behaviors. Points are cost free and convenient for the teacher (McLaughlin & Malaby, 1972a). However, points are more abstract than other more tangible tokens such as chips. Because students may not see when they have earned points, points provide less feedback to students as to their appropriate behaviors.

The probable reasons that token economies have been very effective include (a) tokens themselves immediately follow the behavior the teacher wants to increase; (b) tokens are a tangible record of appropriate behavior and the progress toward earning some back-up consequence; and (c) tokens break up larger consequences into many smaller consequences (Kazdin, 1977). Therefore, tokens should immediately follow target behaviors, successive approximations to target behaviors, and/or task completion to maximize the tokens' effectiveness (Stainback *et al*, 1973). Typically, token economies are used because praise for appropriate behaviors has not been sufficiently reinforcing to promote students' appropriate academic and/or social behavior (McLaughlin & Malaby, 1972a). Pairing praise with tokens, which in turn are paired with a wide variety of back-up consequences, should begin to make praise a generalized conditioned reinforcer (Alberto & Troutman, 1986). Therefore, praise should be used every time a token is delivered but praise may occur at other times without token delivery (Bushell, 1978).

Tokens should be delivered at a relatively high rate, particularly in the early implementation of the token system so that appropriate behaviors are on a relatively dense schedule of reinforcement. Because the token systems break up large consequences into smaller consequences there will be many more opportunities to reinforce appropriate behaviors than if the larger consequence itself was used without tokens (Kazdin, 1977). With increased presentations of tokens contingent upon appropriate behaviors, these behaviors should more likely increase in rate.

When tokens are chips or other discrete tangibles, it is reasonably clear to the student that the teacher presenting a token means the student has performed correctly. Token delivery may also facilitate teacher–student contact and prompt the teacher to praise more frequently (Breyer & Allen, 1975). Unfortunately, when points are used instead of more tangible tokens, a teacher may simply record points without overtly praising the student, thereby losing opportunities to pair praise with points. If the student does not know why or when points have been received, then the token system is probably not functional, though contingent back-up consequences themselves may be somewhwt effective with or without a token system (Payne *et al.*, 1973).

An important decision is the selection of a record-keeping system. This decision is influenced by a number of considerations, such as the type of token used, capabilities of the students, rate of token delivery, and whether tokens can be saved from one exchange to the next or from one day to the next (Stainback *et al.*, 1973). The record keeping can be simple with young children if tangible tokens, such as poker chips or pieces of paper, are used. If the children work primarily at desks, then a receptacle, such as a paper cup or plastic bag, can be taped to the desk or table (Iwata & Bailey, 1974). The teacher or aide would simply put tokens in the cup or bag as they are earned. The tokens would accumulate during the academic earn time until the predetermined exchange time when the child or teacher would count and then exchange the tokens for the selected back-up activity or item (Bushell, 1978).

If children engage in activities away from their desks, then the teacher must decide whether tokens will be given during these activities. If the teacher plans to give tokens, then the receptacles will need to be portable. One method involved kindergarten children wearing aprons with pockets so that the teacher could easily give the children tokens by placing them in the apron pockets wherever the children were at the time the tokens were earned (Bushell, 1978). At the exchange, the children emptied the contents of their cups or aprons and the child or teacher counted the tokens earned.

If the teacher decides to allow students to save unspent tokens from one exchange to the next or from one day to the next, then the record keeping may need to be expanded (McLaughlin & Malaby, 1972a). Students could simply keep the unspent tokens in their receptacles, though this might result in tokens being lost or stolen, particularly if saved beyond one day. To avoid this problem a teacher may record the number of tokens saved in the teacher's record book or on a form at each student's desk. A three-by-five card taped to the student's desk with the school days or dates written on the card makes a practical and functional record.

The use of points usually necessitates a much more elaborate record-keeping system. The teacher may keep a master list of the students' names, target behaviors, and points earned (McLaughlin & Malaby, 1972a). This can be kept at the desk or put on a clipboard so the teacher can move around the classroom instructing the students and conveniently awarding points as they are earned (McLaughlin & Malaby, 1972a). An alternative to the teacher keeping a record on a clipboard or at a desk is publicly posting the record-keeping system at the front of the classroom (Van Houten, 1979). This public posting may add to the incentive of the system, but it is probably less practical than awarding points for social and academic behaviors as they occur in an ongoing fashion. An effective alternative to these two record-keeping systems is to have the record keeping completed at each student's desk with the teacher or student recording the points earned. Students in the primary grades have accurately self-recorded the points they earned for various academic and social behaviors (McLaughlin, 1981a). Initially, teaching self-recording of points will require teacher modeling and frequent monitoring for accuracy, but students can acquire accurate self-recording skills relatively rapidly with only periodic teacher checks to assure accuracy (Alberto & Troutman, 1986).

Behaviors and Token Payment

A token economy may be successfully used individually or in combination to improve most any social or academic behaviors (Kazdin, 1977). A token system can be used with one student, a small group of students, or the entire classroom or school. Teachers are sometimes reluctant to set up a token system with one student because other students may see it as inequitable. If the teacher decides an extrinsic motivation system is needed to improve the behavior of one student or small group of students, then the teacher should matter-of-factly explain the token system and its purpose to all students (Flaman & McLaughlin, 1986). The teacher can let those students who do not need the token system know they are doing well without such a system, and that it is the teacher's way of helping students who are not as successful. Extensive discussions or elaborations to the other students should probably be avoided so as not inadvertently to reinforce complaining.

The teacher may predetermine the number of tokens students will receive for different behaviors, for example, one token for completing an assignment and a second token for 80% accuracy or higher (McLaughlin & Malaby, 1972a, 1975, 1976) or may choose to deliver tokens in an ongoing fashion during an activity or academic period (Bushell, 1973). For younger or less able students, giving tokens in an ongoing fashion is probably preferrable because token delivery can more immediately follow the target behavior or successive approximation to the target behavior. A child might receive a token for reading a word or sentence or for being on-task for two consecutive minutes.

For older or more capable students, the teacher may more easily predetermine the number of tokens for target behaviors because the teacher may be able to delay successfully token delivery until the completion of an activity or an extended period of time (Swain & McLaughlin, in press). This is a more practical procedure for the teacher because token delivery occurs at a specific time and usually after an academic period is over (McLaughlin & Malaby, 1972a). The number of tokens awarded for specific behaviors, and to students with divergent skill levels, should be individualized (Kazdin, 1977). Thus, one student may have to complete five reading comprehension questions accurately to receive a token; whereas a less skilled student might have to make a reasonable attempt at decoding a phonetically regular word before receiving a token. When students are more homogeneously grouped the values assigned to certain behaviors can be more consistent across students. Individualization of token values, particularly for social skills, will often be necessary to maximize all students' development of appropriate behaviors.

If the teacher predetermines the number of tokens or points to award certain behaviors, then these should be made public to the students. If classroom rules are tied into the token system, then the number of tokens earned for following these rules or the number of tokens lost for infractions should be clearly specified (McLaughlin & Malaby, 1974a). This can prompt appropriate behavior and help the teacher avoid drawn out explanations during the class, particularly at the time tokens are taken away for misbehaviors (McLaughlin & Malaby, 1972b).

Once a token system has been implemented, the teacher may find students engaging in behaviors that the teacher had not considered including as target behaviors. For instance, a student may go out of the way to make a new classmate comfortable or come up with a particularly creative answer to a problem; such behavior should be rewarded even if not previously included as a target skill (cf.

McLaughlin, 1981; McLaughlin & Malaby, 1972a, 1975, 1976). Similarly, as students' skills improve, the relationship between the behavior and the tokens should change. Typically, the teacher would give fewer or no tokens for previously mastered skills and give tokens only when the student demonstrates an improvement or higher-level skills. In this way the teacher differentially rewards improvements in the child's behaviors (McLaughlin, 1981b). For example, a student may have previously received one token for attempting to answer five math word problems, but must now complete the five problems with 80% accuracy to earn the one token (Johnston & McLaughlin, 1982). With older or more capable students, the teacher may choose to negotiate the value to be awarded for certain behaviors with students (Lovitt & Curtiss, 1969).

One of the major variables that controls the effectiveness of the token economy is the back-up consequences for which the tokens are exchanged. If the items or activities chosen hold little interest for the students or are not reinforcing, then the token system will be ineffective (K. D. O'Leary & Drabman, 1971). There are several strategies that the teacher can initially use to determine back-up activities. The teacher may (a) make an educated guess as to what may be reinforcing to students, (b) ask students what they wish to earn, or (c) directly observe what behaviors students engage in frequently during recess or free time and make these items or activities back-up consequences. The activities that function as reinforcers will likely vary greatly within a classroom and particularly between disparate age groups of students. Most of the published research on token systems have used a wide variety of back-up consequences for students (Kazdin, 1977). This variety increases the chances that there will be at least one consequence that will be reinforcing for each student at each exchange. Additionally, most of these back-up consequences should be changed systematically to decrease the chances of satiation and to determine other reinforcing activities to maximize student motivation and learning.

If only a brief amount of exchange and back-up time is available, then the teacher may prefer the students to earn discrete items such as stickers, trinkets, or edibles. If at least 10 or 15 minutes can be set aside, then students may earn activities as back-up rewards. Typically, activities allow for greater variety of back-up consequences and are generally cost free and utilize materials that are already available in most classrooms (McLaughlin & Malaby, 1972a). The activities should be appropriate to the students' particular age group. For example, primary-aged pupils might work very hard to earn the privilege of cleaning the blackboard or passing out books or materials, whereas a secondary student might work diligently to earn early dismissal from school (Swain & McLaughlin, in press). Some activities may be effective across age groups, such as early recess (Martin & McLaughlin, 1981).

Back-up activities may be academically related. Teacher-devised or commercially available educational games or books can be highly motivating and extend or facilitate generalization of academic skills. Teacher involvement in the activities may add to the reinforcing effectiveness of back-up activities. For example, the teacher could take part in a baseball game or other special activity with the class (McLaughlin, 1972a).

Students may be unfamiliar with new back-up consequences, and as a result, be unmotivated by them. The teacher may arrange a period of time when the students may sample these new items or activities without cost so that students can experience their reinforcing value and learn the rules governing their use. Ayllon and Azrin (1968) successfully employed such a reinforcer-sampling procedure with mental patients. Alternatives would be to place a relatively low price on the new activity, or present the back-up consequences noncontingently for a few days (McLaughlin & Malaby, 1972a) so that students would be more inclined to try the new activities. If new activities are consistently enjoyable, students may work harder to have access to these novel consequences.

Another alternative is to give the student the opportunity to earn rewards or activities after school that are provided by a parent or guardian contingent on the student's behavior in school (Martin & McLaughlin, 1981). Many consequences not available to the teacher or too costly can be used effectively with such a system (Smith *et al.*, 1984). An added benefit of such a system is increased cooperation and communication between home and school.

A rule of thumb to follow in pricing items is to ensure that the prices of back-up consequences enable those students who put out a reasonable degree of effort or improvement to earn some item or activity during each exchange period. Each student should meet with success in the token system, particularly during the initiation of the system (Bushell, 1973). The longer the token system is used, the more refined and precise the pricing of items can be. There should be a wide range of prices so that a student who tries or who does moderately well at the appropriate skill level will earn something; but a student who puts out little or no effort should earn nothing. A student who does exceptionally well or puts out an inordinate amount of effort should earn something of greater value or a wider selection of choices (Bushell, 1973).

Even after the teacher devises a hierarchy of motivating items, the prices should still be varied periodically so as many students as possible have access to the various consequences. This should also prevent some students from earning just enough tokens for a particular consequence and then stopping or greatly reducing their output (Bushell, 1973).

After students have met with success in a token economy, their social and/or academic behaviors should begin to improve. If the teacher continues to deliver the same number of tokens for the same behaviors then the teacher will likely need to inflate the prices of the back-up consequences so the consequences will retain their same degree of effectiveness (McLaughlin & Malaby, 1976). As an alternative, the teacher may require the students to improve socially or academically in order to receive the same number of tokens they were earning previously.

The teacher should preset the prices for back-up consequences before each academic period (Bushell, 1973). This allows the teacher to deliberate carefully on what prices various items should be and to give a reasonable range of prices across items. The consequences and prices can be written in the form of a back-up menu (a list of the consequences) without prices and displayed at the beginning of the period or day (Bushell, 1973, 1978). One problem with listing prices before the students complete academic activities is that some students may be motivated to earn only enough tokens for the consequences of choice. By not listing prices ahead of exchange times, students should be less likely to stop performing during the academic period (Bushell, 1973).

The teacher needs to decide what to do if students spend fewer tokens than they have earned. One option is for students to start from zero following each exchange (McLaughlin & Malaby, 1972a). If tokens may be saved, there is a potential for stockpiling. Students might earn many tokens during the first academic period(s) and work for fewer tokens during later academic periods. One alternative is to let students save these extra tokens for some extra item or activity at the end of the week. Also, if a student misses school because of illness, the tokens saved may be withdrawn from a bank account (McLaughlin, 1981a; McLaughlin & Malaby 1972a, 1975, 1976). In such systems students will need to work hard to earn tokens for the regular exchanges, but may have an extra incentive to earn more tokens for the special exchange and back-ups and as insurance for days missed.

The Exchange Process

The exchange process can be handled in several ways depending on the age and skills of the students and the personal preference of the classroom teacher. For younger children or developmentally disabled students, the teacher or aide will have to count each student's accumulated tokens. The teacher can require the student to pile neatly the tokens or stack them for easy counting. The student who has earned the most tokens may be allowed to exchange first followed by the student who earned the next greatest number, etc. If this system is used, the teacher should note whether the exchanges are taking place smoothly and rapidly. If some students are taking more than a few seconds to state the back-up activity or item they want, then the teacher may need to switch to calling on the student who is prepared to exchange first (Bushell, 1978). This can greatly reduce the time required for the exchange process (Bushell, 1974). The more quickly students exchange, choose back-up consequences, and exchange, the more time they earn for the back-up activities. As pupils's skills improve, they can take on the responsibility of counting their own tokens. Accuracy should be checked regularly at first, and then only periodically for the pupils who are consistently accurate. Students could earn a bonus token for accurately totaling the tokens earned as an added incentive for accurate self-recording (Drabman *et al.*, 1973). With older students or secondary students, the teacher may shift the conduct of the exchange process from teacher to student. The exchange process should require no more than 5 minutes for an entire class, and in most cases substantially less time is needed (Swain & McLaughlin, in press).

When initiating a token economy or implementing one with younger or less skilled students, such as the moderately to profoundly retarded, exchange and back-up periods should be relatively frequent and immediately follow the period of time during which the students earned the tokens. For instance, in setting up a token system with a severely retarded child who was previously motivated by earning numerous, but small amounts of food, the teacher should place the token beside the student or in the student's hand immediately following an appropriate behavior. The teacher should then verbally and/or physically prompt the student to give the teacher back the token in exchange for the morsel of food. The teacher then gradually increases the number of tokens needed to exchange for food until the student works for a preset amount of time or a certain number of responses are emitted. For young children, such as kindergartners, an exchange time after each academic period seems appropriate because the exchanges and back-ups would be relatively immediate, maximizing the motivational effectiveness of the back-up consequences (Bushell, 1978). If used effectively, the time scheduled for exchanges and back-ups should be more than offset by the increased social skills and academic progress of the students.

The actual exchange can be completed at the desks or tables where the students are seated. The teacher may (a) sit with students if there is a small group, (b) move to the students at their desks as they are ready to exchange, (c) conduct the exchange from the teacher's desk calling upon students one at a time, or (d) conduct the exchange in a designated area of the room (McLaughlin, 1981a). Usually, all students exchange tokens at a designated period of time, though this need not be the case. The teacher may allow students to exchange as soon as a particular assignment (and possibly at some criterion level of accuracy) is completed (Bushell, 1973). In this way, the exchange is staggered and immediately follows the completion of a classroom assignment by each child.

Once student behaviors have improved the teacher may choose to reduce the number of exchange periods. If basic academic skills are the teacher's highest priority, then the exchange period should probably follow immediately the last of the daily periods. In resource rooms for mildly handicapped students or in secondary classrooms that meet only once in the day, the exchange period should occur near the end of the period in order to make the back-up consequences more immediate, and therefore, more effective.

It is probably not wise to schedule initially only weekly exchange periods. It is questionable whether such a large delay will allow the token economy to be very effective (Kazdin, 1977). A token system can result in increased teacher contacts with students and teacher praise for improved student behavior (Breyer & Allen, 1975). These changes in teacher behavior probably contribute to improved student behavior.

If the classroom is self-contained and all students exchange at the same time, then the entire classroom may be used or sectioned off for use of various back-up activities. If the exchanges vary according to when students complete assignments or have earned a specific number of tokens, then a section of the room (sometimes adjacent rooms) will need to be designated for back-up activities, or students will have to engage in activities at their desks. Obviously, if not all students have exchanged for back-ups, then the teacher will need those students who are finished to be relatively quiet until all students have exchanged. Allowing students to have immediate access to back-up activities as soon as they complete assignments can promote students' efficiency (McLaughlin, 1981a).

Clear and concise rules along with consequences for breaking or adhering to rules during the back-up period are important (Alberto & Troutman, 1986). If a student breaks a rule by behaving inappropriately during the back-up period, then the teacher may end the access to the activity or give one warning for the first infraction and then taking away the activity after the second infraction.

For secondary classrooms or resource rooms in which students attend for only 30 to 60 minutes, there is legitimate concern regarding the length of the back-up period. It is important to have daily back-ups at first in order to make the system maximally effective. These periods can later be shortened and/or occur less frequently. In such situations, the teacher may choose to have the students earn discrete items rather than activities so there is very little reduction in instructional time. A nice alternative is to have students earn back-up activities that parents or teachers provide later that same day (Flaman & McLaughlin, 1986; Stewart & McLaughlin, 1986).

Fading Out a Token Economy

Once students have improved their social and/or academic behaviors to the degree the classroom teacher considers acceptable, the token economy may be faded out. There are several effective ways to do this. The teacher may require students to complete progressively more work and/or increase the quality of their work for the same number of tokens or points. The rate of praise should probably be maintained at the original level until tokens are attenuated, and then praise can be gradually attenuated. Similarly, the number of tokens earned by a given behavior could be systematically decreased (Drabman *et al.*, 1973; Turkewitz *et al.*, 1975). The number of exchange and back-up periods could gradually be decreased, from one for each academic period to once or twice per day, to every other day, to once per week, and finally deleted (Drabman *et al.*, 1973; Rhodes *et al.*, 1983; Turkewitz *et al.*, 1975).

A successful and interesting technique is a lottery system used in conjunction with the exchange and back-up periods (McLaughlin, 1981a; McLaughlin & Malaby, 1976). The teacher writes students' names on slips of paper and later draws out a certain number of slips. The students whose names are picked earn the back-up consequences. Students had to continue to work hard to maximize their chances of earning back-up rewards. This effective technique can be used as a method of decreasing the number of back-ups earned and assisting in fading out the token system by progressively drawing fewer names.

When first reducing back-up periods, it may be helpful to ease the transition by letting students earn extra special consequences. It is crucial that the rate at which token delivery is thinned or back-up periods are reduced should be a function of student behavior and not of a predetermined schedule. It may be possible to maintain the token system during one portion of the day without diminishing student improvement in other periods of the day (Colyer, Hernandez-Guzman, & Williams, 1976).

Considerations if Student Behaviors Fail to Improve

Though researchers and teachers have usually found token economies to be very effective for most students, there are some students whose behaviors fail to improve or improve for only a short length of time. There are a few basic areas of the token economy which should be carefully scrutinized if this happens (Kazdin, 1983).

Back-Up Consequences

The chosen back-up activities may not be reinforcing. This is particularly apt to be the case if the teacher has chosen only one back-up consequence or a very limited number of back-up consequences which seldom vary. For instance, if students can only exchange tokens for stickers it is unlikely that students will be highly motivated day in and day out even if the stickers initially had a reinforcing effect. Even if the teacher chooses several reinforcing back-ups, if these consequences do not change they may have a satiating effect on student behavior. It is crucial that the back-up consequences change regularly, particularly those that are seldom chosen by students.

A variety of back-ups, even if they change regularly, will not necessarily be effective reinforcers. A teacher may choose items and activities thought to be reinforcing or were found to be reinforcing for students in the past only to find them ineffective for the current students. Using student suggestions for back-ups may be very helpful, but does not necessarily mean the back-ups will be reinforcing. Activities the students engage in regularly during free-time periods or recess should be effective reinforcers (Premack, 1962). However, if students have a great deal of access to the activities outside of the back-up periods, they may not be effective. Therefore, the teacher needs to control student access to activities thought to be reinforcing.

The involvement of the teacher during back-up periods can be an important variable. Particularly for the younger students, teacher attention can be highly reinforcing and the back-up activities allow the teacher to be paired with a wide variety of fun activities that may facilitate the teacher's attention, praise, and proximity becoming generalized conditioned reinforcers and discriminative for appropriate behavior.

Relationship of Tokens and Back-Up Consequences

An apparent lack of motivation may occur if students are allowed to save tokens from one period to the next or from one day to the next (Kazdin, 1982). For instance, a student may excell at reading and earn so many tokens that later very little work in math needs to be done for the student to have enough tokens for the back-up of choice. Not allowing tokens to be saved or to be saved only for some extra long-term back-up can correct this problem. An alternative procedure is to give fewer tokens in the area of strength and give tokens for smaller approximations to the target behaviors in the area of weakness. Additionally, the teacher could raise the prices of the desirable items so that the student would have to do well in all academic periods to earn a sufficient number of tokens for desirable back-ups (Payne *et al.*, 1975).

A lack of motivation can occur if students earn tokens too easily, thereby giving them access to most or all back-ups without much effort or improvement. A lack of motivation can also occur if students do relatively well yet earn so few tokens that no back-ups or no desirable back-ups are earned. Individualizing token delivery and adjusting the prices of back-up activities can solve these potential problems with the system (Payne *et al.*, 1975).

Relationship of Tokens and Behavior

The timing of token delivery is critical. If tokens are delivered before an appropriate behavior or delivery is delayed for a few seconds, other less appropriate behaviors may be accidentally reinforced (Kazdin, 1983). Descriptive praise paired with the token delivery may help reduce this problem by clarifying what behavior is being rewarded. The teacher should give tokens immediately following the target behavior. A low rate of token delivery may be less effective than a high rate when students are acquiring new skills because there are fewer appropriate behaviors being allowed by token rewards. For some students' behaviors, the tokens should be used to shape new behaviors not currently in the students' repertoires. Frequent presentations for incremental successive approximations to a target behavior may be needed. Token presentation should be scheduled at a much higher rate for newly acquired skills than for maintaining old skills.

If students successfully steal tokens, then there may be little incentive for them to improve academic and social behaviors. However, this probably indicates that the back-up consequences are reinforcing. Obviously, the stealing needs to be stopped. It may be that the work is too difficult for the student to earn tokens for appropriate behavior. A response cost procedure and/or special individualized tokens for the particular student (e.g., color coded tokens) may be needed to monitor and deter the stealing.

Variations and Adaptations of Token Economies

Response Cost

Besides giving tokens for appropriate academic and social behavior, an option that may be added to almost any token economy is a response cost component (Kazdin, 1972; McLaughlin & Scott, 1976). The removal of tokens contingent on certain behaviors is known as response cost (K. D. O'Leary, 1978). Classroom rules should state that certain inappropriate behaviors will result in a student losing a certain number of tokens. If the classroom rules are clear, concise, and specify the amount of response cost, and are periodically reviewed, then lengthy discussions about token removal can be avoided at the time of an infraction. This minimizing of contingent teacher verbalizations should decrease the probability of the teacher's attention inadvertently reinforcing misbehaviors. Two main variations of response cost with a token system are (a) one in which students contingently lose tokens that they have previously earned through appropriate behavior (Kazdin, 1972; K. D. O'Leary, 1978) and (b) one in which students are given a number of tokens at the beginning of the period or day and lose those tokens contingent on inappropriate behaviors rather than losing earned tokens (Iwata & Bailey, 1974).

If a teacher removes a large number or all of the tokens contingent on one misbehavior then there are fewer, if any, opportunities to use the removal of tokens as possible punishers. For this reason, it is probably better to take away relatively few tokens or only one token for each occurrence of a misbehavior, thus allowing up many more opportunities to punish misbehaviors. Unfortunately, some token economies have incorporated response costs that can result in students losing so many tokens or points that the pupils would have to do especially good work for inordinately long periods of time simply to get back to zero. If this happens, the chances seem reasonably high that the student will no longer put out extra effort to do well.

Kaufman and K. D. O'Leary (1972) compared reward and response cost in a remedial after-school program in a psychiatric hospital. During the reward condition, students began each 15-minute period with no tokens, but they could earn from 1 to 10 tokens based on the teacher's evaluation of their social behavior. In the response cost phase, each student began each session with 10 tokens in a jar. Tokens were removed at the end of the 15-minute sessions for various disruptive behaviors. Both systems reduced disruptive behavior and no differences were found between either procedure.

Comparing token response cost and reward systems, Iwata and Bailey (1974) reported similar improvements on rate of math problems completed in a self-contained classroom setting with mildly to moderately mentally retarded school children. During the cost phase, the teacher's behavior was slightly more disapproving. Students were allowed to choose which system they would prefer to have, but no systematic preferences were found.

McLaughlin and Malaby (1972b) found that removing previously earned points for inappropriate verbalizations served to increase rather than decrease such behavior. McLaughlin and Malaby (1974b, 1977) found that a combination of token reinforcement and response cost was more effective in improving academic behavior than either token reinforcement or response cost alone. To date most published research studies on classroom token programs have employed a combination of reward and response cost procedures (Ayllon & Roberts, 1974; Ayllon *et al.*, 1972; McLaughlin, 1981b, 1982b; McLaughlin & Malaby, 1972a, 1975, 1976).

Self-Control Procedures

One of the major goals of education is to teach self-control or self-management skills to students (McLaughlin, 1976; K. D. O'Leary, 1978). Token economies have been successfully used to train students to monitor, evaluate, determine, and administer consequences for their own behaviors (Drabman *et al.*, 1973; McLaughlin, 1976; K. D. O'Leary, 1978; S. G. O'Leary & Dubey, 1979; Rhodes, Morgan, & Young, 1983; Rosenbaum & Drabman, 1979; Turkewitz *et al.*, 1975). Typically, student behavior is initially brought under the control of a token system and then the token system is employed to train students to self-record, self-evaluate, self-determine rewards, and self-administer consequences.

Early research evaluating the effectiveness of students setting their own standards for earning consequences compared to standards imposed externally by the teacher reported no differences between the two procedures. (Felixbrod & O'Leary, 1973, 1974). This finding has also been documented with single-case designs (Glynn, 1970). Other research has found that students may set very low standards for reward (McLaughlin, 1982b; McLaughlin & Malaby, 1979; Santogrossi, O'Leary, Romanczyk, & Kaufman, 1973). Student choice of high performance standards can be established through the use of token reinforcement for the student matching teacher set criteria (Drabman *et al.*, 1973; Turkewitz *et al.*, 1975) or through rewarding high or increasingly higher standards (McLaughlin, 1982b; McLaughlin & Malaby, 1979; Price & O'Leary, 1974).

Students have also been trained to determine their own back-up consequences (Drabman *et al.*, 1973; Rhodes *et al.*, 1983; Turkewitz *et al.*, 1975). In these studies external monitoring by the teacher was gradually faded out until the students alone determined the type and amount of rewards. Santogrossi *et al.* (1973) reported that adolescents in a psychiatric hospital classroom setting had extreme difficulty in the self-determination of the back-up consequences so an externally imposed token system had to be established. Other research has not reported difficulty in teaching students to determine their own back-up consequences (Glynn, 1970; Lovitt & Curtiss, 1969).

Accurate student self-recording has been established with token reinforcement (Drabman *et al.*, 1973; McLaughlin, Burgess, & Sackville-West, 1981; Rhodes *et al.*, 1983; Turkewitz *et al.*, 1975). Other research has found that student recording can be accurate without explicit training (McLaughlin, 1983). Rewards for accurate self-recording also appear to increase on-task behavior and academic performance with behaviorally disordered elementary school children (McLaughlin, 1984).

Little data have been generated regarding the accuracy of students' self-administered consequences. However, if one examines the available data on performance standards, self-evaluation, and self-recording, it appears logical that students might abuse this component of the behavioral self-control paradigm unless externally imposed consequences are employed to train and maintain such a skill. It appears that most successful self-control programs have relied on some form of externally imposed contingencies, such as a token reinforcement program to teach the particular self-management skill (e.g., Drabman *et al.*, 1973; McLaughlin, 1982b, 1984; McLaughlin & Malaby 1974a; Rhodes *et al.*, 1985; Turkewitz *et al.*, 1975).

Group versus Individual Contingencies

More recently, token reinforcement programs have been instituted to compare the effects of rewarding children on an individual versus group basis (Frankosky & Sulzer-Azaroff, 1978; McLaughlin, 1981c, 1982a; McReynolds, Grange, & Speltz, 1981; Speltz, Moore, & McReynolds, 1979; Speltz, Shimamura, & McReynolds, 1982). Several studies have reported that there is little or no difference in effectiveness between group and individual contingency tokens programs (Axelrod, 1973; Drabman, Spitalnik, & Spitalnik, 1974; McLaughlin, Brown, Dolliver, & Malaby, 1977; Speltz *et al.*, 1982). However, some research has indicated that group contigency programs are more effective than individual contingency arrangements (Brown, Reschly, & Saunders, 1974; Hamblin, Hathaway, & Wodarski, 1974; Long & Williams, 1973; McLaughlin, 1981c, 1982a). Teachers have found group contingency arrangements easy to implement, monitor, and manage in their respective classrooms (Drabman *et al.*, 1974; McLaughlin, 1981b, 1982a).

Additional data have been gathered regarding the effects of group versus individual contingencies in terms of student and teacher preference. McLaughlin (1981c, 1982a) reported that students rated group contingencies higher than individual contingency arrangements. Drabman *et al.* (1974) reported that students preferred best the procedure in which all pupils earned consequences based on the highest performing student in the group. Similarly, Speltz *et al.* (1982) found that students favored a procedure in which consequences earned were based on the performance of a particular student.

Some researchers and school personnel are concerned that group contingencies may generate negative peer pressure (Baer & Richards, 1980; Grandy, Madsen, & DeMersseman, 1973; Hayes, 1976; K. D. O'Leary & Drabman, 1971; Packard, 1970). Packard (1970) reported a few minor instances of negative peer comments, but a majority of the research has failed to document such negative pupil behavior (Axelrod, 1973; Hamblin *et al.*, 1974; McLaughlin, 1981c, 1982a).

A novel behavioral intervention developed by Wolter, Pigott, Clement, and Fantuzzo (1985) combined self-control and group contingency procedures. In the program by Wolter *et al.* (1985), students were trained in the role of coach, score keeper, referee, and manager. The coach performed the self-instruction function for the group: he or she set the goals for the group, reminded the group of the techniques to maximize their performance, and encouraged the group during the tasks. The scorekeeper served to monitor pupil output and calculated the average performance for the group. The referee shared the same function as a scorekeeper and served as a reliability check. The manager's role was to compare the group's behavioral outcome with its goal. If the goal was matched or exceeded, the manager declared a win and the group was able to receive back-up consequences. Wolter *et al.* (1985), reported large increased in academic output, reduced disruptive behavior, and improved positive peer interaction.

Conclusions

The token economy is clearly one of the most effective classroom management techniques for improving various social and academic skills with normal and special needs students. Despite the vast body of existing research, many teachers appear unwilling to implement a token economy. It is often stated that a token system may create dependency on extrinsic rewards. The technology exists to fade out effectively token systems, but it should also be kept in mind that the token system is the classroom management technique that most closely approximates the employment system used in most modern Western societies, such as the United States. Typically in our society specific skills, task completion, or hours worked result in a wage, salary, or bonus. Often a token economy is implemented as a last resort and faded out as quickly as possible, once student behavior has improved. However, the token economy, in addition to being an effective classroom intervention, may closely approximate the natural contingencies within our society.

ACKNOWLEDGMENTS

A special note of thanks to Dr. Betty Fry Williams and Nan Roberts for their suggestions and also to Jeannie Mabley and Carrine Van Dyke for their assistance.

References

Alberto, P. A., & Troutman, A. C. (1986). *Applied behavior analysis for teachers* (2nd ed.). Columbus, OH: Merrill.

Axelrod, S. (1973). Comparison of individual and group contingencies in two special classes. *Behavior Therapy, 4*, 83–90.

Ayllon, T., & Azrin, N. (1968). Reinforcer sampling: A technique for increasing behavior of mental patients. *Journal of Applied Behavior Analysis, 1*, 13–20.

Ayllon, T., & Roberts, M. D. (1974). Eliminating discipline problems by strengthening academic performance. *Journal of Applied Behavior Analysis, 7*, 71–76.

Ayllon, T., Layman, D., & Burke, S. (1972). Disruptive behavior and reinforcement of academic performance. *The Psychological Record, 22*, 315–323.

Baer, G. C., & Richards, H. C. (1980). An interdependent group-oriented contingency system for improving academic performance. *School Psychology Review, 9*, 190–193.

Barrish, H. H., Saunders, M., & Wolf, M. M. (1969). Good behavior game: Effects of individual contingencies for group consequences on disruptive behavior in the classroom. *Journal of Applied Behavior Analysis, 2*, 119–124.

Bippes, R., McLaughlin, T. F., & Williams, R. L. (1986). A classroom token system in a detention center: Effects for academic and social behavior. *Techniques: A Journal for Remedial Education and Counseling, 2*, 126–132.

Brigham, T. A., Frinfrock, S. R., Breunig, M. K., & Bushell, D. (1972). The use of programmed materials in the analysis of academic contingencies. *Journal of Applied Behavior Analysis, 5*, 177–182.

Brigham, T. A., Graubrad, P., & Stans, A. (1972). Analysis of the effects of sequential reinforcement contingencies on aspects of composition. *Journal of Applied Behavior Analysis, 5*, 421–429.

Breyer, N. L., & Allen, G. J. (1975). Effects of implementing a token economy on teach attending behavior. *Journal of Behavior Analysis, 8*, 373–380.

Broden, M., Hall, R. V., Dunlap, A., & Clark, R. (1970). Effects of teacher attention and a token reinforcement system in a junior high school special education class. *Exceptional Children, 36*, 341–349.

Brown, D., Reschly, D., & Sabers, D. (1974). Using group contingencies with punishment and positive reinforcement to modify aggressive behaviors in a Head Start classroom. *The Psychological Record, 24*, 491–496.

Bushell, D. (1973). *Classroom behavior: A little book for teachers*. Englewood Cliffs, NJ: Prentice Hall.

Bushell, D. (1974). The design of classroom contingencies. In F. S. Keller & E. Ribes-Inesta (Eds.), *Behavior modification: Applications to education* (pp. 29–42). New York: Academic Press.

Bushell, D. (1978). An engineering approach to the elementary classroom: The behavior analysis follow-through project. In A. C. Catania & T. A. Brigham (Eds.). *Handbook of applied behavior analysis. Social and instructional processes* (pp. 525–563). New York: Irvington.

Chadwick, B. A., & Day, R. C. (1971). Systematic reinforcement: Academic performance of underachieving students. *Journal of Applied Behavior Analysis, 4*, 311–319.

Christensen, D. E. (1975). Effects of combining methylphenidate and a classroom token economy system in modifying hyperactive behavior. *American Journal of Mental Deficiency, 80*, 266–276.

Christensen, D. E., & Sprague, R. L. (1973). Reduction of hyperactive behavior by conditioning procedures alone and combined with methylphenidate (Ritalin). *Behaviour Research and Therapy, 11*, 331–334.

Clark, M., Lachowicz, J., & Wolf, M. M. (1968). A pilot basic education program for school dropouts incorporating a token reinforcement system. *Behaviour Research and Therapy, 8,* 183–188.

Colyer, M. J., Hernandez-Guzman, L., & Williams, R. L. (1976). The effects of tokens in the token economy. In T. A. Brigham, R. P. Hawkins, J. W. Scott, & T. F. McLaughlin (Eds.), *Behavior analysis in education: Self-control and reading* (pp. 235–243). Dubuque, IA: Kendall-Hunt.

Drabman, R. S., Spitalnik, R., & O'Leary, K. D. (1973). Teaching self-control to disruptive children. *Journal of Abnormal Psychology, 82,* 10–16.

Drabman, R. S., Spitalnik, R., & Spitalnik, K. (1974). Sociometric and disruptive behavior as a function of four types of token reinforcement programs. *Journal of Applied Behavior Analysis, 7,* 99–101.

Felixbrod, J. J., & O'Leary, D. K. (1973). Effects of reinforcement on children's academic behavior as a function of self-determined and externally imposed contingencies. *Journal of Applied Behavior Analysis, 6,* 241–250.

Felixbrod, J. J., & O'Leary, K. D. (1974). Self-determination of academic standards by children: Toward freedom from external control. *Journal of Educational Psychology, 66,* 845–850.

Flaman, F., & McLaughlin, T. F. (1986). Token reinforcement: Effects on academic accuracy and generalization to social behavior with an adolescent student. *Techniques: A Journal for Remedial Education and Counseling, 2,* 39–47.

Frankosky, R. J., & Sulzer-Azaroff, B. (1978). Individual and group contingencies and collateral behaviors. *Behavior Therapy, 9,* 313–327.

Gate, J. J. (1972). Overspending (stealing) in a token economy. *Behavior Therapy, 3,* 152–153.

Glynn, E. L. (1970). Classroom applications of self-determined reinforcement. *Journal of Applied Behavior Analysis, 3,* 123–132.

Grandy, G. S., Madsen, C. H., & DeMersseman, L. M. (1973). The effects of individual and interdependent contingencies on inappropriate classroom behavior. *Psychology in the Schools, 10,* 488–493.

Hall, R. V., Panyon, M., Rabon, D., & Broden, M. (1968). Instructing beginning teachers in reinforcement procedures which improve classroom control. *Journal of Applied Behavior Analysis, 1,* 315–322.

Hamblin, R. L., Hathaway, C., & Wodarski, J. (1974). Group contingencies, peer tutoring, and accelerating academic achievement. In R. Ulrich, T. Stachnik, & J. Mabry (Eds.), *Control of human behavior* (Vol. 3, pp. 421–432). Glenview, IL: Scott-Foresman.

Hargreaves, T., & McLaughlin, T. F. (1981). Reducing absences and tardiness in a junior secondary special education classroom: The SCOPE Program. *B.C. Journal of Special Education, 5,* 23–32.

Hayes, L. A. (1976). The use of group contingencies for behavior control: A review. *Psychological Bulletin, 83,* 528–643.

Holland, E., & McLaughlin, T. F. (1982). The use of response cost, public posting, and group consequences to reduce inappropriate behaviors of an entire elementary school population during supervision. *Journal of Educational Research, 76,* 29–34.

Iwata, B., & Bailey, J. S. (1974). Reward versus cost token programs: An analysis of the effects on students and teacher. *Journal of Applied Behavior Analysis, 7,* 567–576.

Johnston, R. J., & McLaughlin, T. F. (1982). The effects of free time on assignment completion and accuracy in arithmetic: A case study. *Education and Treatment of Children, 5,* 33–40.

Kaufman, K. F., & O'Leary, K. D. (1972). Reward, cost, and self-evaluation procedures for disruptive adolescents in a psychiatric hospital school. *Journal of Applied Behavior Analysis, 5,* 293–309.

Kazdin, A. E. (1972). Response cost: The removal of conditioned reinforcers for therapeutic change. *Behavior Therapy, 3,* 533–546.

Kazdin, A. E. (1977). *The token economy: A review and evaluation.* New York: Plenum Press.

Kazdin, A. E. (1982). The token economy: A decade later. *Journal of Applied Behavior Analysis, 15,* 431–446.

Kazdin, A. E. (1983). Failure of persons to respond to the token economy. In E. A. Foa, & Paul M. G. Emmelkamp (Eds.), *Failures in behavior therapy* (pp. 335–354). New York: Wiley-Interscience.

Logan, D. L. (1970). A "paper money" token system as a recording aid in institutional settings. *Journal of Applied Behavior Analysis, 3,* 183–184.

Long, J. D., & Williams, R. L. (1973). The comparative effectiveness of group and individually contingent free-time with inner-city junior high school students. *Journal of Applied Behavior Analysis, 6,* 465–474.

Lovitt, T. C., & Curtiss, K. (1969). Academic response rate as a function of teacher- and self-imposed contingencies. *Journal of Applied Behavior Analysis, 2,* 49–53.

Lovitt, T. C., & Esveldt, K. A. (1970). The relative effects on math performance of single-versus-multiple ratio schedules: A case study. *Journal of Applied Behavior Analysis, 3,* 261–270.

Lovitt, T. C., Guppy, T. E., & Blattner, J. E. (1969). The use of a free-time contingency with fourth grades to increase spelling accuracy. *Behaviour Research and Therapy, 7,* 151–156.

Maloney, K., & Hopkins, B. L. (1973). The modification of sentence structure and its relationship to subjective judgments of creativity in writing. *Journal of Applied Behavior Analysis, 6,* 425–433.

Martin, R. C., & McLaughlin, T. F. (1981). A comparison between the effect of free time and daily report cards on the academic behavior of junior high school students. *B.C. Journal of Special Education, 5,* 303–313.

McKensie, H. S., Clark, M., Wolf, M. M., Kothera, R., & Benson, C. (1968). Behavior modification of children with learning disabilities using grades as tokens and allowances as backup reinforcers. *Exceptional Children, 34,* 745–752.

McLaughlin, T. F. (1975). The applicability of token reinforcement systems in public school systems. *Psychology in the Schools, 12,* 84–89.

McLaughlin, T. F. (1976). Self-control in the classroom. *Review of Educational Research, 46,* 631–663.

McLaughlin, T. F. (1981a). An analysis of token reinforcement: A control group comparison with special education youth employing measures of clinical significance. *Child Behavior Therapy, 3,* 43–51.

McLaughlin, T. F. (1981b). The effects of a classroom token economy on math performance in an intermediate grade school class. *Education and Treatment of Children, 4,* 139–147.

McLaughlin, T. F. (1981c). Effects of individual and group contingencies on the programmed reading performance of special education students. *Contemporary Educational Psychology, 6,* 76–79.

McLaughlin, T. F. (1982a). A comparison of individual and group contingencies on spelling performance with special education students. *Child & Family Behavior Therapy, 4* (2/3), 1–10.

McLaughlin, T. F. (1982b). Effects of self-determined and high performance standards on spelling performance: A multi-element baseline analysis. *Child & Family Behavior Therapy, 4,* 55–61.

McLaughlin, T. F. (1983). Effects of self-recording for on-task and academic responding: A long term analysis. *Journal for Special Education Technology, 6* (3), 5–12.

McLaughlin, T. F. (1984). A comparison of self-recording and self-recording plus consequences for on-task and assignment completion. *Contemporary Educational Psychology, 9,* 185–192.

McLaughlin, T. F., & Malaby, J. E. (1972a). Intrinsic reinforcers in a classroom token economy. *Journal of Applied Behavior Analysis, 5,* 263–270.

McLaughlin, T. F., & Malaby, J. E. (1972b). Reducing and measuring inappropriate verbalizations in a classroom token economy. *Journal of Applied Behavior Analysis, 5,* 329–333.

McLaughlin, T. F., & Malaby, J. E. (1974a). Increasing and maintaining assignment completion with teacher and pupil controlled individual contingency programs: Three case studies. *Psychology, 11* (3), 45–51.

McLaughlin, T. F., & Malaby, J. E. (1974b). Note on the combined and separate effects of token reinforcement and response cost on assignment completion. *Psychological Reports, 35,* 1132.

McLaughlin, T. F., & Malaby, J. E. (1975). The effects of token reinforcement contingencies on the completion and accuracy of assignments under fixed and variable token exchange schedules. *Canadian Journal of Behavioural Science, 7,* 411–417.

McLaughlin, T. F., & Malaby, J. E. (1976). An analysis of assignment completion across time during fixed, variable, and extended exchange periods in a classroom token economy. *Contemporary Educational Psychology, 1,* 346–355.

McLaughlin, T. F., & Malaby, J. E. (1977). The comparative effects of token reinforcement with and without a response cost contingency with special education children. *Educational Research Quarterly, 2,* 34–41.

McLaughlin, T. F., & Malaby, J. E. (1979). Modification of performance standards in elementary special education students. *Education and Treatment of Children, 2,* 31–41.

McLaughlin, T. F., & Scott, J. W. (1976). The use of response cost to reduce inappropriate classroom behavior in classroom settings. *Corrective and Social Psychiatry, 22* (2), 32–34.

McLaughlin, T. F., Brown, D., Dolliver, P., & Malaby, J. E. (1977). The comparative effects of a timing device and group and individual contingencies for on-task behavior and academic responding in a special education class. *Behavioral Engineering, 4,* 11–15.

McLaughlin, T. F., Burgess, N., & Sackville-West, L. (1981). Effects of self-recording and self-recording and matching on academic performance. *Child Behavior Therapy, 3,* 17–27.

McReynolds, W. T., Grange, J., & Speltz, M. L. (1981). Effects of multiple, individual, and group operant contingencies on student performance. *Education and Treatment of Children, 4,* 227–241.

O'Leary, K. D. (1978). The operant and social psychology of token systems. In A. C. Catania & T. A. Brigham (Eds.), *Handbook of applied behavior analysis: Social and instructional processes* (pp. 179–207). New York: Irvington.

O'Leary, K. D., & Becker, W. C. (1967). Behavior modification of an adjustment class: A token reinforcement program. *Exceptional Children, 9,* 637–642.

O'Leary, K. D., & Drabman, R. S. (1971). Token reinforcement programs in the classroom: A review. *Psychological Bulletin, 75,* 379–398.

O'Leary, K. D., Becker, W. C., Evans, M., & Saudargas, R. (1969). A token reinforcement program in a public school: A replication and systematic analysis. *Journal of Applied Behavior Analysis, 2,* 3–13.

O'Leary, S. G., & Dubey, D. R. (1979). Applications of self-control procedures by children: A review. *Journal of Applied Behavior Analysis, 12,* 449–465.

O'Leary, S. G., & O'Leary, K. D. (1976). Behavior modification in the school. In H. Leitenberg (Ed.), *Handbook of behavior modification and behavior therapy* (pp. 475–515). Englewood Cliffs, NJ: Prentice-Hall.

Osborne, J. G. (1969). Free-time as a reinforcer in the management of classroom behavior. *Journal of Applied Behavior Analysis, 2,* 113–118.

Packard, R. G. (1970). The control of classroom attention: A group contingency for complex behavior. *Journal of Applied Behavior Analysis, 3,* 15–28.

Payne, J. S., Polloway, E. A., Kauffman, J. M., & Scranton, T. R. (1975). *Living in the classroom: A currency-based token economy.* New York: Human Sciences Press.

Premack, D. (1962). Reversability of the reinforcement relation. *Science, 136,* 255–257.

Price, G., & O'Leary, K. D. (1974). *Teaching children to*

develop high performance standards. Unpublished manuscript. State University of New York at Stony Brook.

Ravitch, D. (1974). *The great school wars, New York City, 1805–1973: A history of the public schools as a battlefield for social change.* New York: Basic Books.

Rhodes, G., Morgan, D., & Young, K. R. (1983). Generalization and maintenance of treatment gains of behaviorally handicapped students from resource rooms to regular classrooms using self-evaluation procedures. *Journal of Applied Behavior Analysis, 16,* 171–188.

Rosenbaum, M. S., & Drabman, R. S. (1979). Self-control training in the classroom: A review and critique. *Journal of Applied Behavior Analysis, 12,* 467–485.

Santogrossi, D. A., O'Leary, K. D., Romanczyk, R. G., & Kaufman, K. F. (1973). Self-evaluation of by adolescents in a psychiatric hospital school token program. *Journal of Applied Behavior Analysis, 6,* 277–287.

Smith, M., Williams, R. L., & McLaughlin, T. F. (1983). The daily report card as an intervention technique for classroom academic and social behavior: A review. *B.C. Journal of Special Education, 7,* 369–380.

Speltz, M. L., Moore, J. E., & McReynolds, W. T. (1979). A comparison of standardized and interdependent group contingencies in a classroom setting. *Behavior Therapy, 10,* 219–226.

Speltz, M. L., Shimamura, J. W., & McReynolds, W. T. (1982). Procedural variations in group contingencies: Effects of children's academic and social behaviors. *Journal of Applied Behavior Analysis, 15,* 533–544.

Stainback, W., Payne, J. S., Stainback, S., & Payne, R. A. (1973). *Establishing a token economy in the classroom.* Columbus, OH: Merrill.

Stewart, J. P., & McLaughlin, T. F. (1986). The effects of group and individual contingencies on reading performance with Native American junior high school students. *Techniques: A Journal for Remedial Education and Counseling, 2,* 133–143.

Swain, J., & McLaughlin, T. F. (in press). The effects of bonus contingencies on math performance within an ongoing token economy with junior high school special education students. *Adolescence.*

Truhlicka, Swain, J., & McLaughlin, T. F. (in press). Effects of token reinforcement and response cost on the accuracy of spelling performance with adolescent special education students. *Adolescence.*

Turkewitz, H., O'Leary, K. D., & Ironsmith, M. (1975). Generalization of maintenance of appropriate behavior through self-control. *Journal of Consulting and Clinical Psychology, 43,* 577–583.

Van Houten, R. (1979). The performance feedback system: Generalization across time. *Child Behavior Therapy, 1,* 219–236.

Wolf, M. M., Giles, D. K., & Hall, R. V. (1968). Experiments with token reinforcement in a remedial classroom. *Behaviour Research and Therapy, 6,* 51–64.

Wolter, C. F., Pigott, H. E., Clement, P. W., & Fantuzzo, J. W. (1985). Student-administered group oriented contingencies: The application of self-regulation techniques in the context of a group to increase academic productivity. *Techniques: A Journal for Remedial Education and Counseling, 1,* 14–22.

CHAPTER 19

Self-Monitoring

F. Charles Mace and Thomas R. Kratochwill

Most behavioral assessment procedures involve the use of persons other than the target individual to measure student/client behavior. Self-monitoring (SM) differs from these procedures in some important respects. A major difference is the active role the student/client plays in assessing his or her own behavior. Data generated from SM represent self-observation, self-measurement, or self-ratings. From this perspective, SM is consistent with a trend in behavior therapy away from external control of behavior toward greater participation of the client in managing his or her own therapeutic programs (Bandura, 1969; Ciminero, Nelson, & Lipinski, 1977; Mahoney, 1977; Thoresen & Mahoney, 1974). Another distinctive feature of SM is the scope of behavior available for assessment. Numerous child behaviors are inaccessible to external observers, particularly school personnel. Cognitions, toileting, sexual activity, delinquent behavior, and academic strategies are private events by nature or convention. Moreover, self-observers are exposed to the entire population of target responses rather than limited samples under limited conditions (Kazdin, 1974b). Therefore, the potential exists for self-observers to obtain more complete data and data inaccessible to external observations (Nelson, 1977a).

The applications of self-monitoring to school psychology are as diverse as the subspecialty itself. Its utility has been demonstrated with disruptive behavior (Bornstein, Hamilton, & Quevillon, 1977), cheating (Flowers, 1972), nail biting (McNamara, 1972), teacher behavior (Knapczyk & Livingston, 1973), tics (Thomas, Abrams, & Johnson, 1971), and severe behavior problems (Santogrossi, O'Leary, Romanczyk, & Kaufman, 1973), to sample a few. The value of SM as an assessment tool merits considerable attention as do the potential problems associated with its use. This review will examine issues related to definitions, the relationship of SM to self-control, the role of SM in assessment and treatment, SM procedures and methods, methodological concerns, and the relation of SM to other assessment procedures.

Definition of Self-Monitoring

The term *self-monitoring* (SM) refers to a multistage process. First, the child must become aware of or discriminate the presence or

F. Charles Mace • Graduate School of Applied and Professional Psychology, Rutgers University, Piscataway, New Jersey 08854. **Thomas R. Kratochwill** • Department of Educational Psychology, University of Wisconsin-Madison, Madison, Wisconsin 53706.

absence of a target response. The discrimination response itself is controlled by the occurrence of covert or overt stimuli (Thoresen & Mahoney, 1974). As the saliency of the stimuli increases, so does the likelihood of making the appropriate discrimination. Second, the occurrence of the target response is systematically recorded. In contrast to discriminating, self-recording requires overt action on the part of the child to make a permanent record of the event. Both these stages are essential to SM and are considered by some authors to be sufficient to describe the process (Nelson, 1977a; Nelson & Hayes, 1981; Rachlin, 1974, Simkins, 1971). Other authors, however, consider SM to involve a third stage, namely self-evaluation. During this stage, the individual evaluates his or her behavior against some standard (Kanfer, 1977; Mahoney & Arnkoff, 1978; Thoresen & Mahoney, 1974). These standards may represent criteria established by teachers, parents or an agency, or may be self-established goals. Usually, meeting the performance criteria is linked with some form of reinforcement, whereas behavior falling short of the criteria is sometimes associated with self-administered aversive events. Although controversy continues over the stages involved in SM, this review will refer to self-monitoring as a two-stage process of response discrimination and self-recording.

The Relationship of Self-Monitoring to Self-Control

Much of the self-monitoring literature treats SM as a component of self-control procedures (also referred to as self-management and self-regulation). In addition to functioning as a method of assessment, SM is viewed as a key feature of a well-integrated therapeutic strategy. Current behavioral perspectives of self-control include the cognitive-behavioral and operant models (Karoly, 1977).

The cognitive-behavioral perspective considers self-control responses to be a product of self-management of environmental contingencies as well as covert contingencies that are assumed to mediate overt behavior (Kanfer, 1977; Mahoney & Arnkoff, 1978; Meichenbaum, 1979). Kanfer's (1970a, 1975, 1977) three-stage model of self-regulation is representative of this mediational approach, although numerous variations have developed (see Mahoney & Arnkoff, 1978). The first stage of the model is self-monitoring. When the performance criteria are not specified, SM involves response discrimination and self-recording. Once performance criteria are established, either internally or externally, conditions are set for the second stage, self-evaluation. During this stage, the individual compares his or her performance against an a priori set of performance criteria. Persons trained to make this comparison can be expected to direct their behavior toward this standard. Meeting or exceeding the preestablished criterion triggers self-reinforcement. This final stage involves self-delivery of reinforcers contingent on successful performance. Reinforcers may include those available in the external environment, self-generated thoughts or statements, or some combination of the two.

The operant model of self-control (Rachlin, 1974; Skinner, 1953) interfaces with the cognitive-behavioral perspective along several dimensions. First, both consider consequences ultimately to control response frequency (Nelson & Hays, 1981). This implies that the principles of learning operate to determine the self-control response. Second, the individual participates in the management and manipulation of stimulus conditions which influence behavior. That is, the student/client can arrange the environment to maximize the chances that desired responses will occur. For example, a student may position a picture, symbol, or statement on his or her desk that reminds him or her to raise a hand before speaking out. A third dimension common to both models is the self-management of environmental contingencies to increase or decrease target responses. This refers to dispensing reinforcers or punishers to alter behavior in the direction of the performance criteria. Despite these shared characteristics, a fundamental distinction between these two models exists. According to the cognitive-behavioral view, self-evaluation involves cognitive processes that *mediate* the influence of the external environment on behavior (Kanfer & Karoly, 1972). The assumption is that covert self-statements or attitudes (Kanfer, 1977) can be functionally related to the overt self-control response. In contrast, the explanatory power of the operant model rests on the control that environmental contingencies have on behavior. Little recognition is given to mediational processes assumed to contribute to overt behavior.

The role SM plays in self-control strategies will be influenced by the theoretical model adopted. This influence will permeate research and application considerations. From the standpoint of research, issues concerning the accuracy, reliability, and reactivity of SM are affected by theory. Investigators following the cognitive-behavioral model have explained these issues in terms of cognitive variables interacting with environmental events (Kanfer, 1970a, 1975, 1977; Thoresen & Mahoney, 1974). Operant researchers, on the other hand, prefer to restrict their investigation to identifying functional relationships among observable phenomena (Nelson, 1977a; Nelson & Hayes, 1981). School psychologists in educational or clinical settings who avail themselves of SM procedures will be similarly influenced. From the perspective of the mediational model, training youngsters in the use of SM can focus on developing attitudes consistent with behavioral goals, self-evaluative statements comparing performance with specified criteria, and the use of covert rewarding or punishing statements contingent on performance. From the operant perspective, training efforts would emphasize response discrimination and development of the self-recording response. Efforts at behavior change would rely heavily on the self-management of environmental contingencies.

The previous discussion underscores the close link between self-monitoring and self-control. Many of the uses of SM with children will be in the context of self-management programs. A large literature exists in this area to guide the practitioner in the development and application of self-control strategies in a number of settings (see Karoly, 1977; Mahoney & Arnkoff, 1978; McLaughlin, 1976; Meichenbaum, 1979; Ross, 1981; Shapiro, 1984). However, in addition to its application in self-regulation, SM has evolved to become an important vehicle for assessment independent of the therapeutic package to which it is applied. Moreover, numerous researchers have demonstrated that SM can be a significant therapeutic variable exclusive of other interventions (see Nelson, 1977b). The following sections explicate the function of SM in assessment and treatment.

The Role of Self-Monitoring in Assessment and Treatment

The practitioner selecting self-monitoring as an assessment procedure will find it useful for a number of purposes. First, SM is a convenient way to obtain global information regarding child, teacher, or parent functioning at the preintervention stage. Data can take the form of narrations, self-ratings, responses to checklists, or audio recordings of events as they relate to the target problems. Global measures of this nature are useful in identifying potential target behaviors and generating preliminary hypotheses regarding the functional relationship between problematic behavior and antecedent and consequent events (Ciminero *et al.*, 1977). As relationships begin to emerge, global measures can be narrowed to focus on the target behavior and a description of the antecedent and consequent conditions surrounding its occurrence. These data can then lead to establishing baseline measures in addition to providing valuable information toward the development of intervention strategies. Mahoney (1977) pointed out that beginning with global measures, particularly in the form of unstructured narrations, can also be helpful in managing resistance to "structured behavioral programs." Frequently, school psychologists encounter such resistance when dealing with teachers and parents. When it becomes desirable to alter teacher or parent behavior as a means of achieving results with children, Mahoney suggested gradual introduction of structured assessment procedures to maintain vital cooperation.

At this stage of intervention, target behaviors have been defined, baseline measures established, and a therapeutic plan has been developed. The second assessment function of SM can be to obtain measures useful in evaluating the effectiveness of treatment (McFall, 1977). Toward this end, SM measures should be taken repeatedly over the course of treatment and preferably in the context of a time-series design (Kratochwill, 1978).

Third, self-monitoring may be the procedure of choice when covert behaviors are the target of assessment (Haynes & Wilson, 1979). Behaviors such as headaches, muscle tension, nightmares, depressive thoughts, obsessive thoughts, pain, attentiveness, emotions, covert "reinforcers" and covert "punishers" are not readily amenable to external observation. In these cases SM may provide more valid estimates of behavior than indirect methods such as interviews and questionnaires, although empirical support for this assumption remains to be generated (McFall, 1977).

A fourth potential use of SM in assessment is in the area of social validation. Social validation grew out of the movement to develop treatments that are clinically relevant to consumers (Kazdin, 1977; Wolf, 1978). Those receiving services and those impacted by them are typically queried concerning their perception of various facets of treatment (i.e., did therapy achieve what it set out to). This form of assessment has begun to receive attention in the school psychology literature (Witt & Elliot, 1985). Input from teachers, parents, and especially students can be solicited in order to better assess the value of psychological services. In this regard, SM measures could target consumer perceptions of the severity of the problem, collateral changes in other areas of functioning, generalization across settings, and satisfaction with treatment progress. When taken periodically over the course of treatment, SM measures of social validity can be a valuable tool for providers and recipients of therapeutic services in their formative evaluation of intervention.

An equally important role in SM is in the area of treatment. Numerous authors have reported changes in client target behaviors as a function of self-monitoring alone (see Ciminero *et al.*, 1977; McFall, 1977; Nelson, 1977a,b; Shapiro, 1984). This therapeutic aspect of self-monitoring is commonly referred to as reactivity. Alternatively, a number of researchers have failed to obtain reactive effects, suggesting that the phenomena is related to a finite set of variables that influence its occurrence. School psychologists intending to employ self-monitoring for its therapeutic value are advised to include many of the variables associated with reactivity (Nelson, 1977a) and couple self-monitoring with other treatment strategies (Mahoney, 1977). It should be briefly mentioned at this point that an inherent consequence of reactivity is diminished utility of self-monitoring for assessment purposes. The problem is particularly troublesome in research efforts aimed at evaluating discrete treatment variables. Reactivity can confound the data unless its effects are controlled and alternative assessment methods are employed (see section on reactivity in this chapter for further discussion of this topic).

Other potential contributions of self-monitoring to treatment outcome have recently received attention. Haynes and Wilson (1979) speculated that self-monitoring may serve to increase an individual's ability to discriminate and subsequent self-recording may interrupt a well-established behavioral chain, thus interfering with maladaptive behaviors and setting the stage for learning adaptive responses. For example, consider a pupil whose out-of-seat behavior frequently leads to annoying neighboring classmates and eventually culminates in disruptive arguments. Having the child self-monitor out-of-seat responses as they occur engages him or her in an activity incompatible with classroom disruption. Moreover, if the child must return to his or her seat to make the self-recording response, the behavioral chain leading to disruptive arguments is obstructed and academically related behaviors can then be strengthened in the absence of these competing responses. Recording consequent conditions may reveal that students consistently respond with inattention to a given set of instructional materials. This information may function as feedback to the teacher that in turn may affect his or her future use of the materials.

A final consideration is the role self-monitoring may play in enhancing an individual's understanding of the relationship between environmental events and behavior. Learning how the environment controls actions may prompt efforts at self-management of antecedent and consequent events (Karoly, 1977). Similarly, individuals who self-monitor may also develop a greater awareness of the effects their behaviors have on others. At the present time, only the effects of reactivity have been empirically verified. The ideas of Haynes and Wilson (1979) concerning discrimination of target responses await similar scrutiny before their contribution to treatment can be determined.

Self-Recording Procedures

Nelson (1977a) noted that almost no research has been conducted examining the critical features of self-recording procedures. Little progress has been made since that time in identifying the relative effectiveness of procedures, examining components within procedures and client preference among procedures, although some efforts are currently under way (Nelson & Hayes, 1981). A critical issue of importance to school psychology is whether self-recording procedures used with adults are applicable to children. Although Kazdin (1974a) suggested that self-monitoring may be less appropriate for children than adults, self-monitoring has been successfully employed with youth under a variety of circumstances (McLaughlin, 1976). Yet, the parameters of self-recording with children remain to be systematically investigated. In light of the dearth of literature directed at examining self-recording procedures, the following discussion is based on available research, suggested practices, and logical continuity with behavioral assessment methods.

General Considerations

A number of general considerations arise for selecting a self-recording procedure. Foremost among these concerns is that the self-recording procedure be compatible with the target behavior (Mahoney, 1977). Attention should be given to matching the target response with the measurement procedure (e.g., using frequency counts for discrete behaviors). This match should also take into account the frequency of the behavior. When the behavior under analysis occurs at a high frequency, it may not be feasible to record the response continuously. In such cases, a time sampling procedure may be indicated, in which case concern is directed at obtaining representative samples of the target behavior. A further issue affecting compatibility is the way in which treatment is expected to affect the target response. Measures should be selected that will be sensitive to the effects of intervention. For example, Johnson and White (1971) assessed the effects of self-monitoring on student study behavior. These researchers considered using the duration of study time as the dependent variable, but decided against it when they found study output more amenable to change than study time.

Other considerations in the selection of a self-recording procedure include ease of use and acceptability. Recording procedures should be easy to use for several reasons.

First, children may have learned to discriminate the occurrence of the target behavior, but may be unable to accurately self-record because of the complexity or awkwardness of the procedure (Nelson, 1977a). Second, difficult recording procedures may interfere with learning adaptive behavior. A student who is asked to record the number of pages read, as well as the content and the number of reading assignments completed, may do so at the expense of other academic learning time. And third, children may become discouraged if the demands of the recording procedure exceed their ability or willingness to comply. This can result in highly inaccurate data or abandoning self-monitoring altogether. A related factor is the accessibility of the procedure. Frederickson, Epstein, and Kosevsky (1975) found that accuracy increased when subjects self-recorded smoking behavior immediately after it occurred compared to subjects recording at daily or weekly intervals. Having the recording materials immediately available should facilitate accurate self-monitoring, particularly for high-frequency and/or nondiscrete behaviors (Watson & Tharp, 1972).

Direct Methods

Many of the recording procedures available to external observers are applicable to self-recording. Procedures that call on the child to observe the target response as it occurs are termed direct methods. These include narrations, frequency counts, duration measures, and time sampling.

Narrations

During the initial stages of assessment, information regarding the nature of the target behavior and the conditions associated with its occurrence is needed for the selection of formal self-recording procedures and the development of an intervention plan (Nelson, 1977a). A time-honored method of collecting such information is the behavioral diary. Typically, the client is asked to provide a narrative account of the target behavior along with a description of events immediately preceding and following it. Of interest is a description of the target response in objective and, where possible, observable terms. Also important in many cases are estimates of the strength, duration, and degree of unacceptability to the client. Antecedent events of concern are the time, setting, persons present, academic subject and materials, emotional responses, and client–other interactions. Significant changes in these areas following the occurrence of the target behavior are the focus of narrations about consequent conditions. Changes conceived of as reinforcers or punishers form the basis of hypotheses regarding the variables maintaining the target response. Armed with such information, the psychologist can then select a formal self-recording procedure that fits the target problem.

Most of the self-monitoring literature employing narrations or diaries has been conducted with adults. The nature of narrative accounts poses obvious constraints on their use with young children; however, many of these problems may not hold for adolescents. Narrative reports have been used to assess anger (Novaco, 1977), eating behaviors (Stuart & Davis, 1972), sleep disorders (Ribordy & Denny, 1977), marital interactions (Knox, 1972), hair pulling (Horne, 1977), anxiety (Mathews & Shaw, 1977), tension headaches (Feuerstein & Adams, 1977) and migraine headaches (Mitchel & White, 1977). The scope of these behaviors suggests that applications are possible for a broad range of behavior problems. Because most of the previously listed disorders have been reported in adolescents, members of this population would appear to be good candidates for future applications and research.

The formats used in recording narrations vary in terms of their degree of structure. In general, the more structure imposed on narrative accounts, the more readily these data may be used to develop and evaluate interventions. An example of a highly unstructured format is a diary calling for a designation of the date, time, and an anecdotal description of a problematic event. Although this strategy offers the client considerable flexibility, it often yields little useful information toward a behavior analysis. A more fruitful strategy that succeeds in procuring basic and essential data is the ABC format. Bell and Low (1977) have adapted this format for use in self-recording or direct observational recording. In addition to obtaining a description of the target behavior and its antecedent and consequent events, the format provides for operational definitions of the target behaviors, a description of the setting, and observation dates and times. The major advantage of this form is its general purpose application. Numerous problematic behaviors (both excesses and deficits) can be conceptualized and assessed using this structure. Moreover, it can be readily adapted to collect pertinent information on specific disorders. For example, Feuerstein and Adams (1977) had headache sufferers keep a diary of the frequency, duration, and intensity of headaches, and Mitchel and White (1977) asked clients to include a description of symptoms. Mahoney (1977) suggested that structured narrative formats include an open-ended column to allow individuals to self-record significant thoughts, feelings, or perceptions that may shed light on the problem.

Written narratives discussed thus far have applications limited to preadolescents and older; however, this form of assessment need not preclude younger children. Kunzelman (1970) developed a structured pictorial diary designed especially for elementary school populations. "Countoons" depict in pictures the sequence of events surrounding a particular target behavior. A pictorial sequence might include, for example, the events leading up to hitting another child, making him or her cry, and consequently the child being scolded by the teacher. Each time the child observes the sequence, he or she circles consecutive numbers under the "my count" column. This procedure has several advantages worth noting. First, it provides a vehicle for young children to participate in self-monitoring and its associated benefits. Second, it may serve a therapeutic function by helping children learn the relationship between environmental events and their behavior, thus setting the stage for self-management. Moreover, countoons made readily visible to the target child may serve to occasion positive behavior that results in reinforcement.

To summarize, behavioral diaries serve to gather information about the target behavior and the conditions under which it occurs. In the beginning stages of intervention, narrations help to narrow and define client behaviors and their controlling variables. Although available research on behavioral diaries is limited to adults, this procedure holds promise for adolescents and, when modified, younger children (e.g., countoons).

Frequency Counts

Frequency counts are an appropriate method of recording behaviors that are discrete (i.e., have an identifiable start and finish) and of relatively consistent duration. Self-monitoring frequency involves recording each occurrence of the target behavior within a specific period of time (Ciminero *et al.*, 1977). Records may be continuous, that is, reflect every occurrence of the behavior, or sampled from various times and settings throughout the day. Data are often presented as response rates (i.e., the ratio of response count to a time interval), permitting comparisons across measurement occasions of varying duration.

This procedure can also be adapted to suit specific assessment needs. When a finite response class can be identified, such as the number of test items or assignments completed, data can be computed as a percentage of the response class (Skinner, 1953). For example, of the semester's 32 arithmetic assignments, Arthur completed 24 or 75% of the work assigned. Another application of percentages is under conditions where a specific discriminative stimulus can be identified as controlling a target response (Ciminero *et al.*,

1977). For instance, an obese child may find that weight reduction is possible when between-meal snacks are omitted. The denominator is comprised of the number of times he is offered between-meal snacks and the numerator consists of the number of offers accepted.

Frequency counts represent the most prevalent self-recording procedure in the self-monitoring literature. Applications span the gamut of behavior problems encountered in applied psychology. The following examples illustrate applications particularly relevant to behavior therapy in educational settings.

Many academic behaviors appear well-suited for self-recording frequency counts. Broden, Hall, and Mitts (1971) trained an eighth-grade girl to record her study behavior at intermittent and self-determined points in time during class periods. Using an *a priori* definition of studying, the subject recorded a plus or a minus on the basis of her immediately preceding study behavior. Along similar lines, Johnson and White (1971) had college students self-observe and record study output measured by pages read and summarization of readings. In addition, these students calculated points earned for study output and graphed their progress over time. Hundert and Batstone (1978) used a self-scoring procedure with five 9- and 10-year-old boys enrolled in a special education class in a large psychiatric facility. These subjects scored and recorded the number of workbook problems answered correctly and submitted a report slip to the teacher on each occasion. Two of four students also self-recorded academic performance in a study by Piersel and Kratochwill (1979). A second-grade girl monitored worksheet scores on a card taped inside her desk and a ninth-grade boy was able to self-chart the number of language arts units completed. A number of studies have employed self-recording in the context of a programmed instruction paradigm. Piersel, Brody, and Kratochwill (1977) gave 63 children points for correct responses to WISC-R items. During the administration, subjects self-recorded the accuracy of their responses and the number of points earned. Similarly, mechanical counters were used by college students to record accurate responses to test items in separate studies by Mahoney, Moore, Wade, and Moura (1973) and Kirschenbaum and Karoly (1977). Finally, in conjunction with a token program to increase reading performance, Knapczyk and Livingston (1973) had 13 students, grades 7 through 9, self-record the percentage of correct responses on their daily reading assignments. A conversion chart was provided to assist subjects in determining percentage values from the number of correct responses.

The frequency of disruptive and maladaptive behaviors has also been the target of self-recording procedures. Maletzky (1974) had an 11-year-old girl self-monitor out-of-seat behaviors using a wrist counter. A similar device was later used with a 9-year-old boy to self-record incidents of hand raising following teacher questions for which he did not know the answer. Broden *et al.* (1971) employed a self-recording procedure with an eighth-grade boy referred for excessive and disruptive verbalizations. The subject recorded each time he talked out without teacher permission on a sheet of paper on which instructions for self-recording were typed. A more complex procedure was used by Bolstad and Johnson (1972). Twenty-four "predelinquent" males, grades 3 to 6, were instructed in recording their own behavior in three disruptive behavior categories. Each occurrence of talking out, hitting, or leaving their work area without permission was recorded on observation cards. Similar strategies have been used for loud talking (Piersel & Kratochwill, 1979), out-of-seat behavior (Bornstein *et al.*, 1977) and verbal interruptions (Piersel & Kratochwill, 1979).

Self-recording the frequency of more serious behavior problems in school age children has also been reported. Rekers and Varni (1977) taught a 6-year-old "pretransexual" boy to self-record the occurrence of play with masculine toys. In a similar case, Rekers, Amaro-Plotlin, and Low (1977) used self-observation in the treatment of an 8-year-old male having a gender role problem. Videotape was employed as a teaching strategy to increase the child's discrimination of the occurrence of feminine voice inflections and mannerisms. Prior to treatment in a case of trichotillomania, McLaughlin and Nay (1975) asked a 17-year-old female to self-monitor the frequency of eyelash and hair pulling incidents. And in 1977, Lubar and Shouse successfully trained a group of adolescents to self-record measures of seizure activity.

A final area of interest to school psychology is the use of frequency counts in the self-recording of social behavior and activities. Nelson, Kapust, and Dorsey (1978) provided a group of four mentally retarded adolescents training in self-monitoring appropriate classroom verbalizations. These researchers found that retarded youths could successfully use hand-held counters and belt-worn counters to self-record verbalizations. In a similar vein, Gottman and McFall (1972) applied self-monitoring procedures in an intervention to increase classroom participation in a group of inner city high school sophomores characterized as "predelinquent." Half of the subjects were instructed to self-record the frequency of verbal comments whereas the remainder were asked to mark the number of times they "would like to talk but, for any reason, do not."

Prosocial teacher behavior has also been the target of self-monitoring procedures. Nelson, Hay, Hay, and Carstens (1977) also asked two teachers to self-record positive verbal comments during their teaching activities. Each teacher was provided a counter to wear around her neck and was instructed to click the counter each time the target response occurred. In connection with a time out from teacher interaction program, Plummer, Baer, and LeBlanc (1977) taught teachers to discriminate and pace their delivery of instructions and approval behaviors to disruptive children. Finally, McKenzie and Rushall (1974) applied self-recording procedures to members of a swimming team. Youngsters ranging in age from 9 through 16 were instructed to self-record attendance at team practice sessions and laps swum. Recordings were made with a grease marker on a large waterproof display board posted near the swimming pool.

The previously cited literature points to the general utility and wide range of behaviors and populations to which self-recording frequency counts are applicable. Frequency counts have the advantage of being easy to use relative to narrations, duration, and time sampling procedures. Their primary limitation is an insensitivity to changes in intensity and duration of the target response. However, when target behaviors are discrete and the focus of intervention is not to alter the intensity or duration of behavior, frequency counts represent a useful method of self-recording.

Duration Measures

For many behaviors, concern about the frequency or intensity of the response may be secondary to the amount of time spent engaged in the activity. Examples of these behaviors include studying, watching television, exercising, headaches, contact with a feared stimulus, and tantrums. In these cases, duration measures indicate the amount of time consumed by the target behavior (Haynes & Wilson, 1979). Such measures are particularly useful when intervention is aimed at altering the time engaged in the activity. Although frequency and intensity measures may covary with the duration of the response, they are an indirect and potentially invalid index of duration and much less sensitive to change (Nelson, 1977a). Another useful application of duration measures is in combination with frequency or intensity measures (Emmelkamp & Kraanen, 1977; Feuerstein & Adams, 1977). For example, disruptive tantrums may vary along three dimensions: how often, how intense, and how long. Any single measure would not reflect levels in the other and thus may be inadequate to evaluate the effects of treatments.

Although duration measures may be highly desirable in many instances, few studies employing self-monitoring procedures have used them with school-aged populations. A notable exception is a study by Schwartz (1977) in which 240 seventh-grade students were involved in a summer remedial reading program. A component of the program required students to practice reading each night in order to build their stamina. Each student self-recorded the number of minutes spent reading and number of pages read. Students were able to earn points for their performance that were accumulated to form the basis of their final course grade. Other examples of self-monitoring duration measures appear with adult subjects. Johnson and White (1971) asked a large group of college students to self-record time spent in dating activities (i.e., any recreational activity involving the opposite sex). As part of a treatment package for muscle-contraction and migraine headaches, Feuerstein and Adams (1977) had clients record the duration of their headaches along with frequency and intensity measures. Turner, Hersen, and Bellack (1977) employed a self-observation procedure to assess the duration and frequency of hallucinations. Their female subject was instructed to raise her right index finger at the onset of hearing voices and to lower it once the hallucinations ceased. Finally, Leitenberg, Agras, Thompson, and Wright (1968) had a claustrophobic woman use a stop watch to self-monitor the number of seconds spent in a closed room as a measure of fear reduction.

A number of factors can be identified that may explain the scarcity of self-monitoring literature using duration measures, especially with children. First, compared to frequency counts and intensity ratings, obtaining measures of time is more complex (Watson & Tharp, 1972). For behaviors varying in minutes or seconds, timers or clocks are required to obtain accurate readings. In order for children to use effectively these devices, they must be able to coordinate discrimination of the onset and cessation of the behavior with operating the timer. For many children, particularly special populations, the complexity of the task may be prohibitive. Second, the complexity of the procedure may decrease the reliability of the measures. This may frustrate attempts to achieve good interobserver agreement and diminish the experimenter's power to detect differences. A third factor relates to the high potential duration measures may have for reactivity. According to one theory, the act of self-monitoring is responsible for reactive changes (Nelson & Hayes, 1981). Because duration measures involve continuous self-observation, reactivity would tend to be enhanced at the expense of the utility of the measure for assessment purposes; however, empirical support for this hypothesis is needed. The limitations cited earlier should not militate against the use of duration measures, but rather serve as guidelines for minimizing potential problems. Methods for measuring and recording time should be selected for their simplicity (Mahoney, 1977), and adequate preassessment training in the use of devices can enhance reliability (Nelson, 1977b).

Time Sampling Procedures

Time sampling is a convenient strategy for obtaining a representative estimate of the strength of some behavior. These procedures are very useful when the target response occurs at high frequencies. Many times individuals will be unwilling to self-record occurrences of high rate behavior. Moreover, repetitive self-recording may actually interfere with learning adaptive responses. In these cases, samples of behavior can serve as adequate measures and minimize the aversive side effects of continuous recording.

Ciminero *et al.* (1977) have identified four prevalent time sampling procedures used in self-monitoring. The first of these, the all-or-none method (Thoresen & Mahoney, 1974), involves dividing an observation period into equal intervals. During each interval, the client merely records whether the target response occurred. Intervals are coded as 1 =

occurred, or 0 = did not occur, and are thus insensitive to variable frequency rates. The percentage of intervals in which the target behavior occurred is used to assess response strength. Therefore, the length of each interval must be short enough to detect nonoccurrences, yet long enough to avoid tedious recording.

A second procedure is a variation of the all-or-none method. The dichotomous coding system (occurrence/nonoccurrence) is replaced by an ordinal scale that rates the frequency of occurrence. An example reported by Ciminero *et al*. (1977) is a 4-point self-rating scale developed by Stumphauzer (1974). At the end of each interval, the target behavior is rated as 0, 1, 2, or 3 on the basis of whether the behavior occurred "never," "occasionally," "often," or "very often." This procedure has the advantage of providing a more fine-grained measure that retains information lost in a dichotomous system. However, as the length of the interval increases, measurement errors become more common (Tasto, 1977).

Another procedure used to sample high-frequency behaviors involves self-recording target responses in a limited number of observation periods. Ideally, blocks of time are selected randomly from the time available for self-monitoring. For example, class time would be broken down into 10 half-hour periods. Each day, 2 of the 10 periods are chosen via a random procedure. Target responses would only be self-recorded during the selected periods. Because the time of the half-hour periods would vary from day to day, a representative sample of time intervals is assured. Moreover, using random rather than arbitrary methods of interval selection guards against obtaining biased samples resulting from behaviors that may occur at higher frequencies during the day.

The fourth time sampling procedure useful for high-rate behaviors is known as spot checking or momentary time sampling. Typically a timing device is set on a variable interval schedule. Each time the device signals the end of the interval, the subject self-records whether she or he was engaged in the target response at the time of the signal. Data are computed as the percentage of time samples in which the behavior occurred. Because assessment occurs at points in time rather than within time intervals, it is important that the target behavior consume a period of time rather than occur at an instant. For example, momentary time sampling is an appropriate and common strategy for assessing on-task behavior because random checks will likely catch the student engaging in the behavior if it occurs. In contrast, it is unlikely that a behavior occurring for a brief instant (e.g., a facial tic) will coincide with spot checks. For behaviors such as these, an interval sampling procedure will be more sensitive to the behavior's occurrence.

Some examples from literature pertinent to school psychology will help illustrate the application of time sampling procedures. In conjunction with a self-control project, Glynn, Thomas, and Shee (1973) instructed a class of second-grade pupils in self-recording on-task behavior. A tape recorded series of intermittent beeps varied randomly between one and five minutes so that children would be unable to predict when the tone would occur. Each time the beep sounded, the students placed a mark in a box on a self-recording sheet if they were on task. Behavioral definitions of on-task behavior served as the criteria for judging its occurrence. This procedure was later replicated by Glynn and Thomas (1974) with a class of third graders. However, these researchers found it beneficial to operationalize on-task behavior specific to the academic task. Two definitions were printed on cue cards, one relating to teacher lectures and the other to independent seat work. One of the two cards was displayed in the front of the classroom, indicating the target criteria at any given time. In another study, Seymour and Stokes (1976) trained four delinquent girls in a detention center for adolescents to self-record work behavior. Target behaviors were defined and written on index cards and included the following: hands working continuously, looking at work, doing the work set and not something else, not fiddling when getting something, not dawdling, and not talking out of turn. Work periods were divided into 3-minute intervals. Girls were instructed to mark their cards during each interval in which they judged their behavior to be consistent with the work criteria.

Indirect Methods

The self-monitoring procedures discussed thus far involve self-observation and recording of the target response as it occurs. However, in many cases it is not feasible or desirable to obtain direct measures for a variety of reasons. Teachers, students, and parents may find that self-recording narrations, frequency counts, or duration measures may interfere with their primary task. When this occurs, indirect methods are a viable alternative because they require less or no effort during the time in which the target behavior occurs. Another consideration is the potential for reactivity in direct versus indirect methods. Because reactivity is closely associated with the self-recording act (Nelson & Hayes, 1981), recording procedures that are further removed from the behavior may be expected to be less reactive (Mahoney, Moore, *et al.*, 1973; Romanczyk, 1974). These concerns may lead the psychologist to select a self-rating procedure or self-recording of behavioral traces or byproducts.

Self-Ratings

A subtle distinction exists between self-report and self-ratings as part of a self-monitoring procedure. The distinction is one of the degree of removal from the observed behavior. Self-report methods require the subject to engage in retrospective observations of the target behavior and recall it accurately in response to a question or rating scale (Bellack & Hersen, 1977). The time between the occurrence of the behavior and his or her self-report can range anywhere between hours to several years (Tasto, 1977). On the other hand, self-ratings in the context of a self-monitoring procedure are generally closely linked to the actual behavior (Stumphauzer, 1974). Typically, subjects are asked to rate their behavior along some dimension during time intervals or judge the degree to which their behavior approximates a predetermined criterion. Self-rating requires considerably less effort than direct methods calling for a one-to-one correspondence between behavior and self-recording. This characteristic of self-rating makes them particularly attractive for use in the schools where teacher and student time is at a premium.

Several studies demonstrate the application of self-ratings with children and youth. As part of a program to teach children to print, Jones, Trap, and Cooper (1977) trained a group of first grade students to self-rate and record the accuracy of their written letters. Students self-evaluated their performance by tracing over letter strokes that matched the model overlay. Strokes rated as matching were then counted by the students and the number was written at the right edge of the self-recording sheets. Flowers (1972) made use of a self-grading procedure as part of an intervention to eliminate cheating in a school-aged girl. The student was allowed to grade her own daily assignments using the teacher's manual. Accuracy of her self-grading was improved by making her exam grades contingent on agreement between performance on daily assignments and weekly exams (comprised of items from the daily assignments). Hundert and Bucher (1978) found self-rating of arithmetic assignments to be a useful strategy for reducing teacher time spent in grading. As with the Flowers (1972) case, accuracy of student self-rating was enhanced through the application of positive contingencies.

Institutional settings have also been the scene of interventions incorporating self-ratings in assessment. Prior to implementing a teacher-controlled token system, Santogrossi *et al.* (1973) instructed subjects in the self-evaluation of their classroom behavior. Nine adolescent males enrolled in a remedial reading class in a psychiatric hospital self-rated their compliance with classroom rules. At the end of consecutive 15-minute intervals, each youth rated his degree of adherence to rules on a scale from 0 to 2 for each of five rules. Public announcement of their self-ratings was combined with a token system in which students determined the number of tokens they received. Following several phases of a token system, Kaufman and O'Leary (1972) employed a self-evaluation phase to transfer the responsibility for evaluation of pupil behavior from the teacher to the students. Adolescents in a psychiatric hospital school self-rated their disruptive classroom behavior according to 11 behavioral criteria and self-determined the amount of tokens earned for each rating. Finally, Fixen, Phillips, and Wolf (1972) investigated the effects of self-ratings with a group of predelinquent boys placed in a family-style rehabilitation program. Each youth was provided with a list of 21 room cleaning definitions. The boys were instructed to rate the condition of their bedrooms each morning according to each of the 21 criteria.

Behavioral Traces and Archival Records

Another indirect means of self-assessment is by observing the products of one's own behavior. Products of behavior refer to physical traces or records of performance which exist independent of formal assessment efforts (Kazdin, 1979). Behavioral traces or archival records may either serve as the primary dependent measure or as supplements to other direct methods of assessment (Nelson, 1981). For example, worksheet scores can provide an indirect measure of on-task behavior, home study, learning, and motivation. Other applications include a measure of weight as a byproduct of eating (Monti, McCrady, & Barlow, 1977), nurse records as a measure of stomach complaints (Miller & Kratochwill, 1979), hair length as an indicator of hair pulling (Anthony, 1978), fingernail length as a measure of nailbiting (McNamara, 1972), and the number of pills in a prescription bottle to assess compliance with a medical regimen (Dapcich-Miura & Hovell, 1979).

There are a number of advantages in using behavioral traces and archival records for self-monitoring purposes. First, a modicum of effort is required on the part of the client, making it a realistic dependent measure for use in applied settings (Nelson, 1981). Piersel (1985) suggested that psychologists' efforts to trim demands on teachers' time is an effective strategy to bolster support for classroom interventions. Second, as supplemental measures, behavioral traces and records contribute to the validity and reliability of assessment by providing indexes of behavior (Nelson, 1981). Synchronous measures enhance one's confidence in the observed effects, while desynchrony among measures may provide greater conceptual understanding of the problem (Barlow, 1981). A third advantage is that self-monitoring traces and records of behavior may be less reactive than direct measures (Nelson, 1977a). Because subjects are not required to self-observe and record the actual target behavior, the self-recording response is less likely to influence subsequent behavior (Nelson & Hayes, 1981).

Kazdin (1979) observed that the apparent advantages of behavioral traces and archival records should be tempered by their potential shortcomings. Foremost among these is the problem of deciding what is measured. Varying degrees of inference are required to pair the behavioral by-product or record with the behavior that caused it. For instance, using weight gain to make inferences to eating behavior in anorexic children may be erroneous when eating is followed by self-induced vomiting. Similarly, increases in worksheet scores may be a function of teaching strategies, increased study time, or cheating. Such confusion may be reduced by using direct assessment methods initially to identify functionally related variables. Then, a reliably occurring behavioral trace or record may be used to infer the occurrence of the target response. Occasional probes using the original direct methods may be used to ensure that the variables continue to be functionally related (e.g., worksheet scores continue to be a result of teaching methods rather than cheating).

Self-Recording Devices

Several self-recording devices are available to assist clients in obtaining accurate records of their behavior. Ciminero *et al.* (1977) provided a number of considerations for selecting a recording device. The availability of the device at the time the target behavior occurs is a major concern. Particularly with children, errors can be expected to increase the longer the interval is between the occurrence of a behavior and the act of self-recording.

Another consideration is that the self-recording device be easy to use. Elaborate devices may confuse younger or retarded clients rendering the data collected unreliable or invalid. Finally, the obtrusiveness of the self-recording device can affect the quality of the data obtained. A moderately conspicuous device may improve accuracy by serving as a discriminative stimulus for self-recording. However, classmates and teachers are more likely to attend to salient devices and alter the child's use of them. With these considerations in mind, a sampling of devices will be described. For a more detailed discussion the reader is referred to Ciminero *et al.* (1977).

Mechanical Devices

Mechanical devices available for self-monitoring fall into three categories: counters, timers, and tape recorders. Counters are used to record the frequency of some behavior and take a variety of forms. For example, Lindsley (1968) reported the use of a wrist-worn golf counter; Hannum, Thoresen, and Hubbard (1974) used a multiple event wrist counter and Thoresen and Mahoney (1974) described a pipe cleaner wrist counter composed of multiple pipe cleaners, each with nine beads, mounted on a wrist band. A potentially useful counter for children is the "Knit Talley" described by Sheehan and Casey (1974). When mounted on a child's pencil or desk top, this device is a relatively unobtrusive and portable method of event recording. Another innovative device is the pressure sensitive pad and frequency counter. This device may be used for a variety of purposes including out-of-seat behaviors, sleepwalking, and exercising programs. The directional switch can be set to be activated each time the pad is depressed or conversely each time pressure is removed. Timing devices also take on a variety of shapes and sizes and may be used to self-record duration measures or signal recording times using a time sampling procedure. Among the timing instruments available are stopwatches (Ciminero *et al.*, 1977), wrist watches having elapsed time indicators (Katz, 1973), kitchen timers (Rainwater & Ayllon, 1976) and electric clocks with an in-cord/on-off switch (Thoresen and Mahoney, 1974). And finally, with the advent of highly portable video and audiotape recording devices, self-monitoring may occur outside the target setting or time. For example, Litrownik, Freitas, and Franzini (1978) combined videotape and live models in a procedure to train retarded children in self-monitoring.

Graphing Performance

Once self-monitoring data have been collected, it is often useful to transfer the information to a behavior graph or chart (Thoresen & Mahoney, 1974). The client can be instructed in the essentials of graphing and be encouraged to assume responsibility for its maintenance. Graphing performance serves a number of functions. First, the Chinese proverb, "One picture is worth a thousand words," aptly reflects the value of the graphic display of data (Parsonson & Baer, 1978). The graph summarizes performance in a manner that is usually more accurate and easier to comprehend than similar information provided verbally (Bergan, 1977). Second, data points connected by straight lines indicate the level and possible trends in performance. This information is crucial to the task of evaluating the effects of intervention. Moreover, data displayed across time can alert the psychologist and client to possible variables influencing performance and lead to subsequent changes in the treatment strategy. Third, graphs used in conjunction with a self-monitoring procedure can serve a dual purpose: (a) to summarize information, and (b) to provide a means of recording the target behavior as it occurs. For example, Plachetta (1976) used self-charting as part of a treatment package for encopresis in a 6-year-old boy. The graph doubled as a self-recording form plus an illustration of improvement in the child's condition. A fourth function of graphing is as a potential element of treatment. Public display of data may occasion feedback from others or individuals themselves that may have reinforcing or punishing effects (Ciminero *et al.*, 1977). To the extent that this occurs, subsequent performance may be altered.

Bergan (1977) outlined the essentials of graphing in terminology consistent with his consultation model of service delivery. The first characteristic of a readable graph is a title that describes what the graph represents. Included in the title should be a designation of who is being observed and the behavior that is being recorded. Another important graph component is the appropriate labeling of the vertical and horizontal axes. Vertical axis labels should identify the behavior being recorded, the type of strength measure being used (e.g., frequency or duration), and the time period each datum represents. The horizontal axis should specify the dates when observations or self-monitoring occurs. Bergan (1977) suggested using dates rather than days or sessions to avoid losing information regarding interruptions in the monitoring of behavior. A final essential of graphing is to indicate the phase of the intervention in which data were collected. For example, the initial phase may be labeled baseline and may represent self-monitored performance or data collected by an independent observer. Subsequent phases may include various treatment components or follow-up periods. When one uses behavior graphs with younger children, some important steps may be taken to facilitate their use. All graph labels should be completed by the psychologist or person responsible for intervention in order to minimize demands on the child and avert possible confusion.

Summary of Self-Recording Procedures

A broad range of self-monitoring procedures are available to the clinician and researcher. Direct methods in which the client self-records target responses as they occur include narrations, frequency counts, duration measures, and most uses of time-sampling. Narrations or behavioral diaries are useful during the problem identification stage of intervention to identify target behaviors, how they will be measured, and potential environmental variables that control them. Frequency counts are most applicable for discrete target behaviors of relatively consistent duration and when treatment is expected to impact on the number of times a behavior occurs. Duration measures, on the other hand, are appropriate when the time engaged in the behavior is variable or when concern for frequency is secondary to how much time the response consumes (e.g., contact time with a feared object). For high rate or highly variable behaviors, time sampling procedures may provide adequate estimates of response strength and reduce the time required for self-monitoring. Indirect methods discussed in this section include self-ratings, behavioral traces, and archival records. These methods are appropriate when direct assessment is impractical or as supplemental measures.

Several self-recording devices are available to assist children and their caretakers in collecting self-monitoring data. Their value lies in the simplification and organization of complex information, allowing for evaluation of treatment effects. Portable mechanical devices offer a convenient method of recording events as they occur, whereas behavior graphs serve to summarize data across treatment phases. In addition, both kinds of recording devices may influence the reactivity of self-monitored data and consideration should be given to this factor when designing self-assessment strategies (see section on reactivity in this chapter).

Training in Self-Monitoring

An important issue related to any assessment technique is that of training assessors in the proper use of the data collection procedure. Until recently, relatively little attention has been given to training clients, particularly children, in the use of self-monitoring procedures. In the child behavior therapy literature, training has typically consisted of verbal instructions describing the self-recording methods and providing clients with recording forms (e.g., Bornstein *et al.*, 1977; Piersel & Kratochwill, 1979; Sagotsky, Patterson, and Lepper, 1978). Others have indicated praise for appropriate monitoring behavior (Drabman, Spitalnik, & O'Leary, 1973) or modeled the actual recording methods (Anthony, 1978; Hallahan, Lloyd, Kosiewicz, Kauffman, & Graves, 1979). In addition to the above training strategies, Litrownik and Freitas (1980) established performance criteria for each phase of training. Those clients meeting or exceeding the criterion for each phase progressed through subsequent phases until training was completed. Further training was provided to clients whose performance did not reach the performance standard. Jones *et al.* (1977) developed an innovative training procedure to teach children to self-record letter strokes. The experimenter employed verbal instructions, demonstrations, and verbal performance feedback to train subjects to: (a) align the overlay of model letters above practice work samples; (b) identify letter stroke errors on sample training sheets; (c) trace the overlay on practice sheets of target letters; (d) count the number of correct letter strokes for each practice letter and self-record the number on the practice sheet; and (e) apply this procedure to self-monitor the accuracy of their own work samples.

Another issue parallel to the development of training procedures is the effects of training on the accuracy of self-monitored data. Addressing this question, Litrownik *et al.* (1978) assessed the self-monitoring performance of retarded children under three conditions. The group receiving training (i.e., verbal instructions, live and video models, and practice trials with performance criteria) acquired accurate self-monitoring skills compared to subjects in either of the attention or no-contact control groups. In a similar study, Nelson, Lipinski, and Boykin (1978) found that having retarded adolescents practice self-recording from videotapes and in the criterion classroom setting enhanced the accuracy of self-monitoring relative to no-training controls. Interestingly, the effects of training were not found to increase the reactivity of self-recorded measures.

Although recent advances in training strategies have appeared in the applied literature, few authors have proposed a general training sequence of relevance to practitioners and researchers alike. The training sequence proposed here represents an extension of the procedure described by Mahoney (1977). It is based primarily on procedures detailed in the self-monitoring literature, sound behavioral practice, and experience training youth in the use of self-monitoring. Conceptually, self-monitoring, like any other skill, is viewed as a coordinate set of behaviors, each of which can be targeted for acquisition. Usually this involves some sort of task analysis, breaking the entire task into discrete units and their sequential ordering (Sulzer-Azaroff & Mayer, 1977). Because each application of self-monitoring will vary with different subjects, target behaviors, and assessment goals, training should be individualized for each client or group of clients and their specific needs. Yet despite the unique features of each case, some general guidelines can be identified that have broad applications. The proposed training sequence consists of the following.

1. Provide clear and simple definitions of the target events to be self-recorded. Definitions can be written, represented pictorially, or both, depending on the client's level of functioning. Post the definition on the recording form to reduce ambiguity in self-assessment.

2. Provide clear and simple instructions on how to self-monitor. Identify each step and the behavior to be performed [e.g., First, you set the timer for 25 minutes like this (demonstrate). Second, do as many math problems correctly on the worksheet as you can until the timer rings. Third, stop working when the timer rings and mark your answers using the answer key. Fourth, count the number of problems you completed correctly. And fifth, write the number in the box next to today's date on the record form].

3. Demonstrate the self-monitoring procedure using actual record forms or recording devices. Label each step as it is completed.

4. Provide the client with written or pictorial instructions describing the self-monitoring procedure.

5. Ask the client to repeat the target definitions and self-monitoring instructions. Ask the client if he or she has any questions about what is to be done.

6. Test client acquisition of self-monitoring skills by conducting several assessment trials in an analogue or, if possible, the target setting.

7. Specify performance criteria for self-monitoring accuracy. Use an upwardly changing criterion for clients slow to acquire the assessment skills.

8. Provide social and/or tangible reinforcement, as needed, to promote the development and maintenance of self-monitoring.

This sequence can be used to train children, parents, and school personnel to self-monitor a broad spectrum of target behaviors. Although elements were derived from empirical work in the area, research is needed to evaluate the combined effects on the acquisition and occurrence of self-monitoring skills. Also of interest is the contribution of the individual components of the training package to its overall efficacy. Research in this area may help streamline the training sequence for easier use in applied settings.

The Relationship of Self-Monitoring to Other Assessment Procedures

The utility of self-monitoring in child assessment is perhaps best understood relative to other assessment devices. In selecting an assessment procedure, the psychologist is concerned with its objective characteristics as well as its suitability for the specific case. In this regard, self-monitoring has a number of characteristics that merit consideration when choosing among assessment alternatives.

First, self-monitoring can be viewed as a humanistic form of measuring client performance. Compared to other modes of assessment, self-monitoring requires active participation of the client in his or her own evaluation. This essentially eliminates second-party assessor bias from the data. As a result, subsequent diagnosis and/or classification based on self-collected data reflect the client's input and evaluation of his or her functioning. In addition, self-monitoring can be considered a less intrusive form of assessment than the use of external observers (Morris & Hoschouer, 1980). Whenever children record their own behavior, they are aware that assessment is taking place and provide consent to proceed either explicity or implicity. Unfortunately, children are not always accorded this privilege when other forms of assessment are used. Another humanistic aspect of self-monitoring is its emphasis on skill development. Clients who learn to self-record their own behavior acquire valuable skills that have broad application. The child who self-monitors arithmetic performance may extend its use to other target behaviors that he or she may find desirable to change.

A second characteristic of self-monitoring is its relative cost-effectiveness. Continued emphasis on the consultation model of service delivery in school psychology has highlighted the need to involve educational personnel in assessment and treatment (Bergan, 1977; Piersel, 1985). Consistent with this trend, self-monitoring provides the opportunity for the client to share in this responsibility. This prospect has a number of potential advantages. Clearly, enlisting youth in the assessment process reduces the demands on the psychologist and other educational staff. Greater numbers of students can then be served, thereby maximally utilizing the consultant's knowledge (Bergan, 1977). Piersel (1985) has also noted that consultant attention to minimizing teacher time required for assessment is a key variable that can predict the eventual outcome of consultation. From this perspective, self-monitoring appears considerably more cost-effective than other procedures requiring external assessors.

A final aspect of self-monitoring that should influence its selection for assessment is the quality of data it generates. As previously indicated, self-monitored data have a high potential for being inaccurate and reactive relative to other observation methods (Nelson, 1977b; Nelson, Lipinski, & Boykin, 1978). It is strongly recommended, therefore, that the variables shown to enhance the data's validity be included in any self-monitoring procedure. A related issue raised by Haynes and Wilson (1979) is whether even accurate self-monitoring reflects client performance when assessment is not being conducted. For example, a student self-recording on-task behavior during spelling and math may evidence rates near 80%. However, during reading and language arts this rate may be considerably lower (e.g., 30%) and representative of preassessment levels. Discrepancies such as these may be due in large part to the reactivity of the assessment procedure. Consequently, data derived from this method may not be generalizable outside actual assessment occasions. On the positive side, private events such as cognitions, emotions, and certain social relations are perhaps most validly assessed via self-monitoring (Nelson, 1977b). Compared to retrospective methods of self-report, self-monitoring is more direct and less likely to be influenced by bias and limited recall. However, in view of the inherent difficulty in assessing the accuracy of private events, these measures should be supplemented where possible with other sources of information.

Methodological Issues

Many of the issues relating to self-monitoring discussed thus far speak to its advantages as an assessment technique. However, two primary methodological issues must be considered to put its role in assessment into perspective. The first concerns the potential reactive effects associated with self-monitoring, that is, changes in performance occurring as a function of the assessment procedure alone. A second issue pertains to the accuracy or criterion-related validity of the measurement. In the following sections, reactivity and validity will be examined along with the variables which influence them.

Reactivity of Measures

When external observers are introduced into a natural setting, the stimulus conditions exerting control over behavior undergo significant changes. In many cases, the presence of observers has been demonstrated to alter client behavior independent of formal treatment (Kazdin, 1974b; Mercatoris & Craighead, 1974). Yet, other authors have found the reactive effects of observation less problematic (see Nelson, Kapust, & Dorsey, 1978). The issue of reactivity also becomes a factor when clients are engaged in self-monitoring. The act of self-observation and self-recording results in similar changes in the stimulus situation and the sequence of events that would otherwise exist (Ciminero *et al.*, 1977). Resulting behavior changes are referred to as the *reactivity of self-monitoring.*

For the school psychologist employing self-monitoring procedures, the consequences of reactivity are a mixed blessing. On one hand, reactive effects may be therapeutic to the extent that behavior change parallels the goals of treatment. In this regard, self-monitoring may either be used as the sole therapeutic variable or integrated into a comprehensive treatment package. However, when self-monitoring is used primarily to assess and evaluate the effects of a specific treatment, reactivity becomes problematic (Kazdin, 1974). Simultaneous application of self-monitoring and another intervention leads to confounded data, making it impossible to ascertain the contribution of either variable. For example, Hundert and Batstone (1978) had five boys enrolled in a special education class score their own arithmetic workbook. The number of problems answered correctly was self-recorded on a report slip and submitted to the teacher on a daily basis. Concurrently, pupils were awarded points exchangeable for classroom privileges based on their self-reported arithmetic performance. Using a multiple baseline across subjects design, the percentage of correct problems was found to increase under the reinforced self-recording condition relative to teacher scored baseline performance. Although these authors have evidence for a clinically relevant treatment package, the results are ambiguous in terms of the variables responsible for change.

Experimental Controls for Reactivity

In circumstances where there is concern for identifying the source of behavior change, the reactive effects of self-monitoring will need to be accounted for (Nelson, 1977a). Fortunately, there are a number of design options available for this purpose.

When time-series data are collected, Jeffrey (1974) suggested using an A/B/C/A/B/C within-subject experimental design to isolate the effects of reactivity. In this sequence, A is an independently measured baseline, B is self-monitoring and C is a combination of self-monitoring plus another intervention. This design strategy is appropriate when A equals B (i.e., no reactivity is apparent); otherwise the design is confounded by sequence effects (Hersen & Barlow, 1976) and contiguous treatment effects (Kazdin, 1980). When reactivity is present, an A/B/A/C/A/C series provides some control for the problems of continuous treatments, although multiple treatment interference is still a problem. Obtaining data across other settings or subjects in a multiple baseline pattern allows the series to be counterbalanced, thus accounting for sequence effects (e.g., Subject 1 receives A/B/A/C whereas Subject 2 receives A/C/A/B). Nelson (1977a) noted that in some instances acquiring data for the A phase may prove troublesome. The unavailability of independent assessments may prompt the use of client estimates of preintervention levels of behavior (see Berecz, 1972). Obviously, retrospective baseline estimates are less desirable than direct measures; however, they may provide a rough means of gauging the presence of reactivity.

When using between-subject experimental designs, the use of control groups is a common method of examining the contributions of reactivity. Nelson and McReynolds (1971) and Jeffrey (1974) suggested including a self-monitoring only group in addition to no-treatment and experimental treatment plus self-monitoring groups. As Nelson (1977a) pointed out, this strategy does not permit evaluation of the independent effects of treatment, only the interaction between treatment and self-monitoring relative to self-monitoring only. One solution to this problem is the completely crossed factorial design (see Myers, 1979). Four groups of subjects are exposed to separate conditions. In Cell 1, clients receive the package of self-monitoring plus an additional intervention, allowing for examination of their interactive effects. Cells

2 and 3 permit evaluation of the independent contributions of treatment and self-monitoring, respectively. Subjects in the fourth cell serve as no treatment controls against which the experimental conditions are compared. Although subject to the inherent limitations of group designs (see Hersen & Barlow, 1976; Kratochwill, 1978), this design strategy does allow between-condition comparisons in the absence of multiple treatment interference. Furthermore, the design can be strengthened by including a trial factor to facilitate assessment of effects over time.

Evidence of Reactivity

The reactive elements of self-monitoring have been demonstrated across a broad range of subjects, settings, and disorders (Haynes & Wilson, 1979). In the child literature, self-monitoring has been used to initiate desirable behavior change (Broden *et al.*, 1971; Roberts & Dick, 1982), as well as in the maintenance of effects following intervention (Bornstein *et al.*, 1977; Drabman *et al.*, 1973). In addition to playing a supplemental role in treatment, self-monitoring has been used as the primary therapeutic variable. It is in this capacity that the effects of reactivity are most clearly evident.

A case study presented by Hallahan *et al.* (1979) illustrated the therapeutic potential of self-monitoring. A 7-year-old boy with attentional problems was taught to self-monitor his on- and off-task behavior using a tape recorder to occasion self-recording responses. During handwriting and math periods, the child was provided with a self-recording sheet containing a picture of a boy reading a book and the caption, "Was I paying attention?" Each time a tape recorded tone sounded (on a variable interval schedule), the student was to self-record whether he was on or off task at the time of the tone. Using a time-series withdrawal design across handwriting and math periods, on-task behavior increased markedly relative to baseline periods in both settings. In subsequent phases, behavior change remained stable as self-monitoring was phased out and substituted with a covert self-praise procedure.

In another case study by Anthony (1978), a 9-year-old boy referred for trichotillomania (excessive hair pulling) was instructed in the use of a wrist counter to self-record the number of times he pulled his hair and the number of times he started to pull his hair but stopped. The child was also taught to graph his self-recorded data. In addition to self-monitoring, the client wore a baseball cap during waking hours to discourage hair pulling responses. Initially, self-monitoring was to serve primarily as an assessment procedure to be followed by a token economy and relaxation training. However, the client failed to return for treatment following instruction in self-monitoring. Eight weeks later, the therapist received a letter of thanks from the child's mother along with data indicating that hair pulling had ceased. Independent observations made by the mother in addition to measures of hair length were offered in support of her claims. Although lacking an experimental design and control procedures, this case does raise compelling questions about the potential strength of reactive effects.

A series of four single-case studies reported by Piersel and Kratochwill (1978) further exemplify the therapeutic value of reactivity. In the first of these, a 7-year-old girl increased the number of completed worksheets across two academic subjects from a baseline of zero to approximately one per day during self-monitoring. The self-recording strategy involved writing her worksheet scores on a card taped inside her desk. The second referral was a 13-year-old boy who was taught to self-record his disruptive talk in the classroom. Teacher statements to "tone it down" were recorded by the student as an indirect measure of his disruptive verbalizations. Self-recorded data were found to be highly reactive and accurate over the course of intervention. Case 3 involved having a 9-year-old girl identified as hyperactive self-record the frequency of her verbal interruptions. The level of the target behavior dropped significantly with the onset of self-monitoring. Interestingly, independent teacher ratings were found to be more reactive than student self-monitored data. Finally, a 15-year-old hyperactive boy was instructed to monitor the number of language units completed accurately on a sheet of notebook paper. His performance im proved dramatically and was maintained by self-monitoring over a period of 50 consecutive school days. The importance of these cases lies in demonstrating strong and often enduring reactive effects after other staff-planned strategies had failed.

When the therapeutic impact of self-monitoring is compared with conventional treatments, mixed results have occurred. Nelson, Lipinski, and Black (1976) contrasted the effectiveness of a token economy with self-monitoring on increasing community living skills in retarded adults. Across multiple treatment phases, self-recording was found to be superior in altering client behavior. Similarly, Sagotsky *et al.* (1978) found the benefits of self-monitoring to exceed significantly those achieved by goal-setting on children's academic on-task behavior. In contrast to these findings, Mahoney, Moura, and Wade (1973) and Mahoney (1974) reported self-monitoring alone to be less effective for weight reduction than a combination of self-monitoring and self-reward. Moreover, other studies have found minimal or no reactive properties associated with self-monitoring (e.g., Fixen *et al.*, 1972; Miller & Kratochwill, 1979; Romanczyk, 1974).

These notable inconsistencies across studies have important implications for clinical practice and research. For the practicing school psychologist, the primary goal of intervention is to effect clinically significant changes in behavior. In most cases, this is often achieved by integrating a number of therapeutic strategies into a comprehensive treatment package. Concern for the contribution of the individual components is typically subordinate to the need to produce meaningful results. For this reason, the reactive potential of self-monitoring may be best utilized in combination with other treatment approaches, rather than as the solitary therapeutic variable.

Although inconsistent reports of reactivity create ambiguity for the practitioner, these findings have led to a wave of research aimed at explaining these differences (Nelson, 1977b). Efforts have concentrated on identifying the variables that enhance reactive effects. Because the majority of work in this area has been conducted with adults, appropriate caution should be exercised in generalizing to children.

Variables Affecting the Reactivity of Self-Monitoring

Most researchers have conceptualized the occurrence, extent, and duration of reactive effects from self-monitoring as dependent variables under the control of other factors (Haynes & Wilson, 1979). Nelson (1977a,b) has reviewed this literature and identified nine variables implicated in the reactive process. These nine variables are briefly discussed in the following.

Motivation

The extent to which subjects are motivated to alter the target response appears related to reactivity. Evidence for this comes from a number of studies in which smoking behavior was self-monitored. McFall and Hammen (1971) included only those smokers who were motivated to reduce their habit. All four groups in the study decreased their smoking regardless of the smoking measure they self-recorded. In a direct comparison of motivated versus nonmotivated smokers, Lipinski, Black, Nelson, and Ciminero (1974) found that self-recording decreased smoking only in subjects volunteering for an experiment to reduce smoking. Reactivity did not occur in subjects volunteering for a general experiment for smokers.

Valence

Several investigators have determined that the valence associated with the self-monitored target behavior can affect the occurrence and direction of reactivity. Specifically, self-monitoring tends to increase the strength of desirable behaviors and decrease the strength of undesirable ones. For example, Nelson *et al.* (1977) had teachers self-record their positive and negative statements during different phases of a study. Positive verbalizations increased whereas negative comments decreased relative to their baseline rates. Similar results were obtained by Litrownik and Freitas (1980) in a study with moderately retarded adolescents. Participants were divided into four groups: (a) self-record when they finished a bead-string task within a time limit (positive aspect); (b) self-record when they did not finish the task within the time limit (negative aspect); (c) self-record when they strung the beads (neutral aspect); and (d) string beads without self-recording. The results indicated that youths recording positive or neutral aspects of their behavior out-performed the negative aspect and control groups.

Findings obtained by others examining the effects of self-monitoring negatively valenced behaviors indicate a potential for undesirable side-effects. Self-recording negative behaviors was associated with lower self-evaluations and performance (Kirschenbaum & Karoly, 1977), decreased accuracy in performance (Cavior & Marabotto, 1976), and negative affect (Piersel *et al.*, 1977). Similar undesirable concomitants have not been reported with positively valenced target behaviors.

Experimental Instructions

Another variable examined is the effect of experimenter-provided expectations concerning the direction of behavior change to result from self-monitoring. Nelson, Lipinski, and Black (1975) informed different groups of college students that the frequency of face touching would either increase, decrease, or remain unchanged as a function of self-monitoring. However, all groups experienced a decrease in the rate of face touching, suggesting that the salience of experimenter instructions may have been overshadowed by personal valences or motivation (Ciminero *et al.*, 1977). Similar outcomes were reported by Hutzell (1976), Orne (1970), and Nelson *et al.* (1978), suggesting that experimenter induced expectancies have a negligible effect on reactivity. The notable exception is experimenter-assigned valence to target behaviors discussed earlier.

Target Behaviors

The nature of the target behavior used in self-monitoring may also influence the reactivity of the measures. Hayes and Cavior (1977) compared the relative reactivity of self-recording verbal value judgments, verbal nonfluencies, and facial touching. Of the three behaviors, only verbal nonfluencies and facial touching were reactive. In a weight control study, Romanczyk (1974) found that greater weight loss occurred when daily weight and caloric intake were recorded as compared to monitoring daily weight only. And a recent study by Harmon, Nelson, and Hayes (1980) reported improved ratings of depression and involvement in pleasant activities when either mood or activity engaged in were self-monitored. However, recording activity resulted in somewhat greater reactivity than when mood was the target response. Unfortunately, few patterns emerge that allow prediction of which target behaviors will be most reactive, although some authors suggest that nonverbal behaviors are more reactive than verbal ones (Peterson, House, & Alford, 1975) and monitoring urges is more effective than monitoring the actual behavior (Gottman & McFall, 1972).

Goals, Reinforcement, and Feedback

Setting performance goals and the availability of performance feedback and reinforcement tend to enhance reactivity. Kazdin

(1974b) found that providing subjects with a performance standard when self-monitoring was more effective than self-monitoring alone in increasing subjects' use of target pronouns. Response frequency was further increased when feedback was available. Reinforcement contingent on self-monitored performance has similarly heightened reactive effects. Changes in self-recorded behavior were reported when college students were given money for decreasing facial touches (Lipinski *et al.*, 1975) and prompt access to breakfast was made contingent on children's tent cleaning (Lyman, Richard, & Edler, 1975). In short, goals, reinforcement, and feedback have a predictable effect on behavior irrespective of how it is assessed (i.e., via self-monitoring or external observation).

Timing

Reactivity also seems to be a function of the temporal order of self-recording in relation to the occurrence of the target behavior. In general, self-monitoring a behavior prior to its occurrence promotes greater reactivity than recording it after the fact (Kanfer, 1970a). This relationship was demonstrated by Bellack, Rozensky, and Schwartz (1974) when subjects recording their food intake before eating achieved greater weight loss than those monitoring consumption after eating. Similar findings were reported by Gottman and McFall (1972), who found self-monitoring urges to make comments in class more reactive than recording actual comments. The pattern, however, did not hold in a study with young children. Nelson *et al.* (1977) found that self-monitoring prior to or after verbalizations did not differentially influence the reactivity of appropiate or inappropriate classroom verbalizations.

Concurrent Monitoring of Multiple Behaviors

Two studies have examined the effects of concurrently self-monitoring multiple behaviors. Hayes and Cavior (1977) trained subjects to self-record the frequency of face touching, nonfluencies, and value judgments, all considered negatively valenced behaviors. Groups of subjects monitored either one, two, or three of the target behaviors. Tracking of a single behavior produced the greatest reactivity as measured by ratio change score. Similar results were obtained when this study was replicated with positively valenced behaviors (Hayes & Cavior, 1980). In this instance, self-monitoring produced increases in looking, present tense verbs, and feelings statements only when one behavior was recorded. Although decreased reactivity with multiple behaviors may enhance the utility of self-monitoring for assessment purposes, these benefits are offset by the finding that accuracy is also diminished.

Schedule of Self-Monitoring

There is some evidence to indicate that the frequency or schedule of self-monitoring may contribute to reactivity. Frederikson *et al.* (1975) suggested that the optimal schedule for self-monitoring, when reactivity is desirable, is related to the rate and variability of the behavior. High-rate behaviors may require immediate and continuous recording in order to facilitate response discrimination, whereas low-frequency behaviors may still be reactive when apparent in a study by Mahoney, Moore, *et al.* (1973) assessing performance on a standardized general aptitude test. Using a teaching machine, subjects who self-monitored their accuracy on a continuous schedule improved their performance relative to those who monitored accuracy on every third problem. Similarly, Frederiksen *et al.* (1975) found continuous monitoring of each cigarette smoked to be more effective in reducing smoking behavior than nightly or weekly recording of the total number of cigarettes smoked for that time period.

Nature of the Self-Recording Device

A final variable implicated in the reactive process is the type of self-recording device used. According to some authors, obtrusive recording devices may function as a discriminative stimulus for the self-recording response that may cue the individual to the environmental contingencies controlling behavior (Nelson & Hayes, 1981; Rachlin, 1974). Suggestive evidence for this comes from a series of case studies by Maletzky (1974), in which a wrist counter was used to self-record maladaptive behaviors. Reactive effects were demonstrated for all subjects during self-monitoring; however, in each case, when wrist counters were removed and self-recording terminated, response increases were noted. This phenomenon was also reported by Broden *et al.* (1971) when the removal of slips of paper used for self-recording study behavior results in a drop in study rates. The obtrusiveness of the recording device was experimentally manipulated by Nelson *et al.* (1978) with retarded adolescents self-recording appropriate verbalizations. Hand-held counters were found to be more reactive than belt-worn counters, although differences were not statistically significant.

To summarize, equivocal evidence for the reactive effects of self-monitoring has not been treated as whimsical. Systematic evaluation of the self-monitoring process indicates that reactivity may be a function of the specific conditions present during self-assessment. Among the variables affecting reactivity are: (a) client motivation, (b) the valence of the recorded response, (c) experimenter instruction, (d) the nature of the target behavior, (e) goals, reinforcement, and feedback, (f) the timing of self-recording, (g) concurrent monitoring of multiple behaviors, (h) the schedule of self-monitoring, and (i) the nature of the self-recording device. Although empirical support for these variables exists, it should be noted that, with the exception of valence, reinforcement, and feedback, evidence is not strong. In most cases, findings should be considered tentative due to a limited number of studies, conflicting results, and inadequate methodology. Moreover, few investigators have examined these variables with children, thus further limiting the application of these findings to school psychology. Needless to say, future research should target this population as well as the psychological and educational problems they encounter. Finally, the search for the determinants of reactivity should be extended to other potential factors. For example: (a) demographic variables including age, sex, and intellectual functioning, (b) the parameters of training in self-monitoring, (c) behaviors versus behavior products (Haynes & Wilson, 1979), (d) the salience of the contingencies linked to performance, (e) interaction of reactive effects with other treatment strategies, and (f) setting factors.

Theories of Reactivity in Self-Monitoring

Theoretical explanations for the reactive effects of self-monitoring followed on the heels of research documenting the phenomenon. Three theories have been advanced to account for the reactive effects of self-monitoring. These include the cognitive-behavioral model (Kanfer, 1970a,b, 1975, 1977), the operant recording-response model (Rachlin, 1974), and the multiple cueing stimuli model (Nelson & Hayes, 1981). Kanfer accounts for reactive effects in the context of a multistage model of self-regulation. Individuals are said to exert effective control over their own behavior through a process of self-monitoring, self-evaluation, and self-reinforcement. The components of the self-management process occur as a sequential chain of events, each triggered by the occurrence of the preceding component. The reactive chain begins when a child observes and records his or her own behavior (self-monitoring). Inevitably, the individual responds to the self-monitored data by comparing his or her behavior against some performance standard or goal (self-evaluation). Performance equal to or surpassing the criterion leads to self-administration of consequences (which are often presumed to occur covertly).

Rachlin (1974) believed that the search for determinants of behavior change should focus on observable events rather than on hypothetical processes that are not subject to observation and experimental analysis. Accordingly, Rachlin contended that either self-recording responses or self-administered consequences serve as discriminative stimuli for behavior under the ultimate control of often delayed environmental contingencies. "Counting and timing of events with mechanical or written aids and the techniques of self-reinforcement (and self-punishment) are . . . ways to increase the salience of the relationship between behavior and its consequences" (Rachlin, 1974, p. 105). Thus, Rachlin placed emphasis on the self-recording response in the reactive process. Unlike Kanfer, however, environmental contingencies rather than internal and self-determined consequences are believed responsible for self-managed behavior.

Nelson and Hayes' (1981) multiple cuing model shares with the others the assumption that the self-recording response initiates the reactive chain. However, the Rachlin view that reactivity can be precipitated by self-recording alone is extended to implicate the entire self-monitoring process. Stimuli believed to enhance the salience of the relationship between behavior and its controlling environmental consequences include teacher/therapist instructions, training in self-monitoring, the self-monitoring device, feedback from others, and the self-recording response itself. Also acknowledged within this model is the potential contribution of self-evaluation and self-administered consequences. Rather than ascribing causal properties to these private or public events, Nelson and Hayes argue that they too function as cues that help the individual discriminate the environmental contingencies controlling their behavior.

Support for Theories of Reactive Self-Monitoring

Controversy surrounding the mechanisms that underlie reactive self-monitoring centers on behavior's locus of control. Although all three theories view self-monitoring as a catalyst for self-managed behavior change, viewpoints differ on the function of the self-recording response and of the behaviors self-monitoring may precipitate. For Kanfer, self-monitoring triggers self-evaluation and the delivery of response-contingent consequences. Operant theorists, on the other hand, consider self-monitoring (Rachlin, 1974) and related events (Nelson & Hayes, 1981) to be discriminative stimuli for behaviors under the control of delayed environmental contingencies.

Relatively few studies have directly investigated the tenets of the major theories of reactivity. Spates and Kanfer (1977) examined the components of Kanfer's model in a study comparing the math performance of first graders during (a) self-monitoring, (b) criterion setting, (c) self-monitoring plus criterion setting, (d) criterion setting plus self-reinforcement, and (e) a contact control condition. However, the procedures used to represent these components differed from those commonly used in the literature. For example, self-monitoring consisted of having students say aloud the numbers that they were adding (e.g., "Now I am adding these two numbers here . . .") rather than self-recording the accuracy or completion of their work (cf. Hundert & Bucher, 1978; Piersel & Kratochwill, 1979). Also somewhat unorthodox were the criterion-setting procedures employed, which entailed having subjects say aloud a strategy for correctly adding 3-digit numbers (e.g., "First, I should add the two numbers on the right, then I should add the two numbers in the middle," etc.). This procedure differs from most studies in which a criterion or goal is set for accuracy or completion of assignments (cf. Sagotsky *et al.*, 1978). Further, the criterion-setting procedure was very similar to self-instruction training, which has been shown to improve academic behavior independent of self-selection of performance criteria (e.g., Bornstein & Quevillon, 1976; Bryant & Budd, 1982). The results of the study indicated that conditions that included criterion setting, alone or in combination with self-monitoring or self-reinforcement, produced the most accurate math performance. This finding led the authors to conclude that criterion setting is the critical component of reactivity because it triggers the self-evaluation process. However, given that self-monitoring did not involve self-recording of the target behavior and criterion setting approximated self-instruction techniques, additional research is needed before Kanfer's model is supported empirically.

Hayes and Nelson (1983) investigated the validity of their view that self-monitoring functions as a cue that signals the environmental consequences for the target behavior. They hypothesized that the cue function of self-monitoring would be similar to that of an external cue. In a laboratory study, undergraduate students were exposed to one of the following experimental conditions: (a) self-monitoring each occurrence of face touching, (b) contingent external cueing (contingent on face touching a slide was presented stating "please don't touch your face"), (c) noncontingent external cueing (slide presentation on a fixed interval), and (d) a no-treatment control group. As predicted, comparable reductions in face touching were obtained in the self-monitoring and both external cueing groups. Hayes and Nelson noted that these findings cannot rule out the possibility that subjects covertly self-evaluated and delivered consequences to themselves. However, their data enhance the plausibility of a cueing explanation of reactive self-monitoring.

Finally, Mace and Kratochwill (1985) compared procedures associated with the three theories of reactive self-monitoring under uniform conditions. Verbal nonfluencies of undergraduates were monitored under the following conditions: (a) self-monitoring, (b) self-monitoring plus goal setting, (c) self-monitoring, goal setting, and self-reinforcement, (d) goal setting plus self-reinforcement, and (e) self-monitoring training only. Self-monitoring consisted of subjects recording their verbal nonfluencies with an obtrusive counter (cf. Maletzky, 1974) and was designed to represent Rachlin's view which emphasizes the self-recording response. Condition (b) was designed to represent Kanfer's view of the primacy of goal setting (i.e., having subjects set individual goals for reducing nonfluencies). Conditions (c) and (d) reflected Nelson and Hayes' position that components have a cumulative effect by enhancing the response-reinforcer relationship and that the controlling contingencies are external. Because self-reinforcement involved an overt form of reinforcement (i.e., prompting subjects to emit a praise statement aloud contingent on goal attainment in the presence of the experimenter), conditions (c) and (d) were less representative of the Kanfer view that emphasizes covert reinforcement. Results showed that all groups experienced a sizable reduction in nonfluencies following treatment. However, greatest reductions were found in groups that experienced external reinforcement, suggesting that external contingencies play an important role in producing reactive effects. Similar findings were reported with retarded adults (Mace, Shapiro, West, Campbell & Altman, 1986). Mace and Kratochwill suggest that future research examine variables that affect the basic operant processes that appear to be involved, response discrimination and reinforcement.

Validity of Self-Monitoring

As indicated earlier, self-monitoring can serve either a therapeutic or assessment function in the context of behavioral intervention. When used for assessment purposes, the validity of self-monitored data becomes a primary concern. Validity is determined by the degree of association between self-monitored data and concurrent measures of the same target behavior using other methods (Cone, 1981; Haynes, 1978). This type of validity is known as criterion-related validity and refers to the accuracy of measuring a specific behavior compared to some standard or criterion. For example, if interobserver agreement between a teacher and her aide is .90 on some measure of social withdrawal, data from either source can serve as the criterion measure. Validity is assessed by the degree to which the child's self-monitored data correspond to concurrent measures of the criterion (i.e., interobserver agreement between the child and the teacher or aide).

As Nelson (1977a,b) indicated, the accuracy or criterion-related validity of self-monitored data can be evaluated by calculating agreement between: (a) self-monitored data and data obtained concurrently by two or more external observers; (b) self-monitored data and data simultaneously recorded by mechanical devices; and (c) self-monitored data and some product-of-behavior measure directly related to the self-monitored behavior. Using these methods, several studies have directly examined the accuracy of self-recorded data. In reviewing this literature, Ciminero *et al.* (1977), Nelson (1977b), and Haynes and Wilson (1979) found estimates of accuracy to vary widely across studies and target behaviors. In studies with adult subjects, reports ranged from no agreement (.11, Hayes & Cavior, 1977) to excellent accuracy or agreement (.98, Azrin & Powell, 1969). Similar fluctuation is evident in the child literature. At the low end of the continuum were agreement measures of .42 between student and teacher ratings of disruptive behavior (Drabman *et al.*, 1973), and .50 for boys' self-ratings versus teacher ratings of room cleanliness (Fixsen *et al.*, 1974). In contrast, several investigators report good to excellent accuracy (interobserver agreement) when children self-monitored their behaviors. For example, Bornstein *et al.* (1977) obtained 92% agreement between a child's self-monitored data of out-of-seat behavior and data collected by school personnel. Similar accuracy rates (.96) were reported by Miller and Kratochwill (1979) corresponding to agreement between child records of stomach complaints and those kept independently by the child's mother, teacher, and school nurse. Moreover, agreement between the nurse and teacher was .98 in the school, providing a better estimate of the true accuracy of the data.

Variables Affecting the Validity of Self-Monitored Data

Highly variable estimates of validity evident in the studies cited earlier suggest that specific factors operate to affect the accuracy of self-monitored data. Recently, researchers have begun to analyze various conditions of self-monitoring to determine which variables influence accuracy. From a clinical standpoint, this knowledge can be very useful in designing self-monitoring procedures that enhance the data's validity. Accurate self-assessment can obviate the need for costly external observers and/or excessive demands on teacher or parent time. Furthermore, a greater number of children and school personnel can be served when clients participate in assessing their own behavior. Following is a listing of variables that have been empirically demonstrated to affect the accuracy of self-monitored data (McFall, 1977; Nelson, 1977a,b; Haynes & Wilson, 1979). Because much of this literature involves adult subjects, appropriate caution should be exercised in generalizing these findings to children. Clearly needed are replication studies with child populations and exploratory research into the variables endogenous to children that influence accurate self-recording.

Training

In general, training in self-monitoring has been found to improve subjects' accuracy during self-monitoring. This is not surprising because training in the correct use of any behavioral assessment procedure should increase the validity of the data (Haynes, 1978). For example, Hamilton and Bornstein (1975) found that subjects who received training in self-monitoring were more accurate in recording target behaviors than those not provided specific training. Similar results were reported by Nelson, Lipinski, and Boykin (1978) and

Jones *et al.* (1977). In both cases, increases in accuracy paralleled exposure to training.

Reinforcement Contingencies

Administration of reinforcers contingent on accurate self-monitoring has also been shown to enhance accurate data collection. With children, Fixen *et al.* (1972) increased agreement between peer and self-reports of room cleanliness from .76 to .86 when accurate self-ratings were reinforced. For Layne, Richard, Jones, and Lyman (1976) the margin of improvement was even greater, increasing agreement from .67–.75 to .90–.95 following the introduction of contingent rewards for accurate self-recording of cleanliness. Attempts to thin the schedule of accuracy checks and reinforcement for accuracy have met with mixed results. Layne *et al.* (1976) and Turkewitz, O'Leary, and Ironsmith (1975) reported a decline in accuracy measures when the assessment and reinforcement of accuracy were gradually decreased.

Nature of the Target Behavior

Some target behaviors lend themselves to easier and more accurate self-recording than do others. Peterson *et al.* (1975) demonstrated, for example, that accuracies were higher for self-recorded face touches (.64) than for verbal nonfluencies (e.g., "You know", .00; "and all that", .31). Similar findings by Cavior and Marabatto (1976) and Hayes and Cavior (1977) indicated that overt motor behavior may be more accurately self-monitored than verbal response classes depending on the degree to which the verbal behavior is habitual. In addition, the values of the target behavior appear to influence the accuracy of self-monitored data. Nelson, Hay, Devany, and Koslow-Green (1980) found that children self-recorded appropriate classroom verbalizations more accurately (.81) than their inappropriate verbalizations (.57). Similarly, higher accuracy rates were reported when teachers self-recorded their positive comments than when they monitored their negative comments (Nelson *et al.*, 1977). However, Litrownik and Freitas (1980) did not replicate these findings, possibly because of the presence of external observers during self-monitoring.

Schedule of Self-Monitoring

There is some evidence to suggest that the contiguity between the occurrence of the target behavior and the self-recording response may affect the data's accuracy. Frederiksen *et al.* (1975) found that subjects were more accurate when they recorded each cigarette immediately after they smoked it (.93) than waiting until the end of each day (.85) or at the end of each week (.87). This discrepancy would be expected to increase with target behaviors occurring at higher frequencies and/or having no product-of-behavior correlate (i.e., cigarette butts or the number of cigarettes remaining in a pack).

Response Competition

When the number and complexity of responses required of an individual are high, the accuracy of self-monitoring can be expected to decrease. Evidence for this comes from a study by Epstein, Webster, and Miller (1975), in which self-recording accuracy diminished when subjects were engaged in a lever-pressing operant task while concurrently self-monitoring their respiration rates. These findings suggest that self-monitoring is more accurate when clients are not involved in activities that may interfere with their self-observation and self-recording.

Knowledge of Accuracy Assessment

Several studies have demonstrated that self-monitoring accuracy improves when individuals are informed that their accuracy is being assessed. For example, Lipinski and Nelson (1974) achieved marked increases in accuracy of self-recorded face touches when subjects were told that periodic random accuracy checks would be made. Covert assessments of agreement averaged .52 compared to

.86 when subjects were informed that independent measures would also be collected. Similar increases were reported by Nelson *et al.* (1975) and Lipinski *et al.* (1974) using face touches as the target response. Targeting a more clinically relevant behavior, Santogrossi (1974) found the correspondence between pupil's self-recorded reading performance and those obtained concurrently by external observers to increase when either a teacher or peer comonitored pupil reading performance.

In addition to the variables indicated earlier, there are a number of other factors that may be functionally related to the accuracy of self-monitoring. McFall (1977) identified some of these potential factors that await empirical verification. The first of these, client characteristics, is of particular importance to school psychology. Age and type of functional disorder should influence the complexity of the target behavior that can be accurately self-recorded and the amount and type of training needed to obtain high subject-rater agreement. Second, the degree of response effort required in self-monitoring will likely affect client performance. As with other observational procedures, self-monitoring accuracy can be expected to decrease as the recording response becomes more arduous and time consuming (Hersen & Bellack, 1981). A third factor, related to sound scientific practice, is the use of systematic recording methods to enhance the accuracy and reliability of the data. In this regard, the use of recording devices may be effective. Fourth, the type of recording device used in self-monitoring may affect accuracy. Along the dimension of obtrusiveness, Nelson, Lipinski, and Boykin (1978) examined the effects of hand-held versus belt-worn counters on the accuracy of self-monitored data with retarded clients. Although no significant between-group differences were found, accuracy rates were higher for subjects using hand-held counters. A fifth variable not addressed thus far in the research literature is the effect of bias and expectancies on self-monitored data accuracy (Haynes, 1978). For example, a child interested in obtaining positive teacher comments or contingent rewards may overrepresent his or her time on task because of the contingencies operating on that behavior. Similarly, parents may exaggerate the frequency of noncompliant responses on the assumption that a child with more severe problems will have a better chance of being accepted into a treatment program. Thus, the psychologist should always bear in mind the potential for bias in self-monitored data when corroborative data are not available.

Summary

The role of self-monitoring in the assessment and treatment of childhood disorders is expanding rapidly. In the area of assessment, SM may serve the function of obtaining global information at the preintervention stage, providing data on private and unobservable events, or as the primary dependent measure in the evaluation of an intervention. Data systems parallel those used widely in behavioral assessment and include direct methods such as narrations, frequency counts, duration measures, and time sampling, as well as self-ratings, behavioral traces, and archival records considered to be indirect measures of child performance. The therapeutic value of SM is associated with its tendency to be reactive under certain conditions. Factors implicated in the reactive process are the motivation of the client to change, the valence of the self-monitored behavior, the type of experimental instructions provided, the use of goals, reinforcement and feedback, concurrent monitoring of multiple behaviors, the schedule of self-monitoring, and the nature of the self-recording device.

References

Anthony, W. Z. (1978). Brief intervention in a case of childhood trichotillomania by self-monitoring. *Journal of Behavior Therapy and Experimental Psychiatry, 9,* 173–175.

Azrin, N. H., & Powell, J. (1969). Behavioral engineering: The list of response priming to improve prescribed self-medication. *Journal of Applied Behavior Analysis, 2,* 39–42.

Bandura, A. (1969). *Principles of behavior modification.* New York: Holt, Rinehart & Winston.

Barlow, D. H. (1981). On the relation of clinical research to clinical practice: Current issues and new directions. *Journal of Consulting and Clinical Psychology, 49,* 147–155.

Bell, D. R., & Low, R. M. (1977). *Observing and recording children's behavior.* Richland, WA: Performance Associates.

Bellack, A. S., & Hersen, M. (1977). Self-report inventories in behavioral assessment. In J. D. Cone & R. P. Hawkins (Eds.), *Behavioral assessment: New directions in clinical psychology* (pp. 52–76). New York: Brunner/Mazel.

Bellack, A. S., Rozensky, R., & Schwartz, J. (1974). A comparison of two forms of self-monitoring in a behavioral weight reduction program. *Behavior Therapy, 5,* 523–530.

Berecz, J. (1972). Modification of smoking behavior through self-administered punishment of imagined behavior: A new approach to aversive therapy. *Journal of Consulting and Clinical Psychology, 38,* 244–250.

Bergan, J. R. (1977). *Behavioral consultation.* Columbus, OH: Merrill.

Bolstad, O. D., & Johnson, S. M. (1972). Self-regulation in the modification of disruptive behavior. *Journal of Applied Behavior Analysis, 5,* 443–454.

Bornstein, P. H., & Quevillon, R. P. (1976). The effects of a self-instructional package on overactive preschool boys. *Journal of Applied Behavior Analysis, 9,* 179–188.

Bornstein, P. H., Hamilton, S. B., & Quevillon, R. P. (1977). Behavior modification by long distance: Demonstration of functional control over disruptive behavior in a rural classroom setting. *Behavior Modification, 1,* 369–380.

Broden, M., Hall, R. V., & Mitts, B. (1971). The effect of self-recording on the classroom behavior of two eighth-grade students. *Journal of Applied Behavior Analysis, 4,* 191–199.

Bryant, L. E., & Budd, K. S. (1982). Self-instructional training to increase independent work performance in preschoolers. *Journal of Applied Behavior Analysis, 15,* 259–271.

Cavior, N., & Marabotto, C. M. (1976). Monitoring verbal behaviors in a dyadic interaction. *Journal of Consulting and Clinical Psychology, 44,* 68–76.

Ciminero, A. R., Nelson, R. O., & Lipinski, D. P. (1977). Self-monitoring procedures. In A. R. Ciminero, K. S. Calhoun, & H. E. Adams (Eds.), *Handbook of behavioral assessment* (pp. 195–232). New York: Wiley.

Cone, J. D. (1981). Psychometric considerations. In M. Hersen & A. S. Bellack (Eds.), *Behavioral assessment: A practical handbook* (pp. 38–68). New York: Pergamon Press.

Dapcich-Miura, E., & Hovell, M. F. (1979). Contingency management of adherence to a complex medical regimen in an elderly heart patient. *Behavior Therapy, 10,* 193–201.

Drabman, R. S., Spitalnick, R., & O'Leary, K. D. (1973). Teaching self-control to disruptive children. *Journal of Abnormal Psychology, 82,* 10–16.

Emmelkamp, P. M., & Kraanen, J. (1977). Therapist-controlled exposure in vivo versus self-controlled exposure in vivo: A comparison with obsessive compulsive patients. *Behavior Research and Therapy, 15,* 491–495.

Epstein, L. H., Webster, J. S., & Miller, P. M. (1975). Accuracy and controlling effects of self-monitoring as a function of concurrent responding and reinforcement. *Behavior Therapy, 5,* 634–666.

Feuerstein, M., & Adams, H. E. (1977). Cephalic vasomotor feedback in the modification of migraine headaches. *Biofeedback and Self-Regulation, 3,* 241–254.

Fixen, D. L., Phillips, E. L., & Wolf, M. M. (1972). Achievement place: The reliability of self-reporting and peer reporting and their effects on behavior. *Journal of Applied Behavior Analysis, 5,* 19–30.

Flowers, J. V. (1972). Behavior modification of cheating in an elementary school student: A brief note. *Behavior Therapy, 3,* 311–312.

Frederickson, L. W., Epstein, L. H., & Kosevsky, B. P. (1975). Reliability and controlling effects of three procedures for self-monitoring smoking. *Psychological Record, 25,* 255–264.

Glynn, E. L., & Thomas, J. D. (1974). Effect of cueing on self-control of classroom behavior. *Journal of Applied Behavior Analysis, 7,* 229–306.

Glynn, E. L., Thomas, J. D., & Shee, S. M. (1973). Behavioral self-control of classroom behavior in an elementary classroom. *Journal of Applied Behavior Analysis, 6,* 105–113.

Gottman, J. M., & McFall, R. M. (1972). Self-monitoring effects in a program for potential high school dropouts: A time-series analysis. *Journal of Consulting and Clinical Psychology, 39,* 273–281.

Hallahan, D. P., Lloyd, J., Kosiewicz, M. M., Kauffman, J. T., & Graves, A. W. (1979). Self-monitoring of attention as a treatment for a learning disabled boy's off-task behavior. *Learning Disability Quarterly, 2,* 24–32.

Hamilton, S. B., & Bornstein, P. H. (1975). Increasing the accuracy of self-recording in speech anxious undergraduates through the use of self-monitoring training and reliability enhancement procedures. *Journal of Consulting and Clinical Psychology, 43,* 577–583.

Hannum, J. W., Thoresen, C. E., & Hubbard, D. R. (1974). A behavioral study of self-esteem with elementary teachers. In M. J. Mahoney & C. E. Thoresen (Eds.), *Self-control: Power to the person* (pp. 144–155). Monterey, CA: Brooks-Cole.

Harmon, T. M., Nelson, R. O., & Hayes, S. C. (1980). The differential effects of self-monitoring mood versus activity in depressed patients. *Journal of Consulting and Clinical Psychology, 48,* 30–38.

Hayes, S. C., & Cavior, N. (1977). Multiple tracking and

the reactivity of self-monitoring: I. Negative behaviors. *Behavior Therapy, 8*, 819–831.

Hayes, S. C., & Cavior, N. (1980). Multiple tracking and the reactivity of self-monitoring: II. Positive behaviors. *Behavior Therapy, 2*, 283–296.

Hayes, S. C., & Nelson, R. O. (1983). Similar reactivity produced by external areas and self-monitoring. *Behavior Modification, 7*, 183–196.

Haynes, S. N. (1978). *Principles of behavioral assessment.* New York: Halstead Press.

Haynes, S. N., & Wilson, C. C. (1979). *Behavioral assessment: Recent advances in methods, concepts and applications.* San Francisco: Jossey-Bass.

Hersen, M., & Barlow, D. H. (1976). *Single case experimental designs: Strategies for studying behavior change.* New York: Pergamon Press.

Hersen, M., & Bellack, A. S. (1981). *Behavioral assessment: A practical handbook.* New York: Pergamon Press.

Horne, D. J. (1977). Behavior therapy for trichotillomania. *Behavior Research and Therapy, 15*, 192–196.

Hundert, J., & Batstone, D. (1978). A practical procedure to maintain pupils' accurate self-rating in a classroom token program. *Behavior Modification, 2*, 93–111.

Hundert, J., & Bucher, B. (1978). Pupils' self-scored arithmetic performance: A practical procedure for maintaining accuracy. *Journal of Applied Behavior Analysis, 11*, 304.

Hutzel, R. R. (1976). Analogue self-recording therapy: Expectancy effects. *Dissertation Abstracts International, 36*, 4161.

Jeffrey, D. B. (1974). Self-control: Methodological issues and research trends. In M. J. Mahoney & C. E. Thoresen (Eds.), *Self-control: Power to the person* (pp. 166–199). Monterey, CA: Brooks-Cole.

Johnson, S. M., & White, G. (1971). Self-observation as an agent of behavior change. *Behavior Therapy, 2*, 488–497.

Jones, J. C., Trap, J., & Cooper, J. O. (1977). Technical report: Students' self-recording of manuscript letter strokes. *Journal of Applied Behavior Analysis, 10*, 509–514.

Kanfer, F. H. (1970a). Self-regulations: Research, issues, and speculations. In C. Neuringer & J. L. Michael (Eds.), *Behavior modification in clinical psychology* (pp. 178–220). New York: Appleton-Century-Crofts.

Kanfer, F. H. (1970b). Self-monitoring: Methodological limitations and clinical applications. *Journal of Consulting and Clinical Psychology, 35*, 148–152.

Kanfer, F. H. (1975). Self-management methods. In F. H. Kanfer & A. P. Goldstein (Eds.), *Helping people change* (pp. 309–355). New York: Pergamon Press.

Kanfer, F. H. (1977). The many faces of self-control, or behavior modification changes its focus. In R. B. Stuart (Ed.), *Behavior self-management: Strategies, techniques, and outcomes* (pp. 1–48). New York: Brunner/Mazel.

Kanfer, F. H., & Karoly, P. (1972). Self-control: A behavioristic excursion into the lion's den. *Behavior Therapy, 3*, 398–416.

Karoly, P. (1977). Behavioral self-management in children. Concepts. methods, issues and directions. In M. Hersen, R. Eisler, & P. Miller (Eds.), *Progress in behavior modification* (Vol. 5, pp. 197–262). New York: Academic Press.

Katz, R. C. (1973). A procedure for concurrently measuring elapsed time and response frequency. *Journal of Applied Behavior Analysis, 6*, 719–720.

Kaufman, K. F., & O'Leary, K. D. (1972). Reward, cost, and self-evaluation procedures for disruptive adolescents in a psychiatric hospital school. *Journal of Applied Behavior Analysis, 5*, 293–309.

Kazdin, A. E. (1974a). Reactive self-monitoring: The effects of response desirability, goal setting and feedback. *Journal of Consulting and Clinical Psychology, 42*, 704–716.

Kazdin, A. E. (1974b). Self-monitoring and behavior change. In M. J. Mahoney & C. E. Thoresen (Eds.), *Self-control: Power to the person* (pp. 218–246). Monterey, CA: Brooks-Cole.

Kazdin, A. E. (1977). Assessing the clinical or applied importance of behavior change through social validation. *Behavior Modification, 1*, 427–452.

Kazdin, A. E. (1979). Unobtrusive measures in behavioral assessment. *Journal of Applied Behavior Analysis, 12*, 712–724.

Kazdin, A. E. (1980). *Research design in clinical psychology.* New York: Harper & Row.

Kirschenbaum, D. S., & Karoly, P. (1977). When self-regulation fails: Tests of some preliminary hypotheses. *Journal of Consulting and Clinical Psychology, 45*, 1116–1125.

Knapczyk, D. R., & Livingston, G. (1973). Self-recording and student teacher supervision: Variables within a token economy. *Journal of Applied Behavior Analysis, 6*, 481–486.

Knox, D. (1972). *Marriage happiness.* Champaign, IL: Research Press.

Kratochwill, T. R. (1978). *Single subject research: Strategies for evaluating change.* New York: Academic Press.

Kunzelmann, H. D. (Ed.). (1970). *Precision teaching.* Seattle, WA: Special Child Publications.

Layne, C. C., Richard, N. C., Jones, M. T., & Lyman, R. D. (1976). Accuracy of self-monitoring on a variable ratio schedule of observer verification. *Behavior Therapy, 7*, 481–488.

Leitenberg, N., Agras, W. S., Thompson, L. K., & Wright, D. E. (1968). Feedback in behavior modification: An experimental analysis in two phobic cases. *Journal of Applied Behavior Analysis, 1*, 131–137.

Lindsley, O. R. (1968). A reliable wrist counter for recording behavior rates. *Journal of Applied Behavior Analysis, 1*, 77–78.

Lipinski, D. P. & Nelson, R. O. (1974). The reactivity and unreliability of self-recording. *Journal of Consulting and Clinical Psychology, 42*, 118–123.

Lipinski, D. P., Black, J. L., Nelson, R. O., & Ciminero, A. R. (1974). Influence of motivational variables on the reactivity and reliability of self-recording. *Journal of Consulting and Clinical Psychology, 42*, 118–123.

Litrownik, A. J., & Freitas, J. L. (1980). Self-monitoring in moderately retarded adolescents: Reactivity and accuracy as a function of valence. *Behavior Therapy, 11,* 245–255.

Litrownik, A. J., Freitas, J. C., & Franzini, L. R. (1978). Self-regulation in retarded persons: Assessment and training of self-monitoring skills. *American Journal of Mental Deficiency, 82,* 499–506.

Lubar, J. R., & Shouse, M. N. (1977). Use of biofeedback in the treatment of seizure disorders and hyperactivity. In B. Lahey & A. E. Kazdin (Eds.), *Advances in clinical child psychology* (Vol. 1, pp. 203–265). New York: Plenum Press.

Lyman, R. D., Richard, H. C., & Elder, I. R. (1975). Contingency management of self-report and cleaning behavior. *Journal of Abnormal Child Psychology, 3,* 155–162.

Mace, F. C., & Kratochwill, T. R. (1985). Theories of reactivity in self-monitoring: A comparison of cognitive-behavioral and operant models. *Behavior Modification, 9,* 323–343.

Mace, F. C., Shapiro, E. S., West, B. J., Campbell, K., & Altman, J. (1986). The role of reinforcement in reactive self-monitoring. *Applied Research in Mental Retardation, 7,* 315–327.

Mahoney, M. J. (1974). Self-reward and self-monitoring techniques for weight control. *Behavior Therapy, 5,* 48–57.

Mahoney, M. J. (1977). Some applied issues in self-monitoring. In J. B. Cone & R. P. Hawkins (Eds.), *Behavioral assessment: New directions in clinical psychology* (pp. 241–254). New York: Brunner/Mazel.

Mahoney, M. J., & Arnkoff, D. (1978). Cognitive and self-control therapies. In S. L. Garfield & A. E. Bergin (Eds.), *Handbook of psychotherapy and behavior change* (pp. 689–722). New York: Wiley.

Mahoney, M. J., Moore, B. S., Wade, T. C., & Moura, N. (1973). The effects of continuous and intermittent self-monitoring on academic behavior. *Journal of Consulting and Clinical Psychology, 41,* 65–69.

Mahoney, M. J., Moura, N. G., & Wade, T. C. (1973). The relative efficacy of self-reward, self-punishment and self-monitoring techniques for weight loss. *Journal of Consulting and Clinical Psychology, 40,* 404–407.

Maletzky, B. M. (1974). Behavior recording as treatment: A brief note. *Behavior Therapy, 5,* 107–111.

Mathews, A., & Shaw, P. (1977). Cognitions related to anxiety: A pilot study of treatment. *Behavior Research and Therapy, 15,* 503–505.

McFall, R. M. (1977). Parameters of self-monitoring. In J. D. Cone & R. P. Hawkins (Eds.), *Behavior assessment: New directions in clinical psychology* (pp. 152–177). New York: Brunner/Mazel.

McFall, R. M., & Hammen, C. L. (1971). Motivation, structure, and self-monitoring: Role of nonspecific factors in smoking reduction. *Journal of Consulting and Clinical Psychology, 37,* 80–86.

McKenzie, T. L., & Rushall, B. S. (1974). Effects of self-recording on attendance and performance in a competitive swimming training environment. *Journal of Applied Behavior Analysis, 7,* 199–206.

McLaughlin, T. F. (1976). Self-control in the classroom. *Review of Educational Research, 46,* 631–663.

McLaughlin, J. G., & Nay, W. R. (1975). Treatment of trichotillomania using positive coveants and response cost: A case report. *Behavior Therapy, 6,* 87–91.

McNamara, J. R. (1972). The use of self-monitoring techniques to treat nail biting. *Behavior Research and Therapy, 10,* 193–194.

Meichenbaum, D. (1979). Teaching children self-control. In B. Lahey & A. E. Kazdin (Eds.), *Advances in child clinical psychology* (Vol. 2, pp. 1–33). New York: Plenum Press.

Mercatoris, M., & Craighead, W. E. (1974). Effects of nonparticipant observation on teacher and pupil classroom behavior. *Journal of Educational Psychology, 66,* 512–519.

Miller, A. J., & Kratochwill, T. R. (1979). Reduction of frequent stomachache complaints by timeout. *Behavior Therapy, 10,* 211–218.

Mitchel, K. R., & White, R. G. (1977). Behavioral self-management: An application to the problem of migraine headaches. *Behavior Therapy, 8,* 213–221.

Monti, P. M., McCrady, B. S., & Barlow, D. H. (1977). Effect of positive reinforcement, informational feedback, and contingency contracting on a bulimic anorexic female. *Behavior Therapy, 8,* 258–263.

Morris, R. J., & Hoschouer, R. L. (1980). Current issue in applied research with mentally retarded persons. *Applied Research in Mental Retardation, 1,* 85–94.

Myers, J. L. (1979). *Fundamentals of experimental design.* Boston, MA: Allyn & Bacon.

Nelson, C., & McReynolds, W. (1971). Self-recording and control of behavior: Reply to Simkins. *Behavior Therapy, 2,* 594–597.

Nelson, R. O. (1977a). Assessment and therapeutic functions of self-monitoring. In M. Hersen, R. Eisler, & P. Miller (Eds.), *Progress in behavior modification* (Vol. 5, . 263–308). New York: Academic Press.

Nelson, R. O. (1977b). Issues in assessment via self-monitoring. In J. D. Cone & R. P. Hawkins (Eds.), *Behavioral assessment: New directions in clinical psychology* (pp. 217–240). New York; Brunner/Mazel.

Nelson, R. O. (1981). Realistic dependent measures for clinical use. *Journal of Consulting and Clinical Psychology, 49,* 168–182.

Nelson, R. O., & Hayes, S. (1981). Theoretical explanations for reactivity in self-monitoring. *Behavior Modification, 5,* 3–14.

Nelson, R. O., Lipinski, D. P., & Black, J. L. (1975). The effects of expectancy on the reactivity of self-recording. *Behavior Therapy, 6,* 337–349.

Nelson, R. O., Lipinski, D. P., & Black, J. L. (1976). The reactivity of adult retardates' self-monitoring: A comparison among behaviors of different valences and a comparison with token reinforcement. *Psychological Record, 26,* 189–201.

Nelson, R. O., Hay, L. R., Hay, W. M., & Carstens, C. B. (1977). The reactivity and accuracy of teachers' self-monitoring of positive and negative classroom verbalizations. *Behavior Therapy, 8*, 972–985.

Nelson, R. O., Kapust, J. A., & Dorsey, B. L. (1978). Minimal reactivity of overt classroom observations on student and teacher behaviors. *Behavior Therapy, 9*, 695–702.

Nelson, R. O., Lipinski, D. P., & Boykin, A. R. (1978). The effects of self-recorders' training and the obstrusiveness of the self-recording device on the accuracy and reactivity of self-monitoring. *Behavior Therapy, 9*, 200–208.

Nelson, R. O., Hay, L. R., Devany, J., & Koslow-Green, L. (1980). The reactivity and accuracy of children's self-monitoring: Three experiments. *Child Behavior Therapy, 2*, 1–24.

Novaco, R. W. (1977). Stress inoculation: A cognitive therapy for anger and its application to a case of depression. *Journal of Consulting and Clinical Psychology, 45*, 600–608.

Orne, M. T. (1970). From the subject's point of view, when is behavior private and when is it public: Problems and inference. *Journal of Consulting and Clinical Psychology, 35*, 143–147.

Parsonson, B. S., & Baer, D. M. (1978). The analysis and presentation of graphic data. In T. R. Kratochwill (Ed.), *Single subject research: Strategies for evaluating change* (pp. 101–165). New York: Academic Press.

Peterson, G. L., House, A. E., & Alford, H. F. (1975, March). *Self-monitoring: Accuracy and reactivity in a patient's recording of three clinical targeted behaviors.* Paper presented at the meeting of the Southeastern Psychological Association, Atlanta, GA.

Piersel, W. C. (1985). Behavioral consultation: An approach to problem solving. In J. R. Bergan (Ed.), *School psychology in contemporary society* (pp. 252–280). Columbus, OH: Merrill.

Piersel, W. C., & Kratochwill, T. R. (1979). Self-observation and behavior change: Applications to academic and adjustment problems through behavioral consultation. *Journal of School Psychology, 17*, 151–161.

Piersel, W. C., Brody, G. H., & Kratochwill, T. R. (1977). A further examination of motivational influences on disadvantaged minority group children's intelligence test performance. *Child Development, 17*, 151–161.

Plachetta, K. E. (1976). Encopresis: A case study utilizing contracting, scheduling and self-charting. *Journal of Behavior Therapy and Experimental Psychiatry, 7*, 195–196.

Plummer, S., Baer, D. M., & LeBlanc, J. M. (1977). Functional considerations in the use of procedural timeout and effective alternative. *Journal of Applied Behavior Analysis, 10*, 689–705.

Rachlin, H. (1974). Self-control. *Behaviorism, 2*, 94–107.

Rainwater, N., & Ayllon, T. (1976). Increasing academic performance by using a timer as antecedent stimulus: A study of four cases. *Behavior Therapy, 7*, 672–677.

Rekers, G. A., & Varni, J. W. (1977). Self-monitoring and self-reinforcement processes in a pretranssexual boy. *Behavior Research and Therapy, 15*, 177–180.

Rekers, G. A., Amaro-Plotlin, H. D., & Low, B. P. (1977). Sex-typed mannerisms in normal boys and girls as a function of sex and age. *Child Development, 48*, 275–278.

Ribordy, S. C., & Denny, D. R. (1977). The behavioral treatment of insomnia: An alternative to drug therapy. *Behavior Research and Therapy, 15*, 177–180.

Roberts, R., & Dick, L. (1982). Self-control strategies with children. In T. R. Kratochwill (Ed.), *Advances in school psychology* (Vol. 2, pp. 275–314). Hillsdale, NJ: Erlbaum.

Romanczyk, R. G. (1974). Self-monitoring in the treatment of obesity: Parameters of reactivity. *Behavior Therapy, 5*, 531–540.

Ross, A.O. (1981). Of rigor and relevance. *Professional Psychology, 12*, 318–327.

Sagotsky, G., Patterson, C. J., & Lepper, M. R. (1978). Training children's self-control: A field experiment in self-monitoring and goal setting in the classroom. *Journal of Experimental Child Psychology, 25*, 242–253.

Santogrossi, D. A. (1974, May). *Self-reinforcement and external monitoring of performance on an academic task.* Paper presented at the fifth annual Conference on Applied Behavior Analysis in Education, Kansas City, MO.

Santogrossi, D. A., O'Leary, K. D., Romanczyk, R. G., & Kaufman, K. F. (1973). Self-evaluation by adolescents in a psychiatric hospital school token program. *Journal of Applied Behavior Analysis, 6*, 277–287.

Schwartz, G. J. (1977). College students as contingency managers for adolescents in a program to develop reading skills. *Journal of Applied Behavior Analysis, 10*, 645–655.

Seymour, F. W., & Stokes, T. F. (1976). Self-recording in training girls to increase work and evoke staff praise in an institution for offenders. *Journal of Applied Behavior Analysis, 9*, 41–54.

Shapiro, E. S. (1984). Self-monitoring procedures. In T. Ollendick & M. Hersen (Eds.), *Child behavioral assessment: Principles and procedures* (pp. 148–165). New York: Pergamon Press.

Sheehan, D. J., & Casey, B. (1974). Communication. *Journal of Applied Behavior Analysis, 7*, 446.

Simkins, L. (1971). The reliability of self-recorded behaviors. *Behavior Therapy, 2*, 83–87.

Skinner, B. F. (1953). *Science and human behavior.* New York: Macmillan.

Spates, C. R., & Kanfer, F. M. (1977). Self-monitoring, self-evaluation, and self-reinforcement in children's learning: A test of multistage self-regulation model. *Behavior Therapy, 8*, 9–16.

Stuart, R. B., & Davis, B. (1972). *Slim chance in a fat world.* Champaign, IL: Research Press.

Stumphauzer, J. S. (1974). *Daily behavior card.* Vencie, CA: Behaviormetrics.

Sulzer-Azaroff, B., & Mayer, G. R. (1977). *Applying behavior analysis with children and youth.* New York: Holt, Rinehart & Winston.

Tasto, D. L. (1977). Self-report schedules and inventories.

In A. R. Ciminero, K. S. Calhoun, & H. E. Adams (Eds.), *Handbook of behavioral assessment* (pp. 153–193). New York: Wiley.

Thomas, E. J., Abrams, K. S., & Johnson, J. B. (1971). Self-monitoring and reciprocal inhibition in the modification of multiple tics of Gilles de la Tourette's syndrome. *Journal of Behavior Therapy and Experimental Psychiatry, 2,* 159–171.

Thoresen, C. E., & Mahoney, M. J. (1974). *Behavioral self-control.* New York: Holt.

Turkewitz, H., O'Leary, K. D., & Ironsmith, M. (1975). Generalization and maintenance of appropriate behavior through self-control. *Journal of Consulting and Clinical Psychology, 43,* 377–383.

Turner, S. M., Hersen, M., & Bellack, A. S. (1977). Effects of social disruption, stumulus interference, and aversive conditioning on auditory hallucinations. *Behavior Modification, 1,* 249–258.

Watson, D. L., & Tharp, R. G. (1972). *Self-directed behavior change: Self-modification for personal adjustment.* Monterey, CA: Brooks-Cole.

Witt, J. C., & Elliot, S. N. (1985). Acceptability of classroom management strategies. In T. R. Kratochwill (Ed.), *Advances in School Psychology* (Vol. 4, pp. 251–288). Hillsdale, NJ: Erlbaum.

Wolf, M. M. (1978). Social validity: The case for subjective measurement or how applied behavior analysis is finding its heart. *Journal of Applied Behavior Analysis, 11,* 203–214.

CHAPTER 20

Social Skills

Conceptual and Applied Aspects of Assessment, Training, and Social Validation

Frank M. Gresham

Schools represent perhaps the most important setting in which children develop skills in initiating and maintaining interpersonal relationships as well as developing skills that are crucial for peer acceptance. The ability to interact successfully with one's peers and significant adults is one of the most important aspects of a child's development (Gresham & Lemanek, 1983). Prominent developmental theorists (e.g., Erikson, 1963; Kohlberg, 1969; Piaget, 1952) have delineated theories of social and moral development in which social competence evolves in a series of interrelated stages that closely parallel chronological and/or mental age. Apparent in practically all developmental theories is the emphasis each places on the social development of school-age children (see Salkind, 1981, for a review).

Social skills in school settings are important for several reasons. Children and youth who are deficient in social skills and/or who are poorly accepted by peers have a high incidence of school maladjustment, school suspensions/expulsions, dropping out of school, delinquency, childhood psychopathology, and adult mental health difficulties (Asher & Hymel, 1981; Asher, Oden, & Gottman, 1977; Cowen, Pederson, Babigian, Izzo, & Trost, 1973; Gresham, 1981a,b; Gronlund & Anderson, 1963; Hartup, 1983; Kohn & Clausen, 1955; Roff, 1970; Roff, Sells, & Golden, 1972; Ullman, 1957).

Difficulties in peer relationships and social skills have also been related to the social outcomes of mainstreaming. Mainstreamed mildly handicapped children are often poorly accepted, neglected, or socially rejected by nonhandicapped peers and the social interactions between mainstreamed handicapped children and nonhandicapped peers often are negative in nature (Allen, Benning, & Drummond, 1972; Ballard, Corman, Gottlieb, & Kaufman, 1977; Bryan, 1974, 1976, 1978; Gottlieb, 1975, 1981; Gottlieb & Budoff, 1973; Gott-

Frank M. Gresham • Department of Psychology, Louisiana State University, Baton Rouge, Louisiana 70803.

lieb & Leyser, 1981; Gresham, 1981a, 1982a,b, 1985a).

Social skills have been related to other measures of classroom functioning, such as academic achievement, attending behavior, and question asking (Carledge & Milburn, 1978; Walker & Hops, 1976). Several social skills differentiate mainstreamed handicapped children from nonhandicapped peers (Stumme, Gresham, & Scott, 1982) and other social skills are related to positive interactions and acceptance by teachers (Brophy, 1981).

The preceding discussion suggests that social skills and peer acceptance are extremely important for school-age children and youth. The purpose of this chapter is to provide a conceptualization of social skills that places socially skilled behaviors within the domain of social competence. Several definitions of social skills will be presented and critically evaluated along with classification models for social skill deficiencies. Social skills assessment and training procedures will be reviewed as well as procedures for establishing the social significance of target behaviors, the social acceptability of social skills interventions, and evaluating the social importance of the effects of social skills training.

Personal Competence

Personal competence can be described globally as being comprised of three subdomains: (a) academic competence, (b) social competence, and (c) physical competence (Greenspan, 1981). Academic and social competence are most germane to this chapter and will be emphasized. The domain of physical competence will not be addressed. Figure 1 graphically depicts the relationship of academic and social competence to the construct of personal competence. It should be noted that there are at least moderate relationships between the domains of academic and social competence (Reschly, Gresham, & Graham-Clay, 1984). Figure 1 is presented to depict the domains of academic and social competence (and their subcomponents) as they relate to the superordinate domain of personal competence.

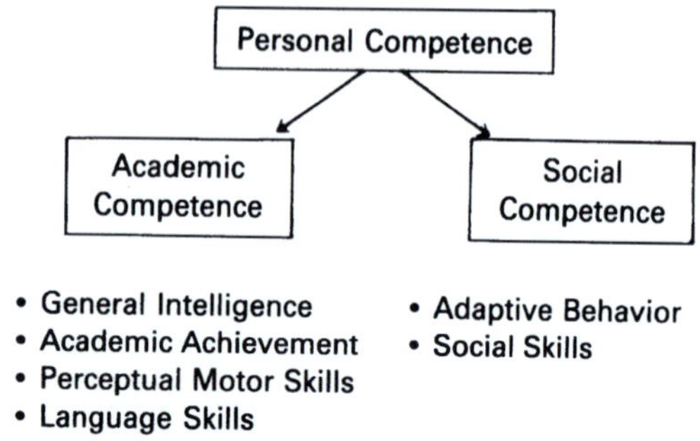

Figure 1. Domains and subdomains of personal competence.

Academic Competence

The construct of academic competence includes skill areas that can be labeled as intellectual/cognitive skills, academic skills, perceptual-motor skills, and language skills. Each of these skill areas can be further subdivided into specific content areas. Figure 1 shows the relationship of these global skill areas to academic competence. Mildly handicapped (MH) students (e.g., learning disabled and mildly mentally retarded) are placed into special education programs primarily on the basis of academic incompetence. Few, if any, MH students get into the special education system primarily on the basis of social incompetence (Reschly *et al.*, 1984). As mentioned earlier, we know a great deal about the assessment and remediation of academic incompetencies of MH learners. School psychologists, by their training and job description, spend the majority of their time assessing the academic incompetencies of students referred to them for evaluation (Keogh, Kukic, Becker, McLoughlin, & Kukic, 1975; Reynolds, Gutkin, Elliott, & Witt, 1984).

Social Competence

Social competence has long been regarded as a fundamental aspect of human capabilities. In an early formulation, Thorndike (1927) suggested three types of intelligence, one of which was social intelligence or social competence. Social competence also has been a fundamental notion associated with the conception of definition and classification criteria with exceptional individuals. This is particularly apparent in the modern classification criteria in the area of mental retardation, which have consistently, through several revisions, emphasized equally the importance of cognitive/academic and social competence (Grossman, 1983).

Various approaches to measuring and defining social competence have been attempted in the past. Social competence is a multidimensional construct that includes demographic (e.g., age, SES, etc.), adaptive behavioral, and social skill variables. Individuals who are high in social competence are considered to be able to meet the demands of everyday functioning and to be equipped to handle participation and responsibility for their own welfare and the welfare of others. Conversely, persons low in social competence are not able to meet such environmental demands nor are they able to assume responsibility for their own as well as others' welfare.

Figure 2 depicts a conceptualization of social competence that is comprised of two subdomains: (a) adaptive behavior and (b) social skills. The general features of the construct of adaptive behavior are widely agreed upon; however, there is widespread disagreement on the emphasis each of these features receive in the assessment of adaptive behavior. Reschly (1982) identified a number of important differences in adaptive behavior conceptions and adaptive behavior instruments. These differences include: (a) the amount of emphasis placed on cognitive competencies, (b) the purpose of the underlying adaptive behavior scale (i.e., program planning/intervention versus classification/placement), (c) the social setting of primary import (e.g., in-school versus out-of-school adaptive behavior), (d) the method of measurement used (e.g., use of third-party informants versus direct administration to the child), and (e) the preferred respondent (e.g., parent versus teacher). These differences in adaptive behavior conceptions exert a great deal of influence on the kind of measure used and subsequent classification and programming decisions.

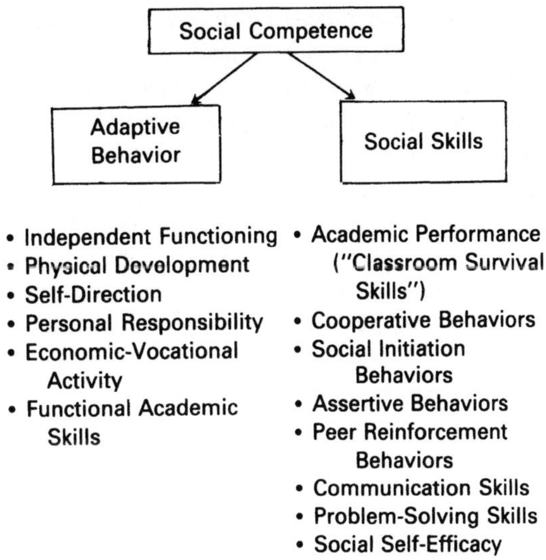

Figure 2. Domains and subdomains of social competence.

I do not suggest by Figure 2 that adaptive behavior and social skills are unrelated, particularly given recent research indicating at least moderate relations between adaptive behavior and social skill domains (Gresham & Elliott, 1987; Gresham & Reschly, 1987). Figure 2 is intended as a heuristic for conceptualizing the domains of adaptive behavior and social skills.

Definitions of Social Skills

Social skills have traditionally received much less emphasis in the classification of and interventions with exceptional children than adaptive behavior (Gresham, 1981a). At least three general definitions of social skills can be found in the literature. One definition can be termed the *peer acceptance* definition in that researchers use indexes of peer acceptance or popularity to define social skill. Thus, children who are accepted by or who are popular with their peers in school and/or community settings can be considered socially skilled. The major drawback of this definition is that it does not identify those specific behaviors that lead to peer acceptance.

A second definition can be termed the *behavioral definition* in which social skills are defined as those situation-specific behaviors that maximize the probability of securing or maintaining reinforcement or decreasing the likelihood of punishment or extinction contingent on one's social behavior. The behavioral definition of social skills has the advantage over the peer acceptance definition in that antecedents and consequences of particular social behaviors can be identified, specified, and operationalized for assessment and intervention purposes. However, this definition does not ensure that the particular social behaviors identified for interventions are in fact socially skilled or socially important behaviors. Merely increasing the frequency or quality of certain behaviors that are defined *a priori* as social skills may not impact on the goals or outcomes valued by schools and teachers (Gresham, 1983a, 1985b).

A final and less frequently discussed definition may be called the *social validity* definition (Gresham, 1983a). According to this definition, social skills are those behaviors that, within given situations, predict important social outcomes for children and youth. In school settings, important social outcomes may include: (a) peer acceptance/popularity, (b) significant others' judgment of social skill (e.g., teachers), (c) academic achievement and (d) other social behaviors known to consistently correlate with (a) through (c). This definition has the advantage of not only specifying behaviors in which a child is deficient, but also can define these behaviors as socially skilled based on their relationship to socially important outcomes in school settings. A more detailed description of specific social skills and important social outcomes are discussed in subsequent sections of this chapter under the rubric of social validity.

Behavioral Classification of Social Skill Deficiencies

Social skill deficiencies can be delineated into four basic types depending on the child's knowledge of how to perform the social skill in question and the presence or absence of interfering cognitive, emotional, or behavioral responses (Gresham, 1981a, 1985a). This conceptualization represents a modification and extension of Bandura's (1977a) distinction between acquisition versus performance deficits.

The four types of social skill deficiencies are: (a) skill deficits, (b) performance deficits, (c) self-control skill deficits, and (d) self-control performance deficits. Figure 3 depicts this four-fold classification system. It should be noted that this classification system is primarily a heuristic framework from which to conceptualize social skill deficits. As such, this classification model requires further empirical investigation

The notion of *interfering responses* is crucial to understanding self-control skill and performance deficits because it is assumed that these responses interfere with or block the acquisition and/or performance of social skills. The term *self-control* is used here to refer to the higher probability of an interfering response than a socially skilled response. This is consistent with Skinner's (1953) distinction between "controlling response" and "controlled response" as well as Catania's (1975) theoretical analysis of self-reinforcement. In this sense, an interfering response can be viewed as a controlling response that controls

	Acquisition Deficit	Performance Deficit
Interfering Response Absent	Social Skills Deficit	Self-Control Skills Deficit
Interfering Response Present	Social Performance Deficit	Self-Control Performance Deficit

Figure 3. Classification of social skills problems.

or prevents the acquisition or performance of a social skill response (i.e., the controlled response).

Interfering responses are perhaps best conceptualized from the perspective of the triple response mode system in behavioral assessment. Nelson and Hayes (1979) indicated that behavior includes the response systems or response modes of cognitive-verbal behaviors, physiological-emotional behaviors, and overt-motoric behaviors. Behaviors expressed through one or any combination of these response systems can interfere with the acquisition or performance of a social skill. For example, anxiety (an emotional response) can either prevent the learning or the performance of a social skill. Similarly, aggressive behavior (an overt-motoric response) can prevent the acquisition or enactment of social skills. The identification of interfering behaviors is critical in the assessment of social skill deficiencies because these competing responses must be eliminated before one can adequately teach social behaviors. Thus, the presence of interfering responses has direct implications for the remediation of social skill deficiencies (Gresham, 1986). The following sections will describe the four types of social skill deficiencies. Table 1 presents several examples of interfering responses under each response mode.

Table 1. Interfering Responses under the Cognitive-Verbal, Overt-Motoric, and Physiological-Emotional Response Modes

Cognitive-verbal
Depressive thoughts
Poor problem-solving ability
Inadequate role-taking skills
Low self-efficacy
Overt-motoric
Disruptive behavior
Aggressive behavior
Excessive motor movement
Impulsive behavior
Physiological-emotional
Anxiety
Anger
Depression
Fear

Skill Deficits

Children with social skill deficits do not have the necessary social skills in their repertoires or they may not know a critical step in the performance of a behavioral sequence. A social skill deficit is similar to what Bandura (1977a) refers to as an acquisition or learning deficit.

Several examples can be cited to elucidate social skill deficits. For example, a child may not know how to cooperate with peers, give a compliment, or initiate a conversation. The barometer to use in determining whether or not a skill deficit exists is based on knowledge or past performance of the behavior. If the child does not know how to perform the behavior or never has been observed to perform the behavior, it is probably a skill deficit. Social skill deficits are most likely the result of an absence of opportunities to learn the skill in question or of deficits in attentional or retentional processes involved in learning social behaviors through vicarious means (Bandura, 1986).

Performance Deficits

A social performance deficit describes an individual who knows how to perform a given behavior, but does not perform the behavior at an acceptable level. Performance deficits can be thought of as a deficiency in the number of times a behavior is emitted and may be related to a lack of motivation (i.e., reinforcement contingencies) or an absence of opportunities to perform the behavior (i.e., a stimulus control problem).

The key in determining whether a social skill deficiency is a performance or skill deficit is whether or not the individual can perform the target behavior in question. Thus, if an individual does not perform the behavior in a classroom situation, but can perform the behavior outside the classroom, it is a performance deficit. Similarly, if the individual has been observed to perform the behavior in the past, it is a performance rather than a skill deficit.

Self-Control Skill Deficits

The self-control skill deficit applies to individauls who have not learned a particular social skill because some type of interfering response (cognitive-verbal, physiological-emotional, and/or overt-motoric) has prevented acquisition of the skill. One way of viewing these deficits is that they are a combination of a behavioral excess (interfering response) and a behavioral deficit (absence of a socially skilled behavior). This conceptualization would suggest that social skills are not learned because interfering behaviors have prevented social skill acquisition.

One interfereing response that impedes learning is anxiety. Anxiety has been shown to prevent the acquisition of appropriate coping responses, particularly in the literature concerning fears and phobias (Bandura, 1977b). Children may not learn appropriate peer interaction skills because social anxiety prevents social approach behaviors. In turn, avoidance of or escape from threatening social situations reduces anxiety, thereby negatively reinforcing social withdrawal or social isolation.

Another interfering response that may prevent social skill acquisition is aggressive behavior. Children who exhibit aggressive behavior toward peers are often socially rejected and avoided by the peer group (Asher & Hymel, 1981). Peers avoid the aggressive child that results in the child not being exposed to models of appropriate social behavior or being placed on an extinction schedule for his or her social responses. In short, the aggressive child may become a discriminative stimulus for avoidance behavior on the part of the peer group.

Self-Control Performance Deficits

Children with self-control performance deficits have specific social skills in their repertoires, but do not perform these skills at acceptable levels because of the presence of interfering responses (i.e., behavioral excesses) and problems in antecedent and/or consequent control. Two criteria are used to determine a self-control performance deficit: (a) the presence of interfering responses and (b) the inconsistent/infrequent performance of the skill.

An example of a self-control performance deficit would be a child who is extremely impulsive. Impulsivity or the tendency toward short response latencies can be considered an interfering behavior. An impulsive child may know how to interact appropriately with peers and teachers, but may do so infrequently because his or her impulsive style of responding is typically inappropriate. Thus, the child's response to another child accidently bumping into him or her may be to scream at and push the offending child rather than to simply ignore the incident.

Perhaps the most understandable way of conceptualizing self-control performance deficits is through the operant learning notion of concurrent schedules. *Concurrent schedules* refer to the reinforcement of two or more responses according to two or more schedules at the same time. Thus, interfering responses may be on a relatively thicker schedule of reinforcement than socially skilled responses. As such, interfering responses will occur more frequently than socially skilled responses. This is known as the Matching Law and has received recent attention in the applied behavior change literature (see McDowell, 1982).

Sociometric Classification Model

Some researchers classify children as deficient in social skills on the basis of their sociometric status. Coie, Dodge, and Coppotelli

(1982) developed a classification system that identifies five sociometric status groups: (a) popular, (b) neglected, (c) rejected, (d) controversial, and (e) average. These sociometric groups are based on standard scores derived from a peer nomination assessment that utilizes positive and negative peer nominations.

Coie *et al.* (1982) used a peer nomination in which children in each class are asked to select from a list of classmates the three peers they like most and the three peers they like least. For each student, all peer nominations are summed to yield like most (LM) and liked least (LL) scores. These scores are then used to calculate social preference or SP scores and social impact or SI scores. Social preference is found by subtracting the liked least score from the liked most score (SP = LM − LL). Social impact is derived by adding the liked most score to the liked least score (SI = LM + LL).

All scores are standardized ($M = 0$, $s = 1$) within each class and the sociometric status groups are categorized according to the following criteria: (a) the *popular group* includes students receiving a social preference (SP) score greater than 1.00, a liked most (LM) score greater than 0, and a liked least (LL) score less than 0; (b) the *controversial group* consists of students who receive social impact (SI) scores greater than 1.0, and liked least (LL) and liked most (LM) scores greater than 0; (c) the *neglected group* consists of students who receive a social impact (SI) score of less than −1.00 and an absolute liked most (LM) score of 0; (d) the *rejected group* includes students receiving a social preference (SP) score less than −1.00, a liked least (LL) score greater than 0, and a liked most (LM) score less than 0; and (e) the *average group* falls at the mean of the social preference and social impact dimensions. Figure 4 presents a visual model of the Coie *et al.* (1982) sociometric classification model.

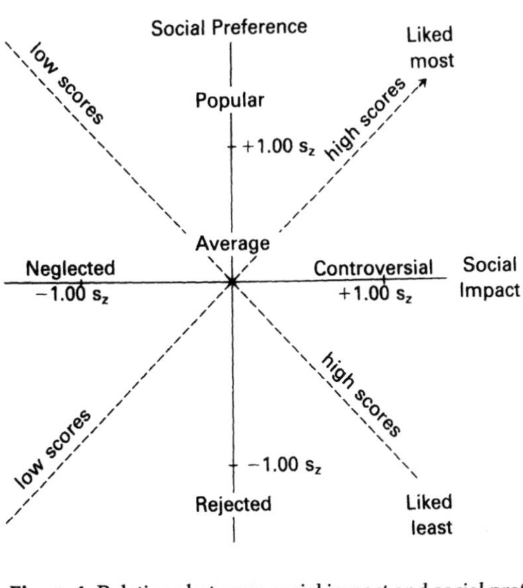

Figure 4. Relations between social impact and social preference. Adapted from "Dimensions and Types of Social Status: A Cross-Age Perspective" by J. D. Coie, K. A. Dodge, and H. Coppotelli, 1982, *Developmental Psychology, 18*, pp. 557–570.

Correlates of Sociometric Status

The correlates of sociometric status can be categorized under three headings: (a) behavioral correlates; (b) cognitive correlates; and, (c) emotional correlates. Each of these areas will be reviewed separately.

Behavioral Correlates

Several researchers have found that popular children, as defined by sociometric assessment, engage in more prosocial interactions than unpopular children. Direct observations of popular and unpopular children have demonstrated that the former group is more likely to contribute relevant conversation during play (Putallaz, 1983), engage in parallel functional play (Rubin & Daniels-Bierness, 1983), receive and initiate more prosocial behavior judged to have positive affect (Dodge, 1983), and use effective group entry strategies (Dodge, Schlundt, Schocker, & Delugach, 1983). Furthermore, peer assessment data have shown that popular children are viewed as leaders and more cooperative than unpopular children when in familiar groups (Coie & Kupersmidt, 1983).

Although it has been the general finding that popular children emit more socially appropriate behavior when compared to unpopular children, exceptions may be expected when more specific sociometric groups are compared. For example, Dodge (1983) found that controversial children displayed more cooperative play and social conversation than other groups including popular children.

One of the most consistent findings in this area of research is that unpopular groups display higher levels of aggressive behavior (Coie & Kupersmidt, 1983; Dodge, 1983; Ladd, 1981; Rubin, 1982). Distinctions among more specific sociometric groups appear to be important when evaluating aggressive behavior. Whereas rejected and controversial children have been found to exhibit excessive amounts of aggression (Coie & Kupersmidt, 1983; Dodge, 1983), neglected children have not been observed to be aggressive (Coie & Kupersmidt, 1983; Dodge, Coie, & Brakke, 1982).

In studies using teacher ratings and direct observations, rejected children also have been reported to display more inattentive, hyperactive, and disruptive behavior than other sociometric groups (Dodge *et al.*, 1983; Green, Vosk, Forehand, & Beck, 1981; Rubin & Daniels-Bierness, 1983; Vosk, Forehand, Parker, & Rickard, 1982). Additionally, there is evidence to suggest that peers view rejected children as least cooperative, most disruptive, and most likely to start fights (Coie & Kupersmidt, 1983). Rejected children receive more negative responses from peers than other children (Dodge, 1983; Gresham, 1982b). The chance for receiving negative responses from peers is greater for the rejected children even when they emit the same behaviors as popular children (Coie, 1983).

As noted by Coie (1985), neglected children most closely resemble socially withdrawn children in behavioral characteristics. These children are labeled by peers as shy and isolated (Dodge *et al.*, 1982). Direct observation studies of children in familiar peer groups support this description (Coie & Kupersmidt, 1983; Dodge, 1983; Dodge *et al.*, 1982; Dodge *et al.*, 1983). The neglected child tends to approach and interact with peers infrequently. Dodge *et al.* (1983) found that neglected children used a low-risk group entry strategy of "waiting and hovering." Gottman (1977) described these children as "tuned out," shy, anxious, and fearful. Evidence exists, however, that is inconsistent with a socially withdrawn description of neglected children. For example, Coie and Kupersmidt (1983) found that when neglected children were in an unfamiliar group of peers they demonstrated more supportive behavior than other status groups and were labeled as leaders by peers. Dodge (1983) reported that neglected children initially received a high rate of positive peer responses when entering a new group; however, within a short time after sociometric status was established in the group most of the peer responses received by neglected children were neutral rather than positive.

Low sociometric status children have been reported also to be poor academic achievers (Green *et al.*, 1981; MacMillan, Morrison, & Silverstein, 1980; Vosk *et al.*, 1982). In a recent review, however, Coie (1985) pointed out that the correlations between academic performance and social standing have been as low as .20 and as high as only .40. This suggests that many children with social skills problems do not necessarily exhibit academic problems. Green *et al.* (1981) found that whereas their rejected group of children obtained standardized achievement scores significantly below accepted children, neglected children did not. Three studies have investigated behavioral differences between low-achieving and high-achieving rejected children (Bursuck & Asher, 1986; Coie & Krehbiel, 1984; Krehbiel, 1983). Generally, these researchers found that children rated low both in social and academic areas were more disruptive, more aggressive, and displayed more inappropriate social behavior than higher achievers.

Cognitive Correlates

Researchers employing a cognitively oriented approach to assessing social competence have focused on identifying covert responses that may influence social behavior. As noted earlier, there is evidence to support the hypothesis that cognitive variables, such as role-taking ability, self-efficacy, problem-solving, and social goal generation may interfere with the performance of socially skilled behavior.

Regarding role-taking ability, Deysach, Keller, Ross, and Hiers (1975) found that social decentering on a role-taking task was significantly related to social competence in a group of 10- to 13-year-olds. Dodge, Murphy, & Buschsbaum (1984) reported that higher sociometric status children performed significantly better on tasks that assessed their ability to identify correctly others' social intentions. These researchers had subjects view videotapes of children exhibiting aggressive behavior. The tapes were designed to express a variety of intentions. Popular and average children were able to identify correctly intentions more frequently than neglected and rejected children. The latter groups tended to associate hostile intentions with the behavior even when prosocial intentions were implied.

In a sample of third through eighth graders, Kurdek and Krile (1983) found a significant correlation between parents' ratings of social skills and three measures of social cognition (i.e., interpersonal understanding, perceived social self-competence, and public self-awareness). Other studies have provided evidence supporting these results. Children's self-report of competence has been found to be associated with sociometric status (Harter, 1982; Wheeler & Ladd, 1982). Pelligrini (1985) found that interpersonal understanding along with problem-solving ability were significant predictors of social competence even when intelligence level was controlled. Problem-solving ability has been linked to socially competent behavior by other authors (e.g., Richard & Dodge, 1982; Spivak & Shure, 1974). Richard and Dodge (1982) reported that the number and variety of solutions generated on a problem-solving task discriminated popular from unpopular children.

Consistent with the hypothesis that problem-solving deficits may interfere with social responding, some authors have proposed that children who have difficulty generating socially appropriate goals may exhibit social skills deficits (Renshaw & Asher, 1983). These researchers found that low status children were less able to generate positive and outgoing social goals in comparison to high status children. Evidence exists to suggest that the goals which predict sociometric status may vary with age. Specifically, Taylor and Asher (1984) found that whereas relationship goals were significantly correlated with sociometric status among third and fourth graders, performance-oriented goals predicted status among fifth and sixth graders.

Emotional Correlates

Few researchers have investigaged emotional correlates of social competence in children. It has been reported that social anxiety is associated with social skills problems (Buhrmester, 1982; Wheeler & Ladd, 1982). The *Children's Concern Inventory* (CCI) (Buhrmester, 1982) is a self-report measure designed to assess children's anxiety in specific social areas, including peer acceptance. Buhrmester (1982) reported significant negative correlations between sociometric status level and children's anxiety regarding peer acceptance as measured by the CCI. Depression also is an emotional response implicated as interfering with social interactions. Helsel and Matson (1984) reported a negative correlation between depression as measured by the *Child Depression Inventory* and social skills level.

Integration of the Behavioral and Sociometric Models

To date, various researchers have operated out of either the behavioral or sociometric models in classifying children's social skills deficits. The emphasis in the behavioral model is to classify social skills problems as being the result of acquisition or skill deficits or performance deficits. In addition, the behavioral model specifies the presence or absence of interfering behaviors that prevent either the acquisition or performance of social skills. In contrast, the sociometric model classifies children according to different dimensions of social status, using the degree of social preference and social impact as anchors. As reviewed earlier, research has demonstrated that different sociometric status groups (e.g., popular, rejected, controversial, and neglected) show different behavioral, cognitive, and emotional correlates.

The advantage of the behavioral classification model is that it is molecular enough to prescribe intervention for specific deficits. However, this model does not adequately associate behavioral deficits with indexes of socially valid outcomes, such as peer acceptance. The sociometric classification model reflects the socially valid outcome of peer acceptance, but does not adequately relate sociometric status to intervention strategies. An integration of these two models is needed in order to provide a more comprehensive and socially valid classification system.

Frentz (1986) suggested that rejected and controversial children are likely to display interfering responses, such as aggressive behavior, poor anger control, impulsive behavior, and the like. In contrast, neglected children are likely to demonstrate behaviors that are more reflective of internalizing interfering responses, such as fear, anxiety, or depression. Based on the research literature, it might be hypothesized that the various sociometric groups differ with respect to acquisition and performance deficits as well as the presence or absence of interfering responses. For example, neglected children might be characterized as having performance deficits (Dodge, 1983) whereas rejected children may be typified as having acquisition deficits (Coie & Dodge, 1983). Controversial children are likely to have a large repertoire of interpersonal skills that are not displayed consistently across persons and settings (Dodge, 1983). As such, controversial children can be said to have performance rather than acquisition deficits.

	Acquisition Deficit	Performance Deficit
Interfering Response Absent	Neglected	Neglected
Interfering Response Present	Neglected Rejected	Neglected Rejected Controversial

Figure 5. Proposed integration of the behavioral and sociometric models.

Currently, there is no research that has directly tested the validity of the integration of the behavioral and sociometric classification models. It would be unreasonable to assume that the various sociometric groups would fit neatly into the categories specified in the behavioral model. Figure 5 shows that the various sociometric groups could have either acquisition or performance deficits and the presence or absence of interfering responses. Future research should investigate the proportions of each sociometric group that have acquisition and performance deficits and the presence and types of interfering responses.

Assessment of Social Skills

Methods for assessing social skills can vary along several dimensions. For example, methods can rely on different sources of information, such as teachers, parents, peers, trained observers, or the child him- or herself. Information produced by assessment procedures can vary in specificity, ranging from global descriptions to quantification of molecular behaviors (McFall, 1982). Methods of assessment can also differ with respect to temporal proximity of performance to assessment. Thus, assessment information may stem from observations of ongoing behavior, ratings of recent behavior in certain situations, or recall of temporally distant social functioning. These three dimensions of source, specificity, and temporal proximity of observation to performance also impact the reliability, validity, accuracy, and practicality of assessment procedures.

Our preference for classifying assessment procedures is decided according to the purpose of assessment: (a) identification/ classification and (b) intervention/programming planning. Some assessment procedures are more useful for identification or classification of social skill deficiencies than for intervention purposes. Most norm-referenced tests (e.g., teacher rating scales) are used primarily for identification and classification purposes. In contrast, other assessment methods are useful for intervention purposes. Direct observations of behavior, behavioral interviews, and self-monitoring are examples of this class of procedures. Table 2 provides an outline of social skills assessment procedures.

Table 2. Assessment of Social Skills

- A. Classification/diagnosis
  - 1. Sociometrics
    - a. Nominations
    - b. Ratings
    - c. Rankings
  - 2. Rating by others
    - a. Teacher
    - b. Parent
    - c. Peer
  - 3. Self-report
  - 4. Behavioral role play
    - a. Analogue
    - b. Naturalistic
- B. Intervention/therapy
  - 1. Behavioral interviews
    - a. Teacher
    - b. Parent
    - c. Target child
    - d. Peers
  - 2. Direct observations
    - a. Classroom
    - b. Playground
    - c. Lunchroom
  - 3. Self-monitoring with functional analysis

The distinguishing feature of any assessment method that classifies it as either an identification or intervention method is based on the extent to which it allows for a *functional analysis of behavior*. That is, the extent to which an assessment procedure provides data concerning the antecedent, sequential, and consequent conditions surrounding behavior determines its classification as an intervention assessment method.

Process and Targets of Social Skills Assessment

Process

As with the psychological assessment of any problem, the process of social skills assessment can be characterized by a series of hypothesis-testing sequences. Hypotheses are generated in an attempt to answer questions related to the following stages of assessment: (a) identification/classification, (b) intervention/program planning, and (c) evaluation of intervention effects. Hypotheses may be generated based on whatever information is available at a given point in the assessment process and then tested at subsequent points through the gathering of additional information. Comprehensive social skills assessments allow one to draw conclusions regarding problem severity, the role of contributory factors, intervention strategies needed, and the degree of intervention success.

A standard procedure for assessing social skills does not exist. Instead, hypotheses are generated that dictate the direction and scope of assessment, questions to be answered, and methods to be used. Assessment should proceed in a manner such that specific information needed for intervention planning is eventually gathered. In contrast, assessment of the effects of social skills training typically proceeds in an opposite direction, moving from examination of immediate and target-specific outcomes toward global analyses of the intervention's impact on important social outcomes (i.e., social validation).

Targets

Social skills assessment focuses on multiple targets. During the identification/classification stage of assessment, children and youth in need of social skills intervention are the focus. After such individuals have beeen identified, more specific foci serve as targets. Subsequent assessment targets are primarily a reflection of one's conceptualization of human behavior, those factors capable of producing ineffective performance, and the type of intervention strategies adopted. The bias here is against personality structures and underlying intrapsychic conflict as useful assessment targets. Instead, observable behaviors occurring in specific situations and influenced by one's learning history as well as current environmental events are seen as the proper focus of assessment.

My bias was reflected in the discussion earlier concerning conceptualizations of social skill problems. Comprehensive social skill assessments should include such targets as performance × situation interactions resulting in judgments of social competency plus any measurable factors contributing to poor social skill performance. Based on the four-category classification outlined previously, specific skill deficits, inadequate reinforcement or opportunity for skilled performance, and interfering behaviors are all important considerations in social skills assessment. The following sections will review specific methods for social skills assessment.

Assessment for Identification/Classification

Several assessment procedures generate information that allows for a determination of the existence of a social skills problem. The most frequently used assessment procedures of this type are sociometrics, rankings or ratings by others (e.g., teachers and parents), self-report, and behavioral role play tasks (Gresham & Elliott, 1984). Hops and Greenwood (1981) consider sociometrics and rankings by others (e.g., teachers) to be selection measures, whereas they consider behavior ratings and checklists to be useful for intervention program planning. According to Hops and Greenwood (1981), the extent to which the assessment procedure yields information about specific behavioral excesses or deficits determines its utility as a screening/identification versus an intervention assessment procedure.

I use a slightly different conceptualization and classification of the various assessment procedures, based on the extent to which the assessment yields information for a functional analysis of behavior. In this view, the extent to which the assessment procedure provides data concerning the antecedent, sequential, and consequent conditions surrounding social behavior determines its classification as an identification/classification or intervention assessment method. As such, behavior ratings would not be an intervention assessment procedure because they do not provide data for functional analyses. Behavioral interviews, on the other hand, would be considered an intervention assessment procedure because they yield data concerning the antecedents and consequences of behavioral excesses or deficits. Similarly, naturalistic observations and self-monitoring yield functional analysis information and, as such, would be classified as intervention assessment procedures.

Assessment for Intervention/Program Planning

Some assessment techniques are better suited than others for obtaining information that is useful in designing social skills training programs. As noted, the extent to which an assessment technique allows for a functional analysis of behavior determines its utility as a behavioral assessment method that yields information for intervention or therapy. Two techniques that allow for such a functional analysis are discussed in the following: (a) behavioral interviews and (b) naturalistic observations.

Behavioral interviews are extremely useful in conducting a functional analysis of social behavior. Research demonstrates that behavioral interviews are effective in defining behaviors in observable terms, identifying the antecedent, sequential, and consequent conditions surrounding target behaviors, and designing observational systems to measure target behaviors (Bergan, 1977; Bergan & Tombari, 1975, 1976; Tombari & Bergan, 1978).

Behavioral observations have been used frequently as selection and outcome measures in social skills training research (Asher & Hymel, 1981; Foster & Ritchey, 1979; Green & Forehand, 1980; Gresham & Elliott, 1984). Observations of social behaviors in naturalistic settings (e.g., classrooms, playground, etc.) have several advantages over other social skills assessment methods. First, naturalistic observations represent the most direct form of behavioral assessment because they measure behavior at the time and place of its actual occurrence. Second, behavioral observations are sensitive to the effects of social skills training interventions (Strain, Cooke, & Apolloni, 1976). Observational data are conducive to repeated measurements, which allow for the monitoring of within-subject variability in social behavior (Gresham, 1981a). This, in turn, allows for a fine-grained functional analysis of behavior in which the antecedent, sequential, and consequent conditions surrounding social behavior can be analyzed. Third, observational data require operational definitions of the social skill being assessed rather than relying on global, nebulous trait descriptions (e.g., friendly, cooperative, etc.).

Conceptualization of Social Skills Training

Social skills training (SST) may be conceptualized as a four-step process: (a) promoting skill acquisition, (b) enhancing skill performance, (c) removing interfering behaviors, and (d) facilitating generalization. These steps are related to the type of social skill deficiency (e.g., skill versus performance deficit), the presence or absence of interfering behaviors, and the functional control of social behaviors in specific situations.

As can be seen in Table 3, modeling and coaching represent the major ways in which social skill acquisition is facilitated. These procedures are typically used to remediate social skill deficits that refer to the child not having the social skill in his or her repertoire or the child not knowing a particular step in the performance of a behavioral sequence.

Modeling represents one of the most effective and efficient ways of teaching social behavior (Gresham, 1981b, 1985a,b). Modeling is efficient in the sense that component behaviors of a particular social skill do not have to be taught using a time-consuming shaping process. Modeling instruction presents the entire sequence of behaviors involved in a particular social skill and teaches how specific behaviors in this sequence can be integrated into a composite behavior.

Table 3. Conceptualization of Teaching Social Skills

I. Promoting Skill Acquisition
   A. Modeling (live and/or symbolic)
   B. Coaching
   C. Instructions/explanations
II. Enhancing Skill Performance
   A. Behavior rehearsal
   B. Reinforcement-based techniques
   C. Peer initiation strategies (antecedents)
   D. Cooperation learning strategies (antecedents and consequences)
III. Removing interfering behaviors
   A. Response cost
   B. Group contingencies
   C. DRO/DRL (Differential reinforcement of other/low rates)
   D. Overcorrection (positive practice and/or restitutional)
   E. Self-instructional procedures/consequential thinking
IV. Facilitating generalization
   A. Take advantage of natural communities of reinforcement
   B. Train diversely
   C. Incorporate functional mediators

Modeling has been used in a variety of formats including videotape/film modeling, live modeling, and verbal modeling (via books, stories, etc.). The crucial aspects of learning through modeling are the observer's attention to the modeling stimulus, the observer's retention of the modeling sequence, the observer's behavioral reproduction of the modeling sequence, and the environment's reinforcement (i.e., motivation) of the modeled behaviors.

Coaching is a direct verbal instruction technique that is comprised of three steps: (a) presentation of rules or standards for behavior, (b) behavioral rehearsal of the social skill, and (c) feedback on behavioral performance (Oden & Asher, 1977).

A number of procedures are designed to enhance the behavioral performance of social skills that are already in the child's repertoire. These procedures are most appropriate for remediation of performance deficits that refer to a deficiency in the number of times a behavior is exhibited (i.e., the behavior is not performed at an acceptable level). Table 3 shows that a variety of antecedent and consequent events have been used to facilitate the performance of social behavior.

The third step in SST is one that is often overlooked in discussions of teaching positive social behaviors. That is, it is often assumed that the child has no interfering behaviors that prevent/block the acquisition or performance of socially skilled behaviors. This is highly unlikely for many children and, as such, one must apply contingencies for the interfering behaviors as well as teach and/or reinforce appropriate social behaviors. As previously mentioned, interfering behaviors are perhaps best conceptualized using the notion of concurrent schedules of reinforcement. Concurrent schedules describe the situation in which two or more behaviors are renforced according to two or more schedules at the same time. If interfering behaviors are on a relatively thicker schedule of reinforcement than the appropriate social skill behaviors, the interfering behaviors will be performed more frequently than the socially skilled behaviors (i.e., they will block the performance of appropriate social skill behaviors).

Finally, generalization of social skills represents a critical component of SST. *Generalization* refers to the occurrence of relevant behaviors under different nontraining conditions (i.e., across settings, subjects, people, behaviors, and times) without the scheduling of these same conditions as had been scheduled in the training conditions (Stokes & Baer, 1977). Stokes and Osnes (1986) provide an in-depth discussion of the technology involved in programming for the generalization of children's social behavior.

Review of the SST Literature

A large number of studies have been published over the past several years that has documented the efficacy of SST in altering the frequency of social behavior and in changing a child's sociometric status (see Cartledge & Milburn, 1983; Gresham, 1981b, 1985a; Gresham & Lemanek, 1983; Ladd & Mize, 1983; Schneider & Byrne, 1985; Strain & Fox, 1981, for comprehensive reviews).

Gresham (1985b) reviewed 33 studies that used cognitive-behavioral SST procedures (i.e., modeling, coaching, treatment packages, and social problem solving) and found that modeling and coaching had the strongest base of empirical support when evaluated on the seven dimensions of subject characteristics, treatment specification, appropriateness of statistical analysis, experimental design, social validity of outcome measures, generalization, and cost-effectiveness. Gresham (1985b) concluded that it is unclear whether the addition of cognitive elements (e.g., self-instruction, problem solving, etc.) enhances the effectiveness of procedures such as modeling, coaching, behavior rehearsal, and operant techniques in teaching social behavior.

The most in-depth review of the SST literature was conducted by Schneider and Byrne (1985), who used a meta-analysis of 51 studies investigating the following seven attributes:

(a) treatment technique, (b) duration of treatment, (c) age and sex of subjects, (d) subject population, (e) therapist characteristics, (f) outcome variable, and (g) reliability of outcome measure. Because of the comprehensiveness and informative nature of the Schneider and Byrne (1985) review, it is discussed in detail in the following sections.

Treatment Technique

Intervention techniques were classified according to four major SST strategies, including modeling, operant procedures, coaching, and social-cognitive techniques. According to Schneider and Byrne (1985), operant procedures had the largest effect size (ES) of .85 followed by modeling (ES = .75), coaching (ES = .65), and social-cognitive techniques (ES = .55). There was a significant difference between the ESs for operant and social-cognitive techniques; however, the differences between operant, modeling, and coaching techniques were not significant. These ESs cannot be taken as equivalent, however, because of the differences in outcome measure, durations of treatment, and other methodological differences.

Outcome Measure and Reliability

Considerable variability can be found in the type of outcome measure used in SST studies. Schneider and Byrne (1985) found the largest ESs for studies using rates of social interaction measured by either naturalistic observation or behavioral role-play tests (M = .86). In addition, the more reliable the outcome measure, the larger the ES (1.01 versus .64). Few studies used self-report and blind teacher ratings as outcome measures in the 51 studies reviewed.

Therapist and Child Characteristics

Schneider and Byrne's (1985) meta-analysis revealed that SST conducted by classroom teachers was less effective than SST conducted by research staff (ESs = .63 versus .80, respectively). This may suggest that SST is more effective when conducted by individuals who have more knowledge in the area of learning theory.

The meta-analysis also showed that SST was more effective for preschoolers (ES = .97) and adolescents (ES = .87) than for elementary-age children (ES = .56). No sex differences in the ESs were noted although few studies treated sex as an independent variable. SST was more effective for withdrawn than for aggressive subjects (ES = 1.04 versus .69, respectively). Schneider and Byrne (1985) hypothesized that problems of social withdrawal may be more related to social skill deficits whereas aggressive behaviors are more related to performance deficits. As such, the use of modeling and coaching (procedures designed to remediate skill deficits) demonstrate greater changes in social skills for withdrawn subjects. This hypothesis, however, requires further investigation because no studies have been conducted in which subjects have been classified as having a skill versus performance deficit.

Duration of Treatment

Opposite to what one might expect, the duration of treatment was negatively related to the outcome of SST. The ES for treatments of less than 5 days was .89 whereas the ES for treatments of more than 50 days was .59. Schneider and Byrne (1985) interpreted this finding by noting that some treatments (e.g., modeling) are always shorter than other treatments (e.g., social-cognitive treatments).

Summary and Implications

Basing my conclusion on the 51 studies reviewed by Schneider and Byrne (1985), it appears that operant procedures and modeling appear to be the most effective SST procedures. This finding is consistent with reviews by Gresham (1981a, 1985b) and Cartledge and Milburn (1983). Social-cognitive procedures were the least effective SST procedures, partially because of the difference in focus of these procedures (i.e., cognitive changes versus behavioral changes). Gresham (1985b) noted that one of the biggest problems with social-cognitive SST procedures is their failure to demonstrate changes on socially valid outcome measures, such as naturalistically observed social behavior and sociometric status.

One problem with the SST literature has been the failure of researchers to classify subjects according to the specific types of social skill deficits prior to the initiation of training. Future research should attempt to classify subjects according to the system mentioned earlier in this chapter (e.g., skill, performance, and self-control deficits) and relate SST strategies to each of these classifications.

Social Validation and Social Skills

Social validity has become an important concept in the behavioral assessment and intervention literature over the past several years (Kazdin, 1977; Van Houten, 1979; Witt & Elliott, 1985; Wolf, 1978). Social validity refers to establishing the social significance of the goals for interventions, creating interventions that are socially acceptable to treatment consumers, and evaluating the social importance of the effects of interventions (Wolf, 1978).

Social Significance

Establishing the social significance of the behavioral goals for social skills interventions is most relevant during the classification/diagnosis phase of the assessment process. The purpose is to target those social skills deficits that are viewed as being most important in the schools. The social significance of behavioral goals is usually based on subjective judgments by teachers (Kazdin, 1977; Wolf, 1978). Subjective evaluations are judgments made by persons who interact with or who are in a special position to judge behavior.

Determining the social significance of the goals of a social skills intervention is vital. One would not want to teach behaviors that are not considered valuable or important. The likely result of teaching socially insignificant behaviors is extinction (i.e., the behaviors simply do not get reinforced). Some years ago, Baer and Wolf (1970) stressed the importance of teaching only those behaviors that have a high probability of being trapped into natural communities of reinforcement.

An interesting study by Black (1985) sheds light on the value of assessing what teachers consider to be socially significant behaviors in their classrooms. Black (1985) asked 125 teachers (43 black and 82 white) to rate the importance of each of the 50 behaviors on the *Social Skills Rating Scale* (SSRS) (Clark, Gresham, & Elliott, 1985; Gresham & Elliott, in preparation). Importance was rated on the following three-point scale: (a) 2—This behavior is *critical* for success in my classroom, (b) 1—This behavior is *important* for success in my classroom, or (c) 0—This behavior is *unimportant* for success in my classroom. Table 4 shows the 10 highest rated and 10 lowest rated behaviors in terms of importance.

As can be seen in Table 4, the 10 most important behaviors deal primarily with classroom order and control. These behaviors, although important, have little to do with the development of peer relationship skills or the ability to cope effectively with peers. These behaviors are what Hersh and Walker (1983) refer to as the model behavioral profile expected by teachers. Many, if not most, MH children were originally referred for assessment and placement in special education because of their divergence from this model behavioral profile (Gresham, 1985a). Conversely, Table 4 shows that the 10 lowest rated behaviors deal primarily with positive peer-to-peer social interactions or social skills, suggesting that teachers view these behaviors as relatively unimportant for classroom success. Interestingly, there was high agreement of this rank ordering for black and white teachers (r = .96), black and white children (r

Table 4. 10 Most Important Social Skills and 10 Least Important Social Skills as Rated By Classroom Teachers on the Social Skills Rating Scales (SSRS)

Top 10: SSRS Importance dimension classroom survival skills

1. Completes classroom assignments in required time
2. Looks at teacher when instructed
3. Follow teacher's verbal directions
4. Requests assistance, explanations, or instructions from teacher
5. Uses time productively while waiting for teacher assistance
6. Asks questions of teacher when unsure of what to do in school work at appropriate times and in an appropriate manner
7. Produces correct academic work
8. Controls temper in conflict situations
9. Attends to class speakers
10. Ignores peer distractions when doing class work

The bottom 10: SSRS Importance dimension

1. Invites peers to play
2. Introduces self to new people on own initiative
3. Praises peers
4. Makes positive statements to other children
5. Presents academic work before class
6. Cooperates with peers without being told
7. Appropriately expresses opinions or beliefs on some issue by giving reasons for expressed opinion or belief
8. Appropriately expresses anger or annoyance when a classmate takes a belonging without asking
9. Attempts classroom tasks before asking for teacher assistance
10. Tolerates peers whose characteristics are different from one's one's own (e.g., ethnic group, handicapped, etc.)

= .96), males and females (r = .93), and MH and nonhandicapped children (r = .98).

What implications does this study have for social skills interventions in regular classrooms? The data would suggest that teachers do not view interpersonal or social competence skills as being important for classroom success. In this sense, these behaviors are socially insignificant and would not be likely candidates for intervention. However, these data may point up the fact that interventions must include task-related as well as interpersonal behaviors. In fact, the 10 highest rated behaviors in Table 4 often are referred to as task-related or academic-related social skills (Gresham, 1984, 1985a; Hersh & Walker, 1983; Stephens, 1978; Walker & Rankin, 1983). The relatively lowest ratings for interpersonal behaviors also may reflect teachers' perceived lack of knowledge and skills in the area of children's social development. More research is needed in order to identify the bases for these ratings.

Social Acceptability

The social acceptability of an intervention procedure forces one to ask the question: Do the ends justify the means? Do the participants, caregivers, and consumers consider the intervention procedure acceptable? Witt and Elliott (1985) indicated that acceptability is a broad term encompassing whether an intervention is appropriate for a given problem, whether it is fair, reasonable, or intrusive, and whether the intervention is consistent with conventional notions of what an intervention should be. In short, acceptability consists of judgments from intervention consumers as to whether or not they like the intervention procedure.

Why should psychologists and educators be concerned with the acceptability of their interventions? One reason is that unacceptable interventions are less likely to be implemented or implemented as planned (Witt & Elliott, 1985). Thus, an unimplemented or poorly implemented intervention has little chance for effectively modifying problem behaviors in classrooms. Variables that relate to the acceptability of interventions are the amount of teacher time involved, effort, and resources. There are currently no data regarding the acceptability of social skills interventions with classroom teachers. However, there is nothing to suggest that the acceptability of these procedures is not related to the same variables (e.g., time, resources, effort, etc.) as other interventions. Future research should address the acceptability issue with social skills interventions with both regular education and special education teachers. It may be that the type of behavior (i.e., social skill deficit versus academic deficit) interacts with the type of intervention producing differences in teachers' acceptability levels.

Social Importance

The final component of social validation is social importance. In other words, does the quantity and quality of behavior change make an educationally significant difference in the individual's functioning. Interventions that produce socially important effects move the individual into normative ranges of functioning on the behaviors of interest and/or are judged by treatment consumers to have produced socially important effects.

Two methods have been discussed as means of establishing the social importance of effects produced by interventions. (a) subjective evaluation and (b) social comparison (Kazdin, 1977; Kazdin & Matson, 1981). Subjective evaluation requires asking persons who are in special position to judge the importance of effects produced by a given intervention. This might entail having teachers rate the magnitude or importance of intervention effects immediately after an intervention and at some future time (e.g., 2 weeks, 4 weeks, etc.) on a Likert-type scale. This procedure would assess the importance of intervention effects as well as the maintenance of these effects over time.

Social comparison consists of comparing the level of behavior of children after intervention to nonreferred peers (i.e., a norm-referenced comparison). Thus, if MH children's behavior rates after intervention are comparable to the rates of nonhandicapped children, the intervention can be said to have produced socially important effects. Social comparisons need not necessarily involve rates or frequencies of behavior. For example, one could use standardized social skills scales to assess behavior change subsequent to an intervention. Similarly, one could use sociometrics to assess changes in sociometric status after intervention. Comparisons could also be made to nonhandicapped or to children not referred for social skills interventions.

Perhaps the best way of socially validating an intervention is to use what Van Houten (1979) calls combined social validation procedures. Combined procedures would use subjective judgments by consumers and social comparisons to assess the social importance of effects produced by interventions. This is important because judgments and empirical comparisons do not necessarily produce the same results (Kazdin & Matson, 1981).

Future Research Directions

Although SST has been shown to facilitate positive social interaction and to increase peer acceptance, much is not known about key issues in this area. Three major areas of knowledge in the social skills area appear to be in need of future research: (a) generalizations; (b) methods of social skill selection, and (c) motivational/affective variables. Each of these areas will be discussed briefly in the following sections pointing toward directions for future research.

Facilitation of Generalization

Generalization represents a key consideration in SST. Obviously, social skills that do not occur outside of the training setting or do not maintain over time would not be functional in obtaining environmental reinforcers for individuals. Moreover, an efficient means of teaching social skills would be to identify pivotal or key response class members, train these pivotal behaviors, and observe generalization to untrained members of these response classes (see Voeltz & Evans, 1982). Hence, generalization across settings, time, and behaviors is crucial to the outcomes of SST.

Stokes and Baer (1977) indicated that specific programming tactics must be implemented in order to ensure that generalized behavior change is accomplished. These authors outlined a number of generalization-programming techniques including (a) the introduction of newly trained behaviors to natural contingencies, (b) the training of multiple stimulus and response exemplars, (c) the use of indiscriminable contingencies, and (d) the use of loose training strategies. More recently, Stokes and Osnes (1986) outlined a number of procedures for facilitating generalization of trained social skills. Table 5 presents an outline of these generalization procedures. Future SST studies should focus on specific procedures to facilitate generalization of trained social skills.

Social Skill Selection

Surprisingly, a number of SST studies have failed to select skills for training on the basis of social validity. That is, targeted social skills have been selected without reference to their relation to important social outcomes for children and youth (Gresham, 1983b, 1986). Hughes (1986) reviewed 32 SST investigations published between 1980 and 1984 and found that 56.5% (18 studies) used nonempirical methods to select social skills for training and 62.5% (20 studies) did not attempt to verify that subjects were in fact deficient on the targeted social skills to be trained.

Table 5. Functional Control of Generalization

I. Take advantage of natural communities of reinforcement
   A. Teach relevant behaviors (i.e., those that are functional in a variety of settings)
   B. Modify enviroments supporting maladaptive behaviors
   C. Recruit "natural communities" of reinforcement (i.e., teach child to ask for reinforcement when deserved)
II. Train diversely
   A. Use sufficient stimulus exemplars (i.e., vary ways of teaching the same response/behavior)
   B. Use sufficient response exemplars (i.e., teach various ways of responding to the same situation)
   C. Train loosely (antecedents: similarity to real-life environments)
   D. Use indiscriminable contingencies (consequences: variable schedules)
   E. Reinforce unprompted generalization (i.e., teach "to generalize")
III. Incorporate functional mediators
   A. Use common physical stimuli (things = discrimination)
   B. Use common social stimuli (people = discrimination)
   C. Use self-mediated stimuli (language as a prompt to promote generalization)

The fact that relatively few SST studies have used a social validity approach to skill selection is perplexing. It appears that many studies have selected social skills for training on the basis of researchers' *a priori* notions of what represents socially significant target behaviors rather than selecting skills on the basis of empirical criteria. Gresham (1986) suggested that a number of empirical criteria could be used to select socially significant target behaviors for SST. First, researchers could compare the rates of observed social behaviors for referred and nonreferred children and select those social skills on which the greatest discrepancy between the two groups existed. Second, targeted social skills could be selected on the basis of teacher ratings of the importance of social skills for classroom success or adjustment. This approach has been taken by Gresham and Elliott (in preparation) in their development of teacher, parent, and self-report versions of the *Social Skills Rating Scales*. Finally, targeted social skills could be selected on the basis of their relation to socially important criteria, such as sociometric status, academic performance, or self-esteem.

Future research should focus on empirical methods for selecting social skills for SST studies. An efficient approach would be to identify social skill response clusters and select targeted social skills on the basis of their relation to socially valid indexes of outcome and generalization to other members of the response class.

Motivation/Affective Variables

There has been a paucity of attention directed toward the role of motivational/affective variables in SST. It may well be the case that certain motivational variables (e.g., learned helplessness, effectance motivation, self-attribution, etc.) and affective varibles (e.g., self-concept, self-esteem, etc.) interact with SST strategies to produce differential effects on measures of social skills and sociometric status. If we were to view motivational and affective variables as dependent measures, it could well be the case that certain SST techniques differentially affect these motivational and affective outcomes.

The theoretical notions of learned helplessness (Seligman, 1975), self-attribution (Weiner, 1979), effectance motivation (Harter, 1982; White, 1959), and self-efficacy (Bandura, 1977b, 1986) all seem relevant to SST. Although there are several differences between these theories of motivation, they all seem to be describing a similar phenomenon in slightly different words.

Learned helplessness, self-attribution, effectance motivation, and self-efficacy all share the common theme regarding an individual's expectancy or belief concerning behavior and its outcomes. For example, learned helplessness describes a situation in which an individual comes to believe that behavior and its outcomes are independent. Similarly, self-attribution theory hypothesizes that there is a relation between an individual's attribution for success or failure (outcomes) on specific tasks and the individual's beliefs (attributions) about the causes of success and failure. Effectance motivation describes an individual's need to be successful or deal effectively with the environment. Harter (1982) suggested that effectance motivation is multidimensional and describes the effects of success and failure on effectance motivation.

Perhaps a more comprehensive and relevant theory of motivation than those discussed earlier is Bandura's (1977b, 1986) theoretical notion of self-efficacy. The basic premise in self-efficacy, as in learned helplessness and effectance motivation, centers on an individual's sense of personal efficacy to produce and regulate events in their lives. Perceived self-efficacy is concerned with judgments of how well one can execute behaviors required to deal with prospective situations.

Perceived self-efficacy affects behavioral functioning by influencing an individual's choice of activities, effort expenditure, and persistence in the face of difficulties. Self-percepts of efficacy can predict not only behavioral choice, but also variations in coping behavior and even specific performance attainments (Bandura, 1986).

Self-efficacy appears to have direct relevance for SST because the level and strength of self-efficacy are based on four major sources of information: (a) performance accomplishments, (b) vicarious experience, (c) verbal persuasion, and (d) emotional arousal. Performance accomplishments represent the strongest basis for efficacy because they are based on personal mastery experiences. That is, repeated success in any setting and/or situation heightens self-efficacy, whereas repeated failure, particularly early on, lowers efficacy (Bandura, 1977b). Several SST strategies are based on performance accomplishments such as participant modeling, behavior rehearsal, and direct reinforcement for behavioral performance (see Gresham, 1984). Other

Table 6. Classification of Social Skills Training Strategies according to Strength of Self-Efficacy Production

- I. Performance accomplishments
  - A. Participant modeling
  - B. Behavior rehearsal
  - C. Direct reinforcement for performance
  - D. Peer initiation strategies
  - E. *In vivo* flooding
  - F. Cooperative learning strategies
- II. Vicarious experience
  - A. Symbolic modeling
  - B. Modeling without participation
  - C. Coaching
  - D. Covert modeling
- III. Verbal persuasion
  - A. Suggestions
  - B. Instructions
  - C. Self-instruction
  - D. Interpretive treatments
- IV. Emotional arousal
  - A. Relaxation
  - B. Desensitization
  - C. Imaginal flooding
  - D. Attribution retraining

SST techniques rely on vicarious experiences (a weaker basis for self-efficacy), including symbolic modeling, modeling without participation, and coaching. Verbal persuasion SST strategies, a still weaker basis for efficacy, include self-instruction, suggestion, and interpretative treatments. Finally, emotional arousal (the weakest basis of self-efficacy) includes techniques such as attribution retraining, imaginal flooding, and desensitization. Table 6 provides an outline of various SST strategies categorized according to the basis of self-efficacy.

Future SST research should focus on changes in levels of self-efficacy as a function of specific training strategies. It may well be the case that there is a relation between the level of self-efficacy an individual possesses in specific social behaviors and the degree of generalization of these behaviors across settings, situations, and time. This hypothesis, however, awaits empirical investigation.

References

Allen, K., Benning, P., & Drummond, T. (1972). Integration of normal and handicapped children in a behavior modification preschool: A case study. In G. Semb (Ed.), *Behavioral analysis and education*. Lawrence, KS: University of Kansas Press.

Asher, S. R., & Hymel, S. (1981). Children's social competence in peer relations: Sociometric and behavioral assessment. In J. D. Wine & M. A. Smye (Eds.), *Social competence* (pp. 125–157). New York: Guilford Press.

Asher, S., Oden, S., & Gottman, J. (1977). Children's friendship in school settings. In L. G. Katz (Ed.), *Current topics in early childhood education* (Vol. 1). Hillsdale, NJ: Erlbaum.

Baer, D., & Wolf, M. (1970). The entry into natural communities of reinforcement. In R. Ulrich, T. Stachnik, & J. Mabry (Eds.), *Control of human behavior* (Vol. 11, pp. 319–324). Glenview, IL: Scott, Foresman.

Ballard, M., Corman, L., Gottlieb, J., & Kaufman, M. (1977). Improving the social status of mainstreamed retarded children. *Journal of Educational Psychology, 69*, 605–611.

Bandura, A. (1977a). *Social learning theory*. Englewood Cliffs, NJ: Prentice-Hall.

Bandura, A. (1977b). Self-efficacy: Toward a unifying theory of behavior change. *Psychological Review, 84*, 191–215.

Bandura, A. (1986). *Social foundations of thought and action: A social cognitive theory*. Englewood Cliffs, NJ: Prentice-Hall.

Bergan, J. R. (1977). *Behavioral consultation*. Columbus, OH: Merrill.

Bergan, J., & Tombari, M. (1975). The analysis of verbal interactions occurring during consultation. *Journal of School Psychology, 13*, 209–226.

Bergan, J., & Tombari, M. (1976). Consultant skill and efficiency and the implementation and outcomes of consultation. *Journal of School Psychology, 14*, 3–14.

Black, F. (1985). *Social skills assessment for mainstreamed handicapped students: The discriminative efficiency of the Teacher Ratings of Social Skills*. Unpublished doctoral dissertation, Louisiana State University.

Brophy, J. (1981). Teacher praise: A functional analysis. *Review of Educational Research, 51*, 5–32.

Bryan, T. S. (1974). Peer popularity of learning disabled children. *Journal of Learning Disabilities, 7*, 621–625.

Bryan, T. S. (1976). Peer popularity of learning disabled children: A replication. *Journal of Learning Disabilities, 9*, 307–311.

Bryan, T. S. (1978). Social relationships and verbal interactions of learning disabled children. *Journal of Learning Disabilities, 11*, 107–115.

Buhrmester, D. (1982). *Children's Concern Inventory Manual*. Unpublished manuscript, University of Denver.

Bursuck, W. D., & Asher, S. R. (1986). The relationship between social competence and achievement in elementary school children. *Journal of Clinical Child Psychology, 15*, 41–49.

Cartledge, G., & Milburn, J. (1983). Social skill assessment and teaching in the schools. In T. R. Kratochwill (Ed.), *Advances in school psychology* (Vol. 3, pp. 175–236). Hillsdale, NJ: Erlbaum.

Catania, C. (1975). The myth of self-reinforcement. *Behaviorism, 3*, 192–199.

Clark, L., Gresham, F. M., & Elliott, S. N. (1985). Development and validation of a social skills assessment measure: The TROSS-C. *Journal of Psychoeducational Assessment, 4*, 347–356.

Coie, J. D. (1985). Fitting social skills intervention to the target group. In B. H. Schneider, K. H. Rubin, & J. E. Ledingham (Eds.), *Children's peer relations: Issues in assessment and intervention*. New York: Springer.

Coie, J. D., & Dodge, K. A. (1983). Continuity of children's social status: A five-year longitudinal study. *Merrill-Palmer Quarterly, 29*, 261–282.

Coie, J. D., & Krehbiel, G. (1984). Effects of academic tutoring on the social status of low-achieving, socially-rejected children. *Child Development, 55*, 1465–1478.

Coie, J. D., & Kupersmidt, J. B. (1983). Behavioral analysis of emerging social status in boys' groups. *Child development, 54*, 1400–1416.

Coie, J. D., Dodge, K. A., & Coppotelli, H. (1982). Dimensions and types of social status: A cross-age perspective. *Developmental Psychology, 18*, 557–570.

Cowen, E., Pederson, A., Babigian, L., & Trost, M. (1973). Long-term follow-up of early detected vulnerable children. *Journal of Consulting and Clinical Psychology, 41*, 438–446.

Deysach, R. E., Keller, H. R., Ross, A. W., & Hiers, T. G. (1975). Social decentering and locus of control in children. *The Journal of Psychology, 90*, 229–235.

Dodge, K. A. (1983). Behavioral antecedents of peer social status. *Child Development, 54*, 1386–1399.

Dodge, K. A., Coie, J. D., & Bradde, N. P. (1982). Behavior patterns of socially rejected and neglected preadolescents: The roles of social approach and aggression. *Journal of Abnormal Child Psychology, 10*, 389–410.

Dodge, K. A., Schlundt, D. C., Schocken, I., & Delugach, J. D. (1983). Social competence and children's sociometric status: The role of peer group entry strategies. *Merrill-Palmer Quarterly, 29*, 309–336.

Erikson, E. (1963). *Childhood and society.* New York: Norton.

Foster, S., & Ritchey, W. (1979). Issues in the assessment of social competence in children. *Journal of Applied Behavior Analysis, 12*, 625–638.

Frentz, C. (1986). *Behavioral correlates of children's social competence: An investigation of two social skills classification models.* Unpublished manuscript, Louisiana State University, Baton Rouge, LA.

Gottlieb, J. (1975). Attitudes toward retarded children: Effects of labeling and behavioral aggressiveness. *Journal of Educational Psychology, 67*, 581–585.

Gottlieb, J., & Budoff, M. (1973). Social acceptability of retarded children in nongraded schools differing in architecture. *American Journal of Mental Deficiency, 78*, 15–19.

Gottlieb, J. (1981). Mainstreaming: Fulfilling the promise. *American Journal of Mental Deficiency, 86*, 115–126.

Gottlieb, J., & Leyser, Y. (1981). Facilitating the social mainstreaming of retarded children. *Exceptional Education Quarterly, 1*, 57–70.

Gottman, J. M. (1977). The effects of a modeling film on social isolation in preschool children: A methodological investigation. *Journal of Abnormal Child Psychology, 5*, 69–78.

Green, K. D., & Forehand, R. (1980). Assessment of children's social skills: A review of methods. *Journal of Behavioral Assessment, 2*, 143–159.

Green, K. D., Vosk, B., Forehand, R., & Beck, S. (1981). An examination of differences among sociometrically identified accepted, rejected, and neglected children. *Child Study Journal, 11*, 117–124.

Greenspan, S. (1981). Social competence and handicapped individuals: Practical implications and a proposed model. *Advances in Special Education, 3*, 41–82.

Gresham, F. M. (1981a). Assessment of children's social skills. *Journal of School Psychology, 19*, 120–133.

Gresham, F. M. (1981b). Social skills training with handicapped children: A review. *Review of Educational Research, 51*, 139–176.

Gresham, F. M. (1982a). Misguided mainstreaming: The case for social skills training with handicapped children. *Exceptional Children, 48*, 420–433.

Gresham, F. M. (1982b). Social skills instruction for exceptional children. *Theory Into Practice, 20*, 129–133.

Gresham, F. M. (1983a). Social skills assessment as a component of mainstreaming placement decisions. *Exceptional Children, 49*, 331–336.

Gresham, F. M. (1983b). Social validity in the assessment of children's social skills: Establishing standards for social competency. *Journal of Psychoeducational Assessment, 1*, 297–307.

Gresham, F. M. (1984). Social skills and self-efficacy for exceptional children. *Exceptional Children, 51*, 253–261.

Gresham, F. M. (1985a). Best practices in social skills training. In J. Grimes & A. Thomas (Eds.), *Best practices manual* (pp. 181–192). Cuyahoga Falls, OH: National Association of School Psychologists.

Gresham, F. M. (1985b). Utility of cognitive-behavioral procedures for social skills training with children: A review. *Journal of Abnormal Child Psychology, 13*, 411–423.

Gresham, F. M. (1986). Conceptual and definitional issues in the assessment of children's social skills: Implications for classification and training. *Journal of Clinical Child Psychology, 15*, 16–25.

Gresham, F. M., & Elliott, S. N. (1984). Assessment and classification of children's social skills: A review of methods and issues. *School Psychology Review, 13*, 292–301.

Gresham, F. M., & Elliott, S. N. (1987). The relationship between adaptive behavior and social skills. *Journal of Special Education, 21*, 167–182.

Gresham, F. M., & Elliott, S. N. (in preparation). *Social Skills Rating Scales.* Circle Pines, MN: American Guidance Service.

Gresham, F. M., & Lemanek, K. L. (1983). Social skills: A review of cognitive-behavioral training procedures with children. *Journal of Applied Developmental Psychology, 4*, 439–461.

Gresham, F. M., & Reschly, D. J. (1987). Dimensions of social competence: Method factors in the assessment of adaptive behavior, social skills, and peer acceptance. *Journal of School Psychology, 25*, 367–387.

Gronlund, H., & Anderson, L. (1963). Personality characteristics of socially accepted, socially neglected, and socially rejected junior high school pupils. In J. Seiderman (Ed.), *Educating for mental health.* New York: Crowell.

Grossman, H. J. (Ed.). (1983). *Classification in mental retardation.* Washington, DC: American Association on Mental Deficiency.

Harter, S. (1982). The perceived competence scale for children. *Child Development, 53*, 87–97.

Hartup, W. W. (1983). Peer relations: In P. Mussen (Series Ed.), & E. Heterington (Vol Ed.), *Handbook of child psychology, Vol. 4: Socialization, personality, and social development* (pp. 103–196). New York: Wiley.

Helsel, W. J., & Matson, J. L. (1984). The assessment of

depression in children: The internal structure of the Child Depression Inventory (CDI). *Behavior Therapy and Research, 22,* 289–298.

Hersh, R. H., & Walker, H. M. (1983). Great expectations: Making schools effective for all students. *Policy Studies Review, 2,* 147–188.

Hops, H., & Greenwood, C. R. (1981). Social skills deficits. In E. J. Mash & L. G. Terdal (Eds.), *Behavioral assessment of childhood disorders* (pp. 347–394). New York: Guilford Press.

Hughes, J. (1986). Methods of skill selection in social skills training: A Review. *Professional School Psychology, 1,* 235–248.

Kazdin, A. (1977). Assessing the clinical or applied importance of behavior change through social validation. *Behavior Modification, 1,* 427–451.

Kazdin, A., & Matson, J. (1981). Social validation in mental retardation. *Applied Research in Mental Retardation, 2,* 39–53.

Keogh, B., Kukic, S., Becker, L., McLoughlin, R., & Kukic, M. (1975). School psychologists' services in special education programs. *Journal of School Psychology, 13,* 142–146.

Kohlberg, L. (1969). Stage and sequence: The cognitive-developmental approach to socialization. In D. A. Goslin (Ed.), *Handbook of socialization theory and research.* Chicago: Rand McNally.

Kohn, M., & Clausen, J. (1955). Social isolation and schizophrenia. *American Sociological Review, 20,* 265–273.

Krehbiel, G. (1983). *Sociometric status and academic achievement-based differences in behavior and peer-assessed reputation.* Unpublished manuscript, Duke University.

Kurdek, L. A., & Krile, D. (1983). The relation between third- through eighth-grade children's social cognition and parents' ratings of social skills and general adjustment. *The Journal of Genetic Psychology, 143,* 201–206.

Ladd, G. W. (1981). Social networks of popular, average, and rejected children in school settings. *Merrill-Palmer Quarterly, 29,* 283–307.

Ladd, G. W., & Mize, J. A. (1983). A cognitive-social learning model of social skill training. *Psychological Review, 2,* 127–157.

MacMillan, D., Morrison, G., & Silverstein, A. (1980). Convergent and discriminant validity of Project PRIME's Guess Who? *American Journal of Mental Deficiency, 85,* 78–81.

McDowell, J. J. (1982). The importance of Herrnstein's mathematical statement of the Law of Effect for behavior therapy. *American Psychologist, 37,* 771–779.

McFall, R. M. (1982). A review and reformulation of the concept of social skills. *Behavioral Assessment, 4,* 1–33.

Nelson, R., & Hayes, S. (1979). Some current dimensions of behavioral assessment. *Behavioral Assessment, 1,* 1–16.

Oden, S. L., & Asher, S. R. (1977). Coaching children in social skills for friendship making. *Child Development, 48,* 496–506.

Pellegrini, D. S. (1985). Social cognition and competence in middle childhood. *Child Development, 56,* 253–264.

Piaget, J. (1952). *The moral judgment of the child.* New York: Collier.

Putallaz, M. (1983). Predicting children's sociometric status from their behavior. *Child Development, 54,* 1417–1426.

Renshaw, P. D., & Asher, S. R. (1983). Children's goals and strategies for social interaction. *Merrill-Palmer Quarterly, 29,* 353–374.

Reschly, D. J. (1982). Assessing mild mental retardation: The influence of adaptive behavior, sociocultural status, and prospects for nonbiased assessment. In C. R. Reynolds & T. B. Gutkin (Eds.), *Handbook of school psychology* (pp. 209–242). New York: Wiley Interscience.

Reschly, D. J., Gresham, F. M., & Graham-Clay, S. (1984). *Multi-factored nonbiased assessment: Convergent and discriminant validity of social and cognitive measures with black and white regular and special education students.* Washington, DC: United States Department of Education, Grant No. G0081101156, Assistance Catalog No. CFDA: 84-023E.

Reynolds, C., Gutkin, T., Elliott, S., & Witt, J. (1984). *School psychology: Essentials of theory and practice.* New York: Wiley.

Richard, B. A., & Dodge, K. A. (1982). Social maladjustment and problem-solving in school-aged children. *Journal of Consulting and Clinical Psychology, 50,* 226–233.

Roff, M. (1970). Some life history factors in relation to various types of adult maladjustment. In M. Ross & D. Ricks (Eds.), *Life history research in psychopathology.* Minneapolis, MN: University of Minnesota Press.

Roff, M., Sells, B., & Golden, M. (1972). *Social adjustment and personality adjustment in children.* Minneapolis, MN: University of Minnesota Press.

Rubin, K. H. (1982). Non-social play in preschoolers: Necessary evil? *Child Development, 53,* 651–657.

Rubin, K. H., & Daniels-Bierness, T. (1983). Concurrent and predictive correlates of sociometric status in kindergarten and grade 1 children. *Merrill-Palmer Quarterly, 29,* 337–351.

Salkind, N. (1981). *Theories of human development* (2nd ed.). New York: Wiley.

Schneider, B. H., & Byrne, B. M. (1985). Children's social skills training: A meta-analysis. In B. Schneider, K. Rubin, & J. Ledingham (Eds.), *Children's peer relations: Issues in assessment and intervention* (pp. 175–192). New York: Springer.

Seligman, M. (1975). *Helplessness: On depression, development, and death.* San Francisco: Freeman.

Skinner, B. F. (1953). *Science and human behavior.* New York: The Free Press.

Spivack, G., & Shure, M. (1974). *Social adjustment of young children.* San Francisco: Jossey-Bass.

Stephens, T. M. (1978). *Social skills in the classroom*. Columbus, Ohio: Cedars Press.
Stokes, T., & Baer, D. (1977). An implicit technology of generalization. *Journal of Applied Behavior Analysis, 19*, 349–367.
Stokes, T., & Osnes, P. (1986). Programming the generalization of children's social behavior. In P. Strain, M. Guralnick, & H. Walker (Eds.), *Children's social behavior: Development, assessment, and modification* (pp. 407–443). New York: Academic Press.
Strain, P. S., & Fox, J. (1981). Peers as behavior change agents for withdrawn classmates. In B. B. Lahey & A. E. Kazdin (Eds.), *Advances in clinical child psychology* (Vol. 4, pp. 167–198). New York: Plenum Press.
Strain, P. S., Cooke, R. P., & Apolloni, T. (1976). *Teaching exceptional children: Assessing and modifying social behavior*. New York: Academic Press.
Stumme, V. S., Gresham, F. M., & Scott, N. A. (1982). Validity of *Social Behavior Assessment* in discriminating emotionally disabled from nonhandicapped students. *Journal of Behavioral Assessment, 4*, 327–342.
Taylor, A., & Asher, S. (1984). Children's interpersonal goals in game situations. In G. Ladd (Chair), *From preschool to high school: Are children's interpersonal goals and strategies predictive of their social competence?* Symposium presented at the meeting of the American Educational Research Association, New Orleans, LA.
Thorndike, E. L. (1927). Intelligence and its uses. *Harper's Magazine, 140*, 227–235.
Tombari, M., & Bergan, J. (1978). Consultant cues and teacher verbalizations, judgments, and expectancies concerning children's adjustment problems. *Journal of School Psychology, 16*, 217–229.
Ullman, C. (1957). Teachers, peers, and tests as predictors of adjustment. *Journal of Educational Psychology, 48*, 257–267.
Van Houten, R. (1979). Social validation: The evolution of standards for competency for target behaviors. *Journal of Applied Behavior Analysis, 12*, 581–591.
Voeltz, L., & Evans, I. (1982). The assessment of behavioral interrelationships in child behavior therapy. *Behavioral Assessment, 4*, 131–166.
Vosk, B., Forehand, R., Parker, J. B., & Rickard, K. (1982). A multimethod comparison of popular and unpopular children. *Developmental Psychology, 18*, 795–805.
Walker, H. M., & Hops, H. (1976). Use of normative peer data as a standard for evaluating classroom treatment effects. *Journal of Applied Behavior Analysis, 9*, 159–168.
Walker, H., & Rankin, R. (1983). Assessing the behavioral expectations and demands of less restrictive settings. *School Psychology Review, 12*, 274–284.
Weiner, B. (1979). A theory of motivation for some classroom experiences. *Journal of Educational Psychology, 71*, 3–25.
Wheeler, V. A., & Ladd, G. W. (1982). Assessment of children's self-efficacy for social interactions with peers. *Developmental Psychology, 18*, 795–805.
White, R. (1959). Motivation reconsidered: The concept of competence. *Psychological Review, 66*, 287–333.
Witt, J. C., & Elliott, S. N. (1985). Acceptability of classroom intervention strategies. In T. R. Kratochwill (Ed.), *Advances in school psychology* (Vol. 4, pp. 251–288). Hillsdale; NJ: Erlbaum.
Wolf, M. M. (1978). Social validity: The case for subjective measurement or how applied behavior analysis is finding its heart. *Journal of Applied Behavior Analysis, 11*, 203–214.

CHAPTER 21

Biofeedback

Donald A. Williamson, Sandra J. McKenzie, and Anthony J. Goreczny

Clinical and educational applications of biofeedback emerged from basic research concerning operant conditioning of visceral responses (Engel & Chism, 1967; Engel & Hansen, 1966; Fowler & Kimmel, 1962; Kimmel & Hill, 1960). This basic research, which was begun in the early 1960s, showed that a wide variety of autonomic responses, for example, heart rate, blood pressure, vasomotor responses, and electrodermal responses, could be voluntarily controlled using instrumental conditioning procedures. This type of learning was demonstrated in humans and animals (Brown, 1970; DiCara & Miller, 1968a; Shapiro, Crider, & Tursky, 1964).

In the early 1970s a number of reports concerning the clinical application of biofeedback were published. These studies reported successful treatment of a variety of psychosomatic and medical disorders of adults, for example, tension headaches (Budzynski, Stoyva, & Adler, 1970) migraine headaches (Sargent, Green, & Walters, 1973), hypertension (Benson, Shapiro, & Tursky, 1971; Kristt & Engel, 1975; Patel, 1973), and circulation disorders (Blanchard & Haynes, 1975). From these initial studies, biofeedback was popularized and further research using much more controlled experimental methods was conducted. By 1986, biofeedback is commonly used for the treatment of a variety of medical, stress, and anxiety problems in adults. Furthermore, there is considerable controlled empirical evidence in support of the efficacy of these procedures (cf. Blanchard & Andrasik, 1982; Blanchard & Miller, 1977; Williamson, 1981).

Biofeedback applications with children have lagged far behind applications with adults. Basic research studying the extent to which children could learn to control visceral responses only emerged in the mid-to-late 1970s (Kator & Spires, 1975; Lynch, Hama, Kohn, & Miller, 1976). Reports of clinical and educational applications of biofeedback began to emerge in the late 1970s and early 1980s (Carlson, 1977; Hampstead, 1979; Labbé & Williamson, 1983, 1984; Omizo, 1980). At present, biofeedback has been reported in the treatment of several childhood medical problems, including pediatric headache, asthma, bladder dysfunction, and cerebral palsy. Also, biofeedback has been used for the remediation of educational and academic prob-

Donald A. Williamson, Sandra J. McKenzie, and Anthony J. Goreczny • Department of Psychology, Louisiana State University, Baton Rouge, Louisiana 70803.

lems, including attention deficit disorder, learning disabilities, and problems of handwriting. This chapter will present basic information about biofeedback learning in children and adolescents and review the literature concerning clinical and educational applications of biofeedback with children and adolescents.

Basic Research

Biofeedback Methodology

Biofeedback involves the presentation of a feedback signal that reflects changes in a physiological response. Typical responses used in biofeedback are skin temperature (measured from a finger), and electroencephalographic (EEG), or brainwave, responses. Feedback is generally produced using either visual or auditory stimuli that change proportionally to visual changes in the needle of a volt meter or a line graph on a computer display. Auditory feedback usually involves changes in the loudness or pitch of a tone. The subject is informed of the meaning of these feedback signals and is instructed to change the feedback signal in a particular direction, thus changing the physiological response in a particular direction. Relaxation or meditative procedures are often combined with biofeedback in order to assist the subject in learning to modify the response. Because of the common usage of relaxation approaches in conjunction with biofeedback, studies using relaxation will also be discussed in the section reviewing applications of biofeedback. Clinical biofeedback training typically involves at least eight one-hour training sessions.

Biofeedback Learning in Children

Most research concerning biofeedback learning in normal children has focused on the learning of skin temperature increases (handwarming) using skin temperature biofeedback. Initial studies (Dikel & Olness, 1980; Hunter, Russell, Russell, & Zimmerman, 1976; Lynch *et al.*, 1976; Suter & Loughry-Machado, 1981) were quite positive, showing that children could learn to warm their hands in as few as two sessions. Suter and Loughry-Machado (1981) found that children were better at handwarming than adults. However, later studies (Kelton & Belar, 1983; Suter, Fredricson, & Portuesi, 1983) failed to show the acquisition of handwarming in children. Using clinical subjects, that is, children migraineurs, Labbé and Williamson (1983, 1984) demonstrated significant increases of skin temperature for most subjects. Other clinical studies have also reported physiological data showing that children can learn to modify EMG (Walton, 1979) and EEG (Tansey & Bruner, 1983). However, these clinical studies did not include appropriate control groups (see Williamson & Blanchard, 1979b, for a discussion of this issue) and therefore no definitive conclusions can be drawn. Thus, at this time there is mixed data on the question of whether children can learn to control visceral responses using biofeedback. It is difficult to compare studies that have found positive results with those negative findings because studies conducted in different laboratories use very different methodologies. Research with adults has shown that procedural variables, such as type of feedback, sensitivity of feedback, delay of feedback, frequency of feedback, and instructions, significantly affect biofeedback learning (Faulstich, Williamson, & Jarrell, 1984; Williamson & Blanchard, 1979a, b). One variable that has never been adequately studied is age of the subject. Biofeedback investigations with children have used children as young as age six. This variable could be one of the significant factors affecting different findings in this area. Thus, there is ample data to conclude that under certain conditions, children and adolescents can learn to modify visceral responses using biofeedback. However, the variables that influence this learning have not been adequately studied in children.

Clinical Applications

Headache

Characteristics

Three types of headaches are common among children and adults: migraine, tension, and combined migraine-tension headache. The primary symptoms of these three types of headache are summarized in Table 1. Childhood migraine headaches are generally described as severe pulsating pain that is located either in the temple or forehead region on one side of the head (although it can occur on both sides of the head). Nausea and/or vomiting commonly occur with the headache. A minority of children report warning signs, for example, flashing lights or blind spots in their visual field that occur approximately 30 minutes prior to the headache.

Tension headaches are generally described as a dull, aching pain that is located across the forehead or around the head, for example, like a hat band that is too tight. Tension headaches are generally less severe than migraine and usually are not accompanied by nausea and vomiting. Over-the-counter medicines, for example aspirin, can usually be used to relieve these headaches.

Combined headache is quite rare among children but is more common in adolescents. Descriptions of combined headache generally involve reports of migraine and tension headaches. The child may report two distinctly different headaches or symptom features of both headaches that occur simultaneously.

Table 1. Diagnostic Characteristics for Migraine, Tension, and Combined Headache

Migraine headache
1. Headache is often one-sided, but may be bilateral
2. Pain is described as pulsating
3. Warning signs that a headache is about to begin
4. Nausea and/or vomiting accompany headache
5. Light and loud noises are very bothersome
6. Headache is relieved after rest
7. Family history of migraine
Tension headache
1. Headache is located across forehead or around head
2. Pain is described as a dull ache
3. No warning sign reported
4. No nausea or vomiting reported
5. Headache is more clearly stress-related
Combined headache
1. Symptom reports of both types of headache
2. Two types of headache may occur simultaneously or separately

Treatment

The literature concerning treatment of childhood migraine is much more well developed than that of tension and combined headache. All treatment studies of migraine headache have used autogenic feedback training, a combination of skin temperature biofeedback and a passive relaxation procedure (autogenic training). The first report of biofeedback treatment of childhood migraines was a single-group outcome study by Diamond and Franklin (1975). These investigators reported that 26 out of 32 treated cases responded to biofeedback therapy. Later, two single-case experiments, one involving two subjects (Andrasik, Blanchard, Edlund, & Rosenblum, 1982) and another involving three subjects (Labbé & Williamson, 1983) reported successful treatment of childhood migraine using skin temperature biofeedback. The Labbé and Williamson (1983) study reported continued improvement at 2-year follow-up. The only published controlled group outcome study for childhood migraine was reported by Labbé and Williamson (1984). In this study, 28 childhood migraineurs, aged 7 to 16 years, were randomly assigned to either a treatment group, autogenic feedback training, or a waiting-list control group. The results of this study are illustrated in Figure 1. As can be seen, biofeedback therapy was very effective in comparison to no treatment. At the end of treatment and at one-month follow-up, 93% of the treated subjects were clinically improved whereas only 7% of the untreated subjects were improved. As shown in Figure 1,

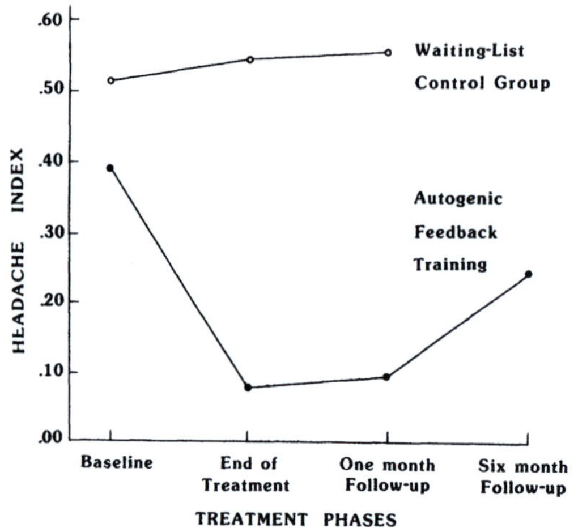

Figure 1. Treatment outcome data for skin temperature biofeedback (autogenic feedback training) treatment of childhood migraine (Labbé & Williamson, 1984).

there was a trend toward relapse at 6-month follow-up. However, 63% of the treated subjects remained clinically improved. These results have recently been replicated in a separate study by Andrasik *et al.* (1984), which is currently in progress. The results of these investigations are very promising. It appears that biofeedback treatment of childhood migraine is even more powerful than it is for adults. Most studies of adult migraine have reported improvement in 40% to 70% of treated subjects (Blanchard & Andrasik, 1982; Blanchard, Theobald, Williamson, Silver, & Brown, 1978; Williamson, 1981).

Only one study has reported biofeedback treatment of tension and combined headache in children (Werder & Sargent, 1984). In this single-group outcome study, 19 migraineurs, 10 tension headache subjects, and 2 combined headache subjects were treated using a combination of skin temperature and EMG biofeedback. The results of this study showed that biofeedback was effective for all three types of headache. Follow-up data at 1 and 2 years showed that improvement continued after treatment ended.

Summary

Treatment studies of headache in children have consistently shown that biofeedback is very effective. Typically, 75% reductions in headache activity have been reported at the end of treatment. Reports of follow-up have yielded inconsistent findings ranging from continued improvement to trends toward relapse. Overall these studies suggest that biofeedback may be a very useful modality of treatment for these disorders.

Asthma

Characteristics

Asthma in children and adolescents is a respiratory disorder involving obstruction of respiratory airways that can be attributed to many causes, ranging from bronchodilation to stress. The changes produced are brought about by spasmogens or some form of a vasoactive substance (e.g., histamine), usually in the process of an allergic reaction. Although the term *asthma* was originally used to refer to general problems of difficult breathing, it has now come to mean bronchial asthma. It is characterized by symptoms such as wheezing, coughing, and difficult breathing. Developmental research has shown that between 50% and 70% of all asthmatic children under age 16 will be asymptomatic within 10 years (Blair, 1977; Rachemanne & Edwards, 1952). Thus, it is possible that much of childhood asthma is intrinsic (i.e., asthma that is not caused by any known circumscribed stimulus). This conclusion has been supported by Ford (1968). He found that of asthmatics under age 14, 60% had intrinsic asthma whereas of those over age 14, only 20% had intrinsic asthma.

Although the disorder often remits, while it is in the active phase it is very debilitating. Medical treatment of asthma most often uses drug therapy. Bronchodilators are the most commonly prescribed medications. However, corticosteroids are also widely used, especially in the treatment of severe cases. One of the reasons psychology began studying asthma is because of the negative side effects produced by these medications.

It has long been recognized that emotions play a large role in the initiation and exacerbation of asthma symptoms. As early as the 12th century, the physician Maimonides alluded to the role of emotions in asthma (Munter, 1968). Much research has been devoted to the specific effects of suggestion and emotions in asthma and to the effect that these may have in its treatment. Several studies have shown that many asthmatics will respond with increased respiratory resistance to the suggestion that a certain drug will produce bronchoconstriction even when the inhaled drug is only an inert placebo (Luparello, Lyons, Bleecker, & McFadden, 1968; Phillip, Wilde, & Day, 1974). Thus, psychological factors may be involved in the etiology and treatment of asthma.

Treatment

It is generally well recognized that anxiety plays a major role in asthma. Biofeedback approaches to the treatment of asthma have centered around the use of biofeedback as a means of reducing the associated anxiety in expectation that the reduced anxiety would lead to more effective breathing and fewer asthmatic attacks.

In one study (Davis, Saunders, Creer, & Chai, 1973), frontalis EMG biofeedback was combined with relaxation. The subjects were divided into three groups: Jacobsonian relaxation with biofeedback, Jacobsonian relaxation alone, and a no-treatment control group. Results showed that for severe asthmatics, there was no difference between the three groups. For the less severe asthmatics, however, Jacobsonian relaxation combined with biofeedback proved superior to the other groups. Jacobsonian relaxation alone did not differ from the control group.

A later study (Kotses, Glaus, Crawford, Edwards, & Scherr, 1976) attempted to identify the specific effects of EMG biofeedback. Results indicated that peak expiratory flow rates (PEFR) increased significantly for the group of children given true feedback whereas no changes were evidenced for a group given false feedback nor for the no-treatment control group. These studies suggest that EMG biofeedback may be a viable treatment for childhood asthma, though the mechanism of its action is unspecified. Unfortunately, the effects of EMG biofeedback on asthma have not been found to be of clinical significance. For this reason, it has not been widely adopted as a treatment for asthma.

Other forms of biofeedback have also been used. Feldman (1976) trained four asthmatic children to lower their respiratory resistance through biofeedback. The results from this study indicated that although peak flow measures remained unchanged, maximum mid-expiratory flow rate and total respiratory resistance improved significantly. Of particular interest was the illustration that changes in these measures were similar to changes brought about by Isoproterenol (a bronchodilator), through Isoproterenol did produce slightly better improvement. These results are confounded, however, by the problem that biofeedback and Isoproterenol treatments were intermixed, thereby leaving open the question of the relative efficacy of each.

An interesting use of biofeedback has been reported by Khan and his associates (Khan, 1974a, b; Khan, 1977; Khan, Staerk, & Bonk, 1974). Khan's theory is one of conditioning. According to conditioning theory, anxiety and/or stress can precipitate an asthma attack. As asthma attacks occur they become conditioned to environmental stimuli associated with the attacks. These stimuli may be a specific circumscribed stimulus or the conditioning may have generalized to many different stimuli (Dekker, Pelsey, & Groen, 1957; Konig & Godfrey, 1973). As conditioning progresses, more and more environmental stimuli come to elicit attacks.

Khan's method of treating asthma has been to attempt to countercondition the asthmatic reaction. This counterconditioning involves two phases and the use of airway resistance biofeedback. The first phase consists of from five to eight sessions. During each of these sessions, baseline forced expiratory volume (FEV) readings are first established. Then the subject is asked to decrease airway resistance and is given feedback concerning how well they have done. The subject is expected to decrease airway resistance by 2% during each of three trials within the session, thus a total of 6% by the end of the session. The subject receives praise for each successful attempt. If a subject has not achieved a 6% decrease by the end of the third session, the subject receives small doses of a bronchodilator. The dosage level is gradually decreased over the next three sessions until in Session 8, no drug is given.

During the second phase, which lasts for 10 sessions, mild bronchoconstriction is induced by one of several methods: recall of a previous asthmatic attack, listening to an audiotape of a wheezing person, inhalation of a bronchoconstrictor, or one of several other methods. After elicitation of an attack, the subject is asked to attempt to relax and to decrease respiratory resistance. The subject is given visual feedback of this resistance. If unable to decrease the resistance within 10 minutes, the subject is given a few inhalations of a bronchodilator. The session ends when the subject reaches baseline FEV levels.

Khan, Staerk, & Bonk (1974) found that a group treated in this manner was significantly improved (i.e., took lower amounts of medication, had a lower number of emergency room visits and had fewer asthmatic attacks) in comparison to a no-treatment control group. However, attempts to replicate these findings have failed (Danker, Miklich, Pratt, & Creer, 1975; Khan, 1977). Therefore, the efficacy of this procedure is currently in question.

Summary

In studies using EMG biofeedback, biofeedback has been found to produce improved respiration in comparison to control groups, though changes in peak expiratory flow rate (PEFR) have been disappointingly low. The amount of change produced by biofeedback treatments range from 2% to about 5%. An increase of about 15% is usually required before any clinically meaningful changes are evident.

Respiratory resistance biofeedback has not fared much better. Feldman (1976) was able to produce large changes in pulmonary functioning measures but biofeedback treatment was confounded with bronchodilator treatment. Conditioning treatment using airway resistance biofeedback initially yielded positive results, but later studies were unable to replicate the findings.

The studies involved in biofeedback treatment of asthma have many shortcomings. Usually no follow-up data are presented. Most studies use either PEFR or FEV in order to assess treatment effectiveness. Both of these measures are effort dependent. What these studies may actually be measuring is subject compliance instead of pulmonary functioning. More importantly, the dependent measures are quite often not clinically relevant. If one has not decreased emergency room visits, asthma attacks, or medication usage, a 5% or 10% or even 30% increase in pulmonary functioning is meaningless. Finally, the theoretical framework that attributes asthma attacks to anxiety has recently been questioned. Instead of anxiety causing the asthma attacks, it may be that the life-threatening and frightening experience of an asthma attack causes the anxiety. All of these problems coupled with poor treatment outcome suggest that biofeedback has not been shown to be clinically efficacious for the treatment of asthma.

In contrast, other behavior modification approaches have yielded consistently positive results (Garner, 1968; Lazar & Jedliczka, 1979). Treatment programs in this area attempt to remove any positive consequences that may have been associated with the exhibition of asthmatic symptoms (e.g., avoiding school or interpersonal conflict and receiving extra attention and special care). However, controlled group outcome studies of these approaches are needed before definitive conclusions can be drawn.

Bladder Incontinence

Characteristics

Bladder incontinence has traditionally been treated strictly by medical intervention. However, due to recent advances in technology and the lack of response to medical intervention by some bladder incontinent children, urodynamic biofeedback has recently become a viable treatment procedure. Urodynamic feedback in children has been restricted to those children who exhibit bladder-sphincter dyssynergia, a learned phenomena involving lack of coordination between the bladder and the urethral sphincter muscle. In normal micturition the bladder contracts and the sphincter relaxes. In spincter dyssynergic patients, both the sphincter and bladder contract.

Factors believed to play a role in the etiology of sphincter dyssynergia include bladder infections, surgery, and harsh toilet training. Urinary tract infections and surgeries are often very painful and can produce pain upon urination. Thus, a child with a history of urinary tract infections may come to associate pain with urination. The child then learns to contract the sphincter muscles in order to avoid pain. The association between contraction of sphincters and avoidance of pain is rapidly conditioned and may persist until treated.

In children whose parents employed harsh toilet training methods, the course is very similar. Children from this background usually are faced with strong punishment and disapproval when they accidentally urinate. Because punishment and disapproval have become associated with urination, children will do most anything to avoid urinating. Many children utilize a squatting posture, which results in contraction of the adductors in the thigh and eventually leads to sphincter tension and contraction.

The long-term effects of sphincter dyssynergia include frequent urination, urinary retention, and enuresis. The contraction of the sphincter does not allow the bladder to void completely. The urinary retention leads to frequent urination because the bladder fills more quickly. It is believed that the sphincter tension leads to enuresis as well. After micturition, an inappropriate relaxation of the sphincter will occur. This, of course, leads to the release of the residual urine. Urine that is not properly released remains in the bladder and can then cause cystitis or other urinary tract infections. This tends to reinforce the maladaptive learning pattern of the child.

Bodily changes occur that accompany the prolonged contraction of the sphincter. Because of the prolonged contraction, a large amount of resistance is encountered during voiding. As a result, the bladder becomes enlarged and layers of supportive tissue build up. This thickening of the bladder leads to increased irritability of the bladder (and therefore an increase in spasms), which then constitutes another possible mechanism of enuresis.

Treatment

Because sphincter dyssynergia is considered to be a learned response, it is generally believed that one can unlearn this response and that a child can be retrained to perform the appropriate response. Urodynamic biofeedback has been used in this process of retraining. Urodynamic biofeedback usually involves the feedback of two signals to the child: urethral sphincter electromyogram (EMG) and urinary flow rates. The dyssynergic response is one in which urinary flow and EMG levels increase. The child is instructed to relax the muscles during micturition, thereby producing the synergystic pattern and allowing the urine to flow unobstructed.

Medical interventions include urethral dilation, pudendal or sacral nerve blocks, sphincterotomy, and pharmacotherapy aimed at relaxing the sphincter muscle. Often sphincter dyssynergic children are refractory to these medical interventions. It is usually after these procedures have been tried and have not worked that biofeedback is attempted. The general procedure is to admit the child to a hospital setting in a private room. Initially therapy is conducted on an inpatient basis and outpatient follow-up sessions are then scheduled. The child is usually taken off of all drugs and then administered some type of water diuresis, causing the child to void very frequently. Before biofeedback is attempted, however, urodynamic studies are performed in order to confirm the presence of sphincter dyssynergia. If sphincter dyssynergia is present, the child is educated about his or her problem and after the child understands the basis for treatment, biofeedback is begun.

In a single-case study attempting urodynamic biofeedback, Sugar (1983) treated a 13-year-old girl with whom neuropharmacologic agents had been ineffective. She had had numerous urinary tract infections and a history of daytime enuresis. After only 2 days of intensive biofeedback, the subject demonstrated a normal synergistic voiding pattern. Several outpatient biofeedback sessions were conducted and after one year, the subject was free from urinary tract infections and was no longer incontinent.

In another single-case study, Libo, Arnold, Woodside, Borden, and Hardy (1983) included urodynamic biofeedback as one part of a treatment regimen. Other treatment components included instructions to tense and relax alternatively noninvolved muscles, EMG biofeedback of noninvolved muscles (especially in the face and head), Kegel-type isometric exercises, and daily monitoring of urinary-related sensations, such as urgency, force, relaxation, and number of times of holding and releasing during urination. One other treatment procedure was to wake the child every evening before the child had a chance to urinate. This procedure was faded by having the child wake herself every 3 hours. Results indicated that over the next 4 to 7 months, an almost complete recovery was evidenced. At a 12-month follow-up, all gains had been maintained. Additionally, there was a concomitant return to a synergistic pattern of voiding. The authors reported that relief of the incontinence resulted in improvements in the child's daily behavior, academic performance, and self-esteem as well.

Somewhat disappointing results were obtained by Maizels, King, and Firlit (1979) in their treatment of three children with sphincter dyssynergia. Only one of the children could be classified as successfully treated. One other child was improved but continued to have some problems. Although the pattern of synergia had returned and urinary continence improved in this child, urinary frequency remained high. The third child was not helped at all by biofeedback. This child could recognize the dyssynergia but was unable to control it.

In the most elaborate study of urodynamic biofeedback done to date, Sugar and Firlit (1982) found that biofeedback facilitated the retraining of the synergistic pattern in 10 children who had been diagnosed as having dyssynergia. Long-term follow-up (6 to 19 months post biofeedback) showed that 8 of the 10 had been completely relieved of incontinence whereas the other two were moderately improved. One of these two exhibited cessation of all symptoms except for stress incontinence (incontinence due to bodily strain, such as coughing, or some sudden voluntary movement). The other had a reduction in incontinency from four times per day to only one or two times per day. Even though dyssynergia continued with this child, nocturnal enuresis had ceased.

Summary

Urodynamic biofeedback has been shown to be very effective in three of four studies reviewed and moderately effective in the other one. However, the field is relatively new and some questions remain concerning its use. No controlled group outcome study has been reported. The studies reported leave open the possibility that other factors, such as maturation and the therapy process itself, may have been responsible for the improvement. Although it is obvious that urodynamic biofeedback is effective in treating some dyssynergic children, future research must use more controlled experimental methodology and should attempt to identify those most likely to be helped by biofeedback.

Cerebral Palsy

Characteristics

Cerebral Palsy is a descriptive term applied to a number of nonprogressive motor disorders. The term is not a diagnosis, but it provides a useful classification for children with motor disorders resulting from gestational or perinatal central nervous system damage and with an impairment of voluntary movement. A number of cerebral palsy syndromes have been described and four general categories have evolved. *Spastic* syndromes are the most common and are characterized by sudden, violent, involuntary contractions. *Athetoid* syndromes are less common and are characterized by slow, writhing, involuntary movements in the extremities (athetoid) or the proximal parts of the limbs and the trunk (dystonic). *Ataxic* syndromes are relatively uncommon and are characterized by weakness, incoordination, and a wide-based gait. *Mixed* syndromes are common; most often, spasticity and athetosis are present together; less often, ataxia and athetosis are present.

There are a number of disorders associated with cerebral palsy that cause the individual to be more incapacitated. Convulsive seizures occur in as many as 25% of patients, especially those with involvement of both limbs on one side (hemiplegia). Mental retardation is also commonly associated and afflicts children with spastic quadriplegia (involvement of all limbs) and mixed forms of cerebral palsy to the greatest degree.

Damage to the motor areas of the brain (particularly the cortex, the basal ganglia of the cerebrum, and the cerebellum), may occur during fetal life, birth, or infancy. Most cerebral palsy victims have at least some damage in all three areas. Anatomical alteration may impair the perception and the integration of sensory information derived from visual, vestibular, proprioceptive, tactile, and pressure receptors normally used for postural orientation.

Treatment

Physical therapy, occupational therapy, bracing orthopedic surgery, and speech training may all be required in the treatment of these individuals. Biofeedback techniques have also been applied to impaired sensorimotor function. Biofeedback concerning movement, tension levels, and postural orientation must be provided to the child through an intact sensory receptor channel. The rationale for biofeedback training in children with cerebral palsy is that systematic, immediate, continual sensory information should augment the child's attempt to consciously control sensory and motor systems.

Electromyographic biofeedback has been utilized to reduce levels of muscle tension in the afflicted arms of cerebral palsy patients. Finley, Etherton, Dickman, Karimian, and Simpson (1981) trained 15 cerebral-palsy children of both sexes to reduce EMG and obtain muscular relaxation with biofeedback procedures. The children had mostly spastic involvement and had varying levels of intelligence. Frontal and forearm flexor EMG was measured during three, 20- to 30-minute baseline recordings prior to biofeedback. Ten children were provided with immediate reinforcement (tangible items such as toys or candy) during feedback training and five children were given feedback without immediate reinforcement. The results of this study showed that all children were able to reduce EMG levels with feedback although those children receiving immediate reinforcement had greater reductions and learning progressed more rapidly. However, the degree to which these children may have been able to reduce tension levels without biofeedback cannot be determined from this data in that no control condition was included.

Several studies have utilized head position training as a biofeedback technique with cerebral-palsied children (Halpern *et al.*, 1970; Maloney, 1980; Wooldridge & Russell, 1976). Although these studies varied in terms of experimental sophistication, the results were encouraging. In a study designed to improve motor performance, Halpern *et al.* (1970) selected 14 children on the basis that poor head posture and poor control of neck muscles were prominent features of their motor difficulties. Four mechanical devices designed to keep the head erect were utilized for training. Positive reinforcement was provided by praise and rewards; negative reinforcement was provided by resistance of the head halter. Positive results were obtained following 6 months of training. Wooldridge and Russell (1976) provided visual and auditory feedback of sagittal and frontal tilt utilizing a head position trainer with mercury switches. Audible feedback was provided when the child moved out of a certain range. The researchers were able to train 6 of 12 individuals to keep their heads within normal ranges. Of the remaining six, three children evidenced learning (maintenance following removal of feedback) and three children evidenced learning in the clinic (some improvement but only with feedback). Although encouraging, these data must be interpreted cautiously. Assessment and training methods varied with the demands of each individual and no experimental control was utilized. However, the clinical utility of this procedure may warrant further investigation. Maloney (1980) utilized a simplified version of a head-control device with six cerebral palsy children and two control children. In spite of the small number of subjects, statistically significant group differences were obtained after training. Advantages of the simplified device include versatility (measures feedback in all directions), portability (can be used in the school, home, or clinic), and relatively low cost of the feedback equipment.

Summary

The efficacy of biofeedback for treating cerebral palsy victims is yet to be firmly established. Although children have been shown to reduce tension levels and control postural orientation, most of the research to date has been uncontrolled. Investigations of biofeedback with larger numbers of subjects and greater experimental control are necessary before definitive utility can be established. Research to date has indicated that the time necessary to teach these individuals the biofeedback procedures may prohibit their general clinical utility.

Educational Applications of Biofeedback

Attention Deficit Disorder

Characteristics

Children displaying signs of developmentally inappropriate inattention and impulsivity have been labeled with a wide variety of terms since 1960. These terms have ranged from Hyperkinesis and Minimal Brain Dysfunction to Attention Deficit Disorder

(ADD) with Hyperactivity (American Psychiatric Association, 1980). According to DSM-III, the essential features of this disorder include inattention (easily distracted and difficulty concentrating on tasks requiring sustained attention), impulsivity (acting without thinking and shifting from one activity to another), and overactivity (difficulty sitting still and excessive running and climbing). Attention Deficit Disorder without Hyperactivity is the correct diagnosis if overactivity is not present. However, attention deficit disorder with hyperactivity is a common disorder in prepubertal children. Belmont (1980) has reported that one to three percent of kindergarten through ninth-grade children demonstrate hyperactive behavior. This prevalence rate translates to 2.5 million children, between the ages of 5 and 14, in the United States.

The problems of ADD children create one of the more perplexing situations faced by teachers and parents. Hyperactive children typically perform poorly in school and create frequent interruptions of regular class activities. Because of the inability to control their behavior, hyperactive children are unable to inhibit impulsive behavior or to exhibit prolonged concentration. Despite average intelligence levels, academic achievement is commonly substandard in these children because diffused attention and distractibility prevent them from learning and reaching their intellectual potential (Werry, 1968). Learning disabilities have been found to occur in 50% to 80% of hyperactive children and as many as 60% to 70% of these children can be expected to fail one or more grades in school by the time they reach their teens (Lambert & Sandoval, 1980). Thus, the magnitude of the problems associated with hyperactivity cannot be overemphasized.

Treatment

Numerous therapeutic interventions, ranging from chemotherapy to manipulations of the environment, have been used to treat the hyperactive child (Wunderlich, 1973). Although drug therapy has tended to be the most frequent form of treatment, earlier research concluded that medication was worthwhile for approximately one half to one third of ADD children (Freedman, 1971). The most common drugs employed have been (a) psychostimulants; (b) tricyclics; and (c) neuroleptics. There are a number of concerns related to drug therapy with hyperactive children. First, side effects have been experienced by approximately one third of the children given drugs to control their hyperactivity (Firestone, Poitras-Wright, & Douglas, 1978). Problems include loss of appetite, sleeplessness, depression, withdrawal, cardiac changes, and retardation of height and weight gain. Additional concerns related to drug therapy include the lack of a long-term effect on the child's school performance, peer relationships, and social problems.

Environmental and curriculum modifications have also been utilized as treatment approaches for hyperactivity. Environmental manipulations involve making adjustments in the environment that is thought to cause the excessive stimulating behavior. Curriculum manipulations may include adjusting the amount of work and the rate at which the child is expected to complete assigned work. Setting short-term tasks and goals has also been recommended by many educators.

Although various drugs and behavior modification techniques have been used to increase attention span (Barkley, 1976) and improve behavior ratings (Pelham, Schneider, Bologna, & Contreras, 1980), none have proven to be exceedingly effective in enhancing academic performance (O'Leary, 1980). It has been hypothesized that drug therapy and behavior modification techniques are ineffective in improving academic achievement because they rely on an external agent to produce behavior change. Nowicki and Strickland (1973) demonstrated that academic achievement is inversely correlated with an external locus of control. Carlson (1977) reported preliminary evidence indicating that electromyographic (EMG) biofeedback seems to shift locus of control internally. Based on this rationale, researchers have begun utilizing biofeedback training as a method of increasing perceptions of self-control with hyperactive children. Numerous studies have been conducted to determine whether biofeedback procedures are effective for increasing internal locus of control, improving academic achievement, and producing motor inhibition in hyperactive children.

Electromyographic (EMG) biofeedback and biofeedback-assisted relaxation training have been the most widely investigated forms of treatment of ADD. Sensorimotor rhythm (SMR) training has also been investigated as a treatment approach for hyperactivity. All of these psychophysiological treatment methods are designed to help hyperactive children gain control over excessive and distractive motor behaviors and to maintain attention in learning situations.

Various studies have been conducted to investigate the effects of EMG biofeedback and relaxation training on hyperactivity and its behavioral concomitants. Hampstead (1979) studied the effects of EMG biofeedback alone and EMG biofeedback coupled with verbal feedback. EMG levels were measured across sessions and found to decrease for both groups. Although the number of children included in the study was small, significant correlations between decreased EMG levels and parent and teacher ratings of behavior were obtained for five of the six children. Hughes, Henry, and Hughes (1980) employed a single-case withdrawal design with three children evidencing activity level problems. Each child was reinforced for both increasing and decreasing EMG levels during auditory feedback. Measures of frontal EMG, percent time on task, and motoric activity rate were obtained during each session. In addition, parent ratings of problem behavior in the home were recorded daily. Results of this study corroborate those of Hampstead (1979), in that each child was able to reduce muscle tension with EMG biofeedback. In addition, academic performance and problem behavior improved with reductions in EMG activity. These studies provided preliminary evidence for the efficacy of EMG feedback as a potential treatment for hyperactivity.

Several controlled group outcome studies have investigated EMG biofeedback and biofeedback-assisted relaxation procedures. Omizo and colleagues have systematically investigated the effects of biofeedback and relaxation on measures of self-concept, locus of control, and teacher and parent behavior ratings, as well as reading and language improvement. In an early study, Omizo (1980) demonstrated that three sessions of relaxation and biofeedback training were effective in reducing EMG activity and increasing five factors of self-concept (as measured by the Dimensions of Self-Concept Scale). Locus of control was added as a dependent measure in a further investigation of biofeedback-assisted relaxation (Omizo, 1980) and again group differences were significant. The group receiving biofeedback evidenced greater internal locus of control and higher level of aspiration scores. Improved parent and teacher behavior ratings were also obtained after biofeedback-assisted relaxation training (Omizo, 1981).

Utilizing the same experimental procedure, Omizo and Michael (1982) measured impulsivity and attention to task in hyperactive children. Again, differences were found between the experimental and no-treatment groups. Measures of academic achievement were included in a further study of biofeedback-assisted relaxation (Denkowski, Denkowski, & Omizo, 1983). Posttreatment measures of reading and language achievement, as measured by the Iowa Test of Basic Skills, showed that the biofeedback group was superior to the control group. The groups also differed on measures of self-esteem and locus of control. In order to determine the extent to which the dependent measures used in this series of studies correlated with the posttreatment EMG levels, Denkowski, Denkowski, & Omizo (1984) entered the cumulative data of several studies into a multiple regression analysis. Locus of control was found to account for

72% of the variance between the experimental and control groups. These researchers concluded that not only is biofeedback-assisted relaxation more effective with "internals" but that its procedures themselves encourage an internal shift in locus of control. Although this finding was repeatedly demonstrated in this series of studies, the increases in academic achievement have not yet been replicated and must be considered tentative at this time.

In addition to EMG biofeedback, sensorimotor rhythm training has been utilized in investigations of hyperactivity. Previous research has suggested a strong relationship between sensorimotor rhythm of 12 Hz to 14 Hz and motor inhibition. In an investigation of the potential therapeutic value of SMR training for hyperactivity, Lubar and Shouse (1976) trained an 11-year-old child to increase 12 Hz to 14 Hz activity and to decrease 4 Hz to 7 Hz activity. Electroencephalographic (EEG) activity was monitored during a no-drug phase, a drug-only phase, and during sensorimotor rhythm training. These investigators showed that SMR training to increase 12 Hz to 14 Hz activity was correlated with decreases in EMG levels and produced improvement in six classroom behaviors related to hyperactivity. This improvement was greater than that observed during the drug-only phase. In a later single-case experiment, Tansey and Bruner (1983) utilized serial application of EMG and SMR biofeedback training with a 10-year-old male presenting with ADD with hyperactivity, developmental reading disorder, and ocular instability. Modification of this child's hyperactivity was accomplished using EMG biofeedback and SMR training effectively remediated the child's reading problems. Lubar and Lubar (1984) reported a single-group outcome study investigating EEG biofeedback of SMR and beta EEG activity for treatment of attention deficit disorders. Six children were provided with long-term biofeedback consisting of two sessions per week for 10 to 27 months. Feedback was provided for either increasing 12 Hz to 15 Hz SMR or 16 Hz to 20 Hz beta activity. Treatment also consisted of combining the feedback with academic training to improve attention. All six children demonstrated improvement in either school grades or achievement test scores and none of the children required medication for hyperactive behavior following treatment. Although encouraging, these results must be interpreted cautiously. First, treatment was of considerable length and may be of little value outside of a clinical setting. Second, the relative contributions of feedback and academic remediation are not discernable in this study. Overall, it has been demonstrated that children can control sensorimotor rhythm, activity, and movement with biofeedback training. However, the degree to which this training affects specific hyperactive behaviors has yet to be established. Research of a more controlled nature must be conducted before EEG biofeedback can be viewed as an effective treatment for hyperactivity.

Summary

From these studies one can conclude that biofeedback and relaxation procedures may have some utility in the remediation of ADD. Studies utilizing EEG biofeedback have been mixed in terms of methodologial procedures, samples studied, and results obtained. Further studies employing rigorous experimental procedures are needed before efficacy of this approach can be concluded. Investigations utilizing EMG biofeedback and biofeedback-assisted relaxation have been more conclusive. Children of varying ages have been trained to reduce levels of muscle tension and associated reductions in activity level have been obtained. Various behavior ratings have been shown to change with treatment, in home and school settings, in the desired direction. Although internal locus of control has been shown to increase, associated improvement in academic achievement has been shown in only one study. Further studies designed to assess changes in academic achievement are necessary before biofeedback-assisted relaxation can be considered a treatment for hyperactive children with educational benefits.

Educational Problems of Children Diagnosed as Learning Disabled, Emotionally Disabled, or Mentally Retarded

Characteristics

One use of biofeedback for more traditional educational goals has been as a stress reduction procedure for learning disabled children, mentally retarded children, and children with emotional disorders. Although each of the disorders are distinctly different, it is generally recognized that children in all of the groups have difficulty in a regularly structured classroom and many of these children display such problems as distractibility and impulsivity.

Although no consistent definition has been used when referring to emotionally disturbed children, Stumme, Gresham, and Scott (1982) defined emotional disturbance as "a behavioral disorder in which situationally inappropriate behavior, observed in a school setting, interferes with the learning process, interpersonal relationships, or personal adjustment of the pupil" (p. 327). The principal difference between emotional disturbance and learning disability is the emphasis, in the latter condition, on behavioral problems that are primarily nonacademic. Although emotionally disturbed children may have learning difficulties, their major problem is a behavioral one, such as trouble controlling their anger.

A learning disabled child, on the other hand, is a child who has average to superior intelligence but whose achievement is much below his or her expected level. Mentally retarded individuals are those whose intelligence and adaptive functioning are both impaired. In order to be classified by DSM-III as mentally retarded, the student's IQ must be below 70.

Treatment

EMG biofeedback has been the primary treatment used for these children. Very few studies have been conducted in this area and those that have been reported have many methodological flaws.

A predominant characteristic among these children is that they are bothered by excessive muscle tension and high anxiety levels (Carter & Russell, 1980; Carter, Lax, & Russell, 1979; Omizo & Williams, 1982; Walton, 1979). It is presumed that this high level of tension and general anxiety interfere with the learning process. This assumption is consistent with the well-established theory proposed by Yerkes and Dodson (1908), which states that after anxiety reaches a certain level, any additional anxiety results in a decrement in performance. Thus, the rationale behind biofeedback and biofeedback-induced relaxation is to reduce the anxiety, thereby decreasing the interference this anxiety has on academic performance.

Walton (1979) combined EMG biofeedback training outside of the classroom with several different relaxation training procedures during class in the treatment of five emotionally disturbed children. The dependent measure of this study was classroom-inappropriate behaviors (e.g., out of seat behavior, off-task, verbal motor). Of five treated subjects, three had reductions in their inappropriate behavior of 65% or more. Additionally, mean EMG levels were significantly reduced from pre- to posttreatment. Although these results are impressive, no control group was included and the small sample size limits the conclusions that can be drawn.

In a study comparing taped relaxation instructions to EMG biofeedback in educably mentally retarded children, Carter *et al.* (1979) found that although the EMG biofeedback group had significant pre- to posttreatment changes on a number of variables (including Slosson IQ, WRAT-Reading Subtest, Bender-Gestalt, auditory memory tasks, and handwriting legibility), children in the taped relaxation group had significant pre- to posttreatment differences only in handwriting legibility. However, comparisons between the groups showed differences on only the Bender-Gestalt.

In one of the best controlled studies concerning learning disabled children (Omizo & Williams, 1982), biofeedback-induced relaxation was effective in reducing attention to task and impulsivity measures when compared with a no-treatment control group. However, no measures of academic performance were presented.

Summary

EMG biofeedback has been used in the treatment of anxiety problems related to academic achievement. The studies that have been reported have yielded promising results. However, all of the studies have methodological flaws that limit their interpretability. Many of the studies used biofeedback as only one component of a treatment package including handwriting training (Carter & Russell, 1980) or some form of relaxation training (Carter *et al.*, 1979; Omizo & Williams, 1982; Walton, 1979). Therefore, it is impossible to determine how much of the treatment effect is due to biofeedback as compared to the other technique and to the interaction between the two. Future research should focus on this problem in order to help make the determination. A second problem, applying to most of the studies, is the lack of a relevant control group. Finally, none of the investigations reported long-term follow-up data. Thus, at this time there is no solid experimental evidence that biofeedback has educational value with emotionally disturbed, learning disabled, or mentally retarded children.

Handwriting Problems

Characteristics

Although the development of legible handwriting is a major objective in the school system, not all children are able to learn to write legibly with standardized instruction. Typically, cursive handwriting is taught via a programmed format beginning with letter formation and progressing to formation of words, sentences, and paragraphs of uniform size and with uniform spacing. For those children who are unable to learn handwriting skills in this manner, other methods, such as training in perceptual motor areas and eye-hand coordination (Barsch, 1967; Frostig & Horne, 1964), have typically been utilized.

Treatment

More recently, methods to improve handwriting skills have focused on procedures that teach children to relax and develop a sense of self-control. For example, Carter and Synolds (1974) administered relaxation training (via audiocassette) to 32 boys who were in special classes for minimally brain-injured children. An equal number of randomly selected age mates were chosen as no-treatment controls. Training consisted of about 7 minutes of instructions on how to relax and was administered to the experimental group 3 days per week for 4 weeks. The children were asked to copy a short paragraph from a chalk board immediately following each relaxation session. The results showed that relaxation training was effective in enhancing the quality of handwriting and that the effects were stable over time. A transfer effect to nonexperimental situations was also observed.

Relaxation training and electromyographic (EMG) biofeedback procedures have also been investigated with children of average intelligence who have poor handwriting. Jackson and Hughes (1978) studied the effects of relaxation on handwriting in fourth grade children. Ten subjects rated as having poor handwriting were included in an experimental treatment group. Ten additional subjects rated as having poor handwriting were included in an experimental control group. A normal control group consisting of 10 children rated as having average handwriting was also included. Only the experimental treatment group received relaxation training, the other groups received an equal number of sessions that involved listening to handwriting instruction given verbally. Handwriting samples were obtained prior to training and immediately following training. Samples of handwriting were rated using the procedures reported by Jackson and Hughes (1978). They found that the experimental treatment group evidenced significantly greater improvement than the experimental control group on each of the five characteristics of handwriting and significantly more improvement than the normal control group on four of the characteristics. The two control groups did not differ. These results supported the efficacy of relaxation as remediation for poor handwriting.

Later, Hughes, Jackson, DuBois, and Erwin (1979) examined the effects of EMG biofeedback training on cursive handwriting using a single-group outcome study. Subjects included four girls and five boys in the fourth grade. Each child was given nine sessions of frontal EMG biofeedback. The procedures developed by Jackson and Hughes (1978) were utilized for analysis of handwriting in this study as well. Pre- and posttreatment measures of handwriting were obtained, but no control group was used. These researchers showed a reduction in muscle tension as well as an improvement in four of the five characteristics of handwriting. Because no control group was included in this study, it is impossible to discern whether treatment effects were due to EMG biofeedback training or other factors, for example, practice or other instructions.

Summary

Two studies conducted by Jackson and colleagues have shown that significant improvements in handwriting can be accomplished using relaxation or EMG biofeedback. However, the procedures utilized by Jackson include suggestions for handwriting improvement as well as self-control instructions. Therefore, it is not clear that biofeedback or relaxation are the principal treatment methods of this treatment package. However, these results are encouraging and should be pursued by other researchers in order to determine their replicability.

Conclusions

Research concerning the application of biofeedback procedures to clinical and educational problems of children has emerged only in the past 10 years. Although much of the research is uncontrolled, some tentative conclusions can be drawn. It appears that older children and adolescents can generally learn to modify a variety of physiological responses, including skin temperature, EMG, and EEG. Data concerning the clinical application of these procedures is very encouraging. For childhood migraine, skin temperature biofeedback combined with autogenic training appears to be very effective for the majority of children treated. Several controlled and uncontrolled studies have shown these therapeutic effects. For bladder incontinence and cerebral palsy, a number of uncontrolled experiments have shown significant improvement to result from the use of EMG biofeedback and urodynamic biofeedback. More controlled research in these areas is needed. Biofeedback treatment of asthma has not yielded clinically significant results and it appears that biofeedback, as it has been used to date, is of little value in treating asthmatics.

Educational applications of biofeedback are very new. The most promising results have been reported with attention deficit disorder. A series of well-controlled studies have shown EMG biofeedback to increase internal locus of control in ADD children. Also, one controlled investigation found EMG biofeedback to improve measures of academic performance. Studies of EEG biofeedback as a treatment for ADD have been uncontrolled, though they have yielded positive results. Studies of biofeedback-assisted relaxation as a treatment for anxiety and tension associated with emotionally disabled, learning disabled, and mentally retarded children have been of relatively poor quality and very little solid evidence has been presented that it offers much promise. Relaxation and biofeedback as treatments for problems of handwriting have been found to be useful in several short-term experiments. However, definitive conclusions about the educational significance of these findings cannot be made given available research.

In conclusion, biofeedback does have a place in the treatment of a variety of clinical and educational problems of childhood and adolescence. What is now needed in most areas of research are more controlled investigations that evaluate the clinical or educational impact of these biofeedback procedures. Until these investigations are completed we can conclude only that biofeedback has promise but lacks extensive empirical validation.

References

American Psychiatric Association. (1980). *Diagnostic and statistical manual of mental disorders.* Washington, DC: Author.

Andrasik, F., Attanasio, V., Blanchard, E. B., Burke, E., Kapela, E., McCarrin, M., Blake, D. D., & Rosenblum, E. L. (1984, November). *Behavioral treatment of Pediatric Migraine Headache.* Paper presented at the annual meeting of the Association for Advancement of Behavior Therapy, Philadelphia, PA.

Andrasik, F., Blanchard, E. B., Edlund, S. R., & Rosenblum, E. L. (1982). Autogenic feedback in the treatment of two children with migraine headache. *Child and Family Behavior Therapy, 4,* 13–23.

Barkley, R. A. (1976). Predicting the response of hyperkinetic children to stimulant drugs: A review. *Journal of Abnormal Child Psychology, 4,* 327–348.

Barsch, R. (1967). *Achieving Perceptual Motor Efficiency.* Seattle, WA: Special Child Publication.

Belmont, L. (1980). Epidemiology. In H. E. Rie & E. D. Rie (Eds.), *Handbook of minimal brain dysfunctions* (pp. 55–74). New York: Wiley.

Bensen, H., Shapiro, D., & Tursky, B. (1971). Decreased systolic blood pressure through operant conditioning techniques in patients with essential hypertension. *Science, 173,* 740–742.

Blair, H. (1977). Natural history of childhood asthma: 20-year follow-up. *Archives of the Diseases of Childhood, 52,* 613–620.

Blanchard, E. B., & Andrasik, F. (1982). Psychological assessment and treatment of headache: Recent developments and emerging issues. *Journal of Consulting and Clinical Psychology, 50,* 859–879.

Blanchard, E. B., & Haynes, M. R. (1975). Biofeedback treatment of a case of Raynaud's disease. *Journal of Behavior Therapy and Experimental Psychiatry, 6,* 230–234.

Blanchard, E. B., & Miller, S. T. (1977). Psychological treatment of cardiovascular disease. *Archives of General Psychiatry, 34,* 1402–1413.

Blanchard, E. B., Theobald, E. E., Williamson, D. A., Silver, B. V., & Brown, D. (1978). Temperature biofeedback in the treatment of migraine headaches. *Archives of General Psychiatry, 35,* 581–588.

Brown, B. (1970). Recognition of aspects of consciousness through association with EEG alpha activity represented by a light signal. *Psychophysiology, 6,* 442.

Budzynski, T., Stoyva, J., & Adler, C. (1970). Feedback induced muscle relaxation: Application to tension headache. *Journal of Behavioral Experimental Psychiatry, 1,* 205.

Carlson, J. G. (1977). Locus of control and frontal electromyographic response training. *Biofeedback and Self-Regulation, 2,* 259–271.

Carter, J. L., & Russell, H. (1980). Biofeedback and academic attainment of LD children. *Academic Therapy, 15,* 483–486.

Carter, J. L., & Synolds, D. (1974). Effects of relaxation training upon handwriting quality. *Journal of Learning Disabilities, 7*(4), 53–55.

Carter, J. L., Lax, B., Russell, H. (1979). Effects of relaxation and EMG training on academic achievement of educable retarded boys. *Education and Training of the Mentally Retarded, 14,* 39–41.

Danker. P. S., Miklich, D. R., Pratt, C., & Creer, T. L. (1975). An unsuccessful attempt to instrumentally condition peak expiratory flow rates in asthmatic children. *Journal of Psychosomatic Research, 19,* 209–213.

Davis, M. H., Saunders, D. R., Creer, T. L., & Chai, H. (1973). Relaxation training facilitated by biofeedback apparatus as a supplemental treatment in bronchial asthma. *Journal of Psychosomatic Research, 17,* 121–128.

Dekker, E., Pelsey, H. E., & Groen, J. (1957). Conditioning as a cause of asthmatic attacks. *Journal of Psychosomatic Research, 2,* 97–104.

Denkowski, K. M., Denkowski, G. C., & Omizo, M. M. (1983). The effects of EMG-assisted relaxation training on the academic performance, locus of control, and self-esteem of hyperactive boys. *Biofeedback and Self-Regulation, 8*(3), 363–375.

Denkowski, K. M., Denkowski, G. C., & Omizo, M. M. (1984). Pedictors of success in the EMG biofeedback training of hyperactive male children. *Biofeedback and Self-Regulation, 9*(2), 253–262.

Diamond, S., & Franklin, M. (1975). Autogenic training with biofeedback in the treatment of children with migraine. In W. Luthe & F. Antonelli (Eds.), *Therapy in psychosomatic medicine: Proceedings of the 3rd Congress of the International College of Psychosomatic Medicine* (pp. 190–192), Rome.

DiCara, L., & Miller, N. (1968a). Instrumental learning of vasomotor responses by rats: Learning to respond differentially in two ears. *Science, 159,* 1485–1486.

Dikel, W., & Olness, K. (1980). Self-hypnosis, biofeed-

back and voluntary peripheral temperature control in children. *Pediatrics, 66*(3), 335–340.
Engel, B., & Chism, R. (1967). Operant conditioning of heart rate speeding. *Psychophysiology, 3*, 418–426.
Engel, B., & Hansen, S. (1966). Operant conditioning of heart rate slowing. *Psychophysiology, 3*, 563–567.
Faulstich, M. E., Williamson, D. A., & Jarrell, M. P. (1984). Differential effects of feedback sensitivity upon learned control of temperature. *International Journal of Neuroscience, 25*, 19–24.
Feldman, G. M. (1976). The effect of biofeedback training on respiratory resistance of asthmatic children. *Psychosomatic Medicine, 38*, 27–34.
Finley, W. W., Etherton, M. D., Dickman, D., Karimian, D., & Simpson, R. W. (1981). A simple EMG - reward system for biofeedback training of children. *Biofeedback and Self-Regulation, 6*(2), 169–180.
Firestone, P., Poitras-Wright, H., & Douglas, V. (1978). The effects of caffeine on hyperactive children. *Journal of Learning Disabilities, 11*, 133–134.
Ford, M. M. (1968). Aetiology of asthma: A review of 11551 cases (1958–1968). *Medical Journal of Australia, 1*, 628–634.
Fowler, R., & Kimmel, H. (1962). Operant conditioning of GSR. *Journal of Experimental Psychology, 63*, 536–567.
Freedman, P. X. (1971). Report of the conference on the use of stimulant drugs in the treatment of behaviorally disturbed young school children. *Journal of Learning Disabilities, 4*, 523–530.
Frostig, M., & Horne, D. (1964). *The Frostig Program for the development of visual perception: Teacher's guide*. Chicago, IL: Follett.
Garner, G. E. (1968). A blending of behavior therapy techniques in an approach to an asthmatic child. *Psychotherapy: Theory, Research, and Practice, 5*, 46–49.
Halpern, D., Kottke, F. J., Burrill, C., Fiterman, C., Popp, J., & Palmer, S. (1970). Training of control of head posture in children with cerebral palsy. *Developmental Medicine and Child Neurology, 12*, 290–305.
Hampstead, W. J. (1979). The effects of EMG-assisted relaxation training with hyperkinetic children: A behavioral alternative. *Biofeedback and Self-Regulation, 4*(2), 113–125.
Hughes, H., Jackson, K., DuBois, K. E., & Erwin, R. (1979). Treatment of handwriting problems utilizing EMG biofeedback training. *Perceptual and Motor Skills, 48*, 603–606.
Hughes, H., Henry, D., & Hughes, A. (1980). The effect of frontal EMG biofeedback training on the behavior of children with activity-level problems. *Biofeedback and Self-Regulation, 5*(2), 207–219.
Hunter, S. H., Russell, H. L., Russell, E. D., & Zimmerman, R. L. (1976). Control of fingertip temperature increases via biofeedback in learning-disabled and normal children. *Perceptual and Motor Skills, 43*, 743–755.
Jackson, K., & Hughes, A. (1978). Effects of relaxation training on cursive handwriting of fourth grade students. *Perceptual and Motor Skills, 47*, 707–712.
Kator, D., & Spires, J. (1975, September). Biofeedback: The beat goes on. *The School Counselor*, pp. 16–21.
Kelton, A., & Belar, C. D. (1983). The relative efficacy of autogenic phrases and autogenic-feedback training in teaching hand warming to children. *Biofeedback and Self-Regulation, 8*(3), 461–475.
Khan, A. U. (1974a). The mechanism of psychogenic asthma attacks in children. *Psychotherapy and Psychosomatics, 27*, 137–140.
Khan, A. U. (1974b). Acquired bronchial hypersensitivity in asthma. *Psychosomatics, 15*, 188–200.
Khan, A. U. (1977). Effectiveness of biofeedback and counterconditioning in the treatment of bronchial asthma. *Journal of Psychosomatic Research, 21*, 97–104.
Khan, A. U., Staerk, M., & Bonk, C. (1974). Role of counterconditioning in the treatment of asthma. *Journal of Psychosomatic Research, 18*, 89–92.
Kimmel, E., & Hill, R. (1960). Operant conditioning of the GSR. *Psychological Reports, 7*, 555–562.
Konig, P., & Godfrey, S. (1973). Prevalence of exercise-induced bronchial lability in families of children with asthma. *Archives of the Diseases of Childhood, 48*, 513–518.
Kotses, H., Glaus, K. D., Crawford, P. L., Edwards, J. E., & Scherr, M. S. (1976). Operant reduction of frontalis EMG activity in the treatment of asthma in children. *Journal of Psychosomatic Research, 20*, 453–459.
Kristt, D. A., & Engel, B. T. (1975). Learned control of blood pressure in patients with high blood pressure. *Circulation, 51*, 370–378.
Labbé, E. E., & Williamson, D. A. (1983). Temperature biofeedback in the treatment of children with migraine headaches. *Journal of Pediatric Psychology, 8*, 317–326.
Labbé, E. E., & Williamson, D. A. (1984). Treatment of childhood migraine using autogenic feedback training. *Journal of Consulting and Clinical Psychology, 52*(6), 968–976.
Lambert, N. M., & Sandoval, J. (1980). The prevalence of learning disabilities in a sample of children considered hyperactive. *Journal of Abnormal Child Psychology, 8*, 33–50.
Lazar, B. S., & Jedliczka, Z. T. (1979). Utilization of manipulative behavior in a retarded asthmatic child. *The American Journal of Clinical Hypnosis, 21*, 287–292.
Libo, L. M., Arnold, G. E., Woodside, J. R., Borden, T. A., & Hardy, T. L. (1983). EMG biofeedback for functional bladder-sphincter dyssynergia: A case study. *Biofeedback and Self-Regulation, 8*, 243–253.
Lubar, J. O., & Lubar, J. F. (1984). Electroencphalographic biofeedback of SMR and Beta for treatment of attention deficit disorders in a clinical setting. *Biofeedback and Self-Regulation, 9*(1), 1–23.
Lubar, J. F., & Shouse, M. N. (1976). EEG and behavioral changes in a hyperkinetic child concurrent with train-

ing of the sensorimotor rhythm (SMR): A preliminary report. *Biofeedback and Self-Regulation*, *1*(3), 293–306.

Luparello, T. J., Lyons, H. A., Bleecker, E. R., & McFadden, E. R. (1968). Influence of suggestion on airway reactivity in asthmatic subjects. *Psychosomatic Medicine*, *30*, 819–825.

Lynch, W. C., Hama, H., Kohn, S., & Miller, N.E. (1976). Instrumental control of peripheral vasomotor responses in children. *Psychophysiology*, *13*(3), 219–221.

Maizels, M., King, L. R., & Firlit, C. F. (1979). Urodynamic biofeedback: A new approach to treat vesical sphincter dyssynergia. *The Journal of Urology*, *122*, 205–209.

Maloney, F. P. (1980). A simplified mercury switch head-control biofeedback device. *Biofeedback and Self-Regulation*, *5*(2), 257–263.

Munter, S. (1968). Maimonides' treatise on asthma. *Disorders of the Chest*, *54*, 48–52.

Nowicki, S., & Strickland, B. (1973). A locus of control scale for children. *Journal of Consulting and Clinical Psychology*, *40*, 148–154.

O'Leary, K. D. (1980). Pills or skills for hyperactive children. *Journal of Applied Behavior Analysis*, *13*(1), 191–204.

Omizo, M. M. (1980). The effects of biofeedback induced relaxation training in hyperactive adolescent boys. *Journal of Psychology*, *105*, 131–138.

Omizo, M. M. (1981). Relaxation training and biofeedback with hyperactive elementary school children. *Elementary School Guidance and Counseling*, *15*(4), 329–332.

Omizo, M. M., & Michael, W. B. (1982). Biofeedback-induced relaxation training and impulsivity, attention to task, and locus of control among hyperactive boys. *Journal of Learning Disabilities*, *15*(7), 414–416.

Omizo, M. M., & Williams, R. E. (1982). Biofeedback-induced relaxation training as an alternative for the elementary school learning-disabled child. *Biofeedback and Self-Regulation*, *7*, 139–148.

Patel, C. H. (1973). Yoga and biofeedback in the management of hypertension. *Lancet*, *2*, 1053–1055.

Pelham, W. E., Schneider, R. W., Bologna, N. C., & Contreras, J. A. (1980). Behavioral and stimulant treatment of hyperactive children: A therapy study with methylphenidate probes in a within-subject design. *Journal of Applied Behavior Analysis*, *13*(2), 221–236.

Phillip, R. L., Wilde, G. J. S., & Day, J. H. (1974). Suggestion and relaxation in asthmatics. *Journal of Psychosomatic Research*, *16*, 193–204.

Rachemanne, F. M., & Edwards, M. D. (1952). Asthma in children. A follow-up study of 688 patients after an interval of twenty years. *New England Journal of Medicine*, *246*, 815–818.

Sargent, J. D., Green, E. E., & Walters, E. D. (1973). Preliminary report on the use of autogenic feedback training in the treatment of migraine and tension headaches. *Psychosomatic Medicine*, *35*, 119–135.

Shapiro, D., Crider, A., & Tursky, B. (1964). Differentiation of an autonomic response through operant reinforcement. *Psychosomatic Medicine*, *1*, 147–148.

Stumme, V. S., Gresham, F. M., & Scott, N. A. (1982). Validity of social behavior assessment in discriminating emotionally disabled from nonhandicapped students. *Journal of Behavioral Assessment*, *4*, 327–341.

Sugar, E. (1983). Bladder control through biofeedback. *American Journal of Nursing*, 1152–1154.

Sugar, E. C., & Firlit, C. F. (1982). Urodynamic biofeedback: A new therapeutic approach for childhood incontinence/infection (vesical voluntary sphincter dyssynergia). *The Journal of Urology*, *128*, 1253–1258.

Suter, S., & Loughry-Machado, G. (1981). Skin temperature biofeedback in children and adults. *Journal of Experimental Child Psychology*, *32*, 77–87.

Suter, S., Fredericson, M., Portuesi, L. (1983). Mediation of skin temperature biofeedback effects in children. *Biofeedback and Self-Regulation*, *8*(4), 567–584.

Tansey, M. A., & Bruner, R. L. (1983). EMG and EEG biofeedback training in the treatment of a 10-year-old hyperactive boy with a developmental reading disorder. *Biofeedback and Self-Regulation*, *8*, 25–37.

Walton, W. T. (1979). The use of a relaxation curriculum and biofeedback training in the classroom to reduce inappropriate behaviors of emotionally handicapped children. *Behavioral Disorders*, *5*, 10–18.

Werder, D. S., & Sargent, J. D. (1984). A study of childhood headache using biofeedback as a treatment alternative. *Headache*, *24*, 122–126.

Werry, J. (1968). Studies of the hyperactive child: IV. An empirical analysis of the minimal brain dysfunction syndrome. *Archives of General Psychiatry*, *19*, 9–16.

Williamson, D. A. (1981). Behavioral treatment of migraine and muscle-contraction headache: Outcome and theoretical explanations. In M. Hersen, R. M. Eisler, & P. M. Miller (Eds.), *Progress in behavior modification* (Vol. 11, pp. 163–201). New York: Academic Press.

Williamson, D. A., & Blanchard, E. B. (1979a). Heart rate and blood pressure biofeedback, I. A review of the recent experimental literature. *Biofeedback and Self-Regulation*, *4*(1), 1–34.

Williamson, D. A., & Blanchard, E. B. (1979b). Heart rate and blood pressure biofeedback, II. A review and integration of recent theoretical models. *Biofeedback and Self-Regulation*, *4*(1), 35–50.

Wooldridge, C. P., & Russell, G. (1976). Head position training with the cerebral palsied child: An application of biofeedback techniques. *Archives of Physical Medicine and Rehabilitation*, *57*, 407–414.

Wunderlich, R. C. (1973). Treatment of the hyperactive child. *Academic Therapy*, *8*, 375–390.

Yerkes, R. M., & Dodson, J. D. (1908). The relation of strength of stimulus to rapidity of habit formation. *Journal of Comparative and Neurological Psychology*, *18*, 458–482.

PART V

The Practice of Behavior Therapy with Specific Problems and Populations

The chapters in this section describe the application of a variety of behavioral procedures to particular populations of children or classes of problems. There will, of course, be some overlap between this and the previous section where the goal was to review the application of specific procedures to a wide array of problems. Thus, some of the procedures reviewed in the previous section will be reviewed in this section as they are applicable to specific classes of problems (e.g., some of the cognitive-behavioral procedures reviewed in the previous section are relevant when working with specific populations, such as learning disabled children, which are reviewed in this section). A review of the behavior therapy literature for specific populations provides another view or perspective of the field and allows the reader to access more conveniently information specific to a particular problem, setting, or diagnosis. In this section reviews are provided of the literature pertaining to early intervention (Paget, Chapter 22), learning disabled children (Kneedler & Meese, Chapter 23), children with mild and moderate mental retardation (Matson & Schaughency, Chapter 24), conduct and attention deficit disorders (Carlson & Lahey, Chapter 25), fears and phobias (Morris, Kratochwill, & Aldridge, Chapter 26), children with severe handicaps (Wacker & Berg, Chapter 27), childhood depression (Kazdin, Chapter 28), and medical problems (Lemanek & Van Buren, Chapter 29).

CHAPTER 22

Early Intervention

Infants, Preschool Children, and Families

Kathleen D. Paget

> The behavioral clinician should be aware of the possible danger of becoming just another partner in a client's cycle of coercion, one more aversive figure to be avoided or submitted to, but only temporarily.
>
> —Dumas & Wahler, 1983, p. 311

The opening passage was written in the context of parent training with socioeconomically disadvantaged mothers. Nevertheless, its application exceeds the boundaries of that particular group. Resistance to a professionally prescribed treatment plan may occur whenever ecological variables related to behavior change are not incorporated into training and the clinician is not sensitive to the side effects of an intervention plan on a family or classroom system. In this respect, Mealiea (1976) commented

> too frequently behavior modifiers develop programs based on the belief that all that is required to change the behavior of individuals and their interaction with their environments is the acceleration or deceleration of a single dimension of performance. (p. 153)

This chapter is based on two premises. The first is that a unidimensional view of behavior change (i.e., where a single treatment is applied to a single behavior) is limited in its usefulness by neglecting multiple causal factors and by ignoring side effects that disturb the system equilibrium within the context where behavior occurs. Following from the first, a second premise is that a multidimensional view, consistent with Shadish's (1986) notion of planned critical multiplism, affords a comprehensive evaluation of the multiple determinants of a problem and the multiple effects of a treatment. Central to this latter view is the examination of various lines of research in various disciplines to attenuate bias and broaden parameters of understanding.

Research with infants and preschool-age children represents a confluence of multiple streams of research and discourse and, thus, is an appropriate forum for illustrating the premises just mentioned. Young children ex-

Kathleen D. Paget • Department of Psychology, University of South Carolina, Columbia, South Carolina 29208.

hibiting both typical and atypical developmental patterns and their families have been of interest to researchers from numerous disciplines, including applied behavioral analysis, applied developmental psychology, early childhood special education, and ecological psychology. In the context of planned critical multiplism, this multidisciplinary marriage is necessary to a complete understanding of early intervention issues. In this respect, multiple definitions of early intervention have evolved, moving from a traditional view consisting only of enrollment in a professional program to a broader-based conceptualization defining it as

> provision of support to families of infants and young children from members of informal and formal social support networks that impact both *directly* and *indirectly* upon parental, family, and child functioning. (Dunst, 1985, p. 179)

Broadly speaking, then, early intervention may consist of many types of assistance and service, including understanding from a friend, child care from a neighbor, participation in a parent support group, and role sharing between a husband and wife (Dunst, 1985).

The purposes of this chapter are to place the use of professionally prescribed behavioral strategies into this broad conceptualization of early intervention and to show that a systemic, multidimensional perspective is critical to intervention effectiveness and generalization. Through a multidisciplinary synthesis of research, the chapter illustrates the complexities involved when using behavioral strategies with infants, preschool-age children, and their families. In so doing, it is intended to assist researchers and clinicians in their efforts to effect positive change in the lives of young children and their families. The chapter is organized to illustrate the ever-widening parameters encompassing early intervention research. First, conceptual issues related to the application of behavioral strategies in infant stimulation programs are discussed. This is followed by a multilevel analysis of issues related to at-risk and handicapped preschoolers. The third section is focused on parent- and family-level interventions and is organized according to the multiple subsystems comprising family systems. Throughout the chapter, limitations of the extant research studies are described in order to delineate questions that need to be addressed through future research efforts.

Behavioral Strategies in Infant Stimulation Programs

Of central importance to any infant intervention program is the issue of how behavioral change occurs. Researchers who have advanced our knowledge about how to intervene effectively have begun their endeavors with a desire to understand the nature of such change. Unfortunately, the philosophy, structure, and techniques used in many infant intervention programs do not reflect systematically the combined results of applied developmental and behavioral research. Nevertheless, at a time when infant intervention programs are proliferating dramatically, it becomes increasingly important to integrate and synthesize this research for individuals who design, implement, and evaluate these programs. Although the myriad issues related to infant intervention are enormously complex, they can be simplified by discussing them in terms of current views of infant competence, quality versus quantity of intervention, and generalization strategies. It should be recognized that this discussion does not attempt to unravel entirely the many issues related to infant programming (see Frank, 1984; Garwood & Fewell, 1983, for more extensive coverage). Rather, the focus is on research employing behavioral strategies with infants and how the use of these strategies blends with current understanding of infant development.

Changing Views of Infant Competence

Operant conditioning procedures have been carried out successfully with very young infants to increase desirable and decrease undesirable behaviors. A representative list would include such behaviors as sucking (Crook, 1976), smiling (Zelazo, 1971), head turning (Vietze, Foster, & Friedman, 1974), vocalization (Finkelstein & Ramey, 1977), visual fixation (Watson, 1969), and manipulation (Millar, 1976a). Advantages of the operant approach include the fact that with training, parents and trainers can carry out the necessary strategies; implementation of some techniques does not require costly or sophisticated materials; and the immediate feedback received by intervenors can serve as reinforcement to continue and broaden their efforts (Lancioni, 1980). Although classical conditioning procedures with infants have not been studied as extensively as operant techniques, it is becoming clear that these procedures also can be used effectively to alter infant behavior (cf. Fitzgerald & Brackbill, 1976).

In contrast to early negative views of infants' capabilities (see Crain, 1980, for an analysis), infants are perceived now to be relatively competent organisms capable of participating in complex interactions with their world (Dunst, 1981). Advances in research methodology, instrumentation, and theory have revealed that normal newborns have a functioning perceptual system capable of intersensory coordination (Bower, 1974) and that they are capable of making multiple categorizations (Carpenter, 1974). They also possess central and peripheral vision at birth (Lewis, Maurer, & Kay, 1978), can coordinate visual and auditory input by 2½ months of age (Field, DiFranco, Dodwell, & Muir, 1979), show recognition memory by 4 months (Olson, 1979), are able to recognize relatively abstract two-dimensional stimuli by 5 months (DeLoach, Strauss, & Maynard, 1979), and by 12 months are able to use pointing behavior to call interesting objects to the attention of others (Leung & Rheingold, 1981). Kaye and Marcus (1981) discovered that over the last half of the first year, infants are able to master the imitation of several complex behaviors, including touching their ear, shaking a toy, and clapping. The body of research on attachment processes developed by Ainsworth (1973) typifies these changes, which

> have tended to shift attention from an almost exclusive concern with environmental control to increased interest in what is inside the organism to start with, how this inner programming affects the response to environmental input, and how it becomes transformed as a consequence of organism-environmental transactions. (p. 99)

Currently adopted models of cognitive development and learning (Bandura, 1977; Bricker & Bricker, 1976) also advance a belief that infants are active initiators rather than passive recipients of learning. Thus, considerable research, model building, and discourse about normal infant development during the last decade have all resulted in a paradigm shift described by Haith (1980) as "a renaissance of sorts . . . a new characterization of man and his infancy as that of a seeker of information rather than of Pavlovian-Thorndikian collater of stimulus events" (p. xx).

Early interventionists face the challenge of translating what is known about typical infant development to atypical infants while data accumulate on intervention effectiveness with specific handicapped and at-risk populations. Germane to the present discussion is the issue that, unlike normally functioning infants, a handicapped or at-risk infant may need to be taught how to explore the environment. Thus, to accomplish desired behavioral change with these infants, it becomes necessary to combine the sophisticated use of behavior change technology with knowledge about the infant's cognitive and motoric mastery of skills. Case (1978) offered a neo-Piagetian model for an instructional technology that incorporates strategies from Piagetian theory and behavioral technology. Through carefully conducted and ongoing evaluation and intervention procedures, the goal is to strike a balance between the infant as a reactor or an initiator of learning and the interventionist as an observer or active planner of learning experiences. For example, techniques of response elicitation, such as modeling, cuing, and prompting need to be changed to response reinforcement if the infant provides evidence of being able to initiate the actual behavior or an approximation of it. In this manner, the interventionist watches for cues from the infant and structures learning experiences around them. Thus, this changing view of infant competence is influencing the manner in which behavioral strategies are implemented.

Quality versus Quantity of Stimulation

The mistaken assumption that larger doses of stimulation lead to more effective intervention for infants has given way to recent evidence that "the presence of too much stimulation may be as detrimental to development as too little stimulation" (Wachs, 1976, p. 26). Thus, it is believed that some early infant intervention programs are potentially harmful if the intensity and type of stimulation are not tailored to the needs of individual infants, such as those with Down Syndrome, who have a particularly low threshold (Gardner, Karmel, & Dowd, 1981). Features that are important to consider are an infant's preparedness for stimulation, the degree to which stimulation (or instruction) is directed by the interventionist, and the relative availability of contingent and noncontingent stimulation.

Preparedness for stimulation

Developmental reviews of the infant operant learning literature (Millar, 1976b; Sameroff & Cavanagh, 1979) emphasize the importance of biological preparedness to the ability to learn operant behavior. Sameroff and Cavanagh (1979), for example, argued that

> certain combinations of stimuli, responses, or reinforcers are biologically prepared such that their association is almost immediate without the apparent necessity of a learning process to occur, while other combinations of stimuli, responses, and reinforcers are unprepared so that a learning process must occur for associations to form. (p. 364)

Dunst and Lingerfelt (1985) and Krafchuk, Sameroff, and Bakow (1976) discovered that individual behavioral differences (i.e., temperament styles) are also related to the ease with which infants acquire operant behavior.

Attentional and arousal states have been found to affect learning such that a stimulus that is preferred when a baby is in a quiet, attending state may not be preferred when the baby is at a different arousal level (Gardner & Karmel, 1983). Field (1977) documented that mothers tend to overstimulate nonresponsive preterm infants, who become overaroused, avert their gaze, and elicit counterproductive efforts from their mothers to attract attention. Similarly, Gardner and Karmel (1983) found greater variability in the behavior of preterm infants than fullterms, with the former displaying more gaze aversion and less gaze fixation. These findings suggest that preterm infants are likely to be vulnerable to overstimulation or being overwhelmed by poorly designed programs that seek simply to provide maximal levels of stimulation as enrichment. Thus, careful observations of a premature infant's arousal and attentional states and modifications of stimulation intensity are necessary to prevent negative side effects of an otherwise well-designed treatment program.

Directed versus Experiential Instruction

Findings from the operant literature that very young infants are aware of contingencies and respond differentially to various stimuli (e.g., Cavanaugh & Davidson, 1977; Siqueland & Lipsitt, 1966) have led to the frequent use of directed instruction in infant intervention programs. Operant techniques have been used with cerebral-palsied infants whose spasticity or athetosis impairs mobility and manipulation capabilities; sensory-impaired infants who have a limited number of sensory input channels with which to explore the environment; autistic children whose stereotypic patterns inhibit accommodation of new behavior patterns; and severely disabled children who have limited capacity for the self-generation of alternatives for problem solving (Alberto, Briggs, & Goldstein, 1983). In addition to these more positive techniques for increasing desirable behavior, extinction procedures have been used frequently to decrease undesirable behaviors such as crying (Hart, Allen, Buell, Harris, & Wolf, 1964) and disruptive behavior (Porterfield, Herbert-Jackson, & Risley, 1976). Punishment has been used to reduce inappropriate language responses (Wulbert, Nyman, Snow, & Owen, 1973), tantrums (Solnick, Rincover, & Peterson, 1979), and oppositional behavior (Wahler & Fox, 1980) in toddlers.

Although directed instructional strategies have been effective with some populations of infants and toddlers, writers in the field of early intervention (e.g., Bailey, Jens, & Johnson, 1983; Dunst, 1981) are asserting the belief that an infant can initiate behavior and learn through provision of appropriate antecedent conditions and reliance on naturally occurring consequences. Thus, they are arguing for a judicious balance between directed and experiential, or less directed techniques. With an experiential approach, the interventionist is responsible for selecting and arranging the particular objects, events, or total environment that facilitate active exploration by the child, through careful study of the behaviors and sensory experiences already in the child's repertoire. Dunst (1986a) offered a model consisting of a three-pronged emphasis on the infant as initiator of learning, the interventionist as nonintrusive facilitator, and the environment as the natural context in which learning occurs. In addition, during the assessment process, Dunst (1986a) suggested that interventionists initially provide the same opportunities for experiential learning to a handicapped infant as to a normal one, keeping a careful eye on the specific physical and cognitive limitations that necessitate more directed strategies.

Contingent and Noncontingent Stimulation

Response-contingent stimulation enables infants to learn that their behavior can affect the environment in a predictable fashion (Dunst, 1981; Ramey, Starr, Pallas, Whitten, & Reed, 1975). Goldberg (1977) contended that early contingency experiences are important for enhancing competence motivation in infants and facilitating predictability and "readability" of children whose signals are unclear. With respect to the effect that prior exposure to noncontingent stimulation has on later infant learning, the results of research are equivocal, with some researchers finding interference (Finkelstein & Ramey, 1977; Seligman & Maier, 1967) and others finding no negative transfer (Gekoski & Fagan, 1984; Ramey & Finkelstein, 1978). The variables to be considered in clarifying this issue are complex and include an infant's age and contingent memory (cf. Millar, 1972; Watson, 1967), the duration and type of contingent stimulation, schedules of reinforcement, features of the setting, and the nature of at-risk or handicapping conditions.

A discussion of Herrnstein's mathematical statement of the law of effect (McDowell, 1982) provides a provocative conceptualization of issues related to noncontingent stimulation. Herrnstein's model asserts that responding is "governed by contingent reinforcement evaluated relative to all reinforcement provided by the environment" (McDowell, 1982, p. 772). By incorporating not only contingent but also noncontingent sources of reinforcement present in human environments, McDowell believes the model is more naturalistic and applicable to human behavior than is Skinner's earlier view. Thus, it is consistent with the shift in infant programming to increased use of naturalistic contingencies. Using the model, an interventionist interested in increasing the frequency of a target behavior (e.g., an infant indicating a desire to be picked up) would decrease the rate of reinforcement for all other concurrently available response alternatives and decrease the rate of free or noncontingent reinforcement in addition to increasing the rate of contingent reinforcement upon the target response. Neither intervention need involve a decrease in the absolute level of reinforcement in the environment; rather, reinforcement already available is redistributed. Similarly, to decrease an undesirable behavior, a viable option to extinction and punishment would be to increase the rate of reinforcement for a concurrently available response alternative and/or increase the rate of free, or noncontingent reinforcement. For more coverage of issues related to concurrent sources of reinforcement and the practical problems related to their implementation, the interested reader is referred to a discussion by Myerson and Hale (1984).

Generalization

In recent years, considerable effort has been devoted to the development of procedures to measure and enhance generalization of infant learning across tasks and/or situations. It is recognized that demonstration of generalization is a practical concern and an ethical issue (Drabman, Hammer, & Rosenbaum, 1979). Thus, it is desirable for intervention effects to demonstrate positive influences on the infant and the family and for the effects to persist when intervention is discontinued.

The definition of generalization provided by Stokes and Baer (1977) serves as a comprehensive guide for research into generalization with infant populations. In their framework, generalization is "the occurrence of relevant behavior under different, nontraining conditions (e.g., across subjects, settings, people, behaviors, and/or time) without the scheduling of the same events in conditions as had been scheduled in the training conditions" (p. 350). Techniques for enhancing generalization consist of using sequential modification; introducing natural maintaining contingencies; training sufficient exemplars (in more than one setting, with more than one person, and with more than one example of the task); training loosely; using indiscriminable contingencies; programming common stimuli; mediating generalization, and training to generalize (See chapter by Rutherford & Nelson, this volume). Similarly, Dunst (1981) emphasized the importance of structured and incidental teaching situations (Hart & Risley, 1975) with infants so that functional skills are taught in functional settings. He advocates that vertical instruction (teaching to the attainment of developmental milestones) be accompanied by horizontal instruction that allows the infant to perform a given behavior under a variety of conditions.

With respect to setting generalization, Drabman *et al.* (1979) noted the importance of the presence of salient discriminative stimuli that were present in the original environment. Thus, in infant intervention, the behavior analyst arranges for similar discriminative stimuli in home and clinic environments. Further, the early interventionist programs for generalization across behaviors so that, for example, the desire to be picked up is accompanied by eye contact and/or smiling from the infant. Generalization across subjects occurs in an early intervention classroom for young toddlers if a peer demonstrates a skill (e.g., smiling) that is applied to a target child. It should be noted here that the principles and techniques related to generalization in infants are also central to the effective use of behavioral strategies with preschool-age children and are discussed in that context in the next section.

In summarizing this section on infant programming in the context of Shadish's (1986) notion of critical multiplism, it can be said that behavioral clinicians who are familiar with applied developmental concepts of infant competence and preparedness for stimulation are more likely to effect meaningful behavioral change than those who are not. Similarly, applied developmentalists who are active consumers of the literature on applied behavioral analysis with infants will approach intervention with a better understanding of contingent and noncontingent stimulation and generalization procedures than those who are not. Thus, the integration of concepts from both fields is essential to an informed approach to infant intervention. In the next section, a similar process is illustrated relative to the confluence of available information on preschool-age children.

Strategies in Classrooms for Preschool-Age Children

The salient conceptual issues related to applied behavioral strategies in classrooms for preschool-age children lend themselves to a multilevel analysis that can be conceptualized on a continuum anchored by direct and mediated strategies. Direct strategies are presented in this chapter as those that are initiated by a teacher to reduce behavioral problems and to teach a child skills in preacademics, communication, social competence, adaptive and motor functioning. Mediated strategies, which do not involve direct instruction from an adult, have resulted from concerns related to generalization and maintenance and have led to an emphasis on the behavioral ecology of preschool classrooms and the training of peers to implement behavioral strategies. Thus, the range of possibility for the locus of preschool intervention has expanded so that intervention with a target child is mediated through another child or environmental arrangement of materials, space, and activities. With this expansion has come a change from a deficit-within-the-child approach to a view that problems and their solutions lie within the transactions between a child and his environment (Sameroff & Chandler, 1975).

Teacher-Directed Strategies

Strategies used by teachers to train skills and reduce inappropriate behaviors have been researched extensively with preschool handicapped children. In general, the strategies have a successful track record when evaluated using short-term, unidimensional research designs. However, maintenance over time and generalization across trainers and settings loom as important issues. Central to the success of teacher-directed instruction is the use of multiple strategies and the matching of strategies to characteristics of individual children (e.g., chronological and developmental age, handicapping condition) and the task (e.g., a domain-specific skill or specific target behavior). Two processes that lay the groundwork for success are task analysis and hierarchical sequencing of skills. In particular, research with autistic preschool children exemplifies a multimethod approach matched to child and task characteristics and based on an analysis of skill sequences. For example, Lovaas, Koegel, and Schreibman (1979) applied stimulus fading and prompting as well as extra stimulus prompts to teach preacademic skills to autistic children. Because the children demonstrated stimulus overselectivity, the researchers found it necessary to introduce stimulus variations to encourage learning on more than one dimension.

Language Skills

A common approach to the development of language skills has been response shaping. With this procedure, the teacher imitates whatever spontaneous vocalizations occur, gradually reinforces vocalizations that sound like a model, and finally reinforces only after immediately occurring verbalizations identical to the teacher's (Lovaas, 1977; McLean & Snyder-McLean, 1978). When children do not respond to these procedures, research support exists for the use of motor imitation (e.g., picking up a cup) prior to verbal imitation (e.g., saying the word cup), because it establishes a stimulus class of behavioral similarity (Baer, Peterson, & Sherman, 1967). Nevertheless, motor imitation may generalize only to other untrained motor responses of similar topography (e.g., picking up a toy) and not to untrained vocal responses (Garcia, Baer, & Firestone, 1971). To enhance generalization, Garcia *et al.* suggested the pairing of a vocalization with a gross motor behavior already imitated consistently by the child. Because speech is often difficult to manipulate physically, teaching another mode learned more easily (e.g., manual signing) and pairing speech with this system ("total communication") is often recommended for high-risk and handicapped children (Bricker & Bricker, 1976; Kahn, 1977). Controversy exists regarding teaching in this manner with nonverbal autistic children, however, because a multisensory message may be more confusing than helpful if the children are tuning in to only one sensory modality through stimulus overselectivity (Lovaas *et al.*, 1979). Nevertheless, these studies illustrate how an interventionist may approach instruction utilizing the child as the initiator and adapting strategies to the limitations created by a specific handicapping condition.

Motor Skills

Numerous studies have been conducted using operant procedures to teach motor behaviors to preschool-age children. For successful completion of tasks that involve a series of steps (e.g., dressing, brushing teeth), forward and backward chaining procedures have been successful (Azrin, Schaeffer, & Wesolowski, 1976). Using verbal cues, physical prompts, and contingent reinforcement, Hardiman, Goetz, Reuter, and LeBlanc (1975) taught a 4-year-old cerebral palsied child a complex series of behaviors, including stepping through the rungs of a ladder, alternating feet while walking up steps, sliding down a slide, and rolling on the ground. O'Brien, Azrin, and Beale (1972) trained four developmentally disabled preschool children to stop crawling and use walking as a means of locomotion. Bragg, Houser, and Schumaker (1975) trained cerebral palsied children to sit in several positions. Although reintroduction of contingencies and reinforcement over time in a variety of situations are often successful in the generalization of motor skills, Russo (1979) suggested the alternative technique of training in a game-like format to incorporate the target skill into a variety of other motor behaviors.

Social Skills

Two social behaviors receiving considerable attention in the preschool literature are smiling and sharing. Many young handicapped children, particularly some retarded children, smile less frequently than their nonhandicapped peers (Cicchetti & Sroufe, 1976; Stone & Chesney, 1978), and relationships with parents and peers may be affected. Social and tangible reinforcement and modeling have been effective in increasing the frequency of these behaviors (Cooke & Apolloni, 1976). For sharing behaviors, Cooke and Apolloni (1976) documented the effectiveness of a combined program utilizing instruction, modeling, and reinforcement, over the singular application of any one of these strategies with nonhandicapped preschoolers (Rogers-Warren & Baer, 1976).

Reduction of Problem Behaviors

In deciding how to intervene to reduce an undesirable behavior exhibited by a preschooler, attention must be given to the age appropriateness of the particular behavior and the variety of factors causing the behavior. For example, increased interest in genitals at 5 years of age is appropriate according to developmental expectations; and the frequency, intensity, and duration of related behaviors should be interpreted within this context. Also, behaviors may develop as an adaptive response to an inability to produce a desired behavior (e.g., in language or motor domains). In this respect, Carr, Newsom, and Binkoff (1980) trained a young boy, who was pinching people as a means of communication, to perform a nonaggressive communication response.

When behavior is deemed to be inappropriate based on developmental and contextual variables, the behavioral clinician has a variety of effective techniques to use with a wide range of behaviors. Combined use of extinction and reinforcement has been found to be effective in decreasing a preschool child's reliance on adults and increasing interactions with peers (Allen, Hart, Buell, Harris, & Wolf, 1964); decreasing disruptive classroom behaviors and increasing on-task behavior (Becker, Madsen, Arnold, & Thomas, 1967), and decreasing aggression (Carr *et al.*, 1980; Pinkston, Reese, LeBlanc, & Baer, 1973). Time out is effective with preschoolers who can distinguish between time out of and time in reinforcement to reduce aggressive and disruptive behaviors (Clark, Rowbury, Baer, & Baer, 1973), inappropriate language (Wulbert *et al.*, 1973), tantrums (Solnick *et al.*, 1977), and oppositional behaviors (Wahler & Fox, 1980).

Overcorrection and positive practice are emerging as increasingly popular behavior reduction techniques with preschool-age children (Matson, Horne, Ollendick, & Ollendick, 1979; Ollendick & Matson, 1978). Noting the lack of responsiveness of some young handicapped children to reinforcement, Foxx (1977) used overcorrection to teach eye contact through a combination of edibles, praise, and a procedure termed functional movement. Conley and Wolery (1980) documented the effectiveness of overcorrection in decreasing the frequency of self-injurious (eye gouging) behavior in blind preschoolers, and Preator, Peterson, Jenson, and Ashcroft (1984) combined overcorrection and alternative response training to reduce inappropriate touching in a 6-year-old boy.

Resulting from the use of teacher-directed strategies, concern has emerged over children's dependence on external controls from an adult, their reduced interactions with peers, and teachers' overreliance on reinforcers that are not part of the child's natural environment. Thus, research interest is growing in self-directed strategies, peer training, and the use of naturalistic features of the classroom environment to train skills and change behavior. Of the techniques mentioned by Stokes and Baer (1977) to enhance generalization and maintenance, this shift capitalizes on natural maintaining contingencies, programming common stimulii, and mediating generalization. Nevertheless, other strategies, such as training sufficient exemplars and using sequential modification, are also being used within the context of this shift to self-instruction, peer mediation, and environmental arrangement.

Despite these advances, attention in the preschool literature to rearrangement of environmental contingencies in line with the recommendation of McDowell (1982) is lacking. In other words, techniques for increasing the rate of free or noncontingent reinforcement to reduce a problem behavior, or for decreasing noncontingent reinforcement to increase a desired behavior, have not been applied systematically to preschool-age children who are handicapped or at risk for later problems. As indicated in the earlier section on infants, studies that investigate the use of these techniques with preschool-age children would contribute significantly to our understanding of the mechanisms of behavior change in this population.

Self-Directed Strategies

Self-control strategies were described and validated initially by Meichenbaum and Goodman (1971) in the training of impulsive children to talk to themselves. Since that time, research interest has occurred in the translation of these and similar techniques to preschool populations, despite a long-held belief that preschool children lacked the necessary prerequisite skills to benefit from cognitively based training programs. Nevertheless, studies conducted thus far have produced equivocal results, and a clear picture has not emerged regarding the requisite variables for successful self-instruction with preschoolers.

Bryant and Budd (1982) documented improved performance of young children on selected assessment tasks, but they found variable changes in classroom behavior and preacademic performance. With less variation in the results, Poth and Barnett (1983) successfully employed self-talk and relaxation techniques to develop internal control mechanisms over a behavioral tic in a 3-year-old disadvantaged boy. Documenting dramatic intervention effectiveness, Bornstein and Quevillon (1976) combined self-praise with tangible reinforcement, modeling by the teacher, a story-like presentation, and a range of task difficulty in teaching 4-year-old disadvantaged children preacademic tasks. However, the results were not replicated when Billings and Wasik (1985) employed similar procedures with similar subjects. Explanations for outcome differences include therapist variables and the differential role of teacher attention in maintaining inappropriate behavior across the two studies.

To advance our rudimentary knowledge of self-directed strategies with preschoolers, numerous variables and the interactions therein warrant closer scrutiny. These include length and intensity of training, the type of task required, and the child's developmental age, gender, intelligence, race, learning history, and cognitive style (Billings & Wasik, 1985; Bornstein, 1985). We need to study these variables in normally functioning and handicapped populations, with an eye toward necessary modifications for the handicapped groups. Because self-instructional strategies developed thus far rely heavily on language, a particularly important avenue for future research involves the development of alternative strategies (e.g., imagery) for language-impaired youngsters.

Peer-Mediated Strategies

Investigations into the effectiveness of using peers to enhance cognitive and social skills in disabled classmates offer promising alternatives to more traditional forms of instruction. In contrast to outcomes produced with adult change agents, peer interventionists have been successful in building skills that generalize more easily to new settings and maintain across time (Hendrickson, Strain, Tremblay, & Shores, 1982). Peer-mediated interventions are attractive also from an efficiency standpoint because nonhandicapped or less handicapped children can provide one-to-one instruction to disabled peers that would not be possible with an "adults only" model. Research in this area can be organized into studies that use peers as behavioral models and those which use peers as direct agents of teaching.

Peers as Behavioral Models

Early studies by R. D. O'Connor (1969) and Evers and Schwartz (1973) were important in showing the effectiveness of filmed models in treating behavioral disorders (e.g., social withdrawal) in preschool children. More recently, other investigations resulted in the development of comprehensive training programs using live peer models in the classroom (Apolloni, Cooke, & Cooke, 1977; Peck, Apolloni, Cooke, & Raver, 1978). To illustrate, Peck *et al.* (1978) investigated the effects of peer imitation training on 3-year-old Down Syndrome children. An important component of the study was that generalization during nontraining occurred more often when training occurred in groups than in one-to-one situations. Other advantages of group versus one-to-one modeling training are that it approximates closely the types of arrangements used in less restrictive settings, allows for more opportunities for vicarious learning and social interaction with peers, and allows for efficient allocation of teacher time and attention to students. Litow and Pumroy's (1975) finding that group-oriented contingencies are as effective as individually based contingencies is relevant to group modeling training and has been replicated recently with autistic and autistic-like preschool children (Odom, Strain, Karger, Smith, 1986; Strain, Hoyson, & Jamieson, 1985).

The results of observational learning studies provide guidelines for the effective use of peers as behavioral models. For example, Garcia *et al.* (1971) emphasized the importance of considering topographical similarity between two behaviors in the facilitation of generalized imitative responding in severely retarded children. An important implication of this study for peer mediated strategies is that modeling examples of each dimension relevant to the desired response (e.g., the verbal and physical components of sharing toys) is an important method for nonhandicapped peers to use to provide sufficient exemplars (Stokes & Baer, 1977) for their handicapped peers. Other conclusions from observational learning studies are that children need to have the opportunity to observe repeated examples of appropriate behavior (Strain, Shores, & Kerr, 1976), the model child's behavior must be reinforced by events that are also reinforcing to the handicapped child (Strain & Kerr, 1979; Strain *et al.*, 1985), and children tend to imitate age-mates and older peer models, or younger peer models who are as competent on the behavioral dimension being modeled (Brody & Stoneman, 1981). Thus, careful selection and training of students is necessary to effective implementation of peer modeling.

An additional consideration in the effective utilization of peer modeling is the training of handicapped (e.g., autistic) children in imitative responding so that they are better able to make use of modeled behavior (Strain *et al.*, 1985). Thus, the mere availability of appropriate models in no way sets the occasion for all handicapped children to imitate behaviors. Employing the Peer Imitation Training program outlined by Peck *et al.* (1978), Strain *et al.* (1985) trained teachers to prompt autistic preschoolers to imitate a modeled behavior, reinforce correct responding, and use prompts and reinforcement. Results supported training effectiveness and underscored the importance of teacher involvement in initial phases of peer modeling strategies.

The conclusions drawn thus far from observational learning studies need to be tested further with populations of preschoolers representing a wider spectrum of handicapping conditions. The work of Strain and his associates with autistic preschoolers offers a workable paradigm to replicate with other populations. Following the lead of Bandura and Menlove (1968), researchers need to vary specific characteristics of the model (e.g., age, sex, and race) when decreasing maladaptive responses and increasing adaptive behaviors in various preschool handicapped populations. Aspects of the environment (e.g., teacher, materials, and dimensions of the training setting) are important foci of research, along with the long-term effects and unanticipated side effects of such training (e.g., imitation of undesirable behavior).

Peers as Teaching Agents

Training nonhandicapped children to teach social skills to their handicapped peers through imitation has been a fruitful avenue of research since the time when integrated preschools were created to meet the "least restrictive" provisions of Public Law 94-142. It has been demonstrated that nonhandicapped children are more likely to play alone than to interact with their handicapped classmates, and that they initiate interactions more frequently with mildly handicapped than severely handicapped preschoolers (Peterson & Haralick, 1977). In this respect, a component of the Strain *et al.* (1985) study was to specify behaviors that, if learned by normally developing preschoolers, would increase rates of social initiation with autistic classmates. An interesting aspect of the training was that nonhandicapped children were trained to expect initial rejection, and, thus, to persist in their efforts. Contrary to the criticism that normally developing preschoolers will pick up the undesirable behavior characteristics of their disabled classmates in mainstreamed settings, the results indicated that the nonhandicapped children exhibited fewer deviant behaviors than were exhibited by highly regarded children in developmentally segregated classrooms. In addition, treatment gains for autistic-like children were equivalent to the level exhibited by their nonhandicapped classmates.

Recent developmental research suggests the nature and effects of peer interaction may vary as a function of same or mixed-age groupings. Lougee, Grueneich, and Hartup (1977) studied social interaction in same- and mixed-age dyads of preschool children and found that when younger children (44 months) were in same-age dyads, they exhibited fewer positive social interactions than older children (58 months). When placed in mixed-age dyads, however, the younger children typically demonstrated more positive social interactions than their counterparts in same-age dyads, and the older children demonstrated fewer positive social interactions than in the same-age dyads. Verbal communication of the younger children was more appropriate in mixed-age than same-age groupings. Goldman (1981) observed the social behavior of 3- and 4-year-olds in same-age and mixed-age classes and found that both groups spent less time in parallel play in the mixed-age classes and more time in positive interactions and solitary play. Four-year-olds spent less time under the direct guidance of an adult in the mixed-age grouping. Furman, Raye, and Hartup (1979) found that when socially withdrawn preschoolers were paired with a younger child, their interaction rates increased more than when they were paired with same-age peers. The authors concluded that play sessions with younger children provided an easier context for the training of socially assertive behaviors. These findings are provocative and carry many implications for intervention and research with handicapped preschoolers, in that peer-mediated teaching and integration in mainstreamed settings can be influenced by greater understanding of mixed-age versus same-age groupings. Research designs need to control effects due to severity and type of handicap and the interaction of these variables with an older child's ability to provide nurturance and reinforcement. A central question to be answered involves sorting out the relative importance of chronological age and developmental level. Thus, an important component of mixed-age grouping in mainstreamed settings may be good models who function higher or lower than another child as a result of developmental level rather than chronological age.

Much remains to be done to advance knowledge regarding the identification of specific characteristics of nonhandicapped preschool children that make them good trainers. Strain *et al.* (1985) recommended the use of teacher nominations, yet the specific criteria used by teachers in this selection process need to be studied. Efforts thus far have been directed primarily toward socially withdrawn preschoolers. In the future, it will be interesting to evaluate the training of manual signing, role play, and puppetry for the classmates of hearing impaired students; auditory cuing for the visually impaired; task analysis and chaining of self-help behaviors for the physically impaired or retarded; and prompting, reinforcement, and aversive techniques for the socially disruptive. Thus, peer training is an endeavor replete with challenges for applied behavior analysts and developmental psychologists to conduct idiographic analyses of handicapped and nonhandicapped children across a spectrum of developmental functioning.

Behavioral Ecology of the Preschool Classroom

Although the effects of physical and environmental differences between classrooms have been part of educational lore for some time, in recent years the systematic study of these variables has increased, particularly in the fields of ecological and environmental psychology. Consequently, we are coming to view each classroom as a unique ecosystem in which variables such as arrangement of space and materials, group size and composition, competencies of teachers and children, and educational activities all interact reciprocally with behavior (Rogers-Warren, 1982; Rogers-Warren & Wedel, 1980). Farbstein and Kantrowitz (1978) stated aptly that

> places . . . are total environments [that form] the settings for all the significant and insignificant events of our lives. More than just containers, they are living, changing systems which support or hinder our actions, please or disturb our emotions. (p. 1)

Attention to these setting variables and the child–environment fit represents a shift from a skill-based, child-focused approach to an ecobehavioral or interactional view of a preschool child's performance (Sameroff & Chandler, 1975). With increased understanding of setting variables that effect behavioral change in specific groups of children, classrooms can be designed appropriately to enhance the effectiveness of intervention efforts. In addition, this approach affords a better understanding of intervention side effects on the classroom ecology. Indeed, a whole new set of questions is created when the environmental variables contributing to specific outcomes are delineated, assessed, and controlled experimentally, rather than taking a unidimensional focus on the outcomes themselves (Carta & Greenwood, 1985). What follows is a discussion of research investigating the effects of variables, such as classroom design and structure, activity schedule, grouping patterns, and toys and materials, on skill acquisition and behavior change in nonhandicapped and handicapped preschool populations. Specific behaviors investigated include engagement in preacademic tasks, social interaction, language production, self-help skills, and types of play.

Physical Design of Classrooms

The use of a large room without walls or high dividers has been advocated as an appropriate design for nonhandicapped preschoolers (Rogers-Warren & Wedel, 1980). Twardosz, Cataldo, and Risley (1974) investigated the effect of an open space design and found that it made supervision easier for teachers, and that it had no adverse effects on sleep patterns or engagement in preacademic tasks. Nevertheless, Danoff, Breitbart, and Barr (1977) cautioned that a preschool classroom should not be like a "child-sized cafeteria" (p. 60), where walls are lined with furniture and materials with an empty area in the middle. Neither should all activity areas be encircled with bookcases, storage units, or other furniture. Rather, boundaries between activity areas should be made fluid, through the use of raised and lowered floor levels, canopies, painted wall space, and the judicious use of dividers and toy shelves.

The appropriateness of open space design for handicapped preschoolers has yet to be demonstrated empirically. Although it has much appeal, many professionals argue that some handicapped children are too distractible and that open spaces increase hyperactivity and stereotypic behavior (Adams, Tallon, & Strangl, 1980; Frankel, Freeman, Ritvo, & Pardo, 1978). The effectiveness of open versus closed designs on the integration of handicapped and nonhandicapped preschoolers is a related area in need of empirical investigation. Bailey and Wolery (1984) suggested that until data exist to support one type of design over the other, the most ethical and least restrictive approach is to assume initially that environments for handicapped preschoolers should be designed similarly to those for nonhandicapped children, with systematic variations made for specific groups of handicapped children as suggested by data. Using this general framework to promote generalization across settings, researchers also must investigate the interactive effectives of classroom design on different behaviors. Thus, an open design may be important to social interaction, whereas a distraction-free design may be important to engagement in preacademic tasks.

Structure of Classrooms and Activities

The effects of various levels of structure in preschool programs have been investigated but are not understood clearly at the present time. Johnson, Ershler, and Bell (1980) compared play behavior of normally functioning preschoolers observed in a discovery-based preschool program with that in a formal education program and found that children in the formal program exhibited more constructive play and more transformations (i.e., changes in use of materials or the identity of people) than children in the discovery-based program. However, discovery program children were observed in nonplay behavior (i.e., unoccupied or onlooking) more often than children in the formal program.

Huston-Stein, Friedrich-Cofer, and Susman (1977) compared highly structured (i.e., high percentages of adult-directed activities) Head Start classrooms with low-structure classrooms and found that children in high-structure classrooms were more attentive in circle time and helped to clean up more often after free play, but did not show more independent task-oriented behavior. Conversely, Doke (1975) investigated the effects of formal (teacher coordinated) versus informal (child-initiated) activity periods in a daycare treatment program for noncompliant preschoolers and found the amount of task engagement to be consistently higher during informal activities than during formal ones. Although engagement alone is an insufficient measure of effectiveness, the results of this study underscore how an activity can be conceptualized to encourage self-initiation, to allow a child to specify his or her reinforcer, and to identify the pace with which he or she is ready to learn.

Doke and Risley (1972) investigated required versus optional activities in organizing a daycare environment, where the former arrangement allowed only one activity area to be open at any given time, and the latter allowed at least two optional activities to be available throughout the day. The authors found no significant differences in the overall percentage of engagement time between the two arrangements. LeLaurin and Risley (1972) investigated zone versus man-to-man staff assignment patterns and found that a zone staffing pattern, in which an adult supervised an area, increased children's level of engagement during planned activities more than man-to-man staffing, where one teacher was responsible for a group of children.

In trying to make sense of these diverse findings, one begins to understand that the structure of a setting exerts differential influences as a result of the particular operational definitions of structure used, the composition of the sample, the behavior being measured, the activity taking place, and the outcome measures used. Although these results for at-risk, behavior-disordered, and normally functioning preschoolers cannot be translated to handicapped populations without empirical justification, they provide useful departure points for conceptualizing the effects of varying degrees of structure on children with differing handicapping conditions. The specific manner in which the severity and type of handicap mediate the influence of structural variables is in need of study. Thus, although a discovery-based classroom may produce desirable outcomes for mildly handicapped or at-risk children, more severely involved youngsters are not as likely to learn through simple manipulation or engage independently in exploratory behaviors without external reinforcement. With these considerations in mind, we need to develop strategies that maximize use of the environment to reinforce the initiating behaviors of handicapped children while also providing effective guidance in the least intrusive manner possible.

Preliminary research into the effect of structure on social interactions between handicapped and nonhandicapped preschoolers in mainstreamed settings has produced equivocal results. Kohl and Beckman (1984) found that the least interaction and the greatest difference between the groups occurred during free play activities, with nonhandicapped children making more verbal statements, looking more frequently at objects and people, and engaging in more body movements than the handicapped children. The structure of other activities (e.g., circle, snack, and fine motor) or the presence of an adult was associated with increased interaction between the two groups. The authors interpret the results to suggest that facilitation of social integration needs to occur during low structure activities but may not be needed during more highly structured periods. Conversely, Burstein (1986) found that interactions had to be promoted by teachers, despite the degree of structure.

In both of these studies, the samples comprised a wide range of severity and type of handicap, the teacher–child ratios were low, and the amount of prior exposure of the children to each other was unclear. Thus, the results cannot be generalized to mainstreamed preschool settings with more homogeneous handicapped populations or higher teacher–child ratios. Following the lead of these two studies, future research efforts need to be directed at assessing the longitudinal effects of classroom structure on more homogeneous groups of handicapped preschoolers, covarying the degree of structure with other contextual variables (e.g., teacher–child ratio, group size, teaching style) to quantify the variance attributable to multiple environmental factors. Time-series analysis with common observation methodologies would contribute to our understanding of how length of time in a mainstreamed setting affects subsequent interaction between groups. Also, the presence of a segregated (nonmainstreamed) setting as a control group (cf. Jenkins, Speltz, & Odum, 1985) would improve the methodologies of the two studies conducted to date. The design principles for planning mainstreamed environments offered by Cohen, Beer, Kidera, and Golden (1979) provide further guidance in identifying the numerous environmental variables that need to be studied.

Activity Schedule

The sequence of activities in a preschool classroom appears to have a less equivocal effect on the children's behavior. For example, gradual rather than sudden decreases in activity level (e.g., from very active play to group instruction), changes in setting (e.g., from outdoors to indoors) and overlapping and staggered activities that eliminate group transitions have been found consistently to be excellent methods for limiting disruptions and increasing children's participation (Doke & Risley, 1972; Krantz & Risley, 1977; LeLaurin & Risley, 1972). In addition, interruptions in the typical schedule are inobtrusive techniques that encourage language and communication. Halle (1985) demonstrated that by delaying the next step of a routine, teachers of handicapped preschoolers could successfully prompt children to verbally request the next step of the routine.

Group versus Individualized Instruction

Considerable research attention is being given to the efficiency and effectiveness of group versus one-to-one instruction with preschoolers. Most of the studies to date have been conducted to identify and validate effective procedures for working with handicapped children in classroom groups, a major requirement of mainstreamed settings. Significantly, in no study has one-to-one instruction been found to be superior to group formats (Biberdoff & Pear, 1977; Favell, Favell, & McGimsey, 1978; Jenkins, Mayhall, Pescha, & Jenkins, 1974). Some of the benefits of group instruction for handicapped preschoolers have been discussed earlier and include the use of other children as behavioral models and the effectiveness of group reinforcement contingencies. Benefits such as these have led program developers to organize instruction using low teacher–child ratios and individualized curricular sequencing within small group settings (Hoyson, Jamieson, & Strain, 1984; Warren, Alpert, & Kaiser, 1986).

With respect to teacher–child ratios, it is surprising how little has been done to clarify the benefits of a low ratio on children's behavior. The studies that have been done (Frankel & Graham, 1976; M. O'Connor, 1975;

Stodolsky, 1974) are fraught with methodological problems because the influence of the teacher–child ratio has not been separated from the array of variables with which it interacts (e.g., staff and child competencies; mixed-age versus same-age grouping). Thus, the disadvantages of low ratios (e.g., reduced interaction with peers), as well as the advantages (e.g., better classroom management) suggested by these studies need to be interpreted with this caveat in mind.

Investigating group size and one-to-one instruction, Sainato and Lyon (1983) found that variation in the size of instructional groups covaried with the degree of teacher direction in effecting on-task behavior of handicapped preschoolers. Although children engaged in a one-to-one instructional activity were found to be significantly more attentive, responsive, and well-behaved than when engaged in a large group activity, increases in the teacher's instructional pace and correction rate to individual children in the group equalized the children's on-task behavior. These findings are not surprising, given the importance of pacing strategies and task variation found in other studies (Koegel, Dunlap, & Dyer, 1980; Dunlap & Koegel, 1980; Plummer, Baer, & LeBlanc, 1977).

Krantz and Risley (1977) found that preschoolers exhibited more on-task behavior in groups as a function of a simple environmental change in seating conditions. That is, children were more likely to attend to the task at hand when required to sit on pieces of masking tape spaced equidistantly than when allowed to sit randomly in a small area. Although similar results were obtained using a contingency management program, the authors suggested that environmental change was superior because it involved less planning and less teacher time for supervision.

The type of skill to be taught has been found to be another variable affecting the impact of group versus individualized instruction for preschool-age children. For example, Alberto, Jones, Sizemore, and Doren (1980) found no significant differences in the effectiveness of group and individual instruction in table top language activities, although there were more opportunities for responding in one-to-one instruction. Individual instruction, however, resulted in more effective acquisition of dressing skills.

In summary, the strategies employed by the teacher and the type of skill being taught are critical variables in understanding the differential effects of group versus individual instruction, and simple manipulations of the setting constitute viable strategies for assessing the effectiveness of group instruction. The jury is still out with respect to the optimum group size or teacher–child ratio that is most conducive to skill acquisition. Much research into the effects of group versus individual instruction remains to be done, with a particular need to identify the process variables and conditions that affect the behavior and skill acquisition of handicapped and at-risk preschoolers.

Toys and Materials

Observations of young children's play behaviors provide support for Lewin's (1931) statement that "objects are not neutral to the child but have an immediate psychological effect on behavior" (p. 6). Since the time this statement was made, researchers have examined the associations between types of materials and types of children's play at different age levels and the structural features of toys and the surrounding physical space that affect play behaviors. For example, Quilitch and Risley (1973) found that some play materials elicit social play whereas others encourage isolated play. Turner and Goldsmith (1976) discovered an association between some toys and antisocial/aggressive behavior, and Cohen, Hulls, and Paige (1978) revealed how some toys affect children's activity level more than others. Investigating the effect of structure on creative play, Pulaski (1973) found that moderately structured materials (e.g., rag dolls and pieces of cloth) elicit more varied and creative play than highly structured, role-specific materials (e.g., cars and trucks). Pepler and Ross (1981) found that with a simple manipulation of materials (separating puzzle pieces from the form board), children's use of the materials took on a more dramatic quality, suggesting that different presentations of the same materials can elicit different play behaviors. Rubin and Seibel (1981) found an interaction between play materials and a child's developmental level and suggested that younger preschoolers with limited cognitive play repertoires may seem less flexible in their play behaviors than older preschoolers who are capable of more varied interactions. Contrasting the behaviors of 3½- and 5-year-olds, McLoyd (1983) found that younger children engaged in more pretend play when realistic dolls were accompanied with relevant props (e.g., doll house, furniture) than when either the realistic dolls were presented alone or when the dolls were less realistic, broomlike figures. Taken together, the studies suggest that when choosing play materials to effect behavior change in young children, it is important that the interventionist consider the child's developmental level of functioning, particular features of the materials, and particular behaviors desired.

Some evidence suggests that social interaction is facilitated by the absence rather than the presence of toys (Eckerman & Whatley, 1977) and a decrease in the amount of play space available (Peck & Goldman, 1978), whereas nonsocial play is facilitated through the availability of many materials in a large space. Also, the storage of materials can be a determinant of the amount of playing that occurs. Montes and Risley (1975) compared the use of open shelves versus toy boxes and found the latter reduced time spent in actual play. Taken together, these findings have important implications for enhancing social interaction of handicapped and nonhandicapped children in mainstreamed settings and raise research questions, such as Does an absence of toys and a decrease in the amount of play space facilitate interaction between the two groups?, and How can the storage of materials be used to facilitate interaction? The effect of play materials on the development of handicapped children is an underinvestigated area that has the potential to provide many ecologically-valid interventions for promoting social and cognitive growth.

Collectively, the intervention studies conducted with preschool-age children provide multiple options to an interventionist for effecting behavioral change. A strong suggestion from the applied developmental and behavioral literature is that strategies intruding minimally on the child, teacher, and overall classroom ecology should be considered before more intrusive techniques. Although few in number, case studies employing self-directed strategies hold promise; and peer-mediated programs for autistic children have been successful enough to warrant experimental application to other handicapped populations. Finally, considerable evidence supports the consideration of classroom-level variables as a workable alternative to an exclusively child-level focus. Research attention must turn to systematic comparisons among these alternative approaches and between them and traditional teacher-directed techniques. In doing so, the capable researcher must have a multiply focused outlook on short- and long-term effectiveness; generalization across behaviors, settings, and subjects; and unanticipated side effects.

Parent and Family Interventions

Parallel to the shift in classroom settings from child-focused strategies to ecobehavioral approaches is the shift in family contexts from a focus on the mother–child dyad to the entire family as a system influenced by other systems. Much discourse in the early intervention literature addresses the many issues related to this shift. (See, for example, Dunst, 1985; Gallagher & Vietze, 1986; Turnbull, Summers, & Brotherson, 1986; Winton, 1986.) Consequently, researchers now are guided by a deeper understanding of the dense interactional texture of family functioning resulting from the many subsystems comprising a family structure. Bristol and Gallagher (1986) illustrated the concepts of family influence that have guided research away from a deficit-within-the-parent approach to a belief that influences from all relationships inside and outside a nuclear family need to be considered in intervention plans. These consist of (a) the *unidirectional dyad,* where the mother was thought to be responsible for a child's developmental problems; (b) the *interactive dyad,* where contributions of the child to mother–child interactions were recognized; (c) *multiple dyads,* where interactions between father and child, mother and father, and mother and child were all considered; (d) the *family system,* where mediational influences of the parent's marital relationship and sibling relationships on a child's development were studied; and (e) the family as an *ecological system* where the entire family is seen as one of an interactive, interdependent set of systems nested within each other. This continuum is conceptualized as being anchored at one end by relatively intrusive strategies in controlled analogue settings and, at the other end, by less intrusive strategies in naturalistic settings. Thus, the continuum illustrates a paradigmatic shift from a focus on isolating single deficits to an interest in capturing multiple transactions. Increased awareness of systemwide reverberations from the birth of an at-risk or handicapped child (see Murphy, 1982, for a review), the side effects of behavioral training (Dubey & Kaufman, 1982; Griest & Forehand, 1982), and Belsky's (1981) assertion that family functioning cannot be understood unless all interactions within and across subsystems are considered, have all served as catalysts for conceptual and technical expansions in research with families.

The purpose of this section is to trace the development of an ecobehavioral paradigm for intervention with families of at-risk and handicapped infants and preschool-age children. The section is organized according to the intrafamily subsystems that have provided the contexts for behavioral training. These include the mother–child and father–child dyads, the mother–child–father triad, and the sibling subsystem. Mediating influences across the major subsystems and from outside the family are also discussed.

Mother–Child Dyad

Because extensive evidence suggests that atypical infants elicit different behaviors from their mothers than normal infants, and that the responsibility of maintaining interactions often falls on mothers (Bell, 1971), the mother–infant dyad has been traditionally the focus of research attention. Studies of infants who are premature (Goldberg, 1979), developmentally delayed (Vietze, Abernathy, Ashe, & Faulstich, 1978), and severely handicapped (Walker, 1982) all suggest a pattern of reduced responsivity during mother–infant interchange. Nevertheless, some studies report heightened responsivity by the mother to a handicapped infant (Peters-Martin & Wachs, 1981). Because some mothers, even when trained, are unable to alter a maladaptive interactional style, researchers are beginning to look more broadly at the disequilibrium within the entire family system when a birth is atypical (Gallagher, Scharfman, & Bristol, 1984).

With respect to preschool-age children, serial studies of child abuse, noncompliance, and aggression that focused initially on the mother–child dyad illustrate how a more ecologically based perspective has been found to be necessary. For example, although documentation exists that abusive mothers differ from nonabusive mothers along several dimensions (Oldershaw, Walters, & Hall, 1986; Wolfe, 1985), Lutzker (1984) proposed that intervention must take place on several aspects of the family ecology, including interactions between parents and family functioning in the community. He found that the inclusion of interpersonal, marital, and job counseling in the design of research increased the effectiveness of training with abusive mothers. Also,

Tertinger, Greene, and Lutzker (1984) found that physical setting variables (i.e., safety hazards) often set the occasion for abusive interactions.

The work of Wahler and his colleagues has led to ecological analyses of noncompliant behavior in the children of single mothers living in poverty. Initially, Wahler (1975) emphasized the role of positive reinforcement (i.e., mother's attention) in shaping deviant behavior. Subsequently, Wahler and Fox (1980) demonstrated that mother-implemented contracts with oppositional children to increase solitary play resulted in concomitant changes in their other children's behaviors. Further, Wahler, Leske, and Rogers (1979) and Wahler (1980) concluded that some mothers, termed insular, experience frequent aversive interactions with extended family members and professional personnel and have fewer positive friendship contacts than middle class noninsular mothers. Moreover, Wahler and Afton (1980) discovered that insular, disadvantaged mothers did not generalize their newly taught observational skills from home to clinic settings. This series of studies led Dumas and Wahler (1983) to emphasize

> the indirect, though powerful, impact of ecological variables upon mother–child behavior change and, consequently . . . the danger of ignoring such variables in parent training. Overlooking the contextual factors in high-risk families may inadvertently turn the experience of treatment into an experience of failure and helplessness for many of them. (p. 311)

The research of Patterson and his associates also exemplifies how an initial focus on the mother–child dyad culminated in a multidimensional paradigm of family functioning (Patterson, 1986). Although the paradigm awaits translation to preschool-age populations, it is still very germane to the present discussion. Patterson's descriptions of coercive cycles in mother–child interaction (cf. Patterson, 1982; Patterson & Bank, 1986) are of an ecological nature in that they (a) describe bidirectional and multidirectional interactions within families; (b) consider multiple levels of the family system concurrently and relate the functioning of family members at two or more levels of analysis; and (c) examine primary and secondary changes in individual behaviors and behavior patterns under contrasting ecological conditions (Kaiser & Fox, 1986).

As an extension of Patterson's coercion hypothesis, Parpal and Maccoby (1985) trained mothers of 3- and 4-year-old children in responsive parenting skills similar to those in Forehand and McMahon's (1981) "Child's Game." Interestingly, they found that (a) setting variables were important to child compliance and (b) maternal compliance with appropriate requests from the child resulted, in turn, in higher levels of child compliance than when the child was simply reinforced for compliance or punished for noncompliance. Given these findings, the authors emphasized the ecological and bidirectional nature of interactive processes and the need to supplement reinforcement theory with reciprocity theory (cf. Gottman, 1979) in understanding mother–child interactions involving a child's noncompliant behavior.

Noncompliant behavior that accompanies developmental disabilities has spawned numerous training studies with handicapped preschoolers. Breiner and Beck (1984) reviewed studies in which mothers were trained as change agents in the management of noncompliance in their developmentally disabled children. By way of critique, the authors stated that only one third of the articles reported data in home settings, less than half reported follow-up assessments, and very few attempted generalization across setting, behavior, or subjects. They concluded "it is imperative that future studies begin to delineate specific marital and parental characteristics that may facilitate or impede the implementation of parent training procedures" (p. 273). In addition, they emphasized, as did Griest and Forehand (1984) and Dubey and Kaufman (1982), that we must develop a methodology for evaluating and anticipating the side effects of behavioral training. For example, changes in a mother's behavior (e.g., less interaction with other family members) may covary with unexpected changes in the target child's behavior (e.g., wanting rewards for all good behaviors) when training is focused exclusively on the mother–child dyad.

Collectively, research on the interactive processes between a mother and her child have set into motion the understanding that a mélange of setting conditions and child, parent, and family system characteristics is likely to be associated with the success or failure of many behavioral training programs.

Father–Child Dyad

In contrast to the large data base on the quality of the mother–child relationshp and its correlates, existing knowledge about the father–child relationship is extremely sparse. Research on the relationship between a father and his normally functioning child has followed two lines of study, establishing that infants become attached to their fathers (e.g., Lamb, 1976) and suggesting that father involvement in child rearing influences developmental outcomes (e.g., Easterbrooks & Goldberg, 1984; Spelke, Zelazo, Kagan, & Kotelchuck, 1973).

Much less is known about these two lines of study with respect to father involvement in the rearing of a handicapped child. For example, evidence regarding the effectiveness of fathers in gaining compliance from their handicapped youngsters is equivocal (Tallman, 1965) but has led to an understanding of the importance of contextual variables in effecting paternal behavior. Thus, much remains to be done to clarify contextual influences on paternal involvement and, in turn, the effects of paternal involvement on child development. In a review of 60 studies of parental involvement in early education programs for young developmentally disabled children (Wiegerink, Hocutt, Posante-Lero, & Bristol, 1980), none were found that assessed the effects of fathers' attitudes, attributes, or behaviors on developmentally disabled children's outcomes. In response to this limited research base, Bristol and Gallagher (1986) asserted "probably the most glaring omission in the literature on fathers of developmentally disabled children at the present time is the lack of consistent evidence that anything that fathers do affects long-term outcomes for their handicapped children" (p. 92).

Lest it be implied that there is no work being done with the fathers of handicapped children, it is important to discuss where the research focus has been. Essentially, the needs of fathers (e.g., Linder & Chitwood, 1984), their emotional reactions to an atypical child (e.g., Cummings, 1976), level of involvement (e.g., Stoneman, Brody, & Abbott, 1983), role adaptations (e.g., Gallagher, Scharfman, & Bristol, 1984), and responsiveness to intervention programs, comprise the bulk of the research with fathers to date.

Intervention programs have emerged only recently and are beginning to produce positive results. Some interventions have taken place immediately after a birth whereas others have been instituted at some other time during the child's preschool years. In-hospital training by Parke, Hymel, Power, and Tinsley (1980) revealed the effectiveness of a short videotape that modeled positive father–infant interactions. In comparison to a control group, fathers who saw the videotape evidenced increased knowledge about infant perceptual abilities, more belief in the value of stimulation, and more responsiveness during feeding and playing.

Dickie and Carnahan (1980) provided training to mothers and fathers of 4- to 12-month-old infants via eight 2-hour weekly training sessions. Training emphasized individual infant variation, knowledge of the infant's temperament and cues, provision of contingent experiences, and awareness of the infant's effect on the parents. Fathers who participated, in contrast to those who did not, increased their interactions by talking, touching, holding, and attending more, as well as giving more contingent responses to infant smiles and vocalizations. Interestingly, mothers in the trained groups decreased their interactions, perhaps to provide more opportunity for their husbands to interact with the child. This finding exemplifies the reciprocal nature of the mother–father relationship and the need to assess the impact of training on the entire family system.

A large project for fathers of handicapped preschoolers has uncovered broad-based intervention results. Participation in an intervention program where fathers could communicate with each other resulted in less stress, less sadness, and fewer problems for them (Fewell, 1983). Again revealing the indirect effects of an intervention, another result was that their wives, who had not participated, benefited in similar ways. Also, a weekly program in which fathers and their children met with male teachers to learn activities and share with other fathers resulted in less depression, more positive feelings about interaction with their children, and greater access to social supports (Vadasy, Fewell, Meyer, & Greenberg, 1985). Recently, promising results were reported regarding the maintenance of these effects over a 1- to 3-year period of time (Vadasy, Fewell, Greenberg, Dermond, & Meyer, 1986). Nevertheless, the results must be interpreted within the limitations of pre-post designs and the lack of a matched control group. Thus, the results are confounded by possible influences from maturation, self-selection, history, or testing effects.

When designing interventions for fathers of handicapped preschoolers, one should place more emphasis on a longitudinal framework for interpreting results, specification of child outcome variables, generalization across settings and behaviors, and comparisons across traditional and nontraditional family contexts of varying social class, number, and ages of children. These considerations need to be operationalized in observational studies of contingent interaction in clinic and home settings to answer the multifaceted question of what roles for which fathers in which families will help promote successful family adaptation while facilitating the development of a disabled child.

Father–Mother–Child Triad

The myriad roles and relationships within a father–mother–child triad highlight the complexities of intrafamily functioning. Broken into its reciprocally related components, the triad encompasses parental and marital relationships and their influence on the child, the father–child relationship and its influence on the mother, the mother–child relationship and its influence on the father, and the child's impact on the mother and father's parental and marital relationships.

Studies with infant and preschool populations that reflect this complexity are few, but growing in number, with some revealing the interdependent nature of the triad's components. For example, as an unexpected finding in a study on father involvement with 2-year-old normally functioning toddlers, Easterbrooks and Goldberg (1984) found high levels of father involvement to be associated with secure attachment between mothers and their sons. The lack of a similar finding with girls led the authors to emphasize the salience of the father–son relationship in family functioning.

In addition, parents have been shown to behave differently when alone with their infant than when interacting with the infant in the presence of the other parent. Parke, Grossman, & Tinsley (1981) found that although the number of interactions between each parent and the child decreased in the triadic context, there was more positive affect (smiling) by each parent in the presence of the spouse. Also, there may be differential effects on each parent. For example, in-home observations of Down Syndrome and nonhandicapped children (ages 4 to 7) and their parents revealed that fathers were more affected by the presence of the mother than vice versa.

Thus, fathers played less active roles when the mothers were present than when alone with their children, although mothers remained consistently involved with their children in both the dyadic and triadic contexts (Stoneman, Brody, & Abbott, 1983). The results suggest either that fathers feel less compliant in the presence of their spouse or that they relinquish more quickly than mothers an active parenting role. In another in-home observational study, Dickie and Matheson (1984) investigated the concept of parental competence and found that feelings of competence on the part of fathers were more dependent on maternal support than was maternal competence dependent on paternal support. Collectively, these two studies suggest that successful paternal parenting may be particularly dependent on a supportive intrafamilial environment. Social class comparisons of paternal and maternal competence and support would consitute a useful extension of these findings.

An interesting result in the Stoneman *et al.* (1983) study was that mothers were more likely than fathers to assume a teaching role when interacting with their impaired child. Nevertheless, existing evidence suggests that one spouse can successfully train the other, an important finding, because only one parent may be able to attend professional sessions (Breiner & Beck, 1984). To illustrate, Adubato, Adams, and Budd (1981) successfully trained the mother of a noncompliant/inattentive developmentally delayed 6-year-old to teach her husband how to give appropriate instructions, sustain positive attention, and teach skills in dressing, eating, and using toys appropriately. Even at a 2-year follow-up, both parents retained their knowledge of skills taught, continued to use the procedures, and found them effective. This study addressed in a practical way the thorny problems of generalization and maintenance by using the involvement of one family member to train another. This is a practical solution for many families where it is found that fathers want to play a more active role with their handicapped offspring but often do not know what that role should be (Gallagher *et al.*, 1984).

Several researchers have investigated the relation between marital quality and parenting during infancy and toddlerhood (e.g., Grossman, Eichler, & Winickoff, 1980) and have found that with normally functioning children, supportive husband–wife relationships facilitate the adaptation of mothers and fathers to their parental roles. Evidence suggests that this kind of support is more difficult to give after the birth of a handicapped child and that the lack or presence of this support is a critical factor in whether such a birth weakens or strengthens a family unit (Bristol & Gallagher, 1986; Friedrich, 1977). It is not surprising, then, that single parents report having more difficulty accepting and adapting to a disabled child (Bristol, 1985) and experiencing more stress (Beckman, 1983) than two-parent families. From a family systems perspective, much remains to be done to identify the mechanisms that strengthen or weaken relationships and activate or deactivate family members to receive training in how to interact optimally with the disabled member.

A major gap in the literature with handicapped children involves the linkages among marital quality, parenting competence, and actual child outcomes. Nevertheless, the emerging studies with parents of normally developing children can be used as guides for research with disabled samples. With parents of toddlers, Reisinger, Frangia, and Hoffman (1976) attributed the lack of generalization of behavioral management training to problems between the parents, and Goldberg and Easterbrooks (1984) found marital quality to be associated with sensitive parenting, which, in turn, was related to secure mother-infant and father-infant attachments. With a sample of school-age children and their parents, Brody, Pellegrini, and Sigel (1986) found that as a marital relationship was perceived to be less satisfactory, fathers behaved in a more intrusive manner than mothers and displayed fewer positive emotions in response to their children's learning attempts. One explanation for these findings is that the mothers responded in a way to compensate for parenting by their husbands that they perceived to be less than satisfactory. If this explanation is true, the mothers' behavior may not have been affected directly by the marital relationship as much as it was indirectly affected by the father's behavior. Thus, marital discontent may directly affect fathering and, thereby, indirectly affect mothering. With provocation from these intricate findings, researchers should proceed to design studies from a longitudinal perspective with families of varying social class, type and severity of handicap, and age of children to clarify further the linkages among marital quality, parenting behavior, and child developmental outcome.

The Sibling Subsystem

Many young handicapped children live in families with brothers and sisters who are younger or older, handicapped or nonhandicapped, of same or different gender, and spaced closely or far apart in age. Thus, many variables make the sibling subsystem a particularly unique one that exerts considerable influence within a family constellation. In fact, existing data suggest that by one year of age, children spend as much time in interaction with their siblings as with their mothers, and far more time than with their fathers (Lawson & Ingleby, 1974). It is surprising, therefore, that little is known about the day-to-day interactions, the environments, and the developmental outcomes of nonhandicapped or handicapped siblings when they are reared together (cf. Brody & Stoneman, 1983). Given this information, it is clear that a focus on this subsystem could advance knowledge regarding the impact of a handicapped child on the family, the side effects and potential effectiveness of interventions, and the interrelatedness among family subsystems.

As with other family subsystems, direct and indirect effects of sibling relationships need to be considered. These are described well by Brody and Stoneman (1986). With respect to direct effects, these authors state that

> ongoing family activities provide opportunities for the [handicapped] sibling to imitate and practice roles performed by an older or younger sibling, as well as for the normal sibling to expand his or her own repertoire to include such important roles as caregiver, teacher, and manager. (p. 198)

Indirect effects result from circumstances that influence the interactions of family members with one another so that "the handicapped sibling may cause the parents to experience stress and fatigue, thereby affecting the parents' socialization practices and the quality of their relationship with the nonhandicapped child" (p. 198). This example reveals how indirect effects are often synonymous with cross-system influences within the family, typifying the interdependent nature of intrafamilial variables. In a similar vein, the relationship between a child and his or her parents, especially the mother, has been found to affect interactions with a young sibling. Dunn (1983) found, for example, that intense and playful relationships between mothers and first-born girls were associated with child hostility soon after the birth of a sibling, a finding that needs to be replicated with handicapped and nonhandicapped siblings of varying ages.

Because interactions between handicapped and nonhandicapped siblings may be similar in some respects to those between peers, the peer interaction research has been looked to for clues regarding sibling relationships. Brody and Stoneman (1986) assert firmly, however, that sibling relationships should be conceptualized differently from peer relationships. Specifically, although the peer literature would support a certain role symmetry in mixed-age groupings, certain emotional needs and attachments to family members of siblings may preclude the expected accommodation to a younger child or imitation of an older one. Thus, contextual features that characterize families in general and the manner in which they are instantiated in specific families are major determinants of the quantity of sibling interactions.

Encouraging results have been found with respect to the effectiveness of training children to teach their handicapped siblings. Most of the studies have been done with school-age siblings (e.g., Colletti & Harris, 1977; Schreibman, O'Neill, & Koegel, 1983), although research is beginning to focus on preschool children. Positive (Cash & Evans, 1975) and negative results (Ferrari, 1984; Harvey & Greenway, 1984; Wellen & Broen, 1982) have been reported for preschool-age siblings of very young handicapped children. A variety of factors explains the variance in effectiveness of these training studies, including family constellation variables (e.g., ordinal position of nonhandicapped sibling), setting influences (e.g., dyadic or triadic context), sibling characteristics (e.g., age or gender), and parental characteristics (e.g., quality of communication). Thus, an automatic adoption of sibling training should not take place as an intervention strategy without consideration of these family system variables, as well as sibling preferences (Simeonsson & Bailey, 1986).

The naturalistic observational research of Brody, Stoneman, and their associates reflects the intensity and persistence of effort that must be displayed to understand the complex interplay of variables within and across a family subsystem. Their investigations of day-to-day interactions within families help to identify the variables that need further study in training and predictive research, and their framework with typical families emphasizing contextual influences, provides a point of departure for work with the siblings of handicapped children. The interested reader is referred to Brody and Stoneman (1986) for more specific explication of conceptual and methodological issues involved in research with the sibling subsystem.

Social Support Networks

Accumulating evidence suggests that the roles played by extended family and community (e.g., neighborhood) members serve to modify family interactions and stress levels and facilitate or interfere with the effectiveness of intervention efforts. Social support has been found to mediate stressors involving divorce (Hetherington, Cox, & Cox, 1982), job loss (Bronfenbrenner & Crouter, 1982), and premature birth (Crnic, Greenberg, Ragozin, Robinsin, & Basham, 1983). Both parental and child outcomes have been produced, including improved attitudes toward childrearing and improved child behavior (Dunst, Trivette, & Cross, 1986). Conversely, the absence of a supportive network has been found to exacerbate problems related to child abuse (Wahler, 1980) and the birth of a handicapped child (Gable & Kotsch, 1981). In addition, Dunst (1986b) found that absence of support, or dissatisfaction with existing relationships, is associated with resistance to professionally prescribed child treatment plans. Thus, on a practical level, the success of intervention efforts may be determined, in part, by an interventionist's ability to create supportive linkages (i.e., create more friendships), to alter the perceptions of existing relationships, or to design an intervention for extended family members (e.g., grandparents) to facilitate their adaptation to the birth of a handicapped child (Berger & Fowlkes, 1980; Gabel & Kotsch, 1981). Without satisfactory support, a family's unmet needs, isolation, and frustration may result in the interventionist becoming just another aversive person to be avoided. Ironically, it may be simple needs, such as respite from caregiving responsibilities and time for oneself and one's spouse, that contribute most to initial and sustained motivation toward a treatment plan. Thus, a wide-angled, systemic view of social support within a family's existing ecology may provide the necessary undergirding for a successful treatment plan. In short, failure to perform a broad-based, multimodal assessment may be the downfall of an otherwise well-designed program (Conger, 1981).

The placement of this discussion does not imply that extended family and community support factors are less important to intervention success than the previously discussed interactions within and across family subsystems. Needed are empirical comparisons of the relative effects of extra- and intrafamilial influences on various intervention strategies within differing family systems. Until this research is done, the salience of support factors to treatment success is determined most effectively through the sensitivity of the interventionist to the idiosyncratic needs of individual family systems.

Conclusions and Future Directions

One risk in presenting an analysis of multidirectional influences exerted by children and adults in various contexts is to do little more than provide a conceptual straitjacket within which the reader feels unable to move. Certainly, the broadening of intervention to be consistent with the notion of multiple transactions presents numerous challenges to clinicians and researchers. Rather than overwhelm the reader, the author hopes to have provided a rationale for well-designed research and competent practice sensitive to the complexities of person–environment transactions from behavioral, developmental, and ecological vantage points.

To advance our understanding of early intervention effectiveness, research efforts must employ multivariate longitudinal designs with a combined molecular and molar focus so as to approximate the natural conditions in which reciprocal interactions and behaviors occur. In addition, there is ample suggestion from past efforts that the following guidelines would help unravel the complexities of early intervention research and bridge the gap between research and practice. First, more case studies are needed in which individual children, classrooms, and families are the units of measurement. To enhance credibility, these case studies should be designed with consideration given to objective and continuous measurement, past and future projections of the dependent variable (before and after intervention), and replication across different cases (Kazdin, 1981). Second, combined time-series, multiple baseline designs across different subjects, settings, and behaviors are needed to avoid the pitfalls of simple pre-post designs and to approximate natural conditions in which several behaviors occur simultaneously. Third, larger samples, adequately matched control groups, random assignment to treatment groups, common observation methods, and prospectively designed studies would lend substance to the conclusions drawn thus far about intervention effectiveness at the preschool level. Finally, selection bias should be avoided, with more attention directed toward the unique needs of nontraditional samples (e.g., single parent families of different ethnic origin), again to approximate reality to the greatest extent possible.

In conclusion, by promoting an understanding of the realities and complexities facing young children and their families, we reduce the likelihood that our efforts will be interpreted as aversive and met with resistance. Rather, we increase the probability that our interventions will tap into the power that family and classroom systems themselves hold to effect meaningful behavioral change.

References

Adams, G. L., Tallon, R. J., & Strangl, J. M. (1980). Environmental influences on self-stimulating behavior. *American Journal of Mental Deficiency, 85,* 171–175.

Adubato, S. A., Adams, K. A., & Budd, K. S. (1981). Teaching a parent to train a spouse in child management techniques. *Journal of Applied Behavior Analysis, 14,* 193–205.

Ainsworth, M. (1973). The development of mother–infant attachment. In B. Caldwell & H. Ricciuti (Eds.), *Review of child development research* (Vol. 3, pp. 1256–1278). Chicago: University of Chicago Press.

Alberto, P., Jones, N., Sizemore, A., & Doran, D. (1980). A comparison of individual and group instruction across response tasks. *Journal of the Association for the Severely Handicapped, 5,* 285-293.

Alberto, P., Briggs, T., & Goldstein, D. (1983). Managing learning in handicapped infants. In S. G. Garwood & R. R. Fewell (Eds.), *Educating handicapped infants* (pp. 417–454). Rockville, MD: Aspen Systems.

Allen, K. E., Hart, B., Buell, J. S., Harris, F. R., & Wolf, M. M. (1964). Effects of social reinforcement on isolate behavior of a nursery school child. *Child Development, 35,* 511–518.

Apolloni, T., Cooke, S. A., & Cooke, T. P. (1977). Establishing a normal peer as a behavioral model for delayed toddlers. *Perceptual and Motor Skills, 44,* 231–241.

Azrin, N. H., Schaeffer, R. M., & Wesolowski, M. D. (1976). A rapid method of teaching profoundly retarded persons to dress. *Mental Retardation, 14,* 29–33.

Baer, D. M., Peterson, R., & Sherman, J. A. (1967). The development of imitation by reinforcing behavioral similarity to a model. *Journal of the Experimental Analysis of Behavior, 10,* 405–416.

Bailey, D. B., & Wolery, M. K. (1984). *Teaching infants and preschoolers with handicaps.* Columbus, OH: Merrill.

Bailey, D. B., Jens, K. G., & Johnson, N. (1983). Curricula for handicapped infants. In S. G. Garwood & R. R. Fewell (Eds.), *Educating handicapped infants* (pp. 387–416). Rockville, MD: Aspen Systems.

Bandura, A. (1977). *Social learning theory.* Englewood Cliffs, NJ: Prentice-Hall.

Bandura, A. & Menlove, F. L. (1968). Factors determining vicarious extinction of avoidance behavior through symbolic modeling. *Journal of Personality and Social Psychology, 8,* 99–108.

Becker, W. C., Madsen, C. H., Arnold, C. R., & Thomas, D. R. (1967). The contingent use of teacher attention and praising in reducing classroom behavior problems. *Journal of Special Education, 1,* 287–307.

Beckman, P. B. (1983). Characteristics of handicapped infants: A study of the relationship between child characteristics and stress as reported by mothers. *American Journal of Mental Deficiency, 88,* 150–156.

Bell, R. (1971). Stimulus control of parent or caregiver behavior by offspring. *Developmental Psychology, 4,* 63–72.

Belsky, J. (1981). Early human experience: A family perspective. *Developmental Psychology, 17,* 3–23.

Berger, M. & Fowlkes, M. (1980). Family intervention project: A family network model for serving young handicapped children. *Young Children, 35,* 22–32.

Biberdoff, J. R., & Pear, J. J. (1977). Two-to-one versus one-to-one student–teacher ratios in the operant verbal training of retarded children. *Journal of Applied Behavior Analysis, 10,* 506.

Billings, D. C., & Wasik, B. H. (1985). Self-instructional training with preschoolers: An attempt to replicate. *Journal of Applied Behavior Analysis, 18,* 61–68.

Bornstein, P. H. (1985). Self-instructional training: A commentary and state-of-the-art. *Journal of Applied Behavior Analysis, 18,* 68–72.

Bornstein, P. H., & Quevillon, R. P. (1976). The effects of a self-instructional package on overactive preschool boys. *Journal of Applied Behavior Analysis, 9,* 179–188.

Bower, T. G. (1974). Competent newborns. *New Scientist, 61,* 672–675.

Bragg, J. H., Houser, C., & Schumaker, J. (1975). Behavior modifications: Effects on reverse tailor sitting in children with cerebral palsy. *Physical Therapy, 55,* 860–868.

Breiner, J., & Beck, S. (1984). Parents as change agents in the management of their developmentally delayed childrens' noncompliant behaviors: A critical review. *Applied Research in Mental Retardation, 5,* 259–278.

Bricker, W. A., & Bricker, D. D. (1976). The Infant, Toddler, and Preschool Research and Intervention Project. In T. D. Tjossem (Ed.), *Intervention strategies for high risk infants and young children* (pp. 545–572). Baltimore, MD: University Park Press.

Bristol, M. M. (1985). Designing programs for young developmentally disabled children: A family systems approach to autism. *Remedial and Special Education, 4,* 46–53.

Bristol, M. M., & Gallagher. J. J. (1986). Research on fathers of young handicapped children: Evolution, review, and some future directions. In J. J. Gallagher & P. M. Vietze (Eds.), *Families of handicapped persons* (pp. 81–100). Baltimore, MD: Paul Brookes.

Brody, G. H., & Stoneman, Z. (1981). Selective imitation of same-age, older, and younger peer models. *Child Development, 52,* 717–720.

Brody, G. H., & Stoneman, Z. (1983). Children with atypical siblings: Socialization outcomes and clinical participation. In B. B. Lahey & A. Kazdin (Eds.), *Advances in clinical child psychology* (Vol. 6, pp. 285–326). New York: Plenum Press.

Brody, G. H., & Stoneman, Z. (1986). Contextual issues in the study of sibling socialization. In J. J. Gallagher & P. M. Vietze (Eds.), *Families of handicapped persons* (pp. 197–218). Baltimore, MD: Paul Brookes.

Brody, G. H., Pellegrini, A. D., & Sigel, I. E. (1986). Marital quality and mother-child and father-child interactions with school-aged children. *Developmental Psychology, 22,* 291–296.

Bronfenbrenner, U., & Crouter, A. C. (1982). Work and family through time and space. In S. B. Kamerman & C. D. Hayes (Eds.), *Families that work: Children in a changing world* (pp. 39–83). Washington, DC: National Academy Press.

Bryant, L. E., & Budd, K. S. (1982). Self-instruction training to increase independent work performance in preschoolers. *Journal of Applied Behavior Analysis, 15*, 259–271.

Burstein, N. D. (1986). The effects of classroom organization on mainstreamed preschool children. *Exceptional Children, 52*, 425–435.

Carpenter, G. (1974). Mother's face and the newborn. *New Scientist, 61*, 742–744.

Carr, E., Newsom, C. D., & Binkoff, J. (1980). Escape as a factor in the aggressive behavior ot two retarded children. *Journal of Applied Behavior Analysis, 13*, 101–117.

Carta, J. J., & Greenwood, C. R. (1985). Eco-behavioral assessment: A methodology for expanding the evaluation of early intervention programs. *Topics in Early Childhood Special Education, 5*, 88–101.

Case, R. (1978). A developmentally based theory and technology of instruction. *Review of Educational Research, 48*, 439–463.

Cash, W. M., & Evans, I. M. (1975). Training preschool children to modify their retarded siblings' behavior. *Journal of Behavioral Therapy and Experimental Psychiatry, 6*, 13–16.

Cavanaugh, P., & Davidson, M. (1977). The secondary circular reaction and response elicitation in the operant learning of six-month-old infants. *Developmental Psychology, 13*, 371–376.

Cicchetti, D., & Sroufe, L. A. (1976). The relationship between affective and cognitive development in Down's Syndrome infants. *Child Development, 46*, 920–929.

Clark, H. B., Rowbury, T., Baer, A. M., & Baer, D. M. (1973). Timeout as a punishing stimulus in continuous and intermittent schedules. *Journal of Applied Behavior Analysis, 6*, 443–455.

Cohen, A. S., Hulls, J., & Paige, R. (1978). The influence of context on activity level of young children. *Journal of Genetic Psychology, 132*, 165–175.

Cohen, Y., Beer, J., Kidera, E., & Golden, W. (1979). *Mainstreaming the handicapped: A design guide*. Milwaukee, WI: Center for Architecture and Urban Planning Research, University of Wisconsin, Milwaukee.

Colletti, G., & Harris, S. L. (1977). Behavior modification in the home: Siblings as behavior modifiers, parents as observers. *Journal of Abnormal Child Psychology, 5*, 21–30.

Conger, R. D. (1981). The assessment of dysfunctional family systems. In B. B. Lahey & A. E. Kazdin (Eds.), *Advances in clinical child psychology* (Vol. 4, pp. 199–242). New York: Plenum Press.

Conley, O. S., & Wolery, M. K. (1980). Treatment by overcorrection of self-injurious eye gouging in preschool blind children. *Journal of Behavior Therapy and Experimental Psychiatry, 11*, 121–125.

Cooke, T. P., & Apolloni, T. (1976). Developing positive social-emotional behaviors: A study of training and generalization effects. *Journal of Applied Behavior Analysis, 9*, 65–78.

Crain, W. C. (1980). *Theories of development*. Englewood Cliffs, NJ: Prentice-Hall.

Crnic, K., Greenberg, M., Ragozin, A., Robinson, N., & Basham, R. (1983). Effects of stress and social support on mothers of premature and full-term infants. *Child Development, 54*, 209–217.

Crook, C. K. (1976). Neonatal sucking: Effects on quantity of the response-contingent fluid upon sucking rhythm and heart rate. *Journal of Experimental Child Psychology, 21*, 539–548.

Cummings, S. J. (1976). The impact of the handicapped child on the father: A study of fathers of mentally retarded and chronically ill children. *American Journal of Orthopsychiatry, 36*, 246–255.

Danoff, J., Brietbart, B., & Barr, E. (1977). *Open for children*. New York: McGraw-Hill.

DeLoach, J. S., Strauss, M. S., & Maynard, J. (1979). Picture perception in infancy. *Infant Behavior and Development, 2*, 77–89.

Dickie, J. R., & Carnahan, S. (1980). Training in social competence: The effects on mothers, fathers, and infants. *Child Development, 51*, 1248–1251.

Dickie, J. R., & Matheson, P. (1984, August). *Mother-father-infant: Who needs support?* Paper presented at the annual meeting of the American Psychological Association, Toronto, Canada.

Doke, L. A. (1975). The organization of day-care environments: Formal versus informal activities. *Child Care Quarterly, 4*, 216–222.

Doke, L. A., & Risley, J. R. (1972). The organization of day-care environments: Required versus optional activities. *Journal of Applied Behavior Analysis, 5*, 405–420.

Drabman, R. S., Hammer, D. S., & Rosenbaum, M. S. (1979). Assessing generalization in behavior modification with children: The generalization map. *Behavioral Assessment, 1*, 203–219.

Dubey, D. R., & Kaufman, K. F. (1982). The "side effects" of parent implemented behavior modification. *Child and Family Behavior Therapy, 4*, 65–71.

Dumas, J. E., & Wahler, R. G. (1983). Predictors of treatment outcome in parent training: Mother insularity and socioeconomic disadvantage. *Behavioral Assessment, 5*, 301–313.

Dunlap, G., & Koegel, R. L. (1980). Motivating autistic children through stimulus variation. *Journal of Applied Behavior Analysis, 13*, 619–627.

Dunn, J. (1983). Sibling relationships in early childhood. *Childhood Development, 54*, 787–811.

Dunst, C. J. (1981). *Infant learning*. Hingham, MA: Teaching Resources.

Dunst, C. J. (1985). Rethinking early intervention. *Analysis and Intervention in Developmental Disabilities, 5*, 165–201.

Dunst, C. J. (1986a, May). *How to select the right teaching techniques*. Paper presented at the Forum on Young Children and Their Families. Morganton, NC.

Dunst, C. J. (1986b). *Measuring parent commitment to profes-*

sionally prescribed child-level interventions. Unpublished paper, Family, Infant, and Preschool Program, Western Carolina Center, Morganton, NC.

Dunst, C. J., & Lingerfelt, B. (1985). Maternal ratings of temperament and operant learning in two- to three-month-old infants. *Child Development, 56,* 555–563.

Dunst, C. J., Trivette, C., & Cross, A. (1986). Mediating influences of social support: Personal, family, and child outcomes. *American Journal of Mental Deficiency, 90,* 403–417.

Easterbrooks, M. A., & Goldberg, W. A. (1984). Toddler development in the family: Impact of father involvement and parenting characteristics. *Child Development, 55,* 740–752.

Eckerman, C. O., & Whatley, J. L. (1977). Toys and social interaction between infant peers. *Child Development, 48,* 1645–1656.

Evers, W. L., & Schwartz, J. S. (1973). Modifying social withdrawal in preschoolers: Filmed modeling and teacher praise. *Journal of Abnormal Child Psychology, 1,* 248–250.

Farbstein, J., & Kantrowitz, M. (1978). *People in places: Experiencing, using, and changing the built environment.* Englewood Cliffs, NJ: Prentice-Hall.

Favell, J. E., Favell, J. E., & McGimsey, J. R. (1978). Relative effectiveness and efficiency of group vs. individual training of severely retarded persons. *American Journal of Mental Deficiency, 83,* 104–109.

Ferrari, M. (1984). Chronic illness: Psychological effects on siblings — I. Chronically ill boys. *Journal of Child Psychology and Psychiatry, 25,* 459–476.

Fewell, R. R. (1983, May). *Supporting extended family members: Summary of research findings.* Paper presented at the 107th meeting of the American Association of Mental Deficiency, Dallas, TX.

Field, J., DiFranco, D., Dodwell, P., & Muir, D. (1979). Auditory-visual coordination in 2 ½ month-old infants. *Infant Behavior and Development, 2,* 113–122.

Field, T. M. (1977). Effects of early separation, interactive deficits, and experimental manipulations on infant-mother face-to-face interaction. *Child Development, 48,* 763–771.

Finkelstein, N. W., & Ramey, C. T. (1977). Learning to control the environment in infancy. *Child Development, 48,* 806–819.

Fitzgerald, H. E., & Brackbill, Y. (1976). Classical conditioning in infancy: Development and constraints. *Psychological Bulletin, 83,* 353–376.

Forehand, R. L., & McMahon, R. J. (1981). *Helping the noncompliant child: A clinician's guide to parent training.* New York: Guilford Press.

Foxx, R. M. (1977). Attention training: The use of overcorrection avoidance to increase the eye contact of autistic and retarded children. *Journal of Applied Behavior Analysis, 10,* 489–499.

Frank, M. (Ed.). (1984). *Infant intervention programs: Truths and untruths.* New York: Haworth Press.

Frankel, F., & Graham, V. (1976). Systematic observation of classroom behavior of retarded and autistic preschool children. *American Journal of Mental Deficiency, 81,* 389–394.

Frankel, F., Freeman, B. S., Ritvo, E., & Pardo, R. (1978). The effect of environmental stimulation upon the stereotyped behavior of autistic children. *Journal of Autism and Childhood Schizophrenia, 8,* 389–394.

Friedrich, W. (1977). Ameliorating the psychological impact of chronic physical disease on the child and the family. *Journal of Pediatric Psychology, 2,* 26–31.

Furman, W., Raye, D. F., & Hartup, W. W. (1979). Rehabilitation of socially withdrawn preschool children through mixed-age and same-age socialization. *Child Development, 50,* 915–922.

Gable, H., & Kotsch, L. S. (1981). Extended families and young handicapped children. *Topics in Early Childhood Special Education, 1,* 29–35.

Gallagher, J. J. & Vietze, P. M. (1986). *Families of handicapped persons.* Baltimore, MD: Paul Brookes.

Gallagher, J. J., Scharfman, W., & Bristol, M. M. (1984). The division of responsibilities in families with preschool handicapped and nonhandicapped children. *Journal of the Division for Early Childhood, 8,* 3–11.

Garcia, E. E., Baer, D. M., & Firestone, I. (1971). The development of generalized imitation within topographically determined boundaries. *Journal of Applied Behavior Analysis, 4,* 101–112.

Gardner, J. M., & Karmel, B. Z. (1983). Attention and arousal in preterm and fullterm neonates. In T. Field & A. Sostek (Eds.), *Infants born at risk: Physiological perceptual, and cognitive processes* (pp. 69–98). New York: Grune & Stratton.

Gardner, J. M., Karmel, B. Z., & Dowd, J. M. (1984). Relationship of infant psychobiological development to infant intervention programs. In M. Frank (Ed.), *Infant intervention programs* (pp. 93–108). New York: Haworth Press.

Garwood, S. G., & Fewell, R. (Eds.). (1983). *Educating handicapped infants.* Rockville, MD: Aspen Systems.

Gekoski, M. J., & Fagan, J. W. (1984). Noncontingent stimulation, stimulus familiarization, and subsequent learning in young infants. *Child Development, 55,* 2226–2233.

Goldberg, S. (1977). Social competence in infancy: A model of parent–infant interaction. *Merrill-Palmer Quarterly, 23,* 163–177.

Goldberg, S. (1979). Premature birth: Consequences for the parent–infant relationship. *American Scientist, 67,* 214–220.

Goldberg, W. A., & Easterbrooks, M. A. (1984). Role of marital quality in toddler development. *Developmental Psychology, 20,* 504–514.

Goldman, J. A. (1981). Social participation of children in same- versus mixed-age groups. *Child Development, 52,* 644–650.

Gottman, J. M. (1979). *Marital interaction: Experimental investigations.* New York: Academic Press.

Griest, D., & Forehand, R. (1982). How can I get any

parent training done with all these other problems going on? The role of family variables in child behavior therapy. *Child and Family Behavior Therapy, 4,* 73–80.

Grossman, F. K., Eichler, L. S., & Winickoff, S. A. (1980). *Pregnancy, birth, and parenthood.* San Francisco: Jossey-Bass.

Haith, M. M. (1980). *Rules that babies look by.* Hillsdale, NJ: Erlbaum.

Halle, J. W. (1985). Enhancing social competence through language: An experimental analysis of a practical procedure for teachers. *Topics in Early Childhood Special Education, 4,* 77–92.

Hardiman, S. A., Goetz, E. M., Reuter, K. E., & LeBlanc, J. M. (1975). Primes, contingent attention, and training: Effects on a child's motor behavior. *Journal of Applied Behavior Analysis, 8,* 399–409.

Hart, B., Allen, K. E., Buell, J. S., Harris, F. R., & Wolf, M. M. (1964). Effects of social reinforcement on operant crying. *Journal of Experimental Child Psychology, 1,* 145–153.

Hart, B., & Risley, T. (1975). Incidental teaching of language in the preschool. *Journal of Applied Behavior Analysis, 8,* 411–420.

Harvey, D. J., & Greenway, A. P. (1984). The self concept of physically handicapped children and their non-handicapped siblings: An empirical investigation. *Journal of Child Psychology and Psychiatry, 25,* 273–284.

Hendrickson, J. M., Strain, P. S., Tremblay, A., & Shores, R.E. (1982). Functional effects of peer social initiations on the interactions of behaviorally handicapped children. *Behavior Modification, 6,* 323–353.

Hetherington, E. M., Cox, M., & Cox, R. (1982). Effects of divorce on parents and children. In M. E. Lamb (Ed.), *Nontraditional families: Parenting and child development* (pp. 233–288). Hillsdale, NJ: Erlbaum.

Hoyson, M., Jamieson, B., & Strain, P. S. (1984). Individualized group instruction of normally developing and autistic-like children. *Journal of the Division for Early Childhood, 8,* 157–172.

Huston-Stein, A., Friedrich-Cofer, L., & Susman, E. J. (1977). The relation of classroom structure to social behavior, imaginative play, and self-regulation of economically disadvantaged children. *Child Development, 48,* 908–916.

Jenkins, J. R., Mayhall, W. F., Pescha, C. M., & Jenkins, L. M. (1974). Comparing small group and tutorial instruction in resource rooms. *Exceptional Children, 40,* 245–250.

Jenkins, J. R., Speltz, M. L., & Odom, S. L. (1985). Integrating normal and handicapped preschoolers: Effects on child development and social interaction. *Exceptional Children, 52,* 7–18.

Johnson, J. E., Ershler, J., Bell, C. (1980). Play behavior in a discovery-based and a formal-education preschool program. *Child Development, 21,* 271–274.

Kahn, J. V. (1977). A comparison of manual and oral training with mute retarded children. *Mental Retardation, 15,* 21–23.

Kaiser, A. P., & Fox, J. J. (1986). Behavioral parent training research: Contributions to an ecological analysis of families of handicapped children. In J. J. Gallagher & P. M. Vietze (Eds.), *Families of handicapped persons* (pp. 219–236). Baltimore: Brookes.

Kaye, K., & Marcus, J. (1981). Infant imitation: The sensory-motor agenda. *Developmental Psychology, 17,* 258–265.

Kazdin, A. E. (1981). Drawing valid inferences from case studies. *Journal of Consulting and Clinical Psychology, 49,* 183–192.

Koegel, R. L., Dunlap, G., & Dyer, K. (1980). Intertrial interval duration and learning in autistic children. *Journal of Applied Behavior Analysis, 13,* 91–99.

Kohl, F. L., & Beckman, P. J. (1984). A comparison of handicapped and nonhandicapped preschoolers' interactions. *Journal of the Division for Early Childhood, 8,* 49–56.

Krafchuk, E., Sameroff, A., & Bakow, H. (1976). *Newborn temperament and operant head turning.* Paper presented at the Southeast Regional Meeting of the Society for Research in Child Development, Nashville, TN.

Krantz, P., & Risley, T. R. (1977). Behavior ecology in the classroom. In K. D. O'Leary & S. O'Leary (Eds.), *Classroom management: The successful use of behavior modification* (pp. 349–366). New York: Pergamon Press.

Lamb, M. E. (1976). Effects of stress and cohort on mother- and father–infant interaction. *Developmental Psychology, 12,* 435–443.

Lancioni, G. E. (1980). Infant operant conditioning and its implications for early intervention. *Psychological Bulletin, 88,* 516–534.

Lawson, A., & Ingleby, J. D. (1974). Daily routines of preschool children: Effects of age, birth order, sex, social class, and developmental correlates. *Psychological Medicine, 4,* 399–415.

LeLaurin, K., & Risley, T. R. (1972). The organization of day-care environments: "Zone" versus "man-to-man" staff assignments. *Journal of Applied Behavior Analysis, 5,* 225–232.

Leung, E. H., & Rheingold, H. L. (1981). Development of pointing as a social gesture. *Developmental Psychology, 17,* 215–220.

Lewin, K. (1931). Environmental forces in child behavior and development. In C. Murchison (Ed.), *A handbook of child psychology* (pp. 590–625). Worcester, MA: Clark University Press.

Lewis, T., Mauer, D., & Kay, D. (1978). Newborns' central vision: Whole or hole? *Journal of Experimental Child Psychology, 26,* 193–203.

Linder, T. N., & Chitwood, D. G. (1984). The needs of fathers of young handicapped children. *Journal of the Division for Early Childhood, 8,* 133–139.

Litow, L., & Pumroy, D. K. (1975). A review of classroom group-oriented contingencies. *Journal of Applied Behavior Analysis, 8,* 341–347.

Lougee, M. D., Grueneich, R., & Hartup, W. W. (1977). Social interaction in same- and mixed-age dyads of preschool children. *Child Development, 48,* 1353–1361.

Lovaas, O. I. (1977). *The autistic child: Language development through behavior modification*. New York: Irvington.

Lovaas, O. I., Koegel, R. L., & Schreibman, L. (1979). Stimulus overselectivity in autism: A review of research. *Psychological Bulletin, 86*, 1236–1254.

Lutzker, J. R. (1984). Project 12-ways: Treating child abuse and neglect from an ecobehavioral perspective. In R. F. Dangel & R. A. Polster (Eds.), *Parent training: Foundations of research and practice* (pp. 260–297). New York: Guilford Press.

Matson, J. L., Horne, A. M., Ollendick, D. G., & Ollendick, T. H. (1979). Overcorrection: A further evaluation of restitution and positive practice. *Journal of Behavior Therapy and Experimental Psychiatry, 10*, 295–298.

McDowell, J. J. (1982). The importance of Herrnstein's mathematical statement of the Law of Effect for behavior therapy. *American Psychologist, 37*, 771–779.

McLean, J. E., & Snyder-McLean, L. K. (1978). *A transactional approach to early language training*. Columbus, OH: Merrill.

McLoyd, V. C. (1983). The effects of the structure of play objects on the pretend play of low-income preschool children. *Child Development, 54*, 626–635.

Mealiea, W. L. (1976). Conjoint-behavior therapy: The modification of family constellations. In E. J. Mash, L. C. Handy, & L. A. Hamerlynck (Eds.), *Behavior modification approaches to parenting* (pp. 152–166). New York: Brunner/Mazel.

Meichenbaum, D. J., & Goodman, J. (1971). Training impulsive children to talk to themselves: A means of developing self-control. *Journal of Abnormal Psychology, 77*, 115–126.

Millar, W. S. (1972). A study of operant conditioning under delayed reinforcement in early infancy. *Monographs of the Society for Research in Child Development, 37*, 1–44.

Millar, W. S. (1976a). Social reinforcement of a manipulative response in six- and nine-month-old infants. *Journal of Child Psychology and Psychiatry, 17*, 205–212.

Millar, W. S. (1976b). Operant acquisition of social behaviors in infancy: Basic problems and constraints. In H. Reese (Ed.), *Advances in child development and behavior* (Vol. 11, pp. 107–141). New York: Academic Press.

Montes, F., & Risley, T. R. (1975). Evaluating traditional day care practices: An empirical approach. *Child Care Quarterly, 4*, 208–215.

Murphy, M. A. (1982). The family with a handicapped child: A review of the literature. *Developmental and Behavioral Pediatrics, 3*, 73–82.

Myerson, J., & Hale, S. (1984). Practical implications of the matching law. *Journal of Applied Behavior Analysis, 17*, 367–380.

O'Brien, F., Azrin, N. H., & Beale, C. (1972). Training profoundly retarded children to stop crawling. *Journal of Applied Behavior Analysis, 5*, 131–137.

O'Connor, M. (1975). The nursery school environment. *Developmental Psychology, 11*, 556–561.

O'Connor, R. D. (1969). Modification of social withdrawal through symbolic modeling. *Journal of Applied Behavior Analysis, 2*, 15–22.

Odom, S., Strain, P. S., Karger, M. A., & Smith, J. (1986). Using single and multiple peers to promote social interactions of preschool children with handicaps. *Journal of the Division for Early Childhood, 10*, 53–64.

Oldershaw, L., Walters, G. C., & Hall, D. K. (1986). Control strategies and noncompliance in abusive mother-child dyads: An observational study. *Child Development, 57*, 722–732.

Ollendick, T. H., & Matson, J. L. (1978). Overcorrection: An overview. *Behavior Therapy, 9*, 830–842.

Olson, G. M. (1979). Infant recognition memory for briefly presented visual stimuli. *Infant Behavior and Development, 2*, 123–124.

Parke, R. D., Hymel, S., Power, T.G., & Tinsley, B. R. (1980). Fathers and risk: A hospital-based model of intervention. In D. B. Sawin, R. C. Hawkins, L. O. Walker, & J. H. Penticuff (Eds.), *Psychosocial risks in infant–environment transactions* (pp. 123–143). New York: Brunner/Mazel.

Parke, R. D., Grossman, K., & Tinsley, B. R. (1981). Father-mother-infant interaction in the newborn period: A German-American comparison. In T. M. Field, A. M. Sostek, P. M. Vietze, & P. H. Leiderman (Eds.), *Culture and early interactions* (pp. 95–114). Hillsdale, NJ: Erlbaum.

Parpal, M., & Maccoby, E. E. (1985). Maternal responsiveness and subsequent child compliance. *Child Development, 56*, 1326–1334.

Patterson, G. (1982). *Coercive family processes*. Eugene, OR: Castalia.

Patterson, G. R., & Bank, L. (1986). Bootstrapping your way in a nomological thicket. *Behavioral Assessment, 8*, 49–73.

Peck, C. A., Apolloni, J., Cooke, T. P., & Raver, S. A. (1978). Teaching retarded preschoolers to imitate the free-play behavior of nonretarded classmates: Trained and generalized effects. *Journal of Special Education, 12*, 195–207.

Peck, J., & Goldman, R. (1978, April). *The behaviors of kindergarten children under selected conditions of the social and physical environment*. Paper presented at the meeting of the American Educational Research Association, Toronto, Ontario.

Pepler, D. J., & Ross, H. S. (1981). The effects of play on convergent and divergent problem-solving. *Child Development, 52*, 1202–1210.

Peters-Martin, P., & Wachs, J. D. (1981, April). *A longitudinal study of temperament and its correlates in the first year of life*. Paper presented at the biennial meeting of the Society for Research in Child Development, Boston.

Peterson, N. L., & Haralick, J. G. (1977). Integration of handicapped and nonhandicapped preschoolers: An analysis of play behavior and social interaction. *Education and Training of the Mentally Retarded, 12*, 235–245.

Pinkston, E. M., Reese, N. M., LeBlanc, J. M., & Baer,

D. M. (1973). Independent control of a preschool child's aggression and peer interaction by contingent teacher attention. *Journal of Applied Behavior Analysis, 6,* 115–124.

Plummer, S., Baer, D. M., & LeBlanc, J. M. (1977). Functional considerations in the use of procedural timeout and an effective alternative. *Journal of Applied Behavior Analysis, 10,* 689–705.

Porterfield, J. K., Herbert-Jackson, E., & Risley, T. R. (1976). Contingent observation: An effective and acceptable procedure for reducing disruptive behavior of young children in a group setting. *Journal of Applied Behavior Analysis, 9,* 55–64.

Poth, R., & Barnett, D. W. (1983). Reduction of a behavioral tic with a preschooler using relaxation and self-control techniques across settings. *School Psychology Review, 12,* 472–475.

Preator, K. K., Jenson, W. R., Peterson. P. B., & Ashcroft, P. (1984). Overcorrection and alternative response training in the reduction of an autistic child's inappropriate touching. *School Psychology Review, 13,* 107–110.

Pulaski, M. A. (1973). Toys and imaginative play. In J. L. Singer (Ed.), *The child's world of make-believe* (pp. 73–103). New York: Academic Press.

Quilitch, H. R., & Risley, T. R. (1973). The effects of play materials on social play. *Journal of Applied Behavior Analysis, 6,* 573–578.

Ramey, C. T., & Finkelstein, N. W. (1978). Contingent stimulation and infant competence. *Journal of Pediatric Psychology, 3,* 89–96.

Ramey, C. T., Starr, R. H., Pallas, J., Whitten, C. I., & Reed, V. (1975). Nutrition, response-contingent stimulation, and the maternal deprivation syndrome: Results of an early intervention program. *Merrill-Palmer Quarterly, 21,* 45–54.

Reisinger, J. J., Frangia, G. W., & Hoffman, E. H. (1976). Toddler management training generalization and marital status. *Journal of Behavior Therapy and Experimental Psychiatry, 7,* 335–340.

Rogers-Warren, A. K. (1982). Behavioral ecology in classrooms for young handicapped children. *Topics in Early Childhood Special Education, 2,* 21–22.

Rogers-Warren, A. K., & Baer, D. M. (1976). Correspondence between saying and doing: Teaching children to share and praise. *Journal of Applied Behavior Analysis, 9,* 335–354.

Rogers-Warren, A. K., & Wedel, J. W. (1980). The ecology of preschool classrooms for the handicapped. *New Directions for Exceptional Children, 1,* 1–24.

Rubin, K. H., Seibel, C. (1981). *The effects of ecological setting on the cognitive and social play behaviors of preschoolers.* Proceedings of the Ninth Annual International Interdisciplinary Conference on Piagetian Theory and the Helping Professions, Los Angeles.

Russo, L. M. (1979). Fun stuff: Having a ball. *The Exceptional Parent, 9,* 55–58.

Sainato, D., & Lyon, S. (1983). A descriptive analysis of the requirements for independent performance in handicapped and nonhandicapped preschool classrooms. In P. S. Strain (Chair), *Assisting behaviorally handicapped preschoolers in mainstream settings: A report of the research from the Early Childhood Research Institute at the University of Pittsburgh.* Presentation at the HCEEP/DEC Conference, Washington, DC.

Sameroff, A., & Cavanagh, P. (1979). Learning in infancy: A developmental perspective. In J. Osofsky (Ed.), *Handbook of infant development* (pp. 344–392). New York: Wiley.

Sameroff, A. J. & Chandler, M. J. (1975). Reproductive risk and the continuum of caretaking casualty. In F. D. Horowitz, M. Hetherington, S. Scarr-Salapateck, & G. Siegel (Eds.), *Review of Child Development Research* (Vol. 4, pp. 187–244). Chicago, IL: University of Chicago Press.

Schreibman, L., O'Neill, R. E., & Koegel, R. L. (1983). Behavioral training for siblings of autistic children. *Journal of Applied Behavior Analysis, 16,* 129–138.

Seligman, M. E., & Maier, S. F. (1967). Failure to escape traumatic shock. *Journal of Experimental Psychology, 74,* 1–9.

Shadish, W. R. (1986). Planned critical multiplism: Some elaborations. *Behavioral Assessment, 8,* 75–103.

Simeonsson, R. J., & Bailey, D. B. (1986). Siblings of handicapped children. In J. J. Gallagher & P. M. Vietze (Eds.), *Families of handicapped persons* (pp. 67–80). Baltimore, MD: Paul Brookes.

Siqueland, E., & Lipsitt, L. (1966). Conditional head turning in newborns. *Journal of Experimental Child Psychology, 3,* 356–376.

Solnick, J. V., Rincover, A., & Peterson, C. R. (1977). Some determinants of the reinforcing and punishing effects of timeout. *Journal of Applied Behavior Analysis, 10,* 415–424.

Spelke, E., Zelazo, P. R., Kagan, J., & Kotelchuck, M. (1973). Father–infant interaction and separation protest. *Developmental Psychology, 9,* 83–90.

Stodolsky, S. S. (1974). How children find something to do in preschool. *Genetic Psychology Monographs, 90,* 245–303.

Stokes, T. F., & Baer, D. M. (1977). An implicit technology of generalization. *Journal of Applied Behavior Analysis, 10,* 349–367.

Stone, N. W., & Chesney, B. H. (1978). Attachment behaviors in handicapped infants. *Mental Retardation, 16,* 8–12.

Stoneman, Z., Brody, G. H., & Abbott, D. (1983). In-home observations of young Down Syndrome children with their mothers and fathers. *American Journal of Mental Deficiency, 87,* 591–600.

Strain, P. S., & Kerr, M. M. (1979). Treatment issues in the remediation of preschool children's social isolation. *Education and Treatment of Children, 2,* 197–208.

Strain, P. S., Shores, R. E., & Kerr, M. M. (1976). An

experimental analysis of "spillover" effects on social interaction among behaviorally handicapped preschool children. *Journal of Applied Behavior Analysis, 9,* 31–40.

Strain, P. S., Hoyson, M., & Jamieson, B. (1985). Normally developing preschoolers as intervention agents for autistic-like children: Effects on class deportment and social interaction. *Journal of the Division for Early Childhood, 9,* 105–115.

Tallman, I. (1965). Spousal role differentiation and the socialization of severely retarded children. *Journal of Marriage and the Family, 27,* 37–42.

Tertinger, D. A., Greene, B. F., & Lutzker, J. R. (1984). Home safety: Development and validation of one component of an ecobehavioral treatment program for abused and neglected children. *Journal of Applied Behavior Analysis, 17,* 159–174.

Turnbull, A. P., Summers, J. A., & Brotherson, M. J. (1986). Family life cycle: Theoretical and empirical implications and future directions for families with mentally retarded members. In J. J. Gallagher & P. M. Vietze (Eds.), *Families of handicapped persons* pp. 45–66). Baltimore, MD: Paul Brookes.

Turner, C. W., & Goldsmith, D. (1976). Effects of toy guns and airplanes on children's antisocial free play behavior. *Journal of Experimental Child Psychology, 21,* 303–315.

Twardosz, S., Cataldo, M. F., & Risley, T. R. (1974). Open environment design for infant and toddler day care. *Journal of Applied Behavior Analysis, 7,* 529–546.

Vadasy, P. F., Fewell, R. R., Meyer, D. T., & Greenberg, M. J. (1985). Supporting fathers of handicapped young children: Preliminary findings of program effects. *Analysis and Intervention in Developmental Disabilities, 5,* 125–137.

Vadasy, P. F., Fewell, R. R., Greenberg, M. T., Dermond, N. L., & Meyer, D. J. (1986). Follow-up evaluation of the effects of involvement in the fathers program. *Topics in Early Childhood Special Education, 6,* 16–31.

Vietze, P. M., Foster, M., & Friedman, S. (1974). Response differentiation in infants: A sex difference in learning. *Perceptual and Motor Skills, 38,* 479–484.

Vietze, P. M., Abernathy, S. R., Ashe, M. L., & Faulstich, G. (1978). Contingent interaction between mothers and their developmentally delayed infants. In G. P. Sackett (Ed.), *Observing behavior: Theory and applications in mental retardation* (pp. 115–132). Baltimore, MD: University Park Press.

Wachs, T. D. (1976). Utilization of a Piagetian approach in the investigation of early experience effects: A research strategy and some illustrative data. *Merrill-Palmer Quarterly, 22,* 11–30.

Wahler, R. G. (1975). Some structural aspects of deviant child behavior. *Journal of Applied Behavior Analysis, 8,* 27–42.

Wahler, R. G. (1980). The insular mother: Her problem in parent–child treatment. *Journal of Applied Behavior Analysis, 13,* 207–219.

Wahler, R. G., & Afton, A. D. (1980). Attentional processes in insular and noninsular mothers: Some differences in their summary reports about child problem behavior. *Child Behavior Therapy, 2,* 25–41.

Wahler, R. G., & Fox, J. (1980). Solitary toy play and time-out: A family treatment package for children with aggressive and oppositional behavior. *Journal of Applied Behavior Analysis, 13,* 23–39.

Wahler, R. G., Leske, G., & Rogers, E. S. (1979). The insular family: A deviance support system for oppositional children. In L. A. Hamerlynck (Ed.), *Behavioral systems for the developmentally disabled: 1. School and family environments* (pp. 102–127). New York: Brunner/Mazel.

Walker, J. A. (1982). Social interactions of handicapped infants. In D. Bricker (Ed.), *Intervention with at-risk and handicapped infants* (pp. 217–232). Austin, TX: PRO-ED.

Warren, S. F., Alpert, C. L., & Kaiser. A. P. (1986). An optimal learning environment for infants and toddlers with severe handicaps. *Focus on Exceptional Children, 18,* 1–11.

Watson, J. S. (1967). Memory and contingency analysis in infant development. *Merrill-Palmer Quarterly, 13,* 55–76.

Watson, J. S. (1969). Operant conditioning of visual fixation in infants under visual and auditory reinforcement. *Developmental Psychology, 1,* 508–516.

Wellen, C., & Broen, P. (1982). The interruption of young children's responses by older siblings. *Journal of Speech and Hearing Disorders, 47,* 204–210.

Wiegerink, R., Hocutt, A., Posante-Loro, R., & Bristol, M. (1980). Parent involvement in early education programs for handicapped children. *New Directions for Exceptional Children, 1,* 67–85.

Winton, P. (1986). The developmentally delayed child within the family context. In B. K. Keogh (Ed.), *Advances in special education* (pp. 219–256). Greenwich, CT: JAI Press.

Wolfe, D. A. (1985). Abusive parents: An empirical review and analysis. *Psychological Bulletin, 97,* 462–496.

Wulbert, M., Nyman, B. A., Snow, D., & Owen, Y. (1973). The efficacy of stimulus fading and contingency management in the treatment of elective mutism: A case study. *Journal of Applied Behavior Analysis, 6,* 435–441.

Zelazo, P. R. (1971). Smiling to social stimuli: Eliciting and conditioning effects. *Developmental Psychology, 41,* 32–42.

CHAPTER 23

Learning-Disabled Children

Rebecca Dailey Kneedler and Ruth Lyn Meese

Among the populations with psychological/learning problems, the newest and fastest-growing area is that of learning disabilities. In the early days of identifying and defining learning disabilites, only a few decades ago, there was a great emphasis on neurological deficits, particularly those resulting in perceptual-motor problems. The major early theories on learning disabilities either emphasized deficits in visual-perceptual processes (Hallahan & Cruickshank, 1973) or the rival hypothesis that learning disabilities are caused by language deficits (Vellutino, 1978).

Children identified as learning disabled were universally seen as having normal intellectual ability (as distinguished from mentally retarded youngsters), but as experiencing great difficulty in learning, particularly when faced with the academic demands of a school setting. The most agreed-upon manifestation of a learning disability, then, was a significant discrepancy between an individual's actual academic achievement and what he or she should be achieving based on intellectual ability (Kneedler, Hallahan, & Kauffman, 1984). Beyond this notion, however, there has been substantial disagreement regarding the identification and classification of youngsters having learning disabilities (Ysseldyke, Algozzine, Richey, & Graden, 1982; Ysseldyke, Algozzine, Shinn, & McGue, 1982).

Despite this controversy, scientific investigations in recent years have continued to delineate common behavioral characteristics of learning-disabled children and to examine instructional techniques designed to lessen the impact of those characteristics in classroom settings. Following a brief description of two major areas within which many learning-disabled students experience difficulty, Attention Deficits and Cognitive Deficits, we will describe two broad approaches to the treatment of learning disabilities in the classroom: (a) teacher-directed interventions, which include applied behavior analysis and direct instruction, and (b) student-directed interventions, which include self-instruction and self-monitoring. Our review of these interventions is admittedly selective; however, the treatment approaches we will present have received empirical support as methods effective in addressing the academic problems of learning-disabled children and are chosen as instructional techniques compatible with what

Rebecca Dailey Kneedler • Department of Curriculum, Instruction, and Special Education, University of Virginia, Charlottesville, Virginia 22903. **Ruth Lyn Meese** • Department of Education, Special Education, and Social Work, Longwood College, Farmville, Virginia 23901.

is presently known concerning the behavioral characteristics of many of these youngsters.

Learning Characteristics of the Learning-Disabled Child

Characteristics of the learning-disabled child that have been reported by teachers and attributed to the population number many dozen. In fact, a national task force identified nearly 100 separate characteristics (Clements, 1966). The 10 characteristics most frequently reported by this task force were hyperactivity, perceptual-motor impairments, emotional lability, general coordination deficits, disorders of attention, impulsivity, disorders of memory and thinking, specific academic problems, disorders of speech and hearing, and equivocal neurological signs and EEG irregularities. With a list so long and varied, it could become difficult to conceptualize the learning-disabled population. Therefore, in describing and understanding this population, two approaches seem logical: dividing the group into smaller, more homogeneous units and identifying a few commonalities throughout the population at large.

Smaller Subtypes

The notion of the heterogeneity of the learning-disabled population has gained strength in the face of recent study (McKinney, 1984). In many ways, learning-disabled children are as individualistic as the nondisabled. Most special educators now agree that the learning disabled are the most heterogeneous group of children within special education. The heterogeneity of the population makes the effectiveness of broad, across-the-board treatments difficult to determine. Confronted with this problem, some researchers have directed their efforts to the identification of subtypes within the learning-disabled population (Speece, McKinney, & Appelbaum, 1985). This work is particularly valuable in creating more homogeneous diagnostic and treatment groups within this category of exceptional children. The future of research into specific subtypes looks very promising.

General Commonalities

The second direction to take in understanding and treating the learning disabled is to examine the few broad and general characteristics that seem to permeate and unify the entire population. Are there common threads that characterize the population of learning disabilities? In answering this question, the initial observation of these children holds true: they all seem to share the characteristic of academic retardation in the face of relatively normal intelligence. Beyond this general discrepancy problem, particular problems within two major areas characterize the majority of learning-disabled children—attention deficits, including problems in selective attention, attention maintenance, and knowledge about attention (Hallahan & Reeve, 1980; Keogh & Margolis, 1976; Pelham, 1981); and cognitive deficits, including deficits in problem-solving strategies, metacognition, and attribution (Baker, 1982; Pearl, 1982; Torgesen, 1979; Toregesen & Kail, 1980). Interestingly although not all individual learning-disabled children necessarily demonstrate these particular characteristics, LD children as a heterogeneous group display persistent patterns of classroom behaviors (e.g., they are less task oriented and independent than peers) that have been associated with their academic failures (McKinney & Feagans, 1983).

Attention Deficits

Among the early observations of learning-disabled children was the comment that they had attention problems—variously described as short attention span, being easily distracted, inattentive, paying attention to the wrong thing, and not persisting in their attention to task. Two early researchers in the 1930s and 1940s, Alfred Strauss and Heinz Werner, reported deficits of attention along with hyperactivity and perceptual-motor problems in their Strauss Syndrome description of the learning-disabled child (Strauss & Werner, 1942; Werner & Strauss, 1939).

The relationship of attention problems to hyperactivity has been extensively studied and debated (Hallahan & Reeve, 1980). Usually, a child who is reported to have one difficulty is also reported to have the other. Although much emphasis has been placed on hyperactivity or the hyperkinetic syndrome, most authorities now believe that the major problems of children who are described as hyperactive are a result of attention deficiencies rather than excessive activity (Hallahan, Kauffman, & Lloyd, 1985). Reflecting the shift in importance to attention from hyperactivity is the change occurring in the American Psychiatric Association's (1980) Diagnostic and Statistical Manual of Mental Disorders (DSM-III). The previous edition of the DSM (1968) provided the category of "Hyperkinetic Reaction of Childhood." The newest edition replaced the single category with two categories emanating from an attention perspective: "Attention Deficit Disorder with Hyperactivity" and "Attention Deficit Disorder without Hyperactivity." In determining the relationship between attention and hyperactivity, Hallahan *et al.* (1985) concluded that virtually all hyperactive children also have attention problems and that a few youngsters have attentional problems without being considered hyperactive.

Many aspects of attention have been examined, and in all areas, the learning-disabled child shows deficits. For example, early work on selective attention by Hagen and his colleagues found that children with learning disabilities performed more poorly than nonlearning-disabled children (a consistent 2- to 3-year developmental lag) when asked to recall central, relevant information versus incidental, irrelevant information on memory tasks (Hagen, 1967; Maccoby & Hagen, 1965). This selective attention deficit affects not only the accuracy of responses to such tasks but also the ability to focus on what the task itself is or on how to approach it. According to Kneedler and Hallahan (1984), a major problem appears to be that learning-disabled children do not use efficient learning strategies, such as verbal rehearsal and categorization, which nonhandicapped peers use spontaneously. These strategic deficits will be discussed further in the subsequent section on cognitive deficits. Selective attention problems, then, cause children to delay in starting a task and handicap what Keogh and Margolis (1976) call "coming to attention." In addition, once they do begin a task, learning-disabled children have difficulty staying with the task. Investigators have found that learning-disabled children do not persist or maintain their attention, as compared to their nonhandicapped peers, on a number of vigilance tasks (Pelham, 1981).

Finally, in talking with learning-disabled children, they seem to lack knowledge about the process of attention itself. Learning-disabled children do not seem to discriminate between situations in which attention demands are greatest (structured academic tasks) and those in which attention demands are lowest (free play) (Krupski, 1981). In addition, they do not appear to know what to do to help themselves stay focused when the high attention demands are present. Little research has been conducted in this area of meta-attention (Loper & Hallahan, 1982; Loper, Hallahan, & Ianna, 1982). The evidence on metacognition and strategy deficits (presented in the next section), however, gives support to the notion that the learning disabled have deficits, not only in attention, but also in knowledge about attention.

In summary, the learning disabled exhibit numerous problems in the attentional domain. Specifically, these individuals attend to the wrong things, do not focus their attention for the necessary duration of time, and do not have accurate information or knowledge about the process of attention or the attentional demands of a situation. The treatment of these deficits in educational settings for the learning disabled will be described in later sections of this chapter. For a further discussion of the nature and treatment of attention disorders, see the chapter by Lahey in this volume.

Cognitive Deficits

The learning disabled also have a variety of problems with cognition. Much early research on this population was focused on two areas of cognition: memory and the cognitive styles of reflectivity-impulsivity. According to Hallahan *et al.* (1985), the research findings on memory have consistently concluded that (a) the performance of learning-disabled children on a variety of memory tasks is poorer than that of their nonhandicapped peers; (b) these memory difficulties seem to be related to a failure to use certain strategies that nonhandicapped children use spontaneously; and (c) those strategies that nonhandicapped children use can be taught to learning-disabled children so that they experience success on the memory tasks similar to that of the nonhandicapped.

A second area of research has been the study of cognitive style along the dimension of impulsivity-reflectivity. Based on children's response time and number of errors, and usually based on their performance on the Matching Familiar Figures Test (MFF) (Kagan, Rosman, Day, Albert, & Phillips, 1964), children are classified as either impulsive—responding too quickly and making errors—or reflective—responding more slowly and making fewer errors. In general, the cognitive style of impulsivity is related to poor academic achievement and seems to characterize a large percentage of the learning-disabled population (Blackman & Goldstein, 1982; Hallahan *et al.* 1985). Again, as in the area of memory, attempts to train for a more reflective approach seem positive. Learning-disabled children can be taught to respond in a more reflective manner on a task such as the MFF. However, these training efforts must go beyond merely getting the child to slow down (i.e., increase his response time). In order for an overall improvement in performance to occur, strategies—such as systematically considering each alternative before responding or using verbal rehearsal—must be taught to the child. Then, the learning-disabled child performs quite well on the MFF, although this improvement does not necessarily generalize to academic tasks in the classroom (Blackman & Goldstein, 1982).

Thus, research on memory and on cognitive styles led to the characterization of the learning-disabled child as one who lacks strategies necessary for successful performance on learning tasks (Hallahan & Bryan, 1981; Torgesen, 1977). Also emanating from both research areas was supporting evidence that such strategies can be taught to this population.

Closely related to an awareness of strategies and the ability to use self-regulatory mechanisms to complete a task successfully is the concept of metacognition. *Metacognition* refers to a person's understanding of cognition. In other words, metacognition is the knowledge a person has about cognitive processes and the factors that may affect these processes. The term also refers to the use of study skills, which include knowledge of how to organize and structure content, an awareness of the need to study longer when material is difficult, and other similar information. As earlier noted, learning-disabled children are deficient in meta-attention—their knowledge about the process of attention (Loper & Hallahan, 1982; Loper *et al*, 1982). Moreover, as Hallahan, *et al.* (1985) pointed out, the learning-disabled child is typically deficient in other aspects of metacognition as well—namely, metamemory, metalistening, and metacomprehension in reading.

In addition to their deficits in problem-solving strategies and metacognition, and perhaps as a result of them, the learning disabled share common beliefs about their own control over events in their lives. This broad area of research includes the study of attributions, motivation, learned helplessness, and locus of control. From a variety of these perspectives, the findings reveal a consistent picture of the learning-disabled child as one who exhibits the belief that he or she has no, or little, control over the outcome of events (Licht, 1983). With a history of frustration and failure, these children display poor motivation and a belief that they do not control their school successes and failures (Licht & Kistner, 1986). They have been described as exhibiting "learned helplessness" (Seligman, 1975), "passivity" (Torgesen, 1977, 1982), and an external locus of control (Hallahan, Gajar, Cohen, & Tarver, 1978). In addition, learning-disabled children's attributions for success and failure differ markedly from those of non-learning-disabled children (Pearl, 1982). For example, they are less likely to credit their success to, or blame their failure on, the amount of their own effort. They simply do not see the relationship between effort and achievement.

It is apparent that these motivation/attribution/personality characteristics of learning-disabled children are the opposite of those characteristics needed for successful academic achievement. Thus, this population seems to have additional handicaps that exacerbate their basic skill deficits (Licht & Kistner, 1986). Learning-disabled youngsters have the additional, debilitating handicap of a faulty perception of personal impact. They lack those beliefs that enable achieving children to attack a task initially, to persist and persevere in the face of difficulty or failure, and to attribute their success to their own effort and concentration (Licht, 1983). Treatments, if they are to be successful on a long-term basis with this population, will need to take into account these self-defeating notions of personal control within the cognitive domain.

Cognitive and Behavior Therapy in Classroom Settings

A variety of treatment approaches have been used with the population of learning-disabled children during the past 25 years. This chapter will review those approaches that have been demonstrated to be effective and that relate closely to the general characteristics described in the previous section. The intervention approaches are organized into two broad areas: (a) teacher-directed interventions, which include applied behavior analysis and direct instruction; and (b) student-directed interventions, which include self-instruction and self-monitoring.

Teacher-Directed Interventions

As noted in the previous section, learning-disabled children and youth exhibit a variety of behavioral characteristics that may affect their performance on academic tasks. Of particular interest is the difficulty these children experience in focusing attention and effectively employing strategies in order to perform tasks more competently (Hallahan, Kneedler, & Lloyd, 1983). Difficulty in acquiring and using academic skills, however, is the most widely accepted manifestation of a learning disability and the characteristic of greatest concern for the classroom teacher (Kirk & Elkins, 1975; Perlmutter & Parus, 1983). Recent research on the components of effective instruction, although conducted primarily as correlational studies in regular classroom settings, indicates that critical teacher behaviors and instructional variables can influence student academic gains.

Stevens and Rosenshine (1981) suggested that effective instruction is highly teacher directed, academically focused, and group oriented. In classrooms in which teachers select and direct academic activities at a brisk pace, either with small groups or with the entire class, students demonstrate higher academic engagement and higher achievement. This process of effective teaching is further characterized by (a) clear demonstration by the teacher of a skill, rule, or general principle, (b) frequent opportunity for controlled practice by the student, with the teacher providing immediate feedback (prompts, hints, or reinforcement) to ensure a high level of success, and (c) independent practice for student mastery of the skill, with continuous teacher monitoring and feedback given (Stevens & Rosenshine, 1981). Furthermore, effective teachers of learning-disabled students also structure lessons to focus student attention on desirable behaviors and the concepts to be learned, provide many examples of new concepts, offer repeated opportunities for successful practice, and precue or prompt student responses to direct attention to relevant aspects of a concept rather than simply telling students correct answers (Englert, 1984).

Modeling, frequent opportunity for correct response, and appropriate consequences, the vital elements of effective instruction, are also the key ingredients of two widely used teacher-directed behavioral approaches to the education of learning-disabled students: applied behavior analysis and direct instruction. Research reveals that both are effective models for improving academic performance, especially the performance of underachieving students (Becker, 1978; Becker, Engelmann, Carnine, & Rhine, 1981; Ramp & Rhine, 1981). Although both approaches share a number of important features, including a reliance on careful analysis of each task into sequential steps, the two models will be discussed separately to elucidate their uses with learning-disabled children. The authors acknowledge the applicability of both models to many academic subject areas, but choose for illustration to present examples from the research literature using applied behavior analysis and direct instruction to effect change in the mathematics skills of learning-disabled students.

Applied Behavior Analysis

The principles of applied behavior analysis are discussed in detail elsewhere (Haring, Lovitt, Eaton, & Hansen, 1978; Kazdin, 1978, 1980; Kunzelman, 1970; Lahey, 1979). Briefly, however, behavior analysis, which evolved from the operant conditioning model proposed by Skinner (1953), relies on the direct, repeated measurement and recording of observable behaviors. When applied to academic tasks, a specific skill is first targeted for change and directly assessed. Next, the environmental events preceding student demonstration of the skill (antecedents) or following student demonstration of the skill (consequences) are carefully manipulated to produce a measured change in the specified skill. Finally, through continuous evaluation of daily student performance information, the teacher can make informed, data-based instructional decisions (Wesson, Skiba, Sevcik, King, & Deno, 1984). Thus, applied behavior analysis operates from the premise that careful structuring of the teaching environment promotes skill acquisition and competence.

Parsons (1972) and Grimm, Bijou, and Parsons (1973) have described the nature of behavior analysis and program development in the area of arithmetic. Complex arithmetic behaviors are broken into smaller sequences of overt response chains, each of which must be elicited and reinforced to produce the terminal behavior. For example, the child might be presented with a group of countable objects (an instructional antecedent event) to which he or she must make a response. This response, the arithmetic behavior of manipulating the objects to form a given set, is then prompted and reinforced verbally or through access to other positive reinforcers. Initially, each of the chained responses (e.g., stating the number, moving an object and saying "one," "two," etc.) is followed by a verbal reinforcer, and errors are corrected immediately as they occur within the chain. As training progresses, however, reinforcement for within-chain responses is systematically eliminated and only the terminal behavior is reinforced. The interface between the instructional antecedent events and the correct performance of a skill and between the performance of a skill and the consequences designed to strengthen or maintain that skill, then, are the two most critical decision points within the applied behavior analysis model.

Consequences

Reinforcement contingencies are effective in fostering proficiency or maintenance of acquired skills (Luiselli & Downing, 1980), but will not increase the use of skills that are not yet within the child's repertoire (Smith & Lovitt, 1976). In a series of experiments, Smith and Lovitt (1976) presented seven learning-disabled boys between the ages of 8 and 11 years, with individually selected computational problems. During the first experiment, three boys exhibiting a zero percent correct baseline level were permitted to earn one point for each correctly answered arithmetic problem in order to purchase a chosen toy. This contingency failed to produce an increase in the number of arithmetic problems correctly solved (i.e., percentage correct remained at zero). After a demonstration by the teacher, however, the boys' level of performance increased dramatically and remained high during a return to baseline conditions with no instructions, feedback, or contingencies given. During the second experiment, the boys' computational proficiency using a previously mastered skill was the target for change. Again, the children earned points for correctly answered items. These points were redeemable first for free time spent in preferred activities and second to purchase toy models. Both the contingent free time and the contingent toy conditions increased the number of problems per minute correctly completed. The authors concluded that reinforcement contingencies alone are not effective when children need to acquire a computational skill, but are effective in improving computational proficiency.

Similarly, Lovitt and Smith (1974) and Smith, Lovitt, and Kidder (1972) used the withdrawal of positive reinforcement (response cost) to increase subtraction performance. An 11-year-old girl who performed erratically on her subtraction problems lost one minute of recess time for each problem she answered incorrectly. Across three classes of subtraction problems, the girl's accuracy increased to nearly 100% with the withdrawal contingency in effect, and some generalization was also noted to classes of problems for which the contingency had been removed. Thus, when children have acquired, but do not use, academic skills, the application or withdrawal of reinforcement contingent on a correct response can enhance performance.

Antecedents

When children have not yet acquired a skill (Smith & Lovitt, 1976) or use a faulty rule to execute a skill (Smith *et al.* 1972), the teacher must analyze the instructional antecedent events as well as the consequences. Instructional antecedent events of particular interest to teachers of learning-disabled students include (a) the selection and sequencing of particular instructional materials, (b) the use of key instructional techniques, such as demonstration or modeling, and (c) the use of prompts or feedback regarding accuracy in order to elicit correct student responses.

Smith and Lovitt (1975), for example, examined the influence of a widely used teaching technique, modeling, on the acquisition of computational arithmetic skills. Seven boys, ages 8 to 11, who all had been labeled learning disabled at some previous time, were given three sets of arithmetic problems that they had the prerequisite skills for, but could not yet solve. During the demonstration-plus-permanent-model condition, the teacher demonstrated a sample problem, outlined by a red box on the child's paper, while verbalizing the steps used. This sample problem remained as a permanent model for the child to use as he completed his arithmetic assignment. Each of the boys obtained 100% accuracy under the demonstration-plus-permanent-model condition and retained this level of performance through the maintenance phase. In two subsequent analyses, the demonstration-plus-permanent-model procedure was more effective than having the teacher mark correct and incorrect answers in the child's presence and more effective than simply providing the child with a permanent model of a correctly solved problem or with a demonstration alone. Although not all of the children required the complete demonstration-plus-permanent-model procedure, the authors recommended that the complete technique be used, as it is effective, yet inexpensive, in terms of teacher time.

Blankenship (1978) also investigated a demonstration-and-modeling-plus-feedback procedure with learning-disabled children making systematic errors on subtraction skills. After a demonstration by the teacher, the child was asked to model the teacher's behavior by solving a similar computational problem from the same class. If students solved the problem correctly, the teacher told them their answer was correct. If a student did not correctly solve the problem, however, the teacher repeated the demonstration and modeling technique using two new problems of the same type. The demonstration-and-modeling-plus-feedback technique increased the level of accuracy for all of the children, and some generalization to noninstructed problem types was also noted.

Blankenship and Lovitt (1976) analyzed the performance of seven 9- to 12-year-old boys of normal intelligence, who were functioning at least one year behind their peers in arithmetic, on 12 classes of story problems using addition, subtraction, and addition/subtraction. The authors determined that these learning-disabled children were troubled by the inclusion and placement of extraneous information in story problems. Furthermore, they maintained that the inability of some learning-disabled students to handle extraneous information in story problems might be explained by the theory of rote computational habit, which suggests that the child reads the problem only until he encounters numbers and then uses those numbers to attempt a solution. Blankenship and Lovitt (1976) proposed a systematic method of teaching story problems to learning-disabled students in which the teacher groups similar types of problems and uses feedback techniques such as rereading, writing, and reexamining solutions to enable students to master that class of problems. Thus, through careful arrangement of instructional sequence and feedback, proficiency can be obtained on more complex, as well as simple, arithmetic tasks.

Effectiveness

Although applied behavior analysis is a powerful approach to the acquisition and maintenance of basic academic skills (Ramp & Rhine, 1981), its critics frequently charge that this methodology has only limited scope, and generalizability. Stokes and Baer (1977) argue that if relevant behaviors are to occur under conditions other than those within the training situation, the teacher must program for that generalization. That is, teachers must train learning-disabled students to use an acquired skill over extended periods of time, in diverse settings, and with increasingly complex problems.

Blankenship and Baumgartner (1982) investigated the extent to which nine 8- to 11-year-old learning-disabled children were able to generalize a computational skill. All of the students had received instruction on computing subtraction problems with borrowing; however, an error analysis revealed that each child was making systematic errors yielding an average accuracy of near 0% correct during baseline. A demonstration-and-modeling-plus-feedback procedure similar to one employed in an earlier study (Blankenship, 1978) was used, except students now received feedback on the instructed and noninstructed classes of problems. Three students increased their accuracy to 100% on the instructed class of problems and also achieved 80% accuracy on the noninstructed class of problems. This high level of accuracy continued throughout the maintenance phase. For those students who failed to reach criteria during the maintenance phase, a reinforcement condition was instituted, during which students could earn points for correct answers toward the purchase of school supplies. This reinforcement condition increased the ability to generalize for three additional students. In a follow-up experiment, demonstration and modeling plus variable reinforcement was given to each of the six students who had failed to achieve criteria during the first experiment. The teacher demonstrated a problem, gave the student a verbal rule for solving the problem, and led the student through a series of identical and similar problems. In addition, students were given the opportunity to earn points for correct answers on some days, but not on other days. The demonstration-and-modeling-plus-variable-reinforcement condition increased pupil accuracy on instructed classes of problems and facilitated across-class generalization. Although a component analysis of the procedures used was not conducted, the authors stated that if students are making systematic errors, the teacher should first consider the demonstration-and-modeling-plus-feedback technique. If students fail to generalize, however, the teacher must program for that generalization by training students to use a verbal rule on several types of problems and under variable reinforcement conditions.

Applied behavior analysis, then, utilizes direct, daily measurement of observable behaviors to assist the teacher in making informed instructional decisions. For those learning-disabled students who have acquired a specific academic skill but fail to use that skill at an acceptable level of proficiency, or for those students who must be encouraged to maintain a skill, the arrangement of appropriate consequences is often an effective instructional intervention. On the other hand, the teacher must attend to the relevant antecedent events (e.g., sequence of task, modeling, prompts) as well as the consequences if students have not yet acquired specific academic skills or if students use a faulty rule when applying a skill. Finally, the teacher must plan for generalization to occur by systematically varying the task, the situation, and the reinforcement contingencies. In summary, the following assumptions underlie the instructional principles derived from behavior analysis (Polsgrove & Nelson, 1982, pp. 170–171):

- Because environmental factors largely control behavior, classroom intervention involves altering teacher behavior, instructional practices, and reward systems to improve a child's functioning.
- Children should receive direct training in specific skills that improve their academic performance.
- Educational goals should be clearly stated in terms of measurable behavioral outcomes.
- Academic tasks must be broken down into small, sequentially arranged steps.
- Instruction should be planned and administered in such a way as to minimize student error.
- Student progress should be measured directly and continuously and these measures should be used in evaluating the effectiveness of the instructional program.
- Measurement of student progress is necessary to develop replicable and reliable teaching procedures.

Direct Instruction

The direct instruction model closely parallels the effective teacher behaviors (i.e., brisk pace, clear demonstration, frequent successful practice, immediate feedback) described earlier in this section (Englert, 1984; Stevens & Rosenshine, 1981). Moreover, the model exemplifies the same underlying assumptions enumerated by Polsgrove and Nelson (1982). Direct instruction grew from the early work of Bereiter and Engelmann (1966) who advocated a structured, repetitive, and highly verbal approach for teaching basic skills to disadvantaged preschoolers. The techniques developed by Engelmann and his associates and used in the Head Start Program were later packaged and published by Science Research Associates under the well-known name of DISTAR (Direct Instruction Systems for Teaching Arithmetic and Reading) (Carnine & Silvert, 1979; Engelmann & Carnine, 1975, 1976). Materials based on the DISTAR program for use with older students and adults are now available under the names Corrective Reading Program (Engelmann *et al.*, 1978) and Corrective Mathematics Program (Engelmann & Carnine, 1982).

Features

Direct instruction is more than a set of scripted materials. As mentioned earlier, direct instruction and behavior analysis are closely related. According to Hallahan, Lloyd, Kauffman, and Loper (1983), both models (a) emphasize the use of positive consequences contingent on pupil performance of correct responses, (b) stress direct, daily assessment of pupil performance as the basis for instructional decision making, and (c) require highly structured and carefully sequenced teaching of specific skills necessary for the performance of academic tasks.

The direct instruction and behavior analysis models differ, however, in their choice of strategies and examples used during the teaching process (Lloyd, Epstein, & Cullinan, 1981). In the direct instruction model, step-by-step systems are devised to emphasize relationships among problems, and the child is taught to use a verbal rule or strategy in order to operate on related items. Examples are carefully chosen so that the child can make only one interpretation from any sequence presented. Hallahan, Lloyd, *et al.* (1983) noted that "Crucial to designing such sequences is the use of examples that are and are not instances of the concept at hand and organization of them so that competing interpretations are discredited" (p. 132). Lloyd (1980) termed this approach, which employs a rule for unifying a specific set of academic skills, "attack strategy training." Direct instruction, then, uses attack strategies, but at a comprehensive, curricular level.

Cullinan, Lloyd, and Epstein (1981) suggested that to implement attack strategy training the teacher must (a) select a group of related problems a student must learn, (b) devise a strategy for solving the problems, (c) analyze the strategy to identify prerequisite skills, (d) assess the student's level of performance on those prerequisite skills, (e) teach the necessary preskills that students lack, (f) model the attack strategy, and (g) provide frequent, controlled, and independent practice opportunities with immediate feedback. That is, the teacher must devise and directly instruct the strategy. An example of an academic attack strategy for simple division is illustrated in Table 1.

Hallahan and his colleagues (Hallahan, Hall, *et al.*, 1983) assert that strategy training is an approach worthy of consideration for remediating the academic achievement deficits of learning-disabled children. Research reveals that learning-disabled children can learn to use attack strategies in a variety of academic areas. Moreover, learning-disabled students can learn very similar strategies without confusion. In addition, the preteaching, rather than concurrent teaching, of necessary preskills is a critical step to ensure rapid strategy acquisition and generalization to untrained problems (Carnine, 1980; Lloyd, Saltzman, & Kauffman, 1981). Finally, the teaching of

Table 1. A Simple Division Strategy and Its Analysis (Using 35 Divided by 5 as an Example)

Strategy	Example
1. Point to the divisor	Points to 5 and . . .
2. Count by the divisor and make a mark for each count	While making marks, counts 5, 10, 15, 20, 25, 30 . . .
3. Stop counting and making marks when the dividend is reached	. . . 35
4. Count the number of marks made	1, 2, 3, 4, 5, 6, 7
5. Write the numeral for the number of marks in the correct quotient place	Writes 7

Preskills: The student would have to know
- By which number to count
- How to count by numbers
- How to stop counting at different points in the counting sequence
- Number–numeral relationships (for counting marks)
- How to write numbers

Note. Adapted from *Academic Strategy Training: A Manual for Teachers* by J. W. Lloyd and L. J. U. deBettencourt, 1982, Charlottesville, VA: University of Virginia Learning Disabilities Research Institute.

strategies requiring the same component skills appears to facilitate the learning of other strategies.

Deshler, Alley, Warner, and Schumaker (1981) also suggested that teachers at the secondary level must employ systematic instructional procedures utilizing learning strategies if learning-disabled adolescents are to acquire and generalize skills. Through the learning strategies approach, developed and field tested at the University of Kansas Institute for Research in Learning Disabilities, students learn a specific skill in isolation, practice this skill using controlled materials, and extend the skill into regular classroom materials and settings. Generalization is conceptualized as a framework on which all phases of instruction are hinged. Although the specific techniques for promoting generalization are still in their infancy, the authors maintain that unless teachers simultaneously attend to the acquisition and generalization components of learning strategies instruction, the performance of adolescent learning-disabled students will be adversely affected (Schumaker, Deshler, Alley, & Warner, 1983).

Effectiveness

The direct instruction model ranked first among nine major approaches investigated in Project Follow Through, a national comparison of instructional programs for young disadvantaged children, in raising the achievement levels of preschool- and primary-level children on measures of basic and cognitive-conceptual skills (Becker *et al.*, 1981). As Nelson and Polsgrove (1984) indicated, it would not be correct to generalize the results from this debated research to higher-order learning tasks or to more advanced students. Nonetheless, direct instruction is effective with young children who require basic skill development.

Of particular interest is the research on the use of direct instruction with special education students. This research reveals that the direct instruction model is also effective in raising the skill levels of handicapped learners. For example, Lloyd, Epstein, and Cullinan (1981) examined instructional procedures from the applied behavior analysis and direct instruction models used with 15 elementary-aged learning-disabled children. Although the authors express several limitations of their study, results indicated that the direct instruction procedures and materials improved performance on measured language arts skills for children in the experimental classrooms as compared with children in the control classroom.

Englert (1984) examined the behavior of 28 effective and less effective teacher interns of elementary-aged learning-disabled and educable mentally retarded children. Observational systems were used to code a number of teacher behaviors, including (a) content coverage and pacing, (b) maintenance of a high level of accuracy, (c) use of feedback strategies (reinforcement, prompts, or hints), (d) statement of lesson rules and objectives, (e) clear presentation of examples of a specific concept, (f) precuing to point out an example's distinctive features, (g) repeated presentations, or error drill, following incorrect responses, and (h) firm-up trials to assure student confidence in a skill. More effective teacher interns maintained a faster pace, obtained higher student accuracy, and prompted rather than told students correct answers following errors. Englert (1984) suggested that these teacher behaviors may be effective with handicapped learners because such students often exhibit deficits in selective attention and memory skills. Thus, strategies for focusing attention and providing for overlearning and mastery of concepts positively affect the performance of learning-disabled children. Englert (1984) cautioned, however, that additional research is required to determine how the complexity of the subject matter and degree of student entry-level skills affect the occurrence of specific teacher–pupil behaviors and the importance of particular lesson components.

Although the results of research on direct instruction and strategy training with learning-disabled students is far from conclusive (Carnine, Darch, Eaves, Hoffman, & Tamarha, 1984), the public and behavioral nature of the direct instruction approach places responsibility for instruction with the teacher and appears to provide a framework for instructional accountability (Brown, 1985). Future research must compare direct instruction and strategy training to other methods of instruction and must address the critical pupil, teacher, and instructional components necessary to optimize the academic performance of learning-disabled students.

Student-Directed Interventions

Given the characteristics of children with learning disabilities discussed in the first section of this chapter, interventions that are student-initiated or student-directed have assumed a growing appeal for educators. Because learning-disabled children lack strategies and approach learning situations as passive, externally controlled recipients (Hallahan & Bryan, 1981; Toregesen, 1977), interventions that provide the learner with ways to generate strategies and to participate more actively with the task would seem to be an excellent match. Thus, in the 1970s, professionals embraced a new approach to the education of the learning disabled well-suited to school settings—cognitive behavior modification (CBM). The rationale for using cognitive behavior modification with learning-disabled children has been provided elsewhere in considerable detail (Hallahan, Kneedler, & Lloyd, 1983; Hallahan, Lloyd, *et al.*, 1983; Kneedler & Hallahan, 1981, 1984); however, the authors of this chapter acknowledge the difficulty in measuring cognitive constructs, in demonstrating a relationship between overt behaviors and unobservable cognitions, and in determining the causal links between cognitive phenomena and behaviors (Gerber, 1983; Harris, 1982; Rooney & Hallahan, 1985). We believe care must be taken to avoid the psychological process trap by focusing instructional efforts on behaviors that are related to academic and to social responding (Hallahan, Kneedler, & Lloyd, 1983). Nevertheless, CBM offers an educational alternative that appears to meet the needs of many learning-disabled children.

Although the terminology, techniques, and populations used in CBM are quite varied, most efforts in this area share three major characteristics. First, the child is provided direct instruction, frequently supplemented with modeling, in a particular cognitive strategy. Unlike many behavior modification studies in which the treatment outcomes remain mysterious to the child, cognitive training programs typically specify what the objectives are, why they are important, and what techniques can be employed to achieve them.

Second, the verbalizations used during the entrenchment of a cognitive strategy are viewed as an essential component. Based on the work of Luria (1961) and Vygotsky (1962), which described the shift in the control of motor behaviors from external to internal language, the controlling power of the child's inner speech is considered a developmental prerequisite for more sophisticated cognitions. Thus, cognitive training does not employ verbalizations as simple parroting exercises, but as crucial tools that enable the child to inhibit impulses, select correct alternatives, and guide his or her behavior toward accurate and appropriate performance.

Finally, the child is seen as an active participant in the learning process. Unlike a number of intervention procedures in which the child is a passive recipient (e.g., drug therapy), cognitive training forces the child into a role of greater responsibility. The child is trained ina specific strategy, such as self-evaluation or self-reinforcement and, therefore, is literally in charge of many aspects of his or her own intervention.

In the adult literature, a variety of CBM techniques have been studied. In the child literature, however, particularly that dealing with children experiencing academic and social learning problems, the most frequently investigated CBM procedures are those involving either self-instructional training or self-monitoring. In this chapter, a review of these two major approaches will be presented. For an in-depth treatment of cognitive behavioral interventions, see the chapter by Kendall in this volume.

Self-Instruction

Self-instructional training regimens were the first CBM procedures to be applied to children with learning and behavioral problems. Donald Meichenbaum of the University of Waterloo is generally recognized as the pioneer in using self-instruction as a remedial technique with children (see Meichenbaum, 1977, for a complete summary of this work). Meichenbaum has relied heavily on the Soviet researchers, Vygotsky and Luria, for his ideas on how to train impulsive children to control their own behavior. Meichenbaum subscribes to the Soviets' theoretical notions regarding the role of language as a controller of motor behavior. Vygotsky's (1962) theory of child development posits that, with age, the child's behavior shifts from being controlled by the external language of adults and others to being under the influence of the child's own inner language. Vygotsky theorizes that true voluntary behavior does not exist until this shift from external to internal language control occurs. This shift is also necessary before the child can engage in higher cognitive functioning. Luria's (1961) three stages of development, too, stress the importance of the child's developing inner language: (1) *adult* speech directs and controls the child's behavior; (2) the child's *overt* speech directs and controls his or her own behavior; and (3) the child's *covert* speech directs and controls his or her own behavior.

Two early studies by Meichenbaum and his colleagues (Meichenbaum & Goodman, 1969, 1971) have served as the impetus for much of the self-instructional literature that has since followed. The first of these studies was a comparison between impulsive and reflective kindergartners, as determined by Kagan's (1966) Matching Familiar Figures Test, on verbal control over motor tasks similar to those used in Soviet studies. One of these tasks, for example, required the child to push a foot pedal whenever a blue light was lit, but not to push it when a yellow light was lit. Meichenbaum and Goodman found that only 40% of the impulsive children, as contrasted with 85% of the reflective children, met a criterion of 90% correct responding. In addition, the magnitude of efforts differed in that the impulsive children, when they made errors by pushing when they should not, evidenced more intense and longer foot depressions. Also, in a condition where the children were instructed to say "push" or "don't push" aloud before responding, Meichenbaum and Goodman observed that the impulsive kindergartners frequently would say "don't push" correctly, but would then push anyway. On a second task, the experimenters instructed the children to modulate their own finger-tapping by saying either "faster" or "slower." Again, the impulsive children, as compared to the reflective children, were less able to control their motor responses appropriately. The impulsive children's tapping was more in sync with the use of words (e.g., in metronome fashion they tended to tap once each time they self-instructed, "faster, faster"). The reflective children, on the other hand, indicated a greater reliance on the semantic content of their self-instructions by being more likely to say "faster" once and then tap several times.

In Meichenbaum and Goodman's (1971) second study, they introduced the following training sequence that has become a model for many of the subsequent studies on self-instruction:

1. The adult models a solution to the problem and verbalizes it aloud while the child watches.
2. The child performs the task while the adult instructs aloud.
3. The child performs the task while instructing him or herself aloud.
4. The child performs the task while instructing him or herself in a whisper.
5. The child performs the task while instructing him- or herself covertly.

Training took place on a variety of tasks. The following is an example of one set of instructions that the adult verbalized:

> Okay, what is it I have to do? You want me to copy the picture with different lines. I have to go slowly and carefully. Okay, draw the line down, down, good; then to the right, that's it; now down some more and to the left. Good, I'm doing fine so far. Remember, go slowly. Now back up again . . . Good. Even if I make an error I can go on slowly and carefully. I have to go down now. Finished. I did it! (Meichenbaum & Goodman, 1971, p. 117)

Using hyperactive second graders as subjects, Meichenbaum and Goodman found that self-instructional training resulted in significant gains relative to attention and assessment control groups on a variety of dependent measures requiring cognitive reflectivity. In a further component analysis of the training regimen, they found evidence that modeling plus self-instructions was superior to modeling alone.

Another study that is closely aligned with those of Meichenbaum and Goodman, because it has served as a precursor to the literature on self-instructional training with children, is that of Palkes, Stewart, and Kahana (1968). These investigators introduced hyperactive boys to a self-instructional routine that focused on teaching them to slow down and think before responding. Using a variety of perceptual and perceptual-motor tasks as training materials, Palkes *et al.* gave the children a set of training pictures that cued them to self-instruct: "This is a stop, listen, look, and think experiment. Before I start any of these tasks I am going to do, I am going to say — 'Stop, listen, look, and think, before I answer.'" Using the Porteus Mazes as a dependent measure, they found quantitative and qualitative differences between the self-instruction and attention control groups. Self-instruction not only resulted in fewer errors, but also those errors that were made were less likely to reflect impulsive responding (i.e., cutting corners, crossing over lines, lifting the pencil from the paper, drawing irregular lines).

The studies of Meichenbaum and Goodman and Palkes *et al.* thus set the stage for a number of studies using dependent measures of more immediate educational relevance. Whereas these early studies focused on changing performance on laboratory-type tasks, a variety of studies have since followed that address problems in academic and social responding. It is to these that we now turn.

Two classroom programs of self-instructional training (Camp, Blom, Hebert, & Van-Doorninck, 1977; Douglas, Parry, Marton, & Garson, 1976), are of interest here. Camp *et al.* (1977) reported that aggressive boys who received "Think Aloud" training tended to have significantly higher ($p < 10$) WRAT reading grade-equivalent scores at posttesting than aggressive boys in a control group. In tests of group-by-time interactions reported by Douglas *et al.* (1976), significant raw score differences on the Durrell Analysis of Reading Difficulty subtest of Listening Comprehension ($p < .05$), and nearly significant differences on the Durrell subtests of Oral Comprehension ($p < .06$) and Spelling ($p < .10$), were found favoring the treated group at posttesting immediately following treatment. At a follow-up assessment, however, significant differences favoring the experimental group were found on oral reading and oral comprehension, whereas the differences found previously had dissipated.

Glenwick and Barocas (1979) compared four self-instructional interventions with fifth and sixth graders identified as impulsive on the basis of MFF scores and as having above average amounts of behavioral difficulties according to teacher ratings. All children in the treated groups received training in self-instructional procedures modeled after the training used by Meichenbaum and Goodman (1971). They were trained for a total of over 6 hours spread across 4 weeks. The major independent variable was who conducted training for children in each group. Children in the four treated groups received training in self-instruction from (a) an experimenter, (b) their parents, (c) their teachers, or (d) their parents and teachers. Although parents and teachers had been made aware of the goals and nature of self-instructional training in previous studies (Douglas *et al.*, 1976), Glenwick and Barocas attempted to use these important people as trainers because including them might enhance the effectiveness of self-instruction. Scores on 16 dependent measures (including reading, arithmetic, and spelling standard scores from the WRAT) were obtained prior to, immediately after, and 5 weeks after the training period. Results indicated that there were no significant between-group differences and only two significant ($p < .05$) groups-by-time of testing interactions (on MFF latency and WRAT arithmetic). Thus, these results reflected very little direct support for self-instruction, although it is noteworthy that there was an indication of effects on arithmetic.

One feature of the previous studies that may have mitigated the likelihood of finding self-instructional effects on academic measures was the generality of the treatments. In most cases, the self-instructional strategy that students were taught to verbalize covertly was broad enough to be applied to virtually any endeavor. Thus, children were taught strategies of the "What's my problem? What's my plan?" type. Such general strategies cannot be directly focused on specific areas of academic performance because the cognitive operations for different academic tasks vary in fairly precise ways.

In order to affect academic performance directly, it is probably necessary to focus self-instruction on narrower areas of competence. In the following studies, self-instructional training procedures have been construed to have more specific functions, and perhaps as a consequence, provide more consistent support for CBM. Additionally, some related studies provide corroboration of self-instruction.

In a study of handwriting performance, a learning-disabled boy in an elementary school special education classroom was taught a self-instructional strategy for improving his copying of written materials (Kosiewicz, Hallahan, Lloyd, & Graves, 1981). The student was taught to guide his copying of words by (a) saying the word to be copied; (b) saying the first (or next) syllable of the word; (c) naming each letter in the syllable three times; (d) naming each letter again as he wrote it; and (e) repeating the actions of steps b through d for each remaining syllable of the word. Percentages of correctly copied letters on lists of unrelated words and on passages of reading material were dependent measures. Self-instructional training was introduced after a period of baseline data collection, first on lists and 5 days later on paragraphs. The percentage of correctly copied letters increased dramatically immediately following the introduction of self-instruction, and high levels of performance were sustained. In later phases of the study, a combination of self-instruction and self-correction (i.e., identification by the student of errors made on the previous day's assignments) was tested. Reversal phases confirmed that the effects observed in the multiple baseline analysis were attributable to treatment variables, and a component analysis revealed that the two treatments had roughly equal effects. Although the study demonstrates that self-instruction (and self-correction) training is an effective means of approaching this boy's handwriting difficulties, it does not reveal whether the procedures are any more or less cumbersome than other procedures such as teacher correction and differential reinforcement (Lahey, Busmeyer, O'Hara, & Beggs, 1977).

A large number of studies have described interventions with academic tasks in which the treatment procedures bear similarity to self-instruction. In one group of investigations, self-verbalizations have been studied as a major part of treatment. In another group, self-verbalizations are of lesser importance, but the application of systematic plans for attacking academic tasks has been emphasized. Because self-verbalizations and systematic plans (i.e., strategies) are important parts of self-instruction, these areas are described briefly.

Self-verbalization of parts of academic tasks has been found to be useful in ameliorating particular academic difficulties experienced by some students. In probably the most well known of these studies, Lovitt and Curtiss (1968) observed that requiring an LD student to verbalize a number sentence (e.g., "Six plus what equals nine?") prior to attempting to solve an arithmetic problem results in substantial improvements in response accuracy. Similarly, Parsons (1972) reported that requiring a student who often performed the wrong arithmetic operation to circle and name the sign (+ = −) of each problem prior to answering it results in increases in accuracy. Knapczyk and Livingston (1974), too, found that prompting students to ask questions during their reading assignments led to greater accuracy on answers to comprehension questions.

Specific strategies for attacking academic tasks have been studied extensively. Attack strategies have been taught to students with a wide range of handicapping conditions and have been found to be effective in teaching students a number of previously unknown academic skills. In general, attack strategies are more narrowly focused than are the strategies used in self-guidance studies, such as that of Douglas *et al.* (1976), and are more similar to the strategies used in directly focused self-instruction studies (Kosiewicz *et al.*, 1981). Strategy training consists of teaching students some limited preskills and then teaching them how to use the preskills in prescribed sequences that lead to the solution of problems within a domain (e.g., addition). Self-verbalization may be incorporated in the strategy (Grimm, Bijou, & Parsons, 1973), although it may not take the form of self-guiding instructions; or self-verbalization may not be formally incorporated at all (Lloyd, Saltzman, & Kauffman, 1981). The use of academic attack strategy training as a guide to basic skill instruction has been discussed elsewhere (Cullinan, Lloyd, & Epstein, 1981), as have descriptions of the general relationship between attack strategy training and CBM (Lloyd, 1980) and the applicability of CBM and attack strategy training principles to reading comprehension (Lloyd, Kosiewicz, & Hallahan, 1982). For additional discussion of attack strategy training, see the section on Direct Instruction in this chapter.

Summary of Self-Instruction Research

CBM interventions, with concomitant measurement of academic performance, have come in several forms. Self-recording, whether focused on attention to task (Hallahan, Lloyd, Kosiewicz, Kauffman, & Graves, 1979) or academic productivity (Piersel & Kratochwill, 1979), has been shown to have effects on academic performance. Self-instruction, which may be combined with self-recording and self-reinforcement to form a multicomponent CBM treatment package, has been found to have somewhat mixed effects on academic performance. Broadly construed, self-instructional strategies, such as those used in studies described in the first part of this section, may have facilitative effects on academic performance because they allow learners who are in possession of required skills to regulate their behaviors in a more reflective and planful manner. On the other hand, broad self-instructional strategies may not have facilitative effects on academic performance for some students because, even though the strategies make it possible to inhibit interfering behaviors, the students may not know the skills required by the academic tasks at hand. In the latter case, we might expect that specific strategies would be more successful because they include demonstrations of overt cognitive operations that lead to solutions of particular tasks. That is, narrower self-instructional strategies may actually be instructional in the same sense that academic attack strategy training has been shown to be instructional: children are taught to solve previously insoluble problems.

In those studies revealing effects of self-instruction on academic performance, types of academic areas treated have varied. For example, two studies (Kosiewicz *et al.*, 1981; Robin, Armel, & O'Leary, 1975) reported the use of self-instruction in training handwriting skills; and another dealt with reading and studying skills (Greiner & Karoly, 1976). It is tempting to conclude that these studies indicate a broad range of applicability for self-instruction, but such a conclusion would not be warranted. Both studies of handwriting used younger children as subjects, whereas the investigation of reading and studying used older subjects. This confounded relationship between area of application and age of subjects prohibits any strong conclusions. Moreover, the area to which self-instructional training is applied may be critical. For example, the development of oral reading skills requires fusion of cognitive operations rather than step-by-step, conscious execution of them. Thus, we might not expect self-instruction to be helpful in this area.

Self-Monitoring

The self-monitoring literature is somewhat confusing in that there is no universally established lexicon of terms used by the various investigators working in this area. For example, different researchers may refer to the very same procedure as self-monitoring, self-recording, self-evaluation, or self-assessment. For our purposes, we will embrace Nelson's (1977) definition of self-monitoring. She views self-monitoring, or self-recording, as involving two stages: (a) the person discriminates when he or she performs a target behavior; and (b) the person him or herself records this event in some way. Another way of stating this is that self-monitoring is composed of self-assessment and self-recording. In addition, self-monitoring is viewed as synonomous with self-recording. In other words, self-recording implies that the person has also self-assessed. Although at first glance such distinctions may appear pedantic, they are actually quite useful. Their utility is especially apparent when researchers conduct component analyses of the self-monitoring process.

Although the last few years have seen a number of self-monitoring studies with children as the focus of treatment, self-monitoring has a much longer history with adults as clients. For example, two areas of behavior in adults that have frequently been the focus of self-monitoring techniques are smoking and obesity. Although our interest in self-monitoring has been in its reactive effects on behavior, it has also been used (with adults in particular) as a nonreactive measure of behavior. In the latter case, the therapist enlists the client as a data collector on him or herself. The client keeps a record, for example, of the number of cigarettes he or she smokes per day. The rationale for using self-monitoring in this kind of situation is that the client is in a better position to keep a record of the target behavior than anyone else, particularly the therapist. Self-monitoring in this context, then, is used as a convenient way of collecting data on a behavior that would otherwise be difficult to obtain. The therapist or researcher, because he or she is evaluating some particular type of treatment (e.g., operant conditioning) used with the client, desires that the self-monitoring procedure be nonreactive (i.e., not result in any change in the target behavior in and of itself). Other researchers, such as Hallahan and his colleagues at the University of Virginia, however, have been interested in the reactive properties of the self-monitoring process. In other words, they are interested in the effects self-monitoring in itself will have on the frequency of a particular behavior. An interesting way of looking at this is that it is taking advantage of a phenomenon that most researchers have dutifully attempted to avoid in these treatment studies. Rather than trying to avoid reactivity, these researchers are attempting to create it.

Before reviewing the self-monitoring research with learing-disabled children, we should mention the prevailing theoretical explanations for the effectiveness of self-monitoring. There are at least three theoretical positions that can be forwarded to explain the efficacy of self-monitoring. Kanfer and Phillips (1970) have argued that the feedback one receives from self-monitoring is the crucial variable that leads to behavior change. According to this conceptualization, self-monitoring allows one to compare one's own performance with a cultural or self-imposed standard. Any deviation from this standard leads to self-adjustive responses in order to come as close as possible to the standard.

Kazdin (1974) believes that operant consequences explain the reactive effects of self-monitoring. Using Kazdin's conceptualization to explain how self-monitoring of on- and off-task behaviors can lead to increased on-task behaviors, one could say that the maladaptive approach behaviors (e.g., off-task behaviors such as looking around the room, staring out the window, closing one's eyes for long periods of time) have immediate reinforcing consequences but delayed aversive consequences. Self-monitoring, in this case, may become a discriminative stimulus for thoughts about the potential aversive consequences. Or, one could say that the adaptive approach behaviors (e.g., on-task behaviors such as looking at one's assigned work, placing one's hands on the desk, writing with a pencil answers to problems on a worksheet) have immediate aversive consequences but delayed reinforcing consequences. Self-monitoring, in this case, may function as a conditioned reinforcer by bridging the delay between the on-task behaviors and the positive consequences that await the individual.

A third possible theoretical explanation that we would like to present for consideration involves the extent to which the activity of self-monitoring influences the individual's metacognition about the behaviors that are being monitored. As we have already discussed, there is more than a hint in the literature that the learning-disabled child has difficulties in the metacognitive arean. It may be that by monitoring his or her own on- and off-task behavior, for example, the child becomes more aware of when he or she is engaging in on- versus off-task behavior. Through clinical observations, it is our opinion that many learning-disabled children who are also identified as inattentive or distractible may not be aware of just how often they engage in off-task behavior. If this is the case, then self-monitoring would help to make more salient for the child when he or she is behaving attentively and inattentively. We hasten to point out that our theoretical position may be applicable only to the particular population (i.e., inattentive learning-disabled children) and particular behaviors (e.g., on- and off-task behaviors) with which we have worked. It is conceivable, however, that even adults who have chronic problems with obesity and smoking may be unaware of how frequently they engage in eating and smoking. For them, too, self-monitoring may serve to heighten their awareness of how much and/or how often they eat and smoke.

Prior to the series of studies conducted by Hallahan and his colleagues at the University of Virginia, there were few investigations of the effects of self-monitoring attentional behavior on learning-disabled children's on-task behavior and academic performance. For those studies that were undertaken, it is difficult to determine exactly what the subject characteristics were. It appears that most of these studies either used children whose learning and behavioral problems may have been less severe (e.g., Glynn & Thomas, 1974; Glynn, Thomas, & Shee, 1973; Reith, Polsgrove, McLesky, Payne, & Anderson, 1978: Sagotsky, Patterson, & Lepper, 1978; Thomas, 1976) or more severe than those of the children in the Virginia studies (Drabman, Spitalnik, & O'Leary, 1973; Kaufman & O'Leary, 1972; Reith *et al.*, 1978; Santogrossi, O'Leary, Romanczyk, & Kaufman, 1973; Turkewitz, O'Leary, & Ironsmith, 1975; Young, Birnbrauer, & Sanson-Fisher, 1977).

Only two studies appeared to involve students who had learning problems severe enough to be classified as learning-disabled, but behavioral problems not severe enough to be considered emotionally disturbed—Broden, Hall, and Mitts (1971) and Cohen, Polsgrove, Reith, and Heinen (1979). The former used a subject who differed in sex (girl) and age (junior high) from the 8- to 11-year-old boys used in the Virginia studies. The Cohen *et al.* study was not directly applicable, in that it was implemented in an afterschool remedial program for underachievers rather than during regular school hours.

Although the methodology does differ somewhat from experiment to experiment, the studies at the University of Virginia have focused on a relatively consistent population throughout most of the investigations. In all of the investigations, the children were (a) learning disabled based on a discrepancy between achievement and IQ; (b) nominated as having attentional problems; (c) between the ages of 7 and 11 years; (d) found to have IQs between 85 and 125; and (5) attending a special class for the learning disabled. In addition, the self-monitoring procedures were implemented by the classroom teacher or aide in all the studies.

In the first of a series of studies (Hallahan *et al.*, 1979), a 7-year, 11-month-old learning-disabled boy with attentional problems was taught to self-monitor his on- and off-task behavior by using an audiotape recorder to cue his self-recording. This study served as a prototype for many of the subsequent studies, which were component analyses of the treatment procedure.

The subject, Edwin, was a bright child (WISC-R IQ = 121) whose primary presenting problem was an inability to stay on task, particularly during seatwork activities. The teacher complained that he was fully capable of doing the work presented to him, but that his daydreaming kept him from completing his assigned work. The assigned work in this case consisted of handwriting and math. For the former, Edwin was given short stories (mean length = 40.92 words, *SD* = 10.96) in manuscript that he was to copy. For the math seatwork, he was given "times tables" (mean number of problems per day = 72.47, *SD* = 18.16) that the teacher judged to be commensurate with his math ability. At the beginning of the study, Edwin worked on the "4 times table"; by the conclusion of the study he was using worksheets containing problems from the "9 times," "10 times," and "11 times table." Edwin engaged in these two types of seatwork activities back to back. Over the 49 days of the study, the mean observation period each day for handwriting was 15.44 minutes and for math was 10.92 minutes. Three dependent variables were measured: on-task behavior, correct words produced per minute in handwriting, and correct answers written per minute for math. Rate rather than percentage correct was used for the academic measures, because Edwin's major difficulty was in output (he rarely made errors). For on-task behavior, an external observer recorded whether or not Edwin's eyes were focused on his work. If he was off task for any portion of a 6-second interval, that interval was scored off task. Thus, the on-task dependent measure, consisting of the percentage of intervals that were scored as on task, was a relatively conservative assessment of his on-task behavior. A total of 14 agreement checks, 7 during math and 7 during handwriting, were made by the second observer. The median percentage of agreement for math was 87% (range = 71%–98%) and for handwriting was 94% (range = 92%–100%).

The experimental design was a combination of multiple-baseline-across-responses (handwriting and math) and reversal designs. There were six phases in the study (ABABCD), with A = baseline, B = self-monitoring with tape, C = self-monitoring without tape, and D = self-praise. No backup reinforcers were used in any phase of the study. The teacher introduced the first treatment condition to Edwin by telling him that she wanted him to help himself be more attentive by keeping track of when he was paying attention and when he was not. She presented him a sheet of paper, with the heading WAS I PAYING ATTENTION? and two columns underneath labeled Yes and No. She also told him that she would place a tape recorder next to him that would play a tape with tones on it. Everytime he heard a tone, he was to ask himself the question, Was I paying attention when I heard the tone? and then make a checkmark in the Yes or No column. The tones were randomly presented, and the mean interval length between tones was 45 seconds (range = 10 to 90 seconds). The general sequence used for presenting the treatment followed the steps recommended by Mahoney (1977). The teacher (a) gave explicit definitions and examples of paying and not paying attention; (b) instructed him in how to mark the sheet; (c) modeled the use of the tape recorder and the self-monitoring sheet by role playing; and (d) asked him to repeat the definitions and instructions.

For the self-monitoring-without-tape condition (Phase C), the teacher told Edwin that he had been doing so well that he no longer needed the tones to help him pay attention. He was instructed to ask himself the question, Was I paying attention? whenever he thought about it and then record a Yes or No.

For the self-praise condition (Phase D), not only was the child's reliance on the cues faded but the recording sheet was also removed. Thus, in response to the question, Was I paying attention?, the child was to say something like, "Yes, I was," or "No, I wasn't. I better start paying attention."

The results for on-task behavior were immediate and dramatic when contrasted with the baseline. For example, in the handwriting session, Edwin jumped from a 58% in baseline of on-task intervals to a mean of 91% in the first self-monitoring phase (Phase B). In addition, the two conditions designed to fade the child's reliance on external factors—self-monitoring without tape and self-praise—were effective in maintaining the child's high level of on-task behavior. A one-month follow-up conducted in math found only that a high level of attention was maintained. The results for academic productivity, although not as dramatic as for on-task behavior, generally supported the notion that the self-monitoring-with-tape condition increased math and handwriting productivity, and that this higher level of productivity was maintained during the self-monitoring-without-tape and self-praise conditions.

From the results of the above study and the results of Glynn and his colleagues, Hallahan *et al.* (1979) concluded that the treatment procedure as implemented in the self-monitoring-with-tape condition had been empirically validated. The next step was to conduct component analyses of the procedure in order to determine what aspect(s) of the technique is (are) crucial for reactivity and to develop a more streamlined procedure. In the first study, Hallahan *et al.* (1979) had faded out the use of the cue (tone) for recording as well as the recording response, so it was logical to turn to an analysis of these components. This study demonstrated that the teacher could successfully eliminate the use of the tone and recording components but, of course, this was done only after both elements had first been implemented. It was not a direct test of either one of these two components. The following two studies—Heins (1980) and Lloyd, Hallahan, Kosiewicz, and Kneedler (1982)—assessed the importance of the self-recording and cues to self-record elements, respectively.

The Lloyd, Hallahan *et al.* (1982) study was composed of two experiments. In Experiment 1, a combination of reversal and multielement (alternating treatments) designs was used with one LD subject. After an initial baseline, an alternating treatments phase was introduced consisting of three conditions—self-assessment, self-assessment plus self-recording, and baseline. For about one third of each session, the child was to assess his own attentional behaviors (i.e., each time he heard a tone, he was to ask himself the question, Was I paying attention? and to answer Yes or No to himself—self-assessment condition). For another third of the session, he was instructed to assess and record his attentional behavior (i.e., he was to do what was required of him in the self-assessment plus self-recording condition). The final third of the session was devoted to a continuing baseline in which neither treatment was in effect. The data showed that both treatments resulted in increases in attention to task and academic productivity (math), but neither procedure was more effective than the other.

The design of Experiment 1, however, did not allow for an uncontaminated test of the self-assessment procedure alone. Because the subject was provided with both treatments each day, it was possible that one of the treatments may have artificially elevated the level of on-task behavior and academic productivity in the other treatment condition. Previous research had already demonstrated the efficacy of self-assessment plus self-recording; therefore, it was logical to assume that the likely direction of any multiple treatment interference would be from the self-assessment plus self-recording condition to the self-assessment condition.

In Experiment 2, designed as a test of self-assessment by itself, we found no treatment effects for the three children in the study. We did find, however, when self-assessment plus self-recording were introduced in multiple-baseline fashion, that on-task behavior was increased dramatically for two of the three subjects and substantially for the third. The results for academic productivity were not as clear-cut in Experiment 2 as they were in Experiment 1, although mean and median levels for two of the subjects were elevated over those during baseline. An additional aspect of Experiment 2 was that we also manipulated the length of intervals between tones as an independent variable. One tape played tones approximately every 22 seconds (range = 5 to 45 seconds), another every 42 seconds (range = 11 to 92 seconds), and the third every 90 seconds (range = 20 to 180 seconds). No differences were found among these intervals.

The Heins (1980) experiment examined the effects of cued versus noncued self-recording on on-task behavior and academic performance of four learning-disabled children. During the cued condition, students checked a self-recording sheet each time they heard a tape-recorded tone. During the noncued self-recording condition, children checked a self-recording sheet whenever they thought about it. A multielement design was used in that each child was placed under each of the two treatment conditions, one for the first half and the other for the second half of the period with the order of conditions randomly determined within weeks. On-task behavior increased dramatically for both treatment conditions; however, the cued condition resulted in a greater increase in on-task behavior compared to the noncued condition. For three of the four subjects, both treatments were equally effective in producing substantial increases in math productivity. The fourth student had a slight increase in math productivity. A 2½-month follow-up found a continued high level of on-task behavior and math productivity for three of the four students.

In a study that was designed to examine whether self-monitoring has an additional effect on behavior beyond the effect that external assessment would have, Hallahan, Lloyd, Kneedler, and Marshall (1982) investigated an aspect of the self-recording procedure that has theoretical as well as practical implications. Specifically, we examined whether it is more effective to have the child himself or the teacher assess whether the child is on- or off-task. Using an ABAC design, where A = baseline, B = multielement treatment phase of internal versus external assessment, and C = the better of the two conditions in B, in this case, internal assessment, we collected data on on-task behavior and arithmetic productivity. For the internal assessment condition, we used the procedure we had followed in our previous studies (i.e, when the child hears the tone he assesses whether he is on- or off-task and then records a Yes or No on the recording sheet). In the external condition, however, whenever the tone sounded the teacher made the judgment about whether the child was on- or off-task and signaled him from where she was in the classroom to record a Yes (with a thumbs up) or a No (with a thumbs down).

A reversal design with alternating treatments during the first intervention phase was used to assess the effects of the two conditions. Later phases were used to reduce the child's reliance on the treatment procedures and to assess maintenance of effects (as had been done in previous studies). Results showed that both treatments (teacher and self-assessment) resulted in sharp slope changes compared with the baseline condition. In addition, the self-assessment condition was superior to that of teacher assessment. Not only was the median for self-assessment (97%) higher than for teacher assessment (88%) but the former was also consistently higher than that of the latter. Across a total of 17 data points (8 for self-assessment and 9 for teacher assessment), there was no overlap between the curves for the two treatments. Reintroduction after reversal of the self-assessment treatment again resulted in immediate and clear improvements in on-task behavior. Data from the next two weaning phases (removal of tape recorder and removal of recording sheet) showed that the external elements of the procedure were successfully withdrawn with no deleterious effect on on-task behavior. In general, the results for academic productivity, although not as dramatic, followed the same trends as those for on-task behavior.

From a practical point of view, of course, these results are encouraging in that the internal assessment treatment requires less teacher time than does the external assessment condition in which the teacher must look up at the sound of the tone, make a judgment regarding the child's attention,and then signal him or her. From a theoretical point of view, the results offer a tentative answer to the question, How important is the "self" in self-monitoring? As discussed by Nelson (1977) and others, it is of some theoretical importance to the entire CBM body of literature to determine whether it makes a difference that the child is administering the treatment himself. Within the limitations of our current study, the data are suggesting that the self is, indeed, an important factor in self-monitoring.

In another experiment, Hallahan, Marshall, and Lloyd (1981) examined the utility of self-recording in other than seatwork situations. Because all of the previous studies had assessed the reactive effects of self-recording during individual seatwork, it was of interest to find out if a self-recording treatment could be successfully implemented during group reading instruction. We employed an ABABCD design with three children during instruction in the SRA Corrective Reading Program (Engelmann, Becker, Hanner, & Johnson, 1979). The three children selected for treatment in this study had been singled out by the teacher as having the most severe attentional problems in a self-contained class for learning disabilities. Two changes in our general methodology were made for this study: (a) on-task behavior was defined for the child as focusing one's eyes on the teacher's face when she was talking and on the teacher's workbook when she was pointing to it (as opposed to child's eyes on seatwork in previous studies), and (b) the child, if he could answer Yes to the question, Was I paying attention? was to press the button on a wristcounter (as contrasted to marking a paper).

The A Phase was baseline; the B Phase was self-recording; and the C and D Phases were designed to assess whether treatment effects could be maintained while fading out reliance on the recording response and the cues respectively. Results showed substantial gains in the percentage of time on task for all three children. The ABAB portion of the design demonstrated clear treatment effects. In the final phases when the wristcounters and taped cues were removed, the children's levels of on-task behavior dropped slightly, but remained substantially higher than those found in the baseline and reversal phases. Moreover, these higher levels of attention were maintained for a 6-week follow-up session. Unfortunately, the open-ended nature of the group instruction did not permit us to collect academic response data. Anecdotal reports by the teacher, however, suggest that the children have improved academically because of the treatment.

In a recent study, Rooney, Polloway, and Hallahan (1985) investigated the effects of self-monitoring procedures on lower ability youngsters with learning disabilities. The procedures were similar to those used by Hallahan and his colleagues in extensive previous research on self-monitoring, involving the use of a tone and a recording sheet. The primary difference in this study was that the subjects had a mean IQ of 76, which was lower than that of subjects in the previous studies. In addition, the children were required to record their academic performance as well as their attention, to determine if one was more effective than the other or if the two in combination were most effective.

Results showed that self-monitoring of attention can be used effectively with lower functioning learning-disabled children, although some adjustments may be needed. The combination of self-monitoring attention and accuracy was more effective in increasing on-task behavior for all the students than was the self-monitoring of attention alone. A need for more extensive self-monitoring training (similar to that used with mentally retarded populations) was suggested.

Rooney, Halahan, and Lloyd (1984) examined the feasibility and effectiveness of the self-monitoring procedures in a mainstream setting. They found that self-monitoring of on- and off-task behavior led to increased attention to task by four learning-disabled children in their regular classrooms. Unlike most of the previous studies using these procedures, this study did not include a measure of academic productivity.

Summary of Self-Monitoring Research

Conclusions emanating from the work of Hallahan and his colleagues with learning-disabled children fall into two broad categories: (a) data-based conclusions—those that are directly related to the results obtained, and (b) non-data-based conclusions—those that are based on clinical intuitions but not yet tested empirically.

Data-based conclusions include the following:

1. Self-monitoring of attention during academic work leads to increases in attentional behavior.
2. Although the results are not as dramatic as for the dependent variable of attention, self-monitoring of attention during academic work also leads to increases in academic productivity.
3. The cue (tone) to record is a necessary element in the procedure, but the child can be weaned from reliance on it.
4. The recording response is also a necessary element in the procedure, but again the child can be weaned from reliance on it.
5. The self-monitoring procedure can be used with a high degree of success with no reliance upon backup reinforcers.
6. Maintenance of effects has been demonstrated for a period of up to 2½ months (this is the longest duration we have tested).

Non-data-based conclusions include the following:

1. The self-monitoring technique seems to work best when children are working on tasks for which they already have the skills. In other words, the success of the procedure has not been demonstrated for children who are in the acquisition stages of learning. The strength of this technique is that it encourages the child to attend to the task at hand. It does not, however, guarantee that the child will learn new skills. Thus, the procedure may be best suited for use with children whose primary problem is attentional in nature.
2. The procedure has been implemented primarily during seatwork; however, it can, with appropriate modifications (e.g., Hallahan *et al.*, 1981), be used in group settings. The latter use, though, requires that the teacher define "paying attention" very narrowly for the children. In any self-monitoring of attention procedure, it is important that the children have a clear understanding of what on- versus off-task behavior is. The more complex the instructional situation, both in terms of task demands and teacher–child and child–child interactions, the more difficult it is for the child to distinguish on- from off-task behavior.
3. It appears that one major reason for the success of self-monitoring is that these procedures attempt to "seduce" the child as

much as possible into believing that he or she is a co-teacher in the instructional process. During the training regimen, the teacher attempts to involve the child in formulating a plan for change. There is no doubt in the teacher's mind regarding what the final outcome will be, but he/she attempts to have the child share in the development of the treatment procedure.

Summary of Student-Directed Interventions

Clinical impressions and laboratory research literature on the psychological characteristics of learning-disabled children corroborate the viewpoint that the learning disabled have problems in applying appropriate task-approach skills. They often seem at a loss when confronted with problems that require strategic behavior for solution. Given this picture of a relatively passive child, we have presented a review of research using two general treatment procedures—self-instruction and self-monitoring—that fall under the rubric of CBM. We look to educational techniques of a CBM nature for use with the learning-disabled child primarily because these procedures: (a) involve direct instruction in the use of strategies necessary for effective learning; and (b) require the child him or herself to become involved actively in the teaching-learning process.

The research we reviewed in the areas of self-instruction of academic and social responding and self-monitoring of attention has shown both techniques to be, for the most part, effective. Two areas for further research in the area of CBM, generally, are component analyses and subject characteristics. More information is needed to know what specific aspects of CBM approaches make them more or less effective, and for what kinds of children these procedures are most beneficial. Within these broad areas, Rooney and Hallahan (1985) enumerated specific guidelines to direct future study in the area of cognitive behavior modification for learning-disabled children.

Summary and Conclusions

Learning-disabled children, although sharing the common characteristic of academic achievement, are a diverse group of youngsters. Deficits in the attentional and cognitive domains, however, are frequently recurring themes in the research literature. Individuals with learning disabilities are often characterized by an impulsive or nonstrategic approach to problem solving, by difficulty in demonstrating task-oriented behaviors, and by self-defeating beliefs about their own personal control over events in their lives. Obviously, these characteristics are antithetical to those adaptive classroom behaviors exhibited by normal peers. Furthermore, we believe that these cognitive and attentional characteristics of learning-disabled children are essential elements of this handicap, elements that exist at the time of identification, that contribute to the child's referral by the classroom teacher, and that have implications for appropriate intervention in the classroom (McKinney, 1984; McKinney & Feagans, 1983).

Teacher-directed interventions (i.e., applied behavior analysis and direct instruction) offer the classroom teacher effective techniques for promoting basic skill acquisition. Critics charge, however, that this methodology is limited in scope and applicability and that the effects produced by these behavioral interventions lack maintenance and generalizability (Harris, 1982). Student-directed interventions, under the rubric of cognitive behavior modification, attempt to engage the student more actively in the learning process. Although techniques such as self-instruction and self-monitoring appear compatible with the needs of the learning disabled and hold promise for fostering generalization, these procedures, too, are receiving increased scrutiny. Rooney and Hallahan (1985), for example, suggested that research is necessary to determine whether cognitive behavior modification does, in fact, result in true cognitive change. Moreover, they maintain that CBM must be examined from a more comprehensive, ecological, and curriculum-oriented viewpoint than has been done previously in order to match the needs of individuals with selected interventions.

The heterogeneity of the learning-disabled population hinders attempts to produce a generalizable body of information regarding these individuals. Traditional group designs in research all too often produce "no significant differences" between the learning disabled and other subjects and fail to reveal the efficacy of various interventions for learning-disabled students. Differences that may exist can be obscured by the variability within the learning-disabled sample. Recent research on cognitive and behavioral subtypes of learning disabilities may prove useful not only for more accurate identification of learning-disabled children, but also for the determination of appropriate placement and intervention for these youngsters (McKinney, 1984).

We suspect that the question of appropriate programming for the learning disabled is not one of either teacher-directed or student-directed intervention, but one of both. Applied behavior analysis and direct instruction may be appropriate, for example, for younger learning-disabled children or for those children first acquiring particular academic skills or task-approach strategies. On the other hand, self-monitoring procedures may be most appropriate for those learning-disabled youngsters whose primary deficit is in the attentional domain or for children who must be encouraged to maintain or to generalize newly acquired skills. These suspicions, of course, await empirical investigation and validation in classroom settings.

References

American Psychiatric Association, (1980). *Diagnostic and statistical manual of mental disorders* (3rd ed.). Washington, DC: Author.

Baker, L. (1982). An evaluation of the role of metacognitive deficits in learning disabilities. *Topics in Learning and Learning* 2(1), 27–35.

Becker, W. C. (1978). The national evaluation of Follow Through: Behavior-theory based programs come out on top. *Education and Urban Society, 10,* 431–458.

Becker, W. C., Engelmann, S., Carnine, D. W., & Rhine, W. R. (1981). Direct instructional model. In W. R. Rhine (Ed.), *Making schools more effective: New directions from Follow Through.* (pp. 95–151). New York: Academic Press.

Bereiter, C., & Engelmann, S. (1966). *Teaching disadvantaged children in the preschool.* Englewood Cliffs, NJ: Prentice-Hall.

Blackman, S., & Goldstein, K. M. (1982). Cognitive styles and learning disabilities. *Journal of Learning Disabilities, 15,* 106–115.

Blankenship, C. (1978). Remediating systematic inversion errors in subtraction through the use of demonstration and feedback. *Learning Disability Quarterly, 1,* 12–22.

Blankenship, C. S., & Baumgartner, M. D. (1982). Programming generalization of computational skills. *Learning Disability Quarterly, 5,* 152–162.

Blankenship, C. S., & Lovitt, T. C. (1976). Story problems: Merely confusing or downright befuddling? *Journal for Research in Mathematics Education, 7,* 290–298.

Broden, M., Hall. V., & Mitts, B. (1971). The effects of self-recording on the classroom behavior of two eighth-grade students. *Journal of Applied Behavior Analysis, 4,* 191–199.

Brown, V. (1985). Direct Instruction Mathematics: A framework for instructional accountability. *Remedial and Special Education,* 6(1), 53–58.

Camp, B. W., Blom, G. E., Hebert, F., & VanDoorninck, W. J. (1977). "Think aloud": A program for developing self-control in young aggressive boys. *Journal of Abnormal Child Psychology, 5,* 157–169.

Carnine, D. (1980). Preteaching vs. concurrent teaching of the component skills of a multiplication algorithm. *Journal for Research in Mathematics Education, 11,* 375–379.

Carnine, D., & Silbert, J. (1979). *Direct instruction reading.* Columbus, OH: Merrill.

Carnine, D., Darch, C., Eaves, R., Hoffman, F., & Tamarha, P. (1984). Minimal differences and analytic assistance during concept-acquisition instruction with LD students.

Clements, S. D. (1966). *Minimal brain dysfunction in children: Terminology and identification.* (NINDB Monograph, No. 3). Washington, DC: U.S. Department of Health, Education and Welfare.

Cohen, R., Polsgrove, L., Reith, H., & Heinen, J. R. K. (1979). The effects of self-monitoring, public graphing, and token reinforcement on the social behaviors of underachieving children. *Education and Treatment of Children, 2,* 36–49.

Cullinan, D., Lloyd, J., & Epstein, M. H. (1981). Strategy training: A structured approach to arithmetic instruction. *Exceptional Education Quarterly,* 2(1), 41–49.

Deshler, D. D., Alley, G. R., Warner, M. M., & Schumaker, J. B. (1981). Instructional practices for promoting skill acquisition and generalization in severely learning disabled adolescents. *Learning Disability Quarterly, 4,* 415–421.

Douglas, V. I., Parry, P., Marton, P., & Garson, C. (1976). Assessment of a cognitive training program for hyperactive children. *Journal of Abnormal Child Psychology, 4,* 389–410.

Drabman, R. S., Spitalnik, R. S., & O'Leary, K. D. (1973). Teaching self-control to disruptive children. *Journal of Abnormal Psychology, 82,* 10–16.

Engelmann, S., Becker, W. C., Hanner, S., & Johnson, G. (1979). *Corrective reading series.* Chicago, IL: Science Research Associates.

Engelmann, S., & Carnine, D. W. (1975). *DISTAR Arithmetic I* (2nd ed.). Chicago, IL: Science Research Associates.

Engelmann, S., & Carnine, D. W. (1976). *DISTAR Arithmetic II* (2nd ed.). Chicago, IL: Science Research Associates.

Engelmann, S., & Carnine, D. (1982). *Corrective mathematics program.* Chicago, IL: Science Research Associates.

Engelmann, S., Johnson, G., Hanner, S., Carnine, D., Meyers, L., Osborne, S., Haddox, P., Becker, W., Osborne, J., & Becker, J. (1978). *Corrective reading program.* Chicago, IL: Science Research Associates.

Englert, C. S. (1984). Effective direct instruciion practices in special education settings. *Remedial and Special Education, 5*(2), 38–47.

Gerber, M. M. (1983). Learning disabilities and cognitive strategies: A case for training or constraining problem-solving? *Journal of Learning Disabilities, 16,* 255–260.

Glenwick, D. S., & Barocas, R. (1979). Training impulsive children in verbal self-control by use of natural change agents. *Journal of Special Education, 13,* 387–398.

Glynn, E. L., & Thomas, J. D. (1974). Effect of cueing on self-control of classroom behavior. *Journal of Applied Behavior Analysis, 7,* 299–306.

Glynn, E. L., Thomas, J. D., & Shee, S. K. (1973). Behavior self-control of on-task behavior in an elementary classroom. *Journal of Applied Behavior Analysis, 6,* 105–118.

Greiner, J. M., & Karoly, P. (1976). Effects of self-control training on study activity and academic performance: An analysis of self-monitoring, self-reward, and systematic-planning components. *Journal of Counseling Psychology, 23,* 496–502.

Grimm, J. A., Bijou, S. W., & Parsons, J. A. (1973). A problem-solving model for teaching remedial arithmetic to handicapped children. *Journal of Abnormal Child Psychology, 1,* 26–39.

Hagen, J. W. (1967). The effect of distraction on selective attention. *Child Development, 38,* 685–694.

Hallahan, D. P., & Bryan, T. H. (1981). Learning disabilities. In J. M. Kauffman & D. P. Hallahan (Eds.), *Handbook of special education* (pp. 141–164). Englewood Cliffs, NJ: Prentice-Hall.

Hallahan, D. P., & Cruickshank, W. M. (1973). *Psycoeducational foundations of learning disabilities.* Englewood Cliffs, NJ: Prentice-Hall.

Hallahan, D. P., & Reeve, R. E. (1980). Selective attention and distractibility. In B. K. Keogh (Ed.), *Advances in special education* (Vol. I, pp. 141–181). Greenwich, CT: JAI Press.

Hallahan, D. P., Gajar, A. H., Cohen, S. B., & Tarver, S. G. (1978). Selective attention and locus of control in learning disabled and normal children. *Journal of Learning Disabilities, 11,* 231–236.

Hallahan, D. P., Lloyd, J., Kosiewicz, M. M., Kauffman, J. M., & Graves, A. W. (1979). Self-monitoring of attention as a treatment for a learning disabled boy's off-task behavior. *Learning Disabilities Quarterly, 2,* 24–32.

Hallahan, D. P., Marshall, K., & Lloyd, J. W. (1981). Self-recording during group instruction: Effects on attention to task. *Learning Disability Quarterly, 4,* 407–413.

Hallahan, D. P., Lloyd, J. W., Kneedler. R. D., & Marshall, K. J. (1982). A comparison of the effects of self- versus teacher-assessment of on-task behavior. *Behavior Therapy, 13,* 715–723.

Hallahan, D. P., Hall, R. J., Ianna, S. O., Kneedler, R. D., Lloyd, J. W., Loper, A. B., & Reeve, R. E. (1983). Summarx of research findings at the University of Virginia Learning Disabilities Research Institute. *Exceptional Education Quarterly, 4*(1), 95–114.

Hallahan, D. P., Kneedler, R. D., & Lloyd, J. W. (1983). Cognitive behavior modification techniques for learning disabled children: Self-instruction and self-monitoring. In J. D. McKinney & L. Feagans (Eds.), *Current topics in learning disabilities* (Vol. 1, pp. 207–244). Norwood, NJ: Ablex.

Hallahan, D. P., Lloyd, J. W., Kauffman, J. M., & Loper, A. B. (1983). Academic problems. In R. J. Morris & T. R. Kratochwill (Eds.), *Practice of child therapy* (pp. 113–141). New York: Pergamon Press.

Hallahan, D. P., Kauffman, J. M., & Lloyd, J. W. (1985). *Introduction to learning disabilities* (2nd ed.). Englewood Cliffs, NJ: Prentice-Hall.

Haring, N. G., Lovitt, T. C., Eaton, M. D., & Hansen, C. (Eds.). (1978). *The fourth R: Research in the classroom.* Columbus, OH: Merrill.

Harris, K. R. (1982). Cognitive-behavior modification: Application with exceptional students. *Focus on Exceptional Children, 15*(2), 1–16.

Heins, E. D. (1980). *Training learning disabled children's self-control: Cued and non-cued self-recording in the classroom.* Unpublished doctoral dissertation, University of Virginia.

Kagan, J. (1966). Reflection-impulsivity: The generality and dynamics of conceptual tempo. *Journal of Abnormal Psychology, 71,* 17–24.

Kagan, J., Rosman, B. L., Day, D., Albert, J., & Phillips, W. (1964). Information processing in the child: Significance of analytic and reflective attitudes. *Psychological Monographs, 78* (1, Whole No. 578).

Kanfer, F. H., & Phillips, J. S. (1970). *Learning foundations of behavior therapy.* New York: Wiley.

Kaufman, K. F., & O'Leary, K. D. (1972). Reward, cost,

and self-evaluation procedures for disruptive adolescents in a psychiatric hospital school. *Journal of Applied Behavior Analysis, 5*, 293–309.

Kazdin, A. E. (1974). Self-monitoring and behavior change. In M. J. Mahoney, & C. E. Thoresen (Eds.), *Self-control: Power to the person*. Monterey, CA: Brooks/Cole.

Kazdin, A. E. (1978). *History of behavior modification: Experimental foundations of contemporary research*. Baltimore, MD: University Park Press.

Kazdin, A. E. (1980). *Behavior modification in applied settings*. Homewood, IL: Dorsey Press.

Keogh, B. K., & Margolis, J. (1976). Learn to labor and wait: Attentional problems of children with learning disorders. *Journal of Learning Disabilities, 9*, 276–286.

Kirk, S. A., & Elkins, J. (1975). Characteristics of children enrolled in the Child Service Demonstration Centers. *Journal of Learning Disabilities, 8*, 630–637.

Knapczyk, D. R., & Livingston, G. (1974). The effects of prompting question asking upon on-task behavior and reading comprehension. *Journal of Applied Behavior Analysis, 7*, 115–121.

Kneedler, R. D., & Hallahan, D. P. (1981). Self-monitoring of on-task behavior with learning-disabled children: Current studies and directions. *Exceptional Education Quarterly, 2*(3), 73–82.

Kneedler, R. D., & Hallahan, D. P. (1984). Self-monitoring as an attentional strategy for academic tasks with learning disabled children. In B. Gholson & T. L. Rosenthal (Eds.), *Applications of cognitive-developmental theory* (pp. 243–260). Orlando, FL: Academic Press.

Kneedler, R. D., Hallahan, D. P., & Kauffman, J. M. (1984). *Special education for today*. Englewood Cliffs, NJ: Prentice-Hall.

Kosiewicz, M. M., Hallahan, D. P., Lloyd, J., & Graves, A. W. (1981). The effects of an LD student's treatment choice on handwriting performance. *Learning Disability Quarterly, 4*, 281–286.

Krupski, A. (1981). An interactional approach to the study of attention problems in children with handicaps. *Exceptional Education Quarterly, 2*(3), 1–10.

Kunzelman, H. P. (Ed.). (1970). *Precision teaching: An initial training sequence*. Seattle, WA: Special Child.

Lahey, B. B. (1979). *Behavior therapy with hyperactive and learning disabled children*. New York: Oxford University Press.

Lahey, B. B., Busmeyer, M., O'Hara, C., & Beggs, V. E. (1977). Treatment of severe perceptual-motor disorders in children diagnosed as learning disabled. *Behavior Modification, 1*(1), 123–140.

Licht, B. (1983). Cognitive-motivational factors that contribute to the achievement of learning-disabled children. *Journal of Learning Disabilities, 16*, 483–490.

Licht, B., & Kistner, J. (1986). Motivational problems of learning-disabled children: Individual differences and their implications for treatment. In J. K. Torgesen & B. Y. L. Wong (Eds.), *Learning disabilities: Some new perspectives*. Orlando, FL: Academic Press.

Lloyd, J. W. (1980). Academic instruction and cognitive-behavior modification: The need for attack strategy training. *Exceptional Education Quarterly, 1*(1), 53–64.

Lloyd, J. W., & deBettencourt, L. J. U. (1982). *Academic strategy training: A manual for teachers*. Charlottesville, VA: University of Virginia Learning Disabilities Research Institute.

Lloyd, J. W., Epstein, M. H., & Cullinan, D. (1981). Direct teaching for learning disabilities. In J. Gottlieb & S. Strichart (Eds.), *Developmental theory and research in learning disabilities* (pp. 278–309). Baltimore, MD: University Park Press.

Lloyd, J. W., Hallahan, D. P., Kosiewicz, M. M., & Kneedler, R. D. (1982). Reactive effects of self-assessment and self-recording on attention to task and academic productivity. *Learning Disability Quarterly, 5*, 216–227.

Lloyd, J. W., Kosiewicz, M. M., & Hallahan, D. P. (1982). Reading comprehension: Cognitive training contributions. *School Psychology Review, 11*, 216–227.

Lloyd, J. W., Saltzman, N. J., & Kauffman, J. M. (1981). Predictable generalization in academic learning as a result of preskills and strategy training. *Learning Disability Quarterly, 4*, 203–216.

Loper, A. B., & Hallahan, D. P. (1982). Meta-attention: The development of awareness of the attentional process. *Journal of General Psychology, 106*, 27–33.

Loper, A. B., Hallahan, D. P., & Ianna, S. O. (1982). Meta-attention in learning disabled and normal children. *Learning Disability Quarterly, 6*, 29–36.

Lovitt, T. C., & Curtiss, K. A. (1968). Effects of manipulating an antecedent event on mathematics response rate. *Journal of Applied Behavior Analysis, 1*, 329–333.

Lovitt, T. C., & Smith, D. D. (1974). Using withdrawal of positive reinforcement to alter subtraction performance. *Exceptional Children, 40*, 357–358.

Luiselli, J. K., & Downing, J. N. (1980). Improving a student's arithmetic performance using feedback and reinforcement procedures. *Education and Treatment of Children, 3*, 45–49.

Luria, A. (1961). *The role of speech in the regulation of normal and abnormal behaviors*. New York: Liveright.

Maccoby, E. E., & Hagen, J. W. (1965). Effects of distraction upon central versus incidental recall: Developmental trends. *Journal of Experimental Child Psychology, 2*, 280–289.

Mahoney, M. J. (1977). Some applied issues in self-monitoring. In J. D. Cone & R. P. Hawkins (Eds.), *Behavioral assessment: New direction in clinical psychology*. New York: Brunner/Mazel.

McKinney, J. D. (1984). The search for subtypes of specific learning disability. *Journal of Learning Disabilities, 17*, 43–50.

McKinney, J. D., & Feagans, L. (1983). Adaptive classroom behavior of learning disabled students. *Journal of Learning Disabilities, 16*, 360–367.

Meichenbaum, D. (1977). *Cognitive-behavior modification: An integrative approach*. New York: Plenum Press.

Meichenbaum, D. M., & Goodman, J. (1969). Reflection-impulsivity and verbal control of motor behavior. *Child Development. 40*, 785–797.

Meichenbaum, D., & Goodman, J. (1971). Training impulsive children to talk to themselves: A means of developing self-control. *Journal of Abnormal Psychology, 77*, 115–126.

Nelson, C. M., & Polsgrove, L. (1984). Behavior analysis in special education: White rabbit or white elephant? *Remedial and Special Education, 5*(4), 6–17.

Nelson, R. O. (1977). Assessment and therapeutic functions of self-monitoring. In M. Hersen, R. M. Eisler, & P. M. Miller (Eds.), *Progress in behavior modification* (Vol. 5, pp. 264–301). New York: Academic Press.

Palkes, H., Stewart, M., & Kahana, B. (1968). Porteus maze performance of hyperactive boys after training in self-directed verbal commands. *Child Development, 39*, 817–826.

Parsons, J. A. (1972). The reciprocal modification of arithmetic behavior and program development. In G. Semb (Eds.), *Behavior analysis and education* (pp. 185–199). Lawrence, KS: Kansas University Department of Human Development.

Pearl, R. (1982). LD children's attributions for success and failure: A replication with a labeled LD sample. *Learning Disability Quarterly, 5*, 173–176.

Pelham, W. E. (1981). Attention deficits in hyperactive and learning-disabled children. *Exceptional Education Quarterly, 2*(3), 13–23.

Perlmutter, B. F., & Parus, M. V. (1983). Identifying children with learning disabilities: A comparison of diagnostic procedures across school districts. *Learning Disability Quarterly, 6*, 321–328.

Piersel, W. C., & Kratochwill, T. R. (1979). Self-observation and behavior change: Applications to academic and adjustment problems through behavioral consultation. *Journal of School Psychology, 17*, 151–161.

Polsgrove, L., & Nelson, C. M. (1982). Curriculum intervention according to the behavioral model. In R. L. McDowell, G. W. Adamson, & F. H. Wood (Eds.), *Teaching emotionally disturbed children* (pp. 169–205). Boston, MA: Little, Brown.

Ramp, E. A., & Rhine, W. R. (1981). Behavior analysis model. In W. R. Rhine (Ed.), *Making schools more effective: New directions from Follow Through* (pp. 155–197). New York: Academic Press.

Reith, H. J., Polsgrove, L., McLeskey, J., Payne, K., & Anderson, R. (1978). The use of self-recording to increase the arithmetic performance of severely behaviorally disordered students. In R. B. Rutherford & A. G. Prieto (Eds.), *Severe behavior disorders of children and youth* (pp. 50–58). Tempe, AZ: Arizona State University, Monographs in Behavioral Disorders Series.

Robin, A. L., Armel, S., & O'Leary, K. D. (1975). The effects of self-instruction on writing deficiencies. *Behavior Therapy, 6*, 178–197.

Rooney, K. J., & Hallahan, D. P. (1985). Future directions for cognitive behavior modification research: The quest for cognitive change. *Remedial and Special Education, 6*(2), 46–51.

Rooney, K. J., Hallahan, D. P., & Lloyd, J. W. (1984). Self-recording of attention by learning disabled students in the regular classroom. *Journal of Learning Disabilities, 17*, 360–364.

Rooney, K. J., Polloway, E. A., & Hallahan, D. P. (1985). The use of self-monitoring procedures with low IQ learning disabled students. *Journal of Learning Disabilities, 18*, 384–389.

Sagotsky, G., Patterson, C. J., & Lepper, M. R. (1978). Training children's self-control: A field experiment in self-monitoring and goal-setting in the classroom. *Journal of Experimental Child Psychology, 25*, 242–253.

Santogrossi, D. Z., O'Leary, K. D., Romanczyk, R. G., & Kaufman, K. F. (1973). Self-evaluation by adolescents in a psychiatric hospital school token program. *Journal of Applied Behavior Analysis, 6*, 267–287.

Schumaker, J. B., Deshler, D. D., Alley, G. R., & Warner, M. M. (1983). Toward the development of an intervention model for learning disabled adolescents: The University of Kansas Institute. *Exceptional Education Quarterly, 4*(1), 45–74.

Seligman, M. E. P. (1975). *Helplessness: On depression, development, and death*. San Francisco: Freeman.

Skinner, B. F. (1953). *Science and human behavior*. New York: Free Press.

Smith, D. D., & Lovitt, T. C. (1975). The use of modeling techniques to influence the acquisition of computational arithmetic skills in learning disabled children. In E. Ramp & G. Semb (Eds.), *Behavior analysis: Areas of research and application* (pp. 283–308). Englewood Cliffs, NJ: Prentice-Hall.

Smith, D. D., & Lovitt, T. C. (1976). The differential effects of reinforcement contingencies on arithmetic performance. *Journal of Learning Disabilities, 9*, 32–40.

Smith, D. D., Lovitt, T. C., & Kidder, J. D. (1972). Using reinforcement contingencies and teaching aids to alter subtraction performance of children with learning disabilites. In G. Semb (Ed.), *Behavior analysis and education* (pp. 342–360). Lawrence, KS: Kansas University Department of Human Development.

Speece, D. L., McKinney, J. D., & Apelbaum, M. I. (1985). Classification and validation of behavioral subtypes of learning disabled children. *Journal of Educational Psychology, 77*, 67–77.

Stevens, R., & Rosenshine, B. (1981). Advances in research on teaching. *Exceptional Education Quarterly, 2*(1), 1–9.

Stokes, T. F., & Baer, D. M. (1977). An implicit technology of generalization. *Journal of Applied Behavior Analysis, 10* 349–367.

Strauss, A. A., & Werner, H. (1942). Disorders of conceptual thinking in the brain-injured child. *Journal of Nervous and Mental Diseases, 96,* 153–172.

Thomas, J. D. (1976). Accuracy of self-assessment of on-task behavior by elementary school children. *Journal of Applied Behavior Analysis, 9,* 209–210.

Torgesen, J. K. (1977). The role of nonspecific factors in the task performance of learning disabled students: A theoretical assessment. *Journal of Learning Disabilities, 10,* 27–34.

Torgesen, J. K. (1979). Factors related to poor performance of memory tasks in reading disabled children. *Learning Disability Quarterly, 2,* 17–23.

Torgesen, J. K. (1982). The learning disabled child as an inactive learner: Educational implications. *Topics in Learning and Learning Disabilities, 2,* 45–52.

Torgesen, J. K., & Kail, R. V. (1980). Memory processes in exceptional children. In B. K. Keogh (Ed.), *Advances in special education: Volume I* (pp. 55–99). Greenwich, CT: JAI Press.

Turkewitz, H., O'Leary, K. D., & Ironsmith, M. (1975). Generalization and maintenance of appropriate behavior through self-control. *Journal of Consulting and Clinical Psychiatry, 43,* 577–583.

Vellutino, F. R. (1978). Toward an understanding of dyslexia. Psychological factors in specific reading disability. In A. L. Benton & D. Pearl (Eds.), *Dyslexia: An appraisal of current knowledge* (pp. 61–111). New York: Oxford University Press.

Vygotsky. L. (1962). *Thought and language.* New York: Wiley.

Werner, H., & Strauss, A. A. (1939). Problems and methods of functional analysis in mentally deficient children. *Journal of Abnormal and Social Psychology, 34,* 37–62.

Wesson, C., Skeba, R., Sevcik, B., King, R. P., & Deno, S. (1984). The effects of technically adequate instructional data on achievement. *Remedial and Special Education,* 5(5), 17–22.

Young, P., Birnbrauer, J. S., & Sanson-Fisher, R. W. (1977). The effects of self-recording on the study of behavior of female juvenile delinquents. In B. C. Etzel, J. M. LeBlanc, & D. M. Baer (Eds.), *New developments in behavior research: Theory, method, and application* (pp. 559–577). Hillsdale, NJ: Erlbaum.

Ysseldyke, J. E., Algozzine, B., Richey, L., & Graden, J. (1982). Declaring students eligible for learning disability service: Why bother with the data? *Learning Disability Quarterly, 5,* 37–43.

Ysseldyke, J. E., Alzoggine, B., Shinn, M. R., & McGue, M. (1982). Similarities and differences between low achievers and students classified learning disabled. *Journal of Special Education, 16,* 73–85.

CHAPTER 24

Mild and Moderate Mental Retardation

Johnny L. Matson and Elizabeth A. Schaughency

Introduction

The field of mental retardation has perhaps the oldest tradition of any area of psychology. For example, the work of Binet attempted to distinguish the mentally retarded from those without handicaps. The development of the Binet, and, later, the Stanford-Binet IQ tests were among the beginnings of psychometry as we know it today. Furthermore, the IQ test played an important part in the separation of children's performance in school and thus the creation of special education was closely linked to this movement. Categorization into regular and special classes was largely associated with the IQ test.

Similarly, behavior therapy has a very strong tradition with mentally retarded persons; the roots of this work lie in early research in learning theory and behaviorism. For example, Skinner, like Thorndike before him, emphasized the necessity of developing a systematic data-based technology of teaching. In a paper entitled "The Science of Learning and the Art of Teaching," presented in 1953, Skinner emphasized a concern for current teaching strategies, a point he has reiterated on numerous occasions since then (see Tawney & Gast, 1984). Recently, Skinner (1984) published an article in the *American Psychologist* entitled "The Shame of American Education," in which he restated the general lack of attention to the implementation of technology and training of teachers in the American school system. He points out that in a review of 70 recently published articles discussing our current "crisis in education," only two mentioned how children could be taught.

These concerns have not gone completely unheeded, though, and is perhaps best exemplifed by the early work of Bijou, a postdoctoral student of Skinner's. Bijou conducted many experiments with the mentally retarded. His work has had a major impact in the behavioral movement, particularly with respect to special educators and school psychologists. For example, in 1957 Bijou argued for systematic laboratory study of child behavior. Bijou studied reinforcement of a simple ball dropping task that resulted in increased performance. In another study (Bijou, 1957),

Johnny L. Matson • Department of Psychology, Louisiana State University, Baton Rouge, Louisiana 70803. **Elizabeth A. Schaughency** • Oregon Health Sciences Center, University of Oregon, Eugene, Oregon 97403.

children were divided into two groups, with one group receiving reinforcement on a continuous basis and the other on an intermittent schedule, with and without extinction. More appropriate responding was noted in the extinction plus reinforcement phase. In yet another study Bijou and Orlando (1961) described a four-phase procedure to establish multiple schedules of performance (responding when a red light but not when a blue light is presented as the appropriate response). From the findings of these and related studies (with a variety of subject populations), it was concluded that behavioral procedures were more effective with infrahuman subjects than with handicapped children. They also revealed, however, that the behavior of normal and mentally retarded children was similar in pattern to that of animals studied in laboratories, demonstrating the lawful nature of behavioral principles. Consequently, these laboratory methods have served as models for later classroom interventions.

Most of the early behavioral research dealt with mentally retarded adults residing in institutional settings. The work of Azrin and associates was particularly striking in this regard. He and his colleagues were able to train basic feeding (Azrin & Armstrong, 1973) and toileting skills (Azrin & Foxx, 1971) while controlling a range of abberant behaviors, including aggression (Ayllon, Layman, & Burke, 1972). Research of this nature encouraged other scientists to use behavioral technology for a broad range of problems with mentally retarded persons and many other populations.

Developments with the mild and moderately mentally retarded have received attention only recently. This research will serve as the major area of attention in our chapter. Efforts relating to the more severely mentally retarded have been covered elsewhere in this volume. In addition, a discussion of disruptive behaviors, academic problems, self-injury, and social skills will be made but to a much lesser degree. We will take this approach because these topics have been addressed in a broader fashion in other chapters but not specifically with mentally retarded persons. Nonacademic topics such as psychopathology, vocational training, and community integration skills with the mentally retarded have been described in detail elsewhere (Matson & Barrett, 1982; Matson & McCartney, 1981; Whitman, Scibak, & Reid, 1983).

Mild Mental Retardation

The mildly mentally retarded combined with the learning disabled make up the vast majority of children with mild academic handicaps and are generally considered to be good candidates for mainstreaming (Madden & Slavin, 1983). Problems with these children are not limited to academic performance. Problems such as inappropriate school interactions and low social status have also been shown to be common. For example, two recent studies found educable mentally retarded (EMR) students to be rated as exhibiting more behavior problems than nonretarded peers by their classroom teacher (Cullinan, Matson, Epstein, & Rosemier, 1984; Kuveke, 1983).

The latter study (Kuveke, 1983) also included direct observations, but these were not found to differentiate the EMR students from their nonretarded classmates. Another recent observational study (Russell & Forness, 1984) found the mean levels of disruptive behavior of both EMR and trainable mentally retarded (TMR) children to be relatively low but comparable to levels found for other academically at-risk or handicapped populations. Moreover, their results were quite variable, leading these authors to conduct further analyses. These analyses led to the identification of a subsample of children (approximately 10%) displaying high levels of disruptive behavior.

The high teacher ratings of problem behaviors do not appear to be a simple result of the EMR label. Aloia and MacMillan (1983) investigated the influence of the EMR label on initial expectations of regular-classroom teachers. Teachers were presented with a vignette portrayed as a child's "cumulative folder" and, in half the cases, the information showed that the child was mentally retarded. Results indicated the label did have an effect on teachers' perceptions of students' academic competence, teacher ability, and general impression of the student, but not behavior. Behavioral ratings, as with other areas of school functioning, were found to be influenced by descriptions of school-related characteristics, such as academic achievement, peer relationships, and respect of authority.

Investigations of social status of mentally retarded students have produced consistent, but disheartening, results. Mentally retarded students are less socially accepted and more socially rejected than their nonhandicapped peers (Bender, Wyne, Stuck, & Bailey, 1984; Jenkinson, 1983; Madden & Slavin, 1983). This finding is of concern because lower social acceptance has been found to be related to deficits in academic competence (Bender *et al.*, 1984; Jenkinson, 1983). Taken together these data suggest a lower overall level of social acumen and adjustment.

Other issues seem to be equally interesting as they relate to the EMR child's performance in school. There is research to suggest that level of cognitive functioning, as assessed by a standardized intelligence test, may improve over time (Carvajal, Lane, & Gay, 1984), but academic deficits appear to remain.

Moderate Mental Retardation

As the degree of mental retardation increases, so does impairment in all aspects of functioning. Genetic and other organic syndromes associated with mental retardation are seen more frequently with the moderately mentally retarded, and the incidence of other physical and medical conditions increases as well. Moderately mentally retarded children are rarely mainstreamed into regular academic classes (Madden & Slavin, 1983).

Although these individuals can profit from training in self-sufficiency skills and are capable of learning many tasks, they are likely to require continued supervision as adults. Graduates from TMR classrooms are commonly placed in day programs, such as sheltered workshops or activity centers, with residential placement in group homes, adult foster care, or semi-independent living programs. A sheltered workshop involves employment for 6 to 8 hours per day and/or training for placement in a community job. A work activity center consists of approximately 5 hours per day, providing support and training to improve independent functioning, community access, and productivity. In addition to vocational/day program and residential services, these individuals often require case management and support services.

Unfortunately, the number of students graduating from TMR classrooms exceed the number of available placement slots in the community, and many of these individuals are placed on waiting lists. Moreover, the demand for community services for MR/DD adults has been heightened by deinstitutionalization, with the return of former residents to the community. As a result, it is likely that the demand for adult placements will greatly outweigh the supply for some time to come. It further points to the need for continuity of services across the age span, particularly for these more handicapped individuals.

We have attempted to provide a brief outline of types of handicapped persons we will be discussing in the remainder of this chapter. Next, we will review some of the major issues involved in the assessment of this group.

Assessment

In the context of service in mental retardation, the principal purposes of assessment include diagnosis, facititation of appropriate placements, and provision of a foundation for individual habilitation or educational programs (Grossman, 1983). Different levels of assessment are indicated to accomplish these purposes. The level of assessment has implications for the procedures deemed appropriate to address these evaluation questions. Given the focus of this particular volume, the relevant intellectual and adaptive behavior measures will not be discussed. This information is available elsewhere (Matson & Mulick, 1983).

Behavioral assessment has for the large part failed to develop sound norm-referenced measures with operationally defined observable items. Although this trend is likely to change, and, we hope, will in the next few years, at present we are primarily confined to operational definitions and recording of a few discrete responses. No effort will be made here to review the sizable literature that exists in this area because it has been covered elsewhere in this volume. However, some effort to give the reader an idea of the topics most frequently covered with mild and moderately mentally retarded persons will be addressed.

For example, Close (1985) first conducted task analyses of daily living skills. The process of task analysis breaks down a specific task into component steps. He then designed training programs for various component skills. As part of this performance-based assessment technique, the individual is provided training in a component skill. The success of this training has been found to be related to responsiveness to habilitative training in daily living skills and adapting to a less restrictive setting (Close, 1985).

Most studies that have been conducted, whether dealing with community living, academic or aggressive behaviors, have used this approach. The reader is referred to Matson and McCartney (1981) for an extensive review and examples of these task-analyzed responses, which are evident for a wide range of behaviors.

Assessment for Intervention Planning

The majority of published instruments in education and psychology are *norm-referenced measures*. Standard intelligence tests and measures of adaptive behavior are examples of these. As such they identify general areas of deficit and are useful in evaluating intervention outcome, but have limited utility in program planning.

Another general type of testing is known as *criterion-referenced testing*. Here the individual's performance is evaluated in terms of a standard, or criterion, that has been set for the individual. Thus, the student's performance is evaluated in terms of whether or not he or she achieved program objectives (cf. Prescott, 1971). If the child does not achieve criterion, possible explanations are that (a) the selected criterion was not appropriate or (b) the student needs additional training (Hallahan & Kaufman, 1976). Because of the direct applicability to specific interventions, criterion-referenced testing has been suggested to offer the following advantages: (a) flexibility in using this type of test for various individual programs; (b) continuous assessment for monitoring individual student progress; and, (c) theoretically, judgment of the student relative to his or her own strengths and weaknesses (Proger & Mann, 1973).

The third general type of assessment technique is *task analysis*. This procedure allows for the identification of specific student errors and subskills that must be learned for adequate task performance (Hallahan & Kaufman, 1976).

Based on the assumption that much behavior is maintained by the contemporary environment (Skinner, 1953), assessment for intervention planning involves conducting a functional analysis of the relationships between a particular behavior and its controlling situational factors. This process, as delineated by Gelfand and Hartmann (1975), involves (a) identifying the specific behavioral deficits or excesses; (b) determining the baseline rate of the behavior; (c) identifying the situational variables surrounding the child's behavior; (d) devising an intervention strategy modifying these environmental factors; (e) monitoring behavior change as part of an ongoing evaluation of the intervention, and, if indicated, (f) making adjustments in the intervention strategy.

The assessment of academic behavior from a behavioral perspective is represented in the four variables identified by Rosenshine (1981) as related to enhanced school performance. He found that time alloted for instruction, time engaged in academic work, content covered, and the instructional procedures employed were particularly instrumental in evaluating improvement in performance on educational tasks. These data should prove to be of considerable pragmatic utility to the behaviorally oriented educator. They suggest particular areas where further analysis may be of considerable value in developing what responses should be operationally defined, assessed, and by so doing, established as targets for intervention.

By viewing these basic areas in more detail the educator may be able to determine more adequately whether the child simply does not possess the skill or whether inadequate reinforcement is the major problem in insuring adequate performance. A case in point is a study conducted by Kazdin, Matson, and Esveldt-Dawson (1981). In their study, normal and emotionally disturbed children were tested on level of social skills with and without reinforcement. Significantly lower levels of appropriate eye contact, facial expression, intonation, and other very discrete skills were evident in both of these groups when reinforcement was not provided, even though the reinforcers were given for doing their best as opposed to reinforcement for specific responses. The conclusion drawn from these data, which have applicability for academic as well as disordered conduct, is that professionals should not too readily assume that the behaviors are not in the person's repertoire. Rather, a fined-grained analysis of the situation is required.

In addition to the types of assessment and goals of evaluation discussed earlier, there are several major methods of behavioral assessment that have been used for selecting target behaviors and for evaluating intervention with the mentally retarded. These methods include direct observation, in naturalistic and role-play analog situations, rating scales, sociometric ratings, and social validation measures (cf. Matson & DiLorenzo, 1986). The multimethod approach to assessment utilizing a combination of procedures is recommended to obtain a valid and reliable picture of the child's behavior.

Direct Observation

This method can take several forms based on the question to be addressed. For example, if the goal is to establish the severity of a given behavior problem, a frequency count or time sampling procedure might be utilized. If the goal is to determine environmental correlates of the behavior an A-B-C (antecedent, behavior, consequence) format might be used to identify the component parts of the behavioral chain. These techniques are addressed elsewhere, and therefore will not be discussed further here.

Role-play interactions provide a means for evaluating the form of the child's response to certain situations. This technique is modeled after similar procedures that have been used with other populations (Bellack, Hersen, & Turner, 1976; Eisler, Hersen, Miller, & Blanchard, 1975). Role-play assessment typically entails providing the child with a narrative depiction of an interpersonal situation, a role-played prompt by a confederate, and the observation of the child's response. The child's response may then be rated on such dimensions as appropriateness of verbal content, intonation, and nonverbal response (e.g., Matson, Kazdin, & Esveldt-Dawson, 1980). Samples of the child's behavior are generally obtained in a variety of situations, such as response to provocation or inappropriate requests, to requests for help, or with giving compliments or making requests as the desired response. Role-play scenes may also be developed to elicit responses to specific problematic situations observed in the classroom.

Rating Scales

Rating scales provide information about the child's behavior outside of the role-play setting and about the informant's perceptions of the child's behavior. To date there has been little research utilizing checklists and rating scales with mentally handicapped persons (Matson & Breuning, 1983). An adaptation of an adult scale, the *Social Skills Performance Survey* (Lowe & Cautela, 1978) has been found to be a sensitive measure of social functioning with mentally retarded persons (Matson, Helsel, Bellack, & Senatore, 1983). A similar measure of childhood social functioning, the *Matson Evaluation of Social Skills with Youngsters* (Matson, Rotatori, & Helsel, 1983), has been recently developed. The MESSY provides information on positive and negative social behaviors and has parallel teacher and self-report forms.

Sociometric Measures

Peer perceptions of their classmates' behavior and social status may be obtained using sociometric measures. Good reliability and validity is the major advantage of this approach, although it has received only brief attention with mentally retarded persons (cf. Hops & Greenwood, 1981).

There are two main forms of sociometric measures. In one, peer nominations, students are given a behavioral descriptor (e.g., fights) and asked to indicate which of their classmates are best described by that word. The other form of sociometric measure is a sociometric rating. Here the student is asked to rate each of their classmates on a given dimension (e.g., How much he or she likes to play with that child) using a five-point Likert-type scale.

Social Validation

Behavioral deficits and excesses are defined relative to social expectations (Kanfer & Saslow, 1965). Social validation, initially described by Wolf (1978) and Kazdin (1977), is a systematic way of assessing the perceptions of others regarding the acceptability of specific target behaviors for treatment and for establishing the clinical significance of treatment effects (Matson & DiLorenzo, 1986). Social comparison and subjective evaluation are two approaches to social validation (Kazdin & Matson, 1981).

Social comparison involves the evaluation of a student's performance relative to a peer comparison group, whereas subjective evaluation involves obtaining the perceptions of significant others (e.g., parent, teacher), not involved in a particular intervention program, regarding the appropriateness of target behaviors or intervention outcome (Matson & DiLorenzo, 1986).

Social comparisons may be on the basis of direct observations in role play or naturalistic classroom settings, rating scales, or sociometric ratings. Matson *et al.* (1980), for example, used this approach with role-play observations in their treatment of two moderately mentally retarded children exhibiting conduct problems. The target children were matched with two normal children on the basis of age and sex. Identical role-play assessment was conducted with all four children. The comparison of children's behavioral performance became the performance criteria established as the intervention objectives, and reassessment was conducted to evaluate progress.

Social comparisons within the classroom help to differentiate specific behavioral difficulties of the target child from general class or teacher effects. For example, this technique may be used in naturalistic classroom observations by coding the behaviors of interest for a comparison child as well as those of the target child in the classroom. Similarly, the classroom teacher may be asked to complete a behavioral rating scale on an average child in his or her classroom of the same age, race, and sex as the target child. Finally, social comparisons of sociometric measures may be made by comparing the target child's total number of nominations to the average for his or her class.

There are a number of methods of assessment that are applicable for mentally retarded persons in school settings. We have made an effort to review some of them here. This area is expanding rapidly with much new technology coming to the forefront. Next, we will discuss treatment issues, another area where rapid expansion is occurring.

Treatment

In this section we have attempted to address the same general topic areas covered in our assessment section; academic performance and the treatment of aggressive and disruptive behavior problems. With children, the latter of these three categories has been heavily researched with mentally retarded children. Various behavioral approaches have been tried and we will make some effort to provide a representative description of each.

Treatment of Academic Behavior

The complementary findings of experimental psychology in the areas of cognition and learning, educational, and behavioral psychological research have important implications for educational interventions with mentally retarded children. Common features of all these approaches are (a) the logical or empirical analysis of component skills of a complex behavior, (b) intervention directly targeting these skills, (c) specification of procedures to allow for systematic implementation, evaluation, and replication, and (d) the goal of developing generalizable skills or behaviors. Moreover, these camps assert that the appropriate first step to analyzing performance failure is a thorough evaluation of training procedures. Consistent with this approach, Weisberg, Packer, and Weisberg (1981) argued that an evaluation of instructional variables is indicated in the remediation of academic deficits (Weisberg *et al.*, 1981). This section will be introduced by an illustrative discussion of these variables. This discussion will be followed by the presentation of examples of specific educational interventions. The section on treatment of academic behavior will then be concluded with the description of a proposed overall educational program for mentally retarded persons.

Instructional Variables

Teaching Concepts and Discriminations

Much of the research on instructional methods with the mentally retarded has been devoted to developing procedures for teaching basic concepts, a difficult task for teachers of mentally retarded children (Weisberg *et al.*, 1981). Concept learning requires that the learner discern the relevant and irrelevant characteristics of the exemplars. Based on their review of the literature, Weisberg *et al.* (1981) recommended that the teacher provide multiple and diverse exemplars of positive and negative instances of the concept. They also suggest that concept training including minimally different pairs (i.e., highly similar except for the relevant feature) seems to be more helpful for the naive learner, especially when the teacher actively transforms instances of a concept into negative instances and vice versa. Another technique they mentioned that has met with some success is stimulus fading.

The effective implementation of each of these seemingly straightforward recommendations, however, depends on careful, systematic programming. The student's failure to demonstrate mastery of the concept at this initial learning stage may be influenced by a host of variables such as stimulus materials, teacher instructions, activity involved in, and rate of presentation. Specificity of instructional procedures is the first step, then, in the analysis of academic difficulties.

Teaching for Generalization

As in the training of specific concepts and skills, programming for expansion and generalization must also be specifically designed and systematically implemented. Before introducing new material, the teacher must determine if the student has attained satisfactory performance on present tasks. The mastery learning approach (Bloom, 1976) is a criterion-referenced approach in which the child must attain some predetermined performance standard before proceeding. Weisberg *et al.* (1981) recommended maintenance of a 95% to 100% accuracy rate for low performers throughout training, as high error rates have been found to be deleterious to learning. New material provided by Weisberg *et al.* (1981) draws heavily on the work of Becker and Carnine (1978) and Carnine (1980).

1. Introduce higher utility material before lower utility material. That is, those concepts that the student is most likely to encounter should be presented early.
2. Introduce easier examples before difficult examples. There is empirical evidence to suggest that some concepts are more difficult to discern than others. Where this evidence is lacking, Weisberg *et al.* (1981) suggest that rational consideration should be given to the problem of presentation order.
3. Separate materials that are similar in sound and/or appearance. To decrease possible confusion, Weisberg *et al.* (1981) recommend that highly similar stimuli are separated by two or more nonsimilar members.
4. Teach regularities before exceptions. Weisberg *et al.* (1981) further recommend that if applicable to a large number of cases the irregular features of a concept should be modified to fit a normal and familiar basis of responding.

An Empirically Based Educational Example

The current focus of academic training is on functional survival skills. With respect to reading, for example, Weisberg *et al.* (1981) noted that it is possible to teach the mentally retarded student, particularly those in the mild range, a number of key functional words through the sight-word technique. Research in cognition and learning, however, posits that although mentally retarded students can profit from item rehearsal, single-item learning is a less efficient learning strategy than training in other cognitive strategies (Glidden, 1979). Moreover, after reviewing the literature on and analyzing the materials of a number of existing reading programs, Weisberg *et al.* (1981) criticized a number of the basal readers and sight-word approaches for violating the empirically derived guidelines for the presentation of material described earlier. Perhaps most important in the long run, however, is the criticism that the sight-word technique does not provide for generalization to other words occurring in the natural environment.

As an alternative, they present DISTAR (Direct Instruction Systems for Teaching and Remediation), based on the work of Englemann and Becker, as an empirically based educational program for use with mentally retarded children. Early reading instruction, using the DISTAR approach, emphasizes the correct decoding of regular words through the teaching of requisite skills and their integration (Carnine & Silbert, 1979). There are programming trade-offs, as Weisberg *et al.* (1981) acknowledge. Introduction of highly discriminable sight words results in word reading more quickly than initial instruction in letter sounds. They assert, however, that teaching the more difficult strategy of sound identification and blending, will eventually result in a greater number of correctly read words.

Weisberg *et al.* (1981) concluded their discussion with the following challenge for behavior analysts: become more knowledgeable about instructional programming; prerequisite academic skills remain to be empirically identified. Instructional programming for the mentally retarded, they argued, must include the integration of related tasks with consideration for long-term goals.

Educational Interventions

The challenge of Weisberg *et al.* (1981) not withstanding, behavioral interventions have been used successfully in the remediation of a variety of academic deficits with mild and moderately retarded students. Matson and colleagues (Beck, Matson, & Kazdin, 1983; Matson & Ollendick, 1979; Matson, Esveldt-Dawson, & Kazdin, 1982; Ollendick, Matson, Esveldt-Dawson, & Shapiro, 1980), for example, have conducted a series of studies in the treatment of spelling deficits in mentally retarded children.

These studies have built on the work of Foxx and Jones (1978) and evaluated the effects of positive practice overcorrection and positive reinforcement on the spelling performance of nonretarded students. These early studies suggested that a combination of positive practice overcorrection and positive reinforcement was more effective than positive reinforcement alone with normal students (Foxx & Jones, 1978). Also, positive practice alone was effective (Matson & Ollendick, 1979); but positive practice plus positive reinforcement proved to be more effective (Ollendick *et al.*, 1980), in the remediation of spelling deficits. And, whereas these data were with learning-disabled students, they would seem to be applicable for mentally retarded persons as well (e.g., Matson *et al.*, 1982). The Matson *et al.* (1982) study examined the effectiveness of the application of these interventions on the spelling performance of students whose level of functioning was in the borderline-to-mild range of mental retardation. The results of this study not only replicated the earlier findings, but also supported the use of these interventions with this population. Therefore, the specific treatment procedures will be described briefly in the following.

Treatment was conducted by trained undergraduate psychology students functioning as teachers' aides. Aide training consisted of approximately 3 hours of direct training by one of the authors plus periodic observation. Treatment consisted of 20 to 35 daily sessions. Treatment was conducted successfully individually and in the classroom setting.

Treatment was introduced to the child via the following script:

> For this set of words, I am going to help you learn those words you misspelled by having you listen while I say the word aloud. Then, I want you to pronounce the word correctly, then say aloud each letter of the word while you write it. I will have you repeat this five times for each word mispelled. I will also place a star or sticker by each word you spell correctly and praise your good work.

Thus, the overcorrection plus reinforcement procedures were as follows: (a) the teachers' aide pronounced the word; (b) the child attempted to spell the word; (c) if correct, the aide reinforced the child by placing a sticker by the word and praising the child; or (d) if incorrect, the child pronounced the incorrectly spelled word and wrote it five times saying each letter as it was written; (e) the child pronounced the next word.

The use of positive practice overcorrection plus reinforcement has also been recently described in the treatment of oral reading errors of moderately mentally retarded students (Singh, Singh, & Winton, 1984). In this study, treatment was conducted in a resource room by the children's teacher, using the children's reading texts. The introductory script was similar to that used in the studies by Matson and associates:

> Here is a story book. I want you to read it. I will help you if you make a mistake. I will tell you the correct word while you listen and point to the word in the book. After that, I want you to say the same word five times. Then you will read the sentence again. Try your best not to make any mistakes, but if you do make one and correct it yourself, I will give you a ______ (an edible reinforcer) and praise you for reading correctly. (Singh *et al.*, 1984)

Earlier work by Singh and colleagues (Singh *et al.*, 1984) suggested that delayed, rather than immediate, attention to oral reading errors was more effective in improving accuracy and self-corrections. In light of this Singh *et al.* (1984) employed a delayed error correction procedure. Specifically, errors were corrected at the end of the sentence in which they occurred. If the child paused after an error, it was corrected after a 10- to 15-second delay.

The results of this study replicate and extend those of the Matson group: positive practice plus positive reinforcement alone was effective, and positive practice plus positive reinforcement was even more effective in decreasing the target behavior of uncorrected oral reading errors and in increasing self-corrections in moderately retarded students. Unfortunately, however, the total number of errors (i.e., uncorrected errors plus self-corrections) did not decrease.

One explanation lies in the targeting of positive behavior, which may be opposite to the target behavior, raising the issue of consideration for the desired long-run treatment outcome. If the treatment goal is accuracy (i.e., error-free) oral reading, perhaps the response selected for reinforcement should have been error-free sentences rather than self-corrected errors. This tentative recommendation is one that awaits experimental support. Nonetheless, the efficacy with which positive practice plus positive reinforcement procedures have modified academic behaviors of mildly and moderately mentally retarded students suggests that this approach merits further research and application.

A pragmatic limitation of behavior modification programs, such as those described earlier, is the staff time involvement required for implementation of the procedures. A less time-consuming alternative is a self-mediated remediation package that requires minimal teacher involvement during spelling instruction (Beck *et al.*, 1983). This package, which provides the student with a self-help manual delineating instructional steps of rehearsal self-assessment, self-reinforcement, etc., has been found to be effective with emotionally disturbed students of low average intelligence who displayed significant academic deficits (Beck *et al.*, 1983). Such promising results suggest that applied research should be undertaken to determine whether the extension of this approach to the mentally retarded is appropriate.

It has been hypothesized that academically handicapped students are deficient in knowing how to approach a task but could improve their performance if given a strategy, suggesting that self-instructional training in task-related areas is a potentially effective remediation procedure with this population (Leon & Pepe, 1983). Initial support for the use of self-instructional training for the remediation of academic deficits of mildly mentally retarded students comes from a study by Johnston, Whitman, and Johnson (1980). Johnston *et al.* (1980) found the teaching of specific addition and subtraction skills using self-instruction training procedures, as outlined by Meichenbaum and Goodman (1971), to be an effective intervention strategy.

A final example of an educational intervention for the academic deficits of mentally handicapped students incorporates aspects of cognitive instruction, educational programming, and reinforcement. Leon and Pepe (1983) compared the effectiveness of systematic instruction plus self-instruction to systematic instruction alone for the remediation of arithmetic deficits with educationally handicapped students. Systematic instruction encompasses several factors considered to be critical elements in educational programming. They include a task-analyzed curriculum, precise assessment procedures, low teacher–student ratio, and the use of reinforcement procedures (Leon & Pepe, 1983). The study controlled for these factors utilizing the same curriculum, assessment procedures, and performance criteria for all students.

As in the Johnston *et al.* (1980) study, the self-instructional sequence was based on the self-instructional model of Meichenbaum and Goodman (1969, 1971), which builds on a cognitive-functional analysis (Meichenbaum & Goodman, 1971). The procedure used by Leon and Pepe (1983) incorporated modeling, self-administration of reinforcement, feedback, coping instructions, and self-instructional dialogue, task analyzed to correspond to each component of the computational process into five stages.

1. The teacher computed the problem using overt self-instruction, providing a model for self-instruction and computation.
2. Teacher and student conjointly computed the problem using overt self-instructions, allowing the teacher to guide the student through computation with self-instructions while ensuring correspondence between the processes.
3. The student computed the problem using overt self-instruction, providing opportunity to monitor the student's independent use of self-instructions as a computation guide.
4. The student computed the problem using whispered self-instructions, allowing the continuation of monitoring while fading self-instructions from the overt level.
5. The student computed the problem using covert self-instructions.

The students, diagnosed as learning disabled or educably mentally handicapped, were seen daily for 15-minute treatment sessions by their resource room teachers for a period of 7 weeks. All of the participating teachers attended a one-day in-service session, the agenda of which included introduction to the study, theory of arithmetic computation and skill development, assessment, and curriculum implementation. Teachers implementing the systematic instruction plus self-instruction procedures also attended a second day in-service session in which they were trained on the self-instructional procedures. The results of this study supported the position that learning-disabled and educably mentally handicapped students benefit from systematic instruction. Furthermore, they supported the notion that systematic instruction plus self-instruction may be an even more effective remediation procedure (Leon & Pepe, 1983).

An Educational Program for the Mentally Retarded

Bijou (1983) proposed a comprehensive program for the mentally handicapped consisting of (a) parent training similar to the Portage Project (Shearer & Shearer, 1976); (b) compulsory preschool education founded on behavior analysis; and (c) an elementary school program based on the Direct Instruction Model developed by Englemann and associates (Becker & Carnine, 1978). Each of these components, Bijou contended, has received empirical support, although the power of an integrated program remains to be measured.

In Bijou's (1983) model, entrance into parent training in behavior management techniques aimed at facilitating development in skills, knowledge, and motivation coincides with the child's enrollment in preschool at age 18 months. The preschool component focuses on social and preacademic developmental activities with the objective of preparing the child for first grade. The first part of its two-part curriculum consists of preschool activities, whereas the second part includes instruction (one to one and small group) in self-care skills, language development, preacademic skills, and knowledge. If the child successfully completes the preschool curriculum, instruction is begun in first-grade academic skills, which will then be continued and extended in the individualized first-grade curriculum.

Strategies for teaching the curriculum content and extinguishing interfering problem behaviors are based on the application of behavior analytic principles. Thus, antecedents (instructions, prompts, and materials), setting factors, and consequences of responses are carefully specified and systematically managed and all responses methodically recorded. In addition to developing accuracy on curriculum items, programming is designed to make performance of school activities reinforcing and to facilitate independence and perseverance.

Building on the earlier two components, the goal of the special elementary school program of Bijou's proposed model (1983) is to develop mastery of the prerequisite social, language, basic academic, and cognitive skills necessary for further development in the academic, recreational, and vocational arenas. To this end, the child ideally moves through the three currently available levels of DISTAR reading, arithmetic, and language, supplementary writing and spelling activities, and a year of a more advanced academic programming designated to prepare the child for a regular fifth-grade class placement. Moreover, systematic programming for the development of independent application of these skills is an integral part of the elementary school component spanning the first through fourth grades. Such programming is reflected in the modification of the staffing pattern delineated in the direct instruction model as proposed by Bijou (1983): two teachers and two aides for a class size of 15 in the first and second grades; one teacher and one aide for 30 pupils in the third and fourth grades.

Salient features of the preschool and elementary school programs as described by Bijou (1983) include:

1. Initial assessment of competencies. Criterion-referenced measures are utilized and repeated to assess programs.
2. Preparing the individualized curricula. Instruction levels of the curricula are determined by the child's performance on the initial assessment.
3. Teaching techniques. Instructional variables, (i.e., scripts, prompts, consequences to response) are systematically managed, including programming for the development of independent study skills.
4. Monitoring individual progress and revising programs. The child's performance is regularly monitored and educational program systematically modified, if indicated.

These data from Bijou (1983) suggest that there is considerable promise for behavior modification with mentally retarded children. The number of studies have not been great but the results have been rather dramatic. Also, procedures that have been found to be effective with other problems, such as aggression and self-help training of the mentally retarded, may also prove effective with academic problems. The use of overcorrection by Matson and associates is one example of this. The primary difficulty has been to get behavioral researchers interested in this area.

Treatment of Aggressive and Disruptive Behaviors

Aggression has been found to be the best predictor of unsuccessful adjustment to community living among mentally retarded persons (Close, 1985). Self-injurious and stereotypic behaviors are found more frequently in children with lower functioning cognitive skills (Baumeister & Forehand, 1973) where these responses often interfere with learning (Dietz, Repp, & Dietz, 1976). Finally, even mildly mentally retarded students enjoy diminished social status, for whatever reason, relative to their nonhandicapped peers (Bender *et al.*, 1984; Jenkinson, 1983; Madden & Slavin, 1983).

In general, discipline is viewed by the American public and administrations as a major problem in public schools (Duke, 1978; Schloss, 1983). Consistent with this concern, school administrators have called for teacher-training curricula to include classroom management techniques (Duke, 1978). Although the prevalence of behavior problems among mentally retarded children may be debated, their existence is not, necessitating the delineation of behavior management strategies appropriate for this population.

Fortunately, perusal of the behavior analysis literature yields many promising and innovative applications of behavioral techniques with the mentally retarded. Reviews of detailed prescriptions with children (Matson, 1983b), social skills interventions (Matson & DiLorenzo, 1986), and self-control strategies (Shapiro, 1981) have been reported. The following discussion will attempt to highlight applications that have relevance for behavior problems interfering with school adjustment. A detailed review of these difficulties can be found elsewhere (Matson & Andrasik, 1983; Matson & McCartney, 1981).

Contingencies

Contingent interventions are operant in nature, that is, a specified consequence is administered contingent upon the emission of the target behavior. In the case of aggression and disruptive behaviors, the goal is to increase the positive, opposite behaviors, while decreasing undesirable behaviors.

Reinforcement Procedures

One reinforcement technique is known as the differential reinforcement of other behavior (DRO). Theoretically, DRO achieves its effects in two ways: (a) DRO places the undesirable behaviors on an extinction schedule, and (b) DRO may be designed to reinforce (and subsequently increase) a specific alternative behavior. As with any operant intervention, a functional analysis of the undesired behavior must be conducted in order to identify and systematically eliminate potential reinforcers present in the environment that may be sustaining the target behavior.

Possible reinforcers for the positive operant behavior must also be identified for the individual child, with consideration of his or her cognitive developmental level. The use of secondary reinforcers (e.g., tokens) involves symbolic thinking and delay of reinforcement (Matson, 1983a). Therefore, primary reinforcers are typically preferred for younger ages, in persons of lower intelligence levels, and with more severe problems (Matson, 1983b).

The progression of behavioral treatment research has been described as moving from initial demonstrations that a technique is effective with a given population to explorations of the parameters or active treatment components of a procedure (Shapiro, 1981). As will be noted with the other interventions to be described in the following, evaluations of the application of DRO, with disruptive behaviors of mentally retarded students has followed such a progression. For example, a recent investigation compared the relative effectiveness of momentary DRO (i.e., reinforcement is administered if no negative target behavior is occurring at the end of the interval) to whole-interval DRO (i.e., reinforcement is delivered if no disruptive behavior occurred throughout the entire interval) with mildly and moderately mentally retarded students (Repp, Barton, & Brulle, 1983). In general, the authors concluded, whole-interval DRO appeared more effective in suppressing disruptive responses, but momentary DRO might be sufficient for maintaining decreased responding (Repp *et al.*, 1983).

Behavior management strategies may be designed for use with individual students or for groups of students in the classroom. A classroom intervention was recently described utilizing a combination of DRO and response cost of inappropriate behavior with learning-disabled and educably mentally handicapped students (Schilling & Cuvo, 1983). The behaviors targeted in this study were determined by the teachers themselves.

Two positive behaviors, remaining in assigned area and class preparation, and one negative behavior, talking without permission, were identified. Students earned points for the positive behaviors and lost points for talking without permission (i.e., response cost). The points could then be used for the purchase of tickets for random lottery drawings held at the end of each week. Lottery drawings were divided into three value categories on the basis of total weekly points earned.

This contingency-based lottery was successful in altering the classroom behavior of individual students and the special education class as a whole in the desired direction, with students and teachers requesting the reinstitution of treatment during baseline, attesting to consumer satisfaction and social validation (Schilling & Cuvo, 1983). Conceptually, this intervention included a number of components for consideration: (a) the use of the point system involves secondary reinforcement; (b) the use of a weekly drawing results in delay of reinforcement; (c) the use of random lottery involves a variable-ratio, intermittent schedule of reinforcement.

Any of these factors may, hypothetically, limit the effectiveness of this treatment strategy with younger and/or lower functioning students. For example, intermittent reinforcement schedules have been recommended for increasing response maintenance because of resistance to extinction (Stokes & Baer, 1977). The results of the research on whole interval versus momentary DRO with mildly and moderately mentally retarded students, however, suggested that whereas momentary DRO seemed sufficient for maintenance, the tighter whole interval schedule was more effective in producing initial behavior change with this population, as noted earlier (Repp *et al.*, 1983). Similarly, the variable ratio reinforcement schedule may prove less effective in altering the behavior of lower functioning and/or younger students. Of course, the test of such speculations is to extend treatment evaluations to the application of such procedures to these populations. Given the promising results reported by Schilling and Cuvo (1983), such endeavors seem warranted.

Aversive Procedures

Stereotypic, self-injurious, and aggressive behaviors are difficult to extinguish and require additional, more direct procedures in order to be effectively suppressed. The procedures available to reduce these inappropriate behaviors involve the application of an aversive consequence contingent upon the occurrence of the behavior. Although use of aversive procedures with these behaviors is justified in order to enhance the student's potential for learning and for the safety of him or herself and others, safeguards against their misuse must be taken. Responsibility for their implementation should rest on a highly trained therapist. In addition, a reinforcement procedure for training the child in an alternative prosocial act should be used in conjunction with the behavior reduction program.

One of the most frequently used procedures is time out from positive reinforcement, which involves removing the child from the positive reinforcement present in the environment, contingent upon the occurrence of misbehavior. Detention, a consequence frequently used in schools, may be thought of as a form of delayed time out. An application of this procedure, combined with the reinforcement of appropriate class behavior, in a special education setting has been recently described (Cousins, Weber, & Dolen, 1984). The level of intellectual functioning of these students ranged from borderline to low average. Clinical diagnosis included autistic features, hyperactive syndrome, severe learning disabilities, emotional disturbance, and behavior disturbance.

The delayed time-out procedure employed by Cousins *et al.* was as follows: each emission of a target negative behavior was consequented with a description of the misbehavior, the resultant forthcoming time out, and a mark on a chart viewed as a token economy. At the end of the school day, each mark was multiplied by the time factor and cumulative detentions were posted. Detentions, ranging from 0 to 60 minutes, were served in the classroom.

This study also included a treatment maintenance component. During the last phase of the study (see description of experimental design below), students were instructed that (a) the delayed time-out procedure could be stopped for an individual if he had 10 consecutive days of two or fewer rule infractions, (b) he could remain exempt from the procedure if rule infractions did not exceed two per day for more than 3 consecutive days.

Thus, the experimental design actually consisted of: (a) A—baseline, (b) B+C—delayed time out + reinforcement of appropriate class behavior, (c) C—reinforcement alone, (d) B+C+D—11 plus programmed maintenance contingency. The results indicated the combined delayed time-out and reinforcement package was an effective behavior reduction strategy with this population (Cousins *et al.*, 1983). Reinforcement alone, however, was found to be ineffective in maintaining treatment gains. During the last phase of the study, frequency of rule infractions per day returned to the previously obtained levels, supporting the use of the delayed time-out procedure. Moreover, 63% of the students successfully earned their way off the delayed time-out program for periods ranging from 6 to 55 days.

Such results are encouraging, although it should be pointed out that this study did not directly evaluate the effectiveness of delayed time out. Nonetheless, further applied evaluations of these procedures seem justified. In particular, the appropriateness of their extension, specifically to the mentally retarded, remains to be examined.

Overcorrection, a technique introduced in this chapter in the context of treatment of academic behaviors, has also been used in the treatment of disruptive and aggressive behaviors. Overcorrection is comprised of two components, restitution and positive practice, which may be used separately or together (Carey & Bucher, 1983). The objective of restitutional overcorrection is to educate the person to accept responsibility for his or her misbehavior by reinstating the environment to a superior condition than existed prior to treatment (Matson, 1983). In positive practice overcorrection, as illustrated in the treatment of spelling and reading errors, the individual is required to practice appropriate forms of responding, contingent upon commission of the target behavior.

The exact procedures employed in an overcorrection intervention plan vary with the individual case. Illustrations of restitutional and positive practice overcorrection in the treatment of aggressive and disruptive behaviors are presented in the following.

DRO was used unsuccessfully in the treatment of object throwing by a chronic psychiatric inpatient (Matson & Stephens, 1977). These authors then instituted a restitutional overcorrection procedure with this patient, by requiring her to apologize to the person at whom she had thrown the object and picking up objects off the floor and throwing them in the trash. The restitutional overcorrection successfully eliminated the object-throwing behavior (Matson & Stephens, 1977).

Replication and extension of these results with the aggressive-destructive behavior of a mildly mentally retarded adolescent have been recently described (Altman & Krupsaw, 1983). As in the Matson and Stephens (1977) case, DRO was attempted, but was ineffective in producing behavior change. DRO with social reinforcement was implemented initially, followed by DRO with secondary reinforcers (i.e., tokens), followed by response cost (i.e., token removal). As these procedures failed to eliminate tantrumming, a restitutional overcorrection procedure was designed.

The only family member who could overpower the boy, and hence ensure enforcement, was the boy's father, so a delayed overcorrection procedure was attempted. When a tantrum episode occurred, an "X" was marked on the kitchen calendar. When his father arrived at home, he examined the calendar. If a tantrum had occurred, the parents would show him the mark and instruct him in the restitution. The procedure was first implemented with severe tantrums, and subsequently mild tantrums were targeted. Significant decreases in tantrum behavior were seen following the introduction of delayed overcorrection. Follow-up indicated that the boy's parents continued to use delayed overcorrection to consequate tantrums. Moreover, the formal token economy had evolved into an informal contractual system in which he had received special privileges following tantrum-free periods of one to four weeks (Altman & Krupsaw, 1983).

Although the previous illustration is a home-based application, its efficacy in suppressing the aggressive behavior of a mildly mentally retarded boy suggests it may be a useful procedure to deal with such behavior in the schools. This hypothesis is supported by the successful application of delayed time out in the school setting. These results suggest it may not only be feasible to implement delayed overcorrection in the school but that delayed overcorrection may also provide school personnel with an effective behavior management procedure, when the classroom teacher is unable to immediately enforce consequences for misbehavior.

The use of relatively brief response-contingent physical restraint has been used to reduce a range of problem behaviors with mentally retarded children, yielding mixed results. Some studies have found it to be effective in reducing target behaviors (e.g., Barrett, Matson, Shapiro, & Ollendick, 1981; Ollendick, Shapiro, & Barrett, 1981; Shapiro, Barrett, & Ollendick, 1980). Others have found it to increase the target behavior (e.g., Singh, Winton, & Ball, 1984) and so to serve as a reinforcer instead of a punisher.

Singh, Winton, and Ball (1984) hypothesized that the differences in effects may depend on the target behavior. In the series of studies by Barrett and colleagues, physical restraint was used in the treatment of stereotypic behavior, whereas the Singh *et al.* (1984) study tried to reduce the out-of-seat behavior of hyperactive, moderately and severely mentally retarded students. These mixed results emphasize the need for careful assessment of intervention impact.

Visual screening is an alternative procedure that has been used in the treatment of self-injurious, disruptive, and stereotypic behaviors. In a recent example with moderately and profoundly mentally retarded students, the therapist briefly covered the child's eyes with his or her hand contingent on the occurrence of the target stereotypic behavior (McConigle, Duncan, Cordisco, & Barrett, 1982). An additional verbal warning component was added to the final intervention phase of one child. In this phase, visual screening was not implemented if the child complied with the therapist's command to stop the stereotypic activity.

The results suggested that visual screening was an effective and durable treatment procedure for stereotypic behaviors with mentally retarded persons. Moreover, the near-zero frequency of stereotypic responding obtained in the visual-screening condition was maintained across the verbal warning phase (McConigle *et al.*, 1982). Such results support future applications. Additional evaluations of pairing the visual screening with verbal warning seem especially warranted.

Social-Learning Methods

Social-learning approaches include a broader range of domains and treatment techniques than those included under operant and classical conditioning learning models (Matson, 1983). Such approaches are aimed at the acquistion of new responses. In the treatment of aggressive and disruptive behavior, the child is trained in an alternative appropriate response to a problematic situation. Procedures employed by the social-learning approach include modeling, role playing, and other forms of vicarious learning and social reinforcement. Such procedures have been found to be useful with mildly and moderately mentally retarded students.

For example, Matson *et al.* (1980) devised a treatment package to improve the social behavior of two conduct-disordered, mentally retarded boys. Social skills training was provided by a special educator in individual sessions. Treatment consisted of practicing responses to problematic situations, the procedure incorporating role-play rehearsal, feedback, and social reinforcement. Results found the children's performance to role-played situations to improve to levels comparable to normal peers during the course of treatment and follow-up (Matson *et al.*, 1980).

Although these results are promising, the ultimate treatment goal is maintenance and generalization to settings outside the training session. An encouraging extension of these procedures to moderately and severely mentally retarded adults has been reported by Matson and Earnhart, (1981). In this study, in addition to the role-play rehearsals in the treatment setting, occurrences of the target behavior on the ward were consequated with rehearsal of the appropriate response on the ward. This added treatment component was effective in promoting the generalization of treatment gains to the natural environment. Other potential adjuncts for facilitating maintenance and generalization are discussed later in the context of self-control procedures.

Self-Control Procedures

Although many of the other behavioral interventions described in this chapter have moved beyond the "it works" stage to component analysis, the application of self-control procedures with the mentally retarded is still in its infancy (Matson, 1983b; Shapiro, 1981). In this section procedures will be presented that relate to changing or maintaining one's own behavior. This definition is consistent with those used by Shapiro (1981) in his review of the topic.

Self-monitoring is defined as a process that includes self-assessment, self-observation, self-evaluation, and self-recording (Shapiro, 1981). Based on his review of the literature, Shapiro (1981) concluded that the retarded can learn self-monitoring in laboratory settings. An application of self-monitoring by an EMR student in a classroom setting has been recently described (Sugai & Rowe, 1984).

In this study the student was instructed to record his out-of-seat behavior on a behavior recording chart. No reinforcement was used. During the initial treatment phase, there was a significant decrease in out-of-seat behavior, with a subsequent increase during return to baseline. The frequency of out-of-seat behavior again decreased with the reinstitution of treatment. In the final phase, a fading procedure was implemented in which recording intervals were gradually lengthened, with out-of-seat behavior remaining low. As the authors noted, social validation of results was also achieved as the teacher and classmates came to view him as less disruptive (Sugai & Rowe, 1984).

Self-reinforcement is another self-management strategy. Again, Shapiro (1981) argued that laboratory studies suggest that mentally retarded children can learn to use this strategy. Moreover, he presents the results of applied classroom studies indicating that self-reinforcement may be incorporated into a self-management package to effectively reduce off-task and disruptive behaviors.

Self-monitoring and self-reinforcement have also been found to hold promise as useful adjuncts to social skills training with mildly and moderately mentally retarded adults in the promotion of generalization beyond the treatment setting (Matson & Andrasik, 1982). Although the ability to self-monitor reliably may be limited by cognitive level, participants expressed positive views at being active participants in their treatment program (Matson & Earnhart, 1981). These promising results call for further innovative combined applications of cognitive-behavioral and social learning approaches with mentally retarded students in a careful and systematic manner.

Another self-management technique is self-instruction training. This technique was introduced earlier in the treatment of academic behaviors. Despite its application to a variety of other problem behaviors with other child populations, limited work has been done with mentally retarded children. A comparison of various cognitive-behavioral self-control training programs for anger management with mildly and moderately mentally retarded adults has been described recently (Benson, Miranti, & Johnson, 1984). This study included progressive muscle relaxation training, self-instructional training, problem-solving skills training, and a combination of the three procedures. The self-instructional training program consisted of training in the use of coping self-statements. Participants were first trained to differentiate between coping and trouble statements. They were provided with a list of coping statements to use in problem situations and practiced using them in role-play situations. Problem-solving skills training involved training participants in a problem-solving strategy that included identification of the problem, possible solutions, the choice of the solution, and self-evaluation. The combined anger management condition proceeded from relaxation training to self-instruction, and concluded with problem-solving skills.

Training was conducted in a group and required 12 sessions. Results indicated that relaxation training and self-instructional training were effective in reducing aggressive behavior with this population, with treatment effects maintained at the one-month follow-up. Included in the assessment measures were work-place supervisors' ratings, indicating generalization of effects as well.

Neither the problem-solving training nor the anger management conditions proved to be successful. As the authors noted, the problem-solving training used here may have been too abstract for this population (Benson *et al.*, 1984). Problem-solving strategies have been taught to mentally retarded students for academic problems in one-to-one settings. Perhaps this type of strategy training requires more intensive, one-to-one training. The authors also hypothesized that "too much, too soon" was attempted in the combined group (Benson *et al.*, 1984). As the researchers in cognitive psychology assert, before a training failure can be blamed on the cognitive deficits of the child, all aspects of the instructional program must be evaluated (Borkowski & Cavanaugh, 1979). In general, these preliminary results argue for further evaluation of cognitive-behavioral treatment of aggression with mentally retarded children. Specifically, extension of these procedures to mentally retarded children remains to be examined.

Current Status and Future Directions

The data presented here are illustrative but certainly not exhaustive. Many conclusions could be drawn from this information but perhaps the most important is that a great deal can definitely be taught to these children. The behaviors successfully remediated in recent years have included spelling, reading, and a variety of inappropriate behaviors that can adversely effect learning and integration in the school and community. These children show a great deal of potential and it would seem that much can be accomplished in addition to what has been achieved to this point.

Much has been made of cognitive psychology and the training of learning and memory strategies that can aid in enhancing academic performance. A considerable amount of excellent research in analogue settings has been conducted. Also, a number of heavily publicized theories of memory and learning have been advanced. Despite this, little promise in direct application has occurred. Clearly, efforts to establish these applied links are needed.

Operant methods have shown promise in the training of applied skills. They have been widely used with academic behavior. Inappropriate social and other disruptive behaviors have almost exclusively involved operant or social-learning procedures. Only a few of the many empirical studies with operant methods are reviewed in the present chapter. Their application is promising and impressive.

Given what has been found to date more research is clearly needed. It is particularly important that more research be performed on academic behaviors. One type of research that is clearly needed is large programmatic studies. These might involve the implementation of programs on academic and social behaviors across entire classes or preferably schools. This approach will require the provision of federal or state funding but could produce very important results. There is precedent for this method of study in some areas of mental retardation; the method is based on multiple-site psychotherapy studies. The first questions (i.e., Do these methods work in educational settings with mentally retarded children?) has been answered in the affirmative. Determining how large-scale implementation can be achieved and better determining the limits of trainability should constitute a major emphasis in the years to come.

References

Aloia, G. F., & MacMillan, D. L. (1983). Influence of the EMR label on initial expectations of regular-classroom teachers. *American Journal of Mental Deficiency, 88,* 255–262.

Altman, K., & Krupsaw, R. (1983). Suppressing aggressive-destructive behavior by delayed overcorrection. *Journal of Behavior Therapy and Experimental Psychiatry, 14,* 359–362.

Ayllon, T., Layman, S., & Burke, S. (1972). Disruptive behavior and reinforcement of academic performance. *The Psychological Record, 22,* 315–323.

Azrin, W. H., & Armstrong, P. M. (1973). "The mini-meal": A method for teaching eating skills to the profoundly retarded. *Mental Retardation, 11,* 9–11.

Azrin, N. H., & Foxx, R. M. (1971). A rapid method of toilet training the institutionalized retarded. *Journal of Applied Behavior Analysis, 4,* 89–99.

Barrett, R. P., Matson, J. L., Shapiro, E. S., & Ollendick, T. A. (1981). A comparison of punishment and RO procedures for treating stereotypic behavior of mentally retarded children. *Applied Research in Mental Retardation, 2,* 247–256.

Baumeister, A. A., & Forehand, R. (1973). Stereotyped acts. In N. R. Ellis (Ed.), *International review of research in mental retardation* (Vol. 6, pp. 55–96). New York: Academic Press.

Beck, S., Matson, J. L., & Kazdin, A. E. (1983). An instructional package to enhance spelling performance in emotionally disturbed children. *Child and Family Behavior Therapy, 4,* 69–77.

Becker, W., & Carnine, D. (1978). *Direct instruction: A behavior theory model for comprehension educational intervention with the disadvantaged.* Paper presented at the VIII Symposium on Behavior Modification, Caracas, Venezuala.

Bellack, A. S., Hersen, M., & Turner, S. M. (1976). Generalization effects of social skills training in chronic schizophrenics: An experimental analysis. *Behavior Research and Therapy, 14,* 391–398.

Bender, W. N., Wyne, M. D., Stuck, G. B., & Bailey, D. B. (1984). Relative peer status of LD, educably mentally handicapped, low achieving, and normally achieving children. *Child Study Journal, 13,* 209–216.

Benson, B. A., Miranti, S. V., & Johnson, C. (1984, November). *Self-control techniques for anger management with mentally retarded adults.* Paper presented at the Annual Convention of the Association for the Advancement of Behavior Therapy, Philadelphia, PA.

Bijou, S. W. (1957). Patterns of reinforcement and resistance to extinction in young children. *Child Development, 28,* 47–54.

Bijou, S. W. (1983). The prevention of mild and moderate retarded development. In F. J. Menolascino, R. Neman, & J. A. Stark (Eds.), *Curative aspects of mental retardation: Biomedical and behavioral advances* (pp. 223–242). Baltimore, MD: Brooks.

Bijou, S. W., & Orlando, R. (1961). Rapid development of multiple-schedule performances with retarded children. *Journal of the Experimental Analysis of Behavior, 4,* 7–16.

Bloom, B. S. (1976). *Human characteristics and school learning.* New York: McGraw-Hill.

Borkowski, J. G., & Cavanaugh, J. C. (1979). Maintenance and generalization of skills and strategies by the retarded. In N. R. Ellis (Ed.), *Handbook of mental deficiency: Psychological theory and research* (2nd ed., pp. 569–618). Hillsdale, NJ: Erlbaum.

Carey, R. G., & Bucher, B. (1983). Positive practice overcorrection: The effects of duration of positive practice on acquisition and response reduction. *Journal of Applied Behavior Analysis, 16,* 101–109.

Carnine, D. W. (1980). *Research on designing and implementing procedures for teaching sounds.* Unpublished manuscript.

Carnine, D. W., & Silbert, J. (1979). *Direct instruction.* Columbus, OH: Merrill.

Carvajal, T. L., Lane, J. M., & Gay, D. A. (1984). Longitudinal comparisons of Wechsler scales in educable mentally retarded handicapped children and adults. *Psychology in the Schools, 21,* 137–140.

Close, D. (1985). *Living and learning in the least restrictive environment.* Interdisciplinary Forum, Crippled Children's Division, Oregon Health Sciences University, University Affiliated Facility.

Cousins, L. S., Weber, E. M., & Dolan, K. (1984). *"How long do I have to stay after school?" Delayed punishment effects in and out of the classroom.* Paper presented at the 18th Annual AABT Convention, Philadelphia, PA.

Cullinan, D., Matson, J. L., Epstein, M. H., & Rosemier, R. A. (1984). Behavior problems of mentally retarded and nonretarded adolescent pupils. *School Psychology Review, 13,* 381–384.

Dietz, S. M., Repp, A. C., & Dietz, D. E. (1976). Reducing inappropriate behavior of retarded students through three procedures of differential reinforcement. *Journal of Mental Deficiency, 20,* 155–170.

Duke, D. (1978). How administrators view the crisis in school discipline. *Phi Delta Kappan, 56,* 325–330.

Eisler, R. M., Hersen, J., Miller, P. M., & Blanchard, E. B. (1975). Situational determinants of assertive behaviors. *Journal of Consulting and Clinical Psychology, 43,* 330–340.

Foxx, R. M., & Jones, J. R. (1978). A remediation program for increasing the spelling achievement of elementary and junior high school students. *Behavior Modification, 2,* 211–230.

Gelfind, D. M., & Hartmann, D. P. (1975). *Child behavior: Analysis and therapy.* New York: Pergamon Press.

Glidden, L. M. (1979). Training of learning and memory in retarded persons: Strategies, techniques, and teaching tools. In N. R. Ellis (Ed.), *Handbook of mental deficiency: Psychological theory and research* (2nd ed., pp. 619–647). Hillsdale, NJ: Erlbaum.

Grossman, H. J. (1983). *Classification in mental retardation.* Washington, DC: American Association on Mental Deficiency.

Hallahan, D. P., & Kaufmann, J. M. (1976). *Introduction to learning disabilities: A psycho-behavioral approach.* Englewood Cliffs, NJ: Prentice-Hall.

Hops, H., & Greenwood, C. R. (1981). Social skills deficits. In E. J. Mash & L. G. Terdal (Eds.), *Behavioral assessment of childhood disorders* (pp. 347–389). New York: Guilford Press.

Jenkinson, J. C. (1983). Correlates of sociometric status among TMR children in regular classrooms. *American Journal of Mental Deficiency, 88,* 332–335.

Johnston, M. B., Whitman, T. L., Johnson, M. (1980). Teaching addition and subtraction to mentally retarded children: A self-motivational program. *Applied Research in Mental Retardation, 1,* 141–160.

Kanfer, F. H., & Saslow, G. (1965). Behavioral analysis: An alternative to diagnostic classification. *Archives of General Psychiatry, 12,* 529–538.

Kazdin, A. E. (1977). Assessing the clinical or applied significance of behavioral change through social validation. *Behavior Modification, 1,* 427–452.

Kazdin, A. E., & Matson, J. L. (1981). Social validation in mental retardation. *Applied Research in Mental Retardation, 2,* 39–54.

Kazdin, A. E., Matson, J. L., & Esveldt-Dawson, K. (1981). Social skills performance among normal and psychiatric inpatient children as a function of assessment conditions. *Behaviour Research and Therapy, 19,* 145–152.

Kuveke, S. H. (1983). School Behaviors of educable mentally retarded children. *Education and Training of the Mentally Retarded, 18,* 134–137.

Leon, J. A., & Pepe, H. J. (1983). Self-instructional training: Cognitive behavior modification for remediating arithmetic deficits. *Exceptional Children, 50,* 54–60.

Lowe, B. R., & Cautela, J. R. (1978). A self-report measure of social skills. *Behavior Therapy, 9,* 535–544.

Madden, N. A., & Slavin, R. E. (1983). Mainstreaming students with mild handicaps: Academic and social outcomes. *Review of Educational Research, 53,* 519–569.

Matson, J. L. (1983a). Independence training versus modeling procedures for teaching phone conversational skills to the mentally retarded. *Behaviour Research and Therapy, 20,* 505–512.

Matson, J. L. (1983b). Mentally retarded children. In R. Morris & T. Kratchowill (Eds.), *The practice of child behavior therapy.* New York: Pergamon Press.

Matson, J. L., & Andrasik, F. (1982). Training leisure-time social-interaction skills to mentally retarded adults. *American Journal of Mental Deficiency, 86,* 533–542.

Matson, J. L., & Barrett, R. P. (1982). *Psychopathology in the mentally retarded.* New York: Grune & Stratton.

Matson, J. L., & Breuning, S. (1983). *Assessing the mentally retarded.* New York: Grune & Stratton.

Matson, J. L., & DiLorenzo, T. M. (1986). Mental handicap and organic impairment. In C. R. Hollin & P. Trower (Eds.), *Handbook of social skills training* (pp. 67–90). Oxford: Pergamon Press.

Matson, J. L., & Earnhart, T. (1981). Programming treatment effects to the natural environment: A procedure for training institutionalized retarded adults. *Behavior Modification, 5,* 27–37.

Matson, J. L., & McCartney, J. R. (1981). *Handbook of behavior modification with the mentally retarded.* New York: Plenum Press.

Matson, J. L., & Mulick, J. A. (1983). *Handbook of mental retardation.* New York: Pergamon Press.

Matson, J. L., & Ollendick, T. H. (1979). *Remediating learn-*

ing deficits of emotionally disturbed children with positive practice overcorrection. Unpublished manuscript.

Matson, J. L., & Stephens, R. M. (1977). Overcorrection of aggressive behavior in a chronic psychiatric patient. *Behavior Modification, 1*, 559–564.

Matson, J. L., Kazdin, A. E., & Esveldt-Dawson, K. (1980). Training interpersonal skills among mentally retarded and socially dysfunctional children. *Behaviour Research and Therapy, 18*, 419–427.

Matson, J. L., Esveldt-Dawson, K., & Kazdin, A. E. (1982). Treatment of spelling deficits in mentally retarded children. *Mental Retardation, 20*, 76–81.

Matson, J. L., Rotatori, A. F., & Helsel, W. J. (1983). Development of a rating scale to measure social skills in children: The Matson Evaluation of Social Skills with Youngsters (MESSY). *Behaviour Research and Therapy, 21*, 335–340.

Matson, J. L., Helsel, W. J., Bellack, A. S. & Senatore, V. (1983). Development of a rating scale to assess social skills deficits in mentally retarded adults. *Applied Research in Mental Retardation, 4*, 399–408.

McGonigle, J. J., Duncan, D., Cordisco, L., & Barrett, R. P. (1982). Visual screening: An alternative method for reducing stereotypic behaviors. *Journal of Applied Behavior Analysis, 15*, 461–467.

Michenbaum, D. H., & Goodman, J. (1969). The developmental control of operant motor responding by verbal operants. *Journal of Experimental Child Psychology, 7*, 553–565.

Meichenbaum, D. H., & Goodman, J. (1971). Training impulsive children to talk to themselves: A means of developing self-control. *Journal of Abnormal Psychology, 77*, 115–126.

Prescott, G. A. (1971). Criterion-referenced test interpretation in reading. *The Reading Teacher, 24*, 347–354.

Proger, B. B., & Mann, L. (1973). Criterion-referenced measurement: The world of gray versus black and white. *Journal of Learning Disabilities, 6*, 72–84.

Repp, A. C., Barton, L. E., & Brulle, A. R. (1983). A comparison of two procedures for programming the differential reinforcement of other behaviors. *Journal of Applied Behavior Analysis, 16*, 435–445.

Rosenshine, R. V. (1981). Academic engaged time, content covered, and direction instruction. *Journal of Education, 3*, 38–66.

Russell, A. T., & Forness, S. R. (1985). Behavioral disturbance in mentally retarded children in TMR and EMR classrooms. *American Journal of Mental Deficiency, 89*, 338–344.

Schilling, D., & Cuvo, A. (1983). The effects of a contingency-based lottery on the behavior of a special education class. *Education and Training of the Mentally Retarded, 18*, 52–58.

Schloss, P. J. (1983). The prosocial response formation technique. *The Elementary School Journal, 83*, 220–229.

Shapiro, E. S. (1981). Self-control procedures with the mentally retarded. *Progress in Behavior Modification, 12*, 265–297.

Shapiro, E. S., Barrett, R. P., & Ollendick, T. H. (1980). A comparison of physical restraint and positive practice overcorrection in treating stereotypic behavior. *Behavior Therapy, 11*, 227–233.

Shearer, D. E., & Shearer, M. S. (1976). The Portage Project: A model for early childhood intervention. In T. D. Tjossen (Ed.), *Intervention strategies for high risk infants and young children*. Baltimore, MD: University Park Press.

Singh, N. N., Singh, J., & Winton, A. S. W. (1984). Positive practice overcorrection of oral reading errors. *Behavior Modification, 8*, 23–27.

Singh, N. N., Winton, A. S. W., & Ball, P. M. (1984). Effects of physical restraint on the behavior of hyperactive mentally retarded persons. *American Journal of Mental Deficiency, 89*, 16–20.

Skinner, B. F. (1953). *Science and human behavior*. New York: MacMillan.

Skinner, B. F. (1984). The shame of American education. *American Psychologist, 39*, 947–954.

Stokes, T. F., & Baer, D. M. (1977). An implicit technology of generalization. *Journal of Applied Behavior Analysis, 10*, 349–367.

Sugai, G., & Rowe, P. (1984). The effect of self-recording on out-of-seat behavior of an EMR student. *Education and Training of the Mentally Retarded, 19*, 23–28.

Tawney, J. W., & Gast, D. L. (1984). *Single subject research in special education*. Columbus, OH: Merrill.

Weisberg, P., Packer, R. A., & Weisberg, R. S. (1981). Academic training. In J. L. Matson & J. R. McCarthey (Eds.), *Handbook of behavior modification with the mentally retarded* (pp. 331–411). New York: Plenum Press.

Whitman, T., Scibak, J., & Reid, D. (1983). *Behavior modification with the severely and profoundly retarded*. New York: Academic Press.

Wolf, M. (1978). Social validity: The case for subjective measurement or how applied behavior analysis is finding its heart. *Journal of Applied Behavior Analysis, 11*, 203–214.

CHAPTER 25

Conduct and Attention Deficit Disorders

Caryn L. Carlson and Benjamin B. Lahey

Behavior Problems of Conduct and Attention Deficit Disorder Children

Currently, one of the most controversial topics in the childhood behavior disorders literature involves the classification and nature of conduct disorders and hyperactivity, or attention deficit disorder with hyperactivity (ADD/H) (American Psychiatric Association, 1980). Despite extensive research, there is much disagreement about whether these two most prevalent of the childhood disorders represent independent syndromes. Although some authors conclude that ADD/H and conduct disorders should be considered similar or identical disorders (i.e., Quay, 1979; Shaffer & Greenhill, 1979), others maintain that it would be premature to abandon separate diagnoses of these two disorders (i.e., Barkley, 1982). Pertinent to the present chapter is the finding that there is a high degree of overlap of symptomatology between ADD/H and conduct disorder children (i.e., Rutter, 1982; Sandberg, Wieselberg, & Shaffer, 1980; Shaffer & Greenhill, 1979; Stewart, deBlois, & Cummings, 1980), and that many of these overlapping problem behaviors are likely to result in school problems. For example, in addition to displaying attention problems, impulsivity, and motor hyperactivity, ADD/H children frequently exhibit stubbornness, bullying, bossiness, low frustration tolerance, temper outbursts, and lack of response to discipline (American Psychiatric Association, 1980). Similarly, conduct-disordered children not only display a wide variety of problem behaviors, ranging from seriously antisocial acts to less severe behaviors such as oppositionalism, bossiness, negativism, and tantrums, but are also frequently impulsive, inattentive, and overactive (Sandberg *et al.*, 1980). Thus, children diagnosed as either hyperactive or conduct disordered are likely to disrupt the class, break rules, engage in aggressive behavior, and have difficulty completing academic assignments. Thus, the two diagnostic groups will generally not be distinguished in this chapter when we discuss treatment strategies.

An important caveat must be made explicit

Caryn L. Carlson • Department of Psychology, Virginia Polytechnic Institute and State University, Blacksburg, Virginia 24061. **Benjamin B. Lahey** • Department of Psychology, Georgia Children's Center, University of Georgia, Athens, Georgia 30602.

concerning the discussion of conduct disorder and ADD/H as highly similar disorders that should be managed in the classroom using the same strategies. Although insufficient evidence now exists to evaluate it fully, a new conceptualization of the relationship of conduct disorder and ADD/H has recently been proposed. August and Stewart (August & Stewart, 1982, 1983; August, Stewart, & Holmes, 1983) and McGee, Williams, and Silva (1984) have proposed that conduct disorder and ADD/H are not highly similar disorders with overlapping behavioral characteristics, but rather are distinct syndromes that frequently co-occur in the same children. Clinical and epidemiological data support this contention by showing that approximately 60% of children diagnosed as ADD/H also qualify for a diagnosis of conduct disorder and vice versa (August & Stewart, 1982, 1983; Lahey, Schaughency, Strauss, & Frame, 1984; McGee *et al.*, 1984). The important finding for the present chapter is that approximately 40% of the ADD/H children do not exhibit the kinds of behavior problems that are most problematic for teachers (those that lead to a diagnosis of conduct disorder). thus, it cannot be assumed that the classroom intervention strategies described in this chapter are appropriate for children who are inattentive, impulsive, and overactive (ADD/H), but are otherwise well behaved. Similarly, it should not be assumed that these strategies would be appropriate for children given the DSM-III diagnosis of attention deficit disorder without hyperactivity. Not only do these children generally not display conduct problems, but some appear to be characterized by problems of anxiety and shyness that might indicate the necessity for very different intervention strategies (Lahey *et al.*, 1984).

Appropriate Target Behaviors for Intervention

Based on the descriptions of the types of disruptive classroom behaviors displayed by conduct disordered and hyperactive children, procedures designed to modify directly these inappropriate behaviors would appear to be the recommended treatment strategies for the classroom management of these two groups of children.

In fact, numerous studies have been published demonstrating the effectiveness of a variety of techniques in decreasing off-task behavior, increasing attentiveness, and modifying a host of other disruptive behaviors presumed to be incompatible with educational goals. However, the practice of designing treatment strategies with the major goal of keeping children quiet and on task has been questioned by a growing number of researchers (i.e., Ayllon & Rosenbaum, 1977; Broughton & Lahey, 1978; Jones & Kazdin, 1981; Keogh & Barkett, 1980; Lahey & Drabman, 1981; Lahey, Hobbs, Kupfer, & Delamater, 1979) for several reasons.

First, criticisms of this approach were voiced in a widely cited article by Winett and Winkler (1972) entitled "Current behavior modification in the classroom: Be still, be quiet, be docile." These authors argued that focusing solely on decreasing disruptive behaviors and increasing on-task behavior may actually be detrimental to academic functioning. They went on to accuse behavior modifiers of fostering the status quo by supporting an educational system that emphasizes orderliness over learning. Despite criticisms that their conclusions were based on a limited sample of behavioral research (O'Leary, 1972), Winett and Winkler's (1972) criticisms prompted a closer analysis of the relationship between on-task or disruptive behavior and academic functioning.

A number of studies have demonstrated, moreover, that academic achievement does not improve as a function of increasing on-task behavior with behavioral techniques (i.e., Ferritor, Buckholdt, Hamblin, & Smith, 1972; Hay, Hay, & Nelson, 1977; Marholin & Steinman, 1977; Marholin, Steinman, McInnis, & Heads, 1975). On the other hand, several studies have found that directly reinforcing academic responding results in increases in academic performance and on-task behavior. For example, Ayllon, Layman, and Kandel (1975) found that reinforcing hyperactive children for accurate classwork increased their academic performance and sharply decreased their inappropriate behavior; in addition, the levels of inappropriate behavior obtained with this method were as low as levels observed while the children were taking stimulant medication. Similar improvements in behavior and academics when academic achievement is reinforced have been consistently reported across a variety of subject populations and behavioral techniques (Aaron & Bostow, 1978; Ayllon & Roberts, 1974; Ayllon, Layman, & Burke, 1972; Broughton & Lahey, 1978; Hay *et al.*, 1977; Marholin & Steinman, 1977; Robinson, Newby, & Ganzell, 1981; Witt, Hannafin, & Martens, 1983).

These findings hold major implications for the classroom management of behavior-problem children. Most importantly, given that academic learning is a primary goal of the educational system, a major emphasis in designing classroom interventions should be placed on academic achievement. Thus, the studies cited clearly support techniques that reinforce academic responding because this approach results in improved academic achievement whereas reinforcing on-task behavior does not. Directly targeting academic behavior is also more efficient because academic and inappropriate behaviors are modified with this single contingency and because reinforcing academic behaviors may be easier than monitoring and controlling inappropriate behaviors (Lahey *et al.*, 1978). Furthermore, techniques that target academic responding are not subject to many of the criticisms made by Winett and Winkler (1972) because only behaviors that are truly incompatible with learning are reduced. As a result, classroom management is more objective and less restrictive. For example, it may be that children can progress academically and still engage in some "inappropriate" behaviors, such as talking to peers or leaving one's seat; if so, it is difficult to defend the use of techniques that attempt to decrease presumably inappropriate behavior as their only goal. Finally, reinforcing academics may result in greater generalization of treatment effects. For example, reinforcing academics has been shown to be superior to reinforcing on-task behavior in maintaining improved behavior when the teacher is out of the room (Marholin & Steinman, 1977) and in maintaining academic and behavioral gains following withdrawal of treatment (Broughten & Lahey, 1978; Hay *et al.*, 1977; Kirby & Shields, 1972).

Although reinforcing academics is clearly the preferred method of simultaneously improving academic achievement and classroom behavior, in some instances it may be necessary or desirable to directly target undesirable behaviors. Children are not engaged in academic activities during the entire school day, for example, during lunch or recess, and behavior problems displayed during these times may necessitate direct reinforcement of good conduct. In addition, certain infrequent and/or serious acts, such as aggression or stealing, may require interventions that place specific contingencies on these behaviors. Perhaps the most troubling constraint to reinforcing solely academic behavior involves the finding that this strategy does not always result in decreases in disruptive behavior. For example, Ferritor *et al.* (1972) found that introduction of a token system to reinforce appropriate classroom behavior resulted in decreased disruption but did not effect academic achievement. When tokens were awarded for academics, work performance improved; however, disruption increased. Only when token reinforcement was made contingent on academic achievement and behavior did both improve. This finding is troubling because although teachers and educators may support techniques that target academic responding if they also decrease disruption, they are probably considerably less likely to support these same techniques when they do not improve classroom behavior. There may be very valid reasons for this position. For example, although no empirical evidence is available concerning this issue, it could be argued that some disruptive behaviors not necessarily incompatible with learning still merit modification if they make the child unpopular or interfere with other children's work or well-being (Lahey *et al.*, 1979). It may also be that, despite the criticisms of Winett and Winkler (1972), some teachers simply do not want classrooms in which children talk freely, walk around, and sit on the floor. In a recent review of research pertaining to the classroom modification of academic performance, Klein (1979) cited the observation by Dietz *et al.* (1978) that public opinion polls suggest classroom discipline remains the major concern of educators and parents. Thus, it may be that consumer interest does not parallel technological advances in classroom management techniques (Klein, 1979; Wolf, 1978).

Clearly, these issues require more attention by developers of behavior management techniques. However, at the present time approaches that target academic responding remain the most ethically and educationally defensible strategies. Whenever possible, studies that utilized this approach will be used to illustrate the various treatment procedures discussed.

Teacher-Mediated Interventions

Of all the agents involved in behavioral interventions, teachers have been by far the most frequent mediators of behavior change strategies. Teacher-mediated techniques include contingent teacher attention, which includes praise, ignoring, and reprimands; token economies; response cost (most frequently used as a component in a token system); and time out.

Teacher Attention

Contingent teacher attention is a frequently employed method of attempting to modify children's behavior problems. Teacher attention includes giving positive attention to appropriate behaviors to increase them, and withdrawing attention (ignoring) or giving negative attention (reprimands) to inappropriate behaviors to decrease them. Research examining the use of contingent teacher attention has often involved some combination of praise, ignoring, and reprimands.

Madsen, Becker, and Thomas (1968) compared the effects of rules, praise, and ignoring on inappropriate classroom behavior. Following a baseline phase, the teacher compiled a list of classroom rules that the children learned (rules). Next, the teacher ignored inappropriate behavior while rules remained in effect (rules and ignoring), and, finally, the teacher additionally praised appropriate behavior (rules, ignoring, and praise). After the initial baseline and treatment phases, the combined program of rules, ignoring, and praise was withdrawn in a return to baseline and then, in the final phase, reintroduced. Results indicated that rules and rules with ignoring were not effective, whereas adding praise to the treatment program resulted in decreased inappropriate behavior. Other studies have also found praise to result in improved conduct, such as reductions in the time required to get ready to work when children were given feedback about their times and praised for decreased times (Struble, 1971), and reductions in off-task behavior when the principal praised individual children or competing teams of children for meeting a specified standard of on-task behavior (Darch & Thorpe, 1977).

McAllister, Stachowiak, Baer, and Conderman (1969) combined praise and reprimands in a study in which teachers verbally praised appropriate behavior and expressed verbal disapproval of talking out and turning around. These procedures substantially reduced inappropriate classroom behavior.

Doleys, Wells, Hobbs, Roberts, and Cartelli (1976) compared social punishment (i.e., holding the child's shoulders, verbally reprimanding, and glaring), positive practice, and time out in reducing noncompliance in four developmentally handicapped children. Social punishment was found to be the most effective procedure. However, it should be noted that the social punishment and time-out procedures lasted 40 seconds, making the social reinforcement longer and time out shorter than is typical for these two procedures.

Some research has suggested that praise is more effective than reprimands and that reprimands may actually increase inappropriate behavior. Madsen, Becker, Thomas, Koser, and Plager (1968) instructed first-grade teachers to triple their baseline rates of telling children to sit down. This procedure resulted in increased out-of-seat behavior and inappropriate verbalizations. However, both of these disruptive behaviors decreased when teachers praised behavior incompatible with standing up. Thomas, Becker, and Armstrong (1968) similarly found that verbal reprimands increased inappropriate behaviors whereas praise for appropriate behavior effectively reduced problem behaviors.

O'Leary and his colleagues (O'Leary & Becker, 1968; O'Leary, Kaufman, Kass, & Drabman, 1970) also found that loud verbal reprimands were ineffective in decreasing children's disruptive behavior, although soft reprimands, which were audible only to the child, reduced rates of inappropriate behavior. In another study investigating variables influencing the effectiveness of reprimands, Van Houten, Nau, MacKenzie-Keating, Sameoto, and Colavecchia (1982) found that delivering reprimands with eye contact while grasping the child's shoulders and reprimands delivered while standing close to the child were more effective.

The results of the studies reviewed here have several implications for the use of contingent attention in the classroom. Social praise may effectively modify disruptive behavior, either alone (Darch & Thorpe, 1977; Struble, 1971) or in combination with other types of teacher attention (Madsen, Becker, & Thomas, 1968; McAllister *et al.*, 1969). On the other hand, verbal reprimands alone may actually increase inappropriate behavior (Madsen, Becker, Thomas, Koser, & Plager, 1968; Thomas *et al.*, 1968), although they may be effective in controlling misbehavior when combined with praise for appropriate behavior (McAllister *et al.*, 1969). When verbal reprimands are used, soft reprimands (O'Leary & Becker, 1968; O'Leary *et al.*, 1970), and reprimands delivered with eye contact and a grasp while standing close to the child (Van Houten *et al.*, 1982) may be more effective. Barkley (1982) suggested that verbal reprimands are less likely to be useful with hyperactive children because they have probably been frequently exposed to the ineffective use of these procedures at home; this may also be true of children with conduct disorders.

Classroom Token Economies

The token economy is a frequently used and extensively studied behavioral technique for the classroom management of children's behavior problems. Token systems involve the use of tokens or points that children may earn for specified behaviors and then exchange for some desired object, privilege, or activity.

O'Leary, Becker, Evans, and Saudergas (1969) implemented a token reinforcement system to decrease disruptive behavior in seven second graders after a combination of rules, educational structure, and praise/ ignore procedures were unsuccessful in reducing disruption in six of the seven children. Results indicated that disruptive behavior decreased in five of the six remaining children during the token program, in which children earned tokens exchangeable for small toys. Many of these gains were maintained during a follow-up phase in which stars and occasional candy were substituted for the token procedures. A number of other studies have also used token programs in which children earn tokens based on their individual performance (i.e., Drabman, 1973; O'Leary & Becker, 1967).

Token systems have also been implemented with entire classrooms of children. An example of a group token system is the good-behavior game developed by Barrish, Saunders, and Wolfe (1969). A class of 24 students was divided into two teams that competed to commit the fewest number of classroom rule violations. The team with the fewest violations, or both teams if violations did not exceed a specified number, received a variety of privileges, such as extra recess time and stars on a name chart. Introduction of the good-behavior game produced substantial decreases in disruptive behavior from baseline levels.

In a study by Brooks and Snow (1972), a combination of individual and group token reinforcement/response-cost procedures were used to reduce stealing by a 10-year-old boy. The subject frequently left his classroom group when they were outside of the classroom and was suspected of stealing during these times. A token system was introduced in which the subject earned points for work completion, staying in the classroom for a specified period, and remaining with the group during outside activities. In addition to receiving a penny for each point he earned, the target child could earn free-time for the entire class when he obtained a specified number of points. In addition, the entire class lost one minute of time during the next desired activity whenever the subject left the classroom or group or did not complete work. During implementation of the token program, the child earned free time for the class each day, increased his rate of assignment completion, and no longer left the group; in addition, stealing incidents stopped. The program was withdrawn after one week and improvements were maintained throughout the remainder of the school year.

Kerr and Nelson (1983) suggested that token systems may be used to manage aggression by rewarding tokens for actions that are incompatible with aggression in addition to removing tokens for aggressive behaviors. Examples of behaviors that could earn tokens might include walking away from a fight, accepting teacher feedback with a nonangry statement, and keeping hands to oneself for a specified time period (Kerr & Nelson, 1983, p. 240).

It can be seen from the studies examined that token systems can be adapted to modify directly a variety of disruptive behaviors as well as more severe behavior problems (e.g., stealing, aggression). Several studies have also used token reinforcement of academics to improve academic performance and indirectly decrease inappropriate behavior.

Robinson *et al.* (1981) used a token system to increase the academic performance of 18 third-grade boys who had been identified as hyperactive by teachers and the school psychologist. In addition to being below grade level in reading, the students displayed a high level of aggressive and disruptive behavior. Tokens were delivered for the successful completion of standardized reading and vocabulary assignments and for helping another student complete an assignment. Tokens were exchangeable for access to a video game. Total assignment completion averaged 35 daily during the initial 14-day treatment phase as compared to 4 daily during a 5-day reversal phase in which tokens and back up reinforcers were withdrawn. When the token program was reinstituted, average assignment completion measured over the next 13 days again rose to 40 daily. In addition, the class rate of passing the school district's standardized weekly reading level exams was four to eight times greater during token phases than during pretreatment and reversal phases. A substantial decrease in disruptive behaviors is also reported although, unfortunately, no objective measures of disruption were obtained.

Ayllon, Layman, & Kandel (1975) utilized an indirect approach of reinforcing academic achievement with a token system to reduce the disruptive behavior of three diagnosed hyperactive children. The children, who were all receiving methylphenidate for hyperactivity, were enrolled in a self-contained learning disability classroom of 10 children. Hyperactivity was assessed by direct observation of inappropriate motor behavior, disturbing others, making disruptive noises, and talking out. Academic performance was measured daily in math, where the percentage correct of 10 math problems was assessed, and in reading, where the percentage correct of workbook questions about reading assignments was assessed. Treatment, which consisted of token reinforcement of academic achievement, was evaluated in a four-phase, multiple baseline design. In the first phase, hyperactivity and academic performance were evaluated while the children were on medication. After a 3-day "wash-out" period, hyperactivity and academic performance were again assessed. During the third phase, the children remained off medication but the token system, whereby children earned tokens that were later exchangeable for backup reinforcers for each correct academic response, was introduced for math performance. In the final phase, the token system was also introduced for reading performance. Results for all three children indicated that hyperactivity averaged 24% and academic achievement averaged 12% during the first phase (medication only). Removal of medication during the second phase resulted in two to three times the rate of hyperactivity observed under the medication phase and a slight improvement in academic performance. During the final two phases, during which children remained off medication and reinforcement of math and reading achievement was initiated, hyperactivity was reduced to about 20% and academic achievement averaged 85%. Thus, reinforcing the competing behavior of academic performance indirectly reduced hyperactive, disruptive classroom behavior.

Ayllon and Roberts (1974) used a similar procedure to decrease indirectly the disruptive behavior of five fifth-grade children by reinforcing academic achievement. The five children, ranked by their teachers as being the most disruptive in the class, displayed baseline rates of disruptive behavior (being out of their seats without permission, talking out, disturbing other students) of approximately 40%. Academic performance in reading, defined as the percentage of correct work on daily reading assignments, initially averaged around 50%. A token economy was introduced whereby children earned two points for a minimum of 80% correct reading work and five points for 100% correct work. Points were exchangeable for a variety of activities and privileges (e.g., having the lowest test grade removed, becoming a teacher's assistant, seeing a movie, having a good-work letter sent home, etc.). Mean reading performance following initial introduction of the token economy increased to 70% and disruption decreased to 15%. Baseline conditions were reinstated and resulted in a decrease in reading accuracy and an increase in disruption. During the final phase of the study, the token system was reinstated. Again, reading performance was increased to about 85% and disruption decreased to about 5%. Thus, by directly strengthening reading accuracy, disruption was indirectly decreased.

In addition to the studies cited, numerous other investigators have used token systems to modify a variety of problem behaviors (see review by Kazdin, 1977). The ease with which diverse behaviors may be targeted in token programs makes them particularly applicable to the wide range of inappropriate behaviors displayed by conduct disorder and hyperactive children. However, despite their demonstrated efficacy, practical issues involving the availability of material resources and teacher time to establish and maintain token systems must be considered drawbacks to their use. These drawbacks are particularly troubling in light of recent evidence that the amount of teacher time involvement significantly influences teacher's judgments of intervention acceptability (Witt, Martens, & Elliott, 1984). Demands for ease of integrating token systems within institutional constraints and disseminating them effectively are major issues dictating the future of the token economy (Kazdin, 1982).

Response Cost

Response cost involves the contingent removal of previously acquired reinforcers. The two most common types of response cost procedures involve removing the opportunity to participate in an activity (e.g., loss of television privileges or recess time) or removing tokens within a token economy system (Rutherford, 1982). For example, Switzer, Deal, and Bailey (1977) used a group response-cost procedure combined with positive reinforcement to reduce stealing in three second grade classrooms. Each day, objects (erasers, nickels, etc.) were placed around the room and observers recorded the number of items stolen or returned every morning. Teachers gave anti-stealing lectures in two classrooms, with no effect. The group contingency was then introduced in which children were told each morning they would have free time if no items were found missing. If something were missing, students were given the opportunity to return the item without suffering a loss of privileges (talking during snack time). This procedure resulted in an immediate reduction of stealing in all three classes.

Rosen and Rosen (1983) similarly used a combination of token reinforcement and response cost to eliminate stealing in a first-grade boy. The child's belongings were marked with green circles, and treatment consisted of contingent praise and tokens for having only marked items and a verbal reprimand and point fine for having unmarked items. Average baseline rates of 6.0 items stolen per day were reduced to .32 during treatment and maintained at .09 during 31 days of follow-up after the token system was eliminated.

Rapport, Murphy, and Bailey (1982) implemented a response-cost procedure that targeted the on-task behavior of two hyperactive boys. The boys worked on academic assignments and were told they would have 20 minutes of free time for "working hard"; each time the teacher saw a child not working, he lost one minute. The response-cost procedure resulted in increases in on-task behavior and academic performance; in addition, these increases were greater than those observed with stimulant medication treatment. This finding that targeting on-task behavior resulted in improved academic performance is somewhat surprising in light of previous research cited; however, the definition of on task used in this study (working on the assignment) is more closely related to academic functioning than definitions used in other studies (i.e., being nondisruptive).

Response-cost procedures have also used loss of 5 minutes of gym time (Schmidt & Ulrich, 1969) or after-school free time (Hall *et al.*, 1971) to decrease out-of-seat behavior; loss of slips of paper to decrease whining and complaining (Hall *et al.*, 1971); and group loss of free time to reduce "naughty finger" behavior and verbalizations about it (Sulzbacher & Houser, 1968).

Several studies have examined the differential effects of reward and response cost on inappropriate behavior. Broughten and Lahey (1978) examined the relative effects of positive reinforcement, response cost, and reinforcement plus response cost on academic performance and on-task behavior when these contingencies were placed on academic accuracy. Through use of a combination of between-group and within-group comparisons, all three academic contingencies were found to increase directly the accuracy of workbook math problems and indirectly decrease off-task behavior. None of the three contingencies was found to be differentially effective.

Iwata and Bailey (1974) divided students into those who received tokens contingent on following rules (reward) and those who began with tokens and were fined for not following rules (response cost). The treatment conditions were then reversed, so that all students received reward and response-cost procedures. The two procedures were found to be equally effective, and no adverse side effects were associated with response cost. In addition, students reported no consistent differences in their preferences for the two systems, although the teacher was found to display higher rates of verbal approval during the reward condition. Other authors have similarly found that response cost is as effective as positive reinforcement and that students report no clearcut preference for one procedure over the other (Hundert, 1976; Kaufman & O'Leary, 1972). Only one study has suggested that positive reinforcement may be more effective than response cost (McLaughlin & Malaby, 1972).

Witt and Elliott (1982) described the use of a response-cost procedure designed to increase effectively on-task behavior and academic achievement with only minimal teacher time and material resources required for implementation. Three fourth-grade boys, identified by the teacher as being the most severe behavior problems in the class, served as subjects in the study. Off-task, disruptive behavior was observed four times weekly during a 30-minute study period that the teacher reported was the time students were most disruptive. Following a one-week baseline phase, the response-cost lottery was implemented. The teacher gave each boy four slips of paper (different color slips were used for each child) at the beginning of the study period and removed one each time a boy violated a classroom rule. At the end of the period, boys deposited their remaining slips in a box for a weekly drawing in which the boy whose slip was drawn could choose a prize (pencils, extra recess time). After 2 weeks, a one-week reversal phase was instituted followed by a one-week return to response-cost procedures. The response-cost lottery was successful in increasing on-task behavior from initial average rates of 10% to 68% during the first treatment phase; on-task behavior decreased to 43% during reversal and again rose to 73% during the return to response-cost procedures. The rates of on-task behavior achieved during response-cost phases compared favorably to the 80% on-task rates observed for randomly selected classmates who were not in the study. Somewhat surprisingly, the percentage of academic work correctly completed also increased during treatment, averaging 27% during baseline, 87% during response cost, 38% during reversal, and 90% during return to response cost. As Witt and Elliott (1982) noted, this improvement in academic performance achieved by reinforcing behavior contradicts findings that contingencies should be on academic behavior (Ferritor *et al.*, 1972; Hay *et al.*, 1977; Marholin & Steinman, 1977) and may have resulted because of the teacher's emphasis on academic behaviors. Thus, although specific classroom rules were not described in the article, slips were evidently removed for not working even when boys were nondisruptive (e.g., "You're looking at your paper, but you're not working.").

Ruggles and LeBlanc (1982) described several drawbacks associated with the use of response cost. These include difficulties involved in maintaining the bookkeeping system (as with token systems) and findings that positive reinforcement systems are equal to (Hundert, 1976; Iwata & Bailey, 1974; Kaufman & O'Leary, 1972) or more effective than (McLaughlin & Malaby, 1972) response-cost procedures. In addressing these issues, it would seem that bookkeeping problems are minimal when response-cost procedures are added to an existing token system. In addition, some response-cost programs have been designed to require minimal teacher time (Witt & Elliott, 1982). Response cost also offers the advantage of being easily incorporated into token systems, thus allowing reinforcement and punishment to be administered along the same reinforcer dimension (i.e., tokens) (Kazdin, 1977), and may actually increase the effectiveness of token programs (McLaughlin & Malaby, 1977). In contrast with what would be expected of children's attitudes toward many punishment techniques, response-cost procedures also appear to be no less preferable to children than reward procedures (Iwata & Bailey, 1974).

Time Out

Time out from positive reinforcement, frequently referred to simply as time out, is a method for reducing undesirable behavior by temporarily denying a child the opportunity to obtain reinforcement contingent on the child's engaging in inappropriate behavior. The use of time out in the classroom usually refers to a social isolation procedure because it typically involves placing the child in an area away from other students (Drabman & Spitalnik, 1973).

In a well-designed multiple baseline study, Drabman and Spitalnik (1973) used time out (social isolation) to reduce the disruptive behavior of three children in a psychiatric hospital classroom. The children were removed from the classroom and taken to another small room for 10 minutes for each occurrence of aggression or out-of-seat behavior. Aggression was reduced from 2.8% during baseline to .37% during social isolation and out-of-seat behavior was reduced from baseline rates of 34% to 11% during the treatment phase. Rates of a third disruptive behavior that was not punished, vocalization, did not change.

A similar social isolation procedure was used by Webster (1976) to reduce the extremely aggressive behavior of a sixth-grade boy. Aggressive acts averaged four daily prior to implementation of social isolation, which involved sending the child to a small room to do schoolwork for the duration of that class period, contingent on the occurrence of aggression. He spent an average of 65 minutes daily in time-out during the first 2 weeks of the program; this time averaged 18 minutes daily during the 3rd week and continued to decrease over the following weeks. At the end of 10 weeks the child was no longer engaging in self-initiated aggressive acts.

Lahey, McNees, and McNees (1973) compared instructed repetition (negative practice) to social isolation time out in reducing obscene language in a boy displaying Tourette-like symptoms. In addition to being more effective, time out was easier for the teacher to implement.

In some time-out procedures, children are placed in a chair within the classroom rather than being sent outside the classroom to an isolated area. LeBlanc, Busby, and Thomson (1973) used a chair time-out procedure to reduce the aggressive and disruptive acts of a preschool child, although a back-up procedure of sending the child to another room contingent on refusal to stay in the chair was initially required on occasion. Porterfield, Herbert-Jackson, and Risley (1976) also used a chair time-out procedure (backed up with room time out) to reduce inappropriate behavior and found it to be more effective than traditional redirection of behavior. In this study, the time-out procedures, which were referred to as contingent observation, differed somewhat from those used in other studies because children were purposefully placed so that they could observe the appropriate behavior of other children.

Another type of time-out procedure involves removing the opportunity to receive reinforcement rather than actually removing the child from the environment. For example, Kubany, Weiss, and Sloggett (1971) reduced disruptive behavior in a hyperactive boy with the use of a good-behavior clock. The child could earn rewards for himself and his class contingent upon the clock running for a specified time. Each time the child displayed inappropriate behavior the clock was stopped for 15 seconds and remained stopped if he continued to misbehave. This procedure was effective in reducing disruptive behavior from baseline rates of 88% to 17% during treatment. Foxx and Shapiro (1978) described a procedure in which ribbons indicating eligibility to participate in activities and receive teacher approval were temporarily removed from children contingent on inappropriate behavior. This procedure, which also constitutes removal of the opportunity to receive reinforcement, effectively reduced disruptive behavior in the children studied. Other studies have also found time out, either alone (e.g., Tyler & Brown, 1967) or in combination with positive reinforcement for appropriate behavior (e.g., Hawkins & Hayes, 1974; Mattos, Wattson, Walker, & Buckley, 1969; Patterson, Shaw, & Ebner, 1969) to be an effective method for reducing various problematic behavior. There is also evidence that children may be able to determine effectively their own time-out durations (Pease & Tyler, 1979) and that time out may vicariously reduce the inappropriate behavior of children who observed, but were not the target of the intervention (Wilson, Robertson, Herlong, & Haynes, 1979).

Overall, time out has been demonstrated to be an effective procedure for reducing inappropriate behavior that can easily be combined with other behavior management techniques. However, in addition to the criticisms aimed at punishment techniques in general, the potential legal implications of time-out procedures (particularly those involving complete isolation) require that they be systematically planned, carefully supervised, and regularly reviewed (Gast & Nelson, 1977).

Peer-Mediated Interventions

Peer attention frequently exerts a major influence on children's behavior. Although this influence is sometimes negative, as when children socially reinforce each other for disruptive behavior, a growing number of studies indicate that peers can serve as positive agents to increase the appropriate behavior of their classmates. Peers have been involved in behavior change programs in several ways: as members of a group who receive consequences dependent on the behavior of classmates; as trained administrators of attention and reinforcement for classmates' appropriate behavior; and, as monitors of tokens in a token economy system.

Some group contingency procedures involve consequence sharing by making rewards or sanctions for the group either partially or completely dependent on the behavior of one or a few individuals. Thus, in addition to the effects of the individual contingency, peer support for target behaviors is elicited.

Speltz, Wenters-Shimamura, and McReynolds (1982) applied individual contingencies and three types of group contingencies (reward based on class average, reward based on the work of a designated, low-achieving child, or reward based on the work of a randomly chosen child) to the academic productivity of the four lowest-performing students in a learning disabilities classroom. All the contingencies resulted in improvements in baseline levels of academic performance. Although individual responses varied greatly, two of the four subjects did their best academic work when class rewards were based on their performance. This contingency was also most preferred by the target children and produced higher levels of positive social interactions than the other contingencies for three of the four student groups. Unfortunately, disruptive behavior was not assessed during the study.

The good-behavior game (described earlier) developed by Barrish *et al.* (1969) utilizes peer influence by dividing children into competing groups who earn reinforcers for surpassing the performance of another group or meeting a specified criteria of appropriate behavior. The good-behavior game and variations of this type of group procedure are quite effective in reducing inappropriate behavior (e.g., Barrish *et al.*, 1969; Darch & Thorpe, 1977; Harris & Sherman, 1973; Hegerle, Kesecker, & Couch, 1979; Medland & Stachnik, 1972; Saigh & Umar, 1983). In some consequence-sharing group strategies, a target child earns rewards that are distributed to the entire classroom. This strategy has been employed to reduce stealing (Brooks & Snow, 1972) and a variety of disruptive behaviors (Carlson, Arnold, Becker, & Madsen, 1968; Coleman, 1970; Patterson, 1965; Walker & Buckley, 1972) and may be effective in some cases when individual contingencies are not (Wolf, Hanley, King, Lachowicz, & Giles, 1970).

Peers have also been used to influence misbehavior by attending to and praising appropriate behaviors. Solomon and Wahler (1973) found that a classroom of elementary school children showed high baseline rates of attending to the disruptive acts of their behavior problem classmates. Some of the children were then trained to praise appropriate classroom behavior (remaining in seat, completing classwork, etc.). When children carried out the program, desirable behaviors increased and problem behaviors decreased; during a reversal phase in which children withdrew contingent attention, disruptive behavior again increased. A similar procedure was effective in reducing inappropriate comments by an elementary school boy when a peer the child particularly liked gave positive attention to him contingent on appropriate talk (Lovitt, Lovitt, Eaton, & Kirkwood, 1973). Grieger, Kauffman, and Grieger (1976) found that aggressive behavior decreased and cooperative play increased in an elementary school classroom through the implementation of a peer-reporting procedure in which children took turns reporting the friendly acts of peers to the class and distributed happy face badges to the peers named.

Peers have also been used to monitor behavior and distribute tokens in token economy systems. This function has been effectively performed by children (Drabman, 1973; Winett, Richards, & Krasner, 1971) even as young as kindergarten age (Carden-Smith & Fowler, 1984). An additional benefit of this procedure is that the position of peer monitor is desired by children and they will work for tokens to exchange for the privilege (Phillips, Phillips, Wolf, & Fixsen, 1973).

Strain, Cooke, and Apolloni (1976) suggested that peers may be even more effective behavior change agents than teachers, because they may be able to monitor children's behavior more continuously and in more settings (i.e., restroom, hallway, etc.) and may promote greater generalization because their presence in the classroom could serve as a discriminative stimulus for appropriate behavior. Peer reinforcement procedures may also have practical advantages because children can relieve teachers of some of the burdens of maintaining treatment programs. However, problems may arise in some group procedures, particularly if children choose to subvert the system, do not have the necessary skills to perform the required behavior, or place undue pressure on an individual child (O'Leary & Drabman, 1971). Jones and Kazdin (1981) suggested that the likelihood that peers will use coercive tactics with an individual child may be reduced if contingencies are arranged such that children gain extra rewards rather than losing them for the target child's performance.

Parent/Home-Mediated Interventions

The use of home-based reinforcement programs to modify children's classroom behavior problems is becoming increasingly popular. In these programs, teachers rate some aspect of the child's behavior and communicate this rating to parents (typically in the form of a letter or report card); parents are then responsible for dispensing rewards or sanctions to the child at home on the basis of the teacher's report. Home-based programs have been effective in modifying disruptive and academic behaviors and offer an important alternative to teacher-mediated programs in some circumstances. Consultants (e.g., school psychologists, clinical child psychologists, child psychiatrists, etc.) frequently find that teachers are unwilling or unable to adopt new classroom management and teaching strategies. Indeed, those teachers who will adopt the methods advocated by the consultant are the exception rather than the rule. Although parent/home-mediated strategies require some degree of teacher involvement, they are far less extensive and are acceptable to far more teachers.

Schumaker, Hovell, and Sherman (1977)

used a daily report card procedure with junior high school students to increase appropriate behavior and classwork completion. Parents administered praise and privileges at home based on teacher ratings of whether their child followed classroom rules and completed assignments. This program resulted in substantial improvements in school performance. Particularly noteworthy is the finding that children participating in the home-based program tended to receive higher grades than comparison children. Other researchers have also employed home-based reinforcement programs to decrease disruptive classroom behavior and increase academic behavior (Bailey, Wolf, & Phillips, 1970; Dougherty & Dougherty, 1977; Lahey *et al.*, 1977).

Ayllon, Garber, and Pisor (1975) used a home-based reinforcement program to decrease children's disruptive behavior after a classroom token system failed to decrease disruption. Subjects were 23 children who showed high rates of disruptive behavior (defined as talking out, being out of their seats, and disturbing other students) and were at least a year behind in reading and math skills. Following a baseline phase, a token program was introduced in which children earned tokens for each page of at least 70% correct academic work completed. Tokens could be exchanged for a variety of tangible (i.e., dolls, comics) and intangible (i.e., recess, game room admittance) reinforcers in the classroom. Although disruptive behavior initially decreased from 85% to 20% with the introduction of the token system, after 2 days disruptiveness increased to baseline levels. The token system was therefore extended to direct reinforcement of good conduct: children earned points for each 15-minute period during which they did not engage in disruptive behavior and lost all points earned that day for two or more disruptions during a 15-minute period. Again, disruption initially decreased but after 7 days rose to baseline levels. Based on an analysis of the experimental procedures, the authors concluded that the classroom back-up reinforcers may have been too weak to maintain behavioral change. A home-based reinforcement system was added to the program in which children earned a good-behavior letter for fewer than two disruptions during any 15-minute period. Parents were instructed to provide rewards and sanctions daily at home based on receipt or nonreceipt of the letter. During a second baseline phase disruption averaged 90%; introduction of the letter decreased this rate to 10%. After 13 days, during which disruptive behavior remained low, a period was initiated during which all children received the letter independent of their behavior. This noncontingent reinforcement phase was implemented to ensure that the letter itself, rather than the novelty of the procedure, was responsible for behavior change. Disruption increased to 50% during the noncontingent letter phase and immediately decreased to zero following reintroduction of the contingent letter, demonstrating that contingent use of the good-behavior letter was responsible for treatment gains. Unfortunately, because the letter was awarded for good conduct, it is not possible to tell whether an indirect approach using the stronger home-based reinforcement—making receipt of the letter contingent on academic performance—would have been sufficient to produce decreased disruption.

A study by Witt *et al.* (1983) suggested that home-based contingencies for academic performance can indirectly decrease disruptive behavior. Subjects were three fourth-grade boys who displayed high rates of inappropriate behavior and performed poorly on in-class assignments. Teachers rated each child daily on accuracy of classwork performance and parents provided praise and privileges to children at home based on good ratings. In a multiple-baseline-across-subjects design, the home reinforcement program was shown to decrease inappropriate behavior and improve academic performance for all three children.

In a review of home-based reinforcement programs, Atkeson and Forehand (1979) concluded that this procedure is an effective strategy for changing behavior across a variety of ages, settings, and target behavior. Home-based strategies also possess several other attractive features; they permit parents to receive feedback about their child's behavior, they can utilize powerful reinforcers from home that may not be available in the classroom (i.e., Ayllon, Garber, & Pisor, 1975), and they require less teacher time and school resources than other techniques (e.g., token systems). In addition, home-based procedures can be designed to indirectly decrease disruptive behavior by reinforcing academics (Witt *et al.*, 1983).

Great care should be exercised in the selection of parents for home-based reinforcement programs, however (Lahey *et al.*, 1977). Although all parents should be cautioned never to punish a child for bringing home a bad daily report card (or failing to bring home the report), some violence-prone parents cannot be trusted to administer such programs. The child's bringing home bad reports may set the occasion for acts of abusive punishment. In such cases, other adults, such as school principals, probation officers, or counselors can sometimes be used to implement the program.

Self-Mediated Interventions

Children have also served as agents to change their own behavior. Several authors have used self-control techniques to attempt to modify the disruptive conduct of behavior problem children. The self-control techniques used can be divided into self-monitoring/self-reinforcement techniques in which children monitor their own behavior and are responsible for rewarding themselves for appropriate behavior, and cognitive self-control techniques, which generally involve a more comprehensive skills training program. The rationale behind both of these types of procedures is that children can be trained to serve as their own behavior change agents, thereby increasing the likelihood that treatment gains may be generalized and maintained.

Self-Monitoring and Self-Reinforcement

Self-reinforcement techniques are frequently implemented within token economies. Some studies have used self-reinforcement procedures as the initial intervention. For example, Glynn and Thomas (1974) asked children to administer themselves checks on a card if their behavior was on task when tape-recorded tones sounded randomly in the classroom. To help them decide if they were on task, the children were instructed to consult a chart posted in the room indicating at any particular time whether children should be doing classwork or listening to the teacher. Checkmarks could later be exchanged for free time. Using an ABAB design, self-administration of points was shown to increase on-task behavior relative to baseline phases. In a replication of this study (Glynn & Thomas, 1974) by Thomas (1976), it was found that treatment gains were maintained at follow-up. Unfortunately, neither the Glynn and Thomas (1974) study nor the Thomas (1976) study provided measures of academic achievement.

Self-reinforcement components are more often added after a period in which externally administered reinforcers have reduced inappropriate behavior. Drabman *et al.* (1973) initially awarded teacher-determined points and backup reinforcers to disruptive boys for academic performance and appropriate behavior. The boys then determined their own point earnings, but were awarded the points only if their estimates closely matched the teacher's, with a bonus point awarded for an exact match. A self-reinforcement phase was then gradually introduced in which children received the number of points they selected. Children's performance improved during the initial introduction of the token system, and treatment gains were maintained during self-reinforcement. Additionally, children's self-evaluations during the self-reinforcement phase were found to match the teacher's as closely as they did during the phase in which reinforcement was contingent on matching. Robertson, Simon, Pachman, and O'Leary (1979) used a similar procedure (Drabman *et al.*, 1973) with disruptive retarded children and also found that inappropriate behavior remained low during self-reinforcement; in addition, children's ratings actually matched teacher's more closely during the self-reinforcement phase than when matching was required for reinforcement.

Santogrossi, O'Leary, Romanczyk, & Kaufman (1973) implemented an experimenter reinforced token system with disruptive adolescents that successfully decreased inappropriate behavior. Next, a self-reinforcement component was added without a phase that required children to match experimenter's ratings of rewards. After only 4 to 5 days, children began awarding themselves the maximum point allowances and disruptive behavior increased. After an unsuccessful attempt to institute a matching phase, experimenter-controlled reinforcers had to be reinstituted. Other studies have also found that children become increasingly lenient in awarding themselves points even when a matching phase was included prior to allowing children to determine their own rewards (Bolstad & Johnson, 1972; Turkewitz, O'Leary, & Ironsmith, 1975). This tendency toward increasing leniency in determining rewards is one problem that may restrict the use of self-reinforcement techniques. In addition, some authors have reported that children may be criticized by peers for not taking the maximum number of points (Kaufman & O'Leary, 1972; Santogrossi *et al.*, 1973). Despite these problems, self-reinforcement procedures offer the advantage of directly involving the student and may be useful as a transitional step between teacher-administered reinforcement and no external reinforcement for good behavior (Jones & Kazdin, 1980).

Cognitive Interventions

A number of cognitive interventions for behavior problem children have been developed and implemented with varying results. Douglas and her colleagues (Douglas, 1980; Douglas, Parry, Marton, & Garson, 1976; Garson, 1977) have developed a comprehensive cognitive training program for hyperactive children based on the conclusion that hyperactivity is related to deficits in abilities to invest attention, inhibit impulsive responding, and appropriately modulate arousal (Douglas & Peters, 1979). The training program involves three levels of intervention. The goal at the first level is helping the child understand the nature of his deficits. At the second level, the goal is increasing the child's understanding of and motivation for the problem-solving role, with a particular emphasis on providing him with success experiences. The third level has the goal of teaching the child specific problem-solving strategies related to the three deficits described previously. At all three levels, self-verbalization, modeling, self-monitoring, and self-reinforcement are emphasized. Based on these methods, Douglas *et al.* (1975) treated 18 hyperactive boys over a 3-month period. Training involved 24 sessions with each child, 12 sessions with his parents, and at least 6 sessions with his teacher. Following completion of the training procedures, the treated children evidenced significantly greater pre- to posttest gains than matched waiting-list control children on a variety of cognitive tests of attention, impulsivity, and some measures of reading achievement. These differences were maintained at the end of a 3-month follow-up period. No significant differences between groups in arithmetic achievement or Conners Teacher Rating Scale (Conners, 1969) scores were found either immediately following treatment or at follow-up.

As Ross and Ross (1982) point out, the use of a waiting-list control group in the Douglas *et al.* (1967) study prohibits drawing firm conclusions about the effectiveness of the cognitive training program because treatment gains due to independent variables such as adult attention cannot be ruled out. Douglas (1980) described a second training study by Garson (1977) that was based on similar methods and in which an "attention control" group was used. Garson (1977) implemented a much briefer training program (three sessions with each child extended over a 3-week period) with 15 "relatively normal" children who displayed attentional and impulsivity problems on a battery of cognitive tests. Following treatment, these children scored significantly better on several cognitive tests of attention and impulsivity than a matched control group who participated in the same number of sessions with the same trainers and materials but did not receive any of the training procedures. Again, these gains were generally maintained at the time of the 3-month follow-up. Unfortunately, it appears that no measures of classroom behavior or academic achievement were obtained.

Camp and her colleagues (Camp, 1980; Camp, Blom, Hebert, & van Doorninck, 1977) have also developed a cognitive behavior modification program for aggressive boys called "Think Aloud." It involves modeling of cognitive strategies and developing self-instruction (similar to procedures described by Meichenbaum & Goodman, 1971). In summarizing the effects of this program, Camp (1980) concluded that, despite some circumscribed "cognitive" improvements, boys in the treatment group continued to display aggression, hostility, distractibility, and hyperactivity. Meichenbaum and his colleagues (Meichenbaum, 1977; Meichenbaum & Goodman, 1971) have also developed a treatment program to teach children to use self-instructions and self-reinforcement. Although some improvements in children's performance on the laboratory cognitive tasks used in the training procedures were obtained, these improvements did not generalize to classroom performance.

Similarly, Barkley, Copeland, and Sivage (1980) implemented a package of self-control procedures including self-monitoring, self-reinforcement, and self-control in a special classroom for hyperactive children and found that misbehavior decreased in some situations, but that academic performance did not improve and there was little treatment generalization.

Hobbs, Moguin, Tyroler, and Lahey (1980) reviewed the literature on cognitive behavior therapy with children and concluded that the clinical utility of these procedures had not yet been adequately demonstrated due to methodological problems and the restricted range of subject populations and outcome measures used. Since that review, some research has yielded more positive findings (i.e., Cameron & Robinson, 1980; Kendall & Braswell, 1982; Rhode, Morgan, & Young, 1983; Varni & Henker, 1979). For example, Cameron and Robinson (1980) demonstrated in a multiple-baseline-across-individuals design that a self-managed cognitive training program improved the mathematics performance and decreased the off-task behavior of three hyperactive children. The study used training procedures designed to promote generalization of treatment effects to classroom performance by using academically relevant tasks (i.e., mathematic activities, visual-perceptual tasks) during training procedures. Similarly, Varni and Henker (1979) found that implementing a cognitive training procedure that emphasized self-reinforcement of academic-type tasks with three disruptive hyperactive boys resulted in improved academic performance and decreased hyperactive behavior.

One major drawback to the use of cognitive training procedures is that they are typically quite time-consuming and impractical as regular classroom interventions because they almost always require implementation by a trained experimenter. It will take continued research of the type described in the preceding paragraph that demonstrates not only treatment generalization, but maintenance of treatment gains (e.g., Cameron & Robinson, 1980, do not report follow-up data) to justify their use on a widespread basis.

Environmental and Task Variables

The issue of how variables such as classroom environments and task demands may affect children's behavior problems has been somewhat neglected in behavioral research. In discussing an optimum school program for hyperactive children, Ross and Ross (1982) cited Cowen's (1973, p. 450) "hypothetical parsimony continuum," which holds that the most parsimonious approaches to treating children's school behavior problems involve engineering settings that optimize adaptation; the next most desirable approaches involve teachers dealing with problems in the classroom; even less preferable are approaches in which help is sought from outside agencies or the child is sent to another class/school; and least parsimonious are approaches that turn the child over to an outside agency for education. As Ross and Ross (1982) pointed out, these latter and less parsimonious approaches are most representative of the school programs developed to date for hyperactive children. Certainly, the research reviewed so far falls primarily in these latter categories.

Within the field of hyperactivity research, there is some historical precedent to examining classroom environments based on particular theories about this disorder. Ross and Ross (1982) provided the rationale and associated interventions for some of these theories. For example, some researchers have held that the brain-injured hyperactive child's major deficit is distractibility, or extreme susceptibility to environmental influences. Based on these theories, minimal stimulation classrooms were advocated as treatment approaches to hyperactivity (Strauss & Lehtinen, 1947). Alternatively, others have proposed that restrictive environments of traditional classrooms are largely responsible for the hyperactive child's school problems (i.e., Ladd, 1970; Nyquist & Hawes, 1970; Silberman, 1970). Proponents of their theory advocate open classrooms, characterized by a greater degree of flexibility and freedom for the child, as an alternative to traditional classrooms for hyperactive children. In reviewing the research on minimal stimulation and open classrooms, Ross and Ross (1982) concluded that little empirical evidence currently exists to support either approach, although hyperactive children may appear less distinguishable in open classrooms (Flynn & Rapoport, 1976). These authors (Ross & Ross, 1982) go on to suggest that future research aimed at developing optimal school programs for hyperactive children must take more complex variables into account (i.e., interactions between stimulation and task demands) and be designed to answer which type of classroom is best for the hyperactive child's achievement, peer acceptance, and overall effective functioning.

In a social ecology framework, Whalen and Henker and their colleagues (Whalen *et al.*, 1978; Whalen, Henker, Collins, Finck, & Dotemoto, 1979) have systematically examined the effects of task (e.g., task difficulty, self- versus other-paced) and classroom environment (e.g., noise level) variables on hyperactive children on and off medication. Among other findings, unmedicated hyperactive boys (on placebo) displayed their highest rates of inattention and inappropriate behavior under noisy conditions and when tasks were difficult and paced by an outside source. In contrast, when conditions such as low noise and easy or self-paced tasks were in effect, hyperactive boys on placebo were as attentive to work as medicated hyperactive and normal peers. Thus, these authors (Whalen *et al.*, 1978; Whalen *et al.*, 1979) found that classrooms could serve as "provocation ecologies" to highlight differences between unmedicated hyperactive boys and their peers or "rarefaction ecologies" to reduce these differences. In summarizing the results of these studies, Henker and Whalen (1980) concluded that unmedicated hyperactive boys were not behaviorally distinctive from peers throughout the day, but only within particular contexts.

It should be noted that the research of Whalen *et al.* (1978) and Whalen *et al.* (1979) has focused on social and behavioral aspects of the classroom performance of hyperactive children. It can be seen from the studies reviewed in this chapter that academic performance does not necessarily correlate with behavioral variables, such as on-task behavior. Thus, another important step may be to examine the task/environmental variables related to the academic achievement of children with behavior problems. Still, the work of Whalen and Henker and their colleagues (Whalen *et al.*, 1978; Whalen *et al.*, 1979) holds important implications for the classroom management of these children. For example, in recognizing that some classroom-environment manipulations (i.e., allowing children to talk) may be impractical because some teachers function best in quiet, orderly environments, Whalen *et al.* (1979) suggested that a relatively simple intervention could involve matching teachers and children according to their styles and characteristics. This suggestion also raises an interesting solution to a problem raised in the section on appropriate target behaviors for modification; that is, some teachers/educators may object to certain inappropriate classroom behaviors even if it can be shown that they are not incompatible with academic achievement. This area holds exciting possibilities for minimally intrusive, maximally beneficial interventions and is deserving of much greater research attention.

Stimulant Medication

Although the primary purpose of this chapter is to discuss the behavioral treatment of children's school behavior problems, the use of stimulant medication with hyperactive children will be briefly discussed because of the prevalence of this practice.

Stimulant medications are currently the treatment of choice of physicians for hyperactivity, with an estimated 60% to 85% of children diagnosed hyperactive receiving psychostimulants (Bosco & Robin, 1980; Lambert, Sandoval, & Sassone, 1978). Among the stimulants, methylphenidate (Ritalin), dextroamphetamine (Dexedrine), magnesium pemoline (Cylert), and caffeine have all been used with hyperactive children. Ritalin is currently the most popular medication prescribed for hyperactivity (Lambert *et al.*, 1978). The beneficial short-term effects of stimulant medication use with hyperactive children are widely documented (Barkley, 1977; Cantwell & Carlson, 1978; Gadow & Loney, 1981; Whalen & Henker, 1976). These effects include decreases in hyperactive behaviors as rated by parents (e.g., Conners, Taylor, Meo, Kurtz, & Fournier, 1972; Hoffman *et al.*, 1974) and teachers (e.g., Arnold *et al.*, 1976; Conners *et al.*, 1972; Gittelman *et al.*, 1980) and improved cognitive performances on laboratory tasks (e.g., Douglas, Barr, O'Neill, & Britton, 1986; Sprague & Sleator, 1977; Swanson, Kinsbourne, Roberts, & Zucker, 1978).

Despite the short-term benefits ascribed to stimulants, however, they are as ineffective as behavioral interventions at ameliorating the poor adult outcome of hyperactive children (Huessy, Metoyer, & Townsend, 1974; Milich & Loney, 1979; Weiss, Hechtman, Perlman, Hopkins, & Werner, 1979). More pertinent to this discussion is that, even though classroom behavior improves with stimulant treatment (e.g., Arnold *et al.*, 1976; Conners *et al.*, 1972; Gittelman *et al.*, 1980), early research suggested that academic performance generally did not (cf. Barkley & Cunningham, 1978). One possible explanation for this seemingly contradictory finding is suggested by the work of Sprague and Sleator (1977). These authors administered placebos and several doses of medication to hyperactive children and examined the effects on a laboratory learning task and teacher ratings of behavior. Whereas teacher ratings showed maximal improvement at the higher dosage level, cognitive performance was optimized by the lower dosage level. Thus, the "best" dosage of medication for a child chosen on the basis of his behavior may not optimize learning. This conclusion holds major implications because most studies of the effects of stimulant medication rely solely on teacher ratings or behavior observations to assess treatment effects.

In a review of the effects of psychostimulants on academic achievement in hyperactive and learning-disabled children, Pelham (1983) described numerous methodological and interpretive problems (such as the differential dose effects on learning and behavior found by Sprague and Sleator (1977), problems in the dependent measures used, individual differences in response to stimulants, and others) that characterize the studies that show no improvements in learning from stimulant treatment. Pelham (1983) concluded that, because these studies did not assess stimulants under optimal conditions, previous negative findings should not be considered conclusive evidence that stimulants do not improve learning. In addition, some recent studies that carefully monitored medication effects have found stimulants to improve classroom learning or performance on academic tasks (i.e., Douglas *et al.*, 1986; Pelham, Bender, Caddell, Booth, & Moorer, 1985; Pelham, Milich, & Walker, 1986; Stephens, Pelham, & Skinner, 1984). It is clear that more research examining the potential benefits of stimulants in improving learning problems is essential.

Rapport (1983) recently reviewed the research comparing stimulant medication, behavior therapy, or combined treatment approaches to hyperactivity and concluded that various design inadequacies (particularly inadequate use of multiple dependent measures) preclude conclusions about the superiority of any of these approaches at the present time. However, promising results have been obtained in studies combining behavior therapy and medication (i.e., O'Leary & Pelham, 1978; Pelham, 1977; Pelham, Schnedler, Bologna, & Contreras, 1980; Pelham *et al.*, 1986; Stableford, Butz, Hasaz, Leitenberg, & Peyser, 1976; Wulbert & Dries, 1977) and future research focusing on the superior qualities of each treatment for different problem areas may result in further treatment refinements (Rapport, 1983).

Summary

A variety of behavior modification techniques have been used in classroom settings to promote the academic learning and appropriate behavior of conduct and attention deficit disorder children. Teachers have been the most frequent mediators of interventions for classroom behavior problems. Teacher-mediated interventions include the use of contingent teacher attention in the form of praise, ignoring, and reprimands, token economy systems, response-cost procedures, and time out. Peers have also been involved in behavior change programs, either as part of a group who receive rewards or sanctions contingent on a classmate's performance, as trained behavior managers for behavior problem children, or as monitors of tokens in token systems. Parents have been involved in home-based procedures by reinforcing their children at home for appropriate school behavior. Children themselves have also been trained to monitor, reinforce, or manage their own behavior. In addition to behavior programs that rely on teachers, peers, parents, or children themselves as agents of change, environmental and task variables have been manipulated to assess their impact on classroom performance. Finally, stimulant medication has been used to treat the behavior problems of hyperactive children. Intervention strategies that reinforce academic achievement are highly recommended because they improve behavior and academics concomitantly and are therefore ethically and educationally defensible. However, some serious or infrequent problem behaviors, such as stealing and aggression, may require more direct treatment techniques.

References

Aaron, B. A., & Bostow, D. E. (1978). Indirect facilitation of on-task behavior produced by contingent free-time academic productivity. *Journal of Applied Behavior Analysis, 11*, 197.

American Psychiatric Association (1980). *Diagnostic and statistical manual of mental disorders* (3rd ed.). Washington, DC: Author.

Arnold, E., Huestis, R., Smeltzer, D., Scheib, J., Wemmer, D., & Colner, G. (1976). Levoamphetamine vs. dextroamphetamine in minimal brain dysfunction. *Archives of General Psychiatry, 33*, 292–301.

Atkeson, B. M., & Forehand, R. (1979). Home-based reinforcement programs designed to modify classroom behavior: A review and methodological evaluation. *Psychological Bulletin, 86,* 1298–1308.

August, G. J., & Stewart, M. A. (1982). Is there a pure syndrome of hyperactivity? *British Journal of Psychiatry, 140,* 305–311.

August, G. J., & Stewart, M. A. (1983). Familial subtypes of childhood hyperactivity. *Journal of Nervous and Mental Disease, 171,* 362–368.

August, G. J., Stewart, M. A., & Holmes, C. S. (1983). A four-year follow-up of hyperactive boys with and without conduct disorder. *British Journal of Psychiatry, 143,* 192–198.

Ayllon, T., & Roberts, M. (1974). Eliminating discipline problems by strengthening academic performance. *Journal of Applied Behavior Analysis, 7,* 71–76.

Ayllon, T., & Rosenbaum, M. S. (1977). The behavioral treatment of disruption and hyperactivity in school settings. In B. B. Lahey & A. E. Kazdin (Eds.), *Advances in clinical child psychology* (Vol. 1, pp. 85–118). New York: Plenum Press.

Ayllon, T., Layman, D., & Burke, S. (1972). Disruptive behavior and reinforcement of academic performance. *Psychological Record, 22,* 315–323.

Ayllon, T., Garber, S., & Pisor, K. (1975). The elimination of discipline problems through a combined school-home motivational system. *Behavior Therapy, 6,* 616–626.

Ayllon, T., Layman, D., & Kandel, H. J. (1975). A behavioral-educational alternative to drug control of hyperactive children. *Journal of Applied Behavior Analysis, 68,* 137–146.

Bailey, J. S., Wolf, M. M., & Phillips, E. L. (1970). Home-based reinforcement and the modification of pre-delinquents' classroom behavior. *Journal of Applied Behavior Analysis, 3,* 223–233.

Barkley, R. A. (1977). A review of stimulant drug research with hyperactive children. *Journal of Child Psychology and Psychiatry, 18,* 137–165.

Barkley, R. A. (1981). *Hyperactive children: A handbook for diagnosis and treatment.* New York: Guilford Press.

Barkley, R. A. (1982). Guidelines for defining hyperactivity in children: Attention deficit disorder with hyperactivity. In B. B. Lahey & A. E. Kazdin (Eds.), *Advances in clinical child psychology* (Vol. 5, pp. 137–180). New York: Plenum Press.

Barkley, R. A., & Cunningham, C. E. (1978). Do stimulant drugs improve the academic performance of hyperkinetic children? A review of outcome studies. *Clinical Pediatrics, 17,* 85–92.

Barkley, R. A., Copeland, A. P., & Sivage, C. (1980). A self-control classroom for hyperactive children. *Journal of Autism and Developmental Disorders, 10,* 75–89.

Barrish, H. H., Saunders, M., & Wolf, M. M. (1969). Good behavior game: Effects of individual contingencies for group consequences on disruptive behavior in a classroom. *Journal of Applied Behavior Analysis, 2,* 119–124.

Bolstad, O. D., & Johnson, S. (1972). Self-regulation in the modification of disruptive classroom behavior. *Journal of Applied Behavior Analysis, 5,* 443–454.

Bosco, J. J., & Robin, S. S. (1980). Hyperkinesis: Prevalence and treatment. In C. K. Whalen & B. Henker (Eds.), *Hyperactive children: The social ecology of identification and treatment* (pp. 173–180). New York: Academic Press.

Brooks, R. B., & Snow, D. L. (1972). Two case illustrations of the use of behavior modification techniques in the school setting. *Behavior Therapy, 3,* 100–103.

Broughton, S. F., & Lahey, B. B. (1978). Direct and collateral effects of positive reinforcement, response cost, and mixed contingencies for academic performance. *Journal of School Psychology, 16,* 126–136.

Cameron, M. I., & Robinson, V. M. J. (1980). Effects of cognitive training on academic and on-task behavior of hyperactive children. *Journal of Abnormal Child Psychology, 8,* 405–419.

Camp, B. W. (1980). Two psychoeducational programs for aggressive boys. In C. K. Whalen & B. Henker (Eds.), *Hyperactive children: The social ecology of identification and treatment* (pp. 191–219). New York: Academic Press.

Camp, B. W., Blom, G. E., Hebert, F., & van Doorninck, W. J. (1977). "Think Aloud": A program for developing self-control in young aggressive boys. *Journal of Abnormal Child Psychology, 5,* 157–169.

Cantwell, D. P., & Carlson, G. A. (1978). Stimulants. In J. S. Werry (Ed.), *Pediatric psychopharmacology* (pp. 171–207). New York: Brunner/Mazel.

Carden-Smith, L. K., & Fowler, S. A. (1984). Positive peer pressure: The effects of peer monitoring on children's disruptive behavior. *Journal of Applied Behavior Analysis, 17,* 213–227.

Carlson, C. S., Arnold, C. R., Becker, W. C., & Madsen, C. H. (1968). The elimination of tantrum behavior in a child in an elementary classroom. *Behavior Research and Therapy, 6,* 117–119.

Coleman, R. A. (1970). Conditioning technique applicable to elementary school classrooms. *Journal of Applied Behavior Analysis, 3,* 293–297.

Conners, C. K. (1969). A teacher rating scale for use in drug studies with children. *American Journal of Psychiatry, 126,* 885–888.

Conners, C. K., Taylor, E., Meo, G., Kurtz, M., & Fournier, M. (1972). Magnesium pemoline and dextroamphetamine: A controlled study in children with minimal brain dysfunction. *Psychopharmacologia, 26,* 321–336.

Cowen, E. L. (1973). Social and community interventions. *Annual Review of Psychology, 24,* 423–472.

Darch, C. B., & Thorpe, H. W. (1977). The principal game: A group consequence procedure to increase classroom on-task behavior. *Psychology in the Schools, 14,* 341–347.

Dietz, S. M., Slack, D. J., Schwarzmueller, E. B., Willander, A. P., Weatherly, T. J., & Hilliard, G. (1978).

Reducing inappropriate behavior in special classrooms by reinforcing average interresponse times: Interval DRL. *Behavior Therapy, 9,* 37–46.

Doleys, D. M., Wells, K. C., Hobbs, S. A., Roberts, M. N., & Cartelli, L. M. (1976). The effects of social punishment on non-compliance: A comparison with timeout and positive practice. *Journal of Applied Behavior Analysis, 9,* 471–482.

Dougherty, E. H., & Dougherty, A. (1977). The daily report card: A simplified and flexible package for classroom behavior management. *Psychology in the Schools, 14,* 191–195.

Douglas, V. I. (1980). Treatment and training approaches to hyperactivity: Establishing internal or external control. In C. K. Whalen & B. Henker (Eds.), *Hyperactive children: The social ecology of identification and treatment* (pp. 283–318). New York: Academic Press.

Douglas, V. I., & Peters, K. G. (1979). Toward a clearer definition of the attentional deficit of hyperactive children. In G. A. Hale & M. Lewis (Eds.). *Attention and cognitive development* (pp. 173–247). New York: Plenum Press.

Douglas, V. I., Parry, P., Marton, P., & Garson, C. (1976). Assessment of a cognitive training program for hyperactive children. *Journal of Abnormal Child Psychology, 4,* 389–410.

Douglas, V. I., Barr, R. G., O'Neill, M. E., & Britton, B. G. (1986). Short-term effects of methylphenidate on the cognitive, learning, and academic performance of children with attention deficit disorder in the laboratory and classroom. *Journal of Child Psychology and Psychiatry, 27,* 191–211.

Drabman, R. S. (1973). Child-versus teacher-administered token programs in a psychiatric hospital school. *Journal of Abnormal Child Psychology, 1,* 68–87.

Drabman, R. S., & Spitalnik, R. (1973). Social isolation as a punishment procedure: A controlled study. *Journal of Experimental Child Psychology, 16,* 236–249.

Drabman, R. S., Spitalnik, R., & O'Leary, K. D. (1973). Teaching self-control to disruptive children. *Journal of Abnormal Psychology, 82,* 10–16.

Ferritor, D. E., Buckholdt, D., Hambin, R. L., & Smith, L. (1972). The noneffects of contingent reinforcement for attending behavior on work accomplished. *Journal of Applied Behavior Analysis, 5,* 7–17.

Flynn, N. M., & Rapoport, J. L. (1976). Hyperactivity in open and traditional classroom environments. *Journal of Special Education, 10,* 285–290.

Foxx, R. M., & Shapiro, S. T. (1978). The timeout ribbon: A nonexclusionary timeout procedure. *Journal of Applied Behavior Analysis, 11,* 125–136.

Gadow, K. D., & Loney, J. (Eds.). (1981). *Psychosocial aspects of drug treatment for hyperactivity.* Boulder, CO: Westview Press.

Garson, C. (1977). *Cognitive impulsivity in children and the effects of training.* Unpublished doctoral dissertation, McGill University.

Gast, D. C., & Nelson, C. M. (1977). Timeout in the classroom: Implications for special education. *Exceptional Children, 43,* 461–464.

Gittelman, R., Abikoff, H., Pollack, E., Klein, D. F., Katz, S., & Mattes, J. (1980). A controlled trial of behavior modification and methylphenidate in hyperactive children. In C. K. Whalen & B. Henker (Eds.), *Hyperactive children: The social ecology of identification and treatment* (pp. 221–243). New York: Academic Press.

Glynn, E., & Thomas, J. (1974). Effect of cueing on self-control of classroom behavior. *Journal of Applied Behavior Analysis, 7,* 299–306.

Grieger, T., Kauffman, J. M., & Grieger, R. M. (1976). Effects of peer reporting on cooperative play and aggression of kindergarten children. *Journal of School Psychology, 14,* 307–313.

Hall, R. V., Axelrod, S., Foundopoulos, M., Shellman, J., Campbell, R., & Cranston, S. (1971). The effective use of punishment to modify behavior in the classroom. *Educational Technology, 1,* 24–30.

Harris, V. W., & Sherman, J. A. (1973). Use and analysis of the "good behavior game" to reduce disruptive classroom behavior. *Journal of Applied Behavior Analysis, 6,* 405–418.

Hawkins, R. P., & Hayes, J. E. (1974). The School Adjustment Program: A model program for treatment of severely maladjustmented children in the public schools. In R. Ulrich, T. Stachnik, & J. Mabry (Eds.), *Control of human behavior: Behavior modification in education* (Vol. 3, pp. 197–208). Glenview, IL: Scott, Foresman.

Hay, W. M., Hay, L., & Nelson, R. O. (1977). Direct and collateral changes in on-task and academic behavior resulting from on-task versus academic contingencies. *Behavior Therapy, 8,* 431–441.

Hegerle, D. R., Kesecker, M. P., & Couch, J. V. (1979). A behavior game for the reduction of inappropriate classroom behavior. *School Psychology Digest, 8,* 339–343.

Henker, B., & Whalen, C. K. (1980). The changing faces of hyperactivity: Retrospect and prospect. In C. K. Whalen & B. Henker (Eds.), *Hyperactive children: The social ecology of identification and treatment* (pp. 321–363). New York: Academic Press.

Hobbs, S. A., Moguin, L. E., Tyroler, M., & Lahey, B. B. (1980). Cognitive behavior therapy with children: Has clinical utility been demonstrated? *Psychological Bulletin, 87,* 147–165.

Hoffman, S., Engelhardt, D., Margolis, R., Polizos, P., Waizer, J., & Rosenfeld, R. (1974). Response to methylphenidate in low socioeconomic hyperactive children. *Archives of General Psychiatry, 30,* 354–359.

Huessy, H., Metoyer, M., & Townsend, M. (1974). Eightten year follow-up of 84 children treated for behavioral disorder in rural Vermont. *Acta Paedopsychiatrica, 40,* 230–235.

Hundert, J. (1976). The effectiveness of reinforcement, response cost, and mixed programs on classroom behaviors. *Journal of Applied Behavior Analysis, 9,* 107.

Iwata, B. A., & Bailey, J. S. (1974). Reward versus cost token systems: An analysis of the effects on students and teachers. *Journal of Applied Behavior Analysis, 7,* 567–576.

Jones, R. T., & Kazdin, A. E. (1981). Childhood behavior problems in the school. In S. M. Turner, K. S. Calhoun, & Adams, H. E. (Eds.), *Handbook of clinical behavior therapy* (pp. 568–606). New York: Wiley.

Kaufman, K. F., & O'Leary, K. D. (1972). Reward, cost, and self-evaluation procedures for disruptive adolescents in a psychiatric hospital school. *Journal of Applied Behavior Analysis, 5,* 293–309.

Kazdin, A. E. (1977). *The token economy: A review and evaluation.* New York: Plenum Press.

Kazdin, A. E. (1982). The token economy: A decade later. *Journal of Applied Behavior Analysis, 15,* 431–445.

Kendall, P. C., & Braswell, L. (1982). Cognitive-behavioral self-control therapy for children: A components analysis. *Journal of Consulting and Clinical Psychology, 50,* 672–689.

Keogh, B. K., & Barkett, C. J. (1980). An educational analysis of hyperactive children's achievement problems. In C. K. Whalen & B. Henker (Eds.), *Hyperactive children: The social ecology of identification and treatment* (pp. 259–282). New York: Academic Press.

Kerr, M. M., & Nelson, C. M. (1983). *Strategies for managing behavior problems in the classroom.* Columbus, OH: Merrill.

Kirby, F. D., & Shields, F. (1972). Modifications of arithmetic response rate and attending behavior in a seventh-grade student. *Journal of Applied Behavior Analysis, 5,* 79–84.

Klein, R. D. (1979). Modifying academic performance in the grade school classroom. In M. Hersen, R. M. Eisler, & P. M. Miller (Eds.), *Progress in behavior modification* (Vol. 8, pp. 293–321). New York: Academic Press.

Kubany, E. S., Weiss, L. E., & Sloggett, B. B. (1971). The good behavior clock: A reinforcement/time out procedure for reducing disruptive classroom behavior. *Journal of Behavior Therapy and Experimental Psychiatry, 2,* 178–179.

Ladd, E. T. (1970, November 21). Pills for classroom peace? *Saturday Review,* pp. 66–68; 81–83.

Lahey, B. B., & Drabman, R. S. (1981). Behavior modification in the classroom. In W. E. Craighead, A. E. Kazdin, & M. J. Mahoney (Eds.), *Behavior modification: Principles, issues, and applications* (2nd ed., pp. 418–433). Boston, MA: Houghton Mifflin.

Lahey, B. B., McNees, M. P., & McNees, M. C. (1973). Control of an obscene "verbal tic" through timeout in an elementary school classroom. *Journal of Applied Behavior Analysis, 6,* 101–104.

Lahey, B. B., Gendrich, J. G., Gendrich, S. I., Schnelle, J. F., Gant, D. S., & McNees, M. P. (1977). An evaluation of daily report cards with minimal teacher and parent contacts as an efficient method of classroom intervention. *Behavior Modification, 1,* 381–394.

Lahey, B. B., Hobbs, S. A., Kupfer, D. L., & Delamater, A. (1979). Current perspectives on hyperactivity and learning disabilities. In B. B. Lahey (Ed.), *Behavior therapy with hyperactive and learning disabled children* (pp. 3–18). New York: Oxford University Press.

Lahey, B. B., Schaughency, E. A., Strauss, C. C., & Frame, C. L. (1984). Are attention deficit disorders with and without hyperactivity similar or dissimilar disorders? *Journal of the American Academy of Child Psychiatry, 23,* 302–309.

Lambert, N. M., Sandoval, J., & Sassone, D. (1978). Prevalence of hyperactivity in elementary school children as a function of social system definers. *American Journal of Orthopsychiatry, 48,* 446–463.

LeBlanc, J. M., Busby, K. H., & Thomson, C. (1973). The functions of timeout for changing aggressive behavior of a preschool child: A multiple baseline analysis. In R. E. Ulrich, T. S. Stachnik, & J. E. Mabry (Eds.), *Control of human behavior: Behavior modification in education* (Vol. 3, pp. 358–364). Glenview, IL: Scott, Foresman.

Lovitt, T. C., Lovitt, A. O., Eaton, M. D., & Kirkwood, M. (1973). The deceleration of inappropriate comments by a natural consequence. *Journal of School Psychology, 11,* 148–154.

Madsen, C. H., Becker, W. C., & Thomas, D. R. (1968). Rules, praise, and ignoring: Elements of elementary classroom control. *Journal of Applied Behavior Analysis, 1,* 139–150.

Madsen, C. H., Becker, W. C., Thomas, D. R., Koser, L., & Plager, E. (1968). An analysis of the reinforcing function of "sit-down" commands. In R. K. Parker (Ed.), *Readings in educational psychology* (pp. 265–278). Boston, MA: Allyn & Bacon.

Marholin, D., & Steinman, W. M. (1977). Stimulus control in the classroom as a function of the behavior reinforced. *Journal of Applied Behavior Analysis, 10,* 465–478.

Marholin, D., Steinman, W. M., McInnis, E. T., & Heads, T. B. (1975). The effect of a teacher's presence on the classroom behavior of conduct-problem children. *Journal of Applied Behavior Analysis, 8,* 11–25.

Mattos, R. L., Mattson, R. H., Walker, H. M., & Buckley, N. K. (1969). Reinforcement and aversive control in the modification of deviant classroom behavior. *Academic Therapy, 5,* 37–52.

McAllister, L. W., Stachowiak, J. G., Baer, D. M., & Conderman, L. (1969). The application of operant conditioning techniques in a secondary school classroom. *Journal of Applied Behavior Analysis, 2,* 277–285.

McGee, R., Williams, S., & Silva, P. A. (1984). Background characteristics of aggressive, hyperactive, and aggressive-hyperactive boys. *Journal of the American Academy of Child Psychiatry, 23,* 280–284.

McLaughlin, T., & Malaby, J. (1972). Reducing and measuring inappropriate verbalizations in a token classroom. *Journal of Applied Behavior Analysis, 5,* 329–333.

Medland, M. B., & Stachnik, T. J. (1972). Good-Behavior

Game: A replication and systematic analysis. *Journal of Applied Behavior Analysis, 5,* 45–51.

Meichenbaum, D. H. (1977). *Cognitive-behavior modification: An integrative approach.* New York: Plenum Press.

Meichenbaum, D. H., & Goodman, J. (1971). Training impulsive children to talk to themselves: A means of developing self-control. *Journal of Abnormal Psychology, 77,* 115–126.

Milich, R. S., & Loney, J. (1979). The role of hyperactive and aggressive symptomatology in predicting adolescent outcome among hyperactive children. *Journal of Pediatric Psychology, 4,* 93–112.

Nyquist, E. B., & Hawes, G. R. (Eds.). (1972). *Open education: A sourcebook for parents and teachers.* New York: Bantam Books.

O'Leary, K. D. (1972). Behavior modification in the classroom: A rejoinder to Winett and Winkler. *Journal of Applied Behavior Analysis, 5,* 505–511.

O'Leary, K. D., & Becker, W. C. (1967). Behavior modification of an adjustment class: A token reinforcement program. *Exceptional Children, 33,* 637–642.

O'Leary, K. D., & Becker, W. C. (1968). The effects of intensity of a teacher's reprimands on children's behavior. *Journal of School Psychology, 7,* 8–11.

O'Leary, K. D., & Drabman, R. (1971). Token reinforcement programs in the classroom. *Psychological Bulletin, 75,* 379–398.

O'Leary, S. G., & Pelham, W. E. (1978). Behavior therapy and withdrawal of stimulant medication with hyperactive children. *Pediatrics, 61,* 211–217.

O'Leary, K. D., Becker, W. C., Evans, M. B., & Saudergas, R. A. (1969). A token reinforcement program in a public school: A replication and systematic analysis. *Journal of Applied Behavior Analysis, 2,* 3–13.

O'Leary, K. D., Kaufman, K. S., Kass, R. E., & Drabman, R. S. (1970). The effects of loud and soft reprimands on the behavior of disruptive students. *Exceptional Children, 37,* 145–155.

Patterson, G. R. (1965). An application of conditioning techniques to the control of a hyperactive child. In L. P. Ullman & L. Krasner (Eds.), *Case studies in behavior modification* (pp. 370–375). New York: Holt, Rinehart & Winston.

Patterson, G. R., Shaw, D. A., & Ebner, M. J. (1969). Teachers, peers, and parents as agents of change in the classroom. In F. H. Benson (Ed.), *Modifying deviant social behaviors in various classroom settings* (pp. 13–48). Eugene, OR: University of Oregon, Department of Special Education.

Pease, G. A., & Tyler, V. O., Jr. (1979). Self-regulation of time-out duration in the modification of disruptive classroom behavior. *Psychology in the Schools, 16,* 101–105.

Pelham, W. E. (1977). Withdrawal of stimulant drug and concurrent behavioral intervention in the treatment of a hyperactive child. *Behavior Therapy, 8,* 473–479.

Pelham, W. E. (1983). The effects of psychostimulants on academic achievement in hyperactive and learning-disabled children. *Thalamus, 3,* 1–47.

Pelham, W. E., Bender, M. E., Caddell, J., Booth, S., & Moorer, S. H. (1985). Methylphenidate and children with attention deficit disorder: Dose effects on classroom academic and social behavior. *Archives of General Psychiatry, 42,* 948–952.

Pelham, W. E., Schnedler, R. W., Bologna, N. C., & Contreras, J. A. (1980). Behavioral and stimulant treatment of hyperactive children: A therapy study with methylphenidate probes in a within subject design. *Journal of Applied Behavior Analysis, 13,* 221–236.

Pelham, W. E., Milich, R., & Walker, J. L. (1986). The effects of continuous and partial reinforcement and methylphenidate on learning in children with attention deficit disorder, *Journal of Abnormal Psychology, 95,* 319–325.

Phillips, E. L., Phillips, E. A., Wolf, M. M., & Fixsen, D. L. (1973). Achievement place: Development of the elected manager system. *Journal of Applied Behavior Analysis, 6,* 541–561.

Porterfield, J. K., Herbert-Jackson, E., & Risley, T. R. (1976). Contingent observation: An effective and acceptable procedure for reducing disruptive behavior of young children in a group setting. *Journal of Applied Behavior Analysis, 9,* 55–64.

Quay, H. C. (1979). Classification. In H. C. Quay & J. S. Werry (Eds.), *Psychopathological disorders of childhood* (2nd ed., pp. 3–42). New York: Wiley.

Rapport, M. D. (1983). Attention deficit disorder with hyperactivity: Critical treatment parameters and their application in applied outcome research. In M. Hersen, R. M. Eisler, & P. M. Miller (Eds.), *Progress in behavior modification* (Vol. 14, pp. 219–298). New York: Academic Press.

Rapport, M. D., Murphy, H. A., & Bailey, J. S. (1982). Ritalin vs. response-cost in the control of hyperactive children: A within-subject comparison. *Journal of Applied Behavior Analysis, 15,* 205–216.

Rhode, G., Morgan, D. P., & Young, K. R. (1983). Generalization and maintenance of treatment gains of behaviorally handicapped students from resource rooms to regular classrooms using self-evaluation procedures. *Journal of Applied Behavior Analysis, 16,* 171–188.

Robertson, S. J., Simon, S. J., Pachman, J. S., & Drabman, R. S. (1979). Self-control and generalization procedures in a classroom of disruptive retarded children. *Child Behavior Therapy, 1,* 347–362.

Robinson, P. W., Newby, T. J., & Ganzell, S. L. (1981). A token system for a class of underachieving children. *Journal of Applied Behavior Analysis, 14,* 307–315.

Rosen, H. S., & Rosen, L. A. (1983). Eliminating stealing. Use of stimulus control with an elementary student. *Behavior Modification, 7,* 56–63.

Ross, D. M., & Ross, S. A. (1982). *Hyperactivity: Current issues, research, and therapy* (Vol. 2). New York: Wiley.

Ruggles, T. R., & LeBlanc, J. M. (1982). Behavior analysis

procedures in classroom teaching. In A. S. Bellack, M. Hersen, & A. E. Kazdin (Eds.), *International handbook of behavior modification and therapy* (pp. 959–996). New York: Plenum Press.

Rutherford, R. B., Jr. (1982). Theory and research on the use of aversive procedures in the education of moderately behaviorally disordered and emotionally disturbed children and youth. In F. Wood & K. C. Lakin (Eds.), *Punishment and aversive stimulation in special education* (pp. 41–64). Reston, VA: Council for Exceptional Children.

Rutter, M. (1982). Syndromes attributed to "minimal brain dysfunction" in childhood. *American Journal of Psychiatry, 139,* 21–33.

Saigh, P. A., & Umar, A. M. (1983). The effects of a good behavior game on the disruptive behavior of Sudanese elementary school students. *Journal of Applied Behavior Analysis, 16,* 339–344.

Sandberg, S. T., Wieselberg, M., & Shaffer, D. (1980). Hyperkinetic and conduct problem children in a primary school population: Some epidemiological considerations. *Journal of Child Psychology and Psychiatry, 21,* 293–311.

Santogrossi, D. A., O'Leary, K. D., Romanczyk, R. G., & Kaufman, K. F. (1973). Self-evaluation by adolescents in a psychiatric hospital school token program. *Journal of Applied Behavior Analysis, 6,* 277–287.

Schmidt, G. W., & Ulrich, R. E. (1969). Effects of group contingent events upon classroom noise. *Journal of Applied Behavior Analysis, 2,* 171–179.

Schumaker, J. B., Hovell, M. F., & Sherman, J. A. (1977). An analysis of daily report cards and parent-managed privileges in the improvement of adolescents' classroom performance. *Journal of Applied Behavior Analysis, 10,* 449–464.

Shaffer, D., Greenhill, L. (1979). A critical note on the predictive validity of "the hyperkinetic child syndrome." *Journal of Child Psychology and Psychiatry, 22,* 375–392.

Silberman, C. E. (1970). *Crisis in the classroom.* New York: Random House.

Solomon, R. W., & Wahler, R. G. (1973). Peer reinforcement control of classroom problem behavior. *Journal of Applied Behavior Analysis, 6,* 49–56.

Speltz, M. L., Wenters-Shimamura, J., & McReynolds, W. T. (1982). Procedural variations in group contingencies: Effects on children's academic and social behaviors. *Journal of Applied Behavior Analysis, 15,* 533–544.

Sprague, R. L., & Sleator, E. K. (1977). Methylphenidate in hyperactive children: Differences in dose effects on learning and social behavior. *Science, 198,* 1274–1276.

Stableford, W., Butz, R., Hasaz, J., Leitenberg, H., & Peyser, J. (1976). Sequential withdrawal of stimulant drugs and use of behavior therapy with two hyperactive boys. *American Journal of Orthopsychiatry, 46,* 302–312.

Stephens, R. S., Pelham, W. E., & Skinner, R. (1984). State-dependent and main effects of methylphenidate and pemoline on paired-associate learning and spelling in hyperactive children. *Journal of Consulting and Clinical Psychology, 52,* 104–113.

Stewart, M. A., deBlois, C. S., & Cummings, C. (1980). Psychiatric disorder in the parents of hyperactive boys and those with conduct disorder. *Journal of Child Psychology and Psychiatry, 21,* 283–292.

Strain, P. S., Cooke, T. P., & Apolloni, T. (1976). The role of peers in modifying classmates' social behavior: A review. *Journal of Special Education, 10,* 351–356.

Strauss, A. A., & Lehtinen, L. E. (1947). *Psychopathology and education of the brain-injured child.* New York: Grune & Stratton.

Struble, J. B. (1971). The application of positive social reinforcement to the behaviors of getting ready to work. *School Applications of Learning Theory, 1,* 34–39.

Sulzbacher, S. I., & Houser, J. E. (1968). A tactic to eliminate disruptive behaviors in the classroom: Group contingent consequences. *American Journal of Mental Deficiency, 73,* 88–90.

Swanson, J. M., Kinsbourne, M., Roberts, W., & Zucker, K. (1978). Time-response analysis of the effect of stimulant medication on the learning ability of children referred for hyperactivity. *Pediatrics, 61,* 21–29.

Switzer, E. B., Deal, T. E., & Bailey, J. S. (1977). The reduction of stealing in second graders using a group contingency. *Journal of Applied Behavior Analysis, 10,* 267–272.

Thomas, J. D. (1976). Accuracy of self-assessment of on-task behavior by elementary school children. *Journal of Applied Behavior Analysis, 9,* 209–210.

Thomas, D. R., Becker, W. C., & Armstrong, M. (1968). Production and elimination of disruptive classroom behavior by systematically varying teacher's behavior. *Journal of Applied Behavior Analysis, 1,* 35–45.

Turkewitz, H., O'Leary, K. D., & Ironsmith, M. (1975). Generalization and maintenance of appropriate behavior through self-control. *Journal of Consulting and Clinical Psychology, 43,* 577–583.

Tyler, V., & Brown, G. (1967). The use of swift, brief isolation as a group control device for institutionalized delinquents. *Behavior Research and Therapy, 5,* 1–9.

Van Houten, R., Nau, P. A., MacKenzie-Keating, S. E., Sameoto, D., & Colavecchia, B. (1982). An analysis of some variables influencing the effectiveness of reprimands. *Journal of Applied Behavior Analysis, 15,* 65–83.

Varni, J. W., & Henker, B. (1979). A self-regulation approach to the treatment of three hyperactive boys. *Child Behavior Therapy, 1,* 171–192.

Walker, H. M., & Buckley, N. K. (1972). Programming generalization and maintenance of treatment effects across time and across settings. *Journal of Applied Behavior Analysis, 5,* 209–224.

Webster, R. E. (1976). A time-out procedure in a public school setting. *Psychology in the Schools, 13,* 72–76.

Weiss, G., Hechtman, L., Perlman, T., Hopkins, J., & Werner, A. (1979). Hyperactives as young adults: A controlled prospective ten-year follow-up of 75 children. *Archives of General Psychiatry, 36,* 675–681.

Whalen, C. K., & Henker, B. (1976). Psychostimulants and children: A review and analysis. *Psychological Bulletin, 83,* 1113–1130.

Whalen, C. K., Collins, B. E., Henker, B., Alkus, S. R., Adams, D., & Stapp, S. (1978). Behavior observations of hyperactive children and methylphenidate (Ritalin) effects in systematically structured classroom environments: Now you see them, now you don't. *Journal of Pediatric Psychology, 3,* 177–184.

Whalen, C. K., Henker, B., Collins, B. E., Finck, D., & Dotemoto, S. (1979). A social ecology of hyperactive boys: Medication effects in systematically structured classroom environments. *Journal of Applied Behavior Analysis, 12,* 65–81.

Wilson, C. C., Robertson, S. J., Herlong, L. H., & Haynes, S. N. (1979). Vicarious effects of time-out in the modification of aggression in the classroom. *Behavior Modification, 3,* 97–111.

Winett, R. A., & Winkler, R. C. (1972). Current behavior modification in the classroom: Be still, be quiet, be docile. *Journal of Applied Behavior Analysis, 5,* 499–504.

Winett, R. A., Richards, C. S., & Krasner, L. (1971). Child-monitored token reading program. *Psychology in the Schools, 8,* 259–262.

Witt, J. C., & Elliott, S. N. (1982). The response cost lottery: A time efficient and effective classroom intervention. *Journal of School Psychology, 20,* 155–161.

Witt, J. C., Hannafin, M. J., & Martens, B. K. (1983). Home-based reinforcement: Behavioral covariation between academic performance and inappropriate behavior. *Journal of School Psychology, 21,* 337–348.

Witt, J. C., Martens, B. K., & Elliott, S. N. (1984). Factors affecting teachers' judgments of the acceptability of behavioral interventions: Time involvement, behavior problem severity, and type of intervention. *Behavior Therapy, 15,* 204–209.

Wolf, M. M. (1978). Social validity: The case for subjective measurement of how applied behavior analysis is finding its heart. *Journal of Applied Behavior Analysis, 11,* 203–214.

Wolf, M. M., Hanley, E. L., King, L. A., Lachowicz, J., & Giles, D. K. (1970). The Timer-Game: A variable-interval contingency for the management of out-of-seat behavior. *Exceptional Children, 37,* 113–117.

Wulbert, M., & Dries, R. (1977). The relative efficacy of methylphenidate (Ritalin) and behavior-modification techniques in the treatment of a hyperactive child. *Journal of Applied Behavior Analysis, 10,* 21–31.

CHAPTER 26

Fears and Phobias

Richard J. Morris, Thomas R. Kratochwill, and Kay Aldridge

Fear is an intense emotion that is associated with cognitive, behavioral, and/or physiological components of anxiety (Morris & Kratochwill, 1983). In the presence of danger, fear can lead an individual to take protective action, and cause the person to behave in a cautious manner (Jersild, 1968). In school-age children transitory fears are common. These fears, which do not typically interfere with the child's daily functioning, are often viewed as integrally tied to normal child development (e.g., Jersild, 1968; Jersild & Holmes, 1935; Morris & Kratochwill, 1983; Smith, 1979).

Fear, on the other hand, can also have a disruptive influence on a child's learning and development, and can set the occasion for the occurrence of mild to severe anxiety and even disabling panic. In the school environment, for example, children may be exposed to particular situations and experiences that are outside of their respective learning histories. This, in turn, may set the occasion for the development of fear reactions. For example, a child who has never learned to be assertive with adults may be reluctant to approach a teacher in class for help on a particular topic. Similarly, the student who has a history of being criticized and negatively evaluated at home for his or her school performance may never adequately demonstrate his or her school knowledge in test situations at school—even though the student has no history of being criticized by the teacher.

Interest in children's fears and phobias has a long tradition among mental health professionals (see, for example, Freud, 1909; Haslam, 1915; Jersild & Holmes, 1935; Jones, 1924; Morris & Kratochwill, 1983; Watson & Rayner, 1920). The trend in this literature over the last 20 years has been away from the strict psychoanalytic formulations of etiology and treatment, and toward more behaviorally based conceptualizations of etiology and treatment (e.g., Morris & Kratochwill, 1983, 1985). Another trend that has emerged from the research and clinical literature involves the locus of treatment changing from the therapist's office to the child's natural environment (Morris & Kratochwill, 1983, 1985). Because the natural environment of most

Richard J. Morris • Department of Educational Psychology, School Psychology Program, University of Arizona, Tucson, Arizona 85721. **Thomas R. Kratochwill** • Department of Educational Psychology, University of Wisconsin-Madison, Madison, Wisconsin 53706. **Kay Aldridge** • Department of Psychology, University of Arizona, Tucson, Arizona 85721.

children includes 5 to 6 hours per weekday in an educational setting, this trend has tremendous implications for school personnel and administrators. In addition, the literature has revealed an increasing number of teachers who are utilizing fear reduction procedures to assist mental health professionals in modifying the fear levels in particular children in their classrooms. This chapter will review the normative and prevalence data on children's school-related fears and phobias, discuss various components of assessment and diagnosis of children's fears, and discuss specific behavioral methods for reducing children's fears within the school setting.

Normative and Prevalence Data

There has been a considerable amount of research on the developmental trends and prevalence of childhood fears and phobias, with several review articles focusing on particular aspects of this literature (e.g., Barrios, Hartmann, & Shigetomi, 1981; Graziano, DeGiovanni, & Garcia, 1979; Johnson & Melamed, 1979; Miller, Barrett, Hampe, & Noble, 1979; Morris & Kratochwill, 1983, 1985; Ollendick, 1979; Rachman, 1968; Smith, 1979). Most of this literature, however, has not focused specifically on school-related fears. Even though this is the case, we do find several trends that are relevant to school-related fears. First, the research literature appears to have centered primarily on infants and preschool children, with these children being studied both in the laboratory setting and natural environment, often with good dependent measures (Smith, 1979). Second, in terms of the assessment of fears, self-report measures appear to be used more frequently with older school-age children and adolescents, whereas parent behavior checklists and rating scales seem to be used with children under 12 years of age, and direct observation methods tend to be used with children below 6 years of age.

The use of these disparate assessment methods across various age ranges results in the measurement of different fear components at different ages, making comparisons across ages very difficult. These assessment procedures also differ on other dimensions, such as the type of data gathered, the type of questions asked, the person responding, and sampling procedures. For example, some researchers asked subjects to report things that were feared by a particular child (e.g., Croake, 1967; Maurer, 1965; Pratt, 1945) whereas in other studies the respondent was asked to report on things feared by other children in the child's own age group (e.g., Angelino, Dollins, & Mech, 1956; Nalvern, 1970). Graziano *et al.* (1979a) criticized this type of list and rank procedure because it (a) does not assure completeness of the fear stimuli being listed, and (b) does not provide information about the intensity of children's fear reactions. For example, the important dimension may not be the number of fears a child has, but the impact that the fear(s) has on the child's life—that is, a single intense fear may be more disabling than numerous minor fears. Another approach has been to use rating scales on which the respondent is asked to indicate the intensity of a particular child's reaction to a list of fearful stimuli (e.g., Bamber, 1974; Miller, 1967; Miller *et al.*, 1971, 1972b; Russell, 1977; Scherer & Nakamura, 1968). The reliability and validity of these types of measures has been found to be equivocal (Graziano *et al.*, 1979).

Definitional issues also sometimes confuse the interpretation of normative and developmental data when multiple terms have been used to describe the fear area being studied (e.g., Kratochwill & Morris, 1985; Morris & Kratochwill, 1983). Although this is more common in infant research, we also find this to occur in fear-related studies with older children. For example, Bowlby (1969, 1973) has made a distinction between *anxiety* (the desire for closer proximity to an attachment figure) and *alarm* (the desire to withdraw or avoid danger). A child could therefore refuse to attend school because (a) separation from the parent was frightening or (b) because something in the school environment was fearful. Whereas some writers would consider both situations to be examples of school phobia or school-related fears, Bowlby (1973) described the first situation as a pseudophobia.

With respect to school-related fears only a small amount of incidence and prevalence literature has been published (e.g., Johnson, 1979; Kennedy, 1965; Phillips, 1978; Trueman, 1984). Johnson (1979), for example, identified three major types of fear that often occur in the school setting. The first, *school phobia*, is a fear of school with associated anxiety so severe as to often prevent school attendance. Onset of the fear can be sudden or gradual (e.g., Baker & Willis, 1978; Coolidge, Hahn, & Peck, 1957; Kennedy, 1965; Trueman, 1984), with an incidence rate, according to Kennedy (1965), of 17 per 1000 school-age children or 1.7%. This rate, however, has been questioned by Trueman (1984a) because no source for this rate was provided by Kennedy. Other estimates of school phobia in those children referred to clinics have ranged from .04% (Eisenberg, 1958) to 8% (Kahn & Nursten, 1962) of all referrals. Although there do not appear to be any sex differences in the occurrence of "school phobia" (Johnson, 1979; Trueman, 1984), there does seem to be a peak incidence period between ages 9 and 11 years of age (e.g., Baker & Willis, 1978; Chazen, 1962)—a similar time period as is found for the occurrence of other children's fears (e.g., Angelino & Shedd, 1953; MacFarlane, Allen, & Hozik, 1954).

A second school-related fear identified by Johnson (1979) was termed *social withdrawal*, a condition in which fearful children seldom interact with their peers and may refuse to speak in class. Within normal preschool samples, the incidence rate has been reported to be 10% to 20% (e.g., Evers & Schwarz, 1974; O'Connor, 1972). Among older children, 2% had excessive or unreasonable fear of reciting in class, whereas almost 10% had an unreasonable or excessive fear regarding being criticized (Miller, Barrett, & Hampe, 1974). Complete mutism in school, on the other hand, is apparently very uncommon (Kratochwill, 1981; Kratochwill, Brody, & Piersal, 1979).

The third common school-related fear identified by Johnson (1979) was *test anxiety*. The incidence figures available come mainly from studies that were designed to measure treatment effects, and included subjects with varying levels of test anxiety. Estimates presented by Johnson (1979) range from 10% to 30% of school populations. Miller *et al*. (1974), on the other hand, indicated that 1.5% of school-age children express extreme fear of tests.

Based on analysis of responses to the Children's School Questionnaire (Phillips, 1966), Phillips (1978) identified four factors of school anxiety: Fear of Assertiveness and Self-Expression, Test Anxiety, Lack of Confidence in Meeting Expectations of Others, and Physiological Reactivity Associated with Low Tolerance of Stress. These factors resembled those earlier reported by Feld and Lewis (1967), based on the Test Anxiety Scale for Children (Sarason, Davidson, & Lighthall, 1960). Two types of stress were also identified by Phillips (1978): achievement and social stress. Interestingly, Phillips found interactional effects between ethnicity and social class, so that neither was adequate to predict anxiety levels among various groups. Actual levels of avoidance behavior and/or intensity of fear were not determined in the Phillips study (1978), but a majority of children responded positively to such anxiety indicators as: "If you made a mistake while reciting would some children laugh at you?" Even academic success was identified as a source of stress because about 40% of the children felt other children were angered by their success.

Although in most studies girls have been reported to have higher fear levels than boys (e.g., Angelino & Shedd, 1957; Bamber, 1974; Croake, 1967; Croake & Knox, 1973; Lapouse & Monk, 1959; Pratt, 1945; Scherer & Nakamura, 1968), this does not appear to be the case with specific school-related fears (e.g., Croake & Knox, 1971; Deffenbacher & Kemper, 1974a,b; Staley & O'Donnell, 1984; Trueman, 1984a). It also appears that there are no clear social class differences, although Lapouse and Monk (1959) reported lower SES students to have more fears and worries about school grades than upper class children, and Phillips (1978) reported higher school anxiety among lower SES Anglos and middle- and upper-class minority children.

Fears not specific to the academic environment also may have a limiting effect on the child at school. For example, an intense fear of animals may cause terror on a child's walk to and from school, cause a child to avoid going on class field trips (McReynolds & Morris, 1985), produce anxiety in a child each time small pets are brought to school by classmates, and/or interfere with a student's performance in such classes as biology in which contact with animals is often required. In addition, a fear of riding a school bus may prevent a child from going on school-sponsored field trips. Some children may also fear catching germs from community drinking fountains or taking a physical education class because they do not want to be seen changing clothes or possibly be seen naked. In the latter case, Miller *et al.* (1974) reported that 8% of females had an excessive fear of being seen naked, whereas the majority of both sexes were found to have at least some fear of being seen naked. Trauma experienced in school-related activities may also have an impact on children within and outside of the school setting. For example, 6 months to one year after the Chowchilla (California) school-bus kidnapping, all 23 child-victims who were interviewed exhibited kidnap-related fears, such as fear of being kidnapped again or fear of being left alone (Terr, 1981). Several of the children involved in the kidnapping also experienced marked personality changes, increased anxiety, and poor school performance.

Because fears occur in children from infancy through adolescence, and tend to be age related, therapists may want to make sure that they are knowledgeable about the developmental course of children's fears—and to use this information in deciding when and if treatment is appropriate. In this regard, Table 1 presents a listing of some of the common fears that are found in children at various age levels. In addition, an awareness of common fears in different age ranges may also assist therapists in identifying fears shared by several children. For example, as is seen in Table 1, fear of examinations is commonly found among 9- to 12-year-olds, and several researchers have therefore used group-treatment methods for reducing test anxiety in adolescents and older elementary school-age children (e.g., Barabasz, 1973, 1975; Deffen-

Table 1. Normative Data on Children's Fears

0–6 months:	Loss of support, loud noises
7–12 months:	Fear of strangers, fear of sudden, unexpected, and looming objects
1 year:	Separation from parent, toilet, injury, strangers
2 years:	A multitude of fears including loud noises (vacuum cleaners, sirens/alarms, trucks, and thunder), animals (e.g., large dog), dark room, separation from parent, large objects/machines, change in personal environment
3 years:	Masks, dark, animals, separation from parent
4 years:	Parent separation, animals, dark, noises (including at night)
5 years:	Animals, "bad" people, dark, separation from parent, bodily harm
6 years:	Supernatural beings (e.g., ghosts, witches, "Darth Vader"), bodily injuries, thunder, and lightning, dark, sleeping or staying alone, separation from parent
7–8 years:	Supernatural beings, dark, fears based on media events, staying alone, bodily injury
9–12 years:	Tests and examinations in school, school performance, bodily injury, physical appearance, thunder and lightning, death, dark (low percentage)

Source: Ilg & Ames, 1955; Jersild & Holmes, 1935; Kellerman, 1981; Lapouse & Monk, 1959; Scarr & Salapatch, 1970. From *Treating Children's Fears and Phobias: A Behavioral Approach* (p. 2) by R. J. Morris and T. R. Kratochwill, 1983, New York: Pergamon Press. Reprinted with permission.

bacher & Kemper, 1974a,b; Kondas, 1967; Mann, 1972).

In the early school years fears that are not specifically school related involve the dark, supernatural figures, and particular persons, objects, and events. With increasing age, common fears turn more toward imaginary figures, objects, and events, as well as the future (Jersild, 1968). Fear of violence and bodily harm is also apparently quite common in pre- and early adolescent youth (e.g., Clemente & Kleeman, 1977; Orton, 1982; Zill, 1977). For example, 52% of the 5th and 6th grade students in the Orton (1982) sample feared getting beaten up in a fight.

Definitions

Although a distinction between fears and phobias may appear clinically useful, the differentiated use of these terms has not been consistent in the literature (Graziano *et al.*, 1979; Kratochwill & Morris, 1985; Morris & Kratochwill, 1983). The terms have been used interchangeably as well as with the terms *anxiety, overanxious, stress, simple phobia,* and *avoidant behavior*. For example, the use of the terms *stress* and *anxiety* as descriptors associated with school-related fears is common (e.g., Foreman & O'Malley 1984; Johnson, 1979; Phillips, 1978). To add to this confusion of terms, we also find "fear" being used at times to describe a "normal" developmental reaction, and at other times as a "clinical problem" (Morris & Kratochwill, 1983).

Generally speaking, however, a phobia is considered to be a fear that is not age specific or developmentally appropriate, and occurs without apparent threat of external danger (Morris & Kratochwill, 1983). When a fear leads to the avoidance of a nondangerous situation, even when such avoidance seems inappropriate, the individual is said to have a phobic reaction (e.g., Knopf, 1979; Morris, 1986). Marks (1969), for example, defined a phobia as a subtype of fear that (a) is out of proportion to the demands of the situation, (b) cannot be explained or reasoned away, (c) is beyond voluntary control, and (d) leads to avoidance of the fear situation (p. 3). Miller, Barrett, and Hempe (1974) have added that a phobia (a) persists over an extended period of time, (b) is maladaptive, and (c) is not age or stage specific (p. 90). Fears that last over 2 years and interfere with a child's ability to function effectively have also been called clinical fears (Graziano *et al.*, 1979).

Phobias may develop as the result of an actual traumatic experience, or as a result of the child's ability to actively imagine danger without obvious antecedent experience. One child may become terrified and refuse to walk to school because a dog once chased the child on the route to school. A second child may have experienced no such trauma associated with the walk to school but may be incapacitated by fears of abduction or injury. Another child may be completely unable to explain what about the walk is frightening, but nonetheless experiences disabling panic when confronted with the task of walking to school. Each child may evidence the same avoidant or phobic behavior.

Diagnosis and Classification

Several approaches have been used in the classification of child psychopathology and there is at this time no single system consistently employed in the diagnosis of children's fears and phobias. The clinically derived categories developed by the American Psychiatric Association (APA, 1987), the Group for the Advancement of Psychiatry, and the World Health Organization (see, for example, Rutter *et al.*, 1969; Rutter, Shaffer, & Shepher, 1975; Yule, 1981) represent one approach to the classification of childhood disorders. Another approach has been to develop empirically derived categories, through the use of multivariate statistics (e.g., Achenbach & Edelbrock, 1978; Quay, 1979). Beyond these two broad classification approaches, there have also been several efforts to classify specifically the fears and phobias of children and adolescents, as well as develop more behaviorally oriented classification systems. Each of these approaches will be briefly reviewed.

Clinically Derived System of the American Psychiatric Association

The *Diagnostic and Statistical Manual* (3rd ed.) of the American Psychiatric Association (1987; DSM-III-R) is widely used in psychiatry and psychology and includes three anxiety disorders of childhood that bear on fears and phobias: Separation Anxiety Disorder, Avoidant Disorder of Childhood or Adolescence, and Overanxious Disorder. These disorders share anxiety as their predominant clinical feature, and like all DSM-III-R categories, were initially developed from the observations of clinicians. In the Overanxious Disorder, anxiety is said to be generalized to a variety of situations, whereas in the former two disorders anxiety is said to focus on specific situations.

Separation Anxiety Disorder

In this disorder "the essential feature . . . is excessive anxiety, for at least two weeks, concerning separation from those to whom the child is attached" (APA, 1987, p. 58). Physical complaints are common, and anxiety may be experienced to the point of panic. Although the disorder represents a form of phobia, it is not included in the Phobic Disorder classification because it has unique features and is typically associated with childhood. The extreme form of Separation Anxiety Disorder, involving school refusal, is said to begin most commonly around ages 11 and 12 and leads to significant impairment in independent functioning, with the disorder apparently occurring with equal frequency in both sexes. The following diagnostic criteria have been advanced for Separation Anxiety Disorder:

A. Excessive anxiety concerning separation from those to whom the child is attached, as evidenced by at least three of the following:
   1. Unrealistic and persistent worry about possible harm befalling major attachment figures or fear that they will leave and not return
   2. Unrealistic and persistent worry that an untoward calamitous event will separate the child from a major attachment figure, e.g., the child will be lost, kidnapped, killed, or be the victim of an accident
   3. Persistent reluctance or refusal to go to school in order to stay with major attachment figures or at home
   4. Persistent reluctance or refusal to go to sleep without being near to a major attachment figure or to go to sleep away from home
   5. Persistent avoidance of being alone, including "clinging" to and "shadowing" major attachment figures
   6. Repeated nightmares involving the theme of separation
   7. Complaints of physical symptoms, e.g., headaches, stomachaches, nausea, or vomiting,on many school days or on other occasions when anticipating separation from major attachment figures
   8. Recurrent signs or complaints of excessive distress in anticipation of separation from home or major attachment figures, e.g., temper tantrums or crying, pleading with parents not to leave
   9. Recurrent signs of complaints of excessive distress when separated from home or major attachment figures, e.g., wants to return home, needs to call parents when they are absent or when child is away from home

B. Duration of disturbance of at least two weeks.

C. Onset before the age of 18.

D. Occurrence not exclusively during the course of a Pervasive Developmental Disorder, Schizophrenia, or any other psychotic disorder. (APA, 1987, pp. 60–61)

Avoidant Disorder of Childhood or Adolescence

In this disorder

"The essential feature . . . is an excessive shirking from contact with unfamiliar people that is of sufficient severity to interfere with social functioning in peer relationships and that is of at least six months' duration. This is coupled with a clear desire for social involvement with familiar peoples, such as peers the person knows well and family members. (APA, 1987, p. 61)

When anxiety is extreme, children with this disorder may appear inarticulate or even mute. Children with this disorder are likely to seem socially withdrawn, embarrassed, and timid when they are with unfamiliar people, and will become anxious when, for example, a trivial demand is made of them to interact with strangers (APA, 1987). Socially reticent children who are slow to warm up, but suffer no impairment of peer relationships, are not diagnosed in this category. The following diagnostic criteria are used for Avoidant Disorder of Childhood or Adolescence (APA, 1987):

A. Excessive shrinking from contact with unfamiliar people, for a period of six months or longer, sufficiently severe to interfere with social functioning in peer relationships.
B. Desire for social involvement with familiar people (family members and peers the person knows well), and generally warm and satisfying relations with family members and other familiar figures.
C. Age at least 2½.
D. The disturbance is not sufficiently pervasive and persistent to warrant the diagnosis of Avoidant Personality Disorder (pp. 62–63)

Overanxious Disorder

In this disorder "The essential feature is . . . excessive or unrealistic anxiety or worry for a period of six months or longer" (APA, 1987, p. 63). Children with this disorder tend to be extremely self-conscious, and worry about such future events as examinations, physical injury, being included in peer group activities, and meeting such expectations as deadlines or keeping appointments, and being concerned about past behavior (APA, 1987). The following diagnostic criteria are used for Overanxious Disorder (APA, 1987):

A. Excessive or unrealistic anxiety or worry, for a period of six months or longer, as indicated by the frequent occurrence of at least four of the following:
   1. Excessive unrealistic worry about future events
   2. Excessive or unrealistic concern about the appropriateness of past behavior
   3. Excessive or unrealistic concern about competence in one or more areas, e.g., academic, athletic, social
   4. Somatic complaints, such as headaches or stomachaches, for which no physical basis can be established
   5. Marked self-consciousness
   6. Excessive need for reassurance about a variety of concerns
   7. Marked feelings of tension or inability to relax
B. If another Axis I disorder is present (e.g., Separation Anxiety Disorder, Phobic Disorder, Obsessive Compulsive Disorder), the focus of the symptoms in A are not limited to it. For example, if Separation Anxiety Disorder is present, the symptoms in A are not exclusively related to anxiety about separation. In addition, the disturbance does not occur during the course of a psychotic disorder or a Mood Disorder.
C. If 18 or older, does not meet the criteria for Generalized Anxiety Disorder.
D. Occurrence not exclusively during the course of a Pervasive Developmental Disorder, Schizophrenia, or any other psychotic disorder. (pp. 64–65)

Other diagnoses within the DSM-III-R system are also relevant to the study of fears and phobias, even though these additional diagnostic categories are not considered specifically to be part of children's anxiety disorders. For example Sleep Terror Disorder is classified under "Sleep Disorders" in DSM-III-R. Because intense anxiety is characteristic of this disorder, it has been discussed in the literature in association with fears and phobias (see, for example, Morris & Kratochwill, 1983). Anxiety Disorders that are not limited to development in childhood or adolescence may also be used to diagnose children's disturbances (APA, 1987). Among these additional diagnostic categories are Obsessive-Compulsive Disorder, Social Phobia, Simple Phobia, and Post-Traumatic Stress Disorder. Each of these is said to sometimes develop in childhood or adolescence.

WHO-ICD-9 Clinically Derived System

The World Health Organization International Classification of Diseases 9 (WHO-ICD-9) also uses a clinically derived classification system for children. This system does not provide specific criteria for diagnosis, but instead provides broad categories under which commonly used psychiatric diagnoses are subsumed. For example, a child with persistent anxiety not associated with a specific stressor would be considered to have a disturbance of emotions specific to childhood and adolescence, with anxiety and fearfulness. The glossary of WHO-ICD-9 lists the specific disorders that are subsumed in any given category. The above category would, for example, include overanxious reaction of childhood or adolescence. Other fear-related disturbances that can be diagnosed in using the ICD-9 system include abnormal separation anxiety, withdrawing reaction of childhood or adolescence, anxiety states, and phobic states. Fine discriminations, though, are sometimes difficult to make in this system (Yule, 1981).

Other Clinically Derived Systems

Another traditional approach to the classification of children's fears has been the labeling of each specific fear based on Greek and Latin prefixes (e.g., "xenophobia" being a fear of strangers). Although this method could result in endless terminology, description and identification of the feared situation could be useful (Marks, 1969).

Still another approach to the problem of classification has been to empirically derive categories through the application of multivariate statistics to group responses, using either general behavioral measures (e.g., Achenbach, 1974; Achenbach & Edelbrock, 1978; Quay, 1979; Yule, 1981) or specific fear measures (e.g., Miller *et al.*, 1974; Scherer & Nakamura, 1968). One of the broad-based studies, conducted with rating scales and checklist assessment, identified several different dimensions of child behavior, namely Conduct Disorder, Anxiety Withdrawal, Immaturity, and Socialized Aggression (Quay, 1979). Of particular interest is the anxiety-withdrawal pattern, which Quay (1979) reported to have been found in all settings in which children have been studied. Similarly, Miller *et al.* (1974) presented a classification scheme based on factor analysis of group responses to specific fear surveys. Three primary factors emerged in their research: physical injury, natural events, and social anxiety. Individual fears were subsumed under the three primary factors.

Finally, behavioral classification systems that focus on information that "can be directly used to develop and guide a treatment program" (Marholin & Bijou, 1978) have also appeared in the fear literature. For example, the *Psychological Response Classification System* (PRCS) is designed to classify responses rather than people (Adams, Doster, & Calhoun, 1977). Although similar to the multivariate approach, Adams *et al.* (1977) conceptualized this classification system within a motor, perceptual, biological, cognitive, and emotional response format—with deviant behavior conceptualized as falling on a continuum with normal behavior.

Diagnosis in the Educational Environment

In the educational setting, the diagnosis of fears and related disorders in students may have implications for both classroom placement and behavioral treatment. For example, Public Law 94-142, The Education for All Handicapped Children Act (1975), includes the following criteria, among others, that may be used to diagnose serious emotional disturbance:

1. An inability to learn which cannot be explained by intellectual, sensory, or health factors;

2. An inability to build or maintain satisfactory interpersonal relationships with peers and teachers;
3. Inappropriate types of behavior or feelings under normal circumstances; or
4. A tendency to develop physical symptoms or fears associated with personal or school problems.

Serious emotional disturbance may be diagnosed only when a student's ability to learn in the regular classroom is significantly impaired because of these difficulties. The diagnostic category of serious emotional disturbance is quite broad, and can include a number of childhood behavior disorders; therefore, more specific and focused diagnoses are probably necessary for development of an appropriate individualized educational program (IEP).

Special education students having various handicapping conditions may also have fears and related problems that must be addressed on the IEP. For example, it has been suggested that mentally retarded individuals may be more susceptible to fears, phobias, and related problems than children of normal IQ (Ollendick & Ollendick, 1982). Fear or anxiety may also exacerbate educational failure in particular special education students, making diagnosis of both the handicapping condition and the fear very important. For example, a 12-year-old learning disabled student may also experience test anxiety or social withdrawal that may need to be addressed on the IEP.

In addition, there may be many children who never come to the attention of school psychologists or counselors because their discomfort is not evident to those around them, or is not severe enough to warrant special education evaluation. Classroom teachers may notice children who choose to fail rather than give a classroom speech, or the school nurse may notice that a child's illnesses are related to school examinations or field trips. Although students with these difficulties may not require special education or school psychological services, identification and diagnosis of their fears and related difficulties, might lead to interventions which could improve their overall academic functioning in the classroom.

Assessment of Fears and Phobias

The assessment of childhood fears and phobias typically involves either a traditional or behavioral approach to conceptualizing children's behavior disorders—with the proponents of the two views differing essentially on their respective basic assumptions about human behavior (Nelson & Hayes, 1979). For example, a traditional assessment approach would generally focus on underlying psychic causes of a student's problem behavior whereas a behavioral approach would focus on identifying those events and persons in the environment that are contributing to the fear and would be relevant to the development of a treatment program. Hartman, Roper, and Bradford (1979), for example, have identified a number of dimensions on which the two approaches differ. Traditional approaches tend to focus on intraorganismic variables in explaining fears and phobias, and, in addition, observed behavior is seen as only a sign of underlying pathology. Traditional assessment is, however, not a uniform approach with consistent models and techniques, and may encompass both psychodynamic and trait models (Korchin & Schulberg, 1981).

Behavioral assessment is also not a set of specific techniques and procedures, but a conceptual approach which focuses on problem-solving strategies (Evans & Nelson, 1977; Mash & Terdall, 1981). General consistency in defining behavioral assessment as well as the possibility for application of a broad range of techniques and procedures is provided by this perspective. Many different methods have been utilized to assess children's fears and phobias within a behavioral framework, and at times, methods originally developed for traditional assessment (e.g., checklists, self-report, rating scales) may be appropriately used in a behavioral assessment. In general, the behavioral approach places considerable emphasis on direct observation and measurement of a target behavior in the environment and the client–environment interaction in which the behavior occurs (Bandura, 1977; Kazdin, 1979; Mischel, 1968, 1973) without reliance on identification of underlying causes.

Given the diversity in available procedures and techniques, a conceptual framework based on the simultaneous consideration of the assessment process outlined by Cone and his associates (e.g., Cone, 1978, 1979; Cone & Hawkins, 1977) will be presented, which should assist the professional with the appropriate selection of a particular procedure or technique. This framework will focus on the contents assessed and the method used to assess the content. For an additional discussion of the methodological features of generalizability (i.e., reliability, validity) the reader is referred to Cone (1977).

Contents

Lang (1968) introduced into the literature a conceptualization of fear that has become increasingly popular, and has been variously labeled triple response mode (e.g., Cone, 1979), multiple response components (e.g., Nietzel & Bernstein, 1981), or three response system (e.g., Kozal & Miller, 1982). This position holds, for example, that fear is not a single response, but a complex multichannel response pattern of behavior or emotion. The three channels of focus are generally the cognitive, physiological, and motor systems. These response patterns are not always perfectly correlated, but are usually related to some extent (Hodgson & Rachman, 1974; Rachman & Hodgson, 1974). This implies that changes in one response may not be reflected by or lead to changes in another response channel, but also that results obtained from one channel may have important implications for the type of data one might obtain from a different channel.

A child may display his or her fear or anxiety in any one or all of the three channels, and a thorough behavioral assessment should tap responses in all three systems. Sometimes the response most troublesome to the adults in a child's life may be somewhat different than the response the child finds most bothersome. For example, a parent may wish only to decrease the motor response components of school refusal, while the child may desire a reduction in the uncomfortable physiological arousal associated with the school stimuli. With adequate assessment, subsequent treatment can be directed at any or all of the response component or channels.

Cognitive Channel

One channel used to define anxiety is the cognitive channel or self-report channel. The existence of this channel cannot be objectively validated through direct observation and is thus a subjective system in that its existence is determined by the child's self-report. The self-report may be made through direct statements, as when the child says, "I'm afraid to give this speech in class" or "School scares me." It may also be determined through such assessment methods as a structured questionnaire or self-monitoring by the child.

Most of the fear reduction methods reviewed in this chapter rely in part upon self-report data to determine the existence of a fear or phobia. Within the field of behavioral treatment, there is, however, a considerable variation in the degree of importance attributed to such data. Cognitive behavior therapists, for example, tend to rely much more heavily on self-report data than do applied behavior analysts (who tend to be critical of the sole reliance on this source of data). Most behavior therapists agree, however, that the cognitive channel provides important information for the definition, assessment, and treatment of fear and related anxieties.

Physiological Channel

A second channel, also referred to as the somatic or visceral system, is the physiological channel, for which measurement usually focuses on the sympathetic portion of the nervous system (e.g., Nietzel & Bernstein, 1981; Paul & Bernstein, 1973). Anxiety and fear in this channel is assessed through various measures of the autonomic nervous system, such as blood pressure, heart and/or respiration rate, muscle tension, galvanic skin response, and temperature. More than one physiological measure is usually used in this system to define anxiety or fear. This is often necessary because different physiological measures are not always highly correlated (Haynes, 1978).

Motor Channel

The third channel is the motor or overt behavior channel, for which measurement is focused on the actual manifest behavior of the child. Measures of this channel may be either direct or indirect (Paul & Bernstein, 1973). Direct measures are those that assess the overt behavioral consequences of physiological arousal. For example, a child trembling in the presence of a particular stimulus (e.g., school bell ringing; teacher discussing an upcoming test) would be a direct measure defining the presence of fear or anxiety. Escape and/or avoidance behaviors (e.g., covering the ears at the sound of a school bell; not going to school on the day of a test) provide indirect evidence of anxiety in the presence of the particular stimulus.

Considerations

Though not universally accepted the popularity of the three-system perspective has grown among behavioral therapists. Kazdin and Hersen (1980) have even suggested that the multiple-response modality framework is one of the major characteristics of behavior therapy. On the other hand, some writers have raised questions about the use of the multiple-response theory (e.g., Cone, 1979; Hugdahl, 1981; Kozak & Miller, 1982). First, as mentioned earlier, measures of the three systems may not be highly correlated (Cone, 1979; Bellack & Hersen, 1977a,b). Second, the use of terms and meanings to define different aspects of the system has not been consistent across writers. Third, the number of dimensions for fear assessment available for use in clinical research and practice is limited. For example, Kozak and Miller (1982) suggested that this may lead the assessor to "think that there are only three things to be measured and that getting a number for each system sufficiently measures fear" (p. 352). A fourth concern is that currently there is insufficient evidence to conclude that specific treatments may be best suited for particular patterns of response within the system.

Methods

Assessment methods utilized within the behavioral framework vary on a continuum of directness defined by the extent to which they measure a clinically relevant target response in the setting and at the time that it would naturally occur (Cone, 1978). Reports by the client or other informant, which are gathered in a different environment or time frame than that in which the response typically occurs, are considered to be indirect methods. For example, interviews, rating scales, checklists, and other self-report measures usually depend on the informant's ability to recall accurately and describe an experience that has occurred in the past in an environment different from that in which the data are gathered. The Cone (1978) conceptualization and a theoretical perspective based on social behaviorism psychometrics (Burns, 1980) have provided a rationale for the use of indirect methods in behavioral assessment.

Direct measures assess the target behavior in either the natural setting or an analogous one. In the use of an analogue, it is useful to remember that a number of dimensions can be separately and systematically varied. These dimensions might include the setting, nature of the stimuli, required response, person doing the assessment, and the instructions given. Self-monitoring, in which the client is both observer and observee, and direct observation by another observer are both forms of direct assessment, because both are utilized in the natural environment (or one analogous to it), and report the behavior at the time at which it occurs. Physiological measures taken in this situation are also a direct method.

Frequently, a single method will tap several channels. For example, a questionnaire might ask the child to report his cognitions in a fearful situation, how he typically responds motorically, and what happens physiologically. This would provide indirect measurement of the target response. When the three systems do not correlate highly, it may have implications for treatment. The therapist may wish to focus on those channels in which problematic responses do occur.

A number of different assessment strategies have been used with children experiencing fear- and phobia-related anxieties. For purposes of this chapter, the devices and procedures have been grouped under the following categories: interview assessment, self-report measures, checklists and rating scales, self-monitoring, direct observation, and psychophysiological techniques. There are many strategies subsumed under each of these categories, and at times it will be obvious that there is considerable overlap among the various categories. This is especially true in regard to the response channel that is assessed.

Interview Assessment

The interview format is probably one of the most popular data gathering techniques used across all therapeutic orientations, and the topic has been reviewed extensively in the behavioral literature (e.g., Ciminero, 1977; Ciminero & Drabman, 1977; Gross, 1984; Haynes & Jensen, 1979; Linehan, 1977; Meyer, Liddel, & Lyons, 1977; Morganstern, 1976). Within the framework of Burke and Demers (1979) it is possible to develop conceptually 27 different interview formats through the combination of three dimensions: predetermination of questions, interviewer response, and breadth of content explored. These dimensions are discussed as they apply to assessment of children's fears and phobias.

Predetermination of Questions

Interviews may range from the standardized interview in which a list of questions or statements is followed, to the unstructured interview in which questions are not predetermined. One standardized format that may be used in the assessment of children's fears is that presented by Morris (1986) and Morris and Kratochwill (1983). Semistructured interviews allow greater flexibility in that exact wording and phrasing are not specified (e.g., Bergan, 1977; Bersoff & Grieger, 1971; Holland, 1970; Wahler & Cormier, 1970). These procedures, such as the Behavioral Analysis System developed by Kanfer and Grimm (1977), do not dictate the script of the interview but do provide structure through the ordering of questions or areas to be discussed. Unstructured formats with no predetermined order or questions probably allow the most flexibility in exploration of the problem.

Each format has associated methodological and conceptual issues. For example, the unstructured interview, although it allows greater flexibility, may compromise the reliability and validity of problem identification. Haynes and Jensen (1979) identified several potential sources of error that could occur in the interview:

1. Differences in race, sex, or social class between interviewer and client
2. The retrospective nature of the interview process and error associated with retrospective data
3. Interviewer knowledge of hypotheses or classification of clients

4. The social sensitivity and type of information elicited
5. The age of the client
6. The population being interviewed
7. The content, format, and structure of the interview
8. Bias in the reports of mediator-clients
9. Bias presumed to be inherent in all self-report measures (p. 103)

Although these problems can occur in any type of interview, a relatively structured standard format tends to provide quantifiable and reliable data, and allow for use by less experienced personnel (Wiens, 1976).

Response Options

Allowable responses of the interviewee determine if the interview is a closed, open, or mixed response option (Burke & DeMers, 1979). In the closed-response option the interview contains at least two thirds closed ended questions, and in the open-response option at least two thirds of the questions are open ended. Whereas open response options tend to increase flexibility in elucidation of a child's problem behaviors, the closed-response option tends to increase reliability of assessment across individuals.

Content Areas Explored

The theoretical persuasion and preferred model of assessment perhaps dictate the breadth of area explored in the interview. For example, the Kanfer and Saslow (1969) model represents a rather broad based analysis of the fear problem.

General Considerations

In general, caution is advised in the use of interview assessment with children's fears and related problems, but there are some positive features to encourage its use in conjunction with other methods of behavioral assessment. Specifically, some advantages are apparent in the behavioral literature (Kratochwill, 1982; Linehan, 1977). First, because of the many options discussed before, the interviewer is allowed much more flexibility than is true of other methods. Second, the interview may promote the development of an interpersonal relationship with the client. Third, the interview may uncover data that would not otherwise be revealed in assessment.

Self-Report Measures

Self-report measures are generally indirect in that they are verbal representations of more clinically relevant behavior occurring in another time and place. Although behavior therapists have used self-report measures for some time in their work with fearful and phobic children, the frequency with which these measures have been used has increased in recent years. Much of this increased use is because the growth of cognitive behavior therapy has increased the credibility of self-reports (e.g., Kendall, 1981; Kendall & Finch, 1979; Kendall & Hollon, 1979), and the recognition that the operational criteria for the existence of a behavior problem such as a fear may lie within the client's self-reported verbalization (Tasto, 1977). Emphasis on the three response channel has also increased the acceptability of such measures. Excellent reviews of the numerous self-report measures relevant to the assessment of children's fears and related problems have appeared in the literature (e.g., Barrios *et al.*, 1981; Finch & Rogers, 1984; Johnson & Melamed, 1979; Miller *et al.*, 1974). Several available measures will be briefly discussed.

Children's Manifest Anxiety Scale

Developed by Castaneda, McCandless, and Palermo (1956), the Children's Manifest Anxiety Scale (CSAS) is a measure of a child's chronic state of anxiety containing 42 items and an additional 11 items composing the Lie scale. It has been used in numerous research studies (see, for example, Reynolds, 1977). The scale has also been revised through reordering, deleting, and adding items, as well as the development of new national norms and reliability data (Reynolds & Paget, 1981; Reynolds & Richmond, 1978). Three anxiety factors have emerged in analysis of the Revised CMAS: Physiological, Worry/Oversensitivity, and Concentration (Reynolds & Paget, 1981; Reynolds & Richmond, 1978). In the Reynolds and Paget (1981) work, a large general anxiety factor was also found, and the Lie scale separated into two distinct factors. The factor structure of the revised CMAS was also found to be generally invariant with respect to race and sex.

Test Anxiety Scale for Children

The Test Anxiety Scale for Children (TASC) developed by Sarason, Davidson, Lighthall, Waite, and Ruebush (1960) is more specific to school-related anxiety than is the CMAS. High-anxious students identified on the 30-item TASC tend to score poorer on intelligence and achievement tests than do less anxious students (Johnson & Melamed, 1979). Actually, the TASC is generally recognized as a multidimensional scale (e.g., Dunn, 1965; Feld & Lewis, 1967). For example, Feld and Lewis (1967) identified four factors: Test Anxiety, Remote School Concern, Poor Self-Evaluation, and Somatic Signs of Anxiety. These factors were essentially the same for males and females.

Children's School Questionnaire

Developed by Phillips (1966, 1978), the 198-question Children's School Questionnaire (CSQ) is read orally to the child and contains questions from the TASC (Sarason *et al.*, 1960) as well as several other sources. Items were also prepared to tap aspects of achievement, social stress, and coping style. Seventy-four questions found to be indicators of school anxiety were analyzed and four factors emerged: Fear of Assertiveness and Self-Expression, Test Anxiety, Lack of Confidence in Meeting Expectations of Others, and Reactivity Associated with Low Tolerance of Stress (Phillips, 1978). Although 26 of the 30 TASC items were among the 74 constituting the measure of school anxiety, Phillips (1978) argued that the CSQ more adequately measured four components of school anxiety.

Fear Survey Schedule for Children

Scherer and Nakamura (1968) developed the 80-item Fear Survey Schedule for Children (FSS-FC). Factor analysis yielded several factors: Fear of Failure or Criticism, Major Fears, Minor Fears—Travel, Medical Fears, Fear of Death, Fear of the Dark, Home–School Fears, and Miscellaneous Fears (Miller, Barrett, Hampe, & Noble, 1972b). A modified version of the FSS-FC for kindergarten through sixth grade consists of 48 items and two blanks in which the child may denote any atypical fears.

Louisville Fear Survey for Children

Miller and his associates (e.g., Miller, 1967; Miller *et al.*, 1972b) developed the 81-item Louisville Fear Survey for Children (LFSC) for children ages 4 through 18. The LFSC can be completed by the child as a self-rating or by an adult (e.g., parent, teacher) as a behavior rating scale, but there is some evidence to suggest that the child and parent ratings may not correspond highly (Miller *et al.*, 1971).

Miscellaneous Measures

A variety of other self-report measures have been used, which include other standardized forms such as the State-Trait Anxiety Inventory for Children (Spielberger, 1973), projective drawings (e.g., Knoff & Proutt, 1985; Melamed & Siegel, 1975; Vernon, 1973), the Fear Thermometer (Walk, 1956) modified by Kelley (1976), which allows the child to indicate one of five levels of fear represented by colors, and a variation of the fear thermometer procedure called the faces test, in which the child is asked to choose the face that best corresponds to how he or she felt during a specific situation.

General Considerations

In considering the use of self-report measures it is important to recognize that these measures vary on several dimensions (Kazdin, 1980). Some scales assess a specific fear stimulus whereas others tap more global aspects, such as general classes of fear or anxiety. The measures may also differ in whether responses are publically observable or private events. Some measures are direct in that the child may know the direct purpose of the assessment, but other measures, such as projective tests, are indirect and obscure the purpose of testing from the child.

Self-report measures have several limitations. One major concern is whether the data obtained are an accurate reflection of the actual fear. Although some instruments, such as the CMAS, include a lie scale to help increase accuracy, whether the scale measures lies has been debated. Kazdin (1980) reported that a range of factors, including social desirability may influence responses. A second concern is that many of the instruments were not originally developed for behavioral assessment, and as Barrios *et al.* (1981) noted, the attempt to assess cross-situational aspects of fear may fail to describe adequately individual situations. Another major limitation is that some scales lack sufficient data on norming, reliability, and validity, which is especially important in view of the developmental nature of fears and related problems (Barrios *et al.*, 1981; Morris & Kratochwill, 1983).

Given the previously cited limitations, self-report measures none the less may prove valuable especially in the school setting. Large numbers of children may be screened with these instruments not only to identify fearful individuals, but also to identify stimuli that may be threatening to several or many students in the same school environment. Self-report methods also allow the child to report personal experiences that may not be observable by others. With the increased emphasis on the three response mode model of fear, they also allow the therapist to tap aspects of fear that cannot be measured in any other way. Assessment of the child's cognitive response to fear may also support hypotheses derived from other assessment methods. At this time, however, there is a lack of instruments specific to school-related fears and phobias.

Behavior Checklists and Rating Scales

Behavior checklists and rating scales are often similar in format to self-report measures but are completed by an informant familiar with the child's behavior (e.g., teacher, parent). These scales are typically of two types: general or specific. A number of the general checklists and rating scales have been used in the study of general child behavior disorders for purposes of classification and diagnosis. Although an Anxiety Withdrawal factor may emerge on the general scales, these scales lack sufficient depth to pinpoint specific fears or phobias that a child may be experiencing.

There are relatively few specific fear rating scales and checklists. The Teacher Rating Scale (Sarason *et al.*, 1960) is one such instrument designed to supplement the Test Anxiety Scale for Children. The 17-item scale is used to assess the motor components of a child's fear or anxiety. Correlations between the TASC and TR are generally low (e.g., $r=.30$). In addition, the Louisville Fear Survey for Children may be completed by an adult familiar with the child's problems. With parent report, three primary factors have emerged: Fear of Physical Injury, Natural and Supernatural Dangers, and Interpersonal Social (e.g., examinations, criticism, making mistakes). In a classification system based on these factors, Miller *et al.* (1974) incorporated school phobia under the category of social anxiety. In addition, the Parent Anxiety Rating Scale and the Teacher's Separation Anxiety Scale (Doris, McIntyre, Kelsey, &

Lehman, 1971) have been used to assess the preschooler's reaction to separation from parents.

There are several disadvantages of behavior checklists and rating scales. One concern is that data are gathered retrospectively, which may compromise validity. The rationale for item selection also varies across these instruments, and often the items used provide little in the way of (a) specificity of a fear and (b) information about the situational conditions under which the child's fears occur. Finally, little is known about the psychometric properties of many informant completed scales.

These methods, however, do have several major advantages in the school setting. Data from these procedures are generally easy to score and quantify. In addition, these scales can be completed relatively easily by parents and teachers, and information about the child's behavior in the natural environment can also be gained easily. As with self-reports it may also be possible to identify situations or events in the school environment that are threatening to several children.

Self-Monitoring

Self-monitoring refers to the process in which the child is required to discriminate and record the occurrence of a particular behavior at the time it occurs. It is therefore a direct method, which distinguishes it from the previous procedures that reported experiences in a different time and place than that in which they naturally occur. Although a fair amount of literature has been published on self-monitoring (e.g., Haynes, 1978; McFall, 1977; Nelson, 1977; Shapiro, 1984), it has been used infrequently in the assessment of children's fears. This is noteworthy because this procedure can be potentially very beneficial in the assessment of children's fears. First, this procedure provides a direct method for gathering information on private cognitions and events. Second, it may be useful in determining not only what a child fears, but also the particular situations in which the fear usually occurs.

Self-monitoring may be quite useful in the assessment of school-related fears and anxiety if the psychologist or clinician makes attempts to maximize the accuracy by reducing reactivity and keeping the task within the child's ability. Reactivity may alter the target behavior and several possible explanations have been offered for such change (e.g., Kanfer, 1977, 1980; Nelson & Hayes, 1981; Rachlin, 1974).

Direct Observation

Direct observation is conducted either in naturalistic, contrived, or analogue settings in which interference by the trained observer-coders is kept to a minimum. Several different classes of direct behavioral observational assessment have been used: behavioral avoidance tests, global behavioral ratings, and direct observation in naturalistic settings.

In the Behavioral Avoidance Test (BAT), the child is usually requested to approach a feared stimulus while observers record the approach responses on a predetermined form. Each BAT is tailored for the particular fear targeted for intervention. The observer might record response latency, number of tasks or steps completed, and distance from the feared stimulus. In a passive version of the BAT, the therapist may move the stimulus toward the child (e.g., Murphy & Bootzin, 1973).

The BAT is an unstandardized procedure and several factors may influence the results obtained across variations of the procedure. For example, segmentation of the BAT into increasingly smaller steps tends to produce greater approach behavior (e.g., Nawas, 1971), and the nature and manner in which instructions are given may affect performance (e.g., Bernstein & Nietzel, 1973, 1974; Kelley, 1976). It is important to realize that a BAT is only analoguous to assessment in the natural environment, and that any threat posed in the BAT may be different from that of the natural environment. A final concern is the general lack of reliability and validity data on this measure (Barrios *et al.*, 1981; Johnson & Melamed, 1979).

Despite these concerns, the use of BATs in conjunction with other measures can provide valuable information. They provide one method of assessment of the motoric channel that may include observation not only of approach behavior, but also facial expressions, trembling, and the time needed to complete the task (cf. Barrios & Shigetomi, 1980). This measure can also be easily used in a school setting for those fears that are clearly specified and observable.

Global Behavior ratings simplify the measurement process by recording observed behavior on a dimensional scale (e.g., "seldom" to "never"), but there is usually a corresponding loss of information. Use of these ratings, however, has typically been outside the school setting (e.g., Peterson & Shigetomi, 1981).

In direct observation in naturalistic settings, the clinician observes and codes target behaviors as they normally occur in the environment. Neisworth, Madle, and Goeke (1975), for example, recorded the duration of crying, screaming, and sobbing during preschool activities in order to assess separation anxiety. On the Preschool Observation Scale of Anxiety (Glennon & Weisz, 1978) the observer rates the occurrence of 30 anxiety indicators (e.g., rigid posture, trembling voice) as the child performs tasks in the presence and absence of the mother. In another study, Wine (1979) used direct observation to study children's anxiety during a time period before an examination and then when no examination was scheduled. Behavior categories included communication, task-related behaviors, attending behaviors, communication, and interpersonal behaviors. Scales have also been developed to measure anxiety related to medical and dental care (e.g., Melamed & Siegel, 1975; Melamed, Hawes, Heiby, & Glick, 1975), which may have application in the school, especially among special education populations.

General Considerations

The literature examining the methodological and conceptual issues of direct observation is quite extensive. Increased standardization of coding should lead to increased accuracy, reliability, and validity. It is also important that the target behaviors chosen for observation adequately represent the actual feared stimulus. Finally, it is important to bear in mind that reactive effects to the obtrusiveness of observation may alter behavior.

Although the practitioner in a school setting may not be able to adhere to such strict methodological requirements, direct observation may be highly valuable in this setting. For example, through classroom observation the clinician or other change agent might better identify the situational variables associated with a child's social withdrawal, selective mutism, test anxiety, and speech anxiety.

Psychophysiological Measures

Psychophysiological measures are generally used to assess directly the physical response channel. The most commonly used measures in the assessment of fear and anxiety are electromyography, cardiovascular monitoring, and electrodermal measures. In electromyography, electrodes attached to the child's skin in several places measure the electrical activity generated when a skeletal muscle is contracted. Muscle tension is then inferred from this measure. Cardiovascular measures include indexes of heart rate, blood pressure, and peripheral blood flow—with heart rate being the most commonly monitored measure. The most common electrodermal measures, skin conductance and skin resistance, are measured by placing electrodes on the skin and passing an electric current between them. The results are then displayed on a polygraph or meter. Neither electromyography nor electrodermal measures have been extensively used with children or in school settings.

The expense and sophistication necessary to obtain reliable physiological measures has limited their use in school or other applied settings. It is possible that alternatives that do not require sophisticated equipment could be used to tap physiological responses. Barrios *et al.* (1981), for example, suggested that the Autonomic Perception Questionnaire (Mandler, Mandler, & Uviller, 1958) could be modified for self-report. A child might also be taught to monitor his own pulse rate. It is also important to realize that physiological measures may not correlate highly with other assessment strategies, and may be influenced by variables other than fear or anxiety.

Methods of Fear Reduction

The behavioral orientation generally assumes that fears and phobias are learned responses to specific stimuli, and fear reduction methods within this orientation are based on the subsequent assumption that more appropriate or desirable responses to the same stimuli may also be learned. Within the behavioral treatment literature, five major fear reduction methods have emerged: systematic desensitization with various modifications, flooding-related therapies, contingency management procedures, modeling, and self-control. Each of these methods will be discussed with an emphasis on its application to the treatment of school-related fears and phobias.

Systematic Desensitization

Systematic desensitization was developed by Joseph Wolpe in the early 1950s and has been reported to be the behavioral therapy procedure that is the most frequently used in the treatment of children's fears and phobias (Ollendick, 1979). It has also been reported to be the most often used procedure for the reduction of test anxiety and school phobia in adolescents (Morris, Kratochwill, & Dodson, 1986). Underlying the desensitization process is a principle termed *reciprocal inhibition* (Wolpe, 1958). Wolpe described reciprocal inhibition in the following way: "If a response inhibitory to anxiety can be made to occur in the presence of anxiety evoking stimuli, it will weaken the connection between these stimuli and the anxiety responses" (Wolpe, 1962, p. 562). Thus, the basic assumption underlying this technique is that a fear response (usually anxiety) can be inhibited by substituting an activity (usually relaxation) that is antagonistic to the fear response.

For example, a child who reported feeling very nervous and tense when asked to recite in front of the class would first be taught to relax and feel calm (an activity antagonistic to anxiety). The child, while continuing to practice relaxation and calmness, would then be exposed in small, graduated steps to the feared classroom situation. This gradual exposure can take place in real life (i.e., *in vivo*) or in the child's cognitions—where the child imagines being exposed to various recitation-related experiences. Thus, the child's avoidance or fear of recitation is desensitized or counterconditioned.

Essentially, there are three phases in systematic desensitization: (a) relaxation training, (b) development of the anxiety hierarchy, and (c) systematic desensitization proper.

The purpose of relaxation training is to help a child learn how to become calm and relaxed and to teach him or her an activity that can be substituted for a fear or anxiety response (Morris & Kratochwill, 1983). The therapist guides the child through a series of steps, such as those presented in Table 2, to induce deep muscle relaxation. The entire procedure typically takes 20 to 25 minutes to administer with the steps in the procedure being adjusted to the child's ease in performing each step (see, for example, Cautela & Groden, 1978; Morris, 1973).

During the relaxation phase, the child and therapist begin to develop an anxiety hier-

Table 2. Program for Teaching Relaxation to Children

1. Take a deep breath and hold it (for about 10 seconds). Hold it. Okay, let it out.
2. Raise both of your hands about half way above the chair or mat, and breathe normally. Now, drop your hands down.
3. Now hold your arms out and make a tight fist. Really tight. Feel the tension in your hands. I am going to count to three and when I say "three" I want you to drop your hands. One . . . Two . . . Three.
4. Raise your arms again, and bend your fingers back the other way (toward your body). Now drop your hands and relax.
5. Raise your arms. Now drop them and relax.
6. Now raise your arms again, but this time "flap" your hands around. Okay, relax again.
7. Raise your arms again. Now relax.
8. Raise your arms above the couch (chair) again and tense your biceps until they shake. Breathe normally, and keep your hands loose. Relax you hands. (Notice how you have a warm feeling of relaxation.)
9. Now hold your arms out to your side a tense your biceps. Make sure that you breathe normally. Relax your arms.
10. Now arch your shoulders back. Hold it. Make sure that your arms are relaxed. Now relax.
11. Hunch your shoulders forward. Hold it, and make sure that you breathe normally and keep your arms relaxed. Okay, relax. (Notice the feeling of relief from tensing and relaxing your muscles.)
12. Now turn you head to the right and tense your neck. Relax and bring your head back again to its natural position.
13. Turn your head to the left and tense your neck. Relax and bring your head back again to its natural position.
14. Now bend your head back slightly toward the chair. Hold it. Okay, now bring your head back slowly to its natural position.
15. This time bring your head down almost to your chest. Hold it. Now relax and let your head come back to its natural resting position.
16. Now open your mouth as much as possible. A little wider; okay, relax. (Mouth must be partly open at end.)
17. Now tense your lips by closing your mouth. Okay, relax.
18. Put your tongue at the roof of your mouth. Press hard. (Pause.) Relax and allow your tongue to come to a comfortable position in your mouth.
19. Now put your tongue at the bottom of your mouth. Press down hard. Relax and let your tongue come to a comfortable position in your mouth.
20. Now just lie (sit) there and relax. Try not to think of anything.
21. To control self-verbalization, I want you to go through the motions of singing a high note—not aloud! Okay, start singing to yourself. Hold that note, and now hard. Relax. (You are becoming more and more relaxed.)
22. Now sing a medium tone and make your vocal cords tense again. Relax.
23. Now sing a low note and make your vocal cords tense again. Relax (Your vocal apparatus should be relaxed now. Relax your mouth.)
24. Now close your eyes. Squeeze them tight and breathe naturally. Notice the tension. Now relax. (Notice how the pain goes away when you relax.)
25. Now let your eyes relax and keep your mouth open slightly.
26. Open your eyes as much as possible. Hold it. Now relax your eyes.
27. Now wrinkle your forehead as much as possible. Hold it. Okay, relax.
28. Now take a deep breath and hold it. Relax.
29. Now exhale. Breathe all the air out . . . all of it out. Relax. (Notice the wondrous feeling of breathing again.)
30. Imagine that there are weights pulling on all your muscles making them flaccid and relaxed . . . pulling your arms and body into the couch.
31. Pull your stomach muscles together. Tighter. Okay, relax.
32. Now extend your muscles as if you were a prize fighter. Make your stomach hard. Relax. (You are becoming more and more relaxed.)
33. Now tense your buttocks. Tighter. Hold it. Now relax.
34. Now search the upper part of your body and relax any part that is tense. First the facial muscles (Pause 3 to 5 seconds.) Then the vocal muscles. (Pause 3 to 5 seconds.) The neck region. (Pause 3 to 5 seconds.) Your shoulder . . . relax any part which is tense. (Pause.) Now the arms and fingers. Relax these. Becoming very relaxed.
35. Maintaining this relaxation, raise both of your legs (about a 45° angle). Now relax. (Notice that this further relaxes you.)
36. Now bend your feet back so that your toes point toward your face. Relax your mouth. Bend them hard. Relax.
37. Bend your feet the other way . . . away from your body. Not far. Notice the tension. Okay, relax.
38. Relax. (Pause) Now curl your toes together as hard as you can. Tighter. Okay, relax. (Quiet . . . silence for about 30 seconds.)

(*continued*)

Table 2. *(Continued)*

39. This completes the formal relaxation procedure. Now explore your body from your feet up. Make sure that every muscle is relaxed. Say slowly—first your toes, your feet, your legs, buttocks, stomach, shoulder, neck, eyes, and finally your forehead—all should be relaxed now. (Quiet . . . silence for about 10 seconds). Just lie there and feel very relaxed, noticing the warmness of the relaxation. (Pause.) I would like you to stay this way for about one more minute, and then I am going to count to five. When I reach five, I want you to open your eyes feeling very calm and refreshed. (Quiet—silence for about one minute.) Okay, when I count to five I want you to open your eyes feeling very calm and refreshed. One . . . feeling very calm; Two . . . very calm, very refreshed; Three . . . very refreshed; Four . . . and Five.

Source: Adapted in part from Jacobson (1938), Rimm (1967, personal communication), and Wolpe and Lazarus (1966). Reprinted from R. J. Morris and T. R. Kratochwill, *Treating Children's Fears and Phobias: A Behavioral Approach*. New York: Pergamon Press, 1983, 135–36.

archy for each fear or phobia that they agree is in need of change. Most hierarchies consist of approximately 20 to 25 items, although it is not uncommon for some hierarchies that represent complex fears (e.g., fear of evaluation) to contain more items.

Even the length of hierarchies that seemingly relate to the same fear in different school children may vary between the children. For example, in some children the number and type of people present in a situation, temporal and/or spatial features, type of setting(s) involved, level of embarrassment a child might experience in the fear situation, and the degree to which a child feels he or she can escape from the fear situation without being noticed by others are all factors that can affect the length of a hierarchy (Morris & Kratochwill, 1983).

The systematic desensitization phase proper begins after the child has gained proficiency at relaxing on command and the hierarchy has been completed. The child is asked to imagine scenes from the hierarchy as clearly and vividly as possible while maintaining a calm, relaxed state. Items on the hierarchy are presented in ascending order, starting with the lowest feared item.

As mentioned earlier, systematic desensitization is the most frequently used procedure for fear reduction in children (see, for example, Graziano *et al.*, 1979; Morris & Kratochwill, 1985; Ollendick, 1979). In terms of supportive research, Mann and Rosenthal (1969) compared children in a no-treatment control group with those receiving direct (systematic) or vicarious (children observing other children in treatment) desensitization in individual and in group treatment settings. Compared to the control group, the treatment groups experienced a significant improvement in reading and a significant reduction in self-reported test anxiety. However, no significant differences were found between the individual or group, direct or vicarious desensitization methods. This latter finding may have implications for school personnel who frequently must deal with children in groups.

Individual systematic desensitization has also been reported to reduce effectively school phobic behavior (e.g., Lazarus, 1960; Miller *et al.*, 1972a; Taylor, 1972). For example, Taylor (1972) reported the successful use of systematic desensitization with a 15-year-old female "school phobic." The case was particularly interesting because the girl engaged in excessive urination during school-related activities that contributed to her avoiding school and withdrawing from social relationships. Four months after desensitization with hierarchies related to riding the school bus, being in school, and participating in class activities, she was experiencing satisfactory relationships in school and no urinary frequency problem.

Variations of Systematic Desensitization

Several variations of systematic desensitization have been developed—many of which have been used, or could be adapted easily, in an educational setting. In *group systematic desensitization* the phases used in individual systematic desensitization are adapted for administration in groups that typically include five to eight people. The fear hierarchy may be entirely developed by the group, or the therapist may provide a list of potential items from which the group may develop an appropriate hierarchy. The desensitization stage proper is generally geared to the slowest progressing person in the group.

In fact, several studies have addressed the effectiveness of group systematic desensitization in the school setting, with a number of these studies focusing on the treatment of test anxiety (e.g., Barabasz, 1973, 1975; Deffenbacher & Kemper, 1974a,b; Kondas, 1967; Laxer, Quarter, Kooman, & Walker, 1969). Each, though using different dependent measures, reported group systematic desensitization to be effective. In one study (Barabasz, 1975), elementary school teachers were trained to administer the desensitization procedure with an automated relaxation method in the regular classroom. Students considered to be highly test anxious showed greater academic gains after treatment than did those in the control and low-anxious treatment groups (Barabasz, 1973, 1975). Muller and Madsen (1970) found that anxious seventh graders with reading problems who were placed in a desensitization or placebo condition showed greater improvement on self-report measures of anxiety than did students in the control condition, but no significant differences were found on reading achievement or teacher ratings. Johnson, Tyler, Thompson, and Jones (1971) also found group systematic desensitization to be as effective as a speech practice/rehearsal condition in reducing the self-report speech anxiety scores of speech anxious middle school children. Cradock, Cotler, and Jason (1978), on the other hand, did not find group desensitization to reduce public speaking anxiety in "high risk" ninth grade girls.

In vivo systematic desensitization involves the exposure of the child to items on the fear hierarchy in the actual situation rather than only in the imagination. The feelings of comfort, security, and trust that emerge out of the therapeutic relationship are used as the counterconditioning agent, instead of relaxation training. The child is encouraged by the therapist, who enters the real-life situations with the child, to go through each item on the hierarchy.

O'Reilly (1971) combined *in vivo* desensitization with an alternative competing response notion with a 6-year-old girl who refused to go to school because she was afraid of the school fire bell. A tape of children's songs and stories was played in the girl's classroom while a tape recording of the school's fire bell was gradually introduced (from barely audible to normal volume). This is similar to the procedure used by Jones (1924) in the treatment of a 3-year-old child who was afraid of a rabbit, in which the boy's eating of food was paired with gradually introducing the rabbit closer and closer to him. In addition, the O'Reilly and Jones studies were conducted in settings where there were other fearless children.

Another variation, *automated systematic desensitization*, allows the client to set the appropriate pace through the desensitization process. Desensitization takes place by the client visualizing scenes from the fear hierarchy, which have been previously recorded on audio tape by the therapist. In a variation of this method called *self-directed desensitization*, the client not only conducts the procedure at his or her own pace, but also develops the treatment program with only minimal help from the therapist. In this procedure, the client typically uses instructional materials developed by the therapist to design the treatment package.

Automated systematic desensitization was used by Wish, Hasazi, and Jurgela (1973) with an 11-year-old boy who had a fear of loud noises. A tape of the child's favorite music with sounds from the fear hierarchy superimposed was utilized in the desensitization phase proper, with the child gradually increasing the volume over the 8-day treatment period. This study, though, appears to be one of the few involving automated systematic desensitization with children.

Emotive imagery was first used by Lazarus and Abramovitz (1962) to adapt the desensitization phase proper for use with children. The procedure begins with development of a fear hierarchy followed by identification of the child's favorite superhero. The child is not asked to imagine himself or herself in the feared situation, but instead the therapist weaves a story about the superhero's increasingly bold involvement with the feared situation, until the highest item on the hierarchy is reached without indications of anxiety. Boyd (1980) reported the successful use of emotive imagery in the reduction of a 16-year-old mentally handicapped boy's school phobia.

Contact desensitization, developed by Ritter (1968, 1969a,b), combines elements of both systematic desensitization and modeling approaches. In this procedure, the therapist first models the particular step on the hierarchy, and then guides the client through physical touch and verbal encouragement in performing the same step. As the client progresses, the therapist gradually withdraws the prompts, until the client can complete each step without assistance.

Ritter (1968) compared contact desensitization and modeling to a no-treatment control condition and found that the two treatment conditions were superior to the no-treatment control condition, and that the subjects in the contact desensitization group improved more than did the subjects in the modeling group. In a later study, Ritter (1969a) found that contact desensitization was superior to a contact desensitization condition that did not include therapist touch. Murphy and Bootzin (1973) also reported the successful use of contact desensitization. McReynolds and Morris (1986) used a contact desensitization procedure for the treatment of a mentally retarded child's severe dog phobia. The child's fear was so pervasive that he would not leave the school bus during field trips because he was afraid that he might come in contact with a dog. The authors found that contact desensitization was effective in reducing the child's fear and that the treatment effects (a) generalized to dogs other than the treatment dog and to settings other than the treatment settings, and (b) were maintained over a 7-month follow-up period.

Finally, in *self-control desensitization,* the child is taught to cope with anxiety and tension (Goldfried, 1971; Meichenbaum & Genest, 1980). Based on the view that clients will not always be able to escape or avoid a situation that arouses fear or tension, the therapist does not ask the child to stop imagining an item on the hierarchy when anxiety is indicated. Instead, the child is encouraged to continue imagining the scene that produces anxiety and to "relax away" the anxiety, or to imagine becoming fearful and then coping with the associated feelings of anxiety and tenseness. A paucity of research exists that supports the efficacy of this procedure in either clinic or school settings (e.g., Bornstein & Knapp, 1981; Morris & Kratochwill, 1983).

General Considerations

There appear to be a substantial number of controlled and uncontrolled studies that support the relative effectiveness of systematic desensitization and its variations. Those procedures that seem to have the most research to support their effectiveness regarding school-related fears and phobias are individual and group systematic desensitization and contact desensitization. Several factors, however, still need to be studied to determine their contribution to treatment outcome. These factors include the following: the age of the child receiving treatment, the child's level of visual imagery, the child's ability to relax, ability to follow instructions, level of acquiescence, and the child's threshold for fatigue (see, for example, Kissel, 1972). Regarding the age factor, there are very few studies that report the successful use of systematic desensitization with children under 9 years of age, so that the therapist treating a young child may wish to choose from those variations that have been successfully utilized with preschool and early elementary school-age children (e.g., *in vivo* and contact desensitization). Regarding the other factors, Morris and Kratochwill (1983) discussed several methods for their evaluation.

In addition, particular variations may be preferred by a therapist working in a school setting. For example, school personnel seldom have the time available that would be necessary to conduct individual therapy with large numbers of students who fear evaluations, taking tests, or giving classroom presentations, and therefore may prefer a group-treatment procedure. In comparison to a therapist outside the school setting, the therapist treating a school-related fear in the school environment may also have better access to the actual fear stimuli necessary to conduct *in vivo* or contact desensitization.

Flooding Therapies

Like systematic desensitization, flooding therapies utilize imaginal presentation of anxiety related material, but unlike systematic desensitization, these methods provide intense and prolonged exposure to frightening imaginal situations (Morris & Kratochwill, 1983). The goal is actually to have the child imagine a fearful experience of such magnitude that continued exposure to the image will result in reduction of the fear associated with that particular event, object, or activity, rather than heighten it. Implosive therapy and flooding therapy are the two major types of flooding therapies that have been discussed in the fear literature.

Implosive therapy, developed by Stampfl (Stampfl, 1961; Stampfl & Levis, 1967) utilizes principles from both learning and psychoanalytic theories. Stampfl maintains that fears and their associated anxiety are learned, and can best be unlearned through a method based on an extinction model. Here, extinction refers to the gradual reduction of a person's feelings of anxiety, as a result of continued exposure to the feared situation in the absence of the reinforcement that perpetuates the fear.

Through consultation with the child and other appropriate persons, the therapist first develops hypotheses about the aspects of the child's life that are contributing to the maintenance of a particular fear or phobia. For example, in the school phobic child these cues might include the sight of the school bus or school building, teacher(s), taking a test, being called upon in class, or hearing school-related noises. Whereas these are situational events that can be identified, the remaining cues are formulated by the therapist, based on psychodynamic theory. According to Stampfl and Levis (1967), these latter cues are usually related to themes of aggression and hostility, oral and anal activity, sexual activity, punishment, rejection, bodily injury, loss of impulse control, and guilt. In addition, it is also these internal dynamic cues that are placed highest on the fear hierarchy that the therapist develops. The purpose, therefore, of this latter hierarchy is to identify scenes for the child that can

> reproduce in the absence of physical pain, as good an approximation as possible, the sights, sounds, and tactual experiences originally present in the primary . . . situation in which the fear was learned. (Stampfl & Levis, 1967, p. 33)

The client is not asked to accept the accuracy of the imagined scenes, nor to agree that they are representative of the actual fear.

Smith and Sharpe (1970) used implosion therapy with a 13-year-old school phobic boy. After the first treatment session, the boy attended his math class the next day and experienced only moderate anxiety. By the end of the sixth session, he attended school full time and reported no anxiety. These results were also found to be maintained at a 13-week follow-up evaluation. Few other studies have been published using this procedure on school-related fears and phobias, although some research has appeared in the literature involving the treatment of fears outside of the school setting (e.g., Handler, 1972; Hersen, 1968; Ollendick & Gruen, 1972).

One variation of implosive therapy is flooding therapy, which also involves intense and prolonged imaginal exposure to frightening events and situations. In this procedure, though, the therapist does not use psychodynamic cues in the formulation of the scenes (Morris, 1986). Instead, only the feared external stimuli are used to prevent the scenes although the scenes are vividly described in a way similar to implosive therapy. An interesting alternative to imaginal flooding is *in vivo* flooding (e.g., Blagg & Yule, 1984; Kandel, Ayllon, & Rosenbaum, 1977; Yule, Sacks, & Jersov, 1974), in which the client is systematically exposed to an exaggerated version of the feared event or object. For example, Kandel *et al.* (1977) worked with two children who had extreme social withdrawal. One boy was an 8-year-old who exhibited bizarre ritualistic behaviors, whereas the other boy was a 4-year-old described as extremely anxious, hyperactive, and aggressive. Treatment consisted of exposing both children to school peers within play situations in the school environment. The results showed an increase in the levels of interaction of the boys as well as the maintenance of their interactional levels at follow-up.

Blagg and Yule (1984) also reported the successful use of this procedure with school refusal children. Specifically, they report that their *in vivo* flooding procedure (consisting of numerous components in addition to the typical *in vivo* flooding method) was significantly more effective in reducing school refusal in preadolescent and adolescent children than either hospital-based inpatient treatment or home tutoring and psychotherapy treatment. This study, however, has a number of methodological problems that preclude drawing any firm conclusions.

General Considerations

Several factors should be considered before choosing to use flooding-related therapies with children. First, with regard to implosive therapy, the therapist should be quite familiar with psychodynamic theory, especially psychoanalytic therapy. Second, because the visual images the child is asked to maintain are initially stress enhancing, some clinicians may be reluctant to use these methods if other appropriate procedures are available (Gelfand, 1978). For example, Gelfand (1978) suggested that the child may find the treatment too aversive, and may refuse to cooperate. Others contend that the therapist must be sensitive to the needs of the client, so that the person may develop sufficient trust and confidence in the therapist in order to associate the anxiety-provoking experience with the feared object or event and not the therapist (Ullmann & Krasner, 1969, 1975). Another consideration has to do with the paucity of research on the use of these therapies with children who have school and non-school-related fears. In addition, virtually no research has been published to date on such client factors as the age of the child, the child's level of visual imagery, or the client's threshold for fatigue. These considerations lead us to the recommendation that these therapies should be used with the utmost caution in the treatment of school-related fears and phobias.

Contingency Management Procedures

The use of contingency management procedures has its roots in the writings of Pavlov (e.g., Pavlov, 1927), Skinner (e.g., Skinner, 1938, 1953), and Watson (e.g., Watson, 1913). In this section we discuss those contingency management procedures most frequently used in the treatment of children's school-related fears, phobias, and associated problems.

Positive Reinforcement

One contingency management procedure that has received considerable attention regarding its application to school-related problems is positive reinforcement. Generally, a positive reinforcer is something that immediately follows a particular behavior and strengthens the number of times it occurs. Positive reinforcement has been used alone and in combination with other behavior therapy procedures in reducing various school-related fears. For example, Sluckin and Jehu (1969) used reinforcement to treat a selectively mute 4-year, 11-month girl who would speak to her mother, but was extremely fearful of strangers. In this case, a social worker visited the home and reinforced the child's talking as the mother was gradually faded out of the home.

In another case, Williamson, Jewell, Sanders, Haney, and White (1977) treated a boy with reluctant speech by utilizing a token reinforcement system. The boy earned tokens contingent on his verbalizations directed toward peers during recess. These tokens were later exchanged for a class party and various privileges, such as being first in line. Williamson *et al.* reported that the child's speech increased and was maintained at a one-year follow-up evaluation. A more extensive discussion of this study, as well as other literature on the treatment of selective mutism in school settings can be found in Kratochwill (1981).

Positive reinforcement procedures have also been used to treat social withdrawal in the school setting, and a comprehensive review of the literature may be found in Conger and Keane (1981). One representative example of the use of positive reinforcement in treating social withdrawal is the procedure used by Simkins (1971). In this study eight girls were assigned points contingent on their interaction with peers. It was found that combining the point system with positive social reinforcement (e.g., praise and attention), special incentives, and instructions, produced significantly greater improvement in social interaction with peers than did the point system alone.

Another school-related fear that has been treated with positive reinforcement procedures is school phobia. To increase the generalization of treatment effects, studies in the area have focused on reinforcement by persons other than the therapist (Trueman, 1984). In this regard, parents and school personnel may be trained to provide the positive reinforcers. For example, Vaal (1973) used a contingency contracting system in which a 13-year-old boy was allowed to engage in various privileges and activities (e.g., attending a basketball game, going bowling) if he met certain target criteria for school attendance that had been agreed on by the child, school personnel, and parents. Edlund (1971) treated a 7-year-old girl who would run away from school and would become extremely disruptive when she did remain in class. Treatment consisted of the parents administering a variety of social, material, and activity reinforcers, contingent upon the teacher's report of appropriate school behavior. Vaal (1973) suggested that privileges already available to the child, regardless of his school attendance should be made available contingent on acceptable behavior during the school day. In fact, Hsia (1984) reported a case in which the mother took the television and stereo to work and locked up the child's bicycle so that enjoyment of these items was made contingent on successful school attendance.

Variations of this positive reinforcement procedure have also been used to treat school phobia. For example, Patterson (1965) used a procedure in which a 7-year-old boy was reinforced in a play situation for making fearless verbal statements about a male doll and not being afraid of being separated from his mother. The mother then reinforced the boy for being away from her. By the ninth session, a visiting teacher was introduced to help the child with his reading. This teacher later accompanied him to school, and then gradually withdrew her involvement until the child was able to ride the school bus and attend school by himself. Positive reinforcement in the form of praise and encouragement was provided by the parents as well as the therapist and teacher. Another variation of the positive reinforcement procedure has been to combine its use with *in vivo* desensitization (e.g., Lazarus, Davison, & Polefka, 1965) or *in vivo* flooding (e.g., Blagg & Yule, 1984) in the natural school setting.

Shaping

In some cases children may not respond to positive reinforcement because the desired approach behavior is too complex for them to master. In these cases, the therapist might consider the use of shaping, in which the child is taught to master the desired behavior in small successive steps. Several studies have reported the effective use of shaping procedures in the treatment of school phobia and selective mutism. In one study, Tahmisian and McReynolds (1971) used shaping to reduce the school phobia of a 13-year-old girl who had previously been treated with systematic desensitization, which was reported to have been ineffective in helping her to attend school. The shaping procedure involved having the parent initially walk around school with the girl after school hours and then later during school hours. This gradually led to her attending one class alone, and finally all of her classes, with reinforcement made contingent on completion of the increasingly more demanding tasks. Brown, Copeland, and Hall (1974) used an elementary school principal to explain and administer a shaping procedure to an 11-year-old school phobic boy. In this case, the boy could initially earn points, which could be traded for tickets to football games, for remaining in the school hall, and then later for attending classes for increasingly longer periods of time.

Rosenbaum and Kellman (1973) also utilized school personnel in the successful treatment of a third grade girl who had remained selectively mute in the school setting. During the initial phase, a speech therapist reinforced the child with M&Ms and praise, for verbalizations in a one-to-one setting. In the second phase, the teacher and peers gradually entered the individual room in the presence of the girl's speech, and in the final phase the girl was encouraged to expand the group by inviting other children from her class to speech sessions. After the entire class had been invited, the girl verbally responded to a question asked in front of the entire class. Bednar (1974), Rasbury (1974), and Semenoff, Park, and Smith (1976) have also reported the successful use of shaping to reduce children's selective mutism.

In another study involving shaping procedures, Luiselli (1978) worked with a 7-year-old boy diagnosed as autistic who was afraid to ride the school bus by himself. In this case, the child was first reinforced for sitting on the bus with his mother while it was parked at school and then for riding the bus with his mother and therapist. The boy next rode without the mother, and subsequently without the therapist. Treatment was reported to last seven days, with continuation of the bus riding behavior one year later.

Extinction

There are times when a child's fear response is maintained by the reinforcement the child receives for exhibiting such responses. Extinction refers to the removal of reinforcing consequences that follow a response. For successful utilization of this procedure within a school or other setting, the therapist must be able to determine (a) when the reinforcing consequences occur, (b) the relative contribution of these consequences to the frequency of the child's fear response, and (c) whether the reinforcing consequences can be reasonably modified (Morris & Kratochwill, 1983). For example, one common reinforcing consequence of fear behavior is increased attention from parents, teachers, school support personnel, and/or peers.

In one study, Hersen (1970) determined that the parents of a 12 ½-year-old school phobic boy were inadvertently reinforcing the child's school phobia by coaxing and cajoling him for approximately 2 hours to attend school. In the three-part treatment procedure, the mother was first taught to (a) ignore the child's crying, and be firm about him attending school, (b) reward him with praise for school-related coping behaviors, and (c) be aware that he might show other school-related avoidance behavior that should also be placed on extinction. Hersen also found that the school counselor reinforced the child's phobia by providing attention to the boy's crying and anxiety. The counselor was therefore asked to limit his contacts with the child to 5 minutes per visit and to firmly insist that the boy return to class. Finally, the therapist worked with the boy individually to (a) reinforce school-coping responses, (b) extinguish inappropriate school-related responses through inattention, and (c) provide the child an opportunity to express his views. The results showed that following treatment the boy was attending school full time and that his academic performance had returned to its prephobia level. A 6-month follow-up evaluation revealed that these results were maintained. A number of other case studies have also been published in which extinction has been used alone or combined with positive reinforcement to reduce school avoidance (e.g., Ayllon, Smith, & Rogers, 1979; Cooper, 1973; Doleys & Williams, 1977; Hsia, 1984).

Stimulus Fading

When a child is able to perform a target behavior in one setting or under certain conditions, but not in other settings, some writers have advocated the use of stimulus fading. In this procedure, as the child performs the target behavior the characteristics of the setting are gradually changed. For example, Lipton (1980) worked with a girl who had a complete absence of speech in kindergarten. First, the child's verbal behavior was shaped through a series of exercises and games with a speech therapist in a room away from the classroom. Gradually, treatment was moved from the therapy room to the school library, and then to the classroom where the girl subsequently engaged in appropriate conversation. In another case, Wulbert, Nyman, Snow, and Owen (1973) combined stimulus fading with a time-out procedure to teach a selectively mute 6-year-old girl to verbalize to persons other than her parents. The authors concluded that this combined procedure was an effective treatment package for modifying selective mutism. As Kratochwill (1981) noted, however, no data are presented by the authors that indicate that normal verbal responding was achieved in the school setting. Others have also reported the successful use of stimulus fading for the treatment of selective mutism (e.g., Clayton, 1981; Conrad, Delk, & Williams, 1974; Reid *et al.*, 1976).

Stimulus fading has also been used for the treatment of separation anxiety. For example, Neisworth, Madles, and Goeke (1975) treated a 4-year-old preschool girl by instructing the mother to stay in the preschool for several sessions before being gradually faded out. At the same time, school personnel reinforced the child for participation in school activities, with treatment lasting 18 hours over an 8-day period.

General Considerations

The contingency management approach to reduction of children's fears and phobias emphasizes the causal relationship between the child's observable behavior and various environmental stimuli (Morris & Kratochwill, 1983). Successful treatment therefore requires the accurate analysis of those factors that contribute to the low rate of approach behavior, and subsequently, the successful manipulation of those factors in order to increase the frequency of the desired behavior. Maintenance of the behavior may then be enhanced through the provision of positive consequences.

It is particularly interesting to note that although the range of children's fears and phobias that have been investigated using the contingency management approach is quite narrow, the overriding majority of the available published studies involve fear behaviors often associated with the school environment. These include school phobia, social withdrawal, and selective mutism.

Modeling

Behavior change that results from observation of another person has been typically referred to as modeling (e.g., Bandura, 1969; Kazdin & Wilson, 1978). The modeling procedure in general consists of an individual called the model (e.g., therapist, parent, peer, sibling) and a person called the observer (i.e., the fearful child). The observer typically watches the model engage in the behavior that is fearful to the observer. Positive behavior change in the observer appears to be enhanced if the model is observed to experience positive and/or safe consequences with the feared situation, event, or object (Perry & Furukawa, 1980). Thus it would be inappropriate to have a socially withdrawn or selectively mute child observe his or her peers modeling interactive behaviors during a time when their teacher was making critical or negative remarks about such interactions. The therapists must therefore be certain that a child can (a) attend to the various aspects of the modeling situation, (b) retain what has been learned in the modeling situation, (c) reproduce motorically or match what has been observed, and (d) be motivated to perform the observed behavior. Most writers also agree with Bandura (1971) that the model's approach to the fear stimulus should be performed in a graduated fashion and with confidence. The two distinct categories of modeling to be discussed are *live modeling* and *symbolic modeling*.

Live modeling involves the actual or live demonstration of a model's approach behavior toward the feared situation. Few studies have been published using this procedure with children and even fewer have appeared involving children with school-related fears and phobias (Morris & Kratochwill, 1983). In one study, however, Mann and Rosenthal (1969) compared the effectiveness of direct systematic desensitization and modeled desensitization in group and individual situations. Students in the study were seventh and eighth graders referred by a counselor for test anxiety. Some children were desensitized individually while they were observed by a peer, and others were desensitized in a group and also observed by a group of peers. In addition, there was a condition in which a group of children observed a peer desensitized individually, and a no-treatment control situation. All of the treatment procedures produced significantly better self-report scores and performance on test-taking samples than the no-treatment condition. In another study, Matson (1981) reported the successful use of participant modeling with mentally retarded children who had a fear of adult strangers.

In the symbolic modeling procedure, the modeling activity is presented either through film, videotape, or imagination. One illustrative example of the use of this procedure is a study by O'Connor (1969), in which 13 socially withdrawn preschool children were each individually shown either a 23-minute modeling film or a 20-minute control film of Marineland dolphins. The results showed that children who watched the modeling film exhibited an increased level of social interaction, whereas children in the control condition showed no such change. Later, O'Connor (1972) found that socially withdrawn children treated with shaping (reinforcement) alone, filmed modeling only, or a combination of shaping and filmed modeling, all demonstrated increased social interaction. However, only the increased interaction among the children exposed to the modeling or combined modeling and shaping condition was stable over time. Using the O'Connor (1969) film, Evers and Schwarz (1973) reported that modeling alone and modeling plus teacher reinforcement conditions produced similar increases in social interaction at posttest and follow-up. Evers-Pasquale and Sherman (1975) and Keller and Carlson (1974) have also reported the successful use of symbolic modeling in reducing children's social withdrawal. Symbolic modeling has also been used effectively in the reduction of non-school-related fears and uncooperative behavior (e.g., Klorman, Hilpert, Michael, LaGana, & Sveen, 1980; Melamed & Siegel, 1975; Melamed, Hawes, Hiegy, & Glick, 1975; Melamed, Yurcheson, Fleece, Hutcherson, & Hawes, 1978) and medical procedures

(Melamed & Siegel, 1975; Vernon & Bailey, 1974).

In addition, several variations in the modeling procedure, as well as combined procedures involving modeling, have been reported in the fear and phobia literature. For example, Whitehall, Hersen, and Bellack (1980) combined instruction, live modeling, behavior rehearsal, performance feedback, and programmed generalization to create a training package to teach conversational behavior to socially isolated children. Morris and Dolker (1974) and Strain, Shores, and Timm (1977), on the other hand, used positive reinforcement and modeling to increase social interaction and cooperative play in socially withdrawn handicapped children.

There is little doubt from the modeling literature that this procedure is an effective means of reducing children's fears and phobias. For school-related fears and phobias, however, the relative effectiveness and efficiency of this procedure has not yet been clearly demonstrated. One of the problems has been the rather narrow range of school-related fears that have been studied using this procedure—the majority of the studies involving the modification of social withdrawal and/or social interaction. Nevertheless, this appears to be a potentially useful procedure and merits much more extensive research.

Self-Control

Self-control can be conceptualized as a treatment strategy in which the therapist teaches the client how, when, and where to use various cognitions in the learning or modification of certain behavior patterns (Kanfer, 1980; Richards & Siegel, 1978). To this end, the "therapist serves as a consultant and expert who negotiates with the client in how to go about change and to what end" (Kanfer, 1980, p. 336). In the area of fear reduction, the focus is on helping the child develop specific thinking skills that can be applied whenever the child is confronted with a particular fear stimulus.

According to Meichenbaum and Genest (1980) the self-control approach involves helping the child:

> (1) become aware of the negative thinking styles that impede performance and that lead to emotional upset and inadequate performance; (2) generate, in collaboration with the trainer, a set of incompatible, specific self-statements, rules, strategies, and so on, which the trainee can then employ; and (3) learn specific adaptive, cognitive and behavior skills. (p. 403)

This demands that the child be aware of the fear or phobia and be able to identify the various motoric, cognitive, and physiological components involved, as well as the conditions that cause the fear (Morris & Kratochwill, 1983). In addition, it demands that the child be able to generate with the therapist a series of incompatible self-statements and rules and be able to apply them in fearful situations (Morris & Kratochwill, 1983).

The first study to demonstrate the relative effectiveness of a self-control procedure was conducted on children's fear of the dark (e.g., Kanfer, Karoly, & Newman, 1975). Fox and Houston (1981) later studied the efficacy of self-instructional training for reducing fear in an analogue evaluative situation in fourth-grade children. Interestingly, in this latter study, subjects who revealed high trait anxiety at pretest and were exposed to the self-instructional training procedure reported and were observed to exhibit more anxiety at the posttest than were those who received either a minimal-treatment or no-treatment control condition.

In another study, test anxious tenth-grade students were taught to recognize inappropriate responses, and replace self-defeating thoughts and self-statements with more positive alternatives (Leal, Baxter, Martin, & Marx, 1981). The effectiveness of this procedure was compared with systematic desensitization and a waiting-list control condition. Self-reported anxiety was significantly reduced in the cognitive modification treatment, whereas the systematic desensitization treatment produced improved performance in the test situation. Leal *et al.* (1981) suggested, however, that because of differences between the two groups in terms of posttest within-group variability, treatment conclusions cannot be drawn from their study. Their finding, on the other hand, of a reduction in self-reported test anxiety is consistent with those obtained with college students (e.g., Holroyd, 1976; Meichenbaum, 1972).

Warren, Deffenbacher, and Brading (1976) also reported decreased self-reported test anxiety in fifth- and sixth-grade students treated with a cognitively focused program, but also failed to find differences between the treatment and no-treatment groups on measures of general anxiety and task performance.

General Considerations

At present, no definitive statements can be made about the use of various self-control strategies in the treatment of children's school-related fears, but given its potential for group application, further well-controlled studies are needed. It may also be that this procedure is particularly appropriate to the classroom setting, which is by nature an instructional setting, but this point also needs further research.

Table 3. Behavior Therapy Procedures Used to Modify Specific School-Related Fears and Phobias

Fear/phobia	Procedure
Test anxiety	Systematic desensitization Group systematic desensitization Modeling Self-control
Public speaking	Systematic desensitization Group systematic desensitization Self-control
Social withdrawal/ social isolation	Positive reinforcement Symbolic modeling Symbolic modeling plus shaping *In vivo* flooding
School phobia	Systematic desensitization *In vivo* desensitization Emotive imagery *In vivo* flooding Implosion therapy Contingency contract Positive reinforcement Shaping Shaping plus extinction
Selective mutism	Positive reinforcement Stimulus fading plus shaping Stimulus fading plus extinction
Separation anxiety	Stimulus fading Stimulus fading plus shaping *In vivo* desensitization
Other: Reading, math anxiety	Systematic desensitization Group desensitization Self-control

Summary and Conclusions

This chapter has presented an overview of the definitions, incidence, diagnosis, and behavioral assessment of school-related fears and phobias, and has provided a review of the five major behavior therapy approaches to the treatment of these school-related behavior problems. Without question the desensitization procedures have been used the most on various school-related fears and phobias, followed next by the use of contingency management and modeling procedures. The procedures that have the least research to support their relative efficacy are the flooding therapies and self-control treatment. Nevertheless, as shown in Table 3, a number of different procedures have been shown in the literature to be useful in the reduction of school-related fears and phobias—with some procedures used more regularly for particular fears. In addition, Table 3 shows that some school-related fears have been researched more heavily than others. For example, it seems clear that school phobia, test anxiety, and social withdrawal have received more attention in the literature than have other school-related fears and phobias.

Major empirical questions are still present regarding school-related fears and phobias. First, although a number of researchers have attempted to determine the incidence and prevalence of general childhood fears and phobias, there has been relatively little research regarding the types, frequency, and intensity of school-related fears and phobias. Little is currently known about the degree to which either fear-related conditions or their subsequent reduction affect academic performance, participation in extracurricular activities, or general school adjustment.

Of the major behavioral fear reduction methods, only systematic desensitization and self-control procedures have been associated with well-controlled research in the school environment. More research, however, is still needed on these procedures because the studies on the effectiveness of these procedures have generally included subjects who were not clinically fearful or anxious, so that generalization to the most severely fearful or anxious students cannot be assumed. Modeling procedures have also been associated with well-controlled research concerning clinically fearful target behaviors, but the scope of this research has been very restricted—typically to fear of dental and medical treatment—rather than centering on school-related fears. Contingency management is also a promising method for use by school personnel, but well-controlled studies utilizing this procedure are relatively rare. Most of the studies are uncontrolled case presentations. No clear statement, therefore, about the relative effectiveness of these procedures can be made at this time.

Another factor to be considered in the evaluation of the effectiveness of each of these methods is the nature of the dependent variables assessed in the efficacy research and the lack of inclusion in research studies of the triple response mode assessment procedure. For example, one method may produce improvement on self-report measures but on no other response channel, another method may produce changes on the motoric channel but no other channels, and so forth. The therapist, in choosing a treatment method, must therefore make a decision about which fear response channel or combination of response channels impact most significantly upon the child's general functioning, and there is currently little research or scholarly writing to assist a therapist in making this decision.

Still to be answered, too, is the question of the conditions under which particular treatment methods are most effective. Conditions that may influence the outcome of a given procedure include the child's age, the type of therapist, the availability of parent and/or teacher support, the setting, and the nature of the fear or phobia.

Another question that still needs to be answered has to do with choosing a treatment method that is cost-effective. School personnel may find the time investment necessary for conducting individual systematic desensitization or the financial investment associated with symbolic modeling to be prohibitive. On the other hand, the therapist in a school setting may find *in vivo* therapy methods far more feasible and cost-effective than would the private clinician.

Related to the cost-effectiveness issue is the issue of fear or anxiety prevention. School environments may provide opportunities for primary prevention of fear-related disorders, but there is currently no research published that uses the various fear reduction methods in a preventative manner on school-related fears and phobias.

Although many questions still remain to be answered regarding the efficacy of fear reduction methods used in the school setting, there has been some very active research conducted on these procedures over the past 15 years, and the methods appear promising.

References

Achenbach, T. M. (1974). *Developmental psychopathology.* New York: Ronald Press.

Achenbach, T. M., & Edelbrock, C. S. (1978). The classification of child psychopathology: A review and analysis of empirical efforts. *Psychological Bulletin, 85,* 1275–1301.

Adams, H. E., Doster, J. A., & Calhoun, K. S. (1977). A psychologically based system of response classification. In A. R. Ciminero, K. A. Calhoun, & H. E. Adams (Eds.), *Handbook of behavioral assessment* (pp. 47–98). New York: Wiley Interscience.

American Psychiatric Association. (1987). *Diagnostic and statistical manual of mental disorders* (3rd ed., revised). Washington, DC: Author.

Angelino, H., & Shedd, C. (1953). Shifts in the content of fears and worries relative to chronological age. *Proceedings of the Oklahoma Academy of Science, 34,* 180–186.

Angelino, H., Dollins, J., & Mech, E. V. (1956). Trends in the "fears and worries" of school children as related to socioeconomic status and age. *Journal of Genetic Psychology, 89,* 263–276.

Ayllon, T., Smith, D., & Rogers, M. (1979). Behavioral management of school phobia. *Journal of Behavioral Therapy and Experimental Psychiatry, 1,* 125–138.

Bamber, J. H. (1974). The fears of adolescents. *Journal of Genetic Psychology, 125,* 127–140.

Bandura, A. (1969). *Principles of behavior modification.* New York: Holt, Rinehart, & Winston.

Bandura, A. (1971). Psychotherapy based upon modeling principles. In A. E. Bergin & S. L. Garfield (Eds.), *Handbook of psychotherapy and behavior change* (pp. 653–708). New York: Wiley.

Bandura, A. (1977). *Social learning theory.* Englewood Cliffs, NJ: Prentice-Hall.

Baker, H., & Willis, U. (1978). School phobia: Classification and treatment. *British Journal of Psychiatry, 132,* 492–499.

Barabasz, A. F. (1973). Group desensitization of test anxiety in elementary schools. *Journal of Psychology, 83,* 295–301.

Barabasz, A. F. (1975). Classroom teachers as paraprofessional therapists in group systematic desensitization of test anxiety. *Psychiatry, 38,* 385–392.

Barrios, B. A., & Shigetomi, C. C. (1980). Coping skills training: Potential for prevention of fears and anxieties. *Behavior Therapy, 11,* 431–439.

Barrios, B. A., & Shigetomi, C. C. (1985). Behavioral assessment of children's fears: A critical review. In T. R. Kratochwill (Ed.), *Advances in school psychology* (Vol. 4, pp. 89–132). Hillsdale, NJ: Erlbaum.

Barrios, B. A., Hartmann, D. P., & Shigetomi, C. C. (1981). Fears and anxieties in children. In E. J. Mash & L. G. Terdal (Eds.), *Behavioral assessment of childhood disorders* (pp. 259–304). New York: Guilford Press.

Bednar, R. A. (1974). A behavioral approach to treating elective mutism in the school. *Journal of School Psychology, 12,* 326–337.

Bellack, A. S., & Hersen, M. (1977a). *Behavior modification: An introductory textbook.* Baltimore, MD: Williams & Wilkinson.

Bellack, A. S., & Hersen, M. (1977b). The use of self-report inventories in behavioral assessment. In J. D. Cone & R. P. Hawkins (Eds.), *Behavioral assessment: New directions in clinical psychology* (pp. 52–76). New York: Bruner/Mazel.

Bellack, A. S., & Hersen, M. (1977b). The use of self-report inventories in behavioral assessment. In J. D. Cone & R. P. Hawkins (Eds.), *Behavioral assessment: New directions in clinical psychology* (pp. 52–76). New York: Bruner/Mazel.

Bergan, J. R. (1977) *Behavior consultation.* Columbus, OH: Merrill.

Bernstein, D. A., & Nietzel, M. T. (1973). Procedural variation in behavioral avoidance tests. *Journal of Consulting and Clinical Psychology, 41,* 165–174.

Bernstein, D. A., & Nietzel, M. T. (1974). Behavioral avoidance tests: The effects of demand characteristics and repeated measures on two types of subjects. *Behavior Therapy, 5,* 184–192.

Bersoff, D. N., & Grieger, R. M. (1971). An interview model for the psychosituational assessment of children's behavior. *American Journal of Orthopsychiatry, 41,* 483–493.

Blagg, N. R., & Yule, W. (1984). The behavioral treatment of school refusal—A comparative study. *Behavior Research and Therapy, 22,* 119–127.

Bornstein, P. H., & Knapp, M. (1981). Self-control desensitization with a multi-phobic boy: A multiple baseline design. *Journal of Behavior Therapy and Experimental Psychiatry, 12,* 281–285.

Bowlby, J. (1969). *Attachment.* New York: Basic Books.

Bowlby, J. (1973). *Attachment and loss* (Vol. 2). New York: Basic Books.

Boyd, L. T. (1980). Emotive imagery in the behavioral management of adolescent school phobias: A case approach. *School Psychology Digest, 9,* 186–189.

Brown, R., Copeland, R., & Hall, R. (1974). School phobia: Effects of behavior modification treatment applied by an elementary school principal. *Child Study Journal, 4,* 125–133.

Burke, J. P., & Demers, S. T. (1979). A paradigm for evaluating assessment interviewing techniques. *Psychology in the Schools, 16,* 51–60.

Burns, G. L. (1980). Indirect measurement and behavioral assessment: A case for social behaviorism psychometrics. *Behavioral Assessment, 2,* 197–206.

Castaneda, A., McCandless, B., & Palermo, D. (1956). The children's form of the Manifest Anxiety Scale. *Child Development, 27,* 317–326.

Cautela, J. R., & Groden, J. (1978). *Relaxation. A comprehensive manual for adults, children, and children with special needs.* Champaign, IL: Research Press.

Chazen, M. (1962). School phobia. *British Journal of Educational Psychology, 32,* 209–217.

Ciminero, A. R. (1977). Behavioral assessment: An overview. In A. R. Ciminero, K. D. Calhoun, & H. E. Adams (Eds.), *Handbook of behavioral assessment* (pp. 3–13). New York: Wiley.

Ciminero, A. R., & Drabman, R. S. (1977). Current developments in the behavioral assessment of children. In B. B. Lahey & A. E. Kazdin (Eds.), *Advances in clinical child psychology* (Vol. 1, pp. 47–82). New York: Plenum Press.

Clemente, F., & Kleiman, M. B. (1977). Fear of crime in the United States: A multivariate analysis. *Social Forces, 56,* 519–531.

Clayton, W. T. (1981). The use of positive reinforcement and stimulus fading in the treatment of an elective mute. *Behavioral Psychotherapy, 9,* 25–33.

Cone, J. D. (1977). The relevance of reliability and validity for behavioral assessment. *Behavior Therapy, 8,* 411–426.

Cone, J. D. (1978). The behavioral assessment grid (BAG): A conceptual framework and taxonomy. *Behavior Therapy, 9,* 882–888.

Cone, J. D. (1979). Confounded comparisons in triple response mode assessment research. *Behavioral Assessment, 1,* 85–95.

Cone, J. D., & Hawkins, R. P. (Eds.). (1977). *Behavioral assessment: New directions in clinical psychology.* New York: Bruner/Mazel.

Conger, J. C., & Keane, S. P. (1981). Social skills intervention in the treatment of isolated or withdrawn children. *Psychological Bulletin, 90,* 478–495.

Conrad, R. D., Delk, J. L., & Williams, C. (1974). Use of stimulus fading procedures in the treatment of a situation specific mutism: A case study. *Journal of Behavior Therapy and Experimental Psychiatry, 5,* 99–100.

Coolidge, J. C., Hahn, P. B., & Peck, A. L. (1957). School phobia. Neurotic crisis or way of life. *American Journal of Orthopsychiatry, 27,* 296–306.

Cooper, J. A. (1973). Application of the consultant role to parent-teacher management of school avoidance behavior. *Psychology in the Schools, 11,* 259–262.

Cradock, C., Cotler, S., & Jason, L. A. (1978). Primary prevention: Immunization of children for speech anxiety. *Cognitive Therapy and Research, 2,* 389–396.

Croake, J. W. (1969). Adolescent fear. *Adolescence, 2,* 459–468.

Croake, J. W., & Knox, F. H. (1971). A second look at adolescent fears. *Adolescence, 6,* 279–284.

Croake, J. W., & Knox, F. H. (1973). The changing nature of children's fears. *Child Study Journal, 3,* 91–105.

Deffenbacher, J. L., & Kempev, C. C. (1974a). Counseling test-anxious sixth graders. *Elementary School Guidance and Counseling, 1,* 22–29.

Deffenbacher, J. L., & Kempev, C. C. (1974b). Systematic desensitization of test anxiety in junior high students. *The School Counselor, 22,* 216–222.

Doleys, D. M., & Williams, S. C. (1977). The use of natural consequences and a make-up period to eliminate school phobic behavior: A case study. *Journal of School Psychology, 45,* 44–49.

Doris, J., McIntyre, J. R., Kelsey, C., & Lehman, E. (1971). Separation anxiety in nursery school children. *Proceedings of the 79th Annual Convention of the American Psychological Association, 6,* 145–146.

Dunn, J. S. (1965). Stability of the factor structure of the test anxiety scale for children across age and sex groups. *Journal of Consulting Psychology, 29,* 187.

Edlund, C. A. (1971). A reinforcement approach to the elimination of a child's school phobia. *Mental Hygiene, 55,* 433–436.

Eisenberg, L. (1958). School phobia: A study in the communication of anxiety. *American Journal of Psychiatry, 114,* 712–718.

Evans, I. M., & Nelson, R. O. (1977). Assessment of child behavior problems. In A. R. Ciminero, K. S. Calhoun, & H. E. Adams (Eds.), *Handbook of behavioral assessment* (pp. 603–668). New York: Wiley.

Evers, W. L., & Schwarz, J. C. (1973). Modifying social withdrawal in preschoolers: The effects of filmed modeling and teacher praise. *Journal of Abnormal Child Psychology, 1,* 248–256.

Evers-Pasquale, W., & Sherman, M. (1975). The reward value of peers: A variable influencing the efficacy of film modeling and modifying social isolation in preschoolers. *Journal of Abnormal Child Psychology, 3,* 179–189.

Feld, S., & Lewis, J. (1967). Further evidence on the stability of the factor structure of the test anxiety scale for children. *Journal of Consulting Psychology, 31,* 434.

Finch, A. J., Jr., & Rogers, T. R. (1984). Self-report instruments. In T. H. Ollendick & M. Hersen (Eds.), *Child behavioral assessment* (pp. 106–123). New York: Pergamon Press.

Forman, S., & O'Malley, A. (1984). School stress and anxiety interventions. *School Psychology Review, 13,* 162–170.

Fox, J., & Houston, B. (1981). Efficacy of self-instructional training for reducing children's anxiety in an evaluative situation. *Behaviour Research and Therapy, 19,* 509–515.

Freud, S. (1909). The analysis of a phobia in a five-year-old boy. In J. Strachey (Ed. and Trans.), *Standard edition of the complete psychological works of Sigmund Freud* (Vol. 10, pp. 3–149). London: Hogarth Press.

Gelfand, D. M. (1978) Behavioral treatment of avoidance, social withdrawal and negative emotional states. In B. B. Wolman, J. Egan, & A. O. Ross (Eds.), *Handbook of treatment of mental disorders in childhood and adolescence* (pp. 330–353). Englewood Cliffs, NJ: Prentice-Hall.

Glennon, B., & Weisz, J. R. (1978). An observational approach to the assessment of anxiety in young children. *Journal of Consulting and Clinical Psychology, 46,* 1246–1257.

Goldfried, M. (1971). Systematic desensitization as training in self-control. *Journal of Consulting and Clinical Psychology, 37,* 228–234.

Graziano, A. M., DeGiovanni, I. S., & Garcia, K. (1979). Behavioral treatments of children's fears: A review. *Psychological Bulletin, 86,* 804–830.

Gross, A. M. (1984). Behavioral interviewing. In T. H. Ollendick & M. Hersen (Eds.), *Child behavioral assessment* (pp. 61–79). New York: Pergamon Press.

Handler, L. (1972). The amelioration of nightmares in children. *Psychotherapy: Theory, Research, & Practice, 9,* 54–56.

Hartmann, D. P., Roper, B. L., & Bradford, D. C. (1979). Source relationships between behavioral and traditional assessment. *Journal of Behavioral Assessment, 1,* 3–21.

Handler, L. (1972). The amelioration of nightmares in children. *Psychotherapy: Theory, Research, & Practice, 9,* 54–56.

Harris, B. (1979). Whatever happened to little Albert? *American Psychologist, 34,* 151–160.

Hartmann, D. P., Roper, B. L., & Bradford, D. C. (1979). Source relationships between behavioral and traditional assessment. *Journal of Behavioral Assessment, 1,* 3–21.

Haslam, J. H. (1915). Nervous fears of children. In The Editorial Board of the University Society, *The child welfare manual (Vol. 2,* pp. 140–142). New York: The University Society.

Haynes, S. N. (1978). *Principles of behavioral assessment.* New York: Gardner Press.

Haynes, S. N., & Jensen, B. J. (1979) The interview as a behavioral assessment instrument. *Behavioral Assessment, 1,* 97–106.

Hersen, M. (1968). Treatment of a compulsive and phobic disorder through a total behavior therapy program: A case study. *Psychotherapy: Theory, Research, and Practice, 5,* 220–225.

Hersen, M. (1970). Behavior modification approach to a school-phobia case. *Journal of Clinical Psychology, 26,* 128–132.

Hodgson, R., & Rachman, S. (1974). Desynchrony in measures of fear. *Behavior Research and Therapy, 12,* 319–326.

Holland, C. J. (1970). An interview guide for behavioral counseling with parents. *Behavior Therapy, 1,* 70–79.

Holroyd, K. A. (1976). Cognition and desensitization in the group treatment of test anxiety. *Journal of Consulting and Clinical Psychology, 42,* 991–1001.

Hsia, H. (1984). Structural and strategic approach to school phobia/school refusal. *Psychology in the Schools, 21,* 360–367.

Hugdahl, K. (1981). The three-system model of fear and emotion—A critical examination. *Behaviour Research and Therapy, 19,* 75–85.

Ilg, F. L., & Aimes, L. B. (1955). *Child behavior.* New York: Dell.

Jersild, A. T. (1968). *Child psychology* (6th ed.). Englewood Cliffs, NJ: Prentice-Hall.

Jersild, A. T., & Holmes, F. B. (1935). Children's fears. *Child Development Monographs,* No. 20.

Johnson, S. B. (1979). Children's fears in the classroom setting. *School Psychology Digest, 8,* 382–396.

Johnson, S. B., & Melamed, B. G. (1979). The assessment and treatment of children's fears. In B. B. Lahey & A. E. Kazdin (Eds.), *Advances in clinical child psychology* (Vol. 2, pp. 108–139). New York: Plenum Press.

Johnson, T., Tyler, V., Thompson, R., & Jones, E. (1971). Systematic desensitization and assertive training in the treatment of speech anxiety in middle school students. *Psychology in the Schools, 8,* 263–267.

Jones, M. C. (1924). A laboratory study of fear: The case of Peter. *Journal of Genetic Psychology, 31,* 308–315.

Kahn, J., & Nursten, J. (1962). School refusal: A comprehensive view of school phobia and other failures of school attendance. *American Journal of Orthopsychiatry, 32,* 707–718.

Kandel, H. J., Ayllon, T., & Rosenbaum, M. S. (1977). Flooding or systematic exposure in the treatment of extreme social withdrawal in children. *Journal of Behavior Therapy and Experimental Psychiatry, 8,* 75–81.

Kanfer, F. H. (1977). The many faces of self-control, or behavior modification changes in focus. In R. B. Stuart (Ed.), *Behavioral self-management: Strategies, techniques, and outcomes* (pp. 1–48). New York: Brunner/Mazel.

Kanfer, F. H. (1980). Self-management methods. In F. H. Kanfer & A. P. Goldstein (Eds.), *Helping people change* (2nd ed., pp. 334–389). New York: Pergamon Press.

Kanfer, F. H., & Grimm, L. G. (1977). Behavioral analysis: Selecting target behaviors in the interview. *Behavior Modification, 1,* 7–28.

Kanfer, F. H., & Saslow, G. (1969). Behavioral diagnosis. In C. M. Franks (Ed.), *Behavior therapy: Appraisal and status* (pp. 417–444). New York: McGraw-Hill.

Kanfer, F. H., Karoly, P., & Newman, A. (1975). Reduction of children's fear of the dark by confidence-related and situational threat-related verbal cues. *Journal of Consulting and Clinical Psychology, 43,* 251–258.

Kazdin, A. E. (1979). Fictions, factions, and functions of behavior therapy. *Behavior Therapy, 10,* 629–654.

Kazdin, A. E. (1980). *Research designs in clinical psychology.* New York: Harper & Row.

Kazdin, A. E., & Hersen, M. (1980). The current status of behavior therapy. *Behavior Modification, 4,* 283–302.

Kazdin, A. E., & Wilson, G. T. (1978) *Evaluation of behavior therapy: Issues, evidence and research strategies.* Cambridge, MA: Ballinger.

Keller, M. F., & Carlson, P. M. (1974). The use of symbolic modeling to promote social skills in preschool children with low levels of social responsiveness. *Child Development, 45,* 912–919.

Kellerman, J. (1981) *Helping the fearful child.* New York: Norton.

Kelley, C. K. (1976). Play desensitization of fear of darkness in preschool children. *Behaviour Research and Therapy, 14,* 79–81.

Kendall, P. C. (1981). Cognitive behavioral interventions with children. In B. B. Lahey & A. E. Kazdin (Eds.), *Advances in clinical child psychology* (Vol. 4, pp. 53–90). New York: Plenum Press.

Kendall, P. C., & Finch, A. J., Jr. (1979). Developing nonimpulsive behavior in children: Cognitive-behavioral strategies for self-control. In P. C. Kendall & S. D. Hollon (Eds.), *Cognitive-behavioral intervention: Theory, research, and problems* (pp. 37–59). New York: Academic Press.

Kendall, P. C., & Hollow, S. D. (Eds.). (1979). *Cognitive*

behavioral intervention: Theory, research, and problems. New York: Academic Press.

Kennedy, W. A. (1965). School phobia: Rapid treatment of fifty cases. *Journal of Abnormal Psychology, 70,* 285–289.

Kipton, H. (1980). Rapid reinstatement of speech using stimulus fading with a selectively mute child. *Journal of Behavior Therapy and Experimental Psychiatry, 11,* 147–149.

Kissel, S. (1972). Systematic desensitization therapy with children: A case study and some suggested modifications. *Professional Psychology, 3,* 164–168.

Klinger, E. (1978). Modes of normal conscious flow. In K. S. Pope & J. L. Singer (Eds.), *The stream of consciousness: Scientific investigations into the flow of human experience* (pp. 75–94). New York: Plenum Press.

Klorman, R., Hilpart, P. L., Michael, R., LaGana, C., & Sveen, L. (1980). Effects on coping and mastery modeling on experienced and inexperienced pedodontic patients' disruptiveness. *Behavior Therapy, 11,* 156–168.

Knoff, H. M., & Prout, H. T. (1985). The kinetic drawing system: A review and integration of the kinetic family and school drawing techniques. *Psychology in the Schools, 22,* 50–59.

Knopf, I. J. (1979). *Childhood psychopathology.* Englewood Cliffs, NJ: Prentice-Hall.

Kondas, O. (1967). Reduction of examination anxiety and "stage fright" by group desensitization and relaxation. *Behaviour Research and Therapy, 5,* 275–281.

Korchin, S. J., & Schulbery, D. (1981). The future of clinical assessment. *American Psychologist, 36,* 1147–1148.

Kozak, M. J., & Miller, G. A. (1982). Hypothetical constructs vs. intervening variables: A re-appraisal of the three-systems model of anxiety assessment. *Behavioral Assessment, 4,* 347–358.

Kratochwill, T. R. (1981). *Selective mutism.* New York: Erlbaum.

Kratochwill, T. R. (1982). Advances in behavioral assessment. In C. R. Reynolds & T. B. Gutkin (Eds.), *Handbook of school psychology* (pp. 314–350). New York: Wiley.

Kratochwill, T. R., & Morris, R. J. (1985). Conceptual and methodological issues in the behavioral assessment and treatment of children's fears and phobias. *School Psychology Review, 14,* 94–107.

Kratochwill, T. R., Brody, G., & Piersel, W. (1979). Elective mutism in children. In B. Lahey & A. Kazdin (Eds.), *Advances in clinical child psychology* (Vol. 2, 194–240). New York: Plenum Press.

Lang, P. J. (1968). Fear reduction and fear behavior: Problems in treating a construct. In J. M. Shlier (Ed.), *Research in psychotherapy* (Vol. 3, pp. 84–120). Washington, DC: American Psychological Association.

Lapouse, R., & Monk, M. A. (1959). Fears and worries in a representative sample of children. *Journal of Orthopsychiatry, 29,* 803–818.

Laxer, R. M., Quarter, J., Kooman, A., & Walker, K. (1969). Systematic desensitization and relaxation of high test-anxious secondary school students. *Journal of Counseling Psychology, 16,* 446–451.

Lazarus, A. A. (1960). The elimination of children's phobias by deconditioning. In H. J. Eysenck (Ed.), *Behavior therapy and the neuroses* (pp. 114–122). Oxford: Pergamon Press.

Lazarus, A. A., & Abramovitz, A. (1962). The use of emotive imagery in the treatment of children's phobias. *Journal of Mental Science, 108,* 191–195.

Lazarus, A. A., Davison, G. C., & Polefka, D. A. (1965). Classical and operant factors in the treatment of school phobias. *Journal of Abnormal Psychology, 70,* 225–229.

Leal, L. L., Baxter, E. G., Martin, J., & Marx, R. W. (1981). Cognitive modification and systematic desensitization with test anxious high school students. *Journal of Counseling Psychology, 28,* 525–528.

Linehan, M. M. (1977). Issues in behavioral interviewing. In J. D. Cone & R. P. Hawkins (Eds.), *Behavioral assessment: New directions in clinical psychology* (pp. 20–51). New York: Bruner/Mazel.

Lipton, H. (1980). Rapid reinstatement of speech using stimulus fading with a selectively mute child. *Journal of Behavior Therapy and Experimental Psychiatry, 11,* 147–149.

Luiselli, J. K. (1978). Treatment of an autistic child's fear of riding a school bus through exposure and reinforcement. *Journal of Behavior Therapy and Experimental Psychiatry, 9,* 169–172.

MacFarlane, J. W., Allen, L., & Hozik, M. P. (1954). *A developmental study of the behavior problems of normal children between twenty-one months and fourteen years.* Berkeley, CA: University of California Press.

Mandler, G., Mandler, J. M., & Uviller, E. T. (1958). Autonomic activity. *Journal of Abnormal and Social Psychology, 56,* 367–373.

Mann, J. (1972). Vicarious desensitization of test anxiety through observation of videotaped treatment. *Journal of Counseling Psychology, 19,* 1–7..

Mann, J., & Rosenthal, T. L. (1969). Vicarious and direct counterconditioning of test anxiety through individual and group desensitization. *Behaviour Research and Therapy, 7,* 359–367.

Marholin, D. II, & Bijou, S. W. (1978). Behavioral assessment: Listen when the data speak. In D. Marholin II (Ed.), *Child behavior therapy* (pp. 13–36). New York: Gardner Press.

Marks, S. M. (1969). *Fears and phobias.* New York: Academic Press.

Mash, E. J., & Terdall, L. G. (1981). Behavioral assessment of childhood disturbance. In E. J. Mash & L. G. Terdall (Eds.), *Behavioral assessment of childhood disorders* (pp. 3–78). New York: Guilford Press.

Matson, J. L. (1981). Assessment and treatment of clinical fears in mentally retarded children. *Journal of Applied Behavior Analysis, 14,* 287–294.

Maurer, A. (1965). What children fear. *Journal of Genetic Psychology, 106,* 265–277.

McFall, R. M. (1977). Parameters of self-monitoring. In R. B. Stuart (Ed.), *Behavioral strategies, techniques, and outcomes* (pp. 196–224). New York: Brunner/Mazel.

McReynolds, R. A., & Morris, R. J. (1986). *Treating a mentally retarded child's dog phobia through contact desensitization.* Unpublished study. University of Arizona, College of Education, Tucson, AZ.

Meichenbaum, D. H. (1972). Cognitive modification of test-anxious college students. *Journal of Consulting and Clinical Psychology, 39,* 370–380.

Meichenbaum, D., & Genest, M. (1980). Cognitive behavior modification: An integration of cognitive and behavioral methods. In F. H. Kanfer & A. P. Goldstein (Eds.), *Helping people change* (2nd ed., pp. 390–422). New York: Pergmon Press.

Melamed, B. G., & Siegel, L. (1975). Reduction of anxiety in children facing hospitalization and surgery by use of filmed modeling. *Journal of Consulting and Clinical Psychology, 43,* 511–521.

Melamed, B. G., Hawes, R. R., Heigy, E., & Glick, J. (1975). Use of film models to reduce uncooperative behavior of children during dental treatment. *Journal of Dental Research, 54,* 797–801.

Melamed, B. G., Yurcheson, R., Fleece, E. L., Hutchenson, S., & Hawes, R. (1978). Effects of film modeling on the reduction of anxiety-related behaviors in individuals varying in levels of previous experience in the stress situation. *Journal of Consulting and Clinical Psychology, 46,* 1357–1367.

Meyer, V., Liddell, A., & Lyons, M. (1977). Behavioral interviews. In A. R. Ciminero, K. S. Calhoun, & H. E. Adams (Eds.), *Handbook of behavioral assessment* (pp. 117–152). New York: Wiley.

Miller, L. C. (1967). Louisville Behavioral Checklist for males 6-12 years of age. *Psychological Reports, 21,* 855–896.

Miller, L. C., Barrett, C. L., Hampe, E., & Noble, H. (1971). Revised anxiety scales for the Louisville Behavior Checklist. *Psychological Reports, 29,* 503–511.

Miller, L. C., Barrett, C. L., Hampe, R., & Noble, H. (1972a). Comparison of reciprocal inhibition, psychotherapy, and waiting list control for phobic children. *Journal of Abnormal Psychology, 79,* 269–279.

Miller, L. C., Barrett, C. L., Hampe, E., & Noble, H. (1972b). Factor structure of childhood fears. *Journal of Consulting and Clinical Psychology, 39,* 264–268.

Miller, L. C., Barrett, C. L., & Hampe, E. (1974). Phobias in children in a prescientific era. In A. Davids (Ed.), *Child personality and psychopathology: Current topics.* New York: Wiley.

Mischel, W. (1968). *Personality and assessment.* New York: Wiley.

Mischel, W. (1973). Toward a cognitive social learning reconceptualization of personality. *Psychological Review, 80,* 252–283.

Morganstern, K. (1976). Behavioral interviewing: The initial stages of assessment. In M. Hersen & A. Bellack (Eds.), *Behavioral assessment: A practical handbook* (pp. 51–76). New York: Pergamon Press.

Morganstern, K. (1976). Behavioral interviewing: The initial stages of assessment. In M. Hersen & A. Bellack (Eds.), *Behavioral assessment: A practical handbook* (pp. 51–76). New York: Pergamon Press.

Morris, R. J. (1973). Shaping relaxation in the unrelaxed client. *Journal of Behavior Therapy and Experimental Psychiatry, 4,* 343–353.

Morris, R. J. (1986). Fear reduction methods. In F. H. Kanfer & A. P. Goldstein (Eds.), *Helping people change* (3rd ed., pp. 145–190). New York: Pergamon Press.

Morris, R. J., & Dolker, M. (1974). Developing cooperative play in socially withdrawn retarded children. *Mental Retardation, 12,* 24–27.

Morris, R. J., & Kratochwill, T. R. (1983). *Treating children's fears and phobias: A behavioral approach.* Elmsford, NY: Pergamon Press.

Morris, R. J., & Kratochwill, T. R. (1985). Behavioral treatment of children's fears and phobias: A review. *School Psychology Review, 14,* 84–93.

Morris, R. J., Kratochwill, T. R., & Dodson, C. L. (1986). Fears and phobias in adolescence: A behavioral perspective. In R. A. Feldman & A. R. Stiffman (Eds.), *Advances in adolescent mental health* (pp. 63–117). Santa Barbara, CA: JAI Press.

Muller, S. D., & Madsen, C. H. (1964). Group desensitization for "anxious" children with reading problems. *Psychology in the Schools, 1,* 184–189.

Murphy, C. M., & Bootzin, R. R. (1973). Active and passive participation in the contact desensitization of snake fear in children. *Behavior Therapy, 4,* 203–211.

Nalvern, F. B. (1970). Manifest fears and worries of ghetto versus middle class suburban children. *Psychological Reports, 27,* 285–286.

Nawas, M. M. (1971). Standardized scheduled desensitization: Some unstable results and an improved program. *Behavior Therapy and Research, 9,* 35–38.

Neisworth, J. T., Madle, R. A., & Goeke, K. E. (1975). Errorless elimination of separation anxiety: A case study. *Journal of Behavior Therapy and Experimental Psychiatry, 6,* 79–82.

Nelson, R. O. (1977). Assessment and therapeutic functions of self-monitoring. In M. Hersen (Ed.), *Progress in behavior modification* (Vol. 5, pp. 264–308). New York: Academic Press.

Nelson, R. P., Hayes, S. C. (1979). The nature of behavioral assessment: A commentary. *Journal of Applied Behavior Analysis, 12,* 491–500.

Nietzel, M. T., & Bernstein, D. A. (1981). Assessment of anxiety and fear. In M. Hersen & A. S. Bellack (Eds.), *Behavioral assessment: A practical handbook* (2nd ed., pp. 215–245). New York: Pergamon Press.

O'Connor, R. D. (1969). Modification of social withdrawal through symbolic modeling. *Journal of Applied Behavior Analysis, 2,* 15–22.

O'Connor, R. D. (1972). Relative efficacy of modeling,

shaping, and the combined procedures for modification of social withdrawal. *Journal of Abnormal Psychology, 79*, 327–334.

Ollendick, T. H. (1979). Behavioral treatment of anorexia nervosa: A five year study. *Behavior Modification, 3*, 124–135.

Ollendick, T. H., & Gruen, G. E. (1972). Treatment of a bodily injury phobia with implosive therapy. *Journal of Consulting and Clinical Psychology, 38*, 389–393.

Ollendick, T. H., & Ollendick, D. G. (1982). Anxiety disorders. In J. L. Matson (Ed.), *Psychopathology in the mentally retarded* (pp. 77–119). New York: Grune & Stratton.

O'Rielly, P. (1971). Desensitization of fire bell phobia. *Journal of School Psychology, 9*, 55–57.

Orton, G. L. (1982). A comparative study of children's worries. *Journal of Psychology, 110*, 153–162.

Patterson, G. R. (1965). A learning theory approach to the treatment of the school phobic child. In L. P. Ullman & L. Krasner (Eds.), *Case studies in behavior modification* (pp. 279–284). New York: Holt, Rinehart, & Winston.

Paul, G. L., & Bernstein, D. A. (1973). *Anxiety and clinical problems: Systematic desensitization and related techniques*. Morristown, NJ: General Learning Press.

Pavlov, I. P. (1927). *Conditioned reflexes* (G. V. Anrep, Trans.). London: Oxford University Press.

Perry, M. A., & Furukawa, M. J. (1980). Modeling methods. In F. H. Kanfer & A. P. Goldstein (Eds.), *Helping people change* (2nd ed., pp. 131–170). New York: Pergamon Press.

Peterson, L., & Shegitomi, C. (1981). The use of coping techniques in minimizing anxiety in hospitalized children. *Behavior Therapy, 12*, 1–14.

Phillips, B. N. (1966). *An analysis of causes of anxiety among children in school*. (Final report, Project No. 2616, U.S.O.E. Cooperative Research Branch), Austin, TX: University of Texas.

Phillips, B. N. (1978). *School stress and anxiety: Theory, research, and intervention*. New York: Human Sciences Press.

Pratt, K. C. (1945). The study of "fears" of rural children. *Journal of Genetic Psychology, 67*, 179–194.

Quay, H. C. (1979). Classification. In H. C. Quay & J. S. Werry (Eds.), *Psychopathological disorders of childhood*. (2nd ed., pp. 1–42). New York: Wiley.

Rachman, S. (1968). *Phobias: Their nature and control*. Springfield, IL: Charles C Thomas.

Rachman, S., & Hodgson, R. (1974). Synchcrony and desynchrony in fear and avoidance. *Behaviour Research and Therapy, 12*, 311–318.

Rasbury, W. C. (1974). Behavioral treatment of selective mutism: A case report. *Journal of Behavior Therapy and Experimental Psychology, 5*, 103–104.

Reid, J. B., Hawkins, N., Keutzer, C., McNeal, S. A., Phelps, R. E., Reid, K. M., & Meas, H. L. (1967). A marathon behavior modification of a selectively mute child. *Journal of Child Psychology and Psychiatry, 8*, 27–30.

Reynolds, C. R. (1977). *A bibliography of research employing the Children's Manifest Anxiety Scale: 1956–1977*. Unpublished manuscript.

Reynolds, C. R., & Paget, K. D. (1981). Factor analysis of the revised Children's Manifest Anxiety Scale for Blacks, Whites, males, and females with a national innovative sample. *Journal of Consulting Clinical Psychology, 49*, 352–359.

Reynolds, C. R., & Richmond, B. O. (1978). What I think and feel: A revised measure of children's manifest anxiety. *Journal of Abnormal Child Psychology, 6*, 271–280.

Richards, C. S., & Siegel, L. J. (1978). Behavioral treatment of anxiety states and avoidance behaviors in children. In D. Marholin II (Ed.), *Child behavior therapy* (pp. 274–338). New York: Guilford Press.

Ritter, B. (1968). The group desensitization of children's snake phobias using vicarious and contact desensitization procedures. *Behaviour Research and Therapy, 6*, 1–6.

Ritter, B. (1969a). Treatment of acrophobia with contact desensitization. *Behaviour Research and Therapy, 7*, 41–45.

Ritter, B. (1969b). The use of contact desensitization, demonstration-plus-participation and demonstration-only in the treatment of acrophobia. *Behaviour Research and Therapy, 7*, 157–164.

Rosenbaum, E., & Kellman, M. (1973). Treatment of a selectively mute third-grade child. *Journal of School Psychology, 11*, 26–29.

Rutter, M., Lebocici, S., Eisenberg, L., Sneznevsky, A. V., Sadoun, R., Brooke, E., & Lin, T. Y. (1969). A triaxial classification of mental disorders in childhood: An international study. *Journal of Child Psychology and Psychiatry, 10*, 41–62.

Rutter, M., Shaffer, D., & Shepherd, M. (1975). *A multiaxial classification of child psychiatric disorders*. Geneva: World Health Organization.

Sarason, S., Davidson, K., Lighthall, F., Waite, R., & Ruebush, B. (1960). *Anxiety in elementary school children*. New York: Wiley.

Scarr, S., & Salapatek, P. (1970). Patterns of fear development during infancy. *Merrill-Palmer Quarterly of Behavior and Development, 16*, 53–90.

Scherer, M. W., & Nakamura, C. Y. (1968). A Fear Survey Schedule for Children (FSS-FC): A factor analytic comparison with manifest anxiety (CMAS). *Behaviour Research and Therapy, 6*, 173–182.

Semenoff, B., Park, C., & Smith, E. (1976). Behavior interventions with a six-year-old elective mute. In J. B. Krumboltz & C. E. Thoreson (Eds.), *Counseling methods* (pp. 89–97). New York: Holt, Rinehart & Winston.

Shapiro, E. S. (1984). Self-monitoring procedures. In T. H. Ollendick & M. Hersen (Eds.), *Child behavioral assessment* (pp. 148–165). New York: Pergamon Press.

Simkins, L. (1971). The reliabity of self-recorded behavior. *Behavior Therapy, 2*, 83–87.

Skinner, B. F. (1938). *The behavior of organisms*. New York: Appleton-Century-Crofts.

Skinner, B. F. (1953). *Science and human behavior*. New York: Macmillan.

Sluckin, A., & Jehu, D. (1969). A behavioral approach in the treatment of elective mutism. *British Journal of Psychiatric Social Work, 10,* 70–73.

Smith, P. K. (1979). The ontogeny of fear in children. In W. Sluckin (Ed.), *Fear in animals and man* (pp. 164–198). New York: Van Nostrand Reinhold.

Smith, R. E., & Sharpe, T. M. (1970). Treatment of a school phobia with implosive therapy. *Journal of Consulting and Clinical Psychology, 35,* 239–243.

Spielberger, C. (1973). *Manual for the State-Trait Inventory for Children.* Palo Alto, CA: Consulting Psychologist Press.

Staley, A. A., & O'Donnell, J. P. (1984). A developmental analysis of mothers' reports of normal children's fears. *Journal of Genetic Psychology, 144,* 165–178.

Stampfl, T. G. (1961). *Implosive therapy: A learning theory derived psychodynamic therapeutic technique.* Paper presented at the University of Illinois, Champaign, IL.

Stampfl, T. G., & Levis, D. J. (1967). Essentials of implosive therapy: A learning-based-psychodynamic behavioral therapy. *Journal of Abnormal Psychology, 72,* 496–503.

Stampfl, T. G., & Levis, D. J. (1968). Implosive therapy—A behavioral therapy? *Behaviour Research and Theray, 6,* 31–36.

Strain, P. S., Shores, R. E., & Temm, M. A. (1977). Effects of peer social initiation on the behavior of withdrawn preschool children. *Journal of Applied Behavior Analysis, 10,* 289–298.

Tahmisian, J., & McReynolds, W. (1971). The use of parents as behavioral engineers in the treatment of a school phobic girl. *Journal of Counseling Psychology, 18,* 225–228.

Tasto, D. L. (1977). Self-report inventions. In A. R. Ciminero, K. S. Calhoun, & H. E. Adams (Eds.), *Handbook of behavioral assessment* (pp. 153–193). New York: Wiley.

Taylor, D. W. (1972). Treatment of excessive frequency of urination by desensitization. *Journal of Behavior Therapy and Experimental Psychiatry, 3,* 311–313.

Terr, L. C. (1981). Psychic trauma in children: Observations following the Chowchilla school bus kidnapping. *American Journal of Psychiatry, 138,* 14–19.

Trueman, D. (1984). What are the characteristics of school phobic children. *Psychological Reports, 54,* R191–202.

Ullmann, L. P., & Krasner, L. (1969). *A psychological approach to abnormal behavior.* Englewood Cliffs, NJ: Prentice-Hall.

Ullmann, L. P., & Krasner, L. A. (1975). *A psychological approach to abnormal behavior* (2nd ed). Englewood Cliffs, NJ: Prentice-Hall.

Vaal, J. J. (1973). Applying contingency contracting to a school phobic: A case study. *Journal of Behavior Therapy and Experimental Psychiatry, 4,* 371–373.

Vernon, D. (1973). Use of modeling to modify children's responses to a natural, potentially stressful situation. *Journal of Applied Psychology, 58,* 351–356.

Vernon, V. T., & Bailey, W. C. (1974). The use of motion pictures in the psychological preparation of children for induction of anesthesia. *Anesthesiology, 40,* 68–72.

Wahler, R. G., & Cormier, W. H. (1970). The ecological interview: A first step in out-patient child behavior therapy. *Journal of Behavior Therapy and Experimental Psychiatry, 1,* 279–289.

Walk, R. D. (1956). Self-ratings of fear in a fear invoking situation. *Journal of Abnormal and Social Psychology, 52,* 171–178.

Warren, R., Deffenbacher, J. L., & Brading, P. (1976). Rational-emotive therapy and the reduction of test anxiety in elementary school students. *Rational Living, 11,* 26–29.

Watson, J. B. (1913). Psychology as the behaviorist views it. *Psychological Review, 20,* 158–177.

Watson, J. B., & Rayner, R. (1970). Conditioned emotional reactions. *Journal of Experimental Psychology, 3,* 1–14.

Whitehall, M. B., Hersen, M., & Bellack, A. S. (1980). Conversation skills training for socially isolated children. *Behaviour Research and Therapy, 18,* 217–225.

Wiens, A. N. (1976). The assessment interview. In I. B. Wiener (Ed.), *Clinical methods in psychology* (pp. 3–60). New York: Wiley.

Williamson, D. A., Jewell, W. R., Sanders, S. H., Haney, J., & White, D. (1977). The treatment of reluctant speech using contingency management procedures. *Journal of Behavior Therapy and Experimental Psychiatry, 8,* 151–156.

Wine, J. D. (1979). Test anxiety and evaluating threat: Children's behavior in the classroom. *Journal of Abnormal Child Psychology, 1,* 45–59.

Wish, P. A., Hasazi, J. E., & Jurgela, A. R. (1973). Automated direct deconditioning of a childhood phobia. *Journal of Behavior Therapy and Experimental Psychiatry, 4,* 279–283.

Wolpe, J. (1958). *Reciprocal inhibition therapy.* Stanford, CA: Stanford University Press.

Wolpe, J. (1962). The experimental foundations of some new psychotherapeutic methods. In A. J. Bachrach (Ed.), *Experimental foundations in clinical psychology* (pp. 554–575). New York: Basic Books.

Wulbert, M., Nyman, B. A., Snow, D., & Owen, Y. (1973). The efficacy of stimulus fading and contingency management in the treatment of elective mutism: A case study. *Journal of Applied Behavior Analysis, 6,* 435–441.

Yule, W. (1981). The epidemiology of child psychopathology. In B. B. Lahey & A. E. Kazdin (Eds.), *Advances in clinical child psychology* (Vol. 4, pp. 1–51). New York: Plenum Press.

Yule, W., Sacks, B., & Jersov, L. (1974). Successful flooding treatment of a noise phobia in an 11-year-old. *Jour-*

nal of Behavior Therapy and Experimental Psychiatry, 5, 209–211.

Zill, B. (1981). When truants and school refusers grow up. *British Journal of Psychiatry, 141,* 208–210.

Zimmerman, B. J. (1977). Modeling. In H. L. Hom, Jr. & P. A. Robinson (Eds.), *Psychological processes in early education* (pp. 00-00). New York: Academic Press.

CHAPTER 27

Behavioral Habilitation of Students with Severe Handicaps

David P. Wacker and Wendy K. Berg

Students with severe handicaps comprise a very heterogeneous group (Sontag, Smith, & Sailor, 1977), ranging from those who engage in remunerative work after school to those who appear completely unresponsive to their environments. In some cases, severely handicapped students attending the same classroom display such diverse behavior as self-injurious behavior, cooperative play on video games with age-appropriate peers, and independent use of public transportation systems. This diversity can make the assessment and treatment of these students seem problematic, at best, and it is not surprising that many psychologists in educational settings question their own competency in providing adequate services to this population of students (Irons, Irons, & Maddux, 1984).

Psychologists who provide services to severely handicapped students in school settings frequently operate outside of the context of the student's educational program. Instead, assessment and treatment protocols are completed in isolated testing rooms, and when observation of ongoing behavior is conducted in the classroom, little if any information has been obtained about the purpose or adequacy of the program being observed. Too often, psychologists find themselves attempting to interpret the data they have collected with no or minimal knowledge about how those data will affect the student's participation in school. In fact, much of the data collected has little to do with a student's program, because the data simply confirm what was already known: the student's overall functioning level or frequency of engaging in a given behavior.

There are, of course, many reasons for conducting descriptive assessments of a student's general level of functioning, whether these are to describe the student's performance in relation to other students (norm referenced) or in relation to a particular activity (criterion referenced). However, a third purpose for psychological assessment and intervention with these students is to prescribe procedures for improving performance, or for selecting target behaviors that will result in greater independence on a specific activity. In other words, the data collected are used to guide ongoing programs for individual students.

David P. Wacker and Wendy K. Berg • Department of Pediatrics, University Hospital School, University of Iowa, Iowa City, Iowa 52242.

This type of assessment, which is sometimes referred to as a prescriptive assessment (Wacker, Kerr, & Carroll, 1983), comprises an ongoing part of the educational treatment package the student receives in school. It is our view that the provision of psychological services in school programs for severely handicapped students must become more prescriptive if psychologists are to affect the overall quality of education these students receive.

The purpose of this chapter is to present an overview for providing prescriptive psychological services in educational programs for severely handicapped students. In the following sections, guidelines for defining, implementing, and evaluating treatment programs for individual students are described, and case studies for each approach are discussed. No attempt is made to distinguish further between assessment and treatment, as both components of a prescriptive program occur simultaneously. Assessment data are continuously collected throughout treatment to provide current information about the effects of treatment.

General Guidelines for Treatment Programs

Two aspects of treatment programs should be considered prior to implementation: (a) the meaningfulness of the proposed treatment outcomes (functional goals), and (b) the continuation of the treatment procedures. Both of these aspects are critical to the overall effectiveness of a treatment program, particularly as it relates to the continued use of the program following any initial success that may be achieved.

Meaningfulness of Treatment Outcomes

Treatment outcomes are typically evaluated solely with respect to the desired increase or decrease of behavior under specific conditions. If a student learns to complete a specific set of responses, or not to display a particular response (self-injurious behavior), treatment is considered successful. Although this type of information provides support for the validity of a treatment package, it is not necessarily sufficient for evaluating the worth of the program.

Functional Utility of the Target Behavior

The first step in establishing treatment procedures is to evaluate the impact that a target behavior will have on the student's ability to function more adequately in normal community and home environments (Brown, Branston, *et al.*, 1979). A common feature of severely handicapped students is the lack of behavior that makes them more independent, or that produces greater acceptance in community settings. In addition, training time for each behavior can be substantial, further necessitating the need for meaningful (functional) target behavior.

Determining functional target behavior can be as simple as asking parents to list behaviors they view as important, or as complex as conducting ecological inventories of the skills students need to acquire to be independent in various community settings (Brown, Branston-McClean, *et al.*, 1979). In general, any skills that are needed in community settings, but that the student does not possess, are functional target responses. This type of analysis, termed a discrepancy analysis by Brown, Branston-McClean, *et al.* (1979), can provide the basis for educational programming. For example, students with profound handicaps are frequently trained in self-feeding skills in school. Determining the feeding skills needed at home and/or in fast-food restaurants may guide the specific feeding responses required.

Determining the Necessary Conditions for the Occurrence of a Response

A related second factor is specifying the conditions under which a behavior is to occur. Self-feeding skills may be prompted in the classroom by discriminative stimuli (Sds), such as the position of the food tray, verbal instructions, and the presence of the teacher. In restaurant settings, these Sds may not be available, making it less likely that the student will engage in the behavior. Therefore, evaluation of the naturally occurring antecedents and consequences to a behavior is as important as defining a functional target behavior. One approach to documenting naturally occurring antecedents and consequences to behavior is first to establish a task analysis of the sequence of behaviors needed to function independently in a given setting. Once the task analysis is established (through an interview or observation), the probable antecedents and consequences that guide each specific response in the chain should be listed.

An example of the potential importance of this procedure is the case of John, a severely mentally retarded adolescent, who was taught to brush his teeth independently at school. Following lunch, John independently went to the restroom, put toothpaste on his toothbrush, and brushed his teeth. However, after weeks of errorless performance at school, no improvement had occurred at home. The solution to the problem was the placement of the toothbrush. When the toothbrush was placed on the sink with the toothpaste next to it, John performed the desired response. At home, his toothbrush was placed in full view, but in a toothbrush holder. Therefore, the antecedent cue of the toothbrush on the sink was available at school but not at home, necessitating that school staff retrain this skill. An analysis of naturally occurring antecedents may have prevented this problem, and in any case, would have provided useful data for designing an effective program.

A second reason for conducting assessments of antecedents and consequences is to evaluate the conditions that motivate current responding by a student. Iwata, Dorsey, Slifer, Bauman, & Richman (1982) reported an excellent example of such a procedure with subjects who engaged in self-injurious behavior. Iwata *et al.* assessed the conditions controlling self-injurious behavior by evaluating the occurrence of this behavior in several analogue situations that manipulated the amount of attention the subject received, the performance demands placed on the subject, and the availability of preferred play materials. This procedure was successful in determining the conditions controlling self-injurious behavior for most of the subjects evaluated, and therefore led to the development of treatment protocols for individual subjects.

Increasing Active Behavior That Results in Reinforcement

A third consideration is the selection of target behavior that results in reinforcement; that is, identification of active behavior by the student that is normally reinforced. In many cases, concern about decreasing inappropriate behavior results in a failure to provide the student with behaviors that are desired (i.e., result in reinforcement) at school or in the community. An obvious example is self-injurious behavior, where the traditional focus for intervention is on decreasing its occurrence. Rather than differentially reinforcing an incompatible response, we instead concentrate exclusively on the reduction of the behavior, sometimes with initially good results. When the focus of a program is almost exclusively on the elimination of behavior, the program is utilizing what can be referred to as the "dead man's criterion," that is, the treatment goals established for a student are easily accomplished by dead people (e.g., be quiet, sit still, quit slapping face). What is needed is a program that removes reinforcement for the undesired behavior while simultaneously providing reinforcement for an alternative, appropriate behavior.

Durand and Carr (1985) provided an excellent description of how an active, functional response can be trained that is incompatible with self-injurious behavior. The treatment program, differential reinforcement of communication, is conducted to increase a response which is incompatible with self-injurious behavior (SIB). A student who engages in SIB is first assessed to determine which of several conditions (social attention, escape from aversive tasks, sensory consequences, etc.) controls the occurrence of this behavior. Following assessment, the students are trained to emit a communicative response that results in the same outcome as engaging in SIB. For example, a student might be trained to solicit attention with a verbal or gestural response if assessment indicates that SIB is controlled by social attention.

Evaluation of Treatment Outcomes

A summary of the three guidelines related to treatment outcomes is provided in Table 1. As shown in Table 1, these guidelines are all proposed to facilitate generalization and maintenance of behavior. The acquisition of separate skills by a student is a needed step in behavioral treatment programs, but a program can be considered successful only if the student continues to engage in desired behavior following the completion of treatment, and generalizes these skills across people, settings, and tasks. Maintenance and generalization may not be of concern only when the treatment results in permanent, ongoing changes in all relevant environments. Because this is almost never the case in public school settings, the treatment protocol must include methods for promoting maintenance and generalization of the behavior.

According to Stokes and Baer (1977), generalization takes place when desired behavior occurs in: "non-training conditions (i.e., across subjects, settings, people, behaviors, and/or time)" and when "no extra training manipulations are needed; or may be claimed when some extra manipulations are necessary, but the cost or extent is clearly less than that of direct intervention" (p. 350).

Most commonly, several types of gener-

Table 1. General Guidelines in Establishing Treatment Programs

Guideline	Focus of guideline	Impact of guideline	Procedure
Functional behavior	Treatment outcome	1. Generalization/maintenance of behavior 2. Improve independence and acceptance of student	1. Parent interview/survey 2. Inventory behavior needed in community settings
Naturally occurring antecedents and consequences	Treatment outcome	1. Generalization of behavior 2. Better specification of effective procedures	1. Task analysis of behavior with antecedents and consequences listed for each step
Active behavior that results in reinforcement	Treatment outcome	1. Maintenance of behavior 2. Focuses treatment on positive behavior	1. Determine normally occurring reinforcers 2. Criterion for treatment is to increase, not decrease, behavior
Social validity of the treatment procedures	Continuation of treatment	1. Maintenance of procedures 2. Consumer satisfaction	1. Establish acceptability of treatment procedures
Feasability of the procedures	Continuation of treatment	1. Maintenance of procedures 2. Carryover of procedures with other students and in other settings	1. Use normally available resources and materials 2. Incorporate treatment procedures into ongoing classroom procedures

alization are required in school-based treatment programs. A common example is that of John, who was described earlier with respect to his toothbrushing skills. Treatment was effective at school, but the program was still unsuccessful because he did not generalize his acquired skills across settings. Although this specific example concerns across-setting generalization, it could also have involved generalization across people (teachers to family) and may have also involved maintenance if the program was ever discontinued at school. Specification of treatment outcomes must include a description of how the proposed treatment procedures will produce generalization and maintenance, and the success of treatment must be evaluated as occurring only when generalization and/or maintenance is achieved. Specific procedures for producing generalization and maintenance of behavior are described briefly in a later section.

Continuation of Treatment

As mentioned previously, treatment of severely handicapped persons can involve relatively extensive amounts of training time. Even when treatment is successful, carryover of the program to other settings, tasks, or people may require additional (although substantially reduced) training time. It is rare in public school programs that the psychologist is able to carry out all or most of the treatment protocol. Instead, once the treatment procedures have been defined, other staff such as teachers or teacher aides will need to provide most of the ongoing treatment, with the psychologist providing ongoing consultation and evaluation.

Teacher Acceptance of Procedures

As shown in Table 1, two general guidelines are proposed for facilitating the continuation of the treatment program. First, the social appropriateness or significance (Kazdin, French, & Sherick, 1981) of the proposed treatment procedures should be established. Witt, Martens, and Elliott (1984) argued that in school settings it is important to evaluate teachers' beliefs concerning what is an acceptable intervention. Witt *et al.* (1984) surveyed 180 teachers regarding their acceptance of various classroom management procedures. The most important finding was that the teachers' acceptance of proposed treatments is influenced by the amount of time needed for planning and implementing specific treatments. Only when teachers viewed the problem to be substantial were they willing to implement even effective treatments that were time-consuming. The implication is that teacher beliefs as to the need for treatment, as well as the effectiveness of proposed treatment procedures, should be established prior to intervention. If the behavior to be treated is not perceived as significant, and the proposed treatment is relatively time-consuming, then there may be a very low probability of treatment continuation.

Utilizing Pragmatic Procedures

A second, interrelated factor is the pragmatic aspects of the proposed treatment. Even when all educational staff agree that the behavior to be treated is important, and that the proposed treatment appears to have a high probability of success, it is still critical that the treatment program be integrated into the student's normal schedule (Wacker, 1984). Elaborate programs that involve unusual resources, no matter how effective, may have very minimal practical value (Kazdin, 1978). Once the need for treatment has been established, and the general outcomes defined, it is critical that treatment consist of normally available materials that are delivered by normally available staff if the treatment protocol is to be continued past relatively brief time periods. In addition, if pragmatic considerations are used to define a treatment package, educational staff may be much more likely to use the established procedures with other students, and other individuals (parents and other educational staff) may also be more likely to utilize the procedures in other settings.

Evaluation of Treatment Continuation

The two guidelines for increasing the probability of treatment continuation can be considered as procedures for facilitating the maintenance of the treatment procedures (see Table 1). Establishing the acceptability of a proposed treatment is important for beginning the treatment process, and utilizing normally available materials and staff helps to ensure its continuation for even extensive time periods. This requires psychologists to be more flexible with respect to the type of treatment proposed, and may sometimes result in the use of a procedure that is not considered to be optimal. However, treatments that can be effectively used in educational settings must be frequently defined as much on their pragmatic value as on their known or anticipated success.

Implementing Treatment Programs

General Goals of Treatment Programs

Treatment programs for severely handicapped students might be evaluated along the two dimensions of behavior proposed by Gifford, Rusch, Martin, and White (1985): adaptability and autonomy. Adaptability refers to the student's generalization of skills, whereas autonomy refers to the student's increased independence. These two general goals of treatment provide a conceptual framework in which the relative success of a treatment program can be evaluated. Following the initial acquisition of skills produced during treatment, the student should be able to generalize those skills to novel conditions (across settings, people, and tasks), and should be able to perform the target behavior without need for extra intervention.

Figure 1 provides an overview of the treatment process that incorporates these two goals. As discussed previously, the treatment process begins by defining meaningful target behavior (behavior needed in community settings) and conditions (antecedents and consequences) necessary for the continued occurrence of the behavior. Once the target behavior and conditions are defined, a treatment protocol is developed that is acceptable to educational staff, parents, and/or individuals in the community (because the behavior is to be ultimately performed in the community). Procedures for producing generalization are incorporated into the protocol, and evaluated based on the student's generalization of skills across novel conditions. In addition, consideration is given to the generalized use of the treatment protocol with other students and/or by other staff (e.g., by using normally available materials). Independence is evaluated by the student's continued performance at acceptable levels following the discontinuation of treatment, and/or by the student's demonstration of skills not directly treated.

This proposed overview is provided to guide professionals who develop treatment programs for persons with severe handicaps. Regardless of the behaviors selected for treatment, the two general goals of generalization and independence remain the same. In addition, the four outcomes of treatment (two each for both goals) provide criteria for evaluating each goal, and for determining when treatment should be initiated or terminated. In the following sections, procedures for facilitating each of these four outcomes are described.

Generalization of Skills across Conditions

Procedures that promote acquisition of skills are not necessarily the same as those that promote generalization (Gifford *et al.*, 1985). Instead, the opposite should be assumed unless specific procedures have been utilized to produce generalization (Stokes & Baer, 1977). The generalization procedures we have found to be most useful with students who are severely handicapped can be divided into two categories based on the stimuli ma-

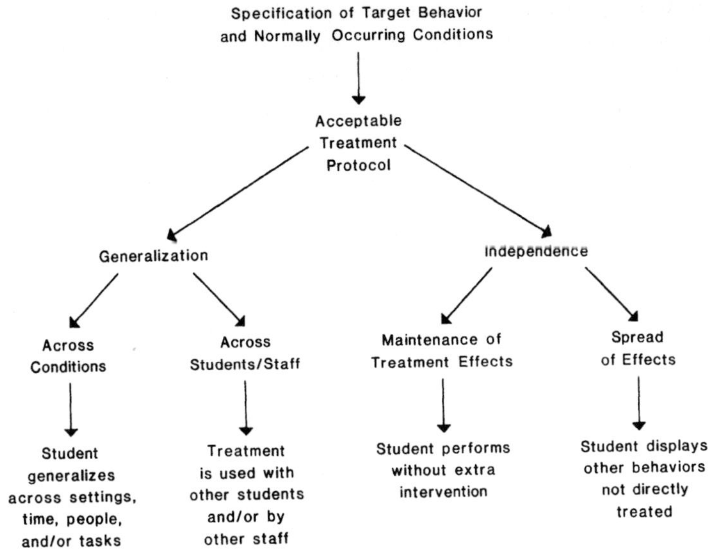

Figure 1. Overview of effective treatment programs.

nipulated during treatment (antecedent or consequence stimuli). These procedures are summarized in Table 2.

Antecedent Procedures

An antecedent stimulus may be any feature of the environment a student is in, including the placement of objects, the presence and position of a particular individual, or the cue or instruction provided. Antecedent stimuli can come to control behavior (become discriminative stimuli) if the response is reinforced only when the stimulus is present and reinforcement does not occur when the stimulus is absent. In many cases, more than one

Table 2. Generalization Procedures

Procedures	Manipulation	Description
1. Common antecedent stimuli[a]	Antecedent cues	Treatment stimuli are selected that closely approximate normally occurring stimuli
2. Sufficient exemplars[a]	Antecedent cues	Treatment is introduced for at least two examples of the desired response
3. General case[b]	Antecedent cues	Treatment is provided for each identified variation of a task or response
4. Antecedent cue regulation[c]	Antecedent cues	Student is trained to control own behavior by manipulating available antecedent stimuli
5. Natural contingencies[a]	Consequences	Treatment contingencies closely approximate normally occurring contingencies
6. Intermittent schedules[a]	Consequences	Reinforcement is shifted from continuous to intermittent schedules
7. Consequence regulation	Consequences	Student is trained to deliver previously defined reinforcers

[a]Based on Stokes and Baer (1977).
[b]Based on Horner and McDonald (1982).
[c]Based on Gifford, Rusch, Martin and White (1985).

discriminative stimulus may control responding because they are provided as a package (e.g., the presence of the teacher, the positioning of play materials, and a verbal or gestural cue). However, it should not be assumed that each of these stimuli are necessary to control responding. In many cases, only one of these stimuli actually control responding, with the other stimuli being "wasted" (Steege, Wacker, Bodensteiner, & Ortina, 1985). Differentiation between discriminative stimuli (those actually controlling behavior) from other antecedent stimuli can be critical for producing generalization.

Steege *et al.* (1985) described a procedure that evaluates which antecedent stimuli set the occasion for the occurrence of the target response. For a given response, these stimuli included verbal cues, gestures, demonstrations, or physical guidance. The students each responded to different types of stimuli when being trained on complex domestic tasks, that is, the antecedent stimuli that served as the discriminative stimuli varied across students. Treatment was made more efficient by systematically including the discriminative stimuli for each student during all training sessions. Pairing the discriminative stimuli with naturally occurring stimuli was then effective in producing generalization.

When a systematic attempt is made to match the antecedent stimuli used during treatment with the stimuli available in the nontreatment (generalization) condition, a *common antecedent stimuli* procedure (Stokes & Baer, 1977) is being utilized. The purpose of treatment is to train a student to respond appropriately to normally occurring antecedent stimuli. Because treatment cannot always be most effectively or efficiently conducted in classroom, residential, or community settings, an attempt is made to utilize the antecedent stimuli usually found in those settings during treatment.

As an example, assume that a referral is made for a student who "only wants to play" and refuses to work. Two antecedent stimuli (placement of play materials and the verbal cue *play*) are normally presented by the classroom teacher to designate the appropriate time for playing. The student is able to play the designated games, and appears to find the games reinforcing. In this case, treatment is conducted to train the student to initiate play following both cues, and to withhold his or her initiation of play behavior when the cues are not provided. An approach to treatment using common antecedent stimuli is systematically to train the student to initiate play when the games are placed on a designated table (but not when the games are on the shelf) and when the word *play* is provided but not when *work* is provided. Three situations are provided during treatment: the desired situation (table—play) and two distractor situations (table—work; shelf—work). In this way, the critical aspects of this situation have been incorporated into treatment, which should improve the probability of generalization. If the student is initially unresponsive to the naturally occurring stimuli, then currently effective stimuli might be paired with the natural stimuli. Once behavior is under the control of these stimuli, the stimuli that originally controlled behavior are gradually removed (faded) until the behavior is under the control of the naturally occurring stimuli.

A relatively frequent difficulty we have experienced with a common stimuli approach is that the antecedent cues vary across settings, and even within the same settings. Teachers and parents use different cues, the same teacher uses different cues at different times, and the position of various other antecedent stimuli varies across settings and time. In these cases, a *sufficient exemplars* (Stokes & Baer, 1977) approach might be used to augment the common antecedent stimuli procedure (normally occurring stimuli should always be used when possible). Sufficient exemplars refers to providing the student with a number of examples of the relevant antecedent stimuli (instructions, people, tasks, materials, etc.). The number of examples needing to be trained is based on an empirical analysis of generalization; when the student generalizes to untrained examples, then the number of examples previously trained is sufficient. Fortunately, in many cases the sufficient number of examples is only two (Stokes & Baer, 1977).

Wacker and Berg (1986) described the use of a sufficient exemplars approach in providing vocational training to four junior high students functioning within the moderate range of mental retardation. The students were trained to perform various cleaning tasks (e.g., windows, sinks, and tables). Rather than train the students to complete all tasks, the students were provided training on two of these tasks, with different types of cleaning materials (paper towels versus sponges) used for each task. In this way, the students received two examples of cleaning tasks and two examples of cleaning materials. Following training, three of four students generalized across a similar cleaning task, and all generalized their responding from the school to an office setting.

An extension of the sufficient exemplars approach is to use what Horner and McDonald (1982) and Sprague and Horner (1984) referred to as general case instruction. In general case programming, the examples trained are defined by variations in the stimulus and response characteristics of a task. For example, spray bottles are frequently used in cleaning tasks, with each type of bottle varying by size and color. In addition, different motoric responses might be required to operate the spray nozzle of different bottles. Rather than selecting at random examples of spray bottles to train, general case training emphasizes that the examples trained represent the variations that are likely to be encountered.

General case instruction is conducted by first defining an instructional or treatment universe and then selecting examples from that universe that are trained sequentially. The instructional universe is defined by determining the stimulus features of a task (stimulus class) that either set the occasion for the occurrence of the same response (response class) or result in different responses. A stimulus class is defined by the characteristics shared by all members. For example, all spray bottles share certain features such as the presence of a nozzle, but the nozzles may vary in color, size, and shape.

A response class can be defined based on two criteria. First, all members result in the same outcome (clean surface). Second, members share similar motoric topographies (spraying and wiping). General case instruction is continued until all members within the stimulus class (spray bottles) produce the designated response (spraying a surface).

Sprague and Horner (1984) taught moderately and severely handicapped students to operate vending machines using a general case approach. An analysis of vending machines in the students' community resulted in ten different types of machines being possible (based on the stimulus characteristics of each machine, such as the location of the coin slot). Training was conducted on vending machines that represented each variation encountered, resulting in generalization across other nontrained vending machines.

The final type of antecedent procedure to be discussed here is referred to as antecedent-cue regulation (Gifford *et al.*, 1985). As discussed previously, multiple antecedent stimuli are available in most settings, any of which may control responding. When students are trained to make specific responses to limit the potential range of discriminative stimuli controlling responding, an antecedent cue regulation procedure is being utilized. There are two general classes of antecedent-cue regulation procedures: self-generated cues and externally generated cues (Gifford *et al.*, 1985).

The use of self-instructions is the most common example of self-generated cues. The self-instructions produced by a student constitute a stimulus that comes to control a previously acquired response (Gifford *et al.*, 1985; Karlan & Rusch, 1982). Students are usually taught first to complete a task to criterion, and then to self-instruct correct performance (say-then-do) prior to completing the task (Wacker & Berg, 1986). Maintenance of responding is improved because the students continue to provide their own cues (verbal instructions) in the absence of any other cue to guide behavior.

With students who are more severely handicapped, the students may be taught to produce a verbal label (instead of a complete instruction) that serves to guide their performance by making certain aspects of the task more salient, rather than explicitly stating what the student should do (Wacker & Greenebaum, 1984). Wacker and Greenebaum (1984) taught seven adolescents with moderate and severe mental retardation to complete a sorting task by training them to verbally label the relevant dimension (shape or color) of the objects being sorted. Following training, the students were able to sort other objects not trained.

Externally generated cues are antecedent stimuli originally provided by staff, but which the student learns to control independently to modify his or her own behavior (Gifford *et al.*, 1985). The most common example of externally generated cues are picture prompts, which have been used extensively to train severely handicapped persons on complex daily living and vocational tasks (Johnson & Cuvo, 1981; Martin, Rusch, James, Decker, & Trtol, 1982; Wacker & Berg, 1983). Training is conducted to teach the student to imitate the performance depicted by each picture representing the task analysis of responses to be completed. In most cases, these pictures are bound together in a sequential order within a picture book, and the student turns to each picture (look-then-do) to complete the task.

In a recently completed study, Berg, Wacker, Berrie, and Swatta (1984) trained students to complete independently dusting and cleaning tasks in the classroom setting with picture prompts. The students learned to imitate the pictures, generalized their use of pictures across other settings (apartments and offices) and tasks, and maintained their behavior over a 3-month period. This study demonstrated that the students learned to rely on their pictures to guide their performance, and to ignore other, potentially distracting stimuli available in other settings. The pictures functioned much like written notes or lists of tasks to be performed that most other people use to guide their behavior. Similar effects have been reported when pretaped instructions or tactual cues were used with severely handicapped adolescents who were blind or deaf/blind respectively (Berg & Wacker, 1983).

Consequence Procedures

Each of the antecedent procedures are used to arrange antecedent events to promote greater generalization of performance. In many cases, once a student learns to use antecedent stimuli to guide performance, treatment can be successfully terminated. For other students, however, the issue is more related to the student's motivation to continue to perform desired behavior, rather than to an inability to complete a task under specific conditions. We have found that successful treatment usually involves both components: (a) use of antecedent procedures to reliably guide behavior, and (b) use of consequence procedures to increase the likelihood of continued responding. Although the antecedent procedures previously described often facilitate maintenance (e.g., picture prompts remove many of the memory demands of a task), the continued performance by students is mostly a function of the consequences delivered for behavior. The following three consequence procedures should be considered in most treatment programs.

As was the case for the selection of antecedent stimuli, normally occurring reinforcers should also be utilized during treatment. Stokes and Baer (1977) termed the use of normally occurring consequences as *natural maintaining contingencies,* because it is through the consistent presentation of these contingencies that behavior can be maintained in nontreatment settings. There are two specific methods that incorporate the use of natural maintaining contingencies within the treatment process.

First, the target behaviors trained must be such that reinforcement for these behaviors occurs in the natural environment (Stokes & Baer, 1977). The program for treating SIB reported by Durand and Carr (1985) is an excellent example. Rather than only focusing on the reduction of SIB, these authors demonstrated that the differential reinforcement of a positive communicative response can serve the same purpose. Because the students' verbal requests or instructions resulted in desired outcomes, there is every reason to believe that long-term maintenance of the incompatible communication behaviors will be achieved.

Another approach to identifying behavior that receives reinforcement is to develop surveys that assess the critical behavior needed within a given setting. Rusch, Schutz, and Agran (1982), for example, reported that community work supervisors frequently have specific behavioral expectations, or entry-level requirements, for their workers. Rusch *et al.* developed a brief survey that listed the expectations of community employers. During training, the students were trained to meet these entry-level requirements, thus increasing the probability of the students receiving routine reinforcement at work (thereby facilitating their maintenance of behavior).

A second method is to train students to solicit reinforcement appropriately in natural settings (Seymore & Stokes, 1976). One of the communicative responses trained by Durand and Carr (1985) was for a student to ask for feedback on a classroom activity, thereby increasing the frequency of social attention and praise. This is incompatible with SIB, if the students engage in SIB as a means of gaining social reinforcement, and social reinforcement is delivered only for the appropriate communicative response.

Most individuals solicit praise and attention from others in their environment by engaging in behavior that has a high probability of resulting in social reinforcement. Unfortunately, severely handicapped students rarely have these skills and must be specifically trained to engage in behaviors that prompt reinforcement. Of equal importance is that they learn to identify appropriate occasions for seeking reinforcement. As an example, one behavior that can promote attention is to engage in acceptable greeting responses. Stokes, Baer, and Jackson (1974) taught four severely handicapped students to produce a greeting response (waving their hands to greet others). Following training, the students generalized this skill to greet others not involved in the training program.

Frequently, this is just the first step of an effective program. Once a skill that solicits attention or praise has been trained, the student must then learn when to engage in the behavior. For example, students might be trained to engage in an acceptable greeting response whenever their teacher or supervisor is in close proximity, and they have completed an assigned task (Wacker & Berg, 1986). When both of these conditions for emitting the greeting response are met, a high probability exists that the behavior will be reinforced. Otherwise, the student may actually engage in behavior that results in punishment (e.g., "finish your assignment").

Naturally occurring consequences, even when solicited, may not initially serve to reinforce behavior. In this case, treatment must continue until natural consequences serve to reinforce behavior, or maintenance of treatment effects is unlikely. This is usually best accomplished by pairing natural consequences with previously established reinforcers. In the Stokes *et al.* (1974) program, food was paired with attention from others during training. Once the subjects began responding to the attention they received, food was faded from the procedures.

In play situations, teacher attention is frequently used as the reinforcer. However, for play to be maintained, the reinforcement delivered by the teacher will either have to be replaced by another reinforcer, or the teacher will have to be available continuously to reinforce the behavior (Wacker, 1984). Strain (1975) avoided this difficulty by instructing a nonhandicapped peer to initiate play (verbally prompt play behavior and provide continued encouragement) with three severely handicapped, preschool boys. A natural reinforcer for engaging in play is contact with peers, and all three boys increased their frequencies of social behavior. More importantly, two of the boys maintained their social behavior when the nonhandicapped child was removed from the setting.

In many situations, we can simply train behavior that provides access to normally available reinforcers. In this case, we have trapped (Baer & Wolf, 1970) the behavior, that is, the behavior will be maintained in natural settings because it results in reinforcement. In other cases, the student does not initially respond to available contingencies as reinforcers, and we must either pair natural consequences with established reinforcers, or augment natural contingencies with additional reinforcers (e.g., a peer-trainer). In either of these situations, the goal of treatment is to fade the need for extra reinforcers.

A related issue concerns the delivery of reinforcement. Behavior in treatment situations often receives a spuriously high amount of reinforcement (continuous reinforcement schedule) as compared to the natural or nontreatment setting. Two aspects of the natural environment are incompatible with this approach: (a) behavior is reinforced on intermittent schedules, and (b) these schedules are often time based (weekly checks; scheduled work breaks or recess times) rather than frequency based. Shifting behavior from continuous to intermittent schedules can promote maintenance, and is referred to as using indiscriminable contingencies (Stokes & Baer, 1977).

An example of this approach is putting change into the coin box on a bus. In many cases, the bus driver and other passengers ignore this response if it is performed correctly. One approach to solving this problem, and to avoid extinction of the response, is to provide social reinforcement on a high frequency, variable schedule. Following training, when the student probably received a great deal of attention, the schedule of reinforcement should be thinned gradually until reinforcement is delivered infrequently and in an unpredictable fashion. In this way, the student cannot discriminate when reinforcement for the behavior is to occur, and there is a greater probability that the student will consistently demonstrate the behavior. In other situations where reinforcement is delivered on an interval schedule (work breaks), a variable frequency schedule can be used to maintain behavior. School staff might drop in at prearranged times that are unpredictable from the students' standpoint. In this situation, the schedule maintaining behavior is indiscriminable, and the student may continue to perform the work task at high rates.

For some students, contingencies can be shifted from external administration to self-administration (Kazdin, 1978), which might be referred to as a consequence regulation procedure (Wacker & Berg, 1986). Consequence regulation procedures offer many of the potential advantages discussed for antecedent-cue regulation procedures. Both procedures result in the development of self-control by students, and both may be effective in the absence of external cues or reinforcers for behavior. The goal of this procedure is to teach students to evaluate their own behavior and to deliver previously defined reinforcers contingent on that behavior.

When the naturally available reinforcers are sufficient to maintain behavior, then the preferred procedure may be to teach students to solicit the occurrence of this reinforcement. By soliciting reinforcement, students can regulate the frequency with which they are reinforced (i.e., increase the density of reinforcement).

For students who do not find available reinforcers to be sufficient to maintain behavior, two alternative approaches may be successful. In the first approach, students are taught to deliver a previously defined reinforcer to themselves to augment naturally occurring reinforcers. Helland, Paluck, and Klein (1976) compared self-delivery of reinforcement (deliver own compliments and select a previously defined reinforcer) with supervisor-delivered reinforcement on the clients' production rates in a workshop setting. Both reinforcement conditions led to higher production levels, but the clients in the self-delivery group worked independently of staff.

Another version of this approach was presented by Berg (1983). A deaf/blind adolescent functioning within the severe range of mental retardation was trained to package various items and to stuff envelopes. To increase her independence on this task, and to maintain her level of performance, a bowl of popcorn (a previously established reinforcer) was placed on the work table. As each assembly or envelope was completed, she ate one piece of popcorn. This procedure was combined with intermittent praise from staff for her contingent delivery of popcorn. The combined use of these procedures proved to be successful over a several month period in maintaining her accuracy of performance.

A second consequence regulation procedure was recently reported by Wacker, Berg, Wiggins, Muldoon, and Cavanaugh (1985). In this investigation, five profoundly/multiply handicapped students were trained to self-deliver sensory reinforcers by engaging in prespecified motoric behavior. Mercury switches were attached to the students' arms or heads, and when the student raised his or her arm/head (these behaviors were defined as having therapeutic value for the students) the mercury switch activated a battery-operated toy or device. The students therefore controlled the delivery of the reinforcer by engaging in a desired behavior. In a follow-up investigation with the switches, the use of prerecorded taped messages were also found to be effective in soliciting social attention. In this case, the students' motoric behavior resulted in a tape recording of the teacher's name, which prompted the teacher to attend to the student. Again, the result was an increase in desired behavior, with the consequences to behavior regulated by the students.

Guidelines for Selecting Generalization Procedures

It is doubtful that any of the procedures discussed is sufficient in isolation to produce generalization across all of the conditions needed. This necessitates the need to combine procedures into packages, based on the treatment goals established. All treatment programs should use natural antecedents and consequences, but the selection of other procedures must be based on additional criteria. Four guidelines for selecting generalization training procedures were described by Wacker and Berg (1986) and are summarized in Table 3.

The first guideline concerns the need for extensive training before a student can begin to learn the actual target task. Spellman, DeBriere, Jarboe, Campbell, and Harris (1978), for example, reported that extensive training time was needed for some of their students to learn picture–object matching. In some cases, this training time may be justified because of the task selected for training (e.g., a task requiring the student to perform a large number of separate activities), or because of the extent of generalization needed for successful performance. Wacker and Berg (1983) made the following recommendations for the use of picture prompts, but these recommendations are applicable to most procedures:

> (a) extensive training time is not required to teach students to use pictures to guide their performance, and (b) once students learn to use picture prompts, the amount of training on other tasks is reduced when pictures are available. (pp. 431–432)

The second guideline in Table 3 refers to the type of generalization needed. General case instruction may be most useful for promoting generalization across tasks, with sufficient exemplars being used for generalization across

Table 3. Guidelines for Selecting Generalization Training Procedures

Guidelines	Explanation
1. Skills of students	Select procedures based on the existing skills of students; avoid extensive training time to teach a student a skill (e.g., picture–object matching) that may be unrelated to the target task.
2. Determine type of generalization needed	The procedures promote different types of generalization. Make sure that the treatment procedures chosen account for the types of generalization needed.
3. Training time	Generalization across multiple tasks, people, and settings may be desirable but not needed. Produce the amount of generalization needed without disrupting the ongoing instruction of other equally important skills.
4. Acceptable procedures	Utilize treatment procedures that are acceptable to others affected by treatment (student, teachers, parents, community supervisors).

people. If both types of generalization are needed, combine the procedures to produce the desired results. The third guideline refers to the training time needed to produce the amount of generalization required. There may be 25 different varieties of board games identified through the use of a general case evaluation. The major question to ask is whether extensive training time should be allocated systematically to produce generalization across each type of board game (at the expense of other skills that might be trained). Finally, the treatment procedures selected might not be acceptable to teachers or parents, and alternative procedures must then be selected. For example, picture prompts are not acceptable to some teachers, and must therefore be replaced by other procedures.

Generalization across Other Students and Staff

A second outcome of treatment procedures is their impact on other students and other staff not involved in the original treatment program. In a typical situation, the psychologist receives a referral for one student, and treatment consists of either directly intervening with that student, or consulting with a few selected staff members who in turn provide intervention. One measure of effective treatment outcome is the use of the treatment procedures by other staff (either with the same student or with other students). Unfortunately, generalized use of established procedures across other students or other staff is infrequently evaluated.

Generalization across other students and staff may be produced using the same procedures for producing the other forms of generalization previously described. Three of these procedures may be especially helpful.

When possible, the use of a sufficient exemplars procedure may produce either type of generalization. If treatment can be implemented with at least two students, educational staff may be more inclined to use similar procedures with other students. If two or more staff implement the procedures, other staff may also become involved. A general case program may be especially useful where students with different presenting behaviors are provided treatment, or staff from different areas are involved (e.g., teacher and speech therapist, or home room teacher and gym teacher). Two examples of students and/or staff may prove sufficient to produce generalization, especially if the students and staff are viewed by others as constituting different examples.

In the program described previously where microswitches were used by students to regulate reinforcers (Wacker *et al.*, 1985), two teachers and a speech therapist were involved originally. Currently, a third teacher routinely uses the switches with different students, and a physical therapist assists in the use of the switches with the original students. Neither staff member was directly trained to use the switches. In addition, all students (N=12) in both of the original classes are routinely evaluated with microswitches by the teachers, an increase of 7 students not directly involved during the original treatment. These generalization effects provide evidence that the treatment program was effective, and also provides data that the time spent in treatment was efficient (as evidenced by the generalization produced by the original treatment program).

A second procedure to consider is to evaluate the natural maintaining contingencies motivating staff, rather than students. In at least some cases, the motivation may derive from negative reinforcement; staff refer students to escape or avoid an aversive event (such as a student engaging in SIB). Analysis of these contingencies may be useful data for facilitating the generalized use of procedures across students, as well as for increasing the probability that the treatment program will be continued or maintained. For example, training multiple staff to assist in the treatment of SIB reduces the amount of time each individual staff member must spend in treating this behavior. If negative reinforcement maintains behavior, the procedures implemented should be continued by trained staff, and used with other students. Other staff may also begin to use the procedures as they observe these effects on staff time.

A final procedure, and one which cannot be overstated, is the use of readily available materials and staff during treatment. Without the acceptance of school staff, the likelihood of any positive effects deriving from treatment are substantially reduced. Again, this requires that we be very flexible in our intervention designs, and that we be prepared to modify our treatment approaches to get a "best fit" with teacher expectations. Our approach has been to offer at least two alternative treatment approaches for any given student, and asking teachers to choose the most acceptable intervention. Offering choices may facilitate acceptance of a proposed treatment because the teachers have actively participated in the selection of treatment procedures, that is, they are now colleagues in the delivery of treatment.

Producing Independence in Students

The second goal of treatment for students with severe handicaps is to increase their independence. There are two treatment outcomes associated with this goal: (a) continued performance at acceptable levels following the discontinuation of treatment (maintenance of performance), and (b) acquisition of skills not directly trained (spread of effects).

Maintenance of Independent Performance

Maintenance of independent performance refers to the student's continued demonstration of acceptable behavior under the natural conditions present in target settings (classroom, community and/or residential settings). If intervention has not been conducted within these settings, then it is necessary first to generalize the behavior into these settings before evaluating independence. It may be helpful to think of the discontinuation of treatment as a fading process that involves two steps: (a) posttreatment, where the student has reached criteria under treatment conditions, and (b) maintenance, where the student is functioning independently following the removal of all extra (i.e., noncontinuing) components of treatment.

Treatment usually consists of a package of procedures that includes critical (e.g., sufficient exemplars of board games) and noncritical (e.g., "it is time to play") components. Specification of critical components is, of course, impossible to predict prior to a systematic evaluation of each separate component. In most cases, however, we make judgments regarding which components are critical. Posttreatment is frequently the removal or withdrawal of the components we assume to be critical, and therefore constitutes a partial withdrawal (Rusch & Kazdin, 1981) from treatment. If the student continues to function independently, we then remove all remaining components and move into a maintenance condition. In addition, maintenance requires that all of these extra conditions be removed for relatively extensive time periods (at least one month), including the removal of any extra person involved in treatment (e.g., the psychologist). If only normally available educational staff have conducted treatment, they must have returned to their routine schedules (or permanent changes in their schedules have been made). Maintenance is conducted until the student continues to display independently the target behavior with no further need for extra assistance, prompting, or reinforcement.

To facilitate maintenance of independent performance, the preferred approach is to (a) train behavior that is normally reinforced in the target setting, and (b) utilize contingencies commonly found in that setting. Thus, the use of natural antecedents and consequences, in addition to facilitating the generalization of behavior, are critical for long-term maintenance of independent performance. However, even when these methods have been used, and the student displays acceptable behavior during posttreatment, lack of maintenance may still be relatively common.

Lack of maintenance can be analyzed as occurring for at least two reasons: (a) the student continues to lack the skills needed for independent functioning (skill deficit), or (b) the student is not reinforced to continue performing the behavior independently (performance deficit). A skill deficit usually occurs because the noncritical components of treatment used during posttreatment are actually critical for continued independence, that is, a stimulus-control problem has occurred. In cooperative game situations, the verbal cue *play* may be a discriminative stimulus for the student. Following posttreatment, the teacher may use this verbal Sd less and less frequently, and the student is unable to discriminate appropriate occasions for playing from inappropriate occasions. As a result, the student becomes increasingly less independent. Another common discriminative stimulus in this situation is that the teacher aid sets the games on a particular table. If this procedure continues during posttreatment but not during maintenance, lack of maintenance may occur. In both of these situations, the student has not acquired the skills necessary to follow normally available Sds, and treatment must be continued.

A performance deficit occurs when the student has acquired all of the necessary skills, but does not find the existing contingencies to be reinforcing. In this situation, the problem may be due to the presence or absence of a trainer. During treatment, when continuous reinforcement is provided, the student may associate the trainer with reinforcement. Although posttreatment shifts this reinforcement from continuous to intermittent schedules, the student is still responding to the trainer rather than to the natural contingencies in the classroom. As a result, maintenance constitutes an extinction condition (the trainer is never present) and lack of independent performance occurs.

Specification of the reasons for the observed lack of maintenance can greatly facilitate the retraining process. It must be assumed from the beginning of treatment that: (a) the critical components of the treatment package are unknown until maintenance is completed successfully, and (b) lack of maintenance is relatively common with these students because we cannot predict which components will be critical. The maintenance condition is therefore the last phase of treatment, and the initiation of this condition should not be a signal to staff that the intervention has been completed. When maintenance does not occur, it is necessary to use this as an error analysis of our judgments regarding the critical components of treatment. Analyzing this situation in terms of skill and performance deficits has proven to be useful to us in prescribing relatively brief remediation plans for producing maintenance. In many cases, this remediation is simply pointing out the need for the continued occurrence of a discriminative stimulus, which the teacher can then consistently incorporate into the program (skill deficit). In other cases, the trainer's withdrawal from the setting must be more gradual, or a different reinforcement system (soliciting attention from other staff) implemented (performance deficit).

Spread of Effects

A second and equally important treatment outcome with respect to independence is the student's new ability to acquire additional skills. In a typical social situation, there may be literally hundreds of separate behaviors that are acceptable, but the intervention focuses on only a small subset of these behaviors. Playing board games with peers requires that the student demonstrate a vast array of behavior, only a few of which concern the game itself. For example, the student may begin to communicate more effectively, be more socially responsive to others, assist in setting up or putting away the game, and engaging in more appropriate social behavior with peers during other situations such as juice time. Prior to treatment, it is common that none of these behaviors are observed. Following treatment, however, a geometric increase in these behaviors may occur, even though none of these behaviors were directly trained. The occurrence of these behaviors demonstrates the spread of effects achieved from treatment and should be documented.

Koegel, Burke, O'Dell, Kern, and Dunlap (1983) discussed this occurrence in terms of independent increases in incidental behavior. Incidental behaviors encompass any response not directly trained, but which directly facilitate independence in a natural setting. Koegel *et al.* (1983) reported a project where students classified as autistic were told to buy items at a grocery store. No training was provided to the students with respect to the use of a shopping cart, picking up dropped items, or using the check-out line appropriately. However, the students acquired these behaviors as a function of the natural antecedents and consequences available in the store setting.

Similar results were obtained from a project where six junior high school students, classified as moderately mentally retarded, were trained to perform two clerical tasks in an office setting (Wacker & Berg, 1984). The students were trained to complete the tasks in their classroom using a sufficient exemplars procedure. Throughout training, the students were taken to an office setting to document generalization. In addition, a checklist was maintained that included all incidental skills demonstrated by the students in the office setting. These behaviors included asking for assistance when needed, picking up dropped items, making appropriate greeting responses, etc. The secretary in the office, who was their work supervisor, was not trained either to encourage or reinforce these behaviors. Instead, she was told simply to treat the students as she would any other clerks working for her.

In addition to acquiring and generalizing the skills necessary to complete the two target tasks, all students independently learned or demonstrated at least 12 other incidental behaviors. As students acquired the behaviors necessary to complete the target tasks, they demonstrated a corresponding increase in their abilities to function as members of the office, that is, they became increasingly independent within the more general context of the setting in which they worked. Because no direct training was provided for these incidental skills, they were demonstrated as a function of the natural antecedents and consequences available in the office.

Providing students with the opportunity to display needed skills in natural settings is therefore important for two reasons. First, experience in natural settings provides generalization probes to evaluate the success of treatment. Second, experience in natural settings permits students to engage the natural antecedents and consequences available in those settings, facilitating their independence through the acquisition of incidental behavior. When incidental behaviors are added to the target behaviors acquired during the treatment process, intervention conducted within the context of classroom, community, or residential settings is more efficient than treatment provided in isolated settings. Even when the extra time needed to trasport students is figured into the equation, the amount of staff time needed for each new behavior observed following treatment is substantially reduced. For example, in the Wacker and Berg (1984) study, the staff time needed to transport the students to and from the office may have been up to three times higher than if all training was conducted in the classroom. However, the additional skills acquired by the students were at least six times higher as a result of the experiences in the office setting where the students worked.

Summary

The treatment model proposed for students with severe handicaps focuses on two major goals (generalization and independence), with two treatment outcomes specified for each goal. The model is prescriptive to the extent that all assessment data directly lead to the establishment of meaningful target behavior, and/or to the selection of treatment procedures that are acceptable to educational staff. Students with severe handicaps are frequently very heterogeneous in the behavior observed, but most display the lack of a well-developed response repertoire. This lack of an extensive behavioral repertoire can be particularly troubling for three interrelated reasons: (a) the substantial training time involved during treatment, (b) lack of generalization of skills, and (c) continued lack of independence following treatment. Providing treatment programs that facilitate generalization and independence is possible; the behavioral technology is available and expanding. However, effective treatment frequently means adjustments in how treatment is provided (e.g., within the classroom or community rather than in a more controlled setting) and in the criteria used to evaluate successful treatment (e.g., generalization and maintenance of skills rather than the initial acquisition of skills).

References

Baer, D., & Wolf, M. M. (1970). The entry into natural communities of reinforcement. In R. Ulrich, T. Stachnik, & J. Mabry (Eds.), *Control of human behavior* (Vol. 2, pp. 319–324). Glenview, IL: Scott Foresman.

Berg, W. K. (1983, October). An overview of permanent prompts. In D. Wacker (Chair), *Use of permanent prompts in vocational training programs*. Symposium at the Iowa Chapter of The Association for Persons With Severe Handicaps, Cedar Falls, IA.

Berg, W. K., & Wacker, D. P. (1983, May). *Effects of permanent prompts on the vocational performance of severely handicapped individuals*. Paper presented at the Association for Behavior Analysis, Milwaukee, WI.

Berg, W. K., Wacker, D. P., Berrie, P., & Swatta, P. (1984, May). *Assessing generalization with picture prompts*. Paper presented at the Association for Behavior Analysis, Nashville, TN.

Brown, L., Branston, M., Hamre-Nietupski, S., Pumpian, I., Certo, N., & Gruenewald, L. (1979). A strategy for developing chronological age-appropriate and functional curricular content for severely handicapped adolescents and young adults. *Journal of Special Education, 13*(1), 81–90.

Brown, L., Branston-McClean, M., Baumgart, D., Vincent, L., Falvey, M., & Schroeder, J. (1979). Using the characteristics of current and subsequent least restrictive environments in the development of curricular content for severely handicapped students. *AAESPH Review*, 4(4), 407–424.

Durand, V. M., & Carr, E. G. (1985). Self-injurious behavior: Motivating conditions and guidelines for treatment. *School Psychology Review, 14*, 171–176.

Gifford, J., Rusch, R., Martin, J., & White, D. (1985). Autonomy and adaptability: A proposed technology for maintaining work behavior. In N. Ellis & N. Bray (Eds.), *International review of research on mental retardation* (Vol. 12, pp. 285–314). New York: Academic Press.

Helland, C., Pauluck, R., & Klein, M. (1976). A comparison of self and external reinforcement with the trainable mentally retarded. *Mental Retardation, 14,* 22–23.

Horner, R., & McDonald, R. (1982). Comparison of single instance and general case instruction in teaching a generalized vocational skill. *Journal of the Association for the Severely Handicapped, 7,* 7–20.

Irons, D., Irons, T., & Maddux, C. D. (1984). A survey of perceived competence among psychologists who evaluate students with severe handicaps. *Journal of the Association for Persons with Severe Handicaps, 9,* 55–60.

Iwata, B. A., Dorsey, M. F., Slifer, K. J., Bauman, K. E., & Richman, G. S. (1982). Toward a functional analysis of self-injury. *Analysis and Intervention in Developmental Disabilities, 2,* 3–20.

Johnson, B., & Cuvo, A. (1981). Teaching mentally retarded adults to cook. *Behavior Modification, 5,* 187–202.

Karlan, G., & Rusch, F. (1982). Correspondence between saying and doing: Some thoughts on defining correspondence and future directions for application. *Journal of Applied Behavior Analysis, 15,* 151–162.

Kazdin, A. (1978). Behavior modification in retardation. In J. Neisworth & R. Smith (Eds.), *Retardation: Issues, assessment, and intervention* (pp. 299–339). New York: McGraw-Hill.

Kazdin, A. E., French, N. H., & Sherick, R. B. (1981). Acceptability of alternative treatments for children: Evaluation of inpatient children, parents, and staff. *Journal of Consulting and Clinical Psychology, 49,* 900–907.

Koegel, R., Burke, J., O'Dell, M., Kern, L., & Dunlap, G. (1983, August). Pivotal responses related to generalization. In D. Baer (Chair), *Generalization and maintenance of treatment gains in severely handicapped clients.* Symposium presented at the American Psychological Association, Anaheim, CA.

Martin, J., Rusch, F., James, V., Decker, P., & Trtol, K. (1982). The use of picture cues to establish self-control in the preparation of complex meals by mentally retarded adults. *Applied Research in Mental Retardation, 3,* 105–119.

Rusch, F., & Kazdin, A. (1981). Toward a methodology of withdrawal designs for the assessment of response maintenance. *Journal of Applied Behavior Analysis, 14,* 131–140.

Rusch, F., Schutz, R., & Agran, M. (1982). Validating entry-level survival skills for service occupations: Implications for curriculum development. *Journal of the Association for the Severely Handicapped, 7,* 32–41.

Seymour, F., & Stokes, T. (1976). Self-recording in training girls to increase work and evoke staff praise in an institution for offenders. *Journal of Applied Behavior Analysis, 9,* 41–54.

Sontag, E., Smith, J., & Sailor, W. (1977). The severely/profoundly handicapped: Who are they? Where are we? *Journal of Special Education, 11,* 5–11.

Spellman, C., DeBriere. T., Jarboe, D., Campbell, S., & Harris, S. (1978). Pictorial instruction: Training daily living skills. In M. Snell (Ed.), *Systematic instruction of the moderately and severely handicapped* (pp. 391–411). Columbus, OH: Merrill.

Sprague, J., & Horner, R. (1984). The effects of single instance, multiple instance, and general case training on generalized vending machine use by moderately and severely handicapped students. *Journal of Applied Behavior Analysis, 17,* 273–278.

Steege, M., Wacker, D. P., Bodensteiner, C., & Ortina, T. (1985, May). *Evaluation of effectiveness and efficiency in using least to most restrictive prompt sequences with severely handicapped students.* Paper presented at the Association for Behavior Analysis, Columbus, OH.

Stokes, T., & Baer, D. (1977). An implicit technology of generalization. *Journal of Applied Behavior Analysis, 10,* 349–367.

Stokes, T., Baer, D., & Jackson, R. (1974). Programming the generalization of a greeting response in four retarded children. *Journal of Applied Behavior Analysis, 7,* 599–610.

Strain, P. (1975). Increasing social play of severely retarded preschoolers through socio-dramatic activities. *Mental Retardation, 13*(6), 7–9.

Wacker, D. P. (1984). Training moderately and severely mentally handicapped children to use adaptive social skills. *School Psychology Review, 13,* 324–330.

Wacker, D. P., & Berg, W. K. (1983). Effects of picture prompts on the acquisition of complex vocational tasks by mentally retarded adolescents. *Journal of Applied Behavior Analysis, 16,* 417–433.

Wacker, D. P., & Berg, W. K. (1984). *Evaluation of response outcome and response topography on generalization of skills.* Unpublished manuscript, Division of Developmental Disabilities, The University of Iowa, Iowa City, IA.

Wacker, D. P., & Berg, W. K. (1986). Developing effective transitional programs: Generalizing and maintaining work behavior. In F. Rusch (Ed.), *Competitive employment issues and strategies* (pp. 129–140). Baltimore, MD: Brookes.

Wacker, D. P., & Greenebaum, F. (1984). Efficacy of a verbal training sequence on the sorting performance of moderately and severely retarded adolescents. *American Journal of Mental Deficiency, 88,* 653–660.

Wacker, D. P., Kerr, N. J., & Carroll, J. L. (1983). Discrimination skill as a predictor of prevocational performance of institutionalized mentally retarded clients. *Rehabilitation Psychology, 28*(1), 45–59.

Wacker, D. P., Berg, W. K., Wiggins, B., Muldoon, M., and Cavanaugh, J. (1985). Evaluation of reinforcer preferences for profoundly handicapped students. *Journal of Applied Behavior Analysis, 18,* 173–178.

Witt, J. C., Martens, B. K., & Elliot, S. N. (1984). Factors affecting teachers' judgement of the acceptability of behavioral interventions: Time involvement, behavior problem severity, and type of intervention. *Behavior Therapy, 15,* 204–209.

CHAPTER 28

Childhood Depression

Alan E. Kazdin

Introduction

Childhood depression is a major area of current research in clinical child psychology and child psychiatry. The current attention can be traced to many factors. Depression as a disorder is quite prevalent in adults. Indeed, depression is often referred to as the common cold of adult psychiatric dysfunction. Because of its relatively high prevalence, considerable attention has been devoted to its empirical investigation. Also, major advances have been made in the research on the diagnosis, assessment, etiology, and treatment of affective disorders (see Clayton & Barrett, 1983; Depue, 1979; Paykel, 1982a). Findings obtained with adults point to areas of research with children where parallel relationships might be found on the nature of the dysfunction or where precursors of adult depression might be identified. Of further significance has been the clarification of psychiatric diagnostic criteria. Recent improvements in diagnosis have facilitated the application of diagnostic criteria to children and adolescents and consequently have enhanced the prospects for research.

Advances have begun to emerge in the investigation of childhood depression. The present chapter discusses the emergence of childhood depression as an area of clinical research. Several topics are reviewed including the characteristics of depression in childhood and adolescence, alternative diagnostic procedures, and models of the causes of depression. Finally, alternative treatments currently in use are reviewed as well.

Background and Alternative Views of Childhood Depression

Research on childhood depression has been delayed because of several different factors. To begin with, the diagnosis of childhood disorders in general has lagged behind the advances with adult disorders. Interrelated efforts in adult psychiatry have carefully delineated specific disorders with explicit descriptive criteria, so that homogeneous diagnostic groups could be investigated (e.g., Feighner *et al.*, 1972; Spitzer, Endicott, & Robins, 1978). Efforts to identify clear diagnostic entities in children have only begun

Alan E. Kazdin • Department of Psychiatry, Western Psychiatric Institute and Clinic, University of Pittsburgh School of Medicine, Pittsburgh, Pennsylvania 15213.
Completion of this chapter was supported by a Research Scientist Development Award (MH00353) and by a grant (MH35408) from the National Institute of Mental Health.

with the application of criteria from the *Diagnostic and Statistical Manual of Mental Disorders* (DSM-III-R, American Psychiatric Association, 1987). The efforts have enhanced research on childhood disorders in general.

A related factor that has delayed research has been the varied conceptualizations of childhood depression. Doubts have been expressed whether depression is manifest in children, and if so, the form(s) that it may take. Although no one has ever doubted that children can show particular symptoms of depression (e.g., sadness), views have varied regarding whether children can suffer from the full set of symptoms similar to major depression in adults.

Elaboration of alternative views requires distinguishing depression as a symptom from depression as a syndrome. As a symptom, depression refers merely to sad affect and obviously is quite common. As a syndrome, depression refers to a group of symptoms that go together. Sadness may only be a part of a larger set of problems that may include loss of interest in activities, feelings of worthlessness, sleep disturbances, changes in appetite, and others. The present chapter discusses depression as a syndrome and alternative models of its development and treatment.[1]

Psychodynamic Views

The dominant conceptual views in child clinical work have been based on variations of psychoanalytic theory that assert that depression as a disorder does not occur in children (e.g., Mahler, 1961; Rie, 1966). Certainly, some forms of depression have been widely acknowledged. For example, Spitz (1946) discussed the reactions in infancy precipitated by separation from the mother. This reaction, referred to as anaclitic depression, may include several signs, such as sadness, withdrawal, apprehension, weepiness, retarded reaction to external stimuli, slowed movement, dejection, loss of appetite and weight, and insomnia. Anaclitic depression is regarded as a result of the experience of object loss. Although many of these symptoms resemble the clinical picture of adult depression, anaclitic depression, as originally formulated, is not parallel to affective disorders in adults. Adult depression goes beyond reactions to specific environmental events.

Depression as a clinical disorder in children, similar to major depression in adults, has not been considered to be possible by prominent psychoanalytic authorities. According to orthodox psychoanalytic theory, depression as a disorder has been considered to be a phenomenon of the superego. Alternative explanations of the emergence of depression have been advanced, including the argument that depression results from inwardly directed aggression against oneself (Rochlin, 1965), from a conflict that arouses guilt (Beres, 1966), and from low self-esteem that results from a discrepancy between the real and ideal self (Rie, 1966). In each of these positions, depression depends on a well-developed superego. Because superego development is hypothesized not to mature until adolescence, the appearance of a full clinical syndrome of depression in childhood is precluded.

Ego-analytic models of depression acknowledge the possible appearance of the disorder in children (Anthony, 1975; Bemporad & Wilson, 1978). Depressive states and approximations of a depressive disorder can emerge in different ages and are considered to vary as a function of psychosexual development, experience, and perceptual and cognitive skills. Thus, contemporary psychoanalytic views are

[1]For the present chapter, the notion of syndrome and disorder will be used in reference to depression. *Syndrome* refers to a constellation of symptoms or behaviors that go together. The notion of a *disorder* suggests that more is known about the constellation of symptoms, such as a characteristic family history, biological correlates, predictable clinical course or outcome, and other factors that suggest the meaningfulness of viewing the syndrome as more than merely a collection of correlated behaviors. Current diagnostic practices consider major depression as a disorder in the sense noted here.

compatible with the appearance of childhood depression as a disorder. Yet the dominant view has been that depression as a disorder does not exist in children. Consequently, it has not been specifically sought clinically nor included as a viable diagnostic category for children.

Masked Depression

A second major conceptual position has acknowledged that depression can exist in children, but that its manifestations differ significantly from adult depression. The essential features, such as dysphoric mood and pervasive loss of interest, may not be present. Rather, this view proposes that there is an underlying depression that is manifest in several other symptoms or forms of psychopathology. Depression is said to be masked or expressed in depressive equivalents. Children may be depressed but their affective disorder can only be inferred from the presence of other complaints evident in childhood (Cytryn & McKnew, 1972, 1974; Glaser, 1968; Malmquist, 1977; Toolan, 1962). The symptoms that putatively mask depression have included the full gamut of psychiatric impairment evident in childhood. As a partial list, temper tantrums, hyperactivity, disobedience, running away, delinquency, phobias, somatic complaints, irritability, separation anxiety, and underachievement have been listed as depressive equivalents (see Kovacs & Beck, 1977).

Despite their limitations, the notions of masked depression and depressive equivalents have indirectly contributed to subsequent conceptual positions and empirical research on childhood depression. The idea that depression is masked at least acknowledges that depression can exist in children. Also, the position implies that depression may frequently be associated with or accompanied by other forms of childhood psychopathology. These other symptoms or syndromes may make depression less clear and readily overlooked. Indeed, recent work has shown that many children who meet DSM-III-R criteria for affective disorders may also have many other symptoms as well (Carlson & Cantwell, 1979). Thus, many of the symptoms that have been considered to mask depression may also be present, but they reflect other symptoms or disorders and can be distinguished from depression. Depression does not necessarily accompany other disorders, but when it does, depression may be overlooked if it is not explicitly sought through careful assessment.

The notions of masked depression and depressive equivalents are also significant because they raise the possibility that depression in childhood will be manifested in ways that differ from depression in adulthood. The differences among children, adolescents, and adults may not be in whether depression is masked but in essential and/or associated features that can be objectively assessed. Developmental differences in the manifestations of clinical depression have yet to be elucidated empirically (Cicchetti & Schneider-Rosen, 1984; Sroufe & Rutter, 1984).

Emergence of Depression as Part of Normal Development

Another conceptual position on the nature of childhood depression also acknowledges that depression may exist (Lefkowitz, 1980; Lefowitz & Burton, 1978). This view suggests that symptoms of depression may emerge in children over the course of normal development but dissipate over time. A premise of this view is that if the clinical symptoms of depression are typical of childhood or relatively prevalent and if they remit with age, they should not be regarded as evidence of psychopathology.

The view that childhood depression may not represent a distinct dysfunction in children has been a partial reaction to the notion of masked depression, which permits virtually any sign of deviance to constitute evidence for depression. Epidemiological research has shown that many so called depressive equivalents, such as temper tantrums, fears, or enuresis are relatively common over the course of childhood (e.g., Lapouse, 1966). These behaviors often are not diagnostically significant, because they are not necessarily related to adjustment in general, and they diminish over time (Lapouse, 1966; Werry & Quay, 1971). Even behaviors that relate more specifically to the syndrome of depression, as defined in current taxonomy, may be relatively common. For example, as a measure of sadness, crying has been shown to vary significantly as a function of age. At 6 years of age, approximately 18% of children have been reported to cry two to three times per week; the percentage decreases markedly by puberty to 2% (Werry & Quay, 1971). Similarly, poor appetite, occasionally a symptom of depression, is relatively common in 5-year-old girls and boys (37% and 29%, respectively) but drops sharply by age 9 (9% and 6%, respectively) (MacFarlane, Allen, & Honzik, 1954).

Despite these findings, there is a major problem with the notion that depression is a developmental phenomenon. Evidence is not available to suggest that the syndrome is present as part of normal development. Depression (dysphoria) as a symptom or other specific symptoms may emerge at different points of development. Whether the group of symptoms that define the syndrome emerges at varying points in childhood is an entirely different matter. Even if the full syndrome were shown to have a relatively high prevalence at a particular age, this does not by itself mean that a disorder does not exist or that it should not be treated (Costello, 1980). Moreover, childhood depression may be a precursor of adolescent and adult depression, in which case its early identification might be important.

As already noted, the notion that depression is part of normal development emerged when the diagnostic criteria for depression were so diffuse that virtually any deviance in the child was taken as a possible sign of depression. The recent specification of diagnostic criteria for the syndrome of depression overcomes many of the concerns which gave rise to this view. Nevertheless, the view that depressive symptoms may emerge over the course of development has been important. The view directs attention to the fact that symptoms of depression may vary over the course of child development and helps to alert clinicians and researchers, so that the developmentally common symptoms are not confused with the full set of symptoms that define the disorder.

Depression as a Syndrome or Disorder

A fourth view is that depression in childhood exists and that the essential features of the disorder are similar in children, adolescents, and adults (e.g., Annell, 1972; Cantwell, 1982; Puig-Antich & Gittelman, 1982). This position is adopted in current psychiatric diagnosis (DSM-III-R), in which criteria for affective disorders are delineated and applied independently of age. The statement that these essential features can be used to diagnose depression in children, adolescents, and adults alike is made *a priori* in DSM-III-R but, by implication, raises the issue as an empirical question; that is, can depression be diagnosed in children, adolescents, and adults using the same criteria? This question has now been answered affirmatively by several investigations in which psychiatric interviews are provided for children or adolescents and their parents (e.g., Carlson & Cantwell, 1980; Chiles, Miller, & Cox, 1980; Kashani, Barbero, & Bolander, 1981; Kashani, Husain, *et al.*, 1981; Puig-Antich, Blau, Marx, Greenhill, & Chambers, 1978; Puig-Antich *et al.*, 1979).

The fact that depression as a clinical syndrome can be diagnosed in children, adolescents and adults does not mean that the manifestations of the disorder are necessarily identical. DSM-III-R recognizes that there may be associated features for different ages and developmental levels. However, as yet these are not well specified and are based on clinical experience rather than empirical research.

Among the major views of depression, the

present one has gained dominance in the last few years largely because of the success in applying unmodified diagnostic adult criteria to children and adolescents. Also, empirical evidence is beginning to emerge that elaborates the affective, cognitive, motivational, and biological components of childhood depression (see Cantwell & Carlson, 1983; Puig-Antich & Gittelman, 1982). Research reviewed in the present chapter is based primarily on the successful application of DSM-III-R criteria to children.

Diagnosis of Depression

Depression has been studied in the population of normal children and adolescents as well as various patient groups. Research has begun to address the prevalence of severe depressive symptoms. For example, using a peer-based measure, Lefkowitz and Tesiny (1985) found severe depression (extreme scores exceeding two standard deviations) in 5.2% of a sample of over 3,000 normal third-, fourth-, and fifth-grade children. In another study, 7.3% and 1.3% of high school students showed moderate and severe levels of depression, respectively, using cutoff criteria developed with adults (Kaplan, Hong, & Weinhold, 1984). These and other studies utilize alternative cutoff scores among different measures and hence their results are difficult to compare.

Other studies have utilized diagnostic criteria to evaluate depression as a disorder. In the general population, approximately 2% have been identified as depressed (in randomly selected child populations ages 7–12) using DSM-III criteria (Kashani & Simonds, 1979; Kashani *et al.*, 1983). In clinical populations, estimates have ranged from approximately 2% to 60% (Kashani, Husain, *et al.*, 1981), although more typical estimates fall between 10% and 20% (Puig-Antich & Gittelman, 1982).

An issue of interest is the possibility of differences in prevalence of depressive disorders as a function of gender. The interest stems from the fact that in adulthood, depression generally is more prevalent among women than among men. To date, research has typically found no sex differences in prevalence of depressive disorders in clinic and nonclinic samples of children (ages 6–12) (e.g., Kashani *et al.*, 1983; Lefkowitz & Tesiny, 1985; Lobovits & Handal, 1985). On the other hand, research has suggested that among adolescents, the prevalence is greater in females than in males (e.g., Mezzich & Mezzich, 1979; Reynolds, 1985). Moreover, differences in severity of depression between males and females appear to begin in early adolescence and to increase over the next several years (Kandel & Davies, 1982). Differences in prevalence rates between adolescent males and females are not always found (Kaplan *et al.*, 1984). Consequently, further work and large-scale epidemiological studies are still needed.

As for the overall prevalence rates for children and adolescents, there remain rather large discrepancies in the currently available studies. The large discrepancies in prevalence rates result in part from the different ages that are studied, the different measures that are used, and perhaps most importantly, the different diagnostic criteria that are invoked. Alternative diagnostic systems have been proposed that have important implications for identifying cases and for investigating the nature of childhood depression.

Development of diagnostic systems for children must be viewed in light of the contemporary evolution of diagnosis for adults. In the area of adult disorders, a significant development occurred in the early 1970s when a group of researchers at Washington University (St. Louis) published diagnostic criteria for use in adult psychiatric research (Feighner *et al.*, 1972). These criteria were designed to specify a uniform set of symptoms or behavioral characteristics for diagnosing particular disorders, so that homogeneous clinical populations could be selected. The criteria required specific core or essential symptoms and a select set of additional symptoms from a larger set that needed to be present for a particular disorder to be diagnosed. The Feighner criteria, as they came to be called, were expanded into the Research Diagnostic Criteria (RDC) (Spitzer *et al.*, 1978), based on the same model but encompassing a wider range of disorders. For present purposes, it is important to note that the approach of the Feighner criteria and RDC served as a model for developing criteria for DSM-III and DSM-III-R. RDC was designed primarily for researchers and restricted to a limited set of disorders. Consequently, many patients who come for treatment would not fall into a particular category of RDC. DSM-III-R was designed to handle the exigencies of clinical practice, which requires a broader range of diagnostic categories. The same operational model used in RDC was adopted for DSM-III-R, but the range of disorders was expanded.[2]

Criteria for Children

Prior to the development of RDC and DSM-III, separate criteria had been proposed for childhood depression (e.g., Ling, Oftedal, & Weinberg, 1970). For example, one of the more well known set of criteria were devised by Weinberg, Rutman, Sullivan, Pencik, and Dietz (1973) who followed the model of the Feighner criteria. The Weinberg criteria are listed in Table 1. The criteria indicate that multiple symptoms can be considered as evidence for depression as a disorder. An interview (Bellevue Index of Depression) was also developed for children and parents to evaluate whether these criteria were met (Petti, 1978). The Weinberg criteria have had marked impact on the diagnosis of childhood depression

[2]There are some differences between RDC and DSM-III-R in the number and duration of symptoms that might be present for the criteria of major depression and also criteria related to whether the patient was referred for help or shows impairment of functioning. The major differences pertain to the different subtypes of depression. RDC permit greater differentiation among alternative subtypes and alternative subtypes are not mutually exclusive (see Williams & Spitzer, 1982).

Table 1. Weinberg Criteria for Depression

A. Both
  1. Dysphoric mood (melancholy)
    a. Statements or appearance of sadness, loneliness, unhappiness, hopelessness, and/or pessimism
    b. Mood swings, moodiness
    c. Irritable, easily annoyed
    d. Hypersensitive, cries easily
    e. Negative, difficult to please
  2. Self-deprecatory ideation
    a. Feeling of being worthless, useless, dumb, stupid, ugly, guilty (negative self-concept)
    b. Beliefs of persecution
    c. Death wishes
    d. Desire to run away or leave home
    e. Suicidal thoughts
    f. Suicidal attempts

B. Two or more of the following eight:
  1. Aggressive behavior (agitation)
    a. Difficult to get along with
    b. Quarrelsome
    c. Disrespectful of authority
    d. Belligerent, hostile, agitated
    e. Excessive fighting or sudden anger
  2. Sleep disturbance
    a. Initial insomnia
    b. Restless sleep
    c. Terminal insomnia
    d. Difficulty waking in morning
  3. Change in school performance
    a. Frequent complaints from teachers re: daydreaming, poor concentration, poor memory
    b. Loss of usual work effort in school subjects
    c. Loss of usual interest in nonacademic school activities
  4. Diminished socialization
    a. Decreased group participation
    b. Less friendly, less outgoing
    c. Socially withdrawing
    d. Loss of usual social interests
  6. Somatic complaints
    a. Nonmigraine headaches
    b. Abdominal pain
    c. Muscle aches or pains
    d. Other somatic concerns or complaints
  7. Loss of usual energy
    a. Loss of usual personal interests or pursuits other than school (e.g., hobbies)
    b. Decreased energy; mental and/or physical fatigue
  8. Unusual change in appetite and/or weight
    a. Anorexia or polyphagia
    b. Unusual weight change in the past 4 months

C. Duration of at least 1 month

D. A change in the child's usual behavior

and have served as the basis for several investigations (Brumback, Dietz-Schmidt, & Weinberg, 1977; Brumback & Weinberg, 1977a, b; Brumback, Jackoway, & Weinberg, 1980; Weinberg *et al.*, 1973).

With the appearance of DSM-III, diagnoses of particular disorders became more clearly associated with specific symptom criteria, whether or not the person was of a particular age. Other diagnostic systems, such as DSM-II, had indicated that diagnostic categories intended for adults could be applied to children. However, this was rarely done. Also, inconsistencies were evident in delineating a disorder (e.g., psychosis) depending on whether the person was an adult or child. In DSM-III-R, major depression and other disorders were more explicitly designed to be applied to children, adolescents, and adults, even though other specific symptoms or syndromes might also be evident at these different stages of development. Although children might evince unique characteristics in their manifestations of depression, the current approach is to apply the diagnosis when the core criteria have been met. The criteria for a DSM-III-R diagnosis of major depression are illustrated in Table 2. With minor exceptions, it is clear that the criteria at least in principle can be applied to patients of different ages.

Table 2. DSM-III-R Criteria for Major Depression

A. Inclusion criteria: At least five of the following symptoms have been present during the same two-week period; at least one of the symptoms was either 1. depressed mood, or 2. loss of interest or pleasure.
   1. Depressed mood more of the day, nearly every day (either by subjective account; e.g., feels "down" or "low" or is observed by others to look sad or depressed)
   2. Loss of interest or pleasure in all or almost all activities nearly every day (either by subjective account or is observed by others to be apathetic)
   3. Significant weight loss or weight gain (when not dieting or binge-eating) (e.g., more than 5% of body weight in a month) or decrease or increase in appetite nearly every day (in children consider failure to make expected weight gains)
   4. Insomnia or hypersomnia nearly every day
   5. Psychomotor agitation or retardation nearly every day (observable by others not merely subjective feelings of restlessness or being slowed down) (in children under six, hypoactivity)
   6. Fatigue or loss of energy nearly every day
   7. Feelings of worthlessness or excessive or inappropriate guilt (either may be delusional) nearly every day (not merely self-reproach or guilt about being sick)
   8. Diminished ability to think or concentrate, or indecisiveness nearly every day (either by subjective account or observed by others)
   9. Thoughts that he or she would be better off dead or suicidal ideation, nearly every day; or suicide attempt

B. Exclusion criteria
   1. An organic etiology has been ruled out, i.e., either there was no new organic factor (or change in preexisting organic factor) that precipitated the disturbance, or the disturbance has persisted for at least one month beyond the cessation of the precipitating organic factor
   2. Not a normal reaction to the loss of a loved one (uncomplicated bereavement)
   3. At no time during the disturbance have there been delusions or hallucinations for as long as two weeks in the absence of prominent mood symptoms
   4. Not superimposed on schizophrenia, schizophreniform disorder or paranoid disorder

Alternative Criteria Compared

The Weinberg and DSM-III-R criteria have dominated research on childhood depression. A comparison of Tables 1 and 2 indicates important differences between these criteria. In the Weinberg criteria, dysphoric mood and self-deprecatory ideation are required. Many of these latter criteria (somatic complaints, change in attitude toward school, and diminished socialization) have no clear counterpart in DSM-III-R. On the whole, the Weinberg criteria, in comparison to DSM-III-R, are more lenient or less selective for reaching a diagnosis of depression. They require fewer number of symptoms and permit a broader range of symptoms to be counted as signs of depression. Moreover, the Weinberg criteria do not specify exclusion criteria. Thus, a major depression might be diagnosed in cases where some other condition or disorder might be present (e.g., bereavement, organic impairment).

Investigations using the Weinberg criteria and DSM-III have found a higher prevalence for depression when the Weinberg criteria are used (e.g., Carlson & Cantwell, 1980; Cytryn, McKnew, Bartko, Lamour, & Hamovitt, 1982). Children who meet the Weinberg criteria tend to have other psychiatric diagnoses as well, which suggests that these criteria do not select as homogeneous a group of patients as does DSM-III. For clinical and research purposes, there is interest in delineating a distinct diagnostic entity to the extent possible. Consequently, DSM-III-R (or RDC) are currently in greater use than are the Weinberg criteria.

Complexities in Identification

When multiple symptoms are present and for protracted periods, major depressive disorder can be readily diagnosed. Difficulties in identifying depression as a disorder exist because of various gradations of the individual symptoms and the events with which they are associated. It is important to discuss alternative ways in which depressive symptoms may be manifest in less extreme forms.

A useful point of departure is DSM-III-R, which describes several conditions in which depressive symptoms may appear. These are important to identify for different reasons. First, manifestations of depressive symptoms may be difficult to delineate from major depression in everyday life. Second, such symptoms are likely to be much more prevalent than major depressive disorder. Finally, identifying different patterns of depressive symptoms has important implications regarding treatment decisions and prediction of outcome.

Apart from major depressive disorder, several DSM-III-R categories acknowledge the presence of depressive symptoms. Table 3 lists several of the major categories along with brief definitions. As evident in the table, mild forms of depression may appear (Dysthymic Disorder) when the full set of symptoms and the severity of symptoms that meet criteria for major depression are not evident. The symptoms may be clinically significant because they are interrupted by only brief periods of normal mood. Also, current evidence suggests that such disorders for many children are likely to become more serious over time (Kovacs *et al.*, 1984).

Table 3. DSM-III-R Diagnostic Categories That Include Depressive Symptoms Other than Major Depressive Disorder

Disorder or condition and key characteristics
Dysthymic disorder
Essentially a depressive disorder in which the symptoms of major depression are evident in less severe form. The symptoms may be chronic lasting for a year or more with periods of a few days or weeks of normal mood interspersed. Impairment in functioning stems more from chronicity of dysfunction than from severity of the symptoms.
Separation anxiety disorder
Many of the symptoms of depression such as sadness, excessive worrying, sleep dysfunction, somatic complaints, apathy, and social withdrawal may emerge as part of fear of separation from the parent or the home. In such cases, the symptoms may be clearly associated with the theme of separation. For example, worrying may have a specific focus on being away from the parent. Similarly, somatic complaints may occur to remain at home or to foster increased attention to the child.
Adjustment disorder with depressed mood
Depressive symptoms may emerge as a maladaptive reaction to a particular stressor such as divorce of the parents, leaving friends during a move away from home, or serious illness of a parent. In such cases, the symptoms are in temporal proximity of the stressor and are viewed as a excessive reaction to the event. The symptoms are likely to remit after a period of adjustment with the new circumstances.
Uncomplicated bereavement
Within DSM-III-R, bereavement resembles an adjustment disorder in terms of its association with a particular event. However, it is not listed as a disorder because it is considered as a normal reaction to the loss of a loved one. Bereavement is often associated with several depressive symptoms and temporary impairment in school and social functioning. Yet, the reaction is not regarded as clinically significant unless the symptoms remain well beyond a "reasonable" period of adjustment or begin to recur with repeated episodes long after the loss.

Other manifestations of depressive symptoms may emerge in response to specific types of precipitants (Adjustment Disorder with Depressed Mood, Uncomplicated Bereavement) or with other sorts of dysfunction where depressive symptoms may relate to a particular area of functioning (Separation Anxiety). In each case, there clearly may be sad affect and loss of interest in usual activities and other symptoms. A careful assessment is required to evaluate the severity and duration of the symptoms and to make judgments about specific events that may have provided the impetus for the symptoms.[3]

Identification of Depression in the Schools

Depressive symptoms may be associated with a variety of conditions even though the child does not fall within any of existing diagnostic categories. A major issue for teachers, school psychologists, and others in everyday life is to distinguish whether the child's characteristics warrant clinical referral or special treatment. The initial concern is what to look for to identify depression in children. There are a variety of signs that might be evident in school performance. Research has suggested that different domains of child performance may reflect depressive symptoms. Thus, peer relations (e.g., unpopularity), poor school work (e.g., disinterest in studying), reduced achievement (e.g., test performance, grades), impairment on cognitive tasks, and acting out in the classroom have all been found to be associated with depression (see Jacobsen, Lahey, & Strauss, 1983; Lefkowitz & Tesiny, 1980; Tesiny, Lefkowitz, & Gordon, 1980). Yet, these characteristics are somewhat nonspecific. They are likely to be associated with all sorts of dysfunction beyond depressive disorders. This does not mean that the type of problems noted above are unimportant. However, as a guide to identification of depression in children, they may be too generic.

Identification of depression in everyday situations, such as at school, needs to focus more specifically on characteristics of the dysfunction. There are some general guidelines that may be helpful. The initial focus of attention, of course, is whether the core symptoms of depression, such as sad affect and loss of interest in activities, are evident. Yet, it is not the presence of one or a few symptoms alone that should be accorded significance. For example, sad affect is very much a part of everyday experience and normal in response to a variety of not well-specified environmental and physiological events. Indeed, studies suggest that as an isolated symptom, depression among elementary school-age children is quite common. For example, one study found 17% of the children were sad, although only 1.9% of the children met criteria for major depression (Kashani & Simonds, 1979). Thus, the presence of sadness alone should not be regarded as necessarily significant.

For a symptom or set of symptoms to take on significance, one should look for different characteristics. First, the symptom should reflect a change in behavior. Many people simply appear moody, apathetic, and slow in their activities in general and these characteristics may not warrant special attention. Depression becomes significant as a change from ordinary behavior. Second, some consistency or continuation of depressed affect is significant. Mood may change rapidly and by definition is short-lived. If there is a period of, say, a week or two where there is depressed affect or other symptoms are sustained, their possible significance is increased. Third, the absence of a clear precipitant often is important. If the child or significant others cannot identify specific events that account for the change in mood, interest, or other symptoms, this is noteworthy. Similarly, the inability to alter the mood or to influence other symptoms

[3]In addition to the problems listed in the table, disorders in which mania is present may also be associated with depression. *Mania* refers to elevated mood, euphoria, and excessive activity. Diagnoses may include mania or mania combined with periods of depression, as in bipolar depressive disorder of cyclothymia (analogous to dysthymic disorder). These are not covered here because mania is relatively rare in children (Rapoport & Ismond, 1984).

with usual ministrations of teachers and parents is important information. Finally, the impact of the symptoms on everyday functioning is a major criterion that is relevant. If changes in school performance, attendance, and participation in activities are associated with the onset of the symptoms, then special attention may be warranted.

As depression receives increased professional attention, there is increased sensitivity to its presence in children and adolescents. It is important, of course, to better identify disorders so that they can be prevented and treated. A potential problem with increased professional attention is that there may be an increased propensity to label dysfunction that does not warrant identification. For these reasons, the specific criteria used in diagnosis and the possible manifestations of depressive symptoms in everyday life that are of the magnitude to warrant possible attention need to be underscored. The difficult task is to judge whether the symptoms appear to impede daily functioning of the child, whether they appear to be stable or emerge repeatedly at different time intervals, or whether they seem to distinguish the child clearly from his or her peers.

An Overview of Etiological Models

Identification of the causes of affective disorders is obviously of great interest. The literature on the etiology of these disorders is complex because of the different subtypes of dysfunction as well as the multiplicity of models proposed to account for them. For present purposes, an overview of models is provided to convey current approaches. The models have been developed and researched in the context of adult dysfunction. Only recently have the models been extended to children.[4] Although the alternative models can be divided into several different overall approaches or schools of thought, they will be highlighted here under two major rubrics, namely, psychosocial and biological models.

Psychosocial Models

Psychosocial models refer to approaches that emphasize intrapsychic, behavioral, and interpersonal underpinnings of depression. There are a number of different views, only some of which are sampled here.

Psychoanalytic Views

Psychoanalytic models of depression have included diverse positions (see Mendelson, 1982). The positions focus on intrapsychic influences beginning with the view of Freud, which emphasized unsatisfied libidinal strivings, particularly object loss (e.g., as reflected in a parent who fails to fulfill the child's needs). The child's identification with the parents' values and ideals has also been accorded an important role. The self-criticism and self-rejection of depressed persons are attributed to the battle of the ego and superego within the individual that reflects these values. The self-directed criticism and internal conflict reflect anger and hostility toward the parent (Freud, 1917).

Freud's views served as a point of departure for several psychoanalytic positions among his followers (e.g., Abraham, Rado, Bibring). Such factors were identified as repeated disappointment in relation to one's parents, fixation at the oral stage, aggression turned inward, excessive craving for narcissistic gratification, loss of self-esteem resulting from the unsatisfied need for affection, feelings of helplessness, and others.

The views cited attribute the causes of depression to experiences in childhood. Constitutional factors were recognized by Freud and his followers as accounting for selected forms of depression and increasing the need for excess gratification and sensitivity to frustrations from inadequate affection. Many specific features of psychoanalytic views, such

[4]Because the models of depression cannot begin to be detailed here, the reader is encouraged to seek other sources (e.g., Paykel, 1982a; Rehm, 1981).

as low self-esteem and helplessness, have played a role in other models and have been the subject of considerable research. However, psychoanalytic views themselves have not generated a great deal of research. Consequently, they cannot be viewed as empirically well-grounded.

Behavioral Views

Several behavioral models of depression have emerged in the last decade (see Rehm, 1981). As a general statement, the models focus on learning, environmental consequences, and skill acquisition and deficits. Symptoms of depression are considered to result from problems in interacting with the environment.

Lewinsohn has offered a social learning view that looks at depression from the standpoint of person–behavior–environment interactions governed by the principles of learning (see Lewinsohn & Arconad, 1981). Depression is attributed to the reduced reinforcement in interpersonal interaction. The person's behavior does not produce sufficient positive reinforcement from others and the individual becomes passive, withdraws from interactions, and shows the affective and cognitive symptoms of depression. Alternatively, punishing and aversive consequences (unpleasant outcomes) may also result from person–environment interactions and lead to the symptoms.

Rehm (1977) has proposed a self-control model of depression which focuses on the individual's maladaptive or deficient self-regulatory processes in coping with stress. Aspects of how individuals self-monitor, self-evaluate, and self-reinforce behavior are central. Persons with deficits in these self-regulatory skills are likely to focus on negative events, to set overly stringent criteria for evaluating their performance, and to administer little reinforcement to themselves, among other characteristics. The model is integrative insofar as it combines and draws upon other psychosocial models. Thus, reduced activity and lack of reinforcement (à la Lewinsohn) are incorporated into the model along with attributions of helplessness and negativism (à la Seligman and Beck), highlighted in the following.

Cognitive Views

Cognitive and behavioral models of depression are not always easily distinguished because versions in each camp often rely on similar constructs, such as attributions and lack of social reinforcement. Also, treatment procedures often overlap considerably as in practice exercises and performance of activities in everyday life. Nevertheless, cognitive views emphasize the perceptual, attributional, and belief systems that underlie depressive symptoms. Beck's (1976) model emphasizes the importance of the cognitive triad of depression, namely, negative views of oneself, the world, and the future. The negative cognitions are considered to affect the person's judgment about the world and interpersonal interactions, and to account for affective, motivational, and behavioral symptoms of depression. Systematic errors in thinking can be identified to reflect the pervasive focus on negative aspects of experience such as overgeneralizing specific events and misinterpreting experience in general.

Seligman (1975) proposed a learned helplessness model of depression. The model proposes that depression results from people's experiences and expectations that their responses do not influence events in their lives. Helplessness leads to passivity, social impairment, slowed activity, and other symptoms of depression. The model grew out of animal laboratory research that showed that animals became helpless after exposure to unavoidable shock. When they could later escape from the shock, they failed to do so. The model was extended by focusing on the perceptions and attributions of depressed persons who often feel they cannot influence their environment (Abramson, Seligman, & Teasdale, 1978). The specific attributions that people have about why they cannot control their environment (e.g., because of internal or external factors) and the pervasiveness of these influences (e.g., specific to a situation or general) affect their specific symptoms, such as self-esteem and other characteristics of their dysfunction.

Another cognitively based position proposes that depression is related to deficits in interpersonal problem-solving skills (D'Zurilla & Nezu, 1982). Persons who are depressed, when compared to nondepressed controls, evince deficits in generating alternative solutions to social problems, engaging in means–end thinking, and in making decisions (Nezu & Ronan, 1985). Problem-solving skills, when present, appear to act as a buffer against the impact of negative life events (Billings & Moos, 1982). In response to negative events or stress, depressive symptoms are more likely to emerge because of deficits in problem-solving skills. This model focuses on the specific cognitive deficits that may mediate management of stress and interpersonal interactions.

Socioenvironmental Views

Socioenvironmental view models have focused on life events that may influence the onset or emergence of symptoms of depression. The view is included here as psychosocial because it is not only the stressful event itself but also the person's perception or cognitive processing of that event. The significance of stressful events as precursors to depressive symptoms is recognized in everyday life. Bereavement, for example, frequently includes multiple symptoms of depressive disorder linked specifically to death of a loved one. Moreover, the risk of suicide is greatly increased following death of a relative or spouse, suggesting that extremes of hopelessness and depression may follow stressful events (Bunch, 1972; MacMahon & Pugh, 1965).

Research has supported the role of stressful life events in depressive disorders. Persons who are depressed or who later meet criteria for depression report significantly more stressful life events than matched controls. Although higher levels of such events characterize other patient groups (schizophrenic or medical patients), depression still seems to be associated with greater levels of such events (Paykel, 1982b). In addition, stressful events appear to precede by a few weeks or months the onset of an episode or relapse (Brown, Harris, & Peto, 1973; Paykel & Tanner, 1976). Attempts to identify the type of events that are uniquely related to depression (e.g., loss of a relative) and severity of the events (e.g., life threatening) have not revealed consistent patterns in the events specifically related to depression.

Biological Models

Biochemical Views

There are a number of biochemical agents that have been implicated in depression, only a few of which can be mentioned here (see Usdin, Asberg, Bertilsson, & Sjoqvist, 1984). Research has focused on the identification of neurotransmitters that may underlie depression (see Zis & Goodwin, 1982). Different transmitters have been studied. Monoamines, especially catecholamine and indoleamine, have received attention in a variety of types of studies. The general view has been that affective disorders are characterized by a deficit (e.g., depression) or excess (e.g., mania) in one or more neurotransmitters or by an imbalance of these transmitters. Support for this view in relation to monoamines comes from several quarters. For example, drugs that increase catecholamine output can act as antidepressants, whereas drugs that decrease output can act as antimanics. Also, concentrations of amines and their metabolites in the urine, cerebrospinal fluid, and plasma indicate altered amine functioning among persons with affective disorders.

Neuroendocrine abnormalities have also been studied (e.g., Sachar, 1982). The focus has a broad-based rationale. Symptoms of depression include disturbances of mood, sex drive, sleep, appetite, and autonomic activity, which as a whole suggest dysfunction of the hypothalamus. Also, neurotransmitters, especially noradrenaline, serotonin, acetylcholine, which have been implicated in depressive disorders, regulate the sorts of neuroendocrine agents that control pituitary function. Deficiencies in these neurotransmitters would be reflected in deficiencies in hormonal responses. Different hormone systems have been studied. For example, depressed patients have been shown to hypersecrete cortisol and not to suppress cortisol secretion in response to drug challenge (administration of dexamethasone) (see Carroll, 1983). Also, hyposecretion of growth hormone has been found in response to insulin-induced hypoglycemia (Carroll, 1978). Growth hormone is believed to be mediated by neurotransmitters which may be deficient among depressed patients.

Genetic Models

The genetic influences in different depressive disorders have been established for some time. Close relatives of persons with major depression are more likely to have the disorder than are unrelated persons (see Depue & Monroe, 1979; Nurnberger & Gershon, 1982). The precise concordance varies with the criteria used to define depression, subtypes of depression, ages of the sample and relatives, and other factors. Different lines of evidence have supported the role of inheritance. The evidence from twin studies has been relatively consistent. Monozygotic twins show about 65% concordance for affective disorders compared to approximately 14% for dizygotic twins (see Gershon, Targum, Kessler, Mazure, & Bunney, 1977). The strong familial ties of affective disorders have also been supported with studies of adoptees and studies of parents and children of index populations.

The genetic evidence has helped foster diverse types of research including the identification of subtypes of affective disorders, with their specific genetic loadings, biological correlates, family histories, and patterns of treatment response. Research has also explored biological markers, that is, genetic, biochemical, or related characteristics that permit identification of who is at risk for affective disorders. Ideally, these markers consist of stable characteristics that can be detected whether or not the person was currently showing the symptoms of depression. Several biological markers have been identified.[5] Another line of work is to identify the mode of genetic transmission (e.g., monogenetic or polygenetic, recessive vs. dominant, X-linked models, and combinations of these views).

The previously cited lines of research are obviously interrelated. The idea of biological markers has implications for different types of affective disorder. Also, if specific markers are identified, they may have implications regarding mode of genetic transmission. If the marker can be traced to a chromosomal location, there may be insights regarding both transmission and the mechanism of action.

General Comments

The foregoing is intended only to highlight selected views of the causes of affective disorders. The above list is by no means exhaustive (see Akiskal & McKinney, 1975). Different models might be presented (e.g., sociological, existential) as well as specific views within particular models (e.g., alternative neurotransmitters and endocrine systems, the models of action through which stress is considered to promote depression).

Few efforts have been provided to integrate

[5]Some of the biological markers that have been studied include urinary metobolites of monoamines (e.g., 3-methoxy-4-hydroxyphenylethylene glycol [MHPG]), measures of blood and plasma (e.g., red blood catechol-o-methyltransferase [COMT] and platelet monamine oxidase [MAO]), cell membrane characteristics (e.g., lithium ion ratio), and neuroendocrine function (e.g., level and diurnal variation of cortisol, resistance to cortisol suppression in response to dexamethasone), and sleep characteristics (e.g., latency to onset of REM sleep and decreased deep sleep as reflected in delta wave).

alternative views that span different models (e.g., psychosocial, biological). Akiskal (1979; Akiskal & McKinney, 1975) provided a biobehavioral model that integrates: (a) genetic vulnerability, (b) developmental events (e.g., early object loss), (c) psychosocial events (e.g., life events as stressors), (d) physiological stressors (e.g., medical conditions, disease, results of childbirth), and (e) personality traits (e.g., stable characteristics that influence reactivity to stress). These influences are proposed to alter the central nervous system, as illustrated in Figure 1. The impact converges on a final common biological pathway that is implicated in the biological substrates of response to environmental reinforcement. Specifically, the areas of the diencephalon are proposed because they mediate arousal, mood, motivation, and psychomotor functions (see Akiskal, 1979). The idea of an integrated model is obviously attractive if for no other reason than the acknowledgement of the legitimacy of alternative perspectives and areas of research.

As for childhood depression, no attempts have been made to subject broad models to empirical test. The initial task has been to evaluate the extent to which models studied primarily with adult samples apply to children. For example, biological evidence on various markers of depression (e.g., cortisol, growth hormone abnormalities) have shown several consistencies between depressed adults and children (Puig-Antich, 1983). Similarly, evidence on various cognitive features of depression also show such consistencies (e.g., Haley, Fine, Marriage, Moretti, & Freeman, 1985; Seligman *et al.*, 1984). Recent research has shown diminished social interaction of depressed children with parents and peers, relative to normal and nondepressed patient control children (Kazdin, Esveldt-Dawson, Sherick, & Colbus, 1985; Puig-Antich *et al.*, 1985a, b). The findings are similar to those

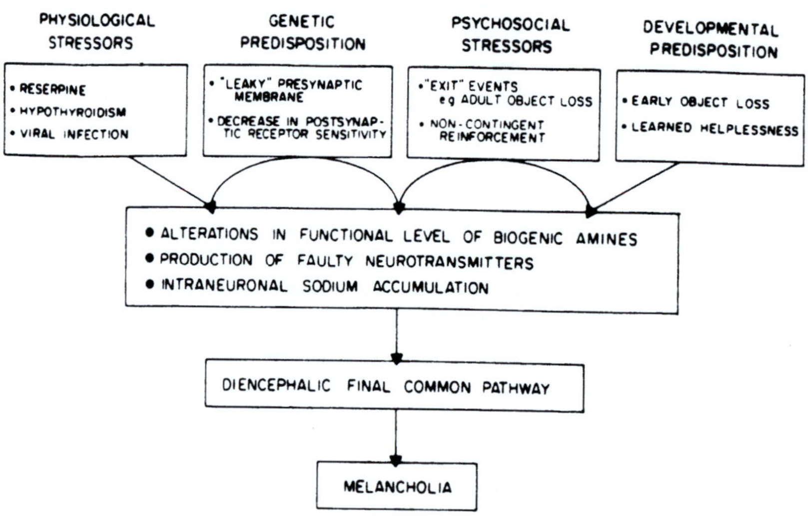

Figure 1. Diagrammatic representation of the biobehavioral model of depression. The model suggests that alternative biological and environmental or interpersonal factors have impact on specific biological processes known to be implicated in depression. The final common pathway is proposed to be the diencephalon which mediates arousal, mood, activation, and psychomotor functions. (From "A Biobehavioral Approach to Depression" by H. S. Akiskal, 1979, in *The Psychobiology of Depressive Disorders* (p. 431), New York: Academic Press.

evident in studies of social behavior among adult samples. Work on the characteristics of children and possible etiological models that these characteristics support are only beginning to be studied programmatically.

Assessment

Alternative Modalities

Major advances have been made in the development of assessment techniques for children and adolescents. The range of measures has increased and data have become available on the psychometric properties of individual measures. The advances are critical because they elaborate specific methods that can be used to identify children who show symptoms of depression and also provide normative information to help identify those departures that warrant special attention. Several different assessment modalities have been identified. The present section highlights alternative modalities, evaluates their current status and the issues they raise. Given the proliferation of assessment devices, the reader is referred to alternative sources for detailed discussion of individual measures (see Cantwell & Carlson, 1983; Kazdin, 1981; Kazdin & Petti, 1982).

Self-Report

Self-report is clearly one of the most widely used assessment modalities. Self-report is important given that key symptoms of depression, such as sadness, feelings of worthlessness, and loss of interest in activities, reflect subjective feelings or perceptions. In addition, self-report measures have been used extensively and successfully for the assessment of depressive symptoms in adults. Consequently, their extension to children is natural. Indeed, some of the measures reflect direct adaptations of adult instruments and the conceptual positions they reflect.

An extraordinarily large number of measures has become available. They are enumerated with key references in Table 4. The measures often are directed toward different goals (e.g., diagnosis vs. assessment of severity of symptoms), assess different facets of dysfunction, and have different status in terms of their empirical base. Also, the measures have been developed in a variety of ways such as direct adaptation from measures developed with adults, reliance upon diagnostic criteria, the ability to discriminate populations, or expert opinions of the item content (see Kazdin & Petti, 1982).

In clinical settings one of the primary purposes of assessment of depression is to attain a diagnosis. For such uses, diagnostic interviews are utilized such as the Schedule for Affective Disorders and Schizophrenia for School-Age Children (Kiddie-SADS or K-SADS; Chambers, Puig-Antich, & Tabrizi, 1978; Chambers *et al.*, 1985). The measure, modeled after the format of the adult diagnostic instrument (Schedule for Affective Disorders and Schizophrenia), provides several diagnoses although the primary emphasis is on affective disorders. The K-SADS has alternative versions depending on whether lifetime or current dysfunction is assessed. The measure consists of an unstructured interview followed by a structured portion where the respondent is asked about the presence, severity, and duration of a number of symptoms. The measure is administered separately to the parent and then the child. Discrepancies are resolved to reach some consensus on the presence of specific symptoms covered in DSM-III. The K-SADS has been utilized in a number of studies and has been shown to reflect treatment effects as well (using ratings of symptom severity) (e.g., Kashani *et al.*, 1983; Puig-Antich *et al.*, 1978). Other diagnostic instruments are available as well (see Table 4) but data are not available attesting to their relative merit.

Although diagnosis of depression is of obvious interest, self-report inventories, ques-

Table 4. Selected Self-Report and Interviews for Childhood and Adolescent Depression

Measure	Response format	Special characteristics
I. Self-report inventories		
1. Children's Depression Inventory (CDI) (Kovacs & Beck, 1977)	27 items, each rated on 0- to 2-point scale	Derivative of Beck Depression Inventory
2. Short Children's Depression Inventory (Short-CDI) (Carlson & Cantwell, 1979)	13 items, rated on a 0- to 4-point scale	Derivative of Short Beck Depression Inventory. Departs slightly from CDI in duration required for symptoms to be endorsed and in response alternatives format
3. Children's Depression Scale (CDS) (Lang & Tisher, 1978)	66 items rated on 1- to 5-point scale	Card sort format: each item on a card is put into 1 of 5 boxes; versions available for parents and teachers, unique feature is inclusion of a positive subscale to measure pleasurable experiences
4. Self-Rating Scale (SRS) (Birleson, 1981)	18 items scored on a 3-point scale	Recently devised scale of childhood depression
5. Modified Zung (M-Zung) (Lefkowitz & Tesiny, 1980)	16 items; yes/no format for presence or absence	Derived from adult scale; modifications include reduced number of items; rewording, and different response format (adult version = 1- to 4-point scale)
6. Face Valid Depression Scale for Adolescents (DSA) (Mezzich & Mezzich, 1979)	35 items scored 0 to 1 (true/false) as characteristic of respondent	Derived from MMPI items from which clinicians selected. Includes items specific to adolescents as well as items common to both adolescents and adults
7. Center for Epidemiological Studies Depression Scale (modified for children) (CES-D) (Weismann *et al.* 1980)	20 items each on 0- to 4-point scale	Derivative of adult scales of same name
8. Beck Depression Inventory (modified for adolescents) (BDI-A) (Chiles *et al.* 1980)	33 items; each on 0- to 3-point scale	Derivative of Beck Depression Inventory
9. Reynolds Adolescent Depression Scale (RADS) (Reynolds & Coats, 1985)	30 items; each on a 4-point scale	Items derived from symptoms included in major, minor, and unipolar depression
II. Interviews		
10. Bellevue Index of Depression (BID) (Petti, 1978)	40 items each rated on 4-point scale of severity and 3-point scale for duration	Items devised on the basis of the Weinberg criteria; interview can be given separately to child, parents, and others; recommendation is to combine scores from different sources
11. Children's Depression Rating Scale (CDRS-R) (Poznanski *et al.*, 1984)	17 items scored after interview; symptoms rated on 7-point scale for severity	Devised from format of Hamilton Depression scale for adults. Administered also to parents and others to combine different sources
12. Children's Affective Rating Scale (CARS) (McKnew *et al.*, 1979)	3 items (mood, verbal behavior, & fantasy) each rated on 10-point	Global clinical ratings rather than self-report of problems by child

(*continued*)

Table 4. *(Continued)*

Measure	Response format	Special characteristics
12. Children's Affective Rating Scale (CARS) *(continued)*	scale for severity following an interview	
13. Interview Schedule for Children (ISC-Form C) (Kovacs, 1978)	Multiple items and subitems covering symptoms of depression, conduct disorders and other symptom constellations; rated for severity; 10-point scale for most items	Current phenomenology of child; duration varies to reflect current condition, specific symptoms queried with varying durations. Child and parent administered interview
14. Kiddie-SADS (K-SADS) (Chambers *et al.*, 1978)	Multiple items covering several disorders based on RDC criteria; depression symptoms rated for degree of severity	Modeled after adult SADS; provides several diagnoses based on RDC criteria

tionnaires, and interviews designed to measure severity of symptoms are used more frequently. The most widely used measure is the Children's Depression Inventory (Kovacs, 1981). The measure, adapted originally from the Beck Depression Inventory, includes 27 items regarding the cognitive, affective, and behavioral signs of depression. Children select one of three alternatives for each item that applies to them in the last 2 weeks. For example, a typical item on the CDI asks the child to select among these alternatives: I feel like crying every day, I feel like crying many days, I feel like crying once in a while. The total score reflects the severity of depressive symptoms.

The CDI has been shown to provide high internal consistency and moderate to high test–retest reliability (from one week up to 6 months), to distinguish clinic from nonclinic groups of children, to correlate in expected directions with other constructs, such as self-esteem, negative cognitive attributions, hopelessness, and others (e.g., Kazdin, French, Unis, Esveldt-Dawson, & Sherick, 1983; Kovacs, 1981; Saylor, Finch, Baskin, Furey, & Kelly, 1984; Saylor, Finch, Spirito, & Bennett, 1984; Seligman *et al.*, 1984). Normative data have appeared in the previously cited studies as well, facilitating evaluation of the level of dysfunction of children relative to their same-age and gender peers. In general, the CDI is one of the more well-researched measures to date. Selected findings in the previously cited studies, such as the general failure to predict ratings from other sources, occasionally low test–retreat correlations, and failure to discriminate depression clearly from other diagnoses make interpretation of CDI performance not entirely problem free.

As Table 4 reflects, there are many different measures. At this point, there have been few attempts to compare their relative merit with regard to a specific purpose (e.g., diagnosis, treatment outcome). Although special measures have been developed for children and adolescents, occasionally measures developed for adults (e.g., Beck Depression Inventory) are also used with adolescents (e.g., Strober, Green, & Carlson, 1981). Thus, for adolescents the range of available measures is broader (see Reynolds, 1984).

Ratings by Adults

Ratings by adults refers primarily to significant others, primarily parents and teachers who are asked to evaluate the child's depression. For present purposes, ratings by clinicians are included here as well. Their significance stems from their expertise rather than their relation to the child. Several different types of measures are available. The most commonly used are general scales that assess a variety of different types of symptoms or constellations of behavior, only one of which is depression. For example, the Personality Inventory for Children is a parent-rated scale that includes multiple areas of child dysfunction (Wirt, Lachar, Klinedinst, & Seat, 1977). A subscale of the instrument includes 46 true-false items to measure depression separately from the larger scale (e.g., Lobovits & Handal, 1985).

A second type of measure by significant others is the adaptation of self-report measures. Essentially, measures such as the CDI (or other measures listed in Table 4) are altered for the parent or adult to convey that the child's depression is evaluated. The alterations are minor with changes in instructions or language of the items. For example, parents and teachers occasionally are asked to complete the CDI for children under their care (e.g., Helsel & Matson, 1984). With alternate forms for child and adult, direct comparisons can be made to evaluate correspondence of responses.

A third type of measure in this category is one specifically made to assess depression and related symptoms and typically is not merely an adaptation of a child scale. One such measure worth highlighting is the Children's Depression Rating Scale (CDRS) (Poznanski, Cook, & Carroll, 1979). The measure is an adaptation of the Hamilton Scale which has been widely used to measure depression in adults. The current revised version (CDRS-R) consists of an interview of 17 items concerning symptoms of depression, each of which is rated on a Likert-type scale for severity of dysfunction. The symptoms may be inferred from the content of the child's verbal report as well as from nonverbal behavior in the interview (e.g., appearance of sad affect, hypoactivity). Evaluation of the symptoms ultimately depends upon the judgment of the clinician. The clinician may rely upon multiple sources of information including interviews of the child, parents, or others. The information is integrated into a single rating. Evaluation of the CDRS in its original or revised form has been sparse. Studies have appeared indicating high interjudge agreement in rating children, high correlations of CDRS with global clinical ratings of depression, and high test-retest performance (over 2 to 6 week intervals) (Poznanski *et al.*, 1979; Poznanski, Cook, Carroll, & Corzo, 1983; Poznanski *et al.*, 1984).

Ratings by Peers

Peer ratings have been utilized to evaluate diverse facets of psychopathology including depression. The advantage of peers is that they observe each other across a wide range of settings and for extended periods and consequently have a reasonably good basis for their evaluations. Peer measures occasionally have been constructed by altering items from self-report inventories so that they can be rated by peers (e.g., Malouff, 1984).

For children, the primary peer-based measure is the Peer Nomination Inventory for Depression (PNID) (Lefkowitz & Tesiny, 1980). The measure depends upon the context of a group because peers within the group (e.g., class) are asked about characteristics of different children. The children must have a sufficient basis for their evaluations. The measure consists of 20 items in which children are asked several specific questions (e.g., Who plays alone? Who doesn't have much fun?). Each child nominates other children for each question. A child's own score is the sum (or proportion) of nominations he or she receives.

The measure has been carefully evaluated in studies that have provided evidence for internal consistency, test–retest stability (over 6 months), and interrater agreement. Validation studies have shown only weak relations between PNID scores and self-report or teacher ratings of depression. Yet, PNID scores correlate with school performance, self-concept, teacher ratings of work skills, social behavior, and peer ratings of happiness and popularity (Lefkowitz & Tesiny, 1985; Lefkowitz, Tesiny, & Gordon, 1980; Tesiny & Lefkowitz, 1982).

Direct Observations of Overt Behavior

Many characteristics of depression refer to overt behaviors or observable characteristics such as diminished social and motor activity, sad facial expression, slowed speech, and others (see Greden & Carroll, 1981; Jacobson, 1981). In the literature with adult populations, some attention has been given to direct observations of overt behavior. The primary focus has been on measures of nonverbal behavior. Research has shown that depressed adults, when compared to normal controls or other patient groups, often show reduced eye contact with others, slower speech, and fewer hand, head, and body movements during conversation (e.g., Jones & Pasna, 1979; Waxer, 1976). Studies have also shown that recovery from a depressive episode and response to antidepressant medication are reflected in changes in nonverbal behaviors (e.g., Fisch, Frey, & Hirsbrunner, 1983; Miller, Ranelli, & Levine, 1977).

Although nonverbal behavior has been rather extensively studied with depressed adults, few direct extensions have been reported with children. In one investigation with psychiatric patients (ages 7–12), nonverbal behaviors were assessed during interviews and evaluated in relation to child and parent report measures of child depression and psychiatric diagnosis (Kazdin, Sherick, Esveldt-Dawson, & Rancurello, 1985). Nonverbal behaviors were assessed as the child answered questions about everyday life or told stories in response to Thematic Apperception Test cards. Nonverbal behaviors included eye contact, facial expressiveness, response latency, bodily movements, gestures, frowning, and others. The results revealed low negative correlations for child and parent reports of depression and selected measures of nonverbal behavior, such as facial expressiveness, body movements, gestures, and a positive correlation with tearfulness. There were, however, important gender differences with girls showing more consistent relationships between nonverbal behaviors and measures of depression.

Nonverbal behavior during interviews does not exhaust the range of options for direct observation. Research with adults has suggested the utility of observing behavior during daily functioning. For example, Williams, Barlow, and Agras (1972) observed talking, smiling, and several motor behaviors of depressed patients. They found moderate-to-high negative correlations of a total sum of these behaviors with clinician and self-report ratings of depression. In addition, overt behavior reflected improvements with treatment and predicted posthospital adjustment better than clinician and self-report ratings.

Direct observations have been made of inpatient children (ages 8–13 years old) who were observed during free-time periods over the course of a week (Kazdin, Esveldt-Dawson, Sherick, & Colbus, 1985). Behaviors were observed to comprise three categories: social activity (e.g., talking, playing a game, participating in a group activity); solitary behavior (e.g., playing a game alone, watching TV by oneself); and affect-related expression (e.g., smiling, frowning, arguing, complaining). Children high in depression, as defined by a parent interview measure (BID-R), engaged in significantly less social behavior and evinced less affect-related expression than children low in depression. These results are consistent with studies of depressed adults that have found deficiencies in social interaction and expressions of affect (e.g., Lewinsohn & Shaffer, 1971; Linden, Hautzinger, & Hoffmann, 1983).

Psychophysiological and Biological Assessments

Psychophysiological and biological assessments encompass a number of laboratory-based measures. Their significance derives from the utility in providing alternative methodologies over and above commonly used rating scales and interviews. Moreover, the measures often have implications for testing etiological views and biological correlates of affective disorders. Much of the work has been guided by parallel studies of adults.

Electrophysiological recordings of adults have been used extensively to evaluate sleep of depressed patients. Sleep characteristics such as decreased total sleep time, decreased delta wave sleep, shortened REM latency, and early morning and intermittent awakenings, are some of the many characteristics shown to distinguish depressed adults (see Kupfer *et al.*, 1983). Evaluations of sleep architecture among depressed children have not shown consistent differences parallel to those obtained with adults (e.g., Young, Knowles, McLean, Boag, & McConville, 1982). Here the absence of differences between depressed and nondepressed children may prove significant given the continuity of many other biological correlates over the developmental spectrum.

Assessment of neuroendocrine functioning has been evaluated more extensively among children than other biological strategies. The research has followed rather extensive exemplars from the literature on adults. Adult depressed patients (endogenous depressives) have been shown to secrete excess cortisol during depressive episodes, a characteristic that returns to normal during recovery (see Depue & Kleiman, 1979). Cortisol hypersecretion is assessed by plasma concentrations obtained repeatedly (e.g., over a 24-hr period) and shows more periods of secretion, higher peak values, and greater amounts of secretion. Research has also shown that endogenous depressed adults hyposecrete growth hormone in response to insulin-induced hypoglycemia. This research has been extended to children showing similar findings with depressed patients (see Puig-Antich, 1983).

These measures do not exhaust the biological correlates that have been studied in children. The primary focus has been the assessment of biological markers that have emerged in research on adult depressives, as noted earlier. Biological assessments make a major contribution in understanding depression and its possible biological substrates. The measures reflect a different level of assessment than symptoms experienced by the child or dysfunction evident to parents and teachers. The relationship between the presence of specific symptoms and results from biological assessments of the sort highlighted here remain to be explored in children.

Other Measures

The previously mentioned modalities reflect the measures most commonly used to assess depression. However, other types of measures have been used as well. Projective techniques have received attention in a few investigations. These techniques, of course, are designed to present ambiguous stimuli and response opportunities to the child. Investigations have evaluated different facets of the Rorschach test (e.g., Decina *et al.*, 1983), the Thematic Apperception Test (e.g., Kazdin, Sherick, Esveldt-Dawson, & Rancurello, 1985; Riddle & Rapoport, 1976), the Children's Apperception Test (Cytryn & McKnew, 1974), and the Draw-A-Person Test (Gordon, Lefkowitz, & Tesiny, 1980). In general, measures derived from these instruments have not yielded significant differences between depressed and nondepressed youths. When differences have emerged, molecular responses have been identified (e.g., number of color responses on the Rorschach) with unclear theoretical or applied significance.

Issues and Limitations

Child Report

The bulk of assessment devices include child self-report measures. A major issue in the use of such measures is the extent to which children are capable or willing to report on their depressive symptoms. This concern does not merely derive from the fact that children might deny symptoms. Rather, measures often ask subtle questions about the presence of specific symptoms, whether children could identify the basis for the symptom, the duration and intensity, and so on. Research has clearly established that both clinic and nonclinic samples can report on their depressive symptoms. However, evidence suggests that children report fewer symptoms and lower bound estimates of symptom severity than do their parents (Kazdin, French, Unis, & Esveldt-Dawson, 1983; Orvaschel, Puig-Antich, Chambers, Tabrizi, & Johnson, 1982; Tisher & Lang, 1983).

The lower bound estimates of symptoms that a child's report is likely to yield is not by itself a bothersome pattern. The questions of interest are the extent to which the measures predict performance in other areas or over time and the relationship of child report to other sources of information designed to assess depressed affect. Evidence to date suggests that self-report among patient and nonpatient samples is related to a number of other areas of performance, such as suicidal attempt and ideation, hopelessness, self-esteem, or negative attributional style, as noted earlier.

Correspondence of Measures

An issue that has frequently emerged is the extent to which measures of depression correspond with each other. The primary issue is the relation of reports from different sources such as parents, teachers, and peers. Reports of children generally do not correlate very well with reports of their parents, teachers, and/or peers (Kazdin, Esveldt-Dawson, Unis, & Rancurello, 1983; Saylor, Finch, Baskin, Furey, & Kelly, 1984; Tesiny & Lefkowitz, 1982). The correlations are occasionally significant but their magnitude typically ranges between .00 and .30. Obviously, the shared variance in ratings of depression from different sources is quite small.

The lack of correspondence, now evident in several studies, raises the question of whose reports are to be believed. For research, the issue is the extent to which child, parent, teacher, peer, or combined reports are better predictors of other criteria, such as family history, long-term prognosis, and treatment course. In everyday experience, reports of depressive symptoms, whether from either the child or an adult, should be attended to. Both reports have shown to be related to other important criteria. For example, as noted earlier, child report of depression correlates with other facets of experience and performance. Parent reports tend to correlate with social behavior and affect-related expression (Kazdin, Esveldt-Dawson, *et al.*, 1985). Peer and teacher reports correlate with popularity and academic performance, respectively (Tesiny & Lefkowitz, 1982; Tesiny *et al.*, 1980).

The major difficulty in validating alternative rater reports has been the absence of independent criteria that are free from the bias or input of one of the raters. For example, psychiatric diagnosis or even clinical judgment may not be independent criteria because they invariably rely on child or parent report. Because ratings of the children's depression from alternative sources correlate with important facets of dysfunction or child behavior, they all may reflect potentially useful information. Yet, for purposes of understanding the relative utility of alternative measures, it will be important to identify alternative sources and measures that predict severity of dysfunction, onset of affective disorders, and response to treatment. Such research remains to be completed.

Inventories to Diagnose Depressive Disorders

An important issue both for research and practice is the use of self-report inventories and questionnaires to diagnose depression or to identify children with relatively severe levels of the symptoms. In studies of nonclinic cases, performance on measures such as the CDI is used to define depressed samples, based on cutoff scores. Although the degree from normal can be clearly delineated with inventories of severity, only the diagnostic interviews specifically address criteria for reaching a psychiatric diagnosis. Children with severe scores on measures such as the CDI may not necessarily meet diagnostic criteria for major depression and vice versa. In general, children with a diagnosis of depression score higher on self-report measures than those without such diagnoses (e.g., Asarnow & Carlson, 1985; Moretti, Fine, Haley, & Marriage, 1985). Yet, self-report measures of depression do not invariably discriminate among children (Yanchyshyn & Robbins, 1980), adolescents (Chiles, Miller, & Cox, 1980), or adults (Myers & Weissman, 1980) who are independently diagnosed as suffering major depression. Thus, self-report inventories are not tantamount to diagnostic interviews in the information they provide.

Biological Assessment

The use of biological assessment raises a number of issues that warrant mention. Because many of the procedures are invasive, concerns emerge about subjecting youths to discomfort and risk. Some techniques currently in use (e.g., insulin-induced hypoglycemia) are risky and simply not feasible for clinical use. Other techniques evaluated with adults (e.g., lumbar puncture) are useful for obtaining information about neurochemistry but have understandably been avoided with children. Some of the biological measures do corroborate diagnoses. It is important to bear in mind that they do not invariably provide confirming evidence. For example, in one study a biological measure (growth hormone secretion during sleep) accurately identified one half of the depressed children (Puig-Antich *et al.*, 1984). Although this finding is highly significant, the measure would not be sufficient for screening or diagnostic purposes until higher levels of identification were obtained. Biological measures nevertheless are likely to be refined and serve multiple functions apart from validation of other assessment techniques. Such measures will help to identify mechanisms underlying depressed symptoms and markers for diagnosis, treatment prescriptions, and prognosis.

Current Status

The assessment of childhood depression is an area of extraordinary research activity. Although many measures are currently available, relatively few have been well tested in studies evaluating some of the obvious forms of reliability and validity. Some measures, such as the CDI, have been frequently evaluated and in diverse contexts. A number of other measures still with little published data to their credit might have rich yield. As a case in point, the Children's Depression Scale is designed to assess many facets of depression, such as social behavior, self-esteem, preoccupation with sickness and death, and others (see Table 4). This measure and several others have only begun to be explored (Tisher & Lang, 1983). The bulk of the measures consist of lists of symptoms that children rate on a Likert-type scale. Among the many such measures, it is likely that some will suffer from disuse and redundancy with more popular measures rather than poor validity. Investigations are emerging at an accelerated rate on specific instruments and typically provide normative data, information on psychometric characteristics of the measure, or correlates of severity of depression. Research has profitted greatly from following the guidelines of research with adults.

Assessment strategies include primarily self- and parent-report measures. Further research is likely to explore alternative modalities to assess depression. Psychophysiological assessment has not been well explored. For example, facial muscle contractions related to expressions of happiness and sadness have been studied with electromyography and have shown to discriminate adult depressives from normals and other patient groups (e.g., Schwartz *et al.*, 1978). Such work has yet to be pursued with children or adolescents. Also, biological assessment procedures such as neuroendocrine evaluation, as one example, are likely to increase given the work with adults in this area. Psychophysiological and biological assessment can be very useful for several purposes, including early diagnosis and treatment evaluation. From the standpoint of assessment, such measures may be especially useful in providing criteria to help evaluate and validate more commonly used self- and parent-report measures. Although such measures are not bias free, they do provide information free from reports of others.

Treatment

Many different therapies have been evaluated for the treatment of depression in adults. Some of these have begun to be extended to children and adolescents. It is useful to convey current progress by grouping techniques as psychosocial or psychopharmacological.[6]

Psychosocial Interventions

Psychosocial interventions refer here to techniques that focus on interpersonal sources of influence as distinct from medical or biological treatments. In adult depression, many psychotherapy techniques have been proposed and investigated (see Klerman & Schechter, 1982). The variation most frequently studied focuses on interpersonal relationships, social adjustment,and mastery of social roles (see Weissman & Paykel, 1974). The version includes nondirective and insight-oriented treatment, although a narrow theoretical framework has not been adopted. Outcome studies have attested to the efficacy of interpersonal psychotherapy relative to no-treatment and minimal-contact control conditions (see Weissman, 1979).

Cognitive therapy has also been applied effectively to adult patients. The technique is based on the model, noted earlier, emphasizing maladaptive and negative cognitions (see Beck, Rush, Shaw, & Emery, 1979). Cognitive therapy has been shown to be as effective as pharmacotherapy and perhaps even more effective over the course of follow-up (see Kovacs, Rush, Beck, & Hollon, 1981; Rush, Beck, Kovacs, & Hollon, 1977).

A more behaviorally oriented treatment focuses on increasing the pleasant or rewarding activities of depressed persons (Lewinsohn, 1974). This treatment requires patients to monitor their daily activities, to increase activities that are reinforcing, and to decrease activities that are aversive. Outcome evidence has shown that this approach is associated with reductions of depression (e.g., Sanchez, Lewinsohn, & Larson, 1980).

In some behavioral techniques, several different behaviors are focused on in treatment. For example, McLean (1981) noted the importance of altering six skill areas: verbal communication, behavioral productivity (engaging specific behaviors), social interaction, assertive behavior, decision making and problem solving in everyday life, and cognitive self-control to identify and controvert maladaptive cognitions. Evidence has suggested that the treatment based on skill development improves depression (McLean & Hakstian, 1979). Other behavioral and cognitive-behavioral treatments have been studied with depressed adults (see Rehm, 1981).

The previously discussed approaches suggest that a wealth of psychosocial techniques are available. To date, very few outcome studies have been reported with depressed children. Uncontrolled case studies have illustrated but not evaluated the effects of psychotherapy with depressed children (Bene, 1975; Sacks, 1977). Also, selected single-case reports have suggested the efficacy of social skills training on specific social behaviors and/or symptoms of depression (e.g., Calpin

[6]There are other treatments that have been used (e.g., electroconvulsive shock) that do not fit this classification. However, such treatments typically are not applied to children and adolescents.

& Cinciripini, 1978; Molick & Pinkston, 1982; Petti, Bornstein, Delamater, & Conners, 1980).

For example, Frame, Matson, Sonis, Fialkov, and Kazdin (1982) evaluated the treatment of a hospitalized 10-year-old boy with a DSM-III diagnosis of major depression. Evaluation of the child revealed several prominent features, including avoidance of social interaction with others as evident in the form of poor eye contact, turning away from others, inaudible and constricted speech, and bland affect. These areas in turn served as the focus of a treatment. The intervention was provided in individual sessions five times per week over a 5-week period. Before and during treatment, interviews were conducted with the child in order to assess the specific social behaviors noted earlier. The treatment consisted of training the child to interact in a variety of interpersonal situations. The therapist modeled specific social behaviors, encouraged the child to practice what was modeled, and provided praise and feedback as needed to improve socially appropriate interaction. The training procedure was introduced across the different social behaviors at different points in time in order to meet the requirements of a multiple baseline design.

Figure 2 shows the effects of treatment, administered in a multiple baseline design across the different behaviors. The figure reveals that marked changes occurred when treatment was introduced. The sequence of changes suggests that it was the intervention that accounted for the change rather than any extraneous factors, such as contact with the therapist or repeated assessment or exposure to social situations in training. A follow-up assessment, conducted 12 weeks after all training had been terminated, indicated that the gains were maintained.

Single-case studies, such as the one illustrated here, can explore alternative treatments and carefully evaluate their impacts. Yet, the single-case studies for childhood depression conducted to date have suffered many different problems. Apart from their application overall to very few individuals, such studies have often confounded multiple treatments, failed to diagnose depression in a standardized manner, used idiosyncratic measures of symptoms, and others. These studies have not clearly identified a treatment that alters depressive symptoms.

Studies with control groups and careful assessment of outcome are beginning to appear and are likely to increase relatively quickly. For example, Butler, Miezitis, Friedman, and Cole (1980) conducted a comparative outcome study of fifth- and sixth-grade school children identified through self-report measures of depression and teacher referral. Children received 10 sessions of either role-play, cognitive restructuring, an attention placebo condition (discussion of teaching rather than depression related topics), or no treatment. Role play focused on interpersonal skills as well as problem-solving techniques. Cognitive restructuring focused on maladaptive cognitions (à la Beck and Ellis). Although the results appeared to favor role play, the precise outcome differences among groups are difficult to discern from the data analyses.

More recently, Reynolds and Coats (1985) compared a cognitive-behavioral treatment, relaxation, and a waiting-list control condition for treatment of depression among adolescents identified in the schools. Treatment was provided in 10 sessions over a 5-week period. Cognitive-behavioral subjects received training that drew on components of cognitive and behavioral models, as reflected in the positions of Beck, Lewinsohn, Seligman, and Rehm, noted earlier. Subjects in the other treatment condition received relaxation training in their sessions and were assigned practice for homework. In general, the results indicated that both active treatments were associated with reductions in depression after treatment and up to a 5-week follow-up. The treatments were not significantly different from each other in outcome.

Notwithstanding the beginnings of promising approaches, psychosocial interventions need a boost with strong tests of treatment.

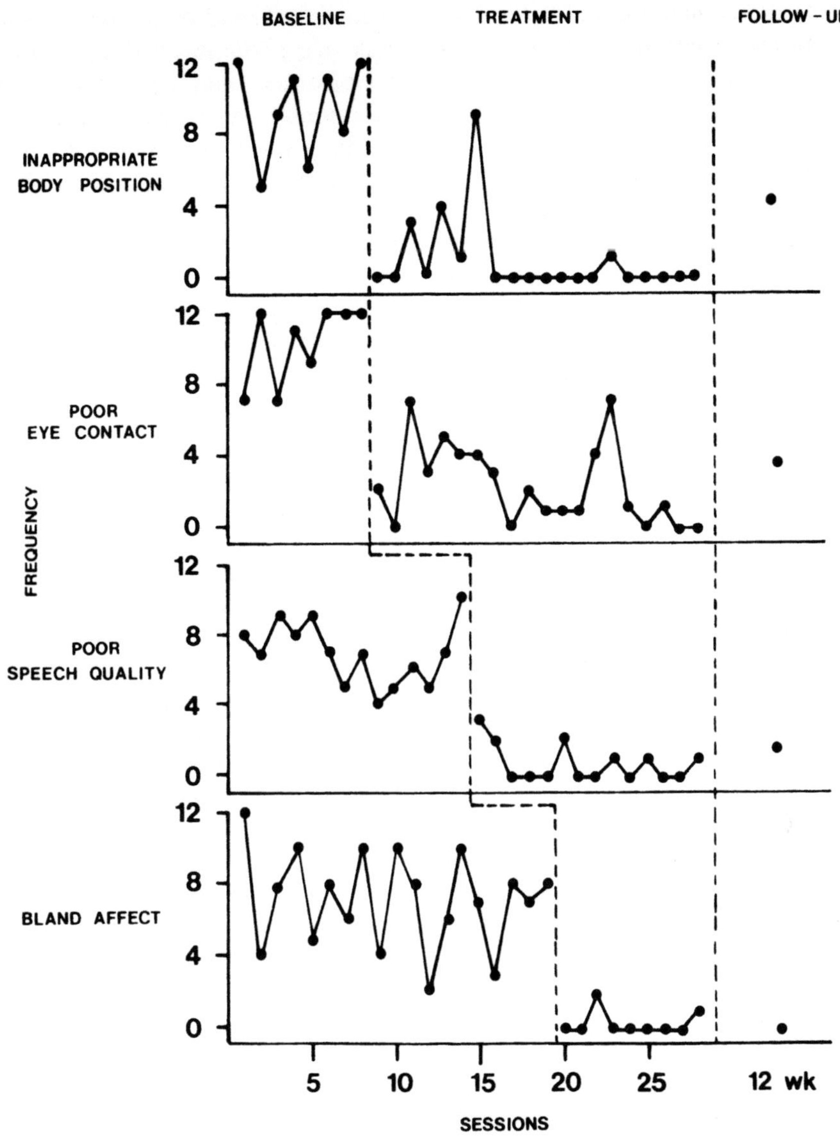

Figure 2. Frequency of social behaviors of a depressed boy as measured during assessment interviews. The treatment was applied to different behaviors at different points in time. From "Behavioral Treatment of Depression in a Prepubertal Child" by C. Frame *et al.*, 1982, *Journal of Behavior Therapy and Experimental Psychiatry*, *3*, p. 241, Fig. 7.

The early evidence reveals a rapid move to comparative outcome studies. The tests are quite weak because of very small sample sizes within alternative groups (e.g., 24 subjects across three groups by the end of treatment; 21 subjects by the end of a 5-week follow-up assessment in Reynolds & Coats, 1985). In addition, the group studies have not yet looked at children who meet criteria (e.g., DSM-III-R, RDC) for major depression. In these methodological features, the work lags behind pharmacotherapy trials, which will be highlighted later. Nevertheless, the models of treatment based on psychosocial approaches have the potential of enjoying widespread use because of the restrictions of applying medications in everyday settings (e.g., the schools).

Pharmacotherapy

Several alternative medications have been used with adult depressed patients. Major types include monoamine oxidase inhibitors (e.g., phenelzine) and tricyclics (e.g., imipramine and amitriptyline) but other medications not of these classes have emerged as well (see Kazdin, Rancurello, & Unis, in press). The literature for adult depression is vast. For example, over 200 placebo controlled trials have appeared on tricyclic antidepressants alone (Elkins & Rapoport, 1983). Not all studies have shown treatment effects nor do all patients respond positively. Tricyclics have been estimated to be more effective than placebos in approximately 60% to 75% of the studies (see Baldessarini, 1977; Elkins & Rapoport, 1983). However, the literature has gone well beyond establishing global effects for groups that receive active medication or placebo. Selective drug effects have been demonstrated showing that some subtypes of depression (e.g., bipolar vs. unipolar, primary vs. secondary) are more likely to respond to some medications rather than others. Also, other variables (e.g., family history, presence of biological markers) have been identified to predict responsiveness to alternative medications. As a general statement, research has progressed greatly on antidepressants for adults.

Many of the medications for adults have begun to be applied to children with affective disorders. Most of the work to date has been with imipramine and amitriptyline. In the 1960s and 1970s, a number of uncontrolled trials appeared but they suffered from such methodological problems as nonblind ratings or unsystematic assessment, unclearly defined groups of children, and so on (e.g., Connell, 1972; Polvan & Cebiroglu, 1972). Control group studies began to appear but also suffered from such problems as nonrandom assignment of children to groups, nonblind ratings (e.g., Weinberg *et al.*, 1973), or small sample sizes and confounding with other treatments (e.g., Petti & Law, 1982). Notwithstanding these and other sorts of criticisms, the demonstrations have been relatively consistent in showing that imipramine and amitriptyline lead to reduction of depressive symptoms.

Placebo-controlled and double-blind studies have begun to appear and have advanced greatly the knowledge about medication effects. Puig-Antich and his colleagues have conducted ongoing studies of the effects of imipramine (see Puig-Antich & Weston, 1983). In one study, imipramine and placebo yielded similar effects in the treatment of depressed children. However, significant differences emerged in the medication group when the group was divided according to median plasma level of imipramine and desipramine (a major metabolite of imipramine). Subjects with higher levels of medication showed 100% response to treatment whereas those with lower levels showed only 33% response. These results suggested that treatment effects are dependent upon a steady state plasma level beyond a particular threshold.

A subsequent report of this work continued to show that plasma level of imipramine and desipramine was related to clinical effects on depressive symptoms (Puig-Antich *et al.*, 1987). Other research on depressed children has shown that remission of symptoms depends on plasma level of medication (Preskorn, Weller, & Weller, 1982). The significance of these findings is great given that dose does not necessarily predict outcome. Apart from plasma level, the study by Puig-Antich *et al.* (1987) indicated that subtype of depression mediated treatment effects. Depressed children with psychotic symptoms responded consistently less well to medication and required higher plasma levels of medication to evince treatment effects. Thus, plasma level and type of depression were related to outcome.

To date, tricyclic antidepressants have been the most widely studied medications for depression in children. Other medications are available and no doubt will be studied. And there are important reasons to do so, such as the need to minimize side effects. For example, a recent study evaluated nortriptiline for childhood depression (Geller, Perel, Knitter, Lycaki, & Farooki, 1983). The results suggest that fewer side effects and lower dose may be required to achieve therapeutic plasma levels compared to imipramine.

Current Status

Given the outcome evidence, medications would seem to be the treatment of choice for depressive disorders. Yet, there are several considerations that must be borne in mind in deciding on medication. To begin, the guidelines for administration of medications to children are not as well worked out as they are with adults. There are significant differences between adults and children in such dimensions as drug absorption and metabolism. Much less research is available in general on the pharmacokinetics of medications with children, so greater caution needs to be exercised in their administration. Indeed, as of this writing the medication evaluated most frequently for treatment of depression in children (imipramine) has yet to receive approval from the Food and Drug Administration.

Second, there are heightened concerns regarding side effects in children. There is concern over the possible permanent effects that drugs may exert on growth, intelligence, and nonsymptomatic behaviors. The impact of medications on developmental changes raises issues not evident with adults. Apart from these effects, there are of course other treatment emergent effects that are likely to be temporary. Obviously, such effects can vary as a function of type of medication, dose, patient age, and other factors. The severity of these effects can vary widely from physiological changes undetectable to the child and of unclear or apparently no clinical significance (e.g., increased variability in heart rate or blood pressure), to minor discomfort (e.g., dry mouth), and to more severe consequences (e.g., seizures and death). In the case of cyclic antidepressants, side effects typically are relatively minor, such as dry mouth, sedation, blurred vision, and constipation. However, cardiovascular changes, reduced thresholds for seizures, cardio-respiratory arrest, and fatalities have been reported as well (see Kazdin *et al.*, in press). Moreover, withdrawal of medication may produce side effects as well (e.g., headaches, abdominal pain, vomitting), although these can be avoided or minimized by tapering withdrawal rather than ceasing medication abruptly.

The side effects of medication obviously raise potential concerns. Parents and their children need to be prepared for these effects. The presence of such side effects may have important implications for treatment efficacy, because parents and children are less likely to comply with medication regimens if even mildly bothersome effects emerge. In treatment settings, such side effects can be closely monitored and changes in treatment can be made in response to their appearance. Such flexibility is reduced slightly in outpatient treatment unless unusually close scrutiny is provided.

At best, current research suggests that medications alone may not address completely the dysfunction of depressed children. Evidence from different quarters might be cited to bolster this point. To begin with, in one study, depressed children showed marked deficiences in communications with their mothers and in peer relations, compared to nondepressed patients and normals (Puig-Antich *et al.*, 1985a,b). After recovery of depression from medication, mother–child interactions had improved although it was not up to the level of normal children. Yet, peer relations had changed very little. These results suggest that medication may not address significant facets of performance relevant to depression. Because social skills deficits have been proposed as a major characteristic of depressed patients (see Lewinsohn, 1974), treatment may be needed to address this area directly.

Research on adult patients has suggested that psychosocial treatments and medications offer unique and complementary advantages. The additive effects of psychosocial treatments and medication have been reasonably well supported in outcome studies with depressed adults (see Klerman & Schechter, 1982). Although there is some overlap in the impact of alternative treatments, medication tends to alter the symptoms of depression with relatively little impact on problems of living, social functioning, and interpersonal relationships. Psychotherapy appears to address these latter problems but with somewhat less impact on depressive symptoms. There are exceptions that fail to show the specific and complementary effects of these alternative treatments (see Murphy, Simons, Wetzel, & Lustman, 1984; Simons, Garfield, & Murphy, 1984).

Psychosocial treatments are likely to contribute significantly because the full range of depressive disorders is not likely to warrant medication nor to be treated by persons in a position to prescribe medication. Mild forms of depression, even if clinically significant, are likely to be detected and treated in everyday life (e.g., at school, with peers). Interventions that can be utilized in such settings would be very helpful to professionals and paraprofessionals alike. Current research has barely begun to explore psychosocial treatments.

Conclusions

Although research on affective disorders has only begun relatively recently, advances are emerging rapidly. The reason is that research on affective disorders in adults has for many years made remarkable gains in several specific areas, including biochemistry, epidemiology, diagnosis, genetics, assessment, and other areas. The work with adults has led to extensions of research paradigms and methods to children.

Findings obtained for adults may not necessarily characterize children. Yet, such findings provide an excellent place to begin to identify what developmental differences exist. To date, studies have shown important consistencies between adults and children in cognitive processes, behavioral repertoires, biological characteristics, and other facets of depression. Not all of the findings show that children and adults are the same in their manifestations of depressive disorders. For example, sleep characteristics obtained with adult depressed patients have not been isolated in children (e.g., Young *et al.*, 1982). Also, suicide, an occasional concomitant of depression in adults, is almost never seen in children. In many obvious ways, because of the different activities and stages of physical and emotional development, it is likely that symptoms of depression and their correlates differ in important ways.

The study on childhood depression has manifold implications. To begin with, it is clear that dysfunction among children goes beyond the occasional sadness evident as part of everyday life. Some children experience severe symptoms that cluster to form a syndrome. It is valuable to alert persons in everyday life to this help in the identification of dysfunction. Also, identification raises the prospect of treatment and prevention. To date, treatments for childhood depression have consisted primarily of alternative medications. Very little work is available on alternative psychosocial treatments. The picture is different in the adult literature, where several different psychotherapy techniques have been investigated. The adult literature has also explored the separate and combined effects of medication and psychosocial intervention. The field greatly needs similar extensions to children and adolescents.

References

Abramson, L. Y., Seligman, M. E. P., & Teasdale, J. D. (1978). Learned helplessness in humans: Critique and reformulation. *Journal of Abnormal Psychology, 87*, 49–74.

Akiskal, H. S. (1979). A biobehavioral approach to depression. In R. A. Depue (Ed.), *The psychobiology of the depressive disorders* (pp. 409–437). New York: Academic Press.

Akiskal, H. S., & McKinney, W. T., Jr. (1975). Overview of recent research in depression: Integration of ten conceptual models into a comprehensive clinical frame. *Archives of General Psychiatry, 32,* 285–305.

American Psychiatric Association. (1980). *Diagnostic and statistical manual of mental disorders* (3rd ed.). Washington, DC: Author.

Annell, A. (Ed.). (1972). *Depressive states in childhood and adolescence.* Stockholm: Almqvist & Wiksell.

Anthony, E. J. (1975). Childhood depression. In E. J. Anthony & T. Benedek (Eds.), *Depression and human existence.* Boston, MA: Little, Brown.

Asarnow, J. R., & Carlson, G. A. (Eds.). (1985). Depression Self-rating Scale: Utility with child psychiatric inpatients. *Journal of Consulting and Clinical Psychology, 53,* 491–499.

Baldessarini, R. J. (1977). *Chemotherapy in psychiatry.* Cambridge, MA: Harvard University Press.

Beck, A. T. (1976). *Cognitive therapy and the emotional disorders.* New York: International Universities Press.

Beck, A. T., Rush, A. J., Shaw, B. F., & Emery, G. (1979). *Cognitive therapy of depression.* New York: Guilford Press.

Bemporad, J. R., & Wilson, A. (1978). A developmental approach to depression in childhood and adolescence. *Journal of the American Academy of Psychoanalysis, 6,* 325–352.

Bene, A. (1975). Depressive phenomena in childhood: Their open and disguised manifestations in analytic treatment. In *Studies in child psychoanalysis* (pp. 33–46). Monograph series of the Psychoanalytic study of the child, No. 5. New Haven, CT: Yale University Press.

Beres, D. (1966). Superego and depression. In R. M. Lowenstein, L. M. Newman, M. Scherr, & A. J. Solnit (Eds.), *Psychoanalysis—A general psychology* (pp. 479–498). New York: International Universities Press.

Billings, A. G., & Moos, R. H. (1982). Psychosocial theory and research on depression: An integrative framework and review. *Clinical Psychology Review, 2,* 213–237.

Birleson, P. (1981). The validity of depressive disorder in childhood and the development of a self-rating scale: A research project. *Journal of Child Psychology and Psychiatry, 22,* 73–88.

Brown, G. W., Harris, T. O., & Peto, J. (1973). Life events and psychiatric disorders. Part II: Nature of causal link. *Psychological Medicine, 3,* 159–176.

Brumback, R. A., & Weinberg, W. A. (1977a). Childhood depression: An explanation of a behavior disorder of children. *Perceptual and Motor Skills, 44,* 911–916.

Brumback, R. A., & Weinberg, W. A. (1977b). Relationship of hyperactivity and depression in children. *Perceptual and Motor Skills, 45,* 247–251.

Brumback, R. A., Dietz-Schmidt, S. R., & Weinberg, W. A. (1977). Depression in children referred to an educational diagnostic center: Diagnosis and treatment and analysis of criteria and literature review. *Diseases of the Nervous System, 38,* 529–535.

Brumback, R. A., Jackoway, M. K., & Weinberg, W. A. (1980). Relation of intelligence to childhood depression in children referred to an educational diagnostic center. *Perceptual and Motor Skills, 50,* 11–17.

Bunch, J. (1972). Recent bereavement in relation to suicide. *Journal of Psychosomatic Research, 16,* 361–366.

Butler, L., Miezitis, S., Friedman, R., & Cole, E. (1980). The effect of two school-based intervention programs on depressive symptoms in preadolescents. *American Educational Research Journal, 17,* 111–119.

Calpin, J. P., & Cinciripini, P. M. (1978, May). *A multiple baseline analysis of social skills training in children.* Paper presented at Midwestern Association for Behavior Analysis, Chicago, IL.

Cantwell, D. P. (1982). Childhood depression. In B. B. Lahey & A. E. Kazdin (Eds.), *Advances in clinical child psychology* (Vol. 5, pp. 39–93). New York: Plenum Press.

Cantwell, D. P., & Carlson, G. A. (Eds.). (1983). *Affective disorders in childhood and adolescence: An update.* New York: Spectrum.

Carlson, G. A., & Cantwell, D. P. (1979). A survey of depressive symptoms in a child and adolescent psychiatric population. *Journal of the American Academy of Child Psychiatry, 18,* 587–599.

Carlson, G. A., & Cantwell, D. P. (1980). Unmasking masked depression in children and adolescents. *American Journal of Psychiatry, 137,* 445–449.

Carroll, B. J. (1978). Neuroendocrine function in psychiatric disorders. In M. A. Lipton, A. DiMascio, & K. F. Killam (Eds.), *Psychopharmacology: A generation of progress* (pp. 487–497). New York: Raven Press.

Carroll, B. J. (1983). Neuroendocrine diagnosis of depression. The dexamethasone suppression test. In P. J. Clayton & J. E. Barrett (Eds.), *Treatment of depression* (pp. 1–30). New York: Raven Press.

Chambers, W. J., Puig-Antich, J., & Tabrizi, M. A. (1978, October). *The ongoing development of the Kiddie-SADS (Schedule for Affective Disorders and Schizophrenia for School-age Children).* Paper presented at the American Academy of Child Psychiatry, San Diego, CA.

Chambers, W. J., Puig-Antich, J., Hirsch, M., Paez, P., Ambrosini, P. J., Tabrizi, M. A., & Davies, M. (1985). The assessment of affective disorders in children and adolescents by semistructured interview: Test–retest reliability. *Archives of General Psychiatry, 42,* 696–702.

Chiles, J. A., Miller, M. L., & Cox, G. B. (1980). Depression in an adolescent delinquent population. *Archives of General Psychiatry, 37,* 1179–1184.

Cicchetti, D., & Schneider-Rosen, K. (1984). Toward a transactional model of childhood depression. In D. Cicchetti & K. Schneider-Rosen (Eds.), *Childhood depres-*

sion: New directions for child development (pp. 5–27). San Francisco: Jossey-Bass.

Clayton, P. J., & Barrett, J. E. (Eds.). (1983). *Treatment of depression*. New York: Raven Press.

Connell, H. M. (1972). Depression in childhood. *Depression, Child Psychiatry and Human Development, 4*, 71–85.

Costello, C. G. (1980). Childhood depression: Three basic but questionable assumptions in the Lefkowitz and Burton critique. *Psychological Bulletin, 87*, 185–190.

Cytryn, L., & McKnew, D. H. (1972). Proposed classification of childhood depression. *American Journal of Psychiatry, 129*, 149–155.

Cytryn, L., & McKnew, D. H. (1974). Factors influencing the changing clinical expression of the depressive process in children. *American Journal of Psychiatry, 131*, 879–881.

Cytryn, L., McKnew, D. H., Bartko, J. J., Lamour, M., & Hamovitt, J. (1982). Offspring of patients with affective disorders: II. *Journal of the American Academy of Child Psychiatry, 21*, 389–391.

Decina, P., Kestenbaum, C. J., Farber, S., Kron, L., Gargan, M., Sackeim, H. A., & Fieve, R. R. (1983). Clinical and psychological assessment of children of bipolar probands. *American Journal of Psychiatry, 140*, 548–553.

Depue, R. A. (Ed.). (1979). *The psychobiology of the depressive disorders: Implications for the effects of stress*. New York: Academic Press.

Depue, R. A., & Kleiman, R. M. (1979). Free cortisol as a peripheral index of central vulnerability to major forms of polar depressive disorders: Examining stress-biology interactions in subsyndromal high-risk persons. In R. A. Depue (Ed.), *The psychobiology of the depressive disorders* (pp. 177–204). New York: Academic Press.

Depue, R. A., & Monroe, S. M. (1979). The unipolar-bipolar distinction in the depressive disorders: Implications for stress-onset interaction. In R. A. Depue (Ed.), *The psychobiology of the depressive disorders* (pp. 23–53). New York: Academic Press.

D'Zurilla, T. J., & Nezu, A. (1982). Social problem solving in adults. In P. C. Kendall (Ed.), *Advances in cognitive-behavioral research and therapy* (Vol. 1, pp. 202–274). New York: Academic Press.

Elkins, R., & Rapoport, J. L. (1983). Psychopharmacology of adult and childhood depression: An overview. In D. P. Cantwell & G. A. Carlson (Eds.), *Affective disorders in childhood and adolescence: An update* (pp. 363–374). New York: Spectrum.

Feighner, J. P., Robins, E., Guze, S. B., Woodruff, R. A., Winokur, G., & Munoz, R. (1972). Diagnostic criteria for use in psychiatric research. *Archives of General Psychiatry, 26*, 57–63.

Fisch, H. U., Frey, S., & Hirsbrunner, H. P. (1983). Analyzing nonverbal behavior in depression. *Journal of Abnormal Psychology, 92*, 307–318.

Frame, C., Matson, J. L., Sonis, W. A., Fialkov, M. J., & Kazdin, A. E. (1982). Behavioral treatment of depression in a prepubertal child. *Journal of Behavior Therapy and Experimental Psychiatry, 3*, 239–243.

Freud, S. (1917). Mourning and melancholia. In J. Strachey (Ed. and Trans.), *The standard edition of the complete psychological works of Sigmund Freud* (Vol. 14, pp. 243–258). London: Hogarth Press.

Geller, B., Perel, J. M., Knitter, E. F., Lycaki, H., Farooki, Z. Q. (1983). Nortriptyline in major depressive disorder in children: Response, steady-state plasma levels, predictive kinetics, and pharmacokinetics. *Psychopharmacology Bulletin, 19*, 62–65.

Gershon, E. S., Targum, S. D., Kessler, L. R., Mazure, C. M., & Bunney, W. E., Jr. (1977). Genetic studies and biologic strategies in the affective disorders. *Progress in Medical Genetics, 2*, 101–164.

Glaser, K. (1968). Masked depression in children and adolescents. In S. Chess & A. Thomas (Eds.), *Annual progress in child psychiatry and child development* (Vol. 1, pp. 345–355). New York: Brunner/Mazel.

Gordon, N., Lefkowitz, M. M., & Tesiny, E. P. (1980). Childhood depression and the Draw-a-Person Test. *Psychological Reports, 47*, 251–257.

Greden, J. F., & Carroll, B. J. (1981). Psychomotor function in affective disorders: An overview of new monitoring techniques. *American Journal of Psychiatry, 138*, 1441–1448.

Haley, G., Fine, S., Marriage, K., Moretti, M., & Freeman, R. (1985). Cognitive bias and depression in psychiatrically disturbed children and adolescents. *Journal of Consulting and Clinical Psychology, 53*, 535–537.

Helsel, W. J., & Matson, J. L. (1984). Assessment of depression in children: The internal structure of the Child Depression Inventory (CDI). *Behaviour Research and Therapy, 22*, 289–298.

Jacobsen, R. H., Lahey, B. B., & Strauss, C. C. (1983). Correlates of depressed mood in normal children. *Journal of Abnormal Child Psychology, 11*, 29–40.

Jacobson, N. S. (1981). The assessment of overt behavior in depression. In L. P. Rehm (Ed.), *Behavior therapy for depression: Present status and future directions* (pp. 279–300). New York: Academic Press.

Jones, I. M., & Pasna, M. (1979). Some nonverbal aspects of depression and schizophrenia occurring during the interview. *Journal of Nervous and Mental Disease, 167*, 402–409.

Kandel, D. B., & Davies, M. (1982). Epidemiology of depressive mood in adolescents: An empirical study. *Archives of General Psychiatry, 39*, 1205–1212.

Kaplan, S. L., Hong, G. K., & Weinhold, C. (1984). Epidemiology of depressive symptomatology in adolescents. *Journal of the American Academy of Child Psychiatry, 23*, 91–98.

Kashani, J. H., & Simonds, J. F. (1979). The incidence of depression in children. *American Journal of Psychiatry, 136*, 1203–1205.

Kashani, J. H., Barbero, G. J., & Bolander, F. D. (1981). Depression in hospitalized pediatric patients. *Journal of* the American Academy of Child Psychiatry, 20, 123–134.

Kashani, J. H., Husain, A., Shekim, W. O., Hodges, K., Cytryn, L., & McKnew, D. H. (1981). Current perspectives on childhood depression: An overview. *American Journal of Psychiatry, 138,* 143–153.

Kashani, J. H., McGee, R. O., Clarkson, S. E., Anderson, J. C., Walton, L. A., Williams, S., Silva, P. A., Robins, A. J., Cytryn, L., & McKnew, D. H. (1983). Depression in a sample of 9-year-old children. *Archives of General Psychiatry, 40,* 1217–1223.

Kazdin, A. E. (1981). Assessment techniques for childhood depression: A critical appraisal. *Journal of the American Academy of Child Psychiatry, 20,* 358–375.

Kazdin, A. E., & Petti, T. A. (1982). Self-report and interview measures of childhood and adolescent depression. *Journal of Child Psychology and Psychiatry, 23,* 437–457.

Kazdin, A. E., Esveldt-Dawson, K., Unis, A. S., & Rancurello, M. D. (1983). Child and parent evaluations of depression and aggression in psychiatric inpatient children. *Journal of Abnormal Child Psychology, 11,* 401–413.

Kazdin, A. E., French, N. H., Unis, A. S., & Esveldt-Dawson, K. (1983). Assessment of childhood depression: Correspondence of child and parent ratings. *Journal of the American Academy of Child Psychiatry, 22,* 157–164.

Kazdin, A. E., French, N. H., Unis, A. S., Esveldt-Dawson, K., & Sherick, R. B. (1983). Hopelessness, depression and suicidal intent among psychiatrically disturbed inpatient children. *Journal of Consulting and Clinical Psychology, 51,* 504–510.

Kazdin, A. E., Esveldt-Dawson, K., Sherick, R. B., & Colbus, D. (1985). Assessment of overt behavior and childhood depression among psychiatrically disturbed children. *Journal of Consulting and Clinical Psychology, 53,* 201–210.

Kazdin, A. E., Sherick, R. B., Esveldt-Dawson, K., & Rancurello, M. D. (1985). Nonverbal behavior and childhood depression. *Journal of the American Academy of Child Psychiatry, 24,* 303–309.

Kazdin, A. E., Rancurello, M., & Unis, A. S. (in press). Childhood depression. In G. D. Burrows & J. S. Werry (Eds.), *Advances in human psychopharmacology* (Vol. 4). Greenwich, CT: JAI Press.

Klerman, G. L., & Schechter, G. (1982). Drugs and psychotherapy. In E. S. Paykel (Ed.), *Handbook of affective disorders* (pp. 329–337). New York: Guilford Press.

Kovacs, M. (1978). *Interview Schedule for Children* (ISC) (10th revision). Pittsburgh, PA: University of Pittsburgh School of Medicine.

Kovacs, M. (1981). Rating scales to assess depression in school aged children. *Acta Paedopsychiatrica, 46,* 305–315.

Kovacs, M., & Beck, A. T. (1977). An empirical clinical approach towards a definition of childhood depression. In J. G. Schulterbrandt & A. Raskin (Eds.), *Depression in children: Diagnosis, treatment, and conceptual models* (pp. 1–25). New York: Raven Press.

Kovacs, M., Rush, A. J., Beck, A. T., & Hollon, S. D. (1981). Depressed outpatients treated with cognitive therapy or pharmacotherapy. *Archives of General Psychiatry, 38,* 33–39.

Kovacs, M., Feinberg, T. L., Crouse-Novak, M., Paulauskas, S. L., Pollock, M., & Finkelstein, R. (1984). Depressive disorders in childhood. *Archives of General Psychiatry, 41,* 643–649.

Kupfer, D. J., Spiker, D. G., Rossi, A., Coble, P. A., Ulrich, R., & Shaw, D. (1983). Recent diagnostic and treatment advances in REM sleep and depression. In P. J. Clayton & J. E. Barrett (Eds.), *Treatment of depression* (pp. 31–52). New York: Raven Press.

Lang, M., & Tisher, M. (1978). *Children's Depression Scale.* Victoria, Australia: Australian Council for Educational Research.

Lapouse, R. (1966). The epidemiology of behavior disorders in children. *American Journal of Diseases of Children, 111,* 594–599.

Lefkowitz, M. M. (1980). Childhood depression: A reply to Costello. *Psychological Bulletin, 87,* 191–194.

Lefkowitz, M. M., & Burton, N. (1978). Childhood depression: A critique of the concept. *Psychological Bulletin, 85,* 716–726.

Lefowitz, M. M., & Tesiny, E. P. (1980). Assessment of childhood depression. *Journal of Consulting and Clinical Psychology, 48,* 43–50.

Lefkowitz, M. M., & Tesiny, E. P. (1985). Depression in children: Prevalence and correlates. *Journal of Consulting and Clinical Psychology, 53,* 647–656.

Lefkowitz, M. M., Tesiny, E. P., & Gordon, N. H. (1980). Childhood depression, family income, and locus of control. *Journal of Nervous and Mental Disease, 168,* 732–735.

Lewinsohn, P. M. (1974). Clinical and theoretical aspects of depression. In K. S. Calhoun, H. E. Adams, & K. M. Mitchell (Eds.), *Innovative treatment methods of psychopathology* (pp. 63–120). New York: Wiley.

Lewinsohn, P. M., & Arconad, M. (1981). Behavioral treatment of depression: A social learning approach. In J. F. Clarkin & H. I. Glazer (Eds.), *Depression: Behavioral and directive intervention strategies* (pp. 33–67). New York: Garland STPM.

Lewinsohn, P. M., & Shaffer, M. (1971). The use of home observations as an integral part of the treatment of depression: Preliminary report and case studies. *Journal of Consulting and Clinical Psychology, 37,* 87–94.

Linden, M., Hautzinger, M., & Hoffmann, N. (1983). Discriminant analysis of depressive interactions. *Behavior Modification, 7,* 403–422.

Ling, W., Oftedal, G., & Weinberg, W. (1970). Depressive illness in childhood presenting as a severe headache. *American Journal of Diseases of Children, 120,* 122–124.

Lobovits, D. A., & Handal, P. J. (1985). Childhood depression: Prevalence using DSM-III criteria and validity of parent and child depression scales. *Journal of Pediatric Psychology, 10,* 45–54.

MacFarlane, J. W., Allen, L., & Honzik, M. P. (1954). *A developmental study of the behavior problems of normal children between 21 months and 14 years.* Berkeley, CA: University of California Press.

MacMahon, B., & Pugh, T. F. (1965). Suicide in the widowed. *American Journal of Epidemiology, 81,* 23–31.

Mahler, M. (1961). On sadness and grief in infancy and childhood. *Psychoanalytic Study of the Child, 16,* 332.

Malmquist, C. P. (1977). Childhood depression: A clinical and behavioral perspective. In J. G. Schulterbrandt & A. Raskin (Eds.), *Depression in children: Diagnosis, treatment and conceptual models* (pp. 33–59). New York: Raven Press.

Malouff, J. (1984). Development and validation of a behavioral peer-rating measure of depression. *Journal of Consulting and Clinical Psychology, 52,* 1108–1109.

McKnew, D. H., Cytryn, L., Efron, A. M., Gershon, E. S., & Bunney, W. E. (1979). Offspring of patients with affective disorders. *British Journal of Psychiatry, 134,* 148–152.

McLean, P. (1981). Remediation of skills and performance deficits in depression: Clinical steps and research findings. In J. F. Clarkin & H. I. Glazer (Eds.), *Depression: Behavioral and directive intervention strategies* (pp. 179–204). New York: Garland STPM.

McLean, P. D., & Hakstian, A. R. (1979). Clinical depression: Comparative efficacy of outpatient treatments. *Journal of Consulting and Clinical Psychology, 47,* 818–836.

Mendelson, M. (1982). Psychodynamics of depression. In E. S. Paykel (Ed.), *Handbook of affective disorders* (pp. 162–174). New York: Guilford Press.

Mezzich, A. C., & Mezzich, J. E. (1979). Symptomatology of depression in adolescence. *Journal of Personality Assessment, 43,* 267–275.

Miller, R. E., Ranelli, C., & Levine, J. M. (1977). Nonverbal communication as an index of depression. In I. Hanin & E. Usdin (Eds.), *Animal models in psychiatry and neurology* (pp. 171–180). New York: Pergamon Press.

Molick, R., & Pinkston, E. M. (1982). Using behavioral analysis to develop adaptive social behavior in a depressed adolescent girl. In E. M. Pinkston, J. L. Levitt, G. R. Green, N. L. Linsk, & T. L. Rzepnicki (Eds.), *Effective social work practice* (pp. 364–375). San Francisco: Jossey-Bass.

Moretti, M. M., Fine, S., Haley, G., & Marriage, K. (1985). Child and adolescent depression: Child-report versus parent-report information. *Journal of the American Academy of Child Psychiatry, 24,* 298–302.

Murphy, G. E., Simons, A. D., Wetzel, R. D., & Lustman, P. J. (1984). Cognitive therapy and pharmacotherapy. *Archives of General Psychiatry, 41,* 33–41.

Myers, J. K., & Weissman, M. M. (1980). Use of a self-report symptom scale to detect depression in a community sample. *American Journal of Psychiatry, 137,* 1081–1084.

Nezu, A. M., & Ronan, G. F. (1985). Life stress, current problems, problem-solving, and depressive symptoms: An integrative model. *Journal of Consulting and Clinical Psychology, 53,* 693–697.

Nurnberger, J. I., & Gershon, E. S. (1982). Genetics. In E. S. Paykel (Ed.), *Handbook of affective disorders* (pp. 109–125). New York: Guilford Press.

Orvaschel, H., Puig-Antich, J., Chambers, W., Tabrizi, M. A., & Johnson, R. (1982). Retrospective assessment of prepubertal major depression with the Kiddie-SADS-E. *Journal of the American Academy of Child Psychiatry, 21,* 392–397.

Paykel, E. S. (Ed.). (1982a). *Handbook of affective disorders.* New York: Guilford Press.

Paykel, E. S. (1982b). Life events and early environment. In E. S. Paykel (Ed.), *Handbook of affective disorders* (pp. 146–161). New York: Guilford Press.

Paykel, E. S., & Tanner, J. (1976). Life events, depressive relapse and maintenance treatment. *Psychological Medicine, 6,* 481–485.

Petti, T. A. (1978). Depression in hospitalized child psychiatry patients: Approaches to measuring depression. *Journal of the American Academy of Child Psychiatry, 17,* 49–59.

Petti, T. A., & Law, W. (1982). Imipramine treatment of depressed children: A double-blind pilot study. *Journal of Clinical Psychopharmacology, 2,* 107–110.

Petti, T. A., Bornstein, M., Delamater, A., & Conners, C. K. (1980). Evaluation and multimodality treatment of a depressed pre-pubertal girl. *Journal of the American Academy of Child Psychiatry, 19,* 690–702.

Polvan, O., & Cebiroglu, R. (1971). Treatment with psychopharmacologic agents in childhood depressions. In A. L. Annell (Ed.), *Depressive states in childhood and adolescence* (pp. 467–472). Stockholm, Sweden: Almqvist & Wiksell.

Poznanski, E. O., Cook, S. C., & Carroll, B. J. (1979). A depression rating scale for children. *Pediatrics, 64,* 442–450.

Poznanski, E. O., Cook, S. C., Carroll, B. J., & Corzo, H. (1983). Use of the Children's Depression Rating Scale in an inpatient psychiatric population. *Journal of Clinical Psychiatry, 44,* 200–203.

Poznanski, E. O., Grossman, J. A., Buchsbaum, Y., Banegas, M., Freeman, L., & Gibbons, R. (1984). Preliminary studies of the reliability and validity of the Children's Depression Rating Scale. *Journal of the American Academy of Child Psychiatry, 23,* 191–197.

Preskorn, S. H., Weller, E. B., & Weller, R. A. (1982). Depression in children: Relationship between plasma imipramine levels and response. *Journal of Clinical Psychiatry, 43,* 450–453.

Puig-Antich, J. (1983). Neuroendocrine and sleep correlates of prepubertal major depressive disorder: Current status of the evidence. In D. P. Cantwell & G. A. Carlson (Eds.), *Affective disorders in childhood and adolescence: An update* (pp. 211–227). New York: Spectrum.

Puig-Antich, J., & Gittelman, R. (1982). Depression in childhood and adolescence. In E. S. Paykel (Ed.), *Handbook of affective disorders* (pp. 379–392). New York: Guilford Press.

Puig-Antich, J., & Weston, B. (1983). The diagnosis and treatment of major depressive disorder in childhood. *Annual Review of Medicine, 34,* 231–245.

Puig-Antich, J., Blau, S., Marx, N., Greenhill, L. L., & Chambers, W. (1978). Prepubertal major depressive disorders: A pilot study. *Journal of the American Academy of Child Psychiatry, 17,* 695–707.

Puig-Antich, J., Perel, J. M., Lupatkin, W., Chambers, W. J., Shea, C., Tabrizi, M. A., & Stiller, R. L. (1979). Plasma levels of imipramine (IMI) and desmethylimipramine (DMI) and clinical response in prepubertal major depressive disorder. *Journal of the American Academy of Child Psychiatry, 18,* 616–627.

Puig-Antich, J., Goetz, R., Davies, M., Fein, M., Hanlon, C., Chambers, W. J., Tabrizi, M. A., Sachar, E. J., & Weitzman, E. D. (1984). Growth hormone secretion in prepubertal children with major depression. II. Sleep-related plasma concentrations during a depressive episode. *Archives of General Psychiatry, 41,* 463–466.

Puig-Antich, J., Lukens, E., Davies, M., Goetz, D., Brennan-Quattrock, J., & Todak, G. (1985a). Psychosocial functioning in prepubertal major depressive disorders. I. Interpersonal relationships during the depressive episode. *Archives of General Psychiatry, 42,* 500–507.

Puig-Antich, J., Lukens, E., Davies, M., Goetz, D., Brennan-Quattrock, J., & Todak, G. (1985b). Psychosocial functioning in prepubertal major depressive disorders. II. Interpersonal relationships after sustained recovery from affective episode. *Archives of General Psychiatry, 42,* 511–517.

Puig-Antich, J., Perel, J., Lupatkin, W., Chambers, W. J., Tabrizi, M. A., King, J., Davies, M., Johnson, R., & Stiller, R. (1987). Imipramine in prepubertal major depressive disorders. *Archives of General Psychiatry, 44,* 81–89.

Rapoport, J. L., & Ismond, D. R. (1984). *DSM-III training guide for diagnosis of childhood disorders.* New York: Brunner/Mazel.

Rehm, L. P. (1977). A self-control model of depression. *Behavior Therapy, 8,* 787–804.

Rehm, L. P. (Ed.). (1981). *Behavior therapy for depression: Present status and future directions.* New York: Academic Press.

Reynolds, W. M. (1984). Depression in children and adolescents: Phenomenology, evaluation, and treatment. *School Psychology Review, 13,* 171–182.

Reynolds, W. M. (1985). Depression in childhood and adolescence: Diagnosis, assessment, intervention strategies, and research. In T. R. Kratochwill (Ed.), *Advances in school psychology* (Vol. 4, pp. 133–189). Hillsdale, NJ: Erlbaum.

Reynolds, W. M., & Coats, K. I. (1985). A comparison of cognitive-behavioral therapy and relaxation training for the treatment of depression in adolescents. *Journal of Consulting and Clinical Psychology, 54,* 653–660.

Riddle, K. D., & Rapoport, J. L. (1976). A 2-year follow-up of 72 hyperactive boys. *Journal of Nervous and Mental Disease, 162,* 126–134.

Rie, H. E. (1966). Depression in childhood: A survey of some pertinent contributions. *Journal of the American Academy of Child Psychiatry, 5,* 653–685.

Rochlin, G. (1965). *Griefs and discontents.* Boston, MA: Little, Brown.

Rush, A. J., Beck, A. T., Kovacs, M., & Hollon, S. (1977). Comparative efficacy of cognitive therapy and pharmacotherapy in the treatment of depressed outpatients. *Cognitive Therapy and Research, 1,* 17–37.

Sachar, E. J. (1982). Endocrine abnormalities in depression. In E. S. Paykel (Ed.), *Handbook of affective disorders* (pp. 191–201.). New York: Guilford Press.

Sacks, J. M. (1977). The need for subtlety: A critical session with a suicidal child. *Psychotherapy: Theory, Research, and Practice, 14,* 434–437.

Sanchez, V., Lewinsohn, P. M., & Larson, D. W. (1980). Assertion training: Effectiveness in the treatment of depression. *Journal of Clinical Psychology, 36,* 526–529.

Saylor, C. F., Finch, A. J., Jr., Baskin, C. H., Furey, W., & Kelly, M. M. (1984). Construct validity for measures of childhood depression: Application of multitrait-multimethod methodology. *Journal of Consulting and Clinical Psychology, 52,* 977–985.

Saylor, C. F., Finch, A. J., Jr., Spirito, A., & Bennett, B. (1984). The Children's Depression Inventory: A systematic evaluation of psychometric properties. *Journal of Consulting and Clinical Psychology, 52,* 955–967.

Schwartz, G. E., Fair, P. L., Mandel, M. R., Salt, P., Meske, M., & Klerman, G. L. (1978). Facial electromyography in the assessment of improvement in depression. *Psychosomatic Medicine, 40,* 355–360.

Seligman, M. E. P. (1975). *Helplessness: On depression, development and death.* San Francisco: Freeman.

Seligman, M. E. P., Peterson, C., Kaslow, N. J., Tanenbaum, R. L., Alloy, L. B., Abramson, L. Y. (1984). Attributional style and depressive symptoms among children. *Journal of Abnormal Psychology, 93,* 235–238.

Simons, A. D., Garfield, S. L., & Murphy, G. E. (1984). The process of change in cognitive therapy and pharmacotherapy for depression. *Archives of General Psychiatry, 41,* 45–51.

Spitz, R. (1946). Anaclitic depression. *Psychoanalytic Study of the Child, 2,* 113–117.

Spitzer, R. L., Endicott, J., & Robins, E. (1978). Research Diagnostic Criteria: Rationale and reliability. *Archives of General Psychiatry, 35,* 773–782.

Sroufe, L. A., & Rutter, M. (1984). The domain of developmental psychopathology. *Child Development, 55,* 17–29.

Strober, M., Green, J., & Carlson, G. (1981). Utility of the Beck Depression Inventory with psychiatrically hospitalized adolescents. *Journal of Consulting and Clinical Psychology, 49,* 482–483.

Tesiny, E. P., & Lefkowitz, M. M. (1982). Childhood depression: A 6-month follow-up study. *Journal of Consulting and Clinical Psychology, 50,* 778–780.

Tesiny, E. P., Lefkowitz, M. M., & Gordon, N. H. (1980). Childhood depression, locus of control, and school achievement. *Journal of Educational Psychology, 72,* 506–510.

Tisher, M., & Lang, M. (1983). The Children's Depression Scale: Review and further developments. In D. P. Cantwell & G. A. Carlson (Eds.), *Childhood depression* (pp. 181–203). New York: Spectrum.

Toolan, J. M. (1962). Depression in children and adolescents. *American Journal of Orthopsychiatry, 32,* 404–414.

Usdin, E., Asberg, M., Bertilsson, L., & Sjoqvist, F. (Eds.). (1984). *Frontiers in biochemical and pharmacological research in depression: Advances in biochemical psychopharmacology* (Vol. 39). New York: Raven Press.

Waxer, P. (1976). Nonverbal cues for depth of depression: Set versus no set. *Journal of Consulting and Clinical Psychology, 44,* 493.

Weinberg, W. A., Rutman, J., Sullivan, L., Pencik, E. C., & Dietz, S. G. (1973). Depression in children referred to an education diagnostic center. *Journal of Pediatrics, 83,* 1065–1072.

Weissman, M. M. (1979). The psychological treatment of depression: Evidence for the efficacy of psychotherapy alone, in comparison with, and in combination with pharmacotherapy. *Archives of General Psychiatry, 36,* 1261–1269.

Weissman, M. M., & Paykel, E. S. (1974). *The depressed woman: A study of social relationships.* Chicago, IL: University of Chicago Press.

Weissman, M. M., Orvaschel, H., & Padian, N. (1980). Children's symptom and social functioning self-report scales: Comparison of mothers' and children's reports. *Journal of Nervous and Mental Disease, 168,* 736–740.

Werry, J. S., & Quay, H. C. (1971). The prevalence of behavior symptoms in younger elementary school children. *American Journal of Orthopsychiatry, 41,* 136–143.

Williams, J. B. W., & Spitzer, R. L. (1982). Research Diagnostic Criteria and DSM III: An annotated comparison. *Archives of General Psychiatry, 39,* 1283–1289.

Williams, J. G., Barlow, D. H., & Agras, W. S. (1972). Behavioral measurement of severe depression. *Archives of General Psychiatry, 27,* 330–333.

Wirt, R. D., Lachar, D., Klinedinst, J. K., & Seat, P. D. (1977). *Multidimensional description of child personality: A manual for the Personality Inventory for Children.* Los Angeles, CA: Western Psychological Services.

Yanchyshyn, G. W., & Robbins, D. R. (1980, October). *The assessment of depression in normal adolescents: A comparison study.* Paper presented at meeting of the American Academy of Child Psychiatry, Chicago, IL.

Young, W., Knowles, J. B., MacLean, A. W., Boag, L., & McConville, B. J. (1982). The sleep of childhood depressives. *Biological Psychiatry, 17,* 1163–1168.

Zis, A. P., & Goodwin, F. K. (1982). The amine hypothesis. In E. S. Paykel (Ed.), *Handbook of affective disorders* (pp. 175–190). New York: Guilford Press.

CHAPTER 29

Medical and Health-Related Disorders

Kathleen L. Lemanek and Dorothy J. Van Buren

An interdisciplinary approach to the total care of chronically ill children and adolescents involves consideration of biomedical, biobehavioral, and psychosocial factors (Varni, 1983). One aspect of this approach is an increasing emphasis on the coordination of services between the medical community and the public schools. There have been two major forces behind linking the care of the chronically ill child's physical health, social development, and educational attainment. First, technical advances in the detection and treatment of acute, infectious diseases have shifted the focus of pediatrics to the management of chronic illnesses and disease prevention (Russo & Varni, 1982). Second, the Education for all Handicapped Children Act of 1975 (P.L. 94-142) has mandated that public schools accept responsibility for providing appropriate educational and supportive services to chronically ill children, that is, administering medications and detailed medical regimens; furnishing physical, occupational, speech, and language therapy; and changing classroom curricula and building structure (Schroeder, Teplin, & Schroeder, 1982; Walker, 1984). As such, pediatricians are seeing a larger number of chronically ill children in their practices and these children are spending more time outside of the family in school (Gortmaker & Sappenfield, 1984; Walker, 1984). The majority of children and adolescents with a chronic illness generally fall into one of two categories specified by P.L. 94-142 as eligible for special education and related services; these categories are the orthopedically impaired and the other health impaired. The category *orthopedically impaired* includes those children whose educational performance is adversely affected by

> impairments caused by congenital anomaly (e.g., clubfoot, absence of some member, etc.), impairments caused by disease (e.g., poliomyelitis, bone tuberculosis, etc.), and impairments from other causes (e.g., cerebral palsy, amputations, and fractures or burns which cause contractures). ("Education of Handicapped Children," 1977)

The definition of *other health impaired* specifies

> limited strength, vitality or alertness, due to chronic or acute health problems such as a heart condi-

Kathleen L. Lemanek • Department of Pediatrics, University of Miami School of Medicine, Miami, Florida 33101. **Dorothy J. Van Buren** • Department of Psychology, Louisiana State University, Baton Rouge, Louisiana 70803.

> tion, tuberculosis, rheumatic fever, nephritis, asthma, sickle-cell anemia, hemophilia, epilepsy, lead poisoning, leukemia, or diabetes, which adversely affects a child's educational performance. ("Education of Handicapped Children," 1977)

Walker (1984) cited data collected by the Office of Special Education indicating that 16% of children (aged 3 to 21) who received special educational or supportive services were orthopedically impaired and 25% were classified as other health impaired during the 1979–1980 school year. Many specialists in the area of pediatric chronic illness assert that only certain children will require placement in a special education classroom (e.g., cerebral palsy, spina bifida) (Gearheart & Weishahn, 1976; Griffiths, 1975). However, most chronically ill children will need some type of related services during the course of their schooling (Walker, 1984). A variety of related services are covered by P.L. 94-142: (a) speech pathology and audiology, (b) psychological services, (c) physical and occupational therapy, (d) recreation, (e) early identification and assessment of disabilities in children, (f) counseling services, (g) medical diagnostic or evaluation services, (h) school health and social work services, and (i) parent counseling and training. Unfortunately, many children who need one or more of these services do not receive them because of the time involved in referring, evaluating, and placing children in special education, the cost of providing these services in underequipped schools, and the availability of these services in the community through Title V and other specialized programs (Walker, 1984).

The need for related services in public schools depends on the number of chronically ill children and adolescents in the United States. Estimates of the prevalence of childhood chronic illness vary according to the definition used, the methods of study, and the population examined (Gortmaker & Sappenfield, 1984). A chronic illness is defined as a condition that remains for a period ranging from 3 months to a lifetime (Magrab & Calcagno, 1978) or that demands hospitalization for one month or more (Pless & Douglas, 1971). Under this definition the prevalence of chronic illness in school-aged children is between 10% and 20%, with the most common being asthma (2%), cardiac disease (0.5%), cerebral palsy (0.5%), orthopedic disorders (0.5%), and diabetes mellitus (0.1%) (Haggerty, Roghmann, & Pless, 1975; Mattson, 1972; Pless & Douglas, 1971; Walker & Gortmaker, 1983). Although the number of children seen in pediatric practices and public schools is still rather small, new responsibilities have developed for the physician, the child, and family, and the school because of improvements in medical treatment and increased life expectancy (e.g., more frequent clinic visits and hospitalizations, special educational services, physical therapy, social services) (Gortmaker & Sappenfield, 1984). To enhance the psychological, cognitive, and physical development of chronically ill children, these new responsibilities need to be taken care of through regular communication between medical specialists (e.g., physicians, nurses), health professionals (e.g., occupational and speech therapists), educational experts (e.g., teachers, school psychologists), and family members.

Based on the NPAS conceptualization of children with a chronic illness, the relative presence or absence of behavioral problems varying across individuals with a particular disorder and across disorders is likely. In addition, the fact that psychological factors and environmental problems may be antecedents to or consequences of medical disorders is highlighted. As such, assessment of children and adolescents with a handicap or chronic illness should emphasize a behavior analytic and idiographic approach. That is, a set of problem behaviors are targeted for change based on an analysis of those behaviors required for effective functioning in situations specific to each individual. To ensure accurate identification and description of the target behaviors, information should be collected on (a) antecendent events and consequences, (b) organismic variables, (c) contingency-related events, and (d) different domains of the behavior (i.e., cognitive, motor, physiological) using multiple methods of assessment (see Cone, 1978; Kanfer & Saslow, 1969). Current behavioral techniques that should be used to conduct such an assessment can be grouped into three categories: (a) operant and social learning procedures (e.g., social/primary reinforcement, response-cost, time out, modeling), (b) cognitive and behavioral self-regulation procedures (e.g., relaxation training, social skills training, systematic desensitization), and (c) biofeedback and physiological self-regulation procedures (Russo & Varni, 1982). Combinations of these techniques should be employed to evaluate four areas of the physical and psychological status of chronically ill children and adolescents: (a) the child's personal growth and development (e.g., tasks of daily living, motor skills, cognitive development), (b) the child's relationships with family members (e.g., parent communication, sibling jealousy), (c) the child's activities outside the home (e.g., school absences, academic performance, classroom behavior, frequency of peer contacts), and (d) the child's adjustment to the illness (e.g., understanding the illness, participation in care) (Leventhal, 1984).

Several studies have shown that children and adolescents with such chronic illnesses as diabetes (Knowles, 1971), cystic fibrosis (Gayton & Friedman, 1973), asthma (Purcell, Weiss, & Hahn, 1972), and juvenile rheumatoid arthritis (McAnarney, Pless, Satterwhite, & Friedman, 1974) evidence a higher incidence of psychopathology compared to healthy children (e.g., poor self-concept, depression, maladaptive family and peer relationships). Much of this earlier research did not study the psychological adjustment of chronically ill children using objective tests, but tended to utilize interviews, clinical observations, and projective techniques (Drotar, 1981). However, results from more controlled research suggest that chronically ill children are as well adjusted as their healthy peers (Kellerman, Zeltzer, Ellenberg, Dash, & Rigler, 1980; Steinhausen, 1981; Zeltzer, Kellerman, Ellenberg, Dash, & Rigler, 1980). In general, the most beneficial model to follow when evaluating and treating chronically ill children is from a "normal person-abnormal situation" conceptualization (NPAS) (Russo & Varni, 1982). That is, children with a chronic illness and their families represent a normal population, but are confronted with numerous, recurring stressors because of their disease (e.g., hospitalizations, aversive treatment procedures, financial expenses, school absences). Such stressors are likely to present frequent opportunities for the learning of aberrant behavior (e.g., temper tantrums, whining, noncompliance) (Varni, Bessman, Russo, & Cataldo, 1980). Furthermore, certain variables are reported to influence the risk of aberrant behaviors occurring in chronically ill children including poor family relationships (e.g., conflicts over managing medical regimens), unstable prognosis (e.g., unpredictable attacks), age of disease onset (e.g., school entry, adolescence), and inappropriate academic and social expectations (Pless, 1984).

Based on the NPAS conceptualization of children with a chronic illness, the relative presence or absence of behavioral problems varying across individuals with a particular disorder and across disorders is likely. In addition, the fact that psychological factors and environmental problems may be antecedents to or consequences of medical disorders is highlighted. As such, assessment of children and adolescents with a handicap or chronic illness should emphasize a behavior analytic and idiographic approach. That is, a set of problem behaviors are targeted for change based on an analysis of those behaviors required for effective functioning in situations specific to each individual. To ensure accurate identification and description of the target behaviors, information should be collected on (a) antecendent events and consequences, (b) organismic variables, (c) contingency-related events, and (d) different domains of the behavior (i.e., cognitive, motor, physiological) using multiple methods of assessment (see

Cone, 1978; Kanfer & Saslow, 1969). Current behavioral techniques that should be used to conduct such an assessment can be grouped into three categories: (a) operant and social learning procedures (e.g., social/primary reinforcement, response-cost, time out, modeling), (b) cognitive and behavioral self-regulation procedures (e.g., relaxation training, social skills training, systematic desensitization), and (c) biofeedback and physiological self-regulation procedures (Russo & Varni, 1982). Combinations of these techniques should be employed to evaluate four areas of the physical and psychological status of chronically ill children and adolescents: (a) the child's personal growth and development (e.g., tasks of daily living, motor skills, cognitive development), (b) the child's relationships with family members (e.g., parent communication, sibling jealousy), (c) the child's activities outside the home (e.g., school absences, academic performance, classroom behavior, frequency of peer contacts), and (d) the child's adjustment to the illness (e.g., understanding the illness, participation in care) (Leventhal, 1984).

The pediatrician, family, and school personnel can operate as a team to develop a profile of each child's needs based on data collected from these four areas. The American Academy of Pediatrics (1977) has outlined the role of the pediatrician when working as a consultant to the schools: (a) identify and refer children with suspected or confirmed problems to the local schools, (b) provide parents information on educational and related services to which they are entitled under federal and states laws, (c) work with the school in assessing children, and (d) help in the appropriate placement of a child and monitoring of a child's program. Education of the child, parents, and school personnel (e.g., teachers, principals) about specific chronic diseases, the child's limitations, capabilities, and medical regimen; and emergency care procedures is one of the most important functions of the pediatrician as a team member (McInerny, 1984; Walker, 1984). Whereas the pediatrician may serve as coordinator of services between the parents and the school, the school nurse frequently fulfills that role directly within the school (Walker, 1984). The school nurse can be responsible for keeping confidential records of each chronically ill child, communicating relevant information to school staff (e.g., classroom and physical education teachers, secretaries), administering medical treatments, and training staff to deal with chronic illnesses and emergency procedures. Staff training on managing a medical emergency (e.g., asthma attacks, insulin reaction, epileptic seizure) should be a priority for inservice workshops because school nurses and physicians usually are not present when emergencies occur (Walker, 1984). The school psychologists and teachers are in unique positions to observe classroom behavior that may be associated with specific illnesses, to implement treatment protocols for modifying aberrant behaviors, and to run individual and group sessions on improving social behaviors and symptom control (e.g., self-management programs). Finally, parents should be included in all phases of the child's medical care and educational program to ensure that appropriate services are being rendered and that various agencies are working together. Employing a team approach with chronically ill children and adolescents will result in the most efficient use of resources and effective care of the child and the family. The next sections describe several chronic illnesses and orthopedic impairments frequently seen in school-aged children with a focus on the behavioral assessment and treatment of these conditions.

Orthopedic Impairments

A variety of conditions result in orthopedic impairments in children. The cause of such impairments range from chronic diseases, such as juvenile rheumatoid arthritis, to traumatic events, such as injuries sustained from severe burns. The issues involved in the behavioral assessment and treatment of the orthopedically impaired child within the educational setting will be illustrated through discussions of these two potentially disabling conditions: Juvenile rheumatoid arthritis and burn injuries.

Juvenile Rheumatoid Arthritis

Juvenile rheumatoid arthritis (JRA) is a chronic disease involving a disorder of the autoimmune system (Achterberg-Lawlis, 1982) that occurs in children between infancy to midadolescence (Calabro, 1970). According to Achterberg-Lawlis, approximately 250,000 children in the United States were affected by JRA in 1982. The mode of onset of JRA varies from patient to patient as does the course of this disease. JRA may be experienced as a relatively mild chronic condition; it can involve periodic, intense exacerbations interspersed with apparent remission of the disease; or it can be a swiftly crippling disease. Because of its frequently erratic course, the treatment for JRA can be quite complicated and is aimed at ameliorating the acute symptoms of the disease as well as at preventing the development of disfigurement and crippling of the joints.

Treatment of JRA is multifaceted. It can involve the use of drugs, such as aspirin, steroids, and gold salts to reduce inflammation, fever, or other systemic symptoms; splints to support joints so that their function is not lost and to minimize deformity during periods of time when the disease is active; and exercise to preserve joint range of motion and to prevent contractures of the joints that could result in crippling and deformity (Baum, 1983; Calabro, 1970). As Rapoff, Lindsley, and Christophersen (1984) pointed out, the complexity of the treatment regimen for JRA coupled with alternating periods of time of apparent healthfulness and active illness, produces the type of disease for which treatment compliance is extremely problematic. Because many children with JRA are of school age, the disease, its treatment, and effective compliance with its treatment are likely to present unique challenges for parents and school personnel as well as for the child with JRA.

McAnarney *et al.* (1974) found that twice as many children with JRA were referred to school psychologists when compared with a group of physically healthy peers. Three times as many children with JRA were also receiving low academic achievement scores when compared with the normal control group. In order further to assess the school adjustment of these children, McAnarney *et al.* (1974) used teacher ratings of adjustment and measures of academic performance to construct an index of overall school adjustment. Of the 42 children with arthritis who participated in this study, one third received low overall adjustment ratings whereas only 9% of the control subjects were so rated. Further, the less obviously disabled the arthritic child was the more likely she or he was to receive lower overall adjustment ratings than was the child with obvious physical handicaps. McAnarney *et al.* (1974) coined the term *marginality* to describe the experience of children who are not obviously physically ill but who are not wholly physically healthy because of a chronic illness or condition that may not be salient to those who interact with the child. The tendency to appear to be other than they are, to be marginal—not quite healthy, not quite sick, is posited by McAnarney *et al.* (1974) to contribute to the poor school adjustment experienced by some children with JRA. The McAnarney *et al.* (1974) findings might lead one to believe that the child with JRA would be better off in school if his or her disease was more salient perhaps through the presence of an obvious handicap or splinting. However, McAnarney *et al.* (1974) made use of teachers' ratings of adjustment only, without regard for the children's peer perceptions of them. Unfortunately, it has been found that, in general, elementary school students have unfavorable attitudes toward children with handicaps.

The awareness of such handicaps develops by 6 years of age and as the child progresses from first to sixth grade his attitudes toward children who are handicapped become increasingly negative (Westervelt, Brantley, & Ware, 1983). Part of the handicapped child's successful classroom adjustment includes the acquisition and use of effective social skills. If able-bodied children are reluctant to interact socially with their disabled peers because of negative perceptions, then the development of social skills in the handicapped school child may be hindered. The use of sociometric techniques (Guidubaldi, Kehle, & Murray, 1984) to assess the social relationships of JRA children have not been used thus far but may provide further information regarding the successful school adjustment of the child with JRA. Despite the apparent appropriateness of applying behavioral assessment techniques to the study of children with JRA at school, few behavioral intervention techniques have been applied to such children in the classroom.

When behavioral treatment techniques have been applied specifically to children with JRA they have been aimed at helping the child comply with his or her medical treatment regimen. Rapoff *et al.* (1984) reported the successful use of contingency management techniques to improve the medical compliance of a 7-year-old arthritic girl. Their intervention occurred within the child's home. Although the child was of school-age, Rapoff *et al.* (1984) make no mention of whether she was in fact attending school. However, based on their single-subject investigation, contingency management techniques are likely to be quite appropriately applied to the child in the classroom to ensure compliance with oral medication ingestion and activity requirements. Medical compliance is but one area in which behavioral interventions can be applied to the child with JRA. Behavioral methods may also prove to be helpful in the assimilation into the classroom of the child with JRA who is wearing splints or is otherwise handicapped.

Despite the presence of effective social skills training techniques for use with children (Gottman, Gonso, & Schuler, 1976), little emphasis has been placed on improving the social skills of the handicapped child in an attempt to enhance school adjustment and peer acceptance (Battle, 1984). Rather, attention has been focused on altering the attitudes of the peers of the handicapped child to more positive perceptions. This has been done with the behavioral technique of peer modeling (Westervelt *et al.*, 1983). The premise behind this emphasis is that increases in the positiveness of the able-bodied child's attitudes toward his disabled peer will result in greater approach behavior by the non-orthopedically impaired student. The subsequent increase in approach behavior is assumed thus to affect the opportunity for the handicapped child to develop and practice appropriate social skills (Westervelt *et al.*, 1983). In an attempt to explore this approach to enhancing peer acceptance of the handicapped child, Westervelt *et al.* (1983) showed a film to fourth graders depicting a handicapped girl's adjustment to school, which was followed by a teacher-led group discussion of the film and the class's reaction to it. The results of this study, based on children's responses toward photographs of various handicapped youngsters and to various questions about hypothetical disabled students, suggest that such an intervention serves to enhance children's attitudes toward the handicapped. These positive results persisted up to one-week follow-up. Unfortunately, the effects of such an intervention on the social assimilation of an actual handicapped peer have not yet been reported. Westervelt *et al.* (1983) suggested that, should the technique they examined be used to prepare a class for the presence of an orthopedically impaired child, the film be shown one week prior to or within the first week of the child's entrance into the classroom.

Burn Injuries

One of the most serious forms of trauma experienced by children is the burn injury. Approximately 2 million burn injuries occur each year with over 50% of these cases being seen in children and adolescents (Crawford, 1981). The largest number of burns occur before the age of 6 years. Thermal burns (e.g., scaldings, flames) are the leading cause of injuries in this age group and for children between the ages of 7 and 15 years (Crawford,

1981). It has been estimated that half of the burn injuries require hospitalization, with the length of hospitalization and rehabilitation averaging 2 years (Crawford, 1981; Shires, 1979).

The pathologic characteristics or severity of a burn injury depends on the extent and depth of the burned area. The extent of an injury is defined as the percentage of the body surface burned (i.e., total body surface area—TBSA). The well-known general classification of burn depth is first degree, second degree, and third degree (Achterberg-Lawlis & Kenner, 1982; Yarbrough, 1981). Flame burns, which appear quite often in school-aged children, usually involve third degree burns (i.e., dry leathery form and little weeping from affected area). More than any other single criteria, the extent of the burn injury determines the prognosis of the child's morbidity and mortality (Yarbrough, 1981).

The nature of psychological complications and precipitating factors in burned children is still unclear. It may, though, be concluded that short-term psychological problems occur in the majority of children, whereas long-term effects are noted in fewer than half of the cases (Achterberg-Lawlis & Kenner, 1982; Wagner, Wolpin, & Forrest, 1981). The intensity, duration, and even presence of psychological complications appear to be based on (a) previous coping skills to stress, (b) nature of the injury, and (c) family interaction or prior psychosocial stressors (e.g., divorce, illness of family members, change in schools) (Achterberg-Lawlis & Kenner, 1982; Jones & Bowden, 1979). Research evaluating the psychological complications of burned children is severely limited in terms of quantity and methodological sophistication. One reason for the paucity of studies is that medical care has priority during the initial phase (i.e., first 72 hours postinjury) and acute phase (i.e., until healing or grafting is completed) of treatment. Unfortunately, few studies have also been conducted during the rehabilitation phase when the children have returned to school. The most often cited psychological complications include delirium (e.g., impaired orientation, insomnia), anxiety (e.g., irritability, decreased appetite and pain tolerance), depression (e.g., withdrawal, hopelessness), regression (e.g., low frustration tolerance, demanding behavior), and anger (e.g., berating, crying, kicking) (Andreasen, Noyes, Hartford, Brodland, & Proctor, 1972; Artz, 1979; Breslin, 1975; Campbell, 1976; Long & Cope, 1961; West & Shuck, 1978). Many of these behavioral reactions result from the constant, prolonged pain experienced by burned children. Pain is produced by virtually all treatment procedures, such as painful medication applied to wounds, debridement, exercise of burned limbs to prevent contractures, air hitting open wounds, and skin grafting, which makes new painful wounds.

The majority of research on burned children has been descriptive accounts of either the presence of psychological complications or the effectiveness of supportive therapy for patients and their families. However, some studies have used behavioral methods to assess the behavior of burned children throughout medical procedures and the recovery process (Kelley, Jarvie, Middlebrook, McNeer, & Drabman, 1984; Varni *et al.*, 1980; Wakeman & Kaplan, 1978; Weinstein, 1976). The assessment methods employed by these studies focused on (a) staff monitoring of medication usage (e.g., analgesics), caloric intake, compliance with physical therapy exercises, and cooperation in the course of dressing changes and on the ward (e.g., swearing, screaming, kicking); (b) behavior rating scales completed by the parent, physical therapist, and child on fear (e.g., "very calm" to "in a panic"), cooperation, and pain (e.g., pictorial scale) after hydrotherapy; and (c) behavioral observations of verbal pain responses (e.g., crying, screaming, pain complaints) and motoric responses (e.g., facial grimaces, not standing, hitting, kicking) during physical therapy and open-treatment sessions. Although pain behaviors and other psychological problems (e.g., anxiety, low frustration tolerance) are typically in reaction to aversive medical techniques, they may generalize to alternate demanding situations (e.g., academic-related tasks, physical education). Similar assessment procedures can be readily transferred to the school setting and used by teachers, school nurses, physical therapists, and school psychologists to determine the extent of the problem behavior (e.g., teasing by peers, frequency and magnitude of aggressive classroom behavior, social attention from teachers).

A multidisciplinary approach to care and management is required due to the lengthy hospitalization and multisystem injuries of burned children (Achterberg-Lawlis & Kenner, 1982; Helm, Head, Pullium, O'Brien, & Cromes, 1978; Wagner *et al.*, 1981). The management of burned children can be grouped into two treatment approaches: medical strategies and psychological strategies. Pharmacologic interventions consist of administering analgesics for pain management (e.g., meperidine), tranquilizers for anxiety reactions (e.g., diazepam), and hypnotic agents for insomnia (e.g., flurazepam) (Miller, Gardner, & Mlott, 1976; Steiner & Clark, 1977; West & Shuck, 1978). However, criteria of adequate amounts for children have not been established and concerns exist over analgesic dependence. Psychological strategies have emphasized either counseling services or behavioral techniques for controlling psychological problems and pain. The goal of counseling is to cope with the stress of the injury by (a) providing repeated written and verbal information on procedures to children and their families to prevent anxiety and fear reactions, (b) allowing children and parents as much control as possible to decrease feelings of dependency (e.g., food selection), and (c) placing burned children on pediatric wards to increase their contact with other children and to desensitize them to negative reactions. Successful behavioral treatments for pain management have included hypnosis (Wakeman & Kaplan, 1978), relaxation (Cromes, Robinson, & Turrentine, 1978), relaxation, visual imagery, and *in-vivo* desensitization (Achterberg & Lawlis, 1980; Weinstein, 1976); token economy plus response cost (Zide & Pardoe, 1976), cartoon viewing (i.e., distraction) and star feedback chart (Kelley *et al.*, 1984), and differential reinforcement of the nonoccurrence of pain behaviors with praise and rewards (e.g., cookies, ice cream) (Varni *et al.*, 1980).

Thus far, the assessment and treatment of burned children have been implemented on pediatric wards or intensive care units. No published studies have evaluated the application of behavioral assessment and treatment procedures in hospital or public schools after the burned child is discharged. Reintegrating the burned child into school as quickly as possible is necessary because of the school's ability to promote social and educational development (Campbell, 1976; Clarke, 1980). Strategies used to facilitate the burned child's return to school are similar to those proposed for children with cancer: (a) the hospital should contact the school to encourage classmates to send cards, visit the child, and supply school work to continue peer interactions and academic progress; (b) the teacher and classmates should be prepared for the child's return through inservices provided by physicians, school nurses, or physical therapists on the complications and treatment of burn injuries; and (c) the teacher, child, and parents should inform classmates on why the burned child may look different and describe the child's physical capabilities (Katz & Jay, 1984). Westervelt *et al.*'s (1983) peer modeling technique may be one method of preparing the school for the burned child's return. However, research is needed to determine whether this technique positively affects the peer acceptance of children with a burn injury. The benefit of combining peer modeling and skills training (e.g., coping) should also be investigated because of possible negative reactions to changes in physical appearance (e.g., disfigurements, Jobst stockings), which can make the burned child feel self-conscious and perhaps reluctant to interact with others (Campbell, 1976; Clarke, 1980).

Other Health Impairments

Recurrent Somatic Complaints

Recurrent Abdominal Pain

Recurrent abdominal pain (RAP) is a common pediatric problem, with a prevalence of 10% to 15% of school-aged children (Apley, 1975; Oster, 1972; Parcel, Nader, & Meyer, 1977). Although pediatric RAP may be a symptom of a physical disorder (e.g., spinal cord tumor, lactose malabsorption) (Varni, 1983), an organic process has been found in less than 10% of children hospitalized for RAP (Apley, 1975) and an even smaller percentage of outpatients reporting abdominal pain (Caghan, McGrath, Morrow, & Pittman, 1978; Liebman, 1978). The RAP syndrome is characterized by pain that (a) is paroxysmal in nature, (b) occurs three or more times over 3 months or more, and (c) results in a change in normal activities at home and in school (Apley, 1975). *Paroxysmal* means that the occurrence of pain is unpredictable, unexpected, and time limited (i.e., lasting less than one hour) (Apley, 1975; Barr & Feuerstein, 1983). Description of the pain is variable, including duration, intensity, frequency, and location (e.g., periumbilical region or area around the umbilicus). Associated symptoms frequently reported are nausea, vomiting, pallor, constipation, and headache (Apley, 1975; Liebman, 1978; Stone & Barbero, 1970). In between episodes of RAP, the children look well and behave as usual. The prognosis of children with RAP is uncertain, yet pain complaints (e.g., gastrointestinal, headache, back) and/or internalizing behaviors (e.g., worrying, timid) may continue in over one third of the children (Apley & Hale, 1973; Christensen & Mortensen, 1975).

The etiology of RAP has not yet been determined. Rectal constipation, disturbances in bowel motility, and lactose intolerance have been suggested as physiological causative factors, but supportive evidence is equivocal (Barr, Levine, & Watkins, 1979; Dimson, 1971; Liebman, 1979). Other investigators have examined the role of psychological factors in the etiology of RAP. A psychogenic theory of RAP has been postulated due to findings that (a) children with RAP are often anxious, shy, fearful, and perfectionistic (e.g., Apley & Naish, 1958; Barr & Feuerstein, 1983); (b) a relationship exists between abdominal pain and psychosocial stressors (e.g., school entrance, family discord) (Liebman, 1978; Michener, 1981; Rubin, Barbero, & Sabinga, 1967; Stone & Barbero, 1970), and (c) a family history of abdominal pain complaints occurs (Christensen & Mortensen, 1975; Stone & Barbero, 1970). However, the lack of objective, valid measurement and the correlational nature of these studies lead to skepticism regarding the psychogenic theory of RAP (Barr & Feuerstein, 1983; McGrath, Goodman, Firestone, Shipman, & Peters, 1983).

Although a behavioral conceptualization of RAP has not been formally proposed, operant and classical conditioning appear to be components in its etiology and maintenance (Finney, Fuqua, Cataldo, Whitehead, & Katz, 1984). Based on an individual's experience with specific life events (e.g., school exams, school entrance, changes in family unit, poor peer relationships) and differences in coping skills, these events may be perceived as stressors. When confronted with future stressors a physiological reaction (e.g., colonic motility) and emotional response (e.g., anxiety) occurs. Whether these reactions are perceived and expressed as pain complaints may depend on the presence of role models (e.g., parents) who complain of somatic problems. Environmental consequences, such as reinforcement (e.g., parental attention, special privileges) or escape/avoidance of aversive responsibilities (e.g., school absences, missed exams, postponed social activities), may serve to maintain the pain complaints, and possibly the underlying pathophysiology (e.g., excessive colonic motility). Experimental support for this conceptualization of RAP is lacking, although studies have shown that individuals with recurrent abdominal or chest pain, headaches, and limb pains perceive more life stress than healthy peers (Greene & Thompson, 1984) and abdominal pain complaints occur at an increased rate in parents and siblings of children who report pain (Apley, 1975; Oster, 1972).

A comprehensive biobehavioral assessment (i.e., involving a physician, family members, and school personnel) is particularly important because RAP accounts for many missed school days annually (Cannon & Compton, 1980) and stressors related to family and school are frequently reported by children with RAP (Apley, 1975; Greene & Thompson, 1984). The first step in a biobehavioral assessment is to rule out an organic cause of the abdominal pain from a detailed history of pain complaints (e.g., diet, bowel habits) and a physical examination (e.g., blood count, urine analysis) (Levine & Rappaport, 1984). The next step is to conduct a functional analysis of pain complaints through behavioral interviews and the collection of monitoring data from the child and the parent. Specifically, the assessment of pain complaints should include information on the description of the pain (i.e., frequency, duration, and intensity), antecedents and consequences of the pain complaint (e.g., school attended and/or left early, methods to relieve pain, activities avoided), frequency of visits to the school nurse and school absences, presence of other physical problems (e.g., headaches), and daily stress ratings (1- to 10-point scale) in school, at home, and with peers. Additional information relevant to the referral problems should be obtained, such as a family history of RAP, current academic functioning, social skills, classroom behavior, and parent–child interactions. The integration of data from such a comprehensive approach will dictate which treatment procedures to incorporate into a joint management program (Varni, 1983).

With the exception of two case studies (Miller & Kratochwill, 1979; Sank & Biglan, 1974), behavioral treatments of RAP have yet to be systematically investigated. Sank and Biglan (1974) used a reinforcement and shaping program with a 10-year-old boy to reduce the frequency of pain episodes and daily pain ratings and to increase school attendance. Points were earned for a gradual decrease in pain episodes and an increase in school attendance, which were later exchanged for a nickel and then items on a reinforcement menu (e.g., favorite meals, books). Limited reinforcement was also provided on sick days by requiring the child to remain in bed for part of the day and to work only on school tasks. Miller and Kratochwill (1979) utilized a multiple baseline design across home and school settings to treat a 10-year-old girl with RAP. Treatment consisted of removing the child from adult attention (e.g., parent, school nurse) and activities (e.g., watching television, playing games, eating snacks) for verbal pain complaints (i.e., contingent time-out procedure). Time out rapidly reduced pain episodes first at home and then in school, with pain episodes remaining at zero levels during a one-year follow-up.

The assessment and treatment of children and adolescents with RAP pose many problems to school personnel because of the uncertainty of its etiology (Greene & Thompson, 1984; Levine & Rappaport, 1984). Cooperation between physicians, the family, and the school would facilitate an extensive assessment and treatment plan being afforded to students with RAP. The potential success of a collaborative approach is described by Greene and Thompson (1984) on a Health Service Team in a Metro Nashville-Davidson County School system. The team (i.e., pediatrician and school psychologist) provides direct service and consultation to high school students and training of residents and fellows from various disciplines (e.g., medicine, nursing, psychology). Prompt referral from either physicians or school personnel is imperative to offset the negative effects of RAP (e.g., academic failure, social isolation) (Greene & Thompson, 1984). Future research is needed to validate the proposed behavioral conceptualization of RAP (e.g., association between "stress" and RAP symptomatology) and to evaluate a variety of treatment issues (e.g., effective treatment components, acceptability of treatment goals).

Pediatric Migraine

Pediatric migraine is a familiar clinical disorder in medical practice, with a prevalence of 4% to 22% in children and adolescents (Bille, 1967; Deubner, 1977). Two diagnostic categories of migraine headache have been proposed: classic and common (Ad Hoc Committee on Classification of Headache, 1962; Jay & Tomasi, 1981). Three phases define the classic migraine: (a) prodromal, (b) headache, and (c) postheadache. During the prodromal phase specific neurological disturbances (e.g., flashing lights, blind spots, vertigo, numbness in particular body parts) and nonspecific problems (e.g., increases in bedwetting, nightmares, sleep walking) occur approximately 30 minutes before the onset of head pain. The headache is described as severe, throbbing/pulsating pain, unilateral (i.e., located on one side of the head), and usually accompanied by nausea, vomiting, diarrhea, and abdominal pain. After the headache ends, the affected area (e.g., right temporal region) is frequently tender and sensitive to touch and feelings of exhaustion to euphoria are reported (Brown, 1977; Thompson, 1980). Common migraine is distinguishable from classic by the absence of clearly defined prodromal symptoms, less association with gastrointestinal symptoms, and bilateral head pain. The frequency and duration of pediatric migraines vary between children, but generally occur once per month and last from 1 to 12 hours (Bille, 1967; Vahlquist & Hackzell, 1949). Common migraines are most often diagnosed in preadolescents, whereas classic migraines and visual auras increase with age (Gascon, 1984; Jay & Tomasi, 1981).

The pathophysiology of classic and common migraine in children is thought to be the same as that proposed for adults. The most widely accepted theory of migraine is based on a biobehavioral approach that emphasizes environmental, biological, and behavioral factors on health and physical problems (Diamond & Dalessio, 1978; Williamson, 1981; Williamson, Ruggiero, & Davis, 1985). According to this theory, a genetic predisposition to respond to stress, hormonal changes, and other environmental events with an abnormal receptivity in the cerebral blood vessels exist. The initial physiological change is intracranial vasoconstriction (i.e., decreased width of blood vessels), leading to reduced blood flow to certain brain areas, anoxia, and acidosis, thus creating the prodromal symptoms of classic migraine. A rebound extracranial vasodilation (i.e., increased width of blood vessels) response follows, along with discharge of histamine and peptide kinins (i.e., hormones), and appearance of inflammation and swelling at the pain site. The severe, throbbing pain is then produced by blood pulsating through an inflamed, swollen blood vessel.

In the past several years the behavioral assessment and treatment of pediatric migraine has developed because of findings that migraines persist from childhood into adulthood (Bille, 1981; Blanchard & Andrasik, 1982). A variety of environmental factors have been identified as provoking migraine headaches in school-aged children, such as emotional factors (e.g., anxiety, anger), physical stress and fatigue (e.g., severe exercise, weather changes), and school-related events (e.g., impending exams, negative peer interactions) (Brown, 1977; Thompson, 1980). These socioenvironmental factors may be important in the etiology of pediatric migraine, whereas a reinforcement paradigm (e.g., social attention from teachers, decrease in anxiety) and/or escape/avoidance paradigm (e.g., missing school exams, adverting parent–child arguments) possibly operate to increase the frequency and intensity of headache perception and pain complaints (Shinnar & D'Souza, 1981; Varni, 1983). Typically, a diagnostic work-up of pediatric migraine includes a physical and neurological examination (e.g., growth parameters, blood pressure, visual acuity), and history taking from both parents and child (e.g., type of pain and location, triggering events) (Gascon, 1984; Shinnar & D'Souza, 1981). If serious intracranial pathology is suspected (e.g., brain tumor), a number of neurodiagnostic procedures (e.g., CAT Scanning) can be completed (Gascon, 1984; Shinnar & D'Souza, 1981). Four assessment methods have generally been used as behavioral process and treatment outcome measures: (a) behavioral interviews, (b) self-monitoring, (c) questionnaires, and (d) psychophysiological recordings (Blanchard & Andrasik, 1982; Williamson, Labbe, & Granberry, 1983). During behavioral interviews with the child, parent, and if possible the teacher, answers to the following questions should be obtained: (a) migraine length, frequency, duration, and intensity; (b) pain location (e.g., unilateral vs. bilateral) and quality (e.g., throbbing vs. constant pressure), (c) antecedents and consequences of head pain (e.g, direct glare from sun, favors from peers), (d) behaviors that relieve or exacerbate the headache (e.g., rest, medication), and (e) medication usage. Most often headache parameters (e.g., intensity, antecedents) are recorded by the child and parent in headache booklets or headache diaries. Ratings are made four times per day (i.e., breakfast, lunch, dinner, and bedtime) on a 0- (no headache) to 5-points (extremely intense headache, incapacitated) scale, which provides several headache measures (e.g., headache and medication index) (see Williamson *et al.*, 1983, for detailed description of these measures). Data from questionnaires and self-report inventories can be helpful in evaluating headache parameters and behavioral problems that contribute to the maintenance of pain, such as depression, social skills deficit, and poor study habits. Psychophysiological assessment has been utilized to evaluate specific physiologic changes during relaxation, biofeedback, or stress testing (e.g., skin temperature, heart rate, muscle tension).

Pharmacologic management and behavior therapy are two components of a multifaceted treatment for pediatric migraine (Gascon, 1984). There are three approaches to the pharmacologic management of migraines: (a) symptomatic treatment with common analgesics (e.g., salicylates), (b) abortive therapy at the time of the headache (e.g., Cafergot), and (c) prophylactic therapy (e.g., propranolol) (Gascon, 1984; Shinnar & D'Souza, 1981). Most often abortive or prophylactic agents are reserved for infrequent and/or debilitating migraines because of the unpredictable drug response of children and possible toxic effects in long-term care (Gascon, 1984; Shinnar & D'Souza, 1981). The behavioral treatment of pediatric migraine is regarded as a primary intervention for symptom reduction after a medical diagnosis (Masek, Spirito, & Fentress, 1984; Varni, 1983). Effective treatment results have been obtained in single-subject studies using self-hypnosis with and without biofeedback (Olness & MacDonald, 1981), progressive muscle relaxation with temperature biofeedback (Houts, 1982), autogenic feedback (Andrasik, Blanchard, Edlund, & Rosenblum, 1983), autogenic training with temperature biofeedback (Labbe & Williamson, 1983), and contingency management (Ramsden, Friedman, & Williamson, 1983). One uncontrolled (Diamond & Franklin, 1975) and three controlled group-outcome studies (Fentress & Masek, 1982; Labbe & Williamson, 1984; Masek, 1982) have reported the successful application of various therapy packages: skin temperature or EMG biofeedback, autogenic training, progressive muscle relaxation or meditative breathing, and home practice for headache activity (e.g., decreased frequency, duration, intensity). Ramsden *et al.* (1983) was the only investigation emphasizing a collaborative approach between the school and home environments. In this study the headache complaints of a 6-year-old girl were significantly reduced, first in school and then at home, when identifiable environmental contingencies were controlled (e.g., excused absences from school, sympathy and attention from teachers and parents).

In comparison to research on migraine headaches in adults, few prospective, controlled studies with children have been published (Blanchard & Andrasik, 1982; Masek *et al.*, 1984; see also Williamson, McKensie, & Goreczny, this volume). Future research is needed to promote health-related behaviors (e.g., diet, exercise habits) and participation in daily activities despite the occurrence of head pain by employing rigorous methods (e.g., multiple dependent measures, large number of subjects, control groups) (Masek *et al.*, 1984). Behavioral interviews, self- and other-monitoring, and questionnaires can be easily employed by school psychologists to conduct a functional analysis of migraines in children and adolescents (e.g., teacher recording of pain complaints, nurse monitoring of medication requests). Stress management (e.g., time management, setting realistic goals), skills training (e.g., social skills, study habits), and relaxation techniques (e.g., progressive muscle relaxation) should also be incorporated into school-based programs to assist those students with pediatric migraines cope with stressful school situations (Masek *et al.*, 1984).

Chronic Illnesses

Sickle-Cell Anemia

Sickle-cell anemia (SCA) is a chronic, hereditary hemoglobinopathy, that is, a disorder of hemoglobin protein or the oxygen-carrying part of red blood cells. In the United States, SCA is found most commonly in the black population, with approximately 50,000 children and adults being affected (Barnhart, Henry, & Lusher, 1974). SCA is characterized by (a) chronic anemia (i.e., deficiency of red blood cells because of excessive destruction), (b) painful crises usually involving the bones, chest, or abdomen, and (c) organ damage because of repeated pain crises (Harkness, 1980; Lukens, 1981). Pain crises result from the rigid, sickle-shaped red blood cells obstructing blood flow (i.e., vasoocclusions), leading ultimately to some tissues becoming anoxic and dying (Bunn, 1982; Lehmann *et al.*, 1977; McFarlane, 1977). Almost all of the clinical symptoms and disabilities linked to SCA are due to these vasoocclusive episodes (McFarlane, 1977).

The clinical manifestations of SCA generally appear between 6 months and 2 years of age and vary in severity among children (e.g., frequency, intensity, duration of pain crises) (Harkness 1980; Lukens, 1981; McFarlane, 1977). In addition to the chronic manifestations of SCA (e.g., anemia, painful crises), various symptoms emerge in certain age groups, such as a high susceptibility to bacterial infections and dactylitis (e.g., joint pains, swelling, limited motion) before age 5; a lag in growth and sexual development especially in adolescent boys; and numerous system complications (e.g., ocular—retinal lesions; hepatobiliary—jaundice; genitourinary—enuresis; cerebrovascular—strokes). Children with SCA will appear relatively healthy and develop normally in between pain crises and system complications (Lehmann *et al.*, 1977).

There is no cure for SCA, so treatment primarily has been symptomatic (Lehmann *et al.*, 1977; Lukens, 1981; McFarlane, 1977). The most common treatment is prevention or management of pain crises by avoiding precipitating environmental factors, for example, overexposure to cold and high altitudes, dehydration, excessive physical activity, and infections. Symptoms of a pain crisis are often a low-grade fever, swelling and limitation of movement, tenderness of affected area, and pain of varying intensity. Management of crises consist of applying heat and massage to the affected area, giving fluids either orally or intravenously, restricting activities, and, if needed, administering medication for pain (e.g., aspirin to intravenous demerol). Home management of a crisis frequently is possible, although hospitalization is required when pain is severe and vomiting or dehydration persists (McFarlane, 1977). Blood transfusions are the most effective treatment of SCA, but reserved for certain conditions, for example, excessive anemia, progressive organ damage (i.e., prevent recurrence of strokes), and during the third trimester of pregnancy. Finally, surgical treatment of complications (e.g., hip replacement, spleen removal, retinal reattachment) is one component of the medical care of SCA.

In addition to the physical complications of SCA, a large percentage of children and adolescents with SCA reportedly evidence serious psychological problems (Alleyne, Wint, & Serjeant, 1976; Conyard, Krishnamurthy, & Dosik, 1980; Kumar, Powers, Allen, & Haywood, 1976; Whitten & Fischhoff, 1974). The most frequent psychological problems cited in the literature include poor self-concept, increased anxiety and depression, aggression or social withdrawal, poor school performance, and maladaptive family and peer relationships. Several authors have attributed these problems to the stress and medical complications of SCA (Gaston, 1973; Conyard *et al.*, 1980; LePontois, 1975; Whitten & Fischhoff, 1974). For example, children and adolescents with SCA develop a poor self-concept because of their small stature, delay in secondary sex characteristics, and other features (e.g., yellow eyes, leg ulcers). The physical problems of SCA also hinder these children's opportunities to interact with their peers by restricting participation in activities (e.g., competitive sports) and requiring numerous clinic visits and hospitalizations, thus leading to social isolation and withdrawal. However, these conclusions should be interpreted with caution because of the various methodological flaws in the research (e.g., objective, standardized dependent measures, matched-control groups, and disease-related variables seldom used). In fact, recent research suggests that children and adolescents with SCA experience the same number and type of problem behaviors as matched normal peers (Lemanek, Gresham, Williamson, & Kelley, 1984a,b; Lemanek, Williamson, Gresham, & Kelley, 1984). Furthermore, there is no indication that sickle-cell anemics are more depressed or have lower self-concepts than healthy children.

Studies on the behavioral assessment and treatment of psychological problems and pain management in SCA is virtually nonexistent. One case study (Zeltzer, Dash, & Holland, 1979) described the use of self-hypnosis techniques with two adolescent sickle cell anemics. The dependent measures included self-reported frequency and intensity of pain crises, analgesic intake, and archival data on the number of pain-related outpatient visits and the number of hospitalizations. Zeltzer *et al.* (1979) instructed the adolescents to employ the following treatment techniques at the perceived onset of a sickling crisis: eye fixation and progressive relaxation as the induction, moving to guided visual imagery of pain-free scenes and increased body warmth. Anecdotal reports showed significant reduction on all measures during an 8-month follow-up period. Guidelines for providing comprehensive care and supportive group counseling to manage the medical, financial, educational, and psychosocial aspects of SCA have generally been described (Conyard *et al.*, 1980; Gaston, 1973; LePontois, 1975; Vavasseur, 1977). Several of these guidelines were applicable to the school setting. They recommend that one should (a) provide school personnel with information on what a crisis consists of, why there are frequent absences and trips to the bathroom, and that SCA does not cause mental retardation or learning disabilities; (b) monitor the academic performance of children with SCA to neutralize any problems because of repeated absences and difficulty completing classwork/homework (i.e., frequent clinic visits, fatigue from anemia), and (c) plan extracurricular and physical education activities based on medical advice and tolerance level (e.g., score keeper for sports team, swimming, learning a musical instrument, joining Scouts), and arrange for vocational training that does not emphasize strenuous manual labor (Gaston, 1973; Prunty, 1975; Tetrault & Scott, 1974).

The bulk of the research in this area has been methodologically flawed because of the use of nonexperimental designs, lack of objective measurement of dependent variables, and nonspecific descriptions of procedures. Future research is needed to evaluate the physical and psychological aspects of SCA within school settings using experimental designs and reliable and valid measurement.

Skills training programs (e.g., social skills, coping skills) and contingency management procedures (e.g., time-out, rewards) should then be implemented to modify targeted problem behaviors. Determining effective pain management techniques (e.g., meditative breathing exercises, distraction, modeling) should also be a priority in which the role of school personnel is clarified.

Diabetes

Diabetes is a chronic illness that involves a disruption in the body's production and/or utilization of the hormone insulin. Approximately 150,000 children are affected by Type I diabetes—the complete or near complete cessation of the body's production of its own insulin (Johnson, 1980). Insulin is important in that it renders glucose capable of entering the cells of the body, where it can be converted into energy. Without sufficient insulin, glucose builds up to dangerously high levels in the bloodstream and the body is unable to create the energy it needs to function from the food it ingests. The body excretes the unusable, excess glucose through the urine. Accordingly, excessive weight loss despite increased food intake, thirst, and frequent urination are common symptoms of the onset of diabetes. Diabetes was invariably fatal until 1922 with the discovery of insulin by Banting and Best and their experiments with the injection of diabetic humans with insulin produced by animals. Today diabetics who follow a complex treatment regimen involving daily injections of insulin, frequent monitoring of blood and urine glucose levels, adherence to a specialized diet, and regular exercise can expect to enjoy relatively normal longevity (Johnson, 1980). Although a great deal of research has been conducted with diabetic children, very little of it has been conducted in the schools.

Diabetes has been associated with school problems, below-average school performance, and decreasing levels of academic achievement with increasing grade (Johnson, 1980). Although children with diabetes have not been found to be on the average of lower intelligence than healthy children, there is some controversy as to whether onset of diabetes before age 5 may negatively impact on brain development producing somewhat lower IQ scores for this subgroup of the diabetic population (Johnson, 1980). Despite evidence to suggest that children with diabetes are at greater risk for school-related problems, very little behavioral assessment of the diabetic child has been conducted in the school setting. Rather, techniques such as self-monitoring, self-report, and behavioral observation have, for the most part, been applied to diabetic children in other settings, such as at summer camps for diabetics or in outpatient clinic settings (Melamed & Johnson, 1981).

Self-monitoring techniques have frequently involved informal diary keeping of urine testing results and other aspects of the diabetic health care regimen. Melamed and Johnson (1981) described the Diabetes Daily Record, which was developed for use at the University of Florida. It provides a structured form for the recording of the child or parent's performance of the primary aspects of daily diabetes care, such as time, type, and amount of insulin injected; results of urine testing, type of food and drink consumed at what times, and the type of exercise in which the child engaged. Although such a structured method for self-monitoring performance of their health care regimen provides important information for the child and those individuals working with him or her, such a form does not allow for the assessment of more subjective reactions to the treatment regimen or to the disease process itself. Melamed and Johnson (1981) described the work of other researchers using self-monitoring techniques that provide the opportunity for the recording of such subjective experiences. The Self-Rated Diabetic Scale (Fowler, Budzynski, & Vandenbergh, 1976) provides an opportunity for a diabetic to rate his or her symptoms of hyper- or hypoglycemia using a 9-point scale. Fowler *et al.* (1976) used the Self-Rated Diabetic Scale with a 20-year-old diabetic. They found that when they also had her monitor her emotions there was a degree of correlation between the experience of emotional fluctuation and her self-reported symptoms of fluctuations in her blood sugar levels. It has long been thought that environmental events can contribute to instability in a diabetic's condition, which is characterized by widely fluctuating blood sugar levels (Greydanus & Hofman, 1979). Using informal self-monitoring techniques, Hinkle and Wolf (1952) described the finding that one diabetic teenager's unstable medical condition was related to the occurrence of stressful tests at school. Therefore, self-monitoring techniques may not only provide important information regarding a child's compliance with and execution of his or her prescribed health care regimen while at school, but such techniques may also be helpful in delineating what role school-related stressors may play in the exacerbation of this disease. Although the daily monitoring of the child's compliance with his or her treatment program is of interest, so is the assessment of the amount of knowledge that the child holds about his or her disease and its care and how such knowledge may affect compliance with the treatment protocol.

The most common self-report assessment techniques of diabetics' knowledge of their disease and its care have been paper-and-pencil quizzes (Melamed & Johnson, 1981). Unfortunately, researchers have generally constructed their own individual quizzes for each of their different studies. Therefore, no standardized knowledge quiz for diabetic children yet exists. However, Dunn *et al.* (1984) presented an attempt at developing a standardized measure of diabetes knowledge consisting of 15 multiple choice items that comes in three different forms. Dunn *et al.*'s (1984) Diabetes Knowledge Scales have been standardized with an adult population and, therefore, it is difficult to determine their usefulness with diabetic children. Melamed and Johnson (1981) described a test of the problem-solving skills of diabetic children in relation to their disease self-management developed at the University of Florida. Many of the items on this paper-and-pencil test relate to problem solving in the school setting or at school-related events. Such an instrument could be quite useful in helping the school psychologist or school nurse determine what school situations may challenge the child's ability to manage his or her disease independently. A behavioral observation checklist has also been developed at the University of Florida that allows for the assessment of the child's knowledge and accuracy in self-injecting insulin (Melamed & Johnson, 1981). Although a child is most likely to inject his or her insulin at home, there may be times when he or she may need to administer additional insulin while at school or when problems in self-injecting at home may lead to insulin reactions or hyperglycemia symptoms at school. For these reasons, the behavioral observation of insulin injection technique may prove to be a valuable assessment instrument for use in the school setting.

Education of the diabetic child and his or her parents has been a frequent intervention aimed at increasing compliance with the diabetic's medical regimen (Etzwiler & Robb, 1972; Johnson, 1980). Other treatment techniques that have been applied to the child with diabetes include modeling (Gilbert *et al.*, 1982) to help school-age children acquire skills necessary for self-injecting their insulin, goal setting and contracting (Schafer, Glasgow, & McCaul, 1982) to improve compliance with the total self-care regimen of adolescent diabetes, and contingency management (Carney, Schecter, & Davis, 1982) to increase compliance with blood glucose testing in three school-age children. All of these behavioral techniques were shown to be useful in improving compliance with medical regimens and health-care skills. However, none of these techniques have been applied to the school setting.

Asthma

Asthma is a respiratory disorder affecting approximagely 5% to 15% of children less than 12 years of age (American Lung Association, 1975). The age of onset is usually between 3 and 8 years and occurs most often in preadolescent boys (i.e., 14 years and younger) (American Lung Association, 1975; Chai, 1975). It is typically defined as recurrent episodes of wheezing or dyspnea (i.e., labored breathing), characterized by a significant increase in airflow resistance and followed by symptom-free periods (Reed & Townley, 1978). Chai (1975) considers three components of this definition to be critical: (a) the *intermittent* component, or attacks that appear on an aperiodic basis, (b) the *variable* component, or attacks that vary in severity from mild (e.g., slight wheeze) to status asthmaticus, and (c) the *reversible* component, or airways that may revert to a normal condition either spontaneously or after treatment. These three components describe the heterogeneous nature of asthma, although some clinical features and pathophysiological factors may be similar (Pearlman, 1984). Bronchial hyperresponsiveness (i.e., irritability of airways) is now considered a characteristic feature of asthma and appears to correlate with severity and frequency of attacks (Pearlman, 1984). The clinical response or symptoms of an asthma attack, such as wheezing, tightness in the chest, chest pains, coughing, labored breathing and anxiety, result from one of three factors: (a) *bronchoconstriction*, which is the contraction or spasms in the smooth muscle surrounding the airways, (b) *edema*, or the swelling of the epithelial lining of the bronchial tubes, or (c) mucus that clogs the narrow airways (Creer, Renne, & Chai, 1982).

Several psychological concomitants of asthma have been examined; these include personality characteristics, family interaction patterns, and emotional precipitants. Controlled studies looking at personality factors and asthma have concluded that (a) there is not a unique personality characteristic of asthmatic children (e.g., anxious, dependent), (b) behavioral problems found in asthmatic children (e.g., temper tantrums, social skills deficits) reflect more a consequence of asthma than any predisposing variable, and (c) that differences detected between children with asthma and healthy peers is because of unreliable and invalid measurement (e.g., Creer & Kotses, 1983; Norrish, Tooley, & Godfrey, 1977; Purcell & Weiss, 1970; Tavormina, Kastner, Slater, & Watt, 1976). Research on the family interaction patterns have suggested both maladaptive relationships (e.g., overprotection, negative childrearing strategies, marital distress) (e.g., Block, Jennings, Harvey, & Simpson, 1964; Meijer, 1979; Purcell, Muser, Miklich, & Dietiker, 1969) and normal relations (e.g., Burbeck, 1979; Gauthier *et al.*, 1977). Definite conclusions cannot be made because of the inadequate assessment instruments employed (e.g., projective tests) and the emphasis on correlational studies (Creer & Kotses, 1983). In addition, several investigators have pointed to the influence of parental behaviors (e.g., increased attention, decreased family responsibilities) on the maintenance of asthmatic symptoms (e.g., Creer, Weinberg, & Molk, 1974; Neisworth & Moore, 1972). Finally, a functional relationship between emotional precipitants and the onset of asthmatic attacks has been shown using hypnosis, emotive imagery, and stress testing (Clarke, 1970; Hahn, 1966; Tal & Miklich, 1976). Yet the opinion of most researchers is that emotions *per se* cannot trigger asthmatic attacks, although such responses as shouting, laughing, coughing, crying, and running often co-occur with emotional expression and can produce bronchospasms (Creer, 1979; Creer *et al.*, 1982).

The heterogeneous pathogenesis and presentation of asthma dictates a multifactorial approach to classification and assessment. A thorough medical evaluation generally consists of a combination of the following procedures: (a) clinical and physical examination (e.g., detailed history, skin and exercise tests), (b) pulmonary function measurement of initial and peripheral airway obstruction (e.g., peak expiratory flow rate, total respiratory resistance), (c) medication scores (e.g., type, frequency, dose), and (d) frequency and duration of hospitalizations (Chai, 1975; Chai, Purcell, Brady, & Falliers, 1968; Creer *et al.*, 1982). These procedures are used to obtain an objective index of the severity and the clinical condition over time. A functional analysis of the antecedents and consequences of asthma attacks and operational definitions of target behaviors are generated through a variety of behavioral assessment methods: (a) behavioral interviews, (b) self-report measures and questionnaires of symptomatology (e.g., Asthma Symptom Checklist), emotional precipitants (e.g., Emotional Precipitant Index), anxiety before or during attacks (e.g., Fear Thermometer), and behavioral disorders (e.g., Asthmatic Potential Scale); (c) psychophysiological measurement (e.g., heart rate, skin temperature in response to shock, problem-solving tests), (d) pulmonary function measurement, (e) self-monitoring of disease-related variables (e.g., frequency of asthmatic attacks, duration of wheezing, medication usage), and (f) direct observation of asthmatic attacks (e.g., anxiety, regimen compliance) and proper use of respiratory equipment (Block *et al.*, 1964; Creer *et al.*, 1982; Kinsman, O'Banion, Resnikoff, Luparello, & Spector, 1973; Lang, Melamed, & Hart, 1970; Melamed & Johnson, 1981; Purcell & Weiss, 1970). An accurate diagnosis and understanding of asthma requires assessment from many areas because of the low correlation between measures and to the problems inherent in each measure (e.g., subjective reporting, observer reactivity, intermittent nature of attacks) (Chai *et al.*, 1968; Creer *et al.*, 1982).

The goal of management is to control asthma symptoms and to maximize pulmonary function, although not necessarily normalize it (Pearlman, 1984). Chai (1975) outlined the medical management of asthma into three phases: (a) maintenance, (b) control of breakthroughs, and (c) status asthmaticus. Continuous, pharmacologic treatment is required to prevent occurrence of asthma attacks with daily use of such drugs as theophylline-based compounds, cromolyn sodium, and corticosteroids. Additional strategies include the prescription of other bronchodilators (e.g., Alupent), antihistamines (e.g., Dimetane), and eye drops on either a fixed schedule or as needed; regular immunotherapy (i.e., injections of allergic extracts), and the removal of precipitants (e.g., pets, stuffed toys, feather pillows) to minimize various symptoms (e.g., throat itching, eye watering, stuffy nose). The role of behavior therapy in the treatment of asthma is primarily an adjunct to medical management with a focus on secondary symptoms (e.g., reducing arousal, developing coping strategies) (Masek *et al.*, 1984). Several self-regulation techniques have been employed either to improve the pulmonary functioning of asthmatics (e.g., PEFR) or to reduce the fear/anxiety associated with an attack: progressive muscle relaxation training (Alexander, 1972; Alexander, Miklich, & Hirshkoff, 1972); relaxation with and without EMG biofeedback (Davis, Saunders, Creer, & Chai, 1973; Scherr, Crawford, Sergent, & Scherr, 1975); autogenic and muscle relaxation training (Alexander, Cropp, & Chai, 1979); and systematic desensitization (Miklich *et al.*, 1977). Results suggest that although the long-term clinical benefits of these procedures on lung functioning is minimal, a reduction in the severity of asthmatic attacks can be achieved by teaching a response opposite to anxiety when confronted with precipitants or the attack itself (Alexander *et al.*, 1979; Creer, 1982). A variety of maladaptive or aberrant behaviors (e.g., extreme use of hospital facilities, improper use of respiratory equipment, excessive wheezing, hyperactivity, tics) have been successfully remediated by contingency management procedures: time out from hospital reinforcers (e.g., television) and social rewards for improved school attendance and performance (Creer, 1979; Creer *et al.*, 1974; Shepard & Hochstadt, 1978), extinction and monetary rewards (Neisworth & Moore, 1972); shaping by repeated instructions and script with back-up reinforcers (Renne & Creer, 1976), and combination of extinction, modeling, and token economy (Creer & Miklich, 1970; Gardner, 1968; Miklich, 1973). In addition, Creer and Yoches (1971) significantly reduced the disruptive classroom behavior (i.e., activity level, nonattendance) of two asthmatic boys using a response-cost contingency for on-task behavior. The majority of treatment studies are noteworthy in that multiple dependent measures were utilized, asthma-related behaviors were examined, and treatment involved different disciplines (Creer & Kotses, 1983).

An interdisciplinary approach to the management of asthma is essential because of its morbidity in terms of school absenteeism and financial expenditure (Creer *et al.*, 1982). That is, asthma accounts for a large number of missed school days (i.e., frequent, brief absences) (Bharani & Hyde, 1976; Douglas & Ross, 1965) and it depletes a family's income from between 2% and 30% (e.g., physician services, drugs, lost work/school time) (Vance & Taylor, 1971). The school psychologist, respiratory therapist, or nurse can be an important member of a health team to teach asthmatic children self-management skills. Specific self-management programs have been developed (e.g., Air Wise, Air Power, Living With Asthma, and Open Airways) and evaluated in the classroom (Parcel & Nader, 1977), with pediatric outpatients (Clark *et al.*, 1980), and in a residential treatment center (Creer & Leung, 1981). Components of these programs generally consist of (a) self-observation and monitoring (e.g., severity of attacks), (b) recording of own responses and behavior (e.g., "Weekly Asthma Diary"), (c) execution of environmental programs (i.e., stimulus and response changes), (d) discrimination between symptoms and other physical changes, (e) self-instruction (i.e., manage asthma attacks through sequence of steps), and (f) problem solving and decision making (Creer, Backiel, & Leung, 1983; Feldman *et al.*, 1983; McNabb, Rodabaugh, Scamagas, & Hughes, 1983a,b). Further application of these management programs in the school should be a priority to determine their effectiveness in decreasing school absences and health care costs for asthmatic children and their families.

Epilepsy

Epilepsy is a term used in reference to a number of central nervous system disorders that produce seizures. Seizures are described as sudden, paroxysmal alterations of brain functioning (Heisler & Friedman, 1981; Krafft & Poling, 1982). Epilepsy is estimated to occur in one in every 50 persons (Heisler & Friedman, 1981). A diagnosis of epilepsy is made when a child has had at least two seizure episodes for which no precipitating condition can account, such as the presence of an unusually high fever, the presence of a toxin in the body, etc. (Sands, 1982). A common form of epilepsy in children is characterized by grand mal seizures. The alterations in brain functioning can be generalized and result in loss of or impairment in consciousness, or the disruption in brain functioning may be focal and result in no alterations in consciousness. A less common form of epilepsy, but one which may be more disruptive to the child's classroom functioning, involves petit mal seizures that may occur a number of times throughout a day. This seizure actively involves periodic, brief alterations in consciousness that begin and end suddenly and that are characterized most often by the child staring off into space.

Some research has suggested that children with epilepsy are more likely to have behavioral and academic problems, concerns about peer relationships, and symptoms of depression (Heisler & Friedman, 1981). Academic achievement is not necessarily impaired in epileptic children. However, Heisler and Friedman (1981) suggested that if the seizure disorder has not been well controlled throughout early childhood, then learning may be delayed in such children. They went on to cite a study that suggests that epileptic boys with persistent spike discharges in the left temporal lobe, as measured by EEG recordings, were prone to be behind their classmates in reading, to be inattentive, and to have other behavioral problems.

Only minimal assessment research has been conducted with epileptic children in the schools. However, Balaschak and Mostofsky (1981) described three assessment instruments that they have developed for use with epileptic children that may be applicable to the school setting. The Seizure Disorder Survey Schedule is administered to the parents of the child with epilepsy and provides detailed information regarding demographic data, the medical history of the seizure disorder, and the presence of additional problems. The Pre-Behavioral Treatment Questionnaire is used to determine the child's own knowledge of his disorder and its potential reinforcing qualities. In addition they describe the Weekly Chart, a seizure monitoring form that is completed by the child's parents. The Weekly Chart may be the most useful assessment instrument for the school setting should the teacher or other observer need to monitor the frequency of a child's seizure activity.

Seizure disorders have traditionally been treated with anticonvulsant medications with which complete or near complete seizure control can be obtained in 10% to 80% of treated patients (Balaschak & Mostofsky, 1981). Some common anticonvulsants are phenobarbitol and dilantin. Although initially low doses of these medications are administered, dosages are gradually increased until adequate control is achieved. Sometimes high doses of these drugs may produce drowsiness or other obvious as well as subtle behavior changes that might affect a child's functioning, particularly in the classroom (Heisler & Friedman, 1981).

More recently behavioral techniques have been applied to the management of seizure disorders with promising results. Contingency management programs, relaxation training, the utilization of self-control techniques, and biofeedback training have all been utilized in attempts to control seizure activity in children (Mostofsky & Balaschak, 1977). Much of the research evaluating contingency management procedures involving various uses of reinforcement of seizure-free periods as well as punishment of seizure activity has been conducted in institutional settings with mentally retarded patients. A notable exception is the study by Balaschak (1976) that investigated teacher administration of reinforcement for seizure-free periods of time, which resulted in a substantial decrease in the observed seizure activity of the targeted child while in school.

Cancer

Cancer is the second leading cause of death in children under 15 years of age (Gogan, O'Malley, & Foster, 1977) and roughly 11 out of every 10,000 children are striken by cancer (Kellerman & Varni, 1982). In children with cancer, 40% are diagnosed with one of the acute leukemias (cancers of the white blood cells), 14% with tumors of the brain, and the remaining 46% have tumors of various organ systems, bones, and soft tissues of the body (Kellerman & Varni, 1982). Survival rates for victims of childhood cancer are improving because of advancements in chemotherapeutic, surgical, and irradiation treatments (Gogan *et al.*, 1977).

Some of the medical techniques used in the diagnosis and treatment of childhood cancer can be painful, such as bone marrow aspirations, lumbar punctures, venipunctures, and the injection of chemotherapeutic agents (Jay, Ozolins, Elliott, & Caldwell, 1983; Kellerman & Varni, 1982). In addition, nausea and vomiting are common side effects of chemotherapy (Morrow, 1984; Redd & Andrykowski, 1982). These frequent, expected reactions to chemotherapy are complicated by the development of anticipatory anxiety, nausea, and vomiting in some cancer patients (Morrow & Morrell, 1982). For these children, stimuli related to medical procedures (e.g., clinic days, arrival at the clinic, clinic personnel, etc.) can produce aversive reactions (Kellerman & Varni, 1982). In addition, cancer treatments can result in temporary, as well as permanent, alterations in the appearance of children. Hair loss is a frequent, temporary result of chemotherapy. Amputations or scars from the removal of cancerous growths are permanent and can also impact on the adjustment of a child to his illness (Pfefferbaum, 1979).

More and more, children with cancer are encouraged to attend school during a large portion of their disease and its treatment.

However, school avoidance is a problem in roughly 10% of children with cancer (Lansky, Lowman, Vats, & Gyulay, 1975). Children with cancer experience anxiety regarding answering questions posed to them by peers about their illness, they fear being teased about changes in their physical appearance because of their cancer treatments, and frequently they are anxious regarding having to catch up on school work they may have missed during the initial diagnosis and treatment of their disease. Complicating the child's desire to avoid school is the fact that parents frequently do not encourage attendance because of their feelings of guilt or fear that the child's health may be affected adversely (Pfefferbaum, 1979).

There has been concern that cranial irradiation and other cancer treatments affecting the nervous system may produce long-term deleterious effects on a child's cognitive functioning. Sound experimental evidence for such effects has not yet been demonstrated (Kellerman & Varni, 1982). However, a recent study by Pavlovsky *et al.* (1983) reported that such occurrences as abnormal CT scans, decreased IQ scores, and soft neurological signs of impairment were present in their sample of 42 children who had received cranial irradiation and chemotherapy injected into the spinal fluid, or chemotherapy only. On the other hand, Tamaroff *et al.* (1982) found no decreases in intellectual functioning in 41 children who were treated with chemotherapy injected into the spinal cord when compared with 33 other children who were treated with chemotherapy not directly involving the nervous system. However, cranial irradiation did not accompany the chemotherapy of either of these groups of children. In another attempt to assess the impact of cancer and its treatment on cognitive functioning, Ott, Webb, Anderson, Kastelic, and Krill (1982) compared 22 children with cancer who were receiving a variety of treatments that did not necessarily involve the nervous system with 22 children without cancer but with behavioral and/or emotional problems. Using McLeod's (1979) statistical method to designate a criterion for underachievement, Ott *et al.* (1982) found that twice as many of the cancer patients met the criteria for underachievement than the physically healthy children. The Ott *et al.* (1982) study did not examine the effects of specific cancer treatments on academic achievement and therefore it is difficult to assess the implications of their research. However, based on this body of literature, it is imperative that the effect of cranial irradiation on the developing intellect of pediatric cancer patients continue to receive attention, particularly in relation to the ways in which any such impairments may later affect the child's school performance.

A variety of treatment techniques have been applied to some of the problems of adjustment facing the school-aged patient with cancer. Contingency management programs have been used to encourage school attendance. Assemblies and other forums encouraging open discussion of changes in a child returning to school as a function of his cancer treatments have been conducted to help decrease interpersonal anxiety. More specific social skills training programs also have been conducted with children with cancer to help them deal with their new interpersonal situations. Additionally, many hospitals provide inpatient classroom instruction and the use of homebound teachers to decrease the likelihood that the child will fall too far behind in coursework during hospitalization and exacerbations of his illness (Kellerman & Varni, 1982). Behavioral treatments have been used most frequently outside the classroom in the treatment of anticipatory anxiety and to decrease perceived pain through the use of biofeedback, relaxation training, hypnosis, and contingency management (LaBaw, Holton, Tewell, & Eccles, 1975; Moore & Altmaier, 1981; Morrow & Morrell, 1982; Redd & Andrykowski, 1982; Zeltzer, LeBaron, & Zelter, 1984). Based on the available literature, it appears as though future systematic applications of behavioral assessment and treatment techniques in the educational system aimed at enhancing the adjustment of the child with cancer are necessary.

Eating Disorders

Anorexia Nervosa

Anorexia nervosa is the least frequently occurring of the eating disorders to be discussed in this section. It is estimated to occur in 1% of women between the ages of 15 and 30 (Dupont, 1984). Anorexia nervosa is also the most fatal of the eating disorders, with a mortality rate of anywhere between 2% and 18% of anorexia (Silber, 1984). Anorexia nervosa is characterized by a decrease in body weight to dangerously low levels, amenorrhea, distortions in perceived body size, and frequently excessive exercising or activity. The presence of the severe weight loss characteristic of anorexia nervosa is quite obvious to the casual observer. Despite its frequent occurrence in adolescent girls, assessment of and intervention with anorexia nervosa have not occurred in the schools.

Behavioral treatments have been successful in producing weight gain in anorexics over the short run (Bellack & Williamson, 1982). Such treatments generally involve hospitalization of the anorexic with reinforcement for eating and weight gain. Maintenance of these weight gains following hospitalization has not been well researched and it is possible that the schools could be utilized in the development of maintenance strategies for use with the outpatient anorexic. An additional involvement of the school includes the early identification of anorexia as suggested by Leon (1984), who requests that educators and other professionals working in the school system be alert to student athletes who may be engaging in excessive exercise as one aspect of anorexia behavior. Also, schools must guard against promotion of athletic training goals and procedures that may induce an anorexic-like eating disorder through overly stringent weight requirements. Another eating disorder that is somewhat more difficult to identify, but which is much more common than anorexia nervosa, is the recently defined eating disorder of bulimia.

Bulimia

Bulimia, although more common than anorexia, is less common than obesity and occurs in an estimated 4% to 10% of women between the ages of 15 and 30 years (Barrios & Pennebaker, 1983; Dupont, 1984). Bulimia occurs at one quarter to one half this rate in males (Anderson, 1984; Dupont, 1984). This disorder is characterized by repeated binge eating and purging (e.g., vomiting, laxative use, diuretic use) in individuals who are generally of average body weight. Bulimia has only recently received its own diagnostic label and is no longer considered to be merely a variant of anorexia nervosa. Unlike obesity or anorexia nervosa, the presence of bulimia is not apparent from the appearance of the sufferer. This eating disorder is generally engaged in quite covertly and the bulimic is very afraid of being discovered (Rosen & Leitenberg, 1982). For these reasons it is difficult for those around the bulimic to know whether an eating disorder does indeed exist. Frequently, somatic complaints such as fatigue, sore throats, hoarseness, amenorrhea, and hair loss are the first signs of the existence of this disorder, which is potentially fatal if severe enough to cause metabolic dysfunction (Barrios & Pennebaker, 1983).

Assessment and treatment of bulimia have not yet occurred in school settings apart from epidemiological studies that have been conducted with high school and college populations (Johnson, Lewis, Love, Lewis, & Stuckey, 1984; Moss, Jennings, McFarland, & Carter, 1984). Such research projects have typically relied on structured interviews, the use of self-report instruments constructed for use with anorexics, such as the Eating Attitudes Test (Garner & Garfinkel, 1979), and/or the use of unstandardized paper-and-pencil tests designed to assess for bulimia using the diagnostic criteria from the *Diagnostic and Statistical Manual of Mental Disorders* (APA, 1980). However, Smith and Thelen

(1984) constructed a 36-item self-report questionaire, called the Bulimia Test (BULIT), that has been found to be a relatively valid and reliable screening instrument for the identification of bulimia in college women. It remains to be seen whether the BULIT has any usefulness with younger adolescents. Self-monitoring techniques have also been used in the assessment of bulimia. Schlundt, Johnson, and Jarrell (1985) described their use of self-monitoring booklets with adult bulimic women. The information that the women recorded in their booklet at each meal included information regarding the social context in which their eating occurred, their mood and degree of hunger prior to eating, the types of food they ate, whether they considered the eating episode a binge, and/or whether purging occurred following the eating episode. Schlundt *et al.* (1985) constructed the self-report booklets in such a way as to provide them with adequate information to allow them to study the antecedent behaviors and consequences associated with bulimia. This type of self-monitoring data can be very useful in designing appropriate behavioral interventions.

Behavioral treatment has begun increasingly to focus on the interruption of the binge–purge cycle through the prevention of the purging behavior (Leitenberg, Gross, Peterson, & Rosen, 1984; Rosen & Leitenberg, 1982). Bulimia has been conceptualized in an anxiety model suggesting that purging relieves not only anxiety from binge eating, but anxiety engendered by other life stressors as well. This reduction in anxiety is reinforcing and thus the binge–purge cycle is perpetuated. Treatment that follows from this conceptualization of bulimia makes use of response-prevention techniques whereby an individual is prevented from purging after eating. This intervention results in a gradual extinction of the anxiety over time (Leitenberg *et al.*, 1984). Although response prevention has been demonstrated to be effective in the treatment of bulimia via single-subject studies, such treatment is impractical for use in educational settings at this time.

Another model of bulimia that may be more easily translated into behavioral intervention strategies that are classroom appropriate has been referred to as the eating habit control model (Johnson & Brief, 1983). This conceptualization of bulimia posits that purging behavior is a result of faulty information and/or a skills deficit regarding how one maintains an appropriate balance between food (energy) needs and energy expenditure. Interventions based on this model have attempted to decrease binge–purge behavior through instructions of bulimics in ways to gain control of their eating habits along with increasing their activity levels. Because adolescents are at high risk for developing bulimia, the school setting may provide an ideal opportunity for training their students in eating-habit-control techniques as a way to impact on this difficult-to-identify eating disorder. Many of the techniques that have been refined in the behavioral treatment of obesity may be applicable to the treatment of bulimia using the eating-habit-control conceptualization.

Obesity

Of the eating disorders discussed thus far, obesity is by far the most prevalent. It is estimated that 10% to 25% of all adolescents are to some extent overweight (Coates, Jeffery, Slinkard, Killen, & Danaher, 1982). Obesity is more common among low socioeconomic status children (Foreyt & Goodrick, 1981) and of all overweight children between 10 to 13 years of age, up to 80% will grow up to be overweight adults (Straw, 1983). The most consistently reported psychological characteristic of obese children is poor self-concept (Straw, 1983). In addition, obese children are stigmatized very early on by their peers, educators, and employers (Straw, 1983).

Behavioral assessment of obesity has traditionally focused on self-monitoring and direct observation of caloric intake and eating habits (Foreyt & Goodrick, 1981). However, researchers have become increasingly aware of the importance of energy expenditure in addition to decreasing energy input in resulting weight loss (Abramson, 1983). Therefore, observational and self-report techniques are beginning to be applied to the assessment of activity level and exercise in children (Abramson, 1983; Foreyt & Goodrick, 1981).

Behavioral treatment of childhood obesity is following the trend of assessment by increasingly focusing on altering and increasing energy expenditure while attempting to decrease caloric intake (Epstein, Wing, Koeske, Ossip, & Beck, 1982). It has been suggested that the schools may provide a viable setting for the provision of weight control programs. Brownell (1982) described two multicomponent weight loss programs that were conducted in schools. These programs produced weight loss in the participants through education, contingency management, and support to promote changes in nutritional intake and exercise. In terms of promoting exercise, Epstein *et al.* (1982) suggested that encouraging changes in lifestyle activity patterns rather than requiring participation in structured exercise classes may be more acceptable to subjects thereby decreasing attrition. However, the additional health benefits of vigorous, regular exercise may be sacrificed.

Coates *et al.* (1982) noted that promoting weight loss in adolescents has been particularly difficult. Results from their research suggest that external motivating factors appear to work best with adolescents especially within the context of a program that provides for frequent therapeutic contact. Although Coates *et al.* (1982) utilized monetary incentives, they contended that a motivational program could be quite applicable in a school setting if something like tokens were utilized that could be exchanged for privileges rather then money. A further rationale for providing weight control programs in the schools comes from recent research suggesting that social support may play an important role in the weight loss process. Schools provide an excellent arena for peer and teacher support (Brownell, 1982). The fact that children eat at least one daily meal at school also provides the opportunity for direct intervention in teaching children to make nutritionally sound food choices as well as providing an excellent opportunity for conducting direct observational assessment of children's food choices and eating habits prior to treatment. Interest in the assessment and treatment of obesity in school children is great because of the link that has been established between obesity and the development of other health problems, particularly the development of cardiovascular disorders.

Cardiovascular Disease

Two areas of interest to the pediatric cardiologist are the primary prevention of risk factors linked to acquired cardiovascular disease and the detection of elevated blood pressure (Coates & Masek, 1982). Risk factors are recognized as those situations (e.g., occupation or environmental), behaviors (e.g., smoking), or conditions (e.g., obesity) that place a person in greater danger of developing a specific disease (Masek, Epstein, & Russo, 1981). Several prospective and epidemiological studies (e.g., Bogalusa Heart Study—Voors, Foster, Freriches, Webber, & Berenson, 1976; Muscatine Study—Lauer, Connor, Leaverton, Reiter, & Clarke, 1975; Western Collaborative Group Study—Rosenman, Brand, Sholtz, & Friedman, 1976) have delineated the most salient risk factors for coronary heart disease (CHD), which involved a behavioral component: (a) Type A or coronary-prone behavior pattern, (b) blood lipids or cholesterol levels, (c) smoking, (d) obesity, (e) diet, and (f) blood pressure. Research on Type A behavior in children indicates that (a) these children are more impatient, aggressive, and competitive than Type B children, (b) it is probably learned through parent modeling and child-rearing practices, and (c) it may operate independently of other risk factors (Blumenthal, Williams, King, Schanberg, & Thompson, 1978; Coates & Masek, 1982; Matthews, 1977, 1978). The mean serum cholesterol level for children of all ages is 182 mg/dl, yet 36% of children in one sample had serum levels greater than 200 mg/dl with black children evidencing greater total cholesterol levels (Frerichs, Srinivasan, Webber, & Berenson, 1976; Lauer *et al.*, 1975). Survey data on the rates of smoking reveal that over one third of all adolescents report cigarette smoking especially if parents, siblings, or peers smoke (i.e., modeling) (Hunter, Webber, & Berenson, 1980; Hymowitz, 1980). Results from the epidemiologic studies show a clear relationship between obesity in children and high serum cholesterol levels, increased blood pressure (i.e., above 90th percentile), and decreased physical activity (Lauer *et al.*, 1975; Voors, Webber, & Berenson, 1978; Waxman & Stunkard, 1980).

Identifying essential hypertension as a significant risk factor for CHD in adults (Blumenthal, 1978; Dowber, Kannel, & Lyell, 1963) has influenced the early detection of high blood pressure in all ages. Based on norms established by the Task Force on Blood Pressure Control in Children (1977), the prevalence of juvenile hypertension is estimated at between 3% and 10% (Voors *et al.*, 1976). Essential hypertension is diagnosed as blood pressure two standard deviations above the mean age norms. Referrals for a diagnosis of essential hypertension are based on fixed blood pressure levels greater than 140 mm Hg for systolic and 90 mm Hg for diastolic. Headaches and visual disturbances frequently accompany signs of essential hypertension, although many children show no overt symptomatology (Schroeder *et al.*, 1982). Hypertension is found more often in adolescents, males, families, and urban populations (Cruz-Coke, Donoso, & Barrera, 1973; Londe, Bourgoignie, Robson, & Goldring, 1971; Zinner, Levy, & Kass, 1971). In general, the cause of essential hypertension is considered to be an interaction of physiological factors (e.g., renin-angiotension system, kidney), psychosocial factors (e.g., occupational stress, low physical activity), and behavioral factors (e.g., Type A pattern) (Harrell, 1980; Shapiro & Goldstein, 1982). Coates and Masek (1982) described one hypothesis that suggests certain children and adolescents respond to environmental or emotional stress by increased release of catecholamines (i.e., epinephrine and norepinephrine) and direct sympathetic stimulation, resulting in greater peripheral resistance and cardiac output. These acute increases in blood pressure may produce changes in anatomical structure, blood pressure regulatory mechanisms, and ultimately in a raised basal level of blood pressure.

Prevention of CHD in adults requires teaching healthy eating, diet, and exercise habits to children and modifying maladaptive behavioral patterns once identified (i.e., preventive medicine) (Masek *et al.*, 1981; Varni, 1983). The need for preventive efforts is highlighted by the fact that risk factors first seen in children (e.g., high blood pressure, obesity) continue into adult life, thus promoting physiological correlates of CHD (Frerichs, Webber, Voors, Srinivasan, & Berenson, 1979; Mobbs, 1970; Voors *et al.*, 1978). Unfortunately, little research has been conducted on the modification of unhealthy life-styles using behavioral techniques (Masek *et al.*, 1981). The assessment of essential hypertension and other risk factors for CHD consist of medical and behavioral methods: (a) repeated self- and other-recording of blood pressure measurements to establish a consistent percentile status because of human and instrumental error (e.g., three readings taken monthly for three or four examinations by the auscultatory method or Doppler principle) (Task Force Report, 1977; Voors *et al.*, 1978); (b) teacher ratings of Type A behavior (e.g., Matthews Youth Test for Health—Matthews & Angulo, 1980) and self-report scales (e.g., Bortner Type A Scale—Spiga & Peterson, 1981); (c) self-monitoring of smoking behavior (e.g., frequency of cigarettes per day, whether cigarettes were offered and/or turned down), knowledge—attitude questionnaires, carbon monoxide breath samples, and nicotine-in-saliva analysis (e.g., Evans *et al.*, 1978; Perry, Killen, Telch, Slinkard, & Danaher, 1980); (d) self- and other-recording of weekly weight loss, daily caloric and salt intake, antecedents of eating (e.g., place, time), and physical activity (e.g., type, duration) (e.g., Aragona, Cassady, & Drabman, 1975; Brownell & Kaye, 1982); (e) direct observation of eating and physical activity patterns at home and/or in school (e.g., Coates, Jeffery, & Slinkard, 1981;

Coates & Thoresen, 1981); and (f) psychophysiological measurement of heart rate and skin temperature during stressful and relaxing laboratory conditions (e.g., Coates & Masek, 1982).

The use of behavioral techniques in prevention programs has been, typically, in primary and secondary prevention efforts (Kasl & Cobb, 1966). Primary prevention efforts are concerned with stopping the occurrence of disease by reducing associated risk factors, whereas secondary prevention strategies attempt to halt the deterioration of disease when identified (Breslow, 1978). Medical management of juvenile hypertension is recommended for children between the ages of 7 and 18 years who show a diastolic elevation above 100 mm Hg (Coates & Masek, 1982; Task Force Report, 1977). A stepped-care titration approach is followed where more potent drugs are added to the regimen (e.g., thiazide diuretic, beta-blocking agent or methylodopa, vasodilator). Recommendations for controlling mild to moderate hypertension involve diet and salt restrictions, and physical activity assignments. Individual cases have shown a reduction in blood pressure to clinically significant levels (i.e., less than 90th percentile) through various behavioral procedures: (a) Bensonian meditative relaxation, pressure and temperature biofeedback, and instructions to limit use of table salt (Coates & Masek, 1982); (b) stress management training (i.e., progressive relaxation training, coping strategies for stress) (Coates, 1980); and (c) skills training (e.g., academic, Type A behavior) (Coates, Parker, & Kolodner, 1982). School-based prevention programs have effectively decreased the onset and frequency of smoking in adolescents employing such strategies as (a) filmed instruction on resisting social pressures to smoke (i.e., from peers, parents, and mass media), (b) group discussion, modeling, and behavior rehearsal of coping methods, (c) poster reminders of social pressures, (d) feedback on the frequency of classroom smoking, and (e) smoking cessation procedures (e.g., self-monitoring of urges to smoke, relaxation techniques, goal setting) (Botvin, Eng, & Williams, 1980; Evans, 1976; Evans *et al.*, 1978; McAlister, Perry, & Maccoby, 1979; McAlister, Perry, Killen, Telch, & Slinkard, 1980; Murray *et al.*, 1979; Perry *et al.*, 1980). Several studies incorporated teachers and peers in running health education sessions on the short- and long-term effects of smoking and skills training on coping with pressures to smoke. Studies demonstrating the benefits of behavioral techniques on altering the eating, exercise, and diet patterns of obese children and adolescents have been described in the section on eating disorders. Two primary prevention programs for CHD have been implemented on a large scale in some schools, for example, "Heart Healthy Program" (Coates *et al.*, 1981) and "Know Your Body" (Williams, Carter, Arnold, & Wynder, 1979). The Heart Healthy Program was designed to change the eating and exercise patterns of fourth and fifth graders based on twelve 45-minute classes within the science curriculum. Results showed significant changes in eating behavior at school, knowledge about heart health, food preferences, and family eating patterns using informative instruction, participatory classroom activities, personal goal setting, parent handouts, systematic feedback, and reinforcement. The Know Your Body program involved screening for major risk factors (e.g., total cholesterol, ing a personal Health Passport, and conducting health education classes with targeted children (ages 11 to 14 years). Preliminary findings suggest that a program emphasizing modeling of appropriate health behaviors, personalized education materials, self-monitoring of health behaviors, and classroom-learning activities can reduce the rate of identified risk factors in children.

Research on the modification of risk factors in children has employed varied populations (i.e., single subjects, classrooms, schools) and multiple dependent measures (e.g., self-monitoring, questionnaires, direct observation). However, future studies should focus on determining effective treatment components and the cost-benefit ratio of school-based programs. In addition, investigation of ways to enhance compliance to medical regimens (e.g., antihypertensive medications) and long-term maintenance of healthy eating and exercise behaviors should be a priority for school psychologists.

Conclusions

In this chapter we have attempted to survey a variety of medical and health related disorders that may occur in the population of school-aged children. With increasingly sophisticated medical treatments and the existence of P.L. 94-142, many children who were once not in public schools because of health problems and decreased longevity are now more likely to be attending school regularly despite their illnesses or physical impairments. However, very little research has been conducted involving the chronically ill or handicapped child in the classroom. Therefore, we have frequently suggested the use of assessment and intervention strategies for use with such children based on their proven usefulness with other populations and/or in other settings. The results of the information covered in this chapter suggest several areas in which the school setting is especially important for work with medically ill or handicapped children, and treatment goals that are applicable to all children with health problems in the school.

The schools can provide an arena for the generalization and maintenance of treatment gains made with the chronically ill or physically handicapped child in other settings, such as the hospital or the home. For these reasons it is important that the means be established for clear and direct communication among parents, medical personnel, and school personnel so that all persons involved in the care of the child with a medical condition can support and promote the treatment goals developed for such a child. In addition to providing an opportunity for the extension of interventions designed to address already existing adjustment, compliance, or health problems, the schools also provide a unique opportunity for the introduction of preventive programs to a large and diverse population of children. Particular programs to promote stress management skills, weight management techniques, and preparation for medical procedures have begun to be applied within the schools (e.g., Ross & Ross, 1985). The long-term efficacy of attempts at generalization, maintenance, and prevention within the schools needs to be continually assessed.

Along the lines of prevention, the school setting may be in a unique position also to note the initial signs of problems in chronically ill and handicapped children, such as drug intoxication in the epileptic child or insulin shock in the diabetic child, that may require immediate medical attention. Difficulties in the child's, as well as the family's, psychological adjustment to the illness can also be detected early in the classroom when evidenced by such behaviors as changes in academic performance or withdrawal from social situations. With early detection, such difficulties in adjustment can be addressed before they become fixed means of coping for the child and his or her family. Along these lines, regular school attendance should be a goal for all such children so that the schools can provide opportunities for children with physical handicaps and chronic illnesses to obtain the socialization experiences necessary to their effective psychological adjustment to their conditions along with their scholastic instruction. However, in order to ensure that appropriate socialization experiences do occur, special attention needs to be paid not only to the implementation of structured programs designed to enhance the social skills of the ill or disabled child but also to the education of school personnel and other students as to the effects of the illness so that such individuals may interact appropriately with the ill or handicapped child.

It is evident from this chapter that work in school settings with children who have a variety of medical problems is an area that holds great promise and in which vigorous research should continue.

References

Abramson, E. E. (1983). Behavioral treatment of obesity: Some good news, some bad news, and a few suggestions. *The Behavior Therapist, 6*, 103–106.

Achterberg, J., & Lawlis, G. F. (1980). *Bridges of the mind*. Champaign, IL: Institute for Personality and Ability Testing.

Achterberg-Lawlis, J. (1982). The psychological dimensions of arthritis. *Journal of Consulting and Clinical Psychology, 50*, 984–992.

Achterberg-Lawlis, J., & Kenner, C. (1982). Burn patients. In D. M. Doleys, R. L. Meredith, & A. R. Ciminero (Eds.), *Behavioral medicine: Assessment and treatment strategies* (pp. 499–525). New York: Plenum Press.

Ad Hoc Committee on Classification of Headache. (1982). *Journal of the American Medical Association, 179*, 717–718.

Alexander, A. B. (1972). Systematic relaxation and flow rates in asthmatic children: Relationship to emotional participants and anxiety. *Journal of Psychosomatic Research, 16*, 405–410.

Alexander, A. B., Miklich, D. R., & Hershkoff, H. (1972). The immediate effects of systematic relaxation on peak expiratory flow rates in asthmatic children. *Psychosomatic Medicine, 34*, 388–394.

Alexander, A. B., Cropp, G. J. A., & Chai, H. (1979). Effects of relaxation training on pulmonary mechanics in children with asthma. *Journal of Applied Behavior Analysis, 12*, 27–35.

Alleyne, S. I., Wint, E., & Serjeant, G. R. (1976). Psychosocial aspects of sickle cell disease. *Health and Social Work, 1*, 105–119.

American Academy of Pediatrics. (1977). *School health: A guide for health professionals*. Evanston, IL: Author.

American Lung Association. (1975). *Introduction to lung diseases* (6th ed.). New York: Author.

American Psychiatric Association. (1980). *Diagnostic and statistical manual of mental disorders* (3rd ed.). Washington, DC: Author.

Andersen, A. E. (1984). Anorexia nervosa and bulimia in adolescent males. *Pediatric Annals, 13*, 901–904, 907.

Andrasik, F., Blanchard, E. B., Edlund, S. R., & Rosenblum, E. L. (1983). Autogenic feedback in the treatment of two children with migraine headache. *Child and Family Behavior Therapy, 4*, 3–23.

Andreasen, N. J. C., Noyes, R., Hartford, C. E., Brodland, G., & Proctor, S. (1972). Management of emotional reactions in seriously burned adults. *New England Journal of Medicine, 286*, 65–69.

Apley, J. (1975). *The child with abdominal pains* (2nd ed.). Oxford: Blackwell Scientific.

Apley, J., & Hale, B. (1973). Children with recurrent abdominal pain. How do they grow up? *British Medical Journal, 3*, 7–9.

Apley, J., & Naish, N. (1958). Recurrent abdominal pain: A field survey of disease in childhood. *Archives of Disease in Childhood, 33*, 165–170.

Aragona, J., Cassady, J., & Drabman, R. S. (1975). Treating overweight children through parental training and contingency contracting. *Journal of Applied Behavior Analysis, 8*, 269–278.

Artz, C. P. (1979). Psychological considerations. In C. P. Artz, J. A. Moncrief, & B. A. Pruitt (Eds.), *Burns: A team approach* (pp. 461–465). Philadelphia, PA: W. B. Saunders.

Balaschak, B. A. (1976). Teacher-implemented behavior modification in a case of organically based epilepsy. *Journal of Consulting and Clinical Psychology, 44*, 218–223.

Balaschak, B. A., & Mostofsky, D. I. (1981). Seizure disorders. In E. J. Mash & L. G. Terdal (Eds.), *Behavioral assessment of childhood disorders* (pp. 601–637). New York: Guilford Press.

Barnhart, M., Henry, R. L., & Lusher, J. (1974). *Sickle cell*. Kalamazoo, MI: Upjohn.

Barr, R. G. & Feuerstein, M. (1983). Recurrent abdominal pain syndrome. How appropriate are our clinical assumptions? In P. J. McGrath & P. Firestone (Eds.), *Pediatric and adolescent behavioral medicine: Issues in treatment* (pp. 13–27). New York: Springer.

Barr, R. G., Levine, M. D., & Watkins, J. W. (1979). Recurrent abdominal pain of childhood due to lactose intolerance, a prospective study. *New England Journal of Medicine, 300*, 1449–1452.

Barrios, B. A., & Pennebaker, J. W. (1983). A note on the early detection of Bulimia Nervosa. *The Behavior Therapist, 6*, 18–19.

Battle, C. U. (1984). Disruptions in the socialization of a young, severely handicapped child. In R. F. Marinelli & A. E. Dell Orto (Eds.), *The psychological and social impact of physical disability* (2nd ed., pp. 67–85). New York: Springer.

Baum, J. (1983). Treatment of juvenile arthritis. *American Family Physician, 27*, 133–139.

Bellack, A. S., & Williamson, D. A. (1982). Obesity and anorexia nervosa. In D. M. Doleys, R. L. Meredith, & A. R. Ciminero (Eds.), *Behavioral medicine: Assessment and treatment strategies* (pp. 295–316). New York: Plenum Press.

Bharani, S. N., & Hyde, J. S. (1976). Chronic asthma and the school. *Journal of School Health, 46*, 24–30.

Bille, B. (1967). Juvenile headache: Its natural history in children. In A. P. Friedman & E. Harms (Eds.), *Headaches in children* (pp. 10–28). Springfield, IL: Charles C Thomas.

Bille, B. (1981). Migraine in childhood and its prognosis. *Cephalalgia, 1*, 71–75.

Blanchard, E. B., & Andrasik, F. (1982). Psychological assessment and treatment of headache: Recent developments and emerging issues. *Journal of Consulting and Clinical Psychology, 50*, 859–879.

Block, J., Jennings, P. H., Harvey, E., & Simpson, E. (1964). Interaction between allergic potential and psychopathology in childhood. *Psychosomatic Medicine, 26*, 307–320.

Blumenthal, J. A., Williams, R. B., King, Y., Schanberg, A. M., & Thompson, L. W. (1978). Type A behavior pattern and coronary atherosclerosis. *Circulation, 58,* 634–639.

Blumenthal, S. (1978). Implications for the future study of hypertension. *Pediatric Clinics of North America, 25,* 183–186.

Botvin, G. J., Eng, A., & Williams, C. L. (1980). Preventing the onset of cigarette smoking through life skills training. *Preventive Medicine, 9,* 135–143.

Breslin, P. W. (1975). The psychological reactions of children to burn traumata: A review. *Illinois Medical Journal, 148,* 519–524.

Brown, J. K. (1977). Migraine and migraine equivalents in children. *Developmental Medicine and Child Neurology, 19,* 683–692.

Brownell, K. D. (1982). Obesity: Understanding and treating a serious, prevalent, and refractory disorder. *Journal of Consulting and Clinical Psychology, 50,* 820–840.

Brownell, K. D., & Kaye, F. S. (1982). Behavioral treatment of obesity in children. *American Journal of Diseases of Children, 132,* 403–412.

Burbeck, T. W. (1979). An empirical investigation of the psychosomatogenic family model. *Journal of Psychosomatic Research, 23,* 327–337.

Bunn, H. F. (1982). Sickle cell disease. Advances in the 1970's and challenges in the 1980's. *American Journal of Pediatric Hematology/Oncology, 4,* 166–171.

Caghan, S., McGrath, M., Morrow, M., & Pittman, L. (1978). When adolescents complain of pain. *Nurse Practitioner, 3,* 19–22.

Calabro, J. J. (1970). Management of juvenile rheumatoid arthritis. *Journal of Pediatrics, 77,* 355–365.

Campbell, L. (1976). Special behavioral problems of the burned child. *American Journal of Nursing, 76,* 220–224.

Cannon, I. P., & Compton, C. L. (1980). School dysfunction in the adolescent. *Pediatric Clinics of North America, 27,* 79–95.

Carney, R. M., Schecter, K., & Davis, T. (1982). Improving adherence to blood glucose testing in insulin-dependent diabetic children. *Behavior Therapy, 14,* 247–254.

Chai, H. (1975). Management of severe chronic perennial asthma in children. *Advances in Asthma and Allergy, 2,* 1–12.

Chai, H., Purcell, K., Brady, K., & Falliers, C. J. (1968). Therapeutic and investigative evaluation of asthmatic children. *Journal of Allergy, 41,* 23–36.

Christensen, M. F., & Mortensen, O. (1975). Long-term prognosis in children with recurrent abdominal pain. *Archives of Disease in Childhood, 50,* 110–114.

Clark, H. M., Feldman, C. H., Freudenberg, N., Millman, E. J., Wasilewski, Y., & Valle, L. (1980). Developing education for children with asthma through study of self-management behavior. *Health Education Quarterly, 7,* 278–297.

Clarke, A. M. (1980). Thermal injuries: The care of the whole child. *Journal of Trauma, 20,* 823–829.

Clarke, P. S. (1970). Effects of emotion and cough on airways obstruction in asthma. *Medical Journal of Australia, 1,* 535–537.

Coates, T. J. (1980). *Stress management for adolescent hypertension.* Paper presented at the Symposium on Hypertension in the Young, Johns Hopkins University, Baltimore, MD.

Coates, T. J., & Masek, B. J. (1982). Pediatric cardiology. Congenital disorders and preventive cardiology. In D. C. Russo & J. W. Varni (Eds.), *Behavioral pediatrics: Research and practice* (pp. 335–374). New York: Plenum Press.

Coates, T. J., & Thoresen, C. E. (1981). Behavior and weight changes in three obese adolescents. *Behavior Therapy, 12,* 383–399.

Coates, T. J., Jeffery, R. W., & Slinkard, L. A. (1981). Heart healthy eating and exercise: Introducing and maintaining changes in health behavior. *American Journal of Public Health, 71,* 15–23.

Coates, T. J., Jeffery, R. W., Slinkard, L. A., Killen, J. D., & Danaher, B. G. (1982). Frequency of contact and monetary reward in weight loss, lipid change, and blood pressure reduction with adolescents. *Behavior Therapy, 13,* 175–185.

Coates, T. J., Parker, F. C., & Kolodner, K. (1982). Stress and heart disease: Does blood pressure reactivity offer a link? In T. J. Coates, A. C. Peterson, & C. Perry (Eds.), *Adolescent health: Crossing the barriers* (pp. 305–321). New York: Academic Press.

Cone, J. D. (1978). The behavioral assessment grid (BAG): A conceptual framework and taxonomy. *Behavior Therapy, 9,* 882–888.

Conyard, S., Krishnamurthy, M., & Dosik, H. (1980). Psychosocial aspects of sickle cell anemia in adolescents. *Health and Social Work, 5,* 20–26.

Crawford, J. L. (1981). Incidence and prevention of burn injuries. In M. M. Wagner (Ed.), *Care of the burn-injured patient: A multidisciplinary involvement* (pp. 1–4). Littleton, MA: PSG.

Creer, T. L. (1979). *Asthma therapy: A behavioral health care system for respiratory disorders.* New York: Springer.

Creer, T. L. (1982). Asthma. *Journal of Consulting and Clinical Psychology, 50,* 912–921.

Creer, T. L., & Kotses, H. (1983). Asthma: Psychological aspects and management. In E. Middleton, Jr., C. E. Reed, & E. F. Ellis (Eds.), *Allergy: Principles and practice* (pp. 1015–1036). St. Louis, MO: Mosby.

Creer, T., & Leung, P. (1981). *The development and evaluation of a self-management program for children with asthma* (Vol. 2: Manuscripts). Bethesda, MD: National Institute of Allergic and Infectious Diseases.

Creer, T. L., & Miklich, D. R. (1970). The application of a self-modeling procedure to modify inappropriate behavior: A preliminary report. *Behaviour Research and Therapy, 8,* 91–92.

Creer, T. L., & Yoches, C. (1971). The modification of an inappropriate behavioral pattern in asthmatic children. *Journal of Chronic Diseases, 24,* 507–513.

Creer, T. L., Weinberg, E., & Molk, L. (1974). Managing a

problem hospital behavior: Malingerling. *Journal of Behavior Therapy and Experimental Psychiatry, 5,* 259–262.

Creer, T. L., Renne, C. M., & Chai, H. (1982). The application of behavioral techniques to childhood asthma. In D. C. Russo & J. W. Varni (Eds.), *Behavioral pediatrics: Research and practice* (pp. 27–66). New York: Plenum Press.

Creer, T. L., Backiel, M., & Leung, P. (1983). *Living with asthma. Manual for teaching children the self-management of asthma* (Contract No. N01-HR-7-2972). Bethesda, MD: National Heart, Lung, and Blood Institute.

Cromes, G. F., Robinson, C., & Turrentine, M. (1978). *The effects of relaxation training on anxiety and pain during wound debridement.* Paper presented at the Annual Assembly of the American Academy of Physical Medicine and Rehabilitation, New Orleans, LA.

Cruz-Coke, R., Donoso, H., & Barrera, R. (1973). Genetic ecology of hypertension. *Clinical Science and Molecular Medicine, 45,* 55–65.

Davis, M. H., Saunders, D. R., Creer, T. L., & Chai, H. (1973). Relaxation training facilitated by biofeedback apparatus as a supplemental treatment in bronchial asthma. *Journal of Psychosomatic Research, 17,* 121–128.

Deubner, D. C. (1977). An epidemiologic study of migraine and headache in 10–20 year olds. *Headache, 17,* 173–180.

Diamond, S., & Dalessio, D. J. (1978) *The practicing physician's approach to headache.* Baltimore, MD: William & Wilkins.

Diamond, S., & Franklin, M. (1975). Biofeedback: Choice of treatment in childhood migraine. In W. Luthe & F. Antonelli (Eds.), *Therapy in psychosomatic medicine* (Vol. 4, pp. 38–56). Rome: Autogenic Therapy.

Dimson, S. B. (1971). Transit time related to clinical findings in children with recurrent abdominal pain. *Pediatrics, 47,* 666–667.

Douglas, J. W. B., & Ross, J. M. (1965). The effects of absence on primary school performance. *British Journal of Education Psychology, 35,* 28–40.

Dowber, T. R., Kannel, W. B., & Lyell, L. P. (1963). An approach to longitudinal studies in a community: The Framingham study. *Annals of the New York Academy of Science, 107,* 539–556.

Drotar, D. (1981). Psychological perspectives in chronic childhood illness. *Journal of Pediatric Psychology, 6,* 211–218.

Dunn, S. M., Bryson, J. M., Hoskins, P. L., Alford, J. B., Handelsman, D. J., & Turtle, J. R. (1984). Development of the Diabetes Knowledge (DKN) Scales: Forms DKNA, DKNB, and DKNC. *Diabetes Care, 7,* 36–40.

DuPont, R. L. (1984). Bulimia: A modern epidemic among adolescents. *Pediatric Annals, 13,* 908–909, 912, 914.

Education of handicapped children: Implementation of Part B of the Education of the Handicapped Act, rules and regulations. (1977, August). *Federal Register, 43,* (163), 427–428.

Epstein, L. H., Wing, R. R., Koeske, R., Ossip, D., & Beck, S. (1982). A comparison of lifestyle change and programmed aerobic exercise on weight and fitness changes in obese children. *Behavior Therapy, 13,* 651–665.

Etzwiler, D. D., & Robb, J. R. (1972). Evaluation of programmed education among juvenile diabetics and their families. *Diabetes, 21,* 967–971.

Evans, R. I. (1976). Smoking in children: Developing a social psychological strategy of deterrence. *Preventive Medicine, 5,* 122–127.

Evans, R. I., Rozelle, R. M., Mittelmark, M. B., Hansen, W. B., Bane, A. L., & Havis, J. (1978). Deterring the onset of smoking in children. Knowledge of immediate physiological effects and coping with peer pressure, media pressure, and parent modeling. *Journal of Applied Social Psychology, 8,* 126–135.

Feldman, C. H., Clark, N., Evans, D., Wasilewski, Y., Millman, E. J., & Valle, I. (1983). *Open airways. Asthma self-management program* (Contract No. N01-HR-7-2973). Bethesda, MD: National Heart, Lung, and Blood Institute.

Fentress, D., & Masek, B. (1982, November). *Behavioral treatment of pediatric migraine.* Paper presented at the Annual Meeting of the Association for Advancement of Behavior Therapy, Los Angeles, CA.

Finney, J. W., Fuqua, R. W., Cataldo, M. F., Whitehead, W., & Katz, H. (1984). *Behavioral treatment and physiological assessment of children with recurrent abdominal pain.* Unpublished manuscript, The Kennedy Institute for Handicapped Children, Baltimore.

Foreyt, J. P., & Goodrick, G. K. (1981). Childhood obesity. In E. J. Mash & L. G. Terdal (Eds.), *Behavioral assessment of childhood disorders* (pp. 573–599). New York: Guilford Press.

Fowler, J. E., Budzynski, T. H., & Vandenbergh, R. L. (1976). Effects of an EMG biofeedback relaxation program on the control of diabetes. *Biofeedback and Self-Regulation, 1,* 105–112.

Frerichs, R. R., Srinivasan, S. R., Webber, L. S., & Berenson, G. S. (1976). Serum cholesterol and triglycerides in 3446 children from a biracial community: The Bogalusa Heart Study. *Circulation, 54,* 302–309.

Frerichs, R. R., Webber, L. S., Voors, A. W., Srinivasan, S. R., & Berenson, G. S. (1979). Cardiovascular disease risk factor variables in children at two successive years: The Bogalusa Heart Study. *Journal of Chronic Diseases, 32,* 251–262.

Gardner, J. E. (1968). A blending of behavior therapy techniques in an approach to an asthmatic child. *Psychotherapy: Therapy, Research, and Practice, 5,* 46–49.

Garner, D. M., & Garfinkel, P. E. (1979). The Eating Attitudes Test: An index of the symptoms of anorexia nervosa. *Psychological Medicine, 9,* 273–279.

Gascon, G. G. (1984). Chronic and recurrent headache in children and adolescents. *Pediatric Clinics of North America, 31,* 1027–1051.

Gaston, M. (1973). Management of children with SCA between crises. *Urban Health, 2,* 24–26.

Gauthier, Y., Fortin, C., Drapeau, P., Breton, J. J., Gosselin, J., Quintal, L., Weisnagel, J., Tatreault, L., & Pinard, G. (1977). The mother–child relationship and the development of autonomy and self-assertion in young (14–30 months) asthmatic children. Correlating allergic and psychological factors. *Journal of the American Academy of Child Psychiatry, 16,* 109–131.

Gayton, W. F., Friedman, S. B. (1973). A review of the psychological aspects of cystic fibrosis. *American Journal of Diseases in Children, 126,* 856–859.

Gearheart, B. R., & Weishahn, M. W. (1976). *The handicapped child in the regular classroom.* St. Louis, MO: C.V. Mosky.

Gilbert, B. O., Johnson, S. B., Spillar, R., McCallum, M., Silverstein, J. H., & Rosenbloom, A. (1982). The effects of a peer-modeling film on children learning to self-inject insulin. *Behavior Therapy, 13,* 183–193.

Gogan, J. L., O'Malley, J. E., & Foster, D. J. (1977). Treating the pediatric cancer patient. A Review. *Journal of Pediatric Psychology, 2,* 42–48.

Gortmaker, S. L., & Sappenfield, W. (1984). Chronic childhood disorders: Prevalence and impact. *Pediatric Clinics of North America, 31,* 3–18.

Gottman, J., Gonso, J., & Schuler, P. (1976). Teaching social skills to isolated children. *Journal of Abnormal Child Psychology, 4,* 179–197.

Greene, J. W., & Thompson, W. (1984). A physician/psychologist team approach to children and adolescents with recurrent somatic complaints. *School Psychology Review, 13,* 204–210.

Greydanus, R., & Hofman, A. D. (1979). Psychological factors in diabetes mellitus: A review of the literature with emphasis on adolescence. *American Journal of Diseases of Children, 133,* 1061–1066.

Griffiths, M. I. (1975). Medical approaches in special education. In R. Wandell (Ed.), *Orientations in special education.* London: Wiley.

Guidubaldi, J., Kehle, T. J., & Murray, J. N. (1984). Assessment strategies for the handicapped. In R. P. Marinelli & A. E. Dell Orto (Eds.), *The psychological and social impact of physical disability* (2nd ed., pp. 288–303). New York: Springer.

Haggerty, R. J., Roghmann, K. G., & Pless, I. B. (1975). *Child health and the community.* New York: Wiley.

Hahn, W. W. (1966). Autonomic responses of asthmatic children. *Psychosomatic Medicine, 28,* 323–332.

Harkness, D. R. (1980). Hematological and clinical features of sickle cell diseases: A review. *Hemoglobin, 4,* 313–334.

Harrell, J. P. (1980). Psychological factors and hypertension: A status report. *Psychological Bulletin, 87,* 482–501.

Heisler, A. B., & Friedman, S. B. (1981). Social and psychological considerations in chronic disease: With particular reference to the management of seizure disorders. *Journal of Pediatric Psychology, 6,* 239–250.

Helm, P. A., Head, M. D., Pullium, G., O'Brien, M., & Cromes, G. F. (1978). Burn rehabilitation—A team approach. *Surgical Clinics of North America, 58,* 1263–1278.

Hinkle, L. E., & Wolf, S. (1952). Importance of life stress in the course and management of diabetes mellitus. *Journal of the American Medical Association, 148,* 513–520.

Houts, A. C. (1982). Relaxation and thermal feedback treatment of child migraine headache: A case study. *American Journal of Clinical Biofeedback, 5,* 154–157.

Hunter, S. MacD., Webber, L. S., & Berenson, G. S. (1980). Cigarette smoking and tobacco usage behavior in children and adolescents: The Bogalusa heart Study. *Preventive Medicine, 6,* 701–702.

Hymowitz, N. (1980). Teenage smoking: A medical responsibility. *Journal of Developmental and Behavioral Pediatrics, 1,* 164–172.

Jay, G. W., & Tomasi, L. G. (1981). Pediatric headaches: A one year retrospective analysis. *Headache, 21,* 5–9.

Jay, S. M., Ozolins, M., Elliott, C. H., & Caldwell, S. (1983). Assessment of children's distress during painful medical procedures. *Health Psychology, 2,* 133–147.

Johnson, C., Lewis, C., Love, S., Lewis, L., & Stuckey, M. (1984). Incidence and correlates of bulimic behavior in a female high school population. *Journal of Youth and Adolescence, 13,* 15–26.

Johnson, S. B. (1980). Psychosocial factors in juvenile diabetes: A review. *Journal of Behavioral Medicine, 3,* 95–116.

Johnson, W. G., & Brief, D. J. (1983). Bulimia. *Behavioral Medicine Update, 4,* 16–21.

Jones, C. A., & Bowden, M. L. (1979). Nurse—Family interface. In W. C. Bailey (Ed.), *Pediatric burns* (pp. 123–136). Chicago, IL: Year Book Medical.

Kanfer, F. H., & Saslow, G. (1969). Behavioral diagnosis. In C. M. Franks (Ed.), *Behavior therapy: Appraisal and status.* New York: McGraw-Hill.

Kasl, S. V., & Cobb, S. (1966). Health behavior, illness behavior, and sick role behavior. *Archives of Environmental Health, 12,* 246–266.

Katz, E. R., & Jay, S. M. (1984). Psychological aspects of cancer in children, adolescents, and their families. *Clinical Psychology Review, 4,* 525–542.

Kellerman, J., & Varni, J. W. (1982). Pediatric hematology/oncology. In D. C. Russo & J. W. Varni (Eds.), *Behavioral pediatrics: Research and practice* (pp. 67–100). New York: Plenum Press.

Kellerman, J., Zeltzer, L., Ellenberg, L., Dash, J., & Rigler, D. (1980). Psychological effects of illness in adolescence. I. Anxiety, self-esteem, and perception of control. *Journal of Pediatrics, 97,* 126–131.

Kelley, M. L., Jarvie, G. J., Middlebrook, J. L., McNeer, M. F., & Drabman, R. S. (1984). Decreasing burned children's pain behavior: Impacting the trauma of hydrotherapy. *Journal of Applied Behavior Analysis, 17,* 147–158.

Kinsman, R. A., O'Banion, K., Resnikoff, P., Luparello, T. J., & Spector, S. L. (1973). Subjective symptoms of acute asthma within a heterogeneous sample of asthmatics. *Journal of Allergy and Clinical Immunology, 52,* 284–296.

Knowles, H. C., Jr. (1971). Diabetes mellitus in childhood and adolescence. *Medical Clinics of North America, 55,* 1007–1019.

Krafft, K. M., & Poling, A. D. (1982). Behavioral treatments of epilepsy: Methodological characteristics and problems of published studies. *Applied Research in Mental Retardation, 3,* 151–162.

Kumar, S., Powars, D., Allen, J., & Haywood, L. J. (1976). Anxiety, self-concept, and personal and social adjustments in children with sickle cell anemia. *Journal of Pediatrics, 88,* 859–863.

LaBaw, W., Holton, C., Tewell, K., & Eccles, D. (1975). The use of self-hypnosis by children with cancer. *American Journal of Clinical Hypnosis, 17,* 233–238.

Labbe, E. E., & Williamson, D. A. (1983). Temperature biofeedback in the treatment of children with migraine headaches. *Journal of Pediatric Psychology, 8,* 317–326.

Labbe, E. L., & Williamson, D. A. (1984). Treatment of childhood migraine using autogenic feedback training. *Journal of Consulting and Clinical Psychology, 52,* 968–976.

Lang, P. J., Melamed, B. G., & Hart, J. A. (1970). A psychophysiological analysis for fear modification using an automated desensitization procedure. *Journal of Abnormal Psychology, 76,* 220–234.

Lansky, S., Lowman, J., Vats, T., & Gyulay, J. (1975). School phobia in children with malignant neuroplasms. *American Journal of Diseases of Children, 129,* 42–46.

Lauer, R. M., Connor, W. B., Leaverton, P. E., Reiter, M. A., & Clarke, W. R. (1975). Coronary heart disease factors in school children: The Muscatine study. *Journal of Pediatrics, 86,* 697–706.

Lehmann, H., Huntsman, G., Casey, R., Lang, A., Lorkin, P. A., & Comings, D. E. (1977). Sickle cell disease and related disorders. In W. J. Williams, E. Beutler, A. J. Erslev, & R. W. Rundles (Eds.), *Hematology* (pp. 495–524). New York: McGraw-Hill.

Leitenberg, H., Gross, J., Peterson, J., & Rosen, J. C. (1984). Analysis of an anxiety model and the process of change during exposure plus response prevention treatment of bulimia nervosa. *Behavior Therapy, 15,* 3–20.

Leon, G. R. (1984). Anorexia nervosa and sports activities. *The Behavior Therapist, 7,* 9–10.

Lemanek, K. L., Gresham, F. M., Williamson, D. A., & Kelley, M. L. (1984a, November). *Investigation of academic and self-reported behavior problems in children with sickle cell anemia.* Paper presented at the Annual Meeting of the Association for Advancement of Behavior Therapy, Philadelphia, PA.

Lemanek, K. L., Gresham, F. M., Williamson, D. A., & Kelley, M. L. (1984b, November). *Multimethod assessment of behavior problems in sickle cell versus normal children.* Paper presented at the Annual Meeting of the Association for Advancement of Behavior Therapy, Philadelphia, PA.

Lemanek, K. L., Williamson, D. A., Gresham, F. M., & Kelley, M. L. (1984, November). *Concurrence of medical and psychological problems in children with sickle cell anemia.* Paper presented at the Annual Meeting of the Association for Advancement of Behavior Therapy, Philadelphia, PA.

LePontois, J. (1975). Adolescents with sickle-cell anemia deal with life and death. *Social Work in Health Care, 1,* 71–80.

Leventhal, J. M. (1984). Psychosocial assessment of children with chronic physical disease. *Pediatric Clinics of North America, 31,* 71–86.

Levine, M. D., & Rappaport, L. A. (1984). Recurrent abdominal pain in school children: The loneliness of the long-distance physician. *Pediatric Clinics of North America, 31,* 969–991.

Liebman, W. M. (1978). Recurrent abdominal pain in children: A retrospective survey of 119 patients. *Clinical Pediatrics, 17,* 149–153.

Liebman, W. M. (1979). Recurrent abdominal pain in children: Lactose and sucrose intolerance, a prospective study. *Pediatrics, 64,* 43–45.

Londe, S., Bourgoignie, J. J., Robson, A. M., & Goldring, D. (1971). Hypertension in apparently normal children. *Journal of Pediatrics, 78,* 569–577.

Long, R. T., & Cope, O. (1961). Emotional problems of burned children. *New England Journal of Medicine, 264,* 1121–1127.

Lukens, J. N. (1981). Sickle cell disease. *Disease-A-Month, 27,* 1–67.

Magrab, P. R., & Calcagno, P. L. (1978). Psychological impact of chronic pediatric conditions. In P. R. Magrab (Ed.), *Psychological management of pediatric problems: Early life conditions and chronic diseases* (Vol. 1, pp. 3–14). Baltimore, MD: University Park Press.

Masek, B. J. (1982, March). *Behavioral medicine treatment of pediatric migraine.* Paper presented at the Annual Meeting of the Society of Behavioral Medicine, Chicago, IL.

Masek, B. J., Epstein, L. H., & Russo, D. C. (1981). Behavioral perspectives in preventive medicine. In S. M. Turner, K. S. Calhoun, & H. E. Adams (Eds.), *Handbook of clinical behavior therapy* (pp. 475–499). New York: Wiley.

Masek, B. J., Spirito, A., & Fentress, D. W. (1984). Behavioral treatment of symptoms of childhood illness. *Clinical Psychology Review, 4,* 561–570.

Matthews, K. A. (1977). Caregiver-child interactions and the Type—A coronary prone behavior patterns. *Child Development, 48,* 1752–1756.

Matthews, K. A. (1978). Assessment and developmental antecedents of the coronary-prone behavior pattern in children. In T. M. Dembroski, S. M. Weiss, J. L. Shields, S. G. Haynes, & M. Feinleib (Eds.), *Coronary-prone behavior* (pp. 207–217). New York: Springer.

Matthews, K. A., & Angulo, J. (1980). Measurement of the Type A behavior: Impatience, anger and aggression. *Child Development, 51,* 466–476.

Mattson, A. (1972). Long-term physical illness in childhood: A challenge to psychosocial adaptation. *Pediatrics, 50,* 801–811.

McAlister, A., Perry, C., & Maccoby, N. (1979). Adolescent smoking: Onset and prevention. *Pediatrics, 63,* 650–658.

McAlister, A., Perry, C. P., Killen, J. D., Telch, M., & Slinkard, L. A. (1980). Pilot study of smoking, alcohol, and drug abuse prevention. *American Journal of Public Health, 70,* 719–721.

McAnarney, E. R., Pless, I., Satterwhite, B., & Friedman,

S. B. (1974). Psychological problems of children with chronic juvenile arthritis. *Pediatrics, 53*, 523–528.

McFarlane, J. (1977). Sickle cell disorders. *American Journal of Nursing, 77*, 1948–1954.

McGrath, P. J., Goodman, J. T., Firestone, P., Shipman, R., & Peters, S. (1983). Recurrent abdominal pain: A psychogenic disorder. *Archives of Disease in Childhood, 58*, 888–890.

McInerny, T. (1984). The role of the general pediatrician in coordinating the care of children with chronic illness. *Pediatric Clinics of North America, 31*, 199–209.

McLeod, J. (1979). Educational underachievement: Toward a defensible psychometric definition. *Journal of Learning Disabilities, 12*, 42–50.

McNabb, W. L., Rodabaugh, B., Scamagas, P., & Hughes, G. W. (1983a). *Air Power. Management of asthma through group education* (Contract No. N01-HR-2974). Bethesda, MD: National Heart, Lung, and Blood Institute.

McNabb, W. L., Rodabaugh, B., Scamagas, P., & Hughes, G. W. (1983b). *Air wise. Self-management of asthma through individual education* (Contract No. N01-HR-2974). Bethesda, MD: National Heart, Lung, and Blood Institute.

Meijer, A. (1979). Maternal feelings towards asthmatic children. *Child Psychiatry and Human Development, 9*, 161–169.

Melamed, B. G., & Johnson, S. B. (1981). Chronic illness: Asthma and juvenile diabetes. In E. J. Mash & L. G. Terdal (Eds.), *Behavioral assessment of childhood disorders* (pp. 529–572). New York: Guilford Press.

Michener, W. M. (1981). An approach to recurrent abdominal pain in children. *Primary Care, 8*, 277–283.

Miklich, D. R. (1973). Operant conditioning procedures with systematic desensitization in a hyperkinetic asthmatic boy. *Journal of Behavior Therapy and Experimental Psychiatry, 4*, 177–182.

Miklich, D. R., Renne, C. M., Creer, T. L., Alexander, A. B., Chai, H., Davis, M. H., Hoffman, A., & Danker-Brown, P. (1977). The clinical utility of behavioral therapy as an adjunctive treatment for asthma. *Journal of Allergy and Clinical Immunology, 60*, 285–294.

Miller, A. J., & Kratochwill, T. R. (1979). Reduction of frequent stomach complaints by time out. *Behavior Therapy, 10*, 211–218.

Miller, W. C., Gardner, N., & Mlott, S. R. (1976). Psychosocial support in the treatment of severely burned patients. *Journal of Trauma, 16*, 722–725.

Mobbs, J. 1970). Childhood obesity. *International Journal of Nursing Studies, 7*, 3–18.

Moore, K., & Altmaier, E. M. (1981, October). Stress inoculation training with cancer patients. *Cancer Nursing*, pp. 389–393.

Morrow, G. R. (1984). The assessment of nausea and vomiting: Past problems, current issues, and suggestions for future research. *Cancer, 53*, 2267–2278.

Morrow, G. R., & Morrell, C. (1982). Behavioral treatment for the anticipatory nausea and vomiting induced by cancer chemotherapy. *New England Journal of Medicine, 307*, 1476–1480.

Moss, R. A., Jennings, G., McFarland, J. H., & Carter, P. (1984). Binge eating, vomiting, and weight fear in a female high school population. *The Journal of Family Practice, 18*, 313, 316, 319–320.

Mostofsky, D. I., & Balaschak, B. A. (1977). Psychobiological control of seizures. *Psychological Bulletin, 84*, 723–750.

Murray, D., Johnson, C. A., Luepker, R., Pechacek, R., Jacobs, D., & Hurd, P. (1979, August). *Social factors in the prevention of smoking in seventh grade students.* Paper presented at the meeting of the American Psychological Association, New York.

Neisworth, J. T., & Moore, F. (1972). Operant treatment of asthmatic responding with the parent as therapist. *Behavior Therapist, 3*, 95–99.

Norrish, M., Tooley, M., & Godfrey, S. (1977). Clinical, physiological, and psychological study of asthmatic children attending a hospital clinic. *Archives of Diseases in Children, 52*, 912–917.

Olness, K., & MacDonald, J. (1981). Self-hypnosis and biofeedback in the management of juvenile migraine. *Developmental and Behavioral Pediatrics, 21*, 168–170.

Oster, J. (1972). Recurrent abdominal pain, headache and limb pains in children and adolescents. *Pediatrics, 50*, 429–436.

Ott, J. S., Webb, T. E., Anderson, C. A., Kastelic, J. E., & Krill, C. E., Jr. (1982). Childhood cancer and vulnerability for significant academic underachievement. *Journal of Learning Disabilities, 15*, 363–364.

Parcel, G. S., & Nader, P. R. (1977). Evaluation of a pilot school health education program for asthmatic children. *Journal of School Health, 47*, 453–456.

Parcel, G. S., Nader, P. R., & Meyer, M. P. (1977). Adolescent health concerns, problems and patterns of utilization in a triethnic urban population. *Pediatrics, 60*, 157–164.

Pavlovsky, S., Castano, J., Leiguarda, R., Fisman, N., Chamoles, N., Moreno, R., & Arizaga, R. (1983). Neuropsychological study in patients with ALL: Two different CNS prevention therapies—Cranial irradiation plus IT methotrexate vs. IT methotrexate alone. *American Journal of Pediatric Hematology/Oncology, 5*, 79–86.

Pearlman, D. S. (1984). Bronchial asthma: A perspective from childhood to adulthood. *American Journal of Diseases in Children, 138*, 459–466.

Perry, C., Killen, J., Telch, M., Slinkard, L., & Danaher, B. G. (1980). Modifying smoking behavior of teenagers: A school-based intervention. *American Journal of Public Health, 70*, 722–725.

Pfefferbaum, B. (1979). Pediatric oncology: A review of the changing psychological aspects. *International Journal of Psychiatry in Medicine, 9*, 289–296.

Pless, I. B. (1984). Clinical assessment: Physical and psychological functioning. *Pediatric Clinics of North America, 31*, 33–45.

Pless, I. B., & Douglas, M. B. (1971). Chronic illness in

childhood: Part I. Epidemiological and clinical characteristics. *Pediatrics, 47,* 405–414.

Prunty, O. (1975). Rehabilitation of the sickle cell anemia patient: A new program. *Rehabilitation Literature, 36,* 179–181.

Purcell, K., & Weiss, J. H. (1970). Asthma. In C. C. Costello (Ed.), *Symptoms of psychopathology* (pp. 597–623). New York: Wiley.

Purcell, K., Muser, J., Miklich, D., & Dietiker, K. E. (1969). A comparison of psychologic findings in variously defined asthmatic subgroups. *Journal of Psychosomatic Research, 13,* 67–75.

Purcell, K., Weiss, J., & Hahn, W. (1972). Certain psychosomatic disorders. In B. B. Wolman (Ed.), *Manual of child psychopathology* (pp. 706–740). New York: McGraw-Hill.

Ramsden, R., Friedman, B., & Williamson, D. (1983). Treatment of childhood headache reports with contingency management procedures. *Journal of Clinical Child Psychology, 12,* 202–206.

Rapoff, M. A., Lindsley, C. B., & Christopherson, E. R. (1984). Improving compliance with Juvenile Rheumatoid Arthritis. *Archives of Physical Medicine and Rehabilitation, 65,* 267–269.

Redd, W. H., & Andrykowski, M. A. (1982). Behavioral intervention in cancer treatment: Controlling aversion reactions to chemotherapy. *Journal of Consulting and Clinical Psychology, 50,* 1018–1079.

Reed, C. E., & Townley, R. G. (1978). Asthma: Classification and pathogenesis. In E. Middleton, Jr., C. E. Reed, & E. F. Ellis (Eds.), *Allergy: Principles and practice* (pp. 659–677). St. Louis, MO: Mosby.

Renne, C. M., & Creer, T. L. (1976). The effects of training on the use of inhalation therapy equipment by children with asthma. *Journal of Applied Behavior Analysis, 9,* 1–11.

Rosen, J. C., & Leitenberg, H. (1982). Bulimia nervosa: Treatment with exposure and response prevention. *Behavior Therapy, 13,* 117–124.

Rosenman, R., Brand, R. J., Sholtz, R. I., & Friedman, M. (1976). Multivariate prediction of coronary heart disease during 8.5 year follow-up in the Western Collaborative Group study. *American Journal of Cardiology, 37,* 902–910.

Ross, D. M., & Ross, S. A. (1985). Pain instruction with third- and fourth-grade children. A pilot study. *Journal of Pediatric Psychology, 10,* 55–63.

Rubin, L. S., Barbero, G. J., & Sabinga, M. A. (1967). Papillary reactivity in children with recurrent abdominal pain. *Psychosomatic Medicine, 29,* 111–120.

Russo, D. C., & Varni, J. W. (1982). Behavioral pediatrics. In D. C. Russo & J. W. Varni (Eds.), *Behavioral pediatrics: Research and practice* (pp. 3–24). New York: Plenum Press.

Sands, H. (1982). *Epilepsy: A handbook for the mental health professional.* New York: Brunner/Mazel.

Sank, L. I., & Biglan, A. (1974). Operant treatment of a case of recurrent abdominal pain in a 10-year-old boy. *Behavior Therapy, 5,* 677–681.

Schafer, L. C., Glasgow, R. E., & McCaul, K. D. (1982). Increasing the adherence of diabetic adolescents. *Journal of Behavioral Medicine, 5,* 353–362.

Scherr, M. S., Crawford, P. L., Sergent, C. B., & Scherr, C. A. (1975). Effect of biofeedback techniques on chronic asthma in a summer camp environment. *Annals of Allergy, 35,* 289–295.

Schlundt, D. G., Johnson, W. G., & Jarrell, M. P. (1985). A naturalistic functional analysis of eating behavior in bulimia and obesity. *Advances in Behavior Research and Therapy, 7,* 149–162.

Schroeder, C. S., Teplin, S., & Schroeder, S. R. (1982). An overview of common medical problems encountered in schools. In C. R. Reynolds & T. B. Gutkin (Eds.), *The handbook of school psychology* (pp. 971–1008). New York: Wiley.

Shapiro, D., & Goldstein, I. B. (1982). Biobehavioral perspectives on hypertension. *Journal of Consulting and Clinical Psychology, 50,* 841–858.

Shepard, J., & Hochstadt, N. J. (1978, April). *Reducing hospitalization in children with asthma.* Paper presented to the Western Psychological Association, San Francisco, CA.

Shinnar, S., & D'Souza, B. U. (1981). The diagnosis and management of headaches in childhood. *Pediatric Clinics of North America, 29,* 79–94.

Shires, G. T. (1979). *Care of the trauma patient.* New York: McGraw-Hill.

Silber, T. (1984). Anorexia nervosa: Morbidity and mortality. *Pediatric Annals, 13,* 851, 855–856, 858–859.

Smith, M. C., & Thelen, M. H. (1984). Development and validity of a test for bulimia. *Journal of Consulting and Clinical Psychology, 52,* 863–872.

Spiga, R., & Peterson, A. C. (1981). *The coronary-prone behavior pattern in early adolescence.* Paper presented at the meeting of the American Educational Research Association, Los Angeles, CA.

Steiner, H., & Clark, W. R. (1977). Psychiatric complications of burned adults: A classification. *Journal of Trauma, 17,* 134–143.

Steinhausen, H. C. H. (1981). Chronically ill and handicapped children and adolescents: Personality studies in relation to disease. *Journal of Abnormal Child Psychiatry, 9,* 291–297.

Stone, R. T., & Barbero, G. J. (1970). Recurrent abdominal pain in childhood. *Pediatrics, 45,* 732–738.

Straw, M. K. (1983). Coping with obesity. In T. G. Burish & L. A. Bradley (Eds.), *Coping with chronic disease: Research and applications* (pp. 219–258). New York: Academic Press.

Tal, A., & Miklich, D. R. (1976). Emotionally induced decreases in pulmonary flow rates in asthmatic children. *Psychosomatic Medicine, 38,* 190–199.

Tamaroff, M., Miller, D. R., Murphy, M. L., Salwen, R., Ghavimi, F., & Nir, Y. (1982). Immediate and long-term posttherapy neuropsychologic performance in children with acute lymphoblastic leukemia treated without central nervous system radiation. *Journal of Pediatrics, 101,* 524–529.

Task Force on Blood Pressure Control Report. (1977). *Pediatrics, 59,* 797–820.

Tavormina, J., Kastner, L. S., Slater, P. M., & Watt, S. L. (1976). Chronically ill children: A psychologically and emotionally deviant population? *Journal of Abnormal Child Psychology, 4,* 99–110.

Tetrault, S. M., & Scott, R. B. (1974). Recreation and hobbies as developmental supports for a child with sickle cell anemia. *Clinical Pediatrics, 13,* 496–497.

Thompson, J. A. (1980). Diagnosis and treatment of headache in the pediatric patient. *Current Problems in Pediatric, 10,* 1–52.

Vahlquist, B. O., & Hackzell, G. (1949). Migraine of early onset. *Acta Pediatrica, 38,* 622–636.

Vance, V. J., & Taylor, W. F. (1971). Status and trends in residential asthma homes in the United States. *Annals of Allergy, 29,* 428–437.

Varni, J. W. (1983). *Clinical behavioral pediatrics: An interdisciplinary biobehavioral approach.* New York: Pergamon Press.

Varni, J. W., Bessman, C. A., Russo, D. C., & Cataldo, M. E. (1980). Behavioral management of chronic pain in children: A case study. *Archives of Physical Medicine and Rehabilitation, 61,* 375–379.

Vavasseur, J. (1977). A comprehensive program for meeting psychosocial needs of sickle cell anemia patients. *Journal of the National Medical Association, 69,* 335–339.

Voors, A. W., Webber, L. S., & Berenson, G. S. (1978). Epidemiology of essential hypertension in youth: Implications for clinical practice. *Pediatric Clinics of North America, 25,* 15–27.

Voors, A. W., Foster, T. A., Frerichs, R. R., Webber, L. S., & Berenson, G. S. (1976). Studies of blood pressure in children ages 5–14 in a total biracial community: The Bogalusa Heart Study. *Circulation, 54,* 319–327.

Wagner, M. M., Wolpin, S., & Forrest, R. F. (1981). An interdisciplinary approach to the care of the burn-injuried patient. In M. M. Wagner (Ed.), *Care of the burn-injuried patient: A multidisciplinary involvement* (pp. 259–288). Littleton, MA: PSG.

Wakeman, R. J., & Kaplan, J. Z. (1978). An experimental study of hypnosis in painful burns. *American Journal of Clinical Hypnosis, 21,* 3–12.

Walker, D. K. (1984). Care of chronically ill children in schools. *Pediatric Clinics of North America, 31,* 221–233.

Walker, D. K., & Gortmaker, S. L. (1983). *Final report: Community child health studies* (Grant MC-R-250-437). Springfield, VA: National Technical Information Service.

Waxman, M., & Stunkard, A. J. (1980). Caloric intake and expenditure of obese boys. *Journal of Pediatrics, 96,* 187–193.

Weinstein, D. L. (1976). Imagery and relaxation with a burn patient. *Behaviour Research and Therapy, 14,* 481.

West, D. A., & Shuck, J. M. (1978). Emotional problems of the severely burned patient. *Surgical Clinics of North America, 58,* 1189–1204.

Westervelt, V. D., Brantley, J., & Ware, W. (1983). Changing children's attitudes toward physically handicapped peers: Effects of a film and teacher-led discussion. *Journal of Pediatric Psychology, 8,* 327–343.

Whitten, C. F., & Fischhoff, J. (1974). Psychosocial effects of sickle cell disease. *Archives of Internal Medicine, 133,* 681–689.

Williams, C. L., Carter, B. J., Arnold, C. B., & Wynder, E. L. (1979). Chronic disease risk factors among children: The "Know Your Body" study. *Journal of Chronic Diseases, 32,* 505–513.

Williamson, D. A. (1981). Behavioral treatment of migraine and muscular contraction headaches: Outcome and theoretical explanations. In M. Hersen, R. M. Eisler, & P. M. Miller (Eds.), *Progress in behavior modification* (Vol. 11, pp. 163–201). New York: Academic Press.

Williamson, D. A., Labbe, E. E., & Granberry, S. W. (1983). Outpatient treatment of somatic disorders in adults. In M. Hersen (Ed.), *Outpatient behavior therapy: A clinical guide* (pp. 109–141). New York: Grune & Stratton.

Williamson, D. A., Ruggiero, L., & Davis, C. J. (1985). Headache. In M. Hersen & A. S. Bellack (Eds.), *Handbook of clinical behavior therapy with adults* (pp. 417–445). New York: Plenum Press.

Yarbrough, D. R. (1981). Pathophysiology of the burn wound. In M. M. Wagner (Ed.), *Care of the burn-injuried patient: A multidisciplinary involvement* (pp. 19–31). Littleton, MA: PSG.

Zeltzer, L., Dash, J., & Holland, J. P. (1979). Hypnotically induced pain control in sickle cell anemia. *Pediatrics, 64,* 533–536.

Zeltzer, L., Kellerman, J., Ellenberg, L., Dash, J., & Rigler, D. (1980). Psychological effects of illness in adolescence. II. Impact of illness in adolescents - crucial issues and coping styles. *Journal of Pediatrics, 97,* 132–138.

Zeltzer, L., LeBaron, S., & Zeltzer, P. M. (1984). The effectiveness of behavioral intervention for reduction of nausea and vomiting in children and adolescents receiving chemotherapy. *Journal of Clinical Oncology, 2,* 683–690.

Zide, B., & Pardoe, R. (1976). The use of behavior modification therapy in a recalcitrant burned child. *Plastic and Reconstructive Surgery, 57,* 378–382.

Zinner, S. H., Levy, P. S., & Kass, E. H. (1971). Familial aggregation of blood pressure in childhood. *New England Journal of Medicine, 284,* 401–404.

PART VI

The Future of Behavior Therapy in Education

What will the future bring for behavior therapy applied in an educational context? If we can use given facts as signs of things to come, then we can predict that behavior therapy will be applied to an ever-expanding array of increasingly more complex problems. In this final section, we conclude the text with two thought-provoking and insightful contributions. In Chapter 30, Greene and Watson-Perczel address the issue of how to utilize behavior analysis to have an impact on our future through educational reform. Chapter 31, the final chapter, comprises Baer's incisive analysis of the school as an organization with implications for the future of behavior therapy in education.

CHAPTER 30

Behavioral Reform of Education

A Venture at Risk

Brandon F. Greene and Edward J. Watson-Perczel

Book chapters usually provide the occasion to review the scope of applied research pertaining to behavioral interventions in the school system. However, this chapter was written in the wake of a spate of nationally commissioned reports that have been critical of public education and, conincidentally, at a time when there are perhaps as many, if not more applied behavioral studies in education as there are in any other area of human service. Therefore, this chapter provides an opportunity to consider the impact behavior analysis has had on public education and to offer some proposals for new intiatives that the field may need to pursue if it is to effect subtantial and sustained improvements in American education.

Perhaps one of the greatest frustrations shared by behavior analysts and other reformers of education is that some of the most useful innovations developed from years of behavioral research have not been assimilated into routine educational practice. One wonders how much different public education in this country would be if it had incorporated innovations reported in the behavioral literature as much as 10 years ago.

The question is worth asking because the National Commission on Excellence in Education has issued a report (1983) concerning issues familiar to behavior analysis: achievement test scores have declined whereas remedial costs have risen; illiteracy is commonplace but proficiency in science is rare; and the ability of teachers to perform their duties has never been more questionable. Moreover, the social and economic costs of these maladies is exacerbated by the fact that they have emerged at a time of enormous need for basic human competence among the general citizenry and specialized technical abilities among various professions.

Some behavioral educators who read this report will be angered, saddened, embarrassed, or humiliated by the fact that its findings and recommendations were conspicuously untouched by the results and implications of two decades of applied behavioral research. While reading the report we found ourselves repeatedly asking, "Haven't

Brandon F. Greene and Edward J. Watson-Perczel • Behavior Analysis and Therapy Program, Southern Illinois University, Carbondale, Illinois 62901.

they heard of ____ " (fill the blank with the behavioral educational innovation of your choice).

It is regrettable that the Commission seems not to have become familiar with behavior approaches to educational problems. Nevertheless, it should now be clear that all hopes to the contrary (e.g., Sulzer-Azaroff, 1985), the next commission's report will not offer any better news or hint of reform if behaviorists do not expand on their present mode of intervention in the educational system.

Nothing that we are about to propose should be construed to suggest that behavioral educators are to blame for the maligned condition of this country's educational system. The efforts of many (most notably the Follow Through participants) have been supererogatory. However, we submit that it would be irresponsible for us to lament the present predicament in education if, after having seen it clearly, we do not begin to make delibrate changes in our efforts to improve it.

Therefore, this chapter will not be an occasion to celebrate recent innovative behavioral research nor to critique the subtleties of its methodological flaws. Rather, this chapter will describe the kinds of activities, in addition to current research efforts, that we believe are necessary to overcome or reform some of the recalcitrant problems in education. Furthermore, although many of these activities would bring us into the arenas of law, politics, and consumer action, the entire adventure should be every bit as behavioral as the Good Behavior Game.

Assumptions regarding the Conditions Necessary to Effect Permanent Behavioral Change in Education

Our proposals for promoting reform of education reflect certain assumptions about the conditions we believe are required to affect change. Therefore, to understand these proposals it may be useful first to state these assumptions explicitly:

1. Reform (i.e., adoption of behavioral innovations) will not be initiated without a sustained source of negative reinforcement impinging on every level of the educational system where important policies and practices are formed. We note this assumption is consistent with Hamerlynck's earlier observations (1980, 1984) that human service agencies, like all political entities, respond to pain or pressure. We agree, and without wishing to offend the good sensibilities of colleagues who prefer softer options, we suggest that this pain must pervade all levels of the educational system including state and federal government, colleges of education, school districts, principals, and classroom teachers. A corollary of this assumption may be stated: the amount of negative reinforcement that must be applied at each level to effect change is inversely correlated with the distance at which that level operates vis-à-vis the consumer (i.e., the student). Thus, a much greater effort must be mounted to shape the behavior of state legislators and the departments of state education than is required to arouse the classroom teacher.

2. The application of pain or pressure must be sustained and uninterrupted. Responses that are not functional to reform should provide neither escape nor avoidance. This statement of basic principle hardly requires elaboration. The point is that pressure bearing on the system should not diminish contingent on feints, balks, pretenses, or merely going through the motions of reform. However, because such responses are expedient and often instrumental to gaining escape, they should be anticipated and reacted to accordingly.

3. A sustained source of negative reinforcement can only emanate from a well-organized source or network of sources. Diverse or unrelated interest groups may occasionaly act cooperatively, or at least concurrently, to press the system toward some semblance of reform.

However, vigilance is more easily sustained by organizations with the singular and explicit mission to reform the system. Merely relying on the strange bedfellows of politics to undertake reform will only produce disappointment. In short, reform-minded efforts must be institutionalized, that is, made a permanent fixture of the political system.

4. Once mobilized, policymakers are most likely to escape or avoid pain by selecting an option that is close at hand. Decision makers typically are not experts at reforming education nor are they necessarily equipped to embark on a critical review of research to select the most effective option. Rather, to escape pain, they must rely on the advice (possibly glib) of experts who are immediately available to them. The quality of the advice may be questionable but that should not detract from the observation that decision making is a social process that can occur readily without the benefit of empirical data. However, because behavior analysts are adamant empiricists we have been slow to appreciate the simple fact that data do not make decisions, people make decisions. In the vernacular, "It ain't what you know, it's who you know." This is not a cynical statement about politics. Rather, it simply is offered to focus attention on relevant contingencies surrounding the decision-making process.

5. An option for reform that appears too simple or simplistic will not be recognized as viable by decision makers. Systemic problems usually require systemic reform; viable options must at least appear to offer such reform. Therefore, one can not hope to persuade the decision maker with glib testimony that the problems of education will be solved by experimental analysis of behavior, or by adoption of behavioral techniques, or by application of learning principles. Such assertions offer no concrete options with distinctive features that decision makers can appreciate. Accordingly, we must be prepared to offer tangible systems representing a synthesis or combination of interrelated behavioral programs. For example, to propose to reduce illiteracy through the application of behavioral principles is sophmoric. On the other hand, it would be legitimate to propose the use of a system of direct instruction involving numerous components whose operations require specific responsibilities of the teacher, the principal, the school district, and so on. Furthermore, we suggest that decision makers will find most attractive those systems requiring visible changes in the behavior of key parties ranking just below them. Therefore, whereas the behavior of the learner may be the bottom line to most behavior analysts, it is not always the line that guides and reinforces certain decisions. If this assumption is correct, it accounts for much of why so many behavioral innovations have gathered dust on shelves.

6. Behavioral reforms that are adopted will not be sustained by the system as it currently exists unless accompanied by ongoing social and technical support and the continuing presence of the aforementioned sources of negative reinforcement. This assumption recognizes that, in general, behavioral reforms tend to promote accountability at all levels of the system through ongoing performance monitoring/evaluation. It further recognizes that there will be an inevitable tendency to escape or avoid accountable systems even if they provide ample positive reinforcement. That is, there always will be attempts to pervert or circumvent the system by obtaining its benefits while escaping its response requirements. Thus, escape/avoidance behaviors will assume various subtle and not so subtle forms that include discrediting the reform, discounting its benefits, questioning its values, distorting its procedures, or abandoning it altogether (Carnine, 1984). In short, the system, if left alone, will drift toward entropy. Therefore, adopting the reform is only the beginning. Its maintenance and its ability to accomodate additional improvements will at least require the same infrastructure that led to its adoption in the first place.

An Infrastructure to Promote and Support Behavioral Reform of Educational Practices

Our proposals for promoting a behavioral reform of education are outlined in subsequent sections. Although they are based on the preceding assumptions, they are not necessarily the only proposals consistent with these assumptions.

In some cases, our proposals may seem a bit far-fetched, perhaps grandiose. We do not apologize for this but simply take it as evidence of the fact that we can hope to accomplish very little without broadening our current set of professional practices. Moreover, as mentioned, we believe these proposals to be eminently behavioral although they may involve more elaborate and somewhat unfamiliar mechanisms or arrangements to overcome the complex and multiple misplaced contingencies that riddle all levels of the present educational system.

Synthesizing Techniques into Technological Systems

A popular topic of discussion in applied behavioral circles these days is dissemination or diffusion. For example, we often speak of the need to "disseminate our research findings" or to promote the "diffusion of behavioral technologies." It is unfortunate that most of us probably nod affirmatively on hearing such statements, considering that they are remarkably imprecise and vague.

The problem begins with the term *disseminate,* which suggests a passive undertaking—a casual scattering of seed. Such terms mislead us about the kind of aggressive effort required to unroot some thoroughly entrenched cultural practices in education. The fact is that not just any dissemination activity should be expected to change current practices.

The term *technology* is also misleading. When we propose to disseminate a behavioral technology, we convey the impression that there exists a specific system of hardware and software for producing educated students much the same way that Japanese technology produces consistently reliable automobiles. In fact, no such ready-to-use technology for all of education exists; nor do the collection of techniques described on the pages of JABA a consumable technology make.

Most behavioral techniques simply are not particularly marketable in their present form. They require synthesis into comprehensive programs or systems designed to attain major educational objectives. For example, techniques such as the pacing of instruction (Carnine, 1976), response signalling (Carnine & Fink, 1978), and the use of reinforcement (Fink & Carnine, 1975) are not marketable programs. What is marketable, however, is a system of direct instruction that combines all of these techniques and specifies how they are to be operationalized for particular educational purposes (Becker, 1978).

Despite a formidable history of behavioral research in education, there has been relatively little systematizing or synthesizing of behavioral procedures into comprehensive programs. This shortcoming partly results from the fact that reinforcement for many behavioral researchers is contingent on their experimental analysis of procedures and the publication of results in esoteric journals. Reinforcers for synthesizing these procedures into programs and forcefully marketing them in the educational system have been more remote and less certain. Therefore, it is worthwhile to consider some possibilities for encouraging a broader range of professional activities that will lead to the reform of educational practices.

A Journal of Applied Behavior Synthesis

Because many behavioral researchers are affiliated with universities, they are expected to publish experimental findings in professional journals. Experimentation typically involves an analysis in which certain limited facets of instructional procedure are splintered or isolated for detailed examination of their effects. The broader social purpose served in all of this is that in breaking things down presumably we may build them back together in more effective ways. However, publication rarely requires (i.e., reinforces) the eventual reconstruction or synthesis of procedures into complete instructional programs.

Accordingly, one way to promote greater synthesis of effective behavioral systems may be to provide distinctive and prestigious publication outlets for their display and for description of the unique experimental process involved in their creation. Such a forum might be the *Journal of Applied Behavior Synthesis.* JABS could publish descriptions and results of effective and comprehensive educational systems that consist of numerous behavioral components (e.g., effective instructional programs, teacher training programs). The character of JABS might best be portrayed by considering some possible dimensions of an applied behavioral synthesis (apologies to Baer, Wolf, & Risley, 1968).

A *synthesis* is achieved when it is demonstrated that several behavioral procedures, when implemented in combination, produce greater or more sustained effects than those that have been produced by any one of the procedures. Thus, a synthesis may involve combining several instructional techniques of a reading program (e.g., enhancing the discriminability of graphemes, pacing the presentation of instructional tasks, signalling responses, etc.) into an instructional system with larger effects on the learner than any single technique can produce.

Alternatively, a synthesis may be achieved by interlocking one fairly complete system with another to insure maintenance of the benefits of either or both. For example, an instructional program for teaching reading may be integrated with a system for supervising reading teachers. Thus, the desired effects of reading instruction, which previously may have been achieved only with the elaborate support researchers provide when attempting to produce an experimental demonstration, can now be produced and sustained on the basis of standard operating procedure.

The authors recognize the proposal for greater synthesis is not in keeping with the generally accepted recommendations for providing component analyses (e.g., more detailed study) of existing behavioral procedures. However, we believe that synthesis should be at least as important as component analysis and that the latter is already generously accomodated by current publication outlets.

A *marketable system* is one with components interlocked in such a way that the behavior of one participant in the system provides reinforcement for other participants. Thus, the behavior (and progress) of the learners must be made sufficiently salient or conspicuous for it to function as a reinforcer for the teacher's effort. In turn, the system must arrange for the results of the teacher to be analyzed, aggregated, and presented in a way that allows principals and school districts to achieve recognition. Finally, the system must be capable of generating cost-effectiveness information that policymakers can use as a basis for promoting the system and justifying their selection of it.

There are other aspects to marketing a system. It is usually necessary, for example, to prepare a presentation (using various media) especially tailored for a particular audience. Thus, a presentation may be prepared for state legislators and superintendents that highlights the fact that the system benefits all students equitably, that it is cost-effective, and that it generates evaluative information about itself on a regular and timely basis. The promotional material for teachers, however, would emphasize the system's ease of implementation, its high probability of success, the array of support services that accompany it, and the fact that it produces information that highlights desirable and achievable teaching outcomes.

Educational programs that produce a .25 standard deviation improvement on achievement tests among the lowest performing students have traditionally been considered effective. However, as a general rule JABS would expect behavioral reforms to produce a gain closer to 1 standard deviation throughout a school district. The magnitude and the breadth of the benefit are important. A system that achieves large gains only with a limited number of students may be promising but it has not yet demonstrated educational effectiveness. The problems of education are pervasive and although their solutions must be developed initially on a small scale (e.g., with a few students), their ultimate test of effectivness must be based on a broader application (e.g., across several districts).

Research Consortiums

Applied behavioral research, as we are accustomed to seeing it, will continue to be essential. However, its impact is likely to be greater and more immediate if it considers a broader range of topics. For example, applied behavioral research in education may command greater attention if it focuses, in part, on nationally visible issues, such as minimum competency exams for students and teachers, vouchers for parents to use to purchase educational alternatives of their choice, merit raises, master teacher plans, and other incentives to promote teaching excellence.

Such issues are not provincial. If their study is to be thorough, with findings intended for national impact, then considerable collaboration will be required among professionals in many different states. Accordingly, consortiums of behavior analysts from various parts of the country could be established. Such consortiums could draw from a wider data base, would have more opportunity to identify model practices and, when occasions arise to offer recommendations on educational practices, will have greater credibilty.

In addition to the aforementioned issues in education, there are many other questions suitable for a consortium of behavioral researchers to raise. For example, what educational benefits have been achieved in states where school districts have specified educational goals and objectives at each grade level? Which states have procedures for screening nonvalidated instructional programs from use in schools? Does this screening program work as intended or has it been perverted as has been the case in Florida (Greene, 1981)? What impact have teacher competency programs had on student achievement or on colleges of education? Which colleges of education deserve national attention for their success at producing competent teachers? Which deserve attention for their notorious failure?

The skeleton of research consortiums may already exist. For example, special interest groups affiliated with professional associations provide the beginnings of such a consortium. Similarly, consortiums may be organized from the ranks of members affiliated with such groups as the Association for Direct Instruction.

Political Initiatives, Litigation, and Consumer Action

Associations of Behavioral Educators

The state is a particularly critical level of government at which educational policy is established. Therefore, it is important for behavioral educators to acquire visibility and influence at this level. One means for doing so may be by organizing state associations of behavioral educators. Such associations can sponsor conferences and other forums to provide behavioral researchers with opportunities to exert influence on decision makers, school personnel, and advocates. More ambitious associations could also develop lobbying efforts and similarly aggressive tactics to influence state legislation.

Behavior analysts in some states have already begun to reap the benefits of having their own state association. In some cases, such as the Florida Association of Behavior Analysis and the Behavior Analysis Society of Illinois, sponsorship and participation regularly involve officials in state government.

These associations provide a forum for behavior analysts to begin exercising some influence on certain human service agencies, particularly, in the case of these two state associations, agencies concerned with the care of developmentally disabled individuals. However, similar associations could operate to influence the state educational system.

A National Bureau of Behavioral/Educational Standards

There are some important similarities between behavioral science and natural science. For instance, innovations in each depend on the capacity to measure phenomena of interest and thereby to predict with greater precision the behavior of the phenomena under a variety of environmental conditions. The capacity for such measurement and prediction provides various fields of science and engineering with a basis for establishing standards, that is, accepted practices for producing and measuring phenomena. The acceptance of these standards worldwide provides an essential degree of consistency or uniformity in operating procedure from one laboratory to the next. Without such standards, scientists and engineers would not have a common basis for describing procedures and for replicating results across different laboratories. In short, without these standards there would be chaos.

Before common standards can be accepted, however, there must be an authoritative source responsible for specifying what these standards should be. This source must represent the state of the art in terms of its capability for precisely measuring and producing phenomena of interest. The authoritative source for the hard sciences (physics, chemistry, etc.) is the National Bureau of Standards (NBS). The NBS is the world's depository for standards related to measurement, testing, and various technical procedures. Its standards are often transmitted to the various fields of engineering through professional associations that represent these specialized fields (e.g., the American Gas Association; the Institute of Electrical and Electronic Engineers). These associations either adopt these standards or approximations to them so that any line of products (e.g., fire retardant insulation) offered by different manufacturers will achieve a degree of uniform quality. No other institution has done more than the NBS for insuring consistent and predictable quality in the products of physical science and engineering.

Unfortunately, no comparable institution exists for the behavioral sciences, including education. However, if such an institution did exist it could establish:

1. Standards for measuring educational achievement (which are somewhat accepted already)
2. Standards for optimal classroom design and instructional procedure
3. Standards regarding what educational outcomes can be expected given that standard operating procedure is followed
4. A basis for recalibrating or adjusting the classroom environment when results fall short of expected outcome

In short, like the NBS, a National Bureau of Behavioral Standards (NBBS) would specify the limits of what is technically possible to achieve under standard operating procedure with different grade levels of children from different backgrounds. Classrooms in the field would then calibrate their instructional procedures for these children according to the standards of the NBBS. Departure from these operating standards or from expected instructional outcomes would indicate the need for recalibration until the anticipated outcomes (e.g., literacy) are attained.

If the proposal has merit it would not necessarily require that the federal government establish a National Bureau of Standards in Behavioral Science (or Education). Rather, the same function could be credibly performed by a trade or professional association (perhaps a federation of the aforementioned state associations) that would establish itself for that purpose and gradually acquire credibility much the way that the Underwriters Laboratory and the American National Standards Institute have done. Something of this idea is reflected in the services provided by the National Teaching Family Association, which certifies (or decertifies) Achievement-Place homes based on calibration checks, that is, the degree to which the homes operate according to the standards of the Teaching-Family model (Kirigin, 1984). A similar function is performed, although less precisely, by the Commission for the Accreditation of Rehabilitation Facitilites and other organizations in human services.

In education there is sufficient evidence from Project Follow Through (Becker, 1978) to establish standards that would simply reject illiteracy rates of 15% among any segment of the poulation. Bold advances can be made in education by an authoritative source that is willing to dispute the present system's foregone conclusion that the tail end of every normal distribution necessarily represents incompetence in the skill under assessment.

Obviously, the functions of NBBS would be more readily fulfilled with the cooperation of school systems. Nevertheless, some quality control tests can be generated regardless of cooperation. That is, the NBBS might take it upon itself to publish data that are typically available in most school districts. This itself might motivate improvements in the system.

Finally, like the NBS, a NBBS would have divisions of specialty. Thus, there may be divisions for special education programs, programs for the gifted, and so forth.

Litigation

It is our assumption that substantial change in education will require the presence of pain or pressure on the system. Such pressure may require political or legal action and advocacy, as well as continued involvement of reform-minded professionals in the mainstream of the educational system. Other areas of human service have been changed by such pressure and it may be useful to consider their experiences as case studies.

For example, systems for providing care and treatment of mentally retarded individuals in this country have been shaped considerably by litigation and legislative action. Reform was by no means painless and much of it occurred despite enormous inertia and resistance from within the system. In fact, because of this resistance, substantive breakthroughs required the involvement of federal courts in some sweeping class action suits.

Reform is not complete but there have been some radical changes. Furthermore, whereas some may question the value of the changes that have occurred, there is no serious argument that these changes would have transpired without judicial and legislative action.

Litigation is no stranger to the school system, as can be seen in the areas of desegregation (*Brown v. Board of Education*, 1954) and the right of mentally retarded children to a public education (*Mills v. Board of Education*, 1972). However, in those cases it was clear that either no education or segregated alternatives had set a class apart; but what of the thousands of children who pass through the mainstream of the classroom only to graduate as illiterates? The difficulty seems to be that their situation is sufficiently common that courts have been reluctant to recognize the culpability of the school system. For example, in the case of *Peter W v. San Francisco Unified School District* (1976), the plaintiff was illiterate upon graduation even though he passed through the mainstream of the education system with no reports of any problems. In fact, intermittent inquiries made by Peter W.'s mother were met with assurances from the school system that he was performing at grade level and was not in need of a remedial program.

Peter's mother brought suit alleging negligence. Defendants responded that there was insufficient knowledge and understanding of the variables influencing learning and therefore it would be impossible to hold the defendant accountable for Peter's illiteracy. Moreover, they suggested that a ruling in favor of the plaintiffs would leave the school system vulnerable to a wave of litigation. The court ruled in favor of the defendants. Other individual law suits alleging negligence and malpractice have met with the same fate (Morucci, 1982).

However, suits brought by individual parties cannot begin to gain the attention or achieve the impact of a class action suit. Moreover, there may be a basis for a class action suit in that a large class is affected by the educational system's failure to make them literate when it can be demonstrated that a much higher literacy rate among disadvantaged, low income children is achievable (Becker, 1978). In particular, the argument can be made that most of those children scoring in the lower 10th to 20th percentile on reading achievement tests could have been taught to read (or at least the illiterate percentage could have been drastically reduced). Imagine the possibility of augmenting that argument in court with evidence from school districts where illiteracy had been overcome, by expert testimony of the proposed state organizations, and by the standards of the NBBS.

We admit that at times we are pessimistic about the realistic chances that a class action suit can be won on the basis that learning failures are really teaching failures. It is at those times that we pinch ourselves to remember how absurd it is that our entire culture has simply resigned itself to accepting (even expecting) gross mediocrity and failure in the educational system. In no other profession—medicine, law, accounting—would such behavior escape prosecution. We also remember that whereas the successes at litigating on behalf of retarded citizens are now taken for granted, there was a time when such success also seemed far-fetched (Rothman & Rothman, 1985).

Finally, we suggest that although such a case, whether won in favor of a right to literacy or not, would have potential benefits. A massive class-action suit would put all state/district school systems on notice that failures in education will not be tolerated.

Consumer Organization/Action

There are other tactics that can be adopted from the experiences of reforming services for mentally retarded individuals. For example, much of that effort was spearheaded by parents and other concerned citizens who organized themselves to become formidable political forces. National and state organizations (most notably ARCs, Associations for Retarded Citizens) are now sustained by membership dues, conference fees, grants, and private contributions. They now represent a political force that must be reckoned with at every level of policy-making. Their influence did not spring forth overnight; it accrued slowly but was substantially bolstered when court cases and legislative initiatives became national flashpoints. These advocacy organizations now hire speicalists, when necessary, in accounting, policy development, and habilitation to exert influence on nearly every state capitol.

Conditions may now be favorable for similar organizations to develop on behalf of education, particularly if they are accompanied by some of the other initiatives discussed here. The core of such groups could include concerned parents and professionals who refuse to accept the status quo, reform-minded researchers, and state and local politicians with a reputaton for innovation in education.

These associations can operate on a variety of levels to promote reform in such areas as funding for education, textbook adoption, hiring and firing of teaching staff, teacher supervison, school discipline problems, competency exams (for teachers and students), and so on.

Another emulable model for organizing such constituents is available from within the broader consumer action movement. The particular model we propose is taken from recent efforts of citizens to achieve political parity with utility companies by forming Consumer's Utility Boards (CUBs) in various states. These organizations have been formed on the recognition that individual consumers are at a political disadvantage vis-à-vis utility companies in such matters as rate cases, legislative affairs, etc. CUBs enable citizens to pool resources and hire thier own accountants, attorneys, and lobbyists.

The mechanism that enables citizens across an entire state to pool their resources is particularly germane to this discussion. Specifically, because utility companies operate as legalized monopolies (presumably under the regulatory reigns of state public service commissions), consumers have no choice in their purchase of service. Thus, when consumers receive their bills they often receive materials (e.g., advertisements and notices) that they have paid for in addition to the actual utility service. This fact provides a basis for consumers to claim a certain ownership of the bill's contents and to insist on being allowed to include their own solicitations in the monthly bill, including solicitations to fund an organization that exists to press utility companies for reform. Legislatures in several states have affirmed this claim of ownership and have allowed citizens to solicit funds through the utility company's monthly bill.

Perhaps an analogous organization with a similar mechanisim for obtaining funding could be established to reform education. In a sense, the public school system is similar to a utility company—it operates as a monopoly inasmuch as private educational alternatives are not affordable to many citizens. Thus, there may be a basis for arguing that consumers have a right to pool their capital through solicitations accompanying their child's report cards, city and county tax bills, and other mail-outs on behalf of the local government and school. This money would be pooled to establish Consumer Education Boards (CEBs). CEBs could act as watchdogs of the educational system, monitor the textbook production and selection process, lobby for legislative reform of education, and identify model educational practices around the country.[1]

Epilogue

As mentioned, the strength of the proposals rests partly on the fact that each can work synergistically with the other. Indeed, we would argue that whereas the quality of education may be improved by enactment of any one proposal, comprehensive and sustained reform requires the fulfillment of all functions served by these proposals.

Nearly all of the national reports agree that American education is in crisis. Therefore, the role of behavior analysis in education must be at an equally crucial crossroad. It seems to us that behavior analysis can continue to patch and prop up any system it is given to operate within. That appears to have been much of what behavior analysis has been willing to do in education so far. That is, we have had to rely on persuasion and the graces of teachers and principals to be permitted to implement slight (often temporary) changes in classroom procedure. If at any time they refused to cooperate we accepted in frustration our apparent inability to press matters further. The proposals offered here, however, may put our energies to a better cause.

Finally, it should be apparent that these proposals strongly emphasize the need for greater accountability in education. That simply reflects our belief that it is the absence of accountability over many years throughout all aspects of education that has debilitated the educational system. This view is fundamentally different from one that ascribes the principal failure of education to the mentalistic interpretations of behavior that pervade the educational establishment (Skinner, 1984). Although we do not argue that mentalistic in-

[1]The authors would like to thank Mary Beth Martin, who first suggested a consumer's group in education similar to CUB.

terpretations abound in education, we suggest that they are popular not because they are cherished *per se* by educators, but because they offer one means of avoiding accountability. A child's "defective mind," "process," "syndrome," or "state" is merely a convenient excuse to avoid taking responsibility for change. The point is that getting rid of the mentalistic metaphor is not enough; another means of escaping or avoiding accountability would soon be found. What is needed are forms of action on our part that insist on accountability and do not allow escape. It could be an interesting predicament if our own preoccupation with battling the mentalistic metaphor has functioned merely to allow us to avoid the demands of our responsibilities in reforming education.

In any case, we predict that eventually there will be attempts at reform, some of them quite drastic, whether we choose to become part of these initiatives or not. If we are not a vital part of such initiatives then the utility of behavior analysis in education will be in serious doubt.

We prefer to be optimistc and suggest that not only is behavior analysis essential to education but that there are many among us prepared to lift both ventures from their crisis. We conclude on this optimistic note by offering the reader a sneak preview of the first issue of the *Journal of Applied Behavioral Synthesis*, side by side with an amalgamated issue of its predecessor.

References

Baer, D. M., Wolf, M. M., & Risley, T. R. (1968). Some current dimensions of applied behavior analysis. *Journal of Applied Behavior Analysis, 1*, 91–97.

Becker, W. C. (1978). The national evaluation of Follow-Through: Behavior-theory-based programs come out on top. *Education and Urban Society, 10*, 431–458.

Brown v. Board of Education, 347 U.S. 483 (1954).

Carnine, D. W. (1976). Effects of two teacher-presentation rates on off-task behavior, answering correctly, and participation. *Journal of Applied Behavior Analysis, 9*, 199–206.

Carnine, D. (1984). *Barriers to student achievement and how to overcome these barriers.* Unpublished manuscript, University of Oregon, Eugene, OR.

Table 1. A Contrast of the *Journal of Applied Behavior Analysis* and the *Journal of Applied Behavior Synthesis*

Journal of Applied Behavior Analysis (1968 to 1986)	*Journal of Applied Behavior Synthesis* (1998)
Madsen, C.H., Becker, W.C., & Thomas, D.R. *University of Illinois.* Rules, praise and ignoring: Elements of elementary classroom control.	Madder, I.S., & Bigger, A.M. *National Behavioral Research Consorsortium.* Validated instructional systems, teacher supervision and publicizing test results: Elements of a sound state educational system.
Cantrell, R.P., *et al. Louisiana Polytechnic Institute.* Contingency contracting with school problems.	Can, D.O. *Louisiana Political Institute.* Performance contracting with school districts.
Hall *et al. University of Kansas.* Teacher & parents as researchers using multiple baseline designs.	Overhall, V. *Illinois Citizens Education Board.* Parents and teachers as reformers using multiple bases of influence.
Murphy *et al. Florida State University.* Behavioral school psychology goes outdoors: The effects of organized games on playground aggression.	Mercy, N.O. *Federation of State Behavioral Education Associations.* Behavioral education goes to Washington: The effects of organized lobbying on Congressional education appropriations
Kazdin, A.E., & Bootzin, R.R. *Pennsylvania State University.* The token economy: An evaluative review.	Surewin, A., & Shoein, A. *Pennsylvania Association of Behavioral Educators.* The voucher system: An evaluative review.
Winett, R.A., & Winkler, R.C. *State University of New York.* Current behavior modification in the classroom: Be still, be quiet, be docile.	Winit, W.E. *National Bureau of Behavioral Standards.* Current behavioral standards in education: Be literate, be scientific, be artistic.

Carnine, D. W., & Fink, W. T. (1978). Increasing the rate of presentation and use of signals in elementary classroom teachers. *Journal of Applied Behavior Analysis, 11,* 35–46.

Fink, W. T., & Carnine, D. W. (1975). Control of arithmetic errors by informational feedback. *Journal of Applied Behavior Analysis, 8,* 461.

Greene, B. F. (1981). The role of evaluation in the development of school curriculum materials. *Catalog of Selected Documents in Psychology, 11,* 59.

Hamerlynck, L. A. (1980). When you pass the behavioral buck—make it contingent. Reflection upon service in state government. *The Behavior Therapist,* 3 (5), 5–9.

Hamerlynck, L. A. (1984). Social engineering for model program adoption: Perspectives of a purchaser. In S. C. Paine, G. T. Bellamy, & B. Wilcox, *Human services that work* (pp. 217–223). Baltimore, MD: Brookes.

Kirigin-Ramp, K. (1984) Effective quality control for social service programs: One piece of the puzzle. In S. C. Paine, G. T. Bellamy, & B. Wilcox, *Human services that work* (pp. 261–268). Baltimore, MD: Brookes.

Mills v. Board of Education, 348 F. Supp. 866 (D.D.C. 1972).

Morucci, M. (1982) Education tort law—Cause of action for education malpractice requires intentional and malicioius conduct by school officials. *University of Baltimore Law Review,* (Fall), 158–164.

The National Commission on Excellence in Education. (1983). *A nation at risk: The imperative for educational reform.* U. S. Government Printing Office, Washington, DC.

Peter W. v. San Francisco Unified School District, 131 Cal. Rptr., 854 (Ct. App. 1976).

Rothman, D. J., & Rothman, S. M. (1984). *The Willowbrook wars.* New York: Harper & Row, Publishers.

Skinner, B. F. (1984). The shame of American education. *American Psychologist, 39,* 947–954.

Sulzer-Azaroff, B. (1985). A behaviorist's response to the report of the National Commission on Excellence in Education. *The Behavior Analyst, 8,* 29–38.

CHAPTER 31

The Future of Behavior Analysis in Educational Settings

Donald M. Baer

In 1980, a national conference (Ysseldyke & Weinberg, 1981) acknowledged a growing crisis of morale and mission in the discipline of school psychology. As part of that conference, Baer and Bushell (1981) described the accomplishments of behavior-analytic approaches to public education. We said of behavior analysis that "It could transform a classroom of shouting, aggressive, destructive, rebellious, out-of-seat vandals into a quiet, seated, attentive, and industrious work force." That work force, we said,

> did assignments quickly and accurately, spoke mainly to ask intelligent questions about the assignments; smiled upon completing them, and upon the teacher's acknowledgements of those completions, and upon the teacher; and given the choice, voted to have school rather than holidays. (p. 259)

We also contrasted the logic of behavior analysis to that of traditional education, and found a striking set of opposites. Finally, we noted the thorough absence of behavior analysis in public schools, despite two decades of documenting its effectiveness there. We wondered why, and guessed that the answer did not lie entirely in the schools, but rather in those arenas of society in which decisions were made about schools. Only a behavioral analysis of that decision making, we hypothesized, would create a future for behavior analysis in the schools.

Only part of that argument is worth repeating here. This book hardly needs another chapter to describe what behavior-analytic procedures have accomplished in educational settings. It will be more useful to consider the remarkable contrast between behavior-analytic and educational assumptions, lest we think that contrast was the major reason for the absence of behavior analysis from public schools. That contrast is certainly part of the problem, but it is far from all of the problem. Look behavior-analytically at the functions of the public schools, and you see a larger problem. Interestingly, that larger problem emerged just as clearly in the 1980 school psychology conference, when that largely non-behavior-analytic discipline tried to see why

Donald M. Baer • Department of Human Development, University of Kansas, Lawrence, Kansas 66045.
This chapter is substantially similar to a paper of the same title read at the tenth annual convention of the Association for Behavior Analysis, Nashville, May 1984, as part of a symposium on *Conceptual and Applied Issues for Behavioral Analysis in Educational Settings*.

its practice in the public schools was so demoralizing to it. We need to guess why behavior analysis is unwelcome in the schools, even though it wants to be there and can be very effective in developing happy and productive scholars. And we also need to guess why school psychology is becoming mandatory in the schools, but so far in ways that make the majority of school psychologists say that if they had it to do over again, they would choose a different profession.

First, consider the contrast in basic assumptions that emerges whenever behavior analysis tries to move systematically into the public schools. Baer and Bushell (1981, pp. 265–266) tabled four instances of paradigm clash.

1. The first is at the level of the organism. Behavior analysis knows that it teaches children's behaviors; Education believes that it teaches children. For education, children are whole; they cannot be taken apart analytically. Unfortunately for the children, they are recognized by education as widely different; and because they are whole, their differences mean that they are intrinsically either easy to teach or difficult to teach. In what it explicitly considers a noble act of democratic public conscience, education has accepted them all as such—and thereby has done its unconscious best to maintain them as such, forever, by segregating them into what now are called resource rooms and tracks. By contrast, behavior analysis is able to consider a child as a collection of behaviors and behavior deficits, each of which can be dealt with separately. It does not accept the children as they are because it assumes that it can make them better children by teaching them the particular behaviors that empower each child to be better.

2. The second clash is at the level of behavior. Behavior analysis assumes that behavior changes because its environmental controls and prerequisites have been programmed for that change, and that programming can be done by teachers and parents. Education assumes that behavior changes because maturation has made the organism ready for that change; given readiness, practice will evoke the change. In this view, teachers need only assign practice; those children who are ready will profit by it, and those who are not will demonstrate that they are not, whereupon they can be accepted as difficult-to-teach children and segregated as such.

3. The third clash follows immediately from the second; it is at the level of strategy. As every student knows, the basic strategy of education is to establish 16 grades of age-appropriate knowledge and skills, the first 12 of which are called grade school and high school, the last four of which are called university. Each grade is divided into a large number of very small linear steps, and these are assigned daily and weekly for practice. Those who teach themselves these assignments are acknowledged as ready and given high grades; those who do not are labeled as unready in maturation, motivation, or both, and are given low grades. Student failure is never the teacher's fault, because the teacher almost certainly made the indicated assignments, and the rest is the student's responsibility. As every behavior analyst knows, the assignment of behavior changes to be accomplished primarily through the student's private resources is probably the most perfect antithesis of behavior analysis. Teaching, in behavior analysis, is the arrangement of various procedures such that behavior change results and can be attributed to those procedures; the more clearly that attribution can be made, the more behavior-analytic the process. In behavior analysis, teaching is something that we aspire to understand only eventually in its total detail; and we expect to accomplish that total understanding only through a great deal of experimental analysis, much of it yet to be done. For education, teaching is so casual a process that all maturationally normal, minimally socialized children can be assigned to do it to themselves.

4. The fourth clash is at the level of technique. The ostensible technique of education is already clear—it is to assign daily and weekly behavior changes and grade the results. But that technique requires a more basic, underly-

ing technique, which is to have a curriculum of such assignments. That problem is solved by buying curricula from curriculum experts, called publishers. By contrast, the techniques of behavior analysis are to arrange contingencies that support a curriculum of behavior changes chosen to fit each child's current set of abilities and deficits. When behavior changes do not occur readily, the behavior analysts assign themselves a failing grade, and make experimental changes in the contingencies and, more important, in the underlying individualized task analyses that generated the curriculum. Curricula are bought only as long as they work; when they fail, new curricula are made and evaluated experimentally, by hand. Failure always is the behavior analyst's failure; all children's behaviors are assumed to be teachable, upon analysis.

That is obviously a lot of clash. Can anything be done about it? Baer and Bushell offered one negative and four positive recommendations, all only vaguely behavioral. They are in fact only invitations to make a truly behavioral analysis of the problem.

The negative recommendation was not to avoid the paradigm clash. We wrote:

> That already is done sometimes. It leads most often to people giving M & Ms to children who do not like M & Ms, reducing task analysis to a paragraph-by-paragraph presentation of what was in the first place a confused book, and giving children pieces of plastic called tokens, which they can trade for pieces of plastic not called tokens—in short, a mindless application of the obvious trappings of behavior analysis, devoid of the logic that alone makes the trappings functional for the children to whom they are applied. You can control a lot of pain by aspirin without understanding physiology; you cannot control much behavior by contingencies without an understanding of behavioral function. You simply cannot. (Baer & Bushell, 1981, p. 267)

Baer and Bushell also offered four positive recommendations. Three of them relied on the universities: (a) teach behavior analysis to education students; (b) especially teach behavior analysis to education's school-psychology students; and (c) continue to maintain a few demonstration projects against a future possibility that they will be seen to be needed (as they manifestly are not seen to be needed now). These three mechanisms were considered very slow acting—appropriate to universities. Our fourth recommendation was a change in target: from schools to politics. We argued that the future of behavior analysis in the schools would be settled

> not in the schools; in the society where decisions about schools are made. The question is, How are those decisions made? What is the behavioral analysis of *that*?" (Baer & Bushell, 1981, p. 268)

A major point must be added to this argument today. If behavior analysis turns to the analysis of societal decisions, it will find that education long ago turned to exactly that arena, and has been working industriously there ever since. Four observations emerge: education is working for decisions (a) against the inclusion of behavior analysis in the schools, and (b) in favor of continuing the presence of school psychology in the schools. And yet (c) so many behavior analysts want to be in the schools, and (d) so many school psychologists want to be out of them. What is the behavioral analysis of those four facts?

I can offer a hypothesis in potential analysis of all of them. This analysis begins with the recognition that the schools are organizations. An organization is a structured collection of people; each person does a particular job in the organization, and the net result of all their behavior is the organization's behavior, ostensibly in pursuit of its mission. But most of the contingencies operating in the organization are for people to do their jobs, not to succeed in the organization's mission.

Most organizations set themselves up to solve some problem; some are set up by other organizations, such as governments, to solve some problem. Sometimes the problem is simply to make money; sometimes it is to improve the quality of our lives. A naive view of any organization is that its mission controls and explains its behavior. A functional view suggests that very early in its life, the first function of any organization's administrators becomes to survive as an organization, and that a second function then emerges almost immediately, which is to grow. To succeed a little in its mission thus becomes their third function: the success reinforces the organization's clients and sponsors; the littleness of the success is the organization's case for growth. To succeed totally in its mission is self-destructive, a flat contradiction of its administrators' first and second functions.

Thus, societies create police for the protection of private property and the organization of public functions like traffic. If the police rid a society of its criminals and create totally automatic mediators of its traffic, they go out of business, too. The most reinforcing outcome, not for the officers but for their organization, will be to catch some criminals, maintain some order, yet constantly be confronted with growing crime and public functions that need their mediation. An organization of police will always need more crime and disorder than it can control with its present resources and personnel. Do we expect such an organization to work hard at eliminating crime and disorder? We should expect it to work hard at falling just the right amount behind: far enough behind to require more personnel, equipment, and pay from us; not so far behind that we decide to abandon it as the tool of our salvation.

Other organizations create themselves to sell us the solution to one of our problems—automobiles, for example. If those organizations created the perfect solution—an automobile that would work well, cost very little, was completely safe, and never broke down—we would each buy a number of them, until we and our families and employees were totally mobile. Then there would be little for the automobile manufacturers to do except wait for a population expansion. That would mean growing much smaller, not larger. Do we expect them to do that? We should expect them to have spent their 70 years of continuous technological research in the development of autos that need replacement more and more often, not less and less, and that at least seem to grow very slightly safer from a baseline of quite dangerous. They need to solve just enough of our transportation problem to reinforce us for buying their solution to it, and to fail to solve just enough of it to keep us investing every few years in what might be better solutions, but for their sake had better not be very much better solutions. A few misjudgments in that delicate matter, and some foreign manufacturer will embarrass them with a slightly more generous adjustment of those parameters, to our momentary delight. But the foreign competitors' organization also must survive and grow; we should expect only momentary generosity in the matter of a solution.

Thus armies are reinforced by victory, but their leaders are more reinforced by the existence or creation of still undefeated and dangerous enemies. Clinicians are reinforced by cures, but more reinforced by the existence or creation of illnesses. Insurance companies urge us to learn health and safety behaviors, but not enough to make the danger of illness, early death, or accident so trivial that we would no longer buy insurance against them.

And schools? School organizations need to succeed in teaching just enough of our children just enough of the skills that we think they need to learn, so that we will be reinforced for maintaining schools. But they should also fail to do that with just enough of our children so that we will fund the schools' growth as they try to do better with that apparently difficult problem (cf. Tucker, 1981). If behavior analysis thinks that problem is not that difficult, what is the function of behavior analysis for the schools' administrators? Punishing: it cancels their best case for increased personnel, better pay for those personnel, more space, and more resources. And if behavior analysis thinks that it can do better with not just the troublesome students, but with all of the schools' students, then the function of behavior analysis for the schools' administrators is even more punishing: it makes a case not only for canceling growth, but for shrinking.

What schools' organizations need from behavioral science is something that is and looks like scientifically validated educational technique, requires more budget and personnel, and looks attractive to the public, who must be persuaded to pay its costs. Behavior analysis is scientifically validated educational technique, and if it has to, it can do the schools' job more expensively than that job is being done at present—especially if it must be added to the schools rather than become integral to the schools. But behavior analysis is not something that looks attractive enough to the public for them to pay more for, and consequently school administrators often tell behavior analysis proponents that their product is too expensive. The same school administrators at the same time do not tell computer salespeople that their product is too expensive. Instead, they say that they will try hard to get the budget increase necessary to buy the microcomputers that they know their classroom teachers will not master sufficiently to make the computers truly educational tools. Surely we have all heard school computers increasingly described as dedicated page-turners. School administrators know that such budget increases remain permanent, and that they can find space to store the soon-to-be unused computers so as to be ready for whatever comes next that is budget and personnel expansive as well as attractive to the tax-hike voters.

In this context, what is a school psychologist, from the schools administrators' point of view? School psychologists are publicly validated specialists who cost a fair amount of money, will always need more space and support personnel, do not burden classroom teachers with the need to manage contingencies all day long, and are seen by the public as media-validated experts wrestling with the problems of difficult-to-teach children. But they are also seen by the school administrators as unlikely to succeed very much with the problem, and when they do succeed, to do so only in expensive ways—that is, ways that require growth of the school system and its budget. Indeed, we should expect that the schools will arrange life for their school psychologists so that this is exactly what happens. In their 1980 conference, Tucker (1981) pointed out to the school psychologists that their role is that of the patsy: their assignment is to fail a lot with the schools' most difficult educational problems, and to be blamed for that failure so that their potential improvement can justify future requests for expanded budgets. Is this the analysis of the fact that the majority of school psychologists were reported in their 1980 conference to prefer to work at any other profession than their present one? Is this the role that behavior analysis aspires to?

Behavior analysis surely does not seek the role of patsy for an organization simply carrying out its life functions. The point is that because those are the schools' life functions, any approach that understands function will see a very serious problem in joining them with what in another context would be the gifts of efficiency, economy, and well-being, but in this context are poison. Perhaps behavior analysis is better equipped to see the magnitude and depth of the problem than any other discipline—function is the essence of its research targets, principles, knowledge, and practice. Perhaps seeing the problem that clearly will let behavior analysts find its solution. Or, perhaps, seeing the problem that clearly will move behavior analysts to show what they can do in alternative schools of their own creation, rather than take on an organizational reform that may be a behavioral impossibility. I have no certainty on this issue, but I will bet on the second strategy rather than the first.

There seems to be a move in our society toward new, different, alternative forms of schooling. That move is in fact a variety of moves serving somewhat different functions, but all based in some part on dissatisfaction with the present public schools. In that multiplicity of social movements, will there not be opportunity for some behavior-analytic schools as well? Bushell and his students have planned one complete, efficient, economical behavior-analytic alternative (Chapter 20); it is totally ready for implementation, awaiting only its moment. Evolutionary theory and behavior-analytic theory suggest that some variety of these alternatives would be desirable. We should design some more, to await their moments.

And we should read the other chapters of this book as potential contributions to those alternatives as well as to the present public schools. I predict that most of the public schools will resist these gifts, after all. True, we may often meet particular teachers and principals who will welcome us and any effectiveness, efficiency, economy, happiness, and social validity that we can program. But if my argument is sound, they will not be able to do that for long—we are antithetical not to their but to their organization's two most basic life functions.

The wry fact in this argument is that if we turn to developing our own behavior-analytic schools, or our own behavior-analytic additions to the present schools, we will have to get organized. Initially, the function of our organizations will be to show education at its current behavioral best. A short time later, two other functions will begin to supplant that function: the administrators of our organizations will start behaving in ways that let the organizations survive and grow, rather than be valid, effective, efficient, and economical. Is the fact that behavior analysts certainly should be able to see that happening sufficient for the planning that might insulate them against its happening, by arranging contingencies that reinforce them all—even their administrators—better for succeeding in their mission than for continuing to fail in some expensive part of it? Today, no one could say with certainty. If awareness is worth that much, that finding will make a remarkable chapter in some future education book—a chapter on the role of self-instruction in the design of contingencies and stimulus controls to prevent classical organizational behavior. If awareness is not that effective, then some other book will have a chapter pointing out that it is time to replace the organized behavior-analytic approaches to schooling.

Meanwhile, we may well be entering an exciting and informative few decades.

ACKNOWLEDGMENT

I am grateful to my long-time colleague, Dr. Don Bushell, Jr., for the experiments, demonstrations, explanations, pointings-out, and arguments that have let me learn this much about behavior analysis and the public schools, behavior analysis in the public schools, and the behavioral analysis of the public schools.

References

Baer, D. M., & Bushell, D., Jr. (1981). The future of behavior analysis in the schools? Consider its recent past, and then ask a different question. [Special issue]. *School Psychology Review, 10,* 259–270.

Tucker, J. A. (1981). The emperor's new clothes are hand-me-downs. [Special issue]. *School Psychology Review, 10,* 271–284.

Ysseldyke, J., & Weinberg, R. A. (Eds.). (1981, spring). The future of psychology in the schools: Proceedings of the Spring Hill Symposium [Special joint issue]. *School Psychology Review, 10* (2).

Index

MIX
Papier aus verantwortungsvollen Quellen
Paper from responsible sources
FSC® C105338

If you have any concerns about our products,
you can contact us on
ProductSafety@springernature.com

In case Publisher is established outside the EU,
the EU authorized representative is:
Springer Nature Customer Service Center GmbH
Europaplatz 3, 69115 Heidelberg, Germany

Printed by Libri Plureos GmbH
in Hamburg, Germany